Eleanora A. Baer

TITLES IN SERIES

A Handbook for Librarians and Students

3d edition

VOLUME 1

Titles in Series A-I

The Scarecrow Press, Inc.
Metuchen, N.J. & London
1978

Library of Congress Cataloging in Publication Data

Baer, Eleanora A
Titles in series.

Bibliography: p.
Includes indexes.
1. Indexes. I. Title.
AI3.B3 1978 011 78-14452
ISBN 0-8108-1043-3

Manufactured in the United States of America

PREFACE

This revised and enlarged edition of Titles in Series: A Handbook for Librarians and Students includes 69,657 book titles published in America and foreign countries prior to January 1975. It includes all books listed in previous editions, but up-dated according to information found in bibliographical tools, publishers' catalogs, and the series catalog at the Library of Congress. Also some series appear for the first time--these are older established ones that have recently been suggested by librarians as worthy of inclusion, as well as newly created series judged by the compiler to warrant inclusion.

The arrangement of publications under each series is in numerical order, if the publisher has assigned numbers to titles in the series; in chronological order, as in the case of lecture series; or in alphabetical order. Individual authors and titles have been verified with the U.S. Library of Congress National Union Catalog in order to establish the official entry to be used in listing works; only slight variations have been made, e.g. the deletion of "Mrs." in name entries. Unlocated titles were checked against other bibliographical tools. The series titles are those used by the Library of Congress; deviations from those appearing in the book are listed in the Series Titles Index. The item number serves as a medium for indexing.

I am grateful to many persons who have offered facilities or suggestions for the work. My thanks go to the different chiefs of the Card Division, who since 1952 have graciously allowed me to use the Special Series File in the Library of Congress, and also to librarians at Chicago, Northwestern, St. Louis, Wisconsin and Washington Universities, and at the St. Louis and Chicago Public Libraries who have furnished materials and assistance. Many librarians have offered suggestions. Societies, organizations, librarians, and publishers have supplied lists and invaluable information.

ELEANORA A. BAER
December 1976

REFERENCE WORKS CONSULTED

Biblio. Paris, 1933-

Bibliografía Hispánica. Madrid, 1942-

Bibliografia Nazionale Italiana. Florence, 1961-

Bibliographie de Belgique. Brussels, 1875-

Bibliographie de la France. Paris, 1811-

Blaser, Fritz, ed. Bibliographie der Schweizer Presse. Basel, 1956-

British Museum. Dept. of Printed Books. General Catalogue of Printed Books. London, 1964-

British National Bibliography. London, 1950-

Canadiana. Ottawa, 1951-

Catálogo General de la Librería Española e Hispanoamericana. Madrid, 1932-

Catalogue de l'Edition Française. Port Washington, N. Y.

Cumulative Book Index. New York, 1898-

Deutsche Bibliographie. Frankfurt, 1947-

Das Deutsche Buch. Frankfurt, 1950-

Deutsche Nationalbibliographie. Leipzig, 1931-

Deutscher Gesamtkatalog. Berlin, 1931-

Deutsches Bücherverzeichnis. Leipzig, 1952-

Edinburgh. University. Library. Catalogue of Printed Books. Edinburgh, 1918-23.

The English Catalogue of Books. London, 1837-

Florence. Biblioteca Nazional Central. Bollettino delle Pubblicazioni Italiane Ricevute per Diritto di Stampa. Florence, 1886-

Gesamtverzeichnis des Deutschsprachigen Schrifttums. 1911-

Halbjährliches Verzeichnis Taschenbücher. Frankfurt, 1951-

Indian National Bibliography. Calcutta, 1958-

Jahres-Verzeichnis der Deutschen Hochschulschriften. Leipzig, 1885-

La Librairie Française. Les Livres de l'Année. Paris, 1930-

El Libro Español. Madrid, 1958-

Libros en Venta en Hispanoamérica y España. Buenos Aires, 1974-

London Library. Catalogue. London, 1913-14. Suppl. 1913-29.

Malclès, L.-N. Les Sources du Travail Bibliographique. Geneva, 1950-

Norsk Bokfortegnelse. Olso, 1814-

Paris. Bibliothèque Nationale. Catalogue Général des Livres Imprimés: Auteurs. Paris, 1900-

Peabody Institute, Baltimore. Catalogue of the Library. Baltimore, 1883-1905.

Publishers Trade List Annual. New York, 1873-

Publishers Weekly. New York, 1872-

Repertorio Bibliografico. Rome, 1958-

Rome (City). Centro Nazionale per il Catalogo Unico delle Biblioteche Italiane e per le Informazioni Bibliografiche. Primo Catalogo Collettivo delle Biblioteche Italiane. Rome, 1962-

Das Schweizer Buch. Zürich, 1948-

Schweizer Bucherverzeichnis/Repertoire du Livre Suisse/Elenco del Libro Svizzero. Zürich, 1951-

Svensk Bokförteckning. Stockholm, 1953-

Svensk Bok-katalog, 1866- Stockholm, 1878-

United States. Library of Congress. Library of Congress Catalog. Washington, 1947-56.

_____ _____ Monographic Series. Washington, 1974-

_____ _____ The National Union Catalog. Washington, 1956-

Verzeichnis Lieferbar Bücher. Frankfurt, 1971-

Whitaker's Cumulative Book List. London, 1924-

TITLES IN SERIES

AGARDograph (Pergamon)

1 Ferri, A. and Bogdonoff, S. M. Design and operation of intermittent supersonic wind tunnels. 1954. A1
2 North Atlantic Treaty Organization. Advisory Group for Aeronautical Research and Development. Methods and criteria for the selection of flying personnel. 1954. A2
3 Kenney, J. T. and Webb, L. M. A summary of the techniques of variable Mach number supersonic wind tunnel nozzle design. 1954. A3
4 Mullins, B. P. Spontaneous ignition of liquid fuels. 1955. A4
5 North Atlantic Treaty Organization. Advisory Group for Aeronautical Research and Development. Anthropometry and human engineering. 1955. A5
6 ____. Collected papers on aviation medicine. 1955. A6
7 Penner, S. S. Introduction to the study of chemical reactions in flow systems. 1955. A7
8 Crocco, L. and Cheng, S. Theory of combustion instability in liquid propellant rocket motors. 1956. A8
9 North Atlantic Treaty Organization. Advisory Group for Aeronautical Research and Development. Combustion researches and reviews. V. 1. 1955. A9
10 Frederick, C. L. and others. Automatic pressure measuring systems used with high-speed wind tunnels. 1955. A10
11 Arnold, L. Dynamic measurements in wind tunnels. 1955. A11
12 Cooper, R. D. and Tulin, M. P. Turbulence measurements with the hot-wire anemometer. 1955. A12
13 Whiteside, T. C. D. The problem of vision in flight at high altitude. 1957. A13
14 Fejér, A. and Clark, J. Compressors for high-speed wind tunnels. 1956. A14
15 Same as no. 9. V. 2. 1957. A15
16 North Atlantic Treaty Organization. Icing problems and recommended solutions. 1957. A16
17 Smolderen, J. J. Condensation effects and air drying systems for supersonic wind tunnels. 1956. A17
18 Malavard, L. C. The use of the rheoelectrical analogies in aerodynamics. 1957. A18
19 North Atlantic Treaty Organization. Fluid physics of hypersonic waves. 2 v. 1967. A19
20 Benecke, T. and Quick, A. W., eds. History of German guided missiles development. 1957. A20
21 AGARD Guided Missiles Seminar. Papers. V. 1. 1956. A21
22 Hill, J. A. F. and others. Mach number measurements in high-speed wind tunnels. 1956. A22
23 North Atlantic Treaty Organization. Advisory Group for Aeronautical Research and Development. Optical methods for examining the flow in high-speed wind tunnels. 1956. A23
24 Morkovin, M. V. Fluctuations and hot-wire anemometry in compressible flows. 1957. A24
25 Lovelace Foundation for Medical Education and Research. Aviation medicine, ed. by White and others. 1958. A25
26 North Atlantic Treaty Organization. Advisory Group for Aeronautical Research and Development. Papers presented at the

61 North Atlantic Treaty Organization. Visual problems in aviation medicine, ed. by Mercier. 1962. A62
62 Material Sciences Symposium, Paris, 1961. Advances in materials research in the NATO nations, ed. by Brooks and others. 1963. A63
63 Nachrichtentechnische Gesellschaft. Radio navigation for aviation and maritime use, ed. by Bauss. 1963. A64
64 North Atlantic Treaty Organization. A review of measurements on AGARD calibration models, ed. by Hills. 1961. A65
65 Clarkson, B. L. Structural aspects of acoustic loads. 1960. A66
66 Leeuwen, H. P. van and Mucuoglu, M. C. Requirements for an axial fatigue machine capable of fast cyclic heating and loading. A67
67 Earl, T. D. Ground effect machines. 1962. A68
68 AGARD-NATO Specialists' Meeting. The high temperature aspects of hypersonic flow, ed. by Nelson. 1963. A69
69 Gallagher, R. H. and others. A correlation study of methods of matrix structural analysis. 1964. A70
70 Maltby, R. L., comp. Flow visualization in wind tunnels using indicators. 1962. A71
71 North Atlantic Treaty Organization. Light and heat sensing, ed. by Merrill. 1963. A72
72 Fraeijs de Veubeke, B., ed. Matrix methods of structural analysis. 1964. A73
73 Anthropometric survey of Turkey, Greece and Italy, by Hertzberg and others. 1963. A74
74 North Atlantic Treaty Organization. Propagation of radio waves at frequencies below 300 kc/s, ed. by Blackband. 1964. A75
75 Markstein, G. H., ed. Nonsteady flame propagation. 1964. A76
76 Campbell, J. P. Free and semi-free model flight-testing techniques used in low-speed studies of dynamic stability and control. 1963. A77
77 Keonjian, E., ed. Micropower electronics. 1964. A78
78 North Atlantic Treaty Organization. Arctic communication, ed. by Landmark. 1964. A79
79 Pindzola, M. Jet stimulation in ground test facilities. 1963. A80
80 Plantema, J. F. Development of a simple runway waviness measuring system. 1963. A81
81 Combustion Colloquium. Combustion and propulsion, ed. by DeGroff and others. 1967. A82
82 AGARD Conference on Refractory Metals. The science and technology of tungsten, tantalum, molybdenum, niobium and their alloys, ed. by Prommisel. 1964. A83
83 Taylor, J. Manual on aircraft loads. 1965. A84
84 U.S. Arnold Engineering Development Center. Arc Heaters and MHD accelerators for aerodynamic purposes. 1964. A85
85 Covey, R. E. Wind tunnel data processing. 1964. A86
86 Jost, W. Low Temperature oxidation. 1965. A87
87 AGARD-NATO Specialists' Meeting. The fluid dynamic aspects of space flight. V. 1. 1966. A88
88 North Atlantic Treaty Organization. Physics and technolgy of ion motors, ed. by Marble and Suruge. 1966. A89
89 North Atlantic Treaty Organization. Advisory group for Aeronautical research and development. Proceedings for a meeting held at NATO headquarters. 1964. A90
90 Laufer, J. and others. Mechanism of noise generation in the turbulent boundary layer. 1964. A91
91 Siegel, A. E. The theory of high speed guns. 1965. A92
92 Orbit optimization and laser applications. 1964. A93
93 North Atlantic Treaty Organization. Space simulation chambers and techniques, ed. by Goethert. 1964. A94
94 Srye, R. Handbook on the properties of niobium, molybdenum,

129 Glassman, I. and Sawyer, R., eds. The performance of chemical propellants. 1970. A130
130 Eckert, E. R. G. and Goldstein, R. J. Measurement techniques in heat transfer. 1970. A131
131 Brown, F. M. Guidance and control for aerospace vehicles. 1969. A132
132 Muntz, E. P. The electron beam fluorescence technique. 1968. A133
133 Glaister, D. H. Effects of gravity and acceleration on the lungs. 1970. A134
134 Obremski, H. J. and others. A portfolio of stability characteristics of incompressible boundary layers. 1967. A135
135 Fluidic control systems for aerospace propulsion. 1969. A136
136 Hancock, G. J. Problems of aircraft behaviour at high angles of attack. 1969. A137
137 Jones, D. J. Tables of inviscid supersonic flow about circular cones at incidence, ed. by Rainbird. 1969. A138
138 Ballistic range technology, ed. by Canning and others. 1970. A139
139 Leondas, C. T., ed. Theory and applications of Kalman filtering. 1970. A140
140 Physiopathology and pathology of the spine in aerospace medicine, by Delahaye and others. 1970. A141
141 Tavernier, P. and others. Propergols hautement energetiques. 1970. A142
142 Hopkin, V. D. Human factors in the ground control of aircraft. 1970. A143
143 Denison, D. M. A non-invasive technique of cardiopulmonary assessment. 1970. A144
144 Bogue, D. C. and White, J. Engineering analysis of non-Newtonian fluids. 1970. A145
145 Bynum, D. S. and others. Wind tunnel pressure measuring techniques. 1970. A146
146 Lomax, H. and others. The numerical solution of partial differential equations governing convection. 1970. A147
147 Nonreacting and chemically reacting viscous flows over a hyperboloid at hypersonic condition, ed. by Lewes. 1971. A148
148 Ziebland, H. and Parkinson, R. C. Heat transfer in rocket engines. 1971. A149
149 Pope, G. G. and Schmit, L. A. Structural design applications of mathematical programming techniques. 1971. A150
150 AGARD. Principles of biodynamics. 1971. A151
151 Guignard, J. C. and King, P. F. Aeromedical aspects of vibration and noise. 1972. A152
152 Dukes, W. H. Handbook of brittle material design technology. 1971. A153
153 Aerospace Medical Panel. Glossary of aerospace medical terms, ed. by Fryer. 1971. A154
154 Dobie, T. G. Aeromedical handbook for aircrew. 1972. A155
155 Ryder, D. A. The elements of fractography. 1971. A156
156 Yoshihara, H. Some recent developments in planar inviscid transonic airfoil theory. 1972. A157
157 Schijve, J. The accumulation of fatigue damage in aircraft materials and structures. 1972. A158
158 Leondes, C. T., ed. Computers in the guidance and control of aerospace vehicles. 1972. A159
159 Perry, C. I. Nomenclature of terrain colour. 1972. A160
160 France, J. T. The measurement of fuel flow. 5 v. 1972. A161
161 Hurwicz, H. and others. Ablation. 1972. A162
162 Thomson, A. G. R. Acoustic fatigue design data. 3 v. 1972. A163
163 Ginoux, J. J., ed. Supersonic ejectors. 1972. A164

164 Surugue, J. Boundary layer effects in turbomachines. 1972. A165
165 Schultz, D. L. and Jones, T. V. Heat-transfer measurements in short-duration hypersonic facilities. 1972. A166
166 Aarons, J., ed. Total electron content and scintillation studies of the Ionosphere. 1972. A167
166A Klobuchar, J. A. and Aarons, J. Numerical models of total electron content over Europe and the Mediterranean and multi-station scintillation comparisons. 1972. A168
167 Pianko, M., ed. Modern methods of testing rotating components of turbomachines. 1973. A169
168 Lengelle, G. and Verdier, C. Gas sampling and analysis in combustion phenomena. 1973. A170
169 Bradshaw, P. Effects of streamline curvature on turbulent flow. 1973. A171
170 Benson, A. J. and Burchard, E. Spatial disorientation in flight. 1973. A172
171 Jacobson, I. D. Magnus characteristics of arbitrary rotating bodies, 1973. A173
172 Crimi, P. Dynamic stall. 1973. A174
173 Spaid, F. W. and Cassel, L. A. Aerodynamic interference by reaction controls. 1973. A175
174 Gibson, C. H. Digital techniques in turbulence research. 1973. A176
175 Structures and Materials Panel of AGARD. Active control systems for load alleviation, flutter suppression and ride control. 1974. A177
176 Liebowitz, H., ed. Fracture mechanics of aircraft structures. 1974. A178
177 Dobie, T. G. Airsickness in aircrew. 1974. A179
178 Holloway, A. H. Guide to the layout of technical publications. 1974. A180
179 Fangmeyer, H. Semi automatic indexing state of art. 1974. A181
182 Glossary of documentation terms, by Gibbs, 2 pts. 1974. A182
184 Bernard, J. J. and Genot, J. Radiation cooling of propulsive nozzles. 1974. A183
185 Horlock, J. H. and Perkins, H. J. Annulus wall boundary layers in turbomachines. 1974. A184
186 Trolinger, J. D. Laser instrumentation for flow field diagnostics, ed. by Bogdonoff. 1974. A185
187 Taylor, T. D. Numerical methods for predicting subsonic, transonic and supersonic flow. 1974. A186
188 McRuer, D. T. and Krendel, E. S. Mathematical models of human pilot behavior. 1974. A187
189 Hartman, B. O. and others. Operational aspects of variations in alertness. 1974. A188
190 Burton, R. R. and others. Man at high sustained G_Z acceleration. 1974. A189
191 Zierep, J. Theory of flows in compressible media with heat additions. 1974. A190
192 Lorenzini, D. A. Testing of precision inertial gyroscopes. 1974. A191
193 Johnson, A. C. and Naitch, P. The operational consequences of sleep deprivation and sleep deficit for flight personnel. 1974. A192
194 Lorentzen, F. V. Cold. 1974. A193
197 Hohenemser, K. H. Hingeless rotorcraft flight dynamics. 1974. A194

A. S. A. MONOGRAPH (Tavistock)

1 Conference on New Approaches in Social Anthropology. 1964. A195
2 Banton, M. P. The political systems and the distribution of power. 1965. A196
3 Conference on Anthropological Approaches to the Study of Religion, ed. by Banton. 1968. A197
4 Conference on the Social Anthropology of Complex Societies,

ed. by Banton. 1966. A198
5 The structural study of myth and totemism, ed. by Leach. 1967. A199
6 Themes in economic anthropology, ed. by Firth. 1967. A200
7 Association for Social Anthropologists of the Commonwealth. History and social anthropology, ed. by Lewis. 1968. A201
8 Socialization, ed. by Mayer. 1970. A202
9 Witchcraft confessions and accusations, ed. by Douglas. 1970. A203
10 Social anthropology and language, ed. by Ardener. 1971. A204
11 Rethinking kinship and marriage, ed. by Needham. 1971. A205
12 Urban ethnicity, ed. by Cohen. 1974. A206

THE A.W. MELLON LECTURES IN THE FINE ARTS (Pantheon)

1952 Maritain, J. Creative intuition in art and poetry. 1953. A207
1953 Clark, K. M. The nude. 1956. A208
1954 Read, H. E. The art of sculpture. 1956. A209
1955 Gilson, E. H. Painting and reality. 1957. A210
1956 Gombrich, E. H. J. Art and illusion. 1960. A211
1957 Giedion, S. The eternal present. V. 1 The beginnings of art. 1962. V. 2 The beginnings of architecture. 1964. A212
1958 Blunt, A. Nicholas Poussin. 2 v. 1966. A213
1959 Gabo, N. Of divers arts. 1962. A214
1960 Lewis, W. S. Horace Walpole. 1961. A215
1961 Grabar, A. Christian iconography. 2 v. 1968. A216
1962 Raine, K. Blake and tradition. 2 v. 1969. A217
1963 Pope-Hennessy, J. The portrait in the Renaissance. 1966. A218
1964 Rosenberg, J. On quality in art. 1967. A219
1966 Cecil, D. Visionary and dreamer. 1969. A220
1967 Praz, M. Mnemosyne. 1969. A221
1968 Barzun, J. The use and abuse of art. 1974. A222

THE A.W. MELLON STUDIES IN THE HUMANITIES (Univ. of Pittsburgh Pr.)

Seymour, C. Michelangelo's David. 1967. A223

ABERDEEN UNIVERSITY STUDIES (1-151 Aberdeen Univ. Pr., 152- Oxford Univ. Pr.)

1 Aberdeen. University and Kings College. Roll of alumni in arts of the University and King's College, 1596-1860, ed. by Anderson. 1900. A224
2 Aberdeen, Scot. Records of old Aberdeen, 1157-1891, ed. by Munro. V. 1. 1900. A225
3 Macdonald, J. Place names of West Aberdeenshire. 1900. A226
4 Burnett, G. The family of Burnett of Leys, ed. by Allardyce. 1901. A227
5 Michie, J. G., ed. The records of Invercauld, 1547-1828. 1901. A228
6 Aberdeen University. Rectorial addresses delivered in the University of Aberdeen, 1835-1900, ed. by Anderson. 1902. A229
7 Albemarle, W. A. K. The Albemarle papers, ed. by Terry. 2 v. 1902. A230
8 Bulloch, J. M., ed. The house of Gordon. V. 1. 1903. A231
9 Elgin, Scot. The records of Elgin, ed. by Cramond. V. 1. 1903. A232
10 Meldrum, A. N. Avogadro and Dalton. 1904. A233
11 Aberdeenshire, Scot. Records of the Sheriff court of Aberdeenshire ed. by Littlejohn. V. 1. 1904. A234
12 Aberdeen University. Anatomical and Anthropological Society. Proceedings of the Aberdeen University anatomical and

and anthropological society. 1904. A235

13 Thomson, J. A. and Henderson, W. S. Report on the Alcyonaria collected by Professor Herdman at Ceylon in 1902. A236

14 Japp, F. R. Researches in organic chemistry. 1905. A237

15 Shewan, A. Meminissee juvat. 1905. A238

16 Morison, A. The Blackhalls of that ilk and Barra. 1905. A239

17 Records of the Scots colleges at Douai, Rome, Madrid, Valladolid and Ratisbon. 1906. A240

18 Aberdeen University. Rolls of the graduates of the University of Aberdeen, 1860-1900. 1906. A241

19 Anderson, P. J. Studies in the history and development of the University of Aberdeen. 1906. A242

20 Ramsay, W. M., ed. Studies in the history and art of the eastern provinces of the Roman Empire. 1906. A243

21 Bulloch, W., ed. Studies in pathology. 1906. A244

22 Same as no. 12. V. 2. 1906. A245

23 Aberdeen. University. Library, Marischal College. Subject catalogues of the Science library and the Law library in Marischal College. 1906. A246

24 Same as no. 11. V. 2. 1906. A247

25 Studies on alcyonarians and antipatharians, by J. A. Thomson and others. 1907. A248

26 Milne, J. S. Surgical instruments in Greek and Roman times. 1907. A249

27 Same as no. 11. V. 3. 1907. A250

28 Harrower, J. Flosculi graeci boreales. 1907. A251

29 Aberdeen. University. Records of the celebration of the quartercentenary of the University of Aberdeen, ed. by Anderson. 1907. A252

30 Same as no. 8. V. 2. 1907. A253

31 New Spalding club, Aberdeen The miscellany of the New Spalding club. 1908. A254

32 Adam, J. The religious teachers of Greece. 1908. A255

33 Driesch, H. A. E. The science and philosophy of the organism. V. 1. 1908. A256

34 Same as no. 12. V. 3. 1908. A257

35 Same as no. 9. V. 2. 1908. A258

36 Tocher, J. F. Pigmentation survey of school children in Scotland. 1908. A259

37 Sames as no. 33. V. 2. 1909. A260

38 Studies on alcyonarians and hydroids, by Thomson and others. 1909. A261

39 Terry, C. S. A catalogue of the publications of Scottish historical and kindred clubs. 1909. A262

40 Anderson, P. J. Aberdeen Friars. 1909. A263

41 Studies on alcyonarians, by Thomson and others. 4th ser. 1909. A264

42 Same as no. 2. V. 2. 1498-1903. 1909. A265

43 Musa latina aberdonensis, ed. by Leask. 1910. A266

44 North of Scotland college of agriculture. Aberdeen. Bulletins of the Aberdeen and North of Scotland college of agriculture. 1910. A267

45 Inverness, Scot. Records of Inverness, ed. by Mackay and Boyd. V. 1. 1911. A268

46 Zoological studies, by Thomson and others. 1911. A269

47 Aberdeen. University. Library, Marischal College. Phillips Library. Subject catalogue of the Phillips library of pharmacology and therapeutics. 1911. A270

48 Zoological studies, by Thomson and others. 1911. A271

49 Lees, J. The Anacreontic poetry of Germany in the eighteenth century. 1911. A272

50 Curtis, W. A. A history of creeds and confessions of faith in Christendom and beyond.

1911. A273
51 Harrower, J., comp. Aberdeen alumni at other universities. 1911. A274
52 Elder, J. R. The royal fishery companies of the seventeenth century. 1912. A275
53 Zoological studies, by Thomson and others. 1912. A276
54 Craib, W. G. The flora of Banffshire. 1912. A277
55 Aberdeen. University. Anthropological Museum. Illustrated catalogue of the Anthropological museum. 1912. A278
56 Bremner, A. The physical geology of the Dee Valley. 1912. A279
57 Craib, W. G. Contributions to the flora of Siam. V. 1. 1912. A280
58 Anderson, P. J. Notes on academic theses. 1912. A281
59 Skelton, C. O. Gordons under arms. 1912. A282
60 Henderson, J. A., ed. History of the Society of advocates in Aberdeen. 1912. A283
61 Same as no. 57. V. 2. 1912. A284
62 Aberdeen. University. Library bulletin. 1911- A285
63 Smith, J. Genealogies of an Aberdeen family. 1913. A286
64 Zoological studies, by Thomson and others. 1914. A287
65 Elder, J. R. The Highland host of 1678. 1914. A288
66 Johnstone, J. F. K. A concise bibliography of the history, topography and institutions of the shires of Aberdeen, Banff and Kincardine. 1914. A289
67 Burnet, G. Bishop Gilbert Burnet as educationalist, ed. by Clarke. 1914. A290
68 Bulloch, J. M. Territorial soldiering in the north-east of Scotland during 1759-1814. 1914. A291
69 Same as no. 12. V. 4. 1915. A292
70 Zoological studies, by Thomson and others. 1915. A293
71 Same as no. 62. V. 2. 1916. A294
72 Physiological studies, by MacWilliam and others. 1st ser. 1916. A295
73 Anderson, P. J. A concise bibliography of the printed and ms. material on the history, topography and institutions of the burgh, parish and shire of Inverness. 1917. A296
74 Seth Pringle Pattison, A. The idea of God in the light of recent philosophy. 1917. A297
75 Leask, W. K. Interamna boreales. 1917. A298
76 Johnston, W. The roll of commissioned officers in the Medical service of the British army. 1917. A299
77 Same as no. 62. V. 3. 1918. A300
78 Sorley, W. R. Moral values and the idea of God. 1918. A301
79 Webb, C. C. J. God and personality. 1919. A302
80 ____. Divine personality and human life. 1920. A303
81 Aberdeen. University. Bulletin of the College of Agriculture, nos. 15-27, 1920. A304
82 Aberdeen. University. Library. Cruickshank science library, subject catalogue. 1921. A305
83 Bremner, A. The physical geology of the Don basin. 1921. A306
84 Aberdeen. University. Roll of service in the great war, 1914-1919, ed. by Allardyce. 1921. A307
85 Aberdeen. University. Library. Catalogue of the Taylor collection of psalm versions. 1921. A308
86 Same as no. 62. V. 4. 1922. A309
87 Banffshire, Scot. Records of the county of Banff, 1660-1760, ed. by Grant and others. 1922. A310
88 McCulloch, W. E., comp. Viri illustres universitatum Abredonensium. 1923. A311
89 Hobson, E. W. The domain of natural science. 1923. A312
90 Rennie, J. Studies in parasitology and general zoology. 1923. A313
91 Traill, J. W. H. James

William Helenus Traill; a memorial volume. 1923. A314
92 Hendrick, J. Agricultural studies. 1st ser. 1924. A315
93 Catholic church. Liturgy and ritual. Epistolare in usum ecclesiae cathedralis aberdonensis, ed. by M'Ewen. 1924. A316
94 Bulloch, J. M. Bibliography of the Gordons. 1924. A317
95 Johnstone, J. F. K. The Alba amicorum of George Strachan... 1924. A318
96 Skene, M. and others. Botanical studies. 1st ser. 1925. A319
97 Same as no. 62. V. 5. 1925. A320
98 Aberdeen. University. Library. A list of the fifteenth century books in the University library of Aberdeen. 1925. A321
99 Same as no. 45. V. 2. 1924. A322
100 Grieg, G., comp. Last leaves of traditional ballads and ballad airs, collected in Aberdeenshire. 1925. A323
101 Milne, C. H. M. A reconstruction of the Old-Latin text or texts of the gospels used in St. Augustine. 1926. A324
102 Same as no. 72. 2d ser. 1926. A325
103 Simpson, W. D. Scottish archaeological studies. V. 1. 1922. A326
104 Aberdeen. University. Library. Catalogue of pamphlets in the King, the Thomson and the Herald collections. 1927. A327
105-107 Same as no. 103. V. 2-4. 1923-26. A328
108 Alexander, W. M. The four nations of Aberdeen university and their European background. 1934. A329
109 Purser, G. L. The early stages of the development of the vertebrates. 1934. A330
110 Getty, R. J. The lost St. Gall ms. of Valerius Flaccus. 1934. A331
111 Simpson, W. D. The Celtic church in Scotland. 1935. A332
112 Findlay, A. The teaching of chemistry in the universities of Aberdeen. 1935. A333
113 Reid, T. Philosophical orations of Thomas Reid, ed. by Humphries. 1937. A334
114 Maclachlan, E. Ewen Maclachlan's Celtic verse, ed. by Macdonald. 1937. A335
115 Simpson, W. D. Ravenscraig Castle. 1938. A336
116 Aberdeen. University. Library. Catalogue of Greek and Latin papyri and ostraca in the possession of the University of Aberdeen, ed. by Turner. 1939. A337
117 Humphries, W. R. William Ogilvie and the projected union of the colleges, 1786-1787. 1940. A338
118 Campbell, D. J. C. Plini Secundi Naturalis historiae, liber secundus. 1936. A339
119 Irvine, J. C. The academic burden in a changing world. 1942. A340
120 Luckwill, L. C. The genus Lycopersicon. 1943. A341
121 Simpson, W. D. The province of Mar. 1943. A342
122 Beattie, J. James Beattie's London diary 1773, ed. by Walker. 1946. A343
123 Henderson, G. D. The founding of Marischal college, Aberdeen. 1947. A344
124 Simpson, W. D. The Earldom of Mar. 1949. A345
125 Kelly, W. A tribute offered by the University of Aberdeen to the memory of William Kelly, L. L. D., A. R. S. A., ed. by Simpson. 1949. A346
126 Aberdeen. University. Library. MacBean collection, comp. by Allardyce. 1949. A347
127 Turnbull, H. W. Bi-centenary of the death of Colin Maclaurin (1698-1746). 1951. A348
128 Raven, C. E. Centenary of the birth on 8th November, 1846 of the Reverend Professor W. Robertson Smith. 1951. A349
129 Read, J. William Davidson of Aberdeen. 1951. A350

130 Thomson, D. S. The Gaelic sources of Macpherson's Ossian. 1952. A351
131 Simpson, W. D. Dundarg Castle. 1954. A352
132 ____, ed. The Viking Congress, Lerwick, July 1950. 1954. A353
133 Hetherington, H. J. W. The British university system, 1914-1954. 1954. A354
134 Mitchell, W. S. A history of Scottish bookbinding 1432 to 1650. 1955. A355
135 Buckley, K. D. Trade unionism in Aberdeen, 1878 to 1900. 1955. A356
136 Eeles, F. C. King's College Chapel, Aberdeen. 1956. A357
137 Findlay, W. M. Oats. 1956. A358
138 Roth, C. The Aberdeen codex of the Hebrew Bible. 1958. A359
139 Porter, I. A. Alexander Gordon, M. D. of Aberdeen. 1958. A360
140 Stein, P. Fault in the formation of contract in Roman law and Scots law. 1958. A361
141 O'Dell, A. C. St. Ninian's Isle treasure. 1960. A362
142 Simpson, W. D. The Castle of Bergen and the Bishop's Palace at Kirkwall. 1961. A363
143-144 Wightman, W. P. D. Science and the Renaissance. 2 v. 1962. A364
145 Smith, J. H. The Gordon's Mill Farming Club, 1758-1764. 1962. A365
146 Simpson, W. D., ed. The fusion of 1860. 1963. A366
147 Duthie, G. I., ed. Papers, mainly Shakespearian. 1964. A367
148 Taylor, T. M. Speaking to graduates, ed. by Hunter and Lillie. 1965. A368
149 Small, A., ed. The fourth Viking congress. 1965. A369
150 Aberdeen. University. Library. Catalogue of incunabula in Aberdeen University Library. 1968. A370
151 Gordon, W. M. Studies in the transfer of property by tradition. 1970. A371
152 Small, A., ed. and others, eds. St. Ninian's Isle and its treasure. 1973. A372
153 Charlton, T. M. Energy principles in the theory of structures. 1973. A373

Some titles were also published as the New Spalding Club. Publications. The number in parentheses indicates their numbering in that series.
2(20), 3(21), 4(22), 5(23), 7(24-25), 8(26), 9(27), 11(28), 16(29), 17(30), 24(31), 27(32), 30(33), 31(34), 35 (35), 42(36), 43(37), 45(38), 59(39), 60(40), 68(41), 87(42), 99(43).

ACADEMY OF AMERICAN FRANCISCAN HISTORY. BIBLIOGRAPHY SERIES.

1 Geiger, M. J., Father. A calendar of documents in the Santa Barbara Archives. 1947. A374
2 Adams, E. B. A bio-bibliography of Franciscan authors in colonial Central America. 1953. A375
3 Santa Fe, N. M. (Archdiocese). Archives, 1678-1900, comp. by Chávez. 1957. A376

ACADEMY OF AMERICAN FRANCISCAN HISTORY. DOCUMENTARY SERIES.

1 Motolinia, T. History of the Indians of New Spain, tr. by Steck. 1951. A377
2 Benavides, A. de. Memorial of 1630; tr. by Forrestal. 1954. A378
3 Palou, F. Life of Fray Junípero Serra, tr. by Geiger. 1955. A379
4-7 Serra, J. Writings, ed. by Tibesar. 4 v. 1956. A380
8 Córdoba y Salinas, D. de. Crónica franciscana de la provincias del Perú, ed. by Canedo. 1957. A381
8-9 De Lasuen, F. F. Writings, ed. by Kenneally. 2 v. 1965. A382
10 Oroz, P. The Oroz Codex, tr. by Chavez. 1972. A383

ACADEMY OF AMERICAN FRANCISCAN HISTORY. MONOGRAPH SERIES.

1 Tibesar, A. Franciscan beginnings in colonial Peru. 1953. A384
2 McCloskey, M. B. The formative years of the Missionary College of Santa Cruz of Querétaro, 1683-1733. 1955. A385
3 Baer, K. Painting and sculpture at Mission Santa Barbara. 1955. A386
4 Greenleaf, R. E. Zumarraga and the Mexican inquisition, 1536-1543. 1962. A387
5-6 Geiger, M. J. The life and times of Fray Junípero Serra. 2 v. 1959. A388
7 Warren, F. B. Vasco de Quiroga and his pueblo-hospitals of Santa Fe. 1963. A389
8 Chavez, A. Coronado's friars. 1968. A390
9 Guest, F. F. Fermin Francisco de Lasuen. 1973. A391
10 Morales, F. Ethnic and social background of the Franciscan Friars in seventeenth century Mexico. 1973. A392

ACADEMY OF AMERICAN FRANCISCAN HISTORY. WRITINGS OF THE PRESIDENTS OF THE CALIFORNIA MISSIONS.

1 Serra, J. Writings, ed. by Tibesar. 4 v. 1956. A393/4

ACADEMY OF NATURAL SCIENCES OF PHILADELPHIA. MONOGRAPHS.

1 Pennell, F. W. The Scrophulariaceae of eastern temperate North America. 1935. A395
2 Fowler, H. W. Fishes of the George Vanderbilt south Pacific expedition, 1938. 1938. A396
3 Pilsbry, H. A. Land Mollusca of North America (north of Mexico). 2 v. in 4. 1939-48. A397
4 Hebard, M. Australian Blattidae of the subfamilies Chorisoneurinae and Ectobiinae (Orthoptera). 1943. A398
5 Pennell, F. W. The Scrophulariaceae of the western Himalayas. 1943. A399
6 George Vanderbilt expedition, 1941. Results of the Fifth George expedition (1941). 1944. A400
7 Fowler, H. W. A study of the fishes of the southern Piedmont and coastal plains. 1945. A401
8 Olsson, A. A. and Harbison, A. Pliocene Molusca of southern Florida. 1953. A402
9 Roback, S. S. The immature tendipedids of the Philadelphia area. 1957. A403
10 MacNeal, D. L. The flora of the Upper Cretaceous Woodbine sand in Denton County, Texas. 1958. A404
11 Abbott, R. T. The marine mollusks of Grand Cayman Island British West Indies. 1958. A405
12 Rehn, J. A. G. and Grant, H. J. A monograph of the Orthoptera of North America. V. 1. 1961. A406
13 Patrick, R. and Reimer, C. W. The diamots of the United States. V. 1. 1966. A407
14 Catherwood Foundation Peruvian-Amazon Expedition. The Catherwood Foundation Peruvian-Amazon Expedition, by Patrick and others. 1966. A408
15 Drouet, F. Revision of the classification of the Oscillatoriaceae. 1968. A409
16 Tyler, J. C. A monograph of plectognath fishes of the super-family Triacanthoidea. 1968. A410
17 Roback, S. S. The adults of the sub-family Tanypodinae (-Pelopiinae) in North America. 1971. A411

ACADEMY OF NATURAL SCIENCES OF PHILADELPHIA. SPECIAL PUBLICATIONS

1 Gordon, S. G. The mineralogy of Pennsylvania. 1922. A412
2 Goldschmidt, V. and Gordon, S. G. Crystallographic tables

for the determination of minerals. 1928 A413
3 Stewart, R. B. Gabb's California cretaceous and tertiary type Lamellibranchs. 1930. A414
4 Clench, W. J. and Turner, R. D. New names introduced by H. A. Pilsbry in the Mollusca and Crustacea. 1962. A415
5 Academy of Natural Sciences of Philadelphia. Guide to the manuscript collections in the Academy of Natural Sciences of Philadelphia, comp. by V. T. and M. E. Phillips. 1963. A416
6 Richards, H. G. and Fairbridge, R. W. Annotated bibliography of quaternary shorelines, 1945-1964. 1965. A417
7 Academy of Natural Sciences of Philadelphia. Minutes and correspondence, 1812-1924, ed. by Phillips. 1967. (Microfilm) Guide to the microfilm publication of the Minutes and Correspondence ... prepared by V. T. and M. E. Phillips. 1967. A418
9 Montgomery, A. The mineralogy of Pennsylvania, 1922-1965. 1969. A419

ADDISON-WESLEY BOOKS IN NUCLEAR SCIENCE AND METALLURGY (Addison-Wesley unless otherwise noted)

Bishop, A. S. Project Sherwood. 1958. A420
Chastain, J. W., ed. U.S. research reactor operation and use. 1958. A421
Claus, W. D., ed. Radiation biology and medicine. 1958. A422
Clegg, J. W. and Foley, D. D., eds. Uranium ore processing. 1958. A423
Cuthbert, F. L. Thorium production technology. 1958. A424
Dietrich, J. R. and Zinn, W. H., eds. Solid fuel reactors. 1958. A425
Goodman, C., ed. The science and engineering of nuclear power. 1952. A426
Holden, A. N. Physical metallurgy of uranium. 1958. A427
Kaplan, I. Nuclear physics. 1962. A428
Keepin, G. R. Physics of nuclear kinetics. 1965. A429
Kramer, A. W., ed. Boiling water reactors. 1958. A430
Lane, J. A. and others, eds. Fluid fuel reactors. 1958. A431
Nuclear Development Corp. of America. Fundamental aspects of reactor shielding, by Goldstein. 1959. A432
Peterson, S. and Wymer, R. G. Chemistry in nuclear technology. 1963. A433
Preston, M. A. Physics of the nucleus. 1962. A434
Seaborg, G. T. The transuranium elements. Yale Univ. Press. 1958. A435
The Shippingport pressurized water reactor. 1958. A436
Starr, C. and Dickinson, R. W. Sodium graphite reactors. 1958. A437

ADVANCES IN CHEMISTRY (Amer. Chemical Soc.)

1 American Chemical Society. Agricultural control chemicals. 1950. A438
2 ____. Chemical factors in hypertension. 1950. A439
3 ____. Analytical methods in the food industry. 1950. A440
4 ____. Searching the chemical literature. 1951. A441
5 ____. Progress in petroleum technology. 1951. A442
6 Dow Chemical Company. Azeotropic data, comp. by Horsley. 2 v. 1952. A443
7 American Chemical Society. Agricultural applications of petroleum products. 1952. A444
8 ____. Chemical nomenclature. 1953. A445
9 ____. Fire retardent paints. 1954. A446
10 ____. Literature resources for chemical process industries. 1954. A447
11 ____. Natural plant hydrocolloids. 1954. A448

12 ____. Uses of sugar and other carbohydrates in the food industry. 1954. A449
13 ____. Pesticides in tropical agriculture. 1955. A450
14 ____. System of nomenclature for terpene hydrocarbons. 1955. A451
15 Dreisbach, R. R. Physical properties of chemical compounds. v. i. 1955. A452
16 American Chemical Society. A key to pharmaceutical and medicinal chemistry. 1956. A453
17 ____. Training of literature chemists. 1956. A454
18 ____. Thermodynamic properties of the elements. 1956. A455
19 Symposium on Handling and uses of Alkali Metals. Handling and uses of alkali metals. 1957. A456
20 International Ozone Conf. Literature of the combustion of petroleum. 1958. A457
21 American Chemical Society. Ozone chemistry and technology. 1959. A458
22 Same as no. 15. V. 2. 1959. A459
23 Symposium on Metal-Organic Compounds. Metal-organic compounds. 1959. A460
24 Symposium on Chemical Marketing in the Competitive Sixties. Chemical marketing in the competitive sixties. 1959. A461
25 American Chemical Society. Physical functions of hydrocolloids. 1960. A462
26 Symposium on Nonmilitary Defense. Nonmilitary defense. 1960. V. 1. A463
27 Symposium on Saline Water Conversion. Saline water conversion. 1960. A464
28 American Chemical Society. Gibberellins. 1961. A465
29 Same as no. 15. V. 3. 1961. A466
30 American Chemical Society. Searching the chemical literature. 1961. A467
31 Francis, A. W. Critical solution temperatures. 1961. A468
32 Symposium from Borax to Boranes. Borax to Boranes. 1961. A469
33 American Chemical Society. Solid surfaces and the gas-solid interface. 1961. A470
34 Symposium on Polymerization and Polycondensation. Polymerization and polycondensation processes. 1962. A471
35 American Chemical Society. Azetropic data-II. 1962. A472
36 Symposium on Inorganic Free Radicals. Free radicals in inorganic chemistry. 1962. A473
37 Reactions of coordinated ligands and homogeneous catalysis. 1963. A474
38 Same as no. 27. V. 2. 1963. A475
39 Symposium on Non-Stoichiometric Compounds. Non-stoichiometric compounds. 1963. A476
40 McLafferty, F. W. Mass spectral correlations. 1963. A477
41 New approaches to pest control and eradication. 1963. A478
42 Symposium on Boron-Nitrogen Chemistry. Boron-nitrogen chemistry. 1964. A479
43 Contact angle, wettability, and adhesion. 1964. A480
44 Richard, J. Block Memorial Symposium. Amino acids and serum proteins. 1964. A481
45 Molecular modification in drug design. 1964. A482
46 American Chemical Society. Patents for chemical inventions. 1964. A483
47 ____. Fuel cell systems. 1965. A484
48 ____. Plasticization and plasticizer processes. 1965. A485
49 Summer Symposium on Mechanisms of Inorganic Reactions. Mechanisms of inorganic reactions. 1965. A486
50 Solvated Electron Symposium. Solvated electron. 1965. A487
51 Symposium on Selected Oxidation Processes. Selective oxidation processes. 1965. A488
52 Symposium on New Aspects

of Elastomer Stereospecific Polymerization. Elastomer stereospecific polymerization. 1966. A489
53 American Chemical Society. Natural pest control agents. 1966. A490
54 ____. Advanced propellant chemistry. 1966. A491
55 American Conference on Coal Science. Coal science. 1966. A492
56 Flavor chemistry. 1966. A493
57 Symposium on Evaluation of World Protein Resources. World protein resources. 1966. A494
58 Iron-molecule reactions in the gas phase. 1966. A495
59 American Chemical Society. Lignin structure and reactions. 1966. A496
60 ____. Organic pesticides in the environment. 1966. A497
61 Kekulé centennial. 1966. A498
62 Werner centennial. 1967. A499
63 Ordered fluids and liquid crystals. 1967. A500
64 Regenerative EFM cells. 1967. A501
65 Radiation preservation of foods. 1967. A502
66 Irradiation of polymers. 1967. A503
67 Equilibrium concepts in natural water systems. 1967. A504
68 The Mossbauer effect and its application in chemistry. 1967. A505
69 Fuel gasification. 1967. A506
70 American Chemical Society. Homogeneous catalysis. 1968. A507
71 Lanthanide/actinide chemistry. 1968. A508
72 American Chemical Society. Mass spectrometry in inorganic chemistry. 1968. A509
73 ____. Trace inorganics in water. 1968. A510
74 Deoxy sugars. 1968. A511
75-77 International Oxidation Symposium. Oxidation of organic compounds. 3 v. 1968-69. A512
78 American Chemical Society. Literature of chemical technology. 1968. A513
79 ____. Adsorption from aqueous solution. 1968. A514
80 Chemical reaction in electrical discharges, ed. by Balustien. 1969. A515
81-82 International Conference on Radiation Chemistry. Radiation chemistry. 2v. 1968. A516
83 American Chemical Society. Chemical marketing. 1968. A517
84 ____. Molecular association in biological and related systems. 1968. A518
85 Stabilization of polymers and stabilizer processes. 1968. A519
86 Pesticidal formulations research. 1969. A520
87 Interaction of liquids at solid substrates. 1969. A521
88 American Chemical Society. Propellants manufacture, hazards, and testing. 1969. A522
89 ____. Isotope effects in chemical processes. 1969. A523
90 ____. Fuel-cell Symposium. 1968. A524
91 Additional and condensation polymerization processes. 1969. A525
92 Epoxy resins. 1970. A526
93 Freiling, E. C. Radionuclides in the environment. 1969. A527
94 Harris, D. S. Dietary chemical vs dental caries. 1969. A528
95 Reese, E. T. Cellulases. 1969. A529
96 Engineering plastics and their commercial development. 1969. A530
97 Refining petroleum for chemicals. 1970. A531
98 Platinum group metals and compounds. 1971. A532
99 Multicomponent polymer systems. 1971. A533
100 Bioinorganic chemistry. 1971. A534
101-102 International Conference on Molecular Sieve Zeolites. Molecular sieve zeolites, by Flanigen and Sard. 2 v. 1971. A535

103 Origin and refining of petroleum, by McGrath and Charles. 1971. A536
104 Pesticides identification at the residue level. Chairman: Biros. 1971. A537
105 Anaerobic biological treatment processes. Chairman: Pohland. 1970. A538
106 Nonequilibrium systems in natural water chemistry. Chairman: Hem. 1971. A539
107 Industrial color technology. Chairmen: Johnston & Saltzman. 1971. A540
108 Drug discovery. Chairmen: Bloom & Ullyot. 1971. A541
109 International Symposium on Chemical Reaction Engineering. Chemical reaction engineering. Chairman: Bischoff. 1972. A542
110 Mardi Gras Symposium. Sulfur research trends. Chairmen: Miller & Wiewiorowski. 1972. A543
111 Fate of organic pesticides in the aquatic environment. Chairman: Faust. 1972. A544
112 Ozone reactions with organic compounds. Chairman: Bailey. 1972. A545
113 Photochemical smog and ozone reactions. 1972. A546
114 Biological correlations--the Hansch approach. Chairman: Van Valkenburg. 1972. A547
115 Extractive and azeotropic distillation. 1972. A548
116 American Chemical Society. Azeotropic data-III. 1973. A549
117 Carbohydrates in solution. Chairman: Isbell. 1973. A550
118 Chemical engineering in medicine. Chairman: Reneau. 1973. A551
119 Electrodeposition of coatings. Chairman: Brewer. 1973. A552
120 Chlorodioxins-origin and fate, ed. by Blair. 1973. A553
121 Molecular sieves, ed. by Meier and Uytterhoeven. 1973. A554
122 Air pollution damage to vegetation, ed. by Naegele. 1973. A555
123 Trace elements in the environment, ed. by Kothny. 1973. A556
124 Solvents theory and practice. 1973. A557
125 Polymer molecular weight methods. 1973. A558
126 Nomenclature of organic compounds: principles and practice. 1974. A559
127 Pollution control and energy needs. 1973. A560
128 Polymerization kinetics and technology. 1974. A561
129 Polymerization reactions and new polymers. 1974. A562
130 Polyamine-chelated alkali metal compounds. 1974. A563
131 Coal gasification. 1974. A564
132 American Chemical Society. Homogeneous catalysis-II. 1974. A565
133 International Symposium on Chemical Reaction Engineering. Chemical reaction engineering-II. 1974. A566
134 Fillers and reinforcements for plastics, ed. by Deanin and Schott. 1974. A567
135 Chemistry of food packaging, ed. by Swalm. 1974. A568
136 Food related enzymes, ed. by Whitaker. 1974. A569
137 Chemistry of winemaking, ed. by Webb. 1974. A570
138 Archaeological chemistry, ed. by Beck. 1974. A571

ADVANCES IN DOCUMENTATION AND LIBRARY SCIENCE (Interscience)

1 American Chemical Society. Division of Chemical Literature. Progress report in chemical literature retrieval, ed. by Peakes and others. 1957. A572
2 Western Reserve University. School of Library Science. Information systems in documentation, ed. by Shera and others. 1958. A573
3 Int'l. Conference for Standards on a Common Language ... Information retrieval and machine translation, ed. by Kent. 2 v. 1960-61. A574

AFFAIRES ET GENS D'AFFAIRES (1-6 Colin; 7- S. E. V. P. E. N.)

1 Sapori, A. Le marchand italien au Moyen Age. 1952. A575
2 Dauvet, J. Les affaires de Jacques Coeur. 2 v. 1952-53. A576
3 Baulant, M. Lettres de negociant Marseillais, ed. by Braudel. 1953. A577
4 De Roover, R. L'evolution de la lettre de change. 1953. A578
5 Sicard, G. Les moulins de Toulouse au Moyen Age, Aux origines des sociétés anonymes. 1953. A579
6 Lapeyre, H. Simon Ruiz et les "asientos" de Philippe II. 1953. A580
7 Mandich, G. Le pacte de ricorsa et le marché italien des changes au XVIIe siècle. 1953. A581
8 Lapeyre, H. Une famille de marchands: les Ruiz. 1955. A582
9 Silva, J. G. da. Stratégie des affaires à Lisbonne entre 1595 et 1607. 1956. A583
10 Berenge, A. Lettres d'un marchand vénitien Andrae Berengo (1553-1556). 1957. A584
11 Schick, L. L. Un grand homme d'affaires au debut du XVIe siècle: Jacob Fugger. 1957. A585
12 Schnapper, B. Les rentes au XVIe siècle. 1957. A586
13 Piccamiglio, G. Le livre de comptes de Giovanni Piccamiglio . . . , by Heers. 1959. A587
14 Silva, J. G. da, ed. Marchandises et finances. V. 2-3. 1959-61. A588
15 Dermigny, L. Cargaisons indiennes. 2 v. 1960. A589
16 Goubert, P. Familles marchandes sous l'Ancien Régime. 1959. A590
17 Gille, B. Recherches sur la formation de la grande enterprise capitaliste (1815-1848). 1959. A591
18 Vazquez de Prada, V. Lettres marchandes 'Anvers. 4 v. A592
19 Lüthy, H. La banque protestante en France, de la révocation de l'Edit de Nantes à la Révolution. 2 v. 1959-61. A593
20 Thuillier, G. Georges Dufand et les débuts du grand capitalisme dans la métallurgie, en Nivernais, au XIXe siècle. 1959. A594
21 Gioffrè, D. Gênes et les foires de change de Lyon à Besancon. 1960. A595
22 Gille, B. Les forges françaises en 1772. 1960. A596
23 Bouvier, J. Le Crédit Lyonnais de 1863 à 1882. 2 v. 1961. A597
24 Heers, J. Gênes au XVe siècle. 1961. A598
25 Gille, B. Le Conseil général des manufactures. 1961. A599
26 Vilar, P. Manual de la Compañva Nova de Gibraltor. 1962. A600
27 Ruiz Martin, F. Lettres marchandes echangees entre Florence et Medina del Campo. 1965. A601
28 Marciani, C. Lettres de change aux foires de Lanciano au XVIe siècle. 1962. A602
29 Bergier, J. F. Gèneve et l'economie européene de la Renaissance. 1963. A603
30 Poliakov, L. Les banchieri juifs et le Saint-Siége du XIII siècle. 1965. A604
31 Cavignac, J. Jean Pellet. 1967. A605
32 Lohmann Villena, G. Les Espinosa. 1968. A606
33 Leleux, F. L'industriel gantois Lievin Bauwens. 1969. A607
34 Bec, C. Il libro degli affari proprii di casa de Lapo di Giovanni Niccolini de Sirigatti. 1969. A608
35 Chaussinand-Nogaret, G. Les financiers de Languedoc au XVIIIe siècle. 1970. A609
36 La Ronciere, C. de. Lippo di Fede del Sega. 1972. A610

AFRICA IN THE MODERN WORLD (Cornell Univ. Pr.)

Hess, R. L. Ethiopia. 1970. A611
LeVine, V. T. The Cameroon Federal Republic. 1971. A612
Leibenow, J. G. Liberia. 1969. A613
Thompson, V. West Africa's Council of the Entente. 1972. A614

AFRICAN HANDBOOKS (Univ. of Pa. Press)

1 Liebesny, H. J. The government of French North Africa. 1943. A615
2 Postel, A. W. The mineral resources of Africa. 1943. A616
3 Githens, T. S. and Wood, C. E. The food resources of Africa. 1943. A617
4 MacDougald, D. The languages and press of Africa. 1944. A618
5 Wieschoff, H. A. Colonial policies in Africa. 1944. A619
6 Noon, J. A. Labor problems of Africa. 1944. A620
7 Buell, R. L. Liberia. 1947. A621
8 Githens, T. S. Drug plants of Africa. 1949. A622

AFRIKA-STUDIEN (Springer)

1 Ahmad, N. Entwicklungsbanken und-gesellschaften in Tropisch-Afrika. 1964. A623
2 Ruthenberg, H. Agricultural development in Tanganyika. 1964. A624
3 Güsten, R. and Helmschrott, H. Volkswirtschaftliche Gesamtrechnung in Tropisch-Afrika. 1965. A625
4 Jürgens, H. S. Beiträge zur Binnenwanderung und Bevölkerung sentwicklung in Liberia. 1965. A626
5 Molnos, A. Die sozialwissenschaftliche Erforschung Ostafrikas, 1954-1963. 1965. A627
6 Rothermund, I. Die politische und wirtschaftliche Rolle der asiatischen minderheit in Ostafrika. 1965. A628
7 Fliedner, H. Die Bodenrechtsreform in Kenya. 1965. A629
8 Schnittger, L. Besteuerung und wirtschaftliche entwicklung in Ostafrika. 1966. A630
9 Güsten, R. Problems of economic growth and planning, tr. by Fruston. 1966. A631
10 Ruthenberg, H. African agricultural production development policy in Kenya, 1952-1965. 1966. A632
11 Rotenham, D. von. Bodennutzung und viehhaltung im Sukumalund, Tanzania. 1966. A633
12 Krauss, H. Die moderne bodengestzgebung in Kamerun, 1884-1964. 1966. A634
13 Pössinger, H. Sidal in Ostafrika. 1967. A635
14 Müller, J. O. Probleme der Auftrags-rinderhaltung durch Fulbe-hirten in Westafrika. 1967. A636
15 Paulus, M. Das genessenshaftswesen in Tanganyika und Uganda. 1967. A637
16 Neuhoff, H. O. Gabun. 1967. A638
17 Jensen, J. Kontinuität und Wandel in der arbeitsteilung bei den Baganda. 1967. A639
18 Kainzbauer, W. Der Handel in Tanzania. 1967. A640
19 Groeneveld, S. Probleme der landwirtschaftlichen entwicklung im Küstengebeit Ostafrikas. 1967. A641
20 Geis, H. G. Die geld-und banksysteme der staaten Westafrikas. 1967. A642
21 Heinze, G. W. Der verkehrssektor in der entwicklungspolitik . . . 1967. A643
22 Ludwig, H. D. Ukara. 1967. A644
23 Clement, W. Angewandte bildungsökonomik. 1967. A645
24 Smallholder farming and small holder development in Tanzania, ed. by Ruthenberg. 1968. A646
25 Attems, M. Bauernbetriebe in tropischen Höhenlangen Ostafrikas. 1967. A647
26 Molnos, A. Attitudes toward

family planning in East Africa. 1968. A648
27 Scheffer, W. Bauerliche produktion unter aufsicht am Beispiel des Tabakanbaus in Tanzania. 1968. A649
28 Jätzold, R. The Kilobero Valley (Tanzania). 1968. A650
29 Jürgens, H. W. Untersuchungen zur Binnenwanderung in Tanzania. 1968. A651
30 Güsten, R. Studies in the staple food economy of western Nigeria. 1968. A652
31 Pössinger. Landwirtschaftliche Entwicklung in Angola und Mocambique. 1968. A653
32 Hellen, J. A. Rural economic development in Zambia, 1890-1964. 1968. A654
33 Vasthoff, J. Small farm credit and development. 1968. A655
34 Schädler, K. Crafts, small-scale industries. 1968. A656
35 Pauw, E. J. Das Bankwesen in Ostafrika. 1969. A657
36 el-Shag, el-Shagi. Neuordnung der Bodennuntzung in Agypten. 1969. A658
37 Amann, H. Energy supply and economic development in East Africa. 1969. A659
38 Gagern, A. von. Die Africanischen Siedler im Projekt Urambo/Tanzania. 1969. A660
39 Golkowsky, R. Bewasserungslandwirtschaft in Kenya. 1969. A661
40 Hieber, H. Wirtschaftsstatistik in Entwicklungsländern. 1969. A662
41 Fischer, W. E. Die Entwicklungsbedingungen Ugandas. 1969. A663
42 Kraut, H. and Cremer, H. D., eds. Investigations into health and nutrition in East Africa. 1969. A664
43 Neuloh, O. Der ostafrikanische industriearbeiter zwischen Shamba and Maschine. 1969. A665
44 Mohr, B. Die Reiskultur in Westafrika. 1969. A666
45 Helmschrott, H. Struktur und Wachstum der Textil- und Bekleidungsindustrie in Ostafrika. 1969. A667
46 Klein, E. C. Sozialer Wandel in Kiteezi/Buganda. 1969. A668
47 Yaffey, M. J. H. Balance of payments problems of a developing country. 1970. A669
48 Bartja, R. Futterpfanzen in der Sahelzane Afrikas. 1970. A670
49 Heine, B. Status and use of African lingua francas. 1970. A671
50 Staewen, C. and Schönberg, F. Kulturwandel und Angstentwicklung bei den Yoruba und Westafrikas. 1970. A672
51 Zajadacz, P., ed. Studies in production and trade in East Africa. 1970. A673
52 Vente, R. E. Planning processes. 1970. A674
53 Financial aspects of development in East Africa, by Marlin and others. 1970. A675
54 Bald, D. Deutsch-Ostafrika, 1900-1914. 1970. A676
55 Sperber, K. W. von. Public administration in Tanzania. 1970. A677
56 Benda-Beckmann, F. von. Rechtspluralismus in Malawi. 1970. A678
57 Ahmad, N. Deficit financing, inflation and capital formation. 1970. A679
58 Blume, H. Organisational aspects of agro-industrial development agencies. 1971. A680
59 Bartha, R. Studien zu Fragen der Zebu-Rinderzucia in den Tropen. 1971. A681
60-62 Schiffers, H. Die Sahara und ihre Randgebiete. 3 v. 1971. A682
63 Bodenstedt, A. A. Staatlich geplante Productionsgenossenschaften. 1971. A683
64 Schultz, J. Agarlandsschaftliche Veränderungen in Tanzania. 1971. A684
65 Harlander, H. Development banking in Africa. 1971. A685
66 Roider, W. Farm settlements for socio-economic development. 1971. A686
67 Moller, T. Bergbau und regionale Entwicklung in Ostafrika.

1971. A687
68 Maguire, G. U. Uhuru. 1971. A688
69 Meek, M. Problems and prospects of social services in Kenya. 1971. A689
70 Bohnet, M. and Reichelt, H. Applied research and its impact on economic development. 1972. A690
71 Simonis, H. and U. E. Socioeconomic development in dual economies. 1971. A691
72 Haugwitz, H. W. von and Thorwart, H. Some experiences with smallholder settlement in Kenya 1963/64 to 1966/67. 1972. A692
73 Popovic, V. Tourism in Eastern Africa. 1972. A693
74 Gotz, E. Siedlerbetriebe im Bewasserungs-gebeit des Unteren Medjerdatales Tunesien. 1972. A694
75 Bernard, F. E. East of Mount Kenya. 1972. A695
76 Ansprenger, F. and others. Die politische Entwicklung Ghanas Von Nkrumah bis Busea. 1972. A696
77 Brandt, H. and others. The industrial town as factor of economic and social development. 1972. A697
78 Hofmeier, R. Transport and economic development in Tanzania. 1973. A698
79 Karsten, D. The economics of handicrafts in traditional societies. 1972. A699
80 Pausewang, S. Methods and concepts of social research in a rural developing society. 1973. A700

AFRICAN STUDIES SERIES (Cambridge)

1 La Fontaine, J. S. City politics. 1970. A701
2 Hill, P. Studies in rural capitalism in West Africa. 1970. A702
3 West, H. W. Land policy in Buganda. 1972. A703
4 Luckham, R. The Nigerian military. 1971. A704
5 Peil, M. The Ghanaian factory worker. 1972. A705
6 Wilson, F. Labour in the South African gold mines. 1972. A706
7 Post, K. W. K. and Jenkins, G. D. The price of liberty. 1973. A707
8 Richards, A. I. and others, eds. Subsistance to commercial farming in present day Buganda. 1973. A708
9 Dunn, J. and Robertson, A. F. Dependence and opportunity. 1973. A709
10 Grillo, R. D. African railwaymen. 1973. A710
11 Bravmann, R. A. Islam and tribal art in West Africa. 1974. A711
12 Cole, P. D. Modern and traditional elites in the politics of lagos. 1974. A712
13 Wilks, I. Asante in the nineteenth century. 1974. A713
14 Obiechina, E. Culture, tradition and society in the West African novel. 1974. A714

AFRICANA COLLECTANEA (Struick)

1 Bowker, J. M. Speeches, letters & selections from important papers of the late John Mitford Bowker. 1962. A715
2 Godlonton, R. and Irving, E. Narratives of the Kaffir War, 1850-1851-1852. 1962. A716
3 Holden, W. C. The past and future of the Kaffir races. 1963. A717
4 ____. History of the colony of Natal. 1963. A718
5 Molema, S. M. The Bantu. 1963. A719
6 Harris, W. C. The wild sports of Southern Africa. 1963. A720
7 Stow, G. W. The native races of Southern Africa. 1963. A721
8-9 Stockenstrom, A. Autobiography. 2 v. 1964. A722
10 Orpen, J. M. Reminiscences of life in South Africa from 1846 to the present day. 1964. A723
11 Godlonton, R. A narrative of the irruption of the Kaffir

Hordes. 1964. A724
12 Collins, W. W. Freestatia. 1965. A724a
13 Bryant, A. T. Olden times in Zululand and Natal. 1965. A725
14-15 Bird, J. The annals of Natal. 2 v. 1965. A726
16 Casalis, E. A. The Basutos. 1965. A727
17-18 Steedman, A. Wanderings and adventures in the interior of Southern Africa. 2 v. 1965. A728
19 Bird, W. State of the Cape of Good Hope in 1822. 1966. A729
20 Pringle, T. Narrative of a residence in South Africa. 1966. A730
21 Gardiner, A. F. Narrative of a journey to the Zoolu country in South Africa. 1966. A731
22-23 Alexander, J. E. An expedition of discovery into the interior of Africa. 2 v. 1967. A732
24 Andersson, K. L. Lake Ngami. 1967. A733
25 Chase, J. C. The Cape of Good Hope and the eastern province of Algoa Bay. 1967. A734
26 Baldwin, W. C. African hunting and adventure. 1967. A735
27 Arbusset, J. T. Narrative of an exploratory tour to the northeast of the colony of the Cape of Good Horn, tr. by Brown. 1968. A736
28 Bleek, W. H. I. and Lloyd, L. C., comps. Specimens of Bushman folklore. 1968. A737
29 Andersson, K. J. The Okavango River. 1968. A738
30 Chase, J. C. The Natal papers. 1968. A739
31 Andersson, C. J. Notes on travel in South Africa. 1968. A740
32-33 Voight, J. C. Fifty years of the history of the republic in South Africa. 1969. A741
34 Shaw, B. Memorials of South Africa. 1969. A742
35 Callaway, H. The religious system of the Amazulu in the Zulu language with translation into English and notes in four parts. 1970. A743
36 McKay, J. Reminiscences of the last Kafir war. 1970. A744
37 Tyler, J. Forty years among the Zulus. 1971. A745
38 Casalis, E. A. My life in Basutoland, tr. by Brierley. 1971. A746
39 Boyce, W. B. Notes on South African affairs. 1971. A747/8
40 Leyland, J. Adventures in the far interior of South Africa. 1972. A749
41 Bellaires, B. S. The Transvaal War, 1880-1881. 1972. A750
42 Nixon, J. The complete story of Transvall. 1972. A751
43 Farini, G. A. Through the Kalahari Desert. 1973. A752
44 Viljoen, B. J. My reminiscence of the Anglo-Boer war. 1973. A753
45 Theal, G. M. History of the Boers in South Africa. 1973. A754
46 Hensman, H. Cecil John Rhodes. 1974. A755
47 Campbell, J. Travels in South Africa. 1974. A756
48 Anderson, A. A. Twenty-five years in a wagon. 1974. A757

ALBERT SHAW LECTURES ON DIPLOMATIC HISTORY (Johns Hopkins Press)

1899 Latané, J. H. The diplomatic relations of the United States and Spanish America. 1900. A758
1900 Callahan, J. M. The diplomatic history of the Southern confederacy. 1901. A759
1906 Reeves, J. S. American diplomacy under Tyler and Polk. 1907. A760
1907 Benton, E. J. International law and diplomacy of the Spanish-American war. 1908. A761
1909 Adams, E. D. British interests and activities in Texas, 1838-1846. 1910. A762
1911 Paullin, C. O. Diplomatic negotiations of American

naval officers, 1778-1833. 1912. A763
1912 Cox, I. J. The West Florida controversy, 1798-1813. 1918. A764
1913 Manning, W. R. Early diplomatic relations between the United States and Mexico. 1916. A765
1914 Updyke, F. A. The diplomacy of the war of 1812. 1915. A766
1917 Treat, P. J. The diplomatic relations between the United States and Japan, 1853-1865. 1917. A767
1921 Martin, P. A. Latin America and the war. 1925. A768
1923 Wriston, H. M. Executive agents in American foreign relations. 1929. A769
1926 Bemis, S. F. Pinckney's treaty. 1926. A770
1927 Williams, B. State security and the League of nations. 1927. A771
1928 Rippy, J. F. Rivalry of the United States and Great Britain over Latin America, 1803-1830. 1929. A772
1930 Belaúnde, V. A. Bolivar and the political thought of the Spanish American Revolution. 1938. A773
1931 Tansill, C. C. The purchase of the Danish West Indies. 1932. A774
1932 Perkins, D. Monroe Doctrine, 1826-1867. 1937. A775
1933 Seymour, C. American diplomacy during the World War. 1934. A776
1935 Simonds, F. H. American foreign policy in post-war years. 1935. A777
1936 Pratt, J. W. Expansionists of 1898. 1936. A778
1937 Perkins, D. The Monroe doctrine, 1867-1907. 1937. A779
1938 Whitaker, A. P. The United States and the independence of Latin America, 1800-1830. 1941. A780
1939 Robertson, W. S. France and Latin-America independence. 1939. A781
1941 Bailey, T. A. The policy of the United States toward the neutrals. 1917-1918. 1942. A782
1942 Callcott, W. H. The Caribbean policy of the United States, 1890-1920. 1942. A783
1946 Graham, M. W. American diplomacy in the international community. 1948. A784
1950 Feis, H. The diplomacy of the dollar, first era, 1919-1932. 1950. A785
1951 Carr, E. H. German-Soviet relations between the two World Wars, 1919-1939. 1951. A786
1953 Beale, H. K. Theodore Roosevelt and the rise of America to world power. 1956. A787
1954 Beloff, M. Foreign policy and democratic process. 1955. A788
1956 Link, A. S. Wilson the diplomat. 1957. A789
1958 Craig, G. A. From Bismarck to Adenauer. 1958. A790
1961 Nicholas, H. G. Britain and the U. S. A. 1963. A791
1968 Divine, R. A. Roosevelt and World War II. 1969. A792

ALLGEMEINE GESCHICHTE IN EINZELDARSTELLUNGEN (Grote)

Hauptabt I:
1 Meyer, E. Geschichte des alten Ägyptens. 1887. A793
2 Hommel, F. Geschichte Babyloniens und Assyriens. 1885. A794
3 Lefmann, S. Geschichte des alten Indiens. 1890. A795
4 Justi, F. Geschichte des alten Persiens. 1879. A796
5 Pietschmann, R. Geschichte der Phönizier. 1889. A797
6 Hertzberg, G. F. Geschichte von Hellas und Rom. 2 v. 1883-84. A798
7 Stade, B. Geschichte des volkes Israel. 2 v. 1888-89. A799
Hauptabt II:
1 Hertzberg, G. F. Geschichte des römischen kaisserreiches. 1880. A800

2 Dahn, F. L. S. Urgeschichte der germanischen und romanischen volker. 4 v. 1881-89. A801
3 Winkelmann, E. Geschichte der Angelsachsen bis zum Tode könig Alfreds. 1883. A802
4 Müller, A. Der Islam im Morgen-und abendlund. 2 v. 1885-87. A803
5 Kugler, B. Geschichte der Kreuzzüge. 1891. A804
6 Prutz, H. Staatengeschichte des Abendlandes im mittelalter von Karl der Gr. bis auf Maximilian. 2 v. 1885-87. A805
7 Hertzberg, G. F. Geschichte der Byzantiner und des osmanischen reiches. 1883. A806
8 Geiger, L. Renaissance und humanismus in Italien und Deutschland. 1882. A807
9 Ruge, S. Geschichte des zeitalters der entdeckungen. 1881. A808
10 Schiemann, T. Russland, Polen und Livland bis ins 17. Jahrh. 2 v. 1886-87. A809

Hauptabt III:
1 Bezold, F. Geschichte der deutschen reformation. 1890. A810
2 Philippson, M. Westeuropa im zeitalter von Philipp II, Elisabeth und Heinrich IV. 1882. A811
3:1 Droysen, G. Geschichte der gegenreformation. 1893. A812
3:2 Winter, G. Geschichte des dreissigjahrigen krieges. 1893. A813
4 Stern, A. Geschichte der revolution in England. 1881. A814
5 Philippson, M. Das zeitalter Ludwigs dis Vierzehnten. 1890. A815
6 Brückner, A. Peter der Grosse. 1888. A816
7 Erdmannsdorffer, B. Deutsche geschichte vom Westfälischen frieden bis zum regierungsantritt Friedrichs des Grossen. 2 v. 1892-93. A817
8 Oncken, W. Das zeitalter Friedrichs des Grossen. 2 v. 1881-82. A818
9 Wolf, A. and Zwiedineck-Sudenhorst, H. von. Österreich unter Maria Theresia, Josef II, und Leopold II. 1884. A819
10 Brückner, A. Katharina II. 1883. A820
Namen-und sachregister. 1893. A821

Hauptabt IV:
1 Oncken, W. Das zeitalter der revolution. 2 v. 1884-86. A822
2 Flathe, T. Das zeitalter der restauration und revolution. 1883. A823
3 Bulle, C. Geschichte des kaisserreiches und des konigreiches Italien. 1890. A824
4 Hopp, E. O. Bundestaat und bundeskrieg in Nordamerika. 1886. A825
5 Bamberg, F. Geschichte der orientalischen angelengenheit im zeitraume des Pariser und der Berliner friedens. 1892. A826
6 Oncken, W. Das zeitalter des kaisers Wilhelm. 2 v. 1890-92. A827
Namen-und sachregister. 1892. A828

ALLGEMEINE STAATEN-GESCHICHTE DER EUROPAISCHEN STAATEN (Perthes)

Abt. I:
1 Pfister, J. C. von. Geschichte der Teutschen. 6 v. 1829-42. A829
2 Leo, H. Geschichte der italienischen staaten. 5 v. 1829-37. A830
3 Stenzel, G. Geschichte der preussischen staats. 5 v. 1830-54. A831
4 Böttiger, C. W. Geschichte der kurstaates und königsreiches Sachsen. 3 v. 1867-73. A832
5 Lembke, F. W. Geschichte von Spanien. 7 v. 1831-1902. A833
6 Wenzelburger, K. T. Geschichte der Niederlande. 2 v. 1879-1886. A834
Van Kampen, N. G. Geschichte der Niederlande. 2 v.

1831-33. A835
7 Strahl, P. Geschichte der russischen staates. 7 v. 1832-66. A836
8 Geijer, E. G. and others. Geschichte Schwedens. 7 v. 1832-1908. A837
9 Lappenberg, J. M. Geschichte von England. 10 v. 1834-98. A838
10 Mailáth, J. G. Geschichte des Östreich. 5 v. 1834-50. A839
11 Schäfer, H. Geschichte von Portugal. 5 v. 1836-54. A840
12 Schmidt, E. A. Geschichte von Frankreich. 4 v. 1835-48. A841
13 Dahlmann, F. C. Geschichte von Dännemark. 5 v. 1840-1902. A842
14 Wachsmuth, W. Geschichte Frankreichs in revolutions-zeitalter. 4 v. 1840-44. A843
15 Zinkeisen, J. W. Geschichte des osmanischen reiches in Europa. 7 v. 1840-63. A844
16 Roepell, R. and others. Geschichte Polens. 6 v. 1840-88. A845
17 Hertzberg, G. F. Geschichte Greichenlands. 4 v. 1876-79. A846
18 Reumont, A. von. Geschichte Toscana's seit dem ende des florentinischen freistaats. 2 v. 1876-77. A847
19 Hillebrand, K. Geschichte Frankreichs von der thronbesteigung Louis Phillip's bis zum falle Napoleon's III. 3 v. 1877-98. A848
20 Riezler, S. Geschichte Baierns. 8 v. 1878-1914. A849
21 Brosch, M. Geschichte der Kirchenstaates. 2 v. 1880-1882. A850
22 Reimann, E. Neuere geschichte des preussischen staates vom Hubertesburger frieden bis zum Wiener Kongress. 2 v. 1882-88. A851
23 Stälin, P. F. Geschichte Wurttembergs. 2 v. 1882-87. A852
24 Dahn, F. L. S. Deutsche geschichte. V. 1, 6. 1883-88. A853
25 Huber, A. Geschichte Österreichs. 6 v. 1885-1921. V. 6 by O. Redlich. A854
26 Dierauer, J. Geschichte der schweizenischen Eidgenossenschaft. 6 v. 1887-1931. A855
27 Kleinschmidt, A. Geschichte des Königsreichs Westfalen. 1893. A856
28 Schybergson, M. G. Geschichte Finnlands. 1896. A857
29 Bruckner, A. Geschichte Russlands bis zum Ende des 18. Jahr. 2 v. 1896-1913. A858
30 Pirenne, H. Geschichte Belgiens. 4 v. 1899-1913. A859
31 Bachmann, A. Geschichte Böh-mens. 2 v. 1899-1905. A860
32 Hartmann, L. M. Geschichte Italiens in Mittelalter. 6 v. 1897-1915. A861
33 Blok, P. J. Geschichte der Niederlande. 6 v. 1902-18. A862
34 Iorga, N. Geschichte des rumänischen volkes im rahmen seiner staatsbildungen. 2 v. 1905. A863
35 Kretschmayr, H. Geschichte von Venedig. 3 v. 1905-34. A864
36 Häbler, K. Geschichte Spaniens unter den Habsburgern. 1907. A865
37 Iorga, N. Geschichte des Osmanischen reiches. 5 v. 1908-13. A866
38 Jirecek, K. Geschichte der Serben. 2 v. 1911-18. A867
39 Zivier, E. Neuere geschichte Polens. 1915. A868
40 Bretholz, B. Neuere geschichte Böhmens. 1920. A869
41 Schybergson, M. G. Politische geschichte Finnlands. 1925. A870

Abt. II: Geschichte der ausser-europäischen staaten.

1. Nachod, O. Geschichte von Japan. 1906. A871
2 Friederici, G. Der charakter der entdeckung und eroberung Amerikas durch die Europäer. 3 v. 1925-36. A872
3 Rein, A. Der kampf Westeuropas um Nordamerika im

15. und 16. Jahr. 1925. A873
Abt. III: Deutsche Landesgeschichten.
1 Lohmeyer, K. Geschichte von Ost-und Westpreussen. 1908. A874
2 Grünhagen, C. Geschichte Schlesiens. 2 v. 1884-86. A875
3 Heinemann, O. von. Geschichte von Braunschweig und Hanover. 3 v. 1884-92. A876
4 Jacobs, E. Geschichte der in der preussischen Provinz Sachsen vereinigten gebiete. 1883. A877
5 Wehrmann, M. Geschichte von Pommern. 2 v. 1904-06. A878
6 Vancsa, M. Geschichte nied-erund oberosterreichs. 2 v. 1905-27. A879
7 Seraphim, E. Geschichte von Livland. 1906. A880
8 Kaindl, R. F. Geschichte der deutschen in den Karpathenländern. 3 v. 1907-11. A881
9 Widmann, H. Geschichte Salzburgs. 3 v. 1907-14. A882
10 Wohlwill, A. Neure geschichte der freien und hansestadt Hamburg. 1914. A883
11 Vitense, O. Geschichte von Mecklenburg. 1920. A884
12 Pirchegger, H. Geschichte der Steiermark. 1920. A885
13 Baasch, E. Geschichte Hamburgs. 2 v. 1924-25. A886

AMERICA IN CRISIS (Wiley)

Divine, R. A. The reluctant belligerent. 1965. A887
Goetzmann, W. When the eagle screamed. 1966. A888
La Feber, W. America, Russia, and the cold war, 1945-1966. 1972. A889
Morgan, H. W. America's road to empire. 1965. A890
Smith, D. M. The great departure. 1965. A891
Smith, G. American diplomacy during the second World War, 1941-1945. 1965. A892
Van Alstyńe, R. W. Empire and independence, 1965. A893
White, P. C. T. A nation on trial. 1965. A894

AMERICAN ACADEMY IN ROME. PAPERS AND MONOGRAPHS (Accademia Americana)

1 Peterson, R. M. The cults of Campania. 1919. A895
2 Taylor, L. R. Local cvlts in Etrvria. 1923. A896
3 Frank, T. Roman buildings of the repvblic. 1924. A897
4 Bryan, W. R. Italic hvt vrn cemeteries. . 1925. A898
5 Holland, L. A. The Faliscans in prehistoric times. 1925. A899
6 Polemten, S. Sicconis Polentoni Scriptorum illustrium latinae libri XVIII, ed. by Ullman. 1928. A900
7 Beatus, St. Beati in Apocalipsin libri duodecim, ed. by Sanders. 1930. A901
8 Rudolphus. Rudolfi Tortarii Carmina, ed. by Ogle and Schullian. 1933. A902
9 Saecvli noni avctoris in Boetii Consolationem philosophiae commentarivs, ed. by Silk. 1935. A903
10 Seneca, L. A. Epistolae Senecae ad Paulum et Pauli ad Senecam, ed. by Barlow. 1938. A904
11 Evans, E. C. The cults of the Sabine territory. 1939. A905
12 Martinus, St. Opera omnia, ed. by Barlow. 1950. A906
13 Kellehar, P. J. The holy cross of Hungary. 1951. A907
14 Shoe, P. J. Profiles of western Greek mouldings. 1952. A908
15 De proprietate sermonum vel rerum. De proprietate sermonum nel rerum, by Uhlfelder. 1954. A909
16 Lewis, M. W. (Hoffman). The official priests of Rome under the Julio-Claudians. 1955. A910
17 Sinnigen, W. G. The officium of the urban prefecture during the later Roman Empire. 1957. A911
18 Arnulfus Aurelianensis. Glosule super Lucanum, ed. by Marti. 1958. A912

19 Hammond, M. The Antonine monarchy. 1959. A913
20 Taylor, L. R. The voting districts of the Roman Republic. 1960. A914
21 Holland, L. A. Janus and the bridge. 1962. A915
22 Scott, R. T. Religion and philosophy in the Histories of Tacitus. 1968. A916
23 Frank, R. I. Scholae palatinae. 1969. A917
24 Forte, B. Rome and the Romans as the Greeks saw them. 1972. A918
25 Wright, J. Dancing in chains. 1974. A919

AMERICAN ACADEMY OF POLITICAL AND SOCIAL SCIENCE, PHILADELPHIA. MONOGRAPH

1 Charlesworth, J. C., ed. The limits of behavioralism in political science. 1962. A920
2 ____. Mathematics and the social sciences. 1963. A921
3 Sweeney, S. B., ed. Achieving excellence in public service. 1963. A922
4 Charlesworth, J. C. Leisure in America. 1964. A923
5 Martindale, D. A., ed. Functionalism in the social sciences. 1965. A924
6 Charlesworth, J. C. A design for political science. 1966. A925
7 Governing urban society, ed. by Sweeney and Charlesworth, 1967. A926
8 Theory and practice of public administration, ed. by Charlesworth. 1968. A927
9 Bierstedt, R., ed. A design for sociology. 1969. A928
10 Palmer, N. D. Design for international relations research. 1970. A929
11 Charlesworth, J. C. Harmonizing technological developments and social policy in America. 1970. A930
12 Riggs, F. W. International studies. 1971. A931
13 Simpson, S. Instruction in diplomacy. 1972. A932
14 Integration of the social sciences through policy analysis, ed. by Charlesworth. 1972. A933
15 Public service professional associations and the public interest, ed. by Bowen. 1973. A934
16 Educating urban administration, ed. by Cleaveland. 1973. A935
17 Lambert, R. D. Language and area studies review. 1973. A936

AMERICAN ACCOUNTING ASSOCIATION MONOGRAPHS
(Foundation Pr.)

1 Mason, P. E. Principles of public-utility depreciation. 1937. A937
2 Daniels, M. B. Financial statements. 1939. A938
3 Paton, W. A. and Littleton, A. C. An introduction to corporate accounting standards. 1940. A939
4 Moonitz, M. The entity theory of consolidated statements. 1944. A940
5 Littleton, A. C. Structure of accounting theory. 1953. A941
6 Mason, P. E. Price-level changes and financial statements, basic concepts and methods. 1956. A942

AMERICAN ANTHROPOLOGICAL ASSOCIATION. MEMOIRS
(Amer. Anthropological Assn. unless otherwise noted)

1:1 Fishberg, M. Materials for the physical anthropology of the eastern European Jews. 1905. A943
1:2 Lewis, A. B. Tribes of the Columbia valley and the coast of Washington and Oregon. 1906. A944
1:3 Laufer, B. Historical jottings on amber in Asia. 1907. A945
1:4 Nichols, J. B. The numerical proportions of the sexes at birth. 1907. A946
1:5 Pittier, H. F. Ethnographic and linguistic notes on the

Paez Indians of Tierra Adentro, Cauca, Columbia. 1907. A947
1:6 Mooney, J. The Cheyenne Indians. 1907. A948
Petter, G. H. Sketch of the Cheyenne grammar. 1907. A949
2:1 Churchill, W. Weather words of Polynesia. 1907. A950
2:2 Speck, F. G. The Creek Indians of Taskigi town. 1907. A951
2:3 Spinden, H. J. The Nez Percé Indians. 1908. A952
2:4 Pepper, G. H. An Hidatsa shrine and the beliefs respecting it. 1908. A953
2:5 Chamberlain, R. V. The ethnobotany of the Gosiute Indians of Utah. 1911. A954
2:6 Kidder, A. V. Pottery of the Pajarito plateau and of some adjacent regions in New Mexico. 1915. A955
3:1 Haeberlin, H. K. The idea of fertilization in the culture of the Pueblo Indians. 1916. A956
3:2 Ferris, H. B. The Indians of Cuzco and the Apurimac. 1916. A957
3:3 Hatt, G. Moccasins and their relation to Arctic footwear. 1916. A958
3:4 Thurnwald, R. Bánaro society. 1916. A959
4:1 Hartland, E. S. Matrilineal kinship and the question of its priority. 1917. A960
4:2 Laufer, B. The reindeer and its domestication. 1917. A961
4:3-4 Parsons, E. W. (Clews). Notes on Zuñi. 2 v. 1917. A962
5:1 Prudden, T. M. A further study of the prehistoric small house ruins in the San Juan watershed. 1918. A963
5:2 An early account of the Choctaw Indians by Swanton. 1918. A964
5:3 Rippen, B. van. Notes on some Bushman implements. 1918. A965
5:4 Colton, M. R. F. and H. S. The little-known small house ruins in the Coconino Forest. 1918. A966
6:1 Speck, F. G. The function of wampum among the Eastern Algonkian. 1919. A967
6:2 Hatt, G. Notes on reindeer nomadism. 1919. A968
6:3 Dumarest, N. Notes on Cochiti New Mexico. 1919. A969
6:4 Speck, F. G. Penobscot Shamanism. 1919. A970
29 Benedict, R. F. The concept of the guardian spirit in North America. 1923. A971
30 Loeb, E. M. The blood sacrifice complex. 1923. A972
31 Parsons, E. W. (Clews). The scalp ceremonial of Zuñi. 1924. A973
32 Crow-wing. A Pueblo Indian journal, ed. by Parsons. 1925. A974
33 Goldfrank, E. S. The social and ceremonial organization of Cochiti. 1927. A975
34 Morss, N. Archaeological explorations on the middle Chinlee. 1927. A976
35 Gower, C. D. The northern and southern affiliations of Antillean culture. 1927. A977
36 Parsons, E. W. (Clews). The social organization of the Tewa of New Mexico. 1929. A978
37 Liang, S. Y. New stone age pottery from the prehistoric site at Hsi-vin-Tsun, Shansi, China. 1930. A979
38 White, L. A. The pueblo of San Felipe. 1932. A980
39 Parsons, E. W. (Clews). Hopi and Zuñi ceremonialism. 1933. A981
40 Lattimore, O. The Gold tribe "Fishskin Tartars" of the lower Sungari. 1933. A982
41 Herskovits, M. J. and F. S. An outline of Dahomean religious belief. 1933. A983
42 Kroeber, A. L. Walapai ethnography. 1935. A984
43 White, L. A. The Pueblo of Santo Domingo, New Mexico. 1935. A985
44 Beaglehole, E. and P. Hopi of the second mesa. 1935. A986
45 Aginsky, B. W. Kinship systems and the forms of marriage. 1935. A987
46 Chona. Papago woman. The

autobiography of a Papago woman, ed. by Underhill. 1936. A988
47 Berreman, J. V. Tribal distribution in Oregon. 1937. A989
48 Turney-High, H. H. The Flathead Indians of Montana. 1937. A990
49 Jenks, A. E. Minnesota's Browns Valley man and associated burial artifacts. 1937. A991
50 Wyman, L. C. and Kluckhohn, C. Navaho classification of their song ceremonials. 1938. A992
51 Mera, H. P. Reconnaissance and excavations in southeastern New Mexico. 1938. A993
52 Opler, M. E. Dirty boy. 1938. A994
53 Kluckhohn, C. and Wyman, L. C. An introduction to Navaho chant practice. 1940. A995
54 Hoebel, E. A. The political organization and by-laws of the Comanche Indians. 1940. A996
55 Siegel, M. The Mackenzie collection: a study of West African carved gambling chips. 1940. A997
56 Turney-High, H. H. The ethnography of the Kutenai. 1941. A998
57 Parsons, E. W. (Clews). Notes on the Caddo. 1941. A999
58 Wagley, C. Economics of a Guatemalan village. 1941. A1000
59 Embree, J. F. Acculturation among the Japanese of Kona, Hawaii. 1941. A1001
60 White, L. A. The Pueblo of Santa Ana, New Mexico. 1942. A1002
61 Franz Boas by Kroeber and others. 1943. A1003
62 Lessa, W. A. An appraisal of constitutional typologies. 1943. A1004
63 Bascom, W. R. The sociological role of the Yoruba cult-group. 1944. A1005
64 Hawthorn, H. D. The Maori. 1944. A1006
65 Barton, R. F. The religion of the Ifugaos. 1945. A1007
66 Siegel, B. J. Slavery during the Third Dynasty of Ur. 1947. A1008
67 Patai, R. On cultural contact and its working modern Palestine. 1947. A1009
68 LaBarre, W. The Aymara Indians of the Lake Titicaca Plateau, Bolivia. ed. by Mason and Donath. 1948. A1010
69 Taylor, W. W. A study of archeology. 1948. A1011
70 Aberle, S. B. de. The Pueblo Indians of New Mexico. 1948. A1012
71 Wagley, C. The social and religious life of a Guatemalan village. 1949. A1013
72 Barnouw, V. Acculturation and personality among the Wisconsin Chippewa, 1950. A1014
73 Watson, J. B. Cayuá culture change. 1952. A1015
74 Hall, R. A. and others. Haitian Creole: grammar, texts, vocabulary. 1953. A1016
75 Wright, A. F., ed. Studies in Chinese thought. Univ. of Chicago. 1953. A1017
76 Von Grunebaum, G. E., ed. Studies in Islamic cultural history. 1954. A1018
77 Spicer, E. H. Potam. 1954. A1019
78 Leacock, E. The Montagnais hunting territory and the fur trade. 1954. A1020
79 Hoijer, H., ed. Language in culture. 1954. A1021
80 Belshaw, C. S. In search of wealth. 1955. A1022
81 Von Grunebaum, G. E., ed. Islam. 1955. A1023
82 Wheat, J. B. Mongollon culture prior to A. D. 1000. 1955. A1024
83 Marriott, M., ed. Village India. 1955. A1025
84 Hencken, H. Indo-European language and archeology. 1955. A1026
85 Salz, B. R. The human element in industrialization. 1955. A1027
86 Spuhler, J. N., ed. Natural selection in man. Wayne Univ. 1958. A1028

87 Nash, M. Machine age Maya. 1958. A1029
88 Caldwell, J. R. Trend and tradition in the prehistory of the eastern United States. 1958. A1030
89 Goldschmidt, W. R., ed. The anthropology of Franz Boas. 1959. A1031
90 Ezell, P. H. The Hispanic acculturation of the Gila River Pimas. 1961. A1032
91 Spindler, L. S. Menomini women culture change. 1962. A1033
92 Hickerson, H. The Southwestern Chippewa. 1962. A1034
93 Gearing, F. Priests and warriors. 1962. A1035
94 Mandelbaum, D. G. and others, eds. The teaching of anthropology. 1963. A1036
95 ____. Resources for the teaching of anthropology. 1963. A1037
96 Shepardson, M. T. Navajo ways in government. 1963. A1038

AMERICAN ASSOCIATION FOR THE ADVANCEMENT OF SCIENCE PUBLICATIONS

1 American Assn. for the Advancement of Science. The protection by patents of scientific discoveries, by Rossman and others. 1934. A1039
2 Hill, A. V. and others. Physical and chemical changes in nerve during activity. 1934. A1040
3 Silcox, F. A. and others. The scientific aspects of flood control. 1936. A1041
4 American Assn. for the Advancement of Science. Some fundamental aspects of the cancer problem, ed. by Ward. 1937. A1042
5 ____. Tuberculosis and leprosy, ed. by Moulton. 1938. A1043
6 ____. Syphilis, ed. by Moulton. 1938. A1044
7 ____. Recent advances in surface chemistry and chemical physics, ed. by Moulton. 1939. A1045
8 ____. The migration and conservation of salmon, ed. by Moulton, 1939. A1046
9 Mental health, ed. by Moulton. 1939. A1047
10 Symposium on Problems of Lake Biology. Problems of lake biology, ed. by Moulton. 1939. A1048
11 American Assn. for the Advancement of Science. The gonococcus and gonococcal infection, ed. by Moulton. 1939. A1049
12 ____. The genetics of pathogenic organisms, ed. by Moulton. 1940. A1050
13 ____. Blood, heart and circulation, ed. by Moulton. 1940. A1051
14 ____. The cell and protoplasm, ed. by Moulton. 1940. A1052
15 ____. A symposium on human malaria, ed. by Moulton. 1941. A1053
16 ____. Liebig and after Liebig, ed. by Moulton. 1942. A1054
17 ____. Aerobiology, ed. by Moulton. 1942. A1055
18 ____. A symposium on relapsing fever in the Americas, ed. by Moulton. 1942. A1056
19 ____. Fluorine and dental health, ed. by Moulton. 1942. A1057
20 ____. Laboratory procedures in studies of the chemical control of insects, ed. by Moulton. 1943. A1058
21 ____. Surface chemistry, ed. by Moulton. 1943. A1059
22 U. S. Nat'l. Cancer Institute. A symposium on mammary tumors in mice, ed. by Moulton. 1945. A1060
23 American Assn. for the Advancement of Science. Mammary tumors in mice. 1945. A1061
24 ____. Cancer. 1945. A1062
25 ____. Dental caries and fluorine. 1946. A1063
26 ____. Approaches to tumor chemotherapy, ed. by Moulton. 1947. A1064
27 ____. Rickettsial diseases

70 Butcher, E. O. and Sognnaes, R. F., eds. Fundamentals of keratinizotion. 1962. A1107
71 Symposium on the Great Lakes Basin. Great Lakes Basin, ed. by Pincus. 1962. A1108
72 Bishop, D. W., ed. Spermatozoan motility. 1962. A1109
73 Thorne, W., ed. Land and water use. 1963. A1110
74 American Assn. for the Advancement of Science. Aridity and man, ed. by Hodge. 1963. A1111
75 Sognnaes, R. F., ed. by Mechanisms of hard tissue destruction. 1963. A1112
76 Moseman, A. H., ed. Agricultural sciences for the developing nations. 1964. A1113
77 Irving, G. W. and Hoover, S. R. Food quality. 1965. A1114
78 Leeds, A. and Vayda, A. P., eds. Man, culture and animals. 1965. A1115
79 Livermore, A. H., ed. Science in Japan. 1965. A1116
80 American Assn. for the Advancement of Science. Air conservation. 1965. A1117
81 Kreshover, S. J. and McClure, F. J., eds. Environmental variables in oral disease. 1966. A1118
82 Eyring, H., ed. Civil defense. 1966. A1119
83 Conference on Estuaries. Estuaries, ed. by Lauff. 1967. A1120
84 Molecular mechanisms of temperature adaptation. 1967. A1121
85 American Assn. for the Advancement of Science. Agriculture and the quality of our environment, ed. by Brady. 1967. A1122
86 Symposium on Ground Level Climatology. Ground level climatology, ed. by Shaw. 1967. A1123
87 Gordon Research Conf. on Formulation of Research Policies. Formulation of research policies, ed. by Bass and Old. 1967. A1124
88 Lomax, A. Folk song style and culture, ed. by Erikson. 1968. A1125
89 Biology of the mouth, ed. by Person. 1968. A1126
90 International Conference on Arid Lands in a Changing World. Arid lands in transition, ed. by Dregne, 1970. A1127
91 Abelson, P. H., ed. Lunar sample analysis. 1970. A1128
92 Research for the world food crisis, ed. by Aldrich. 1970. A1129
93 Antarctic Research Symposium. Research in the Antarctic, ed. by Quam. 1971. A1130

AMERICAN ASSOCIATION OF PETROLEUM GEOLOGISTS. MEMOIRS

1 Ham, W. E., ed. Classification of carbonate rocks. 1962. A1131
2 Childs, O. E. and Beebe, B. W. Backbone of the Americas. 1963. A1132
3 Andel, T. H. van and Shor, G. G., eds. Marine geology of the Gulf of California. 1964. A1133
4 Southwestern Federation of Geological Societies. Fluids in subsurface environments, ed. by Young and Galley. 1965. A1134
5 Source book for petroleum geology, comp. by Dott and others. 1969. A1135
7 Dennis, J. G. International tectonic dictionary. 1967. A1136
8 American Assn. of Petroleum Geologists. Diaperism and diapers, ed. by Braustein and O'Brien. 1968. A1137
9 Beebe, B. W. and Curtis, B. F. Natural gases of North America. V. 1. 1968. A1138
10 Galley, J. E. Subsurface disposal in geologic basins. 1968. A1139
11 Logan, B. W. and others. Carbonate sediments and reefs, Yucatan shelf, Mexico.

1969. A1140
12 International Conference on Stratigraphy and Structure Bearing on the Origin of the North Atlantic Ocean. North Atlantic, ed. by Kay. 1969. A1141
13 Carbonate sedimentation and environment, ed. by Logan and others. 1970. A1142
14 Geology of giant petroleum fields, ed. by Halbouty. 1970. A1143
15 Future petroleum provinces of the United States, ed. by Cram. 2 v. 1971. A1144
16 King, R. E. Stratigraphic and gas fields, ed. by King. 1972. A1145
17 Emery, K. O. and Uchupi, E. Western North Atlantic ocean. 1972. A1146
18 Symposium on Underground Waste Management and Environmental Implications. Underground waste management and environmental implications, ed. by Cook. 1972. A1147
19 International Symposium on Arctic Geology. Arctic geology, ed. by Pitcher. 1973. A1148
20 Black Sea, ed. by Degens and Ross. 1974. A1149

AMERICAN ASSOCIATION OF SCHOOL ADMINISTRATORS. YEARBOOK

1 American Assn. of School Administrators. The status of the superintendent, ed. by Chadsey. 1923. A1150
2 ____. The elementary school curriculum, ed. by Jones. 1924. A1151
3 ____. Research in construction of the elementary school curriculum, ed. by Broome. 1925. A1152
4 ____. The nation at work on the public school curriculum, ed. by Broome. 1926. A1153
5 ____. The junior high school curriculum, ed. by Broome. 1927. A1154
6 ____. The development of the high school curriculum. 1928. A1155
7 ____. The articulation of the units of American education, ed. by West. 1929. A1156
8 ____. The superintendent surveys supervision, ed. by Cook. 1930. A1157
9 ____. Five unifying factors in American education, ed. by West. 1931. A1158
10 ____. Character education, ed. by Treikeld. 1932. A1159
11 ____. Education leadership, ed. by Stoddard. 1933. A1160
12 ____. Critical problems in school administration, ed. by Graham. 1934. A1161
13 ____. Social change, ed. by Studebaker. 1935. A1162
14 ____. The social studies curriculum, ed. by Glenn. 1936. A1163
15 ____. The improvement of education, ed. by Pickell. 1937. A1164
16 ____. Youth education today, ed. by Oberholtzer. 1938. A1165
17 ____. Schools in small communities, ed. by Corning. 1939. A1166
18 ____. Safety education, ed. by Hill. 1940. A1167
19 ____. Education for family life, ed. by Jacobsen. 1941. A1168
20 ____. Health in schools, ed. by Parker. 1942. A1169
21 ____. Schools and manpower. 1943. A1170
22 ____. Morale for a free world, ed. by Reed. 1944. A1171
23 ____. Paths to better schools, ed. by Goslin. 1945. A1172
24 ____. School boards in action, ed. by Carmichael. 1946. A1173
25 ____. Schools for a free world, ed. by Courter. 1947. A1174
26 ____. The expanding role of education, ed. by Hunt. 1948. A1175
27 ____. American school buildings, ed. by White. 1949. A1176
28 ____. Public relations for American schools, ed. by

Misner. 1950. A1177
29 ____. Conservation education in America's schools, ed. by Oberholtzer. 1951. A1178
30 ____. The American school superintendency, ed. by Rogers. 1952. A1179
31 ____. American school curriculum, ed. by Derthick. 1953. A1180
32 ____. Educating for American citizenship, ed. by Willis. 1955. A1181
33 ____. Staff relations in school administration, ed. by Willett. 1956. A1182
34 ____. School board superintendent relationships. 1956. A1183
35 ____. The superintendent as instructional leader, ed. by Trillingham. 1957. A1184
36 ____. The high school in a changing world, ed. by Fischer. 1958. A1185
37 ____. Educational administration in a changing community, ed. by Raubinger. 1959. A1186
38 ____. Professional administrators for America's schools, ed. by Moore. 1960. A1187
Publication suspended.

AMERICAN AUTHORS AND CRITICS SERIES (Barnes & Noble)

1 Walser, R. G. Thomas Wolfe. 1961. A1188
2 Turner, A. Nathaniel Hawthorne. 1961. A1189
3 Baldanza, F. Mark Twain. 1961. A1190
4 Pickard, J. B. John Greenleaf Whittier. 1962. A1191
5 Hochfield, G. Henry Adams. 1962. A1192
6 Walker, W. S. James Fenimore Cooper. 1962. A1193
7 Hazo, S. J. Hart Crane. 1963. A1194
8 Fonterose, J. John Steinbeck. 1964. A1195
10 Thompson, L. William Faulkner. 1967. A1196
Anderson, D. D. Sherwood Anderson. 1967. A1197
Baker, S. W. Ernest Hemingway. 1967. A1198
Hindus, M., ed. F. Scott Fitzgerald. 1968. A1199
McAleer, J. J. Theodore Dreiser. 1968. A1200
Pickard, J. B. Emily Dickinson. 1967. A1201
Powers, L. H. Henry James. 1970. A1202

AMERICAN CATHOLIC HISTORICAL ASSOCIATION. DOCUMENTS.

1 Stock, F. L. ed. United States ministers to the Papal states. 1933. A1203
2 ____ ed. Consular relations between the United States and the Papal states. 1945. A1204

AMERICAN CATHOLIC HISTORICAL ASSOCIATION. PAPERS (Kenedy)

1 Church historians, ed. by Guilday. 1926. A1205
2 The Catholic church in contemporary Europe, 1919-31, ed. by Guilday. 1932. A1206
3 The Catholic philosophy of history, ed. by Guilday. 1936. A1207

AMERICAN CATHOLIC PHILOSOPHICAL ASSOCIATION. PHILOSOPHICAL STUDIES.

Clark, J. T. Conventional logic and modern logic. Woodstock. 1952. A1208
McWilliams, J. A. Physics and philosophy. Amer. Catholic Philosophical Assn. 1945. A1209
Obering, W. F. The philosophy of law of James Wilson. Catholic Univ. Pr. 1938. A1210

AMERICAN CHEMICAL SOCIETY. MONOGRAPH SERIES (Reinhold)

1 Falk, K. G. The chemistry of enzyme action. 1924. A1211
2 Lind, S. C. The chemical effects of alpha particles

and electrons. 1928. A1212
3 Whitmore, F. C. Organic compounds of mercury. 1921. A1213
4 Taylor, H. S. Industrial hydrogen. 1921. A1214
5 Venable, F. P. Zirconium and its compounds. 1922. A1215
6 Sherman, H. C. and Smith, S. L. The vitamins. 1931. A1216
7 Kraus, C. A. The properties of electrical conducting system. 1922. A1217
8 Foote, P. D. and Mohler, F. L. The origin of spectra. 1922. A1218
9 Palmer, L. S. Carotinoids and related pigments. 1922. A1219
10 Tuttle, J. B. The analysis of rubber. 1922. A1220
11 Alexander, J. Glue and gelatin. 1923. A1221
12 Wilson, J. A. The chemistry of leather manufacture. 2 v. 1928-29. A1222
13 Hawley, L. F. Wood distillation. 1923. A1223
14 Lewis, G. N. Valence and the structure of atoms and molecules. 1923. A1224
15 Raiziss, G. W. and Gavron, J. L. Organic arsenical compounds. 1923. A1225
16 Svedberg, T. Colloid chemistry. 1928. A1226
17 Hildebrand, J. H. Solubility. 1924. A1227
____. Solubility of non-electrolytes. 1936. A1228
____ and Scott, R. L. The solubility of non-electrolytes. 3d ed. 1950. A1229
18 Porter, H. C. Coal carbonization. 1924. A1230
19 Wyckoff, R. W. G. The structure of crystals. 1931. A1231
20 Burrell, G. A. The recovery of gasoline from natural gas. 1925. A1232
21 Wells, H. G. The chemical aspects of immunity. 1929. A1233
22 Gillett, H. W. and Mack, E. L. Molybdenum, cerium and related alloy steels. 1925. A1234
23 Armsby, H. P. and Moulton, C. R. The animal as a converter of matter and energy. 1925. A1235
24 Christiansen, W. G. Organic derivatives of antimony. 1925. A1236
25 McKee, R. H. and others. Shale oil. 1925. A1237
26 Bailey, C. H. The chemistry of wheat flour. 1925. A1238
27 Lecomte du Noüy, P. Surface equilibria of biological and organic colloids. 1926. A1239
28 Hawley, F. L. and Wise, L. E. The chemistry of wood. 1926. A1240
29 Spoehr, H. A. Photosynthesis. 1926. A1241
30 Sutermeister, E. Casein and its industrial applications. 1927. A1242
____ and Browne, F. L. Casein and its industrial applications. 1939. A1243
31 Blasdale, W. C. Equilibria in saturated salt solutions. 1927. A1244
32 Tolman, R. C. Statistical mechanics with applications to physics and chemistry. 1927. A1245
33 Thornton, W. M. Titanium. 1927. A1246
34 Waggaman, W. H. Phosphoric acid, phosphates and phosphatic fertilizers. 1952. A1247
35 Henderson, Y. and Haggard, H. W. Noxious gases and the principles of respiration affecting their action. 1943. A1248
36 Laury, N. A. Hydrochloric acid and sodium sulfate. 1927. A1249
37 Sosman, R. B. The properties of silica. 1927. A1250
38 Buswell, A. M. The chemistry of water and sewage treatment. 1928. A1251
39 Rice, F. O. The mechanism of homogeneous organic reactions. 1928. A1252
40 Rawdon, H. S. Protective metallic coatings. 1928. A1253
41 Fundamentals of dairy science, by Rogers and others.

1935. A1254
42 White, W. P. The modern calorimeter. 1928. A1255
43 Kistiakowsky, G. B. Photochemical processes. 1928. A1256
44 Lawrie, J. W. Glycerol and the glycols. 1928. A1257
45 Porter, C. W. Molecular rearrangements. 1928. A1258
46 Vail, J. G. Soluble silicates in industry. 1928. A1259
47 Kendall, E. C. Thyroxine. 1929. A1260
48 Mitchell, H. H. and Hamilton, T. S. The biochemistry of the amino acids. 1929. A1261
49 Teeple, J. E. The industrial development of Searles Lake brines. 1929. A1262
50 Hurd, C. D. The pyrolysis of carbon compounds. 1929. A1263
51 Mantell, C. L. Tin. 1949. A1264
52 Calvert, R. P. Diatomaceous earth. 1930. A1265
53 Corse, W. M. Bearing metals and bearings. 1930. A1266
54 Chittenden, R. H. The development of physiological chemistry in the United States. 1930. A1267
55 Smyth, C. P. Dielectric constants and molecular structure. 1931. A1268
56 Levene, P. A. T. and Bass, L. W. Nucleic acids. 1931. A1269
57 Kassell, L. S. The kinetics of homogeneous gas reactions. 1932. A1270
58 Jamieson, G. S. Vegetable fats and oils. 1943. A1271
59 Curtis, H. A. Fixed nitrogen. 1932. A1272
60 Parks, G. S., and Huffman, H. M. The free energies of some organic compounds. 1932. A1273
61 Marek, F. F. and Hahn, D. A. The catalytic oxidation of organic compounds in the vapor phase. 1932. A1274
62 Laurens, H. The physiological effects of radiant energy. 1933. A1275
63 Kalichevsky, V. A. and Stagner, B. A. Chemical refining of petroleum. 1942. A1276
64 Von Oettingen, W. F. The therapeutic agents of the quinoline group. 1933. A1277
65 Hou, T. P. Manufacture of soda. 1942. A1278
66 Abramson, H. A. Electrokinetic phenomena and their application to biology and medicine. 1934. A1279
67 Gregg, J. L. Arsenical and argentiferous copper. 1934. A1280
68 Franklin, E. C. The nitrogen system of compounds. 1935. A1281
69 Fairlie, A. M. Sulfuric acid manufacture. 1936. A1282
70 Fieser, L. F. The chemistry of natural products related to phenanthrene. 1936. A1283
____ and M. Natural products related to phenanthrene. 1949. A1284
71 McKay, R. J. and Worthington, R. Corrosion resistance of metals and alloys. 1936. A1285
72 Quinn, E. L. and Jones, C. L. Carbon dioxide. 1936. A1286
73 Egloff, G. The reaction of pure hydrocarbons. 1937. A1287
74 Davis, C. C. and Blake, J. T. eds. The chemistry and technology of rubber. 1937. A1288
75 Burk, R. E. and others. Polymerization. 1937. A1289
76 Kalichevsky, V. A. Modern methods of refining lubricating oils. 1938. A1290
77 Morey, G. W. The properties of glass. 1938. A1291
78 Egloff, G. Physical constants of hydrocarbons. 5 v. 1939-53. A1292
79 Burns, R. M. and Schuh, A. E. Protective coatings for metals. 1939. A1293
80 Hibben, T. H. The raman effect and its chemical applications. 1939. A1294
81 Dorsey, N. E. Properties of ordinary water-substance in all its phases. 1940. A1295

82 Shohl, A. T. Mineral metabolism. 1939. A1296
83 Burton, E. F. and others. Phenomena at the temperature of liquid helium. 1940. A1297
84 Patterson, A. M. and Capell, L. T. The ring index. 1940. A1298
85 Blum, H. F. Photodynamic action and disease caused by light. 1941. A1299
86 Noyes, W. A. and Leighton, P. A. The photochemistry of gases. 1941. A1300
87 Thomas, C. A. Anhydrous aluminum chloride in organic chemistry. 1941. A1301
88 Egloff, G. and others. Isomerization of pure hydrocarbons. 1942. A1302
89 Mayer, F. and Cook, A. H. The chemistry of natural coloring matters. 1943. A1303
90 Cohn, E. J. and Edsall, J. T. Proteins, amino acids and peptides. 1943. A1304
91 Turrentine, J. Potash in North America. 1943. A1305
92 Post, H. W. The chemistry of the aliphatic orthoesters. 1943. A1306
93 Bloor, W. R. Biochemistry of the fatty acids and their compounds, the lipids. 1946. A1307
94 Li, K. C. and Wang, C. Tungsten. 1947. A1308
95 Harned, H. S. and Owen, B. B. The physical chemistry of electrolytic solution. 1958. A1309
96 Bailey, C. H. The constituents of wheat and wheat products. 1951. A1310
97 Wise, L. E. and Jahn, E. C. Wood chemistry. 2 v. 1952. A1311
98 Walker, J. Formaldehyde. 1944. A1312
99 Nieuwland, J. A. and Vogt, R. R. The chemistry of acetylene. 1945. A1313
100 Mantell, C. L. and Hardy, C. Calcium metallurgy and technology. 1949. A1314
101 McLaughlin, G. D. and Theis, E. R. The chemistry of leather manufacture. 1945. A1315
102 Steacie, E. W. R. Atomic and free radical reactions. 1954. A1316
103 Elliott, S. B. The alkaline-earth and heavy-metal soaps. 1946. A1317
104 Little, R. W., ed. Flameproofing of textile fabrics. 1947. A1318
105 Migrdichian, V. The chemistry of organic cyanogen compounds. 1947. A1319
106 Northey, E. H. The sulfonamides and allied compounds. 1948. A1320
107 Egloff, G. and Hulla, G. Alkylation of alkanes. V. 1. 1948. A1321
108 Young, R. S. Cobalt. 1948. A1322
109 Kelley, W. P. Cation exchange in soils. 1948. A1323
110 The Biochemistry of B vitamins by Williams and others. 1950. A1324
111 Kelley, W. P. Alkali soils. 1951. A1325
112 Wittcoff, H. The phosphatides. 1951. A1326
113 Zuidema, H. H. The performance of lubricating oils. 1952. A1327
114 Curme, G. O. and Johnston, F. eds. Gycols. 1952. A1328
115 Boundy, R. H. and others, eds. Styrene. 1952. A1329
116 Vail, J. G. and others. Soluble silicates. 2 v. 1952. A1330
117 Miner, C. S. and Dalton, N. N. eds. Glycerol. 1953. A1331
118 Rudolfs, W., ed. Industrial wastes. 1953. A1332
119 Dunlop, A. P. and Peters, F. N. The furans. 1953. A1333
120 Walker, J. F. Formaldehyde. 1956. A1334
121 Rossini, F. D. and others. Hydrocarbons from petroleum. 1953. A1335
122 Butts, A. ed. Copper. 1954. A1336
123 Eckey, E. W. Vegetable fats and oils. 1954. A1337
124 Morey, G. W. The properties of glass. 1954. A1338

125 Steacie, E. W. R. Atomic and free radical reactions. 2 v. 1954. A1339
126 Bear, F. E., ed. Chemistry of the soil. 1955. A1340
127 Lubs, H. A., ed. The chemistry of synthetic dyes and pigments. 1955. A1341
128 Schumb, W. C. and others. Hydrogen peroxide. 1955. A1342
129 Burns, R. M. Protective coating for metals. 1955. A1343
130 Li, K. C., and Wang, C. Tungsten. 1955. A1344
131 Bailar, J. C., ed. The chemistry of the coordination compounds. 1956. A1345
132 Udy, M. J. Chromium. 2 v. 1956. A1346
133 Sitting, M. Sodium. 1956. A1347
134 O'Flaherty, F. and others, eds. The chemistry and technology of leather. 3 v. 1956-62. A1348
135 Becher, P. Emulsions. 1957. A1349
136 Berlow, E. and others. The pentaerythritols. 1958. A1350
137 Harned, H. S. and Owen, B. B. The physical chemistry of electrolytic solutions. 1958. A1351
138 Lovelace, A. M. and others. Aliphatic fluorine compounds. 1958. A1352
139 Cook, M. A. The science of high explosives. 1958. A1353
140 Hannay, N. B., ed. Semiconductors. 1959. A1354
141 Smith, F. and Montgomery, R. The chemistry of plant gums and mucilages and some polysaccharides. 1959. A1355
142 Mathewson, C. H., ed. Zinc. 1959. A1356
143 Zuidema, H. H. The performance of lubricating oils. 1959. A1357
144 Duecker, W. W. and West, J. R., eds. The manufacture of sulfuric acid. 1959. A1358
145 Kaufmann, D. W. ed. Sodium chloride. 1960. A1359
146 Schumacher, J. C., ed. Perchloartes. 1960. A1360
147 Zeiss, H., ed. Organometallic chemistry. 1960. A1361
148 Sauchelli, V., ed. Chemistry and technology of fertilizers. 1960. A1362
149 Young, R. S., ed. Cobalt. 1960. A1363
150 Astle, M. J. Industrial organic nitrogen compounds. 1961. A1364
151 Lind, S. C. and others. Radiation chemistry of gases. 1961. A1365
152 Van Hook, A. Crystallization. 1961. A1366
153 Osipow, L. I. Surface chemistry. 1942. A1367
154 Scone, J. S. Chlorine. 1962. A1368
155 Pavlath, A. E. and Leffler, A. J. Aromatic fluorine compounds. 1962. A1369
156 Tuwiner, S. B. Diffusion and membrane technology. 1962. A1370
157 Moser, F. H. and Thomas, A. L. Phatalocyanine compounds. 1963. A1371
158 LaQue, F. L. and Copson, H. R. eds. Corrosion resistance of metals and alloys. 1963. A1372
159 Walker, F. J. Formaldehyde. 3d ed. 1964. A1373
160 Bear, F. E., ed. Chemistry of soil. 1964. A1374
161 Sauchelli, V., ed. Fertilizer nitrogen. 1964. A1375
162 Becker, P. Emulsions. 1965. A1376
163 Burns, R. M. and Bradley, W. W. Protective coatings for metals. 1967. A1377
164 Fraenkel-Conrat, H., ed. Molecular basis of virology. 1968. A1378
165 Racker, E. Membranes of mitochondria and chloroplasts. 1969. A1379
166 Mathews, C. K. Bacteriophage biochemistry. 1971. A1380
167 Isotope effects in chemical reactions, ed. by Collins and Bowman. 1970. A1381
168 Martell, A. E. Coordination chemistry. 2 v. 1971-72. A1382

AMERICAN CLASSICS (Ungar)

Adams, J. Q. The diary of John Quincy Adams, ed. by Nevins. 1969. A1383
Bancroft, F. Slave trading in the Old South. 1959. A1384
Barnes, V. F. The dominion of New England. 1960. A1385
Beale, H. K. The critical year. 1958. A1386
Beard, C. A. The enduring Federalist. 1959. A1387
Boynton, H. W. James Fenimore Cooper. 1966. A1388
Bruce, P. A. Social life of Virginia in the seventeenth century. 1964. A1389
Callahan, J. M. Diplomatic history of the Southern Confederacy. 1964. A1390
Cheyney, E. P. European background of American history, 1300-1600. 1966. A1391
Cooper, J. F. Notions of the Americans. V. 1. 1963. A1392
Earle, A. (Morse) Colonial Dames and good wives. 1962. A1393
Farrand, L. Basis of American history, 1500-1900. 1964. A1394
The Federalist. The enduring Federalist, ed. by Beard. 1959. A1395
Fite, E. D. Social and industrial conditions in the North during the Civil War. 1963. A1396
Gray, H. D. Emerson. 1957. A1397
Greene, E. B. The foundations of American nationality. 1968. A1398
____. Provincial America, 1690-1740. 1964. A1399
Hall, T. C. The religious background of American culture. 1959. A1400
Hazard, L. L. The frontier in American literature. 1961. A1401
Henry, R. S. The story of the Mexican War. 1961. A1402
Hesseltine, W. B. Civil War prisons. 1964. A1403
____. Ulysses S. Grant. 1957. A1404
Holliday, C. The wit and humor of colonial days. 1960. A1405
____. Woman's life in colonial days. 1960. A1406
Howe, G. F. Chester A. Arthur. 1957. A1407
Jernegan, M. W. The American colonies, 1492-1750. 1959. A1408
____. Laboring and dependent classes in colonial America, 1607-1783. 1960. A1409
Josephson, M. The president makers. 1964. A1410
Labaree, L. W. Royal government in America. 1958. A1411
Maclay, W. The journal of William Maclay, ed. by Beard. 1965. A1412
McClure, S. S. My autobiography, ed. by Filler. 1963. A1413
McMaster, J. B. The acquisition of political, social, and industrial rights of man in America. 1961. A1414
Mather, C. The diary of Cotton Mather, ed. by Ford. 2 v. 1957. A1415
Nevins, A. Frémont, pathfinder of the West. 2 v. 1961. A1416
____. Hamilton Fish. 1957. A1417
Parkman, F. Count Frontenac and New France under Louis XIV, ed. by Nevins. 1965. A1418
____. France and England in North America. 9 v. 1965. A1419
____. A half century of conflict, ed. by Nevins. 2 v. 1965. A1420
____. The Jesuits in North America in the seventeenth century, ed. by Nevins. 1965. A1421
____. LaSalle and the discovery of the Great West, ed. by Nevins. 1965. A1422
____. Montcalm and Wolf, ed. by Nevins. 1965. A1423
____. The old regimé in Canada, ed. by Nevins. 1965. A1424
____. Pioneers of France in the New World, ed. by Nevins. 1965. A1425
Randolph, S. N. The domestic life of Thomas Jefferson. 1958. A1426

Rhodes, J. F. History of the Civil War, 1861-1865, ed. by Long. 1961. A1427
Rusk, R. L. The literature of the middle western frontier. 2 v. 1962. A1428
Schlesinger, A. M. The colonial merchants and the American Revolution. 1957. A1429
Schurz, C. Henry Clay. 2 v. 1968. A1430
Smith, H. E. Colonial days and ways as gathered from family papers. 1967. A1431
Smith, M. (Batard) The first forty years of Washington society in the family letters of Margaret Bayard Smith, ed. by Hunt. 1965. A1432
Smith, W. H. A political history of slavery, ed. by Filler. 1966. A1433
Turner, F. J. The significance of the frontier in American history. 1963. A1434
Tyler, M. C. The literary history of the American Revolution. 2 v. 1957. A1435
____. Patrick Henry. 1966. A1436
Upham, C. W. Salem witchcraft. 2 v. 1959. A1437
Wilson, W. George Washington. 1963. A1438
Wright, R. L. American wags and eccentrics. 1965. A1439
____. Hawkers and walkers in early America. 1965. A1440

AMERICAN COLLEGE AND UNIVERSITY SERIES (Dutton)

1 Coon, H. Columbia. 1947. A1441
2 Sagendorph, K. Michigan. 1948. A1442
3 Hackett, A. P. Wellesley. 1949. A1443
4 Wagner, C. A. Harvard. 1950. A1444
Series discontinued.

AMERICAN COMMONWEALTHS (Houghton)

1 Cooke, J. E. Virginia. 1903. A1445
2 Barrows, W. Oregon. 1892. A1446
3 Browne, W. H. Maryland. 1904. A1447
4 Shaler, N. S. Kentucky. 1888. A1448
5 Cooley, T. M. Michigan. 1905. A1449
6 Spring, L. W. Kansas. 1907. A1450
7 Royce, J. California. 1892. A1451
8-9 Roberts, E. H. New York. 1904. A1452
10 Johnston, A. Connecticut. 1903. A1453
11 Carr, L. Missouri. 1892. A1454
12 Dunn, J. P. Indiana. 1905. A1455
13 King, R. Ohio. 1903. A1456
14 Robinson, R. E. Vermont. 1892. A1457
15 Garrison, G. P. Texas. 1903. A1458
16 Sanborn, F. B. New Hampshire. 1904. A1459
17 Richman, I. B. Rhode Island. 1905. A1460
18 Phelps, A. Louisiana. 1905. A1461
Folwell, W. W. Minnesota. 1908. A1462
Thwaites, R. G. Wisconsin. 1908. A1463

AMERICAN COMMONWEALTHS SERIES (Crowell)

7 Dolan, P. The government and administration of Delaware. 1956. A1464
8 Doyle, W. K. and others. The government and administration of Florida. 1954. A1465
9 Gosnell, C. B. and Anderson, C. D. The government and administration of Georgia. 1956. A1466
11 Garvey, N. F. The government and administration of Illinois. 1958. A1467
13 Ross, R. M. The government and administration of Iowa. 1957. A1468
22 Highsaw, R. B. The government and administration of Mississippi. 1954. A1469
24 Renne, R. R. The

government and administration of Montana. 1958. A1470
28 Rich, B. M. The government and administration of New Jersey. 1957. A1471
30 Caldwell, L. K. The government and administration of New York. 1954. A1472
31 Rankin, R. S. The government and administration of North Carolina. 1955. A1473
33 Aumann, F. R. The government and administration of Ohio. 1956. A1474
48 Trachsel, H. H. and Wade, R. M. The government and administration of Wyoming. 1953. A1475

AMERICAN COUNCIL OF LEARNED SOCIETIES DEVOTED TO HUMANISTIC STUDIES. NEAR EASTERN TRANSLATION PROGRAM. PUBLICATION (Amer. Council of Learned Soc.)

1 Saiyad, J. Social justice in Islam, tr. by Hardie. 1953. A1476
2 Ghali, M. B. The policy of tomorrow, tr. by Faruqi. 1953. A1477
3 Khālid, K. M. From here we start, tr. by Faruqi. 1953. A1478
4 Uthmān Amín. Muhammad 'Abduh, tr. by Wendell. 1953. A1479
5 al-Ghazzāli, M. Our beginning in wisdom, tr. by Faruqi. 1954. A1480
6 Kurd, Ali, M. Memoirs, a selection, tr. by Totah. 1954. A1481
7 'Abdallāh. My memoirs completed (al-Takmilah), tr. by Glidden. 1954. A1482
8 'Allāl al-Fāsī. The independence movement in Arab North Africa, tr. by Nuseibeh. 1954. A1483
9 Taha Husayn. The future of culture in Egypt, tr. by Glazer. 1954. A1484
10 Farrūkh, M. U. The Arab genius in science and philosophy, tr. by Hardie. 1954. A1485

AMERICAN COUNCIL OF LEARNED SOCIETIES DEVOTED TO HUMANISTIC STUDIES. RUSSIAN TRANSLATION PROJECT.

1 Kuz'minskaia, T. A. Tolstoy as I knew him. 1948. A1486
2 Vyshinskiĭ, A. I., ed. The law of the Soviet State, tr. by Babb. 1948. A1487
3 Bal'zak, S. S. and others. Economic geography of the USSR, ed. by Harris, tr. by Hankin and Titelbaum. 1949. A1488
4 Li͡ashchenko, P. I. History of the national economy of Russia, tr. by Herman. 1949. A1489
5 Gudziĭ, N. K. History of early Russian literature, tr. by Jones. 1949. A1490
6 Berg, L. S. Natural regions of the USSR, tr. by Titelbaum, ed. by Morrison and Nikiforoff. 1950. A1491
7 Sokolov, I. M. Russian folklore, tr. by Smith. 1950. A1492
8 Varneke, B. V. History of the Russian theatre, tr. by Brasol, ed. by Martin. 1951. A1493
9 Okuń, B. B. The Russian-American Company, ed. by Grekov, tr. by Ginsburg. 1951. A1494
10 Soviet legal philosophy, tr. by Babb. 1951. A1495
11 Menshutkin, B. N. Russia's Lomonosov. 1952. A1496
12 Zinov'ev, M. A. Soviet methods of teaching history, tr. by Musin-Pushkin. 1952. A1497
13 Andreev, A. I., ed. Russian discoveries in the Pacific and in North America ... tr. by Ginsburg. 1952. A1498
14 Nechkina, M. V., ed. Russia in the nineteenth century (V. 2 of The history of Russia, tr. by Pares and Frederiksen). 1953. A1499
15 Romanov, B. A. Russia in Manchuria, tr. by Jones. 1952. A1500
16 Krachkovskiĭ, I. I. Among

Arabic manuscripts, tr. by Minorsky. 1953. A1501

17-20 Barthold, V. V. Four studies on the history of Central Asia. 4 v. 1956-62. A1502

21 Zen'kóvskiĭ, V. V. Russian thinkers and Europe, tr. by Bodde. 1953. A1503

22 Asaf'ev, B. V. Russian music from the beginning of the nineteenth century, tr. by Swan. 1953. A1504

AMERICAN COUNCIL OF LEARNED SOCIETIES DEVOTED TO HUMANISTIC STUDIES, STUDIES IN CHINESE AND RELATED CIVILIZATIONS.

1 Goodrich, L. C. The literary inquisition of Ch'ien-Lung. 1935. A1505

2 March, B. Some technical terms of Chinese painting. 1935. A1506

3 Creel, H. G. Studies in early Chinese culture. 1937. A1507

4 Bingham, W. The founding of T'ang dynasty. 1941. A1508

5 Naitō, T. The wall-paintings of Hōryūji, tr. by Acker and Rowland. 1943. A1509

6 Kuo, J. Experiences in painting (T'u-hua chien-wên chih), tr. by Soper. 1951. A1510

7 Sun, I. J. and De Francis, J., eds. Chinese social history. 1956. A1511

AMERICAN COUNCIL ON EDUCATION. INTERGROUP EDUCATION IN COOPERATING SCHOOLS. WORK IN PROGRESS SERIES.

American council on education. Intergroup education. Curriculum in intergroup relations. 1949. A1512

____. Elementary curriculum in intergroup relations. 1950. A1513

____. Literature for human understanding. 1948. A1514

____. Reading ladders for human relations. 1947. A1515

____. Sociometry in group relations, by Jennings. 1948. A1516

Chicago. University. Center for Intergroup Education. Diagnosing human relation needs, by Taba and others. 1951. A1517

Taba, H. Leadership training in intergroup education. 1953. A1518

____. School culture. 1955. A1519

____. With perspective on human relations. 1955. A1520

Taba, H. and Elkins, D. With focus on human relations. 1950. A1521

Taba, H. and others. Intergroup education in public schools. 1952. A1522

AMERICAN CULTURE (Braziller)

1 Demos, J., ed. Remarkable providences, 1600-1760. 1971. A1523

2 Wood, G. S., ed. The rising glory of America, 1760-1820. 1971. A1524

3 Grimsted, D., ed. Notions of the Americans, 1820-1860. 1970. A1525

4 Trachtenberg, A., ed. Democratic vistas, 1860-1880. 1970. A1526

5 Harris, N., ed. The land of contrasts, 1880-1901. 1970. A1527

6 Nash, R., ed. The call of the wild, 1900-1919. 1970. A1528

7 Sklar, R. The plastic age, 1919-1929. 1970. A1529

8 Susman, W., ed. Culture and commitment, 1929-1945. 1972. A1530

AMERICAN CULTURE AND ECONOMICS SERIES (Academic Reprints)

1 Chittenden, H. M. The American fur trade of the Far West. 2 v. 1954. A1531

2 Frankfurter, F. The case of Sacco and Vanzetti. 1954. A1532

3 Veblen, T. B. The higher learning in America. 1954. A1533

4 Dunne, F. B. Mr. Dooley:

now and forever, selected by Filler. 1954. A1534

AMERICAN DIPLOMATIC HISTORY SERIES (Macmillan)

Adler, S. The certain giant. 1965. A1535
Dulles, F. Prelude to world power. 1965. A1536
Kaplan, L. S. Colonies into nation. 1972. A1537
Pratt, J. W. Challenge and rejection. 1967. A1538
Savelle, M. The origins of American diplomacy. 1967. A1539

AMERICAN ECONOMIC ASSOCIATION. REPUBLISHED ARTICLES ON ECONOMICS (Irwin)

1 American Economics Association. Readings in the social control of industry. 1942. A1540
2 ____. Readings in business cycle theory. 1944. A1541
3 ____. Readings in the theory of income distribution. 1946. A1542
4 ____. Readings in the theory of internal trade. 1949. A1543
5 ____. Readings in monetary theory. 1951. A1544
6 ____. Readings in price theory. 1952. A1545
7 ____. Readings in fiscal policy. 1955. A1546
8 ____. Readings in industrial organization and public policy. 1958. A1547
9 ____. Readings in the economics of taxation. 1959. A1548
10 ____. Readings in business cycles, ed. by Gordon and Klein. 1965. A1549
11 ____. Readings in international economics, ed. by Caves and Johnson. 1968. A1550
12 ____. Readings in welfare economics, ed. by Arrow and Scitovsky. 1969. A1551
13 ____. Readings in the economics of agriculture, by Fox and Johnson. 1969. A1552

AMERICAN EDUCATION FELLOWSHIP. COMMISSION ON THE RELATION OF SCHOOL AND COLLEGE. ADVENTURE IN AMERICAN EDUCATION (Harper)

1 Aiken, W. M. The story of the eight-year plan. 1942. A1553
2 Giles, H. H. and others. Exploring the curriculum. 1942. A1554
3 Smith, E. R. and others. Appraising and recording student progress. 1942. A1555
4 Chamberlin, C. D. and others. Did they succeed in college? 1942. A1556
5 Thirty schools tell their story. 1942. A1557

AMERICAN EDUCATION FELLOWSHIP. PUBLICATIONS (Appleton-Century)

American education fellowship. Language in general education. 1940. A1558
____. Mathematics in general education. 1940. A1559
____. The personal social development of boys and girls with implications for secondary education. 1940. A1560
____. Science in general education. 1938. A1561
____. The social studies in general education. 1940. A1562
____. The visual arts in general education. 1940. A1563
Blos, P. The adolescent personality. 1941. A1564
Collins, L. B. and Cassidy, R. F. Physical education in the secondary school. 1940. A1565
Heaton, K. L. and others. Bibliography on secondary education. 1940. A1566
Keliher, A. V. Life and growth. 1941. A1567
Langer, W. C. Psychology and human living. 1943. A1568
Lenrow, E. Reader's guide to prose fiction. 1940. A1569
Locke, A. and Stern, B. J., eds. When people meet. 1942. A1570
Rosenblatt, L. M. Literature as exploration. 1938. A1571

Stern, B. J., ed. Family past and present. 1938. A1572
Taylor, K. W. Do adolescents need parents? 1938. A1573
Thayer, V. T. and others. Reorganizing secondary education. 1939. A1574
Wunsch, W. R. and Albers, E., eds. Thicker than water. 1939. A1575
Zachry, C. B. and Lighty, M. Emotion and conduct in adolescence. 1940. A1576

AMERICAN EDUCATION: ITS MEN, IDEAS, AND INSTITUTIONS (Arno)

Series I:
Adams, F. The free school system of the United States. 1969. A1577
Alcott, W. A. Confessions of a school master. 1969. A1578
Bagley, W. C. Determinism in education. 1969. A1579
Barnard, H., ed. Memoirs of teachers, educators, and promoters benefactors of education, literature, and science. 1969. A1580
Bell, S. The Church, the State, and education in Virginia. 1969. A1581
Belting, P. E. The development of a free public school in Illinois to 1860. 1969. A1582
Berkson, I. B. Theories of Americanization. 1969. A1583
Blauch, L. E. Federal cooperation in agricultural extension work, vocational education, and vocational rehabilitation. 1969. A1584
Bloomfield, M. Vocational guidance of youth. 1969. A1585
Brewer, C. H. A history of education in the Episcopal Church to 1835. 1969. A1586
Brown, E. E. The making of our middle schools. 1969. A1587
Burns, J. A. The growth and development of the Catholic school system in the United States. 1969. A1588
____. The principles, origin and establishment of the Catholic school system in the United States. 1969. A1589
Burton, W. The district school as it was. 1969. A1590
Butler, N. M. Education in the United States. 1969. A1591
Butler, V. M. Education as revealed by New England newspapers prior to 1850. 1969. A1592
Campbell, T. M. The movable school goes to the Negro farmer. 1969. A1593
Carter, J. G. Essays upon popular education. 1969. A1594
Channing, W. E. Self-culture. 1969. A1595
Coe, G. A. A social theory of religious education. 1969. A1596
Comm. on Secondary School Studies. Report of the Committee on secondary school studies. 1969. A1597
Counts, G. S. Dare the school build a new social order? 1969. A1598
____. The selective character of American secondary education. 1969. A1599
____. The social composition of Boards of Education. 1969. A1600
Culver, R. B. Horace Mann and religion in Massachusetts public schools. 1969. A1601
Curoe, P. R. V. Educational attitudes and policies of organized labor in the United States. 1969. A1602
Dabney, C. W. Universal education in the South. 1969. A1603
Dearborn, N. H. The Oswego movement in American education. 1969. A1604
DeLima, A. Our enemy the child. 1969. A1605
Dewey, J. The educational situation. 1969. A1606
Dexter, F. B., ed. Documentary history of Yale University. 1969. A1607
Dock, C. Life and works of Christopher Dock, ed. by Brumbaugh. 1969. A1608
Eliot, C. W. Educational reform. 1969. A1609
Ensign, F. C. Compulsory

school attendance and child labor. 1969. A1610
Fitzpatrick, E. A. The educational views and influence of DeWitt Clinton. 1969. A1611
Fleming, S. Children & Puritanism. 1969. A1612
Flexner, A. The American college. 1969. A1613
Foerster, N. The future of the liberal college. 1969. A1614
From servitude to service. 1969. A1615
Gilman, D. C. University problems in the United States. 1969. A1616
Hall, G. A. Adolescence. 2 v. 1969. A1617
Hall, S. R. Lectures on schoolkeeping. 1969. A1618
Hansen, A. O. Early educational leadership in the Ohio Valley. 1969. A1619
Harris, W. T. Psychologic foundations of education. 1969. A1620
Haverson, M. E. Catherine Esther Beecher. 1969. A1621
Jackson, G. L. The development of school support in colonial Massachusetts. 1969. A1622
Kandel, I. L., ed. Twenty-five years of American education. 1969. A1623
Kemp, W. W. The support of schools in colonial New York... 1969. A1624
Kilpatrick, W. H. The Dutch schools of New Netherlands and colonial New York. 1969. A1625
____ and others. The educational frontier. 1969. A1626
Knight, E. W. The influence of reconstruction on education in the South. 1969. A1627
Le Duc, T. H. S. Piety and intellect at Amherst College. 1969. A1628
Maclean, J. History of the College of New Jersey. 1969. A1629
Maddox, W. A. The free school idea in Virginia before the Civil War. 1969. A1630
Mann, H. Lectures on education. 1969. A1631
McCadden, J. J. Education in Pennsylvania, 1801-1835. 1969. A1632
McCallum, J. D. Eleazer Wheelock. 1969. A1633
McCuskey, D. Bronson Alcott, teacher. 1969. A1634
Meiklejohn, A. The liberal college. 1969. A1635
Miller, E. A. The history of educational legislation in Ohio from 1803 to 1850. 1969. A1636
Miller, G. F. The academy system of the State of New York. 1969. A1637
Monroe, W. S. History of the Pestalozzian movement in the United States. 1969. A1638
Mosely Educational Comm. Reports of the Mosely Education Commission to the United States of America. 1969. A1639
Mowry, W. A. Recollections of a New England educator. 1969. A1640
Mulhern, J. A history of secondary education in Pennsylvania. 1969. A1641
Nat'l. Educ. Assn. Report of the Committee of Fifteen on Elementary Education, ed. by Harris and others, 1969. A1642
Nat'l. Society for the Study of Education. Curriculum making, past and present. 1969. A1643
____. Foundations of curriculum making. 1969. A1644
Nearing, S. The new education. 1969. A1645
Neef, J. Sketch of a plan and method of education. 1969. A1646
Nock, A. J. The theory of education in the United States. 1969. A1647
Oviatt, E. The beginnings of Yale. 1969. A1648
Packard, F. A. The daily public school in the United States. 1969. A1649
Page, D. P. Theory and practice of teaching. 1969. A1650
Parker, F. W. Talks on pedagogics. 1969. A1651
Peabody, E. P. Record of a school. 1969. A1652
Pierce, C. and Swift, M. The first state normal school in America, ed. by Norton. 1969. A1653

Porter, N. The American colleges and the American public. 1969. A1654
Reigart, J. F. The Lancasterian system of instruction in the schools of New York City. 1969. A1655
Reilly, D. F. The school controversy. 1969. A1656
Rice, J. M. The public-school system of the United States. 1969. A1657
____. Scientific management in education. 1969. A1658
Ross, E. D. Democracy's college. 1969. A1659
Rugg, H. and Shumaker, A. The child-centered school. 1969. A1660
Seybolt, R. F. Apprenticeship and apprenticeship education in colonial New England and New York. 1969. A1661
____. The private schools of colonial Boston. 1969. A1662
____. The public schools of colonial Boston. 1969. A1663
Sheldon, H. D. Student life and customs. 1969. A1664
Sherrill, L. J. Presbyterian parochial schools. 1969. A1665
Siljestrom, P. A. Educational institutions of the United States. 1969. A1666
Small, W. H. Early New England schools. 1969. A1667
Soltes, M. The Yiddish press. 1969. A1668
Stewart, G. A history of religious education in Connecticut... 1969. A1669
Storr, R. J. The beginnings of graduate education in America. 1969. A1670
Stout, J. E. The development of high-school curricula in the North Central States... 1969. A1671
Suzzallo, H. The rise of local school supervision in Massachusetts. 1969. A1672
Swett, J. Public education in California. 1969. A1673
Tappan, H. P. University education. 1969. A1674
Taylor, H. C. The educational significance of the early federal land ordinance. 1969. A1675
Taylor, J. O. The district school. 1969. A1676
Tewksbury, D. G. The founding of American colleges and universities before the Civil War. 1969. A1677
Thorndike, E. L. Educational psychology. 1969. A1678
True, A. C. A history of agricultural education in the United States. 1969. A1679
____. A history of agricultural extension work in the United States. 1969. A1680
Updegraff, H. The origin of the moving school in Massachusetts. 1969. A1681
Wayland, F. Thoughts on the present collegiate system in the United States. 1969. A1682
Weber, S. E. The Charity school movement in colonial Pennsylvania. 1969. A1683
Wells, G. F. Parish education in colonial Virginia. 1969. A1684
Wickersham, J. P. The history of education in Pennsylvania. 1969. A1685
Woodward, C. M. The manual training school. 1969. A1686
Woody, T. Early Quaker education in Pennsylvania. 1969. A1687
____. Quaker education in the colony and state of New Jersey. 1969. A1688
Wroth, L. C. An American bookshelf. 1969. A1689

Series II:

Adams, E. C. American Indian education. 1971. A1690
American Education Fellowship. Creative education, ed. by Hartman and Shumaker. 1971. A1691
Bailey, J. C. Seaman A. Knapp. 1971. A1692
Beecher, C. E. and Stowe, H. B. The American woman's home. 1971. A1693
Benezet, L. T. General education in the progressive college. 1971. A1694
Boas, L. S. Woman's education begins. 1971. A1695
Bobbitt, F. The curriculum. 1971. A1696

Bode, B. H. Progressive education at the crossroads. 1971. A1697
Bourne, W. O. History of the public school society of the city of New York. 1971. A1698
Bronson, W. C. The history of Brown University. 1971. A1699
Burstall, S. A. The education of girls in the United States. 1971. A1700
Butts, R. F. The college charts its course. 1971. A1701
Caldwell, O. W. and Courtis, S. A. Then & now in education. 1971. A1702
Calverton, V. F. and Schmalhausen, S. D., eds. The new generation. 1971. A1703
Charters, W. W. Curriculum construction. 1971. A1704
Childs, J. L. Education and morals. 1971. A1705
____. Education and the philosophy of experimentation. 1971. A1706
Clapp, E. R. Community schools in action. 1971. A1707
Counts, G. S. The American road to culture. 1971. A1708
____. School and society in Chicago. 1971. A1709
Finegan, T. E. Free schools. 1971. A1710
Fletcher, R. S. A history of Oberlin College. 1971. A1711
Grattan, C. H. In quest of knowledge. 1971. A1712
Kandel, I. L. The cult of uncertainty. 1971. A1713
____. Examinations and their substitutes in the United States. 1971. A1714
Kilpatrick, W. H. Education for a changing civilization. 1971. A1715
____. Foundations of method. 1971. A1716
____. The Montessori system examined. 1971. A1717
Lang, O. H., ed. Educational creeds of the nineteenth century. 1971. A1718
Learned, W. S. The quality of the educational process in the United States and in Europe. 1971. A1719
Meikeljohn, A. The experimental college. 1971. A1720
Middlekauff, R. Ancients and axioms. 1971. A1721
Norwood, W. F. Medical education in the United States before the Civil War. 1971. A1722
Parsons, E. W. C. Educational legislation and administration of the colonial governments. 1971. A1723
Perry, C. M. Henry Philip Tappan. 1971. A1724
Pierce, B. L. Civic attitudes in American school textbooks. 1971. A1725
Rice, E. W. The Sunday-school movement. 1971. A1726
Robinson, J. H. The humanizing of knowledge. 1971. A1727
Ryan, W. C. Studies in early graduate education. 1971. A1728
Seybolt, R. F. The evening school in colonial America. 1971. A1729
____. Source studies in American colonial education. 1971. A1730
Todd, L. P. Wartime relations of the federal government and the public schools. 1971. A1731
Vandewalker, N. C. The kindergarten in American education. 1971. A1732
Ward, F. E. The Montessori method and the American school. 1971. A1733
West, A. F. Short papers on American liberal education. 1971. A1734
Wright, M. M. T. The education of Negroes in New Jersey. 1971. A1735

AMERICAN EDUCATIONAL RESEARCH ASSOCIATION MONOGRAPH SERIES ON CURRICULUM EVALUATION (Rand McNally)

1 Tyler, R. W. and others. Perspectives of curriculum evaluation. 1967. A1736
2 Grobman, H. G. Evaluation activities of curriculum projects. 1968. A1737
3 Instructional objectives, by

Popham and others. 1969. A1738
4 Research strategies for evaluating training, ed. by DuBois and Mayo. 1970. A1739
5 Lindvall, C. M. and others. Evaluation as a tool in curriculum development. 1970. A1740
6 Gallagher, J. J. and others. Classroom observation. 1970. A1741

AMERICAN ENTOMOLOGICAL INSTITUTE. MEMOIRS

1 Townes, H. and others. A catalogue and reclassification of Indo-Australian Ichneumonidae. 1961. A1742
2 ____ and Gupta, V. K. Ichneumonidae of America north of Mexico: Subfamily Gelinea. 1962. A1743
3 Dasch, C. E. Ichneumonidae of America north of Mexico: Subfamily Diplazontinae. 1964. A1744
4 Matusda, R. Morphology and evolution of the insect head. 1965. A1745
5 Townes, H. and others. A catalogue and reclassification of the eastern Palearctic Ichneumonidae. 1965. A1746
6 Cook, D. R. The white mites of Liberia. 1966. A1747
7 Delfinado, M. D. The culicine mosquitoes of the Philippines. 1966. A1748
8 Townes, H. and M. A catalogue and reclassification of the Neotropic Ichneumonidae. 1966. A1749
9 Cook, D. R. Water mites from India. 1967. A1750
10 Porter, C. C. A revision of the South American species of Trachysphyrus. 1967. A1751
11-13 Townes, H. The genera of Ichneumonidae. 3 v. 1969-70. A1752
14 Townes, H. and Chiu, S. C. The Indo Australian species of Xanthopimia. 1970. A1753
15 Fox, R. M. and Real, H. G. A monograph of the Ithomiidae. 1971. A1754
16 Dasch, C. E. Ichneumon-flies of America north of Mexico: 6 subfamily mesochorinae. 1971. A1755
17 Same as no. 11. V. 4. 1971. A1756
18 Prasad, L. and Cook, D. R. The taxonomy of water mite larvae. 1972. A1757
19 Townes, H. and M. A catalogue and reclassification of the Ethiopian Ichneumonidae. 1973. A1758
20 Evans, H. E. Systematics and nesting behavior of Australian Bembix sand wasps. 1973. A1759
21 Cook, D. R. Water mite genera and subgenera. 1974. A1760
22 Dasch, C. E. Neotropic Mesochorinae. 1974. A1761
23 Wilson, T. H. A monographic revision of the Heliothripinae of the world. 1974. A1762

AMERICAN ENVIRONMENTAL STUDIES (Arno)

Agassiz, E. and A. Seaside studies in natural history. 1970. A1763
Agassiz, L. Lake Superior. 1970. A1764
____. Methods of study in natural history. 1970. A1765
____ and Gould, A. A. Principles of zoology. 1970. A1766
Audubon, J. J. Delineations of American scenery and character. 1970. A1767
Bennett, H. H. Soil conservation. 1970. A1768
Bowman, I. Forest physiography. 1970. A1769
Burroughs, J. Camping and tramping with Roosevelt. 1970. A1770
Cory, C. B. Hunting and fishing in Florida. 1970. A1771
Coues, E. The fur-bearing animals of North America. 1970. A1772
Dall, W. H. Alaska and its resources. 1970. A1773
DeKay, J. E. Anniversary address on the progress of the natural sciences of the United

States. 1970. A1774
Ellet, C. The Mississippi and Ohio Rivers. 1970. A1775
Gray, A. The elements of botany. 1970. A1776
Grinnell, G. B. The last of the buffalo. 1970. A1777
____ and Sheldon, C., eds. Hunting and conservation. 1970. A1778
Griscom, J. H. The sanitary condition of the laboring population of New York. 1970. A1779
____. The uses and abuses of air. 1970. A1780
Guyot, A. The earth and man. 1970. A1781
Hallock, C. Our New Alaska. 1970. A1782
Harris, T. W. Report on the insects of Massachusetts injurious to vegetation. 1970. A1783
Herbert, H. W. Frank Forester's fish and fishing in the United States... 1970. A1784
Hornaday, W. T. Our vanishing wildlife. 1970. A1785
____. Thirty years war for wild life. 1970. A1786
Jones, S. Pittsburgh in the year 1826. 1970. A1787
Marshall, G. P. The earth as modified by human action. 1970. A1788
Miller, H. A bird-lover in the West. 1970. A1789
Morse, J. The American geography. 1970. A1790
Nichols, J. R. Chemistry of the farm and the sea. 1970. A1791
Pinchot, G. The Adirondack spruce. 1970. A1792
____. Biltmore forest. 1970. A1793
Porcher, F. P. Resources of the Southern fields and forests. 1970. A1794
Powell, J. J. The golden state and its resources. 1970. A1795
Rafinesque, C. S. Ichthyologia Ohiensis. 1970. A1796
Roosevelt, T. Outdoor pastimes of an American hunter. 1970. A1797
____. Ranch life and the hunting trail. 1970. A1798
Schoolcraft, H. R. Narrative journal of travels through the Northwestern regions of the United States. 1970. A1799
Scott, G. R. Studies of the pollution of the Tennessee River system. 1970. A1800
Whitney, J. D. The metallic wealth of the United States. 1970. A1801
Wilson, A. Wilson's American ornithology. 1970. A1802

AMERICAN ETHNOLOGICAL SOCIETY. MONOGRAPHS (1-25 Augustin, 1956-Univ. of Washington Pr.)

1 Hanks, J. (Richardson) Law and status among the Kiowa Indians. 1940. A1803
2 Spencer, D. M. Disease, religion and society in the Fiji islands. 1941. A1804
3 Mishkin, B. Rank and warfare among the plains Indians. 1940. A1805
4 Bram, J. An analysis of Inca militarism. 1941. A1806
5 Foster, G. M. A primitive Mexican economy. 1942. A1807
6 Lewis, O. The effects of white contact upon Blackfoot culture. 1942. A1808
7 Reichard, G. A. Prayer. 1944. A1809
8 Goldfrank, E. S. Changing configurations in the social organization of a Blackfoot tribe during the reserve period. 1945. A1810
9 Hanks, L. M. Observations on northern Blackfoot kinship. 1945. A1811
10 Greenberg, J. The influence of Islam on a Sudanese religion. 1946. A1812
11 Lantis, M. Alaskan Eskimo ceremonialism. 1947. A1813
12 Gitlow, A. L. Economics of the Mount Hagen tribes, New Guinea. 1947. A1814
13-14 Underhill, R. M. Ceremonial patterns in the greater Southwest. 1948. A1815
15 Eduardo, O. C. The Negro in northern Brazil. 1948. A1816
16 Belo, J. Bali: Rangda and Barong. 1949. A1817

17 Stern, T. The rubber-ball games of the Americas. 1950. A1818
18 Codere, H. Fighting with property. 1950. A1819
19 Jablow, J. The Cheyenne in Plains Indian trade relations, 1795-1840. 1951. A1820
20 Willems, E. Buzios Island. 1952. A1821
21 Secoy, F. R. Changing military patterns on the Great Plains (17th century through early 19th century). 1953. A1822
22 Belo, J. Bali: temple festival. 1953. A1823
23 Róheim, G. Hungarian and Vogul mythology. 1954. A1824
24 Murphy, E. F. and Quain, B. The Trumai of Central Brazil. 1955. A1825
25 Keur, J. Y. and D. L. The deeply rooted. 1955. A1826
26 Krause, A. The Tlingit Indians, tr. by Gunther. 1956. A1827
27 Hutchinson, H. W. Village and plantation life in northeastern Brazil. 1957. A1828
28 Ginsburg, N. and Roberts, C. F. Malaya. 1958. A1829
29 Sahlins, M. D. Social stratification in Polynesia. 1958. A1830
30 Edmonson, M. S. Status terminology and the social structure of North American Indians. 1958. A1831
31 Adams, R. N. A community in the Andes. 1959. A1832
32 Carrasco, P. Land and polity in Tibet. 1959. A1833
33 Lantis, M. Eskimo childhood and interpersonal relationships. 1960. A1834
34 American association for the advancement of science. Caribbean studies, ed. by Rubin. 1960. A1835
35 VanStone, J. W. Point Hope an Eskimo village in transition. 1962. A1836
36 Smith, M. G. West Indian family structure. 1963. A1837
37 Fontana, B. L. and others. Papago Indian pottery. 1963. A1838
38 Ray, V. F. Primitive pragmatists. 1964. A1839
39 Anderson, R. T. and B. G. The vanishing village. 1964. A1840
40 Nurge, E. Life in a Leyte village. 1965. A1841
41 Stern, T. The Klamath Tribe. 1965. A1842
42 Polanyi, K. and Rotstein, A. Dahomey and the slave trade. 1966. A1843
43 Helm, J., ed. Pioneers of American anthropology. 1966. A1844
44 Harding, T. G. Voyages of the Vitiaz Strait. 1967. A1845
45 Meillassoux, C. Urbanization of an African community. 1968. A1846
46 Netting, R. Hill farmers of Nigeria. 1968. A1847
47 Ottenberg, S. Double descent in an African society. 1968. A1848
48 Gonzalez, N. L. Black Carib household structure. 1969. A1849
49 Douglass, W. A. Death in Murelaga. 1969. A1850
50 Mozino, J. M. Noticias de Nutka. 1970. A1851
51 Goodale, J. C. Tiwi wives. 1971. A1852
52 Ottenberg, S. Leadership and authority in an African society. 1971. A1853
53 Waddell, E. The Mound Builders. 1972. A1854
54 Watanabe, H. The Ainu ecosystem. 1973. A1855
55 Oberg, K. The social economy of the Tlingit Indians. 1973. A1856
56 Collins, J. Valley of the spirits. 1974. A1857

AMERICAN ETHNOLOGICAL SOCIETY. PUBLICATIONS (1-10 Amer. Ethnological Soc., 11-16 Stechert, 17-22 Augustin, 1956-Univ. of Washington Pr.)

1 Jones, W. Fox texts. 1907. A1858
2 Sapir, E. Wishram texts. Brill. 1909. A1859
3 Swanton, J. R. Haida songs. 1912. A1860
4 Dixon, R. B. Maidu texts.

1912. A1861
5 Bogoraz, W. Koryak texts. 1917. A1862
6 Chapman, J. W. Ten'a text and tales from Anvik, Alaska. 1914. A1863
7 Jones, W., comp. Ojibwa texts, ed. by Michelson. 2 v. 1917-19. A1864
8 Boas, F. Keresan texts. 2 v. Stechert. 1925-28. A1865
9 Jones, W. comp. Kickapoo tales, tr. by Michelson. 1915. A1866
10 Prince, J. D. Passamoquoddy texts. 1921. A1867
11 Durlach, T. The relationship systems of the Tlingit, Haida and Tsimshian. 1928. A1868
12 Bloomfield, L. Menomini texts. 1928. A1869
13 Wagner, G. Yuchi tales. 1931. A1870
14 Deloria, E. Dakota texts. 1932. A1871
15 Bunzel, R. L., ed. Zuñi texts. 1933. A1872
16 Bloomfield, L. Plains Cree texts. 1934. A1873
17 Weltfish, G. Caddoan texts, Pawnee, South Band dialect. 1937. A1874
18 Garfield, V. E. The Tsimshian, their art and music. 1951. A1875
19 Fortune, R. F. Arapesh. 1942. A1876
20 Voegelin, C. F. and E. W. Map of North American Indian languages. 1941. A1877
21 Reichard, G. A. Navaho grammar. 1952. A1878
22 Bunzel, R. L. Chichicastenango. 1952. A1879
Adams, R. N. A community in the Andes. 1959. A1880
American association for the advancement of science. Caribbean studies, ed. by Rubin. 1960. A1881
Carrasco Pizana, P. Land and polity in Tibet. 1959. A1882
Edmonson, M. S. Status terminology and the social structure of North American Indians. 1958. A1883
Ginsburg, N. S. and others. Malaya. 1958. A1884
Hutchinson, H. W. Village plantation life in Northeastern Brazil. 1957. A1885
Krause, A. The Tlinget Indians, tr. by Gunther. 1956. A1886
Lantis, M., ed. Eskimo childhood and interpersonal relationships. 1960. A1887
Rubin, V. D., ed. Caribbean studies. 1960. A1888
Sahlins, M. D. Social stratification in Polynesia. 1958. A1889
Van Stone, J. W. Point Hope and Eskimo village in transition. 1962. A1890

AMERICAN EXPLORATION AND TRAVEL (Univ. of Okla. Pr.)

1 U. S. War Dept. Adventure on Red river; report on the headwaters of the Red river by Captain Randolph B. Marcy and Captain G. B. McClellan, ed. by Foreman. 1937. A1891
2 Foreman, G. Marcy & the goldseekers. 1939. A1892
3 Tabeau, P. A. Tabeau's narrative of Loisel's expedition to the upper Missouri, ed. by Abel. 1939. A1893
4 Tixier, V. Travels on the Osage prairies, ed. by McDermott. 1940. A1894
5 Croix, T. de. Teodoro de Croix and the Northern frontier of New Spain, 1776-1783, tr. by Thomas. 1941. A1895
6 Whipple, A. W. A pathfinder in the Southwest, ed. by Foreman. 1941. A1896
7 Gregg, J. Diary & letters, ed. by Fulton. 2 v. 1941-44. A1897
8 Irving, W. The western journals, ed. by McDermott. 1944. A1898
9 Dumbauld, E. Thomas Jefferson, American tourist. 1946. A1899
10 Von Hagen, V. W. Maya explorer. 1947. A1900
11 Coulter, E., comp. Travels in the Confederate States. 1948. A1901

12 Hollon, W. E. The lost pathfinder, Zebulon Montgomery Pike. 1949. A1902
13 Ruxton, G. F. A. Ruxton of the Rockies, comp. by C. and M. R. Porter, ed. by Hafen. 1950. A1903
14 ____. Life in the Far West, ed. by Hafen. 1951. A1904
15 Harris, E. Up the Missouri with Audubon, ed. by McDermott. 1951. A1905
16 Stuart, R. On the Oregon Trail, ed. by Spaulding. 1953. A1906
17 Gregg, J. Commerce of the prairies, ed. by Moorhead. 1954. A1907
18 Irving, J. T. Indian sketches taken during an expedition to the Pawnee Tribes, 1833, ed. by McDermott. 1955. A1908
19 Clark, T. D., ed. Travels in the Old South, 1527-1825. 2 v. 1956. A1909
20 Ross, A. The fur hunters of the Far West, ed. by Spaulding. 1956. A1910
21 Bollaert, W. William Bollaert's Texas, ed. by Hollon and Butler. 1956. A1911
22 Conner, D. E. Joseph Reddeford Walker and the Arizona adventure, ed. by Berthrong and Davenport. 1956. A1912
23 Field, M. C. Prairie and mountain sketches, comp. by C. and M. R. Porter, ed. by Gregg and McDermott. 1957. A1913
24 Cox, R. The Columbia River, ed. by E. I. and J. R. Stewart. 1957. A1914
25 Loomis, N. The Texan-Santa Fé pioneers. 1958. A1915
26 Preuss, C. Exploring with Frémont, tr. and ed. by E. G. and E. K. Gudde. 1958. A1916
27 Schiel, J. H. W. Journey through the Rocky Mountains and the Humboldt Mountains to the Pacific Ocean, tr. by Bonner. 1959. A1917
28 Leonard, Z. Adventures of Zenas Leonard, ed. by Ewers. 1959. A1918
29 Field, M. C. Matt Field on the Santa Fe Trail, comp. by C. and M. R. Porter, ed. by Sunder. 1960. A1919
30 Miller, J. K. P. The road to Virginia City, ed. by Rolle. 1960. A1920
31 Harris, B. B. The Gila trail, ed. by Dillon. 1960. A1921
32 Bradley, J. H. The march of the Montana Column, ed. by Stewart. 1961. A1922
33 Lienhard, H. From St. Louis to Sutter's Fort, 1846; ed. by E. G. and E. K. Gudde. 1961. A1923
34 Irving, W. The adventures of Captain Bonneville, U. S. A., ed. by Todd. 1961. A1924
35 Bossu, J. B. Travels in the interior of North America, 1751-1762, tr. by Feiler. 1962. A1925
36 Clark, T. D., ed. Travels in the new South. 2 v. 1962. A1926
37 Stephens, J. L. Incidents of travel in Yucetán, ed. by Von Hagen. 1962. A1927
38 Bartlett, R. A. Great surveys of the American West. 1962. A1928
39 Cline, G. G. Exploring the Great Basin. 1963. A1929
40 Miranda, F. de. The new democracy in America, tr. by Wood. 1963. A1930
41 Mansfield, J. K. F. Mansfield on the condition of the Western forts, 1853-54, ed. by Frazer. 1963. A1931
42 Bougainville, L. A. de. Adventure in the wilderness, tr. by Hamilton. 1964. A1932
43 Simpson, J. H. Navaho expedition, ed. by McNitt. 1964. A1933
44 Irving, W. Astoria, ed. by Todd. 1964. A1934
45 Stanton, R. B. Down the Colorado, ed. by Smith. 1965. A1935
46 Meriwether, D. My life in the mountains and on the plains, ed. by Griffen. 1965. A1936
47 Cook, C. W. and others. The valley of the upper

Yellowstone..., ed. by Haines. 1965. A1937

48 Pike, Z. M. The journals of Zebulon Montgomery Pike, ed. by Jackson. 2 v. 1966. A1938

49 Loomis, N. M. and Nasatir, A. P. Pedro Vial and the roads to Santa Fe. 1966. A1939

50 MacKenzie, A. Journal of travels on the orders of the North West Company, 1786, ed. by McDonald. 1966. A1940

51 Turner, H. S. The original journals of Henry Smith Turner, ed. by Clarke. 1966. A1941

52 Prendergast, D. M. The Walker-Caddy Expedition to Palenque, 1839-40. 1966. A1942

53 Franchère, G. Adventure at Astoria, 1810-1814, tr. by H. Franchère. 1967. A1943

54 Pourtales, A. On the western tour with Irving..., ed. by Spaulding. 1968. A1944

55 Miller, R. R. For science and national glory. 1968. A1945

56 Gale, J. The Missouri Expedition, 1818-1820. 1969. A1946

57 Griffin, G. B. The California coast, ed. by Cutter. 1969. A1947

58 Gage, T. Thomas Gage's travels in the new world, ed. by Thompson. 1969. A1948

59 Work, J. The Snake Country expedition of 1830-1831. John Work's Field journal, ed. by Francis D. Haines. 1971. A1949

60 Des Montaignes, F. The Plains, ed. by Mower and Russell, 1972. A1950

61 Talbot, T. Soldier in the West. 1972. A1951

62 Randolph, J. R. British travelers among the southern Indians, 1660-1763. 1973. A1952

63 Paul Wilhelm. Travels in North America 1822-1824, tr. by Nitske, ed. by Lottinville. 1973. A1953

64 Cline, G. G. Peter Skene Ogden and the Hudson's Bay Company. 1974. A1954

AMERICAN FICTION SERIES (American Bk. Co.)

Bird, R. M. Nick of the woods or the Jibbenainosay, ed. by Williams. 1939. A1955

Brackenridge, H. H. Modern chivalry, ed. by Newlin. 1937. A1956

Brown, C. B. Ormond, ed. by Marchand. 1937. A1957

Cooper, J. F. Satanstoe, ed. by Spiller and Cooper. 1937. A1958

Kennedy, J. P. Horse-shoe Rubinson, ed. by Leisy. 1937. A1959

Simms, W. G. The Yemassee, ed. by Cowie. 1937. A1960

AMERICAN FOLKLORE SOCIETY. BIBLIOGRAPHICAL AND SPECIAL SERIES.

1 Laws, G. M. Native American balladry. 1950. A1961

2 Coffin, T. P. The British traditional ballad in North America. 1951. A1962

3 Ramsey, E. and Howard, D. M., comps. Folklore for children and young people. 1952. A1963

4 Merriam, A. P. and Brenford, R. J. A bibliography of jazz. 1954. A1964

5 Sebeok, T. A., ed. Myth. 1955. A1965

6 Lord, A. B., ed. Slavic folklore. 1956. A1966

7 Journal of American folklore. Analytical index to the journal. V. 1-67, 68, 69, 70, by Coffin. 1958. A1967

8 Laws, G. M. American balladry from British broadsides. 1957. A1968

9 Propp, V. I. Morphology of the folktale. 1958. A1969

10 Singer, M. B. ed. Traditional India. 1959. A1970

11 Folk-Song Society of the Northeast. Bulletin. 1960. A1971

12 Ravenscroft, T., comp. Pammelia. Deutromelia. Melismata. Ed. by Leach. 1961. A1972

13 Coffin, T. P., ed. Indian tales of North America. 1961. A1973

14 Beck, H. P., ed. Folklore in action. 1962. A1974
15 Cox, J. H. Traditional ballads and folksongs mainly from West Virginia, ed. by Boswell. 1964. A1975
16 Elder, J. D. Song games from Trinidad and Tobago. 1962. A1976
17 Jacobs, M., comp. The anthropologist looks at myth, ed. by Greenway. 1966. A1977
18 Jackson, B., comp. The Negro and his folklore in nineteenth-century periodicals. 1967. A1978
19 Combs, J. H. Folk-songs of the southern United States, ed. by Wilgus. 1967. A1979
20 Abrahams, R. D., ed. Jump-rope rhymes. 1969. A1980
21 Krohn, K. Folklore methodology, tr. by Welsch. 1970. A1981
22 Parades, A. and Stekert, E. J. The urban experience and folk tradition. 1971. A1982
23 Parades and Bauman, R., eds., Toward new perspectives in folklore. 1972. A1983
24 Sutton-Smith, B. The folk games of children. 1972. A1984
25 Hassell, J. W. Amorous games. 1974. A1985

AMERICAN FOLKLORE SOCIETY. MEMOIRS.

1 Chatelain, H. Folk-tales of Angola. 1894. A1986
2 Fortier, A. Louisiana folk-tales. 1895. A1987
3 Edwards, C. L. Bahama songs and stories. 1895. A1988
4 Bergen, F., comp. Current superstitions. 1896. A1989
5 Matthews, W. Navaho legends. 1897. A1990
6 Teit, J. A., comp. Traditions of the Thompson river Indians of British Columbia. 1898. A1991
7 Bergen, F., ed. Animal and plant folklore. 1899. A1992
8 Dorsey, G. A., comp. Traditions of the Skidi Pawnee. 1904. A1993
9 Los pastores, ed. by Cole. 1907. A1994
10 Hague, E., ed. Spanish-American folk-songs. 1917. A1995
11 Boas, F., ed. Folk-tales of Salishan and Sahaptin tribes. 1917. A1996
12 Fansler, D. S., ed. Filipino popular tales. 1921. A1997
13 Parsons, E. W. (Clews). The folk-tales of Andros Island, Bahamas. 1918. A1998
14 Journal of American folklore. Index. 1930. A1999
15 Parsons, E. W. (Clews). Folklore from the Cape Verde islands. 2 v. 1923. A2000
16 ____. Folk-lore of the Sea islands, South Carolina. 1923. A2001
17 Beckwith, M. W., comp. Jamaica Anansi stories. 1924. A2002
18 Whitney, A. W. and Bullock, C. C. comp. Folk-lore from Maryland. 1925. A2003
19 Parsons, E. W. (Clews). Tewa tales. 1926. A2004
20 Doke, C. M., comp. Lamba folklore. 1927. A2005
21 Beckwith, M. W. Jamaica folklore. 1928. A2006
22 Parsons, E. W. (Clews). Kiowa tales. 1929. A2007
23 Andrade, M. J. Folk-lore from the Dominican Republic. 1931. A2008
24 Fauset, A. H. Folk-lore from Nova Scotia. 1931. A2009
25 Boas, F. Bella Bella tales. 1932. A2010
26 Parsons, E. W. (Clews). Folk-lore of the Antilles. 3 pts. 1933-43. A2011
27 Adamson, T., comp. Folk-tales of the coast Salish. 1934. A2012
28 Boas, F. Kwakiutl culture as reflected in mythology. 1935. A2013
29 Stout, E. J., ed. Folklore from Iowa. 1936. A2014
30 Espinosa, J. M. Spanish folklore from New Mexico. 1937. A2015
31 Opler, M. E. Myths and tales of the Jicarilla Apache Indians. 1938. A2016

32 Beckwith, M. W. Mandan-Hidatsa myths and ceremonies. 1938. A2017
33 Goodwin, G. Myths and tales of the White Mountain Apache. 1939. A2018
34 Parsons, E. W. (Clews). Taos tales. 1940. A2019
35 Wheeler, H. T. Tales from Jalisco, Mexico. 1943. A2020
36 Opler, M. E. Myths and legends of the Lipan Apache Indians. 1940. A2021
37 ____. Myths and tales of the Chiricahua Apache Indians. 1942. A2022
38 Embree, J. F., comp. Japanese peasant songs. 1943. A2023
39 Bayard, S. P., ed. Hill country tunes. 1944. A2024
40 Métraux, A. Myths and tales of the Toba and Pilaga Indians of the Gran Chaco. 1946. A2025
41 Reichard, G. A. An analysis of Coeur D'Alene Indian myths. 1947. A2026
42 Jakobsen, R. and Simmons, E. J., eds. Russian epic studies. 1950. A2027
43 Hall, R. A. and others. Haitian Creole. 1953. A2028
44 Skendi, S. Albanian and South Slavic oral epic poetry. 1954. A2029
45 Nettl, B. North American Indian musical styles. 1954. A2030
46 Barton, R. F. The mythology of the Ifugaos. 1955. A2031
47 Saucier, C. L. Traditions de la paroisse des Avoyelles en Louisiana. 1956. A2032
48 Spencer, K. Mythology and values. 1957. A2033
49 Gimbutas, M. Ancient symbolism in Lithuanian folk art. 1958. A2034
50 Laski, V. Seeking life. 1958. A2035
51 Patai, R. and others, eds. Studies in Biblical and Jewish folklore. 1960. A2036
52 Goldstein, K. S. A guide for field workers in folklore. 1964. A2037
53 Cheney, T. E., ed. Mormon songs from the Rocky Mountains. 1968. A2038
54 Malone, W. C. Country music, U. S. A. 1968. A2039
55 Fowke, E. Lumbering songs from the northern woods. 1969. A2040
56 Miller, E. K. Mexican folk narratives from Los Angeles area. 1973. A2041
57 Frye, E. The marble threshing floor. 1973. A2042
58 Cohen, A. B. Poor Pearl, poor girl! 1973. A2043
59 Postmas, M. Tales from the Basotho. 1974. A2044
60 Abrahams, R. D. Deep the water, shallow the shore. 1974. A2045
61 Roberts, L. Sang Branch settlers. 1974. A2046

AMERICAN FOLKWAYS (Duell)

Atherton, G. F. Golden Gate country. 1945. A2047
Bracke, W. B. Wheat country. 1950. A2048
Brownell, B. The other Illinois. 1958. A2049
Callahan, N. Smoky mountain country. 1952. A2050
Campbell, W. S. Short grass country. 1941. A2051
Carter, H. and Ragusin, A. Gulf-coast country. 1951. A2052
Corle, E. Desert country. 1941. A2053
____. Listen, bright angel. 1946. A2054
Croy, H. Corn country. 1947. A2055
Day, D. Big-country: Texas. 1947. A2056
Graham, L. Niagara country. 1949. A2057
Henry, R. C. High border country. 1942. A2058
Kane, H. T. Deep delta country. 1944. A2059
Kennedy, S. Pálmetto country. 1942. A2060
Le Suer, M. North star country. 1945. A2061
Lewis, O. High Sierra country. 1955. A2062
Long, H. Piñon country. 1941. A2063
McMeekin, C., pseud. Old Kentucky country. 1957. A2064

McWilliams, C. Southern California country. 1944. A2065
Nixon, H. C. Lower Piedmont country. 1946. A2066
Power, A. Redwood country. 1949. A2067
Putnam, G. P. Death valley and its country. 1946. A2068
Rayburn, O. E. Ozark country. 1941. A2069
Stegner, W. Mormon country. 1942. A2070
Swetnam, G. Pittsylvania country. 1951. A2071
Thomas, J. Blue Ridge country. 1942. A2072
Vestal, S. Short grass country. 1941. A2073
Webster, C. M. Town meeting country. 1945. A2074
White, W. C. Adirondack country, ed. by Caldwell. 1954. A2075
Williams, A. N. Rocky Mountain country. 1950. A2076
Williamson, T. R. Far north country. 1944. A2077

THE AMERICAN FOREIGN POLICY LIBRARY (Harvard Univ. Pr.)

Akenson, D. H. The United States and Ireland. 1973. A2078
Brinton, C. C. The Americans and the French. 1968. A2079
____. The United States and Britain. 1948. A2080
Brown, W. N. The United States and India and Pakistan. 1953. A2081
____. The United States and India, Pakistan and Bangladesh. 1972. A2082
Cline, H. F. The United States and Mexico. 1953. A2083
Craig, G. M. The United States and Canada. 1968. A2084
Dean, V. The United States and Russia. 1948. A2085
Fairbank, J. K. The United States and China. 1958. A2086
Gallagher, C. F. The United States and North Africa. 1963. A2087
Gould, J. W. The United States and Malaysia. 1969. A2088
Grattan, C. H. The United States and the Southwest Pacific. 1961. A2089
Hughes, H. S. The United States and Italy. 1953. A2090
McKay, D. C. The United States and France. 1951. A2091
Perkins, D. The United States and the Caribbean. 1947. A2092
Polk, W. R. The United States and the Arab world. 1965. A2093
Reischauer, E. O. The United States and Japan. 1957. A2094
Safran, N. The United States and Israel. 1963. A2095
Scott, F. D. The United States and Scandinavia. 1950. A2096
Speiser, E. A. The United States and the Near East. 1949. A2097
Thomas, L. V. and Frye, R. N. The United States and Turkey and Iran. 1951. A2098
Whitaker, A. P. The United States and Argentina. 1955. A2099
____. The United States and South America. 1948. A2100
Wolff, R. L. The Balkans in our time. 1956. A2101

AMERICAN FORTS (Prentice-Hall)

Athearn, R. G. Forts of the Upper Mississippi. 1967. A2102
Derleth, A. Vincennes. 1968. A2103
Downey, F. D. Louisbourg. 1965. A2104
Havighurst, W. Three flags at the straits. 1966. A2105
Howard, R. W. Thundergate. 1968. A2106
Lewis, O. Sutter's Fort. 1966. A2107
Nadeau, R. A. Fort Laramie and the Sioux Indians. 1967. A2108
O'Meara, W. Guns at the forks. 1965. A2109
Walton, G. Fort Leavenworth. 1969. A2110
____. Sentinel of the plains: Fort Leavenworth. 1973. A2111

AMERICAN FOUNDATION FOR THE STUDY OF MAN. PUBLICATIONS (Johns Hopkins Pr.)

1 Atiya, A. S. The Arabic manuscript of Mount Sinai. 1955. A2112
2 Bowen, R. L. B. and Albright, F. P. Archaeological discoveries in South Arabia. 1958. A2113
3 Jamme, A. Sabaean inscriptions from Mahram Bilqis. 1962. A2114
4 Cleveland, R. L. An ancient South Arabian necropolis. 1965. A2115
5 Van Beek, G. W. Hajar Bin Humeid. 1969. A2116

AMERICAN GEOGRAPHICAL SOCIETY. MAP OF HISPANIC AMERICA. PUBLICATIONS.

1 Ogilvie, A. G. Geography of the central Andes. 1922. A2117
2 Davis, W. M. The lesser Antilles. 1926. A2118
3 American geographical society of New York. A catalogue of maps of Hispanic America. 4 v. 1930-33. A2119
4 Platt, R. R. and others. The European possessions in the Caribbean area. 1941. A2120
5 American geographical society of New York. Index to map of Hispanic America, ed. by Hanson. 1945. A2121

AMERICAN GEOGRAPHICAL SOCIETY OF NEW YORK. RESEARCH SERIES.

1-2 Golder, F. A. Bering's voyages. 2 v. 1922-25. A2122
3 Johnson, D. W. Battlefields of the world war. 1921. A2123
4 Keltie, J. S. The position of geography in British universities. 1921. A2124
4a Martonne, E. de. Geography in France. 1924. A2125
5 McBride, G. M. The agrarian Indian communities of highland Bolivia. 1921. A2126
6 Jefferson, S. W. Recent colonization in Chile. 1921. A2127
7 ____. The rainfall of Chile. 1921. A2128
8 Babcock, W. H. Legendary islands of the Atlantic. 1922. A2129
9 Sullivan, H. B. A catalogue of geographical maps of South America. 1922. A2130
10 Wright, J. K. Aids to geographical research. 1923. A2131
11 Antevs, E. The recession of the last ice sheet in New England. 1922. A2132
12 McBride, G. M. The land system of Mexico. 1923. A2133
13 Shantz, H. L. and Marbut, C. F. The vegetation and soils of Africa. 1923. A2134
14 Nunn, G. E. The geographical conceptions of Columbus. 1924. A2135
15 Wright, J. K. The geographical lore of the time of the crusades. 1925. A2136
16 Jefferson, S. W. Peopling Argentine pampa. 1926. A2137
17 Antevs, E. The last glaciation. 1928. A2138
18 Thórdarson, M. The Vinland voyages, tr. by Walter. 1930. A2139
19 McBridé, G. M. Chile. 1936. A2140
20 Heidel, W. A. The frame of the ancient Greek maps. 1937. A2141
21 Lattimer, O. Inner Asian frontiers of China. 1951. A2142
22 Wright, J. K. and Platt, E. T. Aids to geographical research. 1947. A2143
23 Lowenthal, D. The West Indies Federation. 1961. A2144
24 Rudolph, W. E. Vanishing trails of Atacama. 1963. A2145
25 Warntz, W. Geography now and then. 1964. A2146
26 Lowenthal, D. West Indian societies. 1972. A2147

AMERICAN GEOGRAPHICAL SOCIETY OF NEW YORK. SPECIAL PUBLICATION.

1 American geographical society

of New York. Memorial volume of the Transcontinental excursion of 1912 of the American geographical society of New York. 1915. A2148

2 Bowman, I. The Andes of southern Peru, geographical reconnaissance along the seventy-third Meridian. 1916. A2149

3 Dominian, L. The frontiers of language and nationality in Europe. 1917. A2150

4 Lee, W. T. The face of the earth as seen from the air. 1922. A2151

5 Bowman, I. Desert trails of Atacama. 1924. A2152

6 Mallory, W. H. China. 1926. A2153

7 American geographical society of New York. Problems of polar research. 1928. A2154

8 Nordenskjöld, O. and Mecking, L. The geography of the polar regions. 1928. A2155

9 Davis, W. M. The coral reef problem. 1928. A2156

10 Parks, G. B. Richard Hakluyt and the English voyages, ed. by Williamson. 1928. A2157

11 Joerg, W. L. G. Brief history of polar exploration since the introduction of flying. 1930. A2158

12 Johnson, G. R. Peru from the air. 1930. A2159

13 Bowman, I. The pioneer fringe. 1931. A2160

14 American geographical society of New York. Pioneer settlement. 1932. A2161

15 Bretz, J. H. The Grand Coulee, ed. by Wright. 1932. A2162

16 American geographical society of New York. New England's prospect. 1933. A2163

17 Carvajal, G. de. The discovery of the Amazon according to the account of Friar Gaspar de Carvajal and other documents, tr. by Lee, ed. by Heaton. 1934. A2164

18 Boyd, L. A. The fiord region of east Greenland. 1935. A2165

19 Sykes, G. G. The Colorado delta. 1937. A2166

20 Boyd, L. A. Polish countrysides. 1937. A2167

21 Antevs, E. Rainfall and tree growth in the Great Basin. 1938. A2168

22 Forbes, A. Northernmost Labrador mapped from the air. 1938. A2169

23 Price, A. G. White settlers in the tropics. 1939. A2170

24 American geographical society of New York. Environment and conflict in Europe. 1940. A2171

25 Light, R. U. Focus on Africa. 1941. A2172

26 Rich, J. L. The face of South America. 1942. A2173

27 Brown, R. H. Mirror for Americans. 1943. A2174

28 Smith, G. H. and others. Japan. 1943. A2175

29 Pelzer, K. J. Pioneer settlement in the Asiatic tropics. 1945. A2176

30 Boyd, L. A. The coast of northeast Greenland. 1948. A2177

31 Pratt, E. and Good, D., eds. World geography of petroleum. 1950. A2178

32 Kimble, G. H. T. and Good, D., eds. Geography of the northlands. 1955. A2179

33 Haden-Guest, S. H. and others, eds. A world geography of forest resources. 1956. A2180

34 American geographical society of New York. Nine glacier maps. 1960. A2181

35 Heusser, C. J. Late-Pleistocene environments of North Pacific North America. 1960. A2182

36 Küchler, A. W. Potential natural vegetation of the conterminous United States. 1964. A2183

____. Manual to accompany the map. 1964. A2184

37 Christie, J. A. Thoreau as world traveler. 1965. A2185

38 Friis, H. R., ed. The Pacific Basin, 1967. A2186

39 Bertrand, J. J. Americans in Antarctica, 1775-1948. 1971. A2187

AMERICAN GEOPHYSICAL UNION. ANTARCTIC RESEARCH SERIES

1 Biology of the Antarctic seas, ed. by Lee. 1914. A2188
2 Antarctic snow and ice studies, ed. by Mellor and Crary. 2 v. 1904. A2189
3 Hartman, O. Polychaeta Errantia of Antarctica. 1964. A2190
4 Waynick, A. H., ed. Geomagnetism and aeronomy. 1965. A2191
5 Llano, G. A., ed. Biology of the Antarctic seas II. 1965. A2192
6 Hadley, J. B., ed. Geology and paleontology of the Antarctic. 1965. A2193
7 Hartman, O. Polychaeta Myzsotomidae and Sedentaria of Antarctica. 1966. A2194
8 Tedrow, J. C. F., ed. Antarctic soil farming processes. 1966. A2195
9 Studies in Antarctic meteorology, ed. by Rubin. 1966. A2196
10 Entomology of Antarctica, ed. by Gressitt. 1967. A2197
11 Llano, G. A., ed. Biology of the Antarctic seas III. 1967. A2198
12 Austin, O. L., ed. Antarctic bird studies. 1968. A2199
13 Kott, P. Antarctic Ascidiacea. 1969. A2200
14 Newman, W. A. and Ross, A. Antarctic Cirripedia. 1970. A2201
15 Antarctic oceanology, ed. by Reed. V. 1. 1971. A2202
16 Crary, A. P. Antarctic snow and ice studies II. 1971. A2203
17 Llano, G. A., ed. Biology of the Antarctic seas IV. 1971. A2204
18 Antarctic pinnipedia, ed. by Burt. 1971. A2205
19 Same as no. 15, ed. by Hayes. V. 2. 1972. A2206
20 Antarctic terrestrial biology, ed. by Llano. 1971. A2207
21 Gunderson, E. K. E., ed. Human adaptability to Antarctic conditions. 1974. A2207a
22 Foster, M. W. Recent Antarctic and subantarctic brachiopods. 1974. A2208
23 Watson, G. Bird handbook. 1974. A2209

AMERICAN GUIDE SERIES.

Berger, J. Cape Cod pilot. Modern Pilgrim pr. 1937. A2210

Federal writers' project. Allegheny co., Pa. Places to play. William Penn Assn. of Phila. 1937. A2211

____. Arizona. The Hopi. Arizona. State Teachers College. 1938. A2212

____. The Navaho. Arizona State Teachers College. 1938. A2213

____. Arkansas. Guide to North Little Rock. Times pr. and pub. co. 1936. A2214

____. Beaver co., Pa. The Harmony society in Philadelphia. William Penn Assn. of Phila. 1937. A2215

____. Berks co., Pa. Hikes in Berks. William Penn Assn. of Phila. 1937. A2216

____. Berks co., Pa. Reading's volunteer fire department. William Penn Assn. of Phila. 1938. A2217

____. California. Balboa park, San Diego, California. Neyensech. 1941. A2218

____. California. Hastings. 1967. A2219

____. Death valley. Houghton. 1939. A2220

____. Festivals in San Francisco. Stanford Univ. Press. 1939. A2221

____. Connecticut. Connecticut. Houghton. 1938. A2222

____. Delaware. Delaware. Hastings. 1955. A2223

____. New castle on the Delaware. New Castle hist. soc. 1936. A2224

____. Dutchess co., N. Y. Dutchess county. William Penn Assn. of Phila. 1937. A2225

____. Erie co., Pa. Erie. William Penn Assn. of Phila. 1938. A2226

____. Florida. Florida. Oxford. 1973. A2227

____. St. Augustine. Seeing St. Augustine. Chamber of commerce. 1937. A2228

____. Georgia. Augusta. Tidwell ptg. supply co. 1938. A2229

____. Savannah. Chamber of Commerce, Savannah, Ga. 1937. A2230

____. Here's New England! Houghton. 1939. A2231

____. Idaho. Idaho. Oxford. 1950. A2232

____. Idaho lore. Caxton pr. 1938. A2233

____. Idaho. Tours in eastern Idaho. 1939. A2234

____. Illinois. Cairo guide. E. V. pub. house. 1938. A2235

____. Illinois. DuPage county..., ed. by Knoblauch. Ruby. 1951. A2236

____. Galena guide. 1937. A2237

____. Princeton guide. Republican pr. co. 1939. A2238

____. Selected bibliography: Illinois, Chicago and its environs. The Program, 433 E. Erie St., Chicago, Ill. A2239

____. Indiana. Hoosier tall tales. 1939. A2240

____. The intracoastal waterway. Govt. Pr. Off. 1937. A2241

____. Iowa. A guide to Burlington, Iowa. Acres-Blackmar co. 1939. A2242

____. Guide to Cedar Rapids and northeast Iowa. Laurance pr. 1937. A2243

____. Guide to Dubuque. Hoermann. 1937. A2244

____. A guide to Estherville, Iowa. Estherville enterprise pr. 1939. A2245

____. Kansas. Kansas. Hastings, 1949. A2246

____. A guide to Salina, Kansas. Advertising sun. 1939. A2247

____. The Larned city guide. Chamber of commerce. 1938. A2248

____. A centennial of the University of Louisville. Standard ptg. co. 1939. A2249

____. Military history of Kentucky. State journal. 1939. A2250

____. Old capitol and Frankfort guide. Kentucky state hist. soc. 1939. A2251

____. Lycoming county, Pennsylvania. Picture of Lycoming county. Commissioners of Lycoming county. 1939. A2252

____. Maine. Houghton, 1937. A2253

____. Maine. Maine's capitol. Kennebec journal. 1939. A2254

____. Massachusetts. The Armenians in Massachusetts. 1937. A2255

____. The Berkshire hills. Funk. 1939. A2256

____. Fairhaven, Massachusetts. 1939. A2257

____. Massachusetts. A historical sketch of Auburn, Massachusetts. Auburn Centennial com. 1937. A2258

____. Massachusetts. Houghton. 1937. A2259

____. Whaling masters. Old Dartmouth hist. soc. 1938. A2260

____. Winter sports and recreation in the Berkshire hills. 1937. A2261

____. Miner county, S. D. Prairie tamers of Miner county. 1939. A2262

____. Minnesota. Minnesota. 1954. A2263

____. Minnesota. St. Cloud guide. 1936. A2264

____. Mississippi. Mississippi. Hastings. 1938. A2265

____. Mississippi gulf coast. Mrs. J. H. Walsh, Box 405, Gulfport, Mississippi. A2266

____. Montana. Montana; a profile in pictures. Fleming. 1941. A2267

____. Montana, a state guide book. Hastings. 1949. A2268

____. Nebraska. Lincoln city guide. Woodruff. 1937. A2269

____. Nebraska. Hastings. 1947. A2270

____. Old Bellevue. Papillion times. 1937. A2271

____. Nevada. Calendar of annual events in Nevada. Nevada Hist. soc. 1939. A2272

____. New England states. Here's New England. Houghton. 1939. A2273

____. New Hampshire. New Hampshire. Houghton. 1938. A2274

____. New Jersey: a guide to its present and past. Hastings. 1939. A2275
____. New Jersey, a profile in pictures. Barrows. 1939. A2276
____. New Jersey. Monroe township. 1938. A2277
____. Ocean highway, New Brunswick, New Jersey to Jacksonville, Florida. McLeod, 1938. A2278
____. The story of Dunellen 1887-1937. Dunellen golden jubilee, inc. 1937. A2279
____. The Swedes and Finns in New Jersey. Jersey pr. co. 1938. A2280
____. New Mexico. Calendar of events. 1937. A2281
____. New Orleans. New Orleans. Houghton. 1952. A2282
____. New Orleans city guide. Houghton. 1952. A2283
____. New York (City). New York city guide. Random. 1939. A2284
____. New York learns. Barrows. 1939. A2285
____. New York panorama. Random. 1938. A2286
____. New York. Albany. 1938. A2287
____. Gli italiani di New York. Labor pr. 1938. A2288
____. The Italians of New York. Random. 1938. A2289
____. North Carolina. Oxford. 1940. A2290
____. North Dakota. Bismarck, North Dakota. 1938. A2291
____. North Dakota. Oxford. 1950. A2292
____. The ocean highway. Modern Age. 1938. A2293
____. Ohio. Chillicothe and Ross county. F. J. Heer pr. co. 1938. A2294
____. Findlay and Hancock county centennial. Findlay College. 1937. A2295
____. Guide to the Lima and Allen county, Ohio. Better business bureau, Lima. Ohio. A2296
____. Martins Ferry sequicentennial... 1938. A2297
____. Zanesville and Muskingum county. Zaneville ?, 1937. A2298
____. Oklahoma. Calendar of annual events in Oklahoma. Tribune. 1938. A2299
____. Tulsa. Midwest ptg. co. 1938. A2300
____. Oregon. Fire prevention in Portland. 1938. A2301
____. Oregon trail. Hastings. 1939. A2302
____. Portland fire alarm system. 1938. A2303
____. Our federal government and how it functions. Hastings. 1939. A2304
____. Our Washington. McClurg. 1939. A2305
____. Pennsylvania. A bid for liberty. William Penn Assn. of Phila. 1937. A2306
____. Northhampton county guide. Times pub. co. 1939. A2307
____. 3 hikes through the Wissahickou. 1936. A2308
____. Philadelphia. The Horseshoe trail. William Penn Assn. of Phila. 1939. A2309
____. Philadelphia. William Penn. Assn. of Phil. 1937. A2310
____. Reading's volunteer fire department. William Penn. Assn. of Phil. 1938. A2311
____. Pittsburgh. Tales of pioneer Pittsburgh. 1937. A2312
____. San Diego, Calif. San Diego. 1937. A2313
____. Skiing in the East. Barrows. 1939. A2314
____. South Carolina. Beaufort and the Sea islands. Review. 1938. A2315
____. Palmetto pioneers. State dept. of education. 1938. A2316
____. Thomas Green Clemson. 193-? A2317
____. South Dakota. Hastings. 1952. A2318
____. Douglas county tales and towns. Armour public library bd., Armour, S. D. A2319
____. Guide to Pierre. State pub. co. 1937. A2320
____. Hamlin Garland memorial. 1939. A2321

____. A South Dakota guide. State pub. 1938. A2322
____. A vacation guide to Custer state park. 1938. A2323
____. Mitchell, South Dakota. A2324
____. Pioneer Mitchell. Hipple pr. co. 1938. A2325
____. Sodbusters. South Dakota writer's league. 1938. A2326
____. Tennessee. Tennessee. Hastings. 1949. A2327
____. Texas. Beaumont. Anson Jones. A2328
____. The Denison guide. Denison Chamber of Commerce. 1939. A2329
____. San Antonio. Clegg. 1941. A2330
____. U. S. one; Maine to Florida. MacLeod. 1938. A2331
____. Utah. Origins of Utah place names. Salt Lake City, Utah. 1940. A2332
____. Vermont. Vermont. Houghton. 1937. A2333
____. Washington. Hastings. 1937. A2334
____. West Virginia. The first census of Hampshire county. West Virginia Schools for the Deaf and the Blind. 1937. A2335
____. Wisconsin. Portage. Portage? n. p. A2336
____. Shorewood. Village Board of Shorewood. 1939. A2337
Raccoon. New Jersey. Swedish Lutheran church. Records of the Swedish Lutheran churches at Raccoon and Penns Neck, 1713-1786. Comm. of Finance. 1939. A2338
U. S. Puerto Rico reconstruction administration. Puerto Rico. Univ. Soc. 1940. A2339
U. S. Works project administration. Kentucky. Libraries and lotteries by Breyer and Kinkade. Hobson Bk. pr. 1944. A2340
Walker, W. , ed. Southern harmony songbook. Hastings. 1939. A2341
Writers' program. Alabama. Alabama. Hastings. 1949. A2342
____. Alaska. A guide to Alaska. Macmillan. 1939. A2343
____. Arizona. Arizona. Hastings. 1956. A2344
____. Mission San Xavier del Bac, Arizona. Hastings. 1940. A2345
____. Arkansas. Arkansas. Hastings. 1941. A2346
____. Boston looks seaward. Humphries. 1941. A2347
____. State forests and parks of Massachusetts. Boston Dept. of Conservation. 1941. A2348
____. Los Angeles. Hastings. 1951. A2349
____. Monterey peninsula. Delkin. 1941. A2350
____. San Francisco, the bay and its cities. Hastings. 1973. A2351
____. Santa Barbara. Hastings. 1941. A2352
____. Colorado. Colorado. Hastings. 1941. A2353
____. Denver. Denver public schools. 1945. A2354
____. Ghost towns of Colorado. Hastings. 1947. A2355
____. District of Columbia. Our federal government and how it functions. Hastings. 1939. A2356
____. Our Washington. McClurg. 1939. A2357
____. A guide to the Key West. Hastings. 1949. A2358
____. Planning your vacation in Florida. Bacon. 1941. A2359
____. Seeing Fernandina. Fernandina News. 1940. A2360
____. Georgia. Atlanta. Smith & Durrell. 1949. A2361
____. Georgia. Univ. of Georgia. 1954. A2362
____. The Macon guide and Ocmulee national monument. Burke. 1939. A2363
____. Savannah River plantations, ed. by Granger. Georgia historical soc. 1947. A2364
____. The Story of Washington-Wilkes. University of Georgia. 1941. A2365
____. Hillsboro guide. Montgomery News. 1940. A2366
____. Illinois. McClurg. 1947. A2367

____. Nauvoo guide. McClurg. 1939. A2368
____. Rockford. Graphic Arts Corp. 1941. A2369
____. Indiana. Indiana. Oxford. 1945. A2370
____. Iowa. Bentonsport memories. Bentonsport. 1940. A2371
____. A guide to McGregor. Widman. 1940. A2372
____. Iowa. Hastings. 1949. A2373
____. Van Buren county. Keith. 1940. A2374
____. Kansas. A guide to Leavenworth, Kansas. Leavenworth Chronicle. 1940. A2375
____. Kentucky. Fairs and fairmakers of Kentucky. 1942. A2376
____. Henderson. Bacon. 1941. A2377
____. In the land of Breathitt. Bacon. 1941. A2378
____. Kentucky. Hastings. 1954. A2379
____. Lexington and the blue grass country. Commercial ptg. co. 1938. A2380
____. Louisville. Hastings. 1941. A2381
____. Union county. Schuhmann. 1941. A2382
____. Louisiana. Louisiana. Hastings. 1941. A2383
____. Maine. Augusta-Hallowell on the Kennebec. Augusta Hallowell Chamber of Commerce. 1940. A2384
____. Portland city guide. Forest City. 1940. A2385
____. Maryland. A guide to the United States Naval Academy. Devin-Adair. 1941. A2386
____. Maryland. Oxford. 1946. A2387
____. Massachusetts. Springfield, Massachusetts. 1941. A2388
____. Michigan. Michigan. Oxford. 1946. A2389
____. Minnesota. Minnesota. Hastings. 1954. A2390
____. Minnesota Arrowhead country. Whitman. 1941. A2391
____. Missouri. Missouri. Duell. 1954. A2392
____. Motor tours in the Berkshire hills. Berkshire Hills conf. 1938. A2393
____. Nevada. Nevada. Binfords. 1940. A2394
____. New Jersey. Progress pub. co. 1939. A2395
____. New Jersey. Bergen county panorama. Colby. 1941. A2396
____. Entertaining a nation. Jersey. 1940. A2397
____. Livingston. Progress Pub. Co. 1939. A2398
____. New Mexico. New Mexico. Hastings. 1962. A2399
____. New York (State). New York. Oxford. 1940. A2400
____. Rochester and Monroe county. Scranton. 1937. A2401
____. The story of five towns. Nassau daily review-star. 1941. A2402
____. Warren county. Glen Falls Post. 1942. A2403
____. North Carolina. Charlotte. News printing co. 1939. A2404
____. Raleigh. Dunn. 1942. A2405
____. Ohio. Bryan and William county. Downtain. 1941. A2406
____. Ohio. Cincinnati. Wiesen-Hart. 1943. A2407
____. Columbus zoo book. Columbus Zoological Society. 1940. A2408
____. Fremont and Sandusky county. C. A. Hochenedel, 6 Masonic block, Fremont. Ohio. A2409
____. Lake Erie. Stephens. 1941. A2410
____. Ohio guide. Oxford. 1946. A2411
____. Springfield and Clark county Ohio. Springfield tribune ptg. co. 1941. A2412
____. Urbana and Champaign county. Urbana Lions club, Urbana, Ohio. 1942. A2413
____. Warren and Trumbull county. Western Reserve hist. celebration comm. 1938. A2414
____. Oklahoma. Oklahoma. Univ. of Okla. 1947. A2415
____. Oregon. Mount Hood. Duell. 1940. A2416

___. Oregon. Binsfords. 1951. A2417
___. Pennsylvania. Oxford. 1940. A2418
___. Pennsylvania cavalcade. Univ. of Pa. 1942. A2419
___. A picture of Clinton county. Comm. of Clinton county. 1942. A2420
___. Erie county, Pennsylvania. Erie. William Penn. Assn. of Phil. 1949. A2421
___. Story of the old Allegheny city. Allegheny Cent. Comm. 1941. A2422
___. Pittsburgh. Tales of pioneer Pittsburgh. William Penn Assn. of Phil. 1937. A2423
___. Rhode Island. Rhode Island. Houghton. 1937. A2424
___. South Carolina. Oxford. 1946. A2425
___. South Carolina state parks. South Carolina state forest service. 1940. A2426
___. A history of the Spartanburg county. Band. 1940. A2427
___. Homesteaders of McPherson county. Writers' project, Mitchell, S.D. 1941. A2428
___. South Dakota place names. Univ. of South Dakota. 1940. A2429
___. South Dakota. Aberdeen. Prairie League work-shop. 1940. A2430
___. Texas. Along the San Antonio river. San Antonio, The city. 1941. A2431
___. Corpus Christi. Corpus Christi caller times, Corpus Christi, Texas. A2432
___. Houston. Anson Jones. 1942. A2433
___. Old Villita. San Antonio. The city. 1939. A2434
___. Port Arthur. Anson Jones. 1940. A2435
___. Texas. Hastings. 1969. A2436
___. Timberline lodge. 1940. A2437
___. Provo. Binfords. 1940. A2438
___. Utah. Hastings. 1954. A2439
___. Origins of the Utah place-names. n.p., 1940. A2440
___. Utah's story. Salt Lake city, Utah. 1942. A2441
___. Virginia. Alexandria. Williams pr. co. 1939. A2442
___. Government of Roanoke. 1939. A2443
___. Industry and commerce in Roanoke. 1939. A2444
___. Jefferson's Albemarle. Jarman's Inc. 1941. A2445
___. Prince William. Whittet. 1941. A2446
___. Protective agencies of Roanoke. 1940. A2447
___. Roanoke. Stone. 1912. A2448
___. Sussex county. Whittet. 1942. A2449
___. Virginia, a guide to the Old Dominion. Oxford. 1946. A2450
___. Virginia, the Old Dominion in pictures. Fleming. 1941. A2451
___. Washington, D.C. Washington. Supt. of Doc. 1937. A2452
___. The new Washington. Binsford. 1941. A2453
___. Washington (State). Washington. Binfords. 1941. A2454
___. West Virginia. Oxford. 1948. A2455
___. Who's Who in the Zoo. McLeod. 1938. A2456
___. Wisconsin. Wisconsin. Hastings. 1954. A2457
___. Wyoming. Wyoming. Oxford. 1941. A2458

AMERICAN HEART ASSOCIATION. MONOGRAPH

1 Symposium on Congestive Heart Failure. 1966. A2459
2 Symposium on Coronary Heart Disease. 1968. A2460
3 Symposium on Antiogtension, ed. by Wood and Ahlquist. 1962. A2461
4 Symposium on Indicator-dilution Technics in the Study of the Circulation. 1968. A2462
5 Moyer, J. H. Application of computers in cardiovascular disease. 1967. A2463
6 American Heart Assn.

Cardiovascular surgery, 1962. 1963. A2464
7 ____ 1963. Ed. by Simone. 1964. A2465
8 Autoregulation of blood flow. 1967. A2466
9 Evans, J. R., ed. Structure and function of heart muscle. 1968. A2467
10 Idiopathic hypertrophic subaortic stenosis. 1968. A2468
11 Same as no. 6. 1964. 1965. A2469
12 DuShane, J. W. and Weidman, W. H., eds. Five congenital cardiac defects. 1967. A2470
13 Same as no. 6. 1965. 1966. A2471
14 Symposium on Cerebrovascular Disease, ed. by Siekert. 1966. A2472
15 Chapman, C. B., ed. Physiology of muscular exercise. 1967. A2473
16 Same as no. 6. 1966. 1967. A2474
17 Catecholamines in cardiovascular physiology and disease, ed. by Reader. 1967. A2475
18 The National diet-heart study. 1968. A2476
19 Same as no. 6. 1967. 1968. A2477
20 Cooperative study of cardiac catherization, ed. by Braunwald and Swan. 1968. A2478
21 Diagrammatic portrayal of variation in cardiac structure, by Stranger and others. 1968. A2479
22 World Congress of Cardiology. Evaluation of results of cardiac surgery, ed. by Dexter and Werko. 1968. A2480
23 Response to exercise after bed rest and after training, by Salton and others. 1968. A2481
24 Same as no. 6. 1968. 1969. A2482
25 Dayton, S. and others. A controlled clinical trial of a diet high in saturated fat in preventing complications of athersclerosis. 1969. A2483
26 Meerson, F. Z. The Myocardium in hyperfunction, hypertrophy and heart failure. 1969. A2484
27 Symposium on Research on acute myocardial infarction. 1969. A2485
28 Ahrens, E. H. Mass field trials of the diet-heart question. 1969. A2486
29 Coronary heart disease in seven countries, ed. by Keys. 1970. A2487
30 Same as no. 6. 1969. A2488
31 Ravin, A. and Frame, F. K. International bibliography of cardiovascular ausculation and phonocardiography. 1971. A2489
32 Conference on Hypertensive. Hypertensive mechanism, ed. by Reader, 1970. A2490
33 Rodbard, S., ed. Local regulation of blood flow. 1971. A2491
34 Same as no. 6. 1970. A2492
35 Same as no. 6. 1971. A2493
36 Myocardial infarction, ed. by Friedberg. 1972. A2494
37 Friedberg, C. K. Angina pectoris. 1972. A2495
38 Coronary Drug Project Group. The coronary drug project. 1973. A2496
39 Sassahara, A. A. The Urokinasepulmonary embolism trial. 1973. A2497

THE AMERICAN HERITAGE SERIES (Liberal Arts)

1 Blau, J. L., ed. Social theories of Jacksonian democracy. 1954. A2497a
2 Franklin, B. Benjamin Franklin: the Autobiography and selections from his writings, ed. by Schneider. 1952. A2498
3 Thoreau, H. D. Selected writings on nature and liberty, ed. by Cargill. 1952. A2499
4 Baudin, M. C., ed. Edgar Allen Poe and others. 1952. A2500
5 Paine, T. Common sense, and other political writings, ed. by Adkins. 1953. A2501
6 Friedrich, C. J. and McCloskey, R. G., eds. From the Declaration of independence to the Constitution.

1954. A2502
7 Federalist. Hamilton, Madison and Jay on the Constitution, ed. by Gabriel. 1954. A2503
8 Adams, J. The political writings of John Adams, ed. by Peek. 1954. A2504
9 Jefferson, T. Political writings, ed. by Dumbauld. 1955. A2505
10 Calhoun, J. C. A disquisition on government, and selections from the discourse, ed. by Post. 1953. A2506
11 Bellamy, E. Selected writings on religion and society, ed. by Schiffman. 1955. A2507
12-14 Baudin, M. C., ed. Contemporary short stories. 3 v. 1954. A2508
15 12-14 considered as a set.
16 Van Nostrand, A. D., ed. Literary criticism in America. 1957. A2509
17 Peirce, C. S. Essays in the philosophy of science, ed. by Tomas. 1957. A2510
18 Hamilton, A. Papers on public credit, commerce and finance, ed. by McKee. 1956. A2511
19 Solberg, W. U., ed. The Federal Convention and the formation of the Union of the American States. 1958. A2512
20 Hamilton, A. Alexander Hamilton selections..., ed. by Aly. 1957. A2513
21 Channing, W. E. Unitarian Christianity and other essays, ed. by Bartlett. 1957. A2514
22 Van Nostrand, A. D. and Watts, C. H., eds. The conscious voice. 1959. A2515
23 Wright, C. Philosophical writings, ed. by Madden. 1958. A2516
24 Quint, H. H. The forging of American Socialism. 1964. A2517
25 not yet published.
26 Filler, L. C. American liberalism of the late 19th century. 1962. A2518
27 Salvadori, M. The American economic system. 1963. A2519
31 Smith, W., ed. Theories of education in early America. 1973. A2520
32 Jacobson, D. L., ed. The English libertarian heritage. 1965. A2521
33 Morgan, E. S., ed. Puritan political ideas, 1558-1794. 1965. A2522
34 Heimert, A. and Miller, P., eds. The great awakening. 1967. A2523
35 Jensen, M., comp. Tracts of the American Revolution, 1763-1776. 1967. A2524
36 Young, A. The American Revolution as a Democratic movement. 1967. A2525
37 U.S. Constitution. The Bill of Rights, ed. by Commager and Levy. 1967. A2526
38 Kenyon, C. M., ed. The antifederalists. 1966. A2527
39 Madison, J. The mind of the founder, ed. by Meyers. 1973. A2528
40 Gallatin, A. Selected writings of Albert Gallatin, ed. by Ferguson, 1967. A2529
41 Levy, L. W., ed. Freedom of the press from Zenger to Jefferson. 1966. A2530
42 Marshall, J. John Marshall, major opinions and other writings, ed. by Roche. 1967. A2531
43 Peterson, M. D., ed. Democracy, liberty and property. 1966. A2532
44 Pease, J. and W. The antislavery argument. 1965. A2533
45 Commager, H. S. The writings of Justice Joseph Story. 1967. A2534
46 Lincoln, A. The political thoughts of Abraham Lincoln, ed. by Current. 1967. A2535
47 Hyman, H. M., ed. The radical Republicans and reconstruction. 1967. A2536
48 Graebner, N., ed. Manifest destiny. 1967. A2537
50 Pollack, N., comp. The Populist mind. 1967. A2538
52 Bryan, W. J. William Jennings Bryan, selections, ed. by Ginger. 1967. A2539
53 Roosevelt, T. The writings of Theodore Roosevelt, ed. by Harbaugh. 1967. A2540

54 Resek, C., ed. The Progressives. 1967. A2541
56 Broderick, F. L. and Meier, A., eds. Negro protest thought in the twentieth century. 1965. A2542
56R Meier, A. and others, eds. Black protest thought in the twentieth century. 1965. A2543
58 Abell, A., ed. American Catholic thought on social questions. 1967. A2544
60 Lynd, S., ed. Nonviolence in America. 1968. A2545
61 Cross, R. D., ed. The church and the city, 1865-1910. 1967. A2546
63 Swados, H., ed. The American writers and the great depression. 1966. A2547
64 Franklin, B. The political thought of Benjamin Franklin, ed. by Ketcham. 1965. A2548
65 Goodrich, C., comp. The government and the economy, 1783-1861. 1967. A2549
67 Ward, L. F. Lester Ward and the Welfare State, ed. by Commager. 1967. A2550
68 Wilson, W. The political thoughts of Woodrow Wilson, ed. by Cronon. 1965. A2551
69 Addams, J. The social thought of Jane Addams, ed. by Lasch. 1965. A2552
70 Zinn, H., ed. The New Deal thought. 1967. A2553
71 McGovern, G., ed. Agriculture policy in the twentieth century. 1967. A2554
72 Mendelson, W., ed. The Supreme Court. 1967. A2555
73 Ahlstrom, S. E., comp. Theology in America. 1967. A2556
74 Nelson, H. L., ed. Freedom of the press from Hamilton to the Warren Court. 1967. A2557
75 Millis, W., ed. American military thought. 1966. A2558
76 Croly, H. The promise of American life. 1965. A2559
77 Clark, T. D., ed. The South since reconstruction. 1973. A2560
78 Auerbach, J. S. American labor. 1969. A2561
79 Rischin, M., ed. Immigration and the American tradition. 1974. A2562
80 Buckley, W. F. American conservative thought in the twentieth century. 1971. A2563
81 Welter, R., ed. The American writings on popular education. 1971. A2564
82 Buckley, W. F., ed. American conservative thought in the twentieth century. 1970. A2565
83 Baritz, L., comp. The culture of the twenties. 1970. A2566/7
84 Miller, W. R., comp. Contemporary American Protestant thought, 1900-1970. A2568
85 Pessen, E., ed. Jacksonian society. 1974. A2569
87 Clark, T. D., ed. The great American frontier. 1974. A2570
89 Bracey, J. and others, eds. Black nationalism in America. 1970. A2571

AMERICAN HERITAGE SERIES (Stratford House)

1 Shaner, D. The story of Joplin. 1948. A2572
2 Butler, M. M. The Lakewood story. 1949. A2573
3 Rohman, D. G. Here's Whiteboro. 1949. A2574
4 Moore, L. W. and others. The story of Eugene. 1949. A2575
5 Allen, H. Rubber's home town. 1949. A2576
Hickey, A. S. The story of Kingston. 1952. A2577
Walton, F. L. Pillars of Yonkers. 1951. A2578

AMERICAN HISTORICAL ASSOCIATION. ALBERT J. BEVERIDGE MEMORIAL FUND (1936-43, Appleton-Century; 1944-Univ. of Pa. unless otherwise stated)

Bentley, G. R. A history of the Freedman's Bureau. 1955. A2579

Bernstein, H. Origins of inter-American interest, 1700-1812. 1945. A2580
Bestor, A. E. Backwoods utopias. 1950. A2581
Binkley, W. C., ed. Official correspondence of the Texan revolution, 1835-1836. 2 v. 1936. A2582
Birney, J. G. Letters, 1831-1857, ed. by Dumond. 2 v. 1938. A2583
Brown, R. E. Middle-class democracy and the Revolution in Massachusetts. 1956. A2584
France. Ministère de la justice. French opinion on the United States and Mexico, 1860-67, ed. by Case. 1936. A2585
Graham, I. C. C. Colonists from Scotland. Cornell Univ. Pr. 1956. A2586
Great Britain. Crown. Royal instructions to British colonial governors, 1670-1776, ed. by Labaree. 2 v. 1935. A2587
Hanke, L. Spanish struggle for justice in the conquest of America. 1949. A2588
Harrington, F. H. Fighting politician, Major General N. P. Banks. 1948. A2589
Hofstadter, R. Social Darwinism in American thought, 1860-1915. 1944. A2590
Hyman, H. M. Era of the oath. 1954. A2591
Johnson, A. The development of American petroleum pipelines. 1956. A2592
Josephson, B. E. Manual of style for publications of the Beveridge fund. 1940. A2593
Kirby, E. W. George Keith. 1942. A2594
McNall, N. A. Agricultural history of the Genesee valley, 1790-1860. 1952. A2595
Perkins, B. The first rapprochement. 1955. A2596
Perkins, H. C., ed. Northern editorials on concession. 1942. A2597
Pomeroy, E. S. Territories and the United States, 1861-1890. 1947. A2598
Twyman, R. W. History of Marshall Field & Co. 1954. A2599
Van Deusen, G. G. Horace Greeley. 1953. A2600
Ver Steeg, C. L. Robert Morris. 1954. A2601
Weld, T. D. and others. Letters of Theodore Dwight Weld, Angelina Grimké Weld and Sarah Grimké, 1822-44. 2 v. 1934. A2602
Wik, R. M. Steam power on the American farm. 1953. A2603
William Augustus, duke of Cumberland. Military affairs in North America, 1748-65, ed. by Pargellis. 1937. A2604

AMERICAN HISTORICAL ASSOCIATION. COMMISSION ON THE SOCIAL STUDIES IN THE SCHOOLS. REPORT (Scribner)

1 American historical ass'n. A charter for the social studies in the schools, by Beard and others. 1932. A2605
2 Johnson, H. An introduction to the history of the social sciences in the schools. 1932. A2606
3 Pierce, B. L. Citizens' organizations and the civic training of youth. 1933. A2607
4 Kelley, T. L. and Krey, A. C. Tests and measurements in the social sciences. 1934. A2608
5 Bowman, I. Geography in relation to the social sciences. 1934. A2609
Clark, R. B. Geography in the schools of Europe. 1934. A2610
6 Merriam, C. E. Civic education in the United States. 1934. A2611
7 Beard, C. A. The nature of the social sciences in relation to objectives of teaching. 1934. A2612
8 Newlon, J. H. Educational administration as social policy. 1934. A2613
9 Counts, G. S. and others. The social foundations of education. 1934. A2614
10 Curti, M. The social ideas of American educators.

1960. A2615
11 Tryon, R. M. The social sciences as school subjects. 1935. A2616
12 Beale, H. K. Are American teachers free? 1936. A2617
13 Marshall, L. C. and Goetz, R. M. Curriculum-making in social studies. 1937. A2618
14 Bagley, W. C. and Alexander, T. The teacher of the social studies. 1937. A2619
15 Horn, E. Methods of instruction in the social studies. 1937. A2620
16 Beale, H. K. A history of the freedom of teaching in American schools. 1946. A2621
17 American historical ass'n. Comm. on the social studies in schools. Conclusions and recommendations of the commission. 1934. A2622

AMERICAN HISTORICAL ASSOCIATION. PUBLICATIONS (1932-49, Appleton-Century, 1950- Univ. of Pa. Pr.)

Allyn, E. Lords versus Commons. 1931. A2623
Barnes, G. H. The antislavery impulse, 1830-44. 1933. A2624
Boyd, C. E. Tithes and parishes in medieval Italy. 1952. A2625
Brown, L. F. The first Earl of Shaftesbury. 1933. A2626
Bruce, K. Virginia iron manufacture in the slave era. 1931. A2627
Cady, J. F. The roots of French imperialism in Eastern Asia. 1954. A2628
Carroll, E. M. French public opinion and foreign affairs, 1870-1914. 1931. A2629
Castel, A. E. A frontier state at war. 1959. A2630
Chitwood, O. P. John Tyler, champion of the old South. 1939. A2631
Clendenen, C. C. The United States and Pancho Villa. Cornell Univ. Pr. 1961. A2632
Conkin, P. K. Tomorrow a new world. Cornell Univ. Pr. 1959. A2633
Davis, C. D. The United States and the first Hague Peace Conference. Cornell Univ. Pr. 1962. A2634
Dietz, F. C. English public finance, 1558-1641. 1932. A2635
Fairchild, B. Messrs. William Pepperell, merchants at Piscataqua. 1954. A2636
Fisher, M. M. Negro slave songs. 1953. A2637
Fleming, D. John William Draper and the religion of science. 1950. A2638
Garrett, M. B. The Estates General of 1789. 1935. A2639
Graham, I. C. C. Colonists from Scotland. 1956. A2640
Gulick, E. V. Europe's classical balance of power. 1955. A2641
Hale, R. W., ed. Guide to the photocopied historical materials in the United States and Canada. Cornell Univ. Pr. 1961. A2642
Heidel, W. A. The day of Yahweh. 1929. A2643
Hoon, E. E. The organization of the English customs system, 1696-1786. 1938. A2644
Horton, J. T. James Kent. 1939. A2645
Hubbart, H. C. The older Middle West, 1840-80. 1936. A2646
Jackson, L. P. Free Negro labor and property holding in Virginia, 1830-60. 1942. A2647
Lanning, J. T. The eighteenth-century enlightenment in the University of San Carlos de Guatemala. 1956. A2648
Miller, N. The enterprise of a free people. Cornell Univ. Pr. 1962. A2649
Motten, C. G. Mexican silver and the enlightenment. 1950. A2650
Paul, A. M. Conservative crisis and the rule of Law. Cornell Univ. Pr. 1960. A2651
Phillips, U. B. The course of the South to secession. 1940. A2652
Pletcher, D. M. Rails, mines, and progress. 1958. A2653

Priestley, H. I. France overseas. 1939. A2654
Ranck, J. B. Albert Gallatin Brown, radical Southern nationalist. 1937. A2655
Sanborn, F. R. Origins of the early English maritime and commercial law. 1930. A2656
Schroeder, P. W. The Axis alliance and Japanese-American relations. 1941. 1958. A2657
Shrycock, J. K. The origin and development of the state cult of Confucius. 1932. A2658
Smith, W. Professors & public ethics. 1956. A2659
Spence, C. C. British investments and the American mining frontier. Cornell Univ. Pr. 1958. A2660
Swann, N. L. Pan Chao. 1932. A2661
Sydnor, C. S. Slavery in Mississippi. 1933. A2662
Whitaker, A. P. The Mississippi question, 1795-1803. 1934. A2663
Wright, C. The beginnings of Unitarianism in America. 1955. A2664

AMERICAN HISTORICAL SOURCES SERIES: RESEARCH AND INTERPRETATION (Prentice-Hall)

Jacob, C. E. Leadership in the New Deal. 1967. A2665
Lovejoy, D. Religious enthusiasm and the great awakening. 1969. A2666
Lubove, R. The urban community. 1967. A2667
Polishook, I. H. Roger Williams, John Cotton, and religious freedom. 1967. A2668
Ratner, L. Antimasonary. 1969. A2669
____. Pre-Civil war reform. 1967. A2670
Silbey, J. H., comp. The transformation of American politics. 1967. A2671
Yellowitz, I. The place of the worker in American society. 1969. A2672

AMERICAN HISTORY RESEARCH CENTER. MADISON, WISC. PUBLICATION.

Bonner, T. N. Medicine in Chicago, 1850-1950. 1957. A2673
Fehrenbacher, D. E. Chicago giant. 1957. A2674
McDonald, F. Let there be light. 1957. A2675
____. We the people. Univ. of Chicago. 1958. A2676
Miller, W. D. Memphis during the progressive era, 1900-1917. 1957. A2677

AMERICAN HOSPITAL ASSOCIATION. MONOGRAPH SERIES

1 American Hospital Assn. Hospitals and the corporate practice of medicine, ed. by Wilcox. 1957. A2678
2 ____. Modernization needs in existing hospital buildings. 1958. A2679
3 Densen, P. M. and others. Prepaid medical care and hospital utilization. 1958. A2680
4 Abdellah, F. G. and Levine, E. Effect of nurse staffing on satisfactions with nursing care. 1958. A2681
5 American Hospital Assn. Physicians' private offices at hospitals. 1959. A2682
6 Roemer, M. I. and Shane, M. Hospital utilization under insurance. 1959. A2683
7 American Hospital Assn. A study of the nonsegregated hospitalization of alcohol patients in a general hospital. 1969. A2684
8 Sturdavant, M. and others. Comparison of intensive nursing service in a circular and rectangular unit. 1960. A2685
9 Littauer, D. and others. Home care. 1961. A2686
10 Treloar, A. E. and Chill, D. Patient care facilities. 1961. A2687
11 Heyman, M. M. Effective utilization of social workers in a hospital setting. 1962. A2688

12 Colbeck, J. C. Control of infections in hospitals. 1962. A2689
13 Littauer, D. and others. A chronic disease unit in a general hospital. 1963. A2690
14 Rosenthal, G. D. The demand for general hospital facilities. 1964. A2691
15 Fry, H. G. The operation of state hospital planning and licensing programs. 1965. A2692

AMERICAN HUMORISTS (Gregg)

1 Ade, G. In pastures new. 1969. A2693
2 Bangs, J. K. R. Holmes & Co. 1969. A2694
3 Burdette, R. J. The rise and fall of the mustache. 1969. A2695
4 Clemens, S. L. The celebrated jumping frog of Calaveras County and other sketches. 1969. A2696
5 Clopper, J. Fragments of the history of Bawlfredonia. 1969. A2697
6 Dunne, F. P. Dissertations by Mr. Dooley. 1969. A2698
7 Field, J. M. The drama in Pokerville. 1969. A2699
8 The galaxy of wit. 1969. A2700
9 Haliburton, T. C. The clockmaker. 1969. A2701
10 Harte, B. Condensed novels. 1969. A2702
11 Holey, M. Samantha on the race problem. 1969. A2703
12 Levison, W. H. Black diamonds. 1969. A2704
13 Lewis, H. C. Odd leaves from the life of a Louisiana swamp doctor. 1969. A2705
14 Locke, D. R. "Swingin' round the cirkle." 1969. A2706
15 ____. The morals of Abou Ben Adhem. 1969. A2707
16 Longstreet, A. B. Georgia scenes. 1969. A2708
17 Nye, E. W. A guest at the Ludlow. 1969. A2709
18 Old Abe's jokes. 1969. A2710
19 Peck, G. W. How Pvt. George W. Peck put down the rebellion. 1969. A2711
20 Pomeroy, M. M. Nonsense. 1969. A2712
21 Shillaber, B. P. Life and saying of Mrs. Partington and others of the family. 1969. A2713
22 Smith, C. H. Bill Arp's peach papers. 1969. A2714
23 Thompson, W. T. Major Jones' chronicles of Pineville. 1969. A2715
24 Thomson, M. N. The witches of New York. 1969. A2716
25 Whitcher, F. M. The Widow Bedott papers. 1969. A2717
26 Minstrel Gags and end men's handbook. 1969. A2718
27 Townsend, C. Negro minstrels with end men's jokes, gags, speeches, etc. 1969. A2719
28 Haverly, J. Negro minstrels. 1969. A2720

AMERICAN IMMIGRATION COLLECTION (Arno)

Abbott, E. Historical aspects of the immigration problem. 1969. A2721
____. Immigration. 1969. A2722
Adamic, L. Laughing in the jungle. 1969. A2723
Babcock, K. C. The Scandinavian element in the United States. 1969. A2724
Balch, E. G. Our Slavic fellow citizens. 1969. A2725
Blegen, F. C. Norwegian migration to America, 1825-1860. 1969. A2726
Bromwell, W. J. History of immigration to the United States. 1969. A2727
Brown, L. G. Immigration. 1969. A2728
Busey, S. C. Immigration. 1969. A2729
Byrne, S. Irish emigration to the United States. 1969. A2730
Capek, T. The Cechs in America. 1969. A2731
Carey, J. P. Deportation of aliens from the United States to Europe. 1969. A2732
Carpenter, N. Immigrants and their children. 1969. A2733

Claghorn, K. The immigrant's day in court. 1969. A2734
Clark, J. P. Deportation of aliens from the United States to Europe. 1969. A2735
Colton, C. Manual for emigrants to America. 1969. A2736
Coolidge, M. E. B. S. Chinese immigration. 1969. A2737
Corsi, E. In the shadow of liberty. 1969. A2738
Davis, J. The Russian immigrant. 1969. A2739
Desmond, H. J. The A. P. A. movement. 1969. A2740
Faust, A. B. The German element in the United States. 2 v. 1969. A2741
Federal Writers' Project. The Italians of New York. 1969. A2742
Foerster, R. F. The Italian immigrants of our times. 1969. A2743
Ford, H. J. The Scotch-Irish in America. 1969. A2744
Franklin, F. G. The legislative history of naturalization in the United States. 1969. A2745
Gamio, M. The Mexican immigrant. 1969. A2746
____. Mexican immigration to the United States. 1969. A2747
Hourwich, I. A. Immigration and labor. 1969. A2748
Ichihashi, Y. Japanese in the United States. 1969. A2749
Joseph, S. Jewish immigration to the United States from 1881 to 1910. 1969. A2750
Kapp, F. Immigration and the commissioners of emigration of the State of New York. 1969. A2751
Lasker, B. Filipino immigration. 1969. A2752
Maguire, J. F. The Irish in America. 1969. A2753
Morse, S. F. B. The imminent dangers to the free institutions of the United States through foreign immigration. 1969. A2754
O'Donovan, J. Immigration in the United States, 1840-1860. A2755
Panunzio, C. The soul of the immigrant. 1969. A2756
Park, R. E. and Miller, H. A. Old world traits transplanted. 1969. A2757
Reid, I. D. The Negro immigrant. 1969. A2758
Steiner, E. A. On the trail of the immigrant. 1969. A2759
Stephenson, G. M. The religious aspects of Swedish immigration. 1969. A2760
Stern, E. G. I am a woman and a Jew. 1969. A2761
Taft, D. R. Two Portuguese communities in New England. 1969. A2762

Series II:

Bogardus, E. S. The Mexican in the United States. 1970. A2763
Bolek, F., ed. Who's who in Polish America. 1970. A2764
Boody, B. M. A psychological study of immigrant children at Ellis Island. 1970. A2765
Burgess, T. Greeks in America. 1970. A2766
Bushee, F. A. Ethnic factors in the population of Boston. 1970. A2767
Child, C. J. The German-Americans in politics. 1970. A2768
Eaton, A. H. Immigrant gifts to American life. 1970. A2769
Ferenczi, I. International migrations. 2 v. 1970. A2770
Fox, P. The Poles in America. 1970. A2771
Grant, M. The passing of the great race. 1970. A2772
Halich, W. Ukrainians in the United States. 1970. A2773
Hansen, M. L. The mingling of the Canadian and American peoples. 2 v. 1970. A2774
Hawgood, J. A. The tragedy of German-America. 1970. A2775
Hrdlicka, A. The old Americans. 1970. A2776
Janson, F. E. The background of Swedish immigration. 1970. A2777
Kallen, H. M. Culture and democracy in the United States. 1970. A2778
Kirkpatrick, C. Intelligence and immigration. 1970. A2779

Kirtak, R. The story of a Bohemian American village. 1970. A2780
Manning, C. The immigrant woman and her job. 1970. A2781
Miller, H. A. The school and the immigrant. 1970. A2782
Mullan, E. H. Mentality of the arriving immigrant. 1970. A2783
Qualey, C. C. Norwegian settlement in the United States. 1970. A2784
Roberts, P. Anthracite coal communities. 1970. A2785
____. The new immigration. 1970. A2786
Seward, G. F. Chinese immigration in its social and economical aspects. 1970. A2787
Smith, W. C. Americans in process. 1970. A2788
____. Americans in the making. 1970. A2789
Strong, E. K. The second generation Japanese problem. 1970. A2790
Taylor, P. S. Mexican labor in the United States. 2 v. 1970. A2791
United States Industrial Comm., 57th Congress. Reports of the Industrial Commission... 1970. A2792
Wessel, B. B. An ethnic survey of Woonsocket. 1970. A2793
Woods, R. A., ed. Americans in process. 1970. A2794
Wright, C. D. The Italians in Chicago. 1970. A2795

THE AMERICAN INDUSTRIES SERIES (Doubleday)

Considine, R. B. Man against fire. 1955. A2796
Denison, M. The power to go. 1956. A2797
Haynes, W. Cellulose. 1953. A2798

AMERICAN INSTITUTE OF BIOLOGICAL SCIENCES. PUBLICATION.

1 Grenell, R. G. and Mullins, L. J. eds. Molecular structure and functional activity of nerve cells. 1956. A2799
2 Pauling, L. C. and Itano, H. A., eds. Molecular structure and biological specificity. 1957. A2800
3 Kelly, E., ed. Ultrasound in biology and medicine. 1957. A2801
4 Brauer, R. W., ed. Liver functions. 1958. A2802
5 Halvorson, H. O. Spores. 1958. A2803
6 Strehler, B. L. and others, eds. The biology of aging. 1960. A2804
7 Symposium on Animal Sounds and Communication. Animal sounds and communication, ed. by Lanyon and Tavalga. 1960. A2805
8 Colloquium on Plant Analysis and Fertilizer Problems. Plant analysis and fertilizer problems, ed. by Reuther. 1961. A2806
9 International Congress on Research in Burns. Research in burns, ed. by Artz. 1962. A2807

AMERICAN JEWISH COMMITTEE. SOCIAL STUDIES SERIES. PUBLICATIONS (Harper)

1 Lowenthal, L. and Guterman, N. Prophets of deceit. 1949. A2808
2 Massing, P. W. Rehearsal for destruction. 1949. A2809
3 The Authoritarian personality, by Adorno and others. 1950. A2810
4 Bettelheim, B. and Janowitz, M. Dynamics of prejudice. 1950. A2811
5 Ackerman, N. W. and Jahoda, M. Anti-semitism and emotional disorder. 1950. A2812

AMERICAN JEWISH COMMUNAL HISTORIES (Amer. Jewish Historical Soc.)

1 Rosenberg, S. E. The Jewish community in Rochester, 1845-1925. 1954. A2813
2 Witnitzer, A. The records of the earliest Jewish community in the new world.

1954. A2814
3 Kohn, S. J. The Jewish community in Utica, New York, 1847-1948. 1959. A2815
4 Plaut, W. G. The Jews in Minnesota. 1959. A2816
5 Korn, B. W. The early Jews of New Orleans. 1969. A2817

AMERICAN LABOR: FROM CONSPIRACY TO COLLECTIVE BARGAINING (Arno)

Series I:
Abbott, E. A woman in industry. 1969. A2818
The accused and the accusers, by Spies and others. 1969. A2819
Aveling, E. B. and E. M. Working class movement in America. 1969. A2820
Beard, M. The American labor movement. 1969. A2821
Blankenhorn, H. The strike for union. 1969. A2822
Blum, S. Labor economics. 1969. A2823
Brandeis, L. D. and Goldmark, J. Women in industry. 1969. A2824
Brooks, J. G. American syndicalism. 1969. A2825
Butler, E. B. Women and the trades. 1969. A2826
Byington, M. F. Homestead. 1969. A2827
Carroll, M. R. Labor and politics. 1969. A2828
Coleman, J. W. The Molly Maguire riots. 1969. A2829
Coleman, M. Men and coal. 1969. A2830
Commons, J. R. Industrial goodwill. 1969. A2831
____ and others. Industrial government. 1969. A2832
Dacus, J. A. Annals of the great strikes in the United States. 1969. A2833
Dealtry, W. The laborer. 1969. A2834
Douglas, P. H. and others. The worker in modern economic society. 1969. A2835
Eastman, C. Work accidents and the law. 1969. A2836
Ely, R. T. The labor movement in America. 1969. A2837
Feldman, H. Problems in labor relations. 1969. A2838
Fitch, J. A. The steel worker. 1969. A2839
Furniss, E. S. and Guild, I. R. Labor problems. 1969. A2840
Gladden, W. Working people and their employers. 1969. A2841
Gompers, S. Labor and the common welfare. 1969. A2842
Hardman, J. B. S., ed. American labor dynamics. 1969. A2843
Higgins, G. G. Voluntarism in organized labor. 1969. A2844
Hiller, E. T. The strike. 1969. A2845
Hollander, J. H. and Barnett, G. E. Studies in American trade unionism. 1969. A2846
Jelley, S. M. The voice of labor. 1969. A2847
Jones, M. The autobiography of Mother Jones. 1969. A2848
Kelley, F. Some ethical gains through legislation. 1969. A2849
LaFollette, R. M., ed. The making of America: Labor. 1969. A2850
Lane, W. D. Civil War in West Virginia. 1969. A2851
Lauck, W. J. and Sydenstricker, E. Conditions of labor in American industries. 1969. A2852
Leiserson, W. M. Adjusting immigration and industry. 1969. A2853
Lescohier, D. D. Knights of St. Crispin. 1969. A2854
Levinson, E. I break strikes. 1969. A2855
Lloyd, H. D. Men, the workers. 1969. A2856
Lorwin, L. L. The women garment workers. 1969. A2857
Markham, E. and others. Children in bondage. 1969. A2858
Marot, H. American labor unions. 1969. A2859
Mason, A. T. Organized labor and the law. 1969. A2860
Newcomb, S. A plain man's talk on the labor question. 1969. A2861

Price, G. M. The modern factory. 1969. A2862
Randall, J. H. Problem of group responsibility to society. 1969. A2863
Rubinow, I. M. Social insurance. 1969. A2864
Saposs, D., ed. Readings in trade unionism. 1969. A2865
Slichter, S. H. Union policies and industrial management. 1969. A2866
Stein, L. and Taft, P., eds. The Pullman strike. 1969. A2867
____. Religion, reform, and revolution. 1969. A2868
____. Wages, hours, and strikes. 1969. A2869
Swinton, J. A momentous question. 1969. A2870
Tannenbaum, F. The labor movement. 1969. A2871
Tead, O. Instincts in industry. 1969. A2872
Vorse, M. H. Labor's new millions. 1969. A2873
Witte, E. E. The government in labor disputes. 1969. A2874
Wright, C. D. The working girls of Boston. 1969. A2875
Wyckoff, V. J. Wage policies of labor organizations in a period of industrial depression. 1969. A2876
Yellen, S. American labor struggles. 1969. A2877

Series II:

Allen, H. J. and Gompers, S. The party of the third part. 1971. A2878
Baker, R. S. The new industrial unrest. 1971. A2879
Barnes, W. E., ed. The labor problem. 1971. A2880
Barnett, G. E. and McCabe, D. A. Meditation, investigation and arbitration in industrial disputes. 1971. A2881
Bing, A. M. War-time strikes and their adjustment. 1971. A2882
Brooks, R. R. R. When labor organizes. 1971. A2883
Calkins, C. Spy overhead. 1971. A2884
Cooke, M. L. and Murray, P. Organized labor and production. 1971. A2885
Creamer, D. and Coulter, C. W. Labor and the shut-down of the Amoskeag textile mills. 1971. A2886
Glocker, T. W. The government of American trade unions. 1971. A2887
Gompers, S. Labor and the employer. 1971. A2888
Haber, W. Industrial relations in the building industry. 1971. A2889
Henry, A. Women and the labor movement. 1971. A2890
Herbst, A. The Negro in the slaughtering and meat-packing industry in Chicago. 1971. A2891
Hicks, O. Life of Richard F. Trevellick. 1971. A2892
Hillquit, M. and others. The double edge of labor's sword. 1971. A2893
Jensen, V. H. Lumber and labor. 1971. A2894
Kampelman, M. M. The Communist party vs. the C. I. O. 1971. A2895
Kingsbury, S. M., ed. Labor laws and their enforcement. 1971. A2896
McCabe, D. A. The standard rate in American trade unions. 1971. A2897
Mangold, G. B. Labor argument in the American protective tariff discussion. 1971. A2898
Millis, H. A., ed. How collective bargaining works. 1971. A2899
Montgomery, R. E. Industrial relations in the Chicago building trades. 1971. A2900
Oneal, J. The workers in American history. 1971. A2901
Palmer, G. L. Union tactics and economic change. 1971. A2902
Penny, V. How women can make money. 1971. A2903
____. Think and act. 1971. A2904
Pickering, J. The working man's political economy. 1971. A2905
Ryan, J. A. A living wage. 1971. A2906

Savage, M. D. Industrian unionism in America. 1971. A2907
Simkhotitch, M. K. The city worker's world in America. 1971. A2908
Spero, S. D. The labor movement in a government industry. 1971. A2909
Stein, L. and Taft, P., eds. Labor politics. 1971. A2910
____. The management of workers. 1971. A2911
____. Massacre at Ludlow. 1971. A2912
____. Workers speak. 1971. A2913
Stolberg, B. The story of the CIO. 1971. A2914
Taylor, P. S. The sailors' union of the Pacific. 1971. A2915
Twentieth Century Fund. How collective bargaining works. 1971. A2916
U. S. Commission on Industrial Relations. Efficiency systems and labor. 1971. A2917
____. The National Erectors' Association and the International Association of Bridge and Structural Ironworkers, by Grant. 1971. A2918
Walker, C. R. American city. 1971. A2919
Walling, W. E. American labor and American democracy. 1971. A2920
Williams, W. What's on the worker's mind. 1971. A2921
Wolman, L. The boycott in American trade unions. 1971. A2922
Ziskind, D. One thousand strikes of government employees. 1971. A2923

AMERICAN LECTURE SERIES (Thomas)

1 Forbus, W. D. Granulomatous inflammation. 1949. A2924
2 Smith, D. T. Fungus diseases of the lungs. 1948. A2925
3 Gross, R. E. Surgical treatment for abnormalities of the heart and great vessels. 1947. A2926
4 Cole, N. H. and Fowler, E. F. The present state of the surgical treatment of hyperthyroidism. 1948. A2927
5 Wolff, H. G. and Wolf, S. Pain. 1951. A2928
6 Karsner, H. T. Acute inflammations of arteries. 1947. A2929
7 Vinson, P. P. Diseases of the esophagus. 1948. A2930
8 Moore, C. R. Embryonic sex hormones and sexual differentiation. 1947. A2931
9 Magoun, H. W. and Rhines, R. Spasticity. 1948. A2932
10 Frank, L. K. Projective methods. 1948. A2933
11 Samuels, L. T. Nutrition and hormones. 1947. A2934
12 Whipple, G. H. Hemoglobin, plasma protein and cell protein. 1948. A2935
13 DuBois, E. F. Fever and the regulation of body temperature. 1948. A2936
14 Goldblatt, D. H. The renal origin of hypertension. 1952. A2937
15 Bradley, S. E. The pathologic physiology of uremia in chronic Bright's disease. 1948. A2938
16 Page, I. H. and Corcoran, A. C. Experimental renal hypertension. 1948. A2939
17 Pappenheimer, A. M. On certain aspects of vitamin E deficiency. 1948. A2940
18 Ernstene, A. C. Coronary heart disease. 1948. A2941
19 Soskin, S. The endocrines in diabetes. 1948. A2942
20 Walker, H. E. Post-traumatic epilepsy. 1949. A2943/4
21 Best, C. H. Diabetes and insulin and the lipotropic factors. 1948. A2945
22 Matson, D. D. The treatment of acute crabiocerebral injuries due to missiles. 1948. A2946
23 ____. The treatment of acute compound injuries of the spinal cord due to missiles. 1948. A2947
24 Sevringhaus, E. L. The management of the climacteric. 1948. A2948
25 Machover, K. Personality

projection in the drawing of the human figure. 1950. A2949
26 Salter, W. T. Chemical developments in thyroidology. 1950. A2950
27 Cannon, P. R. Protein and amino acid deficiencies. 1948. A2951
28 Bell, E. T. Experimental diabetes mellitus. 1948. A2952
29 Thorn, G. W. The diagnosis and treatment of adrenal insufficiency. 1951. A2953
30 Prather, G. C. The urological aspects of spinal cord injuries. 1949. A2954
31 Ficarra, B. J. Diagnostic synopsis of the acute surgical abdomen. 1949. A2955
32 Marriott, H. L. Water and salt depletion. 1952. A2956
33 Kuntz, A. The neuroanatomic basis of surgery of autonomic nervous system. 1949. A2957
34 Farquharson, R. F. Simmond's disease. 1950. A2958
35 Buxton, C. L. and Engle, E. T. Diagnosis and therapy of gynecological endocrine disorders. 1949. A2959
36 Rynearson, E. H. Obesity. 1949. A2960
37 Engel, G. L. Fainting. 1950. A2961
38 Livingstone, R. G. Primary carcinoma of the vagina. 1950. A2962
39 Reeve, D. L. Cranioplasty. 1950. A2963
40 Means, J. H. The function of the thyroid gland. 1949. A2964
41 Edwards, E. A. Thrombosis in arteriosclerosis of the lower extremities. 1950. A2965
42 Comroe, J. H. and Dripps, R. D. The Physiological basis for oxygen therapy. 1950. A2966
43 Heymans, C. Introduction to the regulation of blood pressure and heart rate. 1950. A2967
44 Seidenfeld, M. A. Psychological aspects of medical care. 1949. A2968
45 Thomas, J. E. The external secretions of the pancreas. 1950. A2969
46 Turner, H. H. The clinical use of testosterone. 1950. A2970
47 Dry, T. J. and others. Congenital anomalies of the heart and great vessels, 1949. A2971
48 Souttar, H. S. Physics and the surgeon. 1949. A2972
49 Mushin, W. W. Anesthesia for the poor risk. 1949. A2973
50 Forrester, G. C. Use of chemical tests for alcohol in traffic law enforcement. 1950. A2974
51 Canfield, N. Audiology. 1950. A2975
52 Windle, W. F. Asphyxia neonatorum. 1950. A2976
53 Hotchkiss, R. S. Etiology and diagnosis in the treatment in infertility in men. 1952. A2977
54 Low-Beers, B. V. A. The clinical use of radioactive isotypes. 1950. A2978
55 Cantril, S. T. Radiation therapy in the management of cancer of the uterine cervix. 1950. A2979
56 New, G. B. and Erich, J. B. The use of pedicle flaps of skin in plastic surgery of the head and neck. 1951. A2980
57 Kovâcs, R. Light therapy. 1950. A2981
58 Mayfield, F. H. Causalgia. 1951. A2982
59 Bonin, G. von. Essay on the cerebral cortex. 1950. A2983
60 Evans, J. B. Acute head injury. 1950. A2984
61 Smithwick, R. Surgical measures in hypertension. 1951. A2985
62 Kauffmann, F. The diagnosis of Salmonella types. 1950. A2986
63 Gray, J. S. Pulmonary ventilation and its physiological regulations. 1950. A2987
64 Farr, L. E. Treatment of nephrotic syndrome. 1951. A2988
65 Rovner, L. Infrared radiation therapy sources and their analysis with scanner.

1950. A2989
66 Baur, H. L. Urgent diagnosis, without laboratory aid. 1950. A2990
67 Colwell, A. R. Types of diabetes mellitus and their treatment. 1950. A2991
68 Schmidt, C. F. The cerebral circulation in health and disease. 1950. A2992
69 Newburgh, L. H. Significance of the body fluids in clinical medicine. 1951. A2993
70 Menkin, V. Newer concepts of inflammations. 1950. A2994
71 Harris, J. D. Some relations between vision and audition. 1950. A2995
72 Hellersberg, E. F. The individual's relation to reality in our culture. 1950. A2996
73 Graubard, D. J. and Peterson, M. C. Clinical uses of intravenous procaine. 1950. A2997
74 Seyle, H. and Stone, H. Experimental morphology of the adrenal cortex. 1950. A2998
75 Potter, V. R. Enzymes, growth and cancer. 1950. A2999
76 Segal, M. S. The management of patients with severe bronchial asthma. 1950. A3000
77 Beyer, K. H. Pharmacological basis of penicillin therapy. 1950. A3001
78 Coon, C. S. and others. Races. 1950. A3002
79 Steiner, M. E. The psychologist in industry. 1949. A3003
80 Kendall, H. W. Fever therapy. 1951. A3004
81 Recent advances in diagnostic psychological testing by Harris and others. 1950. A3005
82 Harrower, M. R. and Steiner, M. E. Large scale Rorschach techniques. 1951. A3006
83 Pool, J. L. The neurosurgical treatment of traumatic paraplegia. 1951. A3007
84 Kauffmann, F. The differentiation of Escherichia and Klebsiella types. 1950. A3008
85 Mennell, J. B. Manual therapy. 1951. A3009
86 Coller, F. A. and others. Indications for the results of splenectomy. 1950. A3010
87 Hecht, H. H. Basic principles of clinical electrocardiography. 1950. A3011
88 Youmans, W. B. and Huckins, A. R. Hemodynamics in failure of the circulation. 1950. A3012
89 Lewis, L. A. Electrophoresis in physiology. 1950. A3013
90 McComb, S. J. The preparation of photographic prints for medical publication. 1951. A3014
91 Osborne, S. L. Diathermy. 1950. A3015
92 McMichael, J. The pharmacology of the failing human heart. 1951. A3016
93 Inbau, F. E. Self-incrimination. 1950. A3017
94 Mykebust, H. R. Your deaf child. 1950. A3018
95 Gibson, H. L. The photography of patients. 1951. A3019
96 Grunfeld, F. V. Handwriting. 1952. A3020
97 Weiss, E. Emotional factors in cardiovascular disease. 1951. A3021
98 Peterson, V. W. Gambling. 1951. A3022
99 Keeney, A. H. Chronology of ophthalmic development. 1951. A3023
100 Roth, G. M. Tobacco and cardiovascular system. 1951. A3024
101 Bargen, J. A. Chronic ulcerative colitis. 1951. A3025
102 Hart, V. L. Congenital dysplasia of the hip joint. 1952. A3026
103 Gaunt, R. and Birnie, J. H. Hormones and body water. 1951. A3027
104 Cuneo, H. M. and Rand, C. W. Brain tumors of childhood. 1952. A3028
105 McClellan, W. S. Physical medicine and rehabilitation for the aged. 1951. A3029
106 Moseley, H. F. Ruptures of the rotator cuff. 1952. A3030
107 Snapper, I. Rare manifestations of metabolic bone

disease. 1946. A3031
108 Kountz, W. B. Thyroid function and its possible role in vascular degeneration. 1951. A3032
109 Randall, L. M. and McElin, T. W. Amenorrhea. 1951. A3033
110 Heckel, N. J. The effect of hormones upon the testis and accessory sex organs. 1951. A3034
111 McCulloch, W. S. Finality and form. 1952. A3035
112 Kirk, P. L. Destiny and refractive index. 1951. A3036
113 Rinzler, S. H. Cardiac pain. 1951. A3037
114 Zimmermann, B. Endocrine functions of the pancreas. 1952. A3038
115 Kuntz, A. Visceral innervation and its relation to personality. 1951. A3039
116 Johns, H. E. The physics of radiation therapy. 1952. A3040
117 Horrax, G. Neurosurgery. 1952. A3041
118 Fleischmann, W. Comparative physiology of the thyroid and parathyroid glands. 1952. A3042
119 Conway, E. J. The biochemistry of gastric acid secretion. 1952. A3043
120 Bender, M. B. Disorders in perception. 1952. A3044
121 Biggs, R. Prothrombin deficiency. 1951. A3045
122 Wall, R. L. Practical blood group methods. 1951. A3046
123 Davis, J. E. Clinical applications of recreational therapy. 1952. A3047
124 Katz, L. N. and Stamler, J. Experimental atherosclerosis. 1953. A3048
125 Rantz, L. A. The prevention of rheumatic fever. 1952. A3049
126 Russell, P. F. Malaria. 1952. A3050
127 Andrews, W. Cellular changes with age. 1952. A3051
128 Reynolds, S. R. M. Physiological basis of gynecology and obstetrics. 1952. A3052
129 Williams, H. L. Ménière's disease. 1952. A3053
130 Rifkin, H. L. and others. Diabetic glomerulosclerosis. 1952. A3054
131 Derbes, V. J. and others. Untowards reactions of cortisone and ACTH. 1951. A3055
132 Moore, F. D. and Ball, M. R. The metabolic response to surgery. 1952. A3056
133 Waldbott, G. L. Contact dermatitis. 1953. A3057
134 Sarnat, B. G. ed. The temporomandibular joint. 1951. A3058
135 Holcomb, R. L. Police patrol. 1952. A3059
136 Gibson, H. L. Copying and duplicating medical subjects and radiographs. 1952. A3060
137 Blake, R. G. The present status of antibiotic therapy with particular reference to chloramphenicol, aureomycin and terremycin. 1952. A3061
138 Beecher, H. K. Early care of the seriously wounded man. 1952. A3062
139 ____. Principles, problems, and practices of anesthesia for thoracic surgery. 1958. A3063
140 Wilmer, H. A. This is your world. 1952. A3064
141 Holden, W. D. Acute peripheral arterial occlusion. 1952. A3065
142 Bruetsch, W. L. Syphilitic optic atrophy. 1953. A3066
143 Braunstein, J. R. The ballistocardiogram. 1953. A3067
144 Dubusson, M. Muscular contraction. 1954. A3068
145 Arnold, H. L. Modern concepts of leprosy. 1953. A3069
146 Jukes, T. H. B-vitamins for blood formation. 1952. A3070
147 Selle, W. A. Body temperature. 1952. A3071
148 Patterson, C. H. The Weschler-Bellevue scales. 1953. A3072
149 Grassi, J. R. The Grassi block substitution

test for measuring organic brain pathology. 1953. A3073
150 Dill, L. V. The obstetrical forceps. 1953. A3074
151 Goodman, J. I. and others. The diabetic neuropathies. 1953. A3075
152 Massopust, L. C. Infrared photography in medicine. 1952. A3076
153 Klein, A. Slipped capital femoral epiphysics. 1952. A3077
154 Pullen, R. L. The internship. 1952. A3078
155 Noble, F. W. Electrical methods of blood-pressure recording. 1953. A3079
156 Saklad, M. Inhalation therapy and resuscitation. 1953. A3080
157 Sammis, F. E. The allergic patient and his world. 1953. A3081
158 Reis, R. A. and others. Diabetes and pregnancy. 1952. A3082
159 Greenhill, J. P. Analgesia and anesthesia. 1952. A3083
160 Reimann, H. A. Pnuemonia. 1954. A3084
161 Wikler, A. Opiate addiction. 1953. A3085
162 Gordon, D. M. The clinical use of corticotropin, and cortisone, and hydrocoetisone in eye disease. 1954. A3086
163 Barta, F. R. The moral theory of behavior. 1952. A3087
164 Wyngraf, F. Psychosomatic approach to gynecology and obstetrics. 1953. A3088
165 Womack, N., ed. On burns. 1953. A3089
166 Wolff, H. G. Stress and disease. 1953. A3090
167 Sheehan, H. L. and Moore, H. C. Renal cortical necrosis of the kidney and concealed accidental hemorrhage. 1953. A3091
168 Galloway, T. C. The treatment of respiratory emergencies. 1953. A3092
169 Maurer, D. W. Narcotics and narcotic addiction. 1954. A3093
170 Pulaski, E. J. Surgical infections. 1954. A3094
171 Piers, G. Shame and guilt. 1953. A3095
172 Hoffman, J. G. The size and growth of tissue cells. 1953. A3096
173 Black, B. M. Hyperparathyroidism. 1953. A3097
174 Macgregor, F. M. Facial deformities and plastic surgery. 1953. A3098
175 Sturgis, C. C. Hypersplenism. 1953. A3099
176 DeWesse, D. D. Dizziness. 1953. A3100
177 Spurling, R. G. Lesions of the lumbar intervertebral disc. 1953. A3101
178 Sulzberger, M. B. and Hermann, F. The clinical significance of disturbances and the delivery of sweat. 1954. A3102
179 Ingle, D. J. and Baker, B. L. Physiological and therapeutic effects of corticotropin. 1953. A3103
180 DuBrul, E. L. The adaptive chin. 1954. A3104
181 Rydberg, E. The mechanism of labour. 1954. A3105
182 Downing, J. G. The cutaneous manifestations of systematic diseases. 1954. A3106
183 Wolff, J. W. The laboratory diagnosis of leptospirosis. 1954. A3107
184 Ruskin, A. Physiological cardiology. 1953. A3108
185 Prigogine, I. Introduction to thermodynamics of irreversible processes. 1955. A3109
186 Combes, F. C. Coal tar and cutaneous carcinogenesis in industry. 1954. A3110
187 Faber, F. M. Lung cancer. 1954. A3111
188 Page, E. W. The hypertensive disorders of pregnancy. 1953. A3112
189 McKittrick, L. S. Carcinoma of the colon. 1954. A3113
190 Burch, G. E. A primer of congestive heart failure. 1954. A3114
191 Faust, E. C. Amebiasis.

1954. A3115
192 Grollman, A. Acute renal failure. 1953. A3116
193 Russ, J. D. Resuscitation of the newborn. 1953. A3117
194 Haugaard, N. The action of insulin. 1953. A3118
195 Kauvar, A. J. and Goldner, M. G. Hypoglycemia and hypoglycemic syndrome. 1954. A3119
196 Laughlin, J. S. Physical aspect of betatron therapy. 1954. A3120
197 Seed, L. and Field, T. The treatment of toxic goiter with radioactive iodine. 1953. A3121
198 Atlee, H. B. Chronic iliac pain in women. 1956. A3122
199 Tolstoi, E. The practical management of diabetis. 1953. A3123
200 Jolly, H. Sexual precocity. 1955. A3124
201 Frazier, C. N. and Blank, I. H. A formulary for external therapy of the skin. 1954. A3125
202 Schiff, L. Clinical approach to jaundice. 1954. A3126
203 Wilson, J. M. Pelvic relaxation and herniations. 1954. A3127
204 Gastaut, H. The epilepsies, electro-clinical corrections. 1954. A3128
205 Shirley, H. F. The child, his parents and the physician. 1954. A3129
206 Jones, G. E. S. Management of endocrine disorders of menstruation and fertility. 1954. A3130
207 Brown, J. B. and McDowell, F. Neck dissections. 1954. A3131
208 Bickers, W. Menorrhalgia. 1954. A3132
209 Rocha e Silva, M. Histamine. 1955. A3133
210 Sheppard, L. B. Current concepts of diabetes mellitus with special reference to ocular changes. 1955. A3134
211 Starr, P. Hypothyroidism. 1954. A3135
212 Escamilla, R. F. Laboratory aids in endocrine diagnosis. 1954. A3136
213 Lenzen, V. F. Causality in natural science. 1954. A3137
214 Kaye, S. A handbook of emergency toxicology. 1954. A3138
215 McGill, V. J. Emotions and reason. 1954. A3139
216 Middleton, W. S. Physiological methods in clinical practice. 1954. A3140
217 Roskam, J. Arrest of bleeding. 1954. A3141
218 Kutash, S. B. and Gehl, R. H. The graphometer projection technique. 1954. A3142
219 Fine, J. The bacterial factor in traumic shock. 1954. A3143
220 Simmons, F. A. The diagnosis and treatment of the infertile female. 1954. A3144
221 Héring, J. A good and bad government according to the New Testament. 1954. A3145
222 Davis, L. J. and Brown, A. The magaloblastic anaemias. 1953. A3146
223 Canizares, O. Modern diagnosis and treatment of the minor venereal diseases. 1954. A3147
224 Samter, M. and Durham, O. C., eds. Regional allergy of the United States, Canada, Mexico and Cuba. 1951. A3148
225 Fish, J. S. Hemorrhage of late pregnancy. 1955. A3149
226 Burch, J. C. and Lavely, H. T. Hysterectomy. 1954. A3150
227 Scott, W. W. and Hudson, P. B. Surgery of the adrenal glands. 1954. A3151
228 Singer, M. The human brain in sagittal section. 1954. A3152
229 Riehl, G. F. E. and Köpf, O. The therapy of skin tuberculosis. 1955. A3153
230 Holsopple, J. Q. and Miale, F. R. Sentence

completion. 1954. A3154
231 Derbes, V. J. and Kerr, A. Cough syncope. 1955. A3155
232 Stephen, C. R. Elements of pediatric anesthesia. 1954. A3156
233 Lassek, A. M. The pyramidal tract. 1954. A3157
234 May, C. D. Cystic fibrosis of the pancreas in infants. 1954. A3158
235 Kolb, L. C. The painful phantom. 1954. A3159
236 Durkin, H. E. Group therapy for mothers of disturbed children. 1954. A3160
237 Box, H. K. Oxygen insufflation in periodontal diseases. 1955. A3161
238 Gray, L. A. Vaginal hysterectomy. 1955. A3162
239 Obermayer, M. E. Psychocutaneous medicine. 1955. A3163
240 Minz, L. B. The role of humoral agents in nervous activities. 1953. A3164
241 Ricketts, H. T. Diabetic mellitus. 1955. A3165
242 White, P. D. Clues in the diagnosis and treatment of heart disease. 1955. A3166
243 Ober, L. R. Backache. 1955. A3167
244 Greenfield, J. G. The spinocerebellar degenerations. 1954. A3168
245 Lorhan, P. H. Geriatric anesthesia. 1955. A3169
246 Calkins, L. A. Normal labor. 1955. A3170
247 Berg, J. H. v. d. The phenomenological approach to psychiatry. 1955. A3171
248 Keeney, E. L. Practical medical mycology. 1955. A3172
249 Weinstein, E. A. and Kahn, R. L. Denial of disease. 1955. A3173
250 Hartwell, S. W. Mechanism of healing in human wounds. 1955. A3174
251 Atkinson, W. S. Anesthesia in ophthalmology. 1955. A3175
252 Mack, H. C. The plasma proteins in pregnancy. 1955. A3176
253 Hazen, E. L. and Reed, F. C. Laboratory identification of pathogenic fungi simplified. 1955. A3177
254 Beecher, H. K. and Todd, D. P. A study of the deaths associated with anesthesia and surgery... 1954. A3178
255 Harley, H. R. S. Subphrenic abscess. 1955. A3179
256 Benjamin, A. C. Operationism. 1955. A3180
257 Faber, H. K. The pathogenesis of poliomyelitis. 1955. A3181
258 Parmley, R. T. Saddle block anesthesia. 1955. A3182
259 Postell, W. D. Applied medical bibliography for students. 1955. A3183
260 Glees, P. Neuroglia, morphology and function. 1955. A3184
261 Euler, U. S. Von. Noradrenaline. 1956. A3185
262 Roser, C. M. The relationship between syringomyelia and neuroplasm. 1956. A3186
263 Feuer, L. S. Psychoanalysis and ethics. 1955. A3187
264 Wolff, W. Contemporary psychotherapists examine themselves. 1956. A3188
265 Shefts, L. M. The initial management of thoracic and thoracoabdominal trauma. 1956. A3189
266 Hardy, J. D. Surgical physiology of the adrenal cortex. 1955. A3190
267 Welsh, A. L. Differential diagnosis of leukoplakia, lukokerastosis and cancer in the mouth. 1955. A3191
268 Jackson, R. The cervical syndrome. 1956. A3192
269 Nicola, P. de. The laboratory diagnosis of coagulation defects. 1956. A3193
270 Conway, H. Tumors of the skin. 1956. A3194
271 Holman, E. New concepts of surgery in the vascular system. 1955. A3195
272 Glaser, J. Allergy in childhood. 1956. A3196
273 Gross, E. G. and Schriffrin, M. J. Clinical

analgetics. 1955. A3197
274 Kerr, A. Subacute bacterial endocarditis. 1956. A3198
275 Virtue, R. W. Hypothermic anesthesia. 1955. A3199
276 Harrower, M. B., ed. Medical and psychological teamwork in the care of the chronically ill. 1955. A3200
277 Weller, C. V. Causal factors in cancer of the lung. 1956. A3201
278 Bakay, L. The blood-brain barrier. 1956. A3202
279 Abrams, H. L. and Kaplan, H. S. Angiocardiographic interpretation in congenital heart disease. 1956. A3203
280 Colby, M. C. Postural back pain. 1956. A3204
281 Crowe, F. W. and others. A clinical pathological and genetic study of the multiple neurofibromatosis. 1956. A3205
282 Block, W. D. and Goor, K. V. Metabolism pharmacology and therapeutic use of gold compounds. 1956. A3206
283 Little, D. M. "Controlled hypertension." 1956. A3207
284 Strauss, M. B. and Paiz, L. G. Clinical management of renal failure. 1956. A3208
285 Kuno, Y. Human perspiration. 1956. A3209
286 DeTakats, G. Thromboembolic disease. 1955. A3210
287 Opler, M. K. Culture, psychiatry, and human values. 1956. A3211
288 Menkin, V. Biochemical mechanisms in inflamation. 1956. A3212
289 Hansell, P. A system of ophthalmic illustration. 1957. A3213
290 Ruskin, A. Classics in arterial hypertension. 1956. A3214
291 Atlee, H. B. Natural childbirth. 1956. A3215
292 Caligor, L. A new approach to figure drawing. 1957. A3216
293 Welsh, A. L. The dermatologist's handbook. 1957. A3217
294 Foldes, F. F. Muscle relaxants in anesthesiology. 1956. A3218
295 White, P. D. Clues in the diagnosis and treatment of heart disease. 1956. A3219
296 Evans, F. G. Stress and strain in bones. 1957. A3220
297 Ellis, A. The psychology of sex offenders. 1956. A3221
298 Schwartz, H. and others. Manual of anesthesiology for residents and medical students. 1957. A3222
299 Liddell, H. S. Emotional hazards in animals and man. 1956. A3223
300 Burks, J. W. Wire brush surgery in the treatment of certain cosmetic defects and diseases of the skin. 1956. A3224
301 Spurling, R. G. Lesions of the cervical intervertebral disc. 1956. A3225
302 Bickers, W. Gynecologic therapy. 1957. A3226
303 Pool, J. L. and Pava, A. A. The early diagnosis and treatment of acoustic nerve tumors. 1957. A3227
304 Keown, K. K. Anesthesia for surgery of the heart. 1956. A3228
305 Schroeder, H. A. Mechanism of hypertension. 1957. A3229
306 O'Conor, V. J. Suprapubic closure of vesicovaginal fistula. 1957. A3230
307 Keeney, A. H. Lens materials in the prevention of eye injuries. 1957. A3231
308 Bluefarb, S. M. Kaposi's sarcoma. 1957. A3232
309 De Palma, A. F. Degenerative changes in the sternoclavicular and acromicular joints in various decades. 1957. A3233
310 King, E. L. Occipito-posterior positions. 1957. A3234
311 Barsky, A. J. Congenital anomalies of the hands and their treatment. 1958. A3235
312 Marshall, M. L. The physician's own library. 1957. A3236
313 Roman, M. Reaching delinquents through reading.

1957. A3237
314 Morawitz, P. The chemistry of blood coagulation, tr. by Hartmann and Guenther. 1958. A3238
315 Pearson, O. H., ed. Hypophysectomy. 1957. A3239
316 Nicola, P. de. Thrombelstography. 1957. A3240
317 Roberts, K. E. and others. Electrolyte changes in surgery. 1958. A3241
318 Kramer, E. Art therapy in a children's community. 1958. A3242
319 Senturia, B. H. Diseases of the external ear. 1957. A3243
320 Brown, C. C. and Saucer, R. T. Electronic instrumentation for the behavorial sciences. 1958. A3244
321 Cornu, A. Origins of Marxian thought. 1957. A3245
322 Perry, E. T. The human ear canal. 1957. A3246
323 Gantt, W. A. H., ed. Physiological bases of psychiatry. 1958. A3247
324 Wilson, J. W. Clinical and immunologic aspects of funbous diseases. 1957. A3248
325 Calkins, L. A. Abnormal labor. 1958. A3249
326 Dillon, J. B. Spinal anesthesia. 1958. A3250
327 Alexander, L. Objective approaches to treatment in psychiatry. 1958. A3251
328 DuBrul, E. L. Evolution of the speech apparatus. 1958. A3252
329 Russ, J. D. and Soboloff, H. R. A primer of cerebral palsy. 1958. A3253
330 Bluefarb, S. M. and others. Cutaneous manifestations of the malignant lymphomas. 1958. A3254
331 Zucker, L. J. Ego structure in paranoid schizophrenia. 1958. A3255
332 Bonin, G. von. Some papers on the cerebral cortex. 1960. A3256
333 Wolff, H. G. and Wolf, S. G. Pain. 1958. A3257
334 Jackson, R. The cervical syndrone. 1958. A3258
335 Dornette, W. H. L. Hospital planning for the anesthesiologist. 1958. A3259
336 Carton, C. A. Cerebral angiography in the management of head trauma. 1959. A3260
337 Peck, H. B. A new pattern for mental health services in a children's court. 1958. A3261
338 Leake, C. D. The amphetamines. 1958. A3262
339 Crue, B. L. Medullobastoma. 1958. A3263
340 Adriani, J., comp. The recovery room. 1958. A3264
341 Bunge, M. A. Metascientific queries. 1959. A3265
342 Bonica, J. J. Clinical application of diagnostic and therapeutic nerve blocks. 1959. A3266
343 Rand, R. W. and C. W. Intraspinal tumors of childhood. 1959. A3267
344 Diehl, C. F. Compendium of research and theory on stuttering. 1958. A3268
345 Goldstein, L. A. The surgical treatment of scoliosis. 1959. A3269
346 Cumings, J. N., ed. Heavy metals and the brain. 1959. A3270
347 Handley, C. A. and Moyer, J. H. The pharmacology and clinical use of diuretics. 1959. A3271
348 Kugelmass, I. N. Biochemistry of blood in health and disease. 1959. A3272
349 Wansker, B. A. X-ray and radium in dermatology. 1959. A3273
350 Welsh, A. L. Psychotherapeutic drugs. 1958. A3274
351 Beecher, H. K. Principles, problems and practices of anesthesia for thoracic surgery. 1958. A3275
352 ____. Experimentation in man. 1959. A3276
353 Edel, M. and E. Anthropology and ethics. 1959. A3277
354 Bluefarb, S. M. Leukemia cutis. 1959. A3278
355 Parsons, W. H., ed.

Cancer of the breast. 1959. A3279
356 Goldsmith, G. A. Nutritional diagnosis. 1959. A3280
357 Williams, H. M. and others. Neurological complications of lymphomus and leukemias. 1959. A3281
358 Walder, H. Drive structure and criminality. 1959. A3282
359 Tower, D. B. Neurochemistry of epilepsy. 1960. A3283
360 Berde, B. Recent progress in oxytocin research. 1959. A3284
361 Blandergroen, W. Problems in photosynthesis. 1960. A3285
362 Nyboer, J. Electrical impedance plethusmography. 1959. A3286
363 Bluefarb, S. M., ed. Cutaneous manifestations of the reticuloendotheledl gramelomas. 1960. A3287
364 Mitra, S. Mitra operation for cancer of the cervix. 1960. A3288
365 Zamenhof, S. The chemistry of heredity. 1959. A3289
366 Pitts, R. F. The physiological basis of diuretic therapy. 1959. A3290
367 Farber, M. Naturalism and subjectivism. 1959. A3291
368 Wright, S. E. The metabolism of cardiac glycosedes. 1960. A3292
369 Wilkinson, R. H. Chemical micromethods in clinical medicine. 1960. A3293
370 Hazen, E. L. and Reed, F. C. Laboratory identification of pathogenic fungi simplified. 1960. A3294
371 Foulger, J. H. Chemicals, drugs, and health. 1959. A3295
372 Gibson, H. L. The photography of patients. 1960. A3296
373 Rosen, E. Apotic cataract. 1959. A3297
374 Apley, J. Child with abdominal pain. 1959. A3298
375 Luchins, A. S. A functional approach to training in clinical psychology via study of a mental hospital. 1959. A3299
376 Hurley, H. J. and Shelley, W. B. The human apocrine sweat gland in health and disease. 1960. A3300
377 Busch, H. Chemistry of pancreatic diseases. 1959. A3301
378 Bluefarb, S. M. The cutaneous manifestations of benign inflammatory reticuloses. 1960. A3302
379 Kennedy, R. H. Nonpenetrating injuries of the abdomen. 1960. A3303
380 Winklemann, R. K. Nerve endings in normal and pathologic skin. 1960. A3304
381 King, H. K. The chemistry of lipids in health and disease. 1960. A3305
382 Cronkite, E. P. and Bond, V. P. Radiation injury in man. 1960. A3306
383 Larks, S. D. Electrohysterography. 1960. A3307
384 Jones, R. M. An application of psychoanalysis to education. 1960. A3308
385 Lewis, L. A. Electrophoresis in physiology. 1960. A3309
386 Joseph, J. Man's posture. 1960. A3310
387 Creative variations in the projected techniques, by Harrower and others. 1960. A3311
388 Mackby, M. J. The surgical treatment of portal hypertension. 1960. A3312
389 Moersch, H. J. and Anderson, H. A. Diagnosis and treatment of diseases of the trachea and bronchi. 1960. A3313
390 Schrieber, G. Embolic dispersoids in health and diseases. 1960. A3314
391 Mandarino, M. P. Chemical osteosynthesis in orthopaedic surgery. 1960. A3315
392 Sterling, J. A. Experiences with congential biliary atresia. 1960. A3316
393 Pitts-Rivers, R. and Tata, J. R. The chemistry of thyroid diseases. 1960. A3317
394 Kalmus, H. and Hubbard, S. J. The chemical senses in health disease. 1960. A3318

395 Faulconer, A. and Bickford, R. G. Electrocephalography in anesthesiology. 1960. A3319
396 Linman, J. W. and Bethell, F. H. Factors controlling erythropocesis. 1960. A3320
397 Holland, W. C. and Klein, R. L. Chemistry of heart failure. 1960. A3321
398 Cohn, I. Strangulation obstruction. 1960. A3322
399 Flocks, R. H. and Culp, D. A. Radiation therapy of early prostatic cancer. 1960. A3323
400 Mecham, M. J. and others. Speech therapy in cerebral palsy. 1960. A3324
401 Knoefel, P. K. Radiopaque diagnostic agents. 1961. A3325
402 Hoffer, A. and Osmond, H. The chemical basis of clinical psychiatry. 1960. A3326
403 Ascher, K. W. The aqueous veins. 1961. A3327
404 Bower, E. M. Early identification of emotionally handicapped children in school. 1960. A3328
405 Alexander, L. and others. Multiple sclerosis. 1961. A3329
406 Quastel, J. H. and D. M. J. The chemistry of brain metabolism in health and disease. 1961. A3330
407 Talmage, D. W. and Cann, J. R. The chemistry of immunity in health and disease. 1961. A3331
408 Ambard, L. and Trautmann, S. Ultrafiltration. 1960. A3332
409 Scheffler, I. The language of education. 1960. A3333
410 Bell, E. T. Diabetes mellitus. 1960. A3334
411 Allison, J. B. and Fitzpatrick, W. H. Dietary proteins in health and disease. 1960. A3335
412 Zoffey, J. M. Quantitative cellular haematology. 1960. A3336
413 Bowsher, D. and Kugelmass, I. N. Cerebrospinal fluid dynamics in health and disease. 1960. A3337
414 Rashevsky, N. Mathematical principles in biology and their applications. 1961. A3338
415 Symposium on the Prediction of Overt Behavior ... The prediction of overt behavior through the use of projective techniques, by Carr and others. 1960. A3339
416 Ingram, V. M. Hemoglobin and its abnormalities. 1961. A3340
417 Swank, R. L. A biochemical basis of multiple sclerosis. 1961. A3341
418 Goff, C. W. Surgical treatment of unequal extremities. 1960. A3342
419 Johns, H. E. The physics of radiology. 1961. A3343
420 Frankel, V. H. The femoral neck. 1960. A3344
421 Ratnoff, O. D. Blending syndromes. 1960. A3345
422 Gray, C. H. Bile pigments in health and disease. 1961. A3346
423 Ducasse, C. J. A critical examination of the belief in a life after death. 1961. A3347
424 Bergel, F. Chemistry of enzymes in cancer. 1961. A3348
425 Kaye, S. Handbook of emergency toxicology. 1961. A3349
426 Larks, S. D. Fetal electrocardiography. 1961. A3350
427 Scheflin, A. E. A psychotherapy of schizophrenia. 1961. A3351
428 Botella Llusiá, J. Obstetrical endocrinology. 1961. A3352
429 Manson-Bahr, P. H. and Walters, J. H. The chemotherapy of tropical diseases. 1961. A3353
430 Finean, J. B. Chemical ultrastructure in living tissues. 1961. A3354
431 Gamble, J. R. and Wilbur, D. L. Chemistry of digestive diseases. 1961. A3355
432 Lederman, M. Cancer of the nasopharynx. 1961. A3356
433 Fishman, W. H. Chemistry of drug metabolism. 1961. A3357

434 Pickering, G. W. and others. The treatment of hypertension. 1961. A3358
435 Russell, W. F. and Middlebrook, G. Chemotherapy of tuberculosis. 1960. A3359
436 Josephson, B. Chemistry and therapy of electrolyte disorders. 1961. A3360
437 Allers, R. Existentialism and psychiatry. 1961. A3361
438 Jones, R. J. and Cohen, L. Chemistry and therapy of chronic cardiovascular disease. 1961. A3362
439 Anderson Hospital. Cancer chemotherapy. 1961. A3363
440 Welsh, A. L. The fixed eruption. 1961. A3364
441 Zweifach, B. W. Functional behavior of the microcirculation. 1961. A3365
442 Horowitz, I. L. Philosophy, science, and the sociology of knowledge. 1961. A3366
443 Palmer, E. D. Diagnosis of upper gastrointestinal hemorrhage. 1961. A3367
444 Schwartz, P. Cerebral apoplexy. 1961. A3368
445 Cavanagh, D. Obstetrical emergencies. 1961. A3369
446 Pizzolato, P. and Mannheimer, W. Histopathologic effects of local anesthetic drugs and related substances. 1961. A3370
447 Fletcher, H. and McComb, W. Radiation therapy in the management of cancers of the oral cavity. 1962. A3371
448 Wasmuth, C. E. Anesthesia and the law. 1961. A3372
449 Hagbard, L. Pregnancy and diabetes mellitus. 1961. A3373
450 Mathewson, H. S. Structural forms of anesthetic compounds. 1961. A3374
451 Lerman, S. Glancoma. 1961. A3375
452 Cameron, G. R. and Spector, W. G. The chemistry of the injured cell. 1961. A3376
453 Doyle, J. E. Extracorporeal hemodialysis therapy. 1962. A3377
454 Nakahara, W. and Fukuoka, F. Chemistry of cancer toxin. 1961. A3378
455 Schriener, G. E. and Maher, J. F. Uremia. 1961. A3379
456 Hall, D. A. The chemistry of connective tissue. 1961. A3380
457 Block, J. The Q-sort method in personality assessment and psychiatric research. 1961. A3381
458 Wesolowski, S. A. Evaluation of tissue and prosthetic vascular grafts. 1962. A3382
459 Piccardi, G. The chemical basis of medical climatology. 1962. A3383
460 Jacobson, J. H. Clinical electroritinography. 1961. A3384
461 Harrower, M. R. The practice of clinical psychology. 1961. A3385
462 Ngai, S. H. and Popper, E. M. Metabolic effects of anesthesia. 1962. A3386
463 Moss, A. J. and Adams, F. H. Problems of blood pressure in childhood. 1962. A3387
464 Marble, A. and Cahill, G. F. The chemistry and chemotherapy of diabetes mellitis. 1962. A3388
465 Hoffer, A. Niacin therapy in psychiatry. 1962. A3389
466 Sognnaes, R. F. Chemistry and prevention caries. 1962. A3390
467 Oliver, R. T. Conversation. 1961. A3391
468 Russell, C. S. Visicovaginal fistulas and related matters. 1962. A3392
469 Brechner, V. J. and others. Practica electroencephalography for the anesthesiologist. 1962. A3393
470 Freed, H. The chemistry and therapy of behavior disorders in children. 1962. A3394
471 Astrup, C. Schizophrenia. 1962. A3395
472 Jenkner, F. L. Rheoencephalography. 1962. A3396
473 Engel, G. L. Fainting. 1962. A3397

474 Ullman, M. Behavior changes in patients following strokes. 1962. A3398
475 Arena, J. M. Poisoning. 1963. A3399
476 Schwartz, H. and others. Manual of anesthesiology for residents and medical students. 1962. A3400
477 Fletcher, G. H. and MacComb, W. S. Radiation therapy in the management of cancers of the oral cavity and oropharynx. 1962. A3401
478 Wise, R. E. Intravenous cholangiography. 1962. A3402
479 Tosberg, W. A. Upper and lower extremity protheses. 1962. A3403
480 Snidecor, J. C. and others. Speech rehabilitation of the laryngectomized. 1962. A3404
481 Goldberg, A. and C. Diseases of porphyrin metabolism. 1962. A3405
482 Welsh, A. L. Side effects of anti-obesity drugs. 1961. A3406
483 Bricklin, B. and others. The hand test. 1962. A3407
484 Hauser, E. D. W. Curvatures of the spine. 1962. A3408
485 Millen, J. W. The nutritional basis of reproduction. 1962. A3409
486 Dornette, W. H. L. Anatomy for the anesthesiologist. 1963. A3410
487 Epstein, E. H. and others. Radiodermatitis. 1962. A3411
488 Bishop, P. M. F. Chemistry of the sex hormones. 1962. A3412
489 Greenhill, J. P. Analgesia and anesthesia in obstetrics. 1962. A3413
490 Badger, G. M. The chemical basis of carcinogenic activity. 1962. A3414
491 Dennie, C. C. History of syphilis. 1962. A3415
492 Schwartzman, R. M. and Orkin, M. A comparative study of skin. 1962. A3416
493 Foa, P. P. and Galansino, G. Glucagon. 1962. A3417
494 Humphrey, G. and Coxon, R. V. The chemistry of thinking. 1962. A3418
495 Ostfeld, A. M. The common headache syndromes. 1962. A3419
496 Astrup, C. Prognosis in functional psychoses. 1962. A3420
497 Searcy, R. and Bergquist, L. M. Lipoprotein chemistry in health and disease. 1962. A3421
498 Allen, R. M. and Jefferson, T. W. Psychological evaluation of the cerebral palsied person. 1962. A3422
499 Kroger, W. S., ed. Psychosomatic obstetrics and gynecology. 1962. A3423
500 Rhoads, J. E. and Howard, J. M. The chemistry of trauma. 1962. A3424
501 Brooks, J. R. Endocrine tissue transplantation. 1962. A3425
502 Klarmann, E. G. Cosmetic chemistry for dermatologists. 1962. A3426
503 Adams, J. Q. Chemistry and therapy of diseases of pregnancy. 1962. A3427
504 Blum, R. H. Tranquilizing and antidepressive drugs. 1962. A3428
505 Carruthers, C. Biochemistry of skin. 1962. A3429
506 Oliver, R. T. Culture and communication. 1962. A3430
507 Fazekas, J. F. and Alman, R. W. Coma. 1962. A3431
508 Crowle, A. J. Delayed hypersensitivity. 1962. A3432
509 Greer, A. E. Disseminating fungus diseases of the lungs. 1962. A3433
510 Oliver, R. T. and Barbara, D. A. The healthy mind in communion and communication. 1962. A3434
511 Kahn, E. The past is not past. 1962. A3435
512 Dreyfus, J. C. and Schapira, G. Biochemistry of heredity myopathies. 1962. A3436
513 Maurer, D. W. and Vogel, V. H. Narcotics and

narcotic addiction. 1962. A3437
514 Kallen, H. M. Philosophical issues in adult education. 1962. A3438
515 Marsh, W. H. Automation in clinical chemistry. 1963. A3439
516 Boyland, E. The biochemistry of bladder cancer. 1963. A3440
517 Albert, S. N. Blood volume. 1963. A3441
518 Mackay, I. R. and Burnet, F. M. Autoimmunity in disease. 1963. A3442
519 Feibleman, J. K. Biosocial factors in mental illness. 1962. A3443
520 Neustadt, D. H. Chemistry and therapy of collagen diseases. 1963. A3444
521 Curry, A. S. Poison detection in human organs. 1963. A3445
522 Kerdel-Vegas, F. and others. Rhinoscleroma. 1963. A3446
523 Smith, D. T. Fungus diseases of the lungs. 2d ed. 1963. A3447
524 Ungar, U. C. Excitation. 1963. A3448
525 Rosar, V. W. Perthes and parents. 1963. A3449
526 Zelickson, A. S. Electron microscopy of human skin and oral mucous membrane. 1963. A3450
527 Kinsella, T. J. Tumors of the chest. 1963. A3451
528 Lewis, R. A. Tropical therapeutics. 1963. A3452
529 Edelson, M. The termination of intensive psychotherapy. 1963. A3453
530 Von Kaulla, K. N. Chemistry of thrombolysis. 1963. A3454
531 Enlow, D. H. Principles of bone remodeling. 1963. A3455
532 Verzar, F. Experimental gerontology. 1963. A3456
533 Felson, B. and Wiot, J. F. Case of the day. 1966. A3457
534 Freeman, J. T., ed. Clinical principles and drugs in the aging. 1963. A3458
535 Smith, R. H. Electrical anesthesia. 1963. A3459
536 Smythies, J. R. Schizophrenia. 1963. A3460
537 Beranbaum, S. L. and Meyers, P. H. Special procedures in Roentgen diagnosis. 1964. A3461
538 Ostwald, P. F. Soundmaking. 1963. A3462
539 Reubi, F. C. Clearance tests in clinical medicine. 1963. A3463
540 Dacso, M. M. and others. Restorative medicine in geriatrics. 1963. A3464
541 Furst, A. Chemistry of chelation in cancer. 1963. A3465
542 McHardy, G. The medical treatment of peptic ulcer. 1963. A3466
543 Fiorentino, M. R. Reflex testing methods for evaluating C. N. S. development. 1963. A3467
544 Evans, W. E. D. The chemistry of death. 1963. A3468
545 Jackson, B. B. Occlusion of the superior mesenteric artery. 1963. A3469
546 Smith, J. L. Optokinetic nystagmus. 1963. A3470
547 Dittrich, F. L. and Extermann, R. C. Biophysics of the ear. 1963. A3471
548 Agress, C. M. and Estrin, H. M. The biochemical diagnosis of heart disease. 1963. A3472
549 Lind, J. and others. Human foetal and neonatal circulation. 1964. A3473
550 Rashevsky, N. Some medical aspects of mathematical biology. 1964. A3474
551 Close, J. R. Motor function in the lower extremity. 1964. A3475
552 Keown, K. K. Anesthesia for surgery of the heart. 1963. A3476
553 Torrance, D. J. The chest film in massive pulmonary embolism. 1963. A3477
554 Woodward, E. R. The postgastrectomy syndromes. 1963. A3478

555 Hall, D. A. Elastolysis and ageing. 1964. A3479
556 Lerman, S. Cataracts. 1964. A3480
557 Mason, E. E. Computer applications in medicine. 1964. A3481
558 Ingarden, R. Time and modes of being, tr. by Michajda. 1964. A3482
559 Prunty, F. T. G. Chemistry and treatment of adrenocortical disease. 1964. A3483
560 Catsch, A. Radioactive metal mobilization in medicine, tr. by Kawin. 1964. A3484
561 Hardy, J. D., ed. Physiological problems in space exploration. 1964. A3485
562 Gray, L. A. Vaginal hysterectomy. 2d ed. 1963. A3486
563 Simonson, E. and McGavack, T. H., ed. Cerebral ischemia. 1964. A3487
564 Nishimura, H. Chemistry and prevention of congenital anomalies. 1964. A3488
565 Jokl, E. Physiology of exercise. 1964. A3489
566 Feil, H. Coronary heart disease. 1964. A3490
567 Wright, H. D. Questions and answers in ophthalmology. 1964. A3491
568 Egan, R. L. Mammography. 1964. A3492
569 Jokl, E. Medical sociology and cultural anthropology of sports and physical education. 1964. A3493
570 Miller, M. H. and Polisar, I. A. Audiological evaluation of the pediatric patient. 1964. A3494
571 Jokl, E. Heart and sport. 1964. A3495
572 Greenwood, R. J. and Finkelstein, D. Sinoatrial heart block. 1964. A3496
573 Levine, M. and Spivack, G. The Rorschach index of repressive style. 1964. A3497
574 Jokl, E. Nutrition, exercise and body composition. 1964. A3498
575 Boen, S. T. Peritoneal dialysis in clinical medicine. 1964. A3499
576 Bass, B. H. Pulmonary function in clinical medicine. 1964. A3500
577 Jokl, E. The scope of exercise in rehabilitation. 1964. A3501
578 ____. What is sportsmedicine? 1964. A3502
579 Grigg, E. R. N. The trail of the invisible light... 1965. A3503
580 Browne, R. C. The chemistry and therapy of industrial pulmonary diseases. 1966. A3504
581 Stuart-Harris, C. H. and Dickinson, L. The background of chemotherapy of virus disease. 1964. A3505
582 Birren, J. E., ed. Relations of development and ageing. 1964. A3506
583 Murphy, E. G. The chemistry and therapy of disorders of voluntary muscles. 1964. A3507
584 Kaplan, S. A. Growth disorders in children and adolescents. 1964. A3508
585 Hueper, W. C. and Conway, W. D. Chemical carcinogenesis and cancers. 1964. A3509
586 Kuglemass, I. N. Biochemical diseases. 1964. A3510
587 Lawrence, S. H. The zymogram in clinical medicine. 1964. A3511
588 Oparin, A. I. The chemical origin of life, ed. by Synge. 1964. A3512
589 Pearson, L., ed. The use of written communication in psychotherapy. 1965. A3513
590 Knight, J. A. and Davis, W. E. Manual for the comprehensive community mental health clinic. 1964. A3514
591 Brown, C. C. Instrumentation with semiconductors for medical researches. 1964. A3515
592 Fried, E. and others. Artistic productivity and mental health. 1964. A3516
593 Hayasaka, H. Septic

shock. 1964. A3517
594 Müller, C. Cardiopulmonary hemodynamics in health and disease. 1965. A3518
595 Ingram, G. I. C. and Richardson, J. S. Anticoagulant prophylaxis and treatment. 1964. A3519
596 Lever, W. F. Pemphegus and pemphigold. 1965. A3520
597 Handy, R. Methodology of the behavioral sciences. 1964. A3521
598 Foldes, F. F. and others. Narcotics and narcotic antagonists. 1964. A3522
599 Bacq, Z. M. Chemical protection against ionizing radiation. 1965. A3523
600 Welford, A. T. and Birren, J. E. Behavior, aging and the nervous system. 1965. A3524
601 Jokl, E. and Simon, E., eds. International research in sport and physical education. 1964. A3525
602 Barbara, D. A., ed. New directions in stuttering, theory and practice. 1965. A3526
603 Ziegler, E. The redox potential of the blood in vivo and in vitro, tr. by Smith. 1965. A3527
604 Day, E. D. The immunochemistry of cancer. 1965. A3528
605 Berge, B. S. ten, ed. Pregnancy. 1965. A3529
606 Hecht, E. R. Lipids in blood clotting. 1965. A3530
607 Meerloo, J. A. M. and Nelson, M. C. Transference and trial adaptation. 1965. A3531
608 Griffith, J. D. and Salsbury, A. J. Circulating cancer cells. 1965. A3532
609 Heilmeyer, L. Disturbances in heme synthesis, tr. by Steiner. 1966. A3533
610 Eggen, R. P. Chromosome diagnostics in clinical medicine. 1965. A3534
611 Astrup, C. Pavlovian psychiatry. 1965. A3535
612 Malamud, D. I. and Machover, S. Toward self-understanding. 1965. A3536
613 Albert, S. N. and others. The hematocrit and discovery. 1965. A3537
614 Karlin, I. W. and others. Development and disorders of speech in childhood. 1965. A3538
615 Williams, D. C. Principles of emperical realism, ed. by Ruja. 1966. A3539
616 Harrower, M. R. Psychodiagnostic testing. 1965. A3540
617 Masturzo, A. Cybernetic medicine. 1965. A3541
618 Jaques, L. B. Anticoagulant therapy. 1965. A3542
619 Allen, R. M. Variables in personality theory and personality testing. 1965. A3543
620 Nice, C. M. Clinical roentgenology of collagen diseases. 1966. A3544
621 Bartley, S. H. Fatigue. 1965. A3545
622 Wolken, J. J. Vision. 1966. A3546
623 Atkinson, W. S. Anesthesia in ophthalmology. 1965. A3547
624 Woolf, L. I. Renal tubular dysfunction. 1966. A3548
625 Carlsten, A. and Grimby, G. The circulatory response to muscular exercise in man. 1966. A3549
626 Roland, M. and others. Progestagen therapy. 1965. A3550
627 Marshall, R. Pulmonary embolism. 1965. A3551
628 Boba, A. Death in the operating room. 1965. A3552
629 Barbara, D. A. Questions and answers on stuttering. 1965. A3553
630 Conway, and others. Surgery of tumors of the skin. 1966. A3554
631 Jackson, H. Antifertility compounds in the male and female. 1966. A3555
632 Mullan, H. and Sangiuliano, I. Alcoholism. 1966. A3556
633 Sun, D. C. H. Chemistry and therapy of peptic ulcer. 1966. A3557
634 Leger, L. H. Splenoportography. 1966. A3558
635 Slovenko, R. Psychotherapy, confidentiality and privileged communication.

1966. A3559
636 McConnachie, E. L. F. Lower urinary tract fistulae in the female. 1966. A3560
637 Goldzieher, J. W. and Rice-Wray, E. R. Oral contraception. 1966. A3561
638 Astrup, C. and Noreik, K. Functional psychoses. 1966. A3562
639 Curtis, H. J. Biological mechanisms of aging. 1966. A3563
640 Pittinger, C. B. Hyperbaric oxygenation. 1966. A3564
641 Freud, H. Psychopathology and the problems of stuttering. 1966. A3565
642 Rotenstreich, N. On the human subject. 1966. A3566
643 Hinman, E. H. World eradication of infectious disease. 1966. A3567
644 Jackson, R. The cervical syndrome. 1966. A3568
645 Hayman, M. Alcoholism. 1966. A3569
646 Marshall, R. J. and Darby, T. D. Shock, pharmacological principles in treatment. 1966. A3570
647 Smith, R. H. Pathological physiology for the anesthesiologist. 1966. A3571
648 Costello, M. J. and Gibbs, C. G. The palms and soles in medicine. 1966. A3572
649 Schein, C. J. and others. The common bile duct. 1966. A3573
650 Andrew, W. One world of science. 1966. A3574
651 Brooks, B. N. and Slaney, G. Metabolic derangements in gastrointestinal surgery. 1966. A3575
652 Monge, M. and C. High-altitude diseases. 1966. A3576
653 Henley, K. S. and others. Enzymes in serums. 1966. A3577
654 Lim, T. P. K. Cardiopulmonary function tests in clinical medicine. 1966. A3578
655 Nuzzolo, L. Serological diagnostic. 1966. A3579
656 Manger, W. M. Hormones and hypertension. 1966. A3580
657 Dommeyer, F. C. Current philosophical issues. 1966. A3581
658 Burdick, K. H. Electrosurgical apparatus and their application in dermatology. 1966. A3582
659 Shoemaker, W. C. Shock. 1966. A3583
660 Mecham, M. J. and others. Communication in childhood brain damage. 1966. A3584
661 Gaito, J. Molecular psychobiology. 1966. A3585
662 Gitman, L. Endocrines and aging. 1966. A3586
663 Exner, J. E. A workbook in the rorschach technique emphasizing the Beck and Klopfer systems. 1966. A3587
664 Wang, Y. Clinical radioscope scanning. 1967. A3588
665 Bietti, G. B. and Werner, G. N. Trachoma. 1966. A3589
666 Horosz, W. Escape from destiny. 1966. A3590
667 Sellars, W. Philosophical perspectives. 1966. A3591
668 Maurer, D. W. and Vogel, V. H. Narcotics and narcotic addiction. 1966. A3592
669 Cohen, J. Psychological time in health and disease. 1966. A3593
670 Knock, F. E. Anticancer agents. 1966. A3594
671 Silving, H. Constituent elements of criminal conduct and of crime. 1966. A3595
672 Whelan, R. F. Control of the peripheral circulation in man. 1967. A3596
673 Anderson, J. R. and others. Autoimmunity, clinical and experimental. 1967. A3597
674 Schmitz, A. L. and others. Illustrative cranial neuroradiology. 1967. A3598
675 Physiology of hemostasis and thrombosis, comp. by Johnson and Seegers. 1967. A3599
676 Dawson, J. B. and Heaton, F. W. Spectrochemical analysis of clinical material. 1967. A3600

677 Heironimus, T. W. Mechanical artificial ventilation anesthesiology. 1967. A3601
678 Butt, W. R. The chemistry of gonadotrophins. 1967. A3602
679 Segre, E. J. Androgens, virilization and the hirsute female. 1967. A3603
680 Siddons, H. and Sowton, E. Cardiac pacemakers. 1968. A3604
681 Seegers, W. H. Prothrombin in enzymology, thrombosis and hemophilia. 1967. A3605
682 McGowan, L. Cancer in pregnancy. 1967. A3606
683 Silving, H. Essays on mental incapacity and criminal conduct. 1967. A3607
684 Stevens, K. M. The ecology and etiology of human disease. 1967. A3608
685 Hawkins, C. F. Speaking and writing in medicine. 1967. A3608a
686 Hartmann, E. The biology of dreaming. 1967. A3609
687 Cox, K. R. Planning clinical experiments. 1968. A3610
688 Batsakis, J. G. and Briere, R. O. Interpretive enzymology. 1967. A3611
689 Eysenck, H. J. The biological basis of personality. 1967. A3612
690 Denhoff, E. Cerebral palsy. 1968. A3613
691 Hollister, L. E. Chemical psychoses. 1968. A3614
692 Holt, S. B. The genetics of dermal ridges. 1968. A3615
693 Hewitt, C. R. Law and common man. 1968. A3616
694 Tolansky, S. Inference microscopy for the biologist. 1968. A3617
695 Rubin, P. and Green, J. Solitary metastases. 1968. A3618
696 Barsch, R. H. The parent of the handicapped child. 1968. A3619
697 Philosophical perspectives on punishment, ed. by Madden and others. 1968. A3620
698 Trummer, M. J. and Berg, P. Living transplantation. 1968. A3621
699 Rose, L. E. Aristotle's syllogistic. 1968. A3622
700 Fontaine, W. T. Reflections on segregation, desegration, power and morals. 1967. A3623
701 Moser, S. Absolutism and relativism in ethics. 1968. A3624
702 Bortner, M., ed. Evaluation and education of children with brain damage. 1967. A3625
703 Moskowitz, E. Rehabilitation in extremity fractures. 1968. A3626
704 Geertinger, P. Sudden death in infancy. 1968. A3627
705 Hamelberg, W. and Bosomworth, P. B. Aspiration pneumonites. 1968. A3628
706 Madden, E. H. and Hare, P. H. Evil and the concept of God. 1968. A3629
707 Melchert, N. P. Realism, materialism and the mind. 1968. A3630
708 Rodgers, F. C. and Sinclair, H. M. Metabolic and nutritional eye diseases. 1968. A3631
709 Holt, G. W. The vagi in medicine and surgery. 1968. A3632
710 Sem-Jacobsen, C. W. Depth electrographic stimulation of the human brain and behavior. 1968. A3633
711 Jones, M. V., ed. Special education programs within the United States. 1968. A3634
712 Jokl, E. and P. The physiological basis of athletic records. 1968. A3635
713 Tarnay, T. J. Surgery in the hemophiliac. 1968. A3636
714 Clements, T. S. Science and man. 1968. A3637
715 Brown, H. Hepatic failure. 1969. A3638
716 Harrison, M. and Naftalin, L. Meniere's disease. 1968. A3639
717 Caceres, C. A. and Rikli, A. E. Diagnostic computers. 1969. A3640
718 Craigie, E. H. and Gibson,

W. C. The world of Ramon y Cajal. 1968. A3641
719 Smith, L. D. and Holdeman, L. V. The pathogebic anaerobic bacteria. 1968. A3642
720 Foldi, M. Diseases of lymphatics and lymph circulation. 1969. A3643
721 Rachman, S. Phobias. 1968. A3644
722 Hashimoto, K. and Lever, W. F. Appendage tumors of the skin. 1968. A3645
723 Asao, H. and Oji, K. Hepatocerebral degeneration. 1968. A3646
724 Shingleton, W. W. and Dobbins, W. O. Malabsorption syndromes. 1968. A3647
725 de Silva, C. C. and Baptist, N. G. Tropical nutrition disorders of infants and children. 1969. A3648
726 Heath, D. and others. Corpulmonale in emphysema. 1968. A3649
727 Bierman, H. R. Selective arterial catherization. 1969. A3650
728 Cureton, T. K. The physiological effects of exercise programs on adults. 1968. A3651
729 Bakerman, S. Aging life processes. 1969. A3652
730 Mealey, J. Pediatric head injuries. 1968. A3653
731 The idea of God, comp. by Madden and others. 1968. A3654
732 Sapeika, N. Food pharmacology. 1969. A3655
733 Engle, R. L. and Wallis, L. A. Immunoglobulinopathies. 1969. A3656
734 Bower, E. M. Early identification of emotionally handicapped children in school. 1969. A3657
735 Pearce, J. Migraine. 1969. A3658
736 Taymor, M. L. The management of infertility. 1969. A3659
737 Hoch-Ligeti, C. Laboratory aids in diagnosis of cancer. 1969. A3660
738 Kelsey, J. R. and Beard, E. F. Vascular insufficiency. 1969. A3661
739 Snidecor, J. C. and others. Speech rehabilitation of the laryngectomized. 1969. A3662
740 Handy, R. Value theory and the behavorial sciences. 1968. A3663
741 McGovern, V. J. and Brown, M. M. L. The nature of melanoma. 1969. A3664
742 Bonsett, C. A. Studies of pseudohypertrophic muscular dystrophy. 1969. A3665
743 Johns, H. E. and Cunningham, J. R. The physics of radiology. 1969. A3666
744 Marx, G. F. and Orkin, L. R. Physiology of obstetric anesthesia. 1969. A3667
745 Meszaros, W. T. Cardiac roentgeneology. 1969. A3668
746 Bethke, E. G. Basic drawing for biology students. 1969. A3669
747 Shearman, R. P. Induction of ovulation. 1969. A3670
748 Arens, R. Make mad the guilty. 1969. A3671
749 Curry, A. Poison detection in human organs. 1969. A3672
750 Ferreira, A. J. Prenatal environment. 1969. A3673
751 Miskin, F. S. and Mealey, J. Use and interpretation of the brain scan. 1969. A3674
752 Pedersen, E. Spasticity. 1969. A3675
753 Slough, M. G. Privacy, freedom and responsibility. 1969. A3676
754 Grassi, J. R. The Grassi block substitution test for measuring organic brain pathology. 1969. A3677
755 Alicata, J. E. and Jindrak, K. Angiostrongylosis in the Pacific and Southeast Asia. 1969. A3678
756 Arena, J. M. Poisoning. 1969. A3679
757 Kay, J. M. and Heath, D. Crotalaria spectabilis. 1969. A3680
758 Demetrius, S. R. Mucous and salivary gland tumors. 1969. A3681
759 Seitz, J. F. The

biochemistry of the cells of blood and bone marrow. 1969. A3682
760 Paterson, A. M. The infinite worlds of Giordano Bruno. 1969. A3683
761 Kaye, S. Handbook of emergency toxicology. 1969. A3684
762 Gillette, H. E. Systems of therapy in cerebral palsy. 1969. A3685
763 Hutt, S. J. Direct observation and measurements of behavior. 1969. A3686
764 Miejne, N. G. Hyperboric oxygen and its clinical value. 1970. A3687
765 Poulton, E. C. Environment and human efficiency. 1970. A3688
766 Kugelmass, I. N. The autistic child. 1970. A3689
767 Raab, W. Preventive myocardiology. 1970. A3690
768 Moser, R. H. House of officer training. 1970. A3691
769 Stanley-Jones, D. Hybernetics of mind and brain. 1970. A3692
770 Rice, J. P. The gifted. 1970. A3693
771 Radionuclide applications in neurology and neurosurgery, ed. by Wang and Paoletti. 1970. A3694
772 Riepe, D. The philosophy of India and its impact on American thought. 1970. A3695
773 Amoore, J. E. Nuclear basis of odor. 1970. A3696
774 Berleant, A. The aesthetic field. 1970. A3697
775 Gerbeaux, J. Primary tuberculosis in childhood. 1970. A3698
776 Giroud, A. The nutrition of the embryo. 1970. A3699
777 Caldwell, A. E. Origins of psychopharmacology. 1970. A3700
778 Sinari, R. A. The structure of Indian thought. 1970. A3701
779 Stewart, G. T. and McGovern, J. P. Penicillin allergy. 1970. A3702
780 Hazen, E. L. and others. Laboratory identification of pathogenic fungi simplified. 1970. A3703
781 Silva, M. R. Kinin hormones. 1970. A3704
782 Davison, A. N. and Peters, A. Myelination. 1970. A3705
783 Bahm, A. I. Polarity, dialectic, and organicity. 1970. A3706
784 Darling, D. B. Radiography of infants and children. 1971. A3707
785 Aviado, D. M. Sympathomimetic drugs. 1971. A3708
786 Cruz-Coke, R. Color blindness. 1970. A3709
787 Krikorian, Y. H. The pursuit of ideals. 1970. A3710
788 Lehmann, H. E. and Ban, T. A. Pharmacotherapy of tension and anxiety. 1970. A3711
789 Atria, A. Endocrine function tests. 1970. A3712
790 Porter, C. C. Chemical mechanisms of drug action. 1970. A3713
791 Heironimus, T. W. Mechanical artificial ventilation. 1971. A3714
792 Stephen, C. R. and others. Elements of pediatric anesthesia. 1970. A3715
793 Mathe, G. and others. Bone marrow transplantation and Leucocyte transfusions. 1971. A3716
794 Adventures in medical writing, comp. and ed. by Moser and Cyan. 1970. A3717
795 Ban, T. A. and Lehmann, H. E. Experimental approaches to psychiatric diagnosis. 1971. A3718
796 Frank, S. B. Acne Vulgaris. 1971. A3719
797 Cappon, D. Technology and perception. 1971. A3720
798 Bridges, P. K. Psychiatric emergencies. 1971. A3721
799 Coppleson, M. and others. Colposcopy. 1971. A3722
800 Millar, J. H. D. Multiple sclerosis. 1971. A3723
801 Ferriman, D. Human hair and growth in health and disease. 1971. A3724
802 West, H. F. The chemical pathology of rheumatoid

arthritis. 1970. A3725
803 Parsons, H. L. Humanism and Marx's thought. 1971. A3726
804 Dossetor, J. B. and Gault, M. H. Nephron failure. 1970. A3727
805 Andrews, G. S. Exfoliative cytology. 1971. A3728
806 Bendixen, G. Clinical hypersensitivity disorders. 1971. A3729
807 Albert, S. N. Blood volume and extracellular fluid volume. 1971. A3730
808 National Conference on Histoplasmosis. Histoplasmosis, ed. by Ajello and others. 1971. A3731
809 Colman, A. D. The planned environment in psychiatric treatment. 1971. A3732
810 Dawson, M. Cellular pharmacology. 1972. A3733
811 Clarke, C. A. and McConnell, R. B. Prevention of Rh-Homolytic disease. 1972. A3734
812 Searcy, R. L. Lipopathies. 1971. A3735
813 Priest, J. H. Human cell cultures in diagnosis of disease. 1971. A3736
814 Nelson, N. Workshops for the handicapped in the United States. 1971. A3737
815 Sussman, K. E. Juvenile-type diabetes and its complications. 1971. A3738
816 Finch, S. M. and Poznanski, E. O. Adolescent suicide. 1971. A3739
817 Weil-Malherbe, H. and Szara, S. I. The biochemistry of functional and experimental psychoses. 1971. A3740
818 Molecular aspects of sickle cell hemoglobin, ed. by Nalbandian. 1971. A3741
819 Barbara, D. A. How to make people listen to you. 1971. A3742
820 Tolerance, autoimmunity and aging, comp. and ed. by Sigel and Good. 1972. A3743
821 Polezhaev, L. V. Organ regeneration in animals. 1972. A3744
822 Swineford, O. Asthma and hay fever. 1971. A3745
823 Root, A. W. Human pituitary growth hormone. 1972. A3746
824 Language development, the key to learning. Ed. by Jones. 1972. A3747
825 Brown, F. C. Hallucinogenic drugs. 1972. A3748
826 Hruza, Z. Resistance to trauma. 1971. A3749
827 Aas, K. The biochemical and immunological basis of bronchial asthma. 1972. A3750
828 Chang, T. M. S. Artificial cells. 1972. A3751
829 Lippman, L. Attitudes toward the handicapped. 1972. A3752
830 Egan, R. L. Mammography. 1972. A3753
831 Cull, J. G. and Hardy, R. E. Vocational rehabilitation. 1972. A3754
832 Howell, J. B. Radium recipes for cutaneous cancer. 1972. A3755
833 Cull, J. G. and Colvin, C. R. Contemporary field work practices in rehabilitation. 1972. A3756
834 Jokl, E. Physiology of exercise. 1971. A3757
835 Bicher, H. I. Blood cell aggregation in thrombotic processes. 1972. A3758
836 Stewart, G. T. Trends in epidemiology. 1972. A3759
837 Durant, J. R. and Smalley, R. V. The chronic leukemias. 1972. A3760
838 Gonseth, F. Time and method. 1972. A3761
839 Ban, T. A. Schizophrenia. 1972. A3762
840 Branson, D. Methods in clinical bateriology. 1972. A3763
841 Adams, C. W. M. Research on multiple sclerosis. 1972. A3764
842 York, J. L. The porphyrias. 1972. A3765
843 Schultes, R. E. and Hofmann, A. The botany and chemistry of hallucinogens. 1972. A3766
844 Kost, M. L. Success or

failure begins in the early school years. 1972. A3767
845 Fraser, R. D. B. and others. Keratins. 1972. A3768
846 Hardy, R. E. and Cull, J. G. Social and rehabilitation services for the blind. 1972. A3769
847 Paton, D. The relation of angiois streaks to systemic disease. 1972. A3770
848 Harrower, M. The therapy of poetry. 1972. A3771
849 Cooper, M. Modern techniques of vocal rehabilitation. 1972. A3772
850 Hingerty, D. and O'Boyle, A. Clinical chemistry of the adrenal medulla. 1972. A3773
851 Hall, T. A. and others. Microscopy in clinical and experimental medicine. 1972. A3774
852 Birx, H. J. Pierre Teilhard de Chardin's philosophy of evolution. 1972. A3775
853 Probert, L. Law, language and communication. 1972. A3776
854 Lerner, E. A. The projective use of Bender Gestlat. 1972. A3777
855 Close, J. R. Functional anatomy of the extremities. 1972. A3778
856 Cohen, L. Oral diagnosis and treatment planning. 1972. A3779
857 Morgan, B. Osteomalacia, renal osteodystrophy and osteoporosis. 1972. A3780
858 Sachs, M. The field concept in contemporary science. 1972. A3781
859 Uehling, H. F. Correction of a correctional psychologist in treatment of the criminal offender. 1973. A3782
860 Earle, H. H. Police recruit planning. 1972. A3783
861 Cull, J. G. and Hardy, R. E. Fundamentals of criminal behavior and correctional systems. 1973. A3784
862 Spiro, S. R., ed. Amnesia-analgesia techniques in dentistry. 1972. A3785
863 Ban, T. A. Recent advances in the biology of schizophrenia. 1974. A3786
864 Cooper, B. and Morgan, H. G. Epidemiology psychiatry. 1972. A3787
865 Fiorentino, M. R. Reflex testing methods for evaluating C. S. N. development. 1972. A3788
866 Hardy, R. E. and Cull, J. G. Introduction to correctional rehabilitation. 1973. A3789
867 Rubella, by Friedman and Prier. 1973. A3790
868 Cobb, A. B. Medical and psychological aspects of disability. 1973. A3791
869 Schoenfeld, C. G. Psychoanalysis and the law. 1973. A3792
870 Walsh, S. Z. and others. The human fetal and neonatal circulation. 1974. A3793
871 Arnold, H. L. and Fasal, P. Leprosy. 1973. A3794
872 Klein, H., ed. Polycythemia. 1973. A3795
873 Kugelmass, I. N. Adolescent immaturity. 1973. A3796
874 Dawidoff, D. J. The malpractice of psychiatrists. 1973. A3797
875 Kutscher, A. H. and Goldberg, I. K. Oral care of the aging and dying patient. 1973. A3798
876 Hardy, R. E. and Cull, J. G. eds. Drug dependence and rehabilitation approaches. 1973. A3799
877 ____. Vocational rehabilitation services. 1973. A3800
878 Kimsey, L. R. and Roberts, J. L. Referring the psychiatric patient. 1973. A3801
879 Singh, B. B. The self and the world in the philosophy of Josiah Royce. 1973. A3802
880 Jovanovic, U. J. Psychomotor epilepsy. 1973. A3803
881 Evans, F. G. Mechanical properties of bone. 1973. A3804
882 Hardy, R. E. and Cull, J. G. Applied volunteerism in community development. 1973. A3805
883 Levy, C. M. Liver regeneration in man. 1973. A3806

884 Sanders, R. J. Carcinoids of the gastrointestinal tract. 1973. A3807
885 Cobb, A. B., ed. Special problems in rehabilitation. 1974. A3808
886 Rodin, A. E. The influence of Matthew Baillie's morbid anatomy. 1973. A3809
887 Cull, J. G. and Hardy, R. E. Volunteerism. 1974. A3810
888 ____, eds. The big welfare mess. 1973. A3811
889 Castaneda, H. The structure of morality. 1974. A3812
890 Cull, J. G. and Hardy, R. E., eds. Rehabilitation of the urban disadvantaged. 1973. A3813
891 Drug abuse in industry, by Carone and Krinsky. 1973. A3814
892 Cull, J. G. and Hardy, R. E., eds. Adjustment to work. 1973. A3815
893 Macpherson, A. I. S. The spleen. 1973. A3816
894 Quay, W. G. Pineal chemistry in cellular and physiological mechanisms. 1974. A3817
895 Salkin, J. B. Body ego technique. 1973. A3818
896 Cull, J. G. and Hardy, R. E., eds. Rehabilitation of the drug abuser with delinquent behavior. 1974. A3819
897 Ward, H. L., ed. A periodontal point of view. 1973. A3820
898 Cull, J. G. and Hardy, R. E. The neglected older American. 1973. A3821
899 Sonnenwirth, A. C. Bacteremia. 1973. A3822
900 Bernard, C. Lectures on the phenomena of life common to animals and plants. V. 1. 1974. A3823
901 Hardy, R. E. and Cull, J. G., eds. Mental retardation and physical disability. 1974. A3824
902 Bennett, M. F. Living clocks in the animal world. 1974. A3825
903 Arena, J. M. Poisoning. 1974. A3826
904 Hardy, R. E. and Cull, J. G., eds. Climbing the walls. 1973. A3827
905 ____. Applied psychology in law enforcement and corrections. 1973. A3828
906 Paterson, A. M. Francis Bacon. 1973. A3829
907 Novello, J. R. A practical handbook of psychiatry. 1974. A3830
908 Moose, J. W. The application of comparative morphology in the identification of intestinal parasites. 1973. A3831
909 Cull, J. G. and Hardy, R. E., eds. Law enforcement and correctional rehabilitation. 1973. A3832
910 Aird, R. B. and Woodbury, D. M. The management of epilepsy. 1974. A3833
911 Dummett, C. O. Community dentistry. 1974. A3834
912 Cull, J. G. and Hardy, R. E. Understanding disability for social and rehability services. 1973. A3835
913 Balows, A. and others. Anaerobic bacteria. 1974. A3836
914 Natanson, M. Phenomenology, role and reason. 1974. A3837
915 Maurer, D. W. and Vogel, V. H. Narcotics and narcotic addiction. 1973. A3838
916 Cull, S. G. and Hardy, R. E. Counseling high school students. 1974. A3839
917 Beder, O. E. Fundamentals for maxillofacial prothetics. 1974. A3840
918 Malone, W. F. Electrosurgery in dentistry. 1974. A3841
919 Goshen, C. E. Society and the youthful offender. 1974. A3842
920 Cull, S. G. and Hardy, R. E. Types of drug abusers and their abuses. 1974. A3843
921 Hardy, R. E. and Cull, S. G. Severe disabilities. 1974. A3844
922 Overs, R. P. and others. Avocational activities for handicapped. 1974. A3845
923 Lowbury, E. J. L. and Ayliffe, G. A. J. Drug resistance in antimicrobial therapy. 1974. A3846

924 Friedman, M. Biological clinical basis radiosensitivity. 1974. A3847
925 Darnett, A. J. Scleroderma. 1974. A3848
926 Cull, J. G. and Hardy, R. E. Rehabilitation technique in severe disability cases. 1974. A3849
927 Foster, H. H. "A Bill of Rights" of children. 1974. A3850
928 Hardy, R. E. and Cull, S. G. Group counseling and therapy in special settings. 1974. A3851
929 Cull, S. G. and Hardy, R. E. Counseling and rehabilitating the diabetic. 1974. A3852
930 Fox, S. Freud and education. 1974. A3853
931 Hardy, R. E. and Cull, S. G. Educational and psychosocial aspects of deafness. 1973. A3854
932 Johns, H. E. and Cunningham, J. R. The physics radiology. 1974. A3855
933 Cull, S. G. and Hardy, R. E. Alcohol abuse and rehabilitation approaches. 1974. A3856
934 Hardy, R. E. and Cull, S. G. Therapeutic needs of the family. 1974. A3857
935 Cull, S. G. and Hardy, R. E. Deciding on divorce. 1974. A3858
936 Hardy, R. E. and Cull, S. G. Modification of behavior of mentally ill. 1974. A3859
937 Minton, S. A. Venom diseases. 1974. A3860
938 Baum, L. Operative dentistry for the general practitioner. 1974. A3861
939 Cull, S. G. and Hardy, R. E. Administrative techniques of rehabilitation facility operations. 1974. A3862
940 Balows, A. and others. Anaerobic diseases. 1974. A3863
941 Hardy, R. E. Techniques and approaches in martial and family counseling. 1974. A3864
942 Shields, T. Bronchial acrcinoma. 1974. A3865
943 Hardy, R. E. and Cull, S. G. Creative divorce through social and psychological approaches. 1974. A3866
946 Sinski, J. T. Dermatothytes in human skin, hair and nails. 1974. A3869
947 Cull, S. G. Career guidance for black adolescents. 1974. A3870
948 Hardy, R. E. Modification of behavior of the mentally retarded. 1974. A3871
949 Cull, S. G. Behavior modifications in rehabilitation settings. 1974. A3872
950 Hardy, R. E. Career guidance for young women. 1974. A3873
951 Cullen, J. W. Legacies in the study of behavior. 1974. A3874
952 Hardy, R. E. Psychological and vocational rehabilitation of the youthful delinquent. 1974. A3875
953 Schottenfeld, D. Cancer epidemiology and prevention. 1974. A3876
954 Hardy, R. E. Problems of disadvantaged and deprived youth. 1974. A3877
955 ____. Fundamentals of juvenile criminal behavior and drug abuse. 1974. A3878
956 ____. Problems of adolescents. 1974. A3879
957 Glenn, F. Common duct stones. 1974. A3880
958 Griffin, G. G. The silent misery. 1974. A3881
959 Hardy, R. E. Services of the rehabilitation facility. 1974. A3882
960 ____. Drug language and lore. 1974. A3883
961 Beaudreau, D. E. Atlas of fixed partial prothesis. 1974. A3884
980 Smith, L. D. S. and Holdeman, L. V. Pathogenic anaerobic bacteria. 1974. A3885

The following table is part of this series.

This series has the following subseries. Some subseries have a Bannerstone division, the number refers to the series numbering above.

Bannerstone division: 478, 533, 579, 674, 784, 830.
Social and rehabilitation psychology:
Bannerstone division: 831, 833, 846, 866, 868, 876-7, 882, 885, 887-8, 890, 892, 896, 898, 901, 904-5, 909, 912, 916, 920-2, 926, 928-9, 931, 933-6, 939, 941, 943-5, 947-51, 954-6, 958-9.
Special education: 829.
Bannerstone division: 696, 711, 770, 814, 824, 844.
Speech and hearing: 400, 570, 614, 641, 660, 702-739, 849.
Bannerstone division: 480.
Sportsmedicine: 565, 569, 571, 574, 577-8, 601, 625, 834.
Bannerstone division: 601, 712, 728.
Surgery: 31, 48, 61, 86, 138, 165, 170, 255, 271, 286, 303, 355, 388, 458, 545.
Bannerstone division: 132, 177, 204, 250, 265, 266, 339, 630, 942, 957.
Tests and techniques: 62, 81, 84, 137, 183, 253, 780.
Bannerstone division: 370.
Thoracic surgery: 3.
Tropical diseases: 528.
Tropical medicine: 755.
Tumors: 516, 727.
Bannerstone division: 315, 357.
Urology: 284, 306, 399.

AMERICAN LIBRARY ASSOCIATION. LIBRARY TECHNOLOGY PROJECT. LTP PUBLICATIONS.

1 Fry, G. & Associates. Study of circulation control systems. 1963. A3886
2 American Library Association. Development of performance standards for library binding, phase I. 1961. A3887
3 ____. Permanence and durability of library catalog cards, by Barrows. 1961. A3888
4 Hawkens, W. R. Photocopying from bound volumes. 1962. Supp. 1963. A3889
5 American Library Association. The testing and evaluation of record players for libraries. 1962. A3890
6 Hawkens, W. R. Enlarged prints for library microforms. 1963. A3891
7 American Library Association. Protecting the library and its resources. 1963. A3892
8 ____. Evaluation of record players for libraries, series II. 1964. A3893
9 ____. Catalog card reproduction. 1965. A3894
10 Same as no. 2. V. 2. 1966. A3895
11 Same as no. 4. V. 2. 1966. A3896
12 Horton, C. Cleaning and preserving bindings and related materials. 1967. A3897
13 Berkeley, B. Floors. 1968. A3898
14 Gawrecki, D. Compact library shelving, tr. by Rehak. 1968. A3899
15 Gimbel, H. Work simplification in Danish public libaries. 1969. A3900
____. Same as no. 2. Phase I. 1966. A3901
16 Horton, C. Cleaning and preserving bindings and related materials. 2d ed. 1969. A3902
17 Veaner, A. B. Evaluation of micropublications. 1971. A3903
18 Middleton, B. C. The restoration of leather bindings. 1972. A3904
Library Equipment Institute. Library furniture and equipment. 1963. A3905

AMERICAN LIBRARY PIONEERS (A. L. A.)

1 Lydenberg, H. M. John Shaw Billings. 1924. A3906
2 Shaw, R. K. Samuel Swett Green. 1926. A3907
3 Cutter, W. P. Charles Ammi Cutler. 1931. A3908
4 Eastman, L. A. Portrait of a librarian, William Howard Brett. 1940. A3909
5 Hadley, C. John Cotton Dana. 1943. A3910
6 Rider, F. Melvil Dewey. 1944. A3911

7 Borome, J. A. Charles Coffin Jewett. 1951. A3912
8 Pioneering leaders in librarianship, ed. by Danton. 1953. A3913

AMERICAN MATHEMATICAL SOCIETY; COLLOQUIUM PUBLICATIONS.

1 American mathematical society. The Boston colloquium. 1905. A3914
2 ____. The New Haven mathematical colloquium. 1910. A3915
3 ____. Princeton colloquium. A3916
V. 1 Bliss, G. A. Fundamental existence theorems. 1934. A3917
V. 2 Kasner, E. Differential geometric aspects of dynamics. 1913. A3918
4 American mathematical society. Madison colloquium. 1914. A3919
5 ____. The Cambridge colloquium. 2 v. 1918-22. A3920
6 Evans, G. C. The logarithmic potential. 1927. v. 1 Evans, G. C. Functionals and their application. 1918. v. 2 Veblen, O. Analysis situsitus. 1931. A3921
7 Bell, E. T. Algebraic arithmetic. 1927. A3922
8 Eisenhart, L. P. Non-Riemannian geometry. 1927. A3923
9 Birkhoff, G. D. Dynamical systems. 1927. A3924
10 Coble, A. B. Algebraic geometry and theta functions. 1948. A3925
11 Jackson, D. The theory of approximation. 1930. A3926
12 Lefschetz, S. Topology. 1930. A3927
13 Moore, R. L. Foundations of point set theory. 1962. A3928
14 Ritt, J. F. Differential equations from the algebraic standpoint. 1932. A3929
15 Stone, M. H. Linear transformations in Hilbert space and their application to analysis. 1932. A3930
16 Bliss, G. A. Algebraic functions. 1933. A3931
17 Wedderburn, J. H. M. Lectures on matrices. 1934. A3932
18 Morse, M. The calculus of variations in the large. 1934. A3933
19 Paley, R. E. A. C. and Wiener, N. Fourier transforms in the complex domain. 1934. A3934
20 Walsh, J. L. Interpolation and approximation by rational functions in the complex domain. 1960. A3935
21 Thomas, J. M. Differential systems. 1937. A3936
22 Moore, C. N. Summable series and convergence factors. 1938. A3937
23 Szegö, G. Orthogonal polynominals. 1959. A3938
24 Albert, A. A. Structure of algebras. 1939. A3939
25 Birkhoff, G. Lattice theory. 1960. A3940
26 Levinson, N. Gap and density theorems. 1940. A3941
27 Lefschetz, S. Algebraic topology. 1942. A3942
28 Whyburn, G. T. Analytic topology. 1942. A3943
29 Weil, A. Foundations of algebraic geometry. 1962. A3944
30 Radó, T. Length and area. 1948. A3945
31 Hille, E. and Phillips, R. S. Functional analysis and semigroups. 1957. A3946
32 Wilder, R. L. Topology of manifolds. 1949. A3947
33 Ritt, J. F. Differential algebra. 1950. A3948
34 Walsh, J. L. The location of critical points of analysis and harmonic functions. 1950. A3949
35 Schaeffer, A. C. and Spencer, D. C. Coefficient regions for Schlicht functions. 1950. A3950
36 Gottschalk, W. H. and Hedlund, G. A. Topological dynamics. 1955. A3951
37 Jacobson, N. Structure of rings. 1956. A3952
38 Ore, O. Theory of graphs. V. 1. 1962. A3953
39 Jacobson, N. Structure and representation of Jordan algebras. 1968. A3954

AMERICAN MATHEMATICAL SOCIETY. MATHEMATICAL SURVEYS.

1 Shohat, J. A. and Tamarkin, J. D. The problem of moments. 1950. A3955
2 Jacobson, N. The theory of rings. 1943. A3956
3 Marden, M. The geometry of the zeros of a polynominal in a complex variable. 1949. A3957
4 Schilling, O. F. G. The theory of valuations. 1950. A3958
5 Bergman, S. The kernel function and conformal mapping. 1950. A3959
6 Chevalley, C. Introduction to the theory of algebraic functions of one variable. 1951. A3960
7 Clifford, A. H. and Preston, G. B. The algebraic theory of semigroups. V. 1. 1961. A3961
8 Lehner, J. Discontinuous groups and automorphic functions. 1964. A3962
9 Sard, A. Linear approximation. 1963. A3963
10 Ayoub, R. G. An introduction to the analytic theory of number. 1963. A3964
11 Cronin, J. S. Fixed points and topological degree in non-linear analysis. 1964. A3965
12 Isbell, J. R. Uniform spaces. 1964. A3966

AMERICAN MEN OF LETTERS (Houghton)

Beers, H. A. Nathaniel Parker Willis. 1885. A3967
Bigelow, J. William Cullen Bryant. 1890. A3968
Carpenter, G. R. John Greenleaf Whittier. 1903. A3969
Cary, E. George William Curtis. 1894. A3970
Crothers, S. M. Oliver Wendell Holmes. 1909. A3971
Frothingham, O. B. George Ripley. 1883. A3972
Greenslet, F. James Russell Lowell. 1912. A3973
____. Thomas Bailey Aldrich. 1928. A3974
Higginson, T. W. Henry W. Longfellow. 1902. A3975
____. Margaret Fuller Ossoli. 1884. A3976
Holmes, O. W. Ralph Waldo Emerson. 1885. A3977
Lounsbury, T. R. James Fenimore Cooper. 1883. A3978
McMaster, J. B. Benjamin Franklin. 1887. A3979
Mims, E. Sidney Lanier. 1905. A3980
Ogden, R. William Hickling Prescott. 1904. A3981
Perry, B. Walt Whitman. 1906. A3982
Sanborn, F. B. Henry D. Thoreau. 1882. A3983
Scudder, H. E. Noah Webster. 1883. A3984
Sedgwick, H. D. Francis Parkman. 1904. A3985
Smyth, A. H. Bayard Taylor. 1896. A3986
Trent, W. P. William Gilmore Simms. 1892. A3987
Warner, C. D. Washington Irving. 1881. A3988
Woodberry, G. E. Edgar Allen Poe. 1885. A3989
____. Nathaniel Hawthorne. 1902. A3990

AMERICAN MEN OF LETTERS SERIES (Sloane)

Arvin, N. Herman Melville. 1950. A3991
Berryman, J. Stephen Crane. 1950. A3992
Chase, R. V. Emily Dickinson. 1951. A3993
Dupee, F. W. Henry James. 1951. A3994
Grossman, J. James Fenimore Cooper. 1949. A3995
Howe, I. Sherwood Anderson. 1951. A3996
Krutch, J. W. Henry David Thoreau. 1948. A3997
Matthiessen, F. O. Theodore Dreiser. 1951. A3998
Miller, P. Jonathan Edwards. 1949. A3999
Neff, E. Edwin Arlington Robinson. 1948. A4000
Van Doren, M. Nathaniel Hawthorne. 1949. A4001

AMERICAN MONOGRAPH SERIES (Saunders)

Bland, J. H. The clinical use of fluids and electrolyte. 1952. A4002
Decker, A. Culdoscopy. 1952. A4003
Grishman, A. and Scherlis, L. Spatial vectrocardiography. 1952. A4004
Mainland, D. Elementary medical statistics. 1952. A4005
Moloy, H. C. Clinical and roentgenologic evaluation of the pelvis in obstetrics. 1951. A4006
Series discontinued.

THE AMERICAN MUSEUM OF NATURAL HISTORY. SCIENCE SERIES (Doubleday)

1 Wissler, C. Indians of the United States. 1940. A4007
2 Vaillant, G. C. Aztecs of Mexico. 1962. A4008
3 Radin, P. Indians of South America. 1942. A4009
4 Fisher, G. C. The story of the moon. 1943. A4010
5 Howells, W. W. Mankind so far. 1944. A4011

AMERICAN MUSEUM SOURCE-BOOKS IN ANTHROPOLOGY (Amer. Mus. of Natural History)

Bohannan, P., ed. Law and warfare. 1967. A4012
Bohannan, P. and Curtin, P. Africa and Africans. 1971. A4013
Bohannan, P. and Middleton, J., eds. Kinship and social organization. 1968. A4014
____. Marriage, family and residence. 1968. A4015
Bohannan, P. and Plog, F., eds. Beyond the frontier. 1967. A4016
Carr, A. So excellent a fishe. 1967. A4017
Cohen, R. and Middleton, J., eds. Comparative political systems. 1967. A4018
Dalton, G., ed. Economic development and social change. 1970. A4019
____. Tribal and peasant economics. 1967. A4020
Hunt, R., ed. Personalities and cultures. 1967. A4021
Middleton, J., ed. From child to adult. 1970. A4022
____. Gods and rituals. 1967. A4023
____. Magic, witchcraft, and curing. 1967. A4024
____. Myth and cosmos. 1967. A4025
Otten, C. M., comp. Anthropology and art. 1971. A4026
____, ed. Primitive art. 1970. A4027
Strahler, A. N. A geologist's view of Cape Cod. 1967. A4028
Struever, S., ed. Prehistoric agriculture. 1971. A4029
Vayda, A. P., comp. and ed. Peoples and cultures of the Pacific. 1968. A4030
____, ed. Environment and cultural behavior. 1969. A4031

AMERICAN NATION (Harper)

1 Cheyney, E. P. European backgrounds of American history, 1300-1600. 1904. A4032
2 Farrand, L. Basis of American history. 1500-1900. 1904. A4033
3 Bourne, E. G. Spain in America, 1450-1580. 1904. A4034
4 Tyler, L. G. England in America, 1580-1652. 1904. A4035
5 Andrews, C. M. Colonial self-government, 1652-1689. 1904. A4036
6 Greene, E. B. Provincial America, 1690-1740. 1905. A4037
7 Thwaites, R. G. France in America, 1497-1763. 1905. A4038
8 Howard, G. E. Preliminaries of the revolution, 1763-1775. 1905. A4039
9 VanTyne, C. H. The American revolution, 1776-1783. 1905. A4040
10 McLaughlin, A. C. The confederation and the

Constitution, 1783-1789. 1905. A4041
11 Bassett, J. S. The federalist system, 1789-1801. 1906. A4042
12 Channing, E. The Jeffersonian system, 1801-11. 1906. A4043
13 Babcock, K. C. The rise of American nationality, 1811-1819. 1906. A4044
14 Turner, F. J. Rise of the new West, 1819-1829. 1906. A4045
15 MacDonald, W. Jacksonian democracy, 1829-1837. 1906. A4046
16 Hart, A. B. Slavery and abolition, 1831-1841. 1906. A4047
17 Garrison, G. P. Westward extension, 1841-1850. 1906. A4048
18 Smith, T. C. Parties and slavery, 1850-1859. 1906. A4049
19 Chadwick, F. E. Causes of the civil war, 1859-1861. 1906. A4050
20 Hosmer, J. K. The appeal to arms, 1861-1863. 1907. A4051
21 ____. Outcome of the Civil war, 1863-1865. 1907. A4052
22 Dunning, W. A. Reconstruction, political and economic, 1865-1877. 1907. A4053
23 Sparks, E. E. National development, 1877-1885. 1907. A4054
24 Dewey, D. R. National problems, 1885-1897. 1907. A4055
25 Latané, J. H. America as a world power, 1897-1907. 1907. A4056
26 Hart, A. B. National ideals historically traced, 1607-1907. 1907. A4057
27 Ogg, F. A. National progress, 1907-1917. 1918. A4058
28 Matteson, D. M., comp. Analytic index. 1908. A4059

AMERICAN NEGRO, HIS HISTORY AND LITERATURE (Arno)

Series I:

The Anglo-African magazine. 1968. A4060
Atlantic University. Publications. 12 nos. in 1. 1968. A4061
Botume, E. H. First days among the contrabands. 1968. A4062
Carey, M. Letters of the colonization society. 1968. A4063
Child, L. M. An appeal in favor of Americans called Africans. 1968. A4064
____. The freedman's book. 1968. A4065
Coffin, L. Reminiscences of Levi Coffin. 1968. A4066
Conneau, T. Captain Canot. 1968. A4067
Delany, M. R. The condition, elevation, immigration, and destiny of the colored people of the United States. 1968. A4068
Douglass, F. My bondage and my friends. 1968. A4069
Five slave narratives. 1968. A4070
Fortune, T. T. Black and white. 1968. A4071
Frazier, E. F. The free Negro family. 1968. A4072
Garrison, W. L. Thoughts on African colonization. 1968. A4073
Garvey, M. Philosophy and opinions of Marcus Garvey. V. 1. 1968. A4074
Gibbs, M. W. Shadow and light. 1968. A4075
Gilbert, O. Narrative of Sojourner Truth. 1968. A4076
Haynes, G. E. The Negro at work in New York City. 1968. A4077
Higginson, T. W. Cheerful yesterdays. 1968. A4078
Hinton, R. J. John Brown and his men. 1968. A4079
Illinois. Chicago Comm. on Race Relations. The Negro in Chicago. 1968. A4080
Johnson, J. W. Black Manhattan. 1968. A4081
Keckley, E. Behind the scenes. 1968. A4082
Kerlin, R. T. The voice of the Negro. 1968. A4083
Locke, A. L., ed. The new Negro. 1968. A4084
Love, N. The life and adventure of Nat Love. 1968. A4085
Lynch, J. R. The facts of

reconstruction. 1968. A4086
Massachusetts Colonization Society. American Colonization Society. 1968. A4087
May, S. J. Some recollections of our antislavery conflict. 1968. A4088
Miller, K. Race adjustment . . . 1968. A4089
Nell, W. C. The colored patriots of the American Revolution. 1968. A4090
Ottley, R. New World a-coming. 1968. A4091
Payne, D. A. Recollections of seventy years. 1968. A4092
Siebert, W. H. The underground railroad from slavery to freedom. 1968. A4093
Simmons, W. J. Men at work. 1968. A4094
South Carolina. Constitutional Convention. Proceedings. 2 v. 1968. A4095
Still, W. The underground railroad. 1968. A4096
Stowe, H. E. The key to Uncle Tom's cabin. 1968. A4097
The Suppressed book about slavery. 1968. A4098
Taylor, S. K. Reminiscences of my life in camp. 1968. A4099
U. S. Bur. of the Census. Negro population in the United States, 1790-1915. 1968. A4100
Ward, S. R. Autobiography of a fugitive Negro. 1968. A4101
Weld, T. D. American slavery as it is. 1968. A4102
Williams, G. W. History of the Negro race in America, 1619-1880. 2 v. 1968. A4103
Wilson, J. T. The black phalanx. 1968. A4104
Woodson, C. G. The education of the Negro prior to 1861. 1968. A4105

Series II:

Andrews, S. The South since the war. 1969. A4106
Anti-Negro riots in the North, 1863. 1969. A4107
Baker, H. E. The colored inventor. 1969. A4108
Barnett, I. B. On lynchings. 1969. A4109
Beckworth, J. P. The life and adventures of James P. Beckwith, ed. by Bonner. 1969. A4110
Brown, S. A. The Negro in American fiction and Negro poetry and drama. 1969. A4111
____, ed. and others. The Negro caravan. 1969. A4112
Brown, W. W. Clotel. 1969. A4113
Cashin, H. V. and others. Under fire with the Tenth U. S. Cavalry. 1969. A4114
Chestnutt, C. W. The marrow of tradition. 1969. A4115
Culp, D. W., ed. Twentieth century Negro literature. 1969. A4116
Daniels, J. In freedom's birthplace. 1969. A4117
Dunbar, P. L. Lyrics of lonely life. 1969. A4118
____. The sport of the gods. 1969. A4119
____. The strength of Gideon and other stories. 1969. A4120
Emilio, L. F. A brave black regiment. 1969. A4121
Fisher, R. The walls of Jericho. 1969. A4122
Flipper, H. O. The colored cadet at West Point. 1969. A4123
Foley, A. S. God's men of color. 1969. A4124
Garvey, M. Philosophy and opinions of Marcus Garvey. V. 2. 1969. A4125
Gibson, J. W. Progress of a race. 1969. A4126
Griggs, S. Imperium in imperio. 1969. A4127
Heard, W. H. From slavery to the bishopric in the A. M. E. church. 1969. A4128
Henson, M. A. A Negro explorer at the North Pole. 1969. A4129
Herndon, A. Let me live. 1969. A4130
Higginson, T. W. Black rebellion. 1969. A4131
Holmes, D. O. W. The evolution of the Negro college. 1969. A4132
Howe, S. G. Report to the Freedman's Inquiry

Commission, 1864. 1969. A4133
Katz, B., ed. The social implications of early Negro music in the United States. 1969. A4134
Kester, H. Revolt among the sharecroppers. 1969. A4135
Langston, J. M. From the Virginia plantation to the National Capitol. 1969. A4136
Livermore, G. An historical research respecting the opinions of the founders of the Republic. 1969. A4137
Locke, A. L. The Negro and his music and Negro art. 1969. A4138
McKay, C. A long way from home. 1969. A4139
Miller, K. An appeal to conscience. 1969. A4140
____. Out of the house of bondage. 1969. A4141
National Negro Conference. Proceedings. 1969. A4142
The Negro problem, by Washington and others. 1969. A4143
Ovington, M. W. The walls came tumbling down. 1969. A4144
Payne, D. A. History of the African Methodist Episcopal Church. 1969. A4145
Pearson, E. W., ed. Letters from Port Royal, 1862-1868. 1969. A4146
Penn, I. G. The Afro-American press and its editors. 1969. A4147
Porter, D., ed. Negro protest pamphlets. 1969. A4148
Porter, J. A. Modern Negro art. 1969. A4149
Scott, E. J. Negro migration during the war. 1969. A4150
____. Scott's official history of the American Negro in World War II. 1969. A4151
Silvera, L. D., comp. The Negro in World War II. 1969. A4152
Sinclair, W. A. The aftermath of slavery. 1969. A4153
Smedley, R. C. History of the underground railroad in Chester and the neighboring counties of Pennsylvania. 1969. A4154
Steward, T. G. The colored regulars in the United States Army. 1969. A4155
Thurman, W. The blacker the berry. 1969. A4156
Trowbridge, J. T. The South. 1969. A4157
Turner, E. R. The Negro in Pennsylvania. 1969. A4158
Turner, L. Africanisms in the Gullah dialect. 1969. A4159
U.S. Bur. of the Census. Negroes in the United States, 1920-1932, by Hall. 1969. A4160
U.S. Off. of Education. Negro education, ed. by Jones. 1969. A4161
Walker, D. and Garnet, H. H. Walker's appeal in four articles. 1969. A4162
Walker, M. For my people. 1969. A4163
Washington, B. T. and others. A new Negro for a new century. 1969. A4164
Webb, F. J. The Garies and their friends. 1969. A4165
White, W. F. A man called White. 1969. A4166
____. Rope and faggot. 1969. A4167
Wright, R. 12 million black voices. 1969. A4168
Writers' Program, Va. The Negro in Virginia. 1969. A4169
____. These are our people. 1969. A4170

Series III:

The American Negro Academy. Occasional papers nos. 1-22. A4171
Atlantic University. Atlantic University Publications Nos. 3, 5, 6, 7, 10, 12, 19, 20. 1969. A4172
Bell, H. H. A survey of the Negro convention movement, 1830-1861. A4173
____, comp. Minutes of the Proceedings of the National Negro Conventions, 1830-1864. 1969. A4174
Bruce, J. E. The selected writings of John Edward Bruce, comp. by Gilbert. 1971. A4175
Clark, P. The black brigade of Cincinnati. 1969. A4176
Craft, W. and E. Running a

thousand miles for freedom. 1969. A4177
Cullen, C. Color. 1969. A4178
Donnelly, I. Dr. Huguet. 1969. A4179
DuBois, W. E. B. The Black North in 1901. 1969. A4180
____. The quest of the silver fleece. 1969. A4181
Epstein, A. The Negro immigrant in Pittsburgh. 1969. A4182
Foley, A. S. Bishop Healey. 1969. A4183
The free people of color, by Jay and Clarke. 1969. A4184
Fulton, D. B. Hanover. 1972. A4185
Haynes, G. E. and Brown, S. The Negro newcomers in Detroit and the Negro in Washington. 1969. A4186
Hurston, Z. N. Dust tracks on a road. 1969. A4187
King, E. The great South. 1969. A4188
Larsen, N. Passing. 1969. A4189
Lockwood, L. C. J. and Forten, C. Two black teachers during the Civil War. 1969. A4190
Marks, G. P., comp. The Black press views American imperialism (1898-1900). 1971. A4191
National Association for the Advancement of Colored People. Thirty years of lyching in the United States, 1889-1918. 1969. A4192
O'Connor, E. M. and Miner, M. Myrtille Miner. 1969. A4193
Porter, K. W. The Negro on the American frontier. 1969. A4194
Rollin, F. A. Life and public service of Martin R. Delany. 1969. A4195
Torrence, R. The story of John Hope. 1969. A4196
Turner, H. M. Respect Black, comp. and ed. by Turner. 1971. A4197
Two Black views of Liberia, by Nesbit. Four years on Liberia by Williams. 1969. A4198
U. S. Office of Education. History of schools for the Colored population. 1969. A4199
U. S. President. Report on the conditions of the South, ed. by Schurz. 1969. A4200
Universal Races Congress. Papers on inter-racial problems, ed. by Spiller. 1969. A4201
Warner, R. A. New Haven Negroes. 1969. A4202
Washington, B. T. Working with the hands. 1969. A4203
West, D. The living is easy. 1969. A4204

AMERICAN ORIENTAL SERIES (Amer. Oriental Soc.)

1 Blake, F. R. A grammar of the Tagálog language. 1925. A4205
2-3 Pañchatantra reconstructed, ed. by Edgerton. 2 v. 1924. A4206
4 Vetālapàncavinśati. Jambhaladatta's version of the Vetalapancavinśati, tr. by Emeneau. 1934. A4207
5 Albright, W. F. The vocalization of the Egyptian syllabic orthography. 1934. A4208
6 Pfeiffer, R. H., ed. State letters of Assyria. 1935. A4209
7 Emeneau, M. B., comp. A union list of printed Indic texts and translations in American libraries. 1935. A4210
8 Harris, Z. S. A grammar of the Phoenician language. 1936. A4211
9 Vedas. Atharvaveda. The Kashmirian Atharva Veda, bks. 16, 17, ed. by Barret. 1936. A4212
10 Cross, D. Movable property in the Nuzi documents. 1937. A4213
11 Liu, A. The study of human abilities: the Jen wu chih, tr. by Shryock. 1937. A4214
12 Poleman, H. I. A census of Indic manuscripts in the United States and Canada. 1938. A4215
13 Vasu-bandhu. Wei shih er shih lun, ed. by Hamilton. 1938. A4216
14 Götze, A. The Hittite

ritual of Tunnawi. 1938. A4217
15 Burrows, M. The basis of Israelite marriage. 1938. A4218
16 Harris, Z. S. Development of the Canaanite dialects. 1939. A4219
17 Ssŭ-ma. Statesman, patriot, and general in ancient China, tr. by Bodde. 1940. A4220
18 Same as 9. Bks. 19, 20. 1940. A4221
19 Alī ibn Ismā'īl. A. H. A. Abu'l Hasan Al-ibānah'an usūl addiyānah, tr. by Klein. 1940. A4222
20 Mackay, E. J. H. Chanhu-daro excavations, 1935-36. 1943. A4223
21 Uttarādhyāyana sūtra. Manuscripts illustrations, ed. by Brown. 1941. A4224
22 Coomaraswamy, A. K. Spiritual authority and temporal power in the Indian theory of government. 1942. A4225
23 Wieschhoff, H. A. Anthropological bibliography of Negro Africa. 1948. A4226
24 Pritchard, J. B. Palestinian figurines in relation to certain goddesses known through literature. 1943. A4227
25 Steele, F. R. Nuzi real estate transactions. 1943. A4228
26 Rosenthal, F. Ahmad b. at-Tayyib as-Sarahsi. 1943. A4229
27 Huang, H. Lu Hsiang-shan. 1944. A4230
28 Leslau, W. Gafat documents. 1945. A4231
29 Neugebauer, O. and Sachs, A., eds. Mathematical cuneiform texts. 1945. A4232
30 Whitney, W. D. The roots, verbforms and primary derivatives of the Sanskrit language. 1945. A4233
31 Abû Hayyan. Commentary to the Alfiyya of Ibn Malīk, ed. by Glazer. 1947. A4234
32 Oppenheim, L. Catalogue of the cuneiform tablets of the Wilberforce Eames Babylonian collection in the New York Public Library. 1948. A4235
33 Kent, R. G. Old Persian grammar, text, lexicon. 1953. A4236
34 Ballāla, of Benares. The narrative of Bhoja, ed. by Gray. 1950. A4237
35 al-Tabarī. The reign of al-Mu'tasim, tr. by Marin. 1951. A4238
36 Cross, F. M. and Freedman, D. N. Early Hebrew orthography. 1952. A4239
37 Balkan, K. Kassitenstudien, 1: Die sprachie der Kassiten, tr. by Kraus. 1954. A4240
38 Dentan, R. C., ed. The idea of history in the ancient New East. 1955. A4241
39 Greenberg, M. The Hab/piru. 1955. A4242
40 American Oriental Society. Journal. Index, ed. by Schafer and others. 1955. A4243
41 Bleek, D. F. A Bushman dictionary. 1956. A4244
42 Street, J. C. The language of the Secret history of the Mongols. 1957. A4245
43 Hallo, W. W. Early Mesopotamian royal titles. 1957. A4246
44 Sternbach, L. The Hitopadesa and its sources. 1960. A4247
45 Blair, C. J. Heat in the Rig Veda. 1961. A4248
46 Brown, W. N., ed. and tr. The Vasanta Vilāsa. 1962. A4249
47 American Oriental Society. Indological studies in honor of W. Norman Brown, ed. by Bender. 1962. A4250
48 Huai-nan-tzŭ. The Huai-nan-tzŭ, book eleven, by Wallacker. 1962. A4251
49 Yamauchi, E. M. Mandaic incantation texts. 1967. A4252
50 Oxtoby, W. G. Some inscriptions of the Safaitic Bedouin. 1968. A4253
51 Rocher, R. Alexander Hamilton, 1726-1824. 1968. A4254
52 Stevens, A. M. Madurese phonology and morphology. 1968. A4255
53 Essays in memory of E. A. Speiser, ed. by Hallo. 1968. A4256

54 Vetālapañcavimśati, A. Nepali version of Vetālapañcavimśati, tr. by Riccardi. 1971. A4257
55 Hoffner, H. A. Alimenta Hethaeorum. 1972. A4258
56 George, C. The Canadmaharosana Tantra. 1973. A4259
57 Brown, W. N. and Mayeda, N. Tawi tales. 1974. A4260

AMERICAN PERSPECTIVES (Harper)

Adams, H. The degradation of the democratic dogma. 1969. A4261
Baker, R. S. Following the color line, ed. by Grantham. 1964. A4262
Bourne, R. S. War and the intellectuals, ed. by Resek. 1964. A4263
Brooks, V. W. Van Wyck Brooks. ed. by Sprague. 1968. A4264
Burke, E. On the American Revolution, ed. by Barkan. 1966. A4265
Fox, D. R. The decline of aristocracy in the politics of New York, 1801-1840, ed. by Remini. 1965. A4266
Gilman, C. P. Women and economics. 1966. A4267
Hunter, R. Poverty, ed. by Jones. 1965. A4268
Hutchinson, W. R., comp. American Protestant thought. 1968. A4269
Leonard, A. The American colonial crisis, ed. by Mason. 1972. A4270
McLoughlin, W. G., comp. The American evangelicals. 1968. A4271
Parkman, F. The Seven Years War, ed. by McCallum. 1968. A4272
Rauschenbusch, W. Christianity and the social crisis, ed. by Cross. 1964. A4273
Reid, W. After the war, ed. by Woodward. 1965. A4274
Shinn, C. H. Mining camps, ed. by Paul. 1965. A4275
Smith, J. Captain John Smith's America, ed. by Lankford. 1967. A4276
Tarbell, I. M. The history of the Standard Oil Company, ed. by Chamlers. 1966. A4277
Tindall, G. B., ed. A Populist reader. 1966. A4278
Tourgée, A. W. A fool's errand. 1966. A4279
U. S. Treasury Dept. The reports of Alexander Hamilton, ed. by Cooke. 1964. A4280
Weyl, W. E. The new democracy, ed. by Forcey. 1964. A4281

AMERICAN PHILOLOGICAL ASSOCIATION. MONOGRAPHS.

1 Taylor, L. R. The divinity of the Roman emperor. 1931. A4282
2 Forbes, C. A. Neoi. 1933. A4283
3 Oldfather, W. A. and others. Index Apvleianvs. 1934. A4284
4 Post, L. A. The Vatican Plato and its relations. 1934. A4285
5 Tacitus, C. Germania, a critical edition, ed. by Robinson. 1935. A4286
6 Rogers, R. S. Critical trials and criminal legislation under Tiberius. 1935. A4287
7 Perry, B. E. Studies in the text history of the life and fables of Aesop. 1936. A4288
8 Scholia Platonica contvlervt atqve investigavervnt Fredericvs De Forest Allen, ed. by Greene. 1938. A4289
9 Wolff, H. J. Written and unwritten marriages in Hellenistic and Postclassical Roman law. 1939. A4290
10 Philodemus. Philodemus, ed. by P. H. and E. A. DeLacy. 1941. A4291
11 Pearson, L. I. The local historians of Attica. 1942. A4292
12 Dunchad. Glossae in Martianum, ed. by Lutz. 1944. A4293
13 Fränkel, H. Dichtung und philosophie des fruehen griechentums. 1951. A4294
14 Diller, A. The tradition of

the minor Greek geographers. 1952. A4295
15 Broughton, T. R. S. The magistrates of the Roman Republic. 2 v. 1951-52. A4296
16 Hahn, E. A. Subjunctive and optative: their origin as futures. 1953. A4297
17 Copley, F. O. Exclusus amator. 1956. A4298
18 Eugubine tablets. The bronze tablets of Iguvium. By J. W. Poultney. 1933. A4299
19 Helmbold, W. C. and O'Neil, E. N. Plutarch's quotations. 1959. A4300
20 Pearson, L. I. The lost histories of Alexander the Great. 1960. A4301
21 O'Neil, E. N. A critical concordance of the Tibullan corpus. 1963. A4302
22 Historia de Segundo. Secundus, the silent philosopher, ed. by Perry. 1964. A4303
23 Immerwahr, H. R. Form and thought in Herodotus. 1967. A4304
24 Menander, of Athens. Dyscolus, tr. by Blake. 1966. A4305
25 Cole, A. T. Democritus and the sources of Greek anthropology. 1967. A4306
26 Fink, R. O. Roman military records on papyrus. 1971. A4307
27 Hahn, E. A. Naming constructions in Indo-European languages. 1969. A4308
28 Gerber, D. E. A bibliography of Pindar. 1969. A4309
29 Husselman, E. M., comp. Papyri from Karanis. 3d ser. 1971. A4310
30 Levy, H. L. Claudian's in Rufinum. 1971. A4311
31 Wyatt, W. F. The Greek prothetic vowel. 1972. A4312

AMERICAN PHILOLOGICAL ASSOCIATION. SPECIAL PUBLICATIONS.

1 Servius. Servianorum in Vergilii carmina commentariorum, ed. by Rand. 3 v. 1946. A4313
2 Homerus. Ilias Atheniensium, ed. by Bolling. 1950. A4314

AMERICAN PHILOSOPHICAL SOCIETY, PHILADELPHIA. MEMOIRS.

1 Moore, E. H. and Barnard, R. W. General analysis. 2 pts. 1935. A4315
2 Hyde, W. W. Roman Alpine routes. 1935. A4316
3 Fortune, R. F. Manus religion. 1935. A4317
4 Montgomery, J. A. and Harris, Z. S. The Ras Shamra mythological texts. 1935. A4318
5 Davidson, D. S. Aboriginal Australian and Tasmanian rock carvings and paintings. 1936. A4319
6 ____. Snowshoes. 1937. A4320
7 Speck, F. G. Oklahoma Delaware ceremonies, feasts and dances. 1937. A4321
8 Ramón y Cajal, S. Recollections of my life, tr. by Craigie. 2 pts. 1937. A4322
9 Davidson, D. S. A preliminary consideration of aboriginal Australian decorative art. 1937. A4323
10 Keesing, F. M. The Menomini Indians of Wisconsin. 1939. A4324
11 Caley, E. The composition of ancient Greek bronze coins. 1939. A4325
12 Chamberlain, J. The letters, ed. by McClure. 2 pts. 1939. A4326
13 Ehrich, A. M. (Hoskin). Early pottery of the Jebelah region. 1939. A4327
14 Harrison, B. The correspondence between Benjamin Harrison and James G. Blaine, 1882-1893, ed. by Volwiler. 1940. A4328
15 Nef, J. U. Industry and government in France and England, 1540-1640. 1940. A4329
16 Newby, W. W. The embryology of the echiuroid worm urechis caupo. 1940. A4330
17 Malin, J. C. John Brown and the legend of fifty-six.

1942. A4331
18 Reed, S. W. The making modern New Guinea. 1943. A4332
19 Cailliet, E. La tradition littéraire des idéologues. 1943. A4333
20 Montagu, A. Edward Tyson, 1650-1708. 1943. A4334
21 Kramer, S. N. Sumerian mythology. 1944. A4335
22 Jefferson, T. Thomas Jefferson's Garden book, ed. by Betts. 1944. A4336
23 Sellers, C. C., ed. Charles Willson Peale. Pt. I. Early life, 1741-1790, Pt. II. Later life, 1790-1827. 1947. A4337
24 Franklin, B. Letters and papers of Benjamin Franklin and Richard Jackson, ed. by Van Doren. 1947. A4338
25 Rush, B. The autobiography of Benjamin Rush, ed. by Corner. 1948. A4339
26 Franklin, B. Benjamin Franklin and Catharine Ray Greene; their correspondence, 1755-1790, ed. by Roelker. 1949. A4340
27 ____. The letters of Benjamin Franklin and Jane Mecom, ed. by Van Doren. 1950. A4341
28 Corner, B. C. William Shippen, jr. pioneer in American medical education. 1951. A4342
29 Levy, E. West Roman vulgar law. 1951. A4343
30 Rush, B. Letters, ed. by Butterfield. Pt. I. 1761-1792, Pt. II. 1793-1813. 1951. A4344
31 Rodgers, A. D. Erwin Frink Smith, a story of American plant pathology. 1952. A4345
32 Miner, H. M. The primitive city of Timbuctoo. 1953. A4346
33 Lehman, H. C. Age and achievement. 1953. A4347
34 Servetus, M. Michael Servetus, a translation of his geographical, medical and astrological writings; with introduction and notes by C. D. O'Malley, 1953. A4348
35 Jefferson, T. Thomas Jefferson's Farm book, ed. by Betts. 1953. A4349
36 Keeler, M. F. The Long Parliament, 1640-1641. 1954. A4350
37 Cramer, F. H. Astrology in Roman law and politics. 1954. A4351
38 Rutledge, A. W., ed. Cumulative record of exhibition catalogues. 1955. A4352
39 Tinckom, H. M. and others. Historic Germantown. 1955. A4353
40 Westerman, W. L. The slave system of Greek and Roman antiquity. 1955. A4354
41 Burke, E. Edmund Burke, New York agent, with his letters to the New York Assembly and intimate correspondence with Charles O'Hara, 1761-1776, ed. by Hoffman. 1956. A4355
42 Jameson, J. F. An historian's world, selections from the correspondence of John Franklin Jameson, ed. by Donnan and Stock. 1956. A4356
43 Cohen, I. B. Franklin and Newton. 1956. A4357
44 Harvey, E. N. A history of luminescence from the earliest times until 1900. 1957. A4358
45 Kuznets, S. S. and Thomas, D. S. Popular redistribution and economic growth: United States, 1870-1950. V. 1. 1957. A4359
46 Wertenbaker, T. J. Give me liberty. 1958. A4360
47 Pace, A. Benjamin Franklin and Italy. 1958. A4361
48 Neugebauer, O. and Van Hoesen, H. B. Greek horoscopes. 1959. A4362
49 John, H. J. Jan Evangelista Purkyně. 1959. A4363
50 Jacquemont, V. Letters to Achille Chaper. 1960. A4364
51 Same as no. 45. V. 2. 1960. A4365
52 Poesch, J. Titian Ramsey Peele, 1799-1885. 1961. A4366
53 American Philosophical Society. A catalogue of instruments and models in the possession of the American Philosophical Society, comp. by Multhauf and Davies. 1961. A4367

54 ____. A catalogue of portraits and other works of art in the possession of the American Philosophical Society. 1961. A4368
55 Jacobsson, P. The market economy in the world of today. 1961. A4369
56 Tuckerman, B. Planetary, lunar, and solar positions 601 B. C. to A. D. 1... 1962. A4370
57 Beadle, G. W. Genetics and modern biology. 1963. A4371
58 Murphy, R. C. Fish-shape Paumanok. 1964. A3472
59 Same as no. 56. V. 2. 1962. A4373
60 Stenton, D. M. P. English justice between the Norman Conquest and the Great Charter. 1964. A4374
61 Same as no. 45. V. 3. 1964. A4375
62 Robbins, C. C. David Hosack, citizen of New York. 1964. A4376
63 Waterhouse, E. K. Three decades of British art, 1740-1770. 1965. A4377
64 Markman, S. D. Colonial architecture of Antigua, Guatemala. 1966. A4378
65 Freeman, J. F., comp. A guide to manuscripts relating to the American Indian in the library of the American Philosophical Society. 1965. A4379
66 Bell, W. J. and Smith, M. D. Guide to the archives and manuscript collections of the American Philosophical Society. 1966. A4380
67 Fowler, W. A. Nuclear astrometaphysics. 1967. A4381
68 Sources for history of quantum physics, by Kuhn. 1967. A4382
69 Williram, Abbot of Ebersberg. The "Expositio in Cantica canticorum," ed. by Bartelmez. 1967. A4383
70 Lunt, W. E. Accounts rendered by papal collectors in England, 1317-1378, ed. by Graves. 1968. A4384
71 Raimundus de Agiles. Historica francirum qui ceperunt Iherusaleum, tr. by J. H. and L. L. Hill. 1968. A4385
72 Bush, D. Pagan myth and Christian tradition in English poetry. 1968. A4386
73 Tyler, D. B. The Wilkes expedition. 1968. A4387
74 Bartram, W. Botanical and zoological drawings, ed. by Ewan. 1968. A4388
75 Medawar, P. B. Induction and intuition in scientific thought. 1969. A4389
76 Mason, C. The journal of Charles Mason and Jeremiah Dixon, ed. by A. H. Mason. 1969. A4390
77 American Philosophical Society. Early transactions of the American Philosophical Society published in the American Magazine during 1769. 1969. A4391
78 Dicke, R. H. Gravitation and the universe. 1970. A4392
79 Robson, W. An English view of American Quakerism, ed. by Bronner. 1970. A4393
80 Smith, D. M. Aftermath of war. 1970. A4394
81 Pingree, D. E. Census of the exact sciences in Sanskrit; Ser. A. V. 1. 1970- A4395
82 Wansey, H. Henry Wansey and his American journal, 1794, ed. by Jeremy. 1970. A4396
83 Mitford, T. B. The inscriptions of Kourion. 1972. A4397
84 O'Brien, C. F. Sir William Dawson. 1971. A4398
85 Austin, A. L. The Woolsey sisters of New York. 1971. A4399
86 Same as no. 81. Ser. A. V. 2. 1971. A4400
87 Christiernin, P. N. The Swedish bullionist controversy, ed. by Eagley. 1971. A4401
88 Winslow, J. H. Darwin's Victorian malady. 1971. A4402
89 Scharfe, H. Panini's metalanguage. 1971. A4403
90 Viner, J. The role of providence in the social order. 1972. A4404
91 Newman, W. M. Les seigneurs de Nesle en

Picardie (XIIe-XIIIe siècle)
2 v. 1971. A4405
92 Weber, N. A. Gardening ants. 1972. A4406
93 Thompson, J. E. S. A commentary on the Dresden codex. 1972. A4407
94 Goldstine, H. H. New and full moons 1001 B. C. to A. D. 1651. 1973. A4408
95 Smith, E. H. The diary of Elihu Hubbard Smith, ed. by Cronin. 1973. A4409
96 Blake, M. E. Roman construction in Italy from Nerva through the Antonies, ed. by Bishop. 1973. A4410
97 Gazley, J. G. The life of Arthur Young, 1741-1820. 1973. A4411
98 Cash, P. Medical men at the siege of Boston. 1973. A4412
99 Crucial American elections. 1973. A4413
100 Berkeley, E. and D. S. Zealous partisan in a nation divided. 1973. A4414
101 Tudebode, P. Historia de Hierosolymitano itinere, tr. by J. H. and L. L. Hill. 1974. A4415
102 Miller, C. W. Benjamin Franklin's Philadelphia printing, 1728-1766. 1974. A4416

AMERICAN POLITICS RESEARCH SERIES (Rand)

Alford, R. R. Bureaucracy and participation. 1969. A4417
Barber, J. D. Power in committees. 1966. A4418
____. Social mobility and voting behavior. 1970. A4419
Crecine, J. P. Government problem solving. 1969. A4420
Davis, M. and Weinbaum, M. G. Metropolitan decision processes. 1969. A4421
Devine, D. J. The attentive public. 1970. A4422
Dye, T. R. Politics, economics, and the public. 1967. A4423
Francis, W. L. A comparative analysis of legislative issues in the fifty states. 1967. A4424
Holtzman, A. Legislative liaison. 1970. A4425
Jacob, H. Debtors in court. 1969. A4426
Keech, W. R. The impact of Negro voting. 1968. A4427
Lipsky, M. Protest in city politics. 1970. A4428
McEvoy, J. Radicals or conservatives. 1971. A4429
Schlesinger, J. A. Ambition and politics. 1966. A4430
Sharkansky, I. Spending in the American states. 1968. A4431
Steiner, G. Y. Social insecurity. 1966. A4432

AMERICAN PROCESSION SERIES (Hastings)

Beals, C. Brass-knuckle crusade. 1961. A4433
Fuller, E. Tinkers and genius. 1955. A4434
Havighurst, W. Wilderness for sale. 1956. A4435
Herbst, J. New green world. 1954. A4436
Kramer, D. The wild jackasses. 1956. A4437
Sandoz, M. The beaver men. 1964. A4438
____. The buffalo hunters. 1954. A4439
____. The cattlemen from the Rio Grande across the far Marias. 1958. A4440
Webber, E. Escape to Utopia. 1959. A4441

AMERICAN PROFILE SERIES (Hill & Wang)

Bode, C., ed. Ralph Waldo Emerson. 1968. A4442
Cooke, J. E., ed. Alexander Hamilton. 1967. A4443
Glad, P. W., ed. William Jennings Bryan. 1968. A4444
Harding, W. R., ed. Henry David Thoreau. 1971. A4445
Kaplan, J., comp. Mark Twain. 1967. A4446
Keller, M., ed. Theodore Roosevelt. 1967. A4447
Leuchtenburg, W. E., ed. Franklin D. Roosevelt. 1967. A4448
Levin, D., ed. Jonathan Edwards. 1969. A4449

Lincoln, C. E., ed. Martin Luther King. 1969. A4450
Link, A. S., comp. Woodrow Wilson. 1968. A4451
Logan, R. W., ed. W. E. B. DuBois. 1971. A4452
McKitrick, E. L., ed. Andrew Johnson. 1969. A4453
Peterson, M. D., ed. Thomas Jefferson. 1967. A4454
Sellers, C., ed. Andrew Jackson. 1970. A4455
Smith, J. M., ed. George Washington. 1969. A4456
Thomas, J. L., comp. John C. Calhoun. 1968. A4457
Wright, E., ed. Benjamin Franklin. 1970. A4458

AMERICAN REVOLUTIONARY SERIES (Gregg)

American and French Accounts of the Revolution:

Allen, P. A history of the American Revolution. 1972. A4459
Balch, T. The French in America during the war of independence of the United States. 2 v. 1972. A4460
Bennett, C. Advance and retreat to Saratoga. 2 v. 1972. A4461
Benson, E. Vindication of the captors of Major André. 1972. A4462
Butterfield, W. History of Lt. Col. George Clark's conquest of the Illinois and Wabash towns. 1972. A4463
Fisher, S. G. The true history of the American revolution. 1972. A4464
Goss, E. H. The life of Colonel Paul Revere. 1972. A4465
Haiman, M. Kosciuszko in the American revolution. 1972. A4466
Raynal, G. T. F. The revolution of America. 1972. A4467
Sears, L. John Hancock. 1972. A4468
Sloane, W. M. The French war and the revolution. 1972. A4469
Stark, C. Memoir and official correspondence of General John Stark. 1972. A4470
U. S. Army. General orders issued by Gen. Israel Putnam, ed. by Ford. 1972. A4471
Wolf, S. The American Jew as patriot, soldier, and citizen. 1972. A4472

British Accounts of the American Revolution:

Beatson, R. Naval and military memoirs of Great Britain from 1727-1783. 6 v. 1972. A4473
Burke, E. Speeches on the American war, and letters to the sheriffs of Bristol, ed. by Boston. 1972. A4474
DeFontblanque, E. B. Political and military episodes in the latter half of the eighteenth century. 1972. A4475
Great Britain Historical Manuscripts Comm. Manuscripts of the Earl of Dartmouth. 3 v. 1972. A4476
____. Report on American manuscripts in the Royal Institution of Great Britain. 4 v. 1972. A4477
____. Report on the manuscripts of Mrs. Stofford-Sackville of Drayton House. 1972. A4478
____. Reprint of the manuscripts of Captain H. V. Knox. 1972. A4479
Hadden, J. M. Hadden's journal and orderly books. 1972. A4480
Hannay, D. Rodney. 1972. A4481
The history of the British Empire, from the year 1765, to the end of 1783. By a Society of Gentlemen, ed. by Billias. 2 v. 1972. A4482
Kemble, S. Colonel Stephen Kemble's journal and British Army orders. 1972. A4483
Mundy, G. B. The life and correspondence of the late Admiral Lord Rodney. 2 v. 1972. A4484
Northumberland, H. P. Letters of Hugh, Earl of Percy, ed. by Bolton. 1972. A4485
Ralfe, J. The naval biography of Great Britain... 4 v. 1972. A4486
White, T. Naval researches. 1972. A4487

The Loyalist Library:

Bardley-Wilmot, J. Historical view of the commission for enquiring into the losses, services, and claims of American Loyalists. 1972. A4488

Eaton, A. W. The famous Mather Byles. 1972. A4489

Ellis, G. C. Memoir of Sir Benjamin Thompson. 1972. A4490

Galloway, J. The claims of the American Loyalists reviewed... 1972. A4491

____. Letters to a nobleman. 1972. A4492

____. A reply to the observation of Lieut. Gen. William Howe on a pamphlet entitled letters to a nobleman. 1972. A4493

Gt. Brit. Parliament. The examination of George Galloway, Esq., ed. by Balch. 1972. A4494

Hammond, O. G. Tories of New Hampshire in the war of the revolution. 1972. A4495

Hancock, H. B. The Delaware Loyalists. 1972. A4496

Johnson, J. B. Robert Alexander. 1972. A4497

Jones, E. A. The Loyalists of New Jersey. 1972. A4498

Leonard, D. Massachusettensis. 1972. A4499

Murray, J. N. Letters of James Murray. 1972. A4500

New York (State) Commission for Detecting and Defeating Conspiracies in the State of N. Y. Minutes. 2 v. 1972. A4501

Raymond, W. O., ed. The Winslow papers. 1972. A4502

Siebert, W. H. The legacy of the American revolution to the British West Indies and Bahamas. 1972. A4503

____. Loyalists in East Florida, 1774 to 1785. 1972. A4504

____. The Loyalists of Pennsylvania. 1972. A4505

United Empire Loyalists Centennial Comm. The Centennial of the settlement of Upper Canada by the United Empire Loyalists. 1972. A4506

Wallace, W. S. The United Empire loyalists. 1972. A4507

AMERICAN SHORT STORY SERIES (Garrett)

1 Atherton, G. F. The bell in the fog and other stories. 1968. A4508
2 Bangs, J. K. The water ghost and others. 1968. A4509
3 ____. Ghosts I have met and some others. 1968. A4510
4 Bellamy, E. The blindman's world and other stories. 1968. A4511
5 Bunner, H. C. "Short sixes." 1968. A4512
6 ____. More "short sixes." 1968. A4513
7 Cahan, A. The imported bridegroom and other stories of the New York ghetto. 1968. A4514
8 Chopin, K. A night in Acadie. 1968. A4515
9 Davis, R. H. Silhouettes of American life. 1968. A4516
10 ____. Gallagher and other stories. 1968. A4517
11 ____. The exiles and other stories. 1968. A4518
12 Deming, P. Adirondack stories. 1968. A4519
13 ____. Tompkins and other folks. 1968. A4520
14 Fox, J. 'Hell fer sartain' and other stories. 1968. A4521
15 Fuller, H. B. Under the skylights. 1968. A4522
16 Green, A. K. A difficult problem. 1968. A4523
17 Hale, E. E. If, yes, and perhaps. 1968. A4524
18 ____. His level best and other stories. 1968. A4525
19 ____. Crusoe in New York and other tales. 1968. A4526
20 Hall, J. The wilderness and the warpath. 1968. A4527
21 Harris, J. C. The chronicles of Aunt Minervy Ann. 1968. A4528
22 Hearn, L. Some Chinese ghosts. 1968. A4529
23 Janvier, T. A. In old New York. 1968. A4530
24 London, J. The son of the wolf. 1968. A4531
25 Long, J. L. Madame Butterfly... 1968. A4532

26 O'Brien, F. The poems and stories of Fitz-James O'Brien, ed. by Winter. 1968. A4533
27 Tarkington, B. In the arena. 1968. A4534
28 White, S. E. Blazed trail stories and stories of the wild life. 1968. A4535
29 White, W. A. Stratagems and spoils. 1968. A4536
30 Willis, N. P. Dashes at life with a free pencil. 1968. A4537
31 Wister, O. Red men and white. 1968. A4538
32 ____. The Jimmyjohn boss and other stories. 1968. A4539
33 Alcott, L. M. On picket duty and other tales. 1969. A4540
34 Aldrich, T. B. Two bites at a cherry. 1969. A4541
35 ____. Marjorie Daw and other stories. 1969. A4542
36 Brown, A. Meadow-grass. 1969. A4543
37-38 Bryant, W. C. Tales of Glauber-Spa. 1969. A4544
39 Catherwood, M. H. Mackinac and lake stories. 1969. A4545
40 ____. The queen of the swamp and other plain Americans. 1969. A4546
41 Cooke, R. T. Somebody's neighbors. 1969. A4547
42 ____. The sphinx's children and other people. 1969. A4548
43 ____. Huckleberries gathered from New England hills. 1969. A4549
44 Crane, S. Whilomville stories. 1969. A4550
45 Deland, M. Old Chester tales. 1969. A4551
46 ____. Dr. Lavendar's people. 1969. A4552
47 Edwards, H. S. Two runaways and other stories. 1969. A4553
48 ____. His defense and other stories. 1969. A4554
49 Foote, M. H. In exile and other stories. 1969. A4555
50 ____. A touch of sun and other stories. 1969. A4556
51 Frederic, H. The copperhead and other stories of the North during the American War. 1969. A4557
52 Freeman, M. E. A humble romance and other stories. 1969. A4558
53 ____. The wind in the rose bush and other stories of the supernatural. 1969. A4559
54 ____. The givers. 1969. A4560
55 French, A. Knitters in the sun. 1969. A4561
56 ____. Stories of a western town. 1969. A4562
57 Garland, H. Prairie folks. 1969. A4563
58 Grant, R. The law-breakers and other stories. 1969. A4564
59 Harte, B. Mrs. Skagg's husband and other sketches. 1969. A4565
60 Herrick, R. Literary love-letters and other stories. 1969. A4566
61 Jackson, H. H. Saxe Holm's stories. 1st ser. 1969. A4567
62 ____. ____. 2d ser. 1969. A4568
63 Janvier, T. A. Color studies. 1969. A4569
64 ____. Stories of old new Spain. 1969. A4570
65 Jewett, S. O. Strangers and wayfarers. 1969. A4571
66 ____. The queen's twin and other stories. 1969. A4572
67 King, G. E. Tales of a time and place. 1969. A4573
68 Kirkland, C. S. Western clearings. 1969. A4574
69 Lewis, A. H. Wolfville. 1969. A4575
70 Mitchell, D. G. Seven stories with basement and attic. 1969. A4576
71 Murfree, M. N. The phantoms of the footbridge and other stories. 1969. A4577
72 ____. The mystery of Witch-Face Mountain and other stories. 1969. A4578
73 Page, T. N. The burial of the guns. 1969. A4579
74 Smith, F. H. A gentleman vagabond and some others. 1969. A4580
75 Smith, S. 'Way down East.' 1969. A4581

76 Spofford, H. P. A scarlet poppy and other stories. 1969. A4582
77 Stockton, F. R. The lady, or the tiger? 1969. A4583
78 Stuart, R. M. A golden wedding and other stories. 1969. A4584
79 ____. The second wooing of Salina Sue. 1969. A4585
80 Taylor, B. Beauty and the beast and tales of home. 1969. A4586
81 Thompson, M. Hoosier mosaics. 1969. A4587
82 Townsend, E. W. "Chimmie Fadden," Major Max and other stories. 1969. A4588
83 Trowbridge, J. T. Coupon bonds and other stories. 1969. A4589
84 Ward, E. S. Men, women, and ghosts. 1969. A4590
85 ____. Sealed orders. 1969. A4591
86 Woolson, C. F. Castle nowhere. 1969. A4592
87 ____. Rodman the keeper. 1969. A4593

AMERICAN SOCIETY FOR PUBLIC ADMINISTRATION. COMPARATIVE ADMINISTRATIVE GROUP. COMPARATIVE ADMINISTRATIVE GROUP SERIES (Duke Univ. Pr.)

1 Political and administrative development, ed. by Braibanti. 1969. A4594
2 Temporal dimensions of development administration, ed. by Waldo. 1970. A4595
3 Development administration in Asia, by Abueva and others, ed. by Weidner, 1970. A4596
4 Legislatures in developmental perspective, ed. by Kornberg and Musolf. 1970. A4597
5 Frontiers of development administration, ed. by Riggs. 1971. A4598
6 Seminar on Spatial Aspects of Development Administration. Spatial dimensions of development administration, ed. by Heaphey. 1971. A4599
7 Development administration in Latin America, ed. by Thurber and Graham. 1973. A4600

AMERICAN STATESMEN (Houghton)

1 Morse, J. T. Benjamin Franklin. 1898. A4601
2 Hosmer, J. K. Samuel Adams. 1931. A4602
3 Tyler, M. C. Patrick Henry. 1908. A4603
4-5 Lodge, H. C. George Washington. 2 v. 1909. A4604
6 Morse, J. T. John Adams. 1908. A4605
7 Lodge, H. C. Alexander Hamilton. 1909. A4606
8 Roosevelt, T. Gouverneur Morris. 1898. A4607
9 Pellew, G. John Jay. 1898. A4608
10 Magruder, A. B. John Marshall. 1898. A4609
11 Morse, J. T. Thomas Jefferson. 1911. A4610
12 Gay, S. H. James Madison. 1908. A4611
13 Stevens, J. A. Albert Gallatin. 1909. A4612
14 Gilman, D. C. James Monroe. 1911. A4613
15 Morse, J. T. John Quincy Adams. 1909. A4614
16 Adams, H. John Randolph. 1898. A4615
17 Sumner, W. G. Andrew Jackson. 1910. A4616
18 Shepard, E. M. Martin Van Buren. 1916. A4617
19-20 Schurz, C. Life of Henry Clay. 2 v. 1909. A4618
21 Lodge, H. C. Daniel Webster. 1909. A4619
22 Holst, H. E. von. John C. Calhoun. 1909. A4620
23 Roosevelt, T. Thomas Hart Benton. 1909. A4621
24 McLaughlin, A. C. Lewis Cass. 1909. A4622
25-26 Morse, J. T. Abraham Lincoln. 2 v. 1921. A4623
27 Lothrop, T. K. William Henry Seward. 1917. A4624
28 Hart, A. B. Salmon Portland Chase. 1909. A4625

29 Adams, C. F. Charles Francis Adams. 1909. A4626
30 Storey, M. Charles Sumner. 1909. A4627
31 McCall, S. W. Thaddeus Stevens. 1909. A4628
32 Coolidge, L. A. Ulysses S. Grant. 1917. A4629
33 Burton, T. E. John Sherman. 1909. A4630
34 Stanwood, E. James Gillespie Blaine. 1917. A4631
35 McCall, S. W. Thomas B. Reed. 1914. A4632
36-37 Thayer, W. R. John Hay. 2 v. 1917. A4633
38-39 Olcott, C. S. William McKinley. 2 v. 1916. A4634
40 Smith, T. C. General index. 1917. A4635
Index for V. 1-31 pub. as v. 32 in 1909. V. 32-34 as given in 1917 ed. pub. as v. 1-3, ser. 2 of 1909 ed. V. 40 enlarged by Ives indexes v. 1-39.

AMERICAN THEOLOGICAL LIBRARY ASSOCIATION. ATLA BIBLIOGRAPHY SERIES (Scarecrow)

1 Jones, C. E., ed. A guide to the study of the holiness movement. 1974. A4636
2 Breit, M., ed. Thomas Merton. 1974. A4637

AMERICAN THEOLOGICAL LIBRARY ASSOCIATION. ATLA MONOGRAPH (Scarecrow)

1 Grimes, R. L. The divine imagination. 1972. A4638
2 Kelsey, G. D. Social ethics among Southern Baptists, 1917-1969. 1973. A4639
3 Kring, H. A. The harmonists. 1973. A4640
4 O'Malley, J. S. Pilgrimage of faith. 1973. A4641
5 Jones, C. E. Perfectionist persuasion. 1974. A4642

AMERICAN TRAIL SERIES (A. H. Clark)

1-2 Hebard, G. R. and Brininstool, E. A. The Bozeman trail. 2 v. 1922. A4643
3-5 Conkling, R. P. and M. B. The Butterfield Overland Mail, 1857-1869. 3 v. 1947. A4644
6 Spring, A. The Cheyenne and Black Hills stage and express routes. 1949. A4645
7 Young, O. E. The first military escort on the Santa Fe trail. 1952. A4646
8 Settle, R. W. and M. L., comp. Overland days to Montana in 1865. 1971. A4647
9 Outland, C. P. Stagecoaching on El Camino Real. 1973. A4648

AMERICAN TRAILS SERIES (McGraw)

Carter, H. Doomed road of empire. 1963. A4649
Cushman, D. The Great North Trail. 1966. A4650
Daniels, J. The devil's backbone. 1962. A4651
Egan, F. The El Dorado trail. 1969. A4652
Holbrook, S. H. The Old Post Road. 1962. A4653
Lavender, D. S. Westward vision. 1963. A4654
Riesenberg, F. The Golden Road. 1962. A4655
Rouse, P. The Great Wagon Road. 1973. A4656
Stegner, W. E. The gathering of Zion. 1964. A4657
Stewart, G. R. The California trail. 1962. A4658

AMERICAN VOCATIONAL ASSN. RESEARCH BULL.

1 Amer. vocational assn., inc. Occupational adjustments of vocational school graduates. 1940. A4659
2 ____. A study of industrial teacher education at the graduate level. 1941. A4660
3 ____. Factors affecting the satisfactions of home economic teachers. 1948. A4661
4 ____. Studies in industrial education. 1949. A4662
5 ____. Education of veterans in farming. 1952. A4663

AMERICAN WATERWAYS SERIES (A. H. Clark)

1 Merrick, G. B. Old times on the upper Mississippi. 1908. A4664
2 Blair, W. A. A raft pilot's log. 1930. A4665
3 Ambler, C. H. A history of transportation in the Ohio Valley. 1932. A4666
4 Rector, W. G. Log transportation in the Lake States lumber industry, 1840-1918. 1953. A4667

AMERICAN WILDERNESS SERIES (McGraw)

Douglas, W. O. Farewell to Texas. 1967. A4668

AMERICAN WOMEN: IMAGES AND REALITIES (Arno)

Adams, J. Correspondence between John Adams and Mercy Warren relating to her History of the American Revolution, ed. by Adams. 1972. A4669
Arling, E. S. The terrible siren. 1972. A4670
Beard, M. Woman's work in municipalities. 1972. A4671
Blanc, M. T. The condition of women in the United States. 1972. A4672
Bradford, G. Wives. 1972. A4673
Branagan, T. The excellency of the female character vindicated. 1972. A4674
Breckinridge, S. P. Women in the twentieth century. 1972. A4675
Campbell, H. Women wage-earners. 1972. A4676
Coolidge, M. E. B. S. Why women are so. 1972. A4677
Dall, C. H. The college, the market, and the court. 1972. A4678
D'Arusmont, F. W. Life, letters and lectures, 1834/1844. 1972. A4679
Davis, A. H. The female preacher. 1972. A4680
Ellington, G. The women of New York. 1972. A4681
Farnham, E. Life in prairie land. 1972. A4682
Gage, M. Woman, church and state. 1972. A4683
Gilman, C. S. The living of Charlotte Perkins Gilman. 1972. A4684
Grover, E. R. The American woman. 1972. A4685
Hale, S. J. Manners. 1972. A4686
Higginson, T. W. Women and the alphabet. 1972. A4687
Howe, J., ed. Sex and education. 1972. A4688
LaFollette, S. Concerning women. 1972. A4689
Leslie, E. Miss Leslie's behaviour book. 1972. A4690
Livermore, M. A. My story of the war. 1972. A4691
Logan, M. S. The part taken by women in American history. 1972. A4692
Mann, H. The female review. 1972. A4693
McGuire, J. W. Diary of a Southern refugee during the war. 1972. A4694
Meyer, A., ed. Woman's work in America. 1972. A4695
Myerson, A. The nervous housewife. 1972. A4696
Parsons, E. C. The old-fashioned woman. 1972. A4697
Porter, S. H. The life and times of Anne Royall. 1972. A4698
Pruette, L. Women and leisure. 1972. A4699
Salmon, L. M. Domestic service. 1972. A4700
Sanger, W. W. The history of prostitution. 1972. A4701
Smith, J. E. Abbey Smith and her cows. 1972. A4702
Spencer, A. Woman's share in social culture. 1972. A4703
Sprague, W. F. Women and the West. 1972. A4704
Stanton, E. The woman's Bible. 1972. A4705
Stewart, E. Memories of the crusade. 1972. A4706
Todd, J. Woman's rights. Also Woman's wrongs, by Dodge. 1972. A4707
Van Rensselser, J. K. The Goede Vrouw of Manu-Ha-Ta.

1972. A4708
Velazquez, L. J. The woman in battle, ed. by Worthington. 1972. A4709
Woodbury, H. L. Equal suffrage. 1972. A4710
Young, A. E. Wife no. 19. 1972. A4711
Zahrzewska, M. E. A woman's quest, ed. by Victor. 1972. A4712

AMERICAN WRITERS SERIES (Amer. Bk. Co.)

Bryant, W. C. Representative selections, ed. by McDowell. 1935. A4713
Clemens, S. L. Representative selections, ed. by Patee. 1935. A4714
Cooper, J. F. Representative selections, ed. by Spiller. 1936. A4715
Edwards, J. Representative selections, ed. by Faust and Johnson. 1935. A4716
Emerson, R. W. Ralph Waldo Emerson; representative selections, ed. by Carpenter. 1934. A4717
Franklin, B. Representative selections, ed. by Mott and Jorgenson. 1936. A4718
Hamilton, A. Alexander Hamilton and Thomas Jefferson, ed. by Prescott. 1934. A4719
Harte, B. Bret Harte, representative selections, ed. by Harrison. 1941. A4720
Hawthorne, N. Representative selections, ed. by Warren. 1934. A4721
Holmes, O. W. Representative selections, ed. by Hayakawa and Jones. 1939. A4722
Howells, W. D. Representative selections, ed. by C. M. and R. Kirk. 1950. A4723
Irving, W. Representative selections, ed. by Pochmann. 1934. A4724
James, H. Representative selections, ed. by Richardson. 1941. A4725
Longfellow, H. W. Representative selections, ed. by Shepard. 1934. A4726
Lowell, J. R. Representative selections, ed. by Clark and Foerster. 1947. A4727
Melville, H. Representative selections, ed. by Thorp. 1938. A4728
Motley, J. L. John Lothrop Motley, ed. by Highby and Schantz. 1939. A4729
Paine, G. L., ed. Southern prose writers. 1947. A4730
Paine, T. Representative selections, ed. by Clark. 1944. A4731
Parkman, F. Representative selections, ed. by Schramm. 1938. A4732
Parks, E. W., ed. Southern poets. 1936. A4733
Poe, E. A. Representative selections, ed. by Alterton and Craig. 1935. A4734
Prescott, W. H. William Hickling Prescott, ed. by Charvat and Kraus. 1943. A4735
Taft, K. B., ed. Minor Knickerbockers. 1947. A4736
Thoreau, H. C. Henry David Thoreau, representative selections, ed. by Crawford. 1934. A4737
Whitman, W. Walt Whitman; representative selections, ed. by Stovall. 1939. A4738

AMERICANA CLASSICS (Quadrangle Bks.)

1 Brackenridge, H. M. Views of Louisiana (1814), ed. by Burnette. 1962. A4739
2 Crawford, C. H. Scenes of earlier days (1898), ed. by Burnette. 1962. A4740
3 Lee, H. The campaign of 1781 in the Carolinas, ed. by Burnette. 1962. A4741
4 Beltrami, G. C. A pilgrimage in America (1828), ed. by Burnette. 1962. A4742
5 Lee, R. H. An additional number of letters from the federal farmer to the republican, ed. by Burnette. 1962. A4743
6 Darby, W. A tour from the City of New York, to Detroit ... (1818), ed. by

Burnette. 1962. A4744
7 Ellicott, A. The journal of Andrew Ellicott, ed. by Burnette. 1962. A4745
8 Pearse, J. A narrative of the life of James Pearse, ed. by Burnette. 1962. A4746
9 Krasheninnkov, S. P. The history of Kamtschatka and the Kurilski Islands, tr. by Greive. 1962. A4747
10 Ledyard, J. A journal of Captain Cook's last voyage to the Pacific Ocean... 1963. A4748

AMERICANA LIBRARY (Univ. of Washington Pr.)

1 Howe, F. C. The city, ed. by Pease. 1967. A4749
2 Merrill, H. S. Bourbon democracy of the Middle West. 1967. A4750
3 Kemler, E. The deflation of American ideals, ed. by Graham. 1967. A4751
4 Johnson, C. O. Borah of Idaho. 1967. A4752
5 Pinchot, G. The fight for conservation, ed. by Nash. 1967. A4753
6 Steffens, L. Upbuilders, ed. by Pomeroy. 1968. A4754
7 DeWitt, B. P. The Progressive movement, ed. by Mann. 1968. A4755
8 McMurry, D. L. Coxey's army, ed. by Hicks. 1968. A4756
9 London, J. Jack London and his times. 1968. A4757
10 Walker, F. San Francisco's literary frontier. 1969. A4758
11 Lippman, W. Men of destiny, ed. by Lowitt. 1969. A4759
12 Catt, C. C. and Shuler, N. R. Woman suffrage and politics, ed. by Larson. 1969. A4760
13 Merz, C. The dry decade. 1969. A4761
14 Smythe, W. E. The conquest of arid America, ed. by Lee. 1969. A4762
15 Pomeroy, E. S. The territories and the United States. 1969. A4763
16 Howe, F. C. Why war. 1970. A4764
17 Tucker, R. and Berkley, F. R. Sons of the wild jackass. 1970. A4765
18 Johnson, T. L. and Hauser, E. J., eds. My story. 1970. A4766
19 Lindsey, B. B. and O'Higgins, H. J. The beast. 1970. A4767
20 Ross, E. D. The liberal republican movement. 1970. A4768
21 Smith, J. A. The growth and decadence of constitutional government. 1972. A4769
22 Pinchot, G. Breaking new ground. 1972. A4770
23 Hopkins, H. L. Spending to save. 1972. A4771
24 Hapgood, H. A Victorian in the modern world. 1972. A4772
25 Parker, C. H. The casual laborer and other essays. 1972. A4773
26 Wechsler, J. Revolt on the campus. 1973. A4774
27 Weyl, W. E. American world politics. 1973. A4775
28 Lindsey, B. B. and Evans, W. The revolt of modern youth. 1973. A4776

AMERICANS IN FICTION (Gregg)

Aldrich, T. B. The Stillwater tragedy. 1968. A4777
Allen, J. L. A Kentucky cardinal. 1968. A4778
Atherton, G. F. The aristocrats. 1968. A4779
____. The Californians. 1969. A4780
____. Los Cerritos. 1969. A4781
____. Senator North. 1967. A4782
____. The splendid idle forties. 1968. A4783
Bates, A. The Puritans. 1968. A4784
Beard, O. T. Bristling with thorns. 1968. A4785
Brown, A. The county road. 1969. A4786
____. Tiverton tales. 1967. A4787
Burton, F. Through one

administration. 1967. A4788
Caruthers, W. A. The cavaliers of Virginia. 1967. A4789
____. The Kentuckians in New York. 1968. A4790
Chesnutt, C. W. The conjure woman. 1968. A4791
____. The house behind the cedars. 1969. A4792
____. The wife of his youth. 1967. A4793
Chopin, K. (O'Flaherty). Bayou folks. 1967. A4794
Cooke, J. E. Mohun. 1968. A4795
____. My lady Pokahontas. 1968. A4796
____. Surry of Eagle's nest. 1969. A4797
____. The Virginia comedians. 1968. A4798
Cooke, R. Root-bound. 1968. A4799
Deland, M. W. John Ward, preacher. 1967. A4800
Dixon, T. The clansman. 1967. A4801
____. The leopard's spots. 1967. A4802
Eggleston, E. The faith doctor. 1968. A4803
____. Roxy. 1968. A4804
Foote, M. The Led-Horse Claim. 1968. A4805
Ford, P. L. The honorable Peter Stirling. 1968. A4806
Frederic, H. Seth's brother's wife. 1969. A4807
Freeman, M. E. A New England nun. 1967. A4808
____. The portion of labor. 1967. A4809
Fuller, H. B. The cliff-dwellers. 1968. A4810
Grant, R. Unleavened bread. 1968. A4811
Harris, J. C. Free Joe. 1967. A4812
____. Gabriel Tolliver. 1967. A4813
Hay, J. The bread winners. 1967. A4814
Johnston, R. M. Dukesborough tales. 1968. A4815
King, E. Joseph Zalmonah. 1968. A4816
King, G. E. Balcony stories. 1969. A4817
Kirkland, J. The captain of Company K. 1968. A4818
Lewis, A. H. The boss. 1967. A4819
Lynde, F. The grafters. 1968. A4820
Martin, H. Tillie. 1968. A4821
Merwin, S. The short line war. 1967. A4822
Mitchell, S. W. Hugh Wynne. 1969. A4823
Murfree, M. N. In the Tennessee mountains. 1968. A4824
Page, T. N. In old Virginia. 1969. A4825
____. Red Rock. 1967. A4826
Phillips, D. G. The great god success. 1967. A4827
____. The master rogue. 1969. A4828
Reid, M. Boy hunters of the Mississippi. 1969. A4829
____. The quadroon. 1967. A4830
____. The white chief. 1969. A4831
Remington, F. John Ermine of the Yellowstone. 1968. A4832
Shiel, M. P. Contraband of war. 1969. A4833
Simms, W. G. The partisan. 1968. A4834
____. The scout. 1968. A4835
____. The wigwam and the cabin. 1969. A4836
____. Woodcraft. 1968. A4837
Stowe, H. E. The minister's wooing. 1968. A4838
____. The pearl of Orr's Island. 1967. A4839
____. Sam Lawson's Oldtown fireside stories. 1967. A4840
Tourgée, A. W. Brick's without straw. 1967. A4841
____. The invisible empire. 1968. A4842
____. A royal gentleman. 1967. A4843
Ward, E. S. The silent partner. 1967. A4844
Warner, C. D. A little journey in the world. 1967. A4845
Wister, O. Lord Baltimore. 1967. A4846

AMERIND FOUNDATION. PUBLICATIONS.

1 Fulton, W. S. and Tuthill, C. An archaeological site near Gleeson, Arizona. 1940. A4847
2 Fulton, W. S. A ceremonial cave in the Winchester mountains, Arizona. 1941. A4848
3 Haury, E. W. Painted caves, northeastern Arizona. 1945. A4849
5 Tuthill, C. The Tres Alamos site on the San Pedro river, southeastern Arizona. 1947. A4850
5 DiPeso, C. C. The Babocomari Village site on the Babocomari river, southeastern Arizona. 1951. A4851
6 ____. The Sobaipuri Indians of the Upper San Pedro River valley. 1953. A4852
7 ____. The Upper Pima of San Cayetano del Timacacori. 1956. A4853
8 ____. The Reeve ruin of southeastern Arizona. 1958. A4854

AMSTERDAM. UNIVERSITET. ASTRONOMISCH INSTITUT. PUBLICATIONS (Univ. van Amsterdam)

1 Pannekoek, A. The local star system deduced from the Durchmusterung catalogues. 1924. A4855
2 ____. The space distribution of stars of classes A, K and B, derived from the Draper catalogue, and The Cape photographic Durchmusterung. 1929. A4856
3 ____. Photograf. 1933. A4857
4 ____. The theoretical intensities of absorption lines in stellar spectrum. 1935. A4858
5 Verwey, S. The Stark effect of hydrogen in stellar spectra. 1936. A4859
6 Pannekoek, A. and Van Albada, G. B. A photometric study of some stella spectra. 2 pts. 1936-49. A4860
7 ____. Investigations of dark nebulae. 1942. A4861
8 Walraven, T. The line spectra of δ Cephei. 1948. A4862
9 Pannekoek, A. and Koelbloed, D. Photographic photometry of the Southern milky way. 1949. A4863
10 Koelbloed, D. Line spectra of some giant and dwarf K-type stars. 1953. A4864

ANALECTA BOLLANDIANA. SUBSIDIA HAGIOGRAPHICA (Société des Bollandistes)

1 Catalogus codicum hagiographicorum Bibliotheque Regiae Bruxell. 2 v. 1886-89. A4865
2 Catalogus codicum hagiographicorum latinorum Bibliotheca nationali parisiensi. 3 v. 1889-93. A4866
3a De codicibis hagiographicis Johannis Gielemans adiectis anecdotis. 1895. A4867
3b Anecdota ex codicibus hagiographicorum Johannis Gielemans. 1895. A4868
4 Chevalier, U. Reportorium hymnologicum. V. 4-6. 1912-20. A4869
5 Catalogue codicum hagiographicorum graecorum Bibliotheca nationalis parisiensis. 1896. A4870
6 Bibliotheca hagiographica latina, 1898-1901. 2 v. 1949. A4871
7 Catalogus codicum hagiographicorum graecorum Bibliothecae Vaticanae. 1899. A4872
8 Bibliotheca hagiographica graeca. 1909. A4873
9 Poncelet, A. Catalogus codicum hagiographicorum latinorum bibliothecarum Romanarum. 1909. A4874
10 Bibliotheca hagiographica orientalis. 1910. A4875
11 Poncelet, A. Catalogus codicum hagiographicorum Latinorum Bibliothecae Vaticanae. 1910. A4876
12 Same as 6. Suppl. 1911. A4877
13a Delehaye, H. A travers

trois siècles. 1920. A4878
13b ____. Les passions des martyrs et les genres littéraires. 1921. A4879
14 ____. Les saints stylites. 1923. A4880
15 Plummer, C. Miscellanea hagiographica Hibernica. 1925. A4881
16 Petit, L. Bibliographie des Acolouthies grecques. 1926. A4882
17 Delehaye, H. Sanctus. 1927. A4883
18 ____. Les Légendes hagiographiques. 1927. A4884
19 Halkin, F. Sancti Pachomii vitae graecae. 1932. A4885
20 Delehaye, H. Les origines du culte des martyrs. 1933. A4886
21 ____. Cinq leçons sur la méthode hagiographique. 1934. A4887
22 Grosjean, P. Henrici VI Angliae regis miracula postuma. 1935. A4888
23 Delehaye, H. Etude sur le légendier romain. 1936. A4889
24 Peeters, P. L'Oeuvre des Bollandistes. 1942. A4890
25 Catalogus codicum hagiographicorum Latinorum in bibliothecis publicis Namurci, Gandae, Leodii et Montibus asservatorum... 1948. A4891
26 Peeters, P. Le Tréfonds oriental de l'hagiographie byzantine. 1950. A4892
27 ____. Recherches d'histoire et de philologie orientales. 2 v. 1948. A4893
28 Heist, W. W. and Grosjean, P. Vitae sanctorum Hiberniae. 1953. A4894
29 Laurent, V. La vie merveilleuse de saint Pierre d'Atroa (+837). 1956. A4895
30 Garitte, G. Le calendrier palestino-géorgien du Sinaiticus 34, Xe siècle. 1958. A4896
31 Laurent, V. La vita retractata et les miracles posthumes de S. Pierre d'Atroa. 1958. A4897
32 Van den Ven, P. La vie ancienne de S. Syméon stylite le Jeune. 1962. A4898
33 Strycker, E. de. La forme la plus ancienne du Protevangile de Jacques. 1961. A4899
34 Festugière, A. J. Historia monachorum in Aegypto. 1961. A4900
35 Honigmann, E. Trois mémoires posthumes d'histoire et de géographie de l'Orient chréitien, ed. by Devos. 1961. A4901
36 Guy, J. C. Recherches sur la tradition grecque des Apophthegmata Patrum. 1962. A4902
37 Coens, M. Recueil d'études bollandiennes. 1963. A4903
38 Halkin, F. Inédits byzantine d'Ochrida, Candie et Moscou. 1963. A4904
39 Sargologos, E. La vie de saint Cyrille le Philéote, moine byzantin. 1964. A4905
40 Dubois, J. Le martyrologe d'Usuard. 1965. A4906
41 Halkin, F. Euphémie de Chalcédoine. 1965. A4907
42 Delehaye, H. Mélanges d'hagiographie grecque et latine. 1966. A4908
43 De Gaiffier, B. Etudes critiques d'hagiographie et d'iconologie. 1967. A4909
44 Halkin, F. Manuscrits grec de Paris. 1968. A4910
45 Sauget, J. M. Premières recherches sur l'origine et les caractéristiques des synaxaires melkites. 1969. A4911
46 Van Cranenburgh, H. La vie latine de saint Pachôme traduité du grec par Denys le Petit. 1969. A4912
47 Halkin, F. Auctarium bibliothecae hagiographicae graecae. 1969. A4913
48 Festugière, A. J. Vie de Théodore de Sykeon. 2 v. 1970. A4914
49 Shahîd, I. The martyrs of Najrân. 1971. A4915
50 Van der Straeten, J. Manuscrits hagiographiques d'Arras et de Boulogne-sur-Mer. 1971. A4916
51 Halkin, F. Recherches et documents d'hagiographie

byzantine. 1971. A4917
52 De Gaiffier, B. Recherches d'hagiographie latine. 1971. A4918
53 Festugière, A. J. Historia monac horum in Aegypto. 1971. A4919
54 Duquenne, L. Chronologie des lettres de S. Cyprien. 1972. A4920
55 Halkin, F. Legendes grecques de "martyres romaines." 1973. A4921
56 Van der Straeten, J. Les manuscrits hagiographiques de Charleville, Verdun et Saint Mihiel. 1973. A4922
Hors series:
Peeters, P. Figures bollandiennes contemporaines. 1948. A4923

ANALECTA GREGORIANA (Pontifica Universita Gregoriana)

1 Schwamm, H. Magistri Ioannis de Ripa doctrina de praescientia divina. 1930. A4924
2 Adamczyk, S. De obiecto formali intellectus nostri secundum doctrinam S. Thomae Aquinatis. 1933. A4925
3 Druwé, E. Prima forma inediat operis S. Anselmi "Cur Deus homo." 1933. A4926
4 Bidagor, R. La "Iglesia propria" en Espana. 1933. A4927
5 Madoz, J. El concepto de la tradiciòn en S. Vincente de Lerins. 1933. A4928
6 Keeler, L. The problem of error from Plato to Kant. 1934. A4929
7 De Aldama, J. A. El simbolo Toledano. 1934. A4930
8 Miscellanea iuridica Iustiniani et Gregorii IX legibus commemorandis. 1935. A4931
9-10 Miscellanea Vermeersch. 2 v. 1935. A4932
11 Bévenot, M. S. St. Cyprian's de Unitate. 1938. A4933
12 Gómez Helin, L. Praedestinatio apud Ioannem Cardinalem de Lugo. 1938. A4934
13 Daniele, I. I documenti constantiniani della "Vita Constantini" di Eusebio di Cesarea. 1938. A4935
14 García Villoslada, R. La Universidad de Paris durante los estudios de Francisco de Vitoria, O. P. 1938. A4936
15 Villiger, J. Das bistum basel zur zeit Johanns XXII, Benedikts XII, und Klemens VI. 1939. A4937
16 Schnitzler, T. Im kampfe um Chalcedon. 1938. A4938
17 Sheridan, J. A. Expositio plenior hylemorphismi Fr. Rogeri Baconis. 1938. A4939
18 Boularand, E. La venue de l'homme à la foi d'après Saint Jean Chrysostome. Saint Jean Chrysostome. 1939. A4940
19 Letter, P. de. Le ratione meriti secundum Sanctum Thomam. 1939. A4941
20 Haacke, W. Die glaubensformel des papstes Hormisdas im Acacianischen schisma. 1939. A4942
21 González, S. La fórmula Μια ουσιατρεις ὑποστασε en San Gregorio de Nisa. 1939. A4943
22 Gosso, F. Vita economica delle abbazie Piemontesi. 1940. A4944
23 Mañaricua, A. E. de. El matrimonio de los esclavos. 1940. A4945
24 Mazón, C. Las reglas de los religiosos. 1940. A4946
25 Aguirre Elorriaga, M. El abate de pradt en la emancipación hispano-americana (1800-1830). 1941. A4947
26 Ghiron, M. Il matrimonio canonico delgi italiani all' estero. 1941. A4948
27 Augustinus, Aurelius, St. Sancti Aurelii Augustini doctrina de bonis matrimonii, ed. by Reuter. 1942. A4949
28 Orbán, L. Theologica Guntheriana et Concilium Vaticanum. V. 1. 1950. A4950
29 Conferenze commemorative del... Fondazione della Compagnia di Gesù. La Compagnia di Gesù e le scienze sacre. 1942. A4951

30 Bertrams, W. S. Der neuzeitliche staatsgedanke und die konkordate des ausgenhenden mittelalters. 1950. A4952
31 Izzalini, L. d'. Il principio intellettivo della ragione umana nelle opere de S. Tomaso d'Aquino. 1943. A4953
32 Smulders, P. La doctrine trinitaire de S. Hilaire de Poitiers. 1944. A4954
33 Rambaldi, G. L'oggetto dell' intenzione sacramentale, nei teologi del secoli XVI e XVII. 1944. A4955
34 Munoz, P. Introduction à la sintesis de San Augustin. 1945. A4956
35 Galtier, P. Le Saint Esprit en nous d'apres les Peres Grecs. 1945. A4957
36 Faller, O. De priorum saeculorum silentio circa Assumptionem B. Mariae Virginis. 1946. A4958
37 Elia, P. M. d'. Galileo in Cina. 1947. A4959
38 Alszeghy, G. Grundformen der Liebe, die theorie der gottesliebe bei dem hl. Bonaventura. 1946. A4960
39 Hoenen, P. La théorie du jugement d'apres St. Thomas d'Aquin. 1952. A4961
40 Flick, M. L'attimo della giustificazione secondo S. Tommaso. 1947. A4962
41 Monachino, V. La cura pastorale a Milano, Cartagine e Roma nel sec. IV. 1947. A4963
42 Vollert, C. The doctrine of Hervaeus Natalis on primitive justice and original sin. 1947. A4964
43 Hoenen, P. Recherches de logique formelle: la structure du système des syllogismes... la logique des notions... 1947. A4965
44 Selvaggi, F. Dalla filosofia alla technica: la logica del potenziamento. 1947. A4966
45 Klotzner, J. Kardinal Dominikus Jacobazzi und sein konzilswerk. 1948. A4967
46 Federici, G. C. Il principio animatore della filosopfia vichiana. 1948. A4968
47 Nanni, L. La parrocchia studiata nei documenti lucchesi dei secoli VIII-XII. 1948. A4969
48 Asensio, F. Misericordia et veritas. 1948. A4970
49 Ogiermann, H. A. Hegels gottesbeweise. 1948. A4971
50 Same as no. 28. V. 2. 1949. A4972
51 Beck, G. J. H. The pastoral care of souls in South-East France. 1950. A4973
52 Quadrio, G. Il trattato "De Assumptione B. Mariae Virginis" dello pseudo-Agostino, e il suo influsso nella teologia Assunzionistica latina. 1951. A4974
53 Schmidt, H. A. P. Liturgie et langue vulgaire. Le probleme de la langue liturgique chez kes premiers réformateurs et au Concile de Trente. 1950. A4975
54 Galtier, P. Aux origines du sacrement de pénitence. 1951. A4976
55 Broderick, J. F. The Holy See and the Irish movement for the repeal of the union with England (1829-47). 1951. A4977
56 Williams, M. E. The teaching of Gilbert Porreta on the Trinity as found in the commentaries on Boethius. 1951. A4978
57 Hanssens, J. M. Nature et genèse de l'office des matines; aux origines de la prière liturgique. 1952. A4979
58 Asensio, N. F. Yahveh y su pueblo. 1953. A4980
59 Haes, P. de. Le résurrection de Jésus dans l'apologétique des cinquante dernières années. 1953. A4981
60 Mori, E. G. Il motivo della fede de Gaetano a Suarez. 1953. A4982
61 Laurin, J. R. Orientations maîtresses des apologistes chrétiens de 270 à 361. 1954. A4983
62 Bernini, G. Le preghiera penitenziali del Salterio. 1953. A4984

63 Hoenen, P. De noetica geometriae origine theoriae cognitionis. 1954. A4985
64 Courtney, F. Cardinal Robert Pullen, an English theologian of the twelfth century. 1954. A4986
65 Orbe, A. En aurora de la exegesis del IV Evangelio. 1955. A4987
66 Garcia Villoslada, R. Storia del Collegio romano dal suo inizio (1551) alla soppressione della Campagnia di Gesù (1773). 1954. A4988
67 Rome (City). Pontificia Università Gregoriana. Facoltà di filosofia. Studia filosofici intorno all "esistenza" al mondo, al Trascendenti. 1954. A4989
68 Rome (City). Pontificia Università Gregoriana. Facoltà de teologia. Problemi scelti di teologia contemporanea. 1954. A4990
69 Rome (City). Pontificia Università Gregoriana. Facoltà de canonico. Questioni attuali di diritto canonico. 1954. A4991
70 Rome (City). Pontificia Università Gregoriana. Facoltà di storia ecclesiastica. Studi sulla Chiesa antica e sull'umanesimo. 1954. A4992
71 ____. Nuove richerche storiche sul giansenismo. 1954. A4993
72 Rome (City). Pontificia Università Gregoriana. Facoltà di missiologia. La preghiera e il lavoro apostolico nelle missioni. 1954. A4994
73 Veiga Coutinho, L. da. Tradition et histoire dans la controverse moderniste (1898-1910). 1954. A4995
74 Coathalem, H. Le paralléslisme entre la Sainte Vierge et l'Eglise dans la tradition latine jusqu'a la fin du XIIe siècle. 1954. A4996
75 Van Roo, W. A. Grace and original justice according to St. Thomas. 1955. A4997
76 Bettray, G. Die akkomodations-methode des P. Matteo Ricci, S. J. in Cina. 1955. A4998
77 Fecher, V. J. A study of the movement for German national parishes in Philadelphia and Baltimore (1787-1802). 1955. A4999
78 Baar, P. van der. Die kirchliche Lehre der "Translatio Imperii Romani" bis zur mitte des 13 jahrhunderts. 1955. A5000
79 Belloli, L. La teologia dell'assunzione corporea di Maria SS. dalla definizione dommatica dell' Immaculata Concezione alla fine del secolo XIX. 1956. A5001
80 Rasolo, L. Le dilemme du concours divin: Primat de l'essence ou primat de l'existence. 1956. A5002
81 Alszeghy, Z. Nova creatura. La nozione della grazia nei commentari medievali di S. Paolo. 1956. A5003
82 Sullivan, F. A. The Christology of Theodore of Mopsuestia. 1956. A5004
83 Orbe, A. Los primeros herejes ante la persecucion. 1956. A5005
84 Bartolotti, R. La formazione degli effetti civili del matrimonio nel regime concordatorio italiano. 1956. A5006
85 Teresa, D. Juan de Valdes. 1957. A5007
86 Setien, J. M. Naturaleza jurídica del estado de perfeción en los institutos seculares. 1957. A5008
87 Molinari, F. Teatino Beato Paolo Burali e la riforma tridentina a Piacenza. 1957. A5009
88 Casey, T. F. The Sacred Congregation de Propaganda Fide and the first Provincial Council of Baltimore. 1957. A5010
89 Wright, J. H. The order of the universe in the theology of St. Thomas Aquinas. 1957. A5011
90 Asensio, F. El dios de la luz. 1958. A5012
91 Gambasin, A. Il movimento social nell'opera dei

congressi. 1958. A5013
92 Wetter, F. Die lehre Benedikts vom intensiven wachstum der gottschau. 1958. A5014
93 Gomez Caffarena, J. Ser participado y ser subsistente en la metafisica de Enrique de Gante. 1958. A5015
94 Lotz, J. B. De operatione humana methodo transcendentali explicata. 1958. A5016
95 Egana, A. La teoria del Regio Vicariato español en India. 1958. A5017
96 Rimaldi, A. L'apostolo San pietro nella chiesa primitiva. 1958. A5018
97 De Simone, R. Missioni, repressione e tolleranza. 3 v. 1958. A5019
98 Bennet, A. The functions of the archbishop of Canterbury. 1958. A5020
99-100 Orbe, A. Hacia la primera teologie de la procesión del Verbo. 2 v. 1958. A5021
101-103 Leturia, P. Relaciones entre la Santa Bede e Hispanoamerica. 3 v. 1959-60. A5022
104 Martini, C. M. Il problema storico della risurrezione negli studi recenti. 1959. A5023
105 Navarrete, U. La buena fe de las personas jurídicas en orden a la prescripcion adquisitiva. 1959. A5024
106-107 Blet, P. Le clergé de France et la monarchie. 2 v. 1959. A5025
108 Naus, J. E. The nature of the practical intellect according to St. Thomas Aquinas. 1959. A5026
109 Connelly, J. F. The visit of Archbishop Gaetano Bedini to the United States of America... 1960. A5027
110 Pfammatter, J. Die Kirche als Bau. 1960. A5028
111 Couvreur, G. Les pauvres ontils des droits? 1961. A5029
112 Wolfl, K. Das Heilswirken Gottes durch den Sohn nach Tertullian. 1960. A5030
113 Orbe, A. La unción del Verbo. 1961. A5031
114 Bini, L. L'intervento di Oskar Cullmann nella discussione bultmanniana. 1961. A5032
115 Lynn, W. D. Christ's redemption merit... 1962. A5033
116 Midali, M. Corpus Christi mysticum apud Dominicum Bañez eiusque fontes. 1962. A5034
117 Visintainer, S. La dottrina del peccato in San Girolamo. 1962. A5035
118 Demmer, Ķ. Ius caritatis. 1961. A5036
119 Useros, M. Statuta ecclesias y Sacramenta ecclesiae en la eclesiologia de Santo Tomás de Aquino. 1962. A5037
120 Moynihan, J. M. Papal immunity and liability in the writings of the medieval canonists. 1961. A5038
121 Krenn, K. Vermittlung und differenz? 1962. A5039
122 Cuyas, M. La buena fe en la prescripcion extintiva de deudas desde al Concilio IV de Letran (1215) hasta Bartolo (1357). 1962. A5040
123 Marty, F. La perfection de l'homme selon St. Thomas d'Aquin. 1962. A5041
124 Couture, R. L'imputabilite morale des premiers mouvements de sensualite de Saint Thomas aux Salmanticenses. 1962. A5042
125 Trisco, R. The Holy See and the Nascent Church in middle western United States. 1962. A5043
126 De Finance, J. Essai sur l'agir humain. 1962. A5044
127 Quezada, R. La perseverancia del consentimiento matrimonial en la sanatio in radice. 1962. A5045
128 Schüller, B. Die Herrschaft Christi und das weltlich recht. 1963. A5046
129 Millett, B. The Irish Franciscans, 1651-1665. 1964. A5047
130 Van den Vossenberg, E. T. Die letzten grunde der innerweltlichkeit in Nicolai Hartmanns philosophie. 1963. A5048
131 Richard, L. R. The

problem of an apologetical perspective in the Tritarian theology of St. Thomas Aquinas. 1963. A5049
132 Heitmeyer, H. Sakramentenspendung bei Härtikern und Simonisten nach Huguccio. 1964. A5050
133 Miscellanea Taparelli. 1964. A5051
134 Bolle, A. Die Seminarfrage im Bistum Basel für die zeit vom anfang des 19. jahrhunderts bis zur gegenwart. 1964. A5052
135 Bellucci, D. Fede e giustificazione in Lutero. 1963. A5053
136 Keating, J. R. The bearing of mental impairment on the validity of marriage. 1964. A5054
137 Krahl, J. China missions in crisis. 1964. A5055
138 Russell, J. The Sanatio in radice before the Council of Trent. 1964. A5056
139 Veit, L. M. Pensiero e vita religiosa de Enea Silvio Piccolomini prima della sua Consacrazione Episcopale. 1964. A5057
140-141 Beyer, J. La consécration à Dieu dans les Instituts seculiers. 2 v. 1964. A5058
142 Peter, C. Participated eternity in the vision of God. 1964. A5059
143 Robleda, O. La nulidad del acto jurídico. 1964. A5060
144 Fierro, A. Sobre la gloria en San Hilario. 1964. A5061
145 Scheepers, J. De regime matrimoni disparis. 1964. A5062
146 Cuminetti, M. Elementi cattolici nella dottrina di alcuni teologi calvinisti contemporanei. 1965. A5063
147 Simon, G. Die Achse der weitgeschichte nach Karl Jaspers. 1965. A5064
148 Dhavamony, M. Subjectivity and knowledge in the philosophy of Saint Thomas Aquinas. 1965. A5065
149 Sanclimens a Puig-Reig, M. Conflictus forum interum inter et externum in materia matrimonialis dispensationis. 1965. A5066
150 Brekelmans, A. J. Martyrerkranz. 1965. A5067
151 Vela, L. El derecho natural en Giorgio del Vecchio. 1965. A5068
152 Valkovic, M. L'uomo, la donna e il matrimonio nella teologia di Matthias Joseph Scheeben. 1965. A5069
153 Gerhartz, J. G. Insuper Promitto... 1966. A5070
154 Cronin, T. J. Objective being in Descartes and in Suarez. 1966. A5071
155 De Paolis, V. La natura della posesta del Vicario Generale. 1966. A5072
156 Becker, K. Die rechtertigungskehre nach Domingo De Soto. 1966. A5073
157 Bassett, W. W. The determination of rite, an historical and juridical study. 1966. A5074
158 Orbe, A. La teologia del espíritu santo. 1966. A5075
159 Traets, C. Voir Jesus et le Pere en Lui selon l'Evangile de Saint Jean. 1966. A5076
160 Hoffmann, H. Nature und gnade. 1966. A5077
161 Radrizzani Goñi, J. F. Papa y Obispos en la potestad de jurisdiccion segun el pensamiento en F. de Vitoria. 1966. A5078
162 Maes, B. La loi naturekke selon Ambroise de Milan. 1967. A5079
163 Chiovaro, F. Bernardino Rossignoli S.I. 1967. A5080
164 Daniel, W. The purely penal law theory in the Spanish theologians from Vitoria to Suárez. 1968. A5081
165 Kofler, A. Uber die Beziehung zwischen eheunfahigkeit der personen und dem ehewillen. 1968. A5082
166 Russieri, G. Il figlio di dio Davidico. 1968. A5083
167 Hortal Sanchez, J. De initio potestatis primatialis romani pontificis. 1968. A5084
168 Pastor Pineiro, F. A. La eclesiologia Juanea según E. Schweizer. 1968. A5085
169 Naselli, C. A. La

soppressione napoleonica delle corporazioni religiose. 1969. A5086

170 Mosna, C. S. Storia della Domenica, dalle origini fino agli inizi del V. Secolo. 1969. A5087

171 Voller, A. Einheit der kirche und gemeinschaft des kultes. 1969. A5088

172 Biolo, S. La coscienza nel "De Trinitate" di S. Agostino. 1969. A5089

173 Schulz, W. Dogmenentwicklung als problem der geschichtlichkeit der wahrehitserkenntnis. 1969. A5090

174 Fois, M. Il pensiero cristiano de Lorenzo Valla. 1969. A5091

175 Da Silva Pereira, A. Sacramento da Ordem e munus eclesiastico. 1969. A5092

176 Nothum, A. La rémunération du travail inhérent aux fonctions spirituelles. 1969. A5093

177 Manzaneras Marijuan, J. Liturgia y descentralizacion en el Concilio Vaticano II. 1970. A5094

178 Retinck, P. La cura pastorale in antiochia nel IV secolo. 1970. A5095

179 Figueroa, R. La "Persona standi in iudicio" en la legislación eclesiastica. 1971. A5096

180 Ruini, C. La trascendenza della grazia nella teologia di San Tomasso d'Aquino. 1971. A5097

181 Mullenders, J. Le marriage presumme. 1971. A5098

182 Turtas, R. L'attivita e la politica missionaria della direzione della London Missionary Society. 1971. A5099

183 Angelini, G. L'ortodossia e la grammatica. 1972. A5100

184 Urumpackal, T. P. Organized religion according to Dr. S. Radhakrishnan. 1972. A5101

185 Pittau, F. Il volere umano nei pensiero di Vladimir Jakelevitch. 1972. A5102

186 Brontesi, A. La soteria in Clemente Alessandrino. 1972. A5103

187 Thekedathu, J. The troubled days of Francis Garcia, S. J. Archbishop of Cranganore. 1972. A5104

188 Lotz, J. B. Die identitat von Geist und sein. 1972. A5105

189 Blet, P. Les Assemblees du Clerge et Louis XIV. 1972. A5106

190 Ramallo, V. El derecho y el misterio de la Iglesia. 1972. A5107

191 Holleran, J. W. The synoptic Gethsemane. 1973. A5108

192 Daneels, F. De subiecto officii ecclesiastici attenta doctrina Concilii Vaticani II. 1973. A5109

193 Guerber, J. La ralliement du clergé française a la morale liguorienne. 1973. A5110

194 Bressan, L. Il cacone tridentino sul divorzio per adulterio e l'interpretazione degli autori. 1973. A5111

195 Babolin, S. L'estetica di Maurice Blondel. 1974. A5112

196 Schwarz, R. Die eigenberechtigte Gewalt der kirche. 1974. A5113

197 Preckler, F. G. 'Etat' chez le Cardenal de Bérulle. 1974. A5114

The series has the following subseries which is not always noted on the volume. The number in parentheses refers to the number in the series.

Facultatis historiae ecclesiasticae.
Sectio A. 1(41), 2(66), 3(70), 4(71), 5(101), 6(102), 7(103), 8(106), 9(107)
Sectio B. 1(13), 2(14), 3(15), 4(22), 5(25), 6(45), 7(47), 8(51), 9(55), 10(61), 11(77), 12(78), 13(85), 14(87), 15(88), 16(91), 17(95), 18(96), 19(97), 20(109), 21(125), 22(129), 23(139), 24(149), 25(150), 26(163), 27(169), 28(170), 29(178), 30(182), 31(187), 32(189)

Facultatis Juris Canonici.
Sectio A. 1(4), 2(8), 3(24), 4(69), 5-6(140-141), 7(143)
Sectio B. 1(23), 2(26), 3(30),

4(84), 5(86), 6(98), 7(105), 8(119), 9(120), 10(122), 11(127), 12(132), 13(134), 14(136), 15(138), 16(145), 17(149), 18(151), 19(153), 29(155), 21(157), 22(161), 23(165), 24(167), 25(171), 26(175), 27(176), 28(177), 29(179), 30(181), 31(192), 32(190), 33(194), 34(196)

Facultatis Missiologica.
Sectio A. 1(37), 2(72)
Sectio B. 1(76)

Facultatis philosophica.
Sectio A. 1(6), 2(34), 3(39), 4(43), 5(63), 6(67), 7(94), 8(126), 9(133), 10(154), 11(188)
Sectio B. 1(2), 2(17), 3(31), 4(44), 5(46), 6(49), 7(80), 8(93), 9(108), 10(121), 11(123), 12(130), 13(147), 14(148), 15(174), 16(185), 17(195)

Facultatis theologica.
Sectio A. 1(9), 2(10), 3(29), 4(35), 5(36), 6(54), 7(57), 8(58), 9(62), 10(64), 11(68), 12(65), 13(75), 14(81), 15(83), 16(90), 17(99), 18(100), 19(113), 20(158)
Sectio B. 1(1), 2(2), 3(5), 4(7), 5(11), 6(12), 7(16), 8(18), 9(19), 10(20), 11(21), 12(27), 13(28), 14(32), 15(33), 16(38), 17(40), 18(42), 19(48), 20(50), 21(52), 22(53), 23(56), 24(59), 25(60), 26(73), 27(74), 28(79), 29(82), 30(89), 31(92), 32(104), 33(110), 34(111), 35(112), 36(114), 37(115), 38(116), 39(117), 40(118), 41(124), 42(128), 43(131), 44(135), 45(142), 46(144), 47(146), 48(152), 49(156), 50(154), 51(160), 52(162), 53(164), 54(166), 55(168), 56(173), 57(180), 58(183), 59(184), 60(186), 61(191), 62(193), 63(197)

ANALECTA MEDIAEVALIA NAMURCENSIA (Nauwelaerts)

1 Delhaye, P. Une controverse sur l'âume universelle au IXe siècle. 1950. A5115
2 Lambot, D. C. Ratramme de corbie liber de anima ad odonem bellovacensem. 1951. A5116
3 Delhaye, P. Gauthier de Châtillon est-il l'auteur du Moralium dogma? 1953. A5117
4 Le Chantre, P. Summa de sacramentis et animae consiliis. V. 1. 1954. A5118
5-6 Delhaye, P. Florilegium morale oxoniense. 2 v. 1955-56. A5119
7 Same as no. 4. V. 2. 1957. A5120
8 Geoffroi de Saint Victor. Fons philosophie, ed. by Michaud-Quantin. 1956. A5121
9 Delhaye, P. Le probleme de la conscience moral chez S. Bernard. 1957. A5122
10 ____. Permanence du droit naturel. 1960. A5123
11 Same as no. 4. V. 3:1. 1961. A5124
12 Hamelin, A. M. L'école françiscaine de ses débuts jusqu'à l'occamisme. 1961. A5125
13 Michaud-Quantin, P. Sommes de casuistique et manuels de confessions du XIIe au XVIe siècles. 1962. A5126
14 Alexander de Alexandria. Un traité de morale économique au XIVe siècle, ed. by Hamelin. 1963. A5127
15 Maisonneuve, H. La morale chretienne d'après les Conciles des Xe et XIe siècles. 1963. A5128
16 Same as no. 4. V. 3:2a. 1963. A5129
17-18 Alanus de Insulls. Alain de Lille, ed. by Longere. 2 v. 1965. A5130
19 Conradus Hirsaugiensis. Dialogus de mundi contemptu, ed. by Bultot. 1966. A5131
20 Vandenbroucke, F. La morale monastique du XIe au XVIe siècle. 1966. A5132
21 Petrus Cantor. Summa de sacramentis et animae consiliis, ed. by Dugauquier. 1966. A5133
22-24 Petrus Falcus. Questions disputées ordinaires, ed. by Gondras. 3 v. 1968. A5134
25 Thomas de Chobham.

Thomas de Chobham summa confessorum, ed. by Bloomfield. 1968. A5135
26 Henricus Gandavensis. La "Lectura ordinaria super sacram scripturam" ed. by Macken. 1972. A5136

Hors serie:
1 Delhaye, P. L'organisation scolaire au XIIe siècle. 1952. A5137
2 ____. "Grammatica" et "ethica" au XVIIe siècle. 1958. A5138

ANALECTA ORIENTALIA (Pontificium Institutum Biblicium. Rome)

1 Schneider, N., ed. Die Drehemund Djoha urkunden der Strassburger universitats- und landesbibliothek... 1931. A5139
2 Deimel, A. ed., Sumerische tempelwirtschaft zur zeit Urukaginas und seiner vorgänger. 1931. A5140
3 A catalogue of the provincial capitals of Eranshahr (Pahlavi text, version and commentary) by Markwart, ed. by Messina. 1931. A5141
4 Witzel, M. Texte zum studien sumerischer tempel und kultzentren. 1932. A5142
5 Suys, E. Etude sur le Conte du fellah plaideur, récit egyptien du moyen empire. 1933. A5143
6 Keilschriftliche miscellanea. 1933. A5144
7 Schneider, N. Die Drehem- und Djohatexte im kloster Montserrat (Barcelona). 1932. A5145
8-9 Pohl, A., ed. Neubabylonische rechtsurkunken aus den Berliner Staatlichen museen. 2 v. 1933-34. A5146
10 Witzel, M. Tammuz-litirgien und verwandtes. 1935. A5147
11 Suys, E., ed. and tr. Le sagesse d'Ani. 1935. A5148
12 Miscellanea orientalia. 1935. A5149
13 Schneider, N. Die zeitbestemmungen der wirtschaftsurkunken von Ur III. 1936. A5150
14 Studia arabica, ed. by Rosenthal and others. V. 1. 1937. A5151
15 Witzel, M., ed. and tr. Auswahl sumerischer dichtungen. V. 1. 1938. A5152
16 Monneret de Villard, U. Aksum, richerche di topografia generale. 1938. A5153
17 Studia aegyptiaca. V. 1. 1938. A5154
18 Van Buren, E. The fauna of ancient Mesopotamia as represented in art. 1939. A5155
19 Schneider, N. Die gotternamen von Ur III. 1939. A5156/66
20 Gordon, C. H. Ugaritic grammar. 1940. A5167
21 Rome (City). Pontificio istituto biblico. The cyclinder seals of the Pontifical Biblical Institute. 1940. A5168
22 Ibn Fürak. Baujan muškil alahadit des Ibn Fūrak, ed. by Kobert. 1941. A5169
23 Van Buren, E. Symbols of the gods in Mesopotamian art. 1945. A5170
24 Rosenthal, F. The technique and approach of Muslim scholarship. 1947. A5171
25 Gordon, C. H. Ugaritic handbook. 1948. A5172
26 O'Callaghan, R. T. Aram Nahariam. 1948. A5173
27 Soden, W. von. Das akkadische Syllabar. 1948. A5174
28-29 Falkenstein, A. Grammatik der Sprache Gudeas von Lagaš. 2 v. 1940-50. A5175
30 O'Callaghan, R. T. Aram Nahariam. 1948. A5176
31 Same as no. 17. V. 2. 1950. A5177
32 Friedrich, J. Phonizisch-punische Grammatik. 1951. A5178
33 Soden, W. von. Grundriss der akkadischen Grammatik. 1952. A5179
34 Edel, E. Altägyptische grammatik. V. 1. 1955. A5180
35 Gordon, C. H. Ugaritic manual. 1955. A5181

36 Young, G. D. Concordance of Ugaritic. 1956. A5182
37 Caminos, R. A. The chronicle of Prince Osorkon. 1959. A5183
38 Gordon, C. H. Ugaritic textbook. 1965. A5184
39 Same as no. 34. V. 2. 1964. A5185
40 Fischer, H. G. Inscriptions from the Coptite Nome. 1964. A5186
41 Potratz, J. A. H. Die prezdetetzeusen des alten Orient. 1966. A5187
42 Von Soden, W. and Röllig, W. Das akkadische syllabar. 1967. A5188
43 Brinkman, J. A. A political history of post-Kassite Babylonia. 1968. A5189
44 Hecker, K. Grammatik der Kültepe-texte. 1968. A5190
45 Pettinato, G. Texte zur verwaltrung der landwirtschaft in Ur-III zeit. 1969. A5191
46 Friedrich, J. and Röllig, W. Phonizisch-punische grammatik. 1969. A5192
47 Von Soden, W. Ergänzungsheft zum grundriss der akkadisenen grammatik. 1969. A5193
48 The Claremont Ras Shamra tablets, ed. by Fisher and others. 1972. A5194
49 Ras Shamra parallels, ed. by Fisher. 1972. A5195

ANALECTA ROMANICA; BIEHEFTE ZU DEN ROMANISCHEN FORSCHUNGEN (Klostermann)

1 Lind, G. R. Jorge Guilléns Cántico. 1955. A5196
2 Loos, E. Baldassare Castigliones libro del Cortegiano. 1955. A5197
3 Glasser, R. Studien über die Bildung einer moralischen. 1956. A5198
4 Leo, U. Sehen und Wirklichkeit dei Dante. 1957. A5199
5 Maurer, C. Giacomo Leopardis Canti und die Anflösung der lyrischen Genera. 1957. A5200
6 Leo, U. Zur dichterischen Originaliität des Arcipreste de Hita. 1958. A5201
7 Diderot, D. Correspondance. Diderot et Falconet, ed. by Dieckmann and Seznec. 1959. A5202
8 Schon, P. M. Studien zum Stil der frühen französischen Prosa. 1960. A5203
9 Sckommodau, H. Margarete von Navarra. 1960. A5204
10 Blüher, K. A. Stratégie des Geistes. 1961. A5205
11 Adler, A. Rückzug in epischer Parade. 1963. A5206
12 Keller, A. C. The telling of tales in Rabelais. 1963. A5207
13 Hempel, W. In Onor della Fenice Ibera. 1963. A5208
14 De Booy, J. T. Histoire d'un manuscrit de Diderot, La Promenade du sceptique. 1963. A5209
15 Glasser, R. "Sich finden" in den romanischen Sprachen. 1964. A5210
16 Baader, H. Die Lais. Zur Geschichte einer Gatting der altfranzösischen Kruzerzahlungen. 1965. A5211
17 Nerlich, M. El hombre justo y bueno. 1966. A5212
18 Pollmann, L. Die liebe in der hochmittelalterlichen literatur Frankreichs. 1966. A5213
19 Descouzis, P. Cervantes. 1966. A5214
20 Schalk, F. Praejudicium im Romanischen. 1971. A5215
21 Galiani, F. Dialogues entre M. Marquis de Roquemaure, et Ms le Chevalier Zanobi, ed. by Koch. 1968. A5216
22 Gilman, S. The tower as emblem. 1967. A5217
23 Pitou, S. The text and sources of Chateaubruns "Lost Ajax." 1968. A5218
24 Wunderli, P. Die okzitanischen bibelubersetzungen des mittelalters. 1969. A5219
25 Grimm, J. Die einheit der Ariost'schen satire. 1969. A5220
26 Ages, A. French enlightenment and rabbinic tradition. 1969. A5221

27 Hardt, M. Flaubert's Spätwerk. 1970. A5222
28 Lange, W. D. El fraile trobador. 1971. A5223
29 Daus, R. Der Avantgardismus Ramón Gómêz de la Sernas. 1971. A5224
30 Glasser, R. Retrospektion und Antizipation der Sinne. 1971. A5225
31 Meerts, C. Technique et vision dans "Señas de identidad" de J. Goytisolo. 1972. A5226
32 Trapnell, W. H. Voltaire and his portable dictionary. 1972. A5227
33 Theis, R. Zur sprache der cite in der dichtung. 1972. A5228
34 Stone, D. From tales to truths. 1973. A5229
35 Lope, H. J. Die cartas marruecas von José Cadalso. 1973. A5230

ANCIENT CHRISTIAN WRITERS (Newman)

1 Clemens Romanus. The epistles of St. Clement of Rome and St. Ignatius of Antioch, ed. by Kleist. 1946. A5231
2 Augustinus, Aurelius, St. The first catechetical instruction, ed. by Christopher. 1946. A5232
3 Augustinus, Aurelius, St. Faith, hope and charity, ed. by Arand. 1947. A5233
4 Pomerius, J. The contemplative life, ed. by Suelzer. 1947. A5234
5 Augustinus, Aurelius, St. The Lord's sermon on the mount, ed. by Jepson. 1948. A5235
6 Teaching of the Twelve Apostles. The Didache, The epistle of Barnabas, The epistles and the martyrdom of St. Polycarp, The fragments of Papias, The epistle to Diognetus, ed. by Kleist. 1948. A5236
7-8 Arnobius Afer. The case against the pagans, ed. by McCracken. 2 v. 1949. A5237
9 Augustinus, Aurelius, St. The greatness of the soul, and The teacher, ed. by Colleran. 1950. A5238
10 Athanasius, St. The life of Saint Antony, ed. by Meyer. 1950. A5239
11 Gregorius I, the Great, St. Pastoral Care, ed. by Davis. 1950. A5240
12 Augustinus, Aurelius, St. Against the Academics, ed. by O'Meara. 1951. A5241
13 Tertullianus, Q. S. F. Treatise on marriage and remarriage, ed. by LeSaint. 1951. A5242
14 Prosper, Tiro, Aquitaines, St. The call of all nations, ed. by Letter. 1952. A5243
15 Augustinus, Aurelius, St. Sermons for Christmas and Epiphany, ed. by Lawler. 1952. A5244
16 Irenaeus, St. Proof of the Apostolic preaching, ed. by Smith. 1952. A5245
17 Patrick, St. The works of St. Patrick, tr. by Bieler. 1953. A5246
18 Gregorius, St., Bp. of Nyssa. The Lord's prayer, tr. by Graef. 1954. A5247
19 Origenes. Treatises on prayer and martyrdom, tr. by O'Meara. 1954. A5248
20 Rufinus, T. A. Commentary on the Apostles' Creed, tr. by Kelly. 1955. A5249
21 Maximus Confessor, St. The ascetis life. The four centuries on charity, tr. by Sherwood. 1955. A5250
22 Augustinus, Aurelius, St. The problem of free choice, tr. by Pontifex. 1955. A5251
23 Athenagoras. Embassy for the Christians. The resurrection of the dead, tr. by Crehan. 1956. A5252
24 Tertullianus, Q. S. F. The treatise against Hermogenes, tr. by Waszink. 1956. A5253
25 Cyprianus, St. The lapsed. The unity of the Catholic church, tr. by Bévenot. 1957. A5254
26 Origenes. The Song of songs, ed. by Lawson. 1957. A5255
27 Methodius, St. The

symposium, tr. by Musurillo. 1958. A5256
28 Tertullianus, Q. S. F. Treatise on penance, tr. by LeSaint. 1959. A5257
29-30 Augustine, Aurelius, St. St. Augustine on the Psalms, tr. by Hebgin and Corrigan. 2 v. 1960-61. A5258
31 Chrysostomus, Joannes, St. Baptismal instructions, tr. by Harkins. 1963. A5259
32 Prospero, Tito, Aquitanus, St. Defense of St. Augustine, tr. by Letter. 1963. A5260
33 Hieronymus, St. Letters, tr. by Mierow. V. 1. 1963. A5261
34 Palladius. Palladius: the Lausiac, tr. by Meyers. 1965. A5262
35-36 Paulinus, St. Letters, ed. by Walsh. 2 v. 1966-67. A5263
37 Maternus, F. Error of the pagan religions. 1969. A5264
38 Peregrinatio Aetheriae. Egeria, tr. by Gingras. 1970. A5265
39 Minucius Felix, M. The Octavius of Marcus Minucius Felix, tr. by Clarke. 1974. A5266

ANCIENT CIVILIZATION SERIES (Taplinger)

Cahen, C. Pre-Ottoman Turkey, tr. by Jones-Williams. 1968. A5267

ANCIENT CULTURE AND SOCIETY (Norton)

Adkins, A. W. H. Moral values and political behaviour in ancient Greece. 1972. A5268
Baldry, H. C. The Greek tragic theatre. 1972. A5269
Brunt, P. A. Social conflicts in the Roman Republic. 1972. A5270
Finley, M. I. Early Greece. 1970. A5271
Jones, A. H. M. Augustus. 1970. A5272
Lloyd, G. E. R. Early Greek science. 1970. A5273
____. Greek science after Aristotle. 1973. A5274
Mossé, C. The ancient world at work, tr. by Lloyd. 1970. A5275
Ogilvie, R. M. The Romans and their gods in the age of Augustus. 1970. A5276
Warmington, B. H. Nero. 1970. A5277

ANCIENT PEOPLES AND PLACES (Praeger)

1 Bushnell, G. H. S. Peru. 1957. A5278
2 Rice, T. T. The Scythians. 1957. A5279
3 Brea, L. B. Sicily before the Greeks. 1958. A5280
4 Klindt-Jensen, O. Denmark before the Vikings. 1957. A5281
5 Laet, S. J. de. The Low Countries. 1958. A5282
6 Powell, T. G. E. The Celts. 1958. A5283
7 Bloch, R. The Etruscans, tr. by Hood. 1958. A5284
8 De Paor, M. and L. de. Early Christian Ireland. 1958. A5285
9 Stone, J. F. S. Wessex before the Celts. 1958. A5286
10 Kidder, J. E. Japan before Buddhism. 1959. A5287
11 Evans, J. D. Malta. 1959. A5288
12 Wheeler, R. E. M. Early India and Pakistan: to Ashoka. 1959. A5289
13 Giot, P. R. and others. Brittany. 1960. A5290
14 Clarke, R. R. East Anglia. 1960. A5290a
15 Bloch, R. The origins of Rome. 1960. A5290b
16 Wilson, D. M. The Anglo-Saxons. 1960. A5290c
17 Bosi, R. The Lapps. 1960. A5290d
18 Aldred, C. The Egyptians. 1961. A5290e
19 Gough, M. The early Christian. 1961. A5290f
20 Rice, T. (Abelson). The Seljuks in Asia Minor. 1961. A5290g

21 Arbman, H. The Vikings, tr. by Binns. 1961. A5290h
22 Neustupný, E. and J. Czechoslovakia before the Slavs. 1961. A5290i
23 Watson, W. China before the Han dynasty. 1961. A5290j
24 Cook, R. M. The Greeks until Alexander. 1962. A5291
25 Diringer, D. Writing. 1962. A5292
26 Harden, D. B. The Phoenicians. 1962. A5293
27 Rice, D. T. The Byzantines. 1962. A5294
28 Woodhead, A. G. The Greeks in the West. 1962. A5295
29 Coe, M. Mexico. 1962. A5296
30 Stenberger, M. K. H. Sweden, tr. by Binns. 1962. A5297
31 Cook, J. M. The Greeks in Ionia and the East. 1963. A5298
32 Gimbutas, M. (Alseikaitė). The Balts. 1963. A5299
33 Blegen, C. W. Troy and the Trojans. 1963. A5300
34 Chadwick, N. (Kershaw) Celtic Britain. 1964. A5301
35 Guido, M. Sardinia. 1964. A5302
36 Arribas, A. The Iberians. 1964. A5303
37 Wells, C. Bones, bodies, and disease. 1964. A5304
38 Gray, J. The Canaanites. 1964. A5305
39 Taylour, W. The Mycenaens. 1964. A5306
40 O'Ríordaín, S. P. and Daniel, G. New Grange. 1964. A5307
41 Fox, A. M. (Henderson) South West England. 1964. A5308
42 Culican, W. The Medes and Persians. 1965. A5309
43 Toynbee, J. M. C. The art of the Romans. 1965. A5310
44 Reichel-Dolmatoff, G. Columbia. 1965. A5311
45 Jazdzewski, K. Poland. 1965. A5312
46 Fagan, B. M. Southern Africa during the iron age. 1965. A5313
47 Trump, D. Central and Southern Italy. 1965. A5314
48 Bass, G. F. Archaeology under water. 1966. A5315
49 Meggers, B. J. Ecuador. 1966. A5316
50 McDonald, A. H. Republican Rome. 1966. A5317
51 Lang, D. M. The Georgians. 1966. A5318
52 Coe, M. D. The Maya. 1966. A5319
53 Kivikoski, E. M. Finland, tr. by Binns. 1967. A5320
54 Henderson, I. The Picts. 1967. A5321
55 Shinnie, P. L. Meroe. 1967. A5322
56 Hagen, A. Norway. 1967. A5323
57 Berciw, D. Romania. 1967. A5324
58 Davidson, H. R. E. Pagan Scandinavia. 1967. A5325
59 Colledge, M. A. R. The Parthians. 1967. A5326
60 Maclagan, M. The city of Constantinople. 1968. A5327
61 Savory, H. N. Spain and Portugal. 1968. A5328
62 Hencken, H. Tarquinia and Etruscan origins. 1968. A5329
63 Piggott, S. The Druids. 1968. A5330
64 Phillips, E. D. The Mongols. 1969. A5331
65 Mulvaney, D. J. The prehistory of Australia. 1969. A5332
66 Brothwell, D. and P. Food in antiquity. 1969. A5333
67 Bauml, F. H. Medieval civilization in Germany. 1969. A5334
68 Der Nersessian, S. The Armenians. 1969. A5335
69 Jessup, R. Southeast England. 1970. A5336
70 Lathrop, D. W. The Upper Amazons. 1970. A5337
71 Buxton, D. R. The Abyssinians. 1970. A5338
72 Clark, J. D. The prehistory of Africa. 1970. A5339
73 Sulimirski, T. The Sarmatians. 1971. A5340
74 Gimbutas, M. The Slavs. 1971. A5341
75 Hood, S. The Minoans. 1971. A5342
76 Barfield, L. Northern Italy before Rome. 1971. A5343

77 Alexander, J. Yugoslavia before the Roman Conquest. 1972. A5344
78 Kidder, J. E. Early Buddhist Japan. 1972. A5345
79 Masson, V. M. and Sariandi, V. I. Central Asia. 1972. A5346
80 Bowen, E. G. Britain and the Western seaways. 1972. A5347
81 Pericot García, L. The Balearic Islands, tr. by Brown. 1972. A5348
82 Smail, R. C. The Crusaders in Syria and the Holy Land. 1974. A5349

ANGLICA GERMANICA (Mouton)

1 Wells, G. A. Herder and after. 1959. A5350
2 Urban, G. R. Kinesis and stasis. 1962. A5351
3 Barnett, P. R. Theodore Haak, F. R. S. ... 1962. A5352
4 Benn, M. B. Hölderin and Pindar. 1962. A5353
5 Paul, J. Schulmeisterlein wutz, ed. by Engel. 1962. A5354
6 Bennett, W. German verse in classical metres. 1963. A5355
7 Bock, C. V. Wort-Konkordanz zur Dichtung Stefan Georges. 1964. A5356
8 Trainer, J. Ludwig Tieck. 1964. A5357
9 Sandor, A. I. The exile of Gods. 1968. A5358
10 Klieneberger, H. R. The Christian writers of the inner emigration. 1969. A5359
11 Garland, M. Kleist's Prinz Freudrich von Homburg. 1968. A5360
12 Ellis, J. M. Schiller's Kalliasbriefe and the study of his aesthetic theory. 1969. A5361
13 Bruckner, J. A bibliographical catalogue of seventeenth-century books published in Holland. 1971. A5362

ANGLISTICA (Rosenkilde)

1 Bauer, J. The London magazine, 1820-29. 1953. A5363
2 Everitt, E. B. The young Shakespeare: studies in documentary evidence. 1954. A5364
3 Stene, A. Hiatus in English; problems of catenation and juncture. 1954. A5365
4 Locke, L. G. Tillotson; a study in seventeenth century literature. 1954. A5366
5 Baldwin, R. The unity of the Canterbury Tales. 1955. A5367
6 Whaler, J. Counterpoint and symbol. 1956. A5368
7 Bredsdorff, E. Hans Andersen and Charles Dickens. 1956. A5369
8 Roll-Hansen, D. The Academy, 1869-1879. 1957. A5370
9 Wordsworth, W. Wordsworth's Preface to Lyrical ballads, ed. by Owen. 1957. A5371
10 Jamison, W. S. Arnold and the romantics. 1958. A5372
11 Chandler, E. Pater on style. 1958. A5373
12 Hanzo, T. A. Latitude and restoration criticism. 1961. A5374
13 Widsiǒ. Widsith, ed. by Malone. 1962. A5375
14 Everitt, E. B. and Armstrong, R. L. Six early plays related to the Shakespeare canon. 1965. A5376
15 Brookhouse, C. Sir Amadace and the avowing of Arthur. 1967. A5377
16 Palmer, R. E. Thomas Whythorne's speech. 1968. A5378
17 Eliason, N. E. The language of Chaucer's poetry. 1972. A5379
18 Rogers, W. E. Image and abstraction. 1972. A5380
19 Johnson, L. M. Wordsworth and the sonnet. 1973. A5381
20 Provost, W. The structure of Chaucer's Troilus. 1974. A5382

ANN ARBOR SCIENCE LIBRARY (Univ. of Michigan Pr.)

Buddenbrock, W. von. The senses, tr. by Gaynor. 1958. A5383
Defant, A. Ebb and flow. 1958. A5384
Evans, H. E. and Eberhard, M. J. W. The wasps. 1970. A5385
Evans, L. J. The crisis in medical education. 1964. A5386
Goetsch, W. The ants. 1967. A5387
Heinroth, O. and K. The birds. 1958. A5388
Kiepenheuer, K. The sun, tr. by Pomerans. 1959. A5389
Koenigswald, G. H. von. The evolution of man, tr. by Pomerans. 1973. A5390
Krogman, W. M. Child growth. 1972. A5391
Kruse, W. and Dieckvoss, W. The stars. 1957. A5392
Merrill, P. W. Space chemistry. 1960. A5393
Munroe, M. E. The language of mathematics. 1963. A5394
Portmann, A. Animal camouflage, tr. by Pomerans. 1959. A5395
Rapoport, A. No-person game theory. 1969. A5396
____. Two-person game theory. 1966. A5397
Rüechardt, E. Light, tr. by Gaynor. 1958. A5398
Schaller, F. Soil animals. 1968. A5399
Schmitt, W. L. Crustaceans. 1964. A5400
Slijper, E. J. Whales and dolphins. 1974. A5401
Stumpff, K. Planet earth, tr. by Wayne. 1959. A5402
Thielcke, G. A. Bird sounds. 1974. A5403
Weidel, W. Virus, tr. by Streisinger. 1959. A5404

ANNALES CRYPTOGAMICI ET PHYTOPATHOLOGICI (Chronica Botanica)

1 Garrett, S. D. Root disease fungi. 1944. A5405
2 Horsfall, J. G. Fungicides and their action. 1945. A5406
3 Fulford, M. H. The genus bazzania in Central and South America. 1946. A5407
4 Chester, K. S. The nature and the prevention of the cereal rusts as exemplified in the leaf rust of wheat. 1946. A5408
5 Copeland, E. B. Genera Filicum. 1947. A5409
6 Nickerson, W. J., ed. Biology of pathogenic fungi. 1947. A5410
7-8 Frear, D. E. H. A catalogue of insecticides and fungicides. 2 v. 1947-48. A5411
9 Waksman, S. A. The actinomycetes. 1950. A5412
10 Elliott, C. Manual of bacterial plant pathogens. 1951. A5413
11 McCubbin, W. A. The plant quarantine problem. 1954. A5414
Series discontinued.

ANNALS OF BOTANY MEMOIR (Oxford)

1 Corner, E. J. H. A monograph of Clavaria and allied genera. 1950. A5415
2 ____. A monograph of cantharelloid fungi. 1966. A5416
3 Hawkes, J. G. and Hjerting, J. P. The potatoes of Argentina, Brazil, Paraguay, and Uruguay. 1968. A5417

ANNALS OF MATHEMATICS STUDIES (Princeton Univ. Pr.)

1 Weyl, H. Algebraic theory of numbers. 1940. A5418
2 Tukey, J. W. W. Convergence and uniformity in topology. 1940. A5419
3 Gödel, K. The consistency of the axiom of choice and of the generalized continuum-hypothesis with the axioms of set theory. 1940. A5420
4 Murray, F. J. An introduction to linear transformations in Hilbert space. 1941. A5421
5 Post, E. L. The two-valued

iterative systems of mathematical logic. 1941. A5422
6 Church, A. The calculi of lambda-conversion. 1941. A5423
7 Halmos, P. R. Finite dimensional vector spaces. 1947. A5424
8 Busemann, H. Metric methods in Finsler spaces and in the foundations of geometry. 1942. A5425
9 Sewell, W. E. Degree of approximation by polynomials in the complex domain. 1942. A5426
10 Lefschetz, S. Topics in topology. 1942. A5427
11 Krylov, N. M. Introduction to nonlinear mechanics. 1943. A5428
12 Weyl, H. and J. Meromorphic functions and analytic curves. 1943. A5429
13 Church, A. Introduction to mathematical logic. Pt. 1. 1944. A5430
14 Lefschetz, S. Lectures on differential equations. 1946. A5431
15 Morse, M. Topological methods in the theory of functions of a complex variable. 1947. A5432
16 Siegel, C. L. Transcendental numbers. 1949. A5433
17 Lîapurnov, M. A. Problème général de la stabilité du mouvement. 1949. A5434
18 Truesdell, C. A. A unified theory of special functions. 1948. A5435
19 Bochner, S. and Chadrasekharan, K. Fourier transforms. 1949. A5436
20 Lefschetz, S., ed. Contributions to the theory of nonlinear oscillations. V. 1. 1950. A5437
21-22 Von Neumann, J. Functional operators. 2 v. 1950. A5438
23 Bernstein, D. L. Existence theorems in partial differential equations. 1950. A5439
24 Contributions to the theory of games, ed. by Kuhn and Tucker. V. 1. 1950. A5440
25 Contributions to Fourier analysis, ed. by Zygmund. 1950. A5441
26 Schatten, R. A theory of cross-spaces. 1950. A5442
27 Pólya, G. and Szegö, G. Isoperimetric inequalities in mathematical physics. 1951. A5443
28 Same as no. 24. V. 2. 1952. A5444
29 Same as no. 20. V. 2. 1952. A5445
30 Ahlfors, L. V. and others. Contributions to the theory of Riemann surfaces. 1953. A5446
31 McShane, E. J. Order-preserving maps and integration processes. 1953. A5447
32 Yano, K. and Bochner, S. Curvature and Betti numbers. 1953. A5448
33 Bers, L. and others, eds. Contributions to the theory of partial differential equations. 1954. A5449
34 Shannon, C. E. and McCarthy, J., eds. Automata studies. 1956. A5450
35 Cesari, L. Surface area. 1956. A5451
36 Same as no. 20. V. 3. 1956. A5452
37 Not published.
38 Kuhn, H. W. and Tucker, A., eds. Linear inequalities and related systems. 1956. A5453
39-40 Same as no. 24. V. 3, 4. 1957. A5454
41 Same as no. 20. V. 4. 1958. A5455
42 Bochner, S. Lectures on Fournier integrals. 1959. A5456
43 Abhyanker, S. Ramification theoretic methods in algebraic geometry. 1959. A5457
44 Furstenberg, H. Stationary processes and prediction theory. 1960. A5458
45 Same as no. 20. V. 5. 1960. A5459
46 Borel, A. Seminar on transformation groups. 1960. A5460
47 Smullyan, R. M. Theory of formal systems. 1960. A5461
48 Gunning, R. C. Lectures

on modular forms. 1962. A5462
49 Toda, H. Composition methods in homotopy groups of spheres. 1962. A5463
50 Steenrod, N. E. Cohomology operations, ed. by Epstein. 1962. A5464
51 Milnor, J. Morse theory. 1963. A5465
52 Dresher, M. and others, eds. Advances in game theory. 1964. A5466
53 Auslander, L. and others. Flow on homogeneous spaces. 1963. A5467
54 Munkres, J. R. Elementary differential topology. 1963. A5468
55 Sacks, G. E. Degrees of unsolvability. 1963. A5469
56 Neuwirth, L. P. Knot groups. 1965. A5470
57 Palais, R. S., ed. Seminar on the Atiyah-Singer index theorem, by Atiyah. 1965. A5471
58 Chang, C. C. and Keisler, H. J. Continuous model theory. 1966. A5472
59 Mumford, D. Lectures on curves on an algebraic surface. 1966. A5473
60 Topology seminar, Wisconsin, 1965, ed. by Bing and Bean. 1966. A5474
61 Milnor, J. W. Singular points of complex hypersurfaces. 1969. A5475
62 Speer, E. R. Generalized Feynman amplitudes. 1969. A5476
63 Stein, E. M. Topics in harmonic analysis. 1969. A5477
64 Wu, H. The equidistribution theory of holomorphic curves. 1970. A5478
65 Chung, K. L. Lectures on boundary theory of Markov chains. 1970. A5479
66 Ahlfors, L., ed. and others. Advances in the theory of Riemann surfaces. 1970. A5480
67 Shatz, S. S. Profinite groups, arithmetic, and geometry. 1971. A5481
68 Miller, C. F. On group-theoretic decision problems and their classification. 1971. A5482
69 Symposium on infinite dimensional topology, ed. by Anderson. 1971. A5483
70 Hirzebruch, F. E. P. and others. Prospects in mathematics. 1971. A5484
71 Laufer, H. B. Normal two-dimensional singularities. 1971. A5485
72 Milnor, J. Introduction to algebraic K-theory. 1971. A5486
73 Kumpera, A. and Spencer, D. Lie equations. 1972. A5487
74 Iwasawa, K. Lectures on p-adic L-functions. 1972. A5488
75 Folland, G. B. and Kohn, J. J. The Neumann problem for the Cauchy-Riemann complex. 1972. A5489
76 Milnor, J. W. and Stasheff, J. D. Characteristic classes. 1973. A5490
77 Moser, J. Stable and random motions in dynamical systems with special emphasis on celestial mechanics. 1973. A5491
78 Mostow, G. D. Strong rigidity of locally symmetric spaces. 1973. A5492
79 Discontinuous Groups and Riemann Surfaces. Discontinuous groups and Riemann surfaces, ed. by Greenberg. 1974. A5493
80 Hirsch, M. W. and Mazur, B. Smoothings of piecewise linear manifolds. 1974. A5494
81 Lustig, G. The discrete series of GL_n over a finite field. 1974. A5495
82 Birman, J. S. Braids, links, and mappling class groups. 1974. A5496

THE ANTE-NICENE FATHERS (Christian Literature Pub. Co., 1885-1886)

1 The Apostolic fathers, Justin Martyr, Irenaeus. A5497
2 Fathers of the second century: Hermas, Tatian, Athenagoras, Clement of Alexandria. A5498
3 Latin Christianity: its founder Tertullian. I Apologetic, II Anti-Marcion. III

Ethical. A5499
4 Tertullianus. 4th part: Minucius Felix. Commodian. Origen. Parts 1 and 2. A5500
5 Hippolytus. Cyprian. Caius. Novatian. Appendix. A5501
6 Gregory Thaumaturgus, St. Dionysius the Great. Julian Africanus. Anatolius and minor writers. Methodius. Arnobius. A5502
7 Lactantius, Venantius, Asterius, Victorinus. Dionysius. Apostolic teaching and constitutions, Homily, Liturgies. A5503
8 The twelve patriarchs. Excerpts and epistles. The Clementina. Apocrypha. Decretals, Memoirs of Edessa and Syriac documents. Remains of the first ages. A5504
9 Gospel of Peter. Diatessaron of Tatian. Apocalypse of Peter. Visio Pauli. Apocalypses of the Virgin and Sedrach. Testament of Abraham. Acts of Xanthippe and Polyxena. Narrative of Zosimus. Apology of Aristides. Epistles of Clement. Origen's Commentary. A5505
10 Bibliographic synopsis, by Richardson. A5506

ANTHROPOLOGY OF THE NORTH: TRANSLATIONS FROM RUSSIAN SOURCES (Univ. of Toronto Pr.)

1 Rudenko, S. I. The ancient culture of the Bering Sea and the Eskimo problem. 1961. A5507
2 Michael, H. N., ed. Studies in Siberian ethnogenesis. 1962. A5508
3 Levin, M. G. Ethnic origins of the peoples of Northeastern Asia. 1963. A5509
4 Michael, H. N., ed. Studies in Siberian Shamanism. 1963. A5510
5 ____. The archaeology and geomorphology of northern Asia. 1964. A5511
6 Okladnikov, A. P. The Soviet Far East in antiquity, ed. by Michael. 1965. A5512
7 Zagoskin, L. A. Lieutenant Zagoskin's travels in Russian America, ed. by Michael. 1967. A5513

ANTHROPOS INSTITUTE STUDIA (Anthropos Institute. Distributed by Stechert-Macmillan)

1 Arndt, P. Religion auf Ostflores. 1951. A5514
2 Giet, F. Zur Tonität nordchinesischer Mundarten. 1950. A5515
3 Luzbetak, L. J. Marriage and the family in Caucasia. 1951. A5516
4 Verheijen, J. Het hoogste wezen bij de Manggariers. 1951. A5517
5 Crazzolara, J. P. Zur Gesellschaft und Religion der Nueer. 1953. A5518
6 Schebesta, P. Die Negrito Asiens. V. 1. 1953. A5519
7 Vanoverbergh, M. Songs in Lepanto-Igorot as it is spoken at Bauko. 1954. A5520
8 Arndt, P. Gesellschaftliche Verhältniss der Ngadha. 1954. A5521
9 Rock, J. F. C. The Zsi mä funeral ceremony of the Na-khi of southwest China. 1955. A5522
10 Schmidt, W. Das Mutterrecht. 1954. A5523
11 Drabbe, P. Spraakkunst van het Marind. 1955. A5524
12-13 Same as 6. V. 2-3. 1955-57. A5525
14 Golomb, L. Die Bodenkultur in Ost-Turkistan. 1959. A5526
15 Arndt, P. Wörterbuch der Ngodhasprache. 1961. A5527
16 Huber, H. H. The Krobo. 1963. A5528
18 Festschrift Paul Schebesta zum 75. 1963. A5529
19 Pache, A. Das religiosen Vorstellungen in den Mythen der formosanischen Bergstamme. 1964. A5530
20 Schmidt, W. Wege der Kulturen. 1964. A5531
21 Anthropos Institute. Anthropica. 1969. A5532

ANTIBIOTICS MONOGRAPHS (Medical Encyclopedia)

1 Herrell, W. E. Erythromycin. 1955. A5533
2 Grove, D. C. and Randall, W. A. Assay methods of antibiotics. 1955. A5534
3 Dowling, H. F. Tetracycline. 1955. A5535
4 Jukes, T. H. Antibiotics in nutrition. 1955. A5536
5 Jawetz, E. Polymyxin, neomycin, bacitracin. 1956. A5537
6 Musselman, M. M. Terramycin. 1956. A5538
7 Lepper, M. H. Auremycin. 1956. A5539
8 Woodward, T. E. and Wisseman, C. L. Chloromycetin. 1958. A5540
9 Hirsh, H. L. and Putnam, L. E. Penicillin. 1958. A5541
10 Weinstein, L. and Ehrenkranz, N. J. Streptomycin and dihydrostreptomycin. 1958. A5542
11 Mitchell, R. S. and others. Modern chemotherapy of tuberculosis. 1958. A5543
12 Welch, H. and Finland, M., ed. Antibiotic therapy for staphylococcal diseases. 1959. A5544

Ceased publication.

ANTI-SLAVERY CRUSADE IN AMERICA (Arno)

Adams, J. Q. Argument of John Quincy Adams. 1969. A5545
____. Speech of John Quincy Adams of Massachusetts upon the right of the people. 1969. A5546
Allen, W. G. The American prejudice against color. 1969. A5547
American Anti-Slavery Society. The anti-slavery history of the John Brown year. 1969. A5548
____. The legion of liberty and force of truth. 1969. A5549
____. Proceedings of the Anti-Slavery Society at its third decade. 1969. A5550
Bacon, L. Slavery discussed in occasional essays. 1969. A5551
Barber, J. W., comp. A history of the Amistad captives. 1969. A5552
Bearse, A. Reminiscences of fugitive slave law days in Boston. 1969. A5553
Benezet, A. and Wesley, J. Views of American slavery. 1969. A5554
Birney, J. G. The American churches. 1969. A5555
____, ed. Correspondence between the Hon. F. H. Elmore and James G. Birney. 1969. A5556
____. A letter on the political obligations of abolitionists. 1969. A5557
Blanchard, J. and Rice, N. L. A debate on slavery. 1969. A5558
Bourne, G. The book and slavery irreconcilable. 1969. A5559
Branagan, T. A preliminary essay on the oppression of the exiled sons of Africa. 1969. A5560
Brown, I. V. A. Biography of the Rev. Robert Finley. 1969. A5561
Brown, W. W. The black man. 1969. A5562
Channing, W. E. Emancipation. 1969. A5563
Cheever, G. B. God against slavery. 1969. A5564
Child, L. M. Letters of Lydia Maria Child. 1969. A5565
____. The right way the safe way proved by emancipation in the British West Indies. A5566
Clay, C. M. The writings of Cassius Marcellus Clay, ed. by Greeley. 1969. A5567
Conway, M. D. Testimonies concerning slavery. 1969. A5568
Fee, J. G. An anti-slavery manual. 1969. A5569
Foster, S. S. The brotherhood of thieves. 1969. A5570
Garrison, W. L. and others. Letter to Joseph Kossuth... 1969. A5571

Garrison, W. P. and F. J. William Lloyd Garrison. 4 v. 1959. A5572
____. The new reign of terror in the slaveholding states for 1859-1860. 1969. A5573
Giddings, J. R. The exiles of Florida. 1969. A5574
Goodell, W. The American slave code in theory and practice. 1969. A5575
Grimke, A. E. Appeal to the Christian women of the South. 1969. A5576
____. Letters to Catherine E. Beecher... 1969. A5577
Haven, G. Sermons, speeches, and letters on slavery and its war. 1969. A5578
Haviland, L. S. A woman's life-work. 1969. A5579
Hildreth, R. The white slave. 1969. A5580
Hopkins, S. A dialogue concerning the slavery of the Africans. Also Sewell, S. The selling of Joseph. 1969. A5581
Jay, W. A review of the causes and consequences of the Mexican war. 1969. A5582
Lay, B. All slave keepers that keep the innocent in bondage. 1969. A5583
Lunde, B. The life, travels and opinions of Benjamin Lundy, ed. by Earle. 1969. A5584
Mann, H. Slavery. 1969. A5585
Martineau, H. The martyr age of the United States. 1969. A5586
Parker, T. The Boston kidnapping. 1969. A5587
____. The slave power. 1969. A5588
Pennsylvania Society for Promoting the Abolition of Slavery. An historical memoir, ed. by Needles. 1969. A5589
Phillips, W. Review of Lysander Spooner's essay on the unconstitutionality of slavery. 1969. A5590
____. Speeches, lectures and letters. 1969. A5591
Pierce, E. L. Memoirs and letters of Charles Sumner. 1969. A5592
Pillsbury, P. Acts of the anti-slavery apostles. 1969. A5593
Putnam, M. Record of an obscure man. 1969. A5594
Rankin, J. Letters on American slavery. 1969. A5595
Redpath, J. Echoes of Harper's Ferry. 1969. A5596
Rice, D. Slavery inconsistent with justice and good policy. 1969. A5597
Rush, B. An address to the inhabitants of the British settlements... 1969. A5598
Sandiford, R. A brief examination of the practice of the times. 1969. A5599
Scott, G. The grounds of secession from the M. E. Church. 1969. A5600
Smith, G. Sermons and speeches of Gerrit Smith. 1969. A5601
Smith, T. C. The liberty and free soil parties in the Northwest. 1969. A5602
Stanton, H. B. Remarks of Henry Brewster Stanton. 1969. A5603
Stearns, F. P. Life and public services of George Luther Stearns. 1969. A5604
Stevens, C. E. Anthony Burns. 1969. A5605
Sumner, C. The crime against Kansas. 1969. A5606
Thome, J. A. and Kimball, J. H. Emancipation in the West Indies. 1969. A5607
Walker, J. The branded hand. 1969. A5608
Weld, T. D., ed. Slavery and the internal slave trade in the United States of North America. 1969. A5609
Whittier, J. G. Anti-slavery poems. 1969. A5610
Woolman, J. Some considerations on the keeping of Negroes. 1969. A5611

APPLIED MATHEMATICAL SCIENCES (Springer)

1 John, F. Partial differential equations. 1971. A5612
2 Sirovich, L. Techniques of symptotic analysis. 1971. A5613
3 Hale, H. K. Functional differential equations. 1971. A5614

4 Percus, J. K. Combinatorial methods. 1971. A5615
5 Von Mises, R. and Friedrichs, K. O. Fluid dynamics. 1971. A5616
6 Freiberger, W. F. and Grenander, U. A course on computational probability and statistics. 1971. A5617
7 Pipkin, A. C. Lectures in viscoelasticity theory. 1972. A5618
8 Giacaglia, G. E. O. Perturbation methods in non-linear systems. 1972. A5619
9 Friedrichs, K. O. Spectral theory of operators in Hilbert space. 1973. A5620

APPLIED MATHEMATICS AND MECHANICS (Academic)

1 Oswatitsch, K. Gas dynamics. 1956. A5621
2 Birkhoff, G. and Zarantonello, E. H. Jets, wakes, and cavities. 1957. A5622
3 Von Mises, R. and others. Mathematical theory of compressible fluid flow. 1958. A5623
4 Alt, F. L. Electronic digital computers. 1958. A5624
5 Hayes, W. D. and Probstein, R. F. Hypersonic flow theory. 1959. A5625
6 Brekhovskikh, L. M. Waves in layered media, tr. by Lieberman. 1960. A5626
7 Singer, S. F., ed. Torques and attitude sensing in earth satellites. 1964. A5627
8 Van Dyke, M. D. Perturbation methods in fluid mechanics. 1964. A5628
9 Miele, A., ed. Theory of optimum aerodynamic shapes. 1965. A5629
10 Betchov, R. and Criminale, W. O. Stability of parallel flows. 1967. A5630
11 Burgers, J. M. Flow equations for composite gases. 1969. A5631
12 Lumley, J. L. Stochastic tools in turbulence. 1970. A5632
13 Cabannes, H. Theoretical magneto fluid dynamics, ed. by Holt and Sfeir. 1970. A5633
14 O'Malley, R. E. Introduction to singular perturbations. 1974. A5634

APPLIED MATHEMATICS SERIES (Wiley)

Arley, N. and Buch, K. R. Introduction to the theory of probability and statistics. 1950. A5635
Bickley, W. G. and Gibson, R. E. Via vector to tension. 1962. A5636
Bowman, F. An introduction to determinates and matrices. 1962. A5637
Burnett-Hall, D. G. and others. Computer programming and autocodes. 1964. A5638
Fagg, S. V. Differential equations. 1956. A5639
Forsythe, G. E. and Wasow, W. R. Finite-difference methods for partial differential equations. 1960. A5640
Friedman, B. Principles and techniques of applied mathematics. 1956. A5641
Greig, D. M. and Wise, T. H. Hydrodynamics and vector field theory. 1962. A5642
Hestenes, M. R. Calculus of variations and optimal control theory. 1966. A5643
Lambe, C. G. Statistical methods and formulae. 1967. A5644
Milne, W. E. Numerical solution of differential equations. 1953. A5645
Murnaghan, F. D. Finite deformation of an elastic solid. 1951. A5646
____. Introduction to applied mathematics. 1948. A5647
Prager, W. and Hodge, P. G. Theory of perfectly plastic solids. 1951. A5648
Rainich, G. Y. Mathematics of relativity. 1950. A5649
Redish, K. A. An introduction to computational methods. 1962. A5650
Reid, W. T. Ordinary differential equations. 1971. A5651
Schelkunoff, S. A. Advanced antenna theory. 1952. A5652

____. Antennas. 1952. A5653
Sokolnikoff, I. S. Tensor analysis. 1951. A5654
Whittle, P. Prediction and regulation by linear-least square methods. 1963. A5655
Series discontinued.

APPLIED PHYSICS AND ENGINEERING (Springer)

1 Stupochenko, Y. V. and others. Relaxation of shock waves. 1967. A5656
2-3 Loh, W. H. T., ed. Reentry and planetary entry. 2 v. 1968. A5657
4 Vakman, D. E. Sophisticated signals and the uncertainty principles in radar. 1968. A5658
5 Rapoport, I. M. Dynamics of elastic containers partially filled with liquid. 1968. A5659
6 Moiseev, N. N. and others. Dynamic stability of bodies containing fluid, ed. by Abramson. 1968. A5660
7 Loh, W. H. T., ed. Jet rocket, ion, and electric propulsion. 1968. A5661
8 Houyaux, M. F. Arc physics. 1968. A5662
9 Zimmer, H. G. Geometrical optics. 1969. A5663
10 Bikerman, J. J. Foams. 1973. A5664

APPRECIATION OF THE ARTS (Oxford)

1 Gauldie, S. Architecture. 1969. A5665
2 Rogers, L. R. Sculpture. 1969. A5666
3 Rawson, P. S. Drawing. 1969. A5667
4 Osborne, H. The art of appreciation. 1970. A5668
5 Owen, P. Painting. 1970. A5669
6 Rawson, P. S. Ceramics. 1971. A5670
7 Rice, D. T. The appreciation of Byzantine art. 1972. A5671
8 Rogers, L. R. Relief sculpture. 1973. A5672

ARCHAEOLOGI MUNDI (World)

Alkim, U. B. Anatoli I, tr. by Hogarth. 1968. A5673
Belenitskiĭ, A. M. Central Asia, tr. by Hogarth. 1968. A5674
Groslier, B. P. Indochina, tr. by Hogarth. 1967. A5675
Huot, J. L. Persia I, tr. by Harrison. 1966. A5676
Larco Hoyle, R. Peru, tr. by Hogarth. 1966. A5677
Lukonin, V. G. Persia II, tr. by Hogarth. 1967. A5678
Margueron, J. C. Mesopotamia, tr. by Harrison. 1965. A5679
Platon, N. E. Crete, tr. by Hogarth. 1966. A5680
Soustelle, J. Mexico, tr. by Hogarth. 1967. A5681

ARCHAEOLOGICAL EXPLORATIONS OF SARDIS MONOGRAPHS (Harvard Univ. Pr.)

1 Bates, G. E. Byzantine coins. 1970. A5682
2 Pedley, J. G. Ancient literary sources on Sardis. 1972. A5683
3 Gusmani, R. Neue epichorische schriftzeugnisse aus Sardis. 1974. A5684

ARCHIVES INTERNATIONALES D'HISTOIRE DES IDEES. INTERNATIONAL ARCHIVES OF THE HISTORY OF IDEAS. (Nijhoff)

1 Labrousse, E. Pierre Bayle. 1963. A5685
2 Merlan, P. Monopsychism, mysticism, metaconsciousness. 1963. A5686
3 Leeuwen, H. G. van. The problem of certainty in English thought, 1630-1690. 1963. A5687
4 Janssen, P. W. Les origines de la reforme des Carmes en France au XVIIe siècle. 1963. A5688
5 Sebba, G. Bibliographia Cartesiana. 1964. A5689
6 Same as no. 1. V. 2. 1964. A5690

7 Swart, K. W. The sense of decadence in nineteenth-century France. 1964. A5691
8 Rex, W. Essays on Pierre Bayle and religious controversy. 1965. A5692
9 Heier, E. L. H. Nicolay (1737-1820) and his contemporaries... 1965. A5693
10 Bracken, H. M. The early reception of Berkeley's immaterialism, 1710-1733. 1965. A5694
11 Watson, R. A. The downfall of Cartesianism, 1673-1712. 1966. A5695
12 Descartes, R. Regulae ad directionem ingenii. 1966. A5696
13 Chapelain, J. Soixant-dix-sept lettres inedites à Nicolas Heinsius, ed. by Bray. 1966. A5697
14 Brush, C. B. Montaigne and Bayle. 1966. A5698
15 Neveu, B. Un historien à l'école de Port-Royal. 1966. A5699
16 Faivre, A. Kirchberger et l'illuminisme du dix-huitième siècle. 1966. A5700
17 Clarke, J. A. Huguenot warrior. 1967. A5701
18 Kinser, S. The works of Jacques-Auguste de Thou. 1967. A5702
19 Hirsch, E. F. Damiao de Gois. 1967. A5703
20 Whitmore, P. J. S. The order of Minims in seventeenth century France. 1967. A5704
21 Hillenaar, H. Fénelon et les Jésuites. 1967. A5705
22 Hargreaves-Mawdsley, W. The English Della Cruscans and their time. 1967. A5706
23 Schmitt, C. B. Gianfrancesco Pico della Mirandola. 1967. A5707
24 White, E. B. Peace among the willows. 1968. A5708
25 Apt, L. Louis-Philippe de Ségur. 1969. A5709
26 Kadler, E. H. Literary figures in French drama. 1969. A5710
27 Postel, G. Le Thrésor des Prophéties de l'univers. 1969. A5711
28 Boscherini, E. G. Lexicon Spinozanum. 2 v. 1971. A5712
29 Bolton, C. A. Church reform in 18th century Italy. 1969. A5713
30 Janicaud, D. Une généaologie du spiritualisme française. 1969. A5714
31 Julien Eymard d'Angers, Father. L'Humanisme chrêtien au XVIIe siècle. 1970. A5715
32 White, H. B. Copp'd hills toward heaven. 1970. A5716
33 Olscamp, P. J. The moral philosophy of George Berkley. 1970. A5717
34 Norena, C. G. Juan Luis Vives. 1970. A5718
35 O'Higgins, J. Anthony Collins. 1970. A5719
36 Brechka, F. T. Gerard van Swieten and his world, 1700-1772. 1970. A5720
37 Waddicor, M. H. Montesquieu and the philosophy of natural law. 1970. A5721
38 Bloch, O. R. La philosophie de Gassendi. 1971. A5722
39 Hoyles, J. The waning of the renaissance, 1640-1740. 1971. A5723
40 Dupuy, J. Correspondence de Jacques Dupuy et de Nicolas Heinsuis, 1646-1656, ed. by Bots. 1971. A5724
41 Lehmann, W. C. Henry Home, Lord Kanes, and the Scottish enlightenment. 1971. A5725
42 Kramer, C. Emmery de Lyere et Marnix de Sainte Aldegonde. 1971. A5726
43 Dibon, P. and others. Inventaire de la correspondance d'Andre Rivet. 1971. A5727
44 Kottman, K. A. Law and apocalypse. 1972. A5728
45 Nauen, F. G. Revolution, idealism and human freedom. 1972. A5729
46 Jensen, H. Motivation and the moral sense. 1971. A5730
47 Rosenberg, A. Tyssot de Potot and his work, 1655-1738. 1972. A5731
48 Walton, C. De la recherche

du bien. 1972. A5732
49 Whitmore, P. J. S. A seventeenth-century exposure of superstition. 1972. A5733
50 Sauvy, A. Livres saisis à Paris entre 1678-1701. 1972. A5734
51 Redmond, W. Bibliography of the philosophy in the Iberian colonies of America. 1972. A5735
52 Schmitt, C. B. Cicero scepticus. 1972. A5736
53 Hoyles, J. The edges of Augustianism. 1972. A5737
54 Bruggeman, J. and Ven, A. J. van de. Inventure des pièces d'archives française se rapportant à d'abbaye de Port Royal des Champs... 1972. A5738
55 Montgomery, J. W. Cross and crucible. 2 v. 1973. A5739
56 Lutaud, O. Des révolutions d'Angleterre à la Révolution française. 1973. A5740
57 Duchesneau, F. L'empirisme de Locke. 1973. A5741
58 Boulainvilliers, H. Henry de Boulainviller, ed. by Simon. 1973. A5742
59 Harris, E. E. Salvation from despair. 1973. A5743
60 Battail, J. F. L'avocat philosophe Géraud de Cordemoy. 1973. A5744
61 Liu, T. Discord in Zion. 1973. A5745
62 Strugnell, A. Diderot's politics. 1973. A5746
63 Defaux, G. Pantagruel et les Sophistes. 1973. A5747
64 Bonjour, G. P. Hegel. 1974. A5748
65 Brook, R. J. Berkeley's philosophy of science. 1974. A5749
66 Jessop, J. E. A bibliography of George Berkeley. 1974. A5750
67 Perry, E. I. From theology to history. 1974. A5751
68 Dibon, P. and others. Inventaire de la correspondance de Joh. F. Gronovius. 1974. A5752

Series minor:
1 James, E. D. Pierre Nicole. 1972. A5753
2 Silverblatt, B. G. The maxims in the novels of Duclos. 1972. A5754
3 Allen, E. J. B. Post and courier service in the diplomacy of early modern Europe. 1972. A5755
4 Grey, E. Guevara. 1973. A5756
5 Thompson, R. H. Lothar Franz von Schönborn and the diplomacy of the electorate of Mainz. 1973. A5757
6 Hassler, D. M. The comedian as the letter D. 1973. A5758
7 Kivy, P. Thomas Reid's lectures on the fine arts. 1973. A5759
8 Lindgren, J. R. The social philosophy of Adam Smith. 1973. A5760
9 Hutcheson, F. Francis Hutcheson: An inquiry concerning beauty, order, harmony, design, ed. by Kivy. 1973. A5761
10 Altizer, A. B. Self and symbolism in the poetry of Michelangelo, John Donne, and Agrippa d'Aubigné. 1973. A5762
11 Ruestow, E. G. Physics at seventeenth and eighteenth century Leiden. 1973. A5763
12 Sutch, V. D. Gilbert Sheldon. 1974. A5764

ARCHIVOS HISTORICO DIPLOMATICO MEXICANO (Secretaria de relaciones exteriores)

1 Peña y Reyes, A. de la, ed. La diplomacia mexicana. 1923. A5765
2 Nuñez Ortega, A. Noticia historica de las relaciones politicas y comerciales entre México de el Japón, durante el siglo XVII. 1923. A5766
3 Peña y Reyes, A. de la, ed. Incidente diplomatico con Inglaterra en 1843. 1923. A5767
4 Estrada, G. Las relaciones entre Mexico y Peru. 1923. A5768

5 Peña y Reyes, A. de la, ed. El decreto de Colombia en honor de Juarez. 1923. A5769
6 Mexico. Ministerio de relaciones exteriores. Personas que han tenido a su cargo la Secretaría del relaciones exteriores desde 1821 hasta 1924. 1924. A5770
7 Peña y Reyes, A. de la, ed. Lucas Alaman el reconocimento de nuestra independencia por España y la union de los paises hispanoamericanos. 1924. A5771
8 ____. Don Manuel Eduardo de Gorostiza y la cuestion de Texas. 1924. A5772
9 ____. Leon XII y los paises hispano-americanos. 1924. A5773
10 Fuente, J. A. de la. Notas de don Juan Antonio de la Fuente, ministro de Mexico cerca de Napoleon III, ed. by Peña y Reyes. 1924. A5774
11 Valle, R. H., comp. La anexión de Centro América a México. V. 1. 1924. A5775
12 Iglesias Calderón, F., ed. La concesion Leese. 1924. A5776
13 Peña y Reyes, A. de la, comp. El tratado Mon-Almonte. 1925. A5777
14 González Roa, F., ed. El Dr. Vincenté G. Quesada y sus trabajos diplomaticos sobre Mexico. 1925. A5778
15 Peña y Reyes, A. de la, ed. Lord Aberdeen Texas y California. 1925. A5779
16 Moreno, J. Diario de un escribiente de legacion. 1925. A5780
17 Guzmán y Ray Guzmán, J., comp. Las relaciones diplomaticas de Mexico con Sud-America. 1925. A5781
18 Peña y Reyes, A. de la, ed. El baron Alleye de Cyprey y el Baño de la Delicias. 1926. A5782
19 Peña y Reyes, A. de la. El Congreso de Panama y algunos otros projectos de union hispano-americana. 1926. A5783
20 Fabela, I. Los precusorers de la diplomacia mexicana. 1926. A5784
21 Landaeta Rosales, M. Relaciones entre Mexico y Venezuela. 1927. A5785
22 Peña y Reyes, A. de la. El tratado de pax con España. 1927. A5786
23 ____. La primera guerra entre Mexico y Francia. 1927. A5787
24 Same as no. 11. V. 2. 1924. A5788
25 Estrada, G., comp. Don Juan Prim y su labor diplomatica en Mexico. 1928. A5789
26 Peña y Reyes, A. de la. La insubstistencia de una convención de reclamaciones. 1928. A5790
27 Ramírez Cabañas, J. Las relaciones entre Mexico y el Vaticano. 1928. A5791
28 Peña y Reyes, A. de la. La labor diplomatica de D. Manuel Maria de Zamacona. 1928. A5792
29 Foster, J. W. Las memorias diplomaticas de Mr. Foster sobre Mexico. 1929. A5793
30 Zarco, F. Commentarios de Francisco Zarco sobre la intervencion francesca (1861-63). 1929. A5794
31 Peña y Reyes, A. de la. Algunos documentos sobre el tratado de Guadalupe y la situacion de Mexico durante la invasion americana. 1930. A5795
32 Chávez Orozco, L., comp. Un esfuerzo de Mexico por la independencia de Cuba. 1930. A5796
33 Ramírez Cabañas, J., comp. El emprestito de Mexico a Colombia. 1930. A5797
34 Mestre Ghizliazza, M., comp. Las relaciones diplomáticas entre Mexico y Holanda. 1931. A5798
35 Chávez Orozco, L., comp. La gestión diplomática del doctor Mora. 1931. A5799
36 Vázquez, A. C. Bosquejo histórico de la agregacion a Mexico de Chiapos y

Soconusco. 1932. A5800
37 Azacárate y Lezama, J. F. Un programa de politica internacional. 1932. A5801
38 Ramírez Cabañas, J., comp. Altamirano y el barón de Wagner. 1932. A5802
39 Mexico. Presidente. Un siglo de relaciones internationales de México. 1935. A5803
40 Same as no. 24. V. 2. 1935. A5804

Series 2:

1 Saldívar, G., ed. La misión confidencial de don Jesús Terán en Europa, 1863-66. A5805
2 Valle, R. H., ed. Bolívar en México, 1799-1832. 1946. A5806
3 Same as no. 24. V. 3. 1945. A5807
4 Same as no. 24. V. 4. 1945. A5808
5 Rejón, M. C. Correspondencia inédita de Manuel Crescencio Rejón, ed. by Trujillo. 1948. A5809
6 Magino, F., ed. Un diplomático mexicano en París..., 1848-51, comp. by Valle. 1948. A5810
7 Same as no. 24. V. 5. 1949. A5811
8 Flores, D. J. Lorenzo de Zavala y su misión diplomática en Francia (1834-35). 1951. A5812

ARIZONA. UNIVERSITY OF ARIZONA. ANTHROPOLOGICAL PAPERS (Univ. of Ariz. Pr.)

1 Breternitz, D. A. Excavations at Nantack Village, Point of Pines, Arizona. 1959. A5813
2 Giddings, R. Yaqui myths and legends. 1959. A5814
3 Owen, R. C. Marobavi. 1959. A5815
4 Hinton, T. Survey of Indian assimilation in Eastern Sonora. 1959. A5816
5 Crumrine, L. S. Phonology of Arizona Yaqui. 1961. A5817
6 Ezell, P. The Maricopas. 1963. A5818
7 Getty, H. San Carlos Indian cattle industry. 1964. A5819
8 Crumrine, N. R. House Cross of the Maya Indians of Sonora, Mexico. 1964. A5820
9 Wasley, W. and Johnson, A. Salvage archaeology in painted Rock Reservoir, Western Arizona. 1965. A5821
10 Breternitz, D. A. An appraisal of tree-ring dated pottery in the Southwest. 1966. A5822
11 Hodge, W. H. The Albuquerque Navajos. 1969. A5823
12 Waddell, J. O. Papago Indians at work. 1969. A5824
13 Griffen, W. B. Culture change and shifting populations in Central Northern Mexico. 1969. A5825
14 Crumire, L. S. Ceremonial exchange as a mechanism in tribal integration among the Mayos of Northwest Mexico. 1969. A5826
15 Basso, K. H. Western Apache witchcraft. 1969. A5827
16 Wilmsen, E. N. Lithic analysis and cultural inference. 1970. A5828
17 Longacre, W. Archaeology as anthropology. 1970. A5829
18 Hill, J. N. Broken K. Pueblo. 1970. A5830
19 Carlson, R. L. White Mountain redware. 1970. A5831
20 Hargrave, L. L. Mexican Macaws. 1970. A5832
21 Apachean culture history and ethnology, ed. by Basso and others. 1971. A5833
22 Barker, G. C. Social functions of language in a Mexican-American community. 1972. A5834
23 Bennett, K. A. The Indians of Point of Pines. 1973. A5835
24 Zubrow, E. Population, contact, and climate in New Mexico. 1974. A5836

ARMENIAN TEXTS AND STUDIES (Harvard Univ. Pr.)

2 Sanjian, A. K. Colophons of Armenian manuscripts,

1301-1480. 1969. A5837
3 Gregory, St. The teaching of St. Gregory, ed. by Thomson. 1970. A5838

ARNOLD FOUNDATION STUDIES NEW SERIES (Southern Methodist Univ.)

1 Eister, A. W. The United States and the ABC powers. 1889-1906. 1950. A5839
2 Eagleton, C. The United Nations and the United States. 1951. A5840
3 Smith, O. E. Yankee diplomacy: U.S. intervention in Argentina. 1953. A5841
4 Oost, S. I., Roman policy in Epirus and Acarnania in the age of the Roman conquest of Greece. 1954. A5842
5 Claunch, J. M. The government of Dallas County, Texas. 1954. A5843
6 Sabatino, R. A. Housing in Great Britain. 1956. A5844
7 Powers, R. Edgar Quinet. 1957. A5845
8 Davis, J. and Oden, W. E. Municipal and county government. 1961. A5846
9 Claunch, J. M., ed. Case studies in Latin American politics. 1961. A5847
10 Huey, M. E. Texas constitutional revision, ed. by Claunch. 1962. A5848
11 Taubenfeld, R. and M. J. Man and space. 1964. A5849
12 Conference on Mathematical Applications in Political Science. Mathematical applications in political science, ed. by Claunch. V. 1. 1965. A5850
13 Haggard, L. G. and others. Legislative redistricting in Texas. 1965. A5851
14 Fulbright, J. W. Bridges, east and west, ed. by Claunch. 1965. A5852
15 Claunch, J. M., ed. The 1964 Presidential election in the Southwest. 1966. A5853
16 Same as no. 12. V. 2. Ed. by Bernd. 1966. A5854
17 Cockran, H. From formal to informal international cooperation in the Caribbean, ed. by Claunch. 1967. A5855

ARS HISPANIAE (Salvat)

1 Almagro Basch, M. Arte prehistórico. 1947. A5856
Garcia y Bellido. Colonizaciones púnica y grieca... 1947. A5857
2 Taracena Aguirre, B. Arte romano. 1947. A5858
Huguet, P. B. Arte paleocristiano. 1947. A5859
3 Gomez Moreno, M. El arte árabe español hasta las Almohades y arte mozárabe. 1951. A5860
4 Balbas, L. T. Arte almonhade. 1949. A5861
5 Ricart, J. G. and Gaya Nuño, J. A. Arquitectura y escultura románicas. 1948. A5862

ART CENTERS OF THE WORLD SERIES (World)

Bottral, R., ed. Rome. 1968. A5863
Osman, R. E. New York. 1968. A5864
Watt, A., ed. Paris. 1967. A5865
Whittet, G. S., ed. London. 1967. A5866

ART HISTORY AND REFERENCE SERIES (Burt Franklin)

1 Krumbacher, K. Geschichte der Byzantinischen literatur. 2 v. 1967. A5867
2 Gomme, G. L. Index of archaeological papers, 1665-1890. 2 v. 1965. A5868
3 South Kensington Museum, London. First proofs of the universal catalogue of books on art, ed. by Pollen. 3 v. 1972. A5869
4 Bradley, J. W. Dictionary of miniaturists, illuminators, calligraphers and copyists. 3 v. 1968. A5870
5 Stauffer, D. M. American engravers upon copper and

steel. 2 v. 1964. A5871
6 ____. ____. Supp. by Fielding. 1964. A5872
7 Laborde, L. E. S. J. La Renaissance des arts à la cour de France. 2 v. 1967. A5873
8 Berlin. Staatliche Kunst Bibliothek. Katalog der ornamentstichsammlung der Statlichen Kunstbibliothek Berlin. 2 v. 1961. A5874
9 Diehl, C. Justinien et la civilization Byzantine au VIe siècle. 2 v. 1959. A5875
10 Dionysius. Manual d'econographie chretienne grecque et latine. 1963. A5876
11 Graves, A. A century of loan exhibitions. 5 v. 1969. A5877
12 Passavant, J. D. Le peintre-graveur ... du Oeintregraveur de Adam Bartsch. 1966. A5878
13 Pearson, E. Banbury chapbooks and nursery toy book literature of the 18th and early 19th centuries. 1966. A5879
14 Portalis, R. and H. B. Les graveurs du 18e siécle. 3 v. 1966. A5880
15 Rostenberg, L. Literary, political, religious, legal and scientific publishing, printing and bookselling in England. 2 v. 1964. A5881
16 Savage, W. A dictionary of the art of printing. 1965. A5882
17 White, J. A new century of inventions. 1967. A5883
18 Bonnardot, A. Essai sur l'art de restaurer les estampes et les livres. 1972. A5884
19 Foster, J. J., ed. A dictionary of painters of miniatures. 1968. A5885
20 Carre, L. Lespoicons de l'orfevrerie française du 14e siècle jusqu'au debut 19e siècle. 1967. A5886
21 Venturi, L. Les archives de l'impressionisme. 2 v. 1967. A5887
22 Wildenstein, G., ed. Rapports d'experts, 1712-1791. 1970. A5888
23 Jackson, M. The pictorial press. 1970. A5889
24 Herbert, J. A. Illuminated manuscripts. 1969. A5890
25 Remington, F. Remington's frontier sketches. 1969. A5891
26 Graves, A. A dictionary of artists... 1970. A5892
27 ____. The Royal Academy of Arts. 8 v. 1972. A5893
27 Portalis, R. and Beraldi, H. Les Graveurs de dix-huitiéme siècle. 3 v. 1970. A5894
28 Kondakov, N. P. Histoire de l'art Byzantine considéré principalement dans les miniatures. 2 v. 1970. A5895
28 Pollard, A. W. Old picture books. 1970. A5896
29 Maittaire, M. Historia typographorum aliquot parisiensium vitas et libros complectens. 2 v. 1970. A5897
30 Graves, A. Art sales from early in the eighteenth century to early in the twentieth century. 3 v. 1970. A5898
31 Lattimore, S. B. and Haskell, G. C. Arthur Rackham. 1970. A5899
31 Remington, F. Drawings by Frederic Remington. 1971. A5900
32 Totten, G. O. Maya architecture. 1971. A5901
33 Hugo, T. The Bewick collector. 2 v. 1970. A5902
34 Munsell, J. The typographical miscellany. 1972. A5903
35 Chantelou, P. F. de. Journal de voyage en France du cavalier Bernin. 1971. A5904
36 Goblet d'Alviella, E. F. A. The migration of symbols. 1972. A5905
37 Bertolotti, A. Artisti lombardi a Roma nei secoli XV, XVI, XVII. 2 v. 1972. A5906
38 ____. Artisti bolognesi. 1972. A5907
38 ____. Artisti belgi ed olandesi a Roma nei secoli XVI and XVII. 2 v. 1972. A5908
39 Mosytn-Owen, W. Bibliografia di Bernard Berenson. 1972. A5909
40 Hedicke, R. Methodenlehre der kunstgeschichte. 1972. A5910

41 Fournier, P. S. Fournier on typefounding, tr. by Carter. 1972. A5911
42 Laughton, L. G. C. Old ship figure-heads and sterns. 1972. A5912
43 Tietze, H. Die methode der kunstgeschichte. 1972. A5913
44 Crawford, E. A. E. L. Evolution of Italian sculpture. 1972. A5914
45 Bulfinch, E. S., ed. The life and letters of Charles Bulfinch, architect. 1972. A5915
46 Pollard, A. W. Italian book illustrations. 1972. A5916

ART IDEAS HISTORY (Skira)

Argan, G. C. The Europe of the Capitals, 1600-1700. 1965. A5917
Chastel, A. La crise de la Renaissance, 1420-1520. 1968. A5918
____. The crisis of the Renaissance, tr. by Price. 1968. A5919
____. The myth of the Renaissance, 1420-1520, tr. by Gilbert. 1969. A5920
____. Le mythe de la Renaissance, 1420-1520. 1969. A5921
Delevoy, R. L. Dimensions du XXe siècle. 1965. A5922
____. Dimensions of the 20th century. 1965. A5923
Duby, G. L'Europe des cathédrales, 1140-1280. 1966. A5924
____. The Europe of the cathedrals, 1140-1280. 1965. A5925
____. Fondements d'un nouvels humanisme, 1280-1440. 1966. A5926
____. Foundations of a new humanism, 1280-1440. 1966. A5927
____. The making of the Christian West, 980-1140. 1967. A5928
Keyser, E., ed. The romantic West, 1790-1850. 1965. A5929
Ponente, N. Les structures du monde moderne, 1850-1900. 1965. A5930
____. The structures of the modern world, 1850-1900. 1966. A5931
Starobinski, J. The invention of liberty, 1700-1789. 1965. A5932

ART OF THE WORLD: THE HISTORICAL, SOCIOLOGICAL AND RELIGIOUS BACKGROUNDS (Crown)

Akurgal, E. The art of Greece, tr. by Dynes. 1968. A5933
Art of the stone age, by Bandi and others, tr. by Keep. 1961. A5934
Aubert, M. The art of the High German era, tr. by Gorge. 1965. A5935
Bühler, A. and others. The art of the South Sea Islands. 1962. A5936
De Silva, A. The art of Chinese landscape painting. 1967. A5937
Disselhoff, H. D. and Linné, S. The art of ancient America, tr. by Keep. 1961. A5938
DuBourguet, P. The art of the Copts, tr. by Hay-Shaw, 1971. A5939
Evers, H. G. The art of the modern age, tr. by Foster. 1970. A5940
Fagg, W. B. Tribes and forms in African art. 1966. A5941
Goetz, H. India. 1959. A5942
Grabar, A. The art of the Byzantine Empire, tr. by Forster. 1966. A5943
Griswold, A. B. and others. The art of Burma, Korea, Tibet. 1964. A5944
Groslier, B. P. Indochina, tr. by Laurence. 1962. A5945
Haberland, W. The art of North America. 1964. A5946
Homann-Wedeking, E. The art of archaic Greece, tr. by Crown. 1968. A5947
Jettmar, K. Art of the Steppes, tr. by Keep. 1967. A5948
Kähler, H. The art of Rome and her empire, tr. by Foster. 1962. A5949
Lacy, A. D. Greek pottery in the Bronze age. 1967. A5950
Leuzinger, E. Africa, tr. by Keep. 1960. A5951
____. The art of Africa. 1968. A5952
Mansuelli, G. A. The art of

Etruria and early Rome, tr. by Ellis. 1965. A5953
Matz, F. The art of Crete and early Greece, tr. by Keep. 1962. A5954
Otto-Dorn, K. The art of Islam. 1969. A5955
Porada, E. and Dyson, R. H. The art of ancient Iran, pre-Islamic cultures. 1965. A5956
Schefold, K. The art of classical Greece, tr. by Foster. 1967. A5957
Seckel, D. The art of Buddhism, tr. by Keep. 1964. A5958
Silva-Vigier, A., ed. Chinese Landscape painting in the caves of Tun-huang. 1967. A5959
Speiser, W. The art of China, tr. by Laurence. 1960. A5960
Swann, P. C. The art of Japan. 1968. A5961
Verzone, P. The Dark Ages from Theodoric to Charlemagne. 1968. A5962
Wagner, F. A. Indonesia, tr. by Keep. 1959. A5963
Webster, T. B. L. The art of Greece. 1966. A5964
Wedeking, E. H. The art of archaic Greece. 1962. A5965
Woldering, I. The art of Egypt, tr. by Keep. 1962. A5966
Wooley, C. L. The art of the Middle East, tr. by Keep. 1961. A5967
____. Mesopotamia and the Middle East, tr. by Keep. 1961. A5968
Wuthenau, A. von. The art of terracotta pottery in pre-Columbian Central and South America, tr. by Nicholson. 1969. A5969

THE ARTS OF MANKIND (Golden Pr.)

1 Parrot, A. Sumer, the dawn of art, tr. by Gilbert and Emmons. 1961. A5970
2 ____. The arts of Assyria, ed. by Gilbert and Emmons. 1961. A5971
3 Ghirshman, R. Persian art, the Parthian and Sassanian dynasties, ed. by Gilbert and Emmons. 1962. A5972
4 Guiart, J. The arts of the South Pacific, tr. by Christie. 1963. A5973
5 Ghirshman, R. The arts of ancient Iran, tr. by Gilbert and Emmons. 1964. A5974
6 Demargne, P. The birth of Greek art, tr. by Gilbert and Emmons. 1964. A5975
7 Chastel, A. The flowering of the Italian Renaissance, ed. by Gilbert and Emmons. 1965. A5976
8 ____. The studios and styles of the Italian Renaissance, ed. by Gilbert and Emmons. 1966. A5977
9 Grabar, A. The golden age of Justinian, ed. by Gilbert and Emmons. 1967. A5978
10 ____. The early Christian art, ed. by Gilbert and Emmons. 1968. A5979
11 Leiris, M. and Delange, J., eds. The African art. 1968. A5980
12 Hubert, J. and others. Europe of the invasions. 1969. A5981
13 ____. The Carolingian Renaissance. 1970. A5982
14 Charbonneaux, J. and others. Archaic Greek art, 620-480 B.C. 1971. A5983
15 Bianchi Bandinelli, R. Rome, the center of power. 1970. A5984
16 Charbonneaux, J. and others. Classical Greek art, tr. by Emmons. 1972. A5985
17 Bianchi Bandinelli, R. Rome, the later Empire, tr. by Green. 1971. A5986
18 Charbonneaux, J. and others. Hellenistic art, tr. by Green. 1973. A5987

ASIA HISTORICAL SERIES (Asia Pub. House)

1 Singh, H. L. Problems and policies of the British in India, 1885-1898. 1963. A5988
2 Raj, J. The mutiny and British land policy in North India. 1967. A5989
3 Pandey, B. N. The introduction of English law into India. 1967. A5990

ASIA LIBRARY (Van Nostrand)

Busch, N. F. Thailand. 1964. A5991
McCune, S. B. Korea. 1966. A5992
Mintz, J. S. Indonesia. 1961. A5993
Ravenholt, A. The Philippines. 1962. A5994
Treisidder, A. J. Ceylon. 1960. A5995
Watkins, M. B. Afghanistan. 1963. A5996
Weekes, R. V. Pakistan. 1964. A5997

ASIA MONOGRAPHS (Asia Pub. House)

1 Chatterjee, B. Pulse circuits. 1963. A5998
2 Ganguli, P. K. Radiology of bone and joint tuberculosis... 1963. A5999
3 Chatterjee, B. Propagation of radio waves. 1963. A6000
4 Venkata Rao, P. Transient analysis of single-phase induction motors. 1964. A6001
5 Nair, P. K. K. Pollen grains of Western Himalayan plants. 1965. A6002
6 Ford, J. L. The Ohlin-Heckscher theory of the basis and effects of commodity trade. 1965. A6003
7 Viswanathan, K. S. The many-electron problem. 1966. A6004
8 Bose, P. K. and Choudhury, S. B. On some problems associated with D-2 statistics and p-statistics. 1966. A6005
9 Dasoyan, K. A. and Aguf, I. A. The lead accumulator. 1966. A6006
10 Ramana, D. V. National accounts and input-output account of India. 1969. A6007
11 Sherwani, H. K. Muhammed-Qulī Qutb Shāh. 1967. A6008
12 Venkataraman, K. I. Local finance in perspective. 1965. A6009
13 Freeman, J. B. Assignments in mathematics. 1966. A6010
15 Raghunath, H. M. Dimensional analysis and hydraulic model testing. 1967. A6011
16 Henderson, K. M. Emerging synthesis in American public administration. 1966. A6012
18 Kurien, C. T. A theoretical approach to Indian economy. 1970. A6013
19 Katz, S. S. External assistance and Indian economic growth. 1969. A6014

ASIAN CIVILIZATION (Prentice-Hall)

Bastin, J. S. The emergence of modern Southeast Asia. 1967. A6015
Chavarrin-Aguilar, O. L., ed. Traditional India. 1964. A6016
Feuerwerker, A., ed. Modern China. 1964. A6017
Liu, J. T. C. and Tu, W., eds. Traditional China. 1970. A6018
Stewart-Robinson, J., ed. The traditional Near East. 1966. A6019

ASIATIC SOCIETY OF PAKISTAN. PUBLICATIONS

1 Bessaignet, P. Tribesmen of the Chittagong Tracts. 1958. A6020
2 Karim, A. Social history of the Muslims in Bengal. 1959. A6021
3 Dacca, Pakistan University Library. A descriptive catalogue of Bengali manuscripts in Munshi Abdul Karim's collection, by Karim and Sharif. 1960. A6022
4 Ni'mat Allah. Tarīkh-i Khān Johānī. V. 1. 1960. A6023
5 Bessaignet, P., ed. Social research in East Pakistan. 1964. A6024
6 Karim, A. Corpus of the Muslim coins of Bengal. 1960. A6025
7 Dani, A. H. Muslim architecture in Bengal. 1961. A6026
8 Ahmad Khan, M., ed. Selections from Bengal government records or Wahhabi trials (1863-1870). 1961. A6027

9 Mallick, A. R. British policy and the Muslim in Bengal, 1757-1856. 1961. A6028
10 Same as no. 4. V. 2. 1962. A6029
11 Imamuddin, S. M. The economic history of Spain under the Umayyads, 711-1031 A. D. 1963. A6030
12 Karim, A. Murshid Quli Khān and his times. 1963. A6031
13 Bhuiyan, A. L. Fishes of Dacca. 1964. A6032
14 Huq, M. The East Indian Company's land policy and commerce in Bengal, 1698-1784. 1964. A6033
15 Karim, A. Dacca. 1964. A6034
16 Tarafdar, M. R. Husain Shahi Bengal, 1494-1538. 1965. A6035
17 Muhammad Shahidullah felicitation volume, ed. by Haq. 1966. A6036
18 Huq, M. M. Electorial problems in Pakistan. 1966. A6037
19 Abu Imam. Sir Alexander Cunningham and the beginnings of Indian archaeology. 1966. A6038
20 Harun-er-Rashid. A systematic list of the birds of East Pakistan. 1967. A6039
21 Chowdhury, A. M. Dynastic history of Bengal, c 750-1200 A. D. 1967. A6040
22 Khair, M. A. United States policy in Indo-Pak Sub-continent. 1968. A6041
23 Hussain, S. Everyday life in Pala empire. 1968. A6042
24 Shamsuddin Mish, M. The reign of Al-Mutawakkil. 1969. A6043
25 Ahmed, Z. U. Al-Masnad Min Masa'il Abd Allah B. Muhammed B. Hanbal. 1969. A6044
26 Hussain, A. B. M. The Manara in Indo-Muslim architecture. 1969. A6045

ASPECTS OF GREEK AND ROMAN LIFE (Cornell Univ. Pr.)

Bickerman, E. J. Chronology of the ancient world. 1968. A6046
Burford, A. Craftsmen in Greek and Roman society. 1972. A6047
Crook, J. Law and life of Rome. 1967. A6048
Dicks, A. R. Early Greek astronomy before Aristotle. 1970. A6049
Earl, D. The moral and political tradition of Rome. 1967. A6050
Ferguson, J. The religions of the Roman Empire. 1970. A6051
Ferguson, U. Utopias of the classical world. 1974. A6052
Hands, A. N. Charities and social aid in Greece and Rome. 1968. A6053
Harris, H. A. Sport in Greece and Rome. 1972. A6054
Kurtz, D. C. and Broadman, J. Greek burial customs. 1971. A6055
Lacey, W. K. The family in classical Greece. 1968. A6056
Phillips, E. D. Greek medicine. 1973. A6057
Rossi, L. Trajan's column and the Dacian Wars. 1970. A6058
Salmon, E. T. Roman colonization under the Republic. 1970. A6059
Scarborough, J. Roman medicine. 1970. A6060
Scullard, H. H. The elephant in the Greek and Roman world. 1974. A6061
____. The Etruscan cities and Rome. 1967. A6062
____. Scipio Africanus. 1970. A6063
Snodgrass, A. M. Arms and armour of the Greeks. 1967. A6064
Staveley, E. S. Greek and Roman voting and elections. 1972. A6065
Toynbee, J. M. C. Animals in Roman life and art. 1973. A6066
____. Death and burial in the Roman world. 1970. A6067
Watson, G. R. The Roman soldier. 1969. A6068
White, K. D. Roman farming. 1970. A6069
Witt, R. E. Isis in the Graeco-Roman world. 1971. A6070

ASSOCIATION FOR ASIAN STUDIES. MONOGRAPHS AND PAPERS. (1 and 2 published as FAR EASTERN ASSOCIATION. MONOGRAPHS. 3-10 as ASSOCIATION FOR ASIAN STUDIES. MONOGRAPH AND PAPERS) (1-10 Augustin; 11- Univ. of Arizona Pr.)

1 Brown, D. M. Money economy in medieval Japan. 1951. A6071
2 Ch'ou pan i wu shih mo. China's management of the American barbarians, ed. by Swisher. 1953. A6072
3 Skinner, G. W. Leadership and power in the Chinese community of Thailand. 1958. A6073
4 Vella, W. F. Siam under Rama III, 1824-1851. 1957. A6074
5 Sheldon, C. D. The rise of the merchant class in Tokugawa, Japan, 1600-1868. 1958. A6075
6 Comber, L. Chinese secret societies in Malaya. 1959. A6076
7 Liu, H. The traditional Chinese clan rules. 1959. A6077
8 Beidelman, T. O. A comparative analysis of the jajmani system. 1959. A6078
9 Parmer, J. N. Colonial labor policy and administration. 1960. A6079
10 Kaufman, H. K. Bangkhuad. 1960. A6080
11 Geertz, C. Agricultural involution. Univ. of Calif. Pr. 1964. A6081
12 Gang ārāma. The Mahārāshta Purāna, tr. by Dimock and Gupta. East-West Center Pr., 1964. A6082
13 Henderson, D. F. Conciliation and Japanese law, Tokugawa and modern. 2 v. Univ. of Washington Pr., 1965. A6083
14 Wong, L. K. The Malayan tin industry to 1914. 1965. A6084
15 Weems, B. B. Reform, rebellion, and the heavenly way. 1964. A6085
16 Lee, P. H. Korean literature. 1965. A6086
17 Choe, P. Diary, tr. by Meskill. 1965. A6087
18 Tregonning, K. G. The British in Malaya. 1965. A6088
19 Chambliss, W. J. Chiaraijima village. 1965. A6089
20 Bloom, A. Shinran's gospel of pure grace. 1965. A6090
21 Presseisen, E. L. Before aggression. 1965. A6091
22 Fu, L.-S. A documentary chronicle of Sino-western relations (1644-1820). 2 v. 1966. A6092
23 K'ang Yu-wei; a biography and a symposium, ed. and tr. by Lo. 1967. A6093
24 Wenk, K. The restoration of Thailand under Rama I. 1968. A6094
25 Morrison, B. Political and religious change in Bengal. 1969. A6095
26 Parsons, J. B. Peasant rebellions of the late Ming Dynasty. 1969. A6096
27 Suntharalingam, R. Politics and nationalist awakening in South India. 1974. A6097

THE ASSOCIATION OF AMERICAN GEOGRAPHERS. MONOGRAPHS (Rand McNally)

1 Hartshorne, R. Perspective on the nature of geography. 1959. A6098
2 Meinig, D. W. On the margins of the good earth. 1962. A6099
3 Alexander, L. M. Offshore geography of northwestern Europe. 1963. A6100
4 Thrower, N. J. W. Original survey and land subdivision. 1966. A6101
5 Harris, C. D. Cities of the Soviet Union. 1970. A6102
6 Buttimer, A. Society and milieu in the French geographic tradition. 1971. A6103

ASSOCIATION OF COLLEGE AND RESEARCH LIBRARIES. ACRL PUBLICATIONS IN LIBRARIANSHIP (1-33 published as: ACRL MONOGRAPHS)

1 Kraus, J. W. William Beer and the New Orleans libraries, 1891-1927. 1952. A6104
2 Kaplan, L. The growth of reference service in the United States from 1876 to 1893. 1952. A6105
3 Herner, S. and Heatwole, M. K. The establishment of staff requirements in a small research library. 1952. A6106
4 Association of College and Reference Libraries. Proceedings of the meeting [of the] library building plans institute. V. 1. 1952. A6107
5 Jackson, E. P. Administration of the government documents collection. 1953. A6108
6 Stevens, R. E. Characteristics of subject literatures. 1953. A6109
7 Broadus, R. N. The research literature of the field of speech. 1953. A6110
8 Kinney, M. R. Bibliographical style manuals. 1953. A6111
9 Association of College and Reference Libraries. A recommended list of basic periodicals in engineering and the engineering sciences, comp. by Hyde. 1953. A6112
10-11 Same as 4. V. 2, 3. A6113
12 Esterquest, R. T. Library cooperation in the British Isles. 1955. A6114
13 Conference of Eastern College Librarians. Library instructional integration on the college level. 1955. A6115
14 Rothstein, S. The development of reference service through academic traditions, public library practice and special librarianship. 1955. A6116
15 Same as no. 4. Proceedings 2, 3. 1955. A6117
16 Brown, C. H. Scientific serials. 1956. A6118
17 Conference of Eastern College Librarians. Recruiting of librarians; automation in the library. 1956. A6119
18 Hastings, H. C. Spoken poetry on records and tapes. 1957. A6120
19 Poole's index to periodical literature (Indexes). Poole's index, date and volume key, comp. by Bell and Bacon. 1957. A6121
20 Association of College and Reference Libraries. Comm. on Standards. College and university library standards, comp. by Oboler and others. 1958. A6122
21 Reagan, A. L. A study of factors influencing college students to become librarians. 1958. A6123
22 Downs, R. B., ed. The status of American college and university librarians. 1958. A6124
23 Knapp, P. College teaching and the college library. 1959. A6125
24 Voight, M. J. Scientist's approaches to information. 1961. A6126
25 Erickson, E. W. College and university library surveys, 1938-1952. 1961. A6127
26 Ranz, J. The printed book catalogue in American libraries: 1723-1900. 1964. A6128
27 Archer, H. R., ed. Rare book collections. 1965. A6129
28 Kinney, M. R. The abbreviated citation. 1967. A6130
29 Morrison, P. D. Career of the academic librarian. 1969. A6131
30 Conference on Junior College Libraries. Junior College libraries, ed. by Moore. 1969. A6132
31 Braden, I. A. Undergraduate library. 1969. A6133
32 Thomson, S. K. Interlibrary loan involving academic libraries. 1970. A6134
33 Branscomb, L. C., ed. The case for faculty status for librarians. 1971. A6135
34 Grove, P. S. Nonprint media in academic libraries.

1974. A6136

35 Laugher, C. T. Thomas Bray's grand design. 1973. A6137

36 Churchwell, C. D. Shaping of American library education. 1974. A6138

ATLANTIC POLICY STUDIES (McGraw)

Balassa, B. Trade liberalization among industrial countries. 1967. A6139

Brezezinski, Z. K. Alternative to partition. 1965. A6140

Camps, M. European unification in the sixties. 1966. A6141

Cleveland, H. van B. The Atlantic idea and its European rivals. 1966. A6142

Cooper, R. N. The economics of interdependence. 1968. A6143

Coppock, J. O. Atlantic agricultural unity. 1966. A6144

Geiger, T. The conflicted relationship. 1967. A6145

Hoffmann, S. Gulliver's troubles. 1968. A6146

Kissinger, H. A. The troubled partnership. 1965. A6147

Pincus, J. Trade, aid and development. 1967. A6148

AUGUSTAN REPRINT SOCIETY. PUBLICATIONS.

1 Blackmore, R. Sir Richard Blackmore's Essay upon wit (1716) and Joseph Addison's Freeholder, no. 46(1716), ed. by Boys. 1946. A6149

2 Cobb, S. Discourse on criticism and of poetry from Poems on several occasions (1707) ed. by Bredvold. 1946. A6150

3 A letter to A. H. Esq. [i. e. Anthony Hammond] concerning the stage (1698) and The occasional paper: no. IX (1698), ed. by Swedenberg. 1946. A6151

4 Essay on wit (1748)... Hooker. 1946. A6152

5 Wesley, S. Epistle to a friend concerning poetry (1700) and the Essay on heroic poetry, ed. by Hooker. 1947. A6153

6 Representation of the impiety and the immortality of the English stage (1704)..., ed. by Avery. 1947. A6154

7 Gay, J. The present stage of wit (1711), ed. by Bond. 1947. A6155

8 Rapin, R. De carmine pastorali prefixed to Thomas Creech's translation of the Idylliums of Theocritus (1684), ed. by Congleton. 1947. A6156

9 Hanmer, T. Some remarks on the tragedy of Hamlet..., ed. by Thorpe. 1947. A6157

10 Morris, C. An essay towards fixing the true standards of wit, humour, raillery, satire, and ridicule (1744), ed. by Clifford. 1947. A6158

11 Purney, T. A full enquiry into the true nature of pastoral (1717), ed. by Wasserman. 1948. A6159

12 D'Urfey, T. Preface to The campaigners (1698)..., ed. by Krutch. 1948. A6160

13 Falstaffe, J. The theatre (1720), ed. by Loftis. 1948. A6161

14 Moore, E. The gamester (1753), ed. by Peake. 1948. A6162

15 Oldmixon, J. Reflections on Dr. Swift's letter to Harley (1712); and Arthur Mainwaring, The British Academy (1712), ed. by Landa. 1948. A6163

16 Payne, H. N. The fatal jealousie (1673), ed. by Thorp. 1948. A6164

17 Rowe, N. Some account of the life of Mr. William Shakespear (1709), ed. by Monk. 1948. A6165

18 "Of genius," in The Occasional Paper, ed. by Pahl. 1949. A6166

19 Centlivre, S. The busie body (1709), ed. by Byrd. 1949. A6167

20 Theobald, L. Preface to The works of Shakespeare (1734), ed. by Dick. 1949. A6168

21 Critical remarks on Sir Charles Grandison, Clarissa, and Pamela (1754). 1950. A6169

22 Johnson, S. Samuel Johnson: The vanity of human wishes (1749) and Two Rambler papers (1750), ed. by Bronson. 1950. A6170

23 Dryden, J. His Majesties declaration defended (1681), ed. by Davies. 1950. A6171

24 Nicole, P. An essay on true and apparent beauty in which from settled principles is rendered the grounds for choosing and rejecting epigrams, tr. by Cunningham. 1950. A6172

25 Baker, T. The fine lady's airs (1709), ed. by Smith. 1950. A6173

26 Macklin, C. The man of the world (1792), ed. by MacMillan. 1951. A6174

27 Reynolds, F. An enquiry concerning the principles of taste..., ed. by Clifford. 1951. A6175

28 Evelyn, J. An apologie for the royal party (1659), and A panegyric to Charles the Second (1661), ed. by Keynes. 1951. A6176

29 Defoe, D. A vindication of the press (1718), ed. by Williams. 1951. A6177

30 Cooper, J. G. Essays on taste from Letters concerning taste, 3d edition (1757) & John Armstrong Miscellanies (1770), ed. by Cohen. 1951. A6178

31 Gray, T. An elegy wrote in a country church yard (1751) and The Eton College manuscript, ed. by Sherburn. 1951. A6179

32 Prefaces to fiction..., ed. by Boyce. 1952. A6180

33 Gally, H. A critical essay on characteristic-writings..., ed. by Chorney. 1952. A6181

34 Tyers, T. A biographical sketch of Dr. Samuel Johnson (1785), ed. by Meyer. 1952. A6182

35 Boswell, J. Critical strictures on the New Tragedy of Elvira..., (1763), ed. by Pottle. 1952. A6183

36 Harris, J. The city bride (1696). ed. by Dearing. 1952. A6184

37 Morrison, T. A Pindarick ode on painting, addressed to Joshua Reynolds, Esq. (1767)... intro. by Kirkwood. 1952. A6185

38 Phillips, J. A satyr against hypocrites (1655)... intro. by Howard. 1953. A6186

39 Warton, T. A history of English poetry, ed. by Baine. 1953. A6187

40 Bysshe, E. The art of English poetry (1708)... intro. by Culler. 1953. A6188

41 Mandeville, B. A letter to Dion, 1732... intro. by Viner. 1953. A6189

42 Prefaces to four seventeenth-century romances... intro. by Davies. 1953. A6190

43 Baillie, J. An essay on the sublime (1747)... intro. by Monk. 1953. A6191

44 Sarbiewski, M. K. The odes of Casimire, tr. by Hils (1646). 1953. A6192

45 Scott, J. R. Dissertation on the progress of the fine arts... intro. by Pearce. 1954. A6193

46 Selections from seventeenth-century songbooks... intro. by Angel. 1954. A6194

47 Contemporaries of the Tatler and Spectator... intro. by Bond. 1954. A6195

48 Richardson, S. Samuel Richardson's introduction to Pamela, ed. by Baker. 1954. A6196

49 Estwick, S. The usefulness of church musick, a sermon, 1696... intro. by Phillips. 1955. A6197

50 Aston, H. H. A sermon preached at the Cathedral Church of Saint Paul... intro. by Clifford. 1955. A6198

51 Maidwell, L. An essay upon the necessity and excellency of education (1705)... intro. by Patrick. 1955. A6199

52 Stampoy, P. A collection of Scotch proverbs (1663)... intro. by Taylor. 1955. A6200

53 Oakes, U. The soveraign efficacy of divine providence (1682)... intro. by Blau.

1955. A6201
54 Davys, M. Familiar letters betwixt a gentleman and a lady (1725)... intro. by Day. 1955. A6202
55 Say, S. An essay on the harmony, variety, and power of numbers (1745)... intro. by Fussell. 1956. A6203
56 Theologia ruris, sive schola et scala naturae (1686)... intro. by Ogden. 1956. A6204
57 Fielding, H. An apology for the life of Mrs. Shamela Andrews (1741)... intro. by Watt. 1956. A6205
58 Hofer, P., comp. Eighteenth-century book illustrations. 1956. A6206
59-60 Johnson, S. Notes to Shakespeare, 2 v., ed. by Sherbo. 1956. A6207
61 Elstob, E. An apology for the study of northern antiquities, 1715... intro. by Peake. 1956. A6208
62 Huntley, F. L., ed. Two funeral sermons, 1635. 1956. A6209
63 Parodies of ballad criticism (1711-1787), ed. by Wimsatt. 1957. A6210
64 Prefaces to three eighteenth-century novels (1708-1751-1797), ed. by Jones. 1957. A6211
65-66 Same as 59-60. 2 v. 1957. A6212
67 Fielding, H. The voyages of Mr. Job Vinegar, from the Champion, 1740, ed. by Sackett. 1958. A6213
68 Settle, E. The nctorious impostor; part one (1692), ed. by Peterson. 1958. A6214
69 Marforio pseud. An historical view of the... political writers in Great Britain (1740), ed. by Haig. 1958. A6215
70 Magazine, or, Animadversions on the English spelling (1703), by G. W. 1958. A6216
71-73 Same as 59-60. V. 2, V. 3: Pts. 1-3. 1958. A6217
74 Westcott, I. M., ed. Seventeenth century tales of the supernatural. 1958. A6218
75 Joyne, J. A journal (1769 [i. e.] 1679) ed. by Hughes. 1959. A6219
76 Dacier, A. The preface to Aristotle's Art of poetry (1705). 1959. A6220
77-78 Hartley, D. Various conjectures on the perception, motion, and generation of ideas (1746), tr. by Palmer. 1959. A6221
79 Pembroke, W. H. Poems (1660), ed. by Onderwyzer. 1959. A6222
80 Whalley, P. An essay on the manner of writing history, ed. by Stewart. 1960. A6223
81 Gulick, S. L., ed. Two burlesques of Lord Chesterfield's letters. 1960. A6224
82 Fuseli, H. Remarks on the writing and conduct of J. J. Rousseau (1767), ed. by Guthke. 1960. A6225
83 Jones, W. P., ed. Sawney and Colley (1742) and other Pope pamphlets. 1960. A6226
84 Savage, R. An author to be lett (1729), ed. by Sutherland. 1960. A6227
85-86 Loftis, J. C., ed. Essays on the theatre from eighteenth-century periodicals. 1960. A6228
87 Defoe, D. Of Captain Mission, ed. by Novak. 1961. A6229
88 Butler, S. Three poems, ed. by Spence. 1961. A6230
89 Fielding, H. The lover's assistant, or, new art of love (1790), ed. by Jones. 1961. A6231
90 Needler, H. Works (1728), ed. by Allentuck. 1961. A6232
91-92 Gay, J. Three hours after marriage (1717), ed. by Smith. 2 v. 1961. A6233
93 Norris, J. Cursory reflections upon a book call'd, An essay concerning human understanding (1690), ed. by McEwen. 1961. A6234
94 Collins, A. Divine songs and meditacions (1653), ed. by Stewart. 1961. A6235
95 An essay on the species of writing founded by Mr. Fielding (1751), ed. by

McKillop. 1962. A6236
96 McAleer, J. J., ed. Hanoverian ballads. 1962. A6237
97 Davies, M. Athenae Britannicae, 1716-1719, ed. by Thomas. 1962. A6238
98 Herbert, G. Select hymns taken out of Mr. Herbert's Temple, 1697. 1962. A6239
99 Arne, T. A. Artaxerxes. 1963. A6240
100 Patrick, S. A brief account of the new sect of latitude-men (1662), ed. by Berrill. 1963. A6241
101-102 Hurd, R. de. Letters on chivalry and romance (1762), ed. by Trowbridge. 1963. A6242
103 Richardson, S. Clarissa, ed. by Brissenden. 1964. A6243
104 D'Urfey, T. Wonders in the sun, ed. by Appleton. 1964. A6244
105 Mandeville, B. An enquiry into the causes of the frequent executions at Tyburn (1725), ed. by Zirker. 1964. A6245
106 Defoe, D. A brief history of the poor Palatine refugees (1719), ed. by Moore. 1964. A6246
107-108 Oldmoxon, J. An essay on criticism (1728), ed. by Madden. 1964. A6247
109 Temple, W. An essay upon the original and nature of government (1680), ed. by Steensma. 1964. A6248
110 Tutchin, J. Selected poems, 1685-1700, ed. by Peterson. 1964. A6249
111 Political justice, ed. by Pollin and Wilkes. 1965. A6250
112 Dodsley, R. A. An essay on fable, ed. by Welcher and Dircks. 1965. A6251
113 An essay concerning critical and curious learning by T. R., ed. by Zimansky. 1965. A6252
114 Two poems against Pope, ed. by Guerinot. 1965. A6253
115 Accounts of the apparition of Mrs. Veal, by Defoe, ed. by Schonhorn. 1965. A6254
116 Macklin, C. The Covent Garden Theatre, ed. by Kern. 1965. A6255
117 L'Estrange, R. Citt and Bumpkin (1680), ed. by Rahn. 1965. A6256
118 More, H. Enthusiasmus triumphatus (1662), ed. by De Porte. 1966. A6257
119 Traherne, T. Meditations on the creation (1717), ed. by Guffey. 1966. A6258
120 Mandevilla, B. Aesop dress'd; or a collection of fables (1704), ed. by Shea. 1966. A6259
121 Headley, H. Poems (1786), ed. by Spacks. 1966. A6260
122 Macpherson, J. Fragments of ancient poetry (1760), ed. by Dunn. 1966. A6261
123 Malone, E. Cursory observations on the poems attributed to Thomas Rawlye (1782), ed. by Kuist. 1966. A6262
124 The female wits (1704), ed. by Hook. 1967. A6263
125 The scribleriad (1742). The difference between verbal and practical virtue, by Lord Harvey (1742). 1967. A6264
126 Boileau-Despréaux, N. Le lutrin (1682), ed. by Morton. 1967. A6265
127-128 Macklin, C. A will and no will (1746), ed. by Kern. 1967. A6266
129 Echard, L. Prefaces to Terence's Comedies (1694) and Plautus's Comedies (1694). 1968. A6267
130 More, H. Democritus Platonissans (1646), ed. by Stanwood. 1968. A6268
131 Evelyn, J. The history of... Sabatai Sevi... The suppos'd Messiah of the Jews (1169). 1968. A6269
132 Harte, W. An essay on satire, ed. by Gilmore. 1968. A6270
133 Courtenay, J. A poetical review of the literary and moral character of the late Samuel Johnson (1786), ed. by Kelley. 1969. A6271
134 Downes, J. Roscius

Anglicanus (1708), ed. by Loftis. 1969. A6272
135 Hill, J. Hypochondriasis (1776), ed. by Rousseau. 1969. A6273
136 Sheridan, T. Discourse (1759), ed. by Mohrman. 1969. A6274
137 Murphy, A. The English from Paris (1756), ed. by Trefman. 1969. A6275
138 Trotter, C. Olinda's adventures (1718), ed. by Day. 1969. A6276
139 Ogilvie, J. An essay on the lyric poetry of the ancients, (1762), ed. by Jackson. 1970. A6277
140 Carey, H. A. Learned dissertation on dumpling, ed. by Macey. 1970. A6278
141 L'Estrange, R. Selections from The observator, (1681-1687), ed. by Jordain. 1970. A6279
142 Collins, A. A discourse concerning ridicule and irony in writing (1729), ed. by E. A. and L. D. Bloom. 1970. A6280
143 A letter from a clergyman to his friend (1726), ed. by Kallech. 1970. A6281
144 Gwynn, J. The art of architecture (1742), ed. by Gibson. 1970. A6282
145-146 Shelton, T. A tutor to tachygraphy (1642), ed. by Matthew. 1970. A6283
147-148 Callender, J. T. Deformities of Dr. Samuel Johnson (1782), ed. by Kolb and Congreton. 1971. A6284
149 Poeta de tristibus (1682), ed. by Love. 1971. A6285
150 Langbaine, G. Momus triumphane (1688), ed. by Rodes. 1971. A6286
151-152 Lloyd, E. The Methodist (1766), ed. by Bentman. 1972. A6287
153 Miller, J. Are these things so? (1740), ed. by Gordon. 1972. A6288
154 Arbuthnotiana: The story of the St. Alb-ns ghost (1712), and A catalogue of Dr. Arbuthnot's library (1779). 1972. A6289
155-156 A selection of emblems from Herman Hugo's Pia Desideria (1624), ed. by Quarles and Arwaker. 1972. A6290
157 Mountford, W. The life and death of Doctor Faustus (1697), ed. by Kaufman. 1972. A6291
158 Cibber, C. A letter from Mr. Cibber, to Mr. Pope (1972), ed. by Koon. 1973. A6292
159 Clive, C. The case of Mrs. Clive (1744), ed. by Frushell. 1973. A6293
160 Tyron, T. A discourse... of phrensie, madness of distraction from A treatise of dreams and visions (1689), ed. by DePorte. 1973. A6294
161 Blair, R. The grave (1743), ed. by Means. 1973. A6295
162 Mandeville, B. A modest defence of publick stews (1724), ed. by Cook. 1973. A6296
163 Rider, W. An historical and critical account of the lives and writings of the living authors of Great Britain (1762), ed. by Brack. 1974. A6297
164 Edwards, T. The sonnets of Thomas Edwards (1765, 1780), ed. by Donovan. 1974. A6298
165 Jacob, H. Of the sister arts (1734), ed. by Schweizer. 1974. A6299
166 Miner, E., ed. Poems on the reign of William III (1690, 1696, 1699, 1702). 1974. A6300
167 O'Hara, K. Midas (1766), ed. by Dircks. 1974. A6301
168 Defoe, D. A short narrative history of the life and actions of His Grace John D. of Marlborough (1711), ed. by Backscheider. 1974. A6302

AUGUSTANA COLLEGE, ROCK ISLAND, ILL. DENKMANN MEMORIAL LIBRARY. AUGUSTANA LIBRARY PUBLICATIONS (Augustana Coll.)

1 Udden, J. A. The mechanical composition of wind deposits. 1898. A6303
2 ____. An old Indian village. 1900. A6304
3 Andreen, G. A. A study in the idyl in German literature. 1902. A6305
4 Udden, J. A. On the cyclonic distribution of rainfall. 1905. A6306
5 Anderson, N. C. A preliminary list of fossil mastodon and mammoth remains in Illinois and Iowa. 1905. A6307
Udden, J. A. Proboscidian fossils of the pleistocene deposits in Illinois and Iowa. 1905. A6308
6 Rydberg, P. A. Scandinavians who have contributed to the knowledge of the flora of North America. 1907. A6309
Udden, J. A. A geological survey of lands belonging to the New York and Texas land company, Ltd., in the upper Rio Grande embayment in Texas. 1907. A6310
7 Olsson-Seffer, P. H. Genesis and development of sand formations on marine coasts. 1910. A6311
____. The sand strand flora of marine coasts. 1910. A6312
8 Boström, O. H. Alternative readings in the Hebrew of the books of Samuel. 1918. A6313
9 Cederberg, W. E. On the solution of the differential equations of motion of a double pendulum. 1923. A6314
10 Joranson, E. The danegeld in France. 1923. A6315
11 Lugn, A. L. Sedimentation in the Mississippi River between Davenport, Iowa, and Cairo, Illinois. 1927. A6316
12 Tilberg, F. The development of commerce between the United States and Sweden, 1870-1925. 1930. A6317
13 Fryxell, F. M. Glacial features of Jackson Hole, Wyoming. 1930. A6318
14 Ander, O. F. T. N. Hasselquist, the career and influence of a Swedish-American clergyman, journalist and educator. 1931. A6319
15 Schersten, A. F. The relation of the Swedish-American newspaper to the assimilation of Swedish immigrants. 1935. A6320
16 Horberg, L. Structural geology and physiography of the Teton Pass area, Wyoming. 1938. A6321
17 Johnson, R. A. The Mexican revolution of Ayutla, 1854-1855. 1939. A6322
18 Nelson, V. E. The structural geology of the Cache Creek area, Gros Ventre mountains, Wyoming. 1942. A6323
19 Björck, T. E. The planting of the Swedish church in America. 1943. A6324
20 Bozeman, B. Regional conflicts around Geneva. 1949. A6325
21 Swenson, F. A. Geology of the northwest flank of the Gros Ventre Mountains, Wyoming. 1949. A6326
22 Naeseth, H. C. K. The Swedish theatre of Chicago 1869-1951. 1951. A6327
23 Edmund, R. W. Structural geology and physiography of the northern end of the Teton range, Wyoming. 1951. A6328
24 Nelson, H. E. The resistance of the air to stone-dropping meteors. 1953. A6329
25 Hamming, E. The port of Milwaukee. 1953. A6330
26 Augustana College, Rock Island, Ill. The John H. Hauberg historical essays, comp. and ed. by Ander. 1954. A6331
27 Ander, O. F. The cultural heritage of the Swedish immigrant. 1956. A6332
28 ____. The building of modern Sweden. 1958. A6333
29 Augustana College, Rock Island, Ill. Lincoln images,

ed. by Ander. 1960. A6334
30 Bengston, J. R. Nazi war aims. 1962. A6335
31 Ander, O. F., ed. In the trek of the immigrants. 1964. A6336
32 Arbaugh, G. E. and G. B. Kierkegaard's authorship. 1967. A6337
33 Bergendorff, C. Augustana--a profession of faith. 1969. A6338

AUGUSTANA HISTORICAL SOCIETY. PUBLICATIONS

1 Ander, O. F. T. N. Hasselquist. 1931. A6339
2 Andreen, G. The early missionary work of the Augustana synod in New York City. 1932. A6340
3 Olson, E. W. Augustana book concern. 1933. A6341
4 Norelius, E. Early life of Eric Norelius, tr. by Johnson. 1934. A6342
5 Stephenson, G. M. C. W. Foss. 1935. A6343
6 Swan, G. N. Swedish-American literary publications. 1936. A6344
7 Stephenson, G. M., ed. Letters relating to Gustaf Unonius and the early Swedish settlers in Wisconsin. 1937. A6345
8:1 Hansen, M. L. The problem of the third generation immigrant. 1938. A6346
8:2 Olson, E. W. Olof Olsson. 1941. A6347
9 Ander, O. F. and Nordstrom, O. L. The American origin of the Augustana synod. 1942. A6348
10-11 Augustana Historical Society. Selected documents dealing with the organization of the first congregations, ed. by Northstein. 2 v. 1944-46. A6349
12 Maeseth, H. C. K. The Swedish theatre of Chicago, 1868-1950. 1951. A6350
13 Lindquist, E. K. Smoky Valley people. 1953. A6351
14 Olson, O. N. Olof Christian Telemak Andrén. 1954. A6352
15 ____. Swärd-Johnston. 1955. A6353
16 ____. Anders Jonasson Lindström. 1957. A6354
17 Lawson, E. B. Two primary sources for a study of the life of Jonas Swensson. 1957. A6355
18 Dowie, J. I. Prairie grass dividing. 1959. A6356
19 Lilljeholm, J. E. Pioneering adventures of Johan Edvard Lilljeholm in America, tr. by Wald. 1962. A6357
20 Augustana Historical Society. The Swedish immigrant community in transition, ed. by Dowie and Espelie. 1963. A6358
21 ____. The immigration of ideas, ed. by Dowie and Tredway. 1968. A6359
22 Lindquist, E. Vision for a valley. 1970. A6360
23 ____. An immigrant's two worlds. 1972. A6361

AUSTEN RIGGS CENTER INC., STOCKBRIDGE, MASS. MONOGRAPH (Columbia Univ. Pr.)

Rapaport, D., ed. and comp. Organizations and pathology of thought. Columbia Univ. 1951. A6362
2 Gill, M. M. and Brennan, M. Hypnosis and related states. Int'l. Universities. 1959. A6363
3 Schafer, R. Psychoanalytic interpretation in Rorschach testing. Grune. 1954. A6364
4 Erikson, E. Young man Luther. Norton. 1958. A6365
5 Shapiro, D. Neurotic styles. 1965. A6366
6 Edelson, M. Sociotherapy and psychotherapy. 1970. A6367

AUSTRALIAN NATIONAL UNIVERSITY. SOCIAL SCIENCE MONOGRAPHS (Melbourne Univ. Pr.)

1 McArthur, N. Genetics of twinning. 1953. A6367a
2 Butlin, N. G. and DeMeel, H. Public capital formation

BACKGROUND TO THE BIBLE SERIES (Prentice-Hall)

Hunt, I. The world of the Patriarchs. 1967. B1
McKenzie, J. L. The world of the Judges. 1967. B2
Maly, E. The world of David and Solomon. 1967. B3
Myers, J. The world of the Restoration. 1968. B4
O'Rourke, J. The Johannine world. 1966. B5

BAMPTON LECTURES.

1780 Bandinel, J. Eight sermons preached before the University of Oxford in the year 1780. Prince. 1780. B6
1781 Neve, T. Eight sermons preached before the University of Oxford in the year 1781. Prince. 1781. B7
1782 Holmes, R. On the prophecies and the testimony of John the Baptist. Prince. 1782. B8
1783 Cobb, J. Eight sermons preached before the University of Oxford in the year 1783. Oxford. 1783. B9
1784 White, J. Sermons preached before the University of Oxford in the year 1784. Robinson. 1785. B10
1785 Churton, R. Eight sermons on the prophecies respecting the destruction of Jerusalem. Fletcher. 1785. B11
1786 Croft, G. Eight sermons preached before the University of Oxford in the year 1786. Cooke. 1786. B12
1787 Hawkins, W. Discourses on Scriptur mysteries. Cooke. 1787. B13
1788 Shepherd, R. The grounds and credibility of the Christian religion. Davis. 1788. B14
1789 Tatham, E. The chart and scale of truth. 2 v. Fletcher. 1789. B15
1790 Kett, H. Sermons preached before the University of Oxford at St. Mary's. Fletcher. 1791. B16
1791 Morres, R. Eight sermons preached before the University of Oxford in the year MDCCXCI. Fletcher. 1791. B17
1792 Eveleigh, J. Sermons preached before the University of Oxford in the year 1792. Cooke. 1794. B18
1793 Williamson, J. The truth, inspiration, authority and end of the Scriptures. Cooke. 1793. B19
1794 Wintle, T. The expediency, prediction, and accomplishment of the Christian redemption illustrated. Cooke. 1794. B20
1795 Veysie, D. The doctrine of atonement illustrated and defended. Fletcher. 1795. B21
1796 Gray, R. Sermons on the principles upon which the reformation of the Church of England was established. Rivington. 1796. B22
1797 Finch, W. The objections of infidel historians and other writers against Christianity. Oxford. 1797. B23
1798 Hall, C. H. Sermons preached before the University of Oxford... in the year

MDCCXCVIII. Oxford. 1799. B24

1799 Harrow, W. Eight sermons preached before the University of Oxford in the year 1799. Rivington. 1799. B25

1800 Richards, G. The divine origin of prophecy illustrated and defended in a course of sermons preached before the University of Oxford in the year MDCCC. Oxford. 1800. B26

1801 Faber, G. S. Horae Mosaicae. 2 v. Oxford. 1801. B27

1802 Nott, G. F. Religious enthusiasm considered. Oxford. 1803. B28

1803 Farrer, J. Sermons on the mission and character of Christ. Oxford. 1804. B29

1804 Laurence, R. An attempt to illustrate those articles of the Church of England, which the Calvinists improperly consider as Calvinistical. Parker. 1820. B30

1805 Nares, E. A view of the evidences of Christianity at the close of the pretended age of reason. Oxford. 1805. B31

1806 Browne, J. Sermons preached before the University of Oxford in the year MDCCCVI. Oxford. 1809. B32

1807 LeMesurier, T. The nature and guilt of schism considered. Longman. 1808. B33

1808 Penrose, J. An attempt to prove the truth of Christianity from the wisdom displayed in its original establishment. Oxford. 1808. B34

1809 Carwithen, J. B. S. A view of the Brahminical religion. Cadell. 1810. B35

1810 Falconer, T. Certain principles in Evanson's "Dissonance of the four generally received evangelists." Oxford. 1811. B36

1811 Bidlake, J. The truth and consistency of divine revelation. Longmans. 1811. B37

1812 Mant, R. An appeal to the gospel. Oxford. 1813. B38

1813 Collinson, J. A key to the writings of the principal fathers of the Christian church. Rivington. 1813. B39

1814 Van Mildert, W. An inquiry into the general principles of Scripture-interpretation. Oxford. 1815. B40

1815 Heber, R. The personality and office of the Christian Comforter asserted and explained. Oxford. 1816. B41

1816 Spry, J. H. Christian unity doctrinally and historically considered. Oxford. 1817. B42

1817 Miller, J. The divine authority of Holy Scripture asserted. Oxford. 1817. B43

1818 Moysey, C. A. The doctrines of Unitarians examined. Oxford. 1818. B44

1819 Morgan, H. D. A compressed view of the religious principles and practices of the age. Oxford. 1819. B45

1820 Faussett, G. The claims of the established church to exclusive attachment and support. Oxford. 1820. B46

1821 Jones, J. The moral tendency of divine revelation asserted and illustrated. Oxford. 1821. B47

1822 Whately, R. The use and abuse of party-feeling in matters of religion. Oxford. 1822. B48

1823 Goddard, C. The mental condition necessary to a due inquiry into religious evidence. Oxford. 1824. B49

1824 Conybeare, J. J. The Bampton lectures for the year MDCCCXXIV. Being an attempt to trace the history and to ascertain the limits of the secondary and spiritual interpretation of Scripture. Oxford. 1824. B50

1825 Chandler, G. The scheme of divine revelation considered. Oxford. 1825. B51

1826 Vaux, W. The benefits annexed to a participation in the two Christian sacraments. Oxford. 1826. B52

1827 Milman, H. H. The character and conduct of the apostles considered as an evidence of Christianity.

Oxford. 1827. B53
1828 Horne, T. The religious necessity of the reformation asserted. Oxford. 1828. B54
1829 Burton, E. An inquiry into the heresies of the apostolic age. Parker. 1829. B55
1830 Soames, H. An inquiry into the doctrine of the Anglo-Saxon church. Rivington. 1830. B56
1831 Lancaster, T. W. The popular evidence of Christianity. Parker. 1831. B57
1832 Hampden, R. D. The scholastic philosophy considered in its relation to Christian theology. Marshall. 1848. B58
1833 Nolan, F. The analogy of revelation and science established in a series of lectures. Parker. 1833. B59
1834 No lecture delivered.
1835 No lecture delivered.
1836 Ogilvie, C. A. The divine glory manifested in the conduct and discourses of Our Lord. Parker. 1836. B60
1837 Vogan, T. S. L. Sermons. Parker. 1837. B61
1837 ____. The principle objections against the doctrine of the Trinity. Oxford. 1837. B62
1838 Woodgate, H. A. The authoritative teaching of the church shewn to be in conformity with Scripture. Parker. 1839. B63
1839 Conybeare, W. D. An analytical examination into the character, value, and just application of the writings of the Christian fathers during the ante-Nicene period. Parker. 1839. B64
1840 Hawkins, E. An inquiry into the connected uses of the principal means of attaining Christian truth. Parker. 1840. B65
1841 S. Wilberforce appointed, but domestic calamity prevented lectures. B66
1842 Garbett, J. Christ. 2 v. Oxford. 1842. B67
1843 Grant, A. The past and prospective extension of the gospel by missions to the heathen. Rivington. 1844. B68
1844 Jelf, R. W. An inquiry into the means of grace. Parker. 1844. B69
1845 Heurtley, C. A. Justification. Parker. 1846. B70
1846 Short, A. The witness of the Spirit with our spirit. Parker. 1846. B71
1847 Shirley, W. A. The supremacy of Holy Scripture. Vincent. 1847. B72
1848 Marsh, E. G. The Christian doctrine of sanctification. Seeleys. 1848. B73
1849 Michell, R. The nature and comparative value of the Christian evidences considered generally. Parker. 1849. B74
1850 Goulburn, E. M. The doctrine of the resurrection of the body. Vincent. 1850. B75
1851 Wilson, H. B. The communion of saints. Graham. 1851. B76
1852 Riddle, J. E. The natural history of infidelity and superstition in contrast with Christian faith. Graham. 1852. B77
1853 Thomson, W. The atoning work of Christ. Longman. 1853. B78
1854 Waldegrave, S. New Testament millennarianism. Hamilton. 1855. B79
1855 Bode, J. E. The absence of precision in the formularies of the Church of England, Scriptural, and suitable to a state of probation. 1855. B80
1856 Litton, E. A. The Mosaic dispensation considered as introductory to Christianity. Hatchard. 1856. B81
1857 Jelf, W. E. Christian faith. Parker. 1857. B82
1858 Mansel, H. L. The limits of religious thought examined in eight lectures. Murray. 1858. B83
1859 Rawlinson, G. The historical evidence of the truth of the Scripture records, stated anew. Murray. 1860. B84
1860 Hessey, J. A. Sunday.

1860. B85
1861 Sandford, J. The mission and extension of the church at home. Longman. 1862. B86
1862 Farrar, A. S. A critical history of free thought. Appleton. 1876. B87
1863 Hannah, J. The relation between the divine and human elements in Holy Scripture. Murray. 1863. B88
1864 Bernard, T. D. The progress of doctrine in the New Testament. Macmillan. 1864. B89
1865 Mozley, J. B. Eight lectures on miracles. Dutton. 1879. B90
1866 Liddon, H. P. The divinity of Our Lord and Saviour Jesus. Rivington. 1875. B91
1867 Carbett, E. The dogmatic faith. Rivington. 1867. B92
1868 Moberly, G., Bp. of Salisbury. The administration of the Holy Spirit in the body of Christ. Parker. 1868. B93
1869 Payne Smith, R. Prophecy. Macmillan. 1871. B94
1870 Irons, W. J. Christianity as taught by St. Paul. Parker. 1876. B95
1871 Curteis, G. H. Dissent, in its relation to the Church of England. Macmillan. 1872. B96
1872 Eaton, J. R. T. The permanence of Christianity. Rivington. 1873. B97
1873 Smith, I. G. Characteristics of Christian morality. Parker. 1873. B98
1874 Leathes, S. The religion of Christ. Rivington. 1874. B99
1875 Jackson, W. The doctrine of retribution. Hodder. 1875. B100
1876 Alexander, W. The witness of the Psalms to Christ and Christianity. Dutton. 1877. B101
1877 Row, C. A. Christian evidence viewed in relation to modern thought. Norgate. 1887. B102
1878 Bible. O. T. Zechariah. By Charles Henry Hamilton Wright. Hodder. 1879. B103
1879 Wace, H. The foundations of faith considered in eight sermons. Pickering. 1880. B104
1880 Hatch, E. The organization of the early Christian churches. Longmans. 1918. B105
1881 Wordsworth, J. The one religion. Parker. 1881. B106
1882 Meed, P. G. The one Mediator. Rivington. 1884. B107
1883 Fremantle, W. H. The world as a subject of redemption. Longmans. 1895. B108
1884 Temple, F. The relation between religion and science. Macmillan. 1903. B109
1885 Farrar, F. W. History of interpretation. Baker Book. 1961. B110
1886 Bigg, C. The Christian Platonists of Alexandria. Oxford. 1913. B111
1887 Carpenter, W. B. The permanent elements of religion. Macmillan. 1889. B112
1888 Bartlett, R. E. The letter and the spirit. Rivington. 1888. B113
1889 Cheyne, T. K. The origin and religious contents of the Psalter in the light of the Old Testament criticism and the history of religions. Trubner. 1891. B114
1890 Watkins, H. W. Modern criticism considered in its relation to the Fourth gospel. Murray. 1890. B115
1891 Gore, C. The incarnation of the Son of God. Scribner. 1891. B116
1892 Barry, A. Some lights of science on the faith. Longmans. 1892. B117
1893 Sanday, W. Inspiration. Longmans. 1901. B118
1894 Illingworth, J. R. Personality, human and divine. Macmillan. 1894. B119
1895 Strong, T. B. Christian ethics. Longmans. 1896. B120
1897 Ottley, R. L. Aspects of the Old Testament considered in eight lectures.

Longmans. 1897. B121
1899 Inge, W. R. Christian mysticism considered in eight lectures delivered before the University of Oxford. Methuen. 1933. B122
1901 Robertson, A. Regnum Dei. Macmillan. 1901. B123
1903 Hutton, W. H. The influence of Christianity upon national character illustrated by the lives and legends of the English saints. Dutton. 1903. B124
1905 Bussell, F. W. Christian theology and social progress. Methuen. 1907. B125
1907 Peile, J. H. F. The reproach of the gospel. Longmans. 1907. B126
1909 Hobhouse, W. The church and the world in idea and in history. Macmillan. 1910. B127
1911 Skrine, J. H. Creed and the creeds. Longmans. 1911. B128
1913 Edmundson, G. The church in Rome and in the first century. Longmans. 1913. B129
1915 Rashdall, H. The idea of atonement in Christian theology. Macmillan. 1920. B130
1917, 1919 Lectures suspended.
1920 Headlam, A. C. The doctrine of the church and Christian reunion. Murray. 1920. B131
1922 Pullan, L. Religion since the reformation. Oxford. 1923. B132
1924 Williams, N. P. The idea of the fall and of original sin. Longmans. 1927. B133
1926 Rawlinson, A. E. J. New Testament doctrine of the Christ. Longmans. 1949. B134
1928 Kirk, K. E. The vision of God. Longmans. 1931. B135
1930 Grenstad, L. W. Psychology and God. Longmans. 1930. B136
1932 Streeter, B. H. The Buddha and the Christ. Macmillan. 1932. B137
1934 Lightfoot, R. H. History and interpretation in the Gospels. Hodder. 1935. B138
1936 Brabant, F. H. Time and eternity in Christian thought. Longmans. 1937. B139
1938 Guillaume, A. Prophecy and divination among the Hebrews and other Semites. Hodder. 1938. B140
1940 Prestige, G. L. Fathers and heretics. Macmillan. 1940. B141
1942 Jalland, T. G. The church and the papacy. Morehouse. 1944. B142
1944 Leeson, S. Christian education. Longmans. 1947. B143
1946 Micklem, P. A. The secular and the sacred. Hodder. 1948. B144
1948 Farrar, A. M. The glass of vision. Dacre. 1948. B145
1950 Parker, T. M. Christianity and the state in the light of history. Black. 1955. B146
1952 Milburn, R. E. P. Early Christian interpretations of history. Harper. 1954. B147
1954 Turner, H. E. W. The patterns of Christian faith. Mowbray. 1954. B148
1956 Mascall, E. L. Christian theology and natural science. Longmans. 1956. B149
1958 Davies, J. G. He ascended into Heaven. Assn. Pr. 1958. B150
1960 Kemp, E. W. Counsel and consent. S. P. C. K. 1961. B151
1962 Richardson, A. History, sacred and profane. Westminster. 1964. B152
1964 Neill, S. C. The Church and the Christian union. Oxford. 1968. B153
1966 Jenkins, D. E. The glory of man. Scribner. 1967. B154
1968 Dillistone, F. W. Traditional symbols and the contemporary world. 1973. B155
Note: Lectures biennial after 1895; 1917 and 1919 suspended.

BAMPTON LECTURES IN AMERICA (Columbia Univ. Pr.)

1 Toynbee, A. J. The prospects of western civilization. 1949. B156
2 Hawley, P. R. New discoveries in medicine. 1950. B157
3 Dodd, C. H. Gospel and law. 1951. B158
4 Mumford, L. Art and technics. 1952. B159
5 Conant, J. B. Modern science and modern man. 1952. B160
6 Gregg, A. Challenges to contemporary medicine. 1956. B161
7 Baillie, J. The idea of revelation in recent thought. 1956. B162
8 Venturi, L. Four steps towards modern art. 1956. B163
9 Hildebrand, J. H. Science in the making. 1957. B164
10 Chisholm, G. B. Prescription for survival. 1957. B165
11 Mascall, E. L. The importance of being human. 1958. B166
12 Blunt, A. The art of William Blake. 1959. B167
13 Wood, W. B. From miasmas to molecules. 1961. B168
14 Tillich, P. Christianity and the encounter of the world religions. 1963. B169
15 Frye, N. A natural perspective. 1965. B170
16 Felix, R. H. Mental illness. 1967. B171
17 Hoyle, F. Man in the universe. 1966. B172
18 MacIntyre, A. C. and Ricoeur, P. The religious significance of atheism. 1969. B173
19 Summerson, J. Victorian architecture. 1969. B174

BASLER STUDIEN ZUR DEUTSCHEN SPRACHE UND LITERATUR (Francke)

1 Brand-Sommerfeld, R. J. Zur interpretation des "Ackermann aus Böhmen." 1944. B175
2 Forster, L. W. Georg Rudolf Weckherlin... 1944. B176
3 Salfinger, T. A. Gotthelf und die romantik. 1945. B177
4 Koechlin, E. Wesenszüge des deutschen und des französischen volksmärchens. 1945. B178
5 Weidmann, W. Studien zur entwicklung von Neidharts Lyrik. 1947. B179
6 Wiesmann, L. Das Dionysische bei Hölderlin und in der deutschen romantik. 1948. B180
7 Ludwig, M. Stifter als realist. 1948. B181
8 Riedtmann, M. Jean Pauls briefe. 1950. B182
9 Bindschedler, M. Der lateinische kommentar zum granum sinapis. 1951. B183
10 Oberle, W. Der adelige mensch in der dichtung. 1951. B184
11 Sprenger, U. Praesens historicum und praeteritum in der altisländischen saga. 1952. B185
12 Stoll, R. T. Hölderins Christushymnen. 1952. B186
13 Rippmann, P. Werk und fragment Georg Lichtenberg als Schriftsteller. 1954. B187
14 Müller, E. E. Die Basler mundart im ausgehenden mittelalter. 1953. B188
15 Freivogel, M. Klopstock. 1954. B189
16 Ehrenzeller, H. Studien zur Romanvorrede von Grimmelshausen bis Jean Paul. 1955. B190
17 Dürst, A. Die lyrischen vorstufen des Grünen Heinrich. 1955. B191
18 Block, C. V. Quirinus Kuhlmann als dichter. 1957. B192
19 Wiesmann, L. Conrad Ferdinand Meyer. 1958. B193
20 Gutzwiller, P. Der Narr bei Grimmelshausen. 1959. B194
21 Stiefel, R. Grillparzers (Golden Vliefs). 1959. B195
22 Schweizer, H. Ernst Barlachs Roman (Der gestohlene Mond). 1959. B196
23 Schweizer, H. R. Goethe

und das problem der spache. 1959. B197
24 Wernle, H. Allegorie und Erlebnis bei Luther. 1960. B198
25 Ammann, P. Schicksal und liebe in Goethe's "Wahlverwandtschaften." 1962. B199
26 Dahler, H. Jean Paul Siebenka's. 1965. B200
27 Gessler, L. Lebendig begraben. 1964. B201
28 Gröble, S. Schuld und Sühne im werke Adalbert Stifters. 1965. B202
29 Wehrli, M. Gottfried Kellers Verhältnis zum eigenen schaffen. 1965. B203
30 Zimmerman, H. Zur einen typologie des spontanen Gesprächs. 1965. B204
31 Kulli, M. Die ständestaire in den deutschen geistlichen schauspielen des ausgehenden mittelalters. 1966. B205
32 Hufeland, K. Die deutsche Schwankdichtung des Spätmittelalters. 1966. B206
33 Gass, A. L. Die dichtung im leben und werk Jacob Burckhardts. 1967. B207
34 Graber, H. Alfred Döblins Epos "Manas." 1967. B208
35 Schneider, H. Jakob von Hoddis. 1967. B209
36 Buhne, R. Jeremias Gotthelf und das problem des Armut. 1968. B210
37 Korff, F. W. Diastole und systole. 1969. B211
38 Feldges, M. Grimmelshausens "Landstörtzein Courasche." 1969. B212
39 Leber, E. Das bild des menschen in Schillers und Kleists dramen. 1969. B213
40 Abutille, M. C. Angst und Zynismus bei Georg Büchner. 1969. B214
41 Schnell, R. Rudolf von Ems. 1969. B215
42 Herzog, V. Ironische Erzählformen bei Conrad Ferdinand Meyer, dargestellt am "Jurg Jenatsch." 1971. B216
43 Stadler, U. Der einsame Ort. 1971. B217
44 Wenger, K. Gottfried Kellers auseinandersetzung mit dem Christentum. 1971. B218
45 Schwab, U. Arbeo laosa. 1972. B219
46 Bonati-Richner, S. Der Feuermensch. 1972. B220
47 Jecklin, A. Untersuchungen zu den Satzbauplanen der gesprochenen sprache. 1972. B221
48 Burckhardt, J. Der Mann ohne eigenschaften von Robert Musil. 1973. B222
49 Bonati, P. Die darstellung des Bösen im werk Wilhelm Buschs. 1973. B223
51 Koelliker, B. Reinfrid von Braunschweig. 1974. B224

BASLER STUDIEN ZUR KUNGSTGESCHICHTE (Francke)

1 Murbach, E. Form und material in der spätgotischen plastik. 1943. B225
2 Cahn, H. A. Die Münzer sizileschen Stadt Naxos. 1944. B226
3 Fromer-Im Obersteg, L. Die Entwicklung der schseizerischen Landschaftsmalerei im 18. und fruhen 19. Jahrhundert. 1945. B227
4 Landolt, H. Die Jesuitenkirche in Luzern. 1947. B228
6 Maurer, H. Die romanischen und fruhgotischen Kapitelle der Kathedrale Saint-Pierre in Genf. 1952. B229
7 Maurer, E. Jacob Burckhardt und Rubens. 1951. B230
8 Heyer, H. R. Gaetano Matteo Pisoni. 1967. B231
9 Guth-Dreyfus, K. Transluzides Email in der ersten Hälfte des 14. Jahrhunderts am Ober-, Mittel- und Niederrheim. 1954. B232
11 Licht, F. S. Die Entwicklung der landschaft in den werken von Nicolas Poussin. 1954. B233
13 Bernoulli, C. Die skulpturen der Abtei Conques-en Rourergue. 1956. B234
14 Bloch, P. Das Hornbacher Sakramentar und seine Stellung innerhalb der fruhen reichenauer buchmahrei.

1956. B235
16 Dietschi, P. Der parallelismus Ferdinand Hodlers. 1957. B236
17 Felder, P. Die hofkirche St. Leodegar ind St. Mauritius in Luzern. 1958. B237

Neue folge:

1 Perrig, A. Michelangelo Buonarrotis letzte Pietá-idee. 1960. B238
2 Wyss, A. Die chemalige pro-monstratenserabtei Bellelay. 1960. B239
3 Gasser, H. Das gewand in der formensprache grünewalds. 1962. B240
4 Sieber-Meier, C. Untersuchungen zum "Oeuvre littèraire" von Eugène Delacroix. 1963. B241
5 Brenk, B. Die romanische wandmalerei in der schweiz. 1963. B242
6 Suter-Raeber, R. La charité-sur-Loire. 1964. B243
7 Cahansky, N. Die romanischen wandmalereien der ehemaligen abteikirche St-Chef (Dauphiné). 1966. B244
8 Heyer, H. R. Gaetano Matteo Pisoni. 1967. B245
9 Euler, W. Die architekurde estellung in der Arena-Kapelle. 1967. B246
10 Verzár, C. Die romanischen skulpturen der Abtei Sagra di San Michele. 1968. B247
11 Maurer-Kuhn, F. Romanische kapitellplastik in der schwiez. 1971. B248

BEDFORD HISTORICAL SERIES.

1 Neale, J. E. Queen Elizabeth I. Harcourt. 1959. B249
____. Queen Elizabeth. 1950. B250
2 Chambers, R. W. Thomas More. Newman. 1949. B251
3 Wedgwood, C. V. Strafford, 1593-1641. Cape. 1935. B252
4 Seignobos, C. History of the French people, tr. by Phillips. 1938. B253
5 Bainville, J. Napoleon. Cape. 1938. B254
6 Cooper, D. Talleyrand. Harper. 1932. B255
7 Baskerville, G. English monks and the suppression of the monasteries. Yale. 1937. B256
8 Thomson, G. S. Life in a noble household, 1641-1700. Cape. 1937. B257
9 Rowse, A. L. Sir Richard Grenville of the Revenge. Houghton. 1937. B258
10 Wedgwood, C. V. The thirty years war. Yale. 1939. B259
11 Mattingly, G. Catherine of Aragon. Little. 1941. B260
12 Geyl, P. Napoleon. Yale. 1949. B261

Rowse, A. L. Tudor Cornwall. 1957. B262

BEHAVIOR SCIENCE BIBLIOGRAPHIES (Human Relations Area Files. Distributed by Taplinger)

Burnett, J. H. Anthropology and education. 1974. B263
Chicago. University. Bibliography of Belorussia. 1956. B264
____. Bibliography of British Borneo. 1956. B265
____. Bibliography of Cambodia. 1956. B266
____. Bibliography of Czechoslovakia. 1956. B267
____. Bibliography of Jammu and Kashmir. 1956. B268
____. Bibliography of Laos. 1956. B269
____. Bibliography of Latvia. 1956. B270
____. Bibliography of Lithuania. 1956. B271
____. Bibliography of Poland. 1956. B272
____. Bibliography of Ukraine. 1956. B273
____. Philippine Studies Program. Selected bibliography of the Philippines. 1956. B274
Hazard, H. W. Bibliography of the Arabian peninsula. 1958. B275
Irikura, J. K. Southeast Asia. 1956. B276
Jakobson, R. and others. Paleosiberian peoples and

languages. 1957. B277
Kennedy, R. Bibliography of Indonesian people and cultures, ed. by Maretzki and Fischer. 2 v. 1962. B278
Koh, H. C. Korea. 1971. B279
Murdock, G. P. Ethnographic bibliography of North America. 1960. B280
New York University. Burma Research Project. Annotated bibliography of Burma, ed. by Trager and others. 1960. B281
____. Japanese and Chinese language sources on Burma, ed. by Trager. 1957. B282
O'Leary, T. J. Ethnographic bibliography of South America. 1963. B283
Patai, R. Jordan, Lebanon, and Syria. 1957. B284
Pelzer, K. J. West Malaysia and Singapore. 1970. B285
____. Selected bibliography on the geography of Southeast Asia. 3 v. 1949-56. B286
Sweet, L. E. and O'Leary, T. J., eds. Circum-Mediterranean peasantry. 1968. B287
Theodoratus, R. J. Europe. 1969. B288
Trager, F. N. Burma. 1972. B289
Wilber, D. N. Annotated bibliography of Afghanistan. 1956. B290
Yüan, T'ung-li. Economic and social development of modern China. 1956. B291

BEHAVIOR SCIENCE MONOGRAPHS (Human Relations Area Files. Distributed by Taplinger)

Aberle, D. F. Chahar and Dagor Mongol bureaucratic administration. 1962. B292
Benedict, P. K. Austro-Thai. 1973. B293
Burrows, E. G. and Spiro, M. E. An atoll culture. 1957. B294
Christensen, J. B. Double descent among the Fanti, ed. by Highland. 1954. B295
Fischer, J. L. and A. M. The eastern Carolines. 1957. B296
Hart, D. V. Southeast Asian birth customs. 1965. B297
Kennedy, R. Field notes on Indonesia, ed. by Conklin. V. 1. 1953. B298
Leighton, D. (Cross) and Adair, J. People of the middle place. 1966. B299
Maron, S., ed. Pakistan. 1957. B300
Otterbein, K. F. The evolution of war. 1970. B301
Udy, S. H. Organization of work. 1959. B302
Vreeland, H. H. Mongol community and kinship structure. 1957. B303
Wilson, P. J. A Malay village and Malaysia. 1966. B304

BEHAVIOR SCIENCE OUTLINES (Human Relations Area Files. Distributed by Taplinger)

1 Yale Univ. Institute of Human Relations. Outline of cultural materials, by Murdock and others. 1961. B304a
2 ____. Outline of South American cultures by Murdock and others. 1951. B305
3 ____. Outline of world culture. 1958. B306

BEHAVIOR SCIENCE REPRINTS (Human Relations Area Files. Distributed by Taplinger)

Baden-Powell, B. H. The Indian village community. 1958. B307
Codrington, R. H. The Melanesians. 1957. B308
Morgan, L. H. League of the Ho-de-no-saw-nee or Iroquois. 2 v. 1954. B309
Pospisil, L. Anthropology of law. 1974. B310
Ray, V. F. The Sanpoil and Nespelem. 1954. B311
Roberts, J. M. Zuni daily life. 1965. B312
Schneider, D. M. and Roberts, J. M. Zuni kin terms. 1965. B313

BEHAVIOR SCIENCE TRANSLATIONS (Human Relations Area Files. Distributed by Taplinger)

Anunman Rajathon, P. Life and

ritual in Old Siam, tr. by Gedney. 1961. B314
Dallet, C. Traditional Korea. 1954. B315
Donner, K. Among the Samoyed in Siberia, tr. by Kyler, ed. by Highland. 1954. B316
Gouroy, P. The peasants of the Tonkin Delta. 2 v. 1955. B317
Human Relations Area Files. Vietnamese ethnographic papers by Cadiere and others. 1953. B318
Jirásek, A. Some aspects of Czech culture, tr. by Neuse. 1953. B319
Lin, Y. The Lolo of Liang Shan, tr. by Pan. 1961. B320
Lustéguy, P. The role of women in Tonkinese religion and property, tr. by Messner. 1954. B321
Massé, H. Persian beliefs and customs, tr. by Messner. 1954. B322
Prinkloskii, V. L. and others. Yakut ethnographic sketches. 1953. B323
Spiridonov, N. Snow people (Chukchee). 1954. B324
Stubel, H. The Mewu Fantzu. 1958. B325

BEITRÄGE ZUR GESCHICHTE DER NATIONALOKONOMIE (Fischer)

1 Schreiber, E. Die volkswirtschaftlichen anschauungen der scholastik seit Thomas v. Aquin. 1913. B326
2 Zielenziger, K. Die alten deutschen kameralisten. 1914. B327
3 Hasbach, M. William Thompson. 1922. B328
4 Muziol, R. Karl Rodbertus als begründer der sozialrechtlichen anschauungsweise. 1927. B329
5 Hüter, M. Die methodologie der wirtschafswissenschaft bei Roscher und Knies. 1928. B330
6 Georg. Richelieu als merkantilistischer Wirtschaftspolitiker und der Begriff des Staatsmerkantilismus. 1929. B331
7 Casper, W. Charles Davenant. 1930. B332
8 Binder, H. Das sozialitäre system Eugen Duhrings. 1930. B333

BEITRAGE ZUR HISTORISCHEN THEOLOGIE (Mohr)

1 Lohmeyer, E. Grundlagen paulinischer. 1929. B334
2 Koch, H. Adhuc virgo. 1929. B335
3 Begrich, J. Die chronologie der Könige von Israel und Juda und die Quellen des Rahmes der Königsbücher. 1929. B336
4 Jacob, G. Der Gewissensbegriff in der Theologie Luthers. 1929. B337
5 Schaeder, H. H. Esra der Schreiber. 1966. B338
6 Schlier, H. Christus und der kircheim Epheserbrief. 1930. B339
7 Völker, W. Das Volkommenheitsideal des Origenes. 1931. B340
8 Strothmann, R. Die Koptische kirche in der neuzeit. 1932. B341
9 Käsemann, E. Leib und lieb Christi. 1933. B342
10 Bauer, W. Rechtglaubigkeit und Ketzerei im ältesten Christentum. 1964. B343
11 Bible. N. T. Studien zum Vierten e vangelium. Von Emanuel Hirsch. 1936. B344
12 Lerch, D. Isaaks Opferung, Christlich gedeutet. 1950. B345
13 Kraus, H. J. Die Konigsherrschaft Göttes im Alten Testament. 1951. B346
14 Compenhausen, H. Kirchliches amt und geistliche vollmacht in den ersten drei Jahrhundertan. 1953. B347
15 Ellinger, K. Studien zum Habakuk-kommentar vom Toten Meer. 1953. B348
16 Geschichte und altes Testament. 1953. B349
17 Conzelmann, H. Die Mitte der Zeit. 1954. B350
18 Jetter, W. Die Taufe beim jungen Luther. 1954. B351

19 Ott, H. Geschichte und Heilsgeschichte in der theologie Rudolf Bultmanns. 1955. B352
20 Kraft, H. Kaiser Konstantins religiöse Entwicklung. 1955. B353
21 Kretschmar, G. Studien zur fruhchristlichen Trinitats-theologie. 1956. B354
22 Senft, C. Wahrhaftigkeit und Wahrheit. 1956. B355
23 Westermann, C. Der aufbau des Buches Heob. 1956. B356
24 Brown, H. Spätjudisch-häretischer und frühchristlicher. 1957. B357
25 Gise, H. Der Verfassung-sentwurf der Ezechiel. 1957. B358
26 Wilckens, U. Weisheit und Torheit. 1959. B359
27 Koch, G. Die Auferstehung Jesu Christi. 1959. B360
28 Werbeck, W. Jacobus Perez von Valencia. 1959. B361
29 Schäfer, R. Christologie und Sittichkeit in Melanchthons früher Loci. 1961. B362
30 Wallmann, J. Der theologie-begriff bei Johann Gerhard und Georg Calixt. 1961. B363
31 Raeder, S. Das Hebräische bei Luther. 1961. B364
32 Bonhoeffer, T. Die Gotteslehre des Thomas von Aquin als Sprachproblem. 1961. B365
33 Krause, G. Studien zu Luthers Auslegung der Kleinen Propheten. 1962. B366
34 Kasch, W. F. Die Sozial-philosophie von Ernst Troeltsch. 1963. B367
35 Beyschlag, K. Clemens Romanus und der Fruhkatholizismus. 1966. B368
36 Brecht, M. Die frühe theologie des Johannes Brenz. 1966. B369
37 Betz, H. D. Nachfolge und Nachahmung Jesu Christi im Neuen Testament. 1967. B370
38 Raeder, S. Die Benutzung des masoretischen Textes bei Luther... 1967. B371
39 Campenhausen, H. F. von. Die entstehung der christlichen Bibel. 1968. B372
40 Schmid, H. H. Gerechtigkeit als Weltordnung. 1968. B373
41 Schäfer, R. Ritschl. 1968. B374
42 Wallman, J. Philipp Jakob Spenser und die Anfänge des Pietesmus. 1970. B375
43 Mauser, U. W. Gottesbild und Menschwerdung. 1971. B376
44 Hoffmann, M. Erkenntnis und Verwirklichung der wahren theologie nach Erasmus von Rotterdam. 1972. B377
45 Betz, H. D. Der Apostel Paulus und die sokratische tradition. 1972. B378
46 Mühlen, K. H. Nos extra nos. 1972. B379
47 Osborn, E. F. Justin martyr. 1973. B380
48 Gülzow, H. Cyprian und Novatian. 1974. B381
49 Köpf, U. Die anfange der theologischen wissenschafts-theorie im 13. Jh. 1974. B382
50 Hübner, J. Die theologie Johannes Keplers zwischen Orthodoxie u. naturwissenschaft. 1974. B383

BEITRÄGE ZUR PHILOSOPHIE UND IHRER GESCHICHTE (Mohr)

1 Hönigswald, R. Grundfragen der erkenntnistheorie, kristisches und systematisches. 1931. B383a
2 Adorno, T. W. Kierkegaard. 1933. B384
3 Wind, E. Das experiment und die metaphysik. 1934. B385
4 Binder, J. Grundlegung zur rechtsphilosphie. 1935. B386
5 Boldt, K. Die erkenntnis-beziehung. 1937. B387
6 Zocher, R. Die philosophische grundlehre. 1939. B388
7 Müller, M. Seln und geist. 1940. B389

BELL TELEPHONE LABORATORIES SERIES (Van Nostrand)

Bell Telephone Laboratories,

inc. Radar systems and components. 1949. B390
Bell Telephone Laboratories, inc. Transistor technology, ed. by Bridgers and others. 3 v. 1958. B391
Berry, R. W. and others. Thin film technology. 1968. B392
Black, H. S. Modulation theory. 1953. B393
Bode, H. W. Network analysis and feedback amplifier design. 1945. B394
Bozorth, R. M. Ferromagnetism. 1951. B395
Brotherton, M. Capacitors. 1946. B396
Campbell, G. A. and Foster, R. M. Fourier integrals for practical applications. 1947. B397
Crandall, I. B. Theory of vibrating systems and sound. 1926. B398
Darrow, K. K. Introduction to contemporary physics. 1926. B399
Fletcher, H. Speech and hearing. 1929. B400
____. Speech and hearing in communication. 1953. B401
Fry, T. C. Elementary differential equations. 1929. B402
____. Probability and its engineering uses. 1928. B403
Gewartowski, J. W. and Watson, H. A. Principles of electron tubes. 1965. B404
Harper, A. E., comp. Rhombic antenna design. 1941. B405
Heising, R. A., ed. Quartz crystals for electrical circuits. 1946. B406
Johnson, K. S. Transmission circuits for telephonic communications. 1925. B407
Keister, W. and others. The design of switching circuits. 1951. B408
MacColl, L. A. Fundamental theory of servomechanisms. 1945. B409
Marcuse, D. Light transmission optics. 1972. B410
Mason, W. P. Electromechanical transducers and wave filters. 1948. B411
____. Physical acoustics and the properties of solids. 1958. B412
____. Piezoelectric crystals and their application to ultrasonics. 1950. B413
Molina, E. C. Poisson's exponential binomial limit. 1942. B414
Page, C. H. The algebra of electronics. 1958. B415
Page, H. Principles of aerial design. 1966. B416
Peek, R. L. and Wagar, H. N. Switching relay design. 1955. B417
Pierce, J. R. Theory and design of electronic beams. 1954. B418
____. Traveling-wave tubes. 1950. B419
Potter, R. K. and others. Visible speech. 1947. B420
Rowe, H. E. Signals and noise in communication systems. 1965. B421
Schelkunoff, S. A. Applied mathematics for engineers and scientists. 1948. B422
____. Electromagnetic waves. 1943. B423
Shea, T. E. Transmission networks and wave filters. 1929. B424
Shewhart, W. A. Economic control of quality of manufactured product. 1931. B425
Shive, J. N. The properties, physics, and design of semiconductor devices. 1959. B426
Shockley, W. Electrons and holes in semiconductors. 1950. B427
Slater, J. C. Microwave electronics. 1950. B428
Southworth, G. C. Principles and applications of waveguide transmission. 1950. B429
Sunde, E. D. Earth conduction effects in transmission systems. 1949. B430

THE BELLARMINE SERIES (Burns)

1 Sutcliffe, E. F. A two year public ministry. 1939. B431
2 Cammack, J. S. Moral problems of mental defect. 1939. B432

3 Burrows, E. The oracles of Jacob and Balaam. 1939. B433
4 Bévenot, M. St. Cyprian's De Unitate, chap. 4, in the light of the manuscripts. 1938. B434
5 Goodier, A. An introduction to the study of ascetical and mystical theology. 1938. B435
6 Burrows, E. The gospel of the infancy and other Biblical essays. 1940. B436
7 Copleston, F. Friedrich Nietzsche, philosopher of culture. 1942. B437
8 Sutcliffe, E. F. The Old Testament and the future life. 1947. B438
9 Copleston, F. A history of philosophy. V. 1. Greece and Rome. 1951. B439
10 King, J. L. Sex enlightenment and the Catholic. 1944. B440
11 Copleston, F. Arthur Schopenhauer. 1946. B441
12 Same as no. 9. V. 2. Medieval philosophy. 1954. B442
13 Crehan, J. H. Early Christian Baptism and the creed. 1950. B443
14 Same as no. 9. V. 3. Medieval philosophy. Ockham to Suárez. 1950. B444
15 Same as no. 9. V. 4. Medieval philosophy. Descartes to Leibniz. 1958. B445
16 Same as no. 9. V. 5. Medieval philosophy. Hobbes to Hume. 1959. B446
17 Same as no. 9. V. 6. Wolff to Kant. 1960. B447
18 Same as no. 9. V. 7. Fichte to Nietzsche. 1963. B448
19 Same as no. 9. V. 8. Bentham to Russell. 1964. B449

BENEDICTINE STUDIES (Helicon)

1 Whiting, J. The monk of Forne, ed. by Farmer. 1961. B450
2 Diekmann, G. Come, let us worship. 1961. B451
3 Butler, B. C. Prayer in practice. 1961. B452
4 Marmion, C. English letters. 1962. B453
5 Ellis, J. T. Perspectives in American Catholicism. 1963. B454
6 Schuster, M. F. The meaning of the mountain. 1963. B455
7 Boultwood, A. Alive to God. 1964. B456
8 Ellis, J. T. Catholics in Colonial America. 1965. B457

BERKELEY SERIES IN AMERICAN HISTORY (Rand McNally)

Abrams, R. M., ed. The issues of Federal regulations in the Progressive Era. 1963. B458
Cronon, E. D., ed. Labor and the New Deal. 1963. B459
Diamond, S., ed. The creation of society in the New World. 1963. B460
Dupree, A. H., ed. Science and the emergence of modern America. 1963. B461
Gatell, F. O., comp. The Jacksonians and the money power, 1829-1840. 1967. B462
Holbo, P. S., comp. Isolationism and interventionism, 1932-1941. 1967. B463
Hoogenboom, A. A., ed. Spoilsmen and reformers. 1964. B464
Jacobs, W. R., comp. The Paxton riots and the frontier theory. 1967. B465
Jordan, W. D., comp. The Negro versus equality, 1762-1826. 1969. B466
Koch, A. Adams and Jefferson. 1963. B467
Levin, D., ed. The Puritan in the Enlightenment. 1963. B468
Lowitt, R., comp. The Truman-MacArthur controversy. 1967. B469
McWhitney, G., ed. Reconstruction and the freedmen. 1963. B470
Main, J. T., ed. Rebel versus Tory. 1963. B471
May, E. R. The coming of the war, 1917. 1963. B472
May, H. F., ed. The discontent of the intellectuals. 1963. B473

Middelkauff, R., ed. Bacon's Rebellion. 1964. B474
Rappaport, A., ed. The war with Mexico. 1964. B475
Ross, H., ed. The cold war. 1963. B476
Sellers, C. G., ed. Andrew Jackson, nullification and the state-rights tradition. 1963. B477
____ and May, H. F. A synopsis of American history. 1969. B478
Staudenraus, P. J., ed. The secession crisis, 1860-1861. 1963. B479
Strout, C., ed. Conscience, science and security. 1963. B480
Unger, L., ed. Populism. 1964. B481
Weisberger, B. A., ed. Abolitionism. 1963. B482
Young, A. F., ed. The debate over the Constitution, 1787-1789. 1965. B483

BERKSHIRE STUDIES IN EUROPEAN HISTORY (Holt)

Arragon, R. F. The transition from the ancient to the medieval world. 1936. B484
Baldwin, S. Business in the middle ages. 1937. B485
____. The organization of medieval Christianity. 1929. B486
Bruun, G. The enlightened despots. 1929. B487
Buffinton, A. H. The second hundred years' war, 1689-1815. 1929. B488
Daniels, R. Concentration camps, U.S.A. 1970. B489
Dietz, F. C. The industrial revolution. 1927. B490
Downey, G. The Late Roman Empire. 1969. B491
Fay, S. B. The rise of Brandenburg-Prussia to 1786. 1937. B492
Ferguson, W. K. The renaissance. 1940. B493
Frye, R. N. Iran. 1953. B494
Gershoy, L. The French revolution, 1789-1799. 1932. B495
Gewehr, W. M. The rise of nationalism in the Balkans, 1800-1930. 1931. B496
Gillespie, J. E. A history of geographical discovery, 1400-1800. 1933. B497
Goodenough, E. R. The church in the Roman empire. 1931. B498
Hoskins, H. L. European imperialism, in Africa. 1930. B499
Karpovich, M. M. Imperial Russia, 1801-1917. 1932. B500
Knapton, E. J. France since Versailles. 1952. B501
May, A. J. The age of Metternich, 1814-1848. 1963. B502
Mosse, G. L. The Reformation. 1963. B503
Neilson, N. Medieval agrarian economy. 1936. B504
Newhall, R. A. The crusades. 1963. B505
Nowak, F. Medieval Slavdom and the rise of Russia. 1930. B506
Owen, D. E. Imperialism and nationalism in the Far East. 1929. B507
Packard, L. B. The age of Louis XIV. 1929. B508
____. The commercial revolution, 1400-1776. 1927. B509
Packard, S. R. Europe and the church under Innocent III. 1927. B510
Palm, F. C. Calvanism and the religious wars. 1932. B511
Pauley, B. F. The Hapsburg legacy, 1867-1939. 1972. B512
Remak, J. The origins of World War I. 1966. B513
Salmon, E. D. Imperial Spain. 1931. B514
Salvadori, M. The rise of modern communism. 1963. B515
Schmitt, B. E. Triple alliance and triple entente, 1878-1914. 1934. B516
Schuman, F. L. Germany since 1918. 1937. B517
Skotheim, R. A. Totalitarianism and American social thought. 1972. B518
Smith, T. C. The United States as a factor in world history. 1941. B519
Stavrianos, L. S. The Balkans,

1815-1914. 1963. B520
Trotter, R. G. The British empire-commonwealth. 1932. B521
Vernadskii, G. V. Russian revolution. 1917-1931. 1932. B522
Wallbank, T. W. Indian. 1948. B523
Wren, M. W. The Western impact on Tsarist Russia. 1971. B524
Wright, J. K. The geographical basis of European history. 1928. B525

BERNER UNIVERSITÄTSSCHRIFTEN (Haupt)

1 Vetter, F. Ueber personennamen und namengebung. B526
2 Frankel, J. Wandlungen des Prometheus. B527
3 Schafer, E. A. Die funktionen des Gehirnanhanges. B528
4 Lingner, K. A. Der mensch als organisationsvorbild. 1914. B529
5 Keller, W. Gegenwärtsaufgaben der philosophie. 1945. B530
6 Rudolf, A. and Stein, A. Reden zu Pestalozzis 200 Geburtstag. B531
7 Amstutz, J. Was ist verantwortung? 1947. B532
8 ___. Zweifel und Mystik. 1950. B533
9 Ryffel, H. Philosophie und leben. B534
10 Ansprachen gehalten an der akademischen Gedenkfeier. Bern 600 jahre im bund der Eidgenossen. B535
11 Heimann, H. Prophetie und geisteskrankheit. 1956. B536
12 Naf, W. Collegium generale. 1964. B537
14 Heimann, H. Die Seele-Grenzbegruff der naturwissenschaft und theologie. 1966. B538
15 Dante Alighieri, 1265-1321, by Goldmann and others. 1966. B539
16 Staedtke, J. Vierhundert jahre confessio Helvetica posterior, by Locher and others. 1967. B540
17 Rüegg, W. Die strukturreform der Humboldtschen Universität. 1969. B541
18 Locher, G. Die universität in der gesellschaft. 1969. B542

BIBLIOGRAFIAS MEXICANAS (Secretaria de Relaciones Exteriores)

1 Díaz Mercado, J. Bibliografía general del estado de Veracruz, 1794-1910. 1937. B543
2 ___. Bibliografía sumaria de la Baja California. 1937. B544
3 Gómez Ugarte, E. and Pegaza, A. Bibliografía sumaria del territorio de Quintana Roo. 1937. B545
4-6 Guzmán y Raz Guzmán, J. Bibliografía de la independencia de Mexico. 3 v. 1938-39. B546
7 Not published.
8 Valle, R. H. Bibliografía de Ignacio Manuel Altamirano. 1939. B547
9 Ramos, R. Bibliografía de la revolución Mexicana. V. 3. 1940. (V. 1, 2 published as books independent of the series). B548

BIBLIOGRAPHICAL SOCIETY, LONDON. FACSIMILES AND ILLUSTRATIONS.

1 Johnson, A. F. German renaissance title-borders. 1929. B549
2-3 Isaac, F. S. English & Scottish printing types, 1501-58, 1508-58. 2 v. 1930-32. B550
4 Johnson, A. F. A catalogue of engraved and etched English titlepages down to the death of William Faithorne, 1691. 1933. B551

BIBLIOGRAPHICAL SOCIETY, LONDON. ILLUSTRATED MONOGRAPHS.

1 Redgrave, G. R. Erhard Ratdolt and his work at Venice. 1899. B552
2 Proctor, R. G. C. Jan van

Doesborgh. 1894. B553
3 Ashbee, H. S. An iconography of Don Quixote, 1605-1895. 1895. B554
4 Haebler, K. The early printers of Spain and Portugal. 1897. B555
5 La Marche, O. de. Le chevalier delibere. 1898. B556
6 Claudin, A. The first Paris press... Fichet... Heynlin. 1898. B557
7 Macfarlane, J. Antoine Verárd. 1900. B558
8 Proctor, R. G. C. The printing of Greek in the fifteenth century. 1900. B559
9 Barwick, G. F. A book bound for Mary queen of Scots... Geographia of Ptolemy. 1901. B560
10 Gibson, S. Early Oxford bindings. 1903. B561
11 Steele, R. The earliest English music printing. 1903. B562
12 Madan, F. A chart of Oxford printing, '1468'-1900. 1904. B563
13 Gray, G. J. The earlier Cambridge stationers & bookbinders. 1904. B564
14 Bourdillon, F. W. The early editions of the Roman de la rose. 1906. B565
15 Ricci, S. de. A census of Caxtons. 1909. B566
16 McKerrow, R. B. 'Printers' & sign publishers' devices in England & Scotland 1485-1640. B567
17 Bosanquet, E. F. English printed almanacks and prognostications. 1917. B568
18 Duff, E. G. Fifteenth century English books. 1917. B569
19 Osler, W. Incunabula medica. 1923. B570
20 Thomas-Stanford, C. Early editions of Euclid's Elements. 1926. B571
21 McKerrow, R. B. and Ferguson, F. S. Title-page borders used in England & Scotland, 1485-1640. 1932. B572
22 Hodnett, E. English woodcuts, 1480-1535. 1935. B573
23 Thomas H. Early Spanish bookbindings, XI-XV centuries. 1939. B574
24 Greg, W. W. A bibliography of the English printed drama to the restoration. 4 v. 1929-1959. B575

BIBLIOGRAPHICAL SOCIETY LONDON. PUBLICATIONS.

The Bibliographical Society, 1892-1942. 1945. B576
Blakey, D. The Minerva press, 1790-1820. 1939. B577
Brown, C. F. A register of Middle English religious & didactic verse. 2 v. 1916-20. B578
Case, A. E. A bibliography of English poetical miscellanies, 1521-1750. 1935. B579
Dahl, F. A bibliography of English corantos and periodical newsbooks, 1620-1642. 1952. B580
Day, C. L. and Murrie, E. English song-books, 1651-1702. 1940. B581
Duff, E. G. A century of the English book trade. 1905. B582
Esdaile, A. J. K. A list of English tales and prose romances printed before 1740. 1912. B583
Forman, M. B. A bibliography of the writings in prose and verse of George Meredith. 1922. B584
____. Meredithiana: being a supplement to the bibliography of Meredith. 1924. B585
Gibson, S. Abstracts from the wills and testamentary documents of binders, printers, and stationers of Oxford, from 1493 to 1638. 1907. B586
Gray, G. J. Abstracts from the wills and testamentary documents of printers, binders, and stationers of Cambridge, from 1504 to 1699. 1915. B587
Greg, W. W. A list of English plays written before 1643 and printed before 1700. 1900. B588
____. A list of masques, pageants, & c. supplementary

to a list of English plays. 1902. B589

Greg, W. W. and Boswell, E., eds. Records of the Court of the Stationers' Company, 1576 to 1602, from Register B. 1930. B590

Handlist of the books in the library of the Bibliographical Society. 1935. B591

A hand-list of English books in the library of Emmanuel College, Cambridge, printed before MDCXLI. 1915. B592

Hand-lists of books printed by London printers, 1501-1556. 2 v. 1895-1913. B593

Herbert, W. An index of Dibdin's edition of the Typographical Antiquities, first compiled by Joseph Ames, with some references to the intermediate edition. 1899. B594

Howe, E. A list of London bookbinders, 1648-1815. 1950. B595

____, ed. The London compositor. 1947. B596

London. Stationers' company. Records of the court of the Stationers' company, 1602-1640, ed. by Jackson. 1957. B597

Macdonald, H. and Hargreaves, M. A bibliography of the works of Thomas Hobbes. 1952. B598

McKerrow, R. B., ed. A dictionary of printers and booksellers in England, Scotland and Ireland, 1557-1640. 1910. B599

Marsh's Library, Dublin. A short catalogue of English books in Archbishop Marsh's library, Dublin, printed before MDCXLI, ed. by White. 1905. B600

Masson, I. The Mainz Psalters and Canon Missae, 1457-1459. 1954. B601

Meyer-Baer, K. Liturgical music incunabula. 1962. B602

Morris, B. R. John Cleveland (1613-1658). 1967. B603

Palmer, H. R. List of English editions and translations of Greek and Latin classics printed before 1641. 1911. B604

Plomer, H. R. Abstracts from the wills of English printers and stationers from 1492 to 1630. 1903. B605

____. A dictionary of the booksellers and printers who were at work in England, Scotland and Ireland from 1641 to 1667. 1907. B606

____. A dictionary of the printers and booksellers who were at work in England, Scotland and Ireland from 1668 to 1725. 1922. B607

____. Robert Wyer, printer and bookseller. 1897. B608

Plomer, H. R. and others. A dictionary of the printers and booksellers who were at work in England, Scotland and Ireland from 1726 to 1775. 1932. B609

Pollard, A. W. and Redgrave, G. R., comps. A short-title catalogue of books printed in England, Scotland & Ireland and of English books printed abroad, 1475-1640. 1926. B610

Proctor, R. G. C. A classified index to Serapeum. 1897. B611

Smith, W. C., ed. and comp. A bibliography of the musical works published by John Walsh during the years 1695-1720. 1948. B612

____, and Humphies, C. A bibliography of the musical works published by the firm of John Walsh during the years 1721-1766. 1968. B613

Stevenson, A. H. The problem of the Missale speciale. 1967. B614

Super, R. H. The publication of Landor's works. 1954. B615

Wanley, H. The diary of Humfrey Wanley, 1715-1728. 2 v. 1966. B616

Watson, A. G. The manuscripts of Henry Savile of Banke. 1969. B617

Williams, F. B. Index of dedications and commendatory verses in English books. 1962. B618

Wise, T. J. A bibliography of the writings in prose and verse of Samuel Taylor Coleridge. 1913. B619

Wise, T. J. and Wheeler, S. A bibliography of the writings in prose and verse of Walter Savage Landor. 1919. B620

Worman, E. J. Alien members

of the book-trade during the Tudor period. 1906. B621

BIBLIOGRAPHICAL SOCIETY, LONDON. TRANSACTIONS. SUPPLEMENTS.

1 Dee, J. List of manuscripts formerly owned by Dr. John Dee, ed. by James. 1921. B622
2 Cambridge Univ. Magdalene college. The Spanish books in the library of Samuel Pepys, ed. by Gaselee. 1921. B623
3 Dunn, G. A list of incunabula collected by George Dunn, ed. by Jenkinson. 1923. B624
4 Murphy, G. A bibliography of English character-books, 1608-1700. 1925. B625
5 James, M. R. List of manuscripts formerly in Peterborough abbey library. 1926. B626
6 Harrison, F. M. A bibliography of the works of John Bunyan. 1932. B627
7 Leicester, Earls of. A handlist of manuscripts in the library of the Earl of Leicester at Holkham Hall, ed. by Roscoe and others. 1932. B628
8 Willoughby, E. E. The printing of the First folio of Shakespeare. 1932. B629
9 Lobel, E. The Greek manuscripts of Aristotle's Poetics. 1933. B630
10 Haselden, R. B. Scientific aids for the study of manuscripts. 1935. B631
11 Johnson, A. F. A catalogue of engraved Italian title-pages in the sixteenth century. 1936. B632
12 Sadleir, M. Archdeacon Francis Wrangham, 1796-1842. 1937. B633
13 Bald, R. C. Bibliographical studies in the Beaumont and Fletcher folio of 1647. 1938. B634
14 Pendred, J. The earliest directory of the book trade, ed. by Pollard. 1955. B635
15 Greg, W. W. The variants in the first quarto of 'King Lear.' 1940. B636
16 Goldschmidt, E. P. Medieval texts and their first appearance in print. 1943. B637
17 Hobson, G. B. Blind-stamped panels in the English book trade, 1485-1555. 1944. B638
18 Super, R. H. The publication of Landor's works. 1954. B639
19 Foxon, D. F. Thomas Wise and pre-restoration drama. 1959. B640

BIBLIOGRAPHICAL SOCIETY OF AMERICA. MONOGRAPH SERIES.

1 Stillwell, M. B., ed. Incunabula in American libraries. 1940. B641
2 Ticknor, firm, publishers, Boston. The cost books of Ticknor and Fields, ed. by Tryon and Charvat. 1949. B642

BIBLIOGRAPHIES, FRANÇAISES DE SCIENCES SOCIALES (Colin)

1 Meyriat, J., ed. La science politique en France, 1945-1958, comp. by Maume. 1960. B643
2 Gournay, B. L'administration française. V. 1. 1961. B644
3 France. Centre national de la recherche scientifique. Les societas rurales françaises, ed. by Mendras. 1962. B645

Guides de recherches:

1 Bodiguel, J. L. and Kessler, M. C. L'administration. 1971. B646
2 Marcou, L. L'union soviétique. 1971. B647
3 Coutrot, A. Le unesse et politique. 1971. B648
4 Menudier, H. L'allemagne après 1945. 1972. B649
5 Martin, D. and Yannopoulos, T. L'Afrique noire. 1973. B650

Repertoires documentaires:

1 Guide sommaire des ouvrages de référence en sciences sociales. 1968. B651

2 Fondational nationale des sciences politiques. Catalogue général des périodiques reçus par la Fondation nationale des sciences politique. 1968. B652
3 Charlot, J. Repertoire des publications des partis politiques français. 1970. B653
4 Same as no. 1 Suppl. 1971. B654

BIBLIOGRAPHISCHE EINFÜHRUNGEN IN DAS STUDIUM DER PHILOSOPHIE (Francke)

1 Bocheński, I. M. Allgemeine philosophie Bibliographie. 1948. B655
2 Winn, R. B. Amerikanische Philosophie. 1948. B656
3 Beth, E. W. Symbolische Logik und Grundlegung der exakten Wissenschaften. 1948. B657
4 Joliver, R. Kierkegaard. 1948. B658
5 Gigon, O. A. Antike Philosophie. 1948. B659
6 Menasce, P. J. de. Arabische Philosophie. 1948. B660
7 Sciacca, M. F. Italiensche Philosophie der Gegenwart. 1948. B661
8 Phillipe, M. D. Aristoteles. 1948. B662
9 Jolivet, R. Französische Existenzphilosophie. 1948. B663
10 Sciacca, M. F. Augustinus. 1948. B664
11 Dürr, K. Der logische Positivismus. 1948. B665
12 Gigon, O. A. Platon. 1940. B666
13-14 Wyser, P. Thomas von Aquin. 1950. B667
15-16 ____. Der Thomismus. 1951. B668
17 Steenberghen, F. van. Philosophie des Mittelalters. 1950. B669
18 Perler, O. Patristiche Philosophie. 1950. B670
19 Vajda, G. Jüdische Philosophie. 1950. B671
20-21 Regamey, C. Buddhistische Philosophie. 1950. B672
22 Schäfer, O. Johannes Duns Scotus. 1953. B673
23 Bollnow, O. F. Deutsche Existenzphilosophie. 1953. B674

BIBLIOGRAPHY OF BRITISH HISTORY (Oxford)

Davies, G., ed. Bibliography of British history: Stuart period, 1603-1714. 1928. B675
Pargellis, S. and Medley, D. J., eds. Bibliography of British history: the eighteenth century, 1714-89. 1951. B676
Read, C., ed. Bibliography of British history: Tudor period, 1485-1603. 1959. B677

BIBLIOTECA BIBLIOGRAFICA ITALICA (Sansoni)

1 Parenti, M. Dizionario dei luoghi di stampa falsi, inventati o supposti in opere di autori e traduttori italiani. 1951. B678
2 Prandi, D. Bibliografia di Lazzaro Spallanzani. 1952. B679
3 Santi, A. Bibliografia della enigmistica. 1952. B680
4 Parenti, M. Bibliografia delle opere di Silvio Pellico. 1952. B681
5 Bonacini, C. Bibliografia delle arti scrittorie e della calligrafia. 1953. B682
6-7 Borroni, F. "Il cicognara," bibliografia dell'archeologia classica dell'arte italiana. V. 1:1, V. 1:2. (1954-56). B683
8-9 Aliprandi, G. Bibliografia della stenografia. 2 v. 1956-57. B684
10-11 Same as no. 6-7. V. 2:1, 2. 1957. B685
12 Salvestrini, V. Bibliografia di Giordano Bruno. 1958. B686
13-15 Hall, R. A. Bibliografia della linguistica italiana. 3 v. 1958. B687
16 Giannantonio, P. Bibliografia di Gabriele Rossetti. 1958. B688
17 Moranti, L. Bibliografia

urbinate. 1959. B689
18 Rota Ghibaudi, S. Ricerche su Ludovico Settala. 1959. B690
19 Same as no. 7, V. 2:3. 1959. B691
20 Balsamo, L. Giovann'Angelo Scinzenzeler. 1959. B692
21 Ricottini Marsili Libelli, A. Anton Francesco Doni. 1960. B693
22 Cioni, A. Bibliografia delle sacre rappresentazioni. 1961. B694
23 Same as no. 6-7. V. 2:4. Pt. 1. 1961. B695
24 Ascarelli, F. Annali Tipografica di Giacomo Mazzocchi. 1961. B696
25 Same as no. 6-7. V. 2:4. Pt. 2. 1962. B697
26 Camerini, P. Annali dei Giunti. V. 1. 1962. B698
27 Same as no. 7. V. 4:3. 1963. B699
28 Camerini, P. Annali dei Giunti. V. 1. 1963. B700
29 Same as no. 7. V. 4:4. 1963. B701
30 Cioni, A. Bibliografia della poesia populare dei secoli XIII a XVI. V. 1. 1963. B702
31-32 Same as no. 7. V. 5-6. 1964-1966. B703
33 Schlitzer, F. Salvatore di Giacomo, ed. by Doria and Ricottini. 1966. B704
36-37 Puliatti, P. Bibliografica di Alessandro Tassoni. 2 v. 1969-70. B705

BIBLIOTECA BIOGRAFICA (Editorial AEDOS)

1 García Venero, M. Vida de Cambó. 1952. B706
2 Romero Flores, H. R. Biografia de Sancho Panza. 1969. B707
3 Voltes B. W. P. El archiduque Carlos de Austria. 1953. B708
4 Lorén, S. J. Cajal. 1954. B709
5 Sevilla Andrés, D. Antonio Maura. 1954. B710
6 Onieva, A. J. Bajeza y grandeza de Dostoiewski. 1954. B711
7 Gallego Morell, A. Vida y poesía de Gerardo Diego. 1956. B712
8 Sevilla Andrès, D. Canalejas. 1956. B713
9 Bravo Villasante, C. Vida de Bettina Brentano, de Goethe a Beethoven. 1957. B714
10 Cruset, J. San Juan de Dios. 1958. B715
11 Alfonso, J. Azorin en torno a su vida y a su obra. 1958. B716
12 Pla, J. Grandes tipos. 1959. B717
13 Sánchez Reyes, E. Don Marcelino Menendez Pelayo. 1959. B718
14 Villarrazo, B. Miguel de Unammuno. 1959. B719
15 Bravo Villasante, C. Biografía de don Juan Valera. 1959. B720
16 Oliver Belmas, A. Este orto Rubén Dario. 1960. B721
17 Pérez de Ayala, R. Amistades y recuerdos. 1961. B722
18 Cela, C. Cuarto figuras del 98. 1961. B723
19 Martin-Retortillo, C. Joaquin Costa. 1961. B724
20 Oyarzun, R. Vida de Ramón Cabrera y las guerras carlistas. 1961. B725
21 Martin, E. Tres mujeres gallegas del siglo XIX. 1962. B726
22 Martínez Ruiz, J. Varios hombres y alguna mujer. 1962. B727
23 Brown, R. Becquer. 1963. B728

BIBLIOTECA BIOGRAFICA CATALANA (Editorial AEDOS)

1 Rusiñol de Planas, M. Santiago Rusiñol vist per la seva filla. 1951. B729
2 Soldevila, C. Del llum de gas al llum electric, memòires d'infancia i Joventut. 1952. B730
3 Ráfols, J. F. Gaudi, 1852-1926. 1952. B731
4 Arbó, S. J. Verdaguer. 1952. B732

5 Tasis i Marca, R. La vida del rei En Pere III. 1954. B733
6 Galí, A. Rafel d'Amat i de Cartada. 1954. B734
7 Sagarra, J. M. de. Memòires. 1954. B735
8 (misnumbered 7) Camps y Arboix, J. de. Verntallat. 1955. B736
9 Vendrell de Millas, F. and Masiá de Ros, A. Jaume el Dissortat. 1956. B737
10 Reglá Campistol, J. Felip II i Catalunya. 1956. B738
11 Martínez Ferrando, J. E. Jaume II o El sény catalá. 1956. B739
12 Prat i Ubach, P. Junceda. 1958. B740
13 Miracle, J. Guimerá. 1958. B741
14 Soldevila Zubiburu, F. Vida da Jaume I el Conqueridor. 1958. B742
15 Calvet, A. Tots els camins duen a Roma, historia d'un destí, 1893-1914. 1958. B743
16 Soldevila, C. Records i opinions de Pere Ynglada. 1959. B744
17 Canyameres, F. Josep Oller i la seva època. 1959. B745
18 Camps y Arboix, J. de. La masia Catalana. 1959. B746
19 Tasis i Marca, R. Joan I. 1959. B747
20 Amades, J. El pessebre. 1959. B748
21 Martinez Ferrando, J. E. La tràgica història dels reis de Mallorca. 1960. B749
22 Jardi, E. Antoni Puigblanch. 1960. B750
23 Corredor, J. M. Joan Maragall. 1960. B751
24 Ventura, J. Pere el Catòlic i Simó de Montfort. 1960. B752
25 Guilera, J. M. Una història d'Andorra. 1960. B753
26 Gual, A. Mitja vida de teatre. 1960. B754
27 Camps y Arboix, J. de. Duran i Bas. 1961. B755
28 Ventura Subirats, J. Alfons "el Cast." 1961. B756
29 Reglá Campistol, J. Juan Serrallonga. 1961. B757
31 Oller, N. Memòries literàries. 1962. B758
32 Alavedra, J. Paul Casals. 1962. B759
33 Sales, N. Història dels Mossos d'Esquadra. 1962. B760
34 Díaz Carbonella, R. M. Dom Bonaventura Ubach. 1962. B761
35 Soldevila Zubiburer, F. Vida de Pere el Gran i d'Alfons el Liberal. 1963. B762
36 Calvet, A. Sant Feliu de la Costa Brava. 1963. B763
37 Olivar Bertrand, R. Prat de la Riba. 1964. B764
38 Capdevila Massana, M. Eduard Toldra. 1964. B765
39 Calvet, A. Paris, 1914. 1965. B766
40 Guilera, J. M. Unitat històrica del Pireneu. 1964. B767
41 Nadal y Ferrer, J. M. de. Memòires. 1965. B768
42 Poblet, J. M. Frederic Soler, Serafí Pitarra. 1967. B769
43 Voltes i Bou, P. L'Arxeduc Charles d'Austria, rei dels catalans. 1967. B770
44 Jardi, E. El Dr. Robert i el seu temps. 1968. B771
45 Llates Serrat, R. 30 anys de vida catalana. 1969. B772
46 Fabregas y Barri, E. Josep de Togores. 1970. B773
47 Palau, J. Picasso i els seus amics Catalans. 1970. B774
48 Llates Serrat, R. Esser Cataka no es gens facil. 1971. B775
49 Grabolosa, J. Carlins i liberals. 1971. B776
51 Cogul, E. F. Catalunya i la inquisicio. 1973. B777

BIBLIOTECA DE AUTORES CRISTIANOS (Editorial Catolica. Distributed by Academy Guild Press)

1 Bible, Spanish. Sagrada Biblia, tr. by Nácar Fuster and Colunga. 1953. B778
2 Pemán, J. A. and Herrero García, M., jt. comps.

Suma poética. 1944. B779
3 Léon, L. P. de. Obras completas castellanas, ed. by Garcia. 1951. B780
4 Francesco d'Assisi, St. Escritos completos de San Francisco de Asis, ed. by Legisima and Canedo. 1949. B781
5 Rivadeneira, P. de. Historias de la contrarreforma, ed. by Rey. 1945. B782
6 Bonaventura, St. Obras de San Buenaventura, ed. by Aperribay and Oromi. V. 1. 1945. B783
7 Catholic church. Codex juris canonici. Codigo de derecho canónico y legislacion complementaria by Miguélez and others. 1952. B784
8 Alastruey, D. G. Tratado de la Virgen santisima. 1952. B785
9 Same as no. 6. V. 2. 1946. B786
10-11 Augustinus, Aurelius, St. Obras de San Agustín, ed. by Felix García. V. 1, 2. 1950-51. B787
12-13 Donoso Cortés, J. Obras completas de Donoso Cortes, ed. by Juretschke. 2 v. 1946. B788
14 Bible, Latin. Vulgate. Biblia vulgata latina, ed. by Colunza and Turrado. 1951. B789
15 Juan de la Cruz, St. Vida y obras completas de San Juan de la Cruz, ed. by Crisógono de Jesús. 1950. B790
16 Bover y Oliver, J. M. Teologia de San Pablo. 1952. B791
17-18 González Ruiz, N., ed. Piezas maestros del teatro teológico español. 2 v. 1946. B792
19 Same as no. 6. V. 3. 1947. B793
20 Luis de Granada. Obra selecta de fray Luis de Granada by Francho and others. 1952. B794
21 Same as no. 10-11. V. 3. 1951. B795
22 Domingo de Guzmán, St. Santo Domingo de Guzmán, ed. by María Garganta. 1947. B796
23 Bernard de Clairvaux, St. Obras de San Bernardo, ed. by German Prado. 1947. B797
24 Loyola, Ignace de, St. Obras de San Ignacio de Loyola, ed. by Victoriano Larrañaga. V. 1. 1947. B798
25-26 Bible, Spanish. Sagrada Biblia, ed. by Bover-Cantera. 1951. B799
27 María Bover, P. J. La asuncion de Maria. 1950. B800
28 Same as no. 6. V. 4. 1947. B801
29 Thomas Aquinas, St. Suma teológica, ed. by Muniz. V. 1. 1948. B802
30 Same as no. 10-11. V. 3. 1951. B803
31 Lull, R. Obras literarias de Ramon Lull, ed. by Batllori. 1948. B804
32 Fernández, A. Vida de nuestro señor Jesucristo. 1948. B805
33 Balmes, J. J. Obras completas de Jaime Balmes, ed. by Perelló. V. 1. 1948. B806
34 Sánchez Cantón, F. J. Los grandes temos del arte cristiano en españa. 1948. B807
35 Suárez, F. Misterios de la vida de Cristo, ed. by Galdos. V. 1. 1948. B808
36 Same as no. 6. V. 5. 1958. B809
37 Same as no. 33. V. 2. 1948. B810
38 Gomis, J. B. Misticos Franciscanos españoles. 1948. B811
39 Same as no. 10-11. V. 5. 1948. B812
40 Bible, Spanish. Nuevo testamento, ed. by Nácar-Colunga. 1948. B813
41 Same as no. 29. V. 2. B814
42 Same as no. 33. V. 3. 1948. B815
43 Bible. N. T. Spanish. Nuevo testamento, ed. by Bover. 1948. B816
44-46 Same as no. 38. V. 2, 1, 3. 1948-49. B817
47 Same as no. 34. V. 3. 1949. B818
48 Same as no. 33. V. 4.

1949. B819
49 Same as no. 6. V. 6.
1949. B820
50 Same as no. 10-11. V. 6.
1949. B821
51-52 Same as no. 33. V. 5, 6.
1949-50. B822
53 Same as no. 10-11. V. 7.
1950. B823
54 Historia de la iglesia catolica.
V. 1. Ed. by Llorca. 1950.
B824
55 Same as no. 35. V. 2.
1950. B825
56 Same as no. 29. V. 3.
1950. B826
57 Same as no. 33. V. 7.
1950. B827
58 Prudentius Clemens, A.
Obras completas de Aurelio
Prudencio, ed. by Rodríquez.
1950. B828
59 Bible. N. T. Gospels.
Comentarios a los cuatro
Evangelios, ed. by Font.
1950. B829
60 Jesuits. Cursus philosophicus.
V. 5: Theologia naturalis.
1950. B830
61-62 Jesuits. Sacrae theologica
summa. V. 1. Introductio in
theologiam... 1952. V. 3.
De verbo incarnato. 1950. B831
63 Herrera, J. and Pardo, V.
San Vincente de Paul. 1950. B832
64 Same as no. 34. V. 2.
1950. B833
65 Padres apostolicos, ed. by
Ruiz Bueca. 1950. B834
66 Same as no. 33. V. 8.
1950. B835
67 Isidorus, St. Etimologías,
ed. by Luis Cortés. 1951. B836
68 Jungmann, P. El sacrificio
de la misa. 1951. B837
69 Same as no. 10-11. V. 8.
1951. B838
70 Bover Oliver, J. M. Comentario al sermon de la cena.
1951. B839
71 Alastruey, D. G. Tratado de
la santisima eucarista. 1952.
B840
72 Same as no. 59. V. 2.
1951. B841
73 Jesuits. Sacrae theologiae
summa. V. 4. De sacramentis. 1951. B842
74 Teresa, St. Obras completas de Santa Teresa de
Jesús, ed. by Efrén de la
Madre de Dios. V. 1.
1951. B843
75 Ruiz Bueno, D. Actas de
los martires. 1951. B844
76 Same as no. 54. V. 4.
1951. B845
77 Thomas Aquinas, St. Summa theologica sancti Thomae
Aquinatis. V. 1. Prima
pars. 1951. B846
78 Liguori, A. M. de. Obras
ascéticos de San Alfonso
Maria de Ligorio, ed. by
Goy. V. 1. 1952. B847
79 Same as no. 10-11. V. 9.
1952. B848
80 Same as no. 77. V. 3.
Secunda secundae. 1952. B849
81 Same as no. 77. V. 2.
Prima secundae. 1952. B850
82 Anselm, St. Obras completas, ed. by Alameda.
V. 1. 1952. B851
83 Same as no. 77. V. 4.
Tertia pars. 1952. B852
84 Marín-Sola, F. La evolución homogénea del dogma
catolico. 1952. B853
85 Sauras, E. El Cuerpo
Mistico de Cristo. 1952.
B854
86 Loyola, Ignace de, St.
Obras completas de San Ignacio de Loyola. 1952. B855
87 Same as no. 77. V. 5.
Suppl. Indices. 1952. B586
88 Solano, J., ed. Textus
Eucaristicos primitivos.
V. 1. 1952. B857
89 Avila, J. de. St. Obras
completas del beato maestro
Juan de Avila. 1952. B858
90 Same as no. 73. V. 2.
De Dio uno et trino, ed. by
Dalmau and Segues. V. 2.
1952. B859
91 Arintero, J. G. La evolucion mística. 1952. B860
92 Jesuits. Philosophiae
scholasticae summa. V. 3.
Ed. by Hellín and González.
1952. B861
93 Regatillo, F. and Zalba, M.
Theologiae moralis summa.
V. 1. 1952. B862

94 Thomas Aquinas, St. Summa contra los gentiles. V. 1. 1952. B863
95 Same as no. 10-11. V. 10. 1952. B864
96 Tomás de Villanueva, St. Obras de Santo Tomás de Villanueva, ed. by Santamarta. 1952. B865
97 Herrera Oria, A. La palabra de Cristo, ed. by Aria. V. 1. 1955. B866
98 Same as no. 92. V. 1. Ed. by Salcedo and Iturrioz. 1953. B867
99 Same as no. 10-11. V. 11. Ed. by Cilleruelo. 1953. B868
100 Same as no. 82. V. 2. 1953. B869
101 Francisco Xavier, St. Cartas y escritos de San Francisco Javier, ed. by Zubillaga. 1953. B870
102 Same as no. 94. V. 2. 1953. B871
103 Same as no. 89. V. 2. 1953. B872
104 Same as no. 54. V. 2. Ed. by García Villoslada. 1953. B873
105 Riaza, J. M. Ciencia moderna y filosofía. 1953. B874
106 Same as no. 93. V. 2. 1953. B875
107 Same as no. 97. V. 8. 1953. B876
108 Joseph, St. Teologia de San José, ed. by Llamera. 1953. B877
109 François de Sales, St. Obras selectas de San Francisco de Sales. V. 1. 1953. B878
110 Bernard de Clairvaux, St. Obras completas de San Bernardo. V. 1. 1953. B879
111 Grignon de Montfort, L. M., St. Obras de San Luis Maria Grignion de Montfort, ed. by Perez and Arad. 1954. B880
112 Same as no. 59. V. 3. 1954. B881
113 Same as no. 78. V. 2. 1954. B882
114 Royo Marin, A. Teología de la perfección cristiana, ed. by Menéndez-Reigada. 1954. B883
115 Benedictus, St. San Benito, ed. by Colombás. 1954. B884
116 Ruiz Bueno, D. Padres apologistas griegos. 1954. B885
117 Same as no. 93. V. 3. 1954. B886
118 Same as no. 88. V. 2. 1954. B887
119 Same as no. 107. V. 2. 1954. B888
120 Same as no. 74. V. 2. 1951. B889
121 Same as no. 10-11. V. 12. 1954. B890
122 Same as no. 29. V. 5. 1954. B891
123 Same as no. 97. V. 3. 1954. B892
124 Bible, N. T. Gospels, Spanish. Sinopsis concordada de los cuarto evangelios, ed. by Leal. 1954. B893
125 Kirschbaum, E. and others. La tumba de San Pedro y las catacumbas romanas. 1954. B894
126 Same as no. 29. V. 4. 1954. B895
127 Same as no. 109. V. 2. 1954. B896
128 Doctrina pontifica, by Marin and others. V. 4. 1954. B897
129 Same as no. 97. V. 4. 1954. B898
130 Same as no. 110. V. 2. 1955. B899
131 Same as no. 77. V. 12. 1955. B900
132 Righetti, M. Historia de la liturgia. V. 1. 1955. B901
133 Same as no. 97. V. 5. 1955. B902
134 Same as no. 29. V. 10. 1955. B903
135 Fierro, R. St. Biografia y escritos de San Juan Bosco, ed. by Fierro. 1955. B904
136 Muñoz Iglesias, S. Doctrina pontificia. V. 1. 1955. B905
137 Same as no. 93. V. 2. 1955. B906
138 Same as no. 97. V. 6. 1955. B907
139 Same as no. 10-11. V. 13. 1955. B908
140 Same as no. 97. V. 7.

1955. B909
141 Chrysostomus, Joannes, St. Obras de San Juan Crisostomo. V. 1. 1955. B910
142 Same as no. 29. V. 9. 1955. B911
143 Caterina da Siena, St. Obras de Santa Catalina de Siena, ed. by Morta. 1955. B912
144 Same as no. 132. V. 2. 1956. B913
145 Same as no. 29. V. 15. 1956. B914
146 Same as no. 141. V. 2. 1956. B915
147 Royo Marín, A. Teologia de la salvacion, ed. by Barbado Viejo. 1956. B916
148 Bible. N. T. Apocryphal books. Greek and Latin. Los Evangelios Apocrifos, ed. by Santos Otero. 1956. B917
149 Same as no. 29. V. 6. 1956. B918
150-151 Menéndez y Pelayo, M. Historia de los heterodoxos españoles. 2 v. 1956. B919
152 Same as no. 29. V. 8. 1956. B920
153 Garganta, J. M. St. Biografia y escritos de San Vicente Ferrer. 1956. B921
154 Arintero, J. G. Cuestiones misticas. 1956. B922
155-6 Menéndez y Pelayo, M. Antologia general de Menendez Pelayo, ed. by Sánchez de Muniáin. 2 v. 1956. B923
157 Dante Alighieri, Obras completas, ed. by Ruiz. 1956. B924
158 Pius V, Pope. Catecismo Romano. 1956. B925
159 Sántha, G. Biografia y escritos de San José de Calasanz. 1956. B926
160 Fraile, P. G. Historia de la filosofia. V. 1. 1956. B927
161 Cabodevilla, J. M. Señora nuestra. 1958. B928
162 Castrillo, T. Jesucristo Salvador. 1957. B929
163-4 Same as no. 29. V. 12-13. 1957. B930
165 Same as no. 10-11. V. 14. 1957. B931
166 Royo Marin, A. Teologia moral para seglares. V. 1. 1958. B932
167 Same as no. 97. V. 9. 1957. B933
168 Same as no. 10-11. V. 15. 1957. B934
169 Chrysostomus, Joannes, St. Obras de San Juan Crisostomo, ed. by Bueno. 1958. B935
170 Gregorius I, The Great, St. Obras de San Gregorio Magno, ed. by Gallardo. 1958. B936
171-2 Same as no. 10-11. V. 16-17. 1958. B937
173 Same as no. 166. V. 2. 1958. B938
174 Same as no. 136. V. 2. 1958. B939
175-6 Zalba, M. Theologiae moralis compendium. 2 v. 1958. B940
177 Same as no. 29. V. 3, 2. ed. 1959. B941
178 Same as no. 136. V. 3. 1959. B942
179 Riaza, J. M. El comienzo del mundo. 1959. B943
180 Same as no. 29. V. 7. 1959. B944
181 Vagaggini, C. El sentido teologico de la liturgia. 1959. B945
182 Echeverría, B. and others. Año Cristiano. 1959. B946
183 Same as no. 97. V. 10. 1959. B947
184-6 Same as no. 182. V. 2-4. 1959. B948
187 Same as no. 10-11. V. 18. 1959. B949
188 Claret, Antonio Maria, St. Escritos autobiográficos y espirituales. 1959. B950
189 Same as no. 74. V. 3. 1959. B951
190 Same as no. 160. V. 2. 1960. B952
191 Same as no. 29. V. 11. 1960. B953
192 Royo Marin, A. Teologia de la caridad. 1960. B954
193 Escotto, J. D. Obras del Doctor Sutil. 1960. B955
194 Same as no. 136. V. 5. Ed. by Gutierrez García. 1960. B956
195 Cabodevilla, J. M. Hombre y mujer, ed. by

González. 1960. B957
196 Bible, O. T. Pentateuch. Biblia comentada, ed. by Colunga and Cordero. V. 1. 1960. B958
197 Same as no. 29. V. 14. 1960. B959
198 Francisco de Vitoria. Obras, ed. by Urdánoz. 1962. B960
199 Same as no. 54. V. 3. Ed. by Vjlloslada and Llorca. 1962. B961
200 König, F. Cristo y las religiones de la tierra. V. 1. 1960. B962
201 Same as no. 196. V. 2. Ed. by Arnaldich. 1962. B963
202 Garrido Bonano, M. and Pascual A. Curso de liturgia romana. 1961. B964
203 Same as no. 200. V. 2. 1961. B965
204 Montero Moreno, A. Historia de la persecución religiosa en España. 1961. B966
205 Moriones, P. F. Enchiridion theologicum S. Augustini. 1962. B967
206 Quasten, J. Patrologia. V. 1. 1961. B968
207 Bible, N. T. Evangelists. La sagrada escritura, ed. by Leal and others. V. 1. 1961. B969
208 Same as no. 200. V. 3. 1962. B970
209 Same as no. 196. V. 3. 1961. B971
210 Royo Marin, A. Jesucristo y la vida cristiana. V. 1. 1961. B972
211 Same as no. 207. V. 2. 1962. B973
212 Teresa, St. Obras completas de Santa Teresa de Jesús, ed. by Efrén de la Madre de Dios and Steggink. 1962. B974
213 Catholic Church. Comentarios a la Mater et magistra, by Brugarola and others. 1962. B975
214 Same as no. 207. V. 3. 1962. B976
215 Peinador Navarro, A. Tratado de moral profesional. 1962. B977
216 Lombardi, P. Ejercitaciones por un mundo mejor. 1962. B978
217 Same as no. 206. V. 2. 1962. B979
218 Same as no. 196. V. 4. Ed. by Cordero and Rodriguez. 1962. B980
219-220 Jeronimo, St. Cartas, ed. by Ruiz Bueno. 2 v. 1962. B981
221 De Heredia, V. B. Tratados espirituales. 1962. B982
222 Marin, A. R. Dios y su obra. 1962. B983
223 Catholic Church. Comentarios al Codizo de derecho canonico, ed. by Cabreros de Anta. V. 1. 1963. B984
224 Duque, B. J. Teologia de la mistica. 1963. B985
225 Same as no. 223. V. 2. B986
226 Galve, A. A. La iglesia. 1963. B987
227-228 De Bruyne, E. Historia de la estetica. 2 v. 1963. B988
229 Vizmanos, P. L. B. Teologia fundamental para seglares. 1963. B989
230 Instituto Social Leon XIII. Comentarios a la "Pacem in terris," ed. by Orio. 1964. B990
231 Haas, A. Origen de la vida y del hombre. 1964. B991
232 Cabodevilla, J. M. Cristo vivo. 1964. B992
233 Herrera, A. Obras selectas, ed. by De Muniáin y García. 1964. B993
234 Same as no. 223. V. 3. B994
235 Same as no. 10-11. V. 19. 1964. B995
236 Morales, J. M. R. Azar, Ley, Milagro. 1964. B996
237 Tarsicio de Azcona, Fr. Isabel la Católica. 1964. B997
238 Catholic Church. Concilio Vaticano II. V. 1. 1964. B998
239 Same as no. 196. V. 5. 1964. B999
240 Same as no. 223. V. 4. 1964. B1000
241 San Cipriano, S. Obras,

ed. by Campos. 1964. B1001
242 Carol, J. B., ed. Mariologia. 1964. B1002
243 Same as no. 196. V. 6. 1965. B1003
244 Royo Marin, A. La vida religiosa. 1965. B1004
245 Iparraguirre, L. G. E. Ejercicios espirituales. 1965. B1005
246 Same as no. 10-11. V. 20. 1965. B1006
247 Pascher, J. El año liturgico. 1965. B1007
248 Lopetegui, L. and Zubillaga, F. Historia de la Iglesia en la América Española desde el descubrimiento hasta comienzos del siglo XIX. 1965. B1008
249 Same as no. 196. V. 7. 1965. B1009
250 Plazaola, P. J. El arte sacro actual. 1965. B1010
251 Comentarios a la "Ecclesiam Suam," ed. by Instituto Social León XIII. 1965. B1011
252 Catholic Church. Concilio Vaticano. II: Constituciones. 1966. B1012
253 Same as no. 238. V. 2. 1966. B1013
254 Cabodevilla, J. M. Carta de la Cardidad. 1966. B1014
255 Same as no. 10-11. V. 21. 1966. B1015
256 De Egana, P. A. Historia de la Iglesia en la America española. 1966. B1016
257 Ambrose, St. Obras, ed. by Lucas. 1966. B1017
258 Ambrose, St. Obras, ed. by Garrido. 1966. B1018
259 Crusafont, M. La evolucion. 1966. B1019
260 Garcia, J. M. La nueva cristiandad. 1966. B1020
261 Luis de Palma, P. Obras, ed. by Molero. 1966. B1021
262 Tuya, M. de. and Salguero, J. Introduction a la Biblia. V. 1. 1967. B1022
263 Cabodevilla, J. M. La impaciencia de Job. 1967. B1023
264 Same as no. 10-11. V. 22. 1967. B1024
265 Vatican Council. Constitucions. Declaracions... ed. by Jubany. 1967. B1025
266 Vatican Council. El Concilio de Juan y Pablo, ed. by Descalzo. 1967. B1026
267 Bible. O. T. La sagrada escritura, ed. by profesores de la Compañia de Jesús. V. 1. 1967. B1027
268 Same as no. 262. V. 2. 1967. B1028
269 Curso de doctrina social catolica, por Berna and others. 1967. B1029
270 Brugarola, M. Sociologia y teologia de la tecnica. 1967. B1030
271 Bueno, D. R. Origines contra celso. 1967. B1031
272 Royo Marin, A. Espiritualidad de los seglares. 1967. B1032
273 Maldonado Arenas, L. La plegaria eucaristica. 1967. B1033
274 Lopez Quintas, A. Pensadores cristianos contemporaneos. V. 1. 1968. B1034
275 Floristan, C. and Useros, M. Teologia de la accion pastoral. 1969. B1035
276 Vatican Council. Comentarios a la Constitucion, ed. by Gerrera. 1969. B1036
277 Duns, Joannes, S. Obras del Doctor Sutil Juan Duns Escoto. 1969. B1037
278 Royo Marín, A. La Virgen María. 1968. B1038
279 Salvador, F. R. Introduccion a San Juan de la Cruz. 1969. B1039-79
280 Espinosa, C., ed. Los ejercicios de San Ignacio a la luz del Vaticano II. 1969. B1080
282 Pozo, C. Teologia del mas alla. 1969. B1081
283 De la Madre de Dios, E. and Steggink, O. Tiempo y vida de Santa Teresa. 1969. B1082
284 Vatican Council 2. Comentarios a la Constitucion "Dei Verbum" sobre la divina revelacion, ed. by Schökel. 1969. B1083
285 Molina Martinez, M. A. Diccionario del Vaticano II. 1969. B1084

286 Orbe, A. Anthropologia de San Irenao. 1969. B1085
287 La Sagrada escritura: Antiguo Testamento, ed. by Moriarty. 3 v. 1969. B1086
288 Cabodevilla, J. M. 32 de Diciembre. 1969. B1087
289 Carrasco, J. G. La politica docente. 1969. B1088
290 Alejandro, J. M. de. Dios, hombre y mundo. 1969. B1089
291 Bonaño, M. G. San Leon Magno. 1969. B1090
292 Dalmáu, J. M. and Vergés, S. Dios revelado por Cristo. 1969. B1091
293 Same as no. 267. V. 4. 1969. B1092
294 Nicolau, M. Teologia del signo sacramental. 1969. B1093
295 Zimmermann, H. Los methodos historico-criticos en el nuevo testamento. 1969. B1094
296 Javierre, J. M. Soledad de los enfermos. 1970. B1095
297 Lombardi, P. Para vivir el concilio. 1970. B1096
298 López Quintas, A. Filosofia española contemporanea. 1970. B1097
299 Cencillo, L. Mito. 1970. B1098
300 Aldama, J. A. de. Maria en la patristica de los siglos I y II. 1970. B1099
301 Cabodevilla, J. M. El pato apresurado o apologia de los hombres. 1970. B1100
302-4 Avila, Juan de, St. Obras completas del Santo Maestro Juan de Avila, ed. by Sala Balust and Hernández. V. 1-3. 1970. B1101
305-6 Igartua, J. M. La esperanza ecumenica de la iglesia. 2 v. 1970. B1102
307 Garcia Cordero, M. Teologia de la Biblia. V. 1. 1970. B1103
308 Alejandro, J. M. de. La logica y el hombre. 1970. B1104
309 Delicado Baeza, D. J. Comentarios al decreto "Optatam Totius." 1970. B1105
310-11 Fernández, C. Los filósofos modernos. 1972. B1106
312 Same as no. 267. v. 5. 1970. B1107
313 Same as no. 302. V. 5. 1970. B1108
314 Omachevarriá, I. Escritos de Santa Clara y documentos contemporaneos. 1970. B1109
315 Same as no. 302. V. 4. 1970. B1110
316 Caba, J. De los evangelios al Jesus historico. 1971. B1111
317 Lamadrid, A. G. Los descubrimientos del mar muerto. 1971. B1112
318 García Cordero, M. Problemática de la biblia. 1971. B1113
319 Cabodevilla, J. M. Discurso del padrenuestro. 1971. B1114
320-1 Santos Padres Españoles. V. 1, 2. 1971. B1115
322 Nicolau, M. Ministros de Cristo. 1971. B1116
323 Same as no. 267. V. 6. 1971. B1117
324 Same as no. 302. V. 6. 1971. B1118
325 Turrado, A. Dios en el hombre. 1971. B1119
326 Coppens, J. Sacerdocio y celibato. 1972. B1120
327 Fraile, G. Historia de la filosofia española. V. 1. 1971. B1121
328 Asemblea Conjunta Obispos-Sacredotes. Historia de la Asemblea. 1971. B1122
329 Flórez Garcia, G. La reconcilicacion con dios. 1971. B1123
330 Same as no. 327. V. 2. 1972. B1124
331-2 Orbe, A. Parabolas evangelicas en San Ireneo. 1972. B1125
333 Osuna, F. de. Tercer abecedario espiritual. 1972. B1126
334 Catala, V. H. La expresion de lo divino en las religiones no Cristianas. 1972. B1127
335-6 Same as no. 307. V. 2, 3. 1972. B1128
337 Vischer, L. Textos y documentos de la Comision fe y constitucion. 1972. B1129
338-9 Collantes, J. La iglesia

de la Palabra. 2 v. 1972. B1130
340 Heisenberg, W. Dialogos sobre la fisica atomica. 1972. B1131
341 Martin, M. G. Creo en la iglesia. 1973. B1132
342 Plazaola, J. Introduccion a la estetica. 1973. B1133
343 Damboriena, P. La salvacion en las religiones no Cristianas. 1973. B1134
344 Pironio, E. Escritos pastorales. 1973. B1135
345 Vadillo, L. Al encuentro de la unidad. 1973. B1136
346 Larrabe, J. L. El matrimonio cristiano y la familia. 1973. B1137
347 Royo Marin, A. Los grandes maestros de la vida espiritual. 1973. B1138
348 Manjon, P. Diario, ed. by Prellezo. 1973. B1139
349-50 Velasco, A., ed. Historia eclesiastica. 2 v. 1973. B1140
351 Colombas, G. M. El monacato primitivo. V. 1. 1973. B1141
352 Gabriel, L. Filosofia de la existencia. 1973. B1142
353 O'Callaghan, J. Los papiros griegos de la cueva 7 de qumran. 1974. B1143
354 Trujillo, A. L. Liberacion Marxista y liberacion cristiana. 1974. B1144
355 Iribarren, J. Documentos colectivos del Episcopado Español. 1974. B1145
356 Lopez-Gay, J. La mistica del Budismo. 1974. B1146
357 Schmaus, M. and others. La nueva teologia Holandesa. 1974. B1147
358 Valverde, C. Los origenes del Marxismo. 1974. B1148
359 Cabodevilla, J. M. Feria de Utopias. 1974. B1149
360 Pozo, C. Maria en la obra de la salvacion. 1974. B1150
361 Margerie, B. de. Cristo, vida del mundo. 1974. B1151
362 Javierre, J. M., ed. Sor Angela de la Cruz. 1974. B1152
363 Puga, P. H. Sociedad y delincuencia en el siglo de oro. 1974. B1153
364 Orbe, A. Elevaciones sobre el amor de Cristo. 1974. B1154

Serie maior:

1-2 Comentarios sobre el "Catechismo Christiano" de Bartolome Carranza. 2 v. 1972. B1155
3-4 Martin Lutero, por Ricardo García-Villoslada. 1972. B1156
5-7 Vorgrimler, H. and Gucht, R. V. La teologia en el siglo XX. 3 v. 1973. B1157
8 Capanaga, V. Agustin de Hipona. 1974. B1158

Serie minor:

1 Vatican Council. 2d. Documentos del Vatican II. 1972. B1159
2 ___. Ocho grandes mensajes. 1972. B1160
3 Iribarren, J. El derecho a la verdad. 1972. B1161
4 Bible. N. T. Nuevo Testamento, ed. by Nácar-Colunga. 1971. B1162
5 Zalba, M. La regulacion de la natalidad. 1972. B1163
6 Pozo, C. El credo del pueblo de dios. 1972. B1164
7 Bifet, J. E. Juan de Avila. 1972. B1165
8 Garcia-Villoslada, R. Raices historicas del luteranismo. 1972. B1166
9 Pattino, J. M. M. Nuevas normas de la misa. 1972. B1167
10 Dhanis, E. and others. Las correcciones al catecismo Holandes. 1972. B1168
11 Ple, A. Freud y la religion. 1972. B1169
12 Bermejo, J. M. Juan XXIII. 1972. B1170
13 Royo Marín, A. Teologia de la Esperanza. 1972. B1171
14 Solano, J., ed. La eucaristia. 1972. B1172
15 Antón, A. Primado y colegialidad. 1972. B1173
16 Royo Marín, A. La fe de la iglesia. 1972. B1174
17 ___. Doctoras de la iglesia. 1972. B1175
18 Collantes, J. La cara

oculta del Vaticano I. 1972. B1176
19 De Champouricin, E. Dios en la poesia actual. 1972. B1177
20 Val, J. A. del. El inconformismo de la juventud. 1972. B1178
21 Sanchez Agesta, L. España al encuentro de Europa. 1971. B1179
22 Castán Lacoma, L. Las bienaventuranzas de Maria. 1972. B1180
23 Daniélou, J. and Pozo, C. Iglesia y secularizacion. 1972. B1181
24 Benzo Mestre, M. Sobre el sentido de la vida. 1971. B1182
25 Gómez Heras, J. M. Teologia Protestante. 1972. B1183
26 Camón Heras, J. Arte y pensamiento en San Juan de la Cruz. 1972. B1184
27 Nicoláu, M. La crisis de la Iglesia. 1972. B1185
28 Vega, A. C. La poesia de Santa Teresa. 1972. B1186
29 Royo Marín, A. El gran desconocido. 1972. B1187
30 Hanssler, B. El humanismo en la encrucijada. 1972. B1188
31 De Aldama, J. A. and others. Los movimientos teologicos secularizantes. 1973. B1189
32 Aznar, J. C. Habla el Aguila. 1974. B1190
33 Javierre, J. M. El arzobispo mendigo. 1974. B1191

BIBLIOTECA DE AUTORES ESPAÑOLES (V. 1-71 Rivadeneyra, 72-Ediciones Atlas)

1 Cervantes Saavedra, M. de. Obras de Miguel de Cervantes Saavedra. 1916. B1192
2 Moratín, N. F. de. Obras de don Nicolas y don Leandro Fernández de Moratín. 1898. B1193
3 Aribau, B. C., ed. Novelistas anteriores a Cervantes. 1876. B1194
4 Castellanos, J. de. Elegías de varones ilustres de Indias. 1850. B1195
5 Téllez, G. Comedias escogidas de fray Gabriel Tellez el maestro Tirso de Molina, comp. by Hartzenbush. 1930. B1196
6 Luis de Granada. Obras del v. p. m. fray Luis de Granada. V. 1. 1849. B1197
7 Calderón de la Barca, P. Comedias de don Pedro Calderón de la Barca, ed. by Hartzenbush. V. 1. 1918. B1198
8 Same as no. 6. V. 2. 1850. B1199
9 Same as no. 7. V. 2. 1918. B1200
10 Durán, A., ed. Romancero general. V. 1. 1930. B1201
11 Same as no. 6. V. 3. 1951. B1202
12 Same as no. 7. V. 3. 1918. B1203
13 Ochoa y Ronna, E. de, ed. Epistolario español. V. 1. 1850. B1204
14 Same as no. 7. V. 4. 1918. B1205
15 Isla, J. F. de. Obras escogidas del padre José Francisco de Isla, ed. by Monlau y Roca. 1850. B1206
16 Same as no. 10. V. 2. 1926. B1207
17 Rosell y López, C., ed. Poemas epicos. V. 1. 1851. B1208
18 ____. Novelistas posteriores a Cervantes. V. 1. 1925. B1209
19 Quintana, M. J. Obras completas del excmo. sr. d. Manuel José Quintana. 1867. B1210
20 Ruiz de Alarcón y Mendoza, J. Comedias de don Juan Ruiz de Alarcón y Mendoza. 1931. B1211
21 Rosell y López, C. ed. Historiadores de sucesos particulares. V. 1. 1852. B1212
22 Vedia, E. de, ed. Historiadores primitivos de Indias. V. 1. 1852. B1213
23 Quevedo y Villegas, F. G. de. Obras de don Francisco Quevedo Villegas. V. 1. 1852. B1214
24 Vega Carpio, L. F. de. Comedias escogidas de frey

Lope Félix de Vega Carpio. V. 1. 1928. B1215
25 Saavedra Fajardo, D. de. Obras de don Diego de Saavedra Fajardo y del licenciado Pedro Fernandez Navarrete. 1853. B1216
26 Same as no. 22. V. 2. 1853. B1217
27 Escritos del siglo XVI. V. 1. 1853. B1218
28 Same as no. 21. V. 2. 1853. B1219
29 Same as no. 17. V. 2. 1854. B1220
30-31 Mariana, J. de. Obras del padre Juan de Mariana, ed. by Pi y Margall. 2 v. 1854. B1221
32 Castro y Rossi, A. de, ed. Poetas líricos de los siglos XVI y XVII, V. 1. 1854. B1222
33 Same as no. 18. V. 2. 1932. B1223
34 Same as no. 24. V. 2. 1929. B1224
35 Sancha, J. de. Romancero y cancionero sagrados. 1855. B1225
36 Castro y Rossi, A. de., ed. Curiosidades bibliográficas. 1855. B1226
37 Same as no. 27. V. 2. 1855. B1227
38 Vega Carpio, L. F. de. Colecion escogida de obras no dramáticas de frey Lope Félix de Vega Carpio. 1856. B1228
39 Moreto y Cavana, A. Comedias escogidas de don Agustin Moreto y Cubaña. 1856. B1229
40 Gayangos y Arce, P. de, ed. Libros de caballerias. 1950. B1230
41 Same as no. 24. V. 3. 1933. B1231
42 Same as no. 32. V. 2. 1857. B1232
43 Mesonero y Romanos, R. de, ed. Dramaticos contemporaneos de Lope de Vega. V. 1. 1924. B1233
44 Gran conquista de Ultramar. La gran conquista de Ultramar, ed. by Gayangos y Arce. 1926. B1234
45 Same as no. 43. V. 2. 1933. B1235
46 Jovellanos, C. M. de. Obras publicades e inéditas. V. 1. 1903. B1236
47 Vega Carpio, L. F. de. Dramáticos posteriores a Lope de Vega. V. 1. B1237
48 Same as no. 23. V. 2. 1860. B1238
49 Same as no. 47. V. 2. B1239
50 Same as no. 46. V. 2. B1240
51 Gayangos y Arce, P. de, ed. Escritores in prosa anteriores al siglo XV. 1928. B1241
52 Same as no. 24. V. 4. 1932. B1242
53 Teresa, St. Escritos de Santa Teresa, ed. by Fuente. V. 1. 1861. B1243
54 Rojas Zorrilla, F. de Comedias escogidas de don Francisco de Rojas Zorrilla, ed. by Mesonero y Romanos. 1861. B1244
55 Same as no. 53. V. 2. 1862. B1245
56 Feijóo y Montenegro, B. J. Obras escogidas del padre fray Benito Jerónimo Feijóo y Montenegro. V. 1. 1863. B1246
57 Sánchez, T. A., ed. Poetas castellanos anteriores al siglo XV. 1864. B1247
58 González Pedroso, E., ed. Autos sacramentals desde su origen hasta fines del siglo XVII. 1865. B1248
59 Floridablanca, J. M. y R. Obras originales del conde de Floridablanca, y escritos referentes a su persona. 1867. B1249
60 Rivadeneira, P. de. Obras escogidas del padre Pedro de Rivadeneira. 1868. B1250
61 Cueto, L. A. de. Poetas líricos del siglo XVIII. V. 1. 1869. B1251
62 Same as no. 13. V. 2. 1870. B1252
63 Same as no. 61. V. 2. 1875. B1253
64 Toreno, J. M. Q. de L. R. de S. Historia del levantamiento, guerra y revolucion

de España. 1926. B1254
65 Castro y Rossi, A. de, ed. Obras escogidas de filósofos con un discurso preliminar del excelentísimo e ilustrísimo señor don Adolfo de Castro. 1873. B1255
66 Rosell y López, C., ed. Crónicas de los reyes de Castilla desde don Alfonso el Sabio, hasta los católicos don Fernando y doña Isabel. V. 1. 1919. B1256
67 Same as no. 61. V. 2. 1875. B1257
68 Same as no. 66. V. 2. 1876. B1258
69 Same as no. 23. V. 3. 1877. B1259
70 Same as no. 66. V. 3. 1930. B1260
71 Indices generales. B1261
72 Espronceda, J. de. Obras completas, ed. by Campos. 1954. B1262
73 Acosta, J. de. Obras, ed. by Mateos. 1954. B1263
74 Gil y Carrasco, E. Obras completas, ed. by Campos. 1954. B1264
75-77 Navarete, M. F. de. Obras, ed. by Seco Serrano. 3 v. 1954-55. B1265
78-79 Estébanez Calderon, S. Vida y obra de Serafín Estébanez Calderón "El Solitario," ed. by Campos. 2 v. 1955. B1266
80-82 Sandoval, P. de. Obras. 3 v. 1955-56. B1267
83-84 Alcalá Galiano, A. Obras escogidas, ed. by Campos. 2 v. 1955. B1268
85-87 Same as no. 46. V. 3-5. 1955. B1269
88-89 Godoy Alvarez de Fariá Ríos Sánchez y Zarzosa, M. de. Memorias, ed. by Secco Serrano. 2 v. 1956. B1270
90 Cossío, J. M. de, ed. Autobiografias de soldados (siglo XVIII). 1956. B1271
91-92 Cobo, B. Obras, ed. by Mateos. 2 v. 1956. B1272
93-94 Escalante y Prieto, A. de. Obras escogidas, ed. by Menendez Pelayo. 2 v. 1956. B1273
95-96 Casas, B. de las, Bp. of Chiapa. Obras escogidas. V. 1-2. 1957. B1274
97-98 Artola, M., ed. Memorias de tiempos de Fernando VII. 2 v. 1957. B1275
99 San Felipe, V. B. y S. Commentarios de la guerra de España e historia de su rey Felipe V, ed. Animoso, ed. by Serrano. 1957. B1276
100-102 Rivas, A. P. de S. R. de M. R. de B, 3. Obras completas, ed. by Campos. 3 v. 1957. B1277
103-104 Nieremberg, J. E. Obras escogidas, ed. by Zepeda-Heinriquez. 2 v. 1957. B1278
105-106 Same as nos. 95-96. V. 3, 4. B1279
107 Same as no. 22. V. 2. 1958. B1280
108-109 María de Jesus de Agreda, madre. Cartas de sor María de Jesus de Agreda y de Felipe IV, ed. by Seca Serrano. 2 v. 1958. B1281
110 Same as nos. 95-96. V. 5. 1958. B1282
111 Puente, L. de L. Obras escogidas, ed. by Alvarez. 1958. B1283
112-113 Flórez Estrada, A. Obras, ed. by Artola Gallego. 2 v. 1958. B1284
114-115 Muriel, A. Historia de Carlos IV, ed. by Seco Serrano. 2 v. 1959. B1285
116 Prosita castellanos del siglo XV, ed. by Penna. 1959. B1286
117-121 Oviedo y Valdés, G. F. de. Historia general y natural de las Indias, ed. by Pereza de Tudela Bueso. 5 v. 1959. B1287
122 Relaciones históríco-literarias de la América meridional, ed. by Hanke. 1959. B1288
123-125 Yepes, A. de. Crónica general de la Orden de San Benito, ed. by Perez de Urbel. 3 v. 1959-60. B1289
126 Enríquez de Guizmán, A.

Libro de la vida y costumbres de don Alonso Enríquez de Guzmán, ed. by Keniston. 1960. B1290
127-130 Larra, M. J. de. Obras, ed. by Seco Serrano. 4 v. 1960. B1291
131 Esteve, F., ed. Crónicas del reino de Chile. 1960. B1292
132-135 Garcilaso de la Vega el Inca. Obras completas, ed. by Saenz de Santa Maria. 4 v. 1960. B1293
136-140 Caballero, F. Obras, ed. by Calvo. 5 v. 1961. B1294
141-143 Same as no. 56. V. 2-4. 1961. B1295
144-145 Palma, L. de la. Obras completas, ed. by Abad. 2 v. 1962. B1296
146-147 Espoz y Mina, F. Memorias, ed. by Gallego. 2 v. 1962. B1297
148-155 Martinez de la Rose, F. Obras. 8 v. 1962. B1298
156 Same as no. 1. V. 2. 1962. B1299
157-159 Vega Carpio, L. F. de. Obras, ed. by Menéndez Pelayo. 3 v. 1963. B1300
160 Same as nos. 144-145. V. 3. 1963. B1301
161-163 Pineda, J. de. Diálogos familiares de la agricultura cristiana. 3 v. 1963-66. B1302
164-168 Cronicas del Peru, ed. by Perez de Tudela. 5 v. 1963-66. B1303
169-170 Same as nos. 161-163. V. 4, 5. B1304
171 Same as no. 116. V. 2. 1964. B1305
172-174 Miraflores, M. P. F. de P. Memorias del reinado de Isabel II. 3 v. 1964-67. B1306
175 Remesal, A. de. Historia general de las Indias occidentals y particular de la gobernación de Chiapa y Guatemala, ed. by Sáenz de Santa Maria. V. 1. 1964. B1307
176 Paz y Melia, A., ed. Sales españolas. 1964. B1308
177 Same as nos. 157-159. V. 3. 1964. B1309
178 Same as no. 157-159. V. 4. 1964. B1310
179 Carvajal y Mendoza, L. de. Epistolario y poésias, ed. by González Maranon. 1965. B1311
180-182 López de Ayala, A. Obras completas, ed. by Castro y Calvo. 3 v. 1965. B1312
183-185 Spain. Ministero de Fomento. Relaciones geográficas de Indias, ed. by Martinez Carreras. 3 v. 1965. B1313
186-188 Same as nos. 157-159. 3 v. 1966. B1314
189 Same as no. 175. V. 2. 1966. B1315
190-191 Same as nos. 157-159. 2 v. 1966. B1316
192-193 Fernández de Córdova y Valcárcel, F. Mis memorias intimas. 3 v. in 2. 1966. B1317
194 Martinez Marina, F. Obras escogidas, ed. by Cardos. 1966. B1318
195-196 Same as nos. 157-159. 2 v. 1966. B1319
199-203 Mesonero y Romanos, R. de. Obras, ed. by Serrano. 5 v. 1967. B1320
204 Baralt, R. M. Obras literarias publicades e ineditas, ed. by Diaz-Plaja. 1967. B1321
205-208 Alcedo, A. de. Diccionario geográfico de la Indias Occidentales o America, ed. by Perez-Bustamonte. 4 v. 1967. B1322
209 Barba, F. E. Cronicas Peruanas de interes indigena. 1968. B1323
210 Canga Arguella, J. Diccionario de hacienda, ed. by Huarte y Jáuregui. V. 1. 1968. B1324
211-215 Same as nos. 157-159. 3 v. 1968. B1325
216 Lizarraga, R. de. Descripción breve de toda la tierra del Peru... 1968. B1326
217-218 Palafox y Mendoza, J. de. Tratados mejicanos, ed. by Sánchez Castaner y Mena. 2 v. 1968. B1327
219-220 Same as no. 194. 2 v. 1968. B1328

221-222 Barrinuevo, J. Aviso de don Jerónimo de Barrionuevo (1654-1658), ed. by Paz y Melia. 1968. B1329
223-225 Same as no. 157-159. 2 v. 1969. B1330
226 Indices generale. Tomos XIICCXXV. By De Tena and Bethencourt, 1970. B1331
227-228 Diaz, N-P. Obras completas de don Nicomedes-Pastor Diaz, ed. by Castro y Calvo. 2 v. 1969. B1332
229 Gracián y Morales, B. Obras completas, ed. by Batllori and Peralta. 1969. B1333
230 Fuentas y Guzman, F. A. de. Obras históricas de Francisco Antonio de Fuentes y Guzmán, ed. by Saénz de Santa Maria. 1969. B1334
231 Vazquez de Espinosa, A. Compendio y descripcion de las Indias Occidentales, ed. by Velasco Bayón. 1969. B1335
232 Lobo Lasso de la Vega, G. Mexicana, ed. by Amor y Vazquez. 1970. B1336
233-234 Same as no. 157-159. 2 v. 1970. B1337
235-239 Téllez, G. Obras de Tirso de Molina, ed. by Palomo. 5 v. 1970. B1338
240 Motolina, T. Memoriales e Historia de los indios de la Nueva España, ed. by Lejarza. 1970. B1339
241 Same as nos. 227-228. 1970. B1340
242-243 Same as nos. 235-239. V. 6, 7. 1971. B1341
244-245 Cervantes de Salazar, F. Cronica de la Nueva España, ed. by Millares. 2 v. 1971. B1342
246-247 Same as no. 24. V. 30, 31. 1971. B1343
248 Lopez de Velasco, J. Geografía y descripcion universal de las Indias. 1971. B1344
249-250 Same as no. 24. V. 32, 33. 1972. B1345
251 Same as no. 230. V. 2. 1972. B1346
252-256 Solorzano Pereira, J. de. Politica Indiana, ed. by Ochoa Brun. 5 v. 1972. B1347
260-261 Mendieta, J. de. Historia eclesiastica Indiana, ed. by Solano y Perez-Lila. 1973. B1348

BIBLIOTECA DE IDEAS DEL SIGLO XX (Calpe)

Alder, A. Conocimiento del hombre. 1931. B1349
Hellpach, W. H. Geopsique. 1932. B1350
Hertwig, O. Génesis de la organismos. 2 v. 1929. B1351
Jennings, H. S. Genetica. 1935. B1352
Spengler, O. La decadencia de Occident. 4 v. 1925-27. B1353
Uexküll, J. J. Ideas para una concepcion biologica del mundo. B1354

BIBLIOTECA DEL LEONARDO (Sansoni)

1 Gentile, G. La tradizione Italiana. 1936. B1355
2 Vossler, K. Lingua e nazione in Italia e in Germania. 1936. B1356
3 Gentile, G. Giambattista Vico. 1936. B1357
4 Petronio, G. Poeti del nostro secoli: I crepuscolari. 1937. B1358
5 Migliorini, B. Lingua contemporanea. 1938. B1359
6 Russo, L. Gabriele d'Annunzio. 1938. B1360
7 Parenti, M. Biografia D'annunziana essenziale. 1938. B1361
8 Barbi, M. Poésia popolare italia... 1939. B1362
9 Gentile, G. Poésia e filosofia di Giacomo Leopardi. 1939. B1363
10 Russo, L. Commedie Fiorentine del 500. 1939. B1364
11 Luzzi, G. "Il Padrenostro," studio. 1940. B1365
12 Borrelli, E. Estetica wagneriana. 1940. B1366
13 Wartburg, W. von. La posizione della

lingua italiana. 1940. B1367
14 Gentile, G. Giuseppe Pitrè. 1940. B1368
15 Santoli, V. I canti populari italiani. 1940. B1369
16 Calogero, G. Come ci si orienta nel pensiero contemporaneo? 1940. B1370
17 Toschi, P. Dal dramma liturgico alla rappresentazione sacra, saggi. 1940. B1371
18 Gentile, G. La filosofia Italiana contemporanea. 1940. B1372
19 Spongano, R. Un capitolo di storia della nostra prosa d'arte. 1941. B1373
20 Gentile, G. Il pensiero di Leonardo. 1941. B1374
21 Romano, S. F. Poetica dell'ermetismo. 1942. B1375
22 Palumbo, P. F. L'organizzazione del lavoro nel mondo antico. 1942. B1376
23 Santucci, L. Folgore da San Gimignano. 1942. B1377
24 Gentile, G. La mia religione. 1943. B1378
25 Leonardo da Vinci. L'occhio nell'universo. 1943. B1379
26 Gentile, G. Scritti minori di scienza, filosofia e letteratura. 1943. B1380
27 Sgroi, C. Renato Fucini. 1943. B1381
28 Contini, G. Saggio d'un commento alle correzioni del Petrarca volgare. 1943. B1382
29 Captini, A. Atti della presenza aperta. 1943. B1383
30 Marti, M. La formazione del primo Leopardi. 1944. B1384
31 Momigliano, A. Cinque saggi. 1945. B1385
32 Fazio-Allmayer, V. Commento a Pinocchio. 1945. B1386
33 Ciampini, R. Due campagnoli dell '800. 1947. B1387
34 Spongano, R. Prime interpretazioni dei promessi sposi. 1946. B1388
35 Binni, W. La nuova poetica leonardiana. 1946. B1389
36 Petronio, G. Formazione e storia della lirica manzoniana. 1947. B1390
37 Getto, G. Aspetti della poesia di Dante. 1947. B1391
38 Varese, C. Linguaggio sterniano e linguaggio foscoliano. 1947. B1392
39 Grabher, C. Interpretazioni foscoliane. 1948. B1393
40 Li Gotti, E. La Chanson de Roland e i Normanni. 1949. B1394
41 Santangelo, G. Il Bembo critico e il principo d'imitazione. 1950. B1395
42 Pasquali, G. Universita e scuola. 1950. B1396
43 Garin, E. Dal medioevo al Rinascimento. 1950. B1397
44 Petrocchi, M. Miti e suggestioni nella storia europea. 1951. B1398
45 Fubini, M. Due studi danteschi. 1951. B1399
46 Luzi, M. Studios su Mallarmé. 1952. B1400
47 Pepe, G. Un problema storico: Carlo Magno. 1952. B1401
48 Santoli, V. Goethe e il Faust. 1952. B1402
49 Malcovati, E. Madame Dacier, una gentildonna filologa del gran secolo. 1953. B1403
50 Getto, G. Poeti, critici e cose varie del novecento. 1953. B1404
51 Fazio-Allmyer, V. Moralita dell'arte. 1953. B1405
52 Garbari, R. Lettere d'amore e poesia di giosue carducci. 1953. B1406
53 Noferi, A. I tempi della critica foscoliana. 1953. B1407
54 Spirito, U. Note sul pensiero di Giovanni Gentile. 1954. B1408
55 Pizzorusso, A. Tre studi su Giraudoux. 1954. B1409
56 Gerola, G. Dino campana. 1955. B1410
57 Pesce, D. Citta terrena e città celeste nel pensiero antico: Platone, Cicerone, S. Agostino. 1957. B1411
58 Pascucci, G. I. Fondamenti della filogogia classica. 1957. B1412
59 Gentile, P. Il genio della Grecia. 1958. B1413
60 Apollonio, C. Romantico. 1958. B1414

61 Spirito, U. Cristianesimo e comunismo. 1958. B1415

BIBLIOTECA DELL'ARCHIVIUM ROMANICUM (Olschki)

Series I, Storia, Letteratura, Paleografia.

1 Bertoni, G. Guarino da Verona fra letterati e cortigiani a Ferrara, 1429-1460. 1921. B1416
2 ___. Programma di filologia romanza come scienza idealistica. 1922. B1417
3 Verrua, P. Umanisti ed altri (studiosi viri) italiani e stranieri di qua e di là dalle Alpi e dal Mare. 1924. B1418
4 Zaccagnini, G. Le rime di Cino da Pistoia. 1925. B1419
5 ___. La vita dei maestri e degli scolari nello Studio di Bologna... 1926. B1420
6 Jordan, L. Les idées, leurs rapports et le jugement de l'homme. 1926. B1421
7 Pellegrini, C. Il Sismondi e la storia della letteratura dell'Europa meridionale. 1926. B1422
8 Restori, A. Saggi di Bibliografia teatrale spagnuola. 1927. B1423
9 Santangelo, S. La tenzoni poetiche nella letteratura italiana delle origini. 1928. B1424
10 Bertoni, G. Spunti, scorci e commenti. 1928. B1425
11 Ermini, F. Il dies irae. 1928. B1426
12 Filippini, F. Dante scolaro e maestro. 1929. B1427
13 Lazzarini, L. Paolo de Bernardo e i primordi dell'Umanesimo in Venezia. 1930. B1428
14 Zaccagnini, G. Storia dello Studio di Bologna durante il Rinascimento. 1930. B1429
15 Catalano, M. Vita di Ludovico Ariosto. 2 v. 1931. B1430
16 Ruggueru, J. Il canzoniere di Resende. 1931. B1431
17 Döhner, K. Zeit und Ewigkeit bei Chateaubriand. 1931. B1432
18 Troilo, S. Andrea Giuliano politico e letterato veneziano del Quattrocento. 1932. B1433
19 Ugolini, F. A. I cantari d'argomento classico. 1933. B1434
20 Berni, F. Poesie e prose. 1934. B1435
21 Guilhem, de la Tor. La poesie, ed. by Blasi. 1934. B1436
22 Raimon, P. Le poesie, ed. by Cavaliere. 1935. B1437
23 Toschi, P. La poesie popolare religiosa in Italia. 1935. B1438
24 Catalan, A. La poesia del Trovatore Arnaut, ed. by Blasi. 1934. B1439
25 Gugenheim, S. Madame d'Agoult et la pensée européenne de son époque. 1937. B1440
26 Lewent, K. Zum text der lieder des Giraut de Bornelh. 1938. B1441
27 Kolsen, A. Beiträge zur altprovenzalischen lyrik. 1938. B1442
28 Niedermann, J. Kultur. 1941. B1443
29 Altamura, A. L'Umanesimo net mezzogiorno d'Italia. 1941. B1444
30 Nordmann, P. Gabriel Seigneux de Correvon... 1947. B1445
31 Rosa, S. Poesie e lettere inedite, ed. by Limentani. 1950. B1446
32 Panvini, B. La leggenda di Tristano e Isotta. 1952. B1447
33 Messina, M. Domenico di Giovanno detto il Burchiello. 1952. B1448
34 Panvini, B. Le biografie provanzali. 1952. B1449
35 Moncallero, G. L. Il Cardinale Bernardo Dovizi da Bibbiena umanista e diplomatico. 1953. B1450
36 D'Aronco, G. Indice delle fiabe toscane. 1953. B1451
37 Branciforti, F. Il canzoniere di Lanfranco Cigala. 1954. B1452
38 Moncallero, G. L. L'Arcadia. V. 1. 1953. B1453
39 Galanti, B. M. Le villanelle alla napolitana.

1954. B1454
40 Crocioni, G. Folklore e letteratura. 1954. B1455
41 Vecchi, G. Uffici drammatici padovani. 1954. B1456
42 Vallone, A. Studi sulla Divina Commedia. 1955. B1457
43 Panvini, B. La scuola poetica Siciliana. 1955. B1458
44 Moncallero, G. L. Epistolario di Bernando Dovizi da Bibbiena. V. 1. 1490-1513. 1955. B1459
45 Collina, M. D. Il carteggio letterario di uno scienziato del settecento. 1957. B1460
46 Spaziani, M. Il canzoniere francese di Siena. 1957. B1461
47 Vallone, A. Linea della poesia foscoliana. 1957. B1462
48 Crinò, A. M. Fatti e figure del seicento anglo-toscano. 1957. B1463
49 Panvini, B. La Scuola poetica Siciliana. Le canzoni dei rimatori non siciliani. V. 1. 1957. B1464
50 Crinò, A. M. John Dryden. 1957. B1465
51 Lo Nigro, S. Racconti popolari siciliani. 1958. B1466
52 Musumarra, C. La sacra rappresentazione dalla Natività nella tradizione italiana. 1957. B1467
53 Same as no. 49. V. 2. 1958. B1468
54 Vallone, A. La critica dantesca nell'ottocento. 1958. B1469
55 Crinò, A. M. Dryden, poeta satirico. 1958. B1470
56 Coppola, D. Sacre rappresentazioni aversane del sec XVI, la prima volta edite. 1959. B1471
57 Piramus et Tisbè, ed. by Branciforti. 1959. B1472
58 Gallina, A. M. Contributi alla storia della lessicografia italospagnola dei secoli XVI e XVII. 1959. B1473
59 Piromalli, A. Aurelio Bertola nella letteratura dei settecento. 1959. B1474
60 Gamberini, S. Poeti metafisici e cavalieri in Inghilterra. 1959. B1475
61 Berselli Ambri, P. L'opera di Montesquieu nel Settecento Italiano. 1960. B1476
62 Studi Secenteschi. V. 1. 1960. B1477
63 Vallone, A. La critica Dantesca nel 700. 1961. B1478
64 Same as no. 62. V. 2. 1961. B1479
65 Panvini, B. Le rime della scuola siciliana. V. 1. 1962. B1480
66 Balmas, E. Un poeta francese del Rinascimento, Etienne Jodelle. 1962. B1481
67 Same as no. 62. V. 3. 1963. B1482
68 Coppola, D. La poesia religiosa del secolo XV. 1963. B1483
69 Tetel, B. Etude sur le comique de Rabelais. 1963. B1484
70 Same as no. 62. V. 4. 1964. B1485
71 Bigongiari, D. Essays on Dante and medieval culture. 1964. B1486
72 Same as no. 65. V. 2. 1964. B1487
73 Bax, G. "Nniccu furcedda" farda pastorale in vernaculo salentino a cura di Jurlaro. 1964. B1488
74 Studi di letteratura, storia e filosofia in onore di Bruno Revel. 1965. B1489
75 Gobineau, J. A. de. Poemi inediti di Arthur de Gobineau, ed. by Ambri. 1965. B1490
76 Piromialli, A. Dal Quattrocento al Novecento. 1965. B1491
77 Bascape, A. Arte e religione nei poeti lombardi del Duecento. 1964. B1492
78 Guidubaldi, E. Dante europeo. V. 1. 1965. B1493
79 Same as no. 62. V. 5. 1965. B1494
80 Vallone, A. Studi su Dante medievale. 1965. B1495
81 Same as no. 44. V. 2. 1513-1520. 1965. B1496
82 Machiavelli, N. La mandragola di Niccolò Machiavelli, by Ridolfi. 1965. B1497
83 Same as no. 78. V. 2. 1966. B1498

84 Lorenzo de'Medici. Simposio a cura de Martelli. 1966. B1499
85 Same as no. 62. V. 6. 1966. B1500
86 Studi in onore di Italo Siciliano. 2 v. 1966. B1501
87 Rosetti, G. P. G. Comento analitico al "Purgatorio" di Dante Alighieri. 1967. B1502
88 Piromalli, A. Saggi critici di storia letteraria. 1967. B1503
89 Studi di letteratura francese, ed. by Balmas. V. 1. 1967. B1504
91 Personé, L. M. Scrittori Italiani moderne e contemporanei. 1968. B1505.
92 Same as no. 62. V. 7. 1967. B1506
93 Rodinis, G. T. Glaeazzo Gualdo Priorato. 1968. B1507
94 Guidubaldi, E. Dante Europeo. V. 3. 1968. B1508
95 Distante, C. Giovanni Pascoli poeta inquieto tra '800 e 900. 1968. B1509
96 Renzi, L. Canti narrativi tradizionali romeni. 1969. B1510
97 Vallone, A. L'interpretazione di Dante nel cinquecento. 1969. B1511
98 Piromalli, A. Studi sul rinascimento. 1969. B1512
99 Caccia, E. Tecniche e valori dal Manzone al Verga. 1969. B1513
100 Giannantonio, P. Dante el'allegorismo. 1969. B1514
101 Same as no. 62. V. 9. 1969. B1515
102 Tetel, M. Rabelais et l'Italie. 1969. B1516
103 Reggio, G. Le egoghe di Dante. 1969. B1517
104 Moloney, B. Florence and England. 1969. B1518
105 Same as no. 89. V. 2. 1970. B1519
106 Same as no. 62. V. 10. 1969. B1520
107 Convegno di studi su Matteo Maria Boiardo. Il Boiardo e la critica contemporanea, ed. by Anceschi. 1970. B1521
108 Personé, L. M. Pensatore liberi nell'Italia contemporanea. 1970. B1522
109 Gazzola Staachini, V. La narrativa di Vitaliano Brancati. 1970. B1523
110 Same as no. 62. V. 11. 1970. B1524
111 Bargagli, G. La pellegrina, ed. by Cerrera. 1971. B1525
112 Sarolli, G. R. Prolegomena alla Divina Commedia. 1971. B1526
113 Musumarra, C. La poesia tragica italiana nel rinascimento. 1972. B1527
114 Personé, L. M. Il teatro italiano della Belle èpoque. 1972. B1528
115 Same as no. 62. V. 12. 1972. B1529
116 Lomazzi, A. Rainaldo e Lesengrino. 1972. B1530
117 Perella, N. J. The critical fortune of Battista Guarini's "Il pastor fido." 1973. B1531

Series II: Linguistica.

1 Spitzer, L. Lexikalisches aus dem Katalischen und den übrigen ibero-roma nischen sprachen. 1921. B1532
2 Gamillscheg, E. and Spitzer, I. Beiträge zur romanischen wortbildungslehre. 1921. B1533
3 Miscellanea linguistica, by Riegler and others. 1922. B1534
4 Bertoldi, V. Un ribelle nel regno dei fiori. 1923. B1535
5 Bottiglioni, G. Leggende e tradizioni di Sardegna. 1922. B1536
6 Aebischer, P. Onomastica: Paul Aesbischer, Sur l'origine de famille dans le canton de Fribourg... 1924. B1537
7 Rohlfs, G. Griechen und Romanen in Unteritalien. 1924. B1538
8 Gualzata, M. Studi di dialettologia alto Italiana... 1924. B1539
9 Pascu, G. Rumanische elements in den Balkansprachen. 1924. B1540
10 Farinelli, A. Marrano. 1925. B1541
11 Bertoni, G. Profilo storico

del dialetto di Modena. 1925. B1542
12 Bartoli, M. Introduzione alla Neolinguistica. 1926. B1543
13 Migliorini, B. Dal nome proprio al nome comune. 1927. B1544
14 Keller, O. La flexion du verbe dans le patois genevois. 1928. B1545
15 Spotti, I. Vocabolarietto anconitano-italiano. 1929. B1546
16 Wagner, M. L. Studien über den sardischen Wortschatz. 1930. B1547
17 Soukup, R. Les causes et l'évolution de l'abréviation des pronoms personnels régimes en ancien français. 1932. B1548
18 Rheinfelder, H. Kultsprache und Profansprache in den romanischen Ländern. 1933. B1549
19 Flagge, L. Provenzalisches in den Hochtälern des Verdon und der Bléone. 1935. B1550
20 Sainean, L. Autour des sources indigènes. 1935. B1551
21 Seifert, E. Tenere Haben im Romanischen. 1935. B1552
22 Tagliavini, C. L'Albanese di Dalmazia. 1937. B1553
23 Bosshard, H. Saggio di un Glossario dell'Antico Lombardo. 1938. B1554
24 Vidos, B. E. Storia delle parole marinaresche italiene passate in francese. 1939. B1555
25 Alessio, G. Saggio di Toponmastica calabrese. 1939. B1556
26 Folena, G. La crisi linguistica del '400 e l'Arcadia di I. Sannazaro. 1952. B1557
27 Battisti, C., ed. Miscellanea di Studi Linguistici in ricordo di Ettore Tolomei. 1953. B1558
28 Vidos, B. E. Manuale di linguistica romanza. 1959. B1559
29 Ruggieri, R. Saggi di linguistica italiane e italo-romanza. 1962. B1560
30 Mengaldo, P. V. La lingua del Boiardo lirico. 1963. B1561
31 Vidos, B. E. Prestito, espansione e migrazione dei termini tecnici nelle lingue romanze e non romanze. 1965. B1562
32 Altieri Biagi, M. L. Galileo e la terminologia tecnico-scientifica. 1965. B1563
33 Polloni, A. Toponomastica romagnola. 1966. B1564
34 Ghiglieri, P. La grafia del Machiavelli studiata negli artografi. 1969. B1565

BIBLIOTECA DELLA RIVISTA DI STUDI POLITICI INTERNAZIONALI IN FIRENZE (Sansoni)

1 Narok, Appunti storici sull'etiopia. 1936. B1566
2 Bosco, G. L'Iniquo processo di Ginevra. 1936. B1567
3 Nava, S. Il régime degli stretti turchi dopo la guerra. 1938. B1568
4 ____. La questione del Hatay e la sua soluzione. 1939. B1569
5 Toscano, M. Appunti sulla questione tunisiana. 1939. B1570
6 ____. Francia e Italia di fronte al problema di Gibuti. 1939. B1571
7 Ghersi, E. La questione Marocchina nella politica Europea, 1830-1912. 1939. B1572
8 Vedovato, G. Il non intervento in Spagna. 1939. B1573
9 Nava, S. Processo evolutivo delle relazioni Fra G. Stati Balcanici e medio-Orientali. 1939. B1574
10 Breccia, G. Il problema politico dell'India nel quadro costituzionale. 1941. B1575
11 Cora, G. Il Giappone e la "Grande Asia orientale." 1942. B1576
12 Vedovato, G. Il conflitto Europeo e la non belligeranza dell'Italia. 1943. B1577
13 ____. La protezione internazionale dei monumenti storici contro le offese aeree. 1944. B1578

Second series:
1 Toscano, M. Le origini del patto d'Acciaio. 1948. B1579
2 Socini, R. La protezione

internazionale dei diritti dell'uomo. 1950. B1580
3 Vedovato, G. La comunità internazionale; evoluzione e compiti. 1950. B1581
4 Toscano, M. L'Italia e gli accordi tedesco-sovietici dell' Agosto. 1939. 1952. B1582
5 ____. Una mancata intesa italo-sovietica nel 1940-1941. 1953. B1583
6 Ferrarism L. V. L'amministrazime centrale del Ministero degli esteri italiano nel suo sviluppo storico (1848-1954). 1955. B1584
7 Vedovato, G. Gli accordi italo-etiopica dell'agosto. 1928. 1956. B1585
8 Cana, G. Verso quale avvenire? 1958. B1586
9 Guidi, R. Le conseguenze politische della bomba atomica. 1959. B1587
10 Vedovato, G. Le relazioni Italia-San Marino. 1960. B1588
11 ____. Mercato comune europeo. 1963. B1589
12 Angelini, S. Il tentativo italiano per una colonia nel Borneo. 1965. B1590
13 Pastorelli, P. Italia e Albania. 1966. B1591
14 Vedovato, G. L'Universita europea a Firenza. 1968. B1592

Third series:
1-3 Vedovato, G. Studia africani e asiatici. 3 v. 1964. B1593

BIBLIOTECA DI BIBLIOGRAFIA ITALIANA (Olschki)

1 Bologna. Università. Biblioteca. I codici danteschi della Bibliotheca universitaria di Bologna, ed. by Frati. 1923. B1594
2 Fermi, S. Bibliografia delle lettere a stampa di Pietro Giordani. 1923. B1595
3 Sassari, Sardinia. Università. Biblioteca. Librorvm saec. XV impressorvm qui in Bibliotheca Universitatis stvdiorvm Sassarensis adservantvr catalogvs. 1923. B1596
4 Bustico, G. Bibliografia di Vincenzo Monti. 1924. B1597
5 Pastorello, E. Tipografi, editori, librai a Venezia nel sec. XVI. 1924. B1598
6 Bustico, G. Bibliografia di Vittorio Alfieri, 1927. B1599
7 Moderna Biblioteca Estense. Catalogo degli incunaboli della R. Biblioteca Estense di modena, ed. by Fava. 1928. B1600
8 Sorbelli, A. Opuscóli, stampe alla macchia e fogli volanti rifettenti il pensiero politico italiano, 1830-35. 1927. B1601
9 Bustico, G. Bibliografia di Giuseppe Parini. 1929. B1602
10 Gabrieli, G. Manoscritti e carte orientali nelle biblioteche e negli archivi d'Italia. 1930. B1603
11-12 Bibliografia Leopardiana, comp. by Mazzatini and Menghini. 2 v. 1931-32. B1604
13 Frati, C. Dizionario bio-bibliografico dei bibliotecari e bibliofili italiana dal sec. XIV al XIX. 1933. B1605
14 Fumagalli, G. Bibliografia rodia. 1937. B1606
15 Evola, N. D. Ricerche storiche tipografia siciliana. 1940. B1607
16 Fumagalli, G. Vocabolario bibliografico. 1940. B1608
17 Armao, E. Vincenzo Coronelli. 1944. B1609
18 Sartori, C. Bibliografia delle opere musicali stampate da Ottaviano Petrucci. 1948. B1610
19 Vallone, A. Gli studi danteschi dal 1940 al 1949. 1950. B1611
20 Pinto, O. Repertori bibliografici nazionali. 1951. B1612
21 Rotondi, C. Bibliografie dei periodici toscani, 1847-52. 1952. B1613
22 Lopes Pegna, M. Saggio di bibliografia etrusca. 1953. B1614
23 Sartori, C. Bibliografia delle musica strumentale italiana stampata in Italia fino al 1700. 1952. B1615

24 Crocioni, G. Bibliografia della tradizioni popolari marchigiane. 1953. B1616
25 Baroncelli, U. Catologo degli incunaboli della Biblioteca Ugo da Como di Lonato, a cura del Consiglio della Fondazione. 1953. B1617
26 Same as nos. 11-12. Comp. and ed. by Natali and Musumerra. V. 3. 1953. B1618
27 Mambelli, G. Gil annali delle edizioni virgiliane. 1954. B1619
28 Russo, F. Bibliografia gioachimita. 1954. B1620
29 Pavia. Universita Biblioteca. Librorum saec. XV impressorum qui in Publica Ticinensi Bibliotheca adservantur catalogus, ed. by Ageno. 1954. B1621
30 Pastorello, E. L'epistolario manuziano; inventario cronologicoanalitico, 1483-1597. 1957. B1622
31 Ferrara, M. Bibliografia savonaroliana. 1958. B1623
32 Sartori, C. Dizionario degli editori musicali italiani. 1958. B1624
33 Piloni, L. Bibliografia della posta e filatelia Italiane. 1959. B1625
34 Naples. Università. Biblioteca. La raccolta Dantesca della Biblioteca Universitaria di Napoli, ed. by Manna. 2 v. 1959. B1626
35 Prete, S. I codici della Biblioteca communale di Fermo, catalogo. 1960. B1627
36 Rotondi, C. Bibliografia dei periodici toscani, 1852-1864. 1960. B1628
37 Pastorello, E. Inedita Manutiana 1502-1597. 1960. B1629
38 Zaccaria, G. Catalogo degli incunaboli della Biblioteca comunale di Assisi. 1961. B1630
39 Dona, M. La stampa musicale a Milano fino all'anno 1770. 1961. B1631
40 Genoa. Biblioteca civica Berio. Catalogo degli incunaboli della Biblioteca civica Berio di Genova di Luigi Marchini. 1962. B1632
41 Rhodes, D. E. La stampa a Viterbo, 1488-1800... 1963. B1633
42 Westbury, R. M. T. Handlist of Italian cookery books. 1963. B1634
43 Same as nos. 11-12. V. 4. 1963. B1635
44 Rafanelli, S. Catalogo degli incunaboli delle biblioteche pistoiesi. 1963. B1636
45 Camerani, S. Bibliografia medicae. 1964. B1637
46 Saginati Calcagno, B. La collezione dantesca della biblioteca civica Berio di Genova. 1966. B1638
47 Arnese, R. I codici notati della Biblioteca Nazionale di Napoli. 1966. B1639
48 Vianello, N. La Tipografia di Alvisopoli e gli annali delle sue pubblicazioni. 1967. B1640
49 Moranti, L. L'arte tipografia in Urbino. 1967. B1641
50 Studi bibliografici. 1965. B1642
51 Balsamo, L. La stampa in Sardegna nei secoli XVe-XVIe. 1968. B1643
52 Clubb, L. G. Italian plays (1500-1700) in the Folger Library. 1968. B1644
53 Manzi, P. Annali della stamperia Stigliolia a Porta Reale in Napoli. 1968. B1645
54 Pesante, S. Catalogo degli incunaboli della Biblioteca Civica di Trieste. 1968. B1646
55 Tinto, A. Gli annali tipografici di Eucario e Marcello Silber. 1969. B1647
56 Same as no. 23. V. 2. 1969. B1648
57 Contributi alla storia del libro italiano, by Donati. 1969. B1649
58 Manzi, P. Annali di Giovanni Sultzbach. 1970. B1650
59 Michel, S. and P. H. Répetoire des ouvrages imprimés en langue italienne au XV siècle. V. 1. 1970. B1651
60 Toschi, P. Bibliografia desli ex-voto. 1970. B1652
61 Pinto, O. Nuptialia. 1971. B1653

62 Manzi, P. La tipografia napoletana nel cinquecento. 1971. B1654
63 Bibliografia dell'eta del Risorgimento. V. 1. 1971. B1655
64 Same as no. 21. 1864-1871. V. 3. 1972. B1656
65 Manzi, P. Annali di Mattia Cancer ed eredi. 1972. B1657
66 Same as no. 63. V. 2. 1972. B1658
67 Esposito, E. Annali di Antonio de Rossi Stampatore in Rome. 1972. B1659
68 Milan. Conservatorio di Musica Giuseppe Verdi. Catalogo della biblioteca, ed. by Barbian. V. 1. 1972. B1660
69 Donati, L. Bibliografia della miniatura. 1972. B1661
70 Manzi, P. La tipografia napoletana del '500. 1973. B1662
71 Studi offerti a Roberto Ridolfi direttore de La bibliofilia. 1973. B1663
72 Tortoreto, A. and Rotondi, C. Bibliografia analitica leopandiana. 1973. B1664
73 Manzi, P. Annali di Orazio Salviani. 1974. B1665
74 Zolli, P. Bibliografia dei dizionari specializzati italiana del XIX sécolo. 1974. B1666
75 Lattanzi, A. Bibliografia della Massoneria Italiana e di Cagliostro. 1974. B1667
76 Pine-Coffin, R. S. Bibliography of British and American travel in Italy to 1860. 1974. B1668

BIBLIOTECA DI CULTURA MODERNA (Laterza)

1 Orano, P. Psicologia sociale. 1902. B1669
1b Barone, E. La storia militare della nostra guerra fino a Caporetto. 1919. B1670
2 King, B. and Okey, T. L'Italia d'oggi. 1910. B1671
2b Burzio, F. Politica demiurgica. 1923. B1672
3 Ciccotti, E. Piscologia del movimento socialista. 1903. B1673
3b Fueter, E. La storia del secolo XIXe la guerra mondiale. 1922. B1674
4 Amadori-Virgilj, G. L'Istituto familiare nelle società primordiali. 1903. B1675
4b Naumann, F. Mitteleuropa. 2 v. 1918. B1676
5 Martin, A. L'educazione del carattere. 1915. B1677
6 Lorenzo, G. de. India e buddhismo antico. 1926. B1678
7 Spinazzola, V. Le origini e il cammino dell'arte. 1904. B1679
7b Muri, R. La espansione europea. 1919. B1680
8 Gourmont, R. de. Fisica dell'amore. 1906. B1681
9 Cassola, C. I sindacati industriali. 1905. B1682
9b Ricci, U. Dal protezionismo al sindacolismo. 1926. B1683
10 Marchesini, G. Le finzioni dell'anima. 1905. B1684
10b Ricci, U. Protezionisti e liberisti itáliani. 1920. B1685
11 Reich, E. Il successo delle nazioni. 1905. B1686
12 Barbagallo, C. La fine della Grecia antica. 1905. B1687
12b Smart, G. Il testamento spirituale di un economista. 1921. B1687a
13 Novati, F. Attraverso il medioevo. 1905. B1687b
13b Withers, H. In difesa del capitalismo. 1922. B1688
14 Spingarn, J. E. La critica letteraria nel rinascimento. 1905. B1689
14b Pasquali, G. Socialisti tedeschi. 1919. B1690
15 Carlyle, T. Sartor resartus, tr. by Chimenti. 1924. B1691
16 Carabellese, F. Nord e sud attraverso i secoli. 1905. B1692
17 Spaventa, B. Da Socrate a Hegel. 1905. B1693
17b Weber, M. Parlamento e governo nel nuovo ordinamento della Germania. 1919. B1694
18 Labriola, A. Scritti vari

di filosofia e politica. 1906. B1695
18b Vitale, S. L'estetica dell' architettura. 1928. B1696
19 Balfour, A. J. Le basi della fede. 1906. B1697
19b Azimonti, E. Il mezzogiorno agrario quale è. 1921. B1698
20 Freycinet, C. L. de S. de. Saggio sulla filosofia delle scienze. 1906. B1699
20b Larco, R. La Russia e la sua rivoluzione. 1920. B1700
21 Croce, B. Cio che e vivo e cio che è morto della filosofia di Hegel. 1907. B1701
21b Pantaleoni, M. Politica: criterî ed eventi. 1918. B1702
22 Hearn, L. Kokoro. 1920. B1703
23 Nietzsche, E. La nascita della tragedia, ouvero ellenismo e pessimismo. 1935. B1704
24 Imbriani, V. Studi letterari e bizzarrie satiriche. 1907. B1705
24b Pantaleoni, M. La fine provisoria di un'epopea. 1919. B1706
25 Hearn, L. Spigolature nei campi di Buddho. 1922. B1707
26 Saleeby, C. W. La preoccupazione, ossia la malattia del secolo. 1908. B1708
27 Vossler, K. Positivismo e idealismo nella scienza del linguaggio. 1908. B1709
28 Arcoleo, G. Forme vecchie, e idee nuove. 1909. B1710
28b Pantaleoni, M. Bolcevismo italiano. 1922. B1711
29 Il pensiero dell'abate Galiani-antologia di tutti i suoi scritti editi e inediti. 1909. B1712
29b Prato, G. Riflessi storici della economia di guerra. 1919. B1713
30 Spaventa, B. La filosofia italiana nelle sue relazioni con la filosofia europea. 1926. B1714
31 Sorel, G. Considerazioni sulla violenza. 1926. B1715
32 Labriola, A. Socrate. 1953. B1716
33 Kohler, G. Moderni problemi del diritto. 1909. B1717
34 Vossler, K. La divina commedia studiata nella sua genesi e interpretata. 2 v. 1927. B1718
35 Gentile, G. Il modernismo e i rapporti tra religione e filosofia. 1927. B1719
35b Rathenau, W. L'economia nuova. 1922. B1720
36 Festa, G. B. Un galateo femminile italiano del trecento. 1910. B1721
37 Spaventa, S. La politica della Destra. 1910. B1722
37b Sforza, C. Pensiero e azione di una politica estera italiana. 1923. B1723/4
38 Royce, J. Lo spirito della filosofia moderna. 2 v. 1910. B1725
39 Renier, R. Svaghi critici. 1910. B1726
40 Gebhart, A. L'Italia mistica. 1924. B1727
41 Farinelli, A. Il romanticismo in Germania. 1923. B1728
42 Tari, A. Saggi di estetica e metafisica. 1911. B1729
43 Romagnoli, E. Musica e poesia nell'antica grecia. 1911. B1730
43b Viana, M. Sindacalismo. 1923. B1731
44 Fiorentino, F. Studi e ritratti della rinascenza. 1911. B1732
45 Ferrarelli, G. Memorie militari del mezzogiorno d'Italia. 1911. B1733
46 Spaventa, B. Logica e metafisica. 1911. B1734
47 Anile, A. Vigilie di scienza e di vita. 1921. B1735
48 Royce, J. La filosofia della fedeltà. 1911. B1736
49 Emerson, F. W. Li anima, la natura e la saggezza. 2 v. 1925. B1737
50 Rensi, G. Il genio etico ed altri saggi. 1912. B1738
51 Gentile, G. Bernardino Telesio. 1911. B1739
52 Imbriani, V. Fame usurpate. 1926. B1740
53 Puglisi, M. Gesù il mito di Cristo. 1912. B1741
54 Formichi, C. Açvaghosa poeta del Buddhismo. 1912. B1742
55 Michaelis, A. Un secolo

di scoperte archeologiche. 1912. B1743
56 Cessi, C. La poesia ellenistica. 1912. B1744
57 Martello, T. L'economia politica e la odierna crisi del darwinismo. 1912. B1745
58 Saitta, G. Le origini del neotomismo nel sec. XIX. 1912. B1746
59 Ruggiero, G. de. La filosofia contemporanea. 1951. B1747
60 Maturi, S. Introduzione alla filosofia. 1924. B1748
61 Cumont, F. Le religioni origentali nel paganesimo romano. 1913. B1749
62 Farinelli, A. Hebbel e i suoi drammi. 1912. B1750
63 Gnoli, D. I poeti della scuola romana (1850-1870). 1913. B1751
64 Royce, J. Il mondo e l'individuo. 4 v. 1913-1916. B1752
65 Gentile, G. I problemi della scolastica e il pensiero italiano. 1913. B1753
66 Borgognoni, A. Disciplina e spontaneità nell'arte. 1913. B1754
67 Tommasi, S. Il naturalismo moderno. 1913. B1755
68 Petruccelli della Gattina, F. I. Moribondi del Palazzo Carignano. 1913. B1756
69 Croce, B. Cultura e vita morale. 1914. B1757
70 Tonelli, L. La critica letteraria italiana. 1914. B1758
71 Rohde, E. Psiche. 2 v. 1914. B1759
72 Missiroli, M. La monarchia socialista. 1914. B1760
73 Zumbini, B. W. E. Gladstone nelle sue relazioni con l'Italia. 1914. B1761
74 Bartoli, E. Leggende e novelle de l'India antica. 1914. B1762
75 Morelli, D. and Dalbono, E. La scuola napoletana di pittura nel secolo XIX ed altri scritti d'arte. 1915. B1763
76 Lachelier, G. Psicologia e metafisica. 1915. B1764
77 Carlini, A. La mente di Giovanni Bovio. 1916. B1765
78 Cocchia, E. Introduzione storica allo studio della letteratura latina. 1915. B1766
79 Salandra, A. Politica e legislazione. 1915. B1767
80 Nitti, F. S. Il capitale straniero in Italia. 1915. B1768
81 Parodi, T. Poesia e letteratura. 1916. B1769
82 Abignente, G. La riforma dell'amministrazione pubblica in Italia. 1916. B1770
83 Soragna, A. de. Profezie di Isaia figlio d'Amoz. 1916. B1771
84 Bergson, E. Il riso. 1917. B1772
85 Treitschke, E. La Francia dal primo imperio al 1871. 2 v. 1917. B1773
86 Giovannetti, E. Il tramonto del liberalismo. 1917. B1774
87 Sanctis, F. de. Lettere a Virginia. 1926. B1775
88 Treitschke, E. La politica. 4 v. 1918. B1776
89 Ruggiero, G. de. Storia della filosofia. I: La filosofia greca. 2 v. 1950. B1777
90 Onorato, R. L'Iliade di Omero. 1919. B1778
91 Allason, B. Caroline Schlegel. 1919. B1779
92 Steiner, R. La filosofia della libertà. 1919. B1780
93 Castellano, G. Introduzione allo studio delle opere di Benedetto Croce. 1920. B1781
94 Ruggiero, G. de. Il pensiero politico meridionale nei secoli XVIII e XIX. 1946. B1782
95 Croce, B. Giosuè Carducci. 1953. B1783
96 Dentice di Accadia, C. Il razionalismo religioso di Emanuele Kant. 1910. B1784
97 Lollis, C. de. Saggi di letteratura francese. 1920. B1785
98 Croce, B. Giovanni Pascoli. 1947. B1786
99 Citanna, G. La poesia di U. Foscolo. 1947. B1787
100 Macchioro, V. Zagreus. 1920. B1788
101 Sanctis, F. de Mazzini.

1928. B1789
102 Graziani, L. La poesia moderna in Provenza. 1920. B1790
103 Miranda, L. Da Hegel a Croce e da Jellinek a Chiovenda. 1921. B1791
104 Ruggiero, G. de. Storia della filosofia. II: La filosofia del cristianesimo. 3 v. 1950. B1792
105 Russo, L. Metastasio. 1945. B1793
106 Manacorda, G. Studi foscoliani. 1921. B1794
107 Macchioro, V. Eraclito. 1922. B1795
108 Sanctis, F. de. Manzoni. 1922. B1796
109 Monti, A. L'idea federalista nel risorgimento italiano. 1922. B1797
110 Bardi, P. La poesia di Wordsworth (1770-1808). 1922. B1798
111 Battistelli, L. La bugia. 1923. B1799
112 Gotamo, B. Sette discorsi. 1922. B1800
113 Fubini, M. Alfred de Vigny. 1922. B1801
114 McKenzie, K. Conferenze sulla letteratura americana. 1922. B1802
115 Anile, A. Per la cultura e per la scuola. 1923. B1803
116 Braun, O. Diario e lettere. 1923. B1804
117 Gentile, P. Sommario d'una filosofia della religione. 1923. B1805
118 Spaventa, S. Dal 1848 al 1861. 1923. B1806
119 Cornill, C. E. I profeti d'Israele. 1923. B1807
120 Corte, A. della. L'opera comica italiana nel '700. 2 v. 1923. B1808
121 Guardascione, E. Gioacchimo Toma. 1924. B1809
122 Leopold, H. M. R. La religione dei romani. 1924. B1810
123 Calosso, U. L'anarchia di V. Alfieri. 1949. B1811
124 Piazza, G. L'errore come atto logico. 1924. B1812
125 Moore, G. F. I libri del Vecchio Testamento. 1924. B1813
126 ____. Origine e sviluppo della religione. 1925. B1814
127 Fustel de Coulanges, N. D. La città antica. 2 v. 1925. B1815
128 Capri, A. La musica da camera. Dai clavicembalisti a Debussy. 1925. B1816
129 Croce, B. Shakespeare. 1948. B1817
130 Aeschylus. Le Coefore. 1948. B1818
131 Klaczko, G. Conversazioni fiorentine. 1925. B1819
132 Perito, E. La congiura dei baroni e il conte di Policastro. 1926. B1820
133 Spaventa, E. Lettre politiche (1861-1893). 1926. B1821
134 Lollis, C. de. Alessandro Manzoni e gli storici liberali francesi della restaurazione. 1925. B1822
135 Rho, E. Lorenzo il Magnifico. 1926. B1823
136 Croce, B. Ludovico Ariosto. 1951. B1824
137 Sanctis, F. de. Teoria e storia della letteratura. 2 v. 1926. B1825
138 Ruggiero, G. de. Sommario di storia della filosofia. 1952. B1826
139 Carlyle, T. and Welsh, J. Lettere d'amore. 1926. B1827
140 Jacini, S. Un conservatore rurale della nuova Italia. 2 v. 1916. B1828
141 Costanzi, V. Le costituzioni di Atene e di Sparta. 1927. B1829
142 Gentile, F. Pascal. 1927. B1830
143 Gracían, B. Oracolo manuale e arte della prudenza. 1927. B1831
144 Chatfield-Taylor, H. C. Goldoni. 1927. B1832
145 Olschki, L. Giordano Bruno. 1927. B1833
146 Hopkins, E. W. L'etica nell'India. 1917. B1834
147 Zottoli, A. Leopardi. 1947. B1835
148 Meis, A. C. de. Il sovrano. 1927. B1836
149 Allason, B. Bettina

Brentano. 1927. B1837
150 Okakura, K. Gli ideali dell' Oriente, con speciale riferimento all'arte del Giappone. 1927. B1838
151 Schleiermacher, F. L'amore romantico. 1928. B1839
152 Malagodi, G. F. Le ideologie politiche. 1928. B1840
153 Monti, A. Pio IX nel risorgimento italiano. 1928. B1841
154 Pollard, A. F. Storia d'Inghilterra. 1928. B1842
155 Plato. Il simposio. 1946. B1843
156 Ulloa, P. C. Un re in esilio. 1928. B1844
157 Royce, J. Lineamenti di psicologia. 1928. B1845
158 Gerbi, A. La politica del settercento. 1928. B1846
159 Levi, A. Il positivismo politico di Carlo Cattaneo. 1928. B1847
160 Hume, D. Storia naturale della religione a saggio sul suicidio. 1928. B1848
161 Giordano-Orsini, G. N. La poesia di A. Tennyson. 1928. B1849
162 Momigliano, A. Saggio su l' "Orlando Furioso." 1952. B1850
163 Omodèo, A. Tradizioni morali e disciplina storica. 1929. B1851
164 Amatucci, A. S. Stori della letteratura latina critiana. 1929. B1852
165 Arnaldi, F. Cicerone. 1948. B1853
166 Fradeletto, A. La vita e l'anima. La fantasia e l'arte. 1929. B1854
167 Lollis, C. de. Reisebilder e altri scritti. 1929. B1855
168 Avarna di Gualtieri, C. Ruggero settimo nel risorgimento siciliano. 1928. B1856
169 D'Epinay, J. La signora e l'abate Galiani. 1929. B1857
170 McMahan, A. B. Con Byron in Italia. 1929. B1858
171 Lollis, C. de. Saggi sulla forma poetica italiana dell' ottocento. 1929. B1859
172 Man, H. de. Il superamento del marxismo. 2 v. 1929. B1860
173 Fradeletto, A. L'arte nella vita. 1929. B1861
174 Losacco, M. Introduzione alla storia della filosifia greca. 1929. B1862
175 Salvioli, G. Il capitalismo antico. 1929. B1863
176 Russo, L. Problemi di metodo critico. 1950. B1864
177 Milone, F. Il grano, le condizioni geografiche della produzione. 1929. B1865
178 Zibordi, G. Saggio sulla storia del movimento operaio in Italia. 1930. B1866
179 Ruini, M. Luigi Corvetto, genovese, ministroe restauratore delle finanze di Francia (1756-1821). 1929. B1867
180 Battistelli, L. La vanità. 1929. B1868
181 Bandini, L. Shaftesbury. 1930. B1869
182 Doria, G. Del colore locale e altre interpretazioni napoletane. 1930. B1870
183 Michels, R. Sunto di storia economia germanica. 1930. B1871
184 Ruggiero, G. de. Storia della filosofia. III: Rinascimento, riforma e controriforma. 2 v. 1950. B1872
185 Wells, H. G. Breve storia del mondo. 1945. B1873
186 Tarozzi, G. L'esistenza e l'anima. 1930. B1874
187 Fiore, T. La poesia di Virgilio. 1946. B1875
188 Lodi, L. (Il Saraceno) Giornalisti. 1930. B1876
189 Rigola, R. Il movimento operaio nel Biellese. Autobiografia. 1930. B1877
190 Petrini, D. La poesia e l'arte di G. Parini. 1930. B1878
191 Croce, B. Alessandro Manzoni. 1952. B1879
192 Anzillotti, A. Movimenti e contrasti per l'unità italiana. 1930. B1880
193 Speziale, G. C. Storia militare di Taranto negli ultimi cinque secoli. 1930. B1881
194 Treves, P. La filosofia

politica di Tommaso Campanella. 1930. B1882
195 Cosmo, U. Vita di Dante. 1943. B1883
196 Monti, G. M. Il mezzogiorno d'Italia nel medioevo. 1930. B1884
197 Turolla, E. Saggio su la poesia di Omero. 1949. B1885
198 Ruffini, F. La vita religiosa di Alessandro Manzoni. 2 v. 1931. B1886
199 Terán, G. B. La nascita dell'America spagnuola. 1931. B1887
200 Sophocles. Le donne di Trachis. 1931. B1888
201 Ruini, M. La signora di Staël. 1931. B1889
202 Riguzzi, B. Sindacalismo e riformismo nel Parmense. 1931. B1890
203 Man, H. de. La gioia nel lavoro. 1931. B1891
204 Egidi, P. Mezzogiorno medievale e Piemonte moderno. 1931. B1892
205 Dubreuil, H. Standards. Il lavoro americano veduto da un operaio francese. 1931. B1893
206 Perrotta, G. I. Tragici greci. Eschilo, Sofocle, Euripide. 1931. B1894
207 Lorenzo, G. de. Oriente ed occidente. 1931. B1895
208 Jacini, S. Il tramonto del potere temporale (1860-1870). 1931. B1896
209 Croce, B. Introduzione ad una storia d'Europa nel secolo decimonono. 1931. B1897
210 Jeans, J. L'universo intorno a noi. 1931. B1898
211 Sarlo, F. de. L'uomo nella vita sociale. 1931. B1899
212 Vinciguerra, M. Romanticismo. 1947. B1900
213 Morandi, R. Storia della grande industria in Italia. 1931. B1901
214 Laski, H. J. La libertà nello stato moderno. 1931. B1902
215 Dewey, J. Ricostruzione filosofica. 1931. B1903
216 Nicolini, F. La giovinezza di G. B. Vico (1668-1700). 1932. B1904
217 Grasselli, G. Storia di una mente. 1932. B1905
218 Grassi, E. Il problema della metafisica platonica. 1932. B1906
219 Santonastaso, G. Georges Sorel. 1932. B1907
220 Gerbi, A. La politica del romanticismo. Le origini. 1932. B1908
221 Madariaga, S. de. Spagna. 1932. B1909
222 Julian, the apostate. Degli Dei e degli uomini. 1932. B1910
223 Murray, G. Euripide e i suoi tempi. 1932. B1911
224 Sanctis, G. de. Pröblemi di storia antica. 1932. B1912
225 Cappa, A. Cavour. 1932. B1913
226 Lavagnini, B. Saggio sulla storiografia greca. 1933. B1914
227 Milton, J. Areopagitica, tr. by Breglia. 1933. B1915
228 Mila, M. Il melodramma di Verdi. 1933. B1916
229 Butler, N. M. La crisi della società contemporanea. 1933. B1917
230 Treves, P. Demostene e la libertà greca. 1933. B1918
231 Beloch, G. La monarchie ellenistiche e la Repubblica romana. 1933. B1919
232 Fossi, P. La conversione di Alessandro Manzoni. 1933. B1920
233 Zottoli, A. Il sistema di don Abbondio. 1933. B1921
234 Russo, L. Elogio della polemica. 1933. B1922
235 Madariaga, S. de. Inglesi Francesi Spagnoli. 1933. B1923
236 Valle, E. della. Il ciclope d'Euripide. 1933. B1924
237 Ruggiero, G. de. Storia della filosofia. IV: La filosofia moderna. I: L'età cartesiana. 1950. B1925
238 Bardi, P. Storia della letteratura inglese. 1933. B1926
239 Caramella, S. Senso comune. 1933. B1927
240 Odierno de Lorenzo, A. I. Canti di Shakespeare.

1933. B1928
241 Giuliani, A. de. La cagione riposta delle decadenze e delle rivoluzioni. 1934. B1929
242 D'Epinay, J. Gli ultimi anni della Signora. 1933. B1930
243 Marchesini, M. Omero. L'Iliade e l'Odissea. 1934. B1931
244 Croce, B. Nuovi saggi sul Goethe. 1934. B1932
245 Turolla, E. Saggio sulla poesia di Sofocle. 1948. B1933
246 Flora, F. Civiltà del novecento. 1949. B1934
247 Sanctis, F. de. Pagine sparse. 1936. B1935
248 Russo, L. Giovanni Verga. 1947. B1936
249 Rostovtzeff, M. Città carovaniere. 1934. B1937
250 Ruggiero, G. de. Filosofi del novecento. 1949. B1938
251 Omodèo, A. Momenti della vita di guerra. 1934. B1939
252 Croce, B. La critica e la storia delle arti figurative. 1946. B1940
253 Bignone, E. Teocrito. 1934. B1941
254 Massari, G. Uomini di Destra. 1934. B1942
255 Dazzi, M. Leonardo Giustinian, poeta popolare d'amore. 1934. B1943
256 Pancrazi, P. Scrittori d'oggi. Prima serie. 1946. B1944
257 Piccoli, R. Poesia e vita spirituale. 1934. B1945
258 Monti, G. M. Le corporazioni nell'evo antico e nell'alto medio evo. 1934. B1946
259 Russell, B. Panorama scientifico. 1934. B1947
260 Cataudella, Q. La poesia di Aristofane. 1934. B1948
261 Griffith, G. O. Mazzini. 1935. B1949
262 Mazzucchelli, M. La rivoluzione francese vista dagli ambasciatori veneti. 1935. B1950
263 Corsano, A. Umanesimo e religione in G. B. Vico. 1935. B1951
264 Santonastaso, G. Proudhon. 1935. B1952
265 Jhering, R. La lotta pel diritto. 1935. B1953
266 Bottari, S. La critica figurativa e l'estetica moderna. 1935. B1954
267 Perrotta, G. Saffo e Pindaro. 1935. B1955
268 Ferretti, G. I due tempi della composizione della Divina Commedia. 1935. B1956
269 Eddington, A. S. La natura del mondo fisico. 1935. B1957
270 Petronio, G. Il Decamerone. 1935. B1958
271 Quinet, E. La rivoluzioni d'Italia. 1935. B1959
272 Laski, H. J. Democrazia in crisi. 1935. B1960
273 Rostovtzeff, M. Ricostruzioni storiche greco-romane. 1935. B1961
274 Citanna, G. Il romanticismo a la poesia italiana. 1949. B1962
275 Curtis, L. Civitas Dei. 1935. B1963
276 Lombardo-Radice, G. Pedagogia di apostoli e di operai. 1936. B1964
277 Olschki, L. Struttura spirituale e linguistica del mondo neolatino. 1935. B1965
278 Stenzel, J. Platone educatore. 1936. B1966
279 Berdiaev, N. Il cristianesimo e la vita sociale. 1936. B1967
280 Konrad, N. and others. Breve storia del Giappone. 1936. B1968
281 Parente, A. La musica e le arti. 1946. B1969
282 Schlosser, G. La storia dell'arte nelle esperienze e nei ricordi di un suo cultore. 1936. B1970
283 Ottokar, N. Breve storia della Russia. 1945. B1971
284 Castellano, G. Benedetto Croce. 1936. B1972
285 Flora, F. La poesia ermetica. 1947. B1973
286 Finetti, G. F. Difesa dell'autorità della sacra scrittura contro G. B. Vico. 1936. B1974
287 Fraenkell, A. M. Il problema spirituale del presente e la situazione dell'anima. 1936. B1975

288 Baldacchini, S. Purismo e romanticismo. 1936. B1976
289 Rho, E. La missione teatrale di Carlo Goldoni. 1936. B1977
290 Maggini, F. Introduzione allo studio di Dante. 1948. B1978
291 Ruffini, F. Ultimi studî sul conte di Cavour. 1936. B1979
292 Cosmo, U. L'ultima ascesa. 1936. B1980
293 Natoli, G. Stendhal. 1936. B1981
294 Omodèo, A. Alfredo Loisy. 1936. B1982
295 Corsano, A. Il pensiero religioso italiano. 1937. B1983
296 Leon, P. L'etica della potenza o il problema del male. 1937. B1984
297 Senior, N. W. L'Italia dopo il 1848. 1937. B1985
298 Bignone, E. Poeti apollinei. 1937. B1986
299 Delmer, F. S. Sommario storico della letteratura inglese. 1937. B1987
300 Imbriani, V. Critica d'arte e prose narrative. 1937. B1988
301 Capitini, A. Elementi di un'esperienza religiosa. 1942. B1989
302 Tagliacozzo, E. Voci di realismo politico dopo il 1870. 1937. B1990
303 Russo, L. Ritratti e disegni storici. Serie I: Dall'Alfieri al Leopardi. 1946. B1991
303 ____. Ritarri e disegni storici da Machiavelli a Carducci. 1937. B1992
304 Anagnine, E. G. Pico della Mirandola. 1937. B1993
305 Nicolini, F. Peste e untori nei "Promessi sposi" e nella realta storica. 1937. B1994
306 Pancrazi, P. Scrittori italiani dal Carducci al D'Annunzio. 1943. B1995
307 Forges Davanzati, D. Giovanni Andrea Serrao. 1937. B1996
308 Mosca, G. Storia delle dottrine politiche. 1951. B1997
309 Necco, G. Realismo e idealismo nella letteratura tedesca moderna. 1937. B1998
310 Weill, C. Storia dell'idea laica in Francia nel secolo XIX. 1937. B1999
311 Valdés, G. di. Alfabeto cristiano. 1938. B2000
312 Cione, E. Juan de Valdés. 1938. B2001
313 Sanctis, F. de. Lettere dall'esilio (1853-1860). 1938. B2002
314 Netti, F. Critica d'arte. 1938. B2003
315 Jablonski, W. Goethe e le scienze naturali. 1919. B2004
316 Momigliano, A. Studi di poesia. 1948. B2005
317 Imbriani, V. Sette milioni rubati o "La Croce Sabauda." 1938. B2006
318 Goethe, V. Il primo libro degli anni di viaggio di W. Meister. 1938. B2007
319 Croce, B. Michele Marullo Tarcaniota. 1938. B2008
320 Calandra, E. Breve storia dell'architettura in Sicilia. 1938. B2009
321 Barker, E. La concezione romana dell'impero e altri saggi storici. 1938. B2010
322 De Coigny, A. La jeune captive. La restaurazione francese del 1814. 1938. B2011
323 Labriola, A. La concezione materialistica della storia. 1947. B2012
324 Jacini, S. La crisi religiosa del risorgimentô. La politica ecclesiastica italiana da Villafranca a Porta Pia. 1938. B2013
325 Pepe, G. Lo stato Ghibellino di Federico II. 1951. B2014
326 Rasch, G. Garibaldi e Napoli nel 1860. 1938. B2015
327 Schlosser, G. Xenia. 1938. B2016
328 Ricci, U. Tre economisti italiani. Pantaleoni, Pareto, Loria. 1939. B2017
329 Omodèo, A. Un reazionario: il conte J. de Maistre. 1939. B2018
330 Tocqueville, A. de. Una rivoluzione fallita (1848-1849). 1935. B2019

331 Ruggiero, G. de. Storia della filosofia. IV: La filosofia moderna. II: L'età dell'illuminismo. 2 v. 1950. B2020
332 Leibbrand, W. Medicina romantica. 1939. B2021
333 Marega, M. Il Giappone nei racconti e nelle leggende. 1939. B2022
334 Mazzini, G. Lettere slave. 1939. B2023
335 Mosca, G. Elementi di scienza politica. 2v. 1947. B2024
336 Pirenne, H. Maometto e Carlomagno. 1939. B2025
337 Donadoni, E. Antonio Fogazzaro. 1939. B2026
338 Geremicca, A. V. Spiritualità della natura. 1939. B2027
339 Sainte-Beuve, C. A. Studo su Virgilio. 1939. B2028
340 Johnson, S. Esperienza e vita morale. 1939. B2029
341 Labriola, A. Discorrendo di socialismo e di filosofia. 1947. B2030
342 Scott, G. L'architettura dell'umanesimo. 1933. B2031
343 Carbonara, P. L'architettura in America. 1939. B2032
344 Ricci, U. La politica annonaria dell'Italia durante le Grande Guerra. 1939. B2033
345 Caulaincourt, A. A. L. de. In islitta con l'imperatore. 1939. B2034
346 Poe, E. Le poesie. 1939. B2035
347 Huxley, A. L'Albero d'olivo. 1939. B2036
348 Croce, B. La "Dorotea" di Lope de Vega. 1940. B2037
349 Greenfield, K. R. Economia e liberalismo nel risorgimento. 1940. B2038
350 Roeder, R. Savonarola. 1940. B2039
351 Valgimigli, M. Poeti e filosofi di grecia. 1951. B2040
352 Ruini, C. Economia di guerra. 1940. B2041
353 Cosmo, U. Con madonna povertà. 1940. B2042
354 Agrati, C. Giuseppe Sirtori. 1940. B2043
355 Croce, A., ed. Teatro italiano della seconda metà dell'ottocento. V. 1. 1941. B2044
356 Martino, E. de. Naturalismo storicismo nell'etnologia. 1941. B2045
357 Michelet, J. Dal vespro allo sterminio dei Templari. 1941. B2046
358 Chichiarelli, E. Alexis de Tocqueville. 1941. B2047
359 Pancrazi, P. Ragguagli di Parnaso. 1941. B2048
360 Ruggiero, G. de. Storia della filosifia. IV: La filosifia moderna. II: Da Vico a Kant. 1947. B2049
361 Il Tao-Te-King di Laotse. 1941. B2050
362 Figurelli, F. Giacomo Leopardi. 1941. B2051
363 Eddington, A. S. La filosofia della scienza fisica. 1941. B2052
364 Carcopino, G. La vita quotidiana a Roma all'apogeo del l'impero. 1947. B2053
365 Caizzi, B. La filosofia di A. Cournot. 1942. B2054
366 Romano, P. Silvio Spaventa. 1942. B2055
367 Cione, E., ed. L'opera filosifica, storica e letteraria di Benedetto Croce. 1942. B2056
368 Nardi, B. Dante e la cultura medievale. 1949. B2057
369 Bettini, P. Le poesie. 1942. B2058
370 Pancrazi, P. Scrittori d'oggi. 2d ser. 1946. B2059
371 Croce, B. Storia dell'estetica per saggi. 1942. B2060
372 Russo, L. La critica letteraria contemporanea. 3 v. 1953-4. B2061
373 Bruzzo, S. Il Pensiero di A. Labriola. 1942. B2062
374 Lucarelli, A. Il brigantaggio politico nel mezzogiorno d'Italia (1815-1818). 1942. B2063
375 Ciardo, M. Illuminismo e rivoluzione francese. 1942. B2064
376 Rossi, M. Gusto filologico e gusto poetico. 1942. B2065
377 Moro, T. L'Utopia o, La migliore forma di

republblíca. 1942. B2066
378 Croce, B. Lusia Sanfelice e la conguira dei Baccher. 1942. B2067
379 Flora, F. I miti della parola. 1942. B2068
380 Cassandro, G. I. Storia delle terre comuni e degli usi civici nell'Italia meridionale. 1942. B2069
381 Ruggiero, G. de. Storia della filosofia. IV: La filosofia moderna. IV: L'età del romanticismo. 1949. B2070
382 Fonseca Pimentel, E. de. Il monitore repubblicano del 1799. 1943. B2071
383 Mahābhārata. Bhagavadgita (Il canto del Beato). 1943. B2072
384 Marchesini Gobetti Prospero, A. Il poeta del razionalismo settecentesco. 1943. B2073
385 Sarno, A. Pensiero e poesia. 1943. B2074
386 Russo, L. F. de Sanctis e la cultura napoletana. 1943. B2075
387 Polverini, G. L'estetica di Charles Baudelaire. 1943. B2076
388 Croce, B., ed. La riconquista del regno di Napoli nel 1799. 1943. B2077
389 Teatro italiano della seconda metà dell'ottocento. V. 2. 1944. B2078
390 Matthews, H. L. I frutti de fascismo. 1946. B2079
391 Vischer, R. Raffaello e Rubens. 1945. B2080
392 Croce, B. Pagine politiche. 1945. B2081
393 Russo, L. Scrittori-poeti e scrittori letterati- S. di Giacomo, G. C. Abba. 1945. B2082
394 Croce, B. Elementi di politica. 1946. B2083
395 Ruskin, J. I diritti del lavoro. 1946. B2084
396 Croce, B. Un prelato e una cantante del sec. XVIII. 1946. B2085
397 Goethe, J. W. von. Lirica e gnomica dell'ultimo Goethe, ed. by Amorso. 1946. B2086
398 Ragghianti, C. L. Commenti di critica d'arte. 1945. B2087
399 Palma, L. de. Poesia arcaica italiana. 1946. B2088
400 Croce, B. Pensiero politico e politica attuale. 1946. B2089
401 Russo, L. Vita e disciplina militare. 1946. B2090
402 ____. Ritratti e disegni storici. Serie II: Dal Manzoni al De Sanctis. 1946. B2091
403 Piscicelli-Taeggi, O. Diario di un combattente nell'Africa settentrionale. 1945. B2092
404 Fubini, M. Stile e umanità di Giambottista Vico. 1945. B2093
405 Maranelli, C. Considerazioni geografiche sulla questione meridionale. 1946. B2094
406 Lucarelli, A. Il brigantaggio politico delle Puglie dopo il. 1860. 1946. B2095
407 Rossi, M. Baldassar Castiglione. 1946. B2096
408 Ragghianti, C. L. Miscellanea minore di critica d'arte. 1946. B2097
409 Bernardi, G. Un patriota italiano nella Repubblica argentina, Silvio Olivieri. 1946. B2098
410-411 Pancrazi, P. Scrittori d'oggi. 3d and 4th sers. 1946. B2099
412 Cosmo, U. Con Dante attraverso il seicento. 1946. B2100
413 Ronconi, A. Orazio satiro. 1946. B2101
414 Polverini, G. Saggio sull'immortalità. 1946. B2102
415 Ross, W. D. Aristotele. 1946. B2103
416 Ruggiero, G. de. Il ritorno alla ragione. 1946. B2104
417 Calogero, G. Saggi di etica e di teoria del diritto. 1947. B2105
418 Ciardo, M. Le quattro epoche dello storicismo. 1947. B2106
419 Uexküll, J. L'immortale spirito nella natura. 1947. B2107
420 Sarno, G. L'anarchia. 1947. B2108

421 Fracastoro, G. Il navagero. 1947. B2109
422 Terenzio, V. Da Bach a Debussy. 1942. B2110
423 Fustel de Coulange, N. D. Polibio. 1947. B2111
424 Vitale, S. Attualità dell'architettura. 1947. B2112
425 Carrelli, A. Limiti e possibilità della scienza. 1947. B2113
426 Omodèo, A. Giovanni Calvino e la riforma in Ginevra. 1947. B2114
427 Bruno, A. Religiosità perenne. 1947. B2115
428 Venturi, F. L'antichita svelata e l'idea del progresso in N.A. 1947. B2116
429 Schiavi, A., ed. Filippo Turati attraverso le lettere di corrispondenti. 1947. B2117
430 Petaccia, D. La filosofia e il problema della storia. 1947. B2118
431 Munteano, B. Storia della letteratura romena moderna. 1947. B2119
432 Albèrgamo, F. Storia della logica delle scienze esatte. 1947. B2120
433 Politi, F. La lirica del Minnesang. 1948. B2121
434 Omodèo, A. Religione e civiltà. 1948. B2122
435 Ruggiero, G. de. Storia della filosofia. IV: La filosofia moderna. V: Hegel. 1951. B2123
436 Marsico, A. de. Voci e volti di ieri. 1948. B2124
437 Corsano, A. U. Grozio, l'umanista, il teologo, il giurista. 1948. B2125
438 Calosso, U. Colloqui col Manzoni. 1948. B2126
439 Tivaroni, J. Dialoghi su la moneta. 1948. B2127
440 Mayer, K. A. Vita popolare a Napoli nell'età romantica. 1948. B2128
441 Stefano, F. de. Storia della Sicilia dal secolo XI al XIX. 1948. B2129
442 Croce, B. Due anni di vita politica italiana (1946-1947). 1948. B2130
443 Matthews, H. L. Esperienze della guerra di Spagna. 1948. B2131
444 Marmorale, E. V. La questione petroniana. 1948. B2132
445 Terenzio, V. Chopin. 1948. B2133
446 Orrei, E. J. A. Fichte e i discorsi alla nazione tedesca. 1948. B2134
447 Fortunato, G. Antologia dai suoi scritti. 1948. B2135
448 Polverini, G. Dignità dell'uomo ed altri saggi brevi. 1948. B2136
449 Barmine, A. Uno che sopravvisse. 1948. B2137
450 Richter, J. P. F. Siebenkäs. 1948. B2138
451 Ciardo, M. Un fallito tentativo di riforma dello hegelismo. 1948. B2139
452 Carlini, A. Il problema di Cartesio. 1948. B2140
453 Vossler, K. Civiltà e lingua di Francia. 1948. B2141
454 Whitfield, I. H. Petrarca e il rinascimento. 1949. B2142
455 Menendez Pidal, R. Poesia araba e poesia europea. 1949. B2143
456 Menander, I contendenti. 1949. B2144
457 Del Monte, A. La poesia popolare nel tempo e nella coscienza di Dante. 1949. B2145
458 Galizzi, V. Giolitti e Salandra. 1949. B2146
459 Marmorale, E. V. Cato Maior. 1949. B2147
460 Capograssi, A. Gl'Inglesi in Italia durante le compagne napoleoniche (Lord W. Bentinck). 1949. B2148
461 Ibn Hazm, Alī ibn Ahmad. Il collare della cólomba, sull'amore e gli amanti. 1949. B2149
462 Mosca, G. Partiti e sindacati nella crisi del regime parlamentare. 1948. B2150
463 Salvadori, M. Problemi di libertà. 1949. B2151
464 Ciardo, M. Natura e

storia nell'idealismo attuale. 1949. B2152
465 Turati, F. Uomini della politica e della cultura. 1949. B2153
466 Russo, L. Machiavelli. 1957. B2154
467 Nicolini, F. La religiosità di G. B. Vico. 1949. B2155
468 Goethe, J. W. von. Sette liriche, ed. by Tecchi. 1949. B2156
469 Finanza pubblica contemporanea. 1950. B2157
470 Compagna, F. La lotta politica italiana nel secondo dopoguerra e il mezzogiorno. 1950. B2158
471 Ceci, C. Libertà ideale e libertà storica. 1950. B2159
472 Alfieri, V. E., ed. Studi di filosofia greca. 1950. B2160
473 Goethe, V. La provincia pedagogica. Il secondo libro degli anni di viaggio di W. Meister. 1950. B2161
474 Marmorale, E. V. Giovenale. 1950. B2162
475 Pancrazi, P. Scrittori d'oggi. 5th ser. 1950. B2163
476 Capocci, V. Genio e mestiere. 1951. B2164
477 Chaadaev, P. J. Lettere filosofiche. 1950. B2165
478 Terenzio, V. L'arte di Robert Schumann. 1950. B2166
479 Scivoletto, N. Fra Salimbene da Parma. 1950. B2167
480 Croce, B. Storiografia e idealità morale. 1950. B2168
481 Paparelli, G. Enea Silvio Piccolomini (Pio II). 1950. B2169
482 L'età atomica. 1951. B2170
483 Gigli, G. La seconda guerra mondiale (1939-1945). 1951. B2171
484 Menendez Pidal, R. Gli Spagnuoli nella storia. 1951. B2172
485 Lessing, G. E. L'educazione del genere umano. 1951. B2173
486 Russo, L. Ritratti e disegni storici. 3d ser. : Studî sul due e trecento. 1951. B2174
487 Caretti, L. Saggio sul Sacchetti. 1951. B2175
488 Croce, B. Carteggio Croce-Vosseler (1899-1949). 1951. B2176
489 Capocci, V. Difesa di Orazio. 1951. B2177
490 Craveri-Croce, E. Poeti e scrittori tedeschi dell'ultimo settecento. 1951. B2178
491 Morghen, R. Medioevo cristiano. 1951. B2179
492 Albèrgamo, F. Storia della logica scienze empiriche. 1951. B2180
493 Garin, E. L'umanesimo italiano. 1952. B2181
494 Russo, L. Personaggi dei Promessi sposi. 1956. B2182
495 Valle, E. della. L'Antigone di Sofocle. 1952. B2183
496 Norwood, G. Pindaro. 1952. B2184
497 Parente, A. Il tramonto della logica antica e il problema della storia. 1952. B2185
498 Pancrazi, P. Scrittori d'oggi. 4th ser. 1953. B2186
499 Fubini, M. Romanticismo italiano. 1960. B2187
500 Ashton, T. S. La rivoluzione industriale. 1953. B2188
501 Russo, L. Ritratti e disegni storici. 4th ser. 1953. B2189
502 Ciardo, M. Filosofia dell'arte, e filosofia come totalità. 1953. B2190
503 Mautino, A. La formazione della filosofia politica di Benedetto Croce. 1954. B2191
504 Read, H. H. Breve storia della terra. 1954. B2192
505 Fubini, M. Dal Muratori al Baretti. 1954. B2193
506 Garin, E. Medioevo e Rinascimento. 1954. B2194
507 Croce, B. Il concetto della storia. 1954. B2195
508 Spitzer, L. Critica stilistica e storia del linguaggio. 1954. B2196
509 Garin, E. Cronache di filosofia italiana, 1900-1943. 1955. B2197
510 Rossi, M. Sappio du Berkeley. 1955. B2198
511 Corsano, A. Giambattista Vico. 1956. B2199

512 Gambaro, A. La critica pedagogica di Gino Capponi. 1956. B2200
513 Fubini, M. Critica e poesia. 1956. B2201
514 Russo, L. Lettura antiche del Decameron. 1956. B2202
515 ___. Carducci senza retorica. 1957. B2203
516 Luzzatto, G. Per una storia economia d'Italia. 1957. B2204
517 Rossi, P. Francesco Bacone. 1957. B2205
518 Wirszubski, C. Libertas. 1957. B2206
519 Preti, G. Alle origini dell'etica contemporanea. 1957. B2207
520 Vailati, G. Il metodo della filosofia. 1957. B2208
521 Garin, E. L'educazione in Europa. 1957. B2209
522 Firpo, L. Lo stato ideale della controriforma. 1957. B2210
523 Tucci, G. Storia della filosofia indiana. 1957. B2211
524 Diehl, C. I grandi problemi della storia bizantina. 1957. B2212
525 Pagliaro, A. Poesia giullaresca e poesia popolare. 1958. B2213
526 Surin, Y. Il segreto delgi sputnik. 1958. B2214
527 Norden, E. La letteratura romana. 1958. B2215
528 Lefebvre, G. and others. Sanculotti e contadini nella Rivoluzione francese. 1958. B2216
529 Mila, M. Giuseppe Verdi. 1958. B2217
530 Bloch, M. L. B. Lavoro e tecnica nel Medioevo. 1959. B2218
531 Romero, R. Risorgimento e capitalismo. 1959. B2219
532 Abetti, G. Esplorazione dell'universo. 1959. B2220
533 Garin, E. La filosofia come sapere storico. 1959. B2221
534 Granville-Barker, H. M. Introduzione all'Amleto, tr. by Brunacci. 1959. B2222
535 Pevsner, N. Storia dell'architettura europa. 1959. B2223
536 Gaetano Salvemini by de Sestan and others. 1959. B2224
537 Samonà, G. L'urbanistica e l'avvenire della città negli stati europei. 1959. B2225
538 Chiarini, P. Bertolt Brecht. 1959. B2226
539 Soboul, A. Movimento popolare e rivoluzione borghese. 1959. B2227
540 World Congress of Sociology. La sociologia nel suo contesto sociale, by Aron and others. 1959. B2228
541 ___. Sociologia, by Clemens and others. 1959. B2229
542 ___. Aspetti e problemi sociali dello sviluppo economico in Italia, by Doria and others. 1959. B2230
543 Squarzina, L. Teatro. 1959. B2231
544 Rigutti, M. Il sole e la terra. 1960. B2232
545 Ronga, L. L'esperienza storica della musica. 1960. B2233
546 Hack, M. La radioastronomia alla scoperta di un nuovo aspetto del'universo. 1960. B2234
547 Kaegi, W. Meditazioni storiche. 1960. B2235
548 Russo, I. Il tramonto del letterato. 1960. B2236
549 Jhering, R. La lotta pel diritto. 1960. B2237
550 Cantimori, D. Prospettive di storia ereticale italiana el cinquecento. 1960. B2238
551 Benevolo, L. Una introduzione all'architettura. 1960. B2239
552 Macchia, G. Il paradiso della ragione, studi letterari sulla Francia. 1960. B2240
553 Sapegno, N. Ritratto di Manzoni ed altri saggi. 1961. B2241
554 Bosco, U. Francesco Petrarca. 1961. B2242
555 Piovani, P. Giusnaturalismo de etica moderna. 1961. B2243
556 Borsa, G. L'Estremo Oriento fra due mondi. 1961. B2244
557 Gregory, T. Scetticismo

ed empirismo. 1961. B2245
558 Villardi, R. Mezzogiormo e contadini nell'eta moderna. 1961. B2246
559 Paci, E. Tempo e verita nella fenemenologia di Heisserl. 1961. B2247
560 World Congress of Sociology. La élites politiche atti. 1961. B2248
561 Chabod, F. L'idea di nazione... 1961. B2249
562 ____. Storia dell'idea d'Europa... 1961. B2250
563 Chiarini, P. L'avanguardia el poetica del realismo. 1961. B2251
564 Tenenti, A. Venezia e i corsari 1580-1615. 1961. B2252
565 Sasso, G. Profilo di Federico Chabod. 1961. B2253
566 Corsano, A. Tommaso Campanella. 1961. B2254
567 Casini, P. Diderot 'philosophe.' 1962. B2255
568 Del Monte, A. Breve storia del romanzo poliziesco. 1962. B2256
569 Chiarini, L. Arte e tecnica del film. 1962. B2257
570 Villani, P. Mezzogiorno tra riforme e rivoluzione. 1962. B2258
571 Leone de Castris. Storia di Pirandello. 1962. B2259
572 Garin, E. La cultura italiana tra '800 e '900. 1962. B2260
573 Sociologie e centri di potere in Italia. 1962. B2261
574 Plebe, A. La dodecafonia. 1962. B2262
575 More, T. L'Utopia o la migliore forma di repubblica. 1963. B2263
576 Cesa, C. Il giovane Feuerbach. 1963. B2264
577 Dahrendorf, L. Classi e conflitto di classe nella società industriale. 1963. B2265
578 Caracciolo, A., ed. La formazione dell'Italia industriale. 1963. B2266
579 Taylor, A. J. P. Storia della Germania. 1963. B2267
580 Cilento, V. Primessa storica al pensiero antico. 1963. B2268
581 Morris, W. Architecttura e socialismo. 1963. B2269
582 Binni, W. Poetica, critica e storico letteraria. 1963. B2270
583 Benevolo, L. Le origini dell'ubosnistica moderna di Leonardo Benevolo. 1963. B2271
584 Stefano, F. de and Oddo, F. L. Storia della Sicilia dal 1860 al 1910. 1963. B2272
585 Mauro, T. de. Storia linguistica dell'Italia unita. 1963. B2273
586 De Santillana, G. Fortune di Galileo. 1964. B2274
587 Plebe, A. Introduzione alla logica formale. 1964. B2275
588 Capitini, A., ed. L'educazione civica nella scuola e nella vita sociale, con contributi di Arturo Carlo Jemolo and other. 1964. B2276
589 Bertolini, P., ed. Delinquenza e disabattamento minorile. 1964. B2277
590 Martinoli, G., ed. La formazione sul lavoro. 1964. B2278
591 Visalberglo, A., ed. Educazione e condizionamento sociale. 1964. B2279
592 Bauer, R., ed. L'educazione degli adulti. 1964. B2280
593 Calo, G. Famiglia e educazione oggi en Italia. 1964. B2281
594 Bollea, G., ed. Disadattali e minorati. 1964. B2282
595 Laporta, R. Il tempo libero giovanile e la sua organizzazione educativa. 1964. B2283
596 Mazzetti, R., ed. Assistenza e educazione in una societa in transformazione. 1964. B2284
597 Bongioanni, F. M. Fanciulleza abbandonata. 1964. B2285
598 Motzo Dentice di Accadia, C. Legislazione scolastica e autonomie a cura di Cecilia Motzo Dentice d'Accadia. 1964. B2286
599 Lallo, C. M. di.

Problemi psicopedagogici, scuola e linguaggio. 1964. B2287
600 Borghi, L. Scuola e ambiente. 1964. B2288
601 Agazzi, A. and Zavollini, R. La formazione degli insegnanti. 1964. B2289
602 Bertin, G. M., de. Scuola e societa in Italia. 1964. B2290
603 Adkins, A. W. H. La morale dei Greci. 1964. B2291
604 Buonaiuti, E. Pellegrino di Roma. 1964. B2292
605 Williams, W. A. Storia degli Stati Uniti. 1964. B2293
606 Villari, R. Conservatori e democratici nell'Italia liberale. 1964. B2294
607 Volpicelli, L. Riforme di di struttura. 1964. B2295
608 Flores d'Arcais, G. La ricerca pedagogica. 1964. B2296
609 Valitutti, S. Scuola pubblica e privata. 1965. B2297
610 Ferrarotti, F. Max Weber e il destino della ragione. 1965. B2298
611 Brenner, H. Politica culturale del nazismo. 1965. B2299
612 Pra, M. dal. La dialettica in Marx. 1965. B2300
613 Ventura, A. Nobilita e popolo nella societa venata del '400 e '500. 1964. B2301
614 Mauro, T. de. Introduzione alla semantica. 1965. B2302
615 Plebe, A. Discorso semiserio sul romanzo. 1965. B2303
616 Piovani, P. Filosofia e storia delle idee. 1965. B2304
617 Leroy, M. Profilo storico della linguistica moderna. 1965. B2305
618 Saxl, F. La storia delle immahini. 1965. B2306
619 Covegno su la scuola e la società italiana in transformazione, Milan. La scuola e la società italiana in transformazione; atti... 1965. B2307
620 Martinet, A. Elementi di linguistica generale. 1966. B2308
621 Stenzel, J. Platone educatore. 1966. B2309
622 Meynaud, J. La tecnocrazia. 1966. B2310
623 Luti, G. Cronache letterarie tra le due guerre, 1920-1940. 1966. B2311
624 Rognoni, L. Fenomenologia della musica radicale. 1966. B2312
625 Brandi, C. Le due vie. 1966. B2313
626 Landternari, V. Il sogno e le civilità umane. 1966. B2314
627 Lawson, J. H. Teoria e storia del cinema. 1966. B2315
628 Compagna, F. La politica della città. 1967. B2316
629 Cantimori, D. Conversando di storia. 1967. B2317
630 Vacca, G. Politica e filosofia in Bertrando Spaventa. 1967. B2318
631 Dead Sea scrolls. I manoscritti del Mar Morto, ed. by Michelini Tocci. 1967. B2319
632 Cologero, G. Quaderno laico. 1967. B2320
633 Ragionieri, E. Politica e administrazione nella storia dell'Italia unita. 1967. B2321
634 Lugli, P. M. Storia o cultura della cittá italiana. 1967. B2322
635 Villeri, R. La rivalta antispagnola a Nepoli. 1967. B2323
636 Saussure, F. de. Corso di linguistica generale. 1967. B2324
637 Moriondo, E. L'ideologia della magistratura italiana. 1967. B2325
638 Cellucci, C., comp. La filosofia della matematica. 1967. B2326
639 Giammanco, R. Black power. 1967. B2327
640 Leuchtenburg, W. Roosevelt e il New Deal. 1968. B2328
641 Di Federico, G. La giustizia come organizzazione. 1968. B2329
642 Villani, P. Feudalità, riforme, capitalismo agrario. 1968. B2330
643 Goubert, P. Luigi XIV. 1968. B2331
644 Rossi, E. Elogio della

galera. 1968. B2332
645 Bernstein, E. I presupposti del socialismo e i compiti della socialdemocrazia. 1968. B2333
646 Livshits, B. L'arciere dall'occhio e mezzo. 1968. B2334
647 Moravia, S. Il tramato dell'Illuminismo. 1968. B2335
648 Merker, N. L'Illuminismo tedesco. 1968. B2336
649 Tafuri, M. Teorie e storia dell'architettura. 1968. B2337
650 Benevalo, L. L'architettura delle città nel'Italia contemporanea. 1968. B2338
651 Bouvier, J. I. Rothschild. 1968. B2339
652 Garroni, E. Semiotica ed estetica. 1968. B2340
653 Castellano, C. L'efficenza della guistizea italiana e i suoi effeti economico-sociale. 1968. B2341
654 Laplanche, J. and Pontalis, J. B. Enciclopedia della psicanalisi. 1968. B2342
655 Munari, B. Design e communicazione visiva. 1968. B2343
656 Tranfaglia, N. Carlo Rosselli dall'interventismo a Guistizia e libertà. 1968. B2344
657 Aristophanes. Le commedia, ed. by Marzullo. 1968. B2345
658 Ariès, P. Padri e figli nell'Europa medievale e moderna. 1968. B2346
659 Kraiskj, G., comp. Le poetiche russe del Novocento. 1968. B2347
660 Santucci, A. Sistema e ricerca in David Hume. 1967. B2348
661 Galasso, G. Dal comune medievale all'unità. 1969. B2349
662 Casini, P. L'universo-macchina. 1969. B2350
663 Università di oggi e società di domani. 1969. B2351
664 Robins, R. H. Manuale di linguistica generale. 1969. B2352
665 Colletti, L. Il marxisme e Hegel. 1969. B2353
666 Cesa, C. La filosofia politica de Schelling. 1969. B2354
667 Schmidt, A. Il concetto di natura in Marx. 1969. B2355
668 Bedeschi, G. Alienazione e feticismo nel pensiero di Marx. 1968. B2356
669 Spaventa, B. Unificazione nazionale ed egemonia culturale. 1969. B2357
670 Runcini, R. Illusione e paura nel mondo borghese da Dickens a Orwell. 1968. B2358
671 Le scienze dell'uomo e la riforma universitaria. 1969. B2359
672 Trevor-Roper, H. R. Protestantesimo e trasformazione sociale. 1969. B2360
673 Yates, F. A. Giordano Bruno e la tradizione ermetica. 1969. B2361
674 Di Federico, G. La giustizia come organizzazione. 1969. B2362
675 Quilici, V., comp. L'architettura del costruttivismo. 1969. B2363
676 Macherey, P. Per una teoria della produzione letteraria. 1969. B2364
677 Ziff, P. Itinerari filosofici e linguistici. 1969. B2365
678 Cassese, L. La spedizione di Sapri. 1969. B2366
679 Neppi Modona, G. Sciopero, potere e magistratura. 1969. B2367
680 Habermas, J. Teoria e prassi nella societa tecnologica. 1969. B2368
681 Allsop, K. Ribelli vagabondi nell'America dell'ultima frontiera. 1969. B2369
682 Rossi, A. La festo dei poveri. 1969. B2370
683 Ganapini, L. Il nazionalismo cattolico. 1970. B2371
684 Chiodi, G. M. La giustizia amministrativa nel pensiero politici di Silvio Spaventa. 1969. B2372
685 Weil, J. La frontiera di Mosca. 1970. B2373
686 Isnenghi, M. Il mito della grande guerra da Marinetti a Melaparte. 1970. B2374
687 Madrignani, C. A. Capuana e el naturalismo. 1970. B2375
688 Odorisio, R. and others.

Valori socio-culturali della giurisprudenza. 1970. B2376
689 Cingari, G. Mezzogriorno e Risorgimento. 1970. B2377
690 Governatori, F. Stato e cittadino in tribunale. 1970. B2378
691 Pinzani, C. Jean Jaurès, L'Internazionale e la guerra. 1970. B2379
692 Campa, R. comp. Antologia del pensiero politico latino-americano. 1970. B2380
693 Strappini, L. La classe dei colti. 1970. B2381
694 Forte, F. Costi e benefici della guistizia italiana. 1970. B2382
695 Formigari, L. Linguistica ed empirismo nel Seicento inglese. 1970. B2383
696 Vilar, P. Sviluppo economico e analisi storico. 1970. B2384
697 Moravia, S. La scienza dell'uomo nel settecento. 1970. B2385
698 Gallini, C. Protesta e intergrazione nella Roma antica. 1970. B2386
699 Habermas, J. Conoscenza e interesse. 1970. B2387
700 Saumjan, S. K. Linguistica dinamica. 1970. B2388
701 Sica, P. L'Immagine della città da Sparta a Las Vegas. 1970. B2389
702 Marx, K. Lettere sul Capitale. 1971. B2390
703 Colarizi, S. Dopoguerra e fascismo. 1971. B2391
704 Biani, M. La teoria del valore dai classici a Marx. 1970. B2392
705 Merlin, P. Le città nuove. 1971. B2393
706 Decleva, E. Da Adua a Sarajevo. 1971. B2394
707 Agosti, A. Rodolfo Morandi. 1971. B2395
708 Morghen, R. Civilta medievale al tramonto. 1971. B2396
709 Germani, G. Sociologia della modernizzazione. 1971. B2397
710 Prieto, L. J. Lineamenti di semiologia. 1971. B2398
711 Pepe, A. Storia della CGdL dalla guerra de Libia all'intervento. 1971. B2399
712 Rosdolsky, R. Genesi e struttura del Capitale di Marx. 1971. B2400
713 Habermas, J. Storia e critica dell'opinione pubblica. 1971. B2401
714 Gallini, C. Il consumo del sacro. 1971. B2402
715 Coseriu, E. Teoria del linguaggio e linguistica generale. 1971. B2403
716 Sini, C. Il pragmatismo americano. 1972. B2404
717 Beattie, J. Uomini diversi da noi. 1972. B2405
718 Same as no 711. V. 2. 1971. B2406
719 Herriot, P. La psicologia del linguaggio. 1972. B2407
720 Treves, R. Giustizia e giudici nella società italiana. 1972. B2408
721 Landucci, S. I filosofi e i selvaggi. 1972. B2409
722 Laplanche, J. Vita e morte nella psicoanalisi. 1972. B2410
723 Cera, G. Sarte tra ideologia e storia. 1972. B2411
724 Mannoni, O. La funzione dell'immaginario. 1972. B2412
725 Toynbee, A. La città aggressiva. 1972. B2413
726 Monticone, A. Gli italiani in uniforme. 1972. B2414
727 Jeanneret-Gris, C. E. Arte decorativa e design. 1972. B2415
728 Mead, M. Il futuro senza volto. 1972. B2416
729 Garroni, E. Pragetto di semiotica. 1972. B2417
730 Giolli, R. L'architettura rezionale. 1972. B2418
731 Costa, G. La leggenda dei secoli d'oro nella letteratura italiana. 1972. B2419
732 De Seta, C. La cultura architettonica in Italia fra le due guerre. 1972. B2420
733 Pitocco, F. Utopia e reforma religiosa nel risorgimento. 1972. B2421
734 Boas, F. L'uomo primitivo. 1972. B2422

735 Canfora, L. Totalita e selezione nella storiografia classica. 1972. B2423
736 Bellucci, M. and others. Ricerche sulla cultura dell' Italia moderna. 1973. B2424
737 Casini, P. Introduzione all'illuminismo. 1973. B2425
738 Dardano, M. Il linguaggio dei giornali italiani. 1973. B2426
739 Grassi, F. Il tramonto dell'età giolettiana nell Salento. 1973. B2427
740-1 L'Uso alternativo del diritto, by Blanke and others. 2 v. 1973. B2428
742 Fusco, R. de. Segni, storia e progetto dell'architettura. 1973. B2429
743 Havelock, E. A. Cultura orale e civilità della scrittura. 1973. B2430
744 Forssman, E. Dorico, ionico, corinzio nell'architettura del Rinascimento. 1973. B2431
745 Bedeschi, G. Politica e storia in Hegel. V. 1. 1973. B2432
746 Cappekketti, V. Freud. 1973. B2433
747 Tomeo, V. Il giudice sullo schermo. 1973. B2434
748 Balandier, G. Le società comunicanti. 1973. B2435
749 Dal Pra, M. Hume e la scienza della natura umana. 1973. B2436
750 Pacchi, A. Cartesio in Inghilterra. 1973. B2437
751 Leont'ev, A. A. Teoria dell'attività verbale. 1973. B2438
752 Oldrini, G. La cultura filosofica napoletana dell'ottocento. 1973. B2439
753 Evans-Pritchard, E. E. La donna nelle società primitive. 1973. B2440
754 Nock, A. D. La conversione. 1974. B2441
755 Avineri, S. La teoria begeliana dello stato. 1973. B2442
756 Ullmann, W. Individuo e società nel medioevo. 1974. B2443
757 Pesce, D. Saggio su Epicuro. 1974. B2444
758 Ferguson, J. Le religioni nell'impero romano. 1974. B2445
759 Corradini, D. Storicismo e politicità del diritto. 1974. B2446
760 Sabbatucci, G. I combattenti nel primo dopoguerra. 1974. B2447
761 Techiche giuidiche e sviluppo della persona, ed. by Lipari. 1974. B2448
762 Mangoni, L. L'interventismo della cultura. 1974. B2449
763 Cordova, F. Le origini dei sindacati fascisti. 1974. B2450
764 Etologia e psichiatria, by Balestrieri and others. 1974. B2451
765 Dal Pra, M. Logica e realtà. 1974. B2452
766 Corner, P. R. Il fascismo a Ferrara. 1974. B2453

BIBLIOTECA DI CULTURA STORICA (Einaudi)

1 Salvatorelli, L. Il pensiero politico italiano dal 1700 al 1870. 1959. B2454
2 Bollati, A. I rovesci piu caratteristici delgi eserciti guerra mondiale, 1914-1918. 1936. B2455
3 Bonomi, I. Mazzini, triumviro della repubblica romana. 1936. B2456
4 Santangelo, P. E. Massimo d'Azeglio, politico e moralista. 1937. B2457
5 Cooper, D. Talleyrand. 1937. B2458
6 Salvatorelli, L. Sommario della storia d'Italia dai tempi preistorici ai nostri gionri. 1948. B2459
7 Dawson, C. H. La formazione dell'unità europea dal secolo V all'XI. 1939. B2460
8 Villat, L. La rivoluzione francese e l'impero napoleonico. 1940. B2461
9 Pepe, G. Il medio evo barbico d'Italia. 1945. B2462
10 Valente, A. Gioacchino

Murat e l'Italia meridionale. 1941. B2463
11 Burckhardt, C. J. Richelieu. 1941. B2464
12 Trevelyan, G. M. Storia dell'Inghilterra nel secolo XIX. 1945. B2465
13 Chamberlain, W. H. Storia della rivoluzione russa. 1941. B2466
14 Bono, G. del. Cavour e Napoleone III. 1941. B2467
15 Salvatorelli, L. Profilo della storia d'Europa. 1942. B2468
15 ____. ____. 2 v. ed. 1944. B2469
16 Jaeger, W. W. Demostene. 1943. B2470
17 Loisy, A. F. Le origini del cristianesimo. 1943. B2471
18 Radet, G. A. Alessandro il Grande tr. by Mazziotti. 1944. B2472
19 Wahl, R. Barbarossa. 1945. B2473
20 Bonomi, I. La politica italiana da Porta Pia a Vittorio Veneto (1870-1918). 1944. B2474
21 Rosselli, N. Saggi sul Risorgimento e altri scritti. 1946. B2475
22 Nevins, A. and Commager, H. S. America, la storia di un popolo libero. 1947. B2476
23 Korngold, R. Robespierre e il quarto stato. 1947. B2477
24 Fueter, E. Storia universale degli ultimi cento anni (1815-1920). 1947. B2478
25 Duchesne, L. M. O. I primi tempi dello stato pontificio. 1947. B2479
26 Cusin, F. Antistoria d'Italia. 1948. B2480
27 Mathiez, A. La reazione termidoriana. 1948. B2481
28 Trevelyan, G. M. Storia della societa inglese, tr. by Morra. 1948. B2482
29 Omodèo, A. Il senso della storia. 1948. B2483
30 Bonomi, I. La politica italiana da Porta Pia a Vittorio Veneto, 1870-1918. 1946. B2484
31 Demarco, D. Il tramonto dello stato pontificio. 1949. B2485
32 Jemolo, A. C. Chiesa e Stato in Italia negli ultimi cento anni. 1949. B2486
33 Childe, V. G. Il progresso nel mondo antico. 1949. B2487
34 Groethuysen, B. Origini dello spirito borghese in Francia, tr. by Forti. V. 1. 1949. B2488
35 Mathiez, A. Carovita e lotte sociale sotto il Terrore, tr. by Venturi e Serini. 1949. B2489
36 Bloch, M. L. B. La società feudale. 1949. B2490
37 Bulferetti, L. Socialismo risorgimentale. 1949. B2491
38 Toynbee, A. J. La civiltà nella storia. 1950. B2492
39 Tarle, E. V. La vita economica dell-Italia nell'età napoleonica. 1950. B2493
40 Toscano, M. Guerra diplomatica in Estremo Oriente, 1914-1931. 2 v. 1950. B2494
41 Guignebert, C. A. H. Gesù. 1950. B2495
42 Granet, M. La civiltà cinese antica. 1950. B2496
43 Omodèo, A. Difesa del Risorgimento. 1951. B2497
44 Galante Garrone, A. Filippo Buonarroti e i rivoluzionari dell'Ottocento, 1828-1837. 1951. B2498
45 Pieri, P. Il Rinascimento e la crisi militare italiana. 1952. B2499
46 Venturi, F. Il populismo russo. 2 v. 1952. B2500
47 Glotz, G. La civiltà egea. 1953. B2501
48 Braudel, F. Civiltà e imperi del Mediterraneo nell' età di Filippo II. 1953. B2502
49 Lefebvre, G. La grande paura del 1789. 1953. B2503
50 Rosselli, N. Inghilterra e regno di Sardegna dal 1815 al 1847. 1954. B2504
51 Alatri, P. Lotte politiche in Sicilia sotto il governo della Destra (1866-74). 1954. B2505
52 Carocci, G. Agostino Depretis e la politica interna italiana dal 1876 al 1887. 1956. B2506

53 Salvatorelli, L. and Mira, G. Storia d'Italia nel periodo fascista. 1957. B2507
54 Babinger, F. Ma'omett it Conquistatore e il suo tempo. 1957. B2508
55 Berti, V. Russia e stati italiani nel Risorgimento. 1957. B2509
56 Hauser, H. and Renaudet, A. L'eta del rinascimento e della riforma. 1957. B2510
57 Namier, L. B. La rivoluzione degli intellettuali ed altri saggi sull'ottocento Europeo. 1957. B2511
58 Vaillant, G. C. La civilità azteca. 1957. B2512
59 Panikkar, K. M. Storia della dominazione europea in Asia dal Cinquecento ai nostri giorni. 1958. B2513
60 Lefebvre, G. La rivoluzione francese. 3 v. 1958-62. B2514
61 Mack Smith, D. Garibaldi e Cavour nel 1860. 1958. B2515
62 Battaglia, G. La prima guerra d'Africa. 1958. B2516
63 Cantimori, D. Studi di storia. 1959. B2517
64 Salvemini, G. Magnati e popolani in Firenze dal 1280 al 1295. 1960. B2518
65 Bainton, R. H. Lutero. 1960. B2519
66 Ritter, G. I cospiratori del 20 luglio 1944. B2520
67 Brandi, K. Carlo V. 1961. B2521
68 Felice, R. de. Storia degli ebrei italiani sotto il fascismo. 1961. B2522
69 Ottokar, N. Il comune di firenze alla fine del dugento. 1961. B2523
70 Syme, R. La rivoluzione romana. 1962. B2524
71 Pieri, P. Storia militare del risorgimento. 1962. B2525
72 Maturi, W. Interpretazioni del risorgimento. 1962. B2526
73 Shirer, W. L. Storia del terzo reich. V. 1. 1962. B2527
74 Diaz, F. Filosofia e politica nel settecento francese. 1963. B2528
75 Dangerfield, G. L'Era dei buoni sentimenti. 1963. B2529
76 Deakin, F. W. Storia della repubblica di Salò. 1963. B2530
77 Thomas, H. Storia della guerra civile spagnola. 1963. B2531
78 Carr, E. H. Storia della Russia sovietica. 2 v. 1964-65. B2532
79 Chabod, F. Scritti su Machiavelli. 1964. B2533
80 Vivanti, C. Lotta politica e pace religiosa in Francia fra cinque e seicento. 1963. B2534
81 Battagli, R. Storia della Resistenza italiana, 8 settembre 1943-Aprile 1945. 1964. B2535
82 Berengo, M. Nobili e mercanti nella Lucca del Cinquecento. 1965. B2536
83 De Felice, R. Mussolini. V. 1-2. 1965-66. B2537
84 Gerschenkron, A. Il problema storica dell'arretratezza economica. 1965. B2538
85 Fischer, F. Assalto al potere mondiale. 1965. B2539
86 Febvre, L. Studi su riforma e rinascimento e altri scritti su problemi di metodo e di geografia storica. 1966. B2540
87 Luraghi, R. Storia della guerra civilie Americana. 1966. B2541
88 Eyck, E. Storia della Repubblica di Weimar. 1967. B2542
89 Ginzburg, C. I benandanti. 1966. B2543
90 Lopez, R. S. La nascita dell'Europa. 1968. B2544
91 Runciman, S. Storia delle Crociate. 1966. B2545
92 Same as no. 83. V. 2. 1966. B2546
93 Romano, R. I prezzi in Europa dal XIII secolo a oggi. 1967. B2547
94 Chabod, F. Scritti sul rinascimento. 1967. B2548
95 Spriano, P. Storia del partito commista italiano. 1967. B2549
96 Ritter, G. I militaria e la politica nella Germania

moderna. 1967. B2550
97 Ostrogorsky, G. Storia dell' impero bizantino. 1968. B2551
98 Il confitto tra paganesimo e cristianesimo nel secolo IV. 1968. B2552
99 Spini, G. Autobiografia della giovane America. 1968. B2553
100 Luzzatto, G. L'economia italiana dal 1861 al 1894. 1968. B2554
101 Manacorda, G. Crisi economica e lotta politica in Italia. 1969. B2555
102 Collotti, G. Storia delle due Germanie, 1945-1968. 1969. B2556
103 Venturi, F. Settecento riformatore. 1969. B2557
104 Clark, J. G. D. Europa prestorica. 1970. B2558
105 Vermant, J. P. Mito e pensiero presso i Greci. 1970. B2559
106 Kula, W. Teoria economics del sistema feudale. 1970. B2560
107 Ginzburg, C. Il nicodemismo. 1970. B2561
108 Brenan, G. Storia della Spagna, 1874-1936. 1970. B2562
109 Albertini, R. von. Firenze dalla repubblica al principato. 1970. B2563
110 Lattimore, O. La frontiera. 1972. B2564
111 Léveque, P. La civilità greca. 1970. B2565
113 Chabod, F. Lo stato e la vita religiosa a Milano nell' epoca di Carlo V. 1971. B2566
114 ____. Storia di Milano nell' epoca de Carlo V. 1971. B2567
115 Racconto dei tempi passati, ed. by Lichačëv. 1971. B2568
116 Seton-Watson, H. Storia dell' impero russo. 1971. B2569
117 Brown, P. Agostino d'ippona. 1971. B2570
118 Stone, L. La crisi dell' aristocrazia. 1972. B2571
119 Spriano, P. Storia di Torino operaia e socialista. 1972. B2572
120 Rotelli, C. Una compagna medievale. 1973. B2573

BIBLIOTECA DI "LARES" (Olschki)

1 Toschi, P. "Rappresaglia" di studi di letteratura popolare. 1956. B2574
2 Tassoni, G. Proverbi e indovinelli, folklore mantovano. 1955. B2575
3 Bonaccorsi, A. Il folklore musicale in Toscana. 1956. B2576
4 Moretti, P. Poesia popolare sarda. 1958. B2577
5 Eustacchi-Nardi, A. M. Contributo allo studio delle tradizioni popolari marchigiane. 1958. B2578
6 Alziator, F. Picaro e folklore ed altri saggi di storia delle tradizioni popolari. 1959. B2579
7 Galanti, B. M. Vita tradizionale dell'Abruzzo e del Molise. 1961. B2580
8 Perusini, G. Vita di popolo in Friuli. 1961. B2581
9 Borgatti, M. Canti popolari emiliani raccolti a Cento. 1962. B2582
10 Nobilio, E. Vita tradizionale dei contadini abruzzesi nel territorio di Penne. 1962. B2583
11 Laghezza Ricagni, M. Studi sul canto lirico monostrofico popolare Italiano. 1963. B2584
12 Rohlfs, G. Primitiva costruzioni a cupola in Europa. 1963. B2585
13 Donno, M. del. Poesia popolare religiosa. 1964. B2586
14 Zucchi, F. Del vestire alla marchigiana. 1964. B2587
15 Donno, M. del Poesia popolare religiosa. 1964. B2588
16 Tassoni, G. Tradizioni popalari del Mantovano. 1964. B2589
17 Fontana, S. "Il maggio." 1964. B2590
18 Toschi, P. La leggenda di san Giorgio nei canti popolari italiani. 1964. B2591
19 Radole, G., comp. Canti popolari istriani. 1965. B2592

20 Giardini, M. P. Tradizioni popolari nel Decameron. 1965. B2593
21 Morpurgo, V. La celebre poesia Smrt Najke Jugovíca ed altre due canzoni popolari serbo-croate. 1965. B2594
22 Profeta, G. Canti nuziali nel folklore italiano. 1965. B2595
23 Brozini, G. B. Tradizione di stile aedico dai cantari al "Furioso". 1966. B2596
24 Malecore, I. M. La poesia popolare nel Salento. 1967. B2597
25 Paolucci, L. La Sibilla appenninica. 1967. B2598
26 Vecchi, A. In culto delle immagini nelle stampe popolari. 1968. B2599
27 Borgatti, M. Folklore emiliano raccolto a Cento. 1968. B2600
28 Radole, G. Seconda raccolta di canti popolari sitriani con bibliografia critica. 1968. B2601
29 Crocioni, G. Le tradizioni popolari nella letteratura italiana. 1970. B2602
30 Krekoukias, D. Gli animali nella meterologia popolare degli antichi greci, romani e bizantini. 1970. B2603
31 Soro, G., comp. Folklore, logudorese. 1971. B2604
32 Giancristofaro, E. Il mangiafavole. 1971. B2605
33 Tassoni, G. Fole mantovane. 1971. B2606
34 Del Monte Tammaro, C. Indice delle fiabe abruzzesi. 1971. B2607
35 Bellabarba, R. Proverbi marchigiani illustrati. 1971. B2608
36 Giglioli, L. Natività. 1972. B2609
37 Siracusa Ilacqua, D. I racconti popolari della raccoltà Cannizzaro. 1972. B2610
38 Siracusa Ilacqua, D. I manoscritti di Tommaso Cannizzaro demologo. 1973. B2611
39 Delfino, G. Stregoneria, magia, credenza e superstizioni a Genova e in Liguria. 1973. B2612
40 Battista, P. Vita di antiche tradizioni campane, la sagra dei gigli. 1973. B2613
41 Angarano, F. A. Vita tradizionale dei contadini e pastori colobresi. 1973. B2614
42 Bellabarba, R. Proverbi Toscani illustrati. 1974. B2615
43 Malecore, I. M. Proverbi Francavillesi. 1974. B2616

BIBLIOTECA DI LINGUA NOSTRA (Sansoni)

1 Migliorini, B. Saggi sulla lingua del novecento. 1942. B2617
2 Camilli, A. Pronuncia e grafia dell'Italiano. 1947. B2618
3 Cian, V. La lingua di Baldassarre Castiglione. 1942. B2619
4 Migliorini, B. La lingua contemporanea. 1943. B2620
5 ____. Pronunzia fiorentina o pronunzia romana? 1945. B2621
6 Devoto, G. Dizionari di ieri e di domani. 1946. B2622
7 Malagòli, G. L'accentazione italiana. 1946. B2623
8 Menarini, A. Al margini della lingua. 1947. B2624
9 Fracastoro Martini, O. La lingua e la radio. 1951. B2625
10 Tollemache, F. I deverbali italiani. 1954. B2626
11 Barbi, M. Per un grande vocabolario storico della lingua italiana. 1957. B2627

BIBLIOTECA ESPAÑOLA DE DIVULGACION CIENTIFICA (Suarez)

1 Castro, A. La enseñanza del español en España. 1922. B2628
2 Stolz, F. Historia de la lengua latina, tr. by Castro. 1922. B2629
3 Villena, E. de. Arte de trovar. 1923. B2630
4 Meringer, R. Linguistica

indoeuropea. 1923. B2631
5 Castro, A. Lengua, enseñanza y literatura. 1924. B2632
6 Argote de Molina, G. El "Discurso sobre la poesía castellana," ed. by Tiscornia. 1926. B2633
7 Place, E. B. Manual elemental de novelistica española. 1926. B2634
8 Vera, F. Historia de la matemática en España. V. 1. 1929. B2635
9 Espinosa, A. M. El romancero español. 1931. B2636
10-12 Same as no. 8. V. 2. 1931. V. 3. 1933. B2637
13 Criharsa. Ratnavali o El collar de perlas. 1934. B2638
14 Vera, F. Los historiadores de la matemática española. 1935. B2639

BIBLIOTECA ROMINICA HISPANICA (Gredos)

I. Tratados.
1 Warthburg, W. von. La fragmentación linguistica de la Romania. 1952. B2640
2 Wellek, R. and Warren, A. Teoría literaria. 1953. B2641
3 Kayser, W. J. Interpretación y análisis de la obra literaria. 1954. B2642
4 Peers, E. A. Historia del movimiento romantico español. 2 v. 1954. B2643
5 Alonso, A. De la pronunciación medioeval a la moderna en español. V. 1. 1955. B2644
6 Hatzfeld, H. A. Bibliografía critica de la nueva estilística. 1955. B2645
7 Jungemann, F. H. Le teoría del sustrato y los dialectos hispano-romances y gascones. 1955. B2646
8 Williams, S. T. La huella española en la literatura norteamericana. 2 v. 1957. B2647
9 Wellek, R. Historia de la critica moderna (1750-1950). V. 1. 1959. B2648
10 Baldinger, K. La formación de la dominios linguisticos en la Peninsula Ibérica. 1963. B2649
11 Morley, S. G. and Bruerton, C. Cronologia de las comedias Lope de Vega. 1967. B2650
12 Marti, A. La preceptiva retórica española en el Siglo de Oro. 1972. B2651
13 Aguiar e Silva, V. M. de. Teoría de la literatura. 1972. B2652
14 Hörmann, H. Psicologia del lenguaje. 1972. B2653

II. Estudios y ensayos.
1 Alonso, D. Poesia española. 1950. B2654
2 ____. Estudios lingüísticos tomas españoles. 1951. B2655
3 ____ and Bousoño, C. Seis calas en la expresión literaria española. 1947. B2656
4 García de Diego, V. Lecciones de lingüística española. 1951. B2657
5 Casladuero, J. Vida y obra de Galdós. 1951. B2658
6 Alonso, D. Poetas espanolas contemporáneos. 1952. B2659
7 Bousoño, C. Teoría de la expresión poetica. 1956. B2660
8 Riquer, M. de. Los cantares de gesta franceses. 1952. B2661
9 Menéndez Pidal, R. Toponimia prerrománica hispana. 1952. B2662
10 Clavería, C. Temas de Unamuno. 1953. B2663
11 Sánchez, L. A. Proceso y contenido de la novela Hispano-Americana. 1953. B2664
12 Alonso, A. Estudios lingüísticos temas hispano-americanos. 1953. B2665
13 Catalán Menendez-Pidal, D. Poema de Alfonso XI. 1953. B2666
14 Richthofen Erich, F. von. Estudios épicos medioevales. 1954. B2667
15 Valverde, J. M. Guillermo de Humboldt y la filosofía del lenguaje. 1955. B2668
16 Hatzfeld, H. A. Estudios literarios sobre mística

española. 1955. B2669
17 Alonso, A. Materia y forma en poesia. 1960. B2670
18 ___. Estudios y ensayos gongorinos. 1955. B2671
19 Spitzer, L. Lingüística e historia literaria. 1955. B2672
20 Zamora Vicente, A. La sonatas de Valle Inclán. 1955. B2673
21 Zubiría, R. de. La poesia de Antonio Machado. 1955. B2674
22 Catalán Menendez-Pidal, D. La escuela lingüística española y su concepción del lenguaje. 1955. B2675
23 Flys, J. M. La lenguaje poetica de Federico García Lorca. 1955. B2676
24 Gaos, V. Le poética de Campoamor. 1955. B2677
25 Carballo Calero, R. Aportaciones a la literatura gallega contemporánea. 1955. B2678
26 Ares Montes, J. Góngora y la poesía portuguesa del siglo XVII. 1956. B2679
27 Bousoño, C. La poesia de Vicente Aleixandre. 1956. B2680
28 Sobejano, G. La epíteto en la lirica española. 1956. B2681
29 Alonso, D. Menéndez Pelayo. 1956. B2682
30 Silva Castro, R. Rubén Darío a los veinte años. 1956. B2683
31 Nemes, G. (Palau) Vida y obra de Juan Ramón Jimenez. 1957. B2684
32 Montesions, J. F. Valera, la ficción libre. 1957. B2685
33 Sánchez, L. A. Escritores representativos de América. 2 v. 1957. B2686
34 Asensio, E. Poética y realidad en el cancionero peninsular de la edad media. 1957. B2687
35 Poyán Diaz, D. Enrique Gaspar. 2 v. 1957. B2688
36 Varela, J. L. Poesía y restauración cultural de Galicia en el Siglo XIX. 1958. B2689
37 Alonso, D. De los sigios oscuros al de oro. 1958. B2690
39 Díaz, J. P. Gustavo Adolfo Bécquer. 1958. B2691
40 Carilla, E. El romanticismo en la América hispánica. 1958. B2692
41 Nora, E. de. La novela española contemporánea (1898-1927). 2 v. 1958-62. B2693
42 Eich, C. Federico García Lorca. 1958. B2694
43 Macrí, O. Fernando de Herrera. 1959. B2695
44 Bayo, M. J. Virgilio y la pastoral española del renacimiento (1480-1530). 1959. B2696
45 Alonso, D. Dos españoles del Siglo de Oro. 1960. B2697
46 Criados de Val, M. Teoría de Castilla la Nueva. 1960. B2698
47 Schulman, I. A. Simbolo y color en la obra de José Marti. 1960. B2699
48 Sanchez, J. Academias literarias del Siglo de Oro español. 1961. B2700
49 Casalduero, J. Espronceda. 1961. B2701
50 Gilman, S. Tiempo y formes temporales en el "Poema del Cid." 1961. B2702
51 Pierce, F. W. La poesía épica del Siglo de Oro. 1961. B2703
52 Correa Calderon, E. Baltasar Gracián. 1961. B2704
53 Martin-Gamero, S. Le enseñanza del inglés en España. 1961. B2705
54 Casalduero, J. Estudios sobre el teatro español. 1962. B2706
55 Glendenning, N. Vida y obra de Cadalso. 1962. B2707
56 Galmés de Fuentes, A. Las sibilantes en la Romania. 1962. B2708
57 Casalduero, J. Sentido y forma de las Novelas ejemplares. 1962. B2709
58 Shepard, S. El Pinciano y las teorias literarias del Siglo de Oro. 1962. B2710
59 MacLennan, L. J. El problema del aspects verbal. 1962. B2711
60 Casalduero, J. Estudios de literatura española. 1962. B2712

1967. B2756
105 Rossi, G. C. Estudios sobre las letras en el siglo XVIII. 1968. B2757
106 De Albornoz, A. La presencia de Miguel de Unamuno en Antonio Machado. 1968. B2758
107 Gariano, C. El mundo poético de Juan Ruiz. 1968. B2759
108 Bénichou, P. Creacion poetica en el romancero tradicional. 1968. B2760
109 Fogelquist, D. F. Españoles de America y americanos de España. 1968. B2761
110 Pottier, B. Lingüística moderna y filología hispánica. 1968. B2762
111 De Kock, J. Introduccion al Cancionero de Miguel de Unamuno. 1968. B2763
112 Alazraki, J. La prosa narrative de Jorge Luis Borges. 1968. B2764
113 Debicki, A. P. Estudios sobre poesia española contemporánea. 1968. B2765
114 Zardoya, C. Poesía española del 98 y del 27. 1968. B2766
115 Weinrich, H. Estructura y función de los tiempos en el lenguaje. 1968. B2767
116 Garcia, A. R. El siervo y el senor. 1968. B2768
117 Beser, S. Leopoldo Alas. 1968. B2769
118 Marcos, M. B. Don Juan Valera. 1969. B2770
119 Salinas de Marichal, S. El mundo poetico de Rafael Alberti. 1969. B2771
120 Tacca, O. La historia literaria. 1969. B2772
121 Castillo, H., ed. Estudios criticos el modernismo. 1969. B2773
122 Macrí, O. Ensayo de métrica sintagmatica. 1969. B2774
123 Vicente, A. Z. La realidad esperpéntica. 1969. B2775
124 Gomez, C. B. El "Poema de Mio Cid." 1969. B2776
125 Goode, H. D. La prosa retorica de Fray Luis de Leon en "Los nobres de Cristo." 1969. B2777
126 Green, O. H. España y la tradicion occidental espiritu castellano en la literatura desde "El Cid." 1969. B2778
127 Schulman, I. A. and Gonzalez, M. P. Martí Darío y el modernismo. 1969. B2779
128 Zubizarreta, A. de. Pedro Salinas. 1969. B2780
129 Fernández-Shaw, G. Un poeta de trasicion. 1969. B2781
130 Guizado, E. C. La elegía funeral en la poesía española. 1969. B2782
131 Romeralo, A. S. El villancico. 1969. B2783
132 Rosales, L. Pasión y muerte del Conde de Villamdiana. 1969. B2784
133 Arróniz, O. La influencia italiana en el nacimiento de comedia española. 1969. B2785
134 Catalán, D. Siete siglos de romancero. 1970. B2786
135 Chomsky, N. Lingüistica cartesiana. 1972. B2787
136 Kany, C. E. Sintaxis hispano-americana. 1970. B2788
137 Alvar López, M. Estructuralismo, geograffa lingüística y dialectologia actual. 1969. B2789
138 Richthofen, E. von. Nuevos estudios épicos medievales. 1969. B2790
139 Gullón, R. Una poética para Antonio Machado. 1970. B2791
140 Cohen, J. Estructura dei lenguaje poetico. 1970. B2792
141 Livingstone, L. Tema y forme en las novelas de Azorin. 1970. B2793
142 Catalán Menendez-Pidal, D. Por campos del romancero. 1970. B2794
143 López, M. L. Problemas y métodos en el analisis de preposiciones. 1970. B2795
144 Correa, G. La poesía mitica de Federico García Lorca. 1970. B2796
145 Tate, R. B. Ensayos sobre la historigrafia peninsular del siglo XV. 1970. B2797

146 Barron, C. G. La obra critica y literaria de Don Antonio Alcala Galiano. 1970. B2798
147 Llorach, E. A. Estudios de gramatica funcional del español. 1972. B2799
148 Benítez, R. Becquer tradicionalista. 1971. B2800
149 Araya, G. Cloves filológicas para la compresión de Ortega. 1971. B2801
150 Martinet, A. El lenguaje desde el punto de vista funcional. 1971. B2802
151 Irizarry, E. D. Teoría y creación literaria en Francisco Ayala. 1971. B2803
152 Mounin, G. Los problemas teóricos de la traduccion. 1971. B2804
153 Penuelas, M. C. La obra narrativa de Ramón J. Sender. 1971. B2805
154 Alvar López, M. Estudios y ensayos de literatura contemporánea. 1971. B2806
155 Hjelmslev, L. Prolegómenos a una teoría del lenguaje. 1971. B2807
156 Zuelta, E. de. Cinco poetas españoles. 1971. B2808
157 Fernández Alonso, M del R. Una visión de la muerte en la lirica española. 172. B2809
158 Rosenblat, A. La lengua del "Quijote." 1971. B2810
159 Pollmann, L. La "nueva novela "en Francia y en Ibero-américana. 1971. B2811
160 Capote Benot, J. M. La periodo sevillano de Luis Cunuda. 1971. B2812
161 Garcia Morejon, J. Unamuno y Portugal. 1971. B2813
162 Ribbans, G. W. Niebla y solidad. 1971. B2814
163 Scholberg, K. R. Sátira e invectiva en la España medieval. 1972. B2815
164 Parker, A. A. Los picaros en la literatura. 1972. B2816
165 Rudat, E. M. Las ideas esteticas de Esteban de Arteaga. 1972. B2817
166 San Miguel, A. Sentido y estructura del "Guzmán de Alfarache" de Mateo Alemán. 1971. B2818
167 Marcos Marin, F. Poesía narrativa árabe y épica hispánica. 1971. B2819
168 Cano Ballesta, J. La poesía española entre pureza y revolución. 1972. B2820
169 Corominas, J. Tópica hespérica. 2 v. 1972. B2821
170 Amorós, A. La novelas intelectual de Ramón Pérez de Ayala. 1972. B2822
171 Porqueras Mayo, A. Temas y formas de la literatura española. 1972. B2823
172 Brancaforte, B. Benedetto Croce y su critica de la literatura española. 1972. B2824
173 Martín, C. America en Rubén Darío. 1972. B2825
174 García de la Torre, J. M. G. Analisis temático de "El ruedo ibericos." 1972. B2826
175 Rodriguez-Puértolas, J. De la Edad Media a la Edad conflitiva. 1972. B2827
176 Lopez Estrafa, F. Poetica para un poeta las "Cartas literarias a una mujer" de Becquer. 1972. B2828
177 Hjelmslev, L. Ensayos lingüisticos. 1972. B2829
178 Alonso, D. En torno a Lope... 1972. B2830
179 Pabst, W. La novela corta en la teoria y en la creación literaria. 1972. B2831
180 Rumeu de Armas, A. Alfonso de Ulloa, introductor de la cultura española en Italia. 1972. B2832
181 Leon, P. R. Algunas observaciones sobre Pedro de Cleza de Leon y la Crónica del Perú. 1972. B2833
182 Roberts, G. Temas existenciales en la novela española de postguerra. 1972. B2834
183 Siebenmann, G. Los estilos poéticos en España desde 1900. 1972. B2835
184 Duran, A. Estructura y

técnicas de la novela sentimental y caballeresca. 1972. B2836
185 Beinhauer, W. El humorismo en el español hablado. 1973. B2837
186 Predmore, M. P. La poesía hermética de Juan Ramón Jiménez. 1973. B2838
187 Manent, A. Tres escritores catalanes. 1973. B2839
188 Bratosevich, N. A. S. El estilo de Horacio Quiroga en sus cuentos. 1973. B2840
189 Soldevila Durante, I. La obra narrativa de Max Aub. 1973. B2841
190 Pollmann, L. Sartre y Camus. 1973. B2842
191 Bobes Naves, M. del C. La semiótica como teoría lingüística. 1973. B2843
192 Carilla, E. La creación del Martin Fierro. 1973. B2844
193 Coseriu, E. Sincronia, diacronia e historia. 1973. B2845
194 Tacca, O. Las voces de la novela. 1973. B2846
195 Fortea, J. L. La obra de Andrés Carranque de Rios. 1973. B2847
196 Fernandez, E. N. El diminutivo. 1973. B2848
197 Debicki, A. P. La poesia de Jorge Guillén. 1973. B2849
198 Doménech, R. El teatro de Buero Vallejo. 1973. B2850
199 Villanueva, F. M. Fuentes literarias cervantinas. 1974. B2851
200 Diaz, E. O. Lope y Gongora frente a frente. 1974. B2852
201 Muller, C. Estadistica lingüística. 1974. B2853
202 Kock, J. de. Introducción a la lingüística automática en las lenguas románicas. 1974. B2854
203 Avalle-Arce, J. B. Temas hispánicos medievales. 1974. B2855
204 Quintián, A. R. Cultura y literatura españolas en Rubén Darío. 1974. B2856
205 Trejo, E. C. La poesía de Vicento Huidobro y la vanguardia. 1974. B2857
206 Martin, J. L. La narrativa de Vargus Llosa. 1974. B2858
207 Nolting-Hauff, I. Visión, satira y agudeza en los Sueños de Quevedo. 1974. B2859
208 Phillips, A. W. Temas del modernismo hispánico y otros estudios. 1974. B2860
209 Mayoral, M. La poesía de Rosalia de Castro. 1974. B2861
210 Casalduero, J. Cántico de Jorge Guillén. 1974. B2862
211 Menendez-Pidal, D. C. La tradición manuscrita de la Crónica de Alfonso XI. 1974. B2863
212 Devoto, D. Textos y contextos. 1974. B2864
213 López Estrada, F. Los libros de pastores en la literatura española. 1974. B2865
214 Martinet, A. Economia de los cambios fonéticos. 1974. B2866
215 Sebold, R. P. Cadalso. 1974. B2867
218 Hammarström, G. Unidades lingüísticas en el marco de la lingüística moderna. 1974. B2868

III. Manuales

1 Alarcos Llorach, E. Fonología española. 1961. B2869
2 Gili y Gaya, S. Elementos de fonética general. 1950. B2870
3 Alarcos Llorach, E. Gramática estructural. 1951. B2871
4 López Estrada, F. Introducción a la literatura medioeval española. 1962. B2872
5 Moll y Casasnovas, F. de B. Gramática histórica catalana. 1952. B2873
6 Lázaro Carreter, F. Diccionario de términos filológicos. 1962. B2874
7 Alvar López, M. El dialecto aragonés. 1953. B2875
8 Zamora Vicente, A. Dialectologiá española. 1960. B2876

9 Vázquez Cuesta, P. and Mendes de Luz, M. A. Gramática portuguesa. 1961. B2877
10 Badía Margarit, A. M. Gramática catalana. 2 v. 1962. B2878
11 Porzig, W. El mundo maravilloso del lenguaje. 1964. B2879
12 Lausberg, H. Lingüistica románica. 2 v. 1965. B2880
13 Martinet, A. Elementos de lingüística general. 1965. B2881
14 Wartburg, W. von. Evolución y estructura de la lengua francesca. 1966. B2882
15 Lausberg, H. Manual de retirica literaria. 3 v. 1967. B2883
16 Mounin, G. Historia de la lingüistica. 1968. B2884
17 Martinet, A. La lingüística sincrónica. 1969. B2885
19 Hjelmslev, L. El lenguage. 1969. B2886
20 Melmberg, B. Lingüística estructural y comunicación humana. 1969. B2887
21 Lehmann, W. P. Introducción a la lingüística historica. 1969. B2888
22 Adrados, F. R. Lingüística estructural. 2 v. 1970. B2889
23 Pichois, C. and Rousseau, A. M. La literatura comparada. 1970. B2890
24 Estrada, F. L. Métrica española del siglo XX. 1970. B2891
25 Baehr, R. Manual de versificación española. 1970. B2892
26 Gleason, H. A. Introducción a la lingüística descriptiva. 1971. B2893
27 Greimas, A. J. Semántica estructural. 1971. B2894
28 Robins, R. H. Lingüística general. 1971. B2895
29 Iordan, I. and Manoliu, M. Manual de lingüística románcia. 2 v. 1972. B2896
30 Hadlich, R. L. Gramática transformativa del español. 1974. B2897
31 Ruwet, N. Introducción a la gramatica generativa. 1974. B2898
32 Collado, J. A. Fundamentos de lingüística general. 1974. B2899

IV. Textos
1 Diaz y Diaz, M. C. Antología del latin vulgar. 1962. B2900
2 Canella de Zamora, M. J. Antología de textos foneticos. 1965. B2901
3 Escribano, F. S. and Mayo, A. P. Preceptiva dramática española del renacimiento y el barroco. 1965. B2902
4 Ruiz, J. Libro de buen amor. 1966. B2903
5 Rodriguez-Puertolas, J. Fray Iñigo de Mendoza y sus "Copias de Vita Christi." 1968. B2904
6 Ibn Quzman, M. Todo Ben Quzman. 2 v. 1972. B2905
7 Garcilaso de la Vega. Garcilaso de la Vega y sus comentaristas, ed. by Gallego Morell. 1972. B2906

V. Diccionarios etimológicos
1 Corominas, J. Diccionario critico etimólogico de la lengua castellano. 4 v. 1954. B2907
2 ____. Breve diccionario etimologico de la lengua castellana. 1961. B2908
3 Academia Española, Madrid. Diccionario de autoridades. 3 v. 1963. B2909
4 Alfaro, R. J. Diccionario de anglicismos. 1966. B2910
5 Moliner, M. Diccionario de uso del español. V. 1. 1966. B2911

VI. Antologia hispánica
1 Laforet, C. Mis páginas mejores. 1956. B2912
2 Camba, J. Mis páginas mejores. 1956. B2913
3 Alonso, D., ed. Antologia de la poesia española. 1956. B2914
4 Cela, C. J. Mis páginas preferidas. 1958. B2915
5 Fernández-Floréz, W. Mis páginas mejores. 1956. B2916
6 Aleixandre, V. Mis poemas mejores. 1961. B2917
7 Menéndez Pidal, R. Mis páginas preferidas temas

literarios. 1957. B2918
8 ____ ____, estudios lingüísticos e históricos. 1957. B2919
9 Blecua, J. M. Floresta de lirica española. 2 v. 1963. B2920
10 Gómez de la Serna, R. Mis mejores páginas literarias. 1957. B2921
11 Laín Entralgo, P. Mis páginas preferidas. 1958. B2922
12 Cano, J. L., ed. Antología de la nueva poesía española. 1958. B2923
13 Jiménez, J. R. Pájinas escojidas; prosa, ed. by Gullon. 1958. B2924
14 ____ ____, verso, ed. by Gullon. 1958. B2925
15 Zunzungegui, J. A. de. Mis páginas preferidas. 1958. B2926
16 Garcia Pavon, F., comp. Antología de cuentistas españoles contemporaneos. 1959. B2927
17 Góngora y Argote, L. de. Góngora y el "Polifemo," ed. by Alonso. 2 v. 1961. B2928
18 Antología de poetas ingleses modernos. 1963. B2929
19 Medina, J. R. Antología venezolana: verso. 1962. B2930
20 ____ ____, prosa. 1962. B2931
21 Garcilaso de la Vega. El Inca Garcilaso en sus "Comentarios," ed. by Avalle-Arce. 1964. B2932
22 Ayala, F. Mis páginas mejores. 1965. B2933
23 Guillén, J. Selección de poemas. 1965. B2934
24 Aub, M. Mis páginas mejores. 1966. B2935
25 Puértolas, J. R. Poesía de protesta en Edad Media castellana. 1968. B2936
26 Moreno, C. F. and Becco, H. J. Antología lineal de la poesía argentina. 1969. B2937
27 Scarpa, R. E. and Montes, H. Antología de la poesía chilena contemporánea. 1969. B2938
28 Alonso, D. Poemas escogidos. 1969. B2939
29 Diego, G. Versos escogidos. 1971. B2940
30 Arias y Arias, R. La poesía de los goliardos. 1971. B2941
31 Sender, R. J. Páginas escogidas. 1972. B2942
32 Mantero, M. Los derechos des hombre en la poesía hispánica contemporánea. 1973. B2943

VII. Campo-abierto

1 Zamora Vicente, A. Lope de Vega. 1961. B2944
2 Moreno Báez, E. Nostros y nuestros clásicos. 1961. B2945
3 Alonso, D. Cuatro poetas españoles. 1962. B2946
4 Sánchez Barbundo, A. Le segunda epoca de Juan Ramón Jimenez. 1962. B2947
5 Zamora Vicente, A. Camilo José Cela. 1962. B2948
6 Alonso, D. Del siglo de Oro a este siglo de siglas. 1962. B2949
6 ____. De los siglos oscuros al de Oro. 1964. B2950
7 Sanchez Barbudo, A. Le segunda época de Juan Ramón Jiménez. 1963. B2951
8 Serrano Poncela, S. Formas de vida hispánica. 1963. B2952
9 Ayala, F. Realidad y ensueño. 1963. B2953
10 Baquero Goyanes, M. Perspectivismo y contraste. 1963. B2954
11 Sánchez, L. A. Escritores representativos de América. 3 v. 1963. B2955
12 Gullón, R. Direcciones del modernismo. 1963. B2956
13 Sánchez, L. A. Escritores representativos de América. 2d ser. 3 v. 1963-64. B2957
14 Alonso, D. De los siglos oscuros al' de Oro. 1964. B2958
15 De Pablos, B. El tiempo en la poesía de Juan Ramón Jimenez. 1966. B2959
16 Sender, R. J. Valle-Inclán y la difficultad de la tragedia. 1966. B2960
17 De Torre, G. La dificil universalidad española. 1966. B2961

18 Del Rio, A. Estudios sobre literatura contemporanea española. 1966. B2962
19 Sobejano, G. Forma literaria y sensibilidad sociale. 1967. B2963
20 Serrano Plaja, A. Realismo "magico" en Cervantes. 1967. B2964
21 Diaz-Plaja, G. Soliloquio y coloquio. 1968. B2965
22 DeTorre, G. Del 92 al barraco. 1969. B2966
23 Gullon, R. La invencion del 98 y otras ensayos. 1969. B2967
24 Yndurâin, F. Clasicos modernos. 1971. B2968
25 Connolly, E. Leopoldo Panero. 1972. B2969
26 Blecua, J. M. Sobre poesía de la Edad de Oro. 1971. B2970
27 Boisdeffre, P. de. Los escritores franceses de hoy. 1971. B2971
28 Sopeña Ibanez, F. Arte y sociedad en Galdos. 1970. B2972
29 Garcia-Vino, M. Mundo y trasmundo de las leyendas de Bécquer. 1971. B2973
30 Balseiro, J. A. Expresión de hispanoamérica. 1970. B2974
31 Arrom, J. J. Certedumbre de América. 1971. B2975
32 Ramos, V. Miguel Hernández. 1973. B2976
33 Rodriguez-Alcalá, H. Narrativa hispanoamericana. 1973. B2977

VIII. Documentos
1 Alonso, D. and Galvarriato de Alonso, E. Para la biografía de Gongora. 1962. B2978
2 Marti, J. Epistolario. 1973. B2979

IX. Facsimiles
1 Gallardo, B. J. Ensayo de una biblioteca española de libros raros y curiosus. 4 v. 1968. B2980
2 De la Barrera y Leirado, C. A. Catalogo bibliografico y biográfico del teatro antiguo español. 1969. B2981
3 Sempere y Guarinos, J. Ensayo de una biblioteca española de los mejores escritores del reynado de Carlos III. 3 v. 1969. B2982
4 Amador de los Rios, J. Historia critica de la literatura española. 7 v. 1971. B2983
5 Cejador y Frauca, J. Historia de la lengua y literatura castellana. 5 v. 1972. B2984

BIBLIOTHECA GERMANICA (Francke)

1 Maurer, F. Leid... 1951. B2985
2 Schwarz, E. Goten, Nordgermanen, Angelsachen... 1951. B2986
3 Maurer, F. Nordgermanen und Alemannen... 1952. B2987
4 Glinz, H. Die innere Form des Deutschen... 1952. B2988
5 Henzen, W. Schriftsprache und Mundarten... 1954. B2989
6 Mittner, L. Wurd... 1955. B2990
7 Ruh, K. Bonaventura deutsch... 1956. B2991
8 Müller, E. E. E. Wortgeschichte und Sprachgegensatz im Alemannischen. 1960. B2992
9 Vries, J. de. Kelten und Germanen. 1960. B2993
10 Maurer, F. Dichtung und Sprache des Mittelalters... 1963. B2994
11 Besch, W. Sprachlandschaften und Sprachausgleich im 15. 1967. B2995
12 Ranke, F. Kleinere schriften. 1971. B2996
13 Rupp, H. Deutsche religiöse dichtungen des 11 und 12. jahrhunderts. 1971. B2997
14 Kleiber, W. Otfrid von Weifsenburg. 1971. B2998
15 Kratz, H. Wolfram von Eschenbach's Parzival. 1973. B2999
16 Codex Karlsruhe 408. 1974. B3000
17 Kleinschmidt, E. Herrscherdartstellung. 1974. B3001

BIBLIOTHECA MATHEMATICA, A SERIES OF MONOGRAPHS ON PURE AND APPLIED MATHEMATICS (North-Holland)

1 Kleene, S. C. Introduction to metamathematics. 1952. B3002
2 Zaanen, A. C. Linear analysis. 1956. B3003
3 Yano, K. The theory of Lie derivatives and its applications. 1957. B3004
4 Bruijn, N. G. de. Asymptotic methods in analysis. 1958. B3005
5 Heyting, A. Axiomatic projective geometry. 1963. B3006
6 Nagata, J. Modern dimension theory. 1965. B3007
7 ____. Modern general topology. 1968. B3008
8 Lekkerkerker, C. G. Geometry of numbers. 1969. B3009

BIBLIOTHECA SCRIPTORUM GRAECORUM ET LATINORUM TEUBNERIANA (Blackwell)

Abercius, St. S. Abercii vita, ed. by Nissen. 1912. (1001) Suppl.: Ludtke, Nissen. 1910. (1002) B3010
Achmetis. Oneirocriticon, ed. by Drexl. 1925. B3011
AEgidius, Corbolineses. Egidii Corboliensis viaticus nunc primum, ed. by Rose. 1907. (1907). B3012
AElianus, C. Claudii Aeliani De natura animalium libri XVII, Varia historia, Epistolae fragments, ed. by Hercheri. 2 v. 1864-66. (1006). B3013
____. Claudii Aeliani Varia historia, ed. by Hercheri. 1887. (1005). B3014
Acropolita, G. Georgii Acropolitae Opera, ed. by Heisenberg. 2 v. 1903. (1388). B3015
Aeneas Tacticus. Aeneae Commentarius poliorceticus recensuit Arnoldus Hug. 1874. (1007). B3016
____. Aenae Tacticus De obsidione toleranda commentarius, ed. by Schoene. 1911. (1008). B3017
Aeschines. Aeschinis Orationes, ed. by Franke and Preuss. 1896. (1009). Index. 1926. (1011). B3018
____ ____, ed. by Franke and Blass. 1896. B3019
Aeschines Socraticus. Aeschinis Socratici reliquiae, ed. by Krauss. 1911. (1012). B3020
Aeschylus. Aeschyli Cantica, ed. by Schroeder. 1916. B3021
____. Aeschyli Tragoediae: Weil. 1907. (1013). B3022
____. Agamemnon, ed. by Weil. (1014). B3023
____. Choephoroe. 1930. (1015). B3024
____. Eumenides, ed. by Weil. 1933. (1016). B3025
____. Persae. 1931. (1017). B3026
____. Prometheus, ed. by Weil. 1932. (1018). B3027
____. Septem contra Thebas, ed. by Weil. 1921. (1019). B3028
____. Supplices. 1910. (1020). B3029
AEsopus. Corpus fabularum Aesopicarum, ed. by Hausrath. 1940. (1347) V. 1. Fabulae Aesopicae soluta oratione conscriptae, ed. by Hausrath. Fasc. 1. Praefation. Fabulae 1-181. 1940. (1962). Fasc. 2. Fabulae 182-345. 1940. (1963). V. 2. Fabulae Aesopicae versibus compositae, fabularum Aesopicarum paraphrasis Bodleiana, ed. by Gerstinger. (1964). B3030
Albertus Stadensis. Troilus Alberti Stadensis, ed. by Merzdorf. 1875. (1902). B3031
Alciphron. Alciphronis rhetoris Epistularum libri IV, ed. by Schepers. 1905. (1023). B3032
Alexander of Lycopolis. Alexandri Lycopolitani Contra Manichaei opiniones disputatio, ed. by Brinkmann. 1895. (1024). B3033
Amarcius. Sexti Amarcii Galli

Piosistrati Sermonum libri IV, e codice dresdensi A. 167a nunc primum, ed. by Manitius. 1888. (1903). B3034

Ammianus Marcellinus. Ammiani Marcellini Rerum gestarum libri que supersunt, ed. by Gardthausen. 2 v. 1874-75. B3035

Ampelius, L. Lucii Ampelii Liber memorialis, ed. by Assmann. 1935. (1946). B3036

Anacreon. Anacreontis Teii quae vocantur Σνη ποσιακα ηνιαβια ex Anthologiae palatinae volumine altero nunc parisiensi post Hericum Stephaum et Josephum Spalleti tertium, ed. By Rose. 1876. B3037

____. Carmina Anacreontae e Bybl. nat. par. cod. gr. svppl. 273 post Val. Rosivm, ed. by Preisendanz. 1912. (1025). B3038

Andocides. Andocidis Orationes, ed. by Blass. 1880. (1026). B3039

Anonymi Chronographia syntomos e codici matritensi no. 121 (nunc 4701), ed. by Bauer. 1909. (1029). B3040

Anthimus. Anthimi De observatione ciborum epistula ad Theudericum, regem Francorum, ed. by Rose. 1877. B3041

Anthologia Graeca. Epigrammatum anthologia palatina, ed. by Stadtmveller. 3 v. 1894-1906. (1041-1043). B3042

Anthologia Latina. Anthologia latina. Pars I Carmina in codicibus scripta. Fasc. I. 1894. (1030). Fasc. II. 1906. (1031). Pars II Carmina epigraphica. Fasc. I. 1930. (1032). Fasc. II. (1033). Fasc. III. 1926. (1033a). B3043

Antiphon. Antiphontis Orationes et fragmenta, ed. by Thalhelm. 1914. (1045). B3044

____. Antiphontis Orationes et fragmenta, ed. by Blass. 1892. B3045

Antolycus. Antolyci De sphera quae movetur liber, ed. by Hultsch. 1885. B3046

Apicius. Apicii de re coquinaria, ed. by Vollmer-Giarratano. 1922. (1048). B3047

Apocalypsis Anastasiae. Apocalypsis Anastasiae, ed. by Homburg. 1903. (1049). B3048

Appianus of Alexandria. Appiani historia Romana, ed. by Vierech and Roos. 2 v. 1939, 1905. (1936, 1054). B3049

____. Appiani Historia Romana, ed. by Mendelssohn. 2 v. 1905-39. B3050

Apollinaris, bp. of Laodicea. Apolinari metaphrasis psalmorum, ed. by Ludwick. 1912. (1050). B3051

Apollodorus, of Athens. Apollodori Bibliotheca, ed. by Bekker. 1854. (1543). B3052

Apollonius, P. Apollonii Pergaei, ed. by Heiberg. V. 1. 1891. (1051). V. 2. 1903. (1052). B3053

Apollonius, R. Apolonii Rhodii Argonautica, ed. by Merkel. 1882. (1053). B3054

Appollonius of Tyre. Historia Apollonii, ed. by Riese. 1893. (1425). B3055

Apuleius Madaurensis. Apulei Opera, ed. by Helm. V. 1. Metamorphose on libri XI. 1931. (1055). V. 2. Fasc. 1. Apologia. 1912. (1056). Fasc. 2. Florida. 1921. (1057). V. 3. De pholosophia libri, ed. by Thomas. 1921. (1058). B3056

____. Lvcii Apvlei Madavrensis Apologia, ed. by Vliet. 1900. B3057

Archimedes. Archimedis Opera omnia. 3 v. ed. by Heiberg, 1910-15. (1062-04). B3058

Aristeas' epistle. Aristeae Ad Philocratem epistvla, ed. by Wendland. 1900. (1065). B3059

Aristophanes. Aristophanis comedias, ed. by Bergk. 2 v. 1923. (1066, 1067). B3060

____. Acharnenses. 1923. (1068). B3061

____. Aves. 1929. (1069). B3062

____. Cantica, ed. by Schroeder. 1909. (1079). B3063
____. Ecclesiazusae. 1891. (1070). B3064
____. Eqvites. 1929. (1071). B3065
____. Lysistra. 1918. (1072). B3066
____. Nubes. 1935. (1073). B3067
____. Pax. 1931. (1074). B3068
____. Plutus. 1929. (1075). B3069
____. Ranae. 1934. (1076). B3070
____. Thesmophoriazusae. 1922. (1077). B3071
____. Vespae. 1921. (1078). B3072

Aristoteles. Aristotelis Ars rhetorica, ed. by Romer. 1936. (1080). B3073
____. Aristotelis De anima, ed. by Biehl. 1926. (1081). B3074
____. Aristotelis De animalibus historia, ed. by Dittmeyer. 1907. (1082). B3075
____. Aristotelis De Animalium motione et de animalium incessu, ed. by Yaeger. 1913. (1083). B3076
____. Aristotelis De arte poetica liber, ed. by Christ. 1913. (1084). B3077
____. Athenaion politeca, ed. by Oppermann. 1961. B3078
____. Aristotlis De coelo, et De generatione et corruptione, ed. by Prantl. 1881. B3079
____. Aristotelis De coloribus, De audibilibus, Physiognomonica, ed. by Prantl. 1881. (1085). B3080
____. Aristotelis De partibus animalium, ed. by Langkavel. 1868. (1086). B3081
____. Aristotelis De plantis..., ed. by Gorgia. 1881. (1087). B3082
____. Aristotelis Eudemi Rhodii Ethica, ed. by Susemihl. 1884. (1088). B3083
____. Aristotelis Ethica Nicomachea, ed. by Susemihl. 1912. (1089). B3084
____. Aristotelis Fragmenta, ed. by Rose. 1886. (1090). B3085
____. Aristotelis Magna moralis, ed. by Susemihl. 1883. (1091). B3086
____. Aristotelis Metaphysica, ed. by Christ. 1934. (1938). B3087
____. Aristotelis Oeconomica, ed. by Susemihl. 1887. (1092). B3088
____. Aristotelis Parva naturalia, ed. by Biehl. 1898. (1093). B3089
____. Poleteia Athenaion, ed. Thalheim and Opperman. 1928. (1094). B3090
____. Aristotelis Politica, ed. by Immisch. 1908. B3091
____. Aristotelis Politca post Fr. Susemihlium, ed. by Immisch. 1929. (1095). B3092
____. Aristotelis Πολιτεία Ἀθηναίων; ed. by Thalheim. 1909. B3093
____. ____, ed. by Blass. 1903. B3094
____. Aristotelis quae feruntur De coloribus, De audibililus, Physiognomonica, ed. by Prantt. 1881. B3095
____. Aristotelis quae feruntur De plantis, De mirabilibus auscultationibus..., ed. by Apelt. 1888. B3096
____. Aristotelis que ferebantur librorum fragmenta, ed. by Rose. 1886. B3097
____. Aristotelis quae feruntur Oeconomica, ed. by Susemihl. 1887. B3098
____. Aristotelis quae feruntur Problemata physica, ed. by Ruelle. 1922. (1096). B3099
____. Aristotelis Topica cum libro de sophisticis elenchis, ed. by Strache Wallies. 1923. (1097). B3100

Arrianus, F. Arriani Anabasis, ed. by Roos. V. 1. 1907. (1098, 1099). V. 2. 1928. (1098a). B3101
____. Arriani Nicomediensis Scripta Minora Rudolfus Hercher iterum recognovit, ed. by Eberhard. 1885. B3102

Athenaeus. Athenaei Navcratitae Diposophistarvm libri SV, ed. by Kaibel. V. 1. Libri I-V. 1923. (1101). V. 2. Libri VI-X. 1923. (1102). V. 3. Libri XI-XV. 1927. (1103). B3103

Augustinus, Aurelius, St.

Sancti Aurelii Augustini episcopi De civitate Dei libri XXII, ed. by Dombart. V. 1. Libri X-XIII. 1928. (1104). V. 2. Libri XIV-XXII. 1929. (1105). B3104

____. S. Aureli Augustini Confessionum libri tredecim, ed. by Knoell. 1934. (1106). B3105

Augustus, emperor of Rome. Historiae Augustae, ed. by Hohl. 2 v. (1772, 1772a). B3106

Aurelius, Antoninus, M. D. Imperatoris Marci Antoni commentariorum quos sibi ipsi scripsit libri XII, ed. by Stich. 1903. (1046, 1047). B3107

Ausonius, D. M. Decimi Avsonii Bvdigalensis Opvsvla, ed. by Peiper. 1886. (1109). B3108

Autolycus. Autolyci de sphaera quae movetur liber, ed. by Hultsch. 1885. (1110). B3109

Avienus, R. F. Rvfi Festi Avieni Aratea, ed. by Breysig. 1882. (1111). B3110

Babrius. Babrii Fabviae Aesopeae, ed. by Crvsivs. 1897. (1112). Edition major 1897. (1112). Edition minor 1897. (1114). B3111

Bacchylides. Bacchylidis carmina cum fragmentis, ed. by Suess. 1949. B3112

Baehrens, E., ed. Fragmenta poetarum romanorum. 1886. B3113

____. Poetae Latini minores 5 v. 1879-93. V. 1-3, V. 4. Seneca... 1882. (1706). V. 5. Cl. Rutilius Namatianus... 1883. (1707). Neubearbeitung, ed. by Vollmer. V. 1. Appendix Vergiliana... 1935. (1708). V. 2. 1911-23. (1708a). V. 2. Fasc. 1. Ovidi Halieuticon. Gratti Cynugeticon. 1911. (1709). Fasc. 2. Ovidi Nux. Consolatio ad Liviam. Priapea. 1923. (1710). Fasc. 3. Homerus Latinus. 1913. (1711). V. 5. Dracontius: De laudibus Dei..., 1914. (1712). B3114

Benedictus, St. Benedictii Regula monachorum, ed. by Woelfflin. 1895. B3115

Bible. O. T. Apolinarii metaphrasis Psalmorvm, ed. by Ludwich. 1912. B3116

Bible, N. T. Nonni Panopolitani Paraphrasis S. Evangelii Ioannei, ed. by Scheindler. 1881. B3117

____. Greek. Novvm Testamentvm graece, ed. by Buttmann. 1910. (1848). V. 1. 1892. (1831). V. 2. 1893. (1832). B3118

Bibliotheca scriptorum graecorum et romanorum Teubneriana. Rhetores graeci, ed. Spengel and Hammer. V. 1. De interrogationes et responsione... 1894. (1759). V. 2, 3. V. 5. Aristidis qui feruntur libri rhetorici II, ed. by Schmid. 1926. (1759a). V. 6. Hermogenes, ed. by Rabe. 1913. (1760). V. 10. Aphthonii progymnasmata... 1926. (1760a). V. 11. Nicolai progymnasmata, ed. by Felten. 1913. (1760b). V. 13. Romani Περὶ ἀνειμένου, ed. by Camphausen. 1922. (1761). V. 14. Prolegomenon sylloge, ed. by Rabe. 1931. (1935). V. 15. Ionnis Sardiana in Apthonium, ed. by Rabe. 1928. (1761a). V. 16. Syriani in Hermogenem, ed. by Rabe. 1892-93. (1830). B3119

Bitruvius Pollio. Vitrvii De architectura Libri Decem, ed. by Krohn, 1912. (1883). B3120

Boethius. Anicii Manlii Severini Boetii Commentarii in librum Aristoteli Περὶ ἑρμηνείας.... 2 v. 1877-1880. (1117-1118). B3121

Brandt, S., ed. Ecologae poetarum latinorum. 1910. B3122

Bremer, F. T., ed. Iurisprudentiae antehadrianae. 1896. B3123

Brummer, J., ed. Vitae Vergilianae. 1912. (1881). B3124

Caecilius Calactinus. Caecilii Calactini fragmenta, ed.

by Ofenloch. 1907. (1120). B3125
Caesar, C. J. Iuli Caesaris Belli gallici libri VII, ed. by Dinter. 1899. B3126
____. C. Iuli Caesaris Commentarii, ed. by Klotz. V. 1. Bellum Gallicum. 1938-39. (1121-24). V. 2. Bellum Civile. 1926. (1125, 1125a). V. 3. Bellum Alexandrinum... 1927. (1126). B3127
____. C. Iuli Caesaris Commentarii, ed. by Kuebler-Woelfflin. V. 3. 2. De Bello Hispaniensi. 1898. (1128). B3128
Callinicus. Callinici De Vita s. Hypatii liber. 1895. (1129). B3129
Calpurnius Flaccus. Calpvrnii Flacci Declamationes, ed. by Lehnerdt. 1903. (1130). B3130
Canabutzes, J. Ionnis Canabutzae magistri ad principem Aeni et Samothraces In Dionysium Halicarnasensem commentarius, ed. by Lehnerdt. 1890. (1904). B3131
Canons of Hippolytus. Hippolyti Romani praeter Canonem Paschalem. 1892. (1138). B3132
Cassius Dio Cocceianus. Dionis Casii Cocceiani Historia romana, ed. by Melber and Dindorf. 3 v. 1890-94. (1281-82, 1282a). B3133
Cassius Felix. Cassii Felicis De medicina, ed. by Rose. 1879. (1131). B3134
Cato, M. P. M. Porci Catonis De agri cvltvra liber, ed. by Keil. 1895. (1132). B3135
Catullus, C. V. Catvlli, Tibvlli, Propertii Carmina, ed. by Mveller. 1892. B3136
____. Catulli Veronensis Liber, ed. by Schuster. 1949. B3137
____. Q. Valerii Catulli Veronensis liber, ed. by Rossback. 1867. (1131). B3138
Cebes. Cebetis Tabula, ed. by Praechter. 1893. (1134). B3139
Celsus A. C. A. Cornelii Celsi De medicina libri octa, ed. by Daremberg. 1859. (1135). B3140
Censorinus. Censorini De die natali liber, ed. by Hultsch. 1867. B3141
Charisius. Charisii artis grammaticae libri V, ed. by Barwick. 1925. (1137). B3142
Choricius. Choricii Gazaei opera, ed. by Foerster-Richtsteig. 1929. (1137a). B3143
Christus patiens. Christus patiens, tragoedia christiana, ed. by Brambs. 1885. B3144
Cicero, M. T. De officiis libri tres, ed. by Klotz. 1876. (36). B3145
____, ed. by Atzert. 1949. B3146
____. M. Tullii Ciceronis Scripta quae manserunt omnia, ed. by Muller-Freidrich. 1. Rhetoricorum as C. Herennium libri IV. 1908. (1142). 3. De oratore libre III. 1931. (1142). 9a. Actionis in C. Verren Secundae libri I-III. 1908. (1143). 11. Orationes pro A. Cluentio. 1922. (1149). 16. De provinciis consularibus... 1910. (1153). 19. Epistularum ad familiares libri I-IV. 1897. (1154). 25. Ad Atticum libri V-VIII. 1922. (1157). 26. IX-XII. 1918. (1158). 27. XIII-XVI. 1918. (1159). 33. De divinatione libri II. 1915. (1161). 35. De legibus libri III. 1933. (1128). B3147
____. M. Tullii Ciceronis Scripta quae manserunt omnia, ed. by Atzert and others. V. 1. fasc. 1, 2. 1925. (1162a). V. 4. fasc. 7-10a, 1923. (1163). V. 5. fasc. 11-13a. 1923. (1164). V. 6:1. fasc. 14-16a. 1933. (1949). V. ?:2. fasc. 17-20a. 1933. (1950). V. 7. fasc. 21-25a. 1919. (1165). V. 8. fasc. 26-29a. 1918. (1166). V. 9. fasc. 30-33a. 1925. (1166a). V. 11. Fasc. 37-38a. 1914. (1167). V. 13. fasc. 43-44. 1919. (1168). B3148
____. M. Tullii Ciceronis

Scripta quae manserunt omnia. Rhetorica. V. 1. Fasc. 1. Rhetorica ad Herennium, ed. by Marx. 1923. (1169). Fasc. 2. Rhetorici libri duo qui vocantur de inventione, ed. by Strobel. 1915. (1170). V. 2. Fasc. 3. De oratore, ed. by Stroux. (1171). Fasc. 4. Brutus, ed. by Reis. 1934. (1172). V. 3. Fasc. 5. Orater, ed. by Reis. 1932. (1173). Fasc. 6. De optimo genere oratorum--Partitiones orationiae et topica, ed. by Stroux. (1174). Orationes. V. 4. Fasc. 7. Pro P. Quinctio, ed. by Klotz. 1922. (1175). Fasc. 8. Pro Sex, Roscio Amerino, ed. by Klotz. 1922. (1176). Fasc. 9. Pro Q. Roscio comoedo, ed. by Klotz. 1922. (1177). Fasc. 10. Pro Tullio..., ed. by Schoell. 1921. (1178). Fasc. 10a. Praefatio, Index IV. 1923. (1179). V. 5. Fasc. 11. Divinatio in Qu. Caecilium et in Verrem actio prima, ed. by Klotz. 1923. (1180). Fasc. 12. in verrem actionis secundae libri I-III, ed. by Klotz. 1923. (1181). Fasc. 13. Libri IV-V, ed. by Klotz. 1922. (1182). Fasc. 13a. Praefatio, Index V. 1923. (1183). V. 6:1. Fasc. 14. De imperio Cn. Pompei, ed. by Reis. 1927. (1184). Fasc. 15. Pro A. Cluentio Habito, ed. by Fruchterl. 1931. (1185). Fasc. 16. De lege agraria--Pro Rabirio perduellion--is reo, ed. by Fruchtel. 1931. (1186). Fasc. 16a. Praefatio, Index VI:1. 1933. (1234). V. 6:2. Fasc. 17. In L. Catilinam orat. IV, ed. by Reis. 1936. (1187). V. 6:2. Fasc. 18. Pro L. Murena, ed. by Kasten. 1932. (1188). Fasc. 19. Pro P. Sulla, ed. by Kasten, Pro Archia poeta, ed. by Reis. 1932. (1189). Fasc. 20. Pro Flacco, ed. by Fruchtel. 1932. (1190). Fasc. 20a. Praefatio. Index VI:2, ed. by Reis-Kasten Fruchtel. 1933. (1191). V. 7. Fasc. 21. Orationes: Cum senatui gratias egit--Cum populo gratias egit..., ed. by Klotz. 1915. (1192). Fasc. 22. Pro P. Sestio, ed. by Klotz. 1915. (1194). Fasc. 24. De provinciis consularibus..., ed. by Klotz. 1916. (1195). Fasc. 25. Pro Cn. Plancio..., ed. by Klotz. 1916. (1196). Fasc. 25a. Praefatio, Index VII. 1919. (1197). V. 8. Fasc. 26. Pro T. Annio Milone, ed. by Klotz. 1926. (1198). Fasc. 27. Pro M. Marcello..., ed. by Klotz. 1933. (1199). Fasc. 28. Orationes in M. Antonium Philippicae XIV, ed. by Schoell. 1916. (1200). Fasc. 29. Fragmenta orationum, ed. by Schoell. 1917. (1201). Fasc. 29a. Praefatio, Index VIII, 1918. (1202). Epistulae. V. 9. Fasc. 30. Epistulae ad familiares I-IV, ed. by Sjogren. 1923. (1203). Fasc. 31. V-VIII. 1928. (104). Fasc. 32. IX-XII. 1924. (1205). Fasc. 33. XIII-XVI. 1925. (1208). Fasc. 33a. Praefatio, Index IX. 1925. (1207). V. 10. Fasc. 34. Epistulae ad Atticum I-IV. 1208. Fasc. 35. V-XI. (1209). Fasc. 36. XII-XVI. (1210). V. 11. Fasc. 37. Epistula ad Quintum fratrem..., ed. by Sjogren. 1914. (1212). Fasc. 38. Epistula ad Brutum..., ed. by Sjogren. 1914. (1213). Fasc. 38a. Praefatio, Index XI. 1914. (1214). V. 12. Fasc. 39. De re publica, ed. by Ziegler. 1929. (1215). Fasc. 40. De legibus... (1217). Fasc. 41. Oeconomicus... (1217). Fasc. 42. Academicorum reliquiae cum Lucullo, ed. by Plasberg. 1922. (1218). V. 13.

Fasc. 43. De finibus bonorum et malorum, ed. by Schiche. 1915. (1219). Fasc. 44. Tusculanae disputationes, ed. by Pohlenz. 1918. (1220). V. 14. Fasc. 45. De natura deorum, ed. by Plasberg. 1933. (1221). Fasc. 46. De divinatione. De fato, ed. by Ax. 1938. (1222). Fasc. 47. Cato maior. Laelius, ed. by Simbeck, De gloria, ed. by Plasberg. 1917. (1223). V. 15. Fasc. 48. De officiis, ed. by Atzert, De virtutibus, ed. by Plasberg. 1932. (1224). Fasc. 49. Admiranda.... (1225). V. 16. Fasc. 50. Index Ciceronianus. (1226). B3149

____. M. Tullii Ciceronis Scholarum in usum scripta selecta. Orationes selectae XI. 1937. (1236). Pro Sex. Rosc. Amerino, ed. by Klotz. 1930. (1227). De imperio Cn. Pompei, ed. by Reis. 1936. (1229). In L. Catilianam, ed. by Reis. 1938. (1230). Pro A. Licinio Archia poeta, ed. by Reis. 1929. (1230a). Pro M. Marcello, Pro Q. Ligario, Pro rege deiotaro, ed. by Klotz. 1914. (1231). Tusculanae disputationes, ed. by Pohlenz. 1918. (1232). Cato maior, Laelius, Somnium scripionis, ed. by Simbeck-Ziegler. 1932. (1233). B3150

____. M. Tulli Ciceronis Epistolae, ed. by Wesenberg. 2 v. 1894. (1237). B3151

____. M. Tulli Ciceronis De virtutibus libri fragmenta, ed. by Knollinger. 1908. (1239). B3152

____. M. Tullii Ciceronis Scholia in Ciceronis Bobiensia, ed. by Hildebrandt. 1907. (1238). B3153

Claudianus, C. Claudii Claudiani Carmina, ed. by Koch. 1893. B3154

Cleomedes. Cleomedis De motu circulari corporum caelestium libri duo, ed. by Ziegler. 1891. (1241). B3155

Comnena Anna. Annae Comnenae, Porphyrogenitae, ed. by Reifferscheid. 1884. 2 v. (1027-28). B3156

Comoediae Horatianae, ed. by Jahnke. 1891. (1906). B3157

Commodianus. Commodiani Carmina, ed. by Ludwig. 2 v., 1878, 1877. (1242-43). B3158

Cornutus, L. A. Cornvti Theologiae graecae compendivm, ed. by Lang. 1881. (1244) B3159

Corpus juris civilis. Institutiones. Imp. Ivstiniani Institvtionvm libri qvattvor, ed. by Huschke. 1914. (1465). Pars. I. 1881. (1446). Pars II. 1881. (1467). Appendix. 1884. (1468). Auch geteilt. I. Notanda ad P.I. 1884. (1469). II De diocesi Aegypt. lex. 1891. (1469a) B3160

Corpvs agrimensorvm romanorvm, ed. by Thvlin. V. 1- 1913. (1245) B3161

Corpvs hippiattricorum graecorum, ed. by Oder and Hoppe. V. 1. Hippiatrica Berolinensia. 1924. (1246). Hippiatrica Parisina. 1927. (1246a) B3162

Corpvsvivm poesis epicae graecae lvdibvndae, ed. by Brandt and others. 2 v. 1888, 1885. (1247, 1248) B3163

Curtius Rufus, Q. Q. Curti Rufi Historiarum Alexandri Magni Macedonis libri qui supersunt, ed. by Vogel. 1900. (1249). 1908 ed. (1250) B3164

Dähnhardt, O., ed. Scholia in Aeschyli Persas. 1894. B3165

Damasus I, St. Damisi epigrammata, ed. by Ihm. 1895. (1034) B3166

Dares Phrygius. Daretis Phrygii De excidio Troiae historia, ed. by Meister. 1873. B3167

Demetrius. Démetrii Cydonii De contemnenda morte oratio, ed. by Deckelmann. 1901. (1251) B3168

____. Démetrii Libanii qui feruntur Τμ ποι επγνοτικοι ed. by Weichart. 1910. B3169

____. Phalerei, ed. by Weichert. 1910. (1252) B3170

Demosthenes. Demosthenis orationes, ed. by Fuhr. Editio maior. V. 1. Pars I. Orationes. I-XVII. 1914. (1254). Pars II. Oratio XVIII. 1914. (1255). Pars III. Oratio XIX. 1914. (1256). V. 2. Pars I, ed. by Sykutris. 1937. (1944). Editio minor. V. I. Pars I. Orationes I-XVII. 1928. (1258). V. 1. Orationes I-V. 1933. (1259). V. 2. Orationes VI-IX. 1933. (1260) B3171

____. Demosthenis orationes, ed. by Dindorfii. Ed. maior V. 2 1924. (1261). V. 3. 1927. (1262). Ed. minor V. 2. Orationes XX-XL. 1911. (1263). Pars 1. Orationes XX-XXIII. 1934. (1264). Pars 2. Orationes XXIV-XL. 1927. (1265). V. 3. Pars 1. XLI-LV. 1927. (1266). Pars 2. LVI-LXI. 1923. (1267) B3172

Dictys. Dictys Cretensis Ephemeridos belli troiani libri sex, ed. by Meister. 1872. B3173

Didymus Chalcenterus. Didymi de Demosthene commenta cum anonymi in Aristocrateam lexicon, ed. by Diels and others. 1904. (1269) B3174

Diehl, E. Anthologia lyrica graeca, ed. by Diehl. V. 1. 1936. (1034a). Fasc. 1. Poeta elegiaci. (1035). Fasc. 2. Theognis Megareus. 1934. (1036). Fasc. 3. Iamborum Scriptores. (1036a). Fasc. 4. Poetae Melici. 1935. (1037). V. 2. 1940. (1038). Fasc. 5. Poetae Melici. 1940. (1038a). Fasc. 6. Peplus Aristotelicus. 1924. (1039). Suppl. 1925. (1040). B3175

Dinarchus. Dinarchi Orationes, ed. by Blass. 1888. (1270) B3176

Dindorf, L. A., ed. Historici graeci minores. 2 v. 1870-71. B3177

Dio Coccecianus, Dionis Chrysistomi Orationes, ed. by de Budé. 2 v. 1915-19. (1283-1284) B3178

Diodorus, S. Diodori Bibliotheca historica, ed. by Vogel-Fischer. V. 1. Libri I-IV. 1888. (1271). V. 2. Libri V-XII. 1890. (1272). V. 3. Libri XIII-XV. 1893. (1273). V. 4. Libri XVI-XVIII. 1906. (1274). V. 5. Libri XIX-XX. 1906. (1275) B3179

____. Diodori Bibliotheca historica, ed. by Dindorf. V. 3. Libri XIV-XVIII. 1867. (1277). V. 4. Libri XIX-XXX. 1867. (1278). V. 5. Libri XXXI-XL. 1868. (1279) B3180

Diogenes, Apolloniates. Diogenis Oenoandensis fragmenta, ed. by William. 1907. (1208) B3181

Dionysius. Dionysi Halicarnasensis Antiqvitatvm romanorvm, ed. by Jacoby. V. 1. Liber I-III. 1885. (1285). V. 2. Liber IV-VI. 1888. (1286). V. 3. Liber VII-IX. 1891. (1287). V. 4. Liber X-XX. 1905. (1288). Suppl. 1925. (1291a). V. 5. Opp. I. 1899. (1289). V. 6. Opp. II. 1929. (1933). Indices 1929. (1291) B3182

Diphantus. Diophanti Alexandrini Opera omnia, ed. by Tannery. 2 v. 1893-1895. (1292-93) B3183

Divisiones Aristoteleae, ed. by Mutschmann. 1906. (1294) B3184

Donatus, A. Aeli Donati qvod fertur Commentvm Terenti. Bembina, ed. by Wessner. 3 v. 1902-1908. (1295-1297). Interpretationes Vergilianae, ed. by Georgi. 2 v. 1905-1906. (1298, 1299) B3185

Donatus, T. C. Tiberi Claudi Donati ad Tiberium Claudium Maximum Donatianum filium suum Interpretationes Vergilianae, ed. by Georgii. 2 v. 1905-06. B3186

Drachmann, A. B. Scholia vetera in Pinardi carmina. V. 1. 1969. B3187

Dracontius, B. A. Dracontii Carmina Minora plurima, ed. by Duhn. 1873. (1300) B3188

Eberhard, A., ed. Fabulae romanenses graece conscriptae. 1872. B3189

Endt, J., ed. Adnotationes super Lucanum. 1909. B3190

Epictetus. Epicteti Dissertationes ab Arriano digestae, ed. by Schenkl. Ed. maior 1916. (1302). Ed. minor 1916. (1303) B3191
Epicurus. Epicuri epistulae tres et ratae sententiae e Laertio Diogene servatae, ed. by Muhll. 1922. (1294) B3192
Epistolae obscurorum virorum. Epistolae obscvrorvm virorvm. 3 parts. 1914. (1948) B3193
Euclides. Euclidis Opera omnia. V. 1. Elementa, ed. by Heiberg. Libri I-IV. 1883. (1307). V. 2. Libri V-IX. 1884. (1308). V. 3. Liber X. 1886. (1209). V. 4. Libri XI-XIII. 1885. (1310). V. 5. Libri XIV-XV. 1888. (1311). V. 6. Data: Menge. 1896. (1312). V. 7. Optica, ed. by Heiberg. 1895. (1313). V. 8. Phaenomena, ed. by Menge, 1916. (1314). Suppl. 1899. (1315) B3194
Eudocia, A. Eudociae Augustae, Procli Lycii, Claudiani carminum graecorum reliquiae, ed. by Ludwich. 1897. (1316) B3195
___. Augustae violarum, ed. by Flack. 1880. (1417) B3196
Euripides. Evripidis Cantica novis iisque vltimus curis, ed. by Schroeder. 1928. B3197
___. Evripides tragoediae, ed. by Nauck. V. 1. (No. 1-3, 5-10, 18) 1933. (1318). V. 2. (No. 4, 11,-17, 19). 1921. (1319). V. 3. Fragmenta. 1912. (1320) B3198
___. Evripides. Alcestis. 1930. (1321) B3199
___. Evripides. Andromacha. 1891. (1322) B3200
___. Evripides. Bacche. 1930. (1323) B3201
___. Evripides. Cyclops. 1929. (1324) B3202
___. Evripides. Electra. 1913. (1325) B3203
___. Evripides. Hecuba. 1933. (1326) B3204
___. Evripides. Helena. 1909. (1327) B3205
___. Evripides. Heraclidae. 1929. (1328) B3206
___. Evripides. Hercules. 1930. (1329) B3207
___. Evripides. Hippolytus. 1932. (1330) B3208
___. Evripides. Ion. 1928. (1331) B3209
___. Evripides. Iphigenia Aulidensis. 1934. (1332) B3210
___. Evripides. Iphigena in Tauris. 1939. (1333) B3211
Euripides. Evripides. Medea. 1931. (1334) B3212
___. Evripides. Orestes. 1933. (1335) B3213
___. Evripides. Phoenissae. 1933. (1336) B3214
___. Evripides. Rhesus. 1905. (1337) B3215
___. Evripides. Supplices. 1904. (1338) B3216
___. Evripides. Troades. 1929. (1339) B3217
___. Cantica, ed. by Schroeder. 1928. (1340) B3218
Eusebius Pamphili. Evsebii Caesariensis Opera omnia, ed. by Dindorf. V. 1. Praeparationis evangelicae libri I-X. 1867. (1341). V. 2. Libri XI-XV. 1867. (1342). V. 3. Demonstartiones evangelicae Libri I-X. 1867. (1343). V. 4. Historiae ecclesiasticae Libri I-X. 1890. (1344) B3219
Eutropius. Evtropi Brevarivm ad vrbe condita, ed. by Ruhl. 1897. (1346) B3220
___. Historia Romana, ed. by Dietsch. 1877. (1345) B3221
Favonis Eulogius. Favonii Evlogii Dispvtatio de Somnio Scripionis, ed. by Holder. 1901. B3222
Festus, S. P. Sexti Pompei Festi De verborum significatu quae supersunt, ed. by Lindsay. 1933. (1349) B3223
Firmicius Maternus, J. Iulii Firmici Materini libri VIII, ed. by Kroll and others. 2 v. 1897-1913. (1250, 1251) B3224
___. Iulii Firmici Materini De errore profan. relig., ed. by Ziegler. 1907. (1253) B3225
Florilegivm graecvm in vsvm

primi gymnasiorvm ordinis collectvm a philologis afranis. Fasc. 1. 1898. Fasc. 2. 1893. (1355). Fasc. 3. 1889. Fasc. 4. 1932. (1356). Fasc. 5-7. 1930-31. (1357-9). Fasc. 8. 1901. (1360). Fasc. 9. 10. 1890. (1361-2). Fasc. 11-15. 1901. (1363-1367) B3226

Florilegivm latinum. V. 1. Drama. 1911. (1368). V. 2. Erzahlande Prosa. 1931. (1369). V. 3. Epiku. Lyrik. 1930. (1370). V. 4. Redner Prosa u. Inschriftliches. 1927. (1371) B3227

Florus, L. A. L. Annaei Flori Epitomae libri II. et P. Annii Flori fragmentvm De Vergilio oratore an poeta, ed. by Rossbach. 1896. (1354) B3228

Foerster, R., ed. Scriptores physiognomonici gracaei et latini. V. 1. Pseud aristotelis physiognomonica... 1893. (1780). V. 2. Physiognomonica anonymi... 1893. (1781) B3229

Fragmenta poetarum latinorum epicorum et lyricorum praeter ennium et lucilium, ed. by Morel. 1927. (1371a) B3230

Frick, K., ed. Chronica minora. 1892. B3231

Frontinus, S. J. Ivli Fronti Strapegmaton libri qvattor, ed. by Gvndermann. 1888. (1372) B3232

____. Ivli Fronti Strapegmaton De aquaductu urbis romae liber III, ed. by Krohn. 1922. (1273) B3233

Fulgentius, F. P. Fabii Planciadis Fulgentii Opera, ed. by Helm. 1898. (1374) B3234

Funaioli, G., ed. Grammaticae romanae fragmenta collegit. V. 1. 1907. (1936) B3235

Gaius. Gai Institvtionvm comentarii qvattvor, ed. by Hvschke. 1926. (1375) B3236

____. Gai Institutiones, ed. by Seckel and Kuebler. 1935. B3237

Galenus. Galeni Scripta minora, ed. by Marquardt and others. 3 v. 1884, 1891, 1893. (1376-8) B3238

____. Galeni Institutio logica, ed. by Kalbfeisch. 1896. (1379) B3239

____. Galeni De victu attenuante liber, ed. by Kalbfleisch. 1898. (1380) B3240

____. Galeni De tempementis, ed. by Helmrich. 1904. (1381) B3241

____. Galeni De usu partium libri XVII, ed. by Helmreich. 2 v. 1907-1909. (1382, 1383) B3242

Gellius, A. A. Gellii Noctivm atticarvm Libri XX, ed. by Hosivs. 2 v. 1903. (1384-1385) B3243

Gelzer, H. K. G. and others. Patrum nicaenorum nomina latina, graeca, coptice, syriace, arabice, armentiace. 1898. B3244

Geminus. Gemini Elementa astronomiae ad codicum fidem recensuit, ed. by Manitius. 1898. (1386) B3245

Genevieve, St. Vita Sanctae Genovefae virginis Parisiorum patronae, ed. by Künstle. 1910. (1908) B3246

Geoponica. Geoponica sive Cassiani Bassi scholastici de re rustica eclogae, ed. by Beckh. 1895. (1387) B3247

George, St. Legend. Miracula s. Georgii, ed. by Aufhauser. 1913. (1540) B3248

Georgius monarchus. Georgii monarchi chronicon, ed. by de Boor. 1904. B3249

Georgius, of Cyprus. Georgii Cyprii Descriptio orbis romani, ed. by Gelzer. 1890. (1390) B3250

Georgius Phrantzes. Georgii Phrantzes Chronicon, ed. by de Boor. 2 v. 1904. (1392, 1393) B3251

____, ed. by Papadopoulos. 1935. B3252

Gerland, E. Neue quellen zur geschichte des lateinischen erzbestums Patras. 1903. B3253

Germanicus Caesar. Germanici Caesaris Aratea itervm, ed. by Breysig. 1899. (1395) B3254

Goetz, G. De Plavti vita ae poesi testamonia. 1896. B3255

Graeci minores rerum

1931. (1437) B3287
____. Q. Horati Flacci Romani porcaria, ed. by Lehnerdt. 1907. (1911) B3288
Hrotsvit. Hrotsvithae Opera, ed. by Strecker. 1906. (1912) B3289
Hultsch, F. O., ed. Metrologicorum scriptorum reliquiae, ed. by Hultsch. V. 1. Scriptores graeci. 1864. (1774). V. 2. Scriptores Romani. 1866. (1775) B3290
Huschke, P. E., ed. Ivrisprvdentiae anteistinianae qvae supersvnt. 1866. B3291
____. Ivrisprvdentiae anteistinianae reliqvias in vsvm maxime academicvm. 1908. B3292
Hyginus Gromaticus. Hygini Gromatici Liber De munitionibus castrorum, ed. by Gemoll. 1879. (1943) B3293
Hyperides. Hyperidis Orationes sex cvm ceterarvm fragmentis, ed. by Blass. 1917. (1441) B3294
Incerti auctoris de Constantino Magno eiusque matre Helena libellus, ed. by Heydenreich. 1879. (1447) B3295
Incerti Scriptoris bysantini saeculi X, ed. by Vári. 1901. (1448) B3296
Inscriptores Graecae ad inlustradas dialectos selectae, ed. by Solmsen. 1930. (1449) B3297
Isaeus. Isaei Orationes cum aliquot deperditarum fragments, ed. by Scheibe. 1903. (1456) B3298
Isocrates. Isocratis Orationes, ed. by Benseler and Blass. 2 v. 1879. (1457-1458). Panegyricus. 1930. (1934) B3299
Iurisprundetiae antehadrainae quae supersunt, ed. by Bremer. Pars I. Liberae rei pblicae iuris consulti. 1896. (1459). Pars II. Primi post principatum conctitutum saeculi iuris consulti. Sect. I. 1898. (1460). Sect. II. 1901. (1461) B3300
Iurisprudentiae anteiustinianae quae supersunt Huschke, ed. by Seckel-Kubler. Pars. I. 1908. (1462). Pars. II. Fasc. 1. 1911. (1463). Fasc. 2. 1927. (1463a). Suppl. 1880. (1464) B3301
Jahnke, R., ed. Comoediae Horatianae. 1891. B3302
Jamblichus, of Chalcis. Iamblichi Protrepticus, ed. by Pistelli. 1888. (1442) B3303
____. Iamblichi De commvni mathematica scientic liber, ed. by Festa. 1891. (1443) B3304
____. Iamblichi In Nicomachi arithmeticam introductionem liber, ed. by Pistelli. 1894. (1444) B3305
____. Iamblichi De vita pythcgorica liber, ed. by Deubner. 1937. (1445) B3306
____. Iamblichi theologumena arithmeticae, ed. by De Falco. 1922. (1446) B3307
Jan, K. von, ed. Musici scriptores graeci. 1895. B3308
Joannes Lydus. De magistratibus populi romani libri tres, ed. by Wuensch. 1903. B3309
____. Joannis Laurentii Lydi Liber de mensibus, ed. by Wuensch. 1898. B3310
____. Joannis Lavrentii Lydi Liber de ostentis et calendaria graecaomnia, ed. by Wachsmvth. 1897. (1522) B3311
____. Ioannes Philoponus De aeternitate mundi contra Proclum, ed. by Rabe. 1899. B3312
John of Alexander. I. Philoponi de aeternitate mundi, ed. by Rabe. 1899. (1591) B3313
Josephus, F. Flavii Josephi Opera omnia. V. 1. Antiquitates. Libri I-V. 1888. (1450). V. 2. Libri VI-X. 1889. (1451). V. 3. Libri XI-XV. 1892. (1452). V. 4. Libri XVI-XX. 1893. (1453). V. 5. Bellum Iudauc. Libri I-IV. 1895. (1454). V. 6. Libri V-VII. 1896. (1455) B3314
Julianus. Ivalini imperatoris quae supersunt praeter reliquias apud Cyrillium omnia, ed. by Hertlein. 2 v. 1875-76. B3315
Justinus, M. J. M. Iuniani Iustini Epitoma historiarum Philippicarum Pompei Trogi, ed. by Ruehl. 1935.

(1470) B3316

Juvenalis, D. J. D. Iunii Iuvenalis Satirarum libri quinque, ed. by Hermann. 1890. (1471) B3317

Juvencus, C. V. A. C. Vettii Aquilini luvenci Libri Evangeliorum IIII, ed. by Marold. 1886. B3318

Keller, O., ed. Rervm natrlivm scriptores graeci minores. V. 1. 1877. B3319

Kinkel, G., comp. Epicorum graecorum fragmenta. 1877. B3320

Lactantius Placidus. Lactantii Placidi qui dicitvr Commentarios in Statii Thebaida, ed. by Jahnke. 1898. B3321

Lan, Karl von, ed. Musici scriptores graeci. 1895. (1776). Suppl. 1899. (1777) B3322

Lavagnini, B., ed. Eroticorum graecorum fragmenta papyracea. 1922. B3323

Leipzig. Köningin Carola-gymnasium. Florilegium latinum zusammegestellt von der Philologischen vereingung des Köningin Carola-gymnasiums zu Leipzig. 4 v. 1911-12. B3324

Libanius. Libanii Opera, ed. by Foerster. V. 1. Fasc. 1. Orationes I-V. 1903. (1473). Fasc. 2. Orationes VI-XI. 1903. (1474). V. 2. Orationes XII-XXV. 1904. (1475). V. 3. Orationes XXVI-L. 1906. (1476). V. 4. Orationes LI-LXIV. 1908. (1477). V. 5. Declamationes I-XII. 1909. (1478). V. 6. XIII-XXX. 1911. (1479). V. 7. XXXI-LI. 1913. (1480). V. 8. Progymnasmata... 1915. (1481). V. 9. Qui Feruntur characteres epistolici... ed. by Richtsteig. 1927. (1482). V. 10. Epistulae 1-839. 1921. (1483). V. 11. 840-1544. 1922. (1484). V. 12. Index. 1923. (1485). B3325

Licinianus, G. Grani Liciniani quae supersunt, ed. by Flemisch. 1904. (1397) B3326

Livius, T. Titi Livi Ab urbe condita libri, ed. by Weissenborn and others. Pars 1. Libri 1-10. 1932. (1486). Pars. 2. Libri 21-30. 1939. (1487). Pars 3. Libri 31-40. 1938. (1488). Pars. 4. Libri 41-142. 1930. (1489). Pars 1. Fasc. 1. Libri 1-3. 1936. (1490). Fasc. 2. Libri 4-6. 1931. (1491). Fasc. 3. 7-10. 1925. (1492). Pars. 2. Fasc. 1. Libri 21-23. 1938. (1493). Fasc. 2. Libri 24-26. 1936. (1494). Fasc. 3. Libri 27-30. 1915. (1495). Pars 3. Fasc. 1. Libri 31-35. 1930. (1496). Fasc. 2. Libri 36-38. 1929. (1497). Fasc. 3. Libri 39-40. 1937. (1498). Pars 4. Fasc. 1. Libri 41-42. 1914. (1499). Fasc. 2. Index. 1931. (1500) B3327

____. T. Livi Periochae, ed. by Rossbach. (1501) B3328

Lobkowitz, B. H. Epistulae, ed. by Martinek. V. 1. 1969. B3329

Longus. Longus, ed. by Valley. (1932) B3330

Lucanus, M. A. M. Annaei Lvcani De bello civili libri decem, ed. by Hosivs. 1905. (1502) B3331

____. M. Annei Lvcani Adnotationes super Lucanum, ed. by Endt. 1909. (1503) B3332

____. M. Annei Lvcani Opera, ed. by Jacobitz. V. 1. 1921. (1504). V. 2. 1913. (1505). V. 3. 1913. (1506). V. 1. Pars. 1. De somnio... 1924. (1507). Pars 2. Charon... 1926. (1508). V. 2. Pars. 1. Quomodo historia conscribenda sit... 1913. (1509). Pars 2. Amores... 1939. (1510). V. 3. Pars 1. Bis accusatus... 1913. (1511). Pars 2. Dialogi meretici... 1891. (1512). V. 1. Fasc. 1. Libri I-XIV. 1906. (1513). Fasc. 2. Libri XV-XIX. 1923. (1514). Prolegmonea. 1900. (1515) B3333

____. M. Annei Lvcani Scholia in Lucianum, ed. by Rabe. 1906. (1516) B3334

Lucianus Samosatensis. Luciani Samosatensis Opera, ed. by Jacobsitz. 3 v.

1887-1901. B3335
Lucretius Carus, T. T. Lucreti Cari De rerum natura, ed. by Martin. 1934. (1518) B3336
____. Lucreti Cari De rerum natura libri sex, ed. by Bernaysius. 1852. B3337
____. Ed. by Brieger. 1899. B3338
____. Ed. by Meyer. 1957. B3339
Lycophron. Lycophronis Alexandra, ed. by Kinkel. 1880. (1519) B3340
Lycurgus. Lycurgi Oratio in Leocraten, ed. by Scheibe and Blass. 1899. (1520, 1521) B3341
Lysias. Lysiae Orationes, ed. by Scheibe. 1885. B3342
____. Lysiae Orationes, ed. by Thalheim. 1901. (1525, 1526) B3343
Macrobius, A. A. T. Macrobivs, tr. by Eyssenhardt. 1893. (1527) B3344
Manetho. Manethonis Apotelesmaticorum qui ferunter libri VI, ed. by Köchly. 1858. B3345
Manilius, M. M. Manilii Astronomica, ed. by Wageninger. 1915. (1528) B3346
Mann, O., ed. Anthologie aus römischen dichtern für die obersten klassen der realgymnasien und ähnlichen anstalten. 1883. B3347
Manutius, P. Pavli Manvtii Epistolae seceltae, ed. by Fickelscherer. 1892. (1917) B3348
Marcellus Empiricus. Marcelii De medic amentis liber, ed. by Helmsreich. 1889. (1529) B3349
Marcus Diaconus. Marci Diaconi Vita Prophyrii. 1895. (1530) B3350
Marinus, the philosopher. Euclides. V. 4. B3351
Martialis, M. V. M. Valerii Martialis Epigrammaton libri, ed. by Gilbert. 1896. B3352
____. M. Valerius Martialis Epigrammaton, ed. by Heraeus. 1925. (1531) B3353
Martianus Capella. Martianus Capella, ed. by Dick. 1925. (1532) B3354
____. Martianvs Capella, ed. by Eyssenhardt. 1866. B3355
Maximus. Maximi et Ammonis carminum De actionum auspiciis reliquae, ed. by Ludwich. 1877. (1534) B3356
Maximus Tyrus. Maximi Tyrii Philosophumena, ed. by Hobein. 1910. (1535) B3357
Mela, P. Pomponii Melae De chorographia libri tres, ed. by Frick. 1880. (1536) B3358
Menander. Menandrae ex papyris et membranis vetustissimis, ed. by Koerte. 1912. B3359
____. Menandrea. Fasc. 1. Menandri Reliquiae in papyris et membranis vetustissimis servatae, ed. by Koerte. 1938. (1537) B3360
____. Menandri quae supersunt, ed. by Koerte. V. 1. 1938. B3361
Minucius Felix, M. M. Minucii Felicis Octavius, ed. by Waltzing. 1931. (1539) B3362
____. Octavius, ed. by Boenig. 1903. B3363
Mulomedicina Chironis. Claudii Hermeri Mulomedicina Chironis, ed. by Oder. 1901. (1541) B3364
Muret, M. A. M. Antonii Myreto Scripta selecta, ed. by Frey. V. 1. Orationes. 1887. (1918). V. 2. Epistulae. 1888. (1919) B3365
Musonius Rufus, C. C. Mysonii Rvfi riliqviae, ed. by Hense. 1905. (1542) B3366
Mythographi graeci. 5 v. 1894-1902. B3367
Nemesius. Nemesii Episcopi Premnon physicon, ed. by Burkhard. 1917. (1548) B3368
Nepos, C. Cornelii Nepotis Vitae, ed. by Fleckeisen. 1939. (1549) B3369
Nicephorus, St. Nicephori archiepiscopi constantinopoloitani Opvscvla historica, ed. by Boor. 1880. (1551) B3370
Nicephorus Blemmydes. Nicephori Blemmydae Curriculum vitae et carmina, ed. by Heisenberg. 1896. (1552) B3371
Nicolaus. Nicolai Progymnasmata, ed. by Felten.

1913. B3372
Nicomachus Gerasenus. Nicomachi Geraseni Pythagorei introvctionis arithmeticae libri II, ed. by Hoche. 1866. (1553) B3373
Nonius Marcellus. Nonii Marcelli De compendios a doctrina libri XX, ed. by Lindsay. V. 1. Libri I-III. 1903. (1554). V. 2. Liber IV, 1903. (1555). V. 3. Libri V-XX. 1903. (1556) B3374
Nonnus Panopolitanus. Nonni Panopolitani Dionysiaca, ed. by Lvdwick V. 1. Libri I-XXIV, 1909. (1557). V. 2. Libri XXV-XLVIII. 1911. (1558) B3375
____. Nonni Panopolitani Paraphrasis sancti evangelii Ioannei, ed. by Scheindler. 1881. (1557) B3376
Odo, St. Odonis Abbatis civniacensis Occvpatio, ed. by Swoboda. 1900. (1913) B3377
Olympiodorus. Olympiodori philosophi in Platonis gorgiam, ed. by Norvin. 1936. (1947) B3378
____. Olympiodori Philosophi in Platonis Phaedonem, ed. by Norvin. 1913. (1560) B3379
Onosander. Onosardi De imperatoris officio liber, ed. by Koechly. 1860. B3380
Oratoes panegyrici. XII panegyrici latini, ed. by Baehrens. 1911. B3381
Orosius, P. Pavli Orosii Historiarvm adversvm paganos, ed. by Zangemeister. 1889. (1562) B3382
Ovidius Naso, P. P. Ovidius Naso ex Rudolphi Merkelii recognitione, ed. by Ehwald. V. 1. Amores... 1916. (1563). V. 2. Metamorphosis. 1915. (1564). 1937. (1565). V. 3. Fasc. 1. Tristium Libri V. 1922. (1566). Libri V. 1922. (1567). Fasc. 2. Fasti et fragmenta. 1932. (1568) B3383
____. P. Ovidius Naso Metamorphoseon delectus Siebelisiamus, ed. by Polle 1933. (1570). Fasc. 1. 1930. (1571). Fasc. 2. 1923. (1572) B3384
Palaiokappa, K. Eudociae Augustae Violarium recensuit et emendabot, ed. by Flach. 1880. B3385
Palladius, R. T. A. Palladii Rvtilii Tavri Aemiliani Viri inlvstris Opvs agricvltvrae, ed. by Schmittii. 1898. (1573). B3386
Panegyrici XII, ed. by Beahrens. 1911. (1574) B3387
Parthenius. Parthenii Nicaeni quae svpersvnt, ed. by Martini. 1902. B3388
Paulus Aegineta. Pauli Aeginetae libri tertii interpretatio latina antiqua, ed. by Heiberg. 1912. (1914) B3389
Pausanias. Pausaniae Graeciae descriptio, ed. by Spiro. V. 1. Libri I-IV. 1938. (1575). V. 2. Libri V-VIII. 1903. (1576). V. 3. Libri IX-X. 1903. (1577). V. 2. Libri VII-X, ed. by Schubart, 1900. (1578) B3390
Pelagonius. Pelagonii artis veterinariae quae extent recensvit, ed. by Ihm. 1892. (1579) B3391
Persius Flaccus, A. A. Persii Flacci Satirarum liber, ed. by Hermann. 1900. (1580) B3392
Peter, H. W. G., ed. Historicorum romanorvm fragmenta, ed. by Peter. 1883. B3393
Phaedrus. Phaedri avgvsti liverti Fabvlae Aesopiae, ed. by Muller. Ed. Maior. 1926. (1581a). Ed. Minor. 1928. (1581) B3394
Philodemus. Philodemi Volumina rhetorica, ed. by Sudhaus. 2 v. 1892-96. (1582-83). Suppl. 1895. (1584) B3395
____. Philodemi De ira liber, ed. by Wilke. 1914. (1585) B3396
____. Philodemi de musica Liber, ed. by Kemke. 1884. (1586) B3397
____. Philodemi Περὶ κακιῶν liber decimus, ed. by Jensen. 1911. (1587) B3398
____. Philodemi Περὶ οικονομιας

liber, ed. by Jensen. 1906. (1588) B3399

___. Philodemi Περὶ παρρησίας libellus, ed. by Oliveri. 1914. (1598) B3400

___. Philodemi Περὶ τοῦ καθ' Ὅμηρον ἀγαθοῦ βασιλέως libellus, ed. by Oliveri. 1919. (1590) B3401

Philostratus, F. Flavii Philostrati Opera auctiora, ed. by Kayser. 2 v. 1870-71. B3402

Philostratus. Philostrati Minoris Imagines et Callistrati Descriptiones, ed. by Schenkl and Reisch. 1902. (1593) B3403

___. Philostrati maioris imagines, ed. by Beendorf-Schenklii. 1893. (1592) B3404

Phrynichus, A. Phrynichi sophistae Praeparatio sophistica, ed. by Borries. 1911. B3405

Pindarus. Carmina cum fragmentis, ed. by Snell. 1955. B3406

___. Carmina cum deperditorum fragmentis selectis, ed. by Christ. 1896. B3407

___. Pindari Carmina, ed. by Schroeder. 1914. (1595) B3408

___. Pindari Scholia vetera, ed. by Drachmann. 3 v. 1927. (1597, 1598, 1598a) B3409

Plato. Platonis Dialogi V. 1. ed. by Wohlrab. 1939. (1599). V. 2. ed. by Wohlrab. 1922. (1600). V. 3-6 ed. by Hermann. 1939, 1922, 1934, 1927. (1600-1604). V. 1 no. 1 Euthyphro... ed. by Wohlrab. 1938. (1605). Apolgia... 1932. (1606). No. 2 Cratylus... ed. by Wohlrab. 1925. (1607). No. 3. Sophista, ed. by Wohlrab. 1922. (1608). V. 2. No. 4 Parmenides... ed. by Wohlrab. 1922. (1609). No. 5. Convivium... 1935. (1610). Symposion. 1934. (1611). No. 6 Alcibiades II. ... 1922. (1612). V. 3. No. 7 Charmides... 1931. (1613). No. 8 Euthydemus... 1931. (1614). Protagoras 1930. (1937). No. 9 Gorgias... 1933. (1615). Gorgias. Ed. Ster. 1933. (1615a) No. 10 Hippias. 1937. (1616). V. 4 No. 11 Res publica 1938. (1617). No. 12 Timaeus... 1925. (1618). V. 5. No. 13 Legum libri XII, (Nomoi.)... 1934. (1603). V. 6. No. 14 Platonis epistulae SVIII. 1922. (1620). No. 15 Appendix... 1920. (1621) B3410

___. Platonis Euthyphro... ed. by Hermann. 1906. B3411

Plautus, T. M. T. Macci Plavti Comoediae, ed. by Goetz and Schoell. Fasc. 1-7. 1898-1901. (1622-1628). No. 1. Amphitruo. 1933. (1629). No. 2. Asinaria. 1925. (1630). No. 3. Aulularia. 1931. (1631). No. 4. Bacchides. 1932. (1632). No. 5. Captivi. 1928. (1633). No. 6. Casina. 1914. (1634). No. 7. Cistellaria. 1895. (1635). No. 8. Curuculio. 1929. (1636). No. 9. Epidicus. 1910. (1637). No. 10. Menaechmi. 1935. (1638). No. 11. Mercator. 1932. (1639). No. 12. Miles gloriosus. 1928. (1640). No. 13. Mostellaria. 1927. (1641). No. 14. Persa. 1896. (1642). No. 15. Poenulus. 1896. (1643). No. 16. Pseudolus. 1896. (1644). No. 17. Rudens. 1930. (1645). No. 18. Stichus. 1925. (1646). No. 19. Trinummus. 1929. (1647). No. 20. Truculentus. 1896. (1648). Suppl... 1930. (1649) B3412

Plinius Caecilius Secundus, C. C. Plini Caecili Secundi Epistularum libri novem, ed. by Müller. 1903. B3413

___. C. Plini Caecili epistularem libri novem, ed. by Kukula. 1912. B3414

Plinius Secundus, C. C. Plini Secundi naturalis historiae libri XXXVII, ed. by Mayhoff. V. 1. Libri I-VI. 1933. (1650). V. 2. Libri VII-XV. 1909. (1651). V. 3. Libri XVI-XXII. 1892. (1652). V. 4. Libri XXIII-XXX. 1897. (1653). V. 5. Libri XXXI-XXXVII. 1897.

(1654) B3415

____. C. Plini Secundi librorum dubii sermonis VIII reliquiae, ed. by Beck. 1894. (1655) B3416

____. C. Plini Secundi una cum Gargilii Martialis medicina, ed. by Rose. 1875. (1656) B3417

____. C. Plini Secundi Epistularum ad Traianum liber, Panegyricus, ed. by Schuster. 1933. (1657) B3418

Plotinus. Plotini Enneades, praemisso Porphyrii De vita Plotini deque ordine liborum eius libello, ed. by Volkmann. 2 v. 1883-84. (1658-59) B3419

____. Plotini Opera, ed. by Kirchoff. 2 v. 1856. B3420

Plutarchus. Plutarchi Vitae parallelae, ed. by Sintenis. 6 v. 1881-1902. (1661). Einzein: 1. Theseue et Romulus, Lycurgus et Numa, Solon et Publicola. 1906. (1663). 3. Timoleon et Aemilius Paulus, Pelopias et Marcellus. 1901. (1664). 4. Daraus noch erhaltlich: Philopoemen et Titus Flamininus. 1923. (1665). 6. Nicias et Crassus, Sertorius et Eumenus. 1911. (1666). 7. Agsilaus et Pompeius. 8. Alexander et Caesar. 13. Dion et Brutus. 14. Artaxerxes et Aratus, Galba et Otho. 1911. (1671) B3421

____. Plutarchi Neubearbeitung, ed. by Lindskog and Zeigler. V. 1. Fasc. 1. no. 1-5. 1914. (1672). Fasc. 2. no. 6-9. 1914. (1673). V. 2. Fasc. 1. no. 10-13. 1932. (1674). Fasc. 2. no. 14-16. 1935. (1942). V. 3. Fasc. 1. no. 17-20. 1915. (1675). Fasc. 2. no. 21-23. 1926. (1676). V. 4. Fasc. 1. no. 24. 1935. (1943). Fasc. 2. no. 25. 1939. (1956). In einzelnen heften: 1. Thesei et Romuli. 1914. (1677). 2. Soloni et Publicolae. 1914. (1678). 3. Themistoclis et Camilii. 1914. (1679). 4. Aristidis et Catonis. 1914. (1680). 5. Cimonis et Luculli. 1914. (1681). 6. Pericles et Fabivs Maximvs. 1914. (1682). 7. Niciae et Crassi. 1914. (1683). 8. Alcibiadis et Coriolani. 1914. (1684). 9. Demosthenis et Ciceronis. 1914. (1685). 10. Phocion et Cato Minor. 1931. (1686). 11. Dion et Brutus. 1932. (1687). 12. Aemilius Paulus et Timoleon. 1932. (1688). 13. Sertorius et Eumenes. 1932. (1689). 14. Philopoemen et Titus Flamininus. 1933. (1690). 15. Pelopidas et Marcellus. 1933. (1691). 16. Alexander et Caesar. 1934. (1692). 17. Demetrii et Antonii. 1915. (1693). 18. Pyrrhi et Marii. 1915. (1694). 19. Arati et Artaxeris. 1915. (1695). 20. Agis et Cleomenis, Ti. et. C. Gracchorum. 1915. 21. Lysvrgvs et Nvma. 1926. (1697). 22. Lysander et Svlla. 1926. (1698). 23. Agesilavs et Pompeivs. 1926. (1699). 24. Galba et Otho. 1935. (1700). 25. Indices. 1939. (1956) B3422

____. Plutarchi Chaeronensis Moralia, ed. by Hercheri. 7 v. V. 1-3. 1888-91. V. 4. Quaestionum convivalium libri IX. 1892. (1701). V. 5. Maximi cum principibus philosopho esse disserendum... 1893. (1702). V. 6. Aquane an ignis sit utilior ... 1895. (1703). V. 7. Utrum animae an corporis sit libido et aegritudo... 1896. (1704) B3423

____. Plutarchi Moralia, ed. by Hubert and others. V. 1. 1925. (1705). Fasc. 1. De liberis educandis... 1925. (1705b). Fasc. 2. De fortuna... 1925. (1705c). Praefatio: Pohlenz. 1925. (1705d). V. 2. 1935. (1925). Fasc. 1. Regum et imperatorum apophthegmata... 1934. (1926). Fasc. 2. Parallela Graeca et Romana... 1934. (1927). Fasc. 3. De Iside et Osiride. 1932. (1928). V. 3. De E Apud Delphos... 1929. (1922). Daraus einzeln.

Fasc. 1. De E Apud Delphos ... 1929. (1923). Fasc. 2. An virtus doceri posit... 1929. (1924). V. 4. Quaestionum convivalium libri. Amatorius. Amatoriae narrationes, ed. by Hubert. 1938. (1957) B3424

Polemo, A. Polemonis Declamationes quae exstant duae, ed. by Hinck. 1873. (1713) B3425

Polyaenus. Polyaeni Strategematon libri octo, ed. by Woelfflin, 1877. (1714) B3426

Polybius. Polybii Historiae, ed. by Dindorf. V. 1. Libri I-III. 1922. (1715). V. 2. Libri IV-VIII. 1924. (1716). V. 3. Libri IX-XIX. 1929. (1717). V. 4. Libri XX-XXXVIII. Fragmenta. 1904. (1718). V. 5. Appendix. 1904. (1719) B3427

Polystratus. Polystrati Epicvrei Περια Λαδου Καταφρονήσεως Libelivs, ed. by Wilke. 1905. (1720) B3428

Porphyrio, P. Pomponii Porphyrionis Commentarii in Q. Horatium Flaccum, ed. by Meyer. 1874. (1723) B3429

Porphyrius. Porphyrii Philosophi platonici opscvla, ed. by Nadck. 1886. (1721) B3430

____. Prophyrii Sententiae ad intelligibilia ducentes, ed. by Mommert. 1907. (1722) B3431

Porphyrius. P. Optatiani Porfyrii Carmina, ed. by Kluge. 1926. (1561) B3432

Prantzes, G. Georgios Pharntzes, ed. by Papadopoulos. V. 1. 1935. (1954) B3433

Preger, T., ed. Scriptores originum Constantinopolitarum. Fasc. 1. Hesychii illustrii origines Constantinopolitanae. 1901. (1778). Fasc. 2. PsCodini origines. 1907. (1779) B3434

Priscillianus, bp. of Avila. Priscipi Theodori euporiston libri III cum Physicorum fragmento et additamentis Pseudo-Theodoresis, ed. by Rose. 1894. (1724) B3435

Proclus. Procli Diadochi in primum Euclidis Elementorum librum commentarii, ed. by Friedlein. 1873. (1725) B3436

____. Procli Diadochi in Platonis Rem pvblicam commentari, ed. by Kroll. 2 v. 1899-1901. (1726-27) B3437

____. Procli Diadochi in Platonis Timaeum commentarii, ed. by Diehl. 3 v. 1903-06. (1728-30) B3438

____. Procli Diadochi in Platonis Cratylvm commentaria, ed. by Pasqvali. 1908. (1731) B3439

____. Procli Diadochi Hypotyposis astronomicarum positionum, ed. by Manitius. 1909. (1732) B3440

____. Procli Diadochi Lycii Institutio physica, ed. by Ritzenfeld. 1912. (1733) B3441

Procopius, of Caesarea. Procopii Caesariensis opera omnia, ed. by Haury. V. 1. De bellis libri I-IV. 1936. (1734). V. 2... libri V-VIII. 1936. (1735). V. 3. Fasc. 1. Historia arcana. 1906. (1736). Fasc. 2. De aedificiis. 1913. (1737) B3442

Prodromus, T. Theodori Prodromi Catomyomachia, ed. by Hercheri. 1873. (1853) B3443

Propertius, S. A. Sex. Propertii Elegiarum libri IV, ed. by Hosivs. (1739) B3444

Prophetarum vitae fabulosae, indices apostolorum discipulorumque Domini Dorothea, Epiphenio, Hippolyto aliisque vindicata, ed. by Gelzer and Schermann. 1907. (1740) B3445

Pseudo - Acro. Psevdacronis scholia in Horativm vetvstiora, ed. by Keller. V. 1. In carmina et epodos. 1902. (1741). V. 2. In sermones, epistulas, art, poet. 1904. (1742) B3446

Ptolemaeus, C. Claudii Ptolemaei Opera quae exstant omnia, ed. by Heiberg. V. 1. Syntaxis mathematica. Pars I. Libri I-VI. 1898. (1743). Pars II. Libri VII-XIII. 1903. (1744). V. 2. Opera astronomica minora. 1907. (1745). V. 3. Fasc.

1. Apotelesmatica, ed. by Boll-Boer. 1940. (1746). Fasc. 2. Indices. 1940. (1966) B3447
____. Claudii Ptolemaei Kydus de ostentis, ed. by Heron. V. 2. B3448
____. Claudii Ptolomaei Handbuch der astronomie, ed. by Manitius. V. 1. Books I-VI. 1912. (1747). V. 2. Books VII-XIII. 1913. (1748) B3449
Querolus. Avlvlaria, sive Qvervolvs, Theodosiani aevi comedia Rvtilio dedicta, ed. by Peiper. 1875. (1107) B3450
Quintilianus, M. F. M. Fabi Quintiliani Institutionis oratoriae libri duodecim, ed. by Meister. 2 v. 1886-87. B3451
____. M. Fabi Quintiliani Institutionis oratories libri duodecim, ed. by Rademacher. V. 1. Libri I-VI. 1907. (1751). V. 2. Libri VII-XII. 1935. (1752) B3452
____. M. Fabi Quintiliani Institutio libri X, ed. by Rademacher. 1936. (1753) B3453
____. M. Fabi Quintiliani Declamationes quae aupersunt CXLV, ed. by Ritter. 1884. (1754) B3454
____. M. Fabi Quintiliani Declamationes XIX maiores, ed. by Lehnert. 1905. (1755) B3455
____. Qvintiliani qvae fervntvr Declamationes XIX maiores, ed. by Lehnert. 1905. B3456
Quintus Smyrnaeus. Quinti Smyrnaei Posthomericorum libri XIV, ed. by Zimmermann. 1891. (1749) B3457
Remigius, of Auxerre. Remigii Autissiodorensis In Artem Donati minorem, ed. by Fox. 1902. (1756) B3458
Ribbeck, O., ed. Scaenicae Romanorvm poesis fragamenta. V. 1. Tragicorum fragmenta. 1897. (1769). V. 2. Comicoricum fragmenta. 1898. (1770) B3459
Rowald, P. Repertorium lateinischer wörterverzeichnisse und speziallexika, ed. by Rowald. 1914. (1762) B3460
Ruhnkenius. Ruhnkenii elogium Tiberii Hemsterhusii, ed. by Frey. 1875. (1920) B3461
Rutilius Claudius Namatianus. Clavdii Rotilii Namatiani De reditv suo libri II, ed. by Mueller. 1870. B3462
Sallustius Crispis, C. C. Salusti Crispi Catilina..., ed. by Eussner. 1900. B3463
____. C. Sallusti Crispi Catilina, Iugurtha, ed. by Ahlberg. Ed. minor. 1919. (1763). Ed. minor ster. 1932. (1764). Catilina. Ed. ster. (1765). Iugurtha. Ed. ster. (1766) B3464
____. C. Sallusti In Ciceronem et invicem invectivae, ed. Kurfess. 1914. (1767) B3465
____. C. Sallusti Crispi epistulae ad Caesarem senem de re publica, ed. by Kurfess. 1955. (1768) B3466
Schermann, T., ed. Prophetarum vitae fabulosae. 1907. B3467
Schlee, F. H., comp. and ed. Scholia Terentiana. 1893. B3468
Schöne, H. Repertorium griechischer wörterverzeichnisse und specziallexika. 1907. B3469
Scholia in Lvcianvm, ed. by Rabe. 1906. B3470
Scholia in Theocritum vetera recensuit Carolus Wendel. 1914. B3471
Schroeder, O., ed. Horazens versmasse für anfänger erklärt. 1911. (1438) B3472
Scribonius Largus. Scribonii Largi Compositiones, ed. by Helmreich. 1887. (1771) B3473
Scriptores historiae augustae, ed. by Peter. 2 v. 1884. B3474
Scriptores sacri et profani, ed. by Seminarii philologorum Ienensis. Fasc. 1. Joannes Philoponus de opificio mundi, ed. by Reichardt. 1897. (1782). Fasc. 2. Patrum Nicaenorum nomina graece ..., ed. by Gelzer and others. 1898. (1783). Fasc. 3. Zacharias Rhetor, Kirchengeschichte, ed. by Khrens. 1899. (1784). Fasc. 4. Des Stephanos von Taron

Armenische Geschichte ubersetzet, ed. by Gelzer and Burckhardt. 1907. (1785). Fasc. 5. Neue Quellen zur Geschichte des lateinischen Erzbistums Patras, ed. by Gerland. 1903. (1786) B3475

Seneca, L. A. L. Annaei Senecas opera qvae svpervnt. V. 1. Fasc. 1. Dialogorum Libri XII, ed. by Hermes. 1923. (1787). Pars. 1. De Providentia... 1923. (1788). Pars. 2. Ad Marciam de consolatione... 1923. (1789). Pars. 3. De Brevitate vitae. 1929. (1790). Fasc. 2. De beneficiis, ed. by Hosius. 1915. (1791). V. 2. Naturalium quaestionum Libri VIII, ed. by Gercke. 1939. (1792). V. 3. Epistulae, ed. by Hense. 1938. (1793). V. 4. Fragmenta, index, ed. Bickel. (1795) B3476

____. L. Annaei Senecae Tragoediae, ed. by Piper and Richter. 1937. (1797) B3477

____. L. Annaei Senecas Oratorum et rhetorvm senteniae, divisiones, ed. by Kiessling. 1935. (1798) B3478

____. L. Annaei Senecae patris scripta qvae manservnt, ed. by Müller. 1887. B3479

Serenus, A. Sereni Antinoensis Opuscula, ed. by Heiberg. 1896. (1799) B3480

Sextus Empiricus. Sexti Empirici Opera, ed. by Mutschmann. V. 1. Hypothesis Pyrrhonism Libri III. 1912. (1800). V. 2. Adversus dogmaticos Libri V. 1914. (1801) B3481

Sidonius, C. S. M. A. C. Sollius Apollinaris Sidonius, ed. by Mohr. 1895. (1803) B3482

Silius Italicus, T. C. Sili Italici Punica, ed. by Bauer. V. 1. Libri I-X. 1890. (1804). V. 2. Libri XI-XVII. 1892. (1805) B3483

Simeo Sethus. Simeonis Sethi Syntagma de alimentorum facultatibus, ed. by Langkabel. 1868. (1802) B3484

Simocatta, T. Theophylacti Simocattae Historiae, ed. by Boor. 1887. (1857) B3485

Solmsen, F., comp. and ed. Inscriptiones graecae ad inlustrandes dialectos. 1930. B3486

Sophocles. Sophoclis Oedipus Coloneus, ed. by Mekler. 1898. B3487

____. Sophoclis Tragoediae, ed. by Dindorf and Mekler. Ed. maior. 1925. (1807). Ed. Minor. 1935. (1890). Ed. minor einzeln: Aiax. 1936. (1810). Antigone. 1930. (1811). Electra. 1934. (1812). Oedipus Rex. 1939. (1813). Oedipus Col. 1930. (1814). Philoctetes. (1815). Trachiniae. 1925. (1816) B3488

____. Sophoclis Cantica, ed. by Schroeder. 1907. (1818) B3489

____. Sophoclis Scholia in Sophoclis tragoedias vetera, ed. by Papageorgios. 1888. (1817) B3490

Soranus, of Euphesis. Sorani Gynaeciorum vetus translatio latina..., ed. by Dietz and Rose. 1882. (1819) B3491

Spengel, L. von, ed. Rhetores graeci. 3 v. 1853-56. B3492

Stadtmüller, H., ed. Eclogae poetarum graecorum scholarum in usum. 1883. B3493

Statius P. P. P. Papini Stati Opera. V. 1. Silvae ed. by Klotz. 1911. (1820). V. 2. Fasc. 1. Achilleis, ed. by Klotz. 1926. (1821). Fasc. 2. Thebais, ed. by Klotz. 1908. (1822). V. 3. Lactanti Placidi, ed. by Jahnke. 1898. (1823) B3494

Stephanus. Des Stephanos von Taron Armenische geschichte, ed. by Gelzer. 1907. B3495

Stobaeus, J. Ioannis Stobaei Eclogarum physicarum et ethicarum libro duo, ed. by Meineke. 2 v. 1806-64. B3496

Strabo. Strabonis Geographica, ed. by Meineke. V. 1. Libri I-VI. 1921. (1824). V. 2. Libri VII-XII. 1915. (1825). V. 3. Libri XIII-XVII. 1925. (1826) B3497

Suetonius Tranquillus, C. C.

Suetoni Tranquilli Opera. V. 1. De vita caesarum Libri VIII, ed. by Ihm. 1933. (1827). V. 2. De grammaticis et rhetoribus deperditorum librorum reliquiae, ed. by Roth. 1924. (1829) B3498

Syrianus. Syriani in Hermogenem, ed. by Rabe. 2 v. 1892-93. B3499

Tacitus, C. Cornelii Taciti Libri qui supersunt, ed. by Halm Tome 1. Ab excessu divi Augusti libri. 1938. (1833). Fasc. 1. Libri I-VI. 1938. (1834). Fasc. 2. Libri XI-XVI. 1936. (1835). Tome 2. Historiae... 1936. (1836). Fasc. 1. Historiae. 1935. (1837). Fasc. 2. Germania, Agricola, Dialogus. 1936. (1838). Germania. 1939. (1839) B3500

Terentius Afer, P. P. Terenti Comoediae, ed. by Fleckisen. 1898. (1840). Adelphoe. 1932. (1841). Andria. 1931. (1842). Eunuchus. 1931. (1843). Hauton Timorumenos. 1932. (1844). Hecyra. 1916. (1845). Phormio. 1929. (1846) B3501

____. Scholia Terentiana, ed. by Schlee. 1893. (1847) B3502

____. P. Terenti Afri Comoediae, ed. by Fleckeisen. 1898. B3503

Themistius. Themistii Paraphrases Aristotelis librorum quae supersunt, ed. by Spengel. 2 v. 1866. (1849, 1850) B3504

Theocritus. Bucolicorum graecorum Theocriti..., ed. by Ahrens. 1899. B3505

____. Scholia in Theocritum vetera, ed. by Wendel. 1914. (1851) B3506

Theodoretus, bp. of Cyrrhus. Theodoreti Graecarum affectionum curatio, ed. by Raeder. 1904. (1852) B3507

Theon, of Smyrna. Theonis Smyrnaei, philosophi platonici Expositio rerum mathematicarum ad legendum Platonem utilium, ed. by Hiller. 1878. (1854) B3508

____. Theonis Smyrnaei Euclides. Vol. VII. B3509

Theophrastus. Theophrasti Περὶ λέξεως libri fragmenta, ed. by Mayer. 1910. (1855) B3510

____. Theophrasti Characteres, ed. by Immisch. 1923. (1856) B3511

Thiofridus. Thiofridi Epternacensis Vita Willibrordi Metrica, ed. by Rossberg. 1883. (1914a) B3512

Thucydides. Thucydidis De bello peloponnesiaco, libri octo ed. by Hude. Ed. Maior: V. 1. Libri I-IV. 1913. (1859). V. 2. Libri V-VIII. 1925. (1859). Ed. Minor: V. 1. Libri I-IV. 1938. (1860). V. 2. Libri V-VIII. 1938. (1861). Daraus einzeln: Libri I-II. 1928. (1862). Libri VI-VII. 1930. (1863) B3513

____. Thucydides De bello peloponnesiaco, libri octo, ed. by Boehme. 2 v. 1901. B3514

____. Thucydidis Historiae, ed. by Hude. 2 v. 1903. B3515

____. Thucydidis Scholia in Thucydidem ad optimos coidices collata, ed. by Hude. 1927. (1863a) B3516

Tibullus, A. Tibulli Aliorumque carminum libri tres, ed. by Lenz. 1937. (1864) B3517

Tryphiodorus. Tryphiodori et Collvthi Carmina, ed. by Weinberger. 1896. (1865) B3518

Turpilius, S. Turpilii comici fragmenta, ed. by Rychlewska. 1971. B3519

Ulpianus D. Domitii Vlpiani qvae vvlgo vocantvr Fragmenta..., ed. by Hvschke. 1886. (1866) B3520

Valerius, J. Iuli Valeri Alexandri Polemi Res gestae Alexandri Macedonis..., ed. by Kuebler. 1888. (1867) B3520a

Valerius Flaccus, C. C. Valeri Flacci Setini Balbi Argonauticon libri octo, ed. by Baehrens. 1875. B3521

____. C. Valerii Flacci Setini Balbi Argonauticon libri octo, ed. by Kramer. 1913. (1868) B3522

Valerius Maximus. Valerii Maximi Factorvm et dictorvm memorabilivm libri novem, ed. by Kempf. 1888. (1869) B3523

Varro, M. T. M. Terenti Varronis Rervm rusticarvm libri tres, ed. by Goetz. 1929. (1870) B3524

____. M. Terenti Varronis Rervm rvsticarvm libri tres, ed. by Keil. 1889. B3525

Vegetius Renatus, F. P. Vegeti Renati Digestorum artis mulonedicinae libri, ed. by Lommatzsch. 1903. (1871) B3526

____. P. Vegeti Renati Epitoma rei militaris, ed. by Lang. 1885. (1872) B3527

Velleius Paterculus, C. M. Vellei Patervuli ex Historiae romanae ad M. Vinicium, ed. by Haase. 1870. B3528

____. C. Vellei Paterculi ex Historiae romanae libris doubus quae supersunt, ed. by Stegmann von Pritzwald. 1933. (1873) B3529

____. C. Vellei Paterculi ex Historiae romanae, ed. by Halm. 1876. B3530

Vergilius Maro, P. P. Vergili Maronis Opera, ed. by Janell. Ed. Maior. 1930. (1874). Aeneis. 1920. (1875). Eclogae et Georgica. 1930. (1876). Ed. Minor: Aeneis. 1939. (1877). Libri I-II. 1932. (1878) B3531

____. Vergili Maronis Grammatici Opera, ed. by Huemer. 1886. (1882) B3532

____. P. Vergili Maronis Aeneis in usum scholarum, ed. by Riddeck. 1898. B3533

____. P. Vergili Maronis Opera omnia, ed. by Jahm. 1859. B3534

____. P. Vergili Maronis opera, ed. by Janell. 1930. B3535

Victor, S. A. Sexti Aurelii Victoris Liber de Caesaribus, ed. by Pichlmayr. 1911. (1108) B3536

Vitruvius Pollio. Vitruvii De architectura libri decem, ed. by Rose. 1899. B3537

____. Ed. by Krohn. 1912. B3538

Weber, E., ed. Virorum clarorum saeculi XVI et XVII epistolae selectae. 1894. (1921) B3539

Weis-Liebersdorf, J. E., ed. Diadochi de perfectione spirituali capita Graeca et Latine. 1912. (1268) B3540

Wessner, P., ed. Scholia in Iuvenalem vetustiora collegit. 1931. (1941) B3541

Westphal, R. G. H., ed. Scriptores metrici graeci. V. 1. Hephaestionis. 1866. (1773) B3542

Witkowski, S., ed. Epistvlae priva graecae qvae in papyris aetatis Lagidarvm servantvr. 1911. (1305) B3543

Xenophon. Xenophontis Expeditio Cyri (Anabasis), ed. by Hude. Ed. Maior. 1931. (1939). Ed. Minor. 1939. (1940). Libri I-II, ed. by Hude. 1933. (1886). Libri III-IV, ed. by Gemoll. 1923. (1887) B3544

____. Xenophontis Historia Graeca (Hellenica), ed. by Hude. Ed. Maior. 1930. (1930). Ed. Minor. 1939. (1931) B3545

____. Xenophontis Institutio Cyri (Cyropaedia), ed. by Gemoll. Ed. Maior. 1912. (1889). Ed. Minor. 1912. (1890) B3546

____. Xenophontis Commentarii (Memorabilia), Ed. Maior, ed. by Hude. 1934. (1891). Ed. Minor, ed. by Gilbert. 1928. (1892) B3547

____. Xenophontis Scripta minora, ed. by Dindorfius. 1883. B3548

____. Xenophontis Scripta Minora. Pars. 1. Oecomomicus, ed. by Thalheim. 1915. (1893). Pars. 2. Opuscula politica..., ed. by Ruhl. 1912. (1894) B3549

____. Xenophontis Ἀθηναίων πολιτεία Kalinka. 1934. (1895) B3550

Zacharias. Die segenannte kirchengeschichte des Zacharis, ed. by Ahrens. 1899. B3551

Zonaras J. Ioannis Zonarae

Epitome historiarum, ed. by Dindorf. V. 1. Libri I-V. 1868. (1896). V. 2. Libri VI-X. 1869. (1897). V. 3. Libri XI-XV. 1870. (1898). V. 4. Libri XVI-XVIII. 1871. (1899). V. 5. Annotationes ad voll. I-IV. 1874. (1900). V. 6. Annotationes Ducangii ad voll. I-IV: Schmidt 1875. (1901) B3552

BIBLIOTHECA SCRIPTORUM GRAECORUM ET ROMANORUM TEUBNERIANA AUSGABEN MIT DEUTSCHEN ANMERKUNGEN UNTER DEM TEXT (Blackwell)

Aeschylus. Aeschylus. Agamemnon, ed. by Enger and others. 1895. (2000) B3553

____. Aeschylus. Sieben gegen Theben, ed. by Wecklein. 1902. (2620) B3554

____. Aeschylus Die Schutzflehenden, ed. by Wechlein. 1902. (2621) B3555

____. Aeschylus Orstie, ed. by Wechlein. 1. Agamemnon. 1888. (2562) 2. Die Schoephoren. 1888. (2563). 3. Die Eumeniden. 1888. (2564) B3556

Anthologie aus den Elegikern der Romer, ed. by Jacoby. Heft 1. Catullus, 1917. (2112). Heft. 2. Tibellus, 1918. (2113). Heft 3. Propertius. 1933. (2114). Heft 4. Ovidius. 1915. (2115) B3557

Anthologie aus der Lyrik der Griechen, ed. by Buchholz and others. 1. Elegiker und Iambographen. 1925. (2622). 2. Melische und chorische dichter. 1933. (2623) B3558

Aristophanes. Aristophanes Wolken, ed. by Teuffel and Kaehler. 1887. (2624) B3559

Aristoteles. Aristotles Der staat der Athener, ed. by Hude. 1932. (2013) B3560

Arrianus, F. Arrian Anabasis, ed. by Abicht. Heft 1. Buch I-III. 1871. (2625). Heft 2. Buch IV-VII. 1875. (2626) B3561

Bible, N. T. Greek. Testamentum Novum Graece, ed. by Zelle and Wohlfahrt. Band 1. Matthäus. 1889. (2756). Band 4. Johannes. 1891. (2757). Band 5. Apostelgeschischt. 1893. (2758) B3562

Caesar C. J. Caesar De bello Gallico, ed. by Doberenz and Dinter. Heft 1. Buch I-III. 1918. (2627). Heft 2. Buch IV-VI. 1890. (2628). Heft 2. Buch VII-VIII. 1892. (2629) B3563

____. Caesar De bello civili, ed. by Doberenz and Dinter. 1913. (2630) B3564

Catullus, C. V. Catull, ed. by Kroll. 1939. (2631) B3565

Cicero, M. T. Cicero Briefe Ciceros und seiner zeitgenossen, ed. by Schmidt. Heft 1. 1901. (2078) B3566

____. Cicero Brutus, ed. by Piderit and Friedrich. 1889. (2638) B3567

____. Cicero Cato Maior, ed. by Meissner and Landgraf. 1915. (2091) B3568

____. Cicero Divinatio in Qu. Caecilium, ed. by Richter and Eberhard. 1884. (2642) B3569

____. Cicero Laelius, ed. by Meissner and Wessner. 1931. (2092) B3570

____. Cicero Orator ad M. Brutum, ed. by Piderit. 1876. (2637) B3571

____. Cicero Partitiones oratoriae, ed. by Piderit. 1867. (2639) B3572

____. Cicero Rede für Archias, ed. by Richter. 1926. (2647) B3573

____. Cicero Rede für L. Flaccus, ed. by du Mesnil. 1883. (2643) B3574

____. Cicero Rede für Marcellus, Ligarius und Deiotarus, ed. by Richter and Eberhard. 1904. (2645) B3575

____. Cicero Rede für Milo, ed. by Richter and others. 1907. (2646) B3576

____. Cicero Rede für Mureena, ed. by Kock and Landgraf. 1928. (3647) B3577

____. Cicero Rede für Plancius, ed. by Kopke and Landgraf. 1887. (2649) B3578

____. Cicero Rede für Sulla, ed. by Richter and Landgraf. 1885. (2651) B3579

____. Cicero Rede über das imperium, ed. by Richter and others. 1919. (2644) B3580

____. Cicero Reden gegen Catilina, ed. by Richter and others. 1928. (2641) B3581

____. Cicero Reden gegen Verres Buch IV, ed. by Richter and others. 1908. (2652) B3582

____. Cicero I und II Philippische Rede, ed. by Koch and Eberhard. 1929. (2648) B3583

____. Cicero Rhetorische Schriften: De Oratore, ed. by Piderit and Adler. 1878. (2632). Heft 1. Buch I. 1886. (2633). Heft 2. Buch II. 1889. (2634). Heft 3. Buch III. 1890. (2635). Indices und register. 1890. (2636) B3584

____. Cicero Tusculanarum disputationum libri V, ed. by Heine and Pohlnez. Heft. 1. Libri I-II. 1912. (2653). Heft 2. Libri III-V. 1929. (2654) B3585

Curtius Rufus, Q. Curtius Rufus, ed. by Vogel and Weinhold. Bd. 1. Buch III-V. 1903. (2655). Bd. 2. Buch VI-X. 1906. (2656) B3586

Demosthenes. Demosthenes Ausgewählte reden, ed. by Rehdantz and others. Teil. 1. Die IX. Philippischen reden. Heft. 1. Olynthische reden und gegen Phillippos. 1909. (2657). Heft 2. Abt. 1. Rede über den frieden gegen Philippos, Hegesippos uber Hallones, uber den Cherronnes. 1905. (2659). Heft. 2. Abt. 2 Indices. 1886. (2659). Teil 2. Die rede vom Kranze. 1910. (2660) B3587

Euripides. Euripides Ausgewählte tragodien, ed. by Wecklein. Band. 1. Medea. 1909. (2116). Band 2. Iphigenie im Taurierland. 1904. (2117). Band 3. Bacchen. 1903. (2118). Band 4. Hippolytos. 1908. (2119). Band 5. Phönissen. 1894. (2661). Band 6. Electra. 1906. (2662). Band 7. Orestes. 1906. (2663). Band 8. Helena. 1907. (2664). Band 9. Andromache. 1911. (2665). Band 10. Ion. 1912. (2666). Band 11. Die Schutzflehenden. 1912. (2667). Band 12. Iphigenie im Aulis. 1914. (2120) B3588

Herodotus. Herodotus, ed. by Abicht. Band 1. Heft 1. Buch 1. 1903. (2668). Heft 2. Buch 2. 1926. (2669). Band 3. Heft 1. Buch 3 Nachdr. 1926. (2670). Heft 2. Buch 4. 1886. (2671). Band 3. Heft 5-6. 1906. (2672). Band 4. Heft 7. Buch 4. 1893. (1673). Band 5. Heft 8-9. Buch 4. 1892. (2674) B3589

Homerus. Homerus, Ilias, ed. by La Roche. Teil 1. Gesang 1-4. 1883. (2675). Teil 2. Gesang 5-8. 1886. (2676). Teil 3. Gesang 9-12. 1891. (2677). Teil 4. Gesang 13-16. 1891. (2678) B3590

____. Homerus Ilias, ed. by Ameis and others. Band 1. Heft 1. Gesang 1-3. 1930. (2679). Heft 2. Gesang 4-6. 1927. (2680). Heft 3. Gesang 7-9. 1930. (2681). Heft 4. Gesang 10-12. 1930. (2682). Band 2. Heft 1. Gesang 13-15. 1936. (2683). Heft 2. Gesang 16-18. 1929. (2684). Heft 3. Gesang 19-21. 1932. (2685). Heft 4. Gesang 22-24. 1930. (2686). Anhang: Heft 3. Gesang 7-9. 1887. (2688). Heft 4. Gesang 10-12. 1888. (2689). Heft 5. Gesang 13-15. 1897. (2690) B3591

____. Homerus Odyssee, ed. by Ameis and others. Band 1. Heft 1. Gesang 1-6. 1920. (2693). Heft 2. Gesang 7-12. 1928. (2694). Band 2. Heft 1. Gesang 18-18. 1928. (2695). Heft 2. Gesang 19-24. 1928. (2696). Heft 1. und 2. Gesang 13-24. (2697). Anhang: Heft 2. Gesang 7-12. 1889. (2698). Heft 3. Gesang 13-18. 1895. (2699) B3592

Horatius Flaccus, Q. Q. Horatius Flaccus Sermonen, ed. by Fritzsche, 2 Bd. 1875-76. (2700-01) B3593

____. Q. Horatius Flaccus Oden und epodun, ed. by Nauck and Hoppe. 1926. (2166) B3594

____. Q. Horatius Flaccus Satiren und Episteln, ed. by Krüger and Hoppe. Heft 1. Satiren 1923. (2167). Abt. 2. Episteln. 1920. (2168) B3595

Isocrates. Isokrates Ausgewahlte reden, ed. by Schneider. Band 1. Demonicus, Euagoras, Areopagiticus. 1888. (2702) B3596

Livius, T. Livius Ab urbe condita libri, ed. by Friedersdorff and others. Liber 1. 1921. (2703). Liber 2. 1909. (2704). Liber 3. 1885. (2705). Liber 4. 1886. (2706). Liber 5. 1887. (2707). Liber 6. 1888. (2708). Liber 7. 1889. (2709). Liber 8. 1890. (2710). Liber 9. 1891. (2711). Liber 10. 1892. (2712). Liber 21. 1927. (2713). Liber 22. 1935. (2714). Liber 23. 1906. (2715). Liber 24. 1901. (2716). Liber 25. 1931. (2717). Liber 26. 1880. (2718). Liber 27. 1881. (2719). Liber 28. 1883. (2720). Liber 29. 1893. (2721). Liber 30. 1892. (2722) B3597

Lucanus, M. A. Lucian Ausgewählte schriften, ed. by Jacobitz and Burger. Band 1. Traum, Timon, Premetheus, Charon. 1931. (2505) B3598

Lycurgus. Lukurg Rede gegen Leokrates, ed. by Rehbantz. 1876. (2251) B3599

Lysias. Lysias Orationes, ed. by Frohberger and others. Heft 1. Gegen Eratosthenes..., 1895. (2723). Heft 2. Gegen Alkibiades... 1892. (2724). Grossere Ausgabe: Band 1. Gegen Eratosthenes... 1880. (2725) B3600

Nepos, C. Nepos, ed. by Ebeling. 1870. (2727) B3601

____. Nepos, ed. by Ortmann. 1891. (2728) B3602

____. Nepos, ed. by Siebelis and others. 1897. (2726) B3603

Ovidius Naso, P. Ovid Metamorphosen in auswahl, ed. by Siebelis and others. Heft 1. Buch I-IX. 1930. (2324). Heft 2. Buch X-XV. 1929. (2325) B3604

Phaedrus. Phaedrus Fabulae, ed. by Siebelis and Polle. 1889. (2730) B3605

Plato. Platon Ausgewählte schriften. Teil 1. Verteidigungsrede des Sokrates. Kriton ed. by Struck. 1929. (2731). Teil 2. Gorgias, ed. by Nestle. 1909. (2732). Teil 3. Heft 1. Laches, ed. by Cron. 1891. (2733). Heft 2. Euthyphron, ed. by Wohlrab. 1900. (2734). Teil 4. Protagoras, ed. by Nestle. 1931. (2735). Teil 6. Phaedon, ed. Wohlrab. 1933. (2737). Teil 7. Der Staat, ed. by Wohlrab. 1925. (2738) B3606

Plautus, T. M. Plautus Ausgewählte komödien. Band 1. Trinummus, ed. by Conrad. 1931. (2372). Band 2. Captivi, ed. by Köhler. 1930. (2373). Band 3. Menaechmi, ed. by Conrad. 1929. (2374). Band 4. Miles gloriosus, ed. by Köhler. 1916. (2375) B3607

Plutarchus. Plutarch Ausgewählte biographien, ed. by Seifert and others. Band 1. Philopoemen und Flamininus. 1876. (2740). Band 2. Timoleon und Pyrrhos. 1879. (2741). Band 3. Themistokles und Perikles. 1909. (2613). Band 4. Aristides und Cato, 1931. (2614). Band 5. Agis und Kleomenes. 1875. (2742) B3608

Sallustius Crispus, C. Sallust, ed. by Optiz. Heft 1. Bellum Catilinae. 1939. (2389). Heft 2. Bellum Iugurthinum. 1930. (2390). Heft 3. Orationes et epistulae ex histor. excerptae. 1897. (2391) B3609

Sophocles. Sophokles, ed. by Wolff and Bellerman. Teil 1. Aias. 1913. (2615). Teil 2. Elektra. 1893. (2616). Teil 3. Antigone. 1913. (2617). Teil 4. König

Oedipus. 1908. (2618) B3610
Tacitus, C. Tacitus Annalen, ed. by Draeger and others. Band 1. Heft 1. Buch I-II. 1917. (2745). Heft 2. Buch III-VI. 1914. (2746). Band 2. Heft 1. Buch XI-XIII. 1933. (2747). Heft 2. Buch XIV-XVI. 1930. (2748) B3611
____. Tacitus Historiarum libri, ed. by Heraeus. Band 1. Buch I-II. 1929. (2749). Band 2. Buch III-V. 1927. (2750) B3612
____. Tacitus Dialogus de oratoribus, ed. by Andresen. 1918. (2753) B3613
Terentius Afer, P. Terenz Ausgewählte komödien, ed. by Dziatzko and others. Band 1. Phormio. 1913. (2754). Band 2. Adelphoe. 1921. (2755) B3614
Thucydides. Thykydides, ed. by Böhme and Widmana. Band 1. Buch I. 1929. (2759). Band 2. Buch II. 1894. (2760). Band 3. Buch III. 1894. (2761). Band 4. Buch III. 1894. (2761). Band 4. Buch IV. 1894. (2762). Band 5. Buch V. 1894. (2763). Band 6. Buch VI. 1906. (2764). Band 7. Buch VII. 1908. (2765). Band 8. Buch VIII. 1894. (2766). Band 9. Einleitung. 1894. (2767) B3615
Vergilius Maro, P. Vergil Aeneide, ed. by Kappes and others. Heft 1. Buch I-III. 1930. (2768). Heft 2. Buch IV-VI. 1935. (2769). Einzein: Abt 1. Buch IV-V. 1935. (2770). Abt. 2. Buch V. 1913. (2771). Abt. 3. Buch VI. 1931. (2772). Heft 3. Buch VII-IX. 1931. (2773). Heft 4. Buch X-XII. 1902. (2774). Einzein: Abt. 1. Buch X. 1902. (2775). Abt. 2. Buch XI. 1902. (2776). Abt. 3. Buch XII. 1902. (2777) B3616
Xenophon. Xenophon Agesilaus, ed. by Guthling. 1888. (2788) B3617
____. Xenophon Anabasis, ed. by Wolbrecht. Band 1. Buch I-II. 1926. (2778). Band 2. Buch II-IV. 1912. (2779). Band 3. Buch V-VII. 1907. (2780) B3618
____. Xenophon Anabasis, ed. by Volbrecht. Buch I-IV. Text. 1896. (2781). Kommentar. 1896. (2782) B3619
____. Xenophon Grichische Geschichte, ed. by Buchsenschutz. Heft. 1. Buch I-IV. 1908. (2783). Heft 2. Buch V-VII. 1905. (2784) B3620
____. Xenophon Kyropadie, ed. by Breitenbach and Buchsenschutz. Heft 1. Buch I-IV. 1890. (2786). Heft 2. Buch V-VIII. 1878. (2787) B3621
____. Xenephon Memorabilien, ed. by Kuhner. 1902. (2785) B3622

BIBLIOTHEK DER KLASSISCHEN ALTERTUMSWISSENSCHAFTEN (Francke)

1 Hoppe, E. Mathematik und astronomie im klassischen altertum. 1911. B3623
2 Duhn, F. K. von. Italische gräberkunde. 2 v. 1924. B3624
3 Bilabel, F. and Grohmann, A. Geschichte Vorderasiens und Agyptens vom 16 jahrhundert Chr. bis auf die neuzeit. 1927. B3625
4 Geffcken, J. Griechische literaturgeschichte. 2 v. 1926-34. B3626
5 Schröder, O. Nomenclator metricus. 1929. B3627
6 Willrich, H. Das haus des Herodes. 1929. B3628
7 Schröder, O. Grundriss der griechischen vergeschichte. 1930. B3629
8 Bickel, E. Lehrbuch der geschichte der römanischen literatur. 1937. B3630
9 Böhme, R. Von Sokrates zur ideenlehre. 1959. B3631

BIBLIOTHEQUE D'HISTOIRE CONTEMPORAINE (Alcan prior to 1940; 1940- Presses Universitaires de France)

Adam, J. Guillaume II. 1917. B3632
Alazard, J. L'Italie et le conflit europeen (1914-1916). 1916. B3633
Albin, P. Le conference de la

paix. 1921. B3634
____. Les grandes traités. 1912. B3635
____. Les grandes traités politiques. 1932. B3636
____. La guerre allemande. 1915. B3637
____. La paix armée. 1913. B3638
____. La querelle franco-allemande. 1912. B3639
Aldanov, M. A. Lénine. 1920. B3640
André, L. Les Etats chrétins des Balkans depuis 1815. 1918. B3641
____. Histoire économique depuis l'antiquité jusqú à nos jours. 1931. B3642
Les appétites allemands. 1918. B3643
Auerbach, B. L'Autriche et la Hongrie pendant la guerre... (Août 1914-novembre 1918) 1925. B3644
____. Les races et les nationales en Autriche Hongrie. 1917. B3645
Augier, C. La politique douanière de la France. 1911. B3646
Aulard, F. V. A. La culte de la raison et le culte de la Etre supreme. 1904. B3647
____. Etudes et lecons de la révolution française. 9 v. 1901-24. B3648
____. La révolution française et le régime féodal. 1919. B3649
Aulneau, J. La Turquie et la guerre. 1916. B3650
L'avenir de la France, réformes necessaires. 1918. B3651
Babel, A. La Bessarabie. 1926. B3652
Bagehot, W. Lombard Street. 1874. B3653
Bardoux, J. L'Angleterre radiacle. 1913. B3654
____. De Paris à Spa. 1921. B3655
____. Lloyd George et la France. 1923. B3656
____. La marche à la guerre. 1920. B3657
Barthelemy, J. Démocrate et politique étrangère. 1917. B3658
____. Les institutions politiques de l'-Allgemagne contemporaine. 1915. B3659
Beaussire, E. J. A. La guerre étrangère et la guerre civile en 1870 et en 1871. 1872. B3660
Bèrard, V. La Turquie et l'l'hellenisme contemporain. 1911. B3661
Bernard, A. Le Maroc. 1913. B3662
Bondois, P. Napoleon et la société de son temps. 1895. B3663
Bonet-Maury, G. Histoire de la liberté de conscience en France. 1900. B3664
Bornarel, F. Cambon et la révolution française. 1905. B3665
Bourdeau, J. Le socialisme allemand et le nihilisme russe. 1894. B3666
____. L'evolution du socialisme. 1901. B3667
Bourlier, J. Les Tchèquer et la Bohème contemporaine. 1897. B3668
Bratianu, G. I. Napoléon III et les nationalités. 1934. B3669
____. Origines et formation de l'unité roumaine. 1943. B3670
Brenier, H. and others. Politique coloniale de la France. 1924. B3671
Bruneau, A. Traditions et politique de la France au Levant. 1932. B3672
Cahen, L. Condorcet et la révolution française. 1904. B3673
Carnot, H. La révolution française. 1883. B3674
Challaye, F. Le Congo français. 1909. B3675
Conard, P. Napoleon et la catalogue. 1910. B3676
Cordier, H. L'expédition de Chine de 1857-58. 1905. B3677
____. L'éxpedition de Chine de 1860. 1906. B3678
____. Histoire des relations de la Chine avec les puissances occidentales. 2 v. 1901-02. B3679
Costentini, F. Préliminaires à la Société des nations. 1919. B3680
Courant, M. A. L. M. En Chine. 1901. B3681
Créharrge, G. Histoire de la

Russia. 1896. B3682
Dame, F. Histoire de la Roumaniè contemporaine. 1900. B3683
Deberle, A. J. Histoire de l'Amerique du Sud depuis la coquete jusqu'a à nos jours. 1897. B3684
Debidour, A. L'Eglise catholique et l'état sous la troisieme republique. 2 v. 1906-09. B3685
____. Histoire des rapports de l'église et de l'état en France de 1789 à 1870. 1878. B3686
____. Histoire diplomatique de l'Europe. 3 v. 1925. B3687
Deries, L. Les congrégations religieuses au temps de Napoléon. 1929. B3688
Djuvara, T. G. Cent projets de partage de la Turquie. 1914. B3689
Driault, E. Les leçons de l'histoire. 1921. B3690
____. Le monde actuel. 1909. B3691
____. Napoléon en Italie. 1906. B3692
____. Napoléon et l'Europe. Austerlitz. 1912. B3693
____. Napoléon et l'Europe. La chute de l'empire. 1927. B3694
____. Napoléon et l'Europe. Le grand empire. 1924. B3695
____. Napoléon et l'Europe. Tilsit, France et Russie. 1917. B3696
____. Napoléon et l'Europe, la politique exeterieure, du premier consul. 1910. B3697
____. La politique orientale de Napoléon. 1904. B3698
____. Les problèmes politiques et sociaux à la fin du XIX siècle. 1900. B3699
____. La question d'Extrême-Orient. 1912. B3700
____. La question d'Orient. 1938. B3701
____. Les traditions politiques de la France et les conditions de la paix. 1916. B3702
____. L'unité française. 1914. B3703
Duboscq, A. Syrie, Tripolitaine, Albanie. 1914. B3704
Duhem, J. La question yougoslave. 1918. B3705
Dundulis, B. Napoléon et la Lituanie en 1812. 1940. B3706
Dwelshauvers, G. La Catalogone et le problème catalan. 1926. B3707
Foerster, F. W. Mes combats à l'assaut du militarisme et de l'impérialisme allemands. 1922. B3708
Fribourg, A. La guerre et le passé. 1916. B3709
Fugier, A. Napoléon et l'Espagne (1799-1808). 1930. B3710
Gaffarel, P. L. J. Bonaparte et les républiques italiennes. 1895. B3711
____. Les colonies françaises. 1899. B3712
____. Notre expansion coloniale au Africa de 1870 à nos jours. 1918. B3713
____. La politique coloniale en France. 1908. B3714
Gay, J. Un siècle d'histoire italienne. 1931. B3715
Gillard, M. La Roumanie nouvelle. 1922. B3716
Goblet, Y. M. L'Irlande dans la crise universelle. 1921. B3717
La guerre. 1915. B3718
La guerre et la vie de demain. 2 v. 1916-17. B3719
Guyot, R. Le directiore et la paix de l'Europe. 1911. B3720
Guyot, Y. Les garanties de la paix. 2 v. 1918. B3721
____. Sophismes socialistes et faits économiques. 1908. B3722
Halecki, O. La Pologne de 963 à 1914. 1933. B3723
Handelssman, M. Les idées françaises et la mentalité politique en Pologne au XIXe siècle. 1927. B3724
Hubert, L. L'effort allemand. 1911. B3725
Jaffe, G. M. Le mouvement ouvrier à Paris pendant la revolution française. 1924. B3726
Jaray, G. L. La question sociale et le socialisme en Hongrie. 1909. B3727
Kobayaslin, T. La société japinaise. 1914. B3728

Krichewskiĭ, B. Vers la catastrophe russe. 1919. B3729
Landau-Aldanov, M. A. Lénine. 1920. B3730
Lanessan, J. M. A. de. L'état et les églises en France. 1906. B3731
____. Histoire de l'entente cordiala franco-anglaise. 1916. B3732
____. Les empires germaniques et la politique de la force. 1915. B3733
____. Les missions et leur protectorat... 1907. B3734
Latrielle, A. Napoléon et le Saint-Siege. 1935. B3735
Laugel, A. Les Etats-Unis pendant la guerre. 1866. B3736
____. Lord Palmerston et Lord Russell. 1877. B3737
Laurent, M. L'organisation de la victoire. 1920. B3738
Lebègue, E. La vie et l'oeuvre d'un constituant: Thouret, 1746-1794. 1910. B3739
Leblond, M. La société française sous la troisième république. 1905. B3740
Leger, L. P. M. La renaissance tcheque au dix-neuvieme siècle. 1911. B3741
Lémonon, E. L'Europe et la politique britannique. 1912. B3742
____. L'Italie d'après guerre. 1922. B3743
____. L'Italie économique et sociale. 1913. B3744
Lévy-Bruhl, L. La philosophie d'Auguste Comte. 1900. B3745
Lhéritier, M. La France depuis 1870. 1922. B3746
Lichtenburger, A. Le socialisme et la révolution française. 1899. B3747
Loris-Mélicof, J. La révolution russe et les nouvelles républiques transcausasiennes. 1920. B3748
Louis, P. Le bouleversment mondial. 1920. B3749
____. Histoire du mouvement syndical en France. 1920. B3750
____. L'ouvrier devant létat. 1904. B3751
____. Le syndicalisme contre l'état. 1910. B3752
____. Le syndicalisme européen. 1914. B3753
____. Le syndicalisme français. 1924. B3754
Lourié, O. La Russie en 1914-1917. 1918. B3755
Mansuy, A. Jerome Napoleon et la Pologne en 1812. 1931. B3756
Marcel, R. P. Essai politique sur Alexis de Tocqueville. 1910. B3757
Marcere, E. de. Une ambassade à Constantinople. 2 v. 1927. B3758
Marchand, R. Les grands problemes de la politique intérieure russe. 1912. B3759
Martin, G. L'ere des negriers (1714, 1774). 1931. B3760
____. Nantes au XVIIIe siècle. 2 v. 1931. B3761
Martin, W. La crise politique de l'allemagne contemporaine. 1913. B3762
Marvaud, A. Le Portugal et ses colonies. 1912. B3763
____. La question sociale en Espagne. 1910. B3764
Mathiez, A. Contributions à la histoire religieuse de la révolution française. 1907. B3765
____. Un procès de corruption sous la terreur l'affaire de la Compagnie des Indies. 1920. B3766
____. La théophilanthropie et la culte dé cardaire. 1904. B3767
____. La victoire de l'an II. 1916. B3768
Matter, P. Bismarck et son temps. 3 v. 1905-08. B3769
____. Cavour et l'unité italienne. 3 v. 1922. B3770
____. La dissolution des assemblées parliamentaires. 1898. B3771
____. La Prusse et la révolution de 1848. 1903. B3772
Maurain, J. La politique ecclésiastique du second empire de 1852 à 1869. 1930. B3773
____, ed. Le Saint-siège et la France de décembre 1851 à avril 1853. 1930. B3774
Maury, F. Nos hommes d'Etat

et l'oeuvre de réforme. 1913. B3775
Meggle, A. Le domaine colonial de la France. 1922. B3776
Métin, A. Le socialisme en Angleterre. 1897. B3777
____. La transformation de l'Egypte. 1903. B3778
Milhaud, E. La démocratie socialiste allemande. 1903. B3779
Montandon, G. Deux aus chez Koltchak et ches les Bolchéviques pour la Croux-rouge de Genève (1919-21). 1923. B3780
Montègut, E. Les Pays-Bas. 1869. B3781
Monteilhet, J. Les institutions militaires de la France (1814-1924). 1926. B3782
____. Les institutions militaires de la France (1814-1932). 1932. B3783
Moulin, R. L'année des diplomates. 1919. B3784
____. Vers le redressement. 1927. B3785
Moysset, H. L'esprit public en Allemagne vingt aus après Bismarck. 1911. B3786
Novikov, J. L'Alsace-Lorraine. 1913. B3787
Novion, F. L'Angleterre et sa politique étrangere et interieure, 1900-1914. 1924. B3788
Paris. Ecole libre des sciences politique. Société des anciens ľèves et élèves. L'Afrique du Nord. 1913. B3789
____. Algérie. 1929. B3790
____. La guerre. 1916. B3791
____. Intérêts économiques et rapports internationaux à la veille de la guerre. 1915. B3792
____. L'Islam et la politiqué contemporaine. 1927. B3793
____. Notre diplomatie économique. 1925. B3794
____. Les possibilités économiques de la France. 1927. B3795
____. Les questions actuelles de politique étrangère dans l'Amerique du Nord. 1911. B3796
____. Les questions actuelle de politique étrangère en Asie. 1910. B3797
____. Les questions actuelle de politique étrangère en Europe. 1911. B3798
Patry, R. Le régime de la liberté des cultes dans le departement du Calvados, pendant la premiere séparation (1795 à 1802). 1921. B3799
Paul-Louis, pseud. Histoire du mouvement syndical en Europe. 1922. B3800
____. Le Syndicalisme française d'Amines a Saint-Etienne, (1906-1922). 1924. B3801
Pernot, M. La politique de Pie X. 1910. B3802
Perreau-Pradier, P. La Afrique du Nord et la guerre. 1918. B3803
____. La guerre économique dans nos colonies. 1916. B3804
Phrangaules, A. P. La Grèce et la crise mondiale. 1926. B3805
Piolet, J. B. La France hors de France. 1900. B3806
Polités, A. G. L'hellénisme et l'Egypte moderne. 2 v. 1928-30. B3807
Prezzolini, G. La culture italienne. 1925. B3808
Les questions actuelles de politique étrangère en Europe. 1911. B3809
Questions roumaines du temps present, par Jonesco T. et divers. 1921. B3810
Rabasa, E. L'évolution historique du Mexique. 1924. B3811
Reinach, J. Récits et portraits contemporains. 1915. B3812
____. La vie politique de Léon Gambetta. 1918. B3813
Ristelhueber, R. Les traditions françaises au Liban. 1925. B3814
Robert, A. L'idée nationale autrichienne et les guerres de Napoléon. 1933. B3815
Rodes, J. La Chine nouvelle. 1910. B3816
____. La fin des Mandchous. 1919. B3817
____. Les Chinois. 1923. B3818
Rodrigues, G. La France éternelle. 1919. B3819
Roland-Marcel, P. R. Essai

politique sur Alexis de Tocqueville. 1910. B3820
Ronze, R. La question d'Afrique. 1918. B3821
Sagnac, P. Le Rhin français pendant la révolution et l'empire. 1917. B3822
Schefer, C. La France moderne et les problème colonial. 1907. B3823
Schmidt, C. Le grand-duché de Berg. 1905. B3824
Silvestre, J. De Waterloo à Saint-Hélène. 1904. B3825
La société de geographie, Paris. 1918. B3826
Spuller, E. Education de la democratie. 1892. B3827
____. Figures disparues. 3 v. 1891-94. B3828
Tardieu, A. P. G. A. La conférence d'Algésiras. 1909. B3829
____. La France et les alliances. 1910. B3830
____. Questions diplomatiques de l'année. 1904. 1905. B3831
Tarle, E. Le blocus continental et le royaume d'Italie. 1931. B3832
Tchernoff, J. Les nations et la Société des nations. 1919. B3833
Teste, L. L'Espagne contemporaine. 1872. B3834
Thénard, J. F. Le conventionnel Goujon. 1908. B3835
Verneaux, R. L'idéalisme de Renouvier. 1945. B3836
Vernon, E. Histoire de la Prusse. 1880. B3837
Viallate, A. L'industrie americaine. 1908. B3838
La vie politique dans les deux mondes. 1908. B3839
Villey, D. Ch. Dupont-White. V. 1. 1936. B3840
Wahl, J. A. Etudes kierkegaardiennes. 1949. B3841
Wahl, M. L'Algérie. 1897. B3842
Weill, G. J. Histoire de l'idée laique en France au XIXe siècle. 1929. B3843
____. Histoire du catholicisme libéral en France, 1828-1908. B3844
____. Histoire du mouvement social en France, 1852-1902. 1904. B3845
____. Histoire du mouvement social en France, 1852-1910. 1911. B3846
____. Histoire du mouvement social en France, 1852-1924. 1924. B3847
____. Histoire du parti républicain en France, 1814-1870. 1900. B3848
Welschinger, H. L'Alliance franco-russe. 1919. B3849
____. Bismarck. 1912. B3850
____. L'empereur Frédéric III (1831-1888). 1917. B3851
Woytinsky, W. S. La démocratie géorgienne. 1921. B3852
Zevort, E. Histoire de en troisième république. 1901. B3853

BIBLIOTHEQUE D'HISTOIRE DE LA PHILOSOPHIE (Vrin)

Alquie, F. Le cartésianisme de Malebranche. 1974. B3854
Aristoteles. Aristote: Physique II, tr. by Hamelin. 1931. B3855
Arnaud, P. Le "Nouveau Dieu." 1972. B3856
Aron, R. La philosophie critique de l'histoire. 1950. B3857
Baader, F. von. Lettres... ed. by Susini. 1942. B3858
Baillot, A. Influence de la philosophie de Schopenhauer en France. (1800-1900). 1927. B3859
Basch, V. Essais sur l'esthétique de Kant. 1934. B3860
Bastid, P. Proclus et le crépuscule de la pensée grecque. 1969. B3861
Benz, E. Les sources mystiques de la philosophie romantique allemande. 1968. B3862
Bergasse, L. Un philosophie lyonnais: Nicolas Bergasse.

1938. B3863
Bourgeois, B. Hegel à Francfort. 1970. B3864
Bourgey, L. Observation et expérience chez Aristote. 1955. B3865
Boutroux, E. De l'idée de loi naturelle dans la science et la philosophie contemporaine. 1949. B3866
____. Etude d'histoire de la philosophie allemande. 1926. B3867
____. La nature et l'esprit. 1926. B3868
____. La philosophie allemande au XVIIIe siècle. 1948. B3869
____. La philosophie de Kant. 1926. B3870
____. Des vérités éternelles chez Descartes. 1927. B3871
Bréhier, E. Histoire de la philosophie allemande. 1954. B3872
____. La philosophie de Plotin. 1961. B3873
____. La théorie des incorporels dans l'ancien stoicisme. 1928. B3874
Brochard, V. and Delbos, V. Etudes de philosophie ancienne et de philosophie moderne. 1954. B3875
Brochard, V. C. L. Les sceptique Grecs. 1923. B3876
Brunner, F. Etudes sur la signification historique de la philosophie de Leibniz. 1950. B3877
Bruschvigg, L. Blaise Pascal. 1955. B3878
Burgelin, P. La philosophie de l'existence de Jean-Jacques Rousseau. 1973. B3879
Chevallier, P. La Première profanation du temple maçonnique on Louis XV et la Fraternité, 1737-1755. 1968. B3880
____. Les ducs sous l'acacia. 1964. B3881
Corte, M. de. La doctrine de l'intelligence chez Aristote. 1934. B3882
Courtes, F. Etudes historique et critique sur la fausse subtilité des quartres figures syllogistiques démontrée par Kant. 1972. B3883
Delbos, V. Maine de Biran et son oeuvre philosophique. 1931. B3884
____. La spinozisme. 1926. B3885
Derathé, R. Jean-Jacques Rousseau et la science politique de son temps. 1970. B3886
Dubois, P. Le problème de la connaissance d'auturi dans la philosophie anglaise contemporaine. 1969. B3887
____. Le problème moral dans la philosophie anglaise. 1967. B3888
Dumont, J. P. Le scepticisme et le phénomène. 1972. B3889
DuVergier de Hauranne, J. Lettres, ed. by Barnes. 1962. B3890
Elungu, P. E. Etendue et connaissance dans la philosophie de Malebranche. 1973. B3891
Festugière, A. J. Etudes de religion grecque et héllenistique. 1972. B3892
____. Les trois "Protreptique" de Platon. 1973. B3893
Foucher, L. La jeunesse de Renouvier et sa première philosophie. (1815-1854). 1927. B3894
____. Auguste Comte et Saint-Simon. 1941. B3895
Fraisse, J. C. Philia. 1974. B3896
Ganne de Beaucoudery, E. La psychologie et la métaphysique des idées forces chez Alfred Fouillée. 1936. B3897
Gardet, L. Etudes de philosophie et de mystique comparées. 1972. B3898
Gibelin, J. L'esthetique de Schelling d'après la Philosophie de l'art. 1934. B3899
Gilet, M. Du fondement intellectuel de la morale d'après Aristotle. 1928. B3900
Gilson, L. La psychologie descriptive selon Franz Brentano. 1956. B3901
____. Méthode et métaphysique selon Franz Brentano. 1956. B3902
____. Saint Thomas moraliste.

1974. B3903
Goldschmidt, V. Anthologie et politique. 1974. B3904
____. Questions platoniciennes. 1970. B3905
____. Le système stoicien et l'idée de temps. 1969. B3906
Gouhier, H. G. Blaise Pascal. 1971. B3907
____. Les conversions de Maine de Biran. 1947. B3908
____. La jeunesse d'Auguste Comte et la formation du positivisme. V. 1. 1933. B3909
____. La pensée metaphysique de Descartes. 1962. B3910
____. La philosophie de Malebranche et son experience religieuse. 1948. B3911
____. La vocation de Malebranche. 1926. B3912
____. Les meditations metaphysiques de Jean-Jacques Rousseau. 1970. B3913
____. Pascal et les humanistes chrétiens. 1974. B3914
Gurvitch, G. D. Les tendances actuelles de la philosophie allemande. 1949. B3915
Hamelin, O. Le système de Aristote. 1931. B3916
____. La théorie de l'intellect d'après Aristote et ses commentateurs. 1953. B3917
Harrington, T. M. Vérité et méthode dans les "Penseés" de Pascal. 1972. B3918
Höffding, H. La concept d'analogie. 1931. B3919
Huang, Chia-cheng. De l'humanisme a l'absolutisme. 1954. B3920
____. La néo-hégélianisme en Angleterre. 1954. B3921
Jansen, B. La philosophie religieuse de Kant. 1934. B3922
Jolivet, R. Essai sur les rapports entre la pensée grecque et la pensée chrétienne. 1931. B3923
Joly, H. Le renversement platonicien. 1974. B3924
Klein, Z. La notion de dignité humaine dans la pensée de Kant et de Pascal. 1968. B3925
Koyré, A. Etudes sur l'histoire de la pensée philosophique en Russie. 1950. B3926
____. La philosophie de Jacob Boehme. 1929. B3927
Labrousse, E. Inventaire critique de la correspondance de Pierre Boyle. 1960. B3928
Lachieze-Rey, P. L'idéalisme katien. 1950. B3929
____. Les idées morales, sociales et politiques de Platon. 1951. B3930
____. Les origines cartésiennes du Dieu de Spinoza. 1950. B3931
Lameere, J. L'esthétique de Benedetto Croce. 1936. B3932
Laporte, J. M. F. La doctrine de Port Royal. 1951. B3933
____. Etudes d'histoire de la philosophie française au XVIIe siècle. 1951. B3934
____. La morale, d'après Arnauld. 1951. B3935
Lasbax, E. Le hierarchie dans l'univers chez Spinoza. 1926. B3936
LeBlond, J. M. Logique et methode chez Aristotle. 1939. B3937
LeChevalier, C. Ethique et idéalisme. 1963. B3938
LeChevalier, L. La morale de Leibniz. 1933. B3939
Lecourt, D. L'Epistémologie historique de Gaston Bachelard. 1969. B3940
Lenoble, R. Mersenne. 1943. B3941
Levinas, E. En decouvrant l'existence avec Husserl et Heidegger. 1967. B3942
____. Theorie de l'intuition dans le phénoménologie de Husserl. 1970. B3943
Lewis, G. L'individualité selon Descartes. 1950. B3944
Madkur, I. L'Organan d'Aristote dans le monde arabe. 1934. B3945
Maravall, J. A. La philosophie politique espagnole au XVIIe siècle... 1955. B3946
Merleau-Ponty, M. L'union de l'ame et du corps chez Malebrance, Brian et Bergson. 1968. B3947
Méry, M. La critique du christianisme chez Renouvier.

2 v. 1953. B3948
____. Essai sur la causalité phénoménale selon Schopenhauer. 1948. B3949
Mesnard, P. L'essor de la philosophie politique au XVIe siècle. 1951. B3950
Meyerson, E. Identité et realité. 1951. B3951
Milet, J. Gabriel Tarde et la philosophie de l'histoire. 1970. B3952
Milhaud, G. S. Etudes sur Cournot. 1927. B3953
____. La philosophie de Charles Renouvier. 1927. B3954
____. Les philosophes géomètres de la Grèce. 1934. B3955
Moureau, J. Plotin ou la gloire de la philosophie antique. 1970. B3956
____. Pour ou contre l'insensé? 1967. B3957
Mouy, P. Le développement de la physique cartesienne (1646-1712). 1934. B3958
____. L'idée du progrès dans la philosophie de Renouvier. 1927. B3959
____. Les lois du choc des corps d'après Malebranche. 1927. B3960
Mugnier, R. La théorie du premier moteur et l'évolution de la pensée artisotélicienne. 1930. B3961
Munk, S. Mélanges de philosophie juive et arabe. 1955. B3962
Naert, E. Leibniz et la querelle du pur amour. 1959. B3963
____. Mémoire et conscience de soi selon Leibniz. 1961. B3964
Noel, G. La logique de Hegel. 1967. B3965
Ou Tsuin Chen. La doctrine pédagogique de John Dewey. 1958. B3966
Pang, Ching Jeu. L'idée de Dieu chez Malebranche et l'idée de li, chez Tchou Hi, suives du Du Li et du K'I. 1942. B3967
Parodi, D. Du positivisme à l'idéalisme. 2 v. 1930. B3968
____. La philosophie de l'histoire de la philosophie, ed. by Castelli. 1956. B3969
Philonenko, A. La liberté humaine dans la philosophie de Fichte. 1966. B3970
____. Théorie et proxis dans la pensée morale et politique de Kant de Fichte en 1793. B3971
Poirier, R. Essai sur quelques caractères des notions d'espace et de temps. 1931. B3972
Poisson, J. Le romantisme et la souveraineté. 1932. B3973
____. Le romantisme social de Lamennais. 1931. B3974
Reymond, A. Les principes de la logique et la critique contemporaine. 1957. B3975
Robinet, A. Malebranche de l'Académie des Sciences. 1970. B3976
Rodier, G. Etudes de philosophique greque. 1926. B3977
Rodis-Lewis, G. L'individualité selon Descartes. 1950. B3978
Rolland, E. Le déterminisme monadique et le problème de Dieu dans la philosophie de Leibniz. 1935. B3979
Rousset, B. La doctrine Kantienne de l'objectivaté. 1967. B3980
____. La perspective finale de l'ethique et le problème de la cohérence du spinozisme. 1968. B3981
Savoiz, R. La philosophie de Charles Bonnet de Genève. 1948. B3982
Schlanger, J. E. Les metaphores de l'organisme. 1971. B3983
Segond, J. La sagesse cartésienne et la doctrine de la science. 1932. B3984
Silburn, L. Instant et cause. 1955. B3985
Simon, M. La philosophie de la religion dans l'oeuvre de Schleiermacher. 1974. B3986
Susini, E. Franz Von Baader. 2 v. 1943. B3987
Tatakis, B. N. Panétius de Rhodes. 1931. B3988
Ulmann, J. La nature et l'éducation. 1964. B3989
Ventura, M. Le Kalâm et le

peripatétisme d'après Kuzari. 1934. B3990

____. La philosophie de Saadia gaon. 1934. B3991

Verneaux, R. La idéalisme de Renouvier. 1945. B3992

____. Renouvier. 1945. B3993

Veto, M. La métaphysique religieuse de Simone Weil. 1970. B3994

Wahl, J. A. Etudes sur le Parménide de Platon. 1951. B3995

____. Etudes kiérkegaardiennes. 1949. B3996

____. Du role de l'idée de l'instant dans philosophie de Descartes. 1953. B3997

____. Vers la concret. 1932. B3998

Walch, J. Bibliographie du Saint-Simonisme. 1967. B3999

Wu, C. La doctrine pédagogique de John Dewey. 1958. B4000

BIBLIOTHEQUE DE L'ECOLE DES HAUTES ETUDES. SCIENCES PHILOGIQUES ET HISTORIQUES (3-17 Franck, 18-78 Vieweg, 79-151 Bouillon, 152- Champion)

1 Müller, F. M. La stratification du langage. 1869. B4001

2 Longnon, A. H. Etudes sur les pagi de la Gaule. 2 v. 1869-72. B4002

3 Tournier, E. Notes critiques sur Colluthus. 1870. B4003-4

4 Guyard, S. Nouvel essai sur la formation du pluriel brisé en arabe. 1870. B4005

5 Diez, F. Anciens glossaires romans, tr. by Bauer. 1870. B4006

6 Maspero, G. C. C. Des formes de la conjugaison en égyptien antique. 1871. B4007

7 Alexius, St. Legend. La vie de saint Alexis, ed. by Paris and Pannier. 1872. B4008

8 Monod, G. J. J. Etudes critiques sur les sources de l'histoire mérovingienne. V. 1. 1872. B4009

9 Jagannātha Panditarāja. Le Bhâmini vilâsa, ed. by Bergaigne. 1872. B4010

10 Paris. Ecole pratique des hautes études. Exercises de la Conférence de philologie grecque. 1875. B4011

11 Longnou, A. H. Etudes sur les pagi de la Gaule. 2 v. 1869-72. B4012

12 Maspero, G. C. C. Du genre épistolaire chez les Egyptiens de l'époque pharaonique. 1872. B4013

13 Sohm, R. Etudes sur les institutions germaniques, tr. by Thévenin. 1873. B4014

14 Robiou de la Tréhonnais, F. M. L. J. Itinéraire des deux-mille. 1863. B4015

15 Mommsen, T. Etude sur Pline le Jeune, tr. by Morel. 1873. B4016

16 Joret, C. Du c dans les langues romanes. 1874. B4017

17 Thurot, C. Cicéron Epistolae ad familiares. 1874. B4018

18 Lasteyrie du Saillant, R. C. Etude sur les comtes et vicomtes de Limoges antérieurs à l'an 1000. 1874. B4019

19 Darmesteter, A. Traité de la formation des mots composés dans la langue française... 1874. B4020

20 Châtelain, E. L. M. and Le Coultre, J. Quintellien. 1875. B4021

21 Grébaut, E. Hymne à Ammon-Ra des papyrus égyptiens du musée de Boulaq. 1874. B4022

22 Philippus Solitarius. Les pleurs de Philippe, ed. by Auvray. 1875. B4023

23 Darmesteter, J. Haurvatât et Ameretât. 1875. B4024

24 Buecheler, F. Précis de la déclinaison latine, tr. by Havet. 1875. B4025

25 Sharaf Rāmī. Anîs el'óch-châq. tr. by Huart. 1875. B4026

26 Eugubine tables. Les tables eugubines, ed. by Bréal. 1875. B4027

27 Robiou de la Tréhonnais, F. M. L. J. Questions homériques. 1876. B4028

28 Regnaud, P. Matériaux pour servir a l'histoire de la philosophie de l'Inde. 1876. B4029
29 Darmesteter, J. Ormazd et Ahriman. 1887. B4030
30 Lepsius, R. Les métaux dans les inscriptions égyptiennes. 1877. B4031
31 Giry, A. Histoire de la ville de Saint-Oner et de ses institutions jusqu au XIVe siècle. 1877. B4032
32 La Berge, D. de. Essai sur le règne de Trajan. 1877. B4033
33 Fagniez, G. Etudes sur l'industrie et la classe industrielle à Paris aux XIIIe et au XIVe siècle. 1877. B4034
34 Same as no. 28. V. 2. 1878. B4035
35 Paris. Ecole pratique des hautes études. Mélanges publiés de la Section historique et philologique de l'Ecole des hautes. 1878. B4036
36 Bergaigne, A. H. J. La religion védique d'apres les hymns du Rig-Véda. V. 1. 1878. B4037
37 Junghans, W. Histoire critique des regnes de Childerich et Chlodovech, tr. by Monod. 1879. B4038
38 Ledrain, E. Les monuments égyptiens de la Bibliothèque nationale. V. 1. 1879. B4039
39 Sennacherib, L'inscription de Bavian, ed. by Pognon. V. 1. 1879. B4040
40 Gilliéron, J. Patois de la commune di Vionnaz (Bas-Valais). 1880. B4041
41 Querolus. Le Querolus, tr. by Havet. 1880. B4042
42 Same as no. 39. V. 2. 1880. B4043
43 Havet, L. De saturnio Latinorum versu scripsit Ludovicus Havet. 1880. B4044
44 Clermont-Ganneau, C. S. Etudes d'archéologie orientale. 2 v. 1880-97. B4045
45 Flammermont, J. G. Histoire des institutions municipales de Senlis. 1881. B4046
46 Graux, C. H. Essai sur les origines du fonds grec le l'Escurial. 1880. B4047
47 Same as no. 38. V. 2. 1881. B4048
48 Geneviève, St. of Paris, Legend. Etude critique sur le texte de la vie latine de sainte Geneviève, ed. by Kohler. 1881. B4049
49 Bīdpāī. Deux versions hébraïques du livre de Kalīlâh et Dimnah, ed. by Derenbourg. 1881. B4050
50 Leroux, A. Recherches critiques sur les relations politiques de la France avec l'Allemagne de 1292 à 1378. 1882. B4051
51 Berend, W. B. S. Principaux monuments du Musée égyptien de Florence. 1882. B4052
52 Pannier, L. C. A., ed. Les lapidaires français du moyen âge du XIIe, XIIIe et XIVe siècles. 1882. B4053
53-54 Same as no. 36. V. 2, 3. 1883. B4054
55 Giry, A. Les Establissements de Rouen. V. 1. 1883. B4055
56 Pierson, P. Métrique naturelle du langage. 1884. B4056
57 Loth, J. M. Vocabulaire vieux-breton. 1884. B4057
58 Hincmarus. Hincmar. De ordine palatii. ed. by Prou. 1884. B4058
59 Same as no. 55. V. 2. 1885. B4059
60 Fournier, M. Essai sur les formes et les effets de l'affranchissement dans le droit gallo-franc. 1885. B4060
61-62 Barthélemy. Le romans de Carité et Miserere du rensus de Moiliens, ed. by Hamel. 2 v. 1885. B4061
63 Same as no. 8. V. 2. 1885. B4062
64 Pfister, C. Etudes sur le règne de Robert le Pieux (996-1031). 1885. B4063
65 Meylan, H. Nonius Marcellus. 1886. B4064
66 Marwān ibn Janāh, Abu al-Ualīd. Le livre des parterres fleuris, ed. by Derenbourg. 1886. B4065

67 Ernault, E. J. M. Du parfait en grec et en latin. 1886. B4066
68 Gayet, A. J. Musée du Louvre. 1889. B4067
69 Mātīgān-ī-gudshastak Abālish. Gujastak Abālish, ed. by Barthelémy. 1887. B4068
70 Papyrus Prisse. Etude sur le Papyrus Prisse, ed. by Virey. 1887. B4069
71 Nebuchadnezzar II. Les inscriptions babyloniennes du Wardi Brissa. 1887. B4070
72 Bīdpāī. Arabic version. Kalilâh et Dimnah. Johannis de Capua directionum vitae humanae, alias, parabola antiquorum sapientum, version latine du livre de Kalilâh et Dimnah. 2 v. 1887-89. B4071
73 Paris. Ecole pratique des hautes études. Mélanges Renier. 1887. B4072
74 Nolhac, P. de. La bibliothèque de Fulvio Orsini. 1887. B4073
75 Lefranc, A. J. M. Histoire de la ville Noyon et de ses institutions jusqu'à la fin du XIIIe siècle. 1887. B4074
76 Prou, M. Etude sur les relations politiques du pape Urbain V. avec les rois de France Jean II et Charles V. 1888. B4075
77 Lupus Servatus. Lettres de Servat Loup, abbé de Ferrières, ed. by Dezert. 1888. B4076
78 Porzio, S. Simon Portius, Grammatica linguae graecae vulgaris. 1889. B4077
79 Alexius, St. Le légende syriaque de saint Alexis, l'homme de Dieu, par Amiaud. 1889. B4078
80 Lejay, P. A. A. Les inscriptions antiques de la Côte-d-Or. 1889. B4079
81 Marwan ibn Janah. Le livre des parterres..., ed. by Metzger. 1889. B4080
82 Løseth, E. Le roman en prose de Tristan. 1890. B4081
83 Lévi, S. Le théatre indien. 1890. B4082
84 Brutails, J. A. Documents des archives de la Chambre des comptes de Navarre. 1890. B4083
85 Sefer Yehirah. Commentaire sur le Séfer Yesira, tr. by Lambert. 1891. B4084
86 Compain, L. T. Etudes sur Geoffroi de Vendôme. 1891. B4085
87 Lot, F. Les derniers Caroligiens. 1891. B4086
88 Jacqueton, G. La politique extérieure de Louise de Savoie. 1892. B4087
89 Aristoteles. Constitution d'Athènes, tr. by Haussoullier and others. 1891. B4088
90 Fécamp, A. Le poème de Gudrun. 1892. B4089
91 Nolhac, P. de. Pétrarque et l'humanisme d'après un essai de restitution de sa bibliothèque. 1892. B4090
92 Psichari, J., ed. Etudes de philologie néo-grecque. 1892. B4091
93 Perruchon, J. Les chroniques de Zar'a ya eqôb et de Ba'eda Maryâm. 1893. B4092
94 Havet, L. La prose métrique de Symmaque et les origines métriques du Cursus. 1892. B4093
95-96 Matheolus. Les Lamentations de Matheolus et le Livre de leesce de Jehan le Fèvre de Ressons. 2 v. 1892-1905. B4094
97 Jéquier, G. Le livre de ce qu'il y a dans l'Hadès. 1894. B4095
98 Bédier, J. Les fabliaux. 1895. B4096
99 Favre, E. Etudes. 1893. B4097
100 Paris. Ecole pratique des hautes études. L'Ecole pratique des hautes études (1868-1893), V. 1. 1893. B4098
101 Petit-Dutallis, C. E. Etude sur la vie et le règne de Louis VIII. 1894. B4099
102 Plautus, T. M. Plavti Amphitrvo, ed. by Havet. 1895. B4100
103 Malnory, A. Saint Césaire. 1894. B4101

104 Conzelman, W. E., ed. Chronique de Galâwdêwos. 1895. B4102
105 Ibn al Ṭiḳṭaḳā. Al-Fakhri, ed. by Derenbourg. 1895. B4103
106 Forgeot, H. L. J. Jean Balue. 1895. B4104
107 Blonay, G. J. L., ed. Matériaux pour servir à l'histoire de la déesse buddhique Tarâ. 1895. B4105
108 Mourlot, F. Essai sur l'histoire de l'augustalité dans l'empire romain. 1895. B4106
109 Dianu, J. Tite-Live. 1895. B4107
110 Iorga, N. Philippe de Mézières et la croisade du XIVe siècle. 1896. B4108
111 Finot, L. Les lapidaires indiens. 1896. B4109
112 Dionysius I, of Tell-Mahre. Chronique de Denys de Tell-Mahré, ed. by Chabot. 2 v. 1895. B4110
113 Same as no. 44. V. 2. 1897. B4111
114 Viteau, J. Etude sur le grec du Nouveau Testament comparé avec celui des Septante. 1896. B4112
115 Meillet, A. Recherches sur l'emploi du génitif-accusatif en vieux-slave. 1897. B4113
116 Reuss, R. E. L'Alsace au XVIIe siècle. V. 1. 1897. B4114
117 Same as no. 36. Index. V. 4. 1897. B4115
118 Daumet, G. Etude sur l'alliance de la France et de Castille au XIVe et au XVe siècle. 1898. B4116
119 Monod, C. J. J. Etudes critiques sur les sources de l'histoire carolingienne. V. 1. 1898. B4117
120 Same as no. 116. V. 2. 1897. B4118
121 Bar Hebraeus. Le livre de l'ascension de l'esprit sur la forme du ciel et de la terre, ed. by Nau. 2 v. 1888. B4119
122 Mohl, F. G. Introduction à la chronologie du latin vulgarie. 1899. B4120
123 Guerlin de Guer, C. Essai de dialectologie normade. 1899. B4121
124 Eckel, A. Charles le Simple. 1899. B4122
125 Gavilović, M. Etude sur le traité de Paris de 1259 entre Louis IX, roi de France, et Henri III, roi d'Angleterre. 1889. B4123
126 Dauzat, A. Etudes linguistiques sur la Basse-Auvergne. 1900. B4124
127 Lauer, P. Annales de l'histoire de France à l'époque caroligienne. Le règne de Louis IV d'Outre mer. 1900. B4125
128 Tarafah ibn-al-Abd. Dîwân de Tarafa ibn-al-Abd-al-Bakrî, tr. by Seligsohn. 1901. B4126
129 Dussard, R. Histoire de la religion des Nosairîs. 1900. B4127
130 Martin, F., ed. Textes religieux assyriens et babyloniens. 1900. B4128
131 Poupardin, R. Le royaume de Provence sous les Carolingiens. 1901. B4129
132 Giry, A. Notices bibliographiques sur les archives des églises et des monastères de l'époque carolingienne. 1901. B4130
133 Hermias, of Alexandria. Hermiae Alexandrini in Platonis Phaedrum scholia ad fidem codicis parisini 1810 denuo collati, ed. by Couvreur. 1901. B4131
134 Picarda, E. Les marchands de l'eau, hanse parsienne et compagnie française. 1901. B4132
135 Calmette, J. La diplomatie carolingienne. 1901. B4133
136 Guerlin de Guer, C. Le parler populaire dans la commune de Thaon. 1901. B4134
137 Halévy, J., ed. Tè'ĕzăza sanbat. 1902. B4135
138 Haussoullier, B. C. L. M. Etudes sur l'histoire de Milet et du Didymeion. 1902. B4136
139 Meillet, A. Etudes sur

l'etymologie & le vocabularie de vieux slave. 2 v. 1902-1905. B4137
140 Chavanon, A. Etude sur les sources principales des Mémorables de Xénephon. 1903. B4138
141 Azazaïl, St. Histoire de saunt Azazail, ed. by Macler. 1923. B4139
142 Vaschide, V. Histoire de la conquête romaine de la Dacie et des corps d'armée qui y ont pris part. 1903. B4140
143 Beasley, T. W. Le cautionnement de l'ancien droit grec. 1902. B4141
144 Palanque, C. H. A. Le Nil à l'époque pharaonique. 1903. B4142
145 Dupont-Ferrier, G. Les officiers royaux des bailliages... moyen age. 1902. B4143
146 Gauthiot, R. Le parler de Buividze. 1903. B4144
147 Lot, F. Etudes sur le regne de Hugues Capet et la fin du Xe siècle. 1903. B4145
148 al-Khatib, al-Baghdadi. L'introduction topographique à l'histoire de Bagdâdh d'About Bakr Ahmad ibn Thâbit-al-Khlatîb al-Bagdâdhî. 1904. B4146
149 Gonzalo de Berceo. La vida de Santo Domingo de Silos, ed. by Fitz-Gerald. 1904. B4147
150 Chapot, V. La province romaine proconsulaire d'Asie depuis ses origines jusqu'à la fin du haut-empire. 1904. B4148
151 Périer, J. Vie d'Al-Hadjdjâdj ibn Yousof. 1904. B4149
152 Passy, J. B. L'origine des Ossalois. 1904. B4150
153 Madrid. Biblioteca nacional. La bibliothèque du marquis de Santillane, ed. by Schieff. 1904. B4151
154 Serbat, L. Les assemblées du clergé de France. 1906. B4152
155 Zeiller, J. Les origines chrétiennes dans la province romaine de Dalmatie. 1906. B4153
156 Gauthier, L. Les Lombards dans les deux-Bourgognes. 1907. B4154
157 Grenier, A. Habitations gauloises et villas latines dans la cité des Médiomatrices. 1906. B4155
158 Marouzeau, J. Place du pronom personnel sujet en latin. 1907. B4156
159 Asañga. Māhāyānā-Sūltrālamkāra, ed. by Levi. V. 1. 1907. B4157
160 Bondois, M. Le translation des saints Marcellin et Pierre. 1907. B4158
161 Soehnée, F. Catalogue des actes de Henri Ier, roi de France. 1907. B4159
162 Delaruelle, L. Etudes sur l'humanisme français. 1907. B4160
163 Poupardin, R. Le royaume de Bourgagne. 1907. B4161
164 Monod, B. Essai sur les rapports de Pascal II avec Philippe Ier. 1907. B4162
165 Legendre, P. Etudes tironiennes. 1907. B4163
166 Halphen, L. Etude sur l'administration de Rome au moyen âge. 1907. B4164
167 Bourgin, G. La commune de Soissons... 1908. B4165
168 Mazon, A. Morphologie des aspects du verbe russe. 1908. B4166
169 Babut, E. C. Priscillien et le priscillianisme. 1909. B4167
170 Chatelain, L. Les monuments romains d'Orange. 1908. B4168
171 Weill, R. La presqu'île du Sinai. 1908. B4169
172 Oppinaus. Oppien d'Apamée, ed. by Boudreaux. 1908. B4170
173 Adjarian, H. H. Classification des dialectes arméniens. 1909. B4171
174 France. Parlement (Poitiers) Le comté de la Marche et le parlement de Poitiers, ed. by Thomas. 1909. B4172
175 Lot, F. La règne de Charles le Chauve (840-877). V. 1. 1909. B4173
176-177 Calvin, J. Institution de la religion chrestienne,

ed. by Lefranc and others. 2 v. 1911. B4174

178 Tukulti-Ninip II, roi d'Assyrie. Annales de Tukulti Ninip II, roi d'Assyrie, ed. by Scheil. 1909. B4175

179 Martin, F. Lettres néo-babyloniennes. 1909. B4176

180 Hyginus, C. J. Hygini Astronomica, ed. by Chatelain and Legendre. 1909. B4177

181 Elias bar Shīnāya, metropolitan of Nisibis. La chronographie d'Elie bar Sidaya, ed. by Delaporte. 1910. B4178

182 Joret, C. D'Ansse de Villoison et l'Hellénisme en France pendant le dernier tiers du XVIIIe siècle. 1910. B4179

183 Latouche, R. Histoire du Comté du Maine pendant le Xe et le XIe siècle. 1910. B4180

184 Pouchhenot, M. Le budget communal de Besançon au debut de XVIIIe siècle. 1910. B4181

185 Landry, A. Essai économique sur les mutations des monnaies dans l'ancienne France de Philippe le Bel à Charles VII. 1910. B4182

186 Boüard, A. de. Etudes de diplomatique sur les actes des notaires du Châtelet de Paris. 1910. B4183

187 Faral, E. Les jongleurs en France au moyen âge. 1910. B4184

188 Lauer, P. Annales de l'histoire de France à l'époque carolingienne. Robert Ier et Raoul de Bourogogne, ed. by Lauer. 1910. B4185

189 Cordey, J. Les comtes de Savoie et les rois de France pendant la guerre de cent ans (1329-1391). 1911. B4186

190 Same as no. 159. V. 2. 1911. B4187

191 Brillant, M. Les secrétaires athéniens. 1911. B4188

192 Latouche, R. Mélanges d'histoire de Cornouaille. 1911. B4189

193 Saulnier, E. Le rôle politique du cardinal de Bourbon. 1912. B4190

194 Pagés, A. G. Auzias March et ses prédécesseurs. 1911. B4191

195 Deconinck, J. Essai sur la chaine de l'Octateuque avec une édition des commentaires de Diodore de Tarse. 1912. B4192

196 Auerbach, B. La France et le Saint empire romain germanique depuis la prix Westphalie jusqu'a la revolution française. 1912. B4193

197 Fawtier, R. La vie de Saint Samson. 1912. B4194

198 Godet, M. La congrégation de Montaigue. 1912. B4195

199 Legrain, L. Le temps des rois d'Ur. 1912. B4196

200 Paris, G. B. P. Catalogue de la bibliothèque Gaston Paris, ed. by Barrau-Dihigo. 1913. B4197

201 Maspero, J. Organisation militaire de l'Egypte byzantine. 1912. B4198

202 Morel-Fatio, A. P. V. Historiographie de Charles-Quint. V. 1. 1923. B4199

203 Hogu, L. Jean de l'Espine. 1913. B4200

204 Lot, F. Etude critique sur l'abbaye de Saint-Wandrille. 1913. B4201

205 Sottas, H. La préservation de la propriété funéraire dans l'ancienne Egypte. 1913. B4202

206 Marx, J. L'inquisition en Dauphiné. 1914. B4203

207 Bruneau, C. Enquête linguistique sur les patois d'Ardennes. 1913. B4204

208 Esarhaddon. Le prisme S d'Assaraddon, roi d'Assyrie, ed. by Scheil. 1914. B4205

209 Homburger, L. Etude sur la phonétique historique du bantou. 1913. B4206

210 Coville, H. Etude sur Mazarin et ses démêlés avec le Pape Innocent X. 1914. B4207

211 Foulet, L. Le Roman de Renard. 1914. B4208

212 Terracher, A. L. Etude de géographie linguistique. 1914. B4209

213 Waquet, H. Le bailliage de Vermandois aux XIIe et XIVe siècles. 1919. B4210
214 Havet, L. Notes critiques sur le texte de Festus. 1914. B4211
215 Bloch, J. La formation de la langue marathe. 1915. B4212
216 Mathieu, G. Aristote Constitutions d'Athènes. 1915. B4213
217 Delatte, A. Etudes sur la littérature pythagoricienne. 1915. B4214
218 Alline, H. A. Histoire du texte de Platon. 1915. B4215
219 Contenau, G. Contribution à l'histoire économique d'Umma. 1915. B4216
220 Havet, L. Notes critiques sur Properce. 1916. B4217
221 Le premier divorce de Henri VIII et le schisme d'Angleterre, ed. by Bremont. 1917. B4218
222 Haussoullier, B. C. L. M. Traité entre Delphes et Pellana. 1917. B4219
223 Dauzat, A. Les argots de métiers franco-provençaux. 1917. B4220
224 Adam de la Halle. Les Partures Adan. 1917. B4221
225 Gilliéron, J. L. Généologie des mots qui désignent l'abeille d'après l'Atlas linguistique de la France. 1918. B4222
226 Lot, F. Etude sur le Lancelot en prose. 1918. B4223
227 Nolhac, P. de. Ronsard et l'humanisme. 1921. B4224
228 Pachtere, F. G. de. La table hypothécaire de Veleia. 1920. B4225
229 Brenot, A. Recherches sur l'Ephebie attique et sur la date de l'institution. 1920. B4226
230 Paris. Ecole pratique des hautes études. Cinquantenaire de l'école pratique des hautes-études. 1921. B4227
231 ____. Célebration du cinquantenaire de l'Ecole pratique des hautes-études, by Havet and others. 1922. B4228
232 Bloch, O. La pénétration du français dans les parlers des Vosges méridionales. 1921. B4229
233 Morone, G., cardinal. La légation du Cardinal Morone près l'empereur et le Concile de Trente, ed. by Constant. 1922. B4230
234 Recueil d'études égyptologique dédie a la mémoire de J. F. Champollion. 1922. B4231
235-36 Monod, G. J. J. La vie et la pensée de Jules Michelet. 2 v. 1923. B4232
237 Maspero, J. Histoire des patriarches d'Alexandrie... 1923. B4233
238 Faral, E. Les artes poétiques du XIIe et du XIIIe siècle. 1924. B4234
239 Brenot, A. Les mots et groupes iambiques réduits dans le théâtre latin Plaute-Térence. 1923. B4235
240 Rosetti, A. Etude sur le rhotacisme en roumain. 1924. B4236
241 Tibullus, A. Tibulle et les auteurs du Corpus Tibullianum, ed. by Pichard. 1924. B4237
242 Février, J. G. La date, la composition et les sources de la lettre d'Aristée à Philocrate. 1924. B4238
243 Deck, S. Une commune normande au moyen age, la ville d'Eu son histoire, ses institutions. 1924. B4239
244 Kurylowicz, M. Traces de la place du ton en gathique. 1925. B4240
245 Vasu-bandhu. Vijñaptimātratāsiddhi, ed. by Levi. 1925. B4241
246 Burger, A. Les mots de famille de... en grec ancien. 1925. B4242
247 Pagès, A. G. Commentaire sur les poésies d'Auzias March. 1925. B4243
248 Same as no. 207. V. 2. B4244
249 Skerlj, S. Syntaxe du participe présent et du gérondif en vieil italien. 1926. B4245
250 Lévy, I. La légende de Pythagore de Grèce en Palestine. 1927. B4246
251 Vielliard, J. Le latin des

diplômes, royaux et chartes privées de l'epogue mérovingienne. 1927. B4247
252 Havet, L. Notes critiques sur le texte de l'Orator et sur Isée. 1927. B4248
253 Lot, F. L'impôt foncier et la capitation personnelle sous le Bas-empire et a l'époque franque. 1928. B4249
254 Darmesteter, A. and Blondheim, D. S. Les gloses françaises dans les commentaires talmudiques de Raschi. 2 v. 1929-37. B4250
255-57 Arthur, King. Le légende arthurienne, ed. by Faral. 3 v. 1929. B4251
258 Latin empire. Les assisses de romanie, ed. by Recoura. 1930. B4252
259 Lot, F. Le premier budget de la monarchie française. 1932. B4253
260 Lévi, S. Un système de philosophie bouddhique. 1932. B4254
261 Lîubīmenko, I. I. (Borodīna). Les relations commerciales et politiques de l'Angleterre avec la Russie avant Pierre le Grand. 1933. B4255
262 Le bataille de Caresme et de Charnage, ed. by Lozinski. 1933. B4256
263 Lot, F. , ed. Nennius et l'histoiria Brittonum. 1934. B4257
264 Roques, M. L. , ed. Recueil général des lexiques français du moyen âge. V. 1. 1936. B4258
265 Estienne, C. Le guide des chemins de France de 1553, ed. by Bonnerot. V. 1. 1936. B4259
266 Dupont-Ferrier, G. Les origines et le premier siècle de la cour du trésor. 1936. B4260
267 Same as no. 265. V. 2. 1936. B4261
268 Chapin, E. Les villes de foires de Champagne, des origines au début du XIVe siècle. 1937. B4262
269 Same as no. 264. V. 2. B4263
270 Sjoestedt-Jonval, M. L. Description d'un parler irlandais de Kerry. 1938. B4264
271 Boussard, J. Le comté d'Anjou sous Henri Plantegenêt et ses fils. 1938. B4265
272 Robert, L. Etudes épigraphiques et philologiques. 1938. B4266
273 Rāma Tarka-vāgīsa Bhattacharya. Edition de la première śākha du Prakrtakalpataru de Ramasarman, ed. by Nitti-Dolci. 1939. B4267
274 Bible. O. T. Apocryphal books. La quatrième livre des Macchabées, ed. by Dupont-Sommer. 1939. B4268
275 Cohen, M. Nouvelles études d'éthiopien méridional. 1939. B4269
276 Longnon, J. Recherches sur la vie de Geoffroy de Villehardouin. 1939. B4270
277 Marquant, R. La vie économique à Lille sous Philippe le Bon. 1940. B4271
278 Robert, L. Les gladiateurs dans l'Orient grec. 1940. B4272
279 Goldschmidt, V. Essai sur le "Cratyle." 1940. B4273
280-282 Renou, L. Terminologie grammaticale du sanskrit. 3 v. 1942. B4274
283 Desrousseaux, A. M. Observations critiques sur les livres III et IV d'Athénée. 1942. B4275
284 Dain, A. L'Extrait Tactique tiré de Léon VI le Sage. 1942. B4276
285 Loyen, A. Recherches historiques sur les panégyriques de Sidoine Apollinaire. 1942. B4277
286 Bezzola, R. R. Les origines et la formation de la littérature courtoise en Occident (500-1200). V. 1. 1944. B4278
287 Lot, F. Recherches sur la population et la superficie des cités remontant à la période gallo-romaine. V. 1. 1945. B4279

288 Euripides. Le cyclope d'Euripides, ed. by Duchemim. 1945. B4280

289 Cohen, M. Le français en 1700 d'après le témpoignagne de Gile-Vaudelin. 1946. B4281

290 Tournon, C. F. de. Correspondance du Cardinal François de Tournon, ed. by François. 1946. B4282

291 Cohen, M. Essai comparatif sur le vocabulaire et la phonétique du chamito-sémitique. 1947. B4283

292 Pflaum, H. L. Le marbe de Thorigny. 1948. B4284

293 DeBabione. De Babione, ed. by Faral. 1948. B4285

294 Muhammad Ihrāhim ibn Abū Bakr. La chronique de Dumas d'Al-Jazari, ed. by Sauvaget. 1949. B4286

295 Mahn, J. B. Le Pape Benoit XII et les Cisterciens. 1949. B4287

296 Same as no. 287. V. 2. 1950. B4288

297 Gutun Owain. L'oeuvre poétique de Gutun Owain, ed. by Bachellerv. 2 v. 1950. B4289

298 Académie française. Paris. Observations sur l'orthographe de la langue frse, ed. by Beaulieux. 1951. B4290

299 Guillemain, B. La politique bénéficiale du Pape Benoit XII. 1952. B4291

300 Malinine, M. Choix de textes juridiques en hiératique "anormal" et en démotique (XXVe-XXVIIe dynasties). Part 1. 1953. B4292

301 Same as no. 287. V. 2. 1953. B4293

302 Frank, I. Répertoire métrique de la poésie des troubadours. V. 1. 1954. B4294

303 Redard, G. Recherches sur χρή, χρῆσθαι. 1953. B4295

304 Lot, F. Nouvelles recherches sur impôt foncier et la capitation personnelle sous le Bas-empire. 1955. B4296

305 Duprac-Quioc, S. Le cycle de la croisade. 1955. B4297

306 Marguerite d'Angoulême, Queen of Navarre. La navire, ed. by Marichal. 1956. B4298

307 Posenar, G. Littérature et politique dans l'Egypte de la XIIe dynastie. 1956. B4299

308 Same as no. 302. V. 2. 1957. B4300

309 Assurbanipal, king of Assyria. Le prisme du Louvre AO 19,939, tr. by Aynard. 1957. B4301

310 Irigoin, J. Les scholies metriques de Pindare. 1958. B4302

311 Schneider, R. L'expression des complements de verbe et de nom et la place de l'adjectif epithete en gueze. 1959. B4303

313 Same as no. 286. V. 2. 1947. B4304

314 Callu, J. P. Genio Populi Romani, 295-316. 1960. B4305

315 Solà-Solé, J. M. L'infinitif sémitique. 1961. B4306

316 Vercoutter, J. Textes biographiques du Sérapéum de Memphis. 1962. B4307

317 Jestin, R. R. Notes de graphie et de phonétique sumériennes. 1965. B4308

318 Poulle, E. Un constructueur d'instruments astronomiques au XVe siècle Jean Fusoris. 1963. B4309

319-20 Bezzola, R. R. Les origines et la formation de la littérature courtoise en occident (500-1200). 3 v. 1969. B4310

321 Labat, R. Un calendrier babylonien des travaux des signes et des mois. 1965. B4311

BIBLIOTHEQUE DE LA FACULTE DE PHILOSOPHIE ET LETTRES DE NAMUR (Vrin)

1-2 Ortégat, P. Philosophie de la religion. 2 v. 1948. B4312

3 Willaert, L. Les origines du jansénisme dans les Pay-Bas Catholiques. 1948. B4313

4-5 Ortégat, P. Bibliotheca Janseniana Belgica. 3 v. 1949-1952. B4314

6-7 Sonet, J. Le roman de Barlaam et Josaphat. V. 1. 1949. V. 2, pt. 1. 1950. B4315
8 Grégorie, A. de Leçons de philosophie des sciences expérimentales. 1950. B4316
9 Same as nos. 6-7. V. 2, pt. 2. 1952. B4317
10 Thibaut, R. La mystérieuse prophétie des papes. 1951. B4318
11 Girbet de Metz (chanson de gest). Gerbert de Mez, chanson de geste du XIIe siècle, ed. by Taylor. 1952. B4319
12 Same as no. 4-5. V. 4. 1951. B4320
13 Cloché, P. Thèbes de Béotie, des origines à la conquête romaine. 1951. B4321
14 Johanns, P. La pensée religieuse de l'Inde. 1952. B4322
15 Moretus-Plantin, H. Les passions de Saint Lucien et leurs dérivés céphalophoriques. 1953. B4323
16-17 Troisfontaines, R. De l'existence à l'être. La philosophie de Gabriel Marcel. 1953. B4324
18 Pirlot, J. Destinée et valeur. 1954. B4325
19 Van Ooteghem, J. Pompée le Grand Bâtisseur d'empire. 1954. B4326
20 Willaert, L. Le placet royal dans les anciens pays-bas. 1955. B4327
21 Guillaume, J. Essai sur la valeur exégetique du substantif dans les Entrevisions et La chanson d'Eve de Van Lerberghe. 1956. B4328
23 Ootegham, J. van. Lucius Licinius Lucullus. 1959. B4329
24 Guillaume, J. Le mot-thème dans l'exégèse de Van Lehbreghe. 1965. B4330
25 Willaert, L. L'Eglise au lendemain du concile de Trente. V. 1. 1960. B4331
26 Falise, M. Demande de Monnaie. 1966. B4332
27 Troisfontaines, R. "Je ne meurs pas..." 1960. B4333
28 Willame, G. Sonnets. 1963. B4334
29 Ooteghem, J. van. Lucius Marcius Philippus et sa famille. 1961. B4335
30 Guillaume, J. La poesie de Van Lerberghe. 1967. B4336
31 Chapelle, A. L'ontologie phénoménologique de Heidegger. 1967. B4337
32 Renard, M. Lès-aventures dè Djan d'Nivèle èl fi dè s'pére, ed. by Guillaume. 1963. B4338
33 Troisfantaines, R. ...J'entre dans le vie. 1967. B4339
34 Chapelle, A. Hegel et la religion. V. 1. 1964. B4340
35 Ooteghem, J. van. Caius Marius. 1964. B4341
36 Hambye, E. R. L'aumonerie de la flotte de Flandre au XVIIe siècle, 1623-1662. 1967. B4342
38 Jacques, X. Index de Pline de Jeune. 1966. B4343
39 Hambye, E. L'Aumónerie de la flotte de Flandre au XVIIe siècle. 1968. B4344
40-41 Same as no. 34. V. 2, 3. 1967. B4345
42 Van Parys, J. M. La vocation de la Liberté. 1969. B4346
43 Lebacqz, J. De l'identique au multiple. 1969. B4347
44 Ootegham, J. van. Les Caecilii Metelli de la Rèpublique. 1968. B4348
45 Loreaux, R. Le Phédon de Platon. V. 1. 1969. B4349
46 Léonard, L. Lexique namurois. 1969. B4350
47 Denis, J. Guide de la recherche géographique en Belgique. 1970. B4351
48 Robberechts, L. Essai sur la philosophie réflexive. V. 1. 1971. B4352
51 Guillaume, J. Gerard de Nerval. 1972. B4353
52 Gerard de Nerval, G. L. Lettres a Franz Liszt, ed. by Pichois. 1972. B4354

BIBLIOTHEQUE DE LA REVUE DE LITTERATURE COMPAREE (Champion)

1 Cohen, G. Ecrivains français en Hollande dans la première moitié du XVIIe siècle. 1920. B4355
2-3 Girard, H. Un bourgeois dilettante à l'epoque romantique: Emile Deschamps. 2 v. in 1. 1921. B4356
4 Killen, A. Le roman terrifiant, ou, roman noir de Walpole à Anne Radcliffe et son influence sur la litterature frse jusqu'en 1840. 1923. B4357
5 Esteve, E. Etudes de littérature préromantique. 1923. B4358
6 Roe, F. C. Taine et l'Angleterre. 1923. B4359
7 Faÿ, B. L'esprit revolutionnaire en France et aux Etats-Unis à la fin du XVIIIe siècle. 2 v. 1925. B4360
7:2 ____. Bibliographie critique des ouvrages français relatifs aux Etats-Unis (1770-1800). 1925. B4361
8 Chinard, G. Les amitiés américaines de Madame d'Houdetot. 1924. B4362
9 Larat, L. La tradition et l'exotisme dans l'oeuvre de Charles Nodier (1780-1844). 1923. B4363
10 ____. Bibliographie critique et opuscules inédits de Charles Nodier. 1923. B4364
11 Liebrecht, H. Histoire du théâtre français a Bruxelles aux XVIIe et XVIIIe siècles. 1923. B4365
12 Sells, A. L. Les sources françaises de Goldsmith. 1924. B4366
13 Ferrari, L. Le traduzioni italiane del teatro tragico francese nei secoli XVII° et XVIII°. 1925. B4367
14 Partridge, E. The French romantics' knowledge of English literature (1820-1848). 1924. B4368
15 Goulding, S. Swift en France au XVIIIe siècle. 1924. B4369
16 Larg, D. C. Madame de Staël. 1928. B4370
17 Citoleux, A. Alfred de Vigny. 1924. B4371
18 Trahard, P., ed. Une Revue oubliée: la Revue poetique du XIXe siècle (1835). 1929. B4372
19 Clark, A. F. B. Boileau and the French classical critics in England (1660-1830). 1925. B4373
20 Martin, M. Un aventurier intellectuel sous le restauration... 1925. B4374
21 Gilman, M. Othello in French. 1925. B4375
22 Hunter, J. B. A. Un introducteur de la littérature anglaise en France. 1925. B4376
23 Mapes, E. K. L'influence française dans l'oeuvre de Ruben Dario. 1925. B4377
24 Murris, R. La Hollande et les Hollandais au XVIIe et au XVIIIe siècles vus par les Français. 1925. B4378
25 Fransen, J. Les comédiens français en Hollande au XVIIe et XVIIIe siècles. 1925. B4379
26 Gunnell, D. Sutton Sharpe et ses correspondants français. 1925. B4380
27 Chateaubriand, F. A. R. Les aventures du dernier Abencerage, ed. by Hazard and Durry. 1926. B4381
28 Needham, H. A. Le développement de l'esthétique sociologique en France et en Angleterre au XIXe siècle. 1926. B4382
29 Schoell, F. L. Etudes sur l'humanisme continental en Angleterre à la fin de la renaissance. 1926. B4383
30 Gibb, M. M. Le roman de Basde-Cuir: étude sur Fenimore Cooper et son influence en France. 1927. B4384
31 Baldensperger, F. Orientations étrangères chez Honoré de Balzac. 1927. B4385
32 Palfrey, T. R. L'Europe littéraire (1833-1834) un essai de périodique cosmopolite. 1927. B4386
33 Minderhoud, H. J. La

Henriade dans la littérature hollandaise. 1927. B4387

34 Henry, M. La contribution d'un Américain au symbolisme français, Stuart Merrill. 1927. B4388

35 Smith, M. E. Une Anglaise intellectuelle en France Sous la Restauration, Miss Mary Clarke. 1927. B4389

36 Walter, F. La littérature portugaise en Angleterre a lèpoque romantique. 1927. B4390

37 Cameron, M. M. L'influence des Saisons de Thomson sur la poésie descriptive en France. 1927. B4391

38 Prévost, A. F. Mémoires et aventures d'un homme de qualite, t. v. Séjour en Angleterre; ed. by Robertson. 1927. B4392

39 Purdie, E. The story of Judith in German and English literature. 1927. B4393

40 Schwartz, W. L. The imaginative interpretation of the Far East in modern French literature (1800-1925). 1927. B4394

41 Gill-Mark, G. A. Une femme de lettres au XVIIIe siècle. Anne-Marie Du Bocage. 1927. B4395

42 Lallemand, P. de. Montalembert et ses relations littéraires avec l'étranger. 1927. B4396

43 Guiette, R. La légende de la Sacristine. 1927. B4397

44 Garnier, M-R. Henri James et la France de 1748 à 1798. 1927. B4398

45 Bedarida, H. Parme et la France. 1927. B4399

46-47 Viatte, A. Les sources occultes du romantisme, illuminisme et théosophie. 2 v. 1928. B4400

48 Storer, M. F. Un épisode litteraire de la fin du XVIIe siècle. 1928. B4401

49 Dempsey, M. A contribution to the sources of Genie du christianisme. 1928. B4402

50 Desonay, F. Le rêve hellénique chez les poètes parnassiens. 1928. B4403

51 Thompson, L. F. Kotzebue. 1928. B4404

52 Hartland, R. W. Walter Scott et le roman "frénétique." 1928. B4405

53 Jeffery, V. M. John Lily and the Italian renaissance. 1928. B4406

54 Markovitch, M. I. J-J. Rousseau et Tolstoi. 1928. B4407

55 ____. Tolstoï et Gandhi. 1928. B4408

56 Elkington, M. E. Les relations de société entre l'Angleterre et la France sous la restauration (1814-1830). B4409

57 Lang, D. G. Madame de Staël. 1928. B4410

58 Henning, I. A. L'Allemagne de Mme de Staël et la polémique romantique. 1929. B4411

59 Messac, R. Le "detective novel" et l'influence de la pensée scientifique. 1929. B4412

60 Espiner, J. G. (Scott). Les sonnets elisabéthains. Les sources et l'apport personnel. 1929. B4413

61 Taylor, A. C. Carlyle, sa première fortune littéraire en France (1825-1865). 1929. B4414

62 Taupin, R. L'influence du symbolisme français sur la poésie américaine de 1910 à 1920. 1929. B4415

63 Cours, J. de. Francis Vielé-Griffin. 1930. B4416

64 Woodward, L. D. Une Anglaise amie de la révolution française: Hélène-Maria Williams, et ses amis. 1930. B4417

65 Reque, D. Trois auteurs dramatiques scandinaves: Ibsen, Björnson, Strindberg, devant la critique française. 1930. B4418

66 Summers, V. A. L'orientalisme d'Alfred de Vigny. 1930. B4419

67 Reesnik, H. J. L'Angleterre et la littérature anglaise dans les trois plus anciens périodiques français

de la Hollande. 1931. B4420
68 Beuchat, C. Edouard Rod et le cosmopolitisme. 1930. B4421
69 Bardon, M. "Don Quichotte" en France. 2 v. 1931. B4422
70 Rosenblatt, L. Idée de l'art pour l'art dans la littérature anglaise pendant la période victorienne. 1931. B4423
71 Goethe, J. W. von. Voyage en Italie, ed. by Mutterer. 1930. B4424
72 Audra, E. L'influence française dans l'oeuvre de Pope. 1931. B4425
73 Dechamps, J. Sur la légende de Napoleon. 1931. B4426
74 West, A. H. L'influence française dans la legende burlesque en Angleterre entre. 1660-1700. 1931. B4427
75 Farmer, A. J. La mouvement esthétique et "décadent" en Angleterre (1873-1900). 1931. B4428
76 Brimont, R. (de Beaumont) de. Autour de "Graziella." 1931. B4429
77 Salis, J. R. de. Sismondi, 1777-1842. 1932. B4430
78 Leathers, L. V. L'Espagne et les Espagnols dans l'oeuvre de Honore de Balzac. 1931. B4431
79 Bain, M. I. Les voyaguers français en Ecosse, 1770-1830. 1931. B4432
80 Wright, J. Un intermédiare entre l'esprit germanique et l'esprit français sous le second empire: Camille Selden. 1931. B4433
81 La Vergnas, R. Le chevalier Rutlidge. 1932. B4434
82 Vinant, G. Un esprit cosmopolite au XIXe siècle, Malewida de Meysenbug, (1816-1903). 1932. B4435
83 Fournet, C. Un Genevois cosmopolite, ami de Lamartine: Huber Saladin (1798-1881). 1932. B4436
84 Osborn, A. W. Sir Philip Sidney en France (1932). B4437
85 Tinker, E. L. Les écrits de langue française en Louisiane. 1932. B4438
86 Muralt, B. L. de. Lettres sur les Anglois et les François et sur les voiages (1728). 1933. B4439
87 Rice, H. C. Le Cultivateur américain (1933). B4440
88 Bourl'honne, P. George Eliot. 1933. B4441
89 Sellards, J. Dans le sillage du romantisme: Charles Didier (1805-1864). 1933. B4442
90 Mouraud, M. Le romantisme Français en Angleterre, de 1814 à 1848. 1933. B4443
91 Duthie, E. L. L'influence du symbolisme français dans le renouveau poétique de l'Allemagne. 18933. B4444
92 King, S. M. Maurice Barres. 1933. B4445
93-94 Korwin-Iortrowska, S. de. Balzac en Pologne. 2 v. 1933. B4446
95 Hainsworth, G. Les Novelas exemplaires, de Cervantes en France au XVIIe siècle. 1934. B4447
96 Gibelin, J. L'esthétique de Schelling et l'Allemagne de Madame de Staël. 1934. B4448
97 Rinvolucri, M. J. (Moore) Bernard Shaw et la France. 1934. B4449
98 Duméril, E. Le lied Allemand et ses traductions poétiques en France. 1933. B4450
99 ____. Lieds et ballades germaniques traduits en vers français 1933. 1934. B4451
100 Evans, R. L. Les romantiques français et la musique. 1934. B4452
101 Fuchs, A. Les apports français dans l'oeuvre de Verhaeren. 1934. B4453
102 Charrier, C. Héloïse dans l'histoire et dans la légende. 1934. B4454
103 Mahieu, R. G. Les enquêteurs français aux Etats-Unis de 1830 à 1837. 1935. B4455
104 Vedel, V. Deux classiques Français vus par un critique

etranger. 1936. B4456
105 Joliat, E. Smollett et la France. 1935. B4457
106 Frets, H. L'élément germanique dans l'oeuvre d'Emile Verhaeren. 1935. B4458
107 Savković, M. L'influence du réalisme français dans le roman serbocroate. 1935. B4459
108 Holdworth, F. Joseph de Maistre et L'Angleterre. 1935. B4460
109 Kozko, La fortune de "Quo vadis?" de Sienkiewicz en France. 1935. B4461
110 Linge, T. La conception de l'amour dans le drame de Dumas fils et d'Ibsen. 1935. B4462
111 Tronchon, H. Etudes. France, Allemagne, Italie, Hongrie, pays baltes. 1936. B4463
112 Bauer, H. F. Les ballades de Victor-Hugo. 1936. B4464
113 Pruvost, R. Mattéo Bandello and Elizabeth fiction. 1937. B4465
114 Salvan, J. L. Le romantisme français et l'angleterre victorienne. 1949. B4466
This number completes the series.

BIBLIOTHEQUE DE LA REVUE DES COURS ET CONFERENCES (Boivin)

Bachelard, G. La dialectique de la durée. 1936. B4467
____. Les intuitions atomistiques. 1933. B4468
Bornecque, H. Tite-Live. 1933. B4469
Bray, R. Chronologie du romantisme. 1932. B4470
Bréhier, E. La philosophie de Plotin. 1928. B4471
Carré, J. R. Consistance de Voltaire de philosophie. 1938. B4472
____. Spinoza. 1936. B4473
Chevalier, J. L'habitude. 1929. B4474
Coculesco, P. S. Lyrisme et structures sonores. B4475
____. Principes d'Esthétique. 1935. B4476
____. Les rythmes comme introduction physique à l'esthétique. 1930. B4477
Cohen, G. Ronsard. 1924. B4478
____. Les rythmes. 1930. B4479
Combes, M. Le réve et la personalité. B4480
Connes, G. Le mystére shakespearien. 1926. B4481
Cousin, J. Etudes sur la poésie latine. 1945. B4482
Cresson, A. La représentation. 1936. B4483
Estève, E. Un grand poète de la vie moderne, Emilie Verharen. 1929. B4484
____. Leconte de Lisle. 1923. B4485
____. Sully Prudhomme. 1925. B4486
Feugère, A. Un grand amour romantique. 1927. B4487
____. Le mouvement religieux dans la littérature. 1938. B4488
Fidao-Justiniani, J. E. Discours sur la raison classique. 1937. B4489
Gaiffe, F. A. La rire et la scène française. 1931. B4490
Hauvette, H. La France et la Provence dans l'oeuvre de Dante. 1929. B4491
____. La "morte vivante." 1933. B4492
Hoepffner, E. Les lais de Marie de France. 1935. B4493
Jolivet, A. Le théâtre de Strindberg. 1931. B4494
Jullian, C. Au seuil de notre histoire. 3 v. 1930. B4495
Lachièze-Rey, P. Les idees morales, sociales et politiques de Platon. 1938. B4496
Lalande, A. Les théories de l'induction et la expérimentation. 1929. B4497
LeBreton, A. V. Le théâtre romantique. 1927. B4498
Lejay, P. A. A. Histoire de la littérature latine des origines à Plaute. 1926. B4499
Lejay, P. P. Plaute. B4500
LeRoy, E. L. E. J.

L'exigence idéaliste et la fait de l'évolution. 1927. B4501
____. Les origines humaines et l'évolution de l'intelligence. 1929. B4502
____. La pensée intuitive. 2 v. 1929-30. B4503
Lhéritier, M. L'Europe orientale a l'epoque e contemporaine. 1938. B4504
Lote, R. Explication de la litterature allemande. 1935. B4505
Martino, P. Verlaine. 1944. B4506
Michaud, R. Le roman américain d'aujourd hui. 1926. B4507
Michaut, G. M. A. La Bruyère. 1936. B4508
Millardet, G. Le Roman de Flamenca. 1936. B4509
Mornet, D. Introduction à l'étude des écrivains français d'aujourd'hui. 1939. B4510
Plattard, J. Marot. 1938. B4511
____. Une figure de premier plan dans nos lettres de la renaissance, Agrippa d'Aubigné. 1931. B4512
Poëte, M. Introduction à l'urbanisme. 1929. B4513
Pommier, J. J. M. Diderot avant Vincennes. 1939. B4514
Reymond, A. H. Les principes de la logique et la critique contemporaine. 1932. B4515
Segond, J. L. P. L'esthetique du sentiment. 1927. B4516
Seillière, E. L'évolution morale dans le théâtre d'H. Bataille. B4517
Trahard, P. Le mystère de la sensibilité française au XVIIIe siècle. 1940. B4518
____. La vie intérieure. 1947. B4519
Villard, L. Le théâtre Américain. 1929. B4520
Villey-Desmeserts, P. L. J. Montaigne devant la postérité. 1935. B4521
Wallon, H. Les origines du caractére chez l'enfant les préludes du sentiment de personnalité. 1934. B4522

BIBLIOTHEQUE DE LA SCIENCE POLITIQUE (Presses Universitaires de France)

Series 1: Initiation, méthode, documentation.
Duclos, P. L'évolution des rapports politiques depuis. 1750. 1950. B4523
Mirkine-Guetzévitch, B. Les constitutions europeenes. 2 v. 1950. B4524
Series 2: Les grandes doctrines politique.
Aristotles. Politique, ed. by Prélot. 1950. B4525
Bagge, D. Les idées politique en France sous la Restauration. 1952. B4526
Derathé, R. Jean-Jacques Rousseau et la science politique de son temps. 1950. B4527
Gallouédec-Genuys, F. Le prince selon Fénélon. 1963. B4528
Vlachos, G. Le pensée politique de Kant. 1962. B4529
Series 3: Les grandes formes politique.
Djordjević, J. La Yougoslavie. 1959. B4530
Laski, H. J. Le gouvernement parliamentaire en Angleterre. 1950. B4531
Mouskhely, M. and Jedryka, Z. Le gouvernement de l'U. R. S. S. 1961. B4532
Ogg, F. A. and Ray, P. O. Le gouvernment des Etats-Unis d'Amérique. 1958. B4533
Series 4: Les grandes forces politique.
Duroselle, J. B. Les débuts du catholicisme social en France. (1822-1870). 1951. B4534
No series:
Friedrich, C. J. La démocratie constitutionnelle. 1958. B4535
L'Huillier, F. Les institutions internationales et transnationales. 1961. B4536
Locke, J. Essai sul le pouvoir civil. 1954. B4537
Maritain, J. L'homme et l'etat, tr. by Davril. 1953. B4538

BIBLIOTHEQUE DE PHILOLOGIE GERMANIQUE (Aubier)

1 Jolivet, A. et Mossé, F. Manual de l'alleman du moyen âge des origines au XIVe. 1947. B4539
2 Mossé, F. Manual de la langue gotique. 1942. B4540
3 Wolfram von Eschenbach. Parzival. 1943. B4541
4 Delcourt, J. Initiation à l'étude historique del'anglais. 1944. B4542
5 Hartmann d'Aue. Erec: Iwein. 1944. B4543
6 Nibelungen. La chanson des Nibelungen, ed. by Colleville and Tonnelat. 1944. B4544
7 Le Nibelunglied, ed. by Colleville. 1944. B4545
8 Mossé, F. Manual de l'anglais du moyen âge des origines au XIVe. 2 pts. 1945. B4546
9 Gawain and the Grene knight. Sire Gauvain et le Chavalier Vert, ed. by Pons. 1946. B4547
10 Chaucer, G. Contes de Cantorbéry, ed. by Delcourt. 1948. B4548
11 Gravier, M. Anthologie de l'allemand du XVIe. 1948. B4549
12 Mossé, F. Manual de l'anglais du moyen âge. 2 v. 1949. B4550
13 Moret, A. Anthologie du minnesang. 1949. B4551
14 Zink, G. Le wundereer. 1949. B4552
15 Loey, A. van. Introduction à l'étude du moyen--Néerlandais. 1951. B4553
16 Zink, G. Le cycle de Dietrich. 1952. B4554
17 Gravier, M. La saga d'Eric le Rouge. 1952. B4555
18 Moret, A. Kudrun. 1957. B4556
19 Bizet, J. A. Mystiques allemands du XIVe siècle. 1957. B4557
20 D'Ardenne, S. Le Hibou et le Rossignol. 1961. B4558
21 James, I. Le livre, du roi, attribué à Jacques 1er d'Ecosse, ed. by Simon. 1967. B4559
22 Chaucer, G. Troile et Crisède, ed. by Simon. 1969. B4560
23 Marache, R. Syntaxe structurale allemande. 1971. B4561
24 ____. La saga de Snorri le Godi. 1973. B4562

BIBLIOTHEQUE DE PHILOSOPHIE CONTEMPORAINE (Alcan prior to 1940; 1940- Presses Universitaires de France)

Abramson, J. L'enfant et l'adolescent instables. 1940. B4563
Accambray, L. Un testament philosophique. 1937. B4564
Achille-Delmas, F. Psychologie pathologique du suicide. 1932. B4565
Adam, C. E. La philosophie en France. 1894. B4566
Adolphe, L. La dialectique des images chez Bergson. 1951. B4567
____. La philosophique religieuse de Bergson. 1946. B4568
Aliotta, A. L'Eternite des esprits. 1924. B4569
Alquie, F. La nostalgie de l'etre. 1973. B4570
L'Année pedagogique. 1911-13. B4571
L'Année philosophique. 1890. B4572
L'Année sociologique. 1896-. B4573
Arréat, L. Art de psychologie individuelle. 1906. B4574
____. Psychologie du peintre. 1892. B4575
Aronson, M. J. La philosophie morale de Josiah Royce. 1927. B4576
Aubry, P. La contagion du meurtre. 1896. B4577
Autin, A. Autorité et discipline en matière d'education. 1950. B4578
Avebury, J. L. L'emploi de la vie, par Sir John Lubbock, bart. 1897. B4579
Bachelard, G. La dialectique de la durée. 1950. B4580
____. L'engagement rationaliste. 1972. B4581

____. L'expérience de l'espace dans la physique contemporaine. 1937. B4582
____. La philosophie du non. 1940. B4583
____. La poetique de la reverie. 1960. B4584
Bardoux, J. Essai d'une psychologie de l'Angleterre contemporaine. 1907. B4585
Barthelemy-Madaule, M. Bergson adversaire de Kant. 1966. B4586
Baruzi, J. Saint Jean de la Croix et le problème de l'expérience mystique. 1931. B4587
Barzellotti, G. La philosophie de H. Taine. 1900. B4588
Basch, V. Les doctrines politiques des philosophes classiques de l'Allemagne... 1927. B4589
____. Essai d'esthétique. 1934. B4590
____. La poétique de Schiller. 1911. B4591
Bastide, G. De la condition humaine. 1939. B4592
____. Essai d'ethique fondamentale. 1971. B4593
____. Le moment historique de Socrates. 1939. B4594
Baudouin, C. Psychanalyse de l'art. 1929. B4595
Bayer, R. L'esthetique de la grâce. 1933. B4596
Bayet, A. Histoire de la morale en France. 2 v. 1930. B4597
____. Le suicide et la morale. 1922. B4598
Beauquier, C. Philosophie de la musique. 1865. B4599
Beaussire, E. J. A. Les principes du droit. 1888. B4600
Belot, G. Etudes de moral positive. 1907. B4601
Benrubi, I. L'ideal moral chez Rousseau, Mme de Staël et Amiel. 1940. B4602
____. Les sources et les courants de la philosophie contemporaine en France. 2 v. 1933. B4603
Benzechi, E. La ésprit humain selon Pascal. 1939. B4604
____. Essai sur la nature et la portié de l'attitude métaphysique. 1939. B4605
Berger, G. Recherches sur les conditions de la connaissance. 1941. B4606
Bergson, H. L. Les deux sources de la morale et de la religion. 1948. B4607
____. Durée et simultanéite, à propos de la théorie d'Einstein. 1923. B4608
____. Ecrits et paroles, ed. by Mosse-Bastide. 3 v. 1957-59. B4609
____. L'énergie spirituelle. 1949. B4610
____. Essai sur les données immédiates de la conscience. 1948. B4611
____. L'évolution créatice. 1948. B4612
____. L'rire. 1941. B4613
____. Matière et mémoire. 1941. B4614
____. La pensée et le mouvant. 1941. B4615
Bernard-Leroy, E. Les visions du demisommeil. 1933. B4616
Bernheim, H. Automatisme et suggestion. 1917. B4617
Berr, H. L'histoire traditionnelle et la synthèse historique. 1935. B4618
____. La synthèse en histoire. 1911. B4619
Bertenal, W. Le faux intellectualisme. 1948. B4620
Berthelot, R. Un romantisme utilitaire. 1911. B4621
____. Science et philosophie chez Goethe. 1932. B4622
Bertrand, A. Les études dans la démocratie. 1900. B4623
Bianquis, G. Nietzsche en France. 1929. B4624
Biervliet, J. J. van. La part de l'imagination. 1938. B4625
Binet, A. La psychologie du raisonnement. 1886. B4626
____. Les révelations de l'ecriture d'après un controle scientifique. 1906. B4627
Blanché, R. La notion de fait psychique. 1935. B4628
____. Le raisonnement. 1973. B4629
____. La rationalisme de Whewell. 1935. B4630
Blondel, C. A. A. La

psychophysiologie de Gall. 1914. B4631
Blondel, M. L'action. 1950. B4632
____. L'être et les êtres. 1935. B4633
____. La pensée. 2 v. 1934. B4634
____. La philosophie et l'esprit chrétein. V. 2. 1944. B4635
____. Les premiers écrits de Maurice Blondel. 1956. B4636
____. Premièrs écrits, l'action, 1893- B4637
Boeuf, M. Psychologie de la croyance. 1901. B4638
Bohn, G. La nouvelle psychologie animale. 1911. B4639
Boirac, E. La psychologie inconnue. 1920. B4640
Boissoudy, J. de. Deux réalités, 1936. B4641
____. La phénomène révolution. 1940. B4642
Bonet-Maury, G. L'unite moral des religions. 1913. B4643
Bopp, H. G. Amiel. 1931. B4644
Bouchet, H. L'individualisation de l'enseignement des enfants et son rôle dans l'education. 1933. B4645
Boudot, P. Nietzsche en miettes. 1973. B4646
Bouglé, C. C. A. Essais sur le régime des castes. 1935. B4647
____. Les idées égalitaires. 1925. B4648
____. Qu'est ce que la sociologie? 1925. B4649
Bourdeau, J. L'évolution du socialisme. 1901. B4650
Bourdeau, L. Le problème de la mort. 1904. B4651
____. Le problème de la vie. 1901. B4652
Bourdon, B. L'intelligence. 1926. B4653
Bourgin, H. L'industrie et la marché. 1924. B4654
Boutmy, E. G. Philosophie de l'architecture en Grèce. 1870. B4655
Boutroux, E. De la contingence des lois de la nature. 1915. B4656
____. Nouvelles études d'histoire de la philosophie. B4657
____. De vérités éternelles chez Descartes. 1927. B4658
Boyer, J. Essai d'une definition de la vie. 1939. B4659
Bozzano, E. Les phénonoménès de hantise. 1929. B4660
Bray, L. Du beau. 1902. B4661
Bridel, L. Le droit des femmes et le mariage. 1893. B4662
Brochard, V. C. L. De l'erreur. 1926. B4663
____. Etudes de philosophie ancienne et de philosophie moderne. 1912. B4664
Brocher, H. Le mythe du héros et la mentalité primitive. 1932. B4665
Brugeilles, R. Le droit et la sociologie. 1910. B4666
Brunschvicg, L. De la connaissance de soi. 1931. B4667
____. Escrits philosophiques. 2 v. 1951. B4668
____. Les étapes de la philosophie mathématique. 1947. B4669
____. L'expérience humaine et la causalité physique. 1949. B4670
____. L'idéalisme contemporain. 1921. B4671
____. Introduction à la vie de l'esprit. 1920. B4672
____. La modalité du jugement. 1934. B4673
____. Le progrès de la conscience dans la philosophie occidentale. 2 v. 1927. B4674
____. La raison et la religion. 1939. B4675
____. Le sentiment du beau et la sentiment poétique. 1904. B4676
____. Spinoza. 1894. B4677
____. Spinoza et ses contemporains. 1923. B4678
Bujeau, L. V. La philosophie entomologique de J. H. Fabre. 1943. B4679
____. Le schématisme, psychologie de l'action. 1941. B4680
Burloud, A. La pensée conceptuelle. 1927. B4681
____. La pensée d'après les recherches expérimentales.

1927. B4682
____. Principes d'une psychologie des tendances. 1938. B4683
Busco, P. Les cosmogonies modernes et la theorie de la connaissance. 1924. B4684
Buytendijk, F. J. J. De la douleur. B4685
Cailliet, E. La prohibition de l'occulte. 1930. B4686
Carré, J. R. La philosophie de Fontenelle. 1932. B4687
____. Réflexions sur l'anté-Pascal de Voltaire. 1935. B4688
Casey, D. M. La théorie du subconscient de Morton Prince. 1945. B4689
Cazeneuve, J. Les rites et la condition humaine. 1958. B4690
Cellérier, L. Esquisse d'une sceince pédagogique. 1910. B4691
Cesselin, F. La philosophie organique de Whitehead. 1950. B4692
Chabot, C. Nature et moralitè. 1896. B4693
Chapiro, M. L'illusion comique. 1940. B4694
Chaslin, P. Essai sur le mécanisme psychologique des opérations de la mathématique pure. B4695
Chauchard, P. La matrise du comportement. 1956. B4696
Chide, A. Le mobilisme moderne. 1908. B4697
Cim, A. Le travail intellectuel. 1924. B4698
Cohen-Seat, G. Problèmes du cinema et de l'information visuelle. 1961. B4699
Colestani, G. La morale supérieurs. 1940. B4700
Combris, A. La philosophie des races du comte de Gobineau et sa porteé actuelle. 1937. B4701
Compayre, G. L'adolescence. 1910. B4702
Comte, A. La sociolgie. 1897. B4703
Condillac, E. B. de. Lettres, ed. by Cramer. 1953. B4704
Consentino, A. Temps, Espace, Devenir, Moi. 1938. B4705
Cosentini, F. La sociologie génétique. 1905. B4706
Coste, A. L'expérience des peuples et les prévisions qu'elle autorise. 1900. B4707
Cramaussel, E. Le premier éveil intellectuel de l'enfant. 1909. B4708
Crépieux-Jamin, J. L'ecriture et le caractère. 1934. B4709
Cresson, A. La moral de Kant. 1897. B4710
____. La morale de la raison théorique. 1903. B4711
Cruchet, M. De la méthode en medécine. 1942. B4712
Cyon, E. de. Dieu et science. 1912. B4713
Czarnowski, S. Le culte des heros et ses conditions sociales. 1919. B4714
Danville, G. La psychologie de l'amour. 1907. B4715
Darbon, A. Les catégories de la modalité. 1953. B4716
Daujot, J. L'oeuvre de intelligence en physique. B4717
Dauriac, L. A. Essai sur l'esprit musical. 1904. B4718
____. La psychologie dans l'opéra français. 1897. B4719
Daval, S. Philosophie généale. 1951. B4720
Davy, G. La foi jurée. 1922. B4721
____. Sociologues d'hier et d'aujourd'hui. 1950. B4722
Debesse, M. Comment étudier les adolescents. 1948. B4723
____. La crise d'originalite juvénile. 1941. B4724
Debidour, A. Histoire diplomatique de l'Europe depuis le Congres de Berlin jusqu'a nos jours. 1919. B4725
Dejean, R. L'emotion. 1933. B4726
Delacroix, H. J. L'enfant et le langage. 1934. B4727
____. Les grands mystiques chrétiens. 1938. B4728
____. Psychologie de l'art. 1927. B4729
____. La psychologie de Stendahl. 1918. B4730
Delay, J. P. L. Les dissolutions de la mémoire. 1942. B4731
Delbos, V. La philosophie

pratique de Kant. 1926. B4732
____. Le problème moral dans la philosophie de Spinoza et dans l'histoire du spinozisme. 1893. B4733
Delvaille, J. La vie sociale et l'education. 1907. B4734
Delvolvé, J. Réflexions sur la pensée comtienne. 1932. B4735
____. Religion, critique et philosophie positive chez Pierre Bayle. 1906. B4736
Deschoux, M. Initiation à la philosophie. 1951. B4737
____. La philosophie de Léon Brunschvicq. 1949. B4738
Dide, M. Les émotions et la guerre. 1918. B4739
Dilthey, W. Introduction à l'étude des sciences humaines. 1942. B4740
____. Théorie des conceptions du monde. 1946. B4741
Dorolle, M. Les problèmes de l'induction. 1933. B4742
____. Le raisonnement par analogie. B4743
Draghicescu, D. Du rôle de l'individu dans le déterminisme social. 1904. B4744
____. Vérité et révélation. 2 v. 1934. B4745
Dubois, J. Le problème pedagogique. 1911. B4746
Ducasse, P. Essai sur les origines intuitives du positivisme. 1939. B4747
____. Méthode et intuition chez Auguste Comte. 1939. B4748
Dugas, L. L'éducation du caractère. 1912. B4749
____. Les grands timides. 1922. B4750
____. Le problème de l'education. 1909. B4751
____. Psychologie du rire. 1902. B4752
____. Les timides dans la litterature et l'art. 1925. B4753
____. La timidité. 1898. B4754
Duguit, L. Le droit social... 1922. B4755
Dumas, G. Le sourire. 1948. B4756
____. Le surnaturel et les dieux d'après, les maladies mentales. 1946. B4757
____. Les vie affective. 1948. B4758
Dumas, M. Les instruments scientifiques aux XVIIe et XVIIIe siècle. 1953. B4759
Dunan, C. S. Les deux idéalismes. 1911. B4760
Dupré, E. Le langage musical. 1911. B4761
Dupreél, E. Esquisse d'une philosophie des valeurs. 1939. B4762
Dupuis, L. Les aboulies sociales... 1940. B4763
Durand, G. Les structures anthropologiques de l'imaginaire. 1963. B4764
Durand, J. P. Questions de philosophie morale et sociale. 1901. B4765
Duret, R. Les facteurs pratiques de la croyance dans la perception. 1929. B4766
____. L'objet de la perception. 1929. B4767
Durkheim, E. De la division du travail social. 1960. B4768
____. Education et sociologie. 1934. B4769
____. L'évolution pédegogique en France. 1938. B4770
____. Les formes élémentaires de la vie religieuse... 1937. B4771
____. Leçons en sociologie. 1950. B4772
____. Les Règles de la méthode sociologique. 1895. B4773
____. Le socialisme. 1928. B4774
____. Sociologie et philosophie. 1924. B4775
____. Le suicide. 1897. B4776
Duval, M. La poésie et la principe de transcendance. 1935. B4777
____. Religion, superstition et criminalité. 1935. B4778
Dwelshauvers, G. Les mécanismes subconscient. 1925. B4779
____. La psychologie français contemporaine. 1920. B4780
Ebbinghaus, H. Précis de psychologie. 1912. B4781
Eichthal, E. Pages sociales. 1909. B4782
Espinas, A. V. La philosophie

sociale du XVIIIe siècles et la révolution. 1898. B4783
____. Des sociétés animales. 1878. B4784
Etcheverry, A. L'idéalisme français contemporain. 1934. B4785
Evellin, F. J. M. A. La raison pure et les antinomie. 1907. B4786
Fauconnet, A. L'esthetique de Schopenhauer. 1913. B4787
Faure-Frémiet, P. Pensée et recréation. 1934. B4788
____. La recréation du reél et l'équivoque. 1940. B4789
Féré, C. S. Dégénerescence et criminalité. 1888. B4790
Ferri, E. Les criminels dans l'art et la litterature. 1897. B4791
Fierens-Gevaert, H. Psychologie d'une ville. 1901. B4792
Finot, J. La philosophie de la longevité. 1906. B4793
____. Progrès et bonheur. 2 v. 1914. B4794
Fleury, M. L'âme du criminel. 1898. B4795
Focillon, H. Vie et formes. 1939. B4796
Forti, E. L'emotion, la volonté et le courage. 1952. B4797
Foucault, M. La psychophysique. 1901. B4798
Fouillée, A. J. E. L'avenir de la metaphysique fondée sur l'expérience. 1921. B4799
____. Critique des systèmes de morale contemporaine. 1883. B4800
____. La démocratie politique et sociale en France. 1923. B4801
____. Les éléments sociologiques de la morale. 1928. B4802
____. Esquisse psychologique des peuples europeens. 1903. B4803
____. L'évolutionnisme des idées forces. 1928. B4804
____. La France au point de vue morale. 1900. B4805
____. Humanitaires et libertaires au point de vue sociologique et moral. 1914. B4806
____. La liberté et le déterminisme. 1890. B4807
____. Morale des idées-forces. 1908. B4808
____. La morale, l'art et la religion. 1897. B4809
____. Le mouvement idéaliste et la réaction contre la science positive. 1896. B4810
____. Nietzsche et l'immoralisme. 1902. B4811
____. La pensée et les nouvelles écoles anti-intellectualistes. 1911. B4812
____. La propriété sociale et la démocratie. 1922. B4813
____. Psychologie du peuple français. 1898. B4814
____. La socialisme et la sociologie réformiste. 1909. B4815
____. Tempérament et caractère selon les individus les sexes et les races. 1901. B4816
Fournière, E. Essai sur l'individualisme. 1901. B4817
____. La théories socialistes au XIXe siècle de Babeauf à Proudhon. 1904. B4818
Franck, A. Philosophie du droit penal. 1893. B4819
____. La philosophie mystique en France... 1866. B4820
Freud, S. La science des rêves. B4821
Frutiger, P. Les mythes de Platon. 1930. B4822
Fulliquet, G. Essai sur l'obligation morale. 1898. B4823
Fyot, J. L. Dimensions de l'homme et science économique. 1952. B4824
Gabel, J. Sociologie de l'alienation. 1970. B4825
Gauckler, P. G. Le beau et son histoire. 1873. B4826
Gaultier, J. de. La philosophie officielle et la philosophie. 1922. B4827
____. La sensibilité metaphysique. 1928. B4828
Gentile, G. L'esprit. 1925. B4829
Gerritsen, T. J. La philosophie de Heymans. 1938. B4830
Gille, P. La grand metamorphose. 1947. B4831
Gilson, E. H. La liberté chez Descartes et la théologie. 1913. B4832

Ginestier, P. Le théatre contemporain dans le monde. 1961. B4833
Giran, P. Les origines de la pensee. 1923. B4834
Girard, A. Le journal intime. 1963. B4835
Goblot, E. Justice et liberté. 1902. B4836
Gonseth, F. Les mathématiques et la réalité. 1936. B4837
Gorce, M. M. La politique de l'Eternel. 1941. B4838
Gramont, A. A. A. de. Essai sur le sentiment esthétique. 1941. B4839
Grandjean, G. La raison et la vie. 1920. B4840
Granet, M. Catégories matrimoniales et relations de proximité dans la Chine ancienne. 1939. B4841
____. Danses et légendes de la Chine ancienne. 2 v. 1926. B4842
____. La religion des Chinois. 1951. B4843
Granger, G. G. La mathématique sociale du marquis de Condorcet. 1956. B4844
Grasset, J. Les limites de la biologie. 1902. B4845
Greef, G. J. de. Les lois sociologiques. 1908. B4846
____. La sociologie économique. 1904. B4847
____. La transformisme social. 1901. B4848
Grégoire, A. de. L'apprentissage du langage. 1937. B4849
Grua, G. La justice humaine selon Leibniz. 1956. B4850
Gueroult, M. La philosophie transcendantale de Salomon Maimon. 1929. B4851
Gurvitch, G. La vocation actuelle de la sociologie. 1963. B4852
Gusti, D. La science de la réalité sociale. 1941. B4853
Guthrie, H. Introduction au problème de l'histoire de la philosophie. 1937. B4854
Guy-Grand, G. Le Renaissance religieuse. 1928. B4855
Guyau, J. M. L'art au point de vue sociologique. 1889. B4856
____. Esquisse d'une morale sans obligation ni sanction. 1935. B4857
____. L'irréligion de l'avenir. 1890. B4858
____. La morale anglaise contemporaine. 1900. B4859
____. Les problèmes de l'esthetique contemporaine. 1891. B4860
Halbwachs, M. Les cadres sociaux de la mémoire. 1925. B4861
____. Les causes du suicide. 1930. B4862
____. La classe ouvrière et les nivèaux de vie. 1913. B4863
____. La topographie legendaire des Evangiles en Terre Sainte. 1941. B4864
Halevy, E. La formation du radicalisme philosophique. 3 v. 1901-04. B4865
Hamelin, O. Essai sur éléments principaux de la représentation. 1952. B4866
____. Le système de Descartes. 1921. B4867
Hannequin, A. Etudes d'histoire des sciences et d'histoire de la philosophie. 2 v. 1908. B4868
Hartenberg, P. Physionomie et caractère. 1908. B4869
Heidsieck, F. L'ontologie de Merlau-Ponty. 1971. B4870
Hémon, C. La philosophie de m. Sully Prudhomme. 1907. B4871
Henderson, L. J. L'ordre de la nature. 1924. B4872
Henriot, J. Existence et obligation. 1967. B4873
Hermant, P. Les principales théories de la logique contemporaine. 1909. B4874
Hesnard, A. L. M. La relativité de la conscience de soi. 1924. B4875
Hirth, G. Physiologie de l'art. 1902. B4876
Höffding, H. Le concept d'analogie. 1931. B4877
____. Le conceptions de la vie. 1928. B4878
____. Jean-Jacques Rousseau et sa philosophie. 1912. B4879

____. Philosophies contemporaine. B4880
____. La relativité philosophique. 1924. B4881
Hondt, J. De Hegel a Marx. 1972. B4882
Hubert, H. Mélanges d'histoire des religions. 1909. B4883
Hubert, R. Les sciences socials dans l'Encyclopédie. 1923. B4884
____. Le sens du réel. 1930. B4885
Husson, L. Les transformations de la responsabilité. 1947. B4886
Jaëll, M. L'intelligence et le rhyme dans les mouvements artistiques. 1904. B4887
____. La musique et la psychophysiologie. 1896. B4888
Janet, P. A. R. Le cerveau et la pensée. 1867. B4889
____. Histoire de la science politique. 1925. B4890
____. Le matérialisme contemporain en Allemagne. 1864. B4891
____. Le philosophie de Lamennais. 1890. B4892
____. Saint-Simon et le saint-simonisme. 1878. B4893
Jankélévitch, V. L'alternative. 1938. B4894
____. La mauvoise conscience. 1951. B4895
____. L'odyssée de la conscience dans la denière philosophie de Schelling. 1933. B4896
Kant, I. Critique de la raison pure. 1944. B4897
Keim, A. Helvétius. 1907. B4898
Konczewska, H. L'unité de la matière et le problème des transmutations. 1938. B4899
Konczewski, C. La pensée preconsciente. 1938. B4900
Kornis, G. L'homme d'état. 1938. B4901
Koyré, A. Etudes d'histoire de la pensée scientifique. 1966. B4902
Krinitz, E. La musique en Allemagne. 1867. B4902a
Krzesinski, A. Une nouvelle philosophie de l'immance. 1931. B4903
Lachance, L. Le droit et les droits de l'homme. 1959. B4904
Lachelier, J. E. N. Etudes sur le syllogisme. 1907. B4905
____. Oeuvres de Jules Lachelier, ed. by Brunschvig. 1933. B4906
____. Psychologie et métaphysique. 1949. B4907
Lachièze-Rey, P. L'idéalisme kantien. 1931. B4908
____. Les origines cartésiennes du Dieu de Spinoza. 1932. B4909
Lacombe, P. La psychologie des individus et des sociétés chez Taine. 1906. B4910
Lacombe, R. E. La psychologie bergsonienne. 1933. B4911
Lacroix, J. Marxisme, existentialisme, personalisme. 1971. B4912
Lagache, D. L'unité de la psychologie. 1949. B4913
Lahy, J. M. La morale de Jésus. 1911. B4914
Lalande, A. La dissolution opposée à l'évolution dans les sciences physiques et morales. 1899. B4915
____. Les illusions evolutionnistes. 1930. B4916
Lalo, C. L'art et la morale. 1934. B4917
____. Esquisse d'une esthétique musicale scientifique. 1908. B4918
____. L'esthétique expérimentale contemporaine. 1908. B4919
____. L'expression de la vie dans l'art. 1933. B4920
____. Les sentiments esthétiques. 1909. B4921
Lamperierè, A. Le rôle social de la femme. 1898. B4922
Lamy, P. Claude Bernard et le matérialisme. 1939. B4923
Landry, A. L'idée de chrétienté chez les scolastiques du XIIIe siècle. B4924
____. La responsabilité pénale. 1902. B4925
____. La sensibilité musicale. 1927. B4926
Lanessan, J. M. A. de. Les empire germaniques et la politique de la force. 1915. B4927
____. L'Etat et les églises en

France depuis les origines jusqú à la séparation 1906. B4928
____. Histoire de l'entante cordiale franco-anglaise. 1916. B4929
____. L'idéal moral du materialisme et la guerre. 1918. B4930
____. Les missions et leur protectorat. 1907. B4931
Laporte, J. M. F. Le problème de l'abstraction. 1940. B4932
Lascaris, P. A. L'education esthétique de l'enfant. 1928. B4933
Laugel, A. La voix, l'oreille et la musique. 1867. B4934
Lauvrière, E. Edgar Poe. 1904. B4935
Laveleye, E. L. V. de. De la properiéte et de ses formes primitives. 1891. B4936
____. Le gouvernment dans la démocratie. 1896. B4937
Lavelle, L. De l'être. 1928. B4938
____. La dialectique du monde sensible. 1955. B4939
LeBon, G. Lois psychologiques de l'évolution des peuples. 1898. B4940
____. Psychologie des foules. 1939. B4941
____. Psychologie du socialisme. 1912. B4942
Lechalas, G. Etudes esthetique. 1902. B4943
Lechartier, G. David Hume. 1900. B4944
Leclère, A. Essai critique sur le droit d'affirmer. 1901. B4945
Lecoeur, C. Textes sur la sociologie et l'école au Maroc. 1939. B4946
LeDantec, F. A. Le chaos et l'harmonie universille. 1911. B4947
____. L'unité dans l'être vivant. 1902. B4948
Leenhardt, H. La nature de la connaissance et l'erreur initiale des théories. 1934. B4949
Leeuw, G. van der. L'homme primitif et la religion. 1940. B4950
LeFur, L. E. Races, nationalités. 1922. B4951
LeHénaff, A. Le droit et les forces étude sociologique. 1931. B4952
Leibniz, G. W. freiherr von. Lettres et fragments inédits sur les problèmes philosophiques, théologiques, politiques de la réconciliation des doctrines protestantes (1669-1704): Schrecker. 1934. B4953
Leif, J. La sociologie de Tönnies. 1946. B4954
Lemairé, O. Esquisse d'une philosophie. 1947. B4955
____. Essai sur la personnae. 1936. B4956
Lenoir, R. Condillac. 1924. B4957
____. Les historiens de l'esprit humain. 1926. B4958
Leplae, C. Les finançilles. 1947. B4959
Leroux, E. Le pragmatisme américain & angalis. 1923. B4960
LeRoy, E. L. E. J. Essai d'une philosophie première. V. 1. 1956. B4961
____. Une philosophie nouvelle. 1912. B4962
LeSenne, R. Le devoir. 1930. B4963
____. Le mensonge et le caractère. 1930. B4964
Letourneau, C. J. M. Physiologie des passions. 1868. B4965
Leuba, J. H. La psychologie des phénomènes religieux. 1914. B4966
Leuridon, C. L'idée de liberté morale. 1936. B4967
Levinas, E. La théorie de l'intuition dans la phénoménologie de Husserl. 1930. B4968
Lévy, E. Les fondements due droit. 1933. B4969
Levy-Bruhl, L. L'âme primitive. 1927. B4970
____. Les carnets. 1949. B4971
____. L'expérience mystique et les symboles chez les primitifs. 1938. B4972
____. Les fonctions mentales dans les societés inférieures. 1910. B4973.
____. La mentalité primitive.

1960. B4974
____. La morale et la science des moeurs. 1937. B4975
____. La mythologie primitive. 1935. B4976
____. La philosophie d'Auguste Comte. 1900. B4977
____. La surnaturel et la nature dans la mentalité primitive. 1931. B4978
Lewis, G. Le problème de l'inconscient et le cartésianisme. 1950. B4979
Liard, L. Les logiciens anglais contemporains. 1907. B4980
Lichtenberger, H. Richard Wagner. 1902. B4981
Lodge, O. La vie et la matière. 1930. B4982
Lombroso, C. Le crime politique et les révolutions. 2 v. 1892. B4983
____. La femme criminelle et la prostituee. 1896. B4984
____. L'homme criminel. 1887. B4985
Losskiĭ, N. O. L'intuition. 1928. B4986
Lourié, O. L'arrivisme, essai de psychologie concrète. 1934. B4987
____. La philosophie de Tolstoï. 1931. B4988
____. La philosophie russe contemporaine. 1902. B4989
____. La philosophie sociale dans le theâtre d'Ibsen. 1900. B4990
____. La psychologie des romanciers russes du XIXe siècle. 1905. B4991
____. La Russie en 1914-1917. 1918. B4992
Lubac, E. Le cycle de l'inconscient. 1934. B4993
____. Les niveaux de conscience et d'inconscient et leurs intercommunications. 1929. B4994
____. Present conscient et cycle de dureé. 1936. B4995
Lupasco, S. L'expérience microphysique et la pensée humaine. 1941. B4996
Luquet, G. H. Idées génerale de psychologie. 1906. B4997
Mabille, P. Initiation à la connaissance de l'homme. 1949. B4998
Madinier, G. Conscience et amour. 1938. B4999
Maine de Biran, P. Memoire sur la décomposition de la pensée. 2 v. 1952. B5000
____. O'Euvres. 14 v. 1935-49. B5001
Malapert, P. Les élements du caratère et leurs lois de combinaison. 1906. B5002
Malgand, W. De l'action à la pensée. 1935. B5003
Mamelet, A. L'idée positive de la moralite devant la critique philosophie. 1929. B5004
____. La relativisme philosophique chez Georg Simmel. 1914. B5005
Marcault, J. E. L'education de demain, la biologie de l'esprit et ses applications pedagogiques. 1939. B5006
Marceron, A. La morale por l'Etat. 1912. B5007
Massabuau, J. L'Etat contre la nation. 1922. B5008
Masson-Oursel, P. La philosophie comparèe. 1923. B5009
Matisse, G. La philosophie de la nature. 3 v. 1927. B5010
Mauduit, R. Auguste Comte et la science économique. 1929. B5011
Maugé, F. L'èsprit et le réel dans les limites du nombres et de la grandeur. 1937. B5012
____. L'esprit et le réel perçu. 1954. B5013
Maunier, R. Essais sur les groupements sociaux. 1929. B5014
Maus, I. De la justice pénale. 1891. B5015
Mavit, H. L'intelligence créatice. 1939. B5016
Maxwell, J. Les phénomènes psychiques, recherches, observations, méthodes. 1903. B5017
Medic, P. Le théorie de l'intelligence chez Schopenhauer. 1923. B5018
Medici, A. L'âge de trois ans et l'étude du caractère. 1940. B5019

____. L'éducation nouvelle, ses fondatuers--son évolution. 1940. B5020
Ménard, A. Analyse et critique des Principes de la psychologie de W. James. 1911. B5021
Mendousse, P. L'âme de l'adolescente. 1941. B5022
____. Du dressage à l'éducation. 1910. B5023
Merleau-Ponty, M. La structure du comportement. 1949. B5024
Metzger, H. La concepts scientifiques. 1926. B5025
____. Newton, Stahl, Boerhaave et la doctrine chimique. 1930. B5026
Meyer, H. Le rôle médiateur de la logique. 1956. B5027
Meyerson, E. Du cheminement de la pensée. 1931. 3 v. B5028
Meyerson, I. Identité et realité. 1926. B5029
Michaud, R. L'esthétique d'Emerson. 1927. B5030
Mignard, L. L'unite psychique et les troubles mentaux. 1928. B5031
Milhaud, G. S. Descartes savant. 1921. B5032
____. Essai sur les conditions et les limites de la certitude logique. 1912. B5033
____. Le rationnel. 1939. B5034
Mill, J. S. Lettres inédites de John Stuart Mill à Auguste Comte. 1899. B5035
____. L'utilitarisme. 1883. B5036
Mochi, A. De la connaissance à l'action. 1928. B5037
____. La connaissance scientifique. 1927. B5038
____. Science et morale dans les problèmes sociaux. 1931. B5039
Montagne, R. Les Berbères et le makhzeu dans le sud du Maroc. 1930. B5040
Mouard, Y. L'éveil de intelligence étude de psychologie génétique et comparée. 1939. B5041
Mouloud, N. La peinture et l'espace. 1964. B5042
Mucchielli, R. Le mythe de la cité idéale. 1960. B5043
Müller, M. Individualité, causalité, indéterminisne. 1932. B5044
Naville, A. Nouvelle classification des sciences. 1920. B5045
Naville, E. La définition de la philosophie. 1894. B5046
____. Les systèmes de philosophie. 1909. B5047
Nicolle, C. Biologie de l'invention. 1932. B5048
____. Le destinée humaine. 1941. B5049
____. La nature, conception et morale biologiques. 1934. B5050
Nogué, J. L'activité primitive du moi. 1936. B5051
____. Esquisse d'un système des quitès sensibles. 1943. B5052
____. Le système de l'actualité. 1947. B5053
Nordau, M. S. La biologie de l'éthique. 1930. B5054
____. Dégéréscence. 2 v. 1909, 1907. B5055
____. Les mensonges conventionnels de notre civilisation. 1900. B5056
Novikov, I. A. La critique du Darwinisme social. 1910. B5057
____. Les luttres entre sociétés humaines et leurs phases successives. 1896. B5058
Oechslin, L. L'intitution mystique de Sainte Thérèse. 1946. B5059
Oltramare, P. J. La religion et la vie de l'esprit. 1925. B5060
Ombredone, A. L'aphasie et l'élaboration de la pensée explicite. 1951. B5061
L'orientation actuelle des sciences. 1930. B5062
Ouvré, H. Les formes littéraires de la pensée grecque. 1900. B5063
Pacotte, J. La connaissance. 1934. B5064
____. La pensée mathématique contemporaine. 1931. B5065
____. La pensée technique. 1931. B5066
Palante, G. Les antinomies entre l'individu et la société. 1913. B5067
____. Combat pour l'individu. 1904. B5068

____. Pessimisme et individualisme. 1914. B5069
____. Précis de sociologie. 1921. B5070
Palhories, F. L'héritage de la pensée antique. 1932. B5071
Papaillault, G. Science française, scolastique allemande. 1917. B5072
Parodi, D. Les bases psychologiques de la vie morale. 1928. B5073
____. La philosophie contemporaine de France. 1921. B5074
____. Le problème moral et la pensée contemporaine. 1921. B5075
Paulhan, F. L'activité mentale et les éléments de l'ésprit. 1889- B5076
____. Analystes et esprits synthétique. 1928. B5077
____. La double fonction du langage. 1929. B5078
____. L'esthétique de paysage. 1931. B5079
____. La fonction de la mémoire et la souvenir affectif. 1924. B5080
____. Le mensonge de l'art. 1907. B5081
____. La morale de l'irone. 1925. B5082
____. Les phénomènes affectifs et les lois de leur apparition. 1933. B5083
____. Psychologie de l'invention. 1901. B5084
Paumen, J. Le spiritualisme existentiel de René Le Senne. 1949. B5085
Payot, J. La croyance. 1911. B5086
____. L'éducation de la volonté. 1941. B5087
____. Le travail intellectuel et la volonté. 1921. B5088
Pérès, J. L'art et le réel. 1898. B5089
Perez, B. L'éducation intellectuelle dès le berceau. 1901. B5090
____. L'enfant de trois à sept ans. 1907. B5091
____. Les trois premières années de l'enfant. 1911. B5092
Philippe, L. L'éducation des anormaux. 1910. B5093
La philosophie allemande au XIXe siècle, par Andler and others. 1912. B5094
Picard, J. Essai sur la logique de l'invention dans les sciences. 1928. B5095
____. Essai sur les conditions positives de l'invention dans les sciences. 1928. B5096
____. Le monde du silence. 1954. B5097
Piéron, H. Le développement mental et l'intelligence. 1929. B5098
Pillon, F. La philosophie de Charles Secrétan. 1898. B5099
Pilo, M. La psychologie du beau et de l'art. 1895. B5100
Pioger, J. La vie sociale, la morale et le progrès. 1894. B5101
Polin, R. La compréhension des valeurs. 1945. B5102
Privat, E. Le choc des patriotismes. 1931. B5103
Proal, L. J. C. La criminalité politique. 1895. B5104
____. L'éducation et le suicide des enfants. 1907. B5105
____. La psychologie de Jean-Jacques Rousseau. 1930. B5106
Prudhommeau, M. Le dessin de l'enfant. 1947. B5107
Przyluski, J. Créer. 1943. B5108
____. L'évolution humaine. 1942. B5109
Psychologie du langage. 1933. B5110
Quercy, P. L'hallucination. 2 v. 1930. B5111
Queyrat, F. La curiosite. 1911. B5112
Rabaud, E. Eléments de biologie générale. 1928. B5113
____. Phénomène social et sociétés animales. 1937. B5114
Rabaud, R. Conduite sentiments, pensee des animaux. 1938. B5115
Radhakrishnan, S. L'Hindouisme et la vie. 1929. B5116
Rageot, G. Le succès... 1906. B5117
Rauh, F. Etudes de morale.

1911. B5118
____. La éxperience morale. 1903. B5119
____. De la méthode dans la psychologie des sentiments. 1899. B5120
Ravaisson-Mollien, F. De l'habitude. 1933. B5121
Ray, J. Essai sur la structure logique du Code civil français. 1926. B5122
____. Index du Code civil. 1926. B5123
Regnaud, P. Précis de logique évolutionniste. B5124
Remond, A. La génie littéraire. 1912. B5125
La renaissance religieuse, by Archambault and others. 1928. B5126
Renard, G. F. La méthode scientifique de l'histoire littéraire. 1900. B5127
____. La régime socialiste. 1903. B5128
Renouvier, C. B. Les dilemmes de la métaphysique pure. 1901. B5129
____. Histoire et solution des problèmes métaphysiques. 1901. B5130
____. La personnalisme suivi d'une étude sur la perception externe et sur la force. 1903. B5131
____. Science de la morale. 1908. B5132
Revault d'Allonnes, G. Les inclinations, leur rôle dans la psychologie des sentiments. 1907. B5133
Rey, A. L'énergetique et le mécanisme au point de vue des conditions de la connaissance. 1908. B5134
Ribot, T. A. Essai sur l'imagination créâtice. 1900. B5135
____. Essai sur les passions. 1910. B5136
____. L'évolution des idées générales. 1897. B5137
____. L'héredité psychologique. 1925. B5138
____. Les malades de la mémoire. 1936. B5139
____. Les maladies de la personalité. 1932. B5140
____. Les maladies de la volonté. 1936. B5141
____. La philosophie de Schopenhauer. 1905. B5142
____. Problèmes de psychologie affective. 1910. B5143
____. Psychologie de l'attention. 1938. B5144
____. La psychologie des sentiments. 1939. B5145
Richard, G. Le socialisme et la science sociale. 1909. B5146
Richet, C. R. Essai de psychologie générale. 1930. B5147
____. L'homme et l'intelligence. 1884. B5148
____. L'intelligence et l'homme. 1936. B5149
Rideau, E. Le dieu de Bergson. 1932. B5150
____. Les rapports de la matiere et de l'esprit dans le bergonisme. 1932. B5151
Riese, W. La pensée causale en medecine. 1950. B5152
Rignano, E. Essai de synthèse scientifique. B5153
____. Problèmes de psychologie et de morale. 1928. B5154
____. Qu'est-ce que la vie? 1926. B5155
____. Sur la transmissibilité des caractères acquis. 1906. B5156
Riley, I. W. Le génie américain. 1921. B5157
Rivaud, A. Les notion d'essence et d'existence dans la philosophie de Spinoza. 1906. B5158
Riveline, M. Essai sur le problème le plus général. 1939. B5159
Rivers, W. H. R. L'instinct et l'inconscient. 1926. B5160
Roberty, E. de. Agnosticisme. 1893. B5161
____. L'ancienne et la nouvelle philosophie. 1887. B5162
____. Auguste Comte et Herbert Spencer. 1895. B5163
____. Les concepts de la raison et les lois de l'univers. 1912. B5164
____. L'éthique. Constitution

de l'éthique... 1900. B5165
____. L'éthique. Le psychisme social... 1897. B5166
____. L'éthique. Les fondements de l'éthique... 1899. B5167
____. Frédéric Nietzsche. 1902. B5168
____. Nouveau programme de sociologie. 1904. B5169
____. Sociologie de l'action. 1908. B5170
Robin, L. La pensée hellénique des origines à Epicure. 1942. B5171
Rodrigues, G. Le problème de l'action; la pratique morale. 1909. B5172
Roehrich, E. Philosophie de l'éducation... 1910. B5173
Rogues de Fursac, J. L'avarice. 1911. B5174
Roisel, G. de. L'idée spiritualiste. 1896. B5175
____. La substance. 1881. B5176
Romanes, G. J. L'évolution mentale chez l'homme. 1891. B5177
Rosa, D. L'ologénèse. 1931. B5178
Rosny, J. H. Le pluralisme. 1909. B5179
Rougier, L. A. P. Les paralogismes du rationalisme. 1920. B5180
____. La structure des théories déductives. 1921. B5181
Roussel-Despierres, F. Le hiérachie des principes et des problèmes sociaux. 1912. B5182
____. Hors du scepticisme. 1907. B5183
____. L'idéal esthétique esquisse d'une philosophie de la beauté. 1904. B5184
Roustón, D. La raison et la vie. 1946. B5185
Russier, J. La foi selon Pascal. 2 v. in 1. 1952. B5186
Rusu, L. Essai sur la création artistique. 1935. B5187
Ruyer, R. La conscience et le corps. 1937. B5188
____. Esquisse d'une philosophie de les structure. 1930. B5189
____. L'humanité de l'avenir d'après Cournot. 1930. B5190
Ruyssen, T. De la guerre au croit. 1920. B5191
Sageret, J. Philosophie de la guerre et de la paix. 1919. B5192
Saigey, E. Les sciences au XVIIIe siècle. 1873. B5193
Saint-Paul, G. Le langage intérieur et les paraphasies. 1904. B5194
Saisset, E. E. Critique et histoire de la philosophie. 1865. B5195
Salzi, P. La sensation. 1934. B5196
Sartre, J. P. L'ontologie, ed. by Varet. B5197
Schinz, A. Anti-pragmatisme. 1909. B5198
____. La pensée de Jean-Jacques Rousseau. 1929. B5199
Schoebel, C. Philosophie de la raison pure. 1865. B5200
Schopenhauer, A. Aphorismus sur la sagesse dans la vie. 1943. B5201
____. Le fondement de la morale. 1885. B5202
____. Le monde comme volonté et comme represéntation. 1943. B5203
____. Parerga et Paralepomena. 1912. B5204
Schuhl, P. M. Essai sur la formation de la pensée grecque. 1947. B5205
____. Platon et l'art de son temps. 1952. B5206
Séailles, G. L'origine et les destinées de l'art. 1936. B5207
____. La philosophie de Charles Renouvier. 1905. B5208
____. La philosophie de Jules Lachelier. 1935. B5209
Segond, J. Cournot et la psychologie vitaliste. 1911. B5210
Segond, J. L. P. La guerre mondiale et la vie spirituelle. 1918. B5211
____. L'intuition bergsonienne. 1930. B5212
____. La prière... 1911. B5213
Seillière, E. A. A. L. Introduction à la philosophie de l'impérialisme. 1911. B5214
Serrus, C. L'esthétique transcendantale et la science

moderne. 1930. B5215
Shalom, A. R. G. Collingwood. 1967. B5216
Sighele, S. La foule criminelle... 1901. B5217
Simmel, G. Melanges de philosophie relativiste. 1912. B5218
Solberg, P. C. and Gros, G. C. Le droit et la doctrine de la justice. 1936. B5219
Sollier, P. Morale et moralité. 1912. B5220
____. Les phémonenes d'autocospie. 1903. B5221
____. Le problème de la mémoire. 1900. B5222
Sollier, P. A. La répression mentale. 1930. B5223
Souèges, R. La vie végétale. 1949. B5224
Souriau, E. L'abstraction sentimentale. 1951. B5225
____. L'avenir de l'esthétique. 1929. B5226
____. L'instauration philosophique. 1939. B5227
Souriau, M. La fonction pratique de la finalité. 1925. B5228
____. Pensée vivante et perfection formelle. 1953. B5229
Souriau, P. L'entrainement au courage. 1926. B5230
____. La suggestion dans la art. 1893. B5231
Spaier, A. La pensée concrète. 1927. B5232
____. La pensée et la quantité. 1927. B5233
Spencer, H. Classification des sciences. 1930. B5234
____. Une autobiography: de Varigny. 1907. B5235
____. De l'education intellectuelle, moral et physique. 1912. B5236
Spir, A. Esquisses de philosophie critique. 1930. B5237
Stapfer, P. Question esthétiques et religieuses. 1906. B5238
Stern, A. Philosophie du rire et des pleurs. 1948. B5239
Sully-Prudhomme, R. F. A. Le problème des causes finales. 1902. B5240
____. Psychologie du libre arbitre. 1907. B5241
____. La vraie religion selon Pascal. 1905. B5242
Taine, H. A. Philosophie de l'art. 1865. B5243
Tanon, C. L. L'evolution du droit et la conscience sociale. 1900. B5244
Tarde, G. de. La criminalité comparée. 1890. B5245
____. L'opinion et la foule. 1901. B5246
____. L'opposition universelle. 1897. B5247
____. Psychologie economique. 2 v. 1902. B5248
Tassy, E. L'activité psychique. 1931. B5249
____. Le travail d'ideation. 1911. B5250
Terraillon, E. L'honneur. 1912. B5251
Thomas, P. F. L'éducation des sentiments. 1907. B5252
Tonnies, F. Communauté et société. 1944. B5253
La tradition philosophique et la pensée française. 1922. B5254
Truc, G. Les sacrements. 1925. B5255
Urban, J. L'epithymologie, La desirologie. 1939. B5256
Urtin, H. L'action criminelle. 1911. B5257
Vaucher, G. Le langage affectif et les jugements de valeur. 1925. B5258
Vaysset-Boutbien, R. Stuart Mill et de sociologie française contemporaine. 1941. B5259
Vernon-Lee. Les mensonges vitaux. 1921. B5260
Vialle, L. Defense de la vie. 1938. B5261
____. Introduction à la vie imparfaite. 1947. B5262
Vianne de Lima, A. L'homme selon le transforisme. 1888. B5263
Vidal, A. Conscience de soi et structures mentales. 1943. B5264
Vilar-Fiol, D. L'homme et de milieu social. 1944. B5265
Violet-Concil, M. and Conivet, N. L'exploration expérimentale de la mentalité infantile. 1946. B5266
Vleeschauwer, H. J. de. L'évolution de la pensée

Kantienne. 1939. B5267
Vuillemin, J. Essai sur la signification de la mort. 1949. B5268
Wahl, J. A. La malheur de la conscience dans la philosophie de Hégél. 1951. B5269
____. Les philosophie pluralités d'Angleterre et d'Amérique. B5270
Weber, L. Vers le positivisme absolu par l'idéalisme. 1903. B5271
Wilbois, J. Les nouvelles mèthodes d'éducation. 1914. B5272
Winter, M. La méthode dans la philosophie des mathématiques. 1911. B5273
Zazzo, R. La devenir de l'intelligence. 1946. B5274

BIBLIOTHEQUE DE PHILOSOPHIE CONTEMPORAINE. HISTOIRE DE LA PHILOSOPHIE ET DE PHILOSOPHIE GENERALE (Presses Universitaires de France)

Alquié, F. La découverte métaphysique de l'homme chez Descartes. 1950. B5275
____. La nostalogie de l'être. 1950. B5276
Amado Levy-Valensi, E. La dialogue psychoanalytique. 1962. B5277
Anglès d'Auriac, J. Essai de philosophie générale. 2 v. 1954. B5278
Arbousse-Bastide, P. La doctrine del'education universelle dans la philosophie d'Auguste Comte. 2 v. 1957. B5279
Barcos, M. de. Correspondance, ed. by Goldmann. 1956. B5280
Blondel, M. Exigences philosophique du christianisme. 1950. B5281
Boussoulos, N. I. L'être et la composition des mixtes dans le "Philebe" de Platon. 1952. B5282
____. La peur et l'univers dans l'oeuvre d'Edgar Poe. 1952. B5283
Bréhier, E. Histoire de la philosophie. V. 2. 1957. B5284
Brunschvicg, L. Héritage de mots. 1945. B5285
____. Le progrès de la conscience dans la philosophie occidentale. 2 v. 1953. B5286
Burgelin, P. La philosophie de l'existence de J. J. Rousseau. 1952. B5287
Busson, H. La religion dés classiques (1668-1685). 1948. B5288
Cazeneuve, J. La philosophie médicale de Ravaisson. 1958. B5289
Chastaing, M. L'existence d'autrui. 1951. B5290
____. La philosophie de Virginia Woolf. 1951. B5291
Christoff, D. Recherche de la liberté. 1957. B5292
Clarke, S. Correspondance. 1957. B5293
Darbon, A. Etudes spinozistes. 1946. B5294
____. Une philosophie de l'experience. 1946. B5295
____. Philosophie de la volonté. 1951. B5296
Daudin, H. La liberté de la volonté. 1950. B5297
Daval, R. La métaphysique de Kant. 1950. B5298
Delhomme, J. Vie et conscience de la vie; essai sur Bergson. 1954. B5299
Derathé, R. Le rationalisme de J. J. Rousseau. 1948. B5300
Dumeige, G. Richard de Saint-Victor et l'idée chretienne de l'amour. 1952. B5301
Dussort, H. L'école de Marbowig, ed. by Vuillemin. 1963. B5302
Farber, M., ed. L'activité philosophique contemporaine en France et aux Etats-Unis. 2 v. 1950. B5303
Fauré-Frémiet, P. Equisse d'une philosophie concrète. 1954. B5304
____. L'univers non-dimensionnel et la vie qualitative. 1948. B5305
Garaudy, R. Perspectives de l'homme. 1959. B5306
Gérard, R. Les chemins divers

de la connaissance. 1945. B5307
Goldmann, L. La commuanté numaine et l'univers chez Kant. 1948. B5308
Goldschmidt, V. Les Dialogues de Platon. 1947. B5309
____. La parodigme dans la dialectique platonicienne. 1947. B5310
Gordon, P. L'image du monde dans antiquité. 1949. B5311
____. L'initiation sexuelle et l'évolution religieuse. 1945. B5312
Grua, G. Jurisprudence universelle et theodicée selon Leibniz. 1953. B5313
____. La justice humaine selon Leibniz. 1956. B5314
Husson, L. L'intellectualisme de Bergson. 1947. B5315
Jalabert, J. La théorie leibnizienne de la substance. 1947. B5316
Jankélevitch, V. Philosophie première. 1953. B5317
Kasm, B. L'idée de preuve en métaphysique. 1959. B5318
Krestovskaîa, L. A. Le problème spirituel de la beauté et de la laideur. 1948. B5319
Kucharski, P. Les chemins du savoir dans les derniers dialogues de Platon. 1949. B5320
Lacombe, R. E. L'apologetique de Pascal. 1958. B5321
Lacroix, J. Marxisme, existentialisme personnalisme; présence de l'éternité dans le temps. 1949. B5322
Lagneau, J. Célèbres leçons et fragments. 1950. B5323
Lahbabi, M. A. De l'être a la personne. 1954. B5324
Lamy, P. Le problème de la destinée. 1947. B5325
Laporte, J. M. F. Le rationalisme de Descartes. 1945. B5326
Lefeure, R. La bataille du "cognito." B5327
____. Le criticisme de Descartes. 1958. B5328
____. L'humanisme de Descartes. 1957. B5329
____. La vocation de Descartes. 1956. B5330
Leibniz, G. W. freiherr von. Lettres de Leibniz a Arnauld, ed. by Lewis. 1952. B5331
____. Principes de la nature de la grâce fondés en raison. Principes de la philosophie ou monadologie. 1954. B5332
____. Textes inédits d'après les manuscripts de la Bibliothèque provincale de Hanovre, ed. by Grus. 1948. B5333
LeRoy, E. Essai d'une philosophie première. V. 2. 2 v. 1956-58. B5334
Lewis, G. Le problème de l'inconscient et le cartesianisme. 1950. B5335
Magalhaes-Vilhena, V. de. Le problème de Socrate. 1952. B5336
____. Socrate et la légende platonicienne. 1952. B5337
Matisse, G. L'incoherénce universelle. 3 v. 1953-1956. B5338
Mauchaussat, G. La liberté spirituelle. 1959. B5339
Maydieu, A. J. La désaccord. 1952. B5340
Meyer, F. L'ontologie de Miguel Unamuno. 1955. B5341
Millet, L. Le symbolisme dans la philosophie de Lachelier. 1959. B5342
Moreau, J. L'horizon des esprits... 1960. B5343
Mossé-Bastide, R. M. Bergson et Platin. 1959. B5344
Mourelos, G. Bergson et les niveaux de realité. 1964. B5345
____. L'épistemologie positive et la critique meyersonienne. 1962. B5346
Moutsopoulos, E. La musique dans l'oeuvre de Platon. 1959. B5347
Mucchielli, R. Le mythe de la cité idéale. 1960. B5348
Muralt, A. de. L'idée de la phénoménologie. 1958. B5349
Nicod, J. Le problème logique de l'induction. 1961. B5350
Nogué, J. Le système de l'actualité. 1947. B5351
Paliard, J. La pensée et la vie. 1951. B5352

Papillault, G. Science française, scolastique allemonde. 1917. B5353
Perelman, C. and Olbrechts-Tyteca, L. Rhétorique et philosophie pour une théorie d l'argumentation en philosophie. 1952. B5354
Pètrement, P. Le dualisme chez Platon. 1947. B5355
Polin, R. Politique et philosophie chez Thomas Hobbes. 1952. B5356
____. La politique moral de John Locke. 1960. B5357
Portié, J. F. Essai d'exploration humaine. 1947. B5358
Ralea, M. Explication de l'homme. 1949. B5359
Robinet, A., ed. Correspondance Leibniz-Clarke presentée d'après les manuscrits originaux des bibliothèque de Hanoure et de Londres. 1957. B5360
Russier, J. Sagesse cartesienne et religion. 1958. B5361
Schuhl, P. M. Le dominateur et les possibles. 1960. B5362
____. Etudes platoniciennes. 1960. B5363
____. Etudes sur la fabulation platonicienne. 1947. B5364
____. Imaginer et réalise. 1963. B5365
Sellier, P. Pascal et la liturgie. 1966. B5366
Souriau, E. L'ombre de Dieu. 1948. B5367
Toulemont, R. L'essence de la societé selon Husserl. 1962. B5368
Trouillard, J. La procession plotinienne. 1955. B5369
Vallin, G. Etre et individualité. 1959. B5370
Varet, G. L'ontologie de Sartre. 1948. B5371
Vico, G. B. O'Euvres choises, tr. by Chaix-Ruy. 1946. B5372
Voelke, A. J. L'idee de volonté le stoicisme. 1973. B5373
Vuillemin, J. L'heritage kantien et la révolution copernicienne, Fichte, Cohen, Heidegger. 1954. B5374
____. Physique et metaphysique kantiennes. 1955. B5375

BIBLIOTHEQUE DE PHILOSOPHIE CONTEMPORAINE. LOGIQUE ET PHILOSOPHIE DES SCIENCES. (Presses Universitaires de France)

Bachelard, G. L'activité rationaliste de la physique contemporaine. 1951. B5376
____. La conscience de rationalité. 1958. B5377
____. La matérialisme rationnel. 1952. B5378
____. La poétique de l'espace. 1957. B5379
____. La poétique de la rêverie. 1960. B5380
____. Le rationalisme appliqué. 1949. B5381
Bernard, C. Principes de médecine expérimentale. 1947. B5382
Blanché, R. La science physique et la réalité. 1948. B5383
Boirel, R. Théorie générale de l'invention. 1961. B5384
Bonnot, L. Essai sur les fondaments de la logique et sur la méthodologie causale. 1943. B5385
Bounoure, L. L'autonomie de l'être vivant. 1949. B5386
Bujeau, L. V. La philosophie entomologique de J. H. Fabre. 1943. B5387
Callot, E. La renaissance des sciences de la vie au XVIe siècle. 1951. B5388
Canguilhem, G. La formation du concept de réflexe au XVIIe et XVIIIe siècle. 1955. B5388a
Cavaillès, J. Sur la logique et la théorie de la science. 1960. B5389
Chauchard, P. La maîtrise du comportement. 1956. B5390
Darbon, A. Les catégories de la modalité. 1956. B5391
____. Une doctrine de l'infini. 1951. B5392
____. La philosophie des mathématiques. 1949. B5393
Daujat, J. L'oeuvre de l'intelligence en physique. 1946. B5394
Daumas, M. Les instruments

scientifiques aux XVIIe et XVIIIe siècles. 1953. B5395
____. Lavoisier. 1955. B5396
David, A. Structure de la personne humaine. 1955. B5397
Desargues, G. L'oeuvre mathématique de G. Desargues, ed. by Taton. 1951. B5398
Dorolle, M. Le raisonnement par analogie. 1949. B5399
Garaudy, R. La théorie matérialiste de la connaissance. 1953. B5400
Granger, G. G. Méthodologie economique. 1955. B5401
Herbrand, J. Ecrits logiques. 1968. B5402
LeRoy, E. L. E. J. La pensée mathématique pure. 1960. B5403
Lupasco, S. Logique et contradiction. 1947. B5404
Matisse, G. Le rameau vivant du monde. 3 v. 1947-49. B5405
Meyer, F. Problématique de l'évolution. 1954. B5406
Mierlo, S. van. La science, la raison et la foi. 1948. B5407
Moyse, A. Biologie et physicochimie. 1948. B5408
Nicod, J. La géometrie dans le monde sensible. 1962. B5409
Nogaro, B. La valeur logique des theorie économiques. 1947. B5410
Piaget, J. Essai sur les transformations des opérations logiques. 1952. B5411
____. Introduction à la epistémologie génétique. 3 v. 1950. B5412
Pinel, E. La méthode statistique en médecine. 1945. B5413
Ruyer, R. Eléments de psychobiologie. 1946. B5414
____. Néo-finalisme. 1952. B5415
Taton, R. L'oeuvre scientifique de Monge. 1951. B5416

BIBLIOTHEQUE DE PHILOSOPHIE CONTEMPORAINE. MORALE ET VALEURS (Presses Universitaires de France)

Anglès d'Auriac, J. Essai de philosophie générale. 1954. B5417
Bastide, G. Méditations pour une éthique de la personne. 1953. B5418
Bloch, M. A. Philosophie de l'education nouvelle. 1948. B5419
____. Les tendances de la vie morale. 1948. B5420
Carré, J. B. Le point d'appui pris sur le néant. 1955. B5421
Castelli, E. La temps harclent. 1952. B5422
Chou, Y. La philosophie morale dans le néo-confucianisme. 1954. B5423
Croce, B. La poésie. 1950. B5424
Cuvelier, A. La musique et l'homme. 1949. B5425
Daval, R. La valeur morale. 1950. B5426
Deshaies, G. L'esthétique du pathologie. 1947. B5427
Duméry, H. Blondel et la religion. 1954. B5428
____. Philosophie et la religion. 1957. B5429
Etcheverry, A. La conflict actuel des humanismes. 1955. B5430
Gusdorf, G. Mémoire et personne. 2 v. 1950. B5431
Jankélévitch, V. L'ironie ou la bonne conscience. 1950. B5432
Madinier, G. Conscience et signification. 1953. B5433
Masson-Oursel, P. La morale et l'histoire. 1955. B5434
Nabert, J. Eléments pour une ethique. 1943. B5435
Polin, R. La création des valeurs. 1953. B5436
____. Du laid, du mal, du faux. 1948. B5437
Riesse, W. La pensée morale en medécine. 1954. B5438
Russier, J. Sagesse cartésienne et religion. 1958. B5439

BIBLIOTHEQUE DE PHILOSOPHIE CONTEMPORAINE. PSYCHOLOGIE ET SOCIOLOGIE (Presses Universitaires de France)

Adolphe, L. La dialectique des images chez Bergson.

1951. B5440
Baruk, H. La désorganisation de la personnalité. 1952. B5441
Bize, P. R. L'évolution psycho-physiologique de l'enfant. 1950. B5442
Bonnardel, R. L'adaptation de l'homme à son métier. 1946. B5443
Bouteiller, M. Chamanisme et guérison magique. 1950. B5444
Boutonier, J. L'angoisse. 1945. B5445
____. Les défaillances de la volonté. 1945. B5446
Brelet, G. Le temps musical. 2 v. 1949. B5447
Buytendijk, F. J. J. De la douleur. 1951. B5448
Cavé, M. L'oeuvre paradoxale de Freud. 1945. B5449
Cazeneuve, J. Essai sur la psychologie du prisonnier de guerre. 1944. B5450
Colanéri, L. J. La dénonciation et les dénonciateurs. 1948. B5451
Delay, J. P. L. Les dérèglements de l'humeur. 1946. B5452
Deschoux, M. Essai sur la personalité. 1949. B5453
Deshaies, G. Psychologie du suicide. 1947. B5454
Desoilles, R. Le rêve éveillé en psychothérapie. 1945. B5455
Diel, P. La divinité. 1950. B5456
____. Psychologie de la motivation. 1948. B5457
Forti, E. L'emotion, la volonté et le couràge. 1952. B5458
Galichet, G. Essai de grammaire psychologique. 1947. B5459
____. Méthodologie grammaticale. 1953. B5460
Grappe, J. La genèse réciproque. 1949. B5461-4
Greeff, E. de. Les instincts de défense et de sympathie. 1947. B5465
Gusdorf, G. La découverte de soi. 1948. B5466
____. La expérience humaine du sacrifice. 1948. B5467
Henri, P. Les aveugles et la société. 1958. B5468
Hubert, R. La croissance mentale. 1949. B5469
Inhelder, B. and Piaget, J. De la logique de l'enfant a la logique, de l'adolescent. 1955. B5470
Konczewski, C. La sympathie comme fonctions de progrès et de connaissance. 1951. B5471
Lagache, D. La jalousie amoureuse. 2 v. 1947. B5472
Leplae, C. Les fiancailles. 1947. B5473
Levi-Strauss, C. Les structures élémentaires de la parenté. 1949. B5474
Ley, A. C. Etudes de psychologie instinctive et affective. 1946. B5475
Lucques, C. Un problème de lèxpression. 1948. B5476
Maine de Biran, P. Influence de l'habitude sur la faculté de penséer. 1954. B5477
Malgaud, W. Devant la réalité. 1953. B5478
Malrieu, P. Les origines de la conscience du temps. Les attitudes temporalles de l'enfant. 1952. B5479
Merleau-Ponty, M. La structure du comportement. 1963. B5480
Navratil, M. Introduction critique à une découverte de la pensée. 1954. B5481
____. Les tendences constitutives de la pensée vivante. 2 v. 1954. B5482
Ohana, J. La chance. 1948. B5483
Oldenberg, H. La religion du Véda. 1903. B5484
Piaget, J. La développement de la notion de temps chez l'enfant. 1946. B5485
____. La géometrié spontanée de l'enfant. 1948. B5486
____. Les notions de mouvement et de vitesse chez l'enfant. 1946. B5487
____. La représentation de l'espance chez l'enfant. 1948. B5488
Piaget, J. and Inhelder, B. La genese de l'idée de hasard chez l'enfant. 1951. B5489
Prudhommeau, M. Le dessin

de l'enfant. 1947. B5490
Ruyer, R. L'utopie et les utopies. 1950. B5491
Ruyssen, T. La société internationale. 1950. B5492
Stoetzel, J. L'étude expérimentale des opinions. 1943. B5493
____. Théorie des opinions. 1943. B5494
Victoroff, D. G. H. Mead. 1953. B5495
____. Le rire et le risible. 1953. B5496
Vidal, A. Conscience de soi et structures mentales. 1943. B5497
Vuillard, E. L'être et le travail, les-conditions dialectiques de la psychologie et de la sociologie. 1949. B5498
Wallon, G. H. Les notions morales chez l'enfant. 1949. B5499
____. Les origines de la pensée chez l'enfant. 2 v. 1945. B5500
____. Les origines du caractère chez l'enfant. 1954. B5501
Wallon, H. and Evart-Chemelinski, E. Les mécanismes de la mémoire en rapport avec ses objets. 1951. B5502
Witwicki, W. La foi des éclairés. 1939. B5503
Zazzo, R. Intelligence et quotient d'âges. 1946. B5504

BIBLIOTHEQUE DE PHILOSOPHIE SCIENTIFIQUE (Flammarion)

Achille-Delmas, F. La personnalité humaine. 1935. B5505
Aegerter, E. Le mysticisme. 1952. B5506
Aleksinskiĭ, G. A. La Russie et l'Europe. 1917. B5507
____. La Russie moderne. 1917. B5508
Alquié, F. Philosophie du surréalisme. 1956. B5509
Apert, E. La croissance. 1921. B5510
____. L'hérédité morbide. 1919. B5511
Ardant, H. Les crises économiques. 1948. B5512
Auger, P. L'homme microscopique. B5513
Auriac, J. E. La nationalité française. 1913. B5514
Avenel, G. Découvertes d'histoire sociale, 1200-1910. 1910. B5515
____. L'évolution des moyens de transport. 1919. B5516
____. L'nivellement des jouissances. 1913. B5517
Ayer, A. J. Langage, vérité et logique. 1955. B5518
Bachelier, J. B. B. A. Le jeiv, la chance et la hasard. 1914. B5519
Baldensperger, F. La littérature. 1913. B5520
Barbier, D. Les atmosphères stellaires. B5521
Batiffol, L. Les anciennes républiques alsaciennes. 1918. B5522
Bellet, D. L'évolution de l'industrie. 1914. B5523
____. Le mépris des lois et ses conséquences sociales. 1918. B5524
Berget, A. Les problèmes de l'atmosphère. 1914. B5525
____. Les problèmes de l'ocean. 1920. B5526
____. La vie et la mort du globe. 1912. B5527
Bergson, H. L. Le matérialisme actuel. 1913. B5528
Bertin, L. E. La marine moderne. 1914. B5529
Bertrand, L. Histoire géologique du sol français. 2 v. 1935. B5530
Bigourdan, G. L'astronomie. 1911. B5531
Binet, A. L'âme et le corps. 1907. B5532
____. Les idées modernes sur les enfants. 1909. B5533
Binet, L. and others. Les grandes découvertes françaises en biologie médicale. B5534
Biottot, L. V. Les grands inspires devants la science. 1907. B5535
Blaringhem, L. Les problèmes de la hérédité expérimentale. 1919. B5536
____. Les transformations brusques des êtras vivants. 1911. B5537
Bloch, G. L'empire romain. 1922. B5538

____. L'république romaine. 1913. B5539
Blondel, M. Lutte pour la civilisation et philosophie de la paix. 1947. B5540
Bohn, G. La chimie et la vie. 1920. B5541
____. La naissance de l'intelligence. 1910. B5542
Bonaparte, M. Guerres militaires et guerres sociales. 1920. B5543
Bonnier, G. E. M. Le monde végétal. 1907. B5544
Bonnier, P. Défense organique et centres nerveux. 1914. B5545
Bordet, J. Infection et immunité. 1947. B5546
Borel, E. L'évolution de la mécanique. 1943. B5547
Borghese, G. B. L'Italie moderne. 1913. B5548
Boubier, M. L'oiseau et son milieu. 1922. B5549
Bouché-Leclerq, A. L'intolérance religieuse et la politique. 1911. B5550
Bouchet, H. Introduction à la philosophie de l'individu. 1949. B5551
Bounhoil, J. P. La vie. 1927. B5552
Bournoure, L. Déterminisme et finalité. 1956. B5553
____. Héredité et physiologie du sexe. 1948. B5554
____. Reproduction sexuelle et histoire naturelle du sexe. 1947. B5555
Boutaric, A. M. A. Au seuil de l'ere atomique. 1948. B5556
____. La chaleur et le froid. 1927. B5557
____. Les conceptions actuelles de la physique. 1936. B5558
____. La lumière et les radiations invisibles. 1925. B5559
____. Les ondes hertziennes et la téléphrophie sans fils. 1929. B5560
____. La vie des atomes. 1923. B5561
Boutroux, E. Morale et religion. 1925. B5562
____. Science et religion dans la philosophie contemporaine. 1917. B5563
Bouvier, E. L. Le communisme chez les insectes. 1926. B5564
____. Habitudes et métamorphoses des insectes. 1921. B5565
____. La vie psychique des insectes. 1918. B5566
Bouvier, R. La caoutchouc. 1948. B5567
____. Les migrations végétales. 1945. B5568
Bréhier, E. Transformation de la philosophie française. 1950. B5569
Broglie, L. de. La physique nouvelle et les quanta. 1952. B5570
Broglie, M. de. Atomes, radioactivité, transmutations. 1939. B5571
Brunhes, B. La degradation de l'énergie. 1908. B5572
Bruyssel, E. J. van. La vie sociale et ses évolutions. 1907. B5573
Burnet, E. Microbes et toxines. 1911. B5574
Caullery, M. J. G. C. La conceptions moderne de l'hérédité. 1935. B5575
____. Les problèmes de la sexualité. 1913. B5576
____. Les progrès récents de l'embryologie expérimentale. 1939. B5577
Cazamian, L. L'Angleterre moderne. 1911. B5578
____. La Grande-Bretagne et la guerre. 1917. B5579
Ce que la France a apporte à la médecine depuis le debut du XXe siècle, by Alajouanine and others. B5580
Césari, P. La valeur de la connaissance scientifique. 1960. B5581
Champy, C. La vie cellulaire. 1917. B5582
Chanlaine, P. Les horizons de la science. 1928. B5583
Charles, R. L'âme musulmane. 1958. B5584
Charriaut, H. La Beligique moderne. 1910. B5585
Charriaut, H. and Grossi, A. L'Italie en guerre. 1920. B5586
Chauchard, P. Le sommeil

et les états de sommeil. 1947. B5587
Chavigny, P. M. V. Psychologie de l'hygiene. 1921. B5588
Chevalier, J. L'organisation du travail. 1946. B5589
____. La vie morale et l'au-delà. 1941. B5590
Claparède, E. Comment diagnostiquer les aptitudes chez les écoliers. 1948. B5591
Coculesco, P. S. Science et poésie. 1947. B5592
Colerus, E. De la table de multiplication à l'integrale. 1952. B5593
____. De Pythagore à Hilbert. 1943. B5594
____. Du point à la quatrième dimension. 1957. B5595
Colin, H. La chimie des plantes. 1945. B5596
Colin, J. L. A. Les grandes batailles de l'histoire. 1915. B5597
____. Les transformation de la guerre. 1911. B5598
Colson, A. J. L'essor de la chimie appliquée. 1910. B5599
____. Organisme économique et désorde social. 1912. B5600
Combarieu, J. La musique, ses lois, son évolution. 1907. B5601
Conklin, E. G. L'hérédité et le milely... 1920. B5602
Croiset, A. Les démocraties antiques. 1909. B5603
Cruet, J. La vie du droit et l'impuissance des lois. 1908. B5604
Cuénot, L. C. M. J. Invention finalité en biologie. 1941. B5605
Dastre, A. La vie et la mort. 1920. B5606
Dauvillier, A. La physique cosmique. 1912. B5607
Dauzat, A. La géographie linguistique. 1944. B5608
____. L'philosophie du langage. 1912. B5609
Delage, Y. La parthéonogènese naturelle et expérimentale. 1913. B5610
____. La science et la réalité. 1913. B5611
____. Les théories de l'évolution. 1909. B5612
Delmas, F. A. La personnalité humaine. 1922. B5613
Demolon, A. L'évolution scientifique et l'agriculture française. 1946. B5614
Deonna, W. L'archéologie, son domaine, son but. 1922. B5615
Depéret, C. J. J. Les transformations du monde animal. 1907. B5616
Dide, M. L'hystérie et l'évolution humaine. 1935. B5617
Diehl, C. Byzance. 1919. B5618
____. Une république particienne, Venise. 1915. B5619
Dognon, A. Biologie et médecine devant la science exacte. 1948. B5620
Dromard, G. La rêve et l'action. 1913. B5621
Dubufe, G. La valeur de l'art. 1908. B5622
Duclaux, J. L'homme devant l'univers. 1949. B5623
____. La science de l'incertitude. 1959. B5624
Dugas, L. La mémoire et l'oubli. 1917. B5625
Dumas, G. La vie affective. 1948. B5626
Dumont-Wilden, L. L'évolution de l'espirit européen. 1945. B5627
Dwelshauvers, G. L'inconscient. 1919. B5628
Einstein, A. Comment je vois le monde. 1934. B5629
____. Conceptions scientifiques, morales et sociales. 1954. B5630
Einstein, A. and Infeld, L. L'évolution des idées en physique. 1938. B5631
Enriques, F. Les concepts fond amentaux de la science. 1913. B5632
L'évolution des sciences physiques et mathématiques. 1935. B5633
L'évolution humaine, by Anthony and others. 1957. B5634
Fabry, C. Physique et astrophysique. 1935. B5635
Ferrando, R. Alimentation et équilibre biologique. 1961. B5636
La France et la civilisation

contemporaine. 1941. B5637
Frank, P. Le principe de causalité et ses limites. 1937. B5638
Friedel, J. Personnalité biologique de l'homme. 1921. B5639
Garcia Calderon, E. Les démocraties latines de l'Amérique. 1912. B5640
Gascouin, F. E. L'évolution de l'artillerie pendant la guerre. 1920. B5641
Gaudefroy-Demombynes, M. Les institutions musulmanes. 1921. B5642
Gaultier, P. L'âme française. 1936. B5643
____. Leçons morales de la guerre. 1919. B5644
____. Les défants du caractère. 1957. B5645
Gennep, A. van. La formation des légendes. 1910. B5646
Girardeau, E. F. Les aventures de la science. 1957. B5647
Gramont, A. A. A. de. Problèmes de la vision. 1939. B5648
Grasset, J. La biologie humaine. 1917. B5649
Guiart, J. Les parasites, inoculateurs de maladies. 1911. B5650
Guichard, M. La genèse et la valeur de la connaissance positive. 1950. B5651
Guignebert, C. A. H. Le christianisme antique. 1921. B5652
____. Le Christianisme, médiéval et moderne. 1922. B5653
____. L'évolution des dogmes. 1910. B5654
Guillaume, P. La psychologie de la forme. 1937. B5655
Guilleminot, H. La matière et la vie. 1919. B5656
Guillet, L. Les grands problèmes de la métallurgie moderne. 1943. B5657
Gusdorf, G. Mythe et metaphysique. 1953. B5658
Hachet-Souplet, P. La genèse des instincts. 1912. B5659
Hanotaux, G. La démocratie et de travail. 1910. B5660
Harmand, J. Domination et colonisation. 1910. B5661
Herelle, F. d'. Les defenses de l'organisme. 1923. B5662
Héricourt, J. Les frontières de la maladie. 1904. B5663
____. L'hygiène moderne. 1907. B5664
____. Les maladies des sociétés. 1918. B5665
____. Le terrain dans les maladies. 1927. B5666
Hesnard, A. L. M. Les psychoses et les frontières de la folie. 1924. B5667
Hill, D. J. L'état moderne et l'organisation internationale. 1912. B5668
Hjort, J. La crise de la vérité. 1934. B5669
Homo, L. P. Problèmes sociaux de jardis et d'a présent. 1922. B5670
Hourticq, L. L'art et la science. 1943. B5671
____. L'art et la littérature. 1946. B5672
Houssay, F. A. C. A. Force et acuse. 1920. B5673
____. Nature et sciences naturelles. 1903. B5674
Hovelaque, E. L. Les peuples d'Extrême-Orient. La Chine. 1920. B5675
____. La Japon. 1921. B5676
Howard, L. O. La menace des insectes. 1935. B5677
Hubert, R. Les interpretations de la guerre. 1919. B5678
Humbert, P. Philosophes et savants. 1953. B5679
Les Initiateurs français en pathologie infectieuse, by Bernard and others. 1942. B5680
Introduction a l'étude scientifique du rire, by Berge and others. 1959. B5681
James, E. Histoire des théories économiques. 1950. B5682
James, W. Le pragmatisme, ed. by Bergson. 1911. B5683
Janet, P. M. F. Les débuts de la intelligence. 1935. B5684
____. L'intelligence avant la langue. 1936. B5685
____. La médicine psychologie. 1923. B5686
____. La névroses. 1919. B5687
Jankélévitch, V. L'austérite

et la vie morale. 1956. B5688
Javillier, M. Les éléments chimiques et le monde vivant. 1952. B5689
Joleaud, L. Les temps préhistoriques. 1945. B5690
Jolly, J. Le sang dans la vie de l'organisme. 1946. B5691
Joly, H. Le droit féminin. 1922. B5692
Joteyko, J. La fatigue. 1920. B5693
Joubain, L. M. A. O. E. La vie dans les océans. 1916. B5694
Joussain, A. La loi des révolutions. 1950. B5695
____. Les mystères de la vie... 1958. B5696
____. Les passions humaines. 1928. B5697
____. Psychologie des masses. 1937. B5698
____. Les sentiments et l'intelligence. 1930. B5699
____. La sociologie. 1945. B5700
Juillot, C. L. L'education de la mémoire. 1919. B5701
Lalo, C. Esthétique du rire. 1949. B5702
Lamouche, A. La destinée humaine. 1959. B5703
Lapicque, L. La machine nerveuse. 1943. B5704
Laporte, J. La conscience de la liberté. 1947. B5705
Laskine, E. Le socialisme suivant les peuples. 1920. B5706
Launay, L. de. Le conquête minérale. 1908. B5707
____. L'histoire de la terre. 1906. B5708
Lavelle, L. Les puissances du moi. 1948. B5709
LeBon, G. Bases scientifiques d'une philosophie de l'histoire. 1931. B5710
____. La déséquilibre du monde. 1923. B5711
____. Enseignements psychologiques de la guerre europêene. 1915. B5712
____. L'évolution actuelle du monde. 1927. B5713
____. L'évolution de la matière. 1905. B5714
____. L'évolution des forces. 1907. B5715
____. Hiér et demain, pensées brèves. 1918. B5716
____. Les opinions et les croyances. 1911. B5717
____. Premières conséquences de la guerre. 1916. B5718
____. Psychologie de l'éducation. 1927. B5719
____. Psychologie des temps nouveaux. 1920. B5720
____. La psychologie politique et la défense sociale. révo- 1910. B5721
____. La révolution française et la psychologie des révolutions. 1912. B5722
____. La vie des verités. 1914. B5723
Lecène, P. L'évolution de la chirurgie. 1923. B5724
LeChatelier, H. L. Science et industrie. 1925. B5725
LeClerc du Sablon, M. Les incertitudes de la biologie. 1912. B5726
Lecomte du Noüy, P. L'homme devant la science. 1939. B5727
Lecornu, L. F. A. La mécanique. 1918. B5728
LeDantec, F. A. L'athéisme. 1907. B5729
____. De l'homme à la science. 1907. B5730
____. L'egoïsme seule base de toute société. 1911. B5731
____. Les influences ancestrales. 1914. B5732
____. La lutte universelle. 1906. B5733
____. Savoir! 1917. B5734
____. La science de la vie. 1912. B5735
____. Science et conscience. 1908. B5736
Léger, L. Le panslavisme et l'intérêt français. 1917. B5737
Legrand, M. A. H. A. La longévité à travers les âges. 1911. B5738
Legras, J. L'âme russe. 1934. B5739
Le Lannou, M. La géographie humaine. 1949. B5740
Leprince-Ringuet, F. L'avenir de l'Asia russe. 1951. B5741
Leriche, R. La philosophie

de la chirurgie. 1951. B5742
Le Senne, R. La destinée personnelle. 1951. B5743
Lichtenberger, H. L'allemagne moderne, son évolution. 1908. B5744
____. L'impérialisme économique allemand. 1918. B5745
Locard, E. L'enquête criminelle et les méthodes scientifiques. 1920. B5746
Lombardi, F. Naissance du monde moderne. 1959. B5747
Lombroso, C. Hypnotisme et spiritisme. 1910. B5748
Luchaire, J. Les démocraties italiennes. 1915. B5749
Macdonald, J. R. Le socialisme et la société. 1922. B5750
Mach, E. La connaissance et l'erreur. 1908. B5751
Marchadier, A. L. Les poisons méconnus. 1921. B5752
Marie, A. La psychanalyse et les nouvelles méthodes d'investigation de l'inconscient. 1928. B5753
Marlio, L. Dictature ou liberté. 1940. B5754
____. Le sort du capitalisme. 1938. B5755
Martel, E. A. L'évolution souterraine. 1908. B5756
Martial, R. Les métis. 1942. B5757
Martin, G. and Simon, P. Le chef d'entreprise. 1946. B5758
Maurain, C. La météorologie et ses applications. 1950. B5759
Maurin, L. F. T. L'armée moderne. 1938. B5760
Maxwell, J. Le crime et la société. 1909. B5761
____. La divination. 1927. B5762
____. La magie. 1922. B5763
Mayer, E. La psychologie du commandement. 1924. B5764
Metal'nikov, S. I. Immoralité et rajeunissemént dans la biologie moderne. 1924. B5765
Meunier, S. Les glaciers et les montagnes. 1920. B5766
____. Histoire geologique de la mer. 1917. B5767
Michels, R. Les parties politiques. 1914. B5768
Mireaux, E. Philosophie du libéralisme. 1949. B5769
Moch, G. La relativité des phénomènes. 1921. B5770
Munson, E. L. Le maniement des hommes. 1951. B5771
Muzet, A. Le monde balkanique. 1917. B5772
Naudeau, L. La guerre et la Paix. 1926. B5773
____. Le Japon moderne. 1909. B5774
Ollivier, E. Philosophie d'une guerre. 1911. B5775
Ostwald, W. L'évolution d'une science, la chimie. 1909. B5776
____. Les grands hommes. 1912. B5777
Pasteur, V.-R. Quelques grands problèmes de la médecine contemporaine. 1936. B5778
Paulhan, F. Les transformations sociales des sentiments. 1920. B5779
Pellegrin, F. L. L. La vie d'une armée pendant la grande guerre. 1921. B5780
Perret, J. L'orientation professionnelle. 1926. B5781
Perrier, E. A traverse le monde vivant. 1916. B5782
____. La vie en action. 1918. B5783
Picard, E. Les constantes du droit. 1921. B5784
____. Le droit pur. 1908. B5785
____. La science moderne et son état actuel. 1909. B5786
Picavet, C. Une démocratie historique: la Suisse. 1920. B5787
Piéron, H. L'évolution de la mémoire. 1910. B5788
Pirenne, H. Les anciennes démocraties des Pays-Bas. 1910. B5789
Planck, M. K. E. L. Initiationes a la physique. 1941. B5790
Poincaré, H. Dernières pensées. 1920. B5791
____. Science et méthode. 1908. B5792
____. La science et l'hypothese. 1948. B5793
____. La valeur de la science. 1914. B5794

Poincaré, L. A. Education, science, patrie. 1926. B5795
____. L'électricité. 1907. B5796
____. La physique moderne. 1906. B5797
Porak, R. L'âme chinoise. 1950. B5798
Portier, P. J. Physiologie des animaux marins. 1938. B5799
Pradines, M. L'aventure de l'esprit dans les espèces. 1955. B5800
Rabaud, E. Le hasard et la vie des espèces. 1953. B5801
____. Transformisme et adaptation. 1942. B5802
Rageot, G. La natalité. 1918. B5803
Raphaël, G. L'industrie allemande. 1928. B5804
Reichenbach, H. L'avènement de la philosophie scientifique. 1955. B5805
Renard, P. L'áeronatique. 1909. B5806
____. Le vol mécanique des áeroplanes. 1912. B5807
Renou, L. La civilisation de l'Inde ancienne. 1950. B5808
Rey, A. La philosophie moderne. 1919. B5809
____. Le retour éternel et la philosophie de la physique. 1927. B5810
Reynaud, L. L'âme allemande. 1934. B5811
____. La démocratie en France. 1938. B5812
Rignano, E. La mémoire biologique. 1923. B5813
Roger, G. E. H. Physiologie de l'instinct et de l'intelligence. 1941. B5814
Rothé, E. E. Les tremblements de terre. 1942. B5815
Rouch, J. La Mediterranée. 1946. B5816
____. La mer. 1939. B5817
____. Les mers polaires. 1954. B5818
Rougier, L. A. P. La métaphysique et la langage. 1960. B5819
____. La mystique démocratique. 1929. B5820
Roule, L. Biologie des poissons. 1942. B5821
Roux, E. Energie électrique et civilisation. 1945. B5822
Roz, F. L'Amérique nouvelle. 1923. B5823
____. L'énergie américaine. 1910. B5824
____. L'évolution des idées et des moeurs américaines. 1931. B5825
Russell, B. Signification et vérité. 1959. B5826
Ruyer, R. La cybernétique et l'origine de l'information. 1954. B5827
____. La genèse des formes vivantes. 1958. B5828
Schuhl, P. M. Le merveilleux. 1952. B5829
Sée, H. E. Evolution et révolutions. 1929. B5830
Segond, J. L. P. Le problème du génie. 1930. B5831
Servien, P. Science et poésie. 1948. B5832
Sforza, C. L'âme italienne. 1934. B5833
Simart, M. Interprétation du monde moderne. 1930. B5834
Sorre, M. Les migrations des peuples. 1955. B5835
Souèges, R. La vie végétale. 2 v. 1949. B5836
Souriau, E. La correspondance des arts. 1947. B5837
Stromberg, G. L'âme de l'univers. 1950. B5838
Tissié, P. A. L'éducation physique et la race. 1911. B5839
Ullmo, J. La pensée scientifique moderne. 1958. B5840
Urbain, A. Psychologie des animaux sauvages. 1940. B5841
Vallery-Radot, P. Les grands problèmes de la médecine contemporaine. 1936. B5842
Vaschide, N. Les sommeil et les rêves. 1911. B5843
Vernes, A. Mesure et médecine. 1943. B5844
Vernet, M. L'âme et la vie. 1955. B5845
____. La sensibilité organique. 1949. B5846
____. La vie et la mort. 1952. B5847
Villey-Desmeserets, P. L. J. L'avengle dans le monde

des voyants. 1914. B5848
____. Le monde des aveugles. 1914. B5849
Wahl, J. La pensée de l'existence. 1951. B5850
Wallon, H. De l'acte à la pensée. 1942. B5851
Waltz, R. La création poétique. 1953. B5852
Weizsacker, F. von. Le monde vu par la physique. 1956. B5853
Zolla, D. L'agriculture moderne. 1913. B5854

BIBLIOTHEQUE DE PSYCHIATRIE (Presses Universitaires de France)

Alexander, F. and French, T. M. Psychothérapie analytique. 1958. B5855
Barrucand, D. Histoire de l'hypnose en France. 1967. B5856
Baruk, H. Psychiatrie morale expérimentale, individuelle et sociale. 1950. B5857
____, and Bachet, M. La test "tsedek," le jugement moral et la délinquance. 1950. B5858
Borel, J. Le déséquilibre psychique. 1947. B5859
Clerambauldt, G. G. de. Oeuvre psychiatrique. 2 v. 1942. B5860
Delay, J. P. L. Aspects de la psychiatrie moderne. 1950. B5861
____. Etudes de psychologie médicale. 1953. B5862
____. La test Rorschach et la personalité epilituque. 1954. B5863
English, O. S. and Pearson, G. H. J. Problèmes émotionnels de l'existence. 1955. B5864
Faure, H. Les objets dans le folie. 2 v. 1969. B5865
Gaillat, R. Analyse caractérielle des élèves d'une classe par leur maître. 1952. B5866
Grinker, R. R. and Robbins, F. P. Cliniques psychosomatiques. 1958. B5867
Hebb, D. O. Psycho-physiologie du comportement. 1958. B5868
Henderson, D. K. and Gillespie, R. D. Manuel de psychiatrie pour les étudiants et les practicians. 2 v. 1955. B5869
Jaspers, K. ... De la psychothérapie, tr. by Naef. 1958. B5870
Lanteri-Laura, G. La psychiatrie phenomenlogique. 1963. B5871
Logre, B. J. Psychiatrie clinique. 1962. B5872
Masserman, J. H. Principes de psychiatrie dynamique. 1956. B5873
Mira y Lopez, E. Manuel de psychologie juridique. 1958. B5874
Mucchielli, R. Caractères et visages. 1954. B5875
Oswald, I. Le sommeil et la veille. 1966. B5876
Pichot, P. Les test mentaux en psychiatrie. 1949- B5877
Porot, A. and others. Manuel alpabétique de psychiatrie clinique, thérapeutique et médicolégale. 1953. B5878
Sargant, W. W. Physiologie de la conversion religieuse et politique. 1967. B5879
____ and others. Introduction aux méthodes biologiques de traitement en psychiatrie. 1952. B5880
Schneider, K. Les personalitiés psychopathetiques. 1955. B5881
Schultz, J. H. Le training autogène. 1958. B5882
Schwartz, L. Les névroses et la psychologie dynamique de Pierre Janet. 1955. B5883
Slavson, S. R. Psychotherapie analytique de groupe. 1954. B5884
Szondi, L. Diagnostic expérimental des pulsions. 1953. B5885
Torris, G. L'acte médical et le caractère du malade. 1954. B5886
Tramer, M. Manuel de psychiatrie infantile générale. 1949. B5887
Tullio, B. di. Principes de criminologie clinique. 1967. B5888
Volmat, R. L'art

psychopatholigique. 1955. B5889
Wortis, J. La psychiatrie sovietique, tr. by Thomas. 1950. B5890
Wyrsch, J. La personne du schizophrène. 1956. B5891

BIBLIOTHEQUE DE PSYCHOANALYSE ET DE PSYCHOLOGIE CLINIQUE (Presses Universitaires de France)

Anzieu, D. L'auto-analyse. 1959. B5892
____. Le psychodrame analytique chez l'enfant. 1956. B5893
Balint, M. Le médicin, son malade et la maladie. 1960. B5894
Blum, G. S. Les théories psychanalytiques de la personnalité. 1955. B5895
Bonaparte, M. Chronos, Eros, Thanatos. 1952. B5896
____. De la sexualité de la femme. 1951. B5897
____. Introduction à la théorie des instincts. 1951. B5898
____. Psychanalyse et anthropologie. 1952. B5899
____. Psychanalyse et biologie. 1952. B5900
Boss, M. Introduction à la médicine psychosomatique. 1959. B5901
Bychowski, G. and Despert, J. L. Techniques spécialisées de la psychothérapie. 1958. B5902
Cahn, P. La relation fraternelle chez l'enfant. 1962. B5903
Despert, J. L. Enfants du divorce. 1957. B5904
Deutsch, H. La psychologie des femmes; étude psychoanalytique. 2 v. 1949-53. B5905
Fenichel, O. Problèmes de technique psychoanalytique. 1953. B5906
____. La théorie psychoanalytique de nérvroses. 2 v. 1953. B5907
Freud, A. Le moi et les mécanismes de défense. 1949. B5908
____. La traitement psychoanalytique des enfants. B5909
Freud, S. Abrégé de psychanalyse. 1949. B5910
____. Cinq psychoanalyses, tr. by Lowenstein, 1954. B5911
____. De la technique psychoanalytique. 1953. B5912
____. Inhibition symptôme et angoisse. 1951. B5913
____. La naissance de la psychoanalyse (1887-1902). 1956. B5914
Freud, S. and Breuer, J. Etudes sur l'hystérie. 1956. B5915
Frielander, K. Le délinquance juvénile. 1951. B5916
Garma, A. La psychoanalyse des rêves. B5917
____. Le psychanalyse et les ulcères gastroduodenaux, tr. by W. and M. Baranger. 1957. B5918
____. Les maux de tête. 1962. B5919
Glover, E. Freud ou Jung? 1950. B5920
____. Technique de la psychanalyse. 1958. B5921
Guex, G. La névrose d'abandon. 1950. B5922
Hesnard, A. L. M. Morale sans péché. 1954. B5923
____. Psychanalyse du lien interhumain. 1957. B5924
____. La relativité de la conscience de soi. 1924. B5925
____. L'univers morbide de la faute. 1949. B5926
Isaacs, S. S. Parents et enfants. 1952. B5927
Jones, E. La vie et l'oeuvre de Sigmund Freud. 2 v. 1962. B5928
Klein, M. La psychanalyse des enfants. 1959. B5929
Laplanche, J. Hölderlin et la question du père. 1961. B5930
Lowenstein, R. Psychanalyse de l'antisémitisme. 1952. B5931
Moscovici, S. La psychanalyse. 1961. B5932
Nacht, S. De la pratique à la théorie psychanalytique. 1950. B5933
Nunberg, H. Principes de psychanalyse. 1957. B5934
Rosen, J. N. L'analyse directe. 1960. B5935
Séchehaye, M. A. Introduction à une psychothérapie des

schizophrenes. 1952. B5936
____. Journal d'une schizophrène. 1951. B5937
Seelig, E. Traité de criminologie. 1956. B5938
Spitz, R. A. Le non et le oui. 1962. B5939

BIBLIOTHEQUE DE SYNTHESE HISTORIQUE L'EVOLUTION DE L'HUMANITE SYNTHESE COLLECTIVE (Renaissance du livre; Michel 1947-)

1 Perrier, E. La terre avant l'histoire. 1954. B5940
2 Morgan, J. J. M. de. L'humanité préhistorique. 1921. B5941
3 Vendyres, J. Le langage. 1950. B5942
4 Febvre, L. P. V. La terre et l'évolution humaine. 1949. B5943
5 Pittard, E. Les races et l'histoire. 1953. B5944
6 Moret, A. and Davy, G. Des clans aux empires. 1923. B5945
7 Moret, A. Le Nil et la civilization égyptienne. 1926. B5946
8 Delaporte, L. J. La Méspotamie. 1923. B5947
8 bis. ----Les Hittites. 1936. B5948
9 Glotz, G. La civilasation égéenne. 1937. B5949
10 Jardé, A. F. V. La formation du peuple grec. 1923. B5950
11 Gernet, L. Le génie grec dans la religion. 1937. B5951
12 Ridder, A. H. P. de and Deonna, W. L'art en Grece. 1924. B5952
13 Robin, L. La pensée grecque et los origines de l'espirit scientifique. 1948. B5953
14 Glotz, G. La cite grecque. 1953. B5954
15 Jouguet, P. L'imperialisme macédonien et l'hellenization de l'Orient. 1926. B5955
16 Homo, L. L'Italie primitive et les debuts de impérialisme romain. 1926. B5956
17 Grenier, A. La génie romain dans la religion, la pensée et l'art. 1927. B5957
18 Homo, L. P. Les institutions politiques romaines: de la cite a l'état. 1927. B5958
18 bis. ----Rome imperiale et l'urbanisme dans l'antiquité. 1951. B5959
19 Declareuil, J. Rome et l'organizacíon del derecho. 1924. B5960
20 Toutain, J. F. L'économie antique. 1927. B5961
21 Hubert, H. Les Celtes et l'expansion celtique jusqu'a l'époque de la Tène. 1950. B5962
21 bis. ----Les Celtes depuis l'epogue de la Tène et la civilisation celtique. 1932. B5963
22 Chapot, V. Le monde romain. 1927. B5964
23 Hubert, H. Les Germains. 1952. B5965
24 Huart, C. I. La perse antique et la civilisation iranienne. 1925. B5966
24 bis. Huart, C. I. and Delaporte, L. J. L'Iran antique. 1952. B5967
25 Granet, M. La civilisation chinoise. 1948. B5968
25 bis. ----La pensée chinoise. 1934. B5969
26 Masson-Oursel, P. and others. L'Inde antique et la civilisation indienne. 1951. B5970
27 Lods, A. Israël, des origines au milieu du VIIIe siècle. 1930. B5971
28 ____. Les prophétes d'Israel et les débuts du judaïsme. 1925. B5972
28 bis. Guignebert, C. A. H. Le monde juifs vers le temps de Jesus. 1935. B5973
29 ____. Jesus. 1933. B5974
29 bis. ----Le Christ. 1943. B5975
31 Lot, P. La fin du monde antique et les debut du Moyen âge. 1938. B5976
32 Bréhier, L. Le monde byzantin. 3 v. 1947-50. B5977
32 bis. ----Les institutions de la Empire byzantine.

1949. B5978
32 ter. ----La civilisation byzantine. 1950. B5979
33 Halphen, L. Charlemagne et l'empire carolingien. 1949. B5980
34 Bloch, M. L. B. La société feodale, la formation des lien de dependance. 1949. B5981
34 bis. ----La société feodale, les classes et le gouvernement des hommes. 1949. B5982
36 Gaudefroy-Demombynes, M. Mahomet. 1957. B5983
38 Alphandéry, P. La chrétienté et l'idée de croisade. V. 1. 1954. B5984
40 Reau, L. L'art du moyen âge, arts plastiques, art littérataire, et la civilization française. 1935. B5985
41 Petit-Dutallis, C. E. La monarchie féodale en. France et en Angleterre. 1933. B5986
43 Latouche, R. Les origines de l'economie occidentale. 1945. B5987
44 ____. Les communes françaises. 1947. B5988
45 Bréhier, E. La philosophie de moyen âge. 1937. B5989
48 Schneider, R. La formation du genie moderne dans l'art de l'Occident. 1936. B5990
49 Febvre, L. P. V. and Martin, H. J. L'apparition du livre. 1958. B5991
52 Mandrou, R. Introduction à la France moderne, 1500-1640. 1961. B5992
53 Febvre, L. Le problème de l'incroyance au XVIe siècle. 1942. B5993
58 Guyenot, E. L'évolution de la pensée scientifique. 1941. B5994
64 André, L. Louis XIV et l'Europe. 1950. B5995
65 Cahen, L. and Braure, M. L'évolution politique de l'Angleterre moderne. 1960- B5996
68 Guyenot, E. L'évolution de la pensée scientifiques les sciences de la vie aux XVIIe et XVIIIe siècle. 1941. B5997
70 Réau, L. L'Europe française au siècle des luminères. 1938. B5998
76 Van Tieghem, P. L'ère romantique; dans la litterature europiene. 1948. B5999
76 bis Réau, L. L'ère romantique: the arts plastique. 1949. B6000
76 ter Chantavoine, J. and Gaudefroy-Demombynes, J. L'ère romantique: le romantique: le romantisme dans la musique européene. 1955. B6001
83 Augé-Laribé, M. La révolution agricole. 1955. B6002
84 Weill, G. L'Europe du XIXe siècle et l'idée de nationale. 1938. B6003
88 Hardy, G. La politique coloniale et le partage de la terre. 1939. B6004
94 Weill, G. Le journal. 1939. B6005

Series complementaire:

I. Rey, A. La science dans l'antiquité. B6006
1. La science orientale avante les Grecs. 1930. B6007
2. La jeunesse de la science grecque. 1933. B6008
3. La maturité de la pensée scientifique en Grece. 1939. B6009
4. L'apazee de la science technique grecque. 1946. B6010
5. L'apogée de la science technique grecque. L'essor de la mathematique. B6011

II. Berr, H. En marge de l'histoire universelle. B6012
1. Les problèmes de l'histoire. 1934. B6013
2. Rome et la civilisation romaine. 1953. B6014

____. La montée de l'esprit. 1955. B6015
____. La synthèse en histoire. 1953. B6016

BIBLIOTHEQUE DES ARCHIVES DE PHILOSOPHIE (Beauchesne)

Académie Internationale de Philosophie des Sciences.

Civilisation technique et humanisme. 1968. B6017
____. Science, philosophie, foi. 1974. B6018
Bagot, J. P. Connaissance et amour. 1958. B6019
Balthasar, A. Phenoménologie de la vérité. 1952. B6020
Blondel, M. Blondel et Teilhard de Chardin. 1965. B6021
____. Une énigme historique, le "vinculum substantiale" d'après Leibniz et l'ebauche d'un réalisme supérieur. 1930. B6022
Boyer, C. Essais sur la doctrine de saint Augustin. 1932. B6023
____. L'idée vérité dans la philosophie de saint Augustin. 1945. B6024
Breton, S. Philosophie et mathematique chez Proclus. 1969. B6025
Brière, Y. de la. La communauté des puissances. 1932. B6026
Brunner, A. La personne incarnée. 1947. B6027
Carles, A. Unité et vie. 1948. B6028
Cassirer, E. and Heidegger, M. Debat sur le Kantisme et la philosophie et autres textes de 1929-1931. 1971. B6029
Chaix-Ruy, J. Donoso Cortès, théologien de l'histoire et prophète. 1956. B6030
Corbin, M. Le chemin de la theologie selon Thomas D'Aquin. 1973. B6031
Defourny, M. Aristote. 1932. B6032
De Raymond, J. F. ·Le dynamisme de la vocation. 1974. B6033
Descoqs, P. Essai critique sur l'hylémorphisme. 1924. B6034
Des Places, E. Pindare et Platon. 1949. B6035
Diès, A. Autour de Platon. 2 v. 1927. B6036
Dréano, M. La pensée religieuse de Montaigne. 1937. B6037
Dumont, P. Liberté humaine et le concours divin d'après Suarez. B6038
Evain, F. L'ontologie personnaliste d'Antonio Rosimi. 1971. B6039
Farges, J. Les idées morales et relirieuses de Methode d'Olympe. 1934. B6040
____. Traduction de du libre arbitre par méthode d'Olympe. 1935. B6041
Finance, J. de. Etre et agir dans la philosophie de saint Thomas. 1945. B6042
Fontan, P. L'intention réaliste. 1965. B6043
Forest, A. L'avenement de l'ame. 1973. B6044
Garin, P. Le problème de la causalité et Saint-Thomas d'Aquin. 1958. B6045
Gino, P. N. H. Le verbe dans l'histoire. 1973. B6046
Jolivet, R. La notion de substance. 1929. B6047
Kowalska, G. D. L'Origine. 1972. B6048
Kruger, G. Critique et morale chez Kant, ed. by Regnier. 1961. B6049
LaBrière, Y. de. Le communauté des puissances. 1932. B6050
Lonergan, B. La notion du verbe dans les écrits de Saint Thomas d'Aquin. 1966. B6051
Lotz, J. B. Le jugement et l'etre. 1965. B6052
Martin, G. Leibniz. 1966. B6053
Mentré, F. Pour qu'en lise Cournot. 1927. B6054
Mersenne, M. Correspondance du Père Marin Mersenne, ed. by Tannery. 1932. B6055
Mesnard, P. Le vrai visage de Kierkegaard. 1948. B6056
Parmentier, A. La philosophie de Whitehead et le probleme de Dieu. 1968. B6057
Rimaud, J. Thomisme et méthode. 1925. B6058
Ritter, J. Hegel et la Révolution français. 1970. B6059
Roberts, J. D. Philosophie et science. 1968. B6060
Rohrmoser, G. Théologie et aliénation dans la pensée du jeune Hegel. 1970. B6061
Rolland, E. La finalité morale dans le bergsonisme. 1937. B6062

Rousselot, Le P. L'intellectualisme de St. Thomas. 1924. B6063

Sargi, B. La participation à l'être dans la philosophie de Louis Lavelle. 1957. B6064

Stocker, A. Le traitement moral des nerveux. 1949. B6065

Tardivel, F. La personnalité littéraire de Newman. 1937. B6066

Tonquédec, J. de. La critique de la Connaissance. 1936. B6067

____. Une philosophie existielle. 1945. B6068

Verneaux, C. Esquisse d'un théorie de la connaissance. V. 2. 1956. B6069

____. Les sources cartésiennes et kantiennes de l'idéalisme français. 1936. B6070

Vignon, J. Au souffle de l'esprit créateur. 1946. B6071

BIBLIOTHEQUE DES ECOLES FRANÇAISES D'ATHENES ET DE ROME (1-111 Thorin, 112- Boccard)

1 Duchesne, L. M. O. Etude sur le Liber pontificalis. 1877. B6072

2 Collignon, M. Essai sur les monuments grecs et romains relatifs au mythe de Psyché. 1877. B6073

3 ____, ed. Catalogue des vases, points du Musée de la Société archeologique d'Athènes. 1878. B6074

4 Muntz, E. Les arts à la cour des papes pendant le XVe et le XVIe siècles. 1878-1882. B6075

5 Fernique, N. E. Inscriptions inédites du pays des Marses. 1879. B6076

6 Berger, E. Notice sur divers manuscrits de la Bibliothèque vaticane, Richard le Poitevin. 1879. B6077

7 Clédat, L. Du rôle historique de Bertrand de Born. 1879. B6078

8 Riemann, O. Recherches archéologiques sur les îles Ioniennes. V. 1. Corfou. 1885. B6079

9 Same as no. 4. V. 2. B6080

10 Bayet, C. M. Recherches pour servir a l'histoire de la peinture et de la sculpture chrétienne en Orient. 1897. B6081

11 Riemann, O. Etudes sur la langue et la grammaire de Tite-Live. 1885. B6082

12 Same as no. 8. V. 2. Céphalonie. 1879. B6083

13 Duchesne, L. M. O. De codicubus mss. graecis Pii, II in Bibliotheca alexandrino-vaticana. 1880. B6084

14 Châtelain, E. L. M. Notice sur les manuscrits des poésies de s. Paulin de Nole. 1880. B6085

15 Descemet, C., ed. Inscriptions doliaires latines. 1880. B6086

16 Hellenikè archaiologikē hetairia, Athens. Catalogue des figurines en terre cuite du musée de la société archéologique d'Athènes, par Martha. 1880. B6087

17 Fernique, N. E. Etude sur Prénestre villa du Latium. 1880. B6088

18 Same as no. 8. V. 3. Zante. Cérigo, 1880. B6089

19 Delaborde, H. F., ed. Chartres de Terre Sainte provenant de l'Abbaye de N.-D. de Josaphat. 1880. B6090

20 Cartault, O. G. C. La triere athenienne. 1881. B6091

21 Cuq, E. Etudes d'épigraphie juridique. 1881. B6092

22 Delaborde, H. F. Etude sur la chronique en prose de Guillaume le Breton. 1881. B6093

23 Girard, P. L'Asclépiéion d'Athénes d'après les récentes decouvertes. 1881. B6094

24 Martin, A. Le manuscrit d'Isocrate, Urbinas CXI de la Vaticane. 1881. B6095

25 Thomas, A. Nouvelles recherches sur l'Entrée de Spagne; chanson de geste franco-italienne. 1882. B6096

26 Martha, J. Les sacredoces anthéniens. 1882. B6097
27 Martin, A. Les scolies du manuscrit d'Aristophane à Ravenne. 1882. B6098
28 Same as no. 4. V. 3. 1884. B6099
29 Bloch, M. G. Les origines du Sénat romain. 1884. B6100
30 Pottier, E. Etude sur les lécythes blancs attiques à représentation funéraires. 1883. B6101
31 Albert, M. Le culte de Castor et Pollux en Italie. 1883. B6102
32 Delaville le Roulx, J. M. A. Les archives, la bibliothèque et le trésor de l'Ordre de Saint-Jean de Jérusalem à Malta. 1883. B6103
33 Lafaye, G. L. Histoire du culte des divinités d'Alexandrie. 1884. B6104
34 La Blanchere, R. M. du C. Terracine. 1884. B6105
35 Thomas, A. Francesco de Barberino et la littérature provencale en Italie au Moyen âge. 1883. B6106
36 Beaudouin, M. Etude du dialecte chypriote moderne et médieval. 1884. B6107
37 Jullian, C. L. Les transformations politiques de l'Italie sous les empereurs romains. 1884. B6108
38 Haussoullier, B. C. L. M. La vie municipale en Attique. 1884. B6109
39 Vyriés, A. Les figures criophores dans l'art grec, l'art gréco-romain et l'art chrétien. 1884. B6110
40 Dubois, M. Les ligues Etoliennes et Acheenne. 1885. B6111
41 Hauvette-Besnault, H. Les stratèges athéniens. 1885. B6112
42 Grousset, R. Etude sur l'histoire des sarcophages chrétiens. 1885. B6113
43 Faucon, M. La librairie des papes d'Avignon. V. 1. 1886. B6114
44-45 Delaville Le Roulx, J. M. A. La France en Orient au XIVe siècle. 2 v. 1886. B6115
46 Durrieu, P. Les archives angevines de Naples. V. 1. 1886. B6116
47 Martin, A. Les cavaliers athéniens. 1887. B6117
48 Muntz, E. and Fabre, P. La Bibliothèque du Vatican au XVe siècle. 1887. B6118
49 Homolle, T. Les archives de l'intendance sacrée à Delos. 1887. B6119
50 Same as no. 43. V. 2. 1887. B6120
51 Same as no. 46. V. 2. 1887. B6121
52 Lécrivain, C. A. Le sénat romain depuis dioclétien à Rome et à Constantinople. 1888. B6122
53 Diehl, C. Etudes sur l'administration byzantine dans l'exarchat de Ravenne. 1889. B6123
54 Apostolis, M. Lettres inédites de Michel Apostolis, ed. by Noiret. 1892. B6124
55 Diehl, C. Etudes d'archéologie byzantine. 1889. B6125
56 Auvray, L. H. L. Les manuscrits de Dante des bibliothèques de France. 1892. B6126
57 Dürrbach, F. L'orateur Lycurgue. 1890. B6127
58 Langlois, E. Origines et sources du Roman de la Rose. 1891. B6128
59 Cadier, L. Essai sur l'administration du royaume de Sicile... 1891. B6129
60 Paris, P. Elatée. 1892. B6130
61 Noiret, H., ed. Documents inédits pour servir à l'histoire de la domination vénitienne en Crète de 1380 à 1485. 1892. B6131
62 Fabre, P. Etude sur le Liber censuum de l'Eglise romain. 1892. B6132
63 Radet, G. A. La Lydie et le monde grec au temps des Mermnades. 1893. B6133
64 Clerc, M. A. E. A. Les métèques athéniens. 1893. B6134
65 Gsell, S. Essai sur le règne de l'empereur Domitien. 1894. B6135

66 Enlart, C. Origines françaises de l'architecture gothique en Italie. 1894. B6136
67 Berard, V. De l'origine des cultes arcadiens. 1894. B6137
68 Baudrillart, A. Les divinités de la victoire en Grece et en Italie d'après les textes et les monuments figurés. 1894. B6138
69 Same as no. 16. Par Ridder. 1896. B6139
70 Berger, E. Histoire de Blanche de Castille. 1895. B6140
71 Rolland, R. Les origines du théâtre lyrique moderne. Histoire de l'opéra en Europe avant Lully et Scarlatti. 1895. B6141
72 Toutain, J. Les cités romaines de la Tunisie. 1896. B6142
73 Guiraud, J. L'état pontifical après le grand schisme. 1896. B6143
74 Ridder, A. H. P. de. Catalogue des bronzes trouvés sur l'Acropole d'Athènes. 1896. B6144
75-76 Pélissier, L. G. Recherches dans les archives italienne. 2 v. 1896-97. B6145
77 Ardaillon, E. Les mines du Laurion dans l'antiquité. 1897. B6146
78 Fougères, G. Mantinée et l'Arcadié orientale. 1898. B6147
79 Legrand, P. E. Etude sur Théocrite. 1898. B6148
80 Loye, J. de. Les archives de la chambre apostolique au XIVe siècle. V. 1. 1899. B6149
81 Courbaud, E. Le bas-relief romain à représentations historiques. 1899. B6150
82 Macé, A. Essai sur Suétone. 1900. B6151
83 Dufourcq, A. Etude sur les Gesta martyrum romains. 1900. B6152
84 Audollent, A. M. H. Carthage romaine. 1901. B6153
85-86 bis-85 ter. Athens. Ethnikon archaiologikon mouseion. Catalogue des vases points du mussée national d'Athenes, par Collignon. 3 v. in 1. 1902-04. B6154
86 Déprez, E. Les préliminaires de la guerre de cent ans. La papauté, la France et l'angleterre. 1902. B6155
87 Besnier, M. L'ile Tibérine dans l'antiquité. 1902. B6156
88 Yver, G. Le commerce et les marchands dans l'Italie méridionale au XVIe siècle. 1903. B6157
89 Homo, L. P. Essai sur le règne de l'empereur Aurélien. 1904. B6158
90 Gay, J. L'Italie méridionale et l'Empire byzantin... 1904. B6159
91 Millet, G. and others. Recueil des inscriptions chrétiennes du Mont Athos. 1904. B6160
92 Lechat, H. La sculpture attique avant Phidias. 1904. B6161
93 Colin, G. Le culte d'Apolon Pythien à Athènes. 1905. B6162
94 ____. Rome et la Grèce de 200 à 146 avant Jésus-Christ. 1905. B6163
95 Bourguet, E. L'administration fianancière du sanctuaire pythique au IVe siècle avant. J.-C. 1905. B6164
96 Samaran, C. M. D. and Mollat, G. La fiscalité pontificale en France au XVIe siècle période d'Avignon et du grand schisme d'Occident. 1905. B6165
97 Merlin, A. L'Aventin dans l'antiquité. 1906. B6166
98 Dubois, C. Pouzzoles antiques. 1907. B6167
99 Chapot, V. La frontière de l'Euphrate de Pompée à la conquête arabe. 1907. B6168
100 Cavaignac, E. Etude sur l'histoire financière d'Athènes au VIe siècle le trésor d'Athènes de 480 de 480 à 494. 1907. B6169
101 Perdrizet, P. F. La Vierge de Miséricorde. 1908. B6170
102 Bourgin, G. La France et Rome de 1788-1797.

1909. B6171
103 Celier, L. Les dataires du XVe siècle et les origines de la dataire apostolique. 1910. B6172
104 Jouguet, P. La vie municipale dans l'Egypte romaine. 1911. B6173
105 Hautecoeur, L. Rome et la renaissance d l'antiquité. 1912. B6174
106 Grenier, A. Bologne. 1912. B6175
107 Graillot, H. Le culte de Cybèle, mère des dieux... 1912. B6176
108 Leroux, G. Les origines de l'édifice hypostyle. 1911. B6177
109 Millet, G. Recherches sur l'iconographie de l'évangile aux XIVe, XVe et XVIe siècles. 1916. B6178
111 Roussel, P. Délos, colonie athenienne. 1906. B6179
110 Piganiol, A. Essai sur les origines de Rome. 1917. B6180
112 Zeiller, J. Les origines chrétienne dans les provinces danubiennes de l'Empire romain. 1918. B6181
113 Holleaux, M. Etude sur la traduction en grec du titre consulaire. 1918. B6182
114 Boudreaux, P. Le texte d'Aristophane et ses commentateurs. 1919. B6183
115 Hatzfeld, J. Les trafiquants italiens dans l'Orient hellenique. 1919. B6184
116 Carcopino, J. Virgile et les origines d'ostie. 1919. B6185
117 Laurent, J. L'Arménie entre Byzance et l'Islam depuis la conquête arabi jusqu'en 886. 1919. B6186
118 Boüard, A. de. Le régime politique et les institutions de Rome au moyen âge. 1920. B6187
119 Constans, L. A. Arles antique. 1921. B6188
120 Hirschauer, C. La politique de St. Pie V en France. (1566-1572). 1922. B6189
121 Fawtier, R. Sainte Catherine de Sienne. V. 1. 1921. B6190
122 Roussel, L. Grammaire descriptive du roméique litteraire. 1922. B6191
123 Picard, C. Ephèse et Claros. 1922. B6192
124 Holleaux, M. Rome. 1921. B6193
125 Courby, F. Les vases grecs à reliefs. 1922. B6194
126 Boulanger, A. Aeolius Aristide et la sophistique. 1923. B6195
127 Albertini, E. Le composition dans les ouvrages philosophiques de Sénèque. 1923. B6196
128-128 bis. Constant, G. L. M. J. Concession à l'Allemagne de la communion sous les deux espèces. 2 v. 1923. B6197
129 Dugas, C. La céramique des Cyclades. 1925. B6198
130 Jardé, A. F. V. Les céréales dans l'antiquité grecque. 1925. B6199
131 Bulard, M. La religion domestique dans la colonie italienne de Délos. 1926. B6200
132 Bayet, J. Les origines de l'Hercule romain. 1926. B6201
133 Pocquet du Haut-Jusse, B. Les papes et les ducs de Bretagne. 2 v. 1928. B6202
134 Cahen, E. Callimaque et son oeuvre poétique. 1929. B6203
134 bis ----Les Hymnes de Callimaque. 1930. B6204
135 Same as no. 121. V. 2. B6205
136 Demangel, R. La frise ionique. 1932. B6206
137 Chapouthier, F. Les Dioscures au service d'une déesse. 1935. B6207
138 Frotier de la Coste-Messelière, P. Au Musée de Delphes. III. 1936. B6208
139 Boüard, M. de. Les origines des Guerres d'Italia la France et l'Italie au temps du grand schisme d'occident. 1936. B6209

140 Daux, G. Delphes aux IIe et Ier siècles depuis, l'abaissement de l'Etolie jusqu'à la paix romaine. 1936. B6210
141 Boyancé, P. Le culte des muses chez les philosophies grecs. 1937. B6211
142 Pottier, E. Recueil Edmond Potter études d'art et d'archéologie. 1937. B6212
143 Flacelière, R. Les Aitoliens à Delphes. 1937. B6213
144 Béquignon, Y. La vallée du Spercheios des origines au IVe siècle. 1937. B6214
145-145 bis. Marrou, H. I. Saint Augustin et la fin de la culture antique. 2 v. 1938. B6215
146 Durry, M. Les cohortes pretoriennes. 1938. B6216
147 Robert, F. Thymélé. 1939. B6217
148 Wuilleumier, P. Tarente des origines à la conquête romaine. 1939. B6218
149 Thouvenot, R. Essai sur la province romaine de Bétique. 1940. B6219
150 Berand, J. La colonisation grecque de l'Italie méridionale. 1941. B6220
151 Renouard, Y. Les relations des papes d'Avignon et des compagnies commerciales et bancaires de 1316 à 1378. 1941. B6221
152 Feyel, M. Polybe et l'histoire de la Béotie au IIIe siècle avant notre ère. 1942. B6222
153-153 bis. Guillon, P. Les trepieds du Ptoion. 2 v. 1943. B6223
154 Heurgon, J. Recherches sur l'histoire, la religion et la civilisation de Capoue préromaine. 1942. B6224
155 Grimal, P. Les jardins romains a la fin de la republique... 1942. B6225
156 LeCoq, L. Question es Johannis Galli, ed. by Boulet. 1945. B6226
157 Vallois, R. L'architecture hellénique et helléniste à Delos jusqu'à l'éviction des Déliens. 1944. B6227
157 bis. Planches. B6228
158 Lemerle, P. Philippes et la Macédoine orientale à l'époque chrétienne et byzantine. 1 v. text. 1945. B6229
159 Courcelle, P. Les lettres grecques en Occident, de Macrobe à Cassiodore. 1948. B6230
160 Chatelain, L. Le Maroc des Romains. 1945. B6231
160 bis. -----Planches. B6232
161 Mahn, J. B. L'ordre cistercian et son gouvernement des origines au milieu du XIIIe siècle. 1945. B6233
162 Seston, W. Dioclétien et la tétrarchie. 1946. B6234
163 Effenterre, H. van. Le Crete et le monde grec de Platon a Polybe. 1948. B6235
164 Demargne, P. Le Crete dédalique. 1947. B6236
165 Lapalus, E. Le fronton sculpté en Grèce, des origines à la fin du IVe siècle. 1947. B6237
166 Simon, M. Versus Israël. 1948. B6238
167 Fabre, P. Saint Paulin de Nole et l'amitié chrétienne. 1949. B6239
168 Lesage, G. Marseille angevine. 1949. B6240
169 Launey, M. Recherches sur les armees hellenistiques. 2 v. 1949-51. B6241
170 Amandry, P. La mantique apolinienne à delphes, essai sur le fonctionnement de l'oracle. B6242
171 Aymard, J. Essai sur les chasses romaines, des origines à la fin du siècle des Antonins (cynegetica). 1951. B6243
172 Metzger, H. Les représentations dans la céramique attique du IVe siècle. 1952. B6244
173 François, M. Le cardinal François de Tournon. 1952. B6245
174 Martin, R. Recherches sur l'agora grecque. 1952. B6246

175 Bruhl, A. Liber pater. 1952. B6247
176 Lerat, L. Les Locriens de l'ouest. 2 v. 1952. B6248
177 Chamoux, F. Cyrene sous la monarchie des Battiades. 1953. B6249
178 Schilling, R. La religion romaines de Venus depuis les origines jusqu'au temps d'Auguste. 1954. B6250
179 Pouilloux, J. La fortresse de Rhamnonte. 1954. B6251
180 Elucidarius. L'Elucidarium et las Lucidaires, ed. by LeFèvre. 1955. B6252
181 Jannoray, J. Ensérune. 1955. B6253
182 Gagé, J. Apollon romain. 1955. B6254
183 Will, E. Le relief cultural greco-romain. 1955. B6255
184 Delumeau, J. Vie économique et sociale de Rome dans la second moitié du XVIe siècle. 2 v. 1957-59. B6256
185 Lévêque, P. Pyrrhos. 1957. B6257
186 Dessenne, A. Le sphinx. V. 1. 1957. B6258
187 Charles-Picard, G. Les trophées romains. 1957. B6259
188 Laumonier, A. Les cultes indigènes en Carie. 1958. B6260
189 Vallet, G. Rhégion et Zancle. 1958. B6261
190 Bompaire, J. Lucien écrivain. 1958. B6262
191 Etienne, R. Le culte imperial dans le péninsule iberique d'Auguste a Dioclétien. 1958. B6263
192 Gallet de Santerre, H. Délos primitive et archïque. 1958. B6264
193 Thiriet, F. La romanie vénitienne au moyen-âge. 1959. B6265
194 Festugière, A. J. Antioche païenne et chrétienne. 1959. B6266
195 Villard, F. La céramique grecque de Marseille (VIe-IVe siècle), essai d'histoire economique. 1960. B6267
196 Delorme, J. Gymnasion. 1960. B6268
197 Grenade, P. Essai sur les origines du principat, investiture et renouvellement des pouvoirs impériaux. 1961. B6269
198 Hus, A. Recherches sur la statuaire en pierre etrusque archaïque. 1961. B6270
199 Roux, G. L'Architecture de l'Argolide aux IV° et III° siècle avant J. C. 1961. B6271
200 Ginouves, R. Balaneutiké. 1962. B6272
201 Guillemain, B. La cour pontificale d'Avignon, 1309-1376. 1962. B6273
202 Février, P. A. Le développement urbain en Provence de l'epoque romaine a la fin du XIVe siècle. 1964. B6274
203 Catholic Church. L'administration des Etats de l'Eglise au XIVe siècle, correspondance des légats et vicaires généraux, by Glenisson and Mollat. V. 1. 1964. B6275
204 Boucher, J. P. Etudes sur Properce. 1965. B6276
205 Leglay, M. Saturne Africain. 1955. B6277
206 Cèbe, J. P. La caricature et la parodie. 1966. B6278
207 Nicolet, C. L'ordre équestre à l'epoque républicaine. V. 1. 1966. B6279
208 Courbin, P. La céramique géométrique de l'Argolide. 1966. B6280
209 Ducat, J. Les Vases plastiques rhodiens archaiques en terre cuite. 1966. B6281
210 Turcan, R. Les Sarcophages romains à représentations dionysiaques. 1966. B6282
211 Favier, J. Les Finances pontificales à l'époque du grand schisme d'Occident. 1966. B6283
212 Labrousse, M. Toulouse antique des origines à l'etablissement des Wisigoths. 1968. B6284
213 Bon, A. La Morée

franque. 1969. B6285
214 Callu, J. P. La politique monétaire des empereurs romains de 238 a 311. 1969. B6286
215 Marcade, J. Au musée de Delos. 1969. B6287
216 Vatin, C. Recherches sur le mariage et la condition de la femme mariée à l'époque hellenistique. 1970. B6288
217 Bruneau, P. Recherches sur les cultes de Délos à l'époque hellenistique et à l'époque impériale. 1970. B6289
218 Les Eglises africaines à deux absides. 2 v. 1971-72. B6290
219 Ducat, J. Les Kouroi du Ptolon. 1971. B6291
220 Bloch, R. Recherches archéologiques en territoire volsinien de la protohistoire à la civilisation étrusque. 1972. B6292
221 Toubert, P. Les structures du Latium médieval. 1973. B6293
222 Zehnacker, H. Moneta. 1973. B6294
223 Garlan, Y. Recherches de poliorcétique Grecque. 1974. B6295

BIBLIOTHEQUE DES TEXTES PHILOSOPHIQUES (Vrin)

Abailard, P. Historia calamitatum, ed. by Monfrin. 1959. B6296
Anselm, St. Fides quoerens intellectum, ed. by Koyre. 1930. B6297
Aristotles. De l'âme, tr. by Tricot. 1947. B6298
____. De la génération et de la corruption, tr. by Tricot. 1934. B6299
____. Histoire des animaux, ed. by Tricot. 2 v. 1957. B6300
____. La métaphysique, ed. by Tricot. 2 v. 1953. B6301
____. Les météorologiques, ed. by Tricot. 1941. B6302
____. Organon. 6 v. 1939-47. B6303
____. Parva naturalia (De sensu, De memoria et reminiscentia, De somno e vigilia, De insomniis, De divinatione per somnum, De longitudine et brevitate vitae, De juventute et senectute, De resperatione, De vita et morte) suivis du Traité pseud-aristotelician De spiritu. 1951. B6304
____. Le plaisir, ed. by Festugière. 1947. B6305
____. Traité du ciel suivi du traité pseudo-aristotelician du monde. 1949. B6306
Bachelard, G. Etudes, ed. by Canguilhem. 1970. B6307
____. La formation de l'esprit scientifique, contribution à une psychoanalyses de la connaissance objective. 1969. B6308
Bayle, P. Ce que c'est que la France toute catholique sous le règne de Louis le Grand. 1973. B6309
Berkeley, G. Siris, ed. by Dubois. 1971. B6310
Bonaventura, St. Itinéraire de l'esprit vers Dieu, ed. by Duméry. 1960. B6311
Bonnet, C. Mémoires autobiographiques de Charles Bonnet de Genève, ed. by Savioz. 1948. B6312
Calvin, J. Institution de la religion chrestienne, ed. by Beñoit. 4 v. 1957-61. B6313
Comte, A. Discours sur l'esprit positif. 1974. B6314
____. Lettres inédites à C. de Blignières, ed. by Arbousse-Bastide. 1932. B6315
Condorcet. Esquisse d'un tableau historique des progrès de l'esprit humain. 1970. B6316
Courcelle, P. L'entretien de Pascal et Sacy. 1960. B6317
Descartes, R. Correspondance avec Arnaud et Morus, ed. by Lewis. 1953. B6318
____. Meditationes de prima philosophia, tr. by Luynes. 1945. B6319
____. Les passions de l'âme, ed. by Rodis-Lewis. 1955. B6320

____. Règles pour la direction de l'esprit, tr. by Sirven. 1947. B6321
____. Regulae ad directionem ingenii, tr. by Tannery. 1947. B6322
Destutt de Tracy, A. L. C. Eléments d'idéologie. 2 v. 1970. B6323
DuVair, G. De la sainte philosophie, ed. by Michaut. 1946. B6324
Erasmus, D. Enchiridion militis christiani. 1971. B6325
Fichte, J. G. Conférences sur la destination du savant. 1969. B6326
Gassendi, P. Disquisitio metaphysica seu dubitationes et instantiae adversus Renati Cartesi metaphysicam et responsa, ed. by Rochot. 1962. B6327
____. Exercitationes paradoxicae, ed. by Rochot. 1955. B6328
____. Lettres familières à François Luillier pendant l'hiver, ed. by Rochot. 1944. B6329
Guillaume de Saint-Thierry. Commentaire sur le cantique des cantiques. 1958. B6330
____. Deux traités de l'armour de Dieu. 1959. B6331
____. Meditativae orationes, ed. by Davy. 1934. B6332
Hégél, G. W. F. Différences des systèmes philosophiques de Fichte et de Schelling. 1952. B6333
____. Encyclopédie des sciences philosophiques. 1970. B6334
____. L'esprit du christianisme et son destin. 1948. B6335
____. Leçons sur l'histoire de la philosophie. 7 v. 1971-72. B6336
____. Leçons sur la philosophie de l'histoire, tr. by Gibelin. 1946. B6337
____. Leçons sur la philosophie de la religion, ed. by Gibelin. 3 v. 1946-54. B6338
____. Des manières de traiter scientifiquement du droit naturale. 1972. B6339
____. Précis de encyclopédie des sciences philosophiques. 1952. B6340
____. La relation du scepticisme avec la philosophie. 1972. B6341
Hobbes, T. De la nature humaine. 1971. B6342
Hume, D. Dialogues sur la religion naturelle, tr. by David. 1973. B6343
____. Les essais esthétiques. 2 v. 1973-74. B6344
____. Essai politique. 1972. B6345
____. L'histoire naturelle de la religion et autres essais sur la religion. 1971. B6346
Kant, I. Le conflit des facultés en trois sections, tr. by Gibelin. 1935. B6347
____. Critique de la faculté de juger, tr. by Philosoenko. 1965. B6348
____. Critique de la raison partique, suivie de: Sur le lieu commun, tr. by Gibelin. 1945. B6349
____. Critique du jugement, tr. by Gibelin. 1946. B6350
____. La dissertation de 1770, tr. by Mouy. 1942. B6351
____. Essai pour introduire in philsophie le concept de grandeur négative. 1949. B6352
____. Logique, tr. by Guillermit. 1966. B6353
La métaphysique des moeurs. V. 2. 1968. B6354
____. Observations sur le sentiment du beau et du sublime. 1954. B6355
____. Opus postumum, ed. by Gibelin. 1950. B6356
____. Prèmiere introduction à la "critique de la faculté de juger," tr. by Guillermit. 1968. B6357
____. Première principes métaphysiques de la science de la nature. 1952. B6358
____. Les progrès de la métaphysqieu en Allemagne depuis le temps de Leibniz et de Wolf 1793, tr. by Guillermit. 1968. B6359
____. Projet de paix perpétuelle, tr. by Gibelin. 1948. B6360
____. Prolégomènes à toute

métaphysique future qui pourra se présenter comme science, tr. by Gibelin. 1941. B6361
____. Quelques opuscules précritiques. 1970. B6362
____. Qu'est-ce que s'orienter dans la pensée?, ed. by Philonenko. 1959. B6363
____. La religion dans les limites de la simple raison, tr. by Gibelin. 1943. B6364
____. Résponse à Eberhard, ed. by Kempf. 1959. B6365
Leibniz, G. W., freiherr von. Confessio philosophi, ed. by Belaval. 1961. B6366
____. Discours de métaphysique, ed. by Lestienne. 1946. B6367
____. Discours de métaphysique et Correspondance avec Arnauld, ed. by Roy. 1957. B6368
____. Opuscula philosophiques choisis, tr. by Schrecker. 1954. B6369
____. Opuscula philosophica selecta, ed. by Schrecker. 1959. B6370
Lequier, I. La liberté, tr. by Grenier. 1936. B6371
Locke, J. Deuxieme traite du gouvernement civil, tr. by Gilson. 1967. B6372
____. Draft A première esquisse de l'essai philosophique concernant l'entendement humain. 1974. B6373
____. Essai philosophique concernant l'entedement humain. 1972. B6374
Maine de Brian. De l'aperception immedíate, ed. by Echeverria. 1963. B6375
____. De l'existence, ed. by Gouhier. 1966. B6376
Malebranche, N. Conversations chrétiennes dans lesquelles on justifie la vérité de la religion et de la morale de Jésus-Christ, ed. by Robinet. 1959. B6377
____. Correspondance avec J.-J. Dortous de Mairan, ed. by Moreau. 1947. B6378
____. Correspondance, ed. by Robinet. 2 v. 1961. B6379
____. De la recherche de la vérité, où l'on traite de la nature dé l'esprit de l'homme, et de l'usage qu'il, en droit faire pour eviter l'erreur des sciences, ed. by Lewis. 3 v. 1946. B6380
____. Entretiens sur la métaphysique. ed. by Cuvillier. 1945. B6381
____. Entretiens sur la métaphysique et sur la religion suivis des entretiens sur la mort, ed. by Cuvillier. 1948. B6382
____. Malebranche et Leibniz, ed. by Robinet. 1955. B6383
____. Méditations chrétiennes et métaphysiques, ed. by Gouhier and Robinet. 1959. B6384
____. Méditations pour se disposer a l'humilité et à la pénitence..., tr. by Cuvillier. 1944. B6385
____. Pieces jointes, ed. by Costabel and others. 1960. B6386
____. Reflexions sur la prémotion physique, ed. by Robinet. 1958. B6387
____. Traité de la nature et de la grâce. 1958. B6388
Mandeville, B. La fable des abeilles. 1974. B6389
Montaigne, M. E. de. Trois essais de Montaigne, ed. by Gougenheim. 1951. B6390
Pascal, B. Deux pièces imparfaites sur la grâce et le concile de Trente, ed. by Perier. 1947. B6391
____. L'Entretien de Pascal de Sacy. 1960. B6392
____. Pensées, ed. by Tourneur. 1942. B6393
Porphyrius. Isagoge, tr. by Tricot. B6394
Proclus Diadochus. Commentaire sur la République, ed. by Festugière. 1970. B6395
Ravaisson-Mollien, F. Essai sur la métaphysique d'Aristote. Fragments du tome III. 1953. B6396
Renouvier, C. B. Les derniers entretiens, tr. by Prat. 1930. B6397
Rochot, B. Les travaux de Gassendi sur Epicure et

sur l'atomisme. 1944. B6398
Rousseau, J. J. Lettres philosophiques. 1974. B6399
Saint-Thierry, G. de. Commentaire sur le cantique des cantiques. 1958. B6400
____. Deux traités de l'amour de Dieu. 1953. B6401
____. Deux traités sur la foi. 1954. B6402
____. Meditativae orationes, ed. by Davy. 1934. B6403
Sartre, J. P. La transcendance de l'ego. 1965. B6404
Schopenhauer, A. De la quadruple racine du principe de raison suffisante, ed. by Gibelin. 1946. B6405
Spinoza, B. de. Traité de la réforme de l'entendement et de la meilleure voie à suivre pour parvenir à la vraie connaissance des choses, ed. by Koyre. 1938. B6406
____. Traite politique, ed. by Zac. 1969. B6407
Théophrastus. La métaphysique, tr. by Tricot. 1948. B6408
Thomas Aquinas, St. L'être et l'essence, ed. by Capelle. B6409
Whewell, W. De la construction de la science, tr. by Blanche. 1938. B6410

BIBLIOTHEQUE FRANÇAISE DE PHILOSOPHIE (Desclée)

Avicenna. Introduction à Avicenne. 1933. B6411
Cortes, M. de. Etudes d'histoire de la philosophie ancienne: Aristote de Plotin. 1935. B6412
Defroidmont, J. La science du droit positif. 1933. B6413
Deploige, S. Le conflit de la morale et de sociologie. 1927. B6414
Gardeil, A. La vraie vie chrétienne. 1935. B6415
Garrigou-Lagrange, R. Le réalisme du principe de finalité. 1932. B6416
____. Les sens commun. 1936. B6417
____. Le sens du mystère et le clairobscur intellectuel. 1934. B6418
____. Synthese thomiste. 1946. B6419
Grousset, R. Les philosophies indiennes. c1931. B6420
Haessle, J. Le travail, tr. by Borne and Linn. 1933. B6421
Jolivet, R. Les sources de l'idealisme. 1936. B6422
____. Le thomisme et la critique de la connaissance. 1933. B6423
Journet, C. L'esprit du protestantisme en Suisse. 1925. B6424
Lallemand, M. Le transfini. 1934. B6425
LaVallée Poussin, C. L. de. La morale Bouddhesque. 1927. B6426
Lépicier, A. H. M. Le monde visible, tr. by Grolleau. 1931. B6427
Maritain, J. Distinguer pour unir. 1946. B6428
____. Quatre essais sur l'esprit dans sa condition charnelle. 1939. B6429
____. Réflexions due l'intelligence et sur sa vie propre. 1926. B6430
Richard, T. Etudes de théologie morale. 1933. B6431
Schmitt, C. Romantisme politique. B6432
Simon, Y. Introduction à l'ontologie du connaître. 1934. B6433
Siwek, P. Au coeur du spinozisme. 1952. B6434
____. La problème du mal. 1942. B6435
____. La réincarnation des esprits. 1942. B6436
____. Spinoza et le panthéisme religieux. 1950. B6437
Termier, P. A la gloire de la terre. B6438
____. Joie de connaître. 1938. B6439
____. La vocation de savant. 1929. B6440
Vialatoux, J. Philosophie économique. 1932. B6441

BIBLIOTHEQUE GENERALE D'ECONOMIE POLITIQUE (Rivière)

1 Aftalion, A. Les crises périodiques de suproduction. 2 v. 1913. B6442
2 Antonelli, E. Principes d'économie pure. 1914. B6443
3 Zawadzki, W. Les mathématiques appliquées à l'économie pure. 1914. B6444
4 Ralea, M. L'idée de révolution dans les doctrines socialistes. 1923. B6445
5 Aftalion, A. Les fondements du socialisme. 1923. B6446
6 Ghio, P. La formation historique de l'économie politique. 1926. B6447
7 Montarnal, H. Les salaires, l'inflation et les changes. 1925. B6448
8 Moreau, G. Le syndicalisme. 1925. B6449
9 Lacaombe, E. La prévision en matière de crises économiques. 1926. B6450
10 Zawadzki, W. Théorie de la production. 1927. B6451
11 Bourgeois, N. Les théories du droit international chez. 1927. B6452
12 Bousequet, G. H. Cours d'économie pure. 1928. B6453
13 Weiller, J. L'influence du change sur le commerce. 1929. B6454
14 Laurat, L. L'accumulation du capital... 1930. B6455
15 Seligman, E. Etude économique sur la vente à temperament. 2 v. 1930. B6456
16 Scelle, G. L'Organisation internationale du travail et de B. I. T. 1930. B6457
17 Machali, M. Méthodes scientifiques. 1931. B6458
18 Graziadeli, A. La rente et la propriété de la terre. 1931. B6459
19 Teilhac, E. Les fondements nouveaux de l'économie. 1932. B6460

Anstett, M. La formation de la main--d'oeuvre qualifiée en Union soviétique de 1917 à 1954. 1958. B6461

Antonelli, E. L'économie pure du capitalisme. 1939. B6462

Aupetit, A. Essai sur la théorie générale de la monnaie. 1957. B6463

Barrere, A. Les crises de reconversion et la politique économique d'après-guerre. 1947. B6464

Berard, A. La statistique dans la production et les echanges. 1939. B6465

Bettelheim, C. La planification soviétique. 1945. B6466

____. L'économie allemande sous le nazisme. 1946. B6467

Bousquet, G. H. D'une histoire de la science économique en Italie. 1960. B6468

____. Essai sur l'évolution de la pensée économique. 1927. B6469

____. Institutes de science économique. 3 v. 1930-36. B6470

Closon, F. L. La politique financière du président Roosevelt en sept leçons. 1938. B6471

Ferrara, F. Oeuvres économiques choisies. 1938. B6472

Galiani, F. De la monnaire (1751) traduit et analysè avec bibliographie, ed. by Bosquet and Crisafulli. 1955. B6473

Ibn Khaldour, Abd al Rahman ibn Mohammad. Les textes économiques de l'Youqaddima (1375-1379), ed. by Bousquet. 1962. B6474

Lautman, J. Les aspects nouveaus du protectionnisme. 1933. B6475

Lazarcik, G. Le commerce en matière agricole entre l'Europe de l'ouest et l'Europe de l'Est. 1959. B6476

Levesque, P. Le justa salaire. 1938. B6477

Markovitch, T. Etudes des crises économiques. 1938. B6478

Meade, J. B. Plans et Prix. 1952. B6479

Rădulescu, D. Introduction à l'économie dirigee...

1937. B6480
Sartre, L. Esquisse d'une théorie marxiste des crises périodiques. 1937. B6481
Sriber, J. L'équilibre économique des interêts mondiaux. 1948. B6482
____. La reconstitution économique de la France. 1946. B6483
Weiss, R. Un précurseur de la législation international du travail. 1926. B6484
Wronski, H. Le rôle économique et sociale de la monde dans les démocraties populaires la réforme monétaire polonaise, 1950-53. 1954. B6485

BIBLIOTHEQUE GENERALE DE L'ECOLE PRATIQUE DES HAUTES-ETUDES SCIENCES ECONOMIQUES ET SOCIALES (S. E. V. P. E. N.)

Académie des Sciences de l'U. R. S. S. / E. P. H. E. Au siècle des Lumières. 1970. B6486
____. La Russie et l'Europe, XVIe-XXe siècles. 1970. B6487
Antoniadia-Bibicou, H. Etudes d'histoire maritime de Byzance... 1966. B6488
Ardant, G. Théorie sociologique de l'impôt. 2 v. 1965. B6489
Au siècle des lumières. 1970. B6490
Bernot, L. and Blancard, R. Nouville, un village français. 1953. B6491
Bloch, M. L. Mélanges historiques 1963. B6492
Centre d'études de politique étrangère. Industrialisation de l'Afrique du Nord, ed. by Leduc. 1952. B6493
Charnay, J. P. Société militaire et suffrage politique en France depuis 1789. 1964. B6494
Chatenay, L. Vie de Jacques Esprinchard, Rochelais et Journal de ses voyages au XVIe siècle. 1957. B6495
Colloque international d'histoire maritime. Les aspects internationaux de la découverte océanique aux XVe et XVIe siècles, ed. by Mollat and Adam. 1966. B6496
____. Les grandes voies maritimes dans le monde, XVe-XIXe siècle. 1965. B6497
____. Le navire et l'économie maritime du XVe au XVIIIe siècle, ed. by Mollat. 1957. B6498
____. La navire et l'économie maritime du moyen âge au XVIIIe siècle. 1959. B6499
____. Les routes de l'Atlantique. 1969. B6500
____. Société compagnies de commerce en Orient et dans l'océan Indien. 1970. B6501
____. Les sources de l'histoire maritime en Europe, ed. by Mollat and others. 1962. B6502
David, M. V. Le débat sur les écritures et l'hiéroglyphe. 1965. B6503
Delaunay, R. and Habasque, G. Du cubisme à l'art abstrait. 1957. B6504
Devos, J. P. Description de l'Espagne par Jehan Lhermire et Henri Cock... 1969. B6505
Duby, G. La société au XIe et XIIe siècles dans la région mâconnaise. 1954. B6506
Ehrard, J. L'Idée de nature en France. 2 v. 1960. B6507
Febvre, L. P. V. Au coeur religieux du XVIe siècle. 1957. B6508
____. Pour une histoire à part entiere. 1962. B6509
Flores, X. A. Le Peso politico de todo le mundo d'Anthony Sherley. 1963. B6510
Foreville, R. Le jubile de saint Thomas Becket du XIIIe au XVe siècle (1220-1470). 1959. B6511
Franca, J. A. Une ville des lumières la Lisbonne de Pombal. 1965. B6512
Francastel, P. L'art mosan. 1953. B6513
Gottmann, J. Essais sur l'amenagement de l'espace habité. 1966. B6514

Grillon, P. Un chargé d'affaires au Maric. 2 v. 1970. B6515
Heitz, C. Recherches sur les rapports entre architecture et liturgie à l'epoque carolingienne. 1963. B6516
Ibn Iyās. Journal d'un bourgeois du Caire. 2 v. 1955-60. B6517
La Méditerrannée de 1919 à 1939. 1969. B6518
La Russie et l'Europe. 1970. B6519
LeRoy Ladurie, E. Les Paysans de Languedoc. 2 v. 1966. B6520
Leulliot, P. L'Alsace au debut du XIXe siècle. 3 v. 1959-60. B6521
____. La premiere restauration et les cent jours en Alsace. 1958. B6522
Lot, F. Recherches sur les effectifs des armées françaises des guerres d'Italia aux guerres de religion. 1962. B6523
Mélanges de préhistoire d'archeocivilisation, et d'ethnologie offerts à André Varagnac. 1971. B6524
Menager, L. R. Amiratus-Αμηρας. 1960. B6525
Meyer, J. La noblesse bretonne au XVIIIe siècle. 2 v. 1966. B6526
Meyerson, I. Problèmes de la couleur. 1957. B6527
Mollat, M. Dans les mers du Nord de l'Europe, du moyen âge au XVIIIe siècle. 1960. B6528
____. Les sources de l'histoire maritime en Europe. 1962. B6529
Namer, G. L'abbe le Roy et ses amis. 1962. B6530
Pacant, M. Louis VII et son royaume. 1962. B6531
Personas, L. Le Diocese de La Rochelle. 1963. B6532
Renouard, Y. Etudes d'histoire médiévale... 2 v. 1968. B6533
Rey, M. Le domaine du Roi et les finances extraordinaires sous Charles VI. 1965. B6534
____. Les finances royales sous Charles VI. 1965. B6535
Ronchi, V. Histoire de la lumière. 1956. B6536
Roupnel, G. La ville de la campagne au XVIIe siècle, étude sur les populations du pays dijonnais. 1955. B6537
Schnapper, B. La remplacement militaire en France. 1968. B6538
Semaine sociologique. Industrialisation et technocratie, ed. by Gurvitch. 1949. B6539
____. Villes et campagnes civilisation urbaine et civilisation rurale en France, ed. by Friedman. 1953. B6540
Tenenti, A. Cristoforo da Canal. 1962. B6541
Turin, Y. Miguel de Unamuno, universitaire. 1962. B6542
Vilar, P. La catalogne dans l'Espagne moderne. 3 v. 1962. B6543
Vivero, R. de. Du Japon et du bon gouvernement de l'Espagne et des Indes. 1972. B6544

BIBLIOTHEQUE GENERALE DES SCIENCE ECONOMIQUES (Compatables, Commerciales et Financières)

1 Baude, J. Traité complet de contrôles et expertises compatables. 1958. B6545
2 Hanon de Louvet, C. Analyse et discussion de bilans. 1955. B6546
3 Belvaux, P. A. Procédure d'expertise judiciare. 1941. B6547
4 Rey Alvarez, R. L'inventaire et la formation du bilan... 1942. B6548
5 Dykmans, G. L. La documentation en science économique. 1943. B6549
6 ____. Méthodologie des sciences commerciales. 1943. B6550
7 Mahieu, P. Les réalisations sociales à l'usine. 1943. B6551
8 Dechesne, L. Economie industrielle et sociale. 1949. B6552

9 Jordens, M. Droit et technique des opérations maritimes... 1944. B6553
10 Dechesne, L. Economie géographique. 1948. B6554
11 Pauwels, M. Analyse de l'exploritation. 1947. B6555
12 Dykmans, G. L. Introduction critique à la science économique. V. 1. 1944. B6556
13 Wahlin, C. Le financement du commerce international. 1945. B6557
14 Same as no. 12. V. 2. 1945. B6558
15 Leener, G. de. Traité de principes généraux de l'organisation. 2 v. 1945. B6559
16 Dechesne, L. Economie commerciale. 1945. B6560
17 Claude, G. La composition française à l'usage des affaires. 1947. B6561
18 Dechesne, L. La localisation des diverses productions, règles rationnelles déduites de l'expérience. 1945. B6562
19 ____. Economie internationale. 1946. B6563
20 Valley, J. Amortissement, àutofinancement, dévaluation. 1946. B6564
21 Groote, P. de. Traité d'exploitation des transports. 1946. B6565
22 Blockel, R. Opérations de banque. 1946. B6566
23 Magain, A. Code des finances et de la comptabilité publique. 2 v. 1946. B6567
24 Waleffe, F. Technique et legislation des assurances. 1946. B6568
24 ____. Cours d'assurances privées. 2d ed. 1958. B6569
25 Masoin, M. Théorie économique des finances publiques. 1947. B6570
26 Decoster, E. Initiation bancaire. 1950. B6571
27 Todt, E. L'organisation du service social dans l'entreprise. 1947. B6572
28 Jacques, R. Traité complet de compatabilité des sociétés. 1947. B6573
29 Maes, G. Comment recruter, sélectionner et utiliser le personnel de bureau. 1947. B6574
30 François, L. and Henry, N. Traité des opérations de change-bourse-banque. 1947. B6575
31 Haenens, L. P. F. d'Comment se documenter dans les petites, moyennes et grandes entreprises. 1948. B6576
32 Bovyn, A. Calculs commerciaux et calculs financiers. 1948. B6577
33 Leemans, L. Administration, organisation et compatabilité industrielles. 1949. B6578
34 Maurice, H. Tables pour les operations financières et viagères. 1949. B6579
35 Verbrugge-Baude, H. Traité de comptabilité de banque. 1948. B6580
36 Same as no. 12. V. 3. 1951. B6581
37 Spreutels, M. Théorie et pratique du rapport. 1951. B6582
38 Masoin, M. Précis d'économie politique. 1951. B6583
39 Maurice, H. Les opérations financières et les opérations viagères. 1951. B6584
40 Kirschen, E. S. Conduite financière des entreprises privées et publiques. 1952. B6585
41 Fossoul, A. C. Organisation et technique compatable de l'assurance. 1952. B6586
42 Dykmans, G. L. Législation et règlements consulaires belges. 1952. B6587
43 Belvaux, P. A. Théorie et pratique de l'expertise judicaire. 1953. B6588
44 Buisseret, E. Documents commerciaux et comptabilité commerciale. 1954. B6589
45-46 Baude, J. Cours élémentaire de droit commercial commenté et expliqué. 2 v. 1955. B6590
47 Adriaens, M. and Lennertz, F. J. Guide pratique du

commissionaire-expéditeur maritime. 1955-57. B6591
48-50 Lefebvre, V. Géographie économique. 3 v. 1955. B6592
V. 1 La Belgique et le Congo au milieu du XXe siècle géographie économique. 1955. B6593
V. 2 L'Europe et l'Asie Soviétique au milieu du XXe siècle. géographie économique. 1955. B6594
V. 3 Le monde moins l'Europe et l'Asie Soviétique au milieu du XXe siècle géographie économique. 1957. B6595
51 ____. Psychologie et pratique de la vente. 1957. B6596
52 Brun, J. and others. Pratique de la rédacion. 1957. B6597
53 Laloire, M. Précis theorique et technique de publicité. 1957. B6598
54 Finet, J. Eléments de monnaie et finance à l'usage de la pratique et de l'enseignement. 1957. B6599
55 Peumans, H. Lecture et critique de bilans. 1957. B6600
56 Baude, J. Technique du contrôle et Contrôle comptable et banque. 1960. B6601
57 Desirotte, H. Compatabilité des petotes, moyennes et grands entreprises commerciales. 1961. B6602

BIBLIOTHEQUE HISTORIQUE VAUDOIS (1-10 Rouge, 11- Martin)

1 Martin, C. H. La réglementation bernoise des monnaies au pays de Vaud. 1940. B6603
2 Chapuis, M. Recherches sur les institutions politiques du pays de Vaud du XIe au XIIIe siècle. 1940. B6604
3 Biaudet, J. C. La Suisse et la monarchie de juillet. 1941. B6605
4 Rapp, C. La seisneurie de Prangins du XIIIme siècle à la chute de l'ancien regime. 1942. B6606
5 Mercier-Campiche, M. Le Théâtre de Lausanne de 1871 à 1914. 1944. B6607
6 Chamorel, G. P. La liquidation des droits féodaux dans le canton de Vaud. 1944. B6608
7 Perret, J. P. Les imprimeries d'Yverdon au XVIIe et au XVIIIe siècles. 1945. B6609
8 Déglon, R. Yverdon au moyen âge. 1949. B6610
9 Chevallaz, G. A. Aspects de l'agriculture vaudoise à la fin de l'ancien régime. 1949. B6611
10 Baud, J. P. Le plaict générale de Lausanne de 1368. B6612
11 Pelet, P. L. Le Canal d'Entreroches. 1952. B6613
12 Panchaud, G. Les écoles vaudoises à la fin du régime bernois. 1952. B6614
13 Bugnion, J. Les villes de franchises au pays de Vaud, 1144-1350. 1952. B6615
14 Société vaudoise d'histoire et d'archaéologie. Cent cinquante ans d'histoire vaudoise, 1803-1953. 1953. B6616
15 Monod, H. Souvenirs inédits. 1953. B6617
16 Poget, S. W. Les écoles et le collège d'Orbe. 1954. B6618
17 Dessemontet, O. La seigneurie de Belmont au pays de Vaud, 1154-1553. 1955. B6619
18 Poudret, J. F. La succession testamentaire dans le pays de Vaud à l'époque (XIIIe-XVIe siècle). 1955. B6620
19 Schmidt, M. La Réformation des notaires dans le pays de Vaud, 1717-1723. 1957. B6621
20 Leu, J. J. Le cautionnement dans pays de Vaud, XIIe-XVIe siècle. 1958. B6622
21 Meylan, M. Le grand conseil vaudois sous l'acte de médiation. 1958. B6623
22 Gilliard, C. Pages d'histoire vaudoise. 1959. B6624

23 Mühll, M. von der. Maléfices et cour impériale. 1960. B6625
24 Lasserre, A. Henri Druey... 1960. B6626
25 Michon, F. La condition des gens mariés dans la famille vaudoise au XVIe siècle. 1960. B6627
26 Blaser, A. Les officiers de l'eveque et des couvents du diocese de Lausanne. 1960. B6628
27 Sandoz, H. La procédure ordinaire de saisis et de vente forces a l'époque bernoise dans le Pays de Vaud (XVI-XVIIIe siècle). 1960. B6629
28 Babaiantz, C. L'organisation bernoise des transports en pays romand XVIIIe siècle. 1961. B6630
29-32 Olivier, E. Médecine et santé dans le Pays de Vaud. Pt. 1. 2 v. Pt. 2. 2 v. 1962. B6631
33 La feuille d'avis de Lausanne, 1762-1962, by Junod and others. 1962. B6632
34 Burdet, J. Le musique dans le pays de vaud sous le régime bernois (1536-1798). 1963. B6633
35 Centlivres, R. and Fleury, J. J. De l'Eglise d'Etat à l'Eglise nationale, 1839-1863. 1963. B6634
36 Champoud, P. Les droits seigneuriaux dans le pays de Vaud d'après les reconnaissances reçues par Jean Bolay de 1403 à 1409. 1963. B6635
37 Dubois, F. O. Lonay. 1963. B6636
38 Monnaies au pays de vaud, ed. by Biaudet. 1964. B6637
39 L'abbatiale de Payerne. 1966. B6638
40 Nouvelles pages d'histoire vaudoise, by Poudret and others. 1967. B6639
41 Le Général Antoine-Henri Jomini, by Chuard and others. 1968. B6640
42 Lousonna, by Bogli and others. 1969. B6641
43 Mélanges d'histoire du XVIe siècle, offerts à Henri Meylan. 1970. B6642
44 Burdet, J. La musique dans le canton de Vaud au XIXe siècle. 1971. B6643
45 Gallone, P. Organisation judiciaire et procédure devant les cours laiques du Pays de Vaud. 1972. B6644
46 Paquier, R. Histoire d'un village vaudois. 1972. B6645
47 Anex, D. Le servage au pays de Vaud. 1972. B6646
48 Lasserre, A. La classe ouvrière dans la Société Vaudoise. 1973. B6647
49 Pelet, P. L. Une industrie méconnue fer Charbon Acier dans le pays de vaud. 1973. B6648
50 Martin, C. Trésors et trouvailles monétaires. 1973. B6649
51 Giddey, E. L'angleterre dans la vie intellectielle de la suisse romande. 1974. B6650
52 Ruffieux, R. Les élections au grand conseil vaudois. 1974. B6651
53 Druey, H. Correspondance, ed. by Steiner and Lasserre. V. 1. 1974. B6652
54 Claude, A. Un artisanat minier. 1974. B6653

BIBLIOTHEQUE LITTERAIRE DE LA RENAISSANCE (Bouillon, 1898-1904; Champion 1906-)

Première serie:
1 Cochin, M. D. B. M. La chronologie du Canzoniere de Pétrarque. 1898. B6654
2-3 Gaguini, R. Roberti Gaguini Epistole et orationes. 1903. B6655
4 Cochin, H. La frère de Pétrarque et le livre Du repos des religieux. 1904. B6656
5 Thuasne, L. Etudes sur Rabelais. 1904. B6657
6 Petraca, F. La traité De Sui ipsius et multorum ignorantia. 1906. B6658
7 Zangroniz, J. de. Montaigne, Amyot et Saliat. 1906. B6659

8 Sturel, R. Jacques Amyot. 1908. B6660
9 Villey, P. Les sources italiennes de la "Deffense et illustration de la langue françoise" de Joachim du Bellay. 1908. B6661
10 Schiff, M. L. La fille d'alliance de Montaigne, Marie de Gournay; essai suivi de "L'egalité des hommes et des femmes et du Grief des dames." 1910. B6662
11 Longnon, H. Essai sur Pierre de Ronsard. 1912. B6663
12 Hauvette, H. Etudes sur la Divine comédie, la composition du poème et son rayonnement. 1922. B6664

Deuxième serie:

1-2 Nolhac, H. P. de. Pétrarque et l'humanisme. 1907. B6665
3 Courteault, P. Geoffroy de Malvyn, magistrat et humaniste bordelais (1545-1617). 1907. B6666
4 Guy, H. Histoire de la poesie française au XVIe siècle. 1910. B6667
5 Zanta, L. La renaissance du stoïcime au XVIe siècle. 1914. B6668
6 Busson, H. Charles d'Espinay, évêque de Dol, et son oeuvre poétique. 1923. B6669
7 Franchet, H. Le poète et son oeuvre, d'après Ronsard. 1923. B6670
8 ____. Le philosophie parfait et Le Temple de vertu. 1923. B6671
9 Nolhac, L. de. Un poète rhénan, ami de la Pleiade: Paul Melissus. 1923. B6672
10 Mignon, M. Etudes sur le théâtre français & italien de la renaissance. 1923. B6673
11 Villey-Desmeserts, P. L. J. Les grands écrivains du XVIe siècle. V. 1. Marot et Rabelais. 1923. B6674
12 Guy, H. Histoire de la poesie française au XVIe siècle. Tome II. Clément Marot et son école. 1910. B6675
13 Raffin, L. Saint-Julien de Balleure, historien bourguignon 1519-1593. 1926. B6676
14-15 Raymond, M. L'influence de Ronsard sur le poésie française (1500-1585). 1927. B6677
16 Hauvette, H. L'Arioste et la poesie chevalersque à Ferrare au début du XVIe siècle. 1927. B6678
17 Lebègue, R. La tragédie religieuse en France; les débuts (1514-1573). 1929. B6679
18 Graur, T. Un disciple de Ronsard, Amadis Jamyn. 1929. B6680
19-20 Jourda, P. Marguerite d'Angoulême, duchesse d'Alençon, reine de Navarre (1492-1549). 1930. B6681
21 ____. Répertoire analytique et chronologique de la correspondence de Marguerite d'Angoulême, duchesse d'Alençon, reine de Navarre. 1930. B6682
22 Mann, M. Erasme et les débuts de la réforme française. 1934. B6683

BIBLIOTHEQUE PHILOSOPHIQUE DE LOUVAIN (Univ. of Louvain)

1 Raeymaeker, L. de. Philosophie de l'être; essai de synthese métaphysique. 1947. B6684
2 Waelhens, A. de. La philosophie de Martin Heidegger. 1948. B6685
3 Riet, G. von. L'epistémologie thomiste. 1946. B6686
4 Leclercq, J. Les grandes lignes de la philosophie morale. 1954. B6687
5 Pirlot, J. L'enseignement de la métaphysique. Critiques et suggestions. 1950. B6688
6 Ortegat, P. Intuition et religion, le problème existentialist. 1947. B6689
7 Grégoire, F. Aux sources de la pensée de Marx: Hegel, Feuerbach. 1947. B6690
8 Ortegat, P. Philosophie de la religion. 2 v. 1948. B6691

9 Waelhens, A. de. Une philosophie de l'ambiguité; l'existentialisme de Maurice Merleau-Ponty. 1951. B6692
10 Dondeyne, A. Foi chrétienne et pensée contemporaine. 1961. B6693
11 Asveld, P. La pensée religieuse du jeune Hegel. 1953. B6694
12 Jacques, E. Introduction au problème de la connaissance. 1953. B6695
13 Strasser, S. Le problème de l'âme. 1953. B6696
14 Vanhoutte, M. La philosophie politique de Platon dans les "Lois." 1954. B6697
15 Leclercq, J. La philosophie morale de Saint Thomas devant la pensée contemporaine. 1955. B6698
16 Autor d'Aristotle; recueil d'études de philosophie ancienne et médiévale offert à Msgr. A. Mansion. 1955. B6699
17 Coninck, A., de. L'analytique trancendentale de Kant. V. 1. 1955. B6700
18 Vanhoutte, M. La méthode ontologique de Platon. 1956. B6701
19 Gregoire, F. Etudes hégéliennes. 1958. B6702
20 Riet, G. van. Problèmes d'épistémologie. 1960. B6703
21 Strasser, S. Phénoménologie et sciences de l'homme. 1967. B6704
22 Denissoff, E. Descartes. 1970. B6705
23 Riet, G. van. Philosophie et religion. 1970. B6706
24 Leonard, A. Commentaire littéral de la logique de Hegel. 1974. B6707

BIBLIOTHEQUE SCIENTIFIQUE INTERNATIONALE (Presses Universitaires de France)

Andrews, T. G. Méthodes de la psychologie. 2 v. 1953. B6708
Apostel, L. and others. Les liaisons analytiques et synthétiques dans les comportements de sujets. 1957. B6709
____. Logique, langage et théorie de l'information. 1957. B6710
L'apprentissage sur structure logiques, ed. by Morf and others. 1959. B6711
Association de psychologie scientifique de la langue française. La perception. 1955. B6712
Auerbury, J. L. Fourmis, abeilles et guêpes. 2 v. 1883. B6713
Bagehot, W. Lois scientifique du développement des notions dans leurs rapports avec les principes de la sélection naturelle et de l'héredité. 1875. B6714
Bain, A. La science de l'education. 1882. B6715
Bastian, H. C. Le cerveau organe de la pensée chez l'homme et chez les animaux. 2 v. 1888. B6716
Baumgarten, F. Le psychotechnique dans le monde moderne. 1950. B6717
Bender, L. Un test visuomteur et son usage clinique. 1957. B6718
Berthelot, M. P. E. La synthèse chimique. 1876. B6719
____. La révolution chimique. 1890. B6720
Beth, E. W. and others. Epistémologie génetique et recherche psychologique. 1957. B6721
Binet, A. and Féré, C. La magnétisme animal. 1890. B6722
Bochner, R. and Halpern, F. C. L'application clinique du test Rorshach. 1948. B6723
Bohm, E. Traité de psychodiagnostic de Rorshach. 2 v. 1956. B6724
Bourdeau, L. Histoire de l'habillement et de la parure. 1904. B6725
Brialmont, A. H. La défense des états et les camps retranchés. 1880. B6726
Brücke, E. W. Principes scientifiques des beaux-arts. 1878. B6727
Brunache, P. La centre de

l'Afrique. 1894. B6728
Bruner, J. S. and others. Etudes d'épistemologie génétique. V. 6. 1957. B6729
Brunet, O. and Lézine, L. Le développement psychologique de la première enfance. 1951. B6730
Candolle, A. L. P. P. d. Origine des plantes cultivées. 1883. B6731
Carmichael, L. Manual de psychologie de l'enfant. 3 v. 1952-56. B6732
Cartailhac, E. La France préhistorique d'après les sépultures et les monuments. 1896. B6733
Chauchard, P. Précis de biologie humaine. 1957. B6734
Colajanni, N. Latins et Anglo-Saxons. 1905. B6735
Constantin, N. A. Le rôle sociologique de la guerre et la sentiment national. 1907. B6736
Cottell, R. B. La personnalité. 2 v. 1956. B6737
Demeny, G. E. J. Les bases scientifiques de l'éducation physique. 1902. B6738
____. Mécanisme et éducation des mouvements. 1911. B6739
Demoor, J. and others. L'évolution régressive en biologie et en sociologie. 1897. B6740
Le Diagnostic du caractère, by Klages and others. 1949. B6741
Eysenck, H. L. and others. Les dimensions de la personnalité. 1950. B6742
Faverge, J. M. Introduction aux méthodes statistiques en psychologie appliquée. 1949. B6743
____. Méthodes statistiques en psychologie appliqué. 2 v. 1954. B6744
Fraisse, P. and others. Les attitudes. 1961. B6745
____. Manual pratique de psychologie expérimentale. 1956. B6746
Gellé, M. E. L'audition et ses organes. 1899. B6747
Gesell, A. L. and Ilg, F. L. L'enfant de 5 à 10 ans. 1956. B6748
____. L'orientation du developpement de l'enfant à l'école des toutpetits et à la maison. 1956. B6749
Gesell, A. L. and others. Le jeune enfant dans la civilisation moderne. 1949. B6750
Grosse, E. Les débuts de l'art. 1902. B6751
Guignet, E. and Garnier, E. La céramique ancienne. et moderne. 1899. B6752
Hartmann, R. Les singes anthropoïdes et leur organisation comparée à celle de l'homme. 1886. B6753
Harvey, H. W. Chimie et biologie de l'eau de mer. 1948. B6754
Heitler, W. Elements de mécanique ondulatoire. 1949. B6755
Huxley, T. H. L'ecrevisse. 1890. B6756
International congres de psychotechnique. Psychotechnique dans la monde moderne. 1954. B6757
Jaccard, A. Le pétrole, l'asphalte et le bitume au point de vue géologique. 1895. B6758
Javal, E. Physiologie de la lecture et de l'écriture. 1906. B6759
Jonckheere, A. and others. Etudes d'épistemologie genétique. V. 5. La lecture de l'expérience. 1958. B6760
Klineberg, O. Psychologie sociale. 2 v. 1957. B6761
Kohler, C. Les déficiences intellectuelles chez l'enfant. 1954. B6762
Krech, D. and Crutchfield, R. S. Théorie et problèmes de psychologie sociale. 2 v. 1949. B6763
Lagrange, F. Physiologie des exercises du corps. 1891. B6764
Laloy, L. Parasitisme et mutualisme dans la nature. 1906. B6765
Lanessan, J. M. A. de. Introduction à la botanique. 1885. B6766
____. Principes de colonisation. 1897. B6767
Laurendeau, M. and Pinard, A.

Thomson, G. H. L'analyse factorielle des aptitudes humaines. 1950. B6811
Topinard, P. L'homme dans la nature. 1891. B6812
Trouessart, E. Les microbes. 1891. B6813
Vernon, P. E. La structure des aptitudes humaines. 1952. B6814
Wechsler, D. La mesure de l'intelligence de l'adulte. 1956. B6815
Weil, P. G. L'affectivo-diagnostic. 1953. B6816
Wolff, C. La main humaine. 2 v. 1952. B6817
Woodward, R. S. Psychologie expérimentale, tr. by Ombredane and Lézine. 1949. B6818
Wurtz, C. A. La theorié atomique. 1911. B6819
Zazzo, R. Les jumeaux. 2 v. 1960. B6820
Zulliger, H. Le test Z individuel. 1961. B6821

BIBLIOTHEQUE THEOLOGIQUE (Delachaux)

Allmen, J. J. von. Le Saint ministère selon la conviction et la volontè des Reformes du 16e siècle. 1968. B6822
Amsler, S. L'ancien testament dans l'Eglise. 1960. B6823
Analyse structurale et exégèse biblique, by Barthes and others. 1972. B6824
Aux sources de la tradition chrétienne, by Benoit and others. 1950. B6825
Barth, K. Esquisse d'une dogmatique. 1960. B6826
____. La preuve de l'existence de Dieu d'après Saint Anselme. 1958. B6827
Bovon, F. Exegesis. 1974. B6828
Bridel, C. Aux seuils de l'espérance. 1971. B6829
Bultmann, R. Histoire et eschatalogie. 1958. B6830
Carrez, M. Le la souffrance à la glorie de la δοξα dans la pensée paulinienne. 1964. B6831
____. Lexique grec-français du Nouveau Testament. V. 1. 1966. B6832
Chevallier, M. A. Esprit de dieu. 1965. B6833
Cullmann, O. Christ et le temps. 1947. B6834
____. Christologie du Nouveau Testament. 1959. B6835
____. Des sources de l'evangile à la formation de la théologie chrétienne. 1972. B6836
____. Etudes de théologique biblique. 1968. B6837
____. La foi et le culte de l'Eglise primitive. 1963. B6838
____. Saint Pierre. 1952. B6839
____. Le salut dans l'histoire. 1966. B6840
Cullmann, O. and others. Le dialogue est ouvert I. 1965. B6841
Dix, G. Le ministere dans l'église ancienne. 1955. B6842
Espine, H. La cure d'âme. 1956. B6843
Evdokimov, P. L'orthodoxie. 1959. B6844
Gardeil, A. La crédibilité et l'apologétique. 1928. B6845
____. La structure de l'âme et l'expérience mystique. 1927. B6846
Héring, J. Le royaume de Dieu et sa venue. 1959. B6847
Heussi, K. and Peter, E. Précis d'histoire de l'Eglise. 1972. B6848
Hoffmann, J. G. H. La réforme en Suède, 1523-72. 1945. B6849
Hugede, N. La metaphore du miroir. 1958. B6850
Jacobs, E. Théologie de l'Ancien Testament. 1968. B6851
Kasser, R. L'Evangile selon, saint Jean et les versions coptes de la Bible. 1966. B6852
____. L'evangile selon Thomas. 1961. B6853
Kraemer, H. La foi chrétienne et les religions non-chrétiennes. 1956. B6854
Lecerf, A. Etudes calvinistes. 1949. B6855
Leenhardt, F. J. Parole-Ecriture-Sacrements. 1968. B6856

____. Le sacrement de la Sainte-Cène. 1945. B6857
Leuba, J. L. A la découverte de l'espace occumeneque. 1967. B6858
____. L'institution et l'événement. 1950. B6859
Lindbeck, G. A. Le dialogue est Ouvert. V. 1. 1965. B6860
Lods, M. Précis d'histoire de la théologie chrétienne. 1966. B6861
Martin-Achard, R. Actualité d'Abraham. 1973. B6862
____. De la mort à la resurrection d'après l'ancien testament. 1956. B6863
Masson, C. L'evangile de Marc et l'Eglise de Rome. 1972. B6864
Mehl, R. La condition du philosophie chrétien. 1947. B6865
____. Traité de sociologie du protestantisme. 1965. B6866
Michaeli, F. L'ancien testament et l'église chrétienne d'aujourd'hui. 1956. B6867
____. Dieu à l'image de l'homme. 1950. B6868
Miegge, G. L'evangile et le mythe dans la pensée de R. Bultmann. 1958. B6869
Niebuhr, R. Foi et histoire. 1955. B6870
Paquier, R. Traité de liturgie. 1973. B6871
Preiss, T. La vie en Christ. 1951. B6872
Prenter, R. Connaitre el Christ. 1966. B6873
Rome nous enterpelle, by Cullmann and others. 1972. B6874
Siegwalt, G. La Loi, chemin du Salut. 1971. B6875
Spindler, M. La mission. 1967. B6876
Stauffer, R. Le catholicisme à la découverte de Luther. 1966. B6877
Strohl, H. La pensée de la Réforme. 1973. B6878
Süss, T. La communion au corps du Christ. 1968. B6879
Thurneysen, E. Doctrine de la Cure d'Ame. 1958. B6880
Trocmé, E. Jesus de Nazareth. 1972. B6881
Vignaux, G. P. La théologie de l'histoire chez R. Niebuhr. 1958. B6882
Watteville, J. F. N. de. Le Sacrifice dans les textes eucharistiques des premiers siècles. 1966. B6883
Widmer, G. P. Les valeurs et leur signification théologique. 1950. B6884
Zucher, J. L'homme. 1953. B6885

BIBLIOTHEQUE THOMISTE (1-12 La Saulchoir, 13- Vrin)

1 Mandonnet, P. F. and Destrez, J. Bibliographie thomiste. 1960. B6886
2 Kors, J. B. La justice primitive et le péché originel d'après saint Thomas. 1922. B6887
3 Mélanges thomistes. 1923. B6888
4 Kruitwagen, B. S. Thomae de Aquino Summa opusculorum, anno circiter 1485 typis edita. 1924. B6889
5 Glorieux, P. La littérature quodlibétique, de 1260 à 1320. 1925. B6890
6-7 Théry, G. David de Dínant. 2 v. 1925-26. B6891
8 Thomas Aquinas, St. Le De ente et essentia, ed. by Roland-Gosselin. 1948. B6892
9 Glorieux, P. Les premières polémiques thomiste. V. 1. 1927. B6893
10 Périnelle, J. L'attrition d'après le Concile de Trente et d'après saint Thomas d'Aquin. 1927. B6894
11 Prepositinus. Prepositini cancellarii parisiensis opera omnia. V. 1. 1928. B6895
12 Ulrich von Strassburg. Summa de bono. 1930. B6896
13-14 Mélanges Mandonnet. 2 v. 1930. B6897
15 Penido, M. T. L. Le rôle de l'analogie en théologie dogmatique. 1931. B6898
16 Capelle, G. C. Amaury de Bène. 1932. B6899
17 Roland-Gesselin, M. D. Essai d'une étude critique

de la connaissance. 1932. B6900
18 Destrez, J. Etudes critiques sur les oeuvres de saint Thomas d'Aquin. 1933. B6901
19 Riviere, J. Le dogme de la Rédémption au début du moyen âge. 1934. B6902
20 Vaux, R. de. Notes et textes sur l'aviceenisme latin aux confins des XIIe et XIIIe siècles. 1934. B6903
21 Same as no. 5. V. 2. 1935. B6904
22 Rabeau, G. Species Verbum. L'activité intellectuelle élémentaire selon saint Thomas d'Aquin. 1938. B6905
23 Geiger, L. B. La participation dans la philosophie de S. Thomas d'Aquin. 1942. B6906
24 Mahieu, C. L. Dominique de Flandre (XVe siècle), sa métaphysique. 1942. B6907
25 Dondaine, H. L'attrition suffisante. 1943. B6908
26 Spicq, Le P. Esquisse d'une histoire de l'exégèse latine au moyen âge. 1944. B6909
27 Manteau-Bonamy, H. M. Maternité divine et incarnation. 1949. B6910
28 Gauthier, R. A. Magnanimité. 1951. B6911
29 Isaac, J. Le Peri hermeneias en occident de Boeĉe a Saint Thomas, histoire littéraire d'un traité d'Aristote. 1953. B6912
30 Aubert, J. M. Le droit romain dans l'oeuvre de Saint Thomas. 1955. B6913
31 Same as no. 9. V. 2. 1935. B6914
32 Malet, A. Personne et amour dans le théologie trinitaire de saint Thomas d'Aquin. 1956. B6915
33 Chenu, M. D. La théologie comme science au XIIIe siècle. 1957. B6916
34 Bernard, C. A. Théologie de l'espérance selon saint Thomas d'Aquin. 1961. B6917
35 Ruello, F. Les noms divins et leurs raisons selon saint Albert le Grand. 1963. B6918
36 Michaud-Quantin, P. La psychologie de l'activité chez saint Albert le Grand. 1964. B6919
37 Mélanges offerts à M.-D. Chenu. 1967. B6920
38 Robert d'Orford. Reprobationes dictorum a fratre Egidio in primium sententairum, ed. by Vella. 1968. B6921
39 Laverdiere, R. Le principe de causalité. 1969. B6922
40 Wéber, E. H. La controverse de 1270 à l'Université de Paris et son retentissement sur la pensée de s. Thomas d'Aquin. 1970. B6923
41 Weber, E. H. Dialogue et dissensions entre Saint Bonaventure et Saint Thomas d'Aquin à Paris. 1974. B6924

Some titles in the series are subseries of the series. The numbers in parentheses refer to the above listing.
Section historique: 9(9), 14(16), 15(18), 16(19), 17(20), 18(21).
Section philosophique: 1(17).
Section théologique: 1(10), 2(15).

BICENTENNIAL HISTORY OF COLUMBIA UNIVERSITY (Columbia Univ. Pr.)

Baker, R. T. A history of the Graduate School of Journalism, Columbia University. 1954. B6925
Ballard, C. W. A history of the College of Pharmacy, Columbia University. 1954. B6926
Columbia Univ. Foundation for research. A history of the School of Law, Columbia University, ed. by Goebel. 1955. B6927
Cowan, L. G. A history of the School of International Affairs and associated area institutes, Columbia University. 1954. B6928
Cremin, L. A. and others. A history of Teachers College, Columbia University. 1954. B6929

Finch, J. K. A history of the School of Engineering, Columbia University. 1954. B6930
Fisher, R. M., ed. The metropolis in American life. 1955. B6931
A History of Columbia College on Morningside. 1954. B6932
A History of the Faculty of Philosophy of Columbia University. 1957. B6933
Hoxie, R. G. and others. A history of the Faculty of Political Science, Columbia University. 1955. B6934
Meier, E. G. A history of the New York School of Social Work. 1954. B6935
Rohdenburg, T. K. A history of the School of Architecture, Columbia University. 1954. B6936
Trautman, O. A history of the School of Library Science, Columbia University. 1954. B6937
Van Metre, T. W. A history of the Graduate School of Business, Columbia University. 1954. B6938
White, M. C. A history of Barnard College. 1954. B6939

BILANS DE LA CONNAISSANCE ECONOMIQUE (Rivière)

1 Mossé, R. La monnaie. 1950. B6940
2 Guitton, H. L'objet de l'économie politique. 1951. B6941
3 Mossé, R. Les salaires. 1952. B6942
4 Reynaud, P. L. La psychologie économique. 1954. B6943
5 Moret, M. L'échange international. 1957. B6944
6 Dieterlen, P. L'investissement. 1957. B6945
7 Valarché, J. L'économie rurale [suivi d'observations] de Rene Dumont, Denis Bergmann [et] Carlo Vanzetti. 1959. B6946
8 Austruy, J. Le scandale du developpement. 1965. B6947
9 Crussard, J. L'énergie thermonucléaire. 1963. B6948
10 Lapostalle, P. Les accélérateurs de particules. 1964. B6949

BILATERAL STUDIES IN PRIVATE INTERNATIONAL LAW (Oceana)

1 Nussbaum, A. American-Swiss private international law. 1958. B6950
2 Delaume, G. R. American-French private international law. 1961. B6951
3 Kollewijn, R. D. American-Dutch private international law. 1961. B6952
4 Domke, M. American-German private international law. 1972. B6953
5 Eder, P. J. American-Colombian private international law. 1956. B6954
6 Ehrenzweig, A. A. and others. American-Greek private international law. 1957. B6955
7 Philip, A. American-Danish private international law. 1957. B6956
8 Cowen, Z. American-Austrian private international law. 1957. B6957
9 Garland, P. G. American-Brazilian private international law. 1959. B6958
10 Etcheberry, O. A. American-Chilean private international law. 1960. B6959
11 Seidl-Hohenveldern, I. American-Austrian private international law. 1963. B6960
12 Ehrenzweig, A. A. and others. American-Japanese private international law. 1964. B6961
13 Nial, H. American-Swedish private international law. 1965. B6962
14 Lombard, R. S. American-Venezuelan private international law. 1965. B6963
15 Goldschmidt, W. and Rodriguez-Novas, J. American-Argentine private international law. 1966. B6964
16 Ansay, T. American-Turkish private international

law. 1966. B6965
17 Hecke, G. A. van. American-Belgian private international law. 1968. B6966

BIOGRAPHY AND CRITICISM (St. Martin's)

1 Simpson, L. A. M. James Hogg. 1962. B6967
2 Cowasjee, S. Sean O'Casey. 1963. B6968
3 Thornton, R. D. James Currie. 1963. B6969
4 Jefferson, D. W. Henry James and the modern reader. 1964. B6970
5 Davies, M. Apollinaire. 1964. B6971
6 King, B. A. Dryden's major plays. 1966. B6972
7 Butter, P. H. Edwin Muir. 1966. B6973
8 Spence, G. W. Tolstoy the ascetic. 1968. B6974
9 Godfrey, D. E. M. Forster's other kingdom. 1968. B6975
10 Melchiori, B. Browning's poetry of reticence. 1968. B6976
12 Yudhistav. Conflict in the novels of D. H. Lawrence. 1969. B6977
13 Butterfield, R. W. The broken arc. 1969. B6978
14 Carter, A. John Osborne. 1969. B6979

BIRMINGHAM. UNIVERSITY. DEPARTMENT OF ECONOMICS AND INSTITUTIONS OF THE USSR. MONOGRAPHS ON THE SOVIET ECONOMIC SYSTEM (Blackwell)

1 Barker, G. R. Some problems of incentives and labor productivity in Soviety industry. 1956. B6980

BOLLINGEN SERIES (Pantheon)

1 King, J. Where the two came to their father, recorded by Oakes. 1943. B6981
2 Rougemont, D. de. The devil's share, tr. by Chevalier. 1954. B6982
3 Plato. The Timaeus and the Critias. The Thomas Taylor translation with introduction and notes from the original edition of 1810. 1945. B6983
4 Raphael, M. Prehistoric cave paintings, tr. by Guterman. 1945. B6984
5 Radin, P., ed. and tr. The road of life and death. 1945. B6985
6 Zimmer, H. R. Myths and symbols in Indian art and civilization, ed. by Campbell. 1946. B6986
7 Friedmann, H. The symbolic goldfinch. 1946. B6987
8 Raphael, M. Prehistoric pottery and civilization in Egypt, tr. by Guterman. 1947. B6988
9 Bespaloff, R. On the Iliad, tr. by McCarthy. 1948. B6989
10 Harding, M. E. Psychic energy. 1962. B6990
11 Zimmer, H. R. The king and the corpse, ed. by Campbell. 1948. B6991
12 Cairns, H., ed. The limits of art. 1948. B6992
13 Breasted, J. H. Egyptian servant statues. 1948. B6993
14 Committee of Ancient Near East Seals. Corpus of ancient Near Eastern seals in North American collections. V. 1. The Collection of the Pierpont Morgan Library, ed. by Porada. 1948. B6994
15 Léger, A. S.-L. Exile, and other poems, tr. by Devlin. 1949. B6995
16 Lectures in criticism, by Blackmur and others. 1949. B6996
17 Campbell, J. The hero with a thousand faces. 1949. B6997
18 Reichard, G. A. Navaho religion. 2 v. 1950. B6998
19 I Ching. The I Ching; or Book of changes. The Richard Wilhelm trans., trans. by Baynes. 2 v. 1950. B6999
20 Jung, C. G. Collected works, ed. by Read and

others, tr. by Hull. V. 1 Psychiatric studies. 1970. V. 2 Experimental researches, tr. by Stein and Riviere. 1972. V. 3 The psychogenesis in mental disease. 1960. V. 4 Freud and psychoanalysis. 1961. V. 5 Symbols of transformation. 1967. V. 6 Psychological types. 1971. V. 7 Two essays on analytical psychology. 1966. V. 8 The structure and dynamics of the psyche. 2 v. 1968. V. 9 The archetypes and the collective unconscious. 2 v. 1968. V. 10 Civilization in transition. 1970. V. 11 Psychology and religion. 1969. V. 12 Psychology and alchemy. 1968. V. 13 Alchemical studies. 1968. V. 14 Mysterium coniunctionis. 1970. V. 15 The spirit in man. 1966. V. 16 The practice of psychotherapy. 1966. V. 17 The development of personality. 1954. B7000

21 Schär, H. Religion and the cure of souls in Jung's psychology, tr. by Hull. 1950. B7001

22 Jung, C. G. and Kerényi, C. Essays on a science of mythology, tr. by Hull. 1949. B7002

23 Horapollo. The Hieroglyphics of Horapollo, tr. by Boas. 1950. B7003

24 Malraux, A. The psychology of art, tr. by Gilbert. 3 v. 1949-50. B7004

25 Fierz-David, L. The dream of Poliphilo, tr. by Hottinger. 1950. B7005

26 Zimmer, H. R. The philosophies of India, ed. by Campbell. 1951. B7006

27 Oakes, M. V. C. The two crosses of Todos Santos. 1951. B7007

28 Paracelsus. Selected writings, ed. by Jacobi, tr. by Guterman. 1958. B7008

29 Lu, C. The art of letters, tr. by Hughes. 1951. B7009

30 Eranos-Jahrbuch. Papers from the Eranos Yearbooks, ed. by Campbell. V. 1 Spirit and nature, tr. by Manheim and Hull. 1954. V. 2 The mysteries, tr. by Manheim and Hull. 1955. V. 3 Man and time, tr. by Manheim and Hull. 1956. V. 4 Spiritual disciplines, by Bernoulli, ed. by Campbell, tr. by Manheim. 1960. V. 5 Man and transformation, tr. by Manheim. 1964. V. 6 The mystic vision, ed. by Campbell, tr. by Manheim. 1968. B7010

31 Jung, C. G. Psychological reflexions, ed. by Jacobi. 1953. B7011

32 African folktales & sculpture, ed. by Radin. 1952. B7012

33 Hofmannsthal, H. H. V. 1 Selected prose, tr. by Hottinger and others. 1952. V. 2 Poems and verse plays. 1961. V. 3 Selected plays and libretti, ed. by Hamburger. 1963. B7013

34 Léger, A. S.-L. Winds, tr. by Chisholm. 1953. B7014

35 V. 1 Maritain, J. Creative intuition in art and poetry. 1953. V. 2 Clark, K. M. The nude, a study in ideal form. V. 3 Read, H. The art of sculpture. 1956. V. 4 Gilson, E. H. Painting and reality. 1957. V. 5 Gombrich, E. H. J. Art and illusion. V. 6 Giedion, S. The eternal present. 1: The beginnings of architecture. 1964. V. 7 Blunt, A. Nicolas Poussin. 1966. V. 8 Gabo, N. Of divers arts. 1962. V. 9 Lewis, W. S. Horace Walpole. 1961. V. 10 Grabar, A. Christian iconography. 2 v. 1968. V. 11 Raine, K. Blake and tradition. 2 v. 1968. V. 12 Pope-Hennessy, J. The portrait in the Renaissance. 1966. V. 13 Rosenberg, J. On quality in art. 1967. V. 15 Cecil, D. Visionary and

dreamer. 1968. V. 16 Praz, M. Mnemosyne. 1968. V. 22 Barzun, J. The use and abuse of art. 1973. B7015

36 Curtius, E. R. European literature and the Latin Middle Ages, tr. by Trask. 1953. B7016

37 Goodenough, E. R. Jewish symbols in the Greco-Roman period. V. 1 The archeological evidence from Palestine. 1953. V. 2 The archaeological evidence from the Diaspora. 1953. V. 3 Illustrations for volumes 1 and 2. 1953. V. 4 The problem of method and symbols from Jewish cult. 1954. V. 5-6 Fish, bread and wine. 1956. V. 7-8 Pagan symbols in Judaism. 1958. V. 9-11 Symbolism in the Dura synagogue. 3 v. 1964. V. 12 Summary and conclusion. 1966. V. 13 Indexes and maps. 1968. B7017

38 Seznec, J. The survival of the pagan gods, tr. by Sessions. 1953. B7018

39 Zimmer, H. R. The art of Indian Asia, ed. by Campbell. 2 v. 1955. B7019

40 Egyptian religious texts and representations. V. 1 The tomb of Rameses VI, ed. by Rambova, 2 pts. 1954. The shrines of Tut-Ankh-Amon, tr. by Piankoff, ed. by Rambova. 1955. V. 3 Mythological papyri, tr. by Piankoff. 1956. V. 4 The litany of Re, by Piankoff. 1964. V. 5 The pyramid of Unas, by Piankoff. 1968. B7020

41 Homerus. Chapman's Homer; the Illiad and the Odyssey and the lesser Homerica, ed. by Nicoll. 2 v. 1956. B7021

42 Neumann, E. The origins and history of consciousness, tr. by Hull. 1954. B7022

43 Ibn Khaldūn. The Muqaddimah, ed. by Rosenthal. 3 v. 1958. B7023

44 Zuckerkandl, V. Sound and symbol. V. 1 tr. by Trask, V. 2 tr. by Guterman. 2 v. 1956-73. B7024

45 Valéry, P. The collected works of Paul Valery, ed. by Mathews. V. 1 Poems, tr. by Paul. 1971. V. 2 Prose poems, tr. by Cooke. 1968. V. 3 Plays, tr. by Paul. 1960. V. 4 The dialogues, tr. by Stewart. 1956. V. 5 Idée fixe, tr. by Paul. 1965. V. 6 Monsieur Teste, tr. by Mathews. 1974. V. 7 The art of poetry, tr. by Folliot. 1958. V. 8 Leonardo, Poe, Mallarmé, tr. by Cowley and Lawler. 1972. V. 9 Masters and friends, tr. by Turnell. 1968. V. 10 History and politics, ed. by Mathews. 1962. V. 11 Occasions, tr. by Shattuck and Brown. 1970. V. 12 Dégas, Manet, Morisot, tr. by Paul. 1960. V. 13 Aesthetics, tr. by Manheim. 1964. V. 14 Analects, tr. by Gilbert. 1970. B7025

46 Eliade, M. The myth of the eternal return, tr. by Trask. 1954. B7026

47 Neumann, E. The great Mother, tr. by Manheim. 1955. B7027

48 Simson, O. G. von. The Gothic cathedral. 1962. B7028

49 Wang, K. The tao of painting, ed. by Sze. 2 v. 1956. B7029

50 Coleridge, S. T. The notebooks of Samuel Taylor Coleridge, ed. by Coburn. 2 v. 1957-61. B7030

51 The Interpretation of nature and the psyche, by Jung and Pauli, tr. by Hull. 1955. B7031

52 Panofsky, E. and D. Pandora's box. 1962. B7032

53 Wyman, L. C., ed. Beautyway, tr. by Haile. 1957. B7033

54 Apuleius Mandaurensis. Amor and Psyche, ed. by Neumann. 1956. B7034

55 Léger, A. S.-L. Eloges and other poems, tr. by Varèse. 1956. B7035

56 Eliade, M. Yoga, tr. by Trask. 1958. B7036
57 Jacobi, J. Complex, archetype, symbol in the psychology of C. G. Jung. 1959. B7037
58 Saunders, E. D. Mudrā. 1960. B7038
59 Friedlander, P. Plato, tr. by Meyerhoff. 3 v. 1958-69. B7039
60 V. 1 Lehmann-Hartleben, K. Samothrace, ed. by Lewis. 1958. V. 2:1 Fraser, P. M. The inscriptions on stone. 1960. V. 2:2 Lehmann, K. The inscriptions on ceramics and minor objects. 1960. V. 3 Lehmann, P. W. The Hieron. V. 4:1 Lehmann, K. The hall of votive lights. 1962. 4:2 Lehmann, K. and Spittle, D. The altar court. 1964. B7040
61 Neumann, E. Art and the creative unconscious, tr. by Manheim. 1959. B7041
62 Wilhelm, H. Change, tr. by Baynes. 1960. B7042
63 Adler, G. The living symbol. 1961. B7043
64 Suzuki, D. T. Zen and Japanese culture. 1958. B7044
65 Kerényi, K. Archetypal images in Greek religion, tr. by Manheim. V. 1 Prometheus. 1963. V. 2 Dionysos. 1974. V. 3 Asklepios. 1959. V. 4 Eleusis. 1967. B7045
66 Corbin, H. Avicenna and the visionary recital, tr. by Trask. 1960. B7046
67 Léger, A. S.-L. Seamarks, tr. by Fowlie. 1958. B7047
68 Neumann, E. The archetypal world of Henry Moore, tr. by Hull. 1958. B7048
69 Léger, A. S.-L. Chronique by St.-John Perse pseud, tr. by Fitzgerald. 1961. B7049
70 Underwood, P. A. The Kariye Djami. 4 v. 1966-74. B7050
71 Plato. The collected dialogues of Plato, ed. by Hamilton and Cairns. 1961. B7051
72 Pushkin, A. S. Eugene Onegin, tr. by Nobokov. 4 v. 1964. B7052
72A Nabokov, V. V. Notes on prosody from the commentary to his translation of Pushkin's Eugene Onegin. 1964. B7053
73 Danielou, A. Hindu polytheism. 1964. B7054
74 Auerbach, E. Literary language and its public in late Latin antiquity and in the middle ages, tr. by Manheim. 1965. B7055
75 Coleridge, S. T. Collected works. V. 1 Lectures. 1970. V. 2 The watchman, ed. by Patton. V. 3 Essays on his times, ed. by Erdman. 1974. V. 4 The friend, ed. by Rooke. 1969. V. 6 Lay sermons, ed. by White. 1972. B7056
76 Eliade, M. Shamanism, tr. by Trask. 1964. B7057
77 Thomas Aquinas, St. Aurora consurgens, ed. by Franz, tr. by Hull and Glover. 1966. B7058
78 Raphael, M. The demands of art, tr. by Guterman. 1968. B7059
79 Harding, M. E. The "I" and the "not-I." 1965. B7060
80 Dante Alighieri. The divine comedy, tr. by Singleton. 3 v. 1970-74. B7061
81 Brieger, P. and others. Illuminated manuscripts. 2 v. 1969. B7062
82 Leger, A. S. L. Birds, illus. by Braque. 1966. B7063
83 Kahler, E. The inward turn of narrative, tr. by R. and C. Winston. 1973. B7064
84 Bachofen, J. J. Myth, religion, and mother right, tr. by Manheim. 1967. B7065
85 Unamuno, M. de. Selected works, tr. by Kerrigan. V. 3 Our Lord Don Quixote. 1968. V. 4 The tragic sense of life in men and nations. 1973. B7066
86 Leger, A. S. L. Two addresses, ed. by Auden. 1966. B7067
87 ____. Collected poems, tr. by Auden and

others. 1971. B7068
88 Taylor, T. Thomas Taylor, the Platonist, selected writings, ed. by Raine and Harper. 1968. B7069
91 Corbin, H. Creative imagination in the Sufism of Ibn'arabi, tr. by Manheim. 1970. B7070
92 Lehmann, P. L. and K. Samothracian reflections. 1973. B7071
93 Scholem, G. Sabbatai Sevi, tr. by Werblowsky. 1973. B7072
94 Freud, S. The Freud/Jung letters, tr. by Manheim, ed. by McGuire. 1974. B7073
95 Jung, C. G. Letters, ed. by Adler. V. 1. 1973. B7074
100 Campbell, J. The mythic image. 1974. B7075

BOMBAY. UNIVERSITY. ECONOMIC SERIES (Oxford)

1 Mann, H. H. and Sahasrabuddhe, D. L. Land and labour in a Deccan village. 1917. B7076
2 Ewbank, R. B., ed. Indian co-operative studies. 1920. B7077
3 Mann, H. H. and Kanitkar, N. V. Land and labour in a Deccan village. 1921. B7078
4 Ranadive, B. T. Population problem of India, ed. by Vakil. 1930. B7079
5 Altekar, A. S. A history of village communities in western India. 1927. B7080

BOMBAY. UNIVERSITY. PUBLICATIONS. ECONOMIC SERIES (Oxford)

1 Rangnekar, S. B. Imperfect competition in international trade, ed. by Anjaria. 1947. B7081
2 Desai, M. B. The rural economy of Gujarat. 1948. B7082
3 Krishnamurti, B. V. Pricing in planned economy. 1949. B7083
4 Punekar, S. D. Social insurance for industrial workers in India. 1950. B7084
5 Lakdawala, D. T. International aspects of Indian economic development. 1951. B7085
6 Cirvante, V. R. The Indian capital market. 1956. B7086
7 Rao, K. S. Statistical inference and measurement of structural changes in an economy. 1964. B7087
8 Brahmananda, P. R. Studies in the economics of welfare maximazation. 1959. B7088
10 Lakdawala, D. T. and Sandesara, J. C. Small industry in a big city. 1960. B7089
11 Lakdwala, D. T. Work, wages and well-being in an Indian metropolis. 1963. B7090
12 Joshi, M. S. The national balance sheet of India. 1966. B7091
13 Ezekiel, H. The pattern of investment and economic development. 1967. B7092
14 Rudra, A. Relative rates of growth. 1967. B7093
15 All India Seminar on Foreign Collaboration. Foreign collaboration, ed. by Hazari. 1967. B7094
16 Medhora, P. B. Industrial growth since 1950. 1968. B7095
17 George, P. V. Price behavior in India. 1968. B7096
19 Sandesara, J. C. Size and capital--intensity in India industry. 1969. B7097
20 Seminar on wage policy and wage determination in India, Bombay. Wage policy and wage determination in India, ed. by Sandesara and Deshpande. 1970. B7098

BOMBAY. UNIVERSITY. PUBLICATIONS. SOCIOLOGY SERIES (Oxford)

1 Ghurye, G. S. Culture and society. 1947. B7099
2 Desai, A. R. Social background of Indian nationalism. 1948. B7100
3 Kapadia, K. M. Marriage

and family in India. 1955. B7101
4 Ghurye, G. S. Family and kin in Indo-European culture. 1955. B7102
5 Chapekar, L. N. Thakurs of the Sahyadri. 1960. B7103
6 Venkatarayappa, K. N. Bangalore. 1957. B7104
7 Bopegamage, A. Delni. 1957. B7105
8 Narain, D. Hindu character. 1957. B7106

BOOKMAN MONOGRAH SERIES (Twayne)

Curry, R. W. Woodrow Wilson and Far Eastern policy, 1913-1921. 1957. B7107
Davies, R. M. The humanism of Paul Elmer More. 1958. B7108
De Gorog, R. P. The Scandinavian element in French and Norman. 1958. B7109
Gwinn, W. R. Uncle Joe Cannon. 1957. B7110
Klein, S. The pattern of land tenure reform in East Asia after World War II. 1958. B7111
Kraines, O. Congress and the challenge of big government. 1958. B7112
Low, A. D. Lenin on the question of nationality. 1958. B7113
Moore, J. H. Agriculture in antebellum Mississippi. 1958. B7114
Paden, W. D. An investigation of Gondal. 1958. B7115
Shaw, E. P. François-Augustin Paradis de Moncrif, 1687-1770. 1958. B7116
Woolfolk, G. R. The cotton regency. 1958. B7117
Wunderlich, F. Farmer and farm labor in the Soviet Zone of Germany. 1958. B7118

BOOKS OF THE RENAISSANCE SERIES (Swallow)

Beatty, J. L. Warwick and Holland. 1965. B7119
Cunningham, J. V. Woe or wonder. 1951. B7120
Googe, B. Selected poems, ed. by Stephens. 1961. B7121
King, H. Poems, ed. by Baker. 1960. B7122
Roper, W. The lyfe of Sir Thomas Moore, ed. by Cline. 1950. B7123
Scève, M. Sixty poems of Scève, ed. by Fowlie. 1949. B7124
Vaux, T. V. The poems of Lord Vaux, ed. by Vonalt. 1960. B7125
Wyatt, T. Some poems of Sir Thomas Wyatt, ed. by Swallow. 1949. B7126

BOOKS OF THE THEATRE SERIES (Univ. of Miami Pr.)

1 Serlio, S. The Renaissance stage, tr. by Nicoll and others, ed. by Hewitt. 1958. B7127
2 Appia, A. The work of living art, ed. by Hewitt. 1960. B7128
3 ____. Music and the art of the theatre, tr. by Corrigan and Dirks, ed. by Hewitt. 1962. B7129
4 Grube, M. The story of the Meninger, tr. by Koller, ed. by Cole. 1963. B7130
5 Antoine, A. Memories of the théâtre-libre, tr. by Carlson, ed. by Albright. 1964. B7131
6 McCarthy, D. The court theatre, 1904-07, ed. by Weintraub. 1966. B7132
7 Tairov, A. Notes of a director. 1969. B7133
8 Symons, J. M. Meyerhold's theatre of the grotesque. 1971. B7134

BOOKS THAT MATTER. (Praeger)

Aczél, T. and Méray, T. The revolt of the mind. 1959. B7135
Aldred, C. The Egyptians. 1961. B7136
Almond, G. A. The American people and foreign policy. 1960. B7137
Aron, R. The dawn of universal history, tr. by Pickles.

1961. B7138
Ashley, M. The golden century. 1969. B7139
Avtorkhanov, A. Stalin and the Soviet Communist Party. 1959. B7140
Bailey, S. D., ed. The House of Lords. 1954. B7141
Baldwin, H. W. The great arms race. 1958. B7142
Ballo, G. Modern Italian painting. 1958. B7143
Balys, J. Lithuania and Lithuanians. 1961. B7144
Bandi, H. G. Art in the ice age. 1953. B7145
Banham, R. Theory and design in the first machine age. 1960. B7146
Bartlett, V. Struggle for Africa. 1953. B7147
Battistine, L. H. The United States and Asia. 1955. B7148
Bauer, P. T. Indian economic policy and development. 1961. B7149
Baur, J. I. H. American painting in the nineteenth century. 1953. B7150
____. Philip Evergood. 1960. B7151
____. William Zorach. 1959. B7152
Baxter, R. R. Documents on the St. Lawrence Seaway. 1961. B7153
Becker, H. Man in reciprocity. 1956. B7154
Bereday, G. Z. F. and Pennar, J., eds. The politics of Soviet education. 1960. B7155
Bibbey, H. C. Race, prejudice, and education. 1959. B7156
Bidder, I. Lalibela, tr. by Grabham-Hortmann. 1960. B7157
Bill, V. T. The forgotten class. 1959. B7158
Bilzer, B. and others, eds. Paintings of the world's great galleries. 1960. B7159
Birdwood, C. B. B. India and Pakistan. 1956. B7160
Black, C. E. Rewriting Russian history. 1956. B7161
Bode, C., ed. The great experiment in American literature. 1961. B7162
____. The young rebel in American literature. 1959. B7163
Bolloten, B. The grand camouflage. 1961. B7164
Bosi, R. The Lapps. 1960. B7165
Bossert, H. T., ed. Decorative art of Asia and Egypt. 1956. B7166
____. Folk art of primitive peoples. 1955. B7167
____. Peasant art of Europe and Asia. 1959. B7168
Boyd, R. G. Communist China's foreign policy. 1962. B7169
Brant, S., pseud. The East German rising, 17th June 1957. B7170
Brea, L. B. Sicily before the Greeks. 1958. B7171
Bruhn, W. A pictorial history of costume. 1955. B7172
Brzezinski, Z. K. Ideology and power in Soviet politics. 1962. B7173
____. The Soviet bloc. 1961. B7174
Burn-Murdoch, H. The development of the papacy. 1958. B7175
Buttinger, J. The smallest dragon. 1958. B7176
Butwell, R. A. Southeast Asia today. 1961. B7177
Byrnes, R. F., ed. Yugoslavia. 1957. B7178
Campbell, P. French electoral systems and elections, 1789-1957. 1958. B7179
Cansdale, G. S. Animals and man. 1953. B7180
Carter, G. M. Independence for Africa. 1960. B7181
____. The politics of inequality. 1958. B7182
Carter, G. M. and Herz, J. H. Government and politics in the twentieth century. 1961. B7183
Cetto, M. L. Modern architecture in Mexico, tr. by Stephenson. 1961. B7184
Chandler, E. H. S. The higher tower of refuge. 1960. B7185
Chandrasekhar, S. Red China.

1961. B7186
Charvet, P. E. France. 1955. B7187
Childe, V. G. New light on the most ancient East. 1953. B7188
Clark, M. K. Algeria in turmoil. 1959. B7189
Clarke, R. R. East Anglia. 1960. B7190
Clissold, S. Chilean scrap-book. 1952. B7191
Cole, G. D. H. The post-war condition of Britain. 1957. B7192
Conference on Legal Problems of the European Economic Community. Legal problems of the European Economic Community... 1961. B7193
Cormack, M. L. She who rides a peacock. 1961. B7194
Costa, A. Persia. 1958. B7195
Cowell, F. R. Culture in private and public life. 1959. B7196
Crawford, O. G. S. Archaeology in the field. 1953. B7197
Creighton, T. R. M. South Rhodesia and the Central African Federation. 1960. B7198
Cretzianu, A., ed. Captive Rumania. 1956. B7199
Crossman, R. H. S., ed. New Fabian essays. 1952. B7200
Current digest of the Soviet press. Current Soviet policies, 1952- B7201
Cyriaux, G. and Oakeshott, R. The bargainers. 1960. B7202
Daiken, L. H. Children's toys throughout the ages. 1953. B7203
Dalton, H. Principles of public finance. 1955. B7204
Daniel, G. E. The Megalith builders of western Europe. 1958. B7205
De Gaury, G. The new State of Israel. 1952. B7206
De Graft-Johnson, J. C. African glory. 1955. B7207
De Mare, E. S. Photography and architecture. 1961. B7208
Deniau, J. F. The common market, tr. by Heath. 1960. B7209
Dening, E. Japan. 1961. B7210
Dia, M. The African Nations and world solidarity, tr. by Cook. 1961. B7211
Dinerstein, H. S. War and the Soviet Union. 1959. B7212
Dixon, C. A. and Heilbrunn, O. Communist guerilla warfare. 1954. B7213
Djilas, M. Anatomy of a moral, ed. by Rothberg. 1959. B7214
Draper, T. Castro's revolution. 1962. B7215
Dumont, R. Types of rural economy. 1957. B7216
Ehrstrom, I. Doctor's wife in Greenland. 1955. B7217
Elgar, F. Picasso. 1960. B7218
Elisofon, E. The sculpture of Africa. 1958. B7219
Erhard, L. Prosperity through competition. 1958. B7220
Escholier, R. Matisse, tr. by G. and H. M. Colville. 1960. B7221
European movement. The economic future of Europe. 1954. B7222
Evans, J. D. Malta. 1959. B7223
Eysenck, H. J. The dynamics of anxiety and hysteria. 1957. B7224
____. The psychology of politics. 1955. B7225
Falconer, A. New China, friend or foe? 1950. B7226
Farran, C. d'O. Atlantic democracy. 1957. B7227
Fast, H. M. The naked god. 1957. B7228
Fernau, J. The Praeger encyclopedia of old masters, tr. by Cleugh and Brooksbank. 1959. B7229
50 years of modern art, tr. by Sainsbury and Oliver. 1959. B7230
Fischer-Galati, S. A. Romania. 1957. B7231
Fisher, E. A. An introduction to Anglo-Saxon architecture and sculpture. 1959. B7232
Fitzgerald, C. P. Revolution in China. 1952. B7233
Flemming, E. R. Encyclopedia of textiles. 1958. B7234
Foot, M. R. D. Men in uniforms. 1961. B7235
Foreign Policy Clearing House. Strategy for the 60's, ed.

by Cerf and Pozen. 1960. B7236
Franck, K. Exhibitions. 1961. B7237
Frank, I. The European common market. 1961. B7238
Garthoff, R. L. Soviet strategy in the nuclear age. 1958. B7239
Gelber, L. M. America in Britain's place. 1961. B7240
Georgetown Univ. The Arab Middle East and Muslim Africa, ed. by Kerekes. 1961. B7241
Gibberd, F. Town design. 1959. B7242
Gibbs-Smith, C. H. A history of flying. 1954. B7243
Gillespie, J. Algeria. 1960. B7244
Giot, P. R. and others. Brittany. 1960. B7245
Goblet, Y. M. Political geography and the world map. 1955. B7246
Goodrich, L. Four American expressionists. 1959. B7247
Gordon, S. The British Parliament. 1952. B7248
Greenwood, G., ed. Australia. 1955. B7249
Griffith, E. S. The American system of government. 1954. B7250
Griffiths, P. J. Modern India. 1957. B7251
Grözinger, W. Scribling, drawing, painting. 1955. B7252
Grosser, A. The colossus again. 1955. B7253
Groth-Kimball, I. Mayan terracottas. 1961. B7254
Gruber, K. Between liberation and liberty. 1955. B7255
Guevara, E. Che Guevara on guerrilla warfare. 1961. B7256
Haftmann, W. The mind and the work of Paul Klee. 1954. B7257
____. Painting in the twentieth century. 2 v. 1960. B7258
Halecki, O. Poland. 1957. B7259
Hardt, J. P. and others. The cold war economic gap. 1961. B7260
Harrison, F. L. Music in medieval Britain. 1958. B7261
Hartog, H. European music in the twentieth century. 1957. B7262
Hatch, J. C. Africa today. 1962. B7263
Heilbrunn, O. Partisan warfare. 1962. B7264
____. The Soviet secret services. 1956. B7265
Helmreich, E. C., ed. Hungary. 1957. B7266
Hempstone, S. Africa. 1961. B7267
Hennessy, M. The Congo. 1961. B7268
Heppell, M. Yugoslavia. 1961. B7269
Herberts, K. The complete book of artists techniques. 1958. B7270
Hills, T. L. The St. Lawrence Seaway. 1959. B7271
Hodgkinson, H. Challenge to the Kremlin. 1952. B7272
Horne, A. Return to power. 1956. B7273
Horrabin, J. F. An atlas of Africa. 1960. B7274
Howe, I. and others. The American Communist Party. 1962. B7275
Huizinga, J. H. Mr. Europe. 1961. B7276
International Conference on Sino Soviet Bloc Affairs. Unity and contradiction, ed. by London. 1962. B7277
International Council for Philosophy and Humanistic Studies. The Third Reich. 1955. B7278
James, E. O. The cult of mother goddess. 1959. B7279
____. Prehistoric religion. 1957. B7280
Janouch, G. Conversations with Kafka. 1953. B7281
Jeanneret-Gris, C. E. The chapel at Ronchamp. 1957. B7282
____. Creation is a patient search, tr. by Palmes. 1960. B7283
Jefferies, C. J. Transfer of power. 1960. B7284
Jenks, C. W. The international protection of trade union freedom. 1957. B7285
Jessup, R. F. Anglo-Saxon jewelry. 1953. B7286
Joedicke, J. A history of

modern architecture, tr. by Palmes. 1959. B7287
Joll, J., ed. The decline of the Third Republic. 1959. B7288
Jones, A. H. M. Studies in Roman government and law. 1960. B7289
Jordan, A. A. Foreign aid and the defense of Southeast Asia. 1962. B7290
Jung, A. J., ed. Present trends in American National Government. 1960. B7291
Kahle, P. E. The Cairo Geniza. 1960. B7292
Kann, R. A. A study in Austrian intellectual history. 1960. B7293
Kazakov, G., pseud. The Soviet peat industry. 1956. B7294
Kedourie, E. Nationalism. 1961. B7295
Kellen, K. Khrushchev. 1961. B7296
Kennedy, M. C. A history of communism in East Asia. 1957. B7297
Kent, R. K. From Madagascar to the Malagasy Republic. 1962. B7298
Kenyon, K. M. Archaeology in the Holy Land. 1960. B7299
____. Beginnings in archaeology. 1961. B7300
____. Digging up Jericho. 1957. B7301
Keusen, H. South Asia. 1957. B7302
Kidder, J. E. Japan before Buddhism. 1959. B7303
Kilmarx, R. A. A history of Soviet air power. 1962. B7304
Kimche, J. and D. A clash of destinies. 1960. B7305
King-Hall, S. German parliaments. 1954. B7306
Kingston-McCloughry, E. J. The direction of war. 1955. B7307
Kirk, G. E. Contemporary Arab politics. 1961. B7308
____. A short history of the Middle East. 1960. B7309
Klee, P. Pedagogical sketchbook. 1953. B7310
Klimov, G. P. The terror machine. 1953. B7311
Klindt-Jensen, O. Denmark before the Vikings. 1957. B7312
Kolarz, W. The peoples of the Soviet Far East. 1954. B7313
____. Russia and her colonies. 1955. B7314
Kolko, G. Wealth and power in America. 1962. B7315
Kopf, M. Maxim Kipf. 1960. B7316
Kostiuk, H. Stalinist rule in the Ukraine. 1960. B7317
Kubie, L. S. Practical and theoretical aspects of psychoanalysis. 1960. B7318
Kultermann, U. New Japanese architecture. 1961. B7319
Kyagambiddwa, J. African music from the source of the Nile. 1955. B7320
Labedz, L., ed. Revisionism. 1962. B7321
Labin, S. The anthill, tr. by Fitzgerald. 1960. B7322
Lampert, E. Studies in rebellion. 1957. B7323
Landau, J. M. Parliaments and parties in Egypt. 1954. B7324
Laqueur, W. Z. The Soviet Union and the Middle East. 1959. B7325
____ and L., eds. The future of communist society. 1962. B7326
Lauterpacht, H. The development of international law by the International Court. 1958. B7327
Le Bourdais, D. M. Canada's century. 1952. B7328
Ledermann, A. and Trachsel, A. Creative playgrounds and recreation centers, tr. by Priefert. 1959. B7329
Lee, A. Air power. 1955. B7330
____, ed. The Soviet air and rocket forces. 1959. B7331
Lefevre, E. W., ed. Arms and arms control. 1962. B7332
Leng, S. C. and Palmer, N. D. Sun Yat-sen and communism. 1960. B7333
Leverkuehn, P. German military intelligence. 1954. B7334
Lewe van Edward, E. J. Japan surrender to peace. 1954. B7335
Lewis, G. L. Turkey. 1955. B7336

Leys, C. and Pratt, C., eds. A new deal in Central Africa. 1960. B7337
Lhote, A. Theory of figure painting. 1954. B7338
Lichtheim, G. Marxism. 1961. B7339
Liddell Hart, B. H. Sherman. 1958. B7340
____. Strategy. 1954. B7341
____. The tanks. 2 v. 1959. B7342
Little, T. Egypt. 1958. B7343
Lloyd, S. The art of the ancient Near East. 1961. B7344
Lohse, R. P. New design in exhibitions. 1954. B7345
Low, F. Struggle for Asia. 1955. B7346
Lüthy, H. France against herself. 1955. B7347
MacDonald, M. Angkor. 1959. B7348
McInnes, E. and others. The shaping of postwar Germany. 1960. B7349
Mac Michael, H. A. The Sudan. 1955. B7350
Macmillan, W. M. The road to self-rule. 1959. B7351
Madariaga, S. Spain, a modern history. 1958. B7352
Maki, J. M. Government and politics in Japan. 1962. B7353
Mannoni, D. O. Prospero and Caliban. 1956. B7354
Mansergh, N. South Africa, 1906-1931. 1962. B7355
Mao, T. On guerrilla warfare, tr. by Griffith. 1961. B7356
Marini, M. The sculpture of Marino Marini, text by Trier, tr. by Bullock. 1961. B7357
Marlowe, J. Arab nationalism and British imperialism. 1961. B7358
____. A history of modern Egypt and Anglo-Egyptian relations, 1800-1953. 1954. B7359
Marsh, R. Reginald Marsh. 1956. B7360
Mathey, F. The impressionists, tr. by Steinberg. 1961. B7361
Matthews, R. The death of the Fourth Republic. 1954. B7362
Menhart, K. Soviet man and his world, tr. by Rosenbaum. 1961. B7363
Meulen, D. The wells of Ibn Sa'ud. 1957. B7364
Meyer, A. G. Leninism. 1957. B7365
Meyer, K. E. The Cuban Invasion. 1962. B7366
Middle Eastern affairs. 1959. B7367
Miksche, F. O. Atomic weapons and armies. 1955. B7368
____. The failure of atomic strategy. 1959. B7369
Miller, H. The Communist menace in Malaya. 1954. B7370
Miller, M. O. Archaeology in the U. S. S. R. 1956. B7371
Mills, E. D. The modern church. 1956. B7372
Mitchison, L. Nigeria. 1960. B7373
Modelski, G. A. The theory of foreign policy. 1962. B7374
Montefiore, A. A modern introduction to moral philosophy. 1958. B7375
Moule, A. C. The rulers of China, 291 B. C. -A. D. 1949. 1957. B7376
Muir, P. H. English children's books, 1600 to 1900. 1954. B7377
Mukerjee, R. The culture and art of India. 1959. B7378
Munkman, C. A. American aid to Greece. 1958. B7379
Nair, K. Blossoms in the dust. 1961. B7380
Nash, E. Pictorial history of ancient Rome. V. 1. 1961. B7381
Nervi, P. L. The works of Pier Luigi Nervi. 1957. B7382
Neuenschwander, E. Finnish architecture, and Alvar Aalto. 1954. B7383
Neustupny, E. and J. Czechoslovakia before the Slavs. 1961. B7384
Neutra, R. J. Richard Neutra, ed. by Boesiger. 1959. B7385
New German architecture, selected by Hotje and others. 1956. B7386
Newman, B. Report on Indo-China. 1954. B7387
Nkrumah, K. I speak of freedom. 1961. B7388

Nollau, G. International communism and world revolution, tr. by Anderson. 1961. B7389
Nove, A. The Soviet economy. 1961. B7390
Nutting, A. Europe will not wait. 1960. B7391
Oakeshott, R. E. The archaeology of weapons. 1960. B7392
O'Ballance, E. The Arab-Israeli war. 1957. B7393
____. The Sin'ai Campaign of 1956. 1959. B7394
Paret, P. and Shy, J. W. Guerrillas in the 1960's. 1962. B7395
Parker, R. A guide to labor law. 1961. B7396
Parkin, P. H. Acoustics, noise and buildings. 1958. B7397
Partner, P. A short political guide to the Arab world. 1960. B7398
Paton, A. Hope for South Africa. 1959. B7399
Payne, L. G. S. Air dates. 1958. B7400
Peltz, M. E. (Opdycke) The magic of the opera. 1960. B7401
Pevsner, N. The Englishness of English art. 1956. B7402
Phillips, J. F. V. Agriculture and ecology in Africa. 1960. B7403
____. The development of agriculture and forestry in the tropics. 1961. B7404
____. Kwame Nkrumah and the future of Africa. 1960. B7405
Pickles, D. M. The Fifth French Republic. 1960. B7406
Pistrak, L. The grand tactician. 1961. B7407
Pokrovskiĭ, G. I. Science and technology in contemporary war, tr. by Garthoff. 1959. B7408
Pound, R. and Harmsworth, G. Northcliffe. 1959. B7409
Powell, N. From baroque to rococo. 1959. B7410
Praeger picture encyclopedia of art. 1958. B7411
Preston, R. A. Men in arms. 1956. B7412
Problems of communism. Russia under Communism, ed. by Brumberg. 1962. B7413
Proudfoot, M. Britain and the United States in the Caribbean. 1954. B7414
Qureshi, I. H. The Pakistan way of life. 1956. B7415
Rait, R. S. Scotland. 1955. B7416
Rayner, W. The tribe and its successors. 1962. B7417
Reed, H. E. A concise history of modern painting. 1959. B7418
Reidy, A. E. The works of Affonso Eduardo Reidy, by Franck, tr. by Stephenson. 1960. B7419
Reisky-Dubnic, V. Communist propaganda methods. 1960. B7420
Reshetar, J. S. A concise history of the Communist Party of the Soviet Union. 1960. B7421
Reuter, P. International institutions, tr. by Chapman. 1958. B7422
Rice, T. T. Ancient arts of central Asia. 1965. B7423
____. The Scythians. 1957. B7424
Richards, A. I., ed. East African chiefs. 1959. B7425
Richards, J. M. A guide to Finnish architecture. 1967. B7426
Richards, J. M., ed. New buildings in the Commonwealth. 1961. B7427
Richards, P. G. Honourable members. 1959. B7428
Ripka, H. Eastern Europe in the post-war world. 1961. B7429
Ritter, G. The Schlieffen plan. 1958. B7430
Rivkin, A. Africa and the West. 1962. B7431
Robertson, A. H. The Council of Europe. 1961. B7432
Ronart, S. and N. Concise encyclopaedia of Arabic civilization. 1959. B7433
Roth, A. The new school. 1958. B7434
Saunders, M. G., ed. The Soviet Navy. 1958. B7435
Schlesinger, J. R. The political economy of national security. 1960. B7436

Schneider, R. M. Communism in Guatemala, 1944-1954. 1958. B7437
Schuster, A. B. The art of two worlds. 1959. B7438
Schwartz, H. The red phoenix. 1961. B7439
Scott, D. J. R. Russian political institutions. 1961. B7440
Segal, L. New complete English-Russian dictionary. 1959. B7441
Seton-Watson, H. The decline of imperial Russia, 1855-1914. 1952. B7442
____. From Lenin to Malenkov. 1960. B7443
____. Neither war nor peace. 1960. B7444
Seyid Muhammad, V. A. The legal framework of world trade. 1958. B7445
Sharp, W. R. Field administration in the United Nations system. 1961. B7446
Sheard, J. A. The words we use. 1954. B7447
Shepheard, P. Modern gardens. 1954. B7448
Shepherd, G. Russia's Danubian empire. 1954. B7449
Shwadran, B. The Middle East. 1955. B7450
Simpson, C. Adam in ochre. 1953. B7451
____. Adam with arrows. 1954. B7452
Singh, N. Termination of membership of international organizations. 1958. B7453
Sinor, D. History of Hungary. 1959. B7454
Sispuk, Na Champassak. Storm over Laos. 1961. B7455
Sisson, C. H. The spirit of British administration and some European comparisons. 1959. B7456
Slessor, J. W. What price co-existence? 1961. B7457
Smellie, K. B. The British way of life. 1955. B7458
Smith, K. M. Mumps, measles and mosaics. 1954. B7459
Soviet survey. Hungary today. 1962. B7460
Spanier, J. W. American foreign policy since World War II. 1960. B7461
Speier, H. Divided Berlin. 1961. B7462
Spooner, F. P. South African predicament. 1960. B7463
Stahl, W., ed. Education for democracy in West Germany. 1961. B7464
Staley, E. The future of undeveloped countries. 1961. B7465
Stewart, M. Modern forms of government. 1959. B7466
Stillman, E. O., ed. Bitter harvest. 1959. B7467
Stone, J. F. S. Wessex before the Celts. 1958. B7468
Strang, W. S. Britain in world affairs. 1961. B7469
Strauss, E. The ruling servants. 1960. B7470
Strauz-Hupé, R. Power and community. 1956. B7471
Stucki, L. Behind the great wall. 1965. B7472
Swann, P. C. An introduction to the arts of Japan. 1958. B7473
Swearingen, R. What's so funny comrade? 1961. B7474
Sweeney, J. J. and Sert, J. L. Antoni Gaudi. 1960. B7475
Swettenham, J. A. The tragedy of the Baltic States. 1954. B7476
Talmon, J. L. The origin of totalian democracy. 1960. B7477
____. Political Messianism. 1960. B7478
Tanham, G. K. Communist revolutionary warfare. 1961. B7479
Tapié, A. L. The age of grandeur, tr. by A. Ross Williamson. 1960. B7480
Taylor, F. S. An illustrated history of science. 1955. B7481
Thiel, E. The Soviet Far East. 1957. B7482
Tilke, M. Costume, patterns and designs. 1957. B7483
Toynbee, J. M. C. The art of the Romans. 1965. B7484
Tran-van-Tung. Viet-nam. 1958. B7485
Trier, E. Form and space,

tr. by Ligota. 1962. B7486
Trowell, K. M. African design. 1960. B7487
Trowell, M. Classical African sculpture. 1954. B7488
Turner, G. B. and Challener, R. D., eds. National security in the nuclear age. 1960. B7489
Ubbelohde-Doering, H. The art of ancient Peru. 1952. B7490
U. S. Military Academy. The West Point atlas of American Wars. 2 v. 1959. B7491
Van Rensburg, P. Guilty lands. 1952. B7492
Vatcher, W. H. Panmunjom. 1958. B7493
Vermeil, E. Germany in the twentieth century. 1956. B7494
Von Eckhardt, U. M. The pursuit of happiness in the democratic creed. 1959. B7495
Wadsworth, J. J. The price of peace. 1962. B7496
Walsh, A. H. The urban challenge to government. 1968. B7497
Wanklyn, H. G. Czechoslovakia. 1954. B7498
Warmington, B. H. Carthage. 1960. B7499
Watson, W. China before the Han dynasty. 1961. B7500
Webb, L. Communism and democracy in Australia. 1955. B7501
Webster, T. B. L. Greek art and literature, 700-530 B. C. 1959. B7502
Wheeler, R. E. M. Early India and Pakistan. 1959. B7503
Wheelock, K. Nasser's new Egypt. 1960. B7504
Whitney Museum of American Art. American art of our century, by Goodrich and Baur. 1961. B7505
____. Bernard Reder, by Baur. 1961. B7506
Wilding, N. W. An encyclopedia of Parliament. 1958. B7507
Willemsen, C. A. and Odenthal, D. Apulia, tr. by Woodward. 1959. B7508
Wilson, D. M. The Anglo-Saxons. 1960. B7509
Wint, G. Communist China's crusade. 1965. B7510
____. Dragon and sickle. 1959. B7511
Wolfe, B. D. Khrushchev and Stalin's ghost. 1957. B7512
Wolgensinger, M. Spain. 1957. B7513
Woodhouse, C. M. British foreign policy since the Second World War. 1960. B7514
Woodrow Wilson Foundation. Education in the Nation's service. 1960. B7515
Wooley, C. L. History unearthed. 1958. B7516
Wordmald, F. English drawings of the tenth and eleventh centuries. 1953. B7517
Yershov, P. Comedy in the Soviet theatre. 1957. B7518
Yoshida, T. The Japanese house and garden. 1955. B7519
Yugoslavia. 1957. B7520
Zampaglione, G. Italy. 1956. B7521
Zavalishin, V. Early Soviet writers. 1958. B7522
Zink, H. and others. Rural local government in Sweden, Italy, and India. 1958. B7523

BORDEAUX. UNIVERSITE. PUBLICATIONS (1-9 Delmas; 11- Biere)

1 Bordeaux. Université. Catalogue des périodiques de la bibliothèque universitairé... 1937. B7524
2 Mélanges scientifiques offerts à M. Luc Picart. 1938. B7525
3 Lejeune, M. Les adverbes grecs en $\theta\varepsilon\nu$. 1940. B7526
4 Papy, L. La côte atlantique de la Loire a la Gironde. 1941. Pt. 1 Les aspects naturels... Pt. 2 L'homme et la mer... B7527
5 Lafon, R. Le système du verbe basque au XIVe siècle. 2 v. 1943. B7528
6:1 Charles, A. La révolution de 1848 et la seconde république à Bordeaux. 2 v. 1946. B7529
6:2 ____. Les événements de la péninsule Ibérique et les presses borderlaise sous la monarchie de juillet.

1945. B7530
7 Bordeaux. Université. Conférences du Lundi, 1945-46. 1947. B7531
8 ___. Conférences du Lundi, 1946-47. 1948. B7532
9 ___. Conférences du Lundi, 1948-49. 1950. B7533
10 Fernand Daguin. 1962. B7534
11 Chabe, A. A. La Faculté de Médecine de Bordeaux aux XVe et XVIe siècles. 1962. B7535
12 Vergilius Maro, P. La Ciris, ed. by Haury. 1957. B7536

BOSTON UNIVERSITY. AFRICAN STUDIES PROGRAM. AFRICAN RESEARCH STUDIES (Africana Pub. Corp.)

1 Carter, G. M. and Brown, W. O., eds. Transition in Africa. 1958. B7537
2 Karp, M. The economics of trusteeship in Somalia. 1960. B7538
3 Gulliver, P. H. Social control in an African society. 1963. B7539
4 Bennett, N. R. Studies in East African history. 1963. B7540
5 Gray, R. F. and Gulliver, P. H., eds. The family estate in Africa. 1964. B7541
6 Gabel, C. Stone age hunters of the Kafue. 1965. B7542
7 Bennett, N. R. and Brooks, G. E., eds. New England merchants in Africa. 1965. B7543
8 Gabel, C. and Bennett, N. R., eds. Reconstructing African culture history. 1967. B7544
9 Bennett, N. R., ed. Leadership in Eastern Africa and six political biographies. 1968. B7545
10 Stanley, H. Stanley's despatches to the New York Herald, 1871-1872, 1874-1877. 1970. B7546
11 Brooks, G. E. Yankee traders, old coasters and African middlemen. 1970. B7547

BOWMAN MEMORIAL LECTURES (Amer. Geog. Soc.)

1 Seymour, C. Geography, justice and politics at the Paris conference of 1919. 1951. B7548
2 Sauer, C. O. Agricultural origins and dispersals. 1952. B7549
3 Ahlmann, H. W. Glacier variations and climatic fluctuations. 1952. B7550
4 Gould, L. M. The polar regions in their relation to human affairs. 1958. B7551

BOYD LEE SPAHR LECTURES IN AMERICANA (Revell)

1947-50 Dickinson College, Carlisle, Penna. Bulwark of liberty. 1950. B7552
1951-56 Spahr, B. L. John and Mary's college. 1956. B7553
1964 Brant, I. The free, or not so free, air of Pennsylvania. 1964. B7554

BRANDEIS UNIVERSITY. WALTHAM, MASS. PHILIP W. LOWN INSTITUTE OF ADVANCED JUDAIC STUDIES. STUDIES AND TEXTS (Harvard Univ. Pr.)

1 Altmann, A., ed. Biblical and other studies. 1963. B7555
2 ___. Studies in nineteenth-century Jewish intellectual history. 1964. B7556
3 ___. Biblical motifs. 1966. B7557
4 Jewish medieval and renaissance studies, ed. by Altmann. Harvard Univ. Pr. 1967. B7558

BRIEF LIVES (Macmillan)

1 Williamson, J. A. Sir Francis Drake. 1951. B7559
2 Fulford, R. Queen Victoria. 1951. B7560
3 Wedgwood, C. V. Montrose. 1952. B7561
4 Waldman, M. Queen Elizabeth. 1952. B7562
5 Fergusson, B. Rupert of the

Rhine. 1952. B7563
6 Agar, H. Abraham Lincoln. 1952. B7564
7 Plumb, J. H. Chatham. 1953. B7565
8 Maurois, A. Cecil Rhodes, tr. by Wadham. 1953. B7566
9 Summerson, J. N. Sir Christopher Wren. 1953. B7567
10 Ryan, A. P. Lord Northcliffe. 1953. B7568
11 Andrade, E. N. de C. Sir Isaac Newton. 1954. B7569
12 Lenanton, C. M. A. Lord Nelson. 1954. B7570
13 Ogg, D. William III. 1956. B7571
14 Magnus, P. M. Sir Walter Raleigh. 1956. B7572

BRIGHTON, ENG. COLLEGE OF TECHNOLOGY. AUTOMATIC PROGRAMMING INFORMATION CENTRE STUDIES IN DATA PROCESSING (Academic)

1 Willey, E. L. and others. Some commercial autocodes. 1961. B7573
2 Dijkstra, E. W. A primer of ALGOL 60 programming. 1962. B7574
3 Yershov, A. P. and others. Input language for automatic programming systems. 1973. B7575
4 Wegner, P. and others. Introduction to system programming. 1964. B7576
5 Randell, B. and Russell, L. J. ALGOL 60 implementation. 1964. B7577
6 Breuer, H. Dictionary for computer languages. 1966. B7578
7 Yershov, A. P., ed. The Alpha automatic programming system. 1972. B7579
8 Dahl, O. J. and others. Structured programming. 1972. B7580
9 Hoare, C. A. R. and Perrott, R. H., eds. Operating systems techniques. 1972. B7581
10 Wichmann, B. ALGOL 60 compilation and assessment. 1973. B7582

BRISTOL RECORD SOCIETY. PUBLICATIONS.

1 Bristol, Eng. Bristol charters V. 1. 1155-1375. Ed. by Harding. 1930. B7583
2 ____. The Great red book of Bristol, ed. by Veale. Introduction. V. 1. 1931. B7584
3 ____. Bristol corporation of the poor... 1696-1834, ed. by Butcher. 1932. B7585
4 Same as no. 2. Text V. 1. 1933. B7586
5 Bristol, Eng. The Staple court books of Bristol, ed. by Rich. 1934. B7587
6 ____. The deposition books of Bristol... ed. by Nott. V. 1. 1935. B7588
7 Carus-Wilson, E. M., ed. The oversea trade of Bristol in the later Middle Ages. 1937. B7589
8 Same as no. 2. Text V. 2. 1938. B7590
9 St. Augustine's abbey, Bristol, Eng. Two compotus rolls of Saint Augustine's abbey, Bristol for 1491-2 and 1511-12, ed. by Beachcroft and Sabin. 1938. B7591
10 Bristol, Eng. Proceedings ... of the Company of soapmakers, 1562-1642, ed. by Matthews. 1940. B7592
11 Same as no. 1. V. 2. 1378-1499. Ed. by Cronne. 1946. B7593
12 Same as no. 1. V. 3. 1509-1899. Ed. by Latham. 1947. B7594
13 Same as no. 6. V. 2. 1948. B7595
14 Bristol, Eng. Calendar of the Bristol apprentice book, 1532-1565, ed. by Hollis. V. 1. 1532-1542. 1949. B7596
15 Farr, G. E., ed. Records of Bristol ships, 1800-1838. 1950. B7597
16 Same as no. 2. Text V. 3. 1951. B7598
17 Bristol, Eng. Records relating to the Society of Merchant Venturers of the city of Bristol in the seventeenth century, ed. by McGrath. 1952. B7599

18 Same as no. 2. Text V. 4. 1953. B7600
19 McGrath, P., ed. Merchants and merchandise in seventeenth century Bristol. 1955. B7601
20 Minchinton, W. E. The trade of Bristol in the eighteenth century. 1957. B7602
21 St. Mark's Hospital, Bristol, Eng. Cartulary of St. Mark's Hospital, Bristol, ed. by Ross. 1959. B7603
22 St. Augustine's Abbey, Bristol, Eng. Some manorial accounts of St. Augustine's Abbey, Bristol. 1960. B7604
23 Bristol. Eng. Society of Merchant Venturers of Bristol. Politics and the Port of Bristol in the eighteenth century, ed. by Minchinton. 1963. B7605
24 Livock, D. M. City Chamberlains' account in the sixteenth and seventeenth centuries. 1966. B7606
25 Bristol, Eng. Archives Office. The inhabitants of Bristol in 1969, ed. by Ralph and Williams. 1968. B7607
26 Friends, Society of. Bristol Men's Two-weeks Meetings. Minute book of the Men's Meeting of the Society of Friends in Bristol, 1667-1686, ed. by Mortimer. 1971. B7608
27 Bristol, Eng. Church of Christ, the records of a Church of Christ, 1640-1687, ed. by Hayden. 1974. B7609

BRITAIN IN THE WORLD TODAY (Johns Hopkins Univ. Pr.)

1 Luard, E. Britain and China. 1962. B7610
2 Rose, S. Britain and South-east Asia. 1962. B7611
3 Nicholas, H. Britain and the U.S.A. 1963. B7612
4 Monroe, E. Britain's moment in the Middle East. 1963. B7613
5 Zinkin, M. and T. Britain and India. 1964. B7614
6 Kirkwood, K. Britain and Africa. 1965. B7615
7 Miller, J. D. B. Britain and the Old Dominion. 1966. B7616

BRITISH BATTLES SERIES (Macmillan)

Bennett, G. M. The battle of Jutland. 1964. B7617
____. Coronel and Folklands. 1962. B7618
____. Naval battles of the First World War. 1968. B7619
Carver, M. El Amamein. 1962. B7620
____. Tobruk. 1964. B7621
Collier, B. The battle of Britain. 1962. B7622
Dudley, D. and Webster, G. The Roman conquest of Britain, A.D. 43-57. 1965. B7623
Edwardes, M. The Battle of Plassey and the conquest of Bengal. 1963. B7624
____. Battles of the Indian mutiny. 1963. B7625
Farrar-Hockley, A. H. The Somme. 1964. B7626
Glover, M. Wellington's peninsular victories. 1963. B7627
Grunberger, R. Germany, 1918-1945. 1964. B7628
Hibbert, C. The Battle of Arnhem. 1962. B7629
____. The battle of Corunna. 1961. B7630
Jackson, W. G. F. The battle for Italy. 1967. B7631
Lewis, M. A. The Spanish Armada. 1960. B7632
Lloyd, C. The capture of Quebec. 1961. B7633
____. St. Vincent & Camperdown. 1963. B7634
McGuffie, T. H. The siege of Gibraltar, 1779-1783. 1965. B7635
MacIntyre, D. The battle of the New Atlantic. 1961. B7636
Naylor, J. Waterloo. 1960. B7637
Pack, S. W. C. The Battle of Natapan. 1961. B7638
Pemberton, W. B. Battles of the Boer War. 1964. B7639
____. Battles of the Crimean War. 1962. B7640
Schofield, B. B. The Russian convoys. 1964. B7641
Strawson, J. The battle for

North Africa. 1969. B7642
Terraine, J. Mons. 1960. B7643
Tomasson, K. and Buist, F. Battles of the '45. 1962. B7644
Warner, O. The battle of the Nile. 1960. B7645
____. Glorious first day of June. 1961. B7646
____. Trafalgar. 1959. B7647
Woolrych, A. H. Battles of the English Civil War. 1961. B7648

BRITISH INSTITUTE OF HISTORY AND ARCHAEOLOGY IN EAST AFRICA. MEMOIR (Oxford)

1 Garlake, P. S. The early Islamic architecture of the East African coast. 1966. B7649
2 Sorrensen, M. P. K. Origins of European settlement in Kenya. 1968. B7650

THE BRITISH POLITICAL TRADITION

1 Beloff, M., ed. The debate of the American Revolution, 1761-1783. Barnes & Noble. 1963. B7651
2 Corban, A., ed. The debate on the French Revolution, 1789-1800. Barnes & Noble. 1963. B7652
3 Joll, J., ed. Britain and Europe. Barnes & Noble. 1961. B7653
4 White, R. J., ed. The conservative tradition. New York University Pr. 1964. B7654
5 Maccoby, S., ed. The English radical tradition, 1763-1914. New York University Pr. 1966. B7655
6 Bennett, G., ed. The concept of empire. Barnes & Noble. 1962. B7656
7 Pelling, H. M., ed. The challenge of socialism. Barnes & Noble. 1954. B7657
8 Bullock, A. L. C. and Shock, M., eds. The liberal tradition. Barnes & Noble. 1954. B7658
9 Pelling, H. America and the British Left from Bright to Bevan. Black. 1956. B7659

BROOKINGS INSTITUTION, WASHINGTON, D. C. NATIONAL COMMITTEE ON GOVERNMENT FINANCE, STUDIES OF GOVERNMENT FINANCE

Ando, A. and others, eds. Studies in economic stabilization. 1968. B7660
Barlow, R. and others. Economic behavior of the affluent. 1966. B7661
Blinder, A. S. and others. The economics of public finance. 1974. B7662
Break, G. F. Intergovernmental fiscal relations in the United States. 1967. B7663
Bolton, R. E. Defense purchases and regional growth. 1966. B7664
Brittain, J. A. Corporate dividend policy. 1966. B7665
____. The payroll tax for social security. 1972. B7666
Brookings Conference on the Effects of Tax Policy on Investment. Tax incentives and capital spending, ed. by Fromm. 1971. B7667
Brownlee, O. H. The effects of the 1965 Federal excise tax reductions on prices. 1967. B7668
Buchanan, J. M. The economics of earmarked taxes. 1963. B7669
____. Fiscal choice through time. 1964. B7670
Budget concepts for economic analysis, ed. by Lewis. 1968. B7671
Chase, S. B., ed. Problems in public expenditure analysis. 1968. B7672
Colm, G. and Wagner, P. Federal budget projections. 1966. B7673
Comiez, M. S. A capital budget statement for the U. S. Government. 1966. B7674
David, M. Alternative approaches to capital gains taxation. 1968. B7675
Dorfman, R., ed. Measuring benefits of government investments. 1965. B7676
Eckstein, O., ed. Studies in

the economics of income maintenance. 1967. B7677
Goode, R. B. The individual income tax. 1964. B7678
____. Policy holders' interest income from life insurance under the income tax. 1963. B7679
Green, C. Negative taxes and the poverty problem. 1967. B7680
Groves, H. M. Federal tax treatment of the family. 1963. B7681
Harberger, A. C. and Bailey, M. J. Taxation of income from capital. 1968. B7682
Heller, W. W. and Pechman, J. A. Questions and answers on revenue sharing. 1967. B7683
Jantscher, G. R. Trusts and estate taxation. 1966. B7684
Katona, G. and Mueller, E. Consumer response to income increases. 1968. B7685
Krause, L. B. and Dam, K. W. Federal tax treatment of foreign income. 1964. B7686
Lewis, W. Budget concepts for economic analysis. 1968. B7687
____. Federal fiscal policy in the postwar recessions. 1962. B7688
____. The federal sector in national income models. 1964. B7689
McDonald, S. I. Federal tax treatment of income from oil and gas. 1963. B7690
Maxwell, J. A. Financing State and local governments. 1965. B7691
Musgrave, R. A., ed. Essays in fiscal federalism. 1965. B7692
National Bureau of Economic Research. Foreign tax policies and economic growth. 1966. B7693
____. The role of direct and indirect taxes in the Federal Reserve system. 1964. B7694
Netzer, D. Economics of the property tax. 1966. B7695
Netzer, R. Housing taxation and housing policy. 1967. B7696
Ott, D. J. and A. F. Ott. Federal budget policy. 1965. B7697
Ott, D. J. and Meltzer, A. H. Federal tax treatment of State and local securities. 1963. B7698
Page, D. A. Retraining under the Manpower Development Act. 1964. B7699
Pechman, J. A. Federal tax policy. 1966. B7700
____. Financing state and local government. 1965. B7701
Problems in public expenditure analysis, ed. by Chase. 1968. B7702
Rothenberg, J. Economic evolution of urban renewal. 1967. B7703
Sacks, S. Metropolitan area finances. 1964. B7704
Shoup, C. S. Federal estate and gift taxes. 1966. B7705
Steiner, P. O. Public expenditure budgeting. 1969. B7706
Taussig, M. K. Economic aspects of the personal income tax treatment of charitable contributions. 1967. B7707
The taxation of income from capital, ed. by Harberger and Bailey. 1969. B7708
Tobin, J. and others. Is a negative income tax practical? 1967. B7709
Westwood, A. F. Foreign aid in a foreign policy framework. 1966. B7710

BROOKLYN. POLYTECHNIC INSTITUTE. INSTITUTE OF POLYMER RESEARCH. LECTURES ON PROGRESS IN CHEMISTRY. (Interscience)

Bergmann, E. D. The chemistry of acetylene and related compounds. 1948. B7711
____. Isomerism and isomerization of organic compounds. 1948. B7712
Price, C. C. Mechanisms of reactions at carbon-carbon double bonds. 1946. B7713

BROWN AND HALEY LECTURES (Rutgers Univ. Pr.)

1953 Greenfield, K. R. The historian and the Army. 1954. B7714
1954 Galbraith, J. K. Economics & the art of

controversy. 1955. B7715
1955 Curti, M. E. American paradox: the conflict of thought and activity. 1956. B7716
1956 Shapiro, H. L. Aspects of culture. 1957. B7717
1957 Greene, T. M. Moral, aesthetic and religious insight. 1958. B7718
1958 Jones, H. M. Reflections on learning. 1958. B7719
1959 Fellman, D. The limits of freedom. 1959. B7720
1960 Hauser, P. M. Population perspectives. 1961. B7721
1961 Cantril, H. Human nature and political systems. 1961. B7722
1962 Williams, T. H. McClellan, Sherman, and Grant. 1962. B7723
1963 Smith, H. N. Mark Twain's fable of progress: political and economic ideas in "A Connecticut Yankee." 1964. B7724
1964 Phenix, P. H. Man and his becoming. 1964. B7725
1965 Odegard, P. H. Political power & social change. 1966. B7726
1966 Boulding, K. E. The impact of the social sciences. 1966. B7727
1973 Breé, G. Women writers in France. 1973. B7728

BROWN BIOLOGY READING SERIES (Wm. C. Brown Co.)

Brosseau, G. E. Evolution. 1967. B7729
Flickinger, R. A. Developmental biology. 1966. B7730
Goldstein, L. Cell biology. 1966. B7731
Kormondy, E. J. General biology. 2 v. 1966. B7732
Scheer, B. Comparative physiology. 1968. B7733

BROWN UNIVERSITY STUDIES

1 Robinson, C. A. The ephemerides of Alexander's expedition. 1932. B7734
2 Lowell, M. The poems of Maria Lowell, ed. by Vernon. 1936. B7735
3 Fellows, O. E. French opinion of Molière (1800-1850). 1937. B7736
4 Carlson, C. L. The first magazine. 1938. B7737
5 Wildman, J. H. Anthony Trollope's England. 1940. B7738
6 Braude, W. G. Jewish proselyting in the first five centuries of the common era. 1940. B7739
7 Blyth, J. W. Whitehead's theory of knowledge. 1941. B7740
8 Salvan, A. J. Zola aux Etats-Unis. 1943. B7741
9 Muncy, L. W. Junker in the Prussian administration under William II, 1888-1914. 1944. B7742
10 Newcomb, C. K. The journals of Charles King Newcomb, ed. by Johnson. 1946. B7743
11 Parrington, V. L. American dreams. 1947. B7744
12 Willard, C. B. Whitman's American fame. 1950. B7745
13 Savin, M. Thomas William Robertson. 1950. B7746
14 Hartland, P. C. Balance of interregional payments of New England. 1950. B7747
15 Noyes, R. G. The Thespian mirror. 1953. B7748
16 Robinson, C. A. The history of Alexander the Great. V. 1. 1953. B7749
17 Taylor, R. J. Western Massachusetts in the Revolution. 1954. B7750
18 Pinches, T. G. Late Babylonian astronomical and related texts. 1955. B7751
19 Parker, R. A. and Dubberstein, W. H. Babylonian chronology, 626 B. C. -A. D. 75. 1956. B7752
20 Kindilien, C. T. American poetry in the eighteen-nineties. 1956. B7753
21 Bloom, E. A. Samuel Johnson in Grub Street. 1957. B7754
22 Zola, E. Lettres inédites à Henry Ceard, ed. by

Salvan. 1959. B7755
23 Lovejoy, D. S. Rhode Island politics and the American Revolution, 1760-1776. 1958. B7756
24 Noyes, R. G. The neglected muse. 1958. B7757
25 Haley, G. Vicente Espinel and Marcos de Obregón. 1959. B7758
26 Same as no. 16. V. 2. 1963. B7759

BUFFALO HISTORICAL SOCIETY. PUBLICATIONS.

1-2 Buffalo Historical Soc. Publications. 2 v. 1879-1880. B7760
3 ____. Redjacket. 1884. B7761
4-9 ____. 6 v. 1896-1906. B7762
10-11 ____. Millard Fillmore papers, ed. by Severence. 1907. B7763
12 Hill, H. W. An historical review of waterway canal construction in New York State. 1908. B7764
13 Buffalo Historical Soc. Canal enlargement in New York State. 1909. B7765
14 The Holland Land Co. and canal construction in western New York. 1910. B7766
15 Severence, F. H. Studies of the Niagara frontier. 1911. B7767
16 ____. The picture book of earlier Buffalo. 1912. B7768
17 Buffalo Historical Soc. Publications. 1914. B7769
18 ____. Peace episodes of the Niagara. 1914. B7770
19 ____. Publications. 1915. B7771
20-21 Severence, F. H. An old frontier of France. 2 v. 1917. B7772
22 Buffalo Historical Soc. Publications. 1918. B7773
23 Parker, A. C. The life of General Ely S. Parker. 1919. B7774
24 Buffalo Historical Soc. Publications. 1920. B7775
25 Severence, F. H., ed. The book of the museum. 1921. B7776
26 ____. Recalling pioneer days. 1922. B7777
27 Parker, A. C. Seneca myths and folk tales. 1923. B7778
28 Evans, P. D. The Holland Land company. 1924. B7779
29 Babcock, L. L. The war of 1812 on the Niagara frontier. 1927. B7780
30 Buffalo Historical Soc. Publications. 1930. B7781
31 Bingham, R. W. The cradle of the Queen city. 1931. B7782
32-33 Ellicott, J. Reports of Joseph Ellicott as chief of survey, ed. by Bingham. 2 v. 1937. B7783
34 Buffalo Historical Soc. Niagara frontier miscellany, ed. by Bingham. 1947. B7784
35-39 Niagara frontier. 5 v. 1953-58. B7785
40 Rayback, R. J. Millard Fillmore. 1959. B7786
Niagara Frontier, quarterly magazine continues the numbering.
41 (V. 6, 1959-60) B7787
42 (V. 7, 1960-61) B7788
43 (V. 8, 1961-62) B7789
44 (V. 9, 1962-63) B7790
45 (V. 10, 1963-64) B7791
46 (V. 11, 1964-65) B7792
47 (V. 12, 1965-66) B7793
48 (V. 13, 1966-67) B7794
49 (V. 14, 1967-68) B7795
50 (V. 15, 1968-69) B7796
51 (V. 16, 1969-70) B7797
52 (V. 17, 1970-71) B7798
53 (V. 18, 1971-72) B7799
51 (V. 16, 1969-70) B7800
52 (V. 17, 1970-71) B7801
53 (V. 18, 1971-72) B7802
54 (V. 19, 1972-73) B7803
55 (V. 20, 1973-74) B7804

BUFFALO. UNIVERSITY. UNIVERSITY OF BUFFALO PUBLICATIONS IN PHILOSOPHY.

Farber, M., ed. Philosophic thought in France and the United States. 1950. B7805

BUREAU FOR INTERCULTURAL EDUCATION. NEW YORK. PROBLEMS OF RACE AND CULTURE IN AMERICAN EDUCATION (Harper)

1 Vickery, W. E. and Cole,

S. G. Intercultural education in American schools. 1943. B7806
2 Powdermaker, H. Probing your prejudices. 1944. B7807
3 Brown, S. They see for themselves. 1945. B7808
4 Brameld, T. Minority problems in the public schools. 1946. B7809
5 Brown, I. C. Race relations in a democracy. 1949. B7810
6 Van Til, W. and others. Democracy demands it. 1950. B7811
7 Jaworski, I. D. Becoming American. 1950. B7812
8 Trager, H. C. and Yarrow, M. R. They learn what they live. 1952. B7813
Unnumbered: Cole, S. G. Minorities and the American promise. 1954. B7814

BURT FRANKLIN AMERICAN CLASSICS IN HISTORY AND SOCIAL SCIENCE SERIES

1 Warren, J. Equitable commerce... 1967. B7815
2 Prince Society, Boston. Publications. V. 1-36. 1968. B7816
See listing under Prince Society. Publications
3 Skidmore, T. The rights of man to property. 1967. B7817
4 Mably, G. B. de. Remarks concerning the government and the laws of the United States of America. 1965. B7818
5 Dewees, F. P. The Molly Maguires. 1965. B7819
6 Swank, J. M. History of the manufacture of iron in all ages... 1965. B7820
7 Fitzhugh, G. Sociology for the South. 1965. B7821
8 Adams, H., ed. Documents relating to New England federalism. 1964. B7822
9 Nordhoff, C. The cotton states in Spring and Summer of 1875. 1965. B7823
10 Duane, W. J. Narrative and correspondence concerning the removal of the deposits... 1966. B7824
11 Old South leaflets. 2 v. 1966. B7825
12 Spooner, L. The unconstitutionality of slavery. 1965. B7826
13 Elliot, J., ed. The debates in several state conventions on the adoption of the Federal Constitution... 5 v. 1966. B7827
14 Winship, G. P. Cabot bibliography. 1964. B7828
15 Smith, J. Travels and works of Captain John Smith, ed. by Arber. 2 v. 1966. B7829
16 Carey, H. C. Miscellaneous works. 2 v. 1966. B7830
17 Carey, M. Miscellaneous essays. 2 v. 1966. B7831
18 Warren, J. True civilization and immediate necessity and the last ground of hope for mankind. 1965. B7832
19 Webster, N. Miscellaneous papers on political and commercial subjects. 1967. B7833
20 Byrdsall, F. History of the Locofoco or Equal Rights Party. 1964. B7834
21 Marshall, J. John Marshall's economics, ed. by Oster. 1965. B7835
22 Duane, W. J. Letters addressed to the people of Pennsylvania respecting the internal improvement. 1966. B7836
23 Gordon, T. R. The war on the Bank of the United States... 1966. B7837
24 Martin, E. W. History of the Grange movement... 1967. B7838
25 Bryce, G. The remarkable history of the Hudson's Bay Company. 1967. B7839
26 Bishop, C. F. History of elections in the American colonies. 1967. B7840
27 Scoresby, W. American factories and their female operatives. 1967. B7841
28 Morgan, L. H. The League of Ho-de-no-sau-nee or Iroquois. 2 v. 1966. B7842
29 Joutel, H. Joutel's Journal of LaSalles' last voyage

1684-7. 1967. B7843
30 Winship, G. P., ed. Sailor's narratives of voyages along the New England Coast. 1966. B7844
31 Johnson, E. R. History of domestic and foreign commerce in the U.S. 2 v. 1964. B7845
32 Taussig, F. W., ed. State papers and speeches on the tariff. 1966. B7846
33 Felt, J. B. An historical account of Massachusetts currency. 1967. B7847
34 Morgan, W. S. History of the wheel and alliance and the impending revolution. 1967. B7848
35 Gurowski, A. Diary from March 4, 1861 to November 12, 1862... 2 v. 1966. B7849
36 Cleveland, R. J. Narrative of voyages and commercial enterprises. 1967. B7850
37 Budd, T. Good order established in Pennsylvania and New Jersey in America. 1967. B7851
38 Maclay, E. S. A history of American privateers. 1967. B7852
39 Brisbane, A. The social destiny of man. 1966. B7853
40 Chalmers, G. Political annals of the present United Colonies. 2 v. 1967. B7854
41 Hildeburn, C. R. A century of printing. 1968. B7855
42 Neill, E. D. History of the Virginia Company of London. 1966. B7856
43 Lee, W. Letters, ed. by Ford. 3 v. 1967. B7857
44 Webster, N. A collection of papers on political, literary and moral subjects. 1967. B7858
45 Rich, O. Bibliotheca Americana nova. 2 v. 1963. B7859
46 King, E. The great south. 1967. B7860
47 Wierzbick, F. P. California. 1966. B7861
48 Kirkpatrick, J. B. Timothy Flint. 1968. B7862
49 Lord, E. L. Industrial experiments in the British colonies of North America. 1967. B7863
50 Brisbane, R. Albert Brisbane. 1968. B7864
51 Littlefield, G. E. Early Boston booksellers. 1966. B7865
52 ____. The early Massachusetts press. 2 v. 1967. B7866
53 Schroeder, T. Free speech for radicals. 1967. B7867
54 Schwab, J. C. The Confederate States of America. 1966. B7868
55 Myers, G. History of the Supreme Court. 1967. B7869
56 ____. History of Tammany Hall. 1967. B7870
57 Wood, J. Suppressed history of the administration of John Adams. 1966. B7871
58 Dacus, J. A. Annals of the great strikes. 1967. B7872
59 Winsor, J. The westward movement. 1967. B7873
60 Club for Colonial Reprints. Publications. 6 v. 1967. B7874
61 Phillips, H. Historical sketches of the paper currency of the American colonies prior to the Constitution. 2 v. 1967. B7875
62 Dexter, H. M. The congregationalism of the last three hundred years... 2 v. 1967. B7876
63 Oberholtzer, E. P. Robert Morris. 1967. B7877
64 MacDonald, W. Documentary source book of American history 1606-1926. 1967. B7878
65 MacDonald, W. Select documents illustrative of the history of the United States. 1967. B7879
66 Libby, O. G. Geographical distribution of the vote of the thirteen states on the Federal Constitution. 1968. B7880
67 Bourne, E. G. History of the surplus revenue of 1837. 1967. B7881
68 Schöepf, J. D. Travels in the Confederation. 2 v. 1967. B7882
69 McCook, H. C. The Latimers. 1968. B7883

70 Icazbalceta, J. G. Obras. 11 v. in 8. 1964. B7884
71 Edwards, J. The works of President Edwards, ed. by Williams and Parsons. 10 v. 1968. B7885
72 Dubester, H. J. State censuses. 1967. B7886
73 Phillips, U B. The life of Robert Toombs. 1968. B7887
74 Henry, A. Travels and adventures in Canada and the Indian Territories... 1967. B7888
75 Paine, T. Writings, ed. by Conway. 4 v. 1967. B7889
76 DelMar, A. The history of money in America. 1966. B7890
77 Livermore, G. An historical research respecting the opinion of the founders of the Republic ... 1967. B7891
78 Olmstead, F. L. A journey through Texas. 1967. B7892
79 Chevalier, M. Society, manners, and politics in the United States... 1968. B7893
80 Gouge, W. M. Fiscal history of Texas. 1967. B7894
81 Niles' weekly register (1839-1849). 16 v. 1966. B7895
82 Webster, P. Political essays on the nature and operation of money... 1969. B7896
83 DeVoe, T. F. The market book. 1967. B7897
84 Seybert, A. Statistical animals. 1967. B7898
85 Maclay, W. Sketches of debates in the first Senate of the U S. 1967. B7899
86 Hickox, J. H. A history of the bills of credit or paper money issued by New York. 1967. B7900
87 Maclure, W. Opinions on various subjects. 3 v. B7901
88 Benezet, A. Memoirs of the life of Anthony Benezet, ed. by Vaux. 1969. B7902
89 Stille, C. J. The life and times of John Dickinson. 1967. B7903
90 McLane, L., ed. Report on manufactures. 2 v. 1967. B7904
91 Ballagh, J. C. White servitude in the colony of Virginia. 1969. B7905
92 Henry, W. W. Patrick Henry. 3 v. 1967. B7906
93 Hale, E. E. Franklin in France. 1967. B7907
94 Stevens, H. Historical and geographical notes on the earliest discoveries in America. 1967. B7908
95 Oberholtzer, E. P. Jay Cooke, 2 v. 1967. B7909
96 Carey, M. Brief view of the system of internal improvement of the state of Pennsylvania. 1969. B7910
97 Smith, W. A brief state of the province of Pennsylvania. 1969. B7911
98 Johnson, C. B. Letters from the British settlement in Pennsylvania. 1969. B7912
99 Clung, A. The American traveler. 1969. B7913
100 Davis, J. Calendar of the Jefferson Davis postwar manuscripts in the Louisiana Historical Association collection. 1967. B7914
101 Johnson, A. The Swedish settlements on the Delaware. 2 v. 1970. B7915
102 Tyler, M. C. Literary history of the American Revolution. 2 v. 1970. B7916
103 Doyle, J. Frederick William von Steuren and the American Revolution. 1970. B7917
104 Pickell, J. A new chapter in the early life of Washington. 1970. B7918
105 Lee, H. Memoirs of the war in the Southern Department of the United States. 2 v. 1970. B7919
107 Johnson, A. The speeches of Andrew Jackson. 1970. B7920
109 Thornton, J. W. The pulpit in the American Revolution. 1970. B7921
112 Alcarez, R. The other side, tr. by Ramsey. 1970. B7922
113 Giesecke, A. A. American commercial legislation before 1789. 1970. B7923
114 Haferkorn, H. E. The war with Mexico, 1846-1848.

1970. B7924
115 Tyler, M. C. Patrick Henry. 1970. B7925
116 Miller, J. New York considered and improvised, 1695, ed. by Paltsits. 1970. B7926
117 Winship, G. P., ed. Boston in 1682 and 1699. 1970. B7927
118 Sumner, W. G. The financier and the finances of the American Revolution. 2 v. 1970. B7928
119 Turner, F. J. The character and influence of the Indian trade in Wisconsin. 1970. B7929
120 Madison, J. Calendar of the correspondence of James Madison. 1970. B7930
121 Louisiana Historical Assn. Calendar of the Jefferson Davis post-war manuscripts. 1970. B7931
122 Felt, J. B. The customs of New England. 1970. B7932
123 Brigham, A. P. Geographic influences in American history. 1970. B7933
124 Drake, S G., comp. The witchcraft of delusion in New England. 3 v. 1970. B7934
125 Ripley, W. Z. The financial history of Virginia, 1609-1776. 1970. B7935
126 Wellington, R. G. The political and sectional influence of the public lands, 1828-1842. 1970. B7936
127 Ripley, R. S. The war with Mexico. 2 v. 1970. B7937
128 Cartwright, J. American independence. 1970. B7938
129 U.S. Library of Congress. Calendar of the correspondence of George Washington. 1970. B7939
130 Wierzbicki, F. P. California as it is & as it may be. 1970. B7940
131 Wise, W. H. and Cronin, J. W. A bibliography of Andrew Jackson and Van Buren. 1970. B7941
132 Ford, P. L. Essays on the Constitution of the United States. 1970. B7942
133 Perkins, J. B. France in the American Revolution. 1970. B7943
134 Byrd, W. The writings of Colonel William Byrd of Westover in Virginia. 1970. B7944
135 Ellis, G. E. Puritan age and rule in the colony of the Massachusetts Bay, 1629-1685. 1970. B7945
136 Miner, W. H. Daniel Boone. 1970. B7946
137 Brown, C. B. Novels. 6 v. 1970. B7947
138 Olmsted, F. L. A journey in the back country. 1970. B7948
139 Elliott, J. The American diplomatic code. 2 v. 1970. B7949
140 Cobb, S. H The rise of religious liberty in America. 1970. B7950
141 Hall, J. The West. 1970. B7951
142 Tucker, G. Progress of the U.S. in population and wealth in fifty years. 1970. B7952
143 Dodd, W. E. The life of Nathaniel Macon. 1970. B7953
144 Dunlap, W. History of the New Netherlands. 2 v. 1970. B7954
145 Crosby, S. S. The early coins of America. 1970. B7955
146 Bowden, W. The industrial history of the United States. 1970. B7956
147 Bayley, R. A. The national loans of the United States. 1970. B7957
148 Sears, L. American literature in the colonial and national periods. 1970. B7958
149 Kleeberg, G. S. The formation of the Republican Party as a national organization (1911). 1970. B7959
150 Harbeck, C. T. Contributions to the bibliography of the history of the United States. 1970. B7960
151 Kerr, R. W. History of the Government Printing Office. 1971. B7961
152 Ames, H. V. Proposed amendments to the

Constitution of the U.S. 1970. B7962
153 Allan, F. D. Allan's lone star ballads. 1970. B7963
154 Stevens, H. Historical nuggets. 2 v. in 1. 1971. B7964
155 Miller, S. Retrospect of the eighteenth century. 2 v. 1970. B7965
156 Gaer, J. Bibliography of California literature, fiction of the gold rush period. 1971. B7966
157 Johnston, H. F. The correspondence and public papers of John Jay. 4 v. 1971. B7967
158 American dictionary of printing and bookmaking. 1971. B7968
159 Kelby, W. Notes on American artists, 1754-1820. 1971. B7969
160 Channing, W. E. The works of William E. Channing. 1970. B7970
161 Gaer, J. Jack London. 1971. B7971
163 Channing, W. E. The works of William E. Channing. 1970. B7972
164 Gaer, J. Bibliography of California literature--pre-gold rush. 1971. B7973
165 Ford, F. L. A list of treasury reports and circulars issued by Alexander Hamilton. 1971. B7974
166 Gaer, J. The theatre of the gold rush decade to San Francisco. 1971. B7975
167 Van Tyne, C. H. The loyalists in the American Revolution. 1970. B7976
168 Berthold, A. B. American colonial printing as determined by contemporary cultural forces, 1639-1763. 1970. B7977
169 Day, S. P. Down South. 1971. B7978
170 Bolles, A. S. Pennsylvania. 1970. B7979
171 Fernow, B. The Ohio Valley in colonial days. 1971. B7980
172 Ford, E. S. Notes on the life of Noah Webster. 2 v. 1971. B7981
173 Drake, D. A systematic treatise. 2 v. 1971. B7982
175 Hatch, L. C The administration of the American Revolutionary Army. 1971. B7983
176 Bertrand, M. A historical account of neutrality of Great Britain... 1971. B7984
177 Lahotan, L. A. de. New voyages to North America. 2 v. 1971. B7985
178 Niles, G. Principles and acts of the Revolution in America. 1971. B7986
179 Gibbs, G. Memoirs of the administrators of Washington and John Adams, ed. by Wolcott. 2 v. 1971. B7987
180 Trotter, A. Observations on the financial position and credit of the states of the North American Union... 1971. B7988
181 Hutchinson, T. The diary and letters of His Excellency Thomas Hutchinson, comp. by Peter O. Hutchinson. 2 v. 1971. B7989
182 Ford, P. L., ed. Pamphlets on the Constitution of the United States. 1971. B7990
183 Dyer, W. A. Early American craftsmen. 1971. B7991
184 Neale, W. The sovereignity of the states. 1971. B7992
185 Ames, F. Works of Fisher Ames, ed. by Seth Ames. 1971. B7993
186 Bacon-Foster, G. Early chapters in the development of the Potomac route to the West. 1971. B7994
187 Higginson, F. New-England plantation. 1971. B7995
188 New York (State) Colonial records of the New York Chamber of Commerce, by Stevens. 1971. B7996
189 Keynes, J. M. Indian currency and finance. 1971. B7997
190 U.S. Library of Congress. Catalogue of United States census publications, 1790-1945, ed. by Dubester. 1971. B7998
191 Historic American Buildings Survey. Historic American buildings survey... 1941. 1971. B7999

192 Coke, D. P. The Royal Commission on the losses and services of American Loyalists, 1783 to 1785, ed. by Egerton. 1971. B8000
193 Speed, T. The Wilderness road. 1971. B8001
194 Moore, F. Songs and ballads of the Southern people, 1861-1865. 1971. B8002
195 Nichols, C. L. Isiah Thomas. 1971. B8003
196 Taylor, J. M. The witchcraft delusion in colonial Connecticut, 1647-1697. 1971. B8004
197 Jones, G. N. Florida plantation records, ed. by Phillips and Glunt. 1970. B8005
198 Violette, A. G. Economic feminism in American literature prior to 1848. 1971. B8006
199 Perkins, T. H. Memoir of Thomas Handasyd Perkins, ed. by Cary. 1971. B8007
200 Brigham, A. P. The United States of America. 1971. B8008
201 Bercaw, L. O. Corn in the development of the civilization of the Americas. 1971. B8009
202 Hubbard, W. The history of the Indian wars in New England... 2 v. in 1. 1971. B8010
203 Barre, W. L. The life and public services of Millard Fillmore. 1971. B8011
204 Arymond, G. A connected view of the whole internal navigation of the United States. 1971. B8012
205 Barlow, J. Political writings. 1971. B8013
206 Institute of Jamaica. Bibliographia Jamaicensis, by Cundall. 1971. B8014
207 Buck, S J. Travel and description, 1765-1865. 1971. B8015
208 McCormac, E. I. Colonial opposition to imperial authority during the French and Indian war. 1971. B8016
209 Dellenbaugh, F. S. Breaking the wilderness. 1971. B8017
210 Jefferson, T. A summary view of the rights of British America, ed. by Ford. 1971. B8018
211 Cabet, E. Colonie icarienne aux Etats-Unis d'Amerique. 1971. B8019
212 Duer, W. A. A course of lectures on the constitutional jurisprudence of the United States. 1971. B8020
213 A short history and description of Fort Niagara, ed. by Ford. 1971. B8021
214 Ford, W. C. Washington as an employer and importer of labor. 1971. B8022
215 DeMenil, A. N. The literature of the Louisiana territory. 1971. B8023
216 Nat'l. Assn. of Broadcasters. Broadcasting and the Bill of Rights. 1971. B8024
217 McKee, T. H. The national convention and platforms of all political parties, 1789 to 1905. 1971. B8025
218 Warrington, J. Short-titles of books relating to or illustrating the history and practice of psalmody in the United States, 1620-1820. 1971. B8026
219 Hubbard, J. N. An account of Sa-go-ye-wat-ha. 1971. B8027
220 Pickering, J. A vocabulary. Also Webster, Noah. Letter to John Pickering on his vocabulary. 2 v. in 1. 1971. B8028
221 Jefferson, T. The correspondence of Jefferson and DuPont de Nemours, ed. by Chinard. 1971. B8029
222 Nevins, W. S. Witchcraft in Salem village in 1692. 1971. B8030
223 Carson, H. L. The history of the Supreme Court of the United States. 2 v. 1971. B8031
224 Latrobe, B. The journal of Latrobe. 1971. B8032
225 Ford, P. L. Check-list of American magazines printed in the eighteenth century. 1971. B8033
226 ____. Who was the mother of Franklin's son. 1971. B8034

227 ____. List of some briefs in appeal causes which relate to America... 1971. B8035
228 Lelievre, C. Le travail et l'usure dans l'antiquite. 1971. B8036
230 Ford, P. L. Josiah Tucker and his writings. 1971. B8037
232 Wright, C. D Index to all reports issued by bureaus of labor statistics in the U. S. prior to 1902. 1972. B8038
233 Byington, E. H. The Puritan in England and New England. 1972. B8039
234 Bulloch, J. D. The secret service of the Confederate States in Europe. 1972. B8040
235 Carleton, G. Condition of the Indian trade in North America. 1972. B8041
236 Records of Salem witchcraft. 2 v. in 1. 1972. B8042
237 Drake, S. G. Annals of witchcraft in New England and elsewhere in the United States. 1972. B8043
238 Gross, S. D. History of American medical literature. 1972. B8044
239 Learned, H. B. The President's cabinet. 1972. B8045
240 Poore, B. P. The Federal and State constitutions. 2 v. 1972. B8046
242 Ford, W. C. The Boston book market. 1972. B8047
243 Todd, C. B. Life and letters of Joel Barlow. 1972. B8048
244 Filson, J. Filson's Kentucke. 1972. B8049
245 Doddridge, J Notes on the settlement and Indian wars of the western parts of Virginia and Pennsylvania, ed. by Williams. 1972. B8050
246 Guzman y Raz Guzman, J. Bibliografia de la reforme. 2 v. 1972. B8051
247 Women's Rights Convention... (May 28, 29, 1851) Proceedings. 1972. B8052
248 Henry, A. The trade union woman. 1972. B8053

BURT FRANKLIN BIBLIOGRAPHICAL REFERENCE SERIES (Franklin) 1-19 published as: BURT FRANKLIN BIBLIOGRAPHICAL SERIES.

1 Franklin, B. David Ricardo and Ricardian theory, a bibliographical checklist. 1949. B8054
2 Cordasco, F A Junius bibliography. 1949. B8055
3 Franklin, B. Adam Smith: a bibliographical checklist. 1950. B8056
4 Silberner, E. Moses Hess: an annotated bibliography. 1951. B8057
5 Cordasco, F. The Bohn Libraries. 1951. B8058
6 Novotný, J. M. A library of public finance and economics. 1953. B8059
7 Little, A. G. Initia operum latinorum quae saeculis XIII, XIV, XV disposita. 1958. B8060
8 Bradley, J. W. A dictionary of miniaturists. 1958. B8061
9 Chandler, F. W. The literature of roguery. 2 v. 1958. B8062
10 Fletcher, R. H. The Arthurian material in the chronicles. 1958. B8063
11 Herbert, J. A. Illuminated manuscripts. 1958. B8064
12 Berlin. Staatlichen Kunstbibliothek. Katalog der Ornamentstichsammlung der Staatlichen Kunstbibliothek, Berlin. 2 v. 1958. B8065
13 Krumbacher, K. Geschichte der byzantinischen litteratur von Justinian bis zum ende des Oströmischen reiches. 2 v. 1958. B8066
14 Berger, S. Histoire de la Vulgate pendant les premiers siècles du moyen âge. 1958. B8067
15 Flick, A. C. The rise of the mediaeval church and its influence on the civilisation of western Europe... 1959. B8068
16 Quétif, J. and Echard, J. Scriptores ordinis praedicatorum recensiti notisque historicis et criticis illustrati, opus quo singulorum vita...

2 v. in 4. 1959. B8069
17 Loomis, L. A. Mediaeval romance in England. 1960. B8070
18 Paton, L. A. Studies in the fair mythology of Arthurian romance. 1960. B8071
19 Jourdain, A. L. M. M. B. Recherches critiques sur l'âge et l'origine des traductions latines d'Aristote... ed. by C. Jourdain. 1960. B8072
20 Renouard, A. A. Annales de l'imprimerie des Estienne. 1960. B8073
21 Bernheim, E. Lehrbuch der historischen Methode und der Geschichtsphilosophie. 2 v. 1960. B8074
22 Hall, H. A select bibliography for the study, sources and literature of English mediaeval economic history. 1960. B8075
23a Melzi, G. Dizionario di opere anonime e pseudonime di scrittori italiani. 1960. B8076
23b Passano, G. B. Dizionario di opere anonime e pseudonime in supplemento a quello di Gaetano Melzi. 1960. B8077
24 Rohricht, R., ed. Regesta Regni Hierosolymitani MXCVII-MCCXCI. 2 v. 1960. B8078
25 Gillow, J. Literary and biographical history. 5 v. 1961. B8079
26 Hazlitt, W. C., ed. Handbook to the popular, poetical and dramatic literature from the invention of printing to the Restoration. 8 v. 1961. B8080
27 Crawford, J. L. L. Bibliotheca Lindesiana, catalogue of a collection of English ballads of the 17th and 18th centuries. 2 v. 1961. B8081
28 Pohler, J. Bibliotheca historico-militaris. 4 v. 1961. B8082
29 Reuss, J. D. Repertorium commentationum a societatibus litterariis editarum secundum disciplinarum ordinem digessit. 16 v. 1961. B8083
30 Vaganay, V. Le sonnet en Italie et en France au XVIe siècle. 2 v. 1961. B8084
31 Chandler, F. W. The romance of roguery. 1961. B8085
32 Boehmer, E., ed. Bibliotheca Wiffeniana. 3 v. 1962. B8086
33 Fleay, F. G. A biographical chronicle of the English drama, 1559-1642. 2 v. 1962. B8087
34 Brunet, G. Imprimeurs imaginaires et libraires supposés. 1963. B8088
35 Winfield, P. H. The chief sources of English legal history. 1962. B8089
36 Dunlap, W. History of the American theatre. 3 v. in 1. 1963. B8090
37 Kingsford, C. L. English historical literature of the fifteenth century. 1962. B8091
38 Delaruelie, L. Répertoire analytique et chronologique de la correspondance de Guillaume Budé. 1962. B8092
39 Hurter, H., ed. Nomenclator litterarius recentioris theologiae Catholicae theologos exhibens qui inde a Concilio tridentino florerunt acetate natione, disciplinis distinctos... 5 v. in 6. 1963. B8093
40 McMurtrie, D. C. The invention of printing. 1962. B8094
41 Egli, J. J. Geschichte der geographischen nameskunde. 2 v. 1962. B8095
42 Rostenberg, L. English stationers in the graphic arts, 1599-1700. 1962. B8096
43 Rich, O. Bibliotheca Americana nova. 2 v. 1963. B8097
44 Haebler, K. Bibliografa Iberica dels iglo XV. 2 v. 1963. B8098
45 Hardy, T. D. Descriptive catalogue of materials relating to the history of Great Britain and Ireland... 3 v. in 4. 1964. B8099
46 Boissonnade, P. Les études relatives à l'histoire économique de Espagne et leurs résultats. 1963. B8100
47 Universal catalogue of books on art. 2 v. 1964. B8101
48 Renouard, P. Bibliographie des impressions et des

oeuvres de Josse Bodius Ascenius. 3 v. 1964. B8102
49 Frére, E. B. Manuel du bibliographie normande. 2 v. 1964. B8103
50 Boissonnade, P. Les études relatives à l'histoire économique de la France au moyen age. 1963. B8104
51 Fleay, F. G. Chronicle history London stage, 1559-1642. 1964. B8105
52 Nordenskiold, M. A. E. Periplus. 1964. B8106
53 Egger, E. L'hellénisme en France... 2 v. 1963. B8107
54 Stauffer, D. M. American engravers upon copper and steel. 2 v. 1964. B8108
55 Brown, M. E. A Dedications. 1964. B8109
56 Rostenberg, L. Literary, political, scientific, religious & legal publishing, printing & bookselling in England, 1551-1700. 2 v. 1965. B8110
57 Gilson, E. comp. Index scolastico-cartesien. 1964. B8111
58 Zaccaria, F. A. Bibliotheca ritualis. 3 v. 1964. B8112
59 Praet, J. B. van. Catalogue des livres imprimes sur Velin de la Bibliotheque du Roi. 6 v. 1965. B8113
60 Flick, A. C. The rise of the mediaeval church...1964. B8114
61 Nisard, C. Histoire des livres populaires. 2 v. 1965. B8115
62 Thomas, I. History of printing in America. 2 v. 1964. B8116
63 Fourier, F. M. C. Dictionnaire de sociologie phalanstérienne, ed. by Silberling. 1964. B8117
64 Gross, C. A bibliography of British municipal history... 1964. B8118
65 Paris. Bibliothèque nationale...Inventaire de la collection Anisson sur l'histoire de l'imprimerie et la librairie, ed. by Coyecque. 2 v. 1964. B8119
66 Moreau, C. Bibliographie des Mazarinades. 5 v. 1965. B8120
67 Mira, G. M. Bibliografia Siciliana... 2 v. 1965. B8121
68 A. L. A. portrait index, ed. by Lane and Browne. 3 v. 1964. B8122
69 Graves, A. A century of loan exhibits. 5 v. 1965. B8123
70 Ris-Paquot, O. E. Dictionnaire encyclopedique des Marques et monogrammes. 2 v. 1964. B8124
71 Thompson, E. M. An introduction to Greek and Latin paleography. 1964. B8125
72 Edwards, E. Memoirs of libraries. 2 v. 1964. B8126
73 Adams, W. D. A dictionary of the drama. V. 1. 1965. B8127
74 Blades, W. The life and typography of William Caxton, England's first printer. 2 v. 1965. B8128
75 Watt, R. Bibliotheca Britannica. 4 v. 1965. B8129
76 Roden, R. F. Later American plays, 1831-1900. 1964. B8130
77 Growoll, A. American bookclubs. 1965. B8131
78 Eames, W. Early New England catechisms. 1964. B8132
79 Edmonds, J. P., ed. Catalogue of a collection of 1500 tracts by Martin Luther and his contemporaries. 1964. B8133
80 Molinier, T. A. and Polain, L. Les sources de l'histoire de la France des origines au 1494. 6 v. 1964. B8134
81 Richter, P. E. Biblioteca geographica Germaniae. 2 v. 1965. B8135
82 Savage, W. Dictionary of the art of printing. 2 v. 1965. B8136
83 Soleinne, M. de. Bibliothèque dramatique de M. de Soleinne, ed. by Lacroix, and Tables des pièces de théâtre decrites dans le catalogue. 10 v. 1965. B8137
84 Brueggemann, L. W. A view of English editions. 2 v. 1965. B8138
85 Giry, A. Manuel de

diplomatique. 2 v. 1965. B8139
86 Brigham, C. S., ed. British Royal proclamations relating to America, 1603-1783. 1964. B8140
87 O'Curry, E. Lectures on the manuscript material of ancient Irish history. 2 v. 1965. B8141
88 Fletcher, R. H. The Arthurian material in the chronicles. 1966. B8142
89 Growoll, A. Book trade bibliography in the United States in the 19th century. 1964. B8143
90 Tinker, C. B. Translation of Beowulf: a critical bibliography. 1969. B8144
91 Langbaine, G. An account of the English dramatic poets. 1965. B8145
92 Neve, J. Concordance to the poetical works of William Cowper. 1969. B8146
93 Genest, J. Some account of the English stage from the Restoration in 1660-1830. 10 v. 1964. B8147
94 Viollet Le Duc, E. L. N. Catalogue des livres composant la bibliotheque... 12 v. 1965. B8148
95 Atkinson, G. The extraordinary voyage in French literature before 1700. 2 v. 1965. B8149
96 Rothschild, J. de. Catalogue des livres composant la bibliotheque de feu M. le Baron Rothschild, ed. by Picot. 5 v. 1965. B8150
97 Courant, M. Bibliographie coreene. 4 v. 1965. B8151
98 Meyer, E. S. Machiavelli and the Elizabethan drama. 1964. B8152
99 Winship, G. P. Cabot bibliography. 1964. B8153
100 Notes and queries. Indexes. 12 v. 1964. B8154
101 Walther, J. L. Lexicon diplomaticum abbreviationes syllabarum et vocum in diplomatibus... 3 v. 1965. B8155
102 Cicogna, E. A. Saggio di bibliografia Veneziana. 1965. B8156
103 Soranzo, G. Bibliografia Veneziana... 1965. B8157
104 Forman, H. B. The books of William Morris described. 1966. B8158
105 Crawford, C. Marlowe concordance. 2 v. 1964. B8159
106 Cordier, H. Bibliotheca indosinica. 5 v. 1965. B8160
107 Collier, J. P., ed. Broadside black-letter ballads. 1968. B8161
108 Williams, I. A. Seven bibliographies of the 18th century. 1967. B8162
109 Hazlitt, W. C., ed. A manual for the collector and amateur of Old English plays. 1965. B8163
110 Sonneck, O. G. T. Catalog of opera librettos printed before 1800. 4 v. in 3. 1965. B8164
111 Denis, F. Le monde enchanté. 1965. B8165
112 Ricci, S. de. A bibliography of Shelley's letters. 1967. B8166
113 McMurtie, D. C. A history of printing in the United States. 2 v. 1969. B8167
114 Stourm, R. Bibliographie historique des finances de la France au dix-huitieme siècle. 1966. B8168
115 California. University. Library. Spain and Spanish America in the libraries of the University of California. 2 v. 1967. B8169
116 Cristophersen, H. O. A bibliographical introduction to the study of John Locke. 1967. B8170
117 Littlefield, G. E. Early Boston booksellers, 1642-1711. 1966. B8171
118 ____. The early Massachusetts press, 1638-1711. 2 v. 1967. B8172
119 Gosse, P. The pirate's who's who. 1967. B8173
120 LePetit, J. Bibliographie des principales éditions originales d'écrivains français du XVe au XVIIIe siècle. 1966. B8174
121 Wood, A. A. Athenae oxinienses. 3d ed. 4 v.

1967. B8175
122 Hidalgo, D. Diccionario general de bibliografía española. 7 v. 1967. B8176
123 Masson, D. Wordsworth, Shelley and Keats. 1969. B8177
124 Moore, M. F. Two select bibliographies of medieval historical study. 1967. B8178
125 Passavant, J. D. Le peintre-graveur... du Oeintre-graveur de Adam Bartsch. 1966. B8179
126 Bonnardot, A. Essai sur l'art de restaurer les estampes et les livres...1965. B8180
127 Ruelens, C. L. and Backer, A. de. Annales Plantiniennes depuis la fondation de l'imprimerie Plantinienne...1965. B8181
128 Crawford, J. L. L. A bibliography of royal proclamations... 2 v. 1965. B8182
129 Phillips, P. L. A list of maps of America. 1966. B8183
130 Boissonnade, P. Etude relatives à l'histoire économique de la revolution française. 1967. B8184
131 Green, H. Andre Alciati and his books of emblems. 1965. B8185
132 Gomme, G. L. Index of archaeological papers, 1665-1890. 1965. B8186
133 Flick, A. C. The decline of the medieval church. 1967. B8187
134 Courtney, W. P. A register of national bibliography. 3 v. 1966. B8188
135 Griswold, W. M. A descriptive list of international novels and tales of America, France, Great Britain, Italy, Russia, Germany and Norway. 1967. B8189
136 Foster, J. J. Dictionary of painters of miniatures, 1525-1850. 1966. B8190
137 Plomer, H. R. William Caxton. 1968. B8191
138 Bonnafee, E. Dictionnaire des amateurs français au XVIIe siècle. 1967. B8192
139 Crawford, J. L. L. Catalogue of English broadsides, 1505-1897. 1965. B8193
140 Barre, A. Le symbolisme. 2 v. 1968. B8194
141 Courtney, W. P. Dodsley's collection of poetry. 1968. B8195
142 Pollard, A. W. An essay on colophons. 1967. B8196
143 Rimbault, E. F. Bibliotheca madrigaliana. 1966. B8197
144 Lalanne, L. Dictionnaire historique de la France contenant l'histoire civile, politique et litteraire. 1967. B8198
145 Thompson, J. W., ed. The Frankfort book fair. 1967. B8199
146 Plomer, H. R. English printer's ornaments. 1967. B8200
147 Barroux, M. Essai de bibliographie critique des généralites de l'histore de Paris. 1967. B8201
148 Parfaict, F. and C. Histoire du théâtre françois despuis son origine. 15 v. 1966. B8202
149 Bernays, J. Joseph Justus Scalinger. 1966. B8203
150 Yost, K. A bibliography of the works of Edna St. Vincent Millay. 1967. B8204
151 Wilkins, W. C. First and early American editions of the works of Charles Dickens. 1967. B8205
152 Hubbard, L. L. Contribution towards a bibliography of Gulliver's travels. 1967. B8206
153 Symington, J. A. Catalogue of the museum and library, the Bronte Society. 1967. B8207
154 McDonald, E. D. A bibliography of the writings of Theodore Dreiser. 1968. B8208
155 Cutler, B. D. Sir James Barrie. 1967. B8209
156 Cuthbertson, J. Complete glossary to the prose and poetry of Robert Burns. 1967. B8210
157 Weber, C. J. The first hundred years of Thomas

Hardy. 1968. B8211
158 Keynes, G. L. Jane Austen. 1967. B8212
159 Smart, T. B. The bibliography of Matthew Arnold. 1967. B8213
160 Ford, P. L. Franklin bibliography. 1966. B8214
161 Gaer, J., ed. Ambrose Gwinett Bierce. 1967. B8215
162 ____. Bret Harte. 1967. B8216
163 Murray, F. E. A bibliography of Austin Dobson. 1967. B8217
164 Sturges, H. C. Chronologies of the life and writings of William Cullen Bryant. 1967. B8218
165 Skeat, W. W. A glossary of Tudor and Stuart words, ed. by Mayhew. 1967. B8219
166 Pillet, A. and Carstens, H. Bibliographie des troubadours. 1967. B8220
167 Moore, J. W. Moore's historical, biographical and miscellaneous notes relative to printers... 1967. B8221
168 Marquet de Vasselot, A. J. Repertoire des catalogues du Musée du Louvre. 1968. B8222
169 Schmoller, G. Zur literargeschichte der staats und sozialwissenchaften. 1967. B8223
170 Weulersee, G. Les manuscrits économiques de François Quesnay et du marquis de Mirabeau aux Archives nationales. 1967. B8224
171 Warner, B., ed. Famous introductions to Shakespeare's plays. 1967. B8225
172 Winship, G. P. From Gutenberg to Plantin. 1967. B8226
173 Alberts, S. S. A bibliography of the works of Robinson Jeffers. 1967. B8227
174 Babington, P. L. Bibliography of the writings of John Addington Symonds. 1967. B8228
175 Brushfield, T. N. The bibliography of Sir Walter Raleigh. 1967. B8229
176 Cook, J. Bibliography of Captain James Cook. 1967.
177 Dyer, I. W. A bibliography of Thomas Carlyle's writings and annotations. 1967. B8231
178 Hoppé, A. J. A bibliography of the writings of Samuel Butler. 1967. B8232
179 Schroeder, T. Free speech bibliography. 1969. B8233
180 Irwin, M. L. Anthony Trollope. 1967. B8234
181 Livingston, F. V. M. Bibliography of the workds of Rudyard Kipling. 2 v. 1968. B8235
182 Livingston, L. S. A bibliography of the first editions in book form of the writings of Henry Wadsworth Longfellow. 1967. B8236
183 ____. A bibliography of the first editions in book form of the writings of James Russell Lowell. 1967. B8237
184 Marrot, H. V. A bibliography of the works of John Galsworthy. 1968. B8238
185 Palsits, V. H. A bibliography of the separate and collected works of Philip Freneau. 1967. B8239
186 Parrish, M. L. and Miller, E. V. Wilkie Collins and Charles Reade. 1967. B8240
187 Perkins, P. D. and I. Lafcadio Hearn. 1967. B8241
188 Allen, F. H. A bibliography of the writings of Henry David Thoreau. 1967. B8242
189 Phillips, L. A bibliography of the writings of Henry James. 1967. B8243
190 Prideaux, W. F. A bibliography of the works of Robert Louis Stevenson. 1967. B8244
191 ____. Notes for a bibliography of Edward Fitzgerald. 1967. B8245
192 Searle, T. Sir William Schwenck Gilbert. 1967. B8246
193 Wells, C. and Goldsmith, A. F. A concise bibliography of the works of Walt Whitman. 1967. B8247
194 Wells, G. H. The works

of H. G. Wells. 1967. B8248
195 Zetterlund, R. Bibliografiska anteckningar om August Strindberg. 1967. B8249
196 Jackson, S. W. LaFayette. 1967. B8250
197 Browne, N. E. A bibliography of Nathaniel Hawthorne. 1967. B8251
198 Franklin, A. Dictionnaire historique des arts... 1967. B8252
199 Essertier, D. Psychologie et sociologie. 1967. B8253
200 Granier, C. Essai de bibliographie charitable. 1967. B8254
201 Blanc, H. Bibliographie des corporations ouvrières âvant 1789. 1967. B8255
202 Edwards, E. Lives of founders and benefactors of the British Museum. 1969. B8256
203 Hunter, D. The literature of paper-making, 1390-1800. 1967. B8257
204 Hoffmans, J. La philosophie et les philosophes. 1967. B8258
205 Fay, B. Bibliographie critique des ouvrages français relatifs aux Etats-Unis. 1968. B8259
206 Mehnert, K. Die Soviet-Union 1917-1932. 1967. B8260
207 Maunier, R. Manuel bibliographique des sciences sociales et économiques. 1966. B8261
208 Ryland, F. Chronological outlines of English literature. 1967. B8262
209 Fletcher, W. Y. English book collectors. 1967. B8263
210 John Crerar Library. A list of bibliographies on special subjects. 1968. B8264
211 Hildeburn, C. R. A century of printing. 2 v. 1966. B8265
212 Furnivall, F. Bibliography of Browning. 1967. B8266
213 Atkinson, G. The extraordinary voyage in French literature before 1700. 2 v. and supp. 1965. B8267
214 Marion, M. Dictionnaire des institutions de la France aux XVIIe et XVIIIe siècles. 1968. B8268
215 Williamson, G. C. Milton tercentenary. 1967. B8269
216 Besterman, T. The beginnings of systematic bibliography. 1966. B8270
217 McDonald, D. Agricultural writers from Sir Walter Henley to Arthur Young. 1967. B8271
218 Hunter, D. Handmade paper and its watermarks. 1967. B8272
219 Nettlau, M. Bibliographie de l'ancharie. 1967. B8273
220 Mexico. Bibliotheca Mejicana. A catalogue of an extraordinary collection of books and manuscripts. 1968. B8274
221 Masui, M., ed. A bibliography of finance. 3 v. 1967. B8275
222 John Crerar Library. A catalogue of the French economic documents from the 16th, 17th, and 18th centuries. 1966. B8276
223 Belgium. Chambres des Representatives Library. Catalog systematiques de. 1968. B8277
224 Paltsits, V. H. and others. Bibliographical essays. 1968. B8278
225 Upcott, W. Bibliographical account of the principal works relating to English topography. 3 v. 1967. B8279
226 Ireland, J. N. Records of the New York stage from 1750 to 1860. 1968. B8280
227 Marouzeau, J. Dix années de bibliographie classique. 2 v. 1967. B8281
228 Nield, J. A guide to the best historical novels and tales. 1967. B8282
229 Quaritch, B. A contribution towards a list of English book collectors. 13 parts. 1967. B8283
230 Benton, J. H. John Baskerville. 1966. B8284
231 Heartman, C. F. A bibliography of the writings of Hugh Henry Brackenridge prior to 1825. 1967. B8285
232 Lockwood, L. E. Lexicon to the poetical works of

Milton. 1966. B8286
233 Leroux, E. Bibliothèque méthodique de pragmatisme américain. 1967. B8287
234 Jessop, T. E. A bibliography of George Berkeley... 1967. B8288
235 Stevens, H. Bibliotheca Americana... 2 v. in 1. 1969. B8289
236 Kircheisen, F. M. Bibliographie du temps de Napoléon comprenant l'histoire des Etats-Unis. 2 v. 1967. B8290
237 Ellis, F. S. Lexical concordance to the poetical works of Percy Bysshe Shelley. 1967. B8291
238 U.S. Library of Congress. Census Library Project. State censuses, comp. by Dubester. 1967. B8292
239 ____. National Census and vital statistics in Europe. 2 v. in 1. 1967. B8293
240 Smith, F. S. The classics in translation. 1967. B8294
241 Mantz, R. E. Critical bibliography of Katherine Mansfield. 1969. B8295
242 Spiller, R. E. and Blackburn, P. C. A descriptive bibliography of the writings of James Fenimore Cooper. 1969. B8296
243 Tokyo. Handels-Universität. Carl Menger Bibliothek. Katalog. 1967. B8297
244 Fernandez de Navarrete, M. Bibliotheca maritima Española. 2 v. 1966. B8298
245 Walther, P. A. F. Systematisches repertorium über die schriften samtlicher historischer gesellschafter deutschlands. 1965. B8299
246 Savage, A. E. The story of libraries and book collecting. 1969. B8300
247 Klussmann, R. C. Systematisches verziechnis der abhandlungen welche in den schulschriften samtlicher an dem programmaustausche teilnehmenden lehranstalten erschienen sind 1876-85. 1967. B8301
248 VarHagen, H. Systematisches verseichnis der programmabhandlungen, ed. by Martin. 1968. B8302
249 Mourier, A. and Deltour, F. Notice sur le doctrat des lettres... 1966. B8303
250 Cordier, H. Bibliotheca sinica. 6 v. in 5. 1965. B8304
251 Parrish, M. L. Victorian lady novelists. 1967. B8305
252 Reid, J. B. Word and phrase concordance to the poems and songs of Robert Burns. 1969. B8306
253 Baker, E. A. Guide to historical fiction. 1969. B8307
255 Kerner, R. J. Northeastern Asia. 2 v. 1967. B8308
256 Tutin, J. R. Concordance to Fitzgerald's translation of the Rubaiyat of Omar Khayyam. 1967. B8309
257 Collins, W. E., ed. Archbishop Laud commemoration, 1895. 1968. B8310
258 Paris. Bibliotheque de l'universite. Catalogue de la reserve XVIe siècle. 1968. B8311
259 Cordier, H. Bibliographie stendhalienne. 1967. B8312
260 Edwards, E. Libraries and founders of libraries. 1969. B8313
261 Carré, L. Les poinçons de l'orfèvrerie française. 1967. B8314
262 Holmes, W. Introduction to the bibliography of Captain James Cook. 1969. B8315
263 Ireland, W. H. Confessions with particulars of his Shakespeare fabrications. 1967. B8316
264 Corson, J. C. A bibliography of Sir Walter Scott. 1967. B8317
265 Phillips, U. B. The life of Robert Toombs. 1968. B8318
266 Peers, E. A. Ramon Lull: a bibliography. 1967. B8319
267 Tutin, J. R. The Wordsworth dictionary of persons and places. 1968. B8320
268 Ricci, S. de. English

collectors of books and manuscripts, 1530-1930. 1969. B8321
269 Corn, A. R. and Sparke, A. A bibliography of unfinished books in the English language. 1969. B8322
270 Ross, F. A. and Kennedy, L. V. A bibliography of Negro migration. 1969. B8323
271 Peck, W. E. Shelley. 2 v. 1969. B8324
273 Dokumente des sozialismus. 5 v. 1969. B8325
274 Blades, W. Shakespeare and topography. 1969. B8326
275 Taylor, F. I. A bibliography of unemployment and the unemployed. 1969. B8327
276 McMurtrie, D. C. A history of printing in the United States. 1969. B8328
277 Salley, A. S. Catalogue of the Salley collection of the works of Wm. Gilmore Simms. 1969. B8329
278 Schroeder, T. A. Free speech bibliography. 1969. B8330
279 Jackson, M. The pictorial press. 1969. B8331
280 Scott, M. A. Elizabethan translations from the Italians. 1969. B8332
281 Ast, L. Lexicon Platonicum. 3 v. 1969. B8333
282 Laumonier, P. Tableaux chronologique des oeuvres de Ronsard. 1969. B8334
283 Keynes, G. L. William Pickering. 1969. B8335
284 U. S. Supt. of Documents, Reports of explorations printed in the documents of the United States, comp. by Hasse. 1969. B8336
285 Weeks, L. H. History of paper manufacturing in the U. S. 1970. B8337
286 Shaw, W. A. A bibliography of the historical works of Dr. Creighton... 1969. B8338
287 Grismer, R. L. A reference index to twelve thousand Spanish American authors. 1970. B8339
288 East India Co. A catalogue of the library of the Hon. East India Company. 2 v. 1969. B8340
289 Dionne, N. E. Inventaire chronologique... 5 v. 1969. B8341
290 Munsell, J. Bibliotheca munselliana. 1970. B8342
291 Young, W. A. A dictionary of the characters and scenes in the stories and poems of Rudyard Kipling. 1969. B8343
292 Gulliver, L. Louisa May Alcott. 1972. B8344
293 Esdaile, A. The sources of English literature. 1970. B8345
294 Peddie, R. A. Fifteenth-century books. 1969. B8346
295 Pulver, J. A biographical dictionary of old English music. 1969. B8347
296 Hall, H., comp. A formula book of English official historical documents. 2 v. 1969. B8348
297 Hall, H. Studies in English official historical documents. 1969. B8349
298 William, A. and Starrett, V., ed. Stephen Crane. 1970. B8350
299 Graves, A. Art sales from early in the 18th century to early in the 20th century. 3 v. 1970. B8351
300 Bédier, J. Bibliographie des travaux de Gaston Paris. 1969. B8352
301 Cobden-Sanderson, F. Shakespearian punctuation. 1970. B8353
302 Hart, W. H. Index expurgatorius Anglicanus. 1969. B8354
303 U. S. Treasury Dept. Documents relative to the manufactures in the United States. 3 v. 1969. B8355
304 Fresca, F. Catalogo de la causas contre la fe seguidas ante el Tribunal des Santo Oficio de la Inquisición de Toledo. 1969. B8356
305 Kracauer, I., ed. Urkundenbuch z. geschichte der juden in Frankfurt am Main von. 1150-1400. 2 v. 1969. B8357

306 Campbell, W. J. The collection of Franklin imprints in the museum of the Curtis publishing company. 1969. B8358
307 Ellinger, E. P. The southern war poetry of the Civil War. 1970. B8359
308 MacDonald, W., ed. Select documents illustrative of the history of the United States, 1776-1861. 1968. B8360
309 ____. ____. 1606-1926. 1968. B8361
310 Jefferson, T. Calendar of the correspondence of Thomas Jefferson. 3 v. 1970. B8362
311 Brown, S. J. M. Ireland in fiction. 1970. B8363
312 Wroot, H. E. The persons and places of the Brontë novels. 1970. B8364
313 Philip, A. J. and Gadd, W. L. A Dickens dictionary. 1970. B8365
314 Hugo, T. The Bewick collector. 2 v. 1970. B8366
315 Broughton, I. N. Robert Browning. 1970. B8367
316 Tompkins, H. B. Burr bibliography. 1970. B8368
317 Boyne, W. Trade tokens issued in the seventh century in England, Wales and Ireland. 2 v. 1970. B8369
318 Johnson, T. H. The printed writings of Jonathan Edwards, 1703-1758. 1970. B8370
319 Forrer, L. Bibliographical dictionary of meallists. 8 v. 1970. B8371
320 Graves, A. The Royal Academy of Arts. 8 v. 1972. B8372
321 Plan, P. P. Bibliographie rabelaissenne. 1970. B8373
322 Burton, M. A bibliography of librarianship. 1970. B8374
323 Haferkorn, H. E. The war with Mexico, 1846-1848. 1970. B8375
324 Streeter, B. H. The chained library. 1970. B8376
325 Laban, F. Die Schopenhauer literatur. 1970. B8377
326 Brewer, L. A. My Leigh Hunt library. 1970. B8378
327 Ricci, S. de. The bank collector's guide. 1970. B8379
328 Madison, J. Calendar of the correspondence of James Madison. 1970. B8380
329 Louisiana Historical Assn. Calendar of the Jefferson Davis postwar manuscripts. 1970. B8381
330 Norton, J. E. A bibliography of the works of Edward Gibbon. 1970. B8382
331 Corson, L. A finding list of political poems referring to English affairs of the XII. and XIV. centuries. 1970. B8383
332 Harris, W. J. The first printed translations into English of the great foreign classics. 1970. B8384
333 Aldis, H. G. A list of books printed in Scotland before 1700. B8385
334 Luce, M. A handbook to the works of Alfred Lord Tennyson. 1970. B8386
335 García Icazbalceta, J. Apuntes para un catalogo de escritores en lenguas indígenas de América. 1970. B8387
336 Maittaire, M. Historia typographorum aliquot perisiensium vitas et libros complectens. 2 v. 1970. B8388
337 Penzer, N. M. An annotated bibliography of Sir Richard Francis Burton. 1970. B8389
338 Woodward, C. J. Bibliography of the cotton manufacture. 1970. B8390
339 U. S. Library of Congress. Calendar of the correspondence of George Washington. 1970. B8391
340 Graves, A. Art sales from early in the eighteenth century to early in the twentieth century. 3 v. 1970. B8392
341 Cowley, J. D. Bibliographical description and cataloguing. 1970. B8393
342 Wise, W. H. and Cronin, J. W. A bibliography of Andrew Jackson and Van

Buren. 1970. B8394
343 Desfeuilles, A. O'Euvres de Molière. 1970. B8395
343b Wells, G. H. The works of H. G. Wells, 1887-1925. 1970. B8396
344 Williams, S. T. A bibliography of the writings of Washington Irving. 1970. B8397
345 Gardner, C. S., comp. A union list of selected western books on China in American libraries. 1970. B8398
346 Edwards, E. E. A bibliography of the history of agriculture in the United States. 1970. B8399
347 Adickes, E. German Kantian bibliography. 1970. B8400
348 Lattimore, S. B. Arthur Rackham. 1970. B8401
349 Rius y de Llosellas, L. Bibliografía crítica de las obras de Miguel de Cervantes Saavedra. 3 v. 1970. B8402
350 Cannon, H. G. T. Bibliography of library economy. 1970. B8403
351 Raymond, F. C. Les personnages des Rougon-Macquart. 1970. B8404
352 Wharton, F. State trials of the United States during the administration of Washington and Adams. 1970. B8405
353 Miner, W. H. Daniel Boone. 1970. B8406
354 Dobson, A., comp. A bibliography of the first editions of published and privately printed books and pamphlets by A. Dobson. 1970. B8407
355 Garrett, R. Essays on librarianship and bibliography. 1970. B8408
356 Fortescue, G. K. List of the contents of three collections of books, pamphlets and journals in the British Museum relating to the French Revolution. 1970. B8409
357 Martin, J. Bibliographical catalogue of privately printed books. 1970. B8410
358 Louitt, C. M. Bibliography of bibliographies on psychology. 1900-1927. 1970. B8411
359 Duff, E. G. William Caxton. 1970. B8412
360 Dublin. Univ. Library. Catalogue of fifteenth-century books in the Library of Trinity College, Dublin... by Abbott. 1970. B8413
361 Price, F. Handbook of London bankers, 1677-1876. 1970. B8414
362 Manchester, Eng. Public Libraries. List of glees, madrigals, partsongs, etc. in the Henry Watson Music Library, ed. by Cartledge. 1970. B8415
363 Abeling, T. Das Nibelungenlied und seine literatur. 1970. B8416
364 Pierre-Quint, L. Comment travaillait Proust. 1970. B8417
365 Rochambeau, E. A. L. V. Bibliographie des oeuvres de LaFontaine. 1970. B8418
366 Whitcomb, S. L. Chronological outlines of American literature. 1970. B8419
367 Verga, E. Bibliografia vinciana, 1493-1930. 1970. B8420
368 Harbeck, C. T. Contributions to the bibliography of the history of the United States. 1970. B8421
369 Monterde Garcia Icazbalceta, F. Bibliografia del teatro en Mexico. 1971. B8422
370 Brivois, J. J. B. L. Essai de bibliographie des oeuvres de M Alphonse Daudet avec fragments inedits. 1971. B8422
371 Duff, E. G. Early English printing. 1971. B8423
372 Graves, A. Dictionary of artists who have exhibited works in the principal London exhibitions from 1760 to 1893. 1971. B8425
373 Kerr, R. W. History of the Government Printing Office. 1971. B8426
374 Eldredge, H. J. "The stage" cyclopedia. 1970. B8427
375 Mesnard, P. Notice biographique sur J. Racine.

1971. B8428
376 Leroux de Lincy, A. J. V. Researches concerning Jean Grolier, ed. by Portalis, tr. by Shipman. 1971. B8429
377 Charles Louis de Bourbon. Bibliotheque liturgique. 1971. B8430
378 Gaer, J. Bibliography of California literature, fiction of the gold rush period. 1971. B8431
379 ____, ed. Franklin Norris. 1970. B8432
380 Langfors, A. I. E. Les incipit des poemes français anterieurs au XVIe siècle, ed. by Meyer. 1971. B8433
381 Gosse, P. A bibliography of the works of Captain Charles Johnson. 1970. B8434
382 American dictionary of printing and bookmaking. 1971. B8435
383 Gaer, J. Jack London. 1971. B8436
384 Roden, R. F. The Cambridge press, 1638-1692. 1971. B8437
385 Shorter, C. K. Victorian literature. 1971. B8438
386 Valle, R. H. Bibliografia de Hernan Cortes. 1971. B8439
387 Hill, F. P. American plays printed 1714-1830. 1971. B8440
388 Maries, L. Frederick Cornwallis Conybeare. 1971. B8441
389 Gaer, J. Bibliography of California literature--pre-gold rush. 1971. B8442
390 Ford, P. L. A list of treasury reports and circulars issued by Alexander Hamilton. 1971. B8443
391 Gaer, J. The theatre of the gold rush decade in San Francisco. 1971. B8444
392 LeVerdier, P. J. G. Additions à la bibliographie cornelienne. 1971. B8445
393 Baranowski, H. Bibliografia Kopernikowska, 1509-1955. 1971. B8446
394 Paris. Bibliothèque Nationale. Catalogue des ouvrages de Chateaubriand. 1971. B8447
395 Brebion, A. Bibliographie des voyages dans l'Indochine française du IXe au XIXe siècle. 1971. B8448
396 Russell, J. C. Dictionary of writers of thirteenth century England. 1971. B8449
397 Iguiniz, J. B. Bibliografía de novellistas mexicanos, 1971. B8450
398 Faider, P. Repertoire des index et lexiques d'auteurs latins. 1971. B8451
399 Fitzgerald, E. Dictionary of Madame de Sevigne, ed. by Kerrich. 1971. B8452
400 Esdaile, A. J. K. List of English tales and prose romances printed before 1740. 1971. B8453
401 Finotti, J. M. Bibliografía catholica americana. 1971. B8454
402 Dix, E. R. M., comp. Catalogue of early Dublin-printed books, 1601 to 1700. 4 v. in 2. 1971. B8455
403 Van Winkle, W. M., comp. Henry William Herbert. 1971. B8456
404 Van Duzer, H. Thackeray library. 1970. B8457
405 Dufour, T. A. Recherches bibliographiques sur les oeuvres imprimes de J. J. Rousseau... 2 v. 1971. B8458
406 Lacroix, P. Bibliographie of iconographie de tous les ouvrages de Restif de la Bretonne. 1971. B8459
407 Maunier, R. Bibliographie economique, juridique et sociale de l'Egypte moderne. 1971. B8460
408 Dubois, P. Bio-bibliographie de Victor Hugo de 1802 à 1825. 1971. B8461
409 Raynaud, G. Bibliographie des chansonniers français des XIIIe et XIVe siècles... 1971. B8462
410 Stevens, H. Historical nuggets. 2 v. in 1. 1971. B8463
411 Hunter, D. The literature of papermaking, 1390-1800. 1971. B8464
412 Paris. Bibliotheque Nationale. Dept. des imprimés. Catalogue de l'histoire de

l'Afrique. 1971. B8465
413 Eisler, R. Kant-lexikon. 1971. B8466
414 Mendes, C. Le mouvement poetique français de 1867 à 1900. 1971. B8467
415 U. S. Library of Congress. Catalogue of United States census publications, 1790-1945, ed. by Dubester. 1971. B8468
416 Historic American Buildings Survey. Historic American buildings survey...1941. 1971. B8469
417 Jeanroy, A. Bibliographie sommaire des chansonniers français du moyen âge. 1971. B8470
418 Moore, J. W. A dictionary of musical information. 1971. B8471
419 Comte, A. The positivist library of Auguste Comte, tr. by Harrison. 1971. B8472
420 Trahard, P. Bibliographie des oeuvres de Prosper Merimee. 1971. B8473
421 Rudolph, L. Schiller-lexikon. 2 v. 1971. B8474
422 MacLean, J. P. A bibliography of Shaker literature. 1971. B8475
423 Jeanroy, A. Bibliographie sommaire des chansonniers provençaux. 1971. B8476
424 Abbott, E. A subject-index to the Dialogues of Plato. 1971. B8477
425 Scott, W. R. Scottish economic literature to 1800. 1971. B8478
426 Marty-Laveaux, C. J. Lexique de la langue de Pierre Corneille... 1971. B8479
427 Paris. Université. Bibl. Catalogue des incunables de la Bibliotheque de l'Université de Paris, comp. by Chatelain. 1971. B8480
428 Gautier, L. Bibliographie des chansons de geste...1971. B8481
429 Spoelberch de Lovenjoul, C. V M. A. de. George Sand. 1971. B8482
430 Works Progress Administration. Bibliography on incineration. 1971. B8483
431 Hazlitt, W. C. A roll of honour. 1971. B8484
432 Ferrazzi, G. J. Torquato Tasso. 1971. B8485
433 Institute of Jamaica. Library. Bibliographia jamaicensis. 1971. B8486
434 Aarne, A. The types of the folk-tale. 1971. B8487
435 Langlois, E. Table des noms propres de toute nature compris dans les chansons de geste imprimées. 1971. B8488
436 Valle, R. H. Bibliografia maya. 1971. B8489
437 Kappes, M. Aristoteles-lexikon. 1971. B8490
438 Warrington, J. Short-titles of books relating to or illustrating the history and practice of psalmody in the United States, 1620-1820. 1971. B8491
439 Gaer, J. Upton Sinclair. 1971. B8492
440 Joannides, A. Le comedie-française de 1680 à 1900...1971. B8493
441 Ford, P. L. Check-list of American magazines printed in the eighteenth century. 1971. B8494
442 ____. Bibliotheca Chaunciana. 1971. B8495
443 Baxter, J. H. An index of British and Irish Latin writers, 400 to 1520. 1972. B8496
444 N. Y. State Library. Checklist of books and pamphlets in the social sciences... 1972. B8497
445 Ford, P. L. Josiah Tucker and his writings. 1972. B8498
446 U. S. Bureau of Labor. Index of all reports issued by bureaus of labor statistics in the United States prior to March 1902, comp. by Wright. 1972. B8499
447 Palmer, S. A general history of printing. 1971. B8500
448 Spurgeon, C. F. E. Chaucer devant la critique en Angleterre et en France depuis son temps jusqu'à

nos jours. 1972. B8501
449 Ribera y Tarrago, J. Bibliofilos y bibliotecas en la Espana mululmana. 1972. B8502
450 Goto, R. Robert Owen. 2 v. 1972. B8503
451 Gross, S. D. History of American medical literature. 1972. B8504
452 Lasteyrie de Saillant, R. C. Bibliographie générale des travaux historiques et archaeologiques publicés par les sociétés savantes de la France... 6 v. 1972. B8505
453 Pitre, G. Bibliografia delle tradizioni popolari d'Italia. 1972. B8506
454 Richardson, E. A list of printed catalogues of manuscript books. 1972. B8507
455 Baldensperger, F. Bibliographie critique de Goethe en France. 1972. B8508
456 McCoy, J. Jesuit relations of Canada, 1632-1673. 1972. B8509
457 Boutiere, J. and Schutz, A. H. Bibliographie des troubadours. 1972. B8510
458 Henslow, G. Medical works of the fourteenth century. 1972. B8511
459 Ford, W. C. The Boston book market, 1679-1700. 1972. B8512
460 Moore, E. R. Bibliografía de novelistas de la revolución mexicana. 1972. B8513
461 Blanc, E. Dictionnaire de philosophie ancienne, moderne et contemporaine, 1972. Supp. 1972. B8514
462 Barr, M. M. H. A century of Voltaire study. 1972. B8515
463 Mostyn-Owen, W. Bibliografía de Bernard Berenson. 1972. B8516
464 King & Son. Catalogue of parliamentary papers, 1801-1902. 1972. B8517
465 Morgan, W. T. A bibliography of British history, 1700-1715. 5 v. 1972. B8518
466 Regnier, H. Lexique de la langue de Jean de la Fontaine. 2 v. 1972. B8519
467 Cogrinton, O. Manual of Muselman numismatics. 1972. B8520
468 Fournier, P. S. Fournier on typefounding, tr. by Carter. 1972. B8521
469 Raynaud, G. Bibliographie des chansonniers français des XIIIe et XIVe siècles... 1972. B8522
470 Gaudin, L. F. Bibliography of Franco-Spanish literary relations. 1972. B8523
471 Desfeuilles, A. Notice bibliographique de Molière. 1972. B8524
472 Vaganay, H. Amadis en français. 1972. B8525
473 Eames, W. A list of editions of the Bay Psalm book, or, New England version of the Psalms. 1972. B8526
474 Vicaire, G. Manuel de l'amateur de livres du XIXe siècle. 8 v. 1972. B8527
475 Fournal, H. Bibliographie Saint-Simonienne... 1972. B8528
476 Guzman y Raz Guzman, J. Bibliografia de la reforme... 2 v. 1972. B8529
477 Manwaring, G. E. A bibliography of British naval history. 1972. B8530
478 France. Assemblée Nationale. Catalogue général des manuscrits des bibliothèques publiques en France, comp. by Coyecque and Debraye. 1972. B8531
479 Villey-Desmeserets, P. L. J. Lexique de la langue des Essais de Michel de Montaigne. 1972. B8532
480 Lion, J. Bibliographie des oeuvrages consacrés à Anatole France. 1972. B8533
481 Forcella, R. D'Annunzio. 4 v. 1972. B8534
482 Traversari, G. Bibliografia boccaccesca. 1972. B8535
483 Chassant, A. A. L. Dictionnaire des abbreviations latines et françaises usitées dans les inscriptions .. 1972. B8536
484 Clouard, M. Bibliographie des oeuvres d'Alfred de

Musset. 1972. B8537
485 Harrisse, H. Bibliographie de Manon Lescaut et notes pour servir à l'histoire du livre. 1972. B8538
486 Pollard, A. W. Italian book illustrations. 1972. B8539
487 Longnon, A. H. Les noms de lieu de la France. 1972. B8540
488 Peterson-Dyggve, H. Onomastique des trouvères. 1972. B8541

BURT FRANKLIN ESSAYS IN HISTORY AND SOCIAL SCIENCE (Franklin)

1 Malthus, T. R. The occasional papers of Malthus on population & political economy, ed. by Semmel. 1962. B8542

BURT FRANKLIN RESEARCH AND SOURCE WORKS SERIES.

1 Diehl, C. Justinien et la civilisation byzantine au VIe siècle. 2 v. 1960. B8543
2 Thompson, J. W. The literacy of the laity in the Middle Ages. 1960. B8544
3 Chalandon, F. Jean II Comnène, 1118-1143. Et Manuel I. Comnène, 1143-1180. 2 v. 1960. B8545
4 Guilhiermoz, P. E. Essai sur l'origine de la noblesse en France au moyen âge. 1960. B8546
5 Gay, J. L'Italie meridionale et l'empire byzantin. 2 v. 1960. B8547
6 Chakandon, F. Histoire de la domination normande de Italie et en Sicile. 2 v. 1960. B8548
7 Werner, K. Die Scholatik des späteren Mittelalters. 4 v. in 5. 1960. B8549
8 Dollinger, J. J. I. Beiträge zur Sektengeschichte des Mittelalters. 2 v. 1960. B8550
9 Makower, F. The Constitutional history and the constitution of the Church of England. 1960. B8551
10 Rockinger, L. R. von. Briefsteller und Formebücher des eilften bis vierzehnten Jahrhunderts. 1961. B8552
11 Round, J. K. Geoffrey de Mandeville. 1960. B8553
12 Jordan, E. Les origines de la domination angevine en Italie. 2 v. 1960. B8554
13 Tawney, R. H. The agrarian problem in the sixteenth century. 1960. B8555
14 Riezler, S. Die literarischen widersacher der papste zur zeit Ludwig des Bayers. 1962. B8556
15 Werunsky, E. Geschichte Kaiser Karls IV und seiner zeit. 2 v. 1960. B8557
16 Watkins, O. D. A history of penance. 1961. B8558
17 Hopf, K. Geschichte Griechenlands vom Beginne des Mittelalters bis auf die Neure Zeit. 2 v. 1960. B8559
18 LeClerc, L. Histoire de la médecine arabe. 2 v. 1961. B8560
19 Cam, H. M. The hundred and the Hundred rolls. 1960. B8561
20 Bennett, J. W. The evolution of "The Faerie Queene." 1962. B8562
21 Liebermann, F. The National Assembly in the Anglo-Norman period. 1961. B8563
22 Wolff, S E. Greek romances in Elizabethan fiction. 1962. B8564
23 Gildersleeve, V. C. Government regulations of the Elizabethan drama. 1962. B8565
24 Beard, C. A. The office of the Justice of Peace in England. 1962. B8566
25 Werner, K. Giambattista Vico als philosoph und gelehrter Forscher. 1962. B8567
26 Einstein, L. The Italian renaissance in England. 1962. B8568
27 Belin, F. P. Le mouvement philosophique en France de 1748-1789. 1962. B8569
28 ____. Le commerce des livres prohibités à Paris

de 1750-1789. 1962. B8570
29 Allen, J. Inquiry into the rise and growth of the Royal prerogative in England. 1962. B8571
30 Werner, K. Franz Suarez und der scholastik d. letzten jahrhunderts, 2 v. 1962. B8572
31 Dunlap, W. History of the American theatre. 1962. B8573
34 Brunet, G. Imprimeurs imaginaires et libraires supposés. 1962. B8574
36 Dunlap, W. The history of the American theatre, by Hodgkinson. 3 v. in 1. 1963. B8575
37 Rambaud, A. De Byzantino Hippodromo et circebsibus factionibus. 1962. B8576
38 Hobbes, T. Behemoth. 1962. B8577
39 Diehl, C. Etudes Byzantines. 1962. B8578
40 Werner, K. Beda und seine zeit. 1962. B8579
42 Rambaud, A. N. L'Empire grec au dixième siècle. 1962. B8580
43 Small, A. W. The Cameralists. 1962. B8581
44 Werner, K. Der heilige Thomas Von Acquino. 3 v. 1963. B8582
45 Dionysius, of Fourna d'Agrapha. Manuel d'econographie chretiénne Grecque et Latine. 1963. B8583
46 Tolstoy, G., ed. The first forty years of intercourse between England and Russia. 1964. B8584
47 Montaiglon, A. de and Raymond, G., eds. Recueil général et complet des fabliaux du XIII et du XIV siècles. 6 v. 1964. B8585
48 Hazlitt, W. C., ed. The English drama and stage under the Tudor and Stuart princes, 1543-1663. 1964. B8586
49 ____. Inedited tracts. 1964. B8587
50 ____. Shakespeare jest books. 3 v. 1964. B8588
50 Wustenfeld, H. F. Die geschichtschreiber der Araber und ihre werke. 1964. B8589
51 The boke of noblesse, ed. by Nichols. 1966. B8590
52 Lenient, C. F. La satire en France... 1966. B8591
53 Egger, E. L'Hellenisme en France. 1964. B8592
54 Arber, E. An introductory sketch to the Martin Marprelate controversy. 1964. B8593
55 Hannay, D. The later renaissance. 1965. B8594
56 Blanchet, L. Campanella. 1964. B8595
57 Texte, J. Jean-Jacques Rousseau and the original of literary cosmopolitanism, tr. by Matthews. 1964. B8596
58 Pierce, W. An historical introduction to the Marprelate tracts. 1964. B8597
59 Mornet, D. Le sentiment de la nature en France de J. J. Rousseau à Bernardin de Saint Pierre. 1964. B8598
60 Baddeley, J. F. Russia, Mongolia, China. 2 v. 1964. B8599
61 Biese, A. The development of feeling for nature in the Middle Ages. 1964. B8600
62 Chatelain, E. Introduction à la lecture des notes Tironiennes. 1964. B8601
63 Mas-Latrie, L. de. Traites de paix et de commerce et documents concernant les relations des Chrétiens avec les Arabs... 1964. B8602
64 Pike, L. O. The constitutional history of the House of Lords. 1964. B8603
65 Valois, N. De arte scribendi epistolae apud Gallicis medii aevii scriptores rheotoresque. 1964. B8604
67 Thun, A. Geschichte der revolutionaren bewegungen in Russland. 1964. B8605
68 Analecta byzantino-russica, ed. by Regel. 1964. B8606
69 Meyer, E. S. Machiavelli and the Elizabethan drama. 1964. B8607
70 Fournier, M. E. Le théâtre français. 1965. B8608
71 Stephen, J. F. History of the criminal law of England.

1964. B8609
72 Johnson, E. R. History of domestic and foreign commerce in the U.S. 2 v. 1964. B8610
73 Raleigh, W. Works, ed. by Oldys and Birch. 8 v. 1965. B8611
74 Bennett, R. and Elton, J. History of corn milling. 4 v. 1964. B8612
75 Bates, E. S. Touring in 1600. 1964. B8613
76 Schwab, J. B. Johannes Gerson. 2 v. 1967. B8614
77 Thomsen, W. L. P. The relations between ancient Russia and Scandinavia, and the origin of the Russian state. 1964. B8615
78 Gofflot, L. V. Le théâtre au college du moyen âge à nos jours. 1964. B8616
79 Juster, J. Les Juifs dans l'Empire romain. 2 v. 1965. B8617
80 Busch, W. England under the Tudors. 1965. B8618
83 Molinier, C. L'inquisition dans la France au XIII et au XIV siècle. 1965. B8619
84 Gairdner, J. and Hunt, W. Lollardy and the Reformation in England. 4 v. 1965. B8620
85 Howorth, H. H. History of the Mongols from the 9th to the 19th century. 4 v. 1965. B8621
86 Hartmann, L. M. Untersuchungen zur geschichte der byzantinischen verwaltung in Italien. 1965. B8622
87 Domesday studies, ed. by Dove. 2 v. 1965. B8623
88 Corbett, J. S. Drake and the Tudor navy. 1965. B8624
89 Adams, H., ed. Documents relating to New England federalism. 1964. B8625
90 Nordhoff, C. The cotton states in Spring and Summer of 1875. 1965. B8626
91 Kydd, W. H. G. The history of the factory movement from the year 1802 to the enactment of the ten hours bill in 1847. 1965. B8627
92 Spooner, L. The unconstitutionality of slavery. 1965. B8628
93 Genest, J. Some account of the English stage from the Restoration to 1660-1830. 10 v. 1965. B8629
94 Ross, E. G. History of the impeachment of Andrew Jackson. 1965. B8630
95 Freeman, E. A. A history of Sicily. 1965. B8631
96 Beazley, C. R. John and Sebastian Cabot. 1964. B8632
97 Brown, L. F. The political activities of the Baptists and the Fifth Monarchy men in England during the Interregnum. 1965. B8633
98 Pearson, E. Banbury chapbooks and nursery toy book literature. 1966. B8634
99 Hervieux, A. L. Les fabulistes Latins depuis le siècle D'Auguste jusqu'à la fin du moyen âge. 5 v. 1965. B8635
100 Reeves, A. M. The finding of Wineland the good. 1966. B8636
101 White, J. A new century of inventions. 1965. B8637
102 Fitzhugh, G. Sociology for the South. 1965. B8638
103 Green, H. Shakespeare and the emblem writers. 1966. B8639
104 Dasent, A. I. The speakers of the House of Commons. 1965. B8640
105 Delisle, L. Etudes sur la condition de la classe agricole et l'état de l'agriculture en normandie au Moyen Age. 1965. B8641
106 Old South leaflets. 8 v. 1966. B8642
107 Brehaut, E. An encyclopedist of the Dark Ages. 1965. B8643
108 Henry, J. T. The early and later history of petroleum. 1965. B8644
109 Elliot, J., ed. The debates in several state conventions on the adoption of the Federal Constitution... 5 v. 1966. B8645
110 Mill, J. S. The occasional papers of, ed. by Semmel. 1965. B8646

111 Laborde, L. E. S. J. de. La Renaissance des arts à la cour de France. 2 v. 1967. B8647
112 Thomas, G. M. Diplomatarium Veneto-Levantinum... 2 v. 1965. B8648
113 Denis, F. Le monde enchanté. 1965. B8649
114 Errera, A. Economica politica nei secoli XVII e negli Stati della Veneta. 1965. B8650
115 Haureau, B. Histoire de la philosophie scholastique. 3 v. 1965. B8651
116 Charriere, E. Negociations de la France dans le Levant ou correspondance memories et actes diplomatiques des ambassadeurs... 4 v. 1965. B8652
117 Nichols, J. The progresses and public processions of Queen Elizabeth... 3 v. 1966. B8653
118 ____. The progresses and processions and magnificent festivities of King James the First... 4 v. 1967. B8654
119 Clinton, H. F. Fasti Hellenici. 3 v. 1965. B8655
120 ____ Fasti Romani. 2 v. 1965. B8656
121 Byrdsall, F. History of the Locofoco or Equal Rights Party. 1964. B8657
122 Strype, J. Annals of the Reformation and establishment of religion and other various occurrences in the Church of England. 1968. B8658
123 Burgon, J. W. The life and times of Sir Thomas Gresham. 1965. B8659
124 Ibn'Abd-al-Hakem. Ibn-abd-el Hayem's History of the conquest of Spain, ed. by Jones. 1964. B8660
125 Comte, A. System of positive polity. 4 v. 1966. B8661
126 Rigault, E. Histoire de la quérelle des anciens et des modernes. 1967. B8662
127 Eisler, M. Vorlesungen über die judischen philosophen der Mittelalters. 1966. B8663
128 Atkinson, G. The extraordinary voyage in French literature. 2 v. 1968. B8664
129 Pfaff, R. F. Die unterschiede zwischen d. naturphilosophie Descartes u. Gassendis... 1965. B8665
130 Smith, J. Travels and works of Captain John Smith, ed. by Arber. 2 v. 1966. B8666
131 Adams, C. F. Antinomianism in Massachusetts Bay. 1966. B8667
132 Zawaszki, W. Les mathématiques appliquées à l'économie politique. 1965. B8668
133 Carey, H. C. Miscellaneous works. 2 v. 1966. B8669
134 Ducros, L. Jean-Jacques Rousseau. 3 v. 1966. B8670
135 Carey, M. Miscellaneous essays. 2 v. 1966. B8671
136 Oster, J. E. John Marshall's economics. 1965. B8672
137 Duane, W. J. Narrative and correspondence concerning the removal of the deposites. 1965. B8673
138 Warren, J. Equitable commerce... 1967. B8674
139 Boissonnade, P. Les études relatives à l'histoire economique de la Revolution française. 1967. B8675
140 Pattison, M. Essays by the late Mark Pattison collected and arranged by Henry Nettleship. 2 v. 1965. B8686
141 Shaw, W. A. The history of currency, 1252-1894. 1967. B8687
142 Oman, C. The unfortunate Colonel Despard and other studies. 1967. B8688
143 Hackwood, F. W. William Hone. 1967. B8689
144 McCloy, S. T. Gibbon's antagonism to Christianity. 1967. B8690
145 Webster, N. Miscellaneous papers on political and commercial subjects. 1967. B8691
146 Thomas, P. F. La philosophie du Gassendi. 1965. B8692

147 Warren, J. True civilization and immediate necessity and the last ground of hope for mankind. 1965. B8693
148 Felkin, W. History of the machine-wrought hosiery and lace manufactures. 1967. B8694
149 Bernays, J. Joseph Justis Scalinger. 1965. B8695
150 Spencer Society. Publications, 1867-1894. 55 v. 1967. B8696
151 Gomel, C. Les causes financieres de la Révolution française. V. 1-2. 1965-66. B8697
152 ____. ____. V. 3-4. 1965-66. B8698
153 ____. ____. V. 5-6. 1965-66. B8699
154 Caxton Society. Publications. 16 v. 1966. B8700
155 Hanauer, C. A. Les paysans de l'Alsace au moyen âge. 1965. B8701
156 Girard, A. Le commerce français à Séville et Cadix au temps des Habssbourg. 1965. B8702
157 Kaeppelin, P. Les origines de l'Inde Française. 1965. B8703
158 Masson, P. Histoire du commerce français dans le Levant au 17e siècle. 1966. B8704
159 Maugis, E. Histoire du parlement de Paris de l'avenement des rois Valois à la mort d'Henri IV. 1966. B8705
160 Masson, P. Histoire du commerce français dans le Levant au 18e siècle. 1966. B8706
161 Duane, W. J. Letters addressed to the people of Pennsylvania respecting the internal improvement. 1966. B8707
162 Gordon, T. R. The war on the Bank of the United States... 1966. B8708
163 Walford, C. Fairs, past and present. 1967. B8709
164 Martin, E. W. History of the Grange movement... 1967. B8710
165 Elyot, T. The boke named the governour devised by Sir Thomas Elyot, knight. 2 v. 1966. B8711
166 Leib, B. Rome, Kiev, et Byzance du XIe siècle. 1967. B8712
167 Ducros, L. Les encyclopédistes. 1967. B8713
168 Teuffel, W. S. Teuffel's history of Roman literature, tr. by Warr. 2 v. 1967. B8714
169 Gelzer, H. K. G. Sextus Julius Africanus U. D. byzantinische chronologie. 2 v. 1964. B8715
170 Cawston, G. and Keane, A. H. The early chartered companies. 1967. B8716
171 Bryce, G. The remarkable history of the Hudson's Bay Company. 1967. B8717
172 Stephen, L. Some early impressions. 1967. B8718
173 Cooper, L. Theories of style. 1966. B8719
174 Koyré, A. La philosophie de Jacob Boehme. 1967. B8720
Wilberforce, W. Private papers, ed. by A. M. Wilberforce. 1967. B8721
175 Cardozo, J. L. The contemporary Jew in Elizabethan drama. 1967. B8722
176 Corbett, J S. The successors of Drake. 1967. B8723
177 Dargan, E. C. A history of preaching. 2 v. 1965. B8724
178 Baldensperger, F. Le mouvement des idees dans l'émigration française, 1789-1815. 2 v. 1967. B8725
179 Pieri, M. Le Pétrarquisme au XVIe siècle... 1967. B8726
180 Schelling, F. E. The English chronicle play. 1967. B8727
181 Dargan, E. P. The aesthetic doctrine of Montesquieu. 1968. B8728
182 Corbett, J. S. Fighting instructions, 1530-1816. 1967. B8729
183 Bishop, C. F. History of elections in the American

colonies. 1967. B8730
184 Scoresby, W. American factories and their female operatives. 1967. B8731
185 Morgan, L. H. The League of Ho-de-no-sau-nee or Iroquoise. 2 v. 1966. B8732
186 Burton, J. H Life and correspondence of David Hume. 1967. B8733
187 Joutel, H. Joutel's journal of LaSalle's last voyage, ed. by Stiles. 1967. B8734
188 Winship, G. P., ed. Sailor's narratives of voyages along the New England Coast. 1966. B8735
189 Underhill, E. B., ed. Tracts on liberty of conscience and persecution. 1965. B8736
190 Tovey, D. Anglia Judaica. 1967. B8737
191 Weill, G. J. Les theories sur le pouvoir royal en France pendant les guerres de religion. 1966. B8738
192 Cartwright, J. Life and correspondence of Major (John) Cartwright, ed. by F D. Cartwright. 2 v. 1967. B8739
193 Epstein, M. The English Levant Company. 1967. B8740
194 Cartwright, J. The commonwealth in danger... 1968. B8741
195 Carmack, E. M. Price sources. 1967. B8742
196 Marion, M. Histoire financiere de la France despuis 1715. 6 v. 1965. B8743
197 Miller, G. M. The historical point of view in English literary criticism from 1570-1770. 1968. B8744
198 Kahn, L. Les juifs à Paris pendant la Revolution. 1967. B8745
199 Pareto, V. La liberté économique et les evènements d'Italie. 1968. B8746
200 Mossion, E. Dupont de Nemours et la question de la Compagnie des Indes. 1967. B8747
201 Partridge, E. The French Romantics' knowledge of English literature, 1820-1848. 1968. B8748
202 Chailley-Bert, J. Les Compagnies de colonization sous l'ancien régime. 1967. B8749
203 Stourm, R. Les finances de l'ancien régime et de la revolution. 2 v. 1967. B8750
204 Bunge, N. C. Esquisses litterature politico-économique. 1967. B8751
205 Clements, P. Histoire du systeme protecteur in France... 1967. B8752
206 Schöepf, J. D. Travels in the Confederation, tr. by Morrison. 2 v. 1968. B8753
207 Chambers, E. K. Notes on the history of the revels office under the Tudors. 1966. B8754
208 Schwab, M. Bibliographie d'Aristote. 1967. B8755
209 Chambers, E. K. History and motives of literary forgeries. 1967. B8756
210 Bücher, C. Industrial evolution. 1967. B8757
211 Cadet, F Pierre de Boisguilbert. 1967. B8758
212 Avenel, G. Histoire de tours les prix. 6 v. 1968. B8759
213 Manhart, G. B. and Rowland, A. L. Studies in English commerce and exploration in the age of Elizabeth. 2 v. 1967. B8760
214 Carlyle, A. J. The Christian church and liberty. 1967. B8761
215 Sicot, L. Le marquis de Chastellux. 1967. B8762
216 Taussig, F. W., ed. State papers and speeches on the tariff. 1966. B8763
217 Hall, H. Antiquities and curiosities of the exchequer. 1968. B8764
218 Worms, E. Histoire commerciale de la Ligue Hanséatique. 1967. B8765
219 Cavalli, F. La scienza politica in Italia. 4 v. 1965. B8766
220 McCullough, J. R. A treatise on the principles and practical influence of taxation and the funding system. 1967. B8767
221 Picot, E. Les Français

Italianisants au XVIe siècle. 1968. B8768
222 Popper, W. The censorship of Hebrew books. 1967. B8769
223 Felt, J. B. An historical account of Massachusetts currency. 1967. B8770
224 Maunier, R. L'origine et la function des villes. 1967. B8771
225 See, H. The economic interpretation of history. 1966. B8772
226 Strieder, von J. Zur Genesis des modernen kapitalismus... 1968. B8773
227 DelMar, A. A history of money in ancient countries from the earliest times to the present. 1967. B8774
228 Morgan, W. S. History of the wheel and alliance and the impending revolution. 1967. B8775
229 Gurowski, A. Diary from March 4, 1861 to November 12, 1862... 2 v. 1968. B8776
230 Cleveland, R. J. Narrative of voyages and commercial enterprises. 1967. B8777
231 Beard, C. A. Introduction to the English historians. 1967. B8778
232 Budd, T. Good order established in Pennsylvania and New Jersey in America. 1967. B8779
233 Holcroft, T. Theatrical recorder. 2 v. 1967. B8780
234 Maclay, E. S. A history of American privateers. 1967. B8781
235 Shortt, A. Documents relating to Canadian currency. 2 v. 1967. B8782
236 Avenel, G. d'. La fortune privée à travers sept siècles. 1968. B8783
237 Brisbane, A. The social destiny of man. 1966. B8784
238 Chalmers, G. Political annals of the present United Colonies. 2 v. 1967. B8785
239 Stephens, A. Memoirs of John Horne Tooke. 2 v. 1967. B8786
240 Neill, E. D. History of the Virginia Company of London. 1966. B8787
241 Weber, M. Schriften zur theoretischen soziologie zur soziologie der politik und verfassung. 1968. B8788
242 Alem, A. Le Marquis d'Argenson et l'économie politique au debut du XVIIIe siècle. 1967. B8789
243 Prior, J. Memoirs of the life and character of the Right Honorable Edmund Burke. 2 v. 1967. B8790
244 Jackson, T. A. Trials of British freedom. 1968. B8791
245 Lea, H. C. Chapters from the religious history of Spain connected with the Inquisition. 1967. B8792
246 Brentano, L. Eine geschichte d. wirtschaftlichen entwicklung England. 3 v. 1968. B8793
247 Quetelet, A. A treatise on man and the development of his faculties. 1967. B8794
248 Lee, W. Letters, ed. by Ford. 3 v. 1967. B8795
249 Webster, N. A collection of papers on political, literary and moral subjects. 1967. B8796
250 Bisschop, W. R. The rise of the London money market. 1967. B8797
251 Carlile, W. W. Evolution of modern money. 1967. B8798
252 Pringle-Pattison, A. S. The philosophical radicals. 1967. B8799
253 Acloque, G. Les corporations, l'industrie et le commerce à Chartres... 1967. B8800
254 O'Brien, G. An essay on medieval economic teaching. 1966. B8801
255 The Phalanx, nos. 1-23. 1966. B8802
256 Lamansky, V. Secrets d'état de Venise. 2 v. 1965. B8803
257 Brentano, L. On the history and development of guilds and the origin of trade unions. 1966. B8804
258 Brazier, N. Histoire des petits theatres de Paris depuis leur origine. 2 v.

1967. B8805
259 Akerman, J. Y. Tradesmen's tokens. 1969. B8806
260 Seybert, A. Statistical annals. 1967. B8807
261 Sharman, J. A cursory history of swearing. 1968. B8808
262 Coutourat, L. De l infini mathematique. 1967. B8809
263 Wierzbick, F. P. California. 1966. B8810
264 Moxon, J. A tutor to astronomy and geography. 1968. B8811
265 Henry, J. Aeneidea. 4 v. 1967. B8812
266 Society of the Arts. Preventing the forgery of bank notes. 1968. B8813
267 Kirkpatrick, J. E. Timothy Flint. 1968. B8814
268 Summers, M. Mallerus Malificorum. 1968. B8815
269 Acton, J. E. E. D. A. Lord Acton and his circle, ed. by Gasquet. 1968. B8816
270 Lottin, J. Quetelet. 1968. B8817
271 Edwards, J. The works of President Edwards, ed. by Williams and Parsons. 1966. B8818
272 Lea, H. C. The Moriscos of Spain. 1967. B8819
273 Lord, E. L. Industrial experiments in the British colonies of North America. 1967. B8820
274 Thesaurus novus anecdotorum..., ed. by Martene and Durand. 5 v. 1964. B8821
275 Veterum scriptorium et monumentorum historicorum dogmaticorum moralium amplissima collectio. 9v. 1965. B8822
276 Coleridge, S. T. Seven lectures on Shakespeare and Milton. 1968. B8823
277 Martin, J. B. The grasshopper in Lombard Street. 1967. B8824
278 Allain, E. L'oeuvre scolaire de la Révolution. 1968. B8825
279 Marx, K., ed. The Eastern question. 1966. B8826
280 Brisbane, R. Albert Brisbane. 1968. B8827
281 Schroeder, T. Free speech for radicals. 1967. B8828
282 Brehier, L. Le schisme oriental du XIe siècle. 1968. B8829
283 Evans, D. M. Speculative notes and notes on speculation, ideal and real. 1968. B8830
284 See, H. Modern capitalism. 1966. B8831
285 Cobden-Sanderson, T. J. Journals, 1879-1922. 2 v. 1967. B8832
286 Thompson, W. An inquiry into the principles of the distribution of wealth... 1968. B8833
287 Giles, J. A., ed. Memorials of King Alfred. 1968. B8834
289 Johnson, D. C. Pioneers of reform. 1967. B8835
290 Tracy, A. L. C. D. A commentary and review of Montesquieu's Spirit of laws from the original manuscript. 1967. B8836
291 Moustoxdës, T. M. Histoire de l'esthétique française... 1967. B8837
292 Gosse, E. From Shakespeare to Pope. 1967. B8838
293 Gosse, P. History of piracy. 1968. B8839
294 Schwab, J. C. The Confederate States of America. 1966. B8840
295 Wirth, M. Geschichte d. Handelskrisen. 1967. B8841
296 Bonassieux, J. L. and Pierre, M. Les grandes compagnies de commerce. 1967. B8842
297 Myers, G. History of the Supreme Court. 1967. B8843
298 ____. History of Tammany Hall. 1967. B8844
299 Yver, G. Le commerce et les marchands dans l'Italie méridionale au XIIIe et au XIVe siècles. 1967. B8845
300 Docoudray, G. Les origines du parlement de Paris et la justice aus XIIIe et

XIVe siècles. 1967. B8846
301 Wood, J. Suppressed history of the administration of John Adams. 1966. B8847
302 Juglar, C. Des crises commerciales et de leur retour périodique en France, Angleterre, et Etates-Unis. 1967. B8848
303 Wright, T. The life of William Blake. 2 v. 1968. B8849
304 ____. Life of Sir Richard Burton. 2 v. 1967. B8850
305 Straus, R. Robert Dodsley. 1967. B8851
306 Dacus, J. A. Annals of the great strikes. 1967. B8852
307 Winsor, J. The westward movement. 1967. B8853
308 MacDonald, W. Select documents illustrative of the history of the United States, 1776-1861. 1967. B8854
309 ____. Documentary source book of American history, 1606-1926. 1967. B8855
310 Sargent, A. J. The economic policy of Colbert. 1967. B8856
311 Hammer-Purgstall, J. von. History of the assassins, tr. by Wood. 1968. B8857
312 Club for Colonial Reprints. Publications. 6 v. 1967. B8858
313 Livermore, G. An historical research respecting the opinion of the founders of the Republic... 1967. B8859
314 Phillips, H. Historical sketches of the paper currency of the American colonies prior to the Constitution. 2 v. 1967. B8860
315 Dexter, H. M. The congregationalism of the last three hundred years... 2 v. 1967. B8861
316 Beazley, C. R. Prince Henry the Navigator. 1966. B8862
317 Oberholtzer, E. P. Robert Morris. 1967. B8863
318 Guillaume, J. L'internationale. 4 v. 1965-66. B8864
319 DuBoys, A. Catherine of Aragon and the sources of the English Reformation. 2 v. 1966. B8865
320 Ashton, J. The history of gambling in England. 1968. B8866
321 Benjamin, L. S. The South Sea bubble. 1967. B8867
322 DelMar, A. The science of money. 1967. B8868
323 ____. The history of money in America. 1966. B8869
324 ____. A history of the precious metals from earliest times to the present. 1967. B8870
325 Davidson, T. Aristotle and ancient educational ideals. 1967. B8871
326 Garcin de Tassy, J. H. Histoire de la literature Hindoui et Hindoustani. 3 v. 1966. B8872
327 Bourne, E. G. History of the surplus revenue of 1837. 1967. B8873
328 Chadwick, W. Life and times of Daniel Defoe. 1967. B8874
329 Douce, F. Illustrations of Shakespeare. 1967. B8875
330 Baudrillart, H. Jean Bodin et son temps. 1967. B8876
331 Scofield, C. I. A study of the Court of the Star Chamber... 1967. B8877
332 Drake, N. Shakespeare and his times... 2 v. 1968. B8878
333 Pendzig, P. Pierre Gasendi Metaphysik... 2 v. 1966. B8879
334 Lescure, J. Les crises generales et periodiques de la surproduction. 2 v. 1967. B8880
335 McCook, H. C. The Latimers. 1968. B8881
336 Icazbelceta, J. G. Obras. 10 v. in 8. 1964. B8882
337 Villey, P. Les sources et l'evolution des essais de Montaigne. 2 v. 1967. B8883
338 Venturi, L. Les archives de l'impressionisme. 2 v. 1967. B8884
339 Howard, C. English travellers of the Renaissance. 1967. B8885
340 Maitland, F. W. Roman canon law in the Church of England. 1967. B8886
341 Esmein, A. Le mariage

en droit canonique. 2 v. 1968. B8887
342 Henry, A. Travels and adventures in Canada and the Indian territories between 1760 and 1776. 1967. B8888
343 Paine, T. Works, ed. by Conway. 4 v. 1967. B8889
344 Brehier, L. La querelle des images. 1965. B8890
345 Ure, A. The philosophy of manufactures. 2 v. 1961. B8891
346 Cattermole, R. Sacred poetry of the 17th century. 2 v. 1969. B8892
347 Code. 1967. B8893
348 Olmsted, F. L. A journey through Texas. 1967. B8894
349 Juglar, C. Des crises commerciales et de leur retour periodique en France, Angleterre, et Etates-Unis. 1967. B8895
350 Mann, H. Slavery. 1969. B8896
351 Norgate, K. England under the Angevin kings. 2 v. 1966. B8897
352 Chevalier, M. Society, manners and politics in the United States. 1969. B8898
353 Gouge, W. H. Fiscal history of Texas, 1834-1852. 1968. B8899
354 Webster, P. Political essays on the nature and operation of money, public finances and other subjects. 2 v. in 1. 1967. B8900
355 Niles' Weekly Register. 16 v. 1966. B8901
356 Evans, D. M. The history of the commercial crises. 1967. B8902
357 DeVoe, T. F. The market book. 1967. B8903
358 Ib-Abd-el-Hayem. History of the conquest of Spain, ed. by Jones. 1964. B8904
359 Libby, O. G. Geographical distribution of the vote of the thirteen states on the Federal Constitution. 1966. B8905
360 Oman, C. History of the art of war in the Middle Ages. 2 v. 1969. B8906
361 Martinson, P. Les strophes. 1969. B8907
362 Longman, W. History of the life and times of Edward III. 1967. B8908
363 MacLay, W. Sketches of debates in the first senate of the U. S., ed. by MacLay. 1967. B8909
364 Hickcox, J. H. A history of the bills of credit or paper money issued by New York, 1709-1789. 1967. B8910
365 Chipman, N. Principles of government. 1969. B8911
366 Sombart, W. Jews and modern capitalism. 1969. B8912
367 Novicow, J. War and its alleged benefits. 1969. B8913
368 Wildenstein, G., ed. Rapports d'experts, 1712-1791. 1967. B8914
369 Lee, R. E. Recollections and letters of General Robert E. Lee. 1969. B8915
370 Picot, G. Histoires des Etats-Generaux. 8 v. 1969. B8916
371 Krueger, G. History of early Christian literature in the first three centuries, tr. by Gillet. 1970. B8917
372 Holme, L. R. The extinction of the Christian churches in North Africa. 1969. B8918
373 Helvétius, C. A. A treatise on man, tr. by Hooper. 2 v. 1969. B8919
374 McDonald, J. Secrets of the great whiskey ring. 1969. B8920
375 Jessopp, A. Studies by a recluse. 1969. B8921
376 Hodgson, G. E. Studies in French education from Rabelais to Rousseau. 1969. B8922
377 Radcliffe, W. Fishing from the earliest times. 1969. B8923
378 Botha, C. G. The public archives of South Africa, 1652-1910. 1969. B8924
379 Craik, H. The life of Jonathan Swift. 2 v. 1970. B8925
380 Fortescue, A. The Orthodox Eastern Church. 1969. B8926

381 King, E. The great South. 2 v. 1969. B8927
382 Blake, W. Observations on the principles which regulate the course of exchange. 1969. B8928
383 Maclure, W. Opinions on various subjects. 3 v. 1969. B8929
384 Vaux, R. Memoirs of the life of Anthony Benezet. 1969. B8930
385 Mitchell, W. Essays on the early history of the law merchant. 1969. B8931
386 Starr, J. The Jews in the Byzantine Empire, 641-1204. 1970. B8932
387 Brown, T. A. History of the American stage. 1969. B8933
388 Stille, C. The life and times of John Dickinson, 1732-1808. 1969. B8934
389 Chaboseau, A. De Babeuf à la commune. 1969. B8935
390 Baxter, R. The panic of 1866 with its lessons on the Currency Act. 1970. B8936
391 Flach, J. Les origines de l'ancienne France. 4 v. 1969. B8937
392 Del Mar, A. Money and civilization. 1969. B8938
393 Phillips, U. B., ed. Plantation and frontier, 1649-1863. 3 v. 1969. B8939
394 Bucknill, J. C. The mad folk of Shakespeare. 1969. B8940
395 Quesnay, F. Oeuvres economiques et philosophiques de F. Quesnay, ed. by Oncken. 1969. B8941
396 Moorman, F. W. William Browne. 1970. B8942
397 Ballagh, J. C. White servitude in the colony of Virginia. 1970. B8943
398 Remington, F. Remington's frontier sketches. 1969. B8944
399 McKinley, A. L. The suffrage franchise in the thirteen English colonies in America. 1970. B8945
400 Mandon, L. Etude sur le Syntagma philosophicum de Gassendi. 1969. B8946
401 Collier, J. P. Notes and emendations to the text of Shakespeare plays... 1970. B8947
402 Dunton, J. Life and errors of John Dunton, ed. by Nichols. 2 v. 1970. B8948
403 Stapfer, P. Shakespeare and classical antiquity. 1970. B8949
404 Wright, T. Essays on subjects connected with the literature, popular superstitions, and history of England in the Middle Ages. 2 v. 1969. B8950
405 Eisner, S. A tale of wonder. 1969. B8951
406 Guy, H. Essai sur la vie et les oeuvres litteraires du trouvere Adan de Le Hale. 1969. B8952
407 Henry, W. W. Patrick Henry. 3 v. 1969. B8953
408 Richardson, J. D. Compilation of messages and papers of the Confederacy including diplomatic correspondence. 2 v. 1970. B8954
409 Hale, E. E. Franklin in France. 1970. B8955
410 Tuckerman, B. William Jay and the Constitutional movement for the abolition of slavery. 1970. B8956
411 Robertson, J. M. Shakespeare and other essays on cognate questions. 1970. B8957
412 Taylor, J. M. The witchcraft delusion in colonial Connecticut, 1647-1697. 1971. B8958
413 Kirchoff, A. Die Dandschriftenhändler der Mittelalters. 1971. B8959
414 Hall, H. A history of the custom revenue in England. 1970. B8960
415 L'Estrange, A. G. K. History of English humour. 2 v. 1970. B8961
416 Mitchell, W. C. Business cycles. 1970. B8962
417 Phillips, U. B. The economic and political essays of the ante bellum South. 1970. B8963
418 Watson, D. S. History

of American coinage. 1970. B8964
419 Oberholtzer, E. P. Jay Cooke. 2 v. 1970. B8965
420 Carey, M. Brief view of the system of internal improvements in the state of Pennsylvania. 1970. B8966
421 Smith, W. A brief history of the province of Pennsylvania. 1970. B8967
422 Johnson, C. B. Letters from the British settlement in Pennsylvania. 1970. B8968
423 Cluny, A. Observations on the present state, culture and commerce of the British colonies in America. 1970. B8969
424 Bauer, O. The Austrian revolution, tr. by Stenning. 1970. B8970
425 Depping, G. Histoire du commerce entre la levant et l'Europe. 2 v. 1969. B8971
426 Løseth, E. Le roman en prose de Tristan. 1970. B8972
427 Johnson, A. The Swedish settlements on the Delaware. 2 v. 1970. B8973
428 Jelley, S. M. The voice of labor. 1970. B8974
429 Jenks, E. Law and politics in the Middle Ages. 1970. B8975
430 Tyler, M. C. Literary history of the American Revolution. 2 v. 1970. B8976
431 Ashton, J. Humour, wit and satire of the 17th century. 1970. B8977
432 Doyle, J. Frederick William Von Steuren and the American Revolution. 1970. B8978
433 Pickell, J. A new chapter in the early life of Washington. 1970. B8979
434 Lee, H. Memoirs of the war in the Southern Department of the United States. 2 v. 1970. B8980
435 Ayer, J. C. Some of the usages and abuses in the management of our manufacturing corporations. 1971. B8981
436 Wilkes, J. The correspondence of the late John Wilkes, ed. by Almon. 5 v. 1970. B8982
437 Johnson, A. The speeches of Andrew Jackson. 1970. B8983
438 Nichols, C. L. Isiah Thomas. 1971. B8984
439 LeBrun, R. Corneille devant trois siècles. 1970. B8985
440 Thornton, J. W. The pulpit in the American Revolution. 1970. B8986
441 Wharton, F. The revolutionary diplomatic correspondence of the United States. 6 v. 1970. B8987
442 Stevens, H. Historical and geographical notes on the earliest discoveries in America, 1453-1530. 1970. B8988
443 Greene, R. Groats Worth of Witte bought with a million of repentance. 1970. B8989
444 Meyer, J. M. Official publications of European governments. 1971. B8990
445 Defoe, D. The complete English tradesman. 2 v. 1970. B8991
446 Fowell, F. and Palmer, F. Censorship in England. 1970. B8992
447 Laughton, J. K , ed. State papers relating to the defeat of the Spanish Armada. 2 v. 1970. B8993
448 Root, W. T. The relations of Pennsylvania with the British government, 1696. 1970. B8994
449 Goodnow, F. J. Social reform and the Constitution. 1970. B8995
450 Alcarez, R. The other side, tr. by Ramsey. 1970. B8996
450 Giesecke, A. A. American commercial legislation before 1789. 1970. B8997
451 (Giesecke misnumbered 450)
452 Pollock, F. The first book of jurisprudence for students of the common law. 1970. B8998
453 Koren, J. The history of statistics. 1970. B8999

454 Pope, J. E. The clothing industry in New York. 1970. B9000
455 Hack, R. K. God in Greek philosophy to the time of Socrates. 1970. B9001
456 Tyler, M. C. Patrick Henry. 1970. B9002
457 Evans, D. M. The commercial crisis, 1847-1848. 1970. B9003
458 Miller, J. New York considered and improvised, 1695, ed. by Paltsits. 1970. B9004
459 Wafer, L. A new voyage and description of the Isthmus of America, ed. by Winship. 1970. B9005
460 Winship, G. P. Boston in 1682 and 1699. 1970. B9006
461 AEsopus. The fables of AEsop, tr. by Caxton, ed. by Jacobs. V. 1. 1970. B9007
462 Sumner, W. G. The financier and the finances of the American Revolution. 2 v. 1970. B9008
463 Goodnow, F. J. Comparative administrative law. 2 v. 1970. B9009
464 Kondakov, N. P. Histoire de l'art Byzantine considere principalement dans les miniatures. 2 v. 1970. B9010
465 Hamilton, W. The poet laureate of England. 1970. B9011
466 Capell, E. Notes and various readings to Shakespeare. 1970. B9012
467 Turner, F. J. The character and influence of the Indian trade in Wisconsin. 1970. B9013
468 Felt, J. B. The customs of New England. 1970. B9014
469 Dunlop, J. C. History of prose fiction. 2 v. 1970. B9015
470 Brigham, A. P. Geographic influences in American history. 1970. B9016
471 Drake, S. G., comp. The witchcraft of delusion in New England. 3 v. 1970. B9017
472 Bodin de Saint-Laurent, J. de. Les idées monetaires et commerciales de Jean Bodin. 1970. B9018
473 Ripley, W. Z. The financial history of Virginia, 1609-1776. 1970. B9019
474 Wellington, R. G. The political and sectional influence of the public lands, 1828-1842. B9020
475 Baird, H. M. Theodore Baza. 1970. B9021
476 Corwin, E. S. French policy and the American alliance of 1778. 1970. B9022
477 Dedieu, J. Montesquieu et la tradition politique anglaise en France. 1970. B9023
478 Lindo, E. H. The history of the Jews of Spain and Portugal. 1970. B9024
479 Clyde, W. M. The struggle for freedom of the press from Caxton to Cromwell. 1970. B9025
480 Ferris, J. A. The financial economy of the United States and some of the causes which retarded the progress of California demonstrated. Also A searching analysis of the action of paper money... 1970. B9026
481 Kellogg, E. A new monetary system, ed. by Putnam. 1970. B9027
482 Murray, A. E. A history of the commercial and financial relations between England and Ireland from the period of the Revolution. 1970. B9028
483 Tunison, J. S. Dramatic traditions of the Dark Ages. 1970. B9029
484 Ripley, R. S. The war with Mexico. 2 v. 1970. B9030
485 Merrill, E. The dialogue in English literature. 1970. B9031
486 Black, W. G. Folk-medicine. 1970. B9032
487 Cartwright, J. American independence. 1970. B9033
488 Wierzbicki, F. P. California as it is & as it may be. 1970. B9034
489 Masson, D. Wordsworth, Shelley, Keats. 1970. B9035
490 Dutt, R. G. The economic history of India. 2 v.

1970. B9036
491 Montgomery, J. The cotton manufacture of the United States. 1970. B9037
492 Garnier, G. Histoire de la monnale. 2 v. 1970. B9038
493 Edgeworth, F. Y. Papers relating to political economy. 3 v. in 1. 1970. B9039
494 Ford, P. L. Essays on the Constitution of the United States. 1970. B9040
495 Ditchfield, P. H. Books fatal to their authors. 1970. B9041
496 Calhoun, G. M. Athenian clubs in politics and litigations. 1970. B9042
497 Pearse, J. B. A concise history of the iron manufacture of the American colonies up to the Revolution. 1970. B9043
498 Adams, H. C. Taxation in the United States, 1789-1816. 1970. B9044
499 Bouzinac, J. Les doctrines économiques au XVIIIe siècle. 1970. B9045
500 Brocard, L. Les doctrines économiques et sociale marquis de Mirabeau dans l'ami des hommes. 1970. B9046
501 Guiraud, P. Etudes économiques sur l'antiquité. 1970. B9047
502 Jones, G. N. Florida plantation records, ed. by Phillips and Glunt. 1970. B9048
503 Cadet, F. Histoire de l'economie politique. 1970. B9049
504 Perkins, J. B. France in the American Revolution. 1970. B9050
505 Clark, V. S. The labour movement in Australia. 1970. B9051
506 Pigeonneeau, H. Histoire du commerce de la France. 2 v. 1970. B9052
507 Neeser, R. W. Statistical and chronological history of the United States Navy, 1775-1907. 2 v. 1970. B9053
508 Chambers, E. K. The history and motives of literary forgeries. 1970. B9054
509 Morgan, L. H. The American beaver and his works. 1970. B9055
510 Brants, V. L. J. L. L'economie politique au moyen âge. 1970. B9056
511 Cooley, A. J. The toilet in ancient and modern times. 1970. B9057
512 Toussaint, P. Memoirs, ed. by Lee. 1970. B9058
513 Totten, G. O. Maya architecture. 1970. B9059
514 Lightner, O. C. History of business depressions. 1970. B9060
515 Helvétius, C. A. De l'esprit. 1970. B9061
516 Olmsted, F. L. A journey in the back country. 1970. B9062
517 Defoe, D. An account of the conduct and proceedings of the pirate Gow. 1970. B9063
518 Byrd, W. The writings of Colonel William Byrd of Westover in Virginia. 1970. B9064
519 Dexter, H. M. The Congregationalism of the last three hundred years as seen in its literature. 2 v. 1970. B9065
520 Hughes, S. C. The pre-Victorian drama in Dublin. 1970. B9066
521 Eliason, A. O. The rise of commercial banking institutions in the United States. 1970. B9067
522 Ellis, G. E. Puritan age and rule in the colony of the Massachusetts Bay, 1629-1685. 1970. B9068
523 Brown, C. B. Novels. 6 v. 1970. B9069
524 Ford, J. W., ed. Some correspondence between the Governors... 1970. B9070
525 Gibbons, J. S. The public debt of the United States. 1970. B9071
526 Horn, I. E. L'economie politique avant les physiocrates. 1971. B9072
527 Martin, G. La grande industrie sous le règne de Louis XIV. 1971. B9073

528 Kuslūm, N. Customs and manners of the women of Persia and their domestic superstitions, tr. by Atkinson. 1971. B9074
529 Cobb, S. H. The rise of religious liberty in America. 1970. B9075
530 Babelon, E. C. F. Les origines de la monnaie. 1970. B9076
531 Hall, J. The West. 1970. B9077
532 Tucker, G. Progress of the U.S. in population and wealth in fifty years. 1970. B9078
533 Heinrich, P. La Louisians sous la Compagnie des Indes, 1717-1731. 1970. B9079
534 Latimer, J. The history of the Society of Merchant Venturers of the city of Bristol. 1970. B9080
535 Scott, W. The journal of Sir Walter Scott. 2 v. 1970. B9081
536 Ellery, E. Brissot de Warville. 1970. B9082
537 Dodd, W. E. The life of Nathaniel Macon. 1970. B9083
538 Dunlap, W. History of the New Netherlands... 2 v. 1970. B9084
539 Webster, N. A history of epidemic and pestilential national periods. 2 v. 1970. B9085
540 Hecker, J. F. C. The dancing mania of the Middle Ages. 1970. B9086
541 Schoepperle, G. Tristan and Isolt, ed. by Loomis. 1970. B9087
542 Kovalevsky, M. Modern customs and ancient laws of Russia. 1970. B9088
543 Zorn, F. A. Grammar of the art of dancing. 1970. B9089
544 Crosby, S. S. The early coins of America. 1970. B9090
545 Cilleuls, A. des. Histoire et regime de la grande industrie en France aux XVIIe et XVIIIe siècle. 1970. B9091
546 Hooker, R. The works of that learned and judicious Divine Mr. Richard Hooker... 3 v. 1970. B9092
547 Thomas, P. Essai sur quelques theories economiques dans le corpus juris civilis. 1970. B9093
548 Jaubet, C. Montesquieu economiste. 1970. B9094
549 Shillington, V. M. and A. B. Wallis Chapman. 1970. B9095
550 Caillaud, E. Les idées économiques de Condorcet. 1970. B9096
551 Carr, C. T. Select charters of trading companies, A.D. 1530-1707. 1970. B9097
552 Bowden, W. The industrial history of the United States. 1970. B9098
553 Arnould, L. Racan. 2 v. 1970. B9099
554 Bayley, R. A. The national loans of the United States. 1970. B9100
555 Sears, L. American literature in the colonial and national periods. 1970. B9101
556 Walford, C. The famines of the world. 1970. B9102
557 Evans, E. Historical, descriptive and analytical account of the entire works of Johannes Brahms. 4 v. 1971. B9103
558 Walras, L. L'economie politique et la justice. 1970. B9104
559 Ducrocq, T. G. A. Etudes d'histoire financiers et monetaire. 1970. B9105
560 Smith, E. Foreign visitors in England... 1970. B9106
561 Kleeberg, G. S. The formation of the Republican Party as a national political organization. 1970. B9107
562 Corbett, J. S., ed. Papers relating to the Navy during the Spanish War, 1585-1587. 1970. B9108
563 Newton, A. P. The great age of discovery. 1970. B9109
564 Rambaud, A. N. La Russie epique. 1970. B9110
565 Robespierre, M. I. de. Oeuvres, ed. by Laponneraye. 3 v. 1970. B9111
566 Fagniez, G. C. Etudes

sur l'industrie et la classe industrielle à Paris au XIIIe et au XIVe siècle. 1970. B9112

567 Thompson, W. Appeal of one half the human race. 1970. B9113

568 Auber, P. Analysis of the constitution of the East-India Company. 2 v. 1970. B9114

569 Austin, J. The province of jurisprudence determined. 1970. B9115

570 Marechal, H. Les conceptions économiques d'Auguste Comte. 1970. B9116

571 Stevens, H. The dawn of British trade to the East Indies. 1970. B9117

572 Ward, C. O. The ancient lowly. 2 v. 1970. B9118

573 Dunlap Society. Publications. 30 v. 1971. B9119

574 Charbonnard, R. Les idées économiques de Voltaire. 1970. B9120

575 Grimke, S. M. Letters on equality of the sexes and conditions of women. 1970. B9121

576 Ames, H. V. Proposed amendments to the Constitution of the U. S. 1970. B9122

577 Portalis, R. and Beraldi, H. Les graveurs de dix-huitième siècle. 3 v. 1970. B9123

578 Allan, F. D. Allan's lone star ballads. 1970. B9124

579 Altmeyer, J. J. Histoire des relations commerciales et diplomatiques des Pays-Bas. 1970. B9125

580 Chaucer, G. The works of Geoffrey Chaucer and others, ed. by Skeats. 1970. B9126

581 Cooke, G. W., ed. The poets of transcendentalism. 1971. B9127

582 Pollen, J. H. English Catholics in the reign of Queen Elizabeth. 1970. B9128

583 Tocqueville, A. de. Etudes économiques, politiques et litteraires. 1971. B9129

584 Harington, J. A tract on the succession to the crown, A. D. 1602, ed. by Markham. 1971. B9130

585 Beccaria and others. Discourse on public economy and commerce. 1970. B9131

586 Fagan, L. Life of Andrew Panizzi. 2 v. 1970. B9132

587 Miller, S. Retrospect of the eighteenth century. 2 v. 1970. B9133

588 Southey, R. History of Brazil. 3 v. 1970. B9134

589 Wright, T., ed. Songs and ballads... 1970. B9135

590 Schumacher, E. Thomas Otway. 1970. B9136

591 Cary, T. G. Memoirs of Thomas Handasyd Perkins. 1970. B9137

592 Levasseur, E. Recherches historiques sur le systeme de law. 1970. B9138

593 Albert, M. Les theatres de la foire. 1970. B9139

594 Demangeon, A. Les sources de la geographie de la France archives nationale. 1970. B9140

595 Johnston, H. F. The correspondence and public papers of John Jay. 4 v. 1971. B9141

596 Guillaume de Palerne. The ancient English romance of William and the werewolf, ed. by Madden. 1970. B9142

597 Michel, F. X. Histoire du commerce et de la navigation à Bordeaux. 2 v. 1971. B9143

598 Alexander, D. A. S. History and procedure of the House of Representatives. 1971. B9144

599 Loomis, R. Studies in medieval literature. 1971. B9145

600 Gruhn, A. Die byzantinische politik... 1971. B9146

601 Kelby, W. Notes on American artists, 1754-1820. 1971. B9147

602 Gomes, F. L. Essai sur la théorie de l'économie politique et de ses rapports avec la morale et le droit. 1970. B9148

603 Loisel, E. Essai sur la legislation economique des

Carolingiens d'après les capitularies. 1971. B9149
604 Lodge, L. D. A study in Corneille. 1971. B9150
605 Elliott, J. The American diplomatic code. 2 v. 1971. B9151
606 Faral, E. Les jongleurs en France au moyen âge. 1971. B9152
607 Haney, J. L., ed. Early reviews of the English poets. 1971. B9153
608 Pollard, A. W. Old picture books. 1971. B9154
609 Woodberry, G. E. Makers of literature. 1970. B9155
610 Tournyol du Clos, J. Les idées financieres de Montesquieu. 1970. B9156
611 Schluter, H. The brewing industry and the Brewery Workers' Movement in America. 1970. B9157
612 Spencer, A. and Hutchins, E. L. A history of factory legislation. 1970. B9158
613 Ward, C. O. The equilibrium of human attitudes and powers of adaptation. 1970. B9159
614 Scrutton, T. E. Commons and common fields. 1970. B9160
615 Gothein, E. Wittschaftsgeschichte des Schwarzwaldes. 1970. B9161
616 Ward, A. Works. 1970. B9162
617 Cavaignac, C. E. Etudes sur l'histoire financiere d'Athenes au Ve siècle. 1970. B9163
618 D'Holbach, P. H. T. System of nature. 1970. B9164
619 Gosse, P. My pirate library. 1970. B9165
620 Loiseau, G. Les doctrines economiques de Cournot. 1970. B9166
621 Lebeau, A. Condillac. 1970. B9167
622 Allen, W. and McClure, E. Two hundred years. 1970. B9168
623 Deloche, M. La crise economique au XVIe siècle et la crise actuelle. 1970. B9169
624 Dessaix, P. Montchretian et l'economie politique nationale. 1970. B9170
625 Dionnet, G. Le neomercantilisme au 18e siècle et au debut du 19e siècle. 1970. B9171
626 Channing, W. E. The works of William E. Channing. 1970. B9172
627 Alcedo, D. A. de. The geographical and historical dictionary of America and the West Indies, tr. by Thompson. 1970. B9173
628 Toner, J. M. Contributions to the annals of medical progress and medical education in the United States... 1970. B9174
629 Vrau, J. Proudhon et son systeme economique. 1970. B9175
630 Gerber, A. Great Russian animal tales. 1970. B9176
631 Copley, T. Letters to Queen Elizabeth and her ministers. 1970. B9177
632 Rupin, C. Les idées economiques de Sully et leurs applications à l'agriculture, aux finances et à l'industrie. 1970. B9178
633 Aftalion, A. L'oeuvre economique de Simonde de Sismondi. 1970. B9179
634 Van Tyne, C. H. The loyalists in the American Revolution. 1970. B9180
635 Berthold, A. B. American colonial printing as determined by contemporary cultural forces, 1639-1763. 1970. B9181
636 Grote, H. The philosophical radicals of 1832. 1970. B9182
637 Binet, H. Le style de la lyrique courteoise en France... 1970. B9183
638 Keep, A. B. The library in colonial New York. 1970. B9184
639 Villey-Desmeserets, P. L. J. Les sources italiennes de la "Deffense et illustration de la langue françoise" de Joachim du Bellay. 1970. B9185
640 Desourteaux, R. Les idées

de William Thompson. 1970. B9186
641 Boiteau, D. A. P. Les traites de commerce... 1970. B9187
642 Anghiera, P. M. d'. De orbe novo. 2 v. 1970. B9188
643 Fischer, J. The discoveries of the Norsemen in America. 1970. B9189
644 Mantoux, P. and Alfassa, M. La crise du trade-unionisme. 1970. B9190
645 Audiganne, A. Les populations ouvrieres et les industries de la France. 2 v. 1970. B9191
646 Enfantin, P. Economie politique. 1970. B9192
647 Teyssendier de la Serve, P. Mably et les physiocrates. 1970. B9193
648 Gueneau, L. Lyon et le commerce de la soie. 1970. B9194
649 Cornelissen, C. Theorie de la valeur. 1971. B9195
650 Brown, P. H. Early travelers in Scotland. 1970. B9196
651 Clark, A. F. B. Boileau and the French classical critics in England. 1971. B9197
652 Bolles, A. S. Pennsylvania. 1970. B9198
653 Mesnil-Marigny, J. du. Histoire de l'economie politique des anciens peuples de l'Inde. 1971. B9199
654 Whitford, N. E. History of the canal system of the state of New York. 1970. B9200
655 Daehnhardt, A. O., ed. Natursagen. 4 v. in 2. 1971. B9201
656 Held, A. Zwei bucher zur socialen geschichte Englands. 1971. B9202
657 Dix, E. R. M. Printing in Dublin prior to 1691. 1971. B9203
658 Fernow, B. The Ohio Valley in colonial days. 1971. B9204
659 Mille, J. G.-F. Le Trosne. 1971. B9205
660 Ford, E. E. Notes on the life of Noah Webster. 2 v. 1971. B9206
661 Everett, A. H. America. 1971. B9207
662 Drake, D. A systematic treatise. 2 v. 1971. B9208
663 Janson, C. W. The stranger in America, 1793-1806, ed. by Driver. 1971. B9209
664 Hatch, L. C. The administration of the American Revolutionary Army. 1971. B9210
665 Brebion, A. Livre d'or du Cambodge. 1971. B9211
666 Niles, H. Principles and acts of the Revolution in America. 1971. B9212
667 Pasquier, M. Sir William Petty. 1971. B9213
668 Pollard, A. W. Last words on the history of the title-page. 1971. B9214
669 Roy, E. Etudes sur le theatre français XIVe et du XVe siècle. 1970. B9215
670 Steck, F. B. A tentative guide to historical materials on the Spanish borderlands. 1971. B9216
671 Bertrand, M. A historical account of neutrality of Great Britain... 1971. B9217
672 Chodzko, A. B., comp. Specimens of the popular poetry of Persia. 1971. B9218
673 Hildreth, R. Theory of politics. 1971. B9219
674 Joubleau, F. Etudes sur Colbert. 2 v. 1971. B9220
675 Lahontan, L. A. de. New voyages to North America. 2 v. 1971. B9221
676 Elliot, J. The funding system of the United States and Great Britain. 2 v. 1971. B9222
677 Gibbs, G. Memoirs of the administrators of Washington and John Adams, ed. by Wolcott. 2 v. 1971. B9223
678 Goris, J. A. Etude sur les colonies marchandes merionales. 2 v. in 1. 1971. B9224
679 Trotter, A. Observations on the financial position and credit of the states of the North American Union...

1971. B9225
680 Walker, F. A. Discussions in economics and statistics. 2 v. 1971. B9226
681 Wright, C. Philosophical discussions. 1971. B9227
682 Schmoller, G. and Hintze, O., eds. Politikerund Nationalokonomen. 2 v. 1971. B9228
683 Centre international de synthese, Paris. L'encyclopedie et les encyclopedistes. 1971. B9229
684 Hutchinson, T. The diary and letters of His Excellency Thomas Hutchinson, comp. by Peter O. Hutchinson. 2 v. 1971. B9230
685 Cherniss, H. F. The Platonism of Gregory of Nyssa. 1971. B9231
686 Elson, L. C. A history of American music. 1971. B9232
687 Carvalho, D. N. Forty centuries of ink. 1971. B9233
688 Rodbertus, J. K. Overproduction and crises, tr. by Franklin. 1971. B9234
689 Ford, P. L., ed. Pamphlets on the Constitution of the United States. 1971. B9235
690 West, A. H. L'influence française dans la poesie burlesque en Angleterre entre 1660 et 1700. 1971. B9236
691 Houtte, H. V., ed. Documents pour servir l'histoire des prix de 1381 à 1794. 1971. B9237
692 Seeber, E. D. Anti-slavery opinion during the second half of the 18th century. 1971. B9238
693 Dyer, W. A. Early American craftsmen. 1971. B9239
694 Rousseau, J. J. A discourse upon the origin and foundation of the inequality among mankind. 1971. B9240
695 Harvey, W. Scottish chapbook literature. 1971. B9241
696 Ducros, L. French society in the eighteenth century, tr. by de Geijer. 1971. B9242
697 Bunge, N. K. Esquisses de litterature politico-economique. 1971. B9243
698 Neale, W. The sovereignty of the states. 1971. B9244
699 Freund, E. Administrative power over persons and places. 1971. B9245
700 Leonard, E. M. The early history of English poor relief. 1971. B9246
701 Robertson, J. M. A short history of morals. 1971. B9247
702 Seth Pringle Pattison, A. Hegelianism and personality. 1971. B9248
703 ____. Scottish philosophy. 1971. B9249
704 Whewell, W. On the philosophy of discovery. 1971. B9250
705 Drake, M. Saints and their emblems. 1971. B9251
706 Pecqueur, C. Theorie nouvelle d'economie sociale et politique, ou études sur l'organization des sociétés. 1971. B9252
707 Revue Historique, by Bataillon and others. 2 v. in 1. 1971. B9253
708 Moride, P. Le produit net des physiocrates et la plus-value de Karl Marx. 1971. B9254
709 Seth Pringle Pattison, A. and Haldane, R. B., eds. Essays in philosophical criticism. 1971. B9255
710 Thompson, W. Labour rewarded. 1971. B9256
711 Ames, F. Works of Fisher Ames, ed. by Seth Ames. 1971. B9257
712 Villey-Desmeserets, P. L. J. L'influence de Montaigne sur les idées pedagogiques de Locke et de Rousseau. 1971. B9258
713 Walker, J. H. Banking and currency. 1971. B9259
714 Woodward, W. H. Desiderius Erasmus concerning the aim and method of education. 1971. B9260
715 Wedderburn, A. D. O. and Collingwood, W. G. The economist of Xenophon. 1971. B9261
716 Bird, R. M. The life and dramatic works of Robert Montgomery Bird, ed. by

Foust. 1971. B9262
717 Belote, T. T. The Scioto speculation and the French settlement at Gallipolis. 1971. B9263
718 Bacon-Foster, C. Early chapters in the development of the Potomac route to the West. 1971. B9264
719 Higginson, F. New England plantation. 1971. B9265
720 Fowler, W. W. Ten years in Wall Street. 1971. B9266
721 Swinton, J. A momentous question. 1971. B9267
722 Humboldt, A. von. The fluctuations of gold.... The law of payment by F. Grimaudet. 2 v. in 1. 1971. B9268
723 Levy-Bruhl, L. History of modern philosophy in France. 1971. B9269
724 Freund, E. The legal nature of corporations. 1971. B9270
725 Chatelain, H. L. Recherches sur le vers français au XVe siècle. 1971. B9271
726 Fling, F. M. Outline of the historical method. 1971. B9272
727 Generides. A royal historie of the excellent knight Generides, ed. by Furnivall. 1971. B9273
728 Leibell, J. F. Anglo-Saxon education of women. 1971. B9274
729 New York (State). Colonial records of the New York Chamber of Commerce, by Stevens. 1971. B9275
730 Jaffe, W. Les theories economiques et sociales et Thorstein Veblen. 1971. B9276
731 Ogle, A. The canon law in mediaeval England. 1971. B9277
732 Brissended, P. F. Earnings of factory workers, 1899 to 1927. 1971. B9278
733 Thompson, J. An essay on English municipal history. 1971. B9279
734 Jackson, T. A. Dialectics. 1971. B9280
735 Hunter, D. Papermaking through eighteen centuries. 1971. B9281
736 The oracle of reason, ed. by Southwell and others. 2 v. 1971. B9282
737 Martin, F. A history of Lloyds and of marine insurance in Great Britain. 1971. B9283
738 Masson, G. The early chroniclers of Europe. 1971. B9284
739 Keynes, J. M. Indian currency and finance. 1971. B9285
740 LaFontainerie, F. de., ed. French liberalism and education in the eighteenth century. 1971. B9286
741 Graham, W. English political philosophy from Hobbes to Maine. 1971. B9287
742 Crane, T. F. The exempla. 1971. B9288
743 Dunand-Henry, A. Les doctrines et la politique economiques du comte de Cavour. 1971. B9289
744 Mantoux, P. Notes sur les comptes rendus des seances di Parlement anglais au 18e siècle. 1971. B9290
745 Marsan, J. La pastorale dramatique en France à la fin du XVIe et au commencement du XVIIe siècle. 1971. B9291
746 Mathiez, A. Un proces de corruption sous la terreur. 1971. B9292
747 Collmann, H. L., ed. Ballads & broadsides. 1971. B9293
748 Fesch, P. Constantinople aux derniers jours d'Abdul-Hamid. 1971. B9294
749 Hamilton, W. Parodies of the works of English and American authors. 6 v. 1971. B9295
750 Faguet, E. La politique comparee de Montesquieu, Rousseau et Voltaire. 1971. B9296
751 Kent, C. B. P. The English radicals. 1971. B9297
752 Redfern, O. The wisdom of Sir Walter Scott. 1971. B9298
753 Lehmann-Brockhaus, O. Schriftquellen zur kunstgeschichte des 11. und 12.

jahrhunderts für Deutsch-
land... 2 v. 1971. B9299
754 Strieder, J. Studien zur geschichte kapitalistischer organisationformen. 1971. B9300
755 Henry, J. Aeneidea. 4 v. 1971. B9301
756 Coke, D. P. The Royal Commission on the losses and services of American Loyalists, 1783 to 1785, ed. by Egerton. 1971. B9302
757 Tarde, A. de. L'idee du juste prix. 1971. B9303
758 Dexter, E. G. A history of education in the United States. 1971. B9304
759 Lambert, E. L'art gotheque en Espagne aux XIIe et XIIIe siècles. 1971. B9305
760 Turgot, A. R. J. The life and writings of Turgot, ed. by Stephens. 1971. B9306
761 Speed, T. The Wilderness road. 1971. B9307
762 Leroux de Lincy, A. J. V. Researches concerning Jean Grolier, ed. by Shipman. 1971. B9308
763 Remington, F. Drawings by Frederic Remington. 1971. B9309
764 Grellier, J. J. The history of the national debt. 1971. B9310
765 Mill, J. The principles of toleration. 1971. B9311
766 Stephen, L. Studies of a biographer. 1971. B9312
767 Moore, F. Songs and ballads of the Southern people, 1861-1865. 1971. B9313
768 Clergue, H. The salon. 1971. B9314
769 Wittek, J. The rise of the Ottoman empire. 1971. B9315
770 Nieboer, H. J. Slavery as an industrial system. 1971. B9316
771 Rousseau, J. J. The reveries of a solitary, tr. by Fletcher. 1971. B9317
772 Davidson, T. The education of the wage-earners, ed. by Bakewell. 1971. B9318
773 Jevons, W. S. Pure logic and other minor works, ed. by Adamson and H. A. Jevons. 1971. B9319
774 Wilson, H. W. The downfall of Spain. 1971. B9320
775 Wright, C. Letters, ed. by Thayer, 1971. B9321
776 Franklin, A. L. A. Les corporations ouvrieres de Paris du XIIe au XVIIIe siècle. 1971. B9322
777 Pargoire, J. L'eglise byzantine de 527 à 847. 1971. B9323
778 Venn, J. Symbolic logic. 1971. B9324
779 Brigham, A. P. The United States of America. 1971. B9325
780 Brunot, F. La doctrine de Malherbe d'apres son commentaire sur Desportes. 1971. B9326
781 Rogers, R. Ponteach, ed. by Nevins. 1971. B9327
782 Compayre, G. Montaigne and the education of the judgment, tr. by Mansion. 1971. B9328
783 Cyrano de Bergerac, S. Les oeuvres libertines, ed. by Lachevre. 2 v. 1971. B9329
784 Bardon, M. "Don Quichotte" en France au XVIIe et au XVIIIe siècle. 2 v. 1971. B9330
785 Atkinson, G. Les relations de voyages au XVIIe siècle et l'evolution des idées. 1971. B9331
786 Picavet, F. J. Les idéologues. 1971. B9332
787 Chasles, E. La comedie en France au siezieme siècle. 1971. B9333
788 DuPuynode, M. G. Les grandes crises financiers de la France. 1971. B9334
789 Mettrier, H. L'impot et la milice dans J. J. Rousseau et Mably. 1971. B9335
790 Thieme, H. P. Essai sur l'histoire du vers français. 1971. B9336
791 Diderot, D. Diderot's thoughts on art and style, tr. by Tollemache. 1971. B9337
792 Bercaw, L. O. Corn in the development of the

civilization of the Americas. 1971. B9338
793 Bachman, A. Censorship in France from 1715-1750. 1971. B9339
794 Bourne, R. S. Youth and life. 1971. B9340
795 Ducros, L. Diderot. 1971. B9341
796 Hubbard, W. The history of the Indian wars in New England... 2 v. in 1. 1971. B9342
797 Cahen, L. Concorcet et la revolution française. 1971. B9343
798 Cushing, M. P. Baron d'Holbach. 1971. B9344
799 Smith, H. E. The literary criticism of Pierre Bayle. 1971. B9345
800 Lenient, C. La poesie patriotique en France au moyen âge. 1971. B9346
801 Perrens, F. T. Les libertins en France au XVIIe siècle. 1971. B9347
802 Barre, W. L. The life and public services of Millard Fillmore. 1971. B9348
803 MacCarthy, J. P. The rise of Dennis Hathnaught. 1971. B9349
804 Smith, A. L. Frederick William Maitland. 1971. B9350
805 Gooch, G. P. Annals of politics and culture. 1971. B9351
806 Arymoyd, G. A connected view of the whole internal navigation of the United States. 1971. B9352
807 Forsyth, W. History of trial by jury. 1971. B9353
808 Bertrand, L. M. E. La fin du classicisme et le retour à l'antique dans la seconde moitie du XVIIIe siècle. 1971. B9354
809 Martino, P. L'Orient dans la litterature française au XVIIe et au XVIIIe siècle. 1971. B9355
810 Lanson, G. Nivelle de la Chausee et la comedie larmoyante. 1971. B9356
811 Monod, A. De Pascal à Chateaubriand. 1971. B9357
812 Barlow, J. Political writings. 1971. B9358
813 Davis, J. P. Corporations. 2 v. 1971. B9359
814 Ross, D. W. The early history of landholding among the Germans. 1971. B9360
815 Hainsworth, G. Les "Novelas exemplares" de Cervantes en France au XVIIe siècle. 1971. B9361
816 Laborde, L. E. S. J. Les comptes des batiments du roi. 2 v. 1971. B9362
817 Lee, S. The travels of Batuta. 1971. B9363
818 Locke, J. Of the conduct of the understanding, ed. by Fowler. 1971. B9364
819 Ford, P. L. Some notes towards an essay on the beginnings of American dramatic literature. 1971. B9365
820 Hammond, W. A., ed. Polydori Vergilii, tr. by Langley. 1971. B9366
821 Bapst, G. Essai sur le histoire du theatre. 1971. B9367
822 Heynen, R. Zur entstehung des kapitalismus in Venedig. 1971. B9368
823 Cuny, L. Le role de DuPont de Nemours en nature fiscale à l'Assemblee constituante. 1971. B9369
824 Briaune, M. Des crises commercials. 1971. B9370
825 Bastide, C. The Anglo-French entente in the seventeenth century. 1971. B9371
826 Landry, A. Essai economique sur les mutations des monnaies dans l'ancienne France de Philippe Bel à Charles VII. 1971. B9372
827 Buck, S. J. Travel and description, 1765-1865. 1971. B9373
828 McCormac, E. I. Colonial opposition to imperial authority during the French and Indian war. 1971. B9374
829 Crotch, W. J. B. Prologues and epilogues of William Caxton. 1971. B9375

830 Dellenbaugh, F. S. Breaking the wilderness. 1971. B9376
831 Shepherd, R. P. Turgot and the six edicts. 1971. B9377
832 Paris, G. Melanges de litterature française du moyen âge publies par Mario Roques. 1971. B9378
833 Jefferson, T. A summary view of the rights of British America, ed. by Ford. 1971. B9379
834 Reynaud, L. L'influence allemande en France au XVIIIe et au XIXe siècle. 1971. B9380
835 Davidson, T. A history of education. 1971. B9381
836 Delvolve, J. Religion, critique et philosophie positive chez Pierre Bayle. 1971. B9382
837 Egli, J. J. Nomina geographica. 1971. B9383
838 Cohen, G. Histoire de la mise en scène dans le thèâtre religieux française du Moyen âge. 1971. B9384
839 Melvill, D. The Melvill book of roundels, ed. by Bantock and Anderton. 1971. B9385
840 Cabet, E. Colonie icarienne aux Etats-Unis d'Amerique. 1971. B9386
841 Raymond, M. L'influence de Ronsard sur la poesie française. 1971. B9387
842 Chalmers, G. Opinions of eminent lawyers. 1971. B9388
843 A century of American medicine, 1776-1876, ed. by Clarke and others. 1971. B9389
844 Duer, W. A. A course of lectures on the constitutional jurisprudence of the United States. 1971. B9390
845 Feilbogen, S. Smith und Turgot. 1971. B9391
846 McCullough, J. R., ed. The overstone tracts. 8 v. 1972. B9392
847 A short history and description of Fort Niagara, ed. by Ford. 1971. B9393
848 Ford, W. C. Washington as an employer and importer of labor. 1971. B9394
849 Duval, J. Histoire d'emigration europeene... 1971. B9395
850 Dureau de la Malle, A. J. C. A. Economie politique des Romains. 2 v. 1971. B9396
851 Gouraud, C. Histoire de la politique commerciale de la France et de son influence sur le progrès de la richesse publique depuis le Moyen âge jusqu'a nos jours. 2 v. 1971. B9397
852 Reynaud, L. Histoire générale de l'influence française en Allemagne. 1971. B9398
853 Mornet, D. Le romantisme en France au XVIIIe siècle. 1971. B9399
854 ____. Le sciences de la nature en France. 1971. B9400
855 DeMenil, A. N. The literature of the Louisiana territory. 1971. B9401
856 Bouchard, L. Systeme financiere de l'ancienne monarchie. 1971. B9402
857 Blanqui, J. A. De la liberte du commerce et de la protection de l'industrie. 1971. B9403
858 Graf, A. Miti, leggende e superstizioni del medio evo. 1971. B9404
859 Jameson, R. P. Montesquieu et l'esclavage. 1971. B9405
860 Mitchell, S. W. The early history of instrumental precision in medicine. 1971. B9406
861 Du Cange, C. du F. Histoire de l'empire de Constantinople. 2 v. 1971. B9407
862 Hodgkin, T. The dynasty of Theodosius. 1971. B9408
863 Linguet, S. H. N. Theorie des lois civiles. 1971. B9409
864 Du Cange, C. du F. Familles d'outre-mer. 1971. B9410
865 Lingelbach, W. E. The merchant adventurers of England. 1971. B9411
866 Bonno, G. Constitution Britannique devant l'opinion française. 1971. B9412
867 Rousseau, J. J. The

reveries of a solitary. 1971. B9413
868 Nat'l. Assn. of Broadcasters. Broadcasting and the Bill of Rights. 1971. B9414
869 Havens, G. R. Voltaire's marginalia on the pages of Rousseau. 1971. B9415
870 Strowski, F. Montaigne. 1971. B9416
871 Lone, E. M. Some noteworthy firsts in Europe during the 15th century. 1971. B9417
872 Hill, J. The bookmakers of Old Birmingham. 1971. B9418
873 McKee, T. H. The national conventions and platforms of all political parties, 1789 to 1905. 1971. B9419
874 Hardy, E. G. Christianity and the Roman government. 1971. B9420
875 Rousselt, P. Histoire de l'education des femmes en France. 2 v. 1971. B9421
876 Lodge, E. C. Sully, Colbert, and Turgot. 1971. B9422
877 Compayré, G. Jean Jacques Rousseau and education from nature, tr. by Jago. 1971. B9423
878 Pickering, J. A vocabulary. Also Webster, Noah. Letter to John Pickering on his vocabulary. 2 v. in 1. 1971. B9424
879 Newton, A. E. The format of the English novel. 1971. B9425
880 Hubbard, J. N. An account of Sa-go-ye-wat-ha. 1971. B9426
881 Hales, J. A discourse of the Common Weal of this realme of England, ed. by Lamond. 1971. B9427
882 Grote, G. Fragments on ethical subjects. 1971. B9428
883 Jefferson, T. The correspondence of Jefferson and DuPont de Nemours, ed. by Chinard. 1971. B9429
884 Bedier, J. Les chansons des croisade avec leur melodies publiess par Pierre Aubry. 1971. B9430
885 Letronne, A. J. Considerations generales sur l'evaluation des monnaies... 1971. B9431
886 Nevins, W. S. Witchcraft in Salem village in 1692. 1971. B9432
887 Carson, H. L. The history of the Supreme Court of the United States. 2 v. 1971. B9433
888 Latrobe, B. The journal of Latrobe. 1971. B9434
889 Talbot, A. Les theories de Boisguilbert et leur place dans l'histoire des doctrines economiques. 1971. B9435
890 Ford, P. L. Who was the mother of Franklin's son? 1971. B9436
891 ____. List of some briefs in appeal causes which relate to America... 1971. B9437
892 Guillois, A. Le salon de Madame Helvetius. 1971. B9438
894 Lelievre, C. Le travail et l'usure dans l'antiquite. 1971. B9439
895 Gaer, J. California in juvenile literature. 1971. B9440
896 Mackenzie, J. S. Lectures on humanism. 1971. B9441
897 Baynes, T. S. An essay on the new analytic of logical forms. 1971. B9442
898 Leroy, A. A. Walrus. 1971. B9443
899 Faguet, E. Drame ancien; drame moderne. 1971. B9444
900 Allen, E. Reason the only oracle of man. 1971. B9445

BURT FRANKLIN SELECTED PAPERS IN LITERATURE AND CRITICISM (Franklin)

1 Loomis, L. H. Mediaeval romance in England. 1959. B9446

- C -

CAHIERS DE LA NOUVELLE JOURNEE (Bloud)

1 Lanzac de Laborie, G. de and others. Paul Bureau. 1924. C1
2 Le témoignage d'une génération, by Manteuil and others. 1924. C2
3 Qu'est-ce que la mystique?, by Blondel and others. 1925. C3
4 La cité moderne et les transformations du droit, by Hauriou and others. 1925. C4
5 Qu'est-ce que la science?, by Manville and others. 1926. C5
6 Bureau, P. Le bon citoyen de la cité moderne. 1926. C6
7 Jeunes maîtres. C7
8 L'âme russe, by Berdiaef and others. 1927. C8
9 Où chercher le réel?, by Chevalier and others. 1927. C9
10 Vialatoux, J. and others. Un grand débat catholique et français. 1927. C10
11 Yver, C. and others. George Fonsegrive. 1928. C11
12 Chambault, P. L'oeuvre philosophique de Maurice Blondel. C12
13 France et allemagne, by Pange and others. 1928. C13
14 Fidao-Justiniani, J. E. Qu'est-ce qu'un classique? 1929. C14
15 Continu et discontinu, by Chevalier and others. 1930. C15
16 De Renan à Jacques Riviere. C16
17 Saint Augustin, by Blondel and others. 1930. C17
18 Sturzo, L. La communauté internationale et le droit de guerre. 1931. C18
19 Eugénisme et morale. C19
20 Blondel, M. Problème de la philosophie catholique. 1932. C20
21 Lafitte, J. Réflexions sur la science des machines. 1932. C21
22 Bremond, H. La querelle du pur Amour au temps de Louis XIII. 1932. C22
23 Hauriou, M. Aux sources du droit. 1933. C23
24 Archambault, P. Témoins du spirituel. 1933. C24
25 La révolution allemande. C25
26 Nédoncelle, M. La philosophie religieuse en Grande-Bretagne. 1934. C26
27 Marrou, H. I. Fondements d'une culture chrétienne. 1934. C27
28 L'oeuvre exégétique et historique du r. p. Lagrange. 1935. C28
29 Archambault, P. Pierres d'attente pour une cité meilleure. 1935. C29
30 Le belle aventure de la route. 1935. C30
31 Destins de la personne. C31
32 Sturzo, L. Essai de sociologie. 1935. C32
33 Armoudru, B. La vie posthume des Pensées. 1936. C33
34 Paliard, J. Le monde des idoles. 1936. C34
35 Lacroix, J. Itinéraire spirituel. 1937. C35
36 Wilbois, J. La nouvelle organisation du travail. 1937. C36
37 Magnin, E. Un demi-siècle de pensée catholique. 1937. C37
38 Duhamel et nous. 1938. C38
39 Feesard, G. Le méthode

de reflexion chez Maine de Biran. 1938. C39
40 Sturzo, L. Politique et morale. 1938. C40

CAHIERS DE LA NOUVELLE REVUE THEOLOGIQUE (Casterman)

1 Catholic church. Pope. Le Pape Pie XII et la guerre, ed. by Levie and Bergh. 1945. C41
2 Ranwez, P. and others. Problèmes de formation religieuse. 1946. C42
3 Charles, P. and others. Prédication et prédicateurs. 1947. C43
4 Coninck, L. de. Problèmes de l'adaptation en apostolat. 1948. C44
5 DeBauche, R. and others. Les exercices spirituels de saint Ignace. 1948. C45
6 Coppens, J. Les harmonies des deux Testaments. 1949. C46
7 ____. Le problème des réfugiés, ed. by Levie and others. 1950. C47
8 Levie, J. L'encycliqué Humani generis. 1951. C48
9 Jean, C. F. Six campagnes de fouilles à Mari, 1933-1939. 1952. C49

CAHIERS DE PHILOSOPHIE DE LA NATURE (Vrin)

1 Le transformisme. 1927. C50
2 Mélanges, par Termier et als. 1929. C51
3 Collin, R. Réflexions sur le psychisme. 1929. C52
4 André, H. and others. Vues sur la psychologie animale. 1930. C53
5 Manquat, M. Aristote naturaliste. 1932. C54
6 Oldekop, E. Le principe de hiérarchie dans la nature et ses rapports avec le problème du vitalisme et du mécanisme. 1933. C55
7 Rutkiewicz, B. L'individualisation, l'évolution et le finalisme biologique. 1933. C56
8 Thomas, M. La notion de l'instinct et ses bases scientifiques. 1936. C57

CAHIERS SCIENTIFIQUES (Gauthiers-Villars)

1 Picard, E. Leçons sur quelques types simples d'équations aux dérivées partielles. 1950. C58
2 Cartan, E. J. Leçons sur la géométrie des espaces de Riemann. 1963. C59
3 Picard, E. Leçons sur quelques équations fonctionnelles. 1950. C60
4 Janet, M. Leçons sur les systèmes d'équations aux dérivées partielles. 1929. C61
5 Picard, E. Leçons sur quelques problèmes aux limites de la théorie des équations différentielles. 1930. C62
6 Julia, G. Principes géométriques d'analyse. Pt. 1. 1930. C63
7 Volterra, V. Leçons sur la théorie mathématique de la lutte pour la vie. 1931. C64
8 Julia, G. Leçons sur la représentation conforme des aires simplement connexes. 1950. C65
9 Picard, E. Quelques applications analytiques de la théorie des courbes et surfaces algébriques. 1931. C66
10 Cartan, E. J. Leçons sur la géométrie projective complexe. 1950. C67
11 Same as no. 6. Pt. 2. 1952. C68
12 Wavre, R. Figures planétaires et géodésie. 1932. C69
13 Favard, J. Leçons sur les fonctions presque périodiques. 1933. C70
14 Julia, G. Leçons sur la représentation conforme des aires multiplement connexes. Pt. 1. 1934. C71
15 Humbert, P. Potentiels et prépontentiels. 1936. C72
16 Julia, G. Introduction mathématique aux théories quantiques. V. 1. 1955. C73

17 Cartan, E. J. Leçons sur la théorie des espaces à connexion projective. 1937. C74
18 ___. La théorie des groupes finis et continues et la géométrie différentielle traitées par la méthode du repère mobile. 1951. C75
19 Same as no. 16. V. 2. 1955. C76
20 Dubreil, P. Algèbre. V. 1. 1954. C77
21 Dubreil-Jacotin, M. L. and others. Leçons sur la théorie des treillis des structures algébriques ordonnées et des treillis géométriques. 1953. C78
22 Lelong-Ferrand, J. Représentation conformé et transformations à intégrale de Dirichlet bornée. 1955. C79
23 Lagrange, R. Produits d'inversions et métrique conforme. 1956. C80
24 Favard, J. Cours de géométrie différentielle locale. 1957. C81
25 Dixmier, J. Les algèbres d'opérateurs dans l'espace Hilbertien (algèbres de Von Neumann). 1969. C82
26 Favard, J. Cours d'analyse de l'Ecole Polytechnique. 3 v. 1960-63. C83
27 Artin, E. Algèbre géométrique. 1962. C84
28 Dieudonné, J. Elements d'analyse. V. 1. Fondements de l'analyse moderne, tr. by Huet. 1971. C85
29 Dixmier, J. Les C*-algèbres et leurs représentations. 1969. C86
30 Dixmier, J. Cours de mathématiques du premier cycle... 1967. C87
31 Same as no. 28. V. 2. 1969. C88
32 Same as no. 30. 2d ed. 1968. C89
33-34 Same as no. 28. V. 2, 3. 1970-1. C90
35-36 MacLane, S. and Birkhoff, G. Algèbre. 2 v. 1971. C91

CAHIERS THEOLOGIQUES DE L'ACTUALITE PROTESTANTE (Delachaux & Mestlé)

1 Cullmann, O. Le retour du Christ. 1944. C92
2 Barth, K. La confession de foi de l'Eglise. 1943. C93
3 Menoud, P.-H. L'Evangile de Jean. 1943. C94
4 Leenhardt, F.-J., Le baptême chrétien. 1944. C95
5-6 ___. La confession hélvetique posterieure, ed. by Courvoisier-Patry. 1944. C96
7 Espine, H. d'. Les anciens, conducteurs de l'Eglise. 1944. C97
8 Cullmann, O. Le culte dans l'Eglise primitive. 1944. C98
9 Menoud, P.-H. Le sort des trépassés. 1945. C99
10 Asmussen, H. Le ministère de l'intercession. 1945. C100
11 Masson, C. Les paraboles de Marc IV. 1945. C101
12 Leuba, J.-L. Résumé analytique de la dogmatique ecclésiastique de Karl Barth. V. 1. 1946. C102
13 Preiss, T. Le témoignage intérieur du Saint-Esprit. 1946. C103
14 De Pury, R. La Maison de Dueu. 1946. C104
15-16 Ellul, J. Le fondement théologique du droit. 1946. C105
17 Pidoux, G. Le Dieu qui vient, esperance d'Israël. 1947. C106
18 Roux, H. L'argent dans la communauté de l'Eglise. 1947. C107
19-20 Cullmann, O. Le baptême des enfants et la doctrine biblique du baptême. 1948. C108
21 Bonnard, P. Jesus-Christ édifiant son Eglise. 1948. C109
22 Menoud, P.-H. L'Eglise et les ministères. 1949. C110
23-24 Prenter, R. Le Saint-Esprit et le renouveau de l'Eglise. 1949. C111
25 Cullmann, O. Noël dans

l'Eglise ancienne. 1949. C112
26 Barth, K. La prière d'après les catéchismes de la Réformation. 1949. C113
27 Mauris, E. Le travail de l'homme et son oeuvre. 1950. C114
28 Mehl-Kohnlein, H. L'homme selon l'apôtre Paul. 1950. C115
29 Allmen, J. J. von. Maris et femmes d'après saint Paul. 1951. C116
30 Crespy, G. La guérison par lafoi. 1952. C117
31 Menoud, P. H. La vie de l'Eglise naissante. 1952. C118
32 Pidoux, G. L'homme dans l'ancien testament. 1953. C119
33 Cullman, O. La tradition. 1953. C120
34 Ortigues, E. Le temps de la parole. 1954. C121
35 Torrance, T. F. Les Réformateurs et la fin des temps. 1954. C122
36 Mehl, R. La rencontre d'autrui. 1954. C123
37 Leenhardt, F. J. Ceci est mon corps. 1955. C124
38 Barth, K. Hegel. 1955. C125
39 Jeremias, J. Jésus et les paiens. 1956. C126
40 Mehl, R. Du Catholicisme Romain. 1958. C127
41 Lods, M. Confesseurs et martyrs. 1958. C128
42 Martin-Achard, R. Israel et les nations. 1958. C129
43 Stamm, J. J. Le décalogue. 1959. C130
44 Vischer, L. La confirmation au cours des siècles. 1959. C131
45 Vuillemier-Bessard, R. La tradition cultuelle d'Israel dans la prophétie d'Amos et d'Osée. 1960. C132
46 Michaud, H. Jésus selon le Coran. 1960. C133
47 Benoit, A. L'actualite des Pères de l'Eglise. 1961. C134
48 Grimm, R. Amour et sexualité. 1962. C135
49 Amsler, S. David, roi et Messie. 1963. C136
50 Widmer, G. Gloire au père, au fils, au Saint-Esprit. 1963. C137
51 Stauffer, R. L'humanité de Calvin. 1964. C138
52 Prigent, P. Apocalypse et liturgie. 1964. C139
53 Courvoisier, J. Zwingli. 1965. C140
54 Crespy, G. De la science à la théologie. 1966. C141
55 Allmen, J. J. van. Essai sur le repar du Seigneur. 1966. C142
56 Mehl, R. Pour une ethique sociale chrétienne. 1967. C143
57 Robert, P. de. Le Berger d'Israël. 1968. C144
58 Barth, K. Entretiens à Rome après le Concile, tr. by von Allmen and Jegge. 1968. C145
59 Spindler, M. Pour une théologie de l'espace. 1969. C146
60 Martin-Achard, R. Approche des psaumes. 1969. C147
61 Mehl, R. Ethique catholique et ethique. 1970. C148
62 Cullmann, O. Vrai et faux oecuménisme. 1972. C149
63 Leenhardt, F. J. Parole visible. 1971. C150

Hors series:

1 Deluz, G. and others. La Sainte-Cène. 1945. C151
2 Hommage et reconnaissance ...du soixantième anniversaire de Karl Barth, by Bonnard and others. 1946. C152
3 Allmen, J. J. von. L'Eglise et ses fonctions d'après J. F. Ostervald. 1947. C153
4 Florovsky, G. and others. La sainte Eglise universelle. 1948. C154

CALENDARS OF AMERICAN LITERARY MANUSCRIPTS (Ohio State Univ. Pr.)

1 Lohf, K. A., comp. The literary manuscripts of Hart Crane, comp. by Lohf. 1967. C155
2 Gottesman, R. and Silet, C., comp. The literary manuscripts of Upton Sinclair.

1972. C156
3 Howarth, W. L. The literary manuscripts of Henry David Thoreau. 1974. C157

CALIFORNIA NATURAL HISTORY GUIDE (Univ. of Cali. Pr.)

1 Smith, A. C. Introduction to the natural history of San Francisco Bay Region. 1959. C158
2 Berry, W. D. and E. Mammals of the San Francisco Bay Region. 1959. C159
3 Stebbins, R. C. Reptiles and amphibians of the San Francisco Bay Region. 1959. C160
4 Metcalf, W. Native trees of the San Francisco Bay Region. 1959. C161
5 Bowen, O. E. Rocks and minerals of the San Francisco Bay Region. 1962. C162
6 Gilliam, H. Weather of the San Francisco Bay Region. 1962. C163
7 Howard, A. D. Evolution of the landscape of the San Francisco Bay Region. 1962. C164
8 Orr, R. T. and D. B. Mushrooms and other common fungi of the San Francisco Bay Region. 1968. C165
9 Hedgpeth, J. W. Introduction to seashore life of the San Francisco Bay Region and the coast of northern California. 1962. C166
10 Balls, E. K. Early uses of California plants. 1962. C167
11 Sharsmith, H. K. Spring wildflowers of the San Francisco Bay Region. 1965. C168
12 Wilden, J. W. Butterflies of the San Francisco Bay Region. 1965. C169
13 Jaeger, E. C. and Smith, A. C. Introduction to the natural history of Southern California. 1966. C170
14 Peterson, V. P. Native trees of Southern California. 1966. C171
15 Raven, P. H. Native shrubs of Southern California. 1966. C172
16 Grillos, S. J. Ferns and fern allies of California. 1966. C173
17 Bailey, H. P. The climate of Southern California. 1966. C174
18 Dawson, E. Y. Cacti of California. 1966. C175
19 ____. Seashore plants of Southern California. 1966. C176
20 ____. Seashore plants of Northern California. 1966. C177
21 Booth, E. S. Mammals of Southern California. 1968. C178
22 Orr, R. T. and D. B. Mushrooms and other fungi of Southern California. 1968. C179
23 Downs, T. Fossil vertebrates of Southern California. 1968. C180
24 Ferris, R. J. Native shrubs of the Southern Basin region. 1968. C181
25 Fitch, J. E. and Lavenberg, R. J. Deep-water telestean fishes of California. 1968. C182
26 Hinton, S. Seashore life of Southern California. 1969. C183
27 Metcalf, W. Introduced trees of central California. 1968. C184
28 Fitch, J. E. and Lavenberg, R. J. Marine food and game fishes of California. 1971. C185
29 Orr, R. T. Marine mammals of California. 1972. C186
30 Gross, P. P. and Railton, E. P. Teaching science in an outdoor environment. 1972. C187
31 Stebbins, R. C. Reptiles and amphibians of California. 1972. C188
32 Niehaus, T. F. Sierra wildflowers. 1974. C189
33 Crampton, B. Grasses in California. 1974. C190
34 Thomas, J. H. and Parnell, D. R. Native shrubs of the Sierra Nevada. 1974. C191

35 Ornduff, R. Introduction to California plant life. 1974. C192
36 Peterson, V. P. Native trees of the Sierra Nevada. 1974. C193
37 Hill, M. Geologies of the Sierra Nevada. 1974. C194

CALIFORNIA STUDIES IN THE HISTORY OF ART. (Univ. of California Pr.)

1 Sullivan, M. The birth of landscape painting in China. 1962. C195
2 Boggs, J. S. Portraits by Degas. 1962. C196
3 Leonardo da Vinci on painting, ed. and tr. by Pedretti. 1964. C197
4 Randall, L. M. C. Images in the margins of Gothic manuscripts. 1966. C198
5 Rosenfeld, J. M. The dynastic art of the Kushans. 1966. C199
6 Delaisse, L. M. J. A century of Dutch manuscript illumination. 1968. C200
7 Bloch, E. M. George Caleb Bingham. 2 v. 1967. C201
8 Roethlisberger, M. Claude Lorrain: the drawings. 2 v. 1969. C202
9 Schulz, J. Venetian painted ceilings of the Renaissance. 1968. C203
10 de Leiris, A. The drawings of Edouard Manet. 1968. C204
11 Chipp, H. B., comp. and others. Theories of modern art. 1968. C205
12 Frankenstein, A. After the hunt. 1969. C206
13 Blum, S. N. Early Netherlandish triptychs. 1969. C207
14 Mellinkoff, R. The horned Moses in medieval art and thought. 1970. C208
15 Cohen, K. G. Metamorphosis of a death symbol. 1974. C209
16 McKillop, S. R. Franciabigio. 1974. C210
17 Branner, R. Manuscript painting in Paris during the reign of St. Louis. 1974. C211

CALIFORNIA. UNIVERSITY. CENTER FOR CHINESE STUDIES. RESEARCH SERIES.

1 Scalapino, R. A. and Yu, G. T. The Chinese anarchist movement. 1961. C212
2 Hsia, T. A. Enigma of the five martyrs... 1962. C213
3 Schurmann, F. Ideology and organization in Communist China. 1966. C214

CALIFORNIA. UNIVERSITY. CENTER FOR JAPANESE AND KOREAN STUDIES. PUBLICATIONS.

Araki, J. T. The ballad-dream of medieval Japan. 1964. C215
Cho, S. S. Korea in world politics, 1940-1950. 1967. C216
Cooper, M., ed. They came to Japan. 1965. C217
Craig, A. M. and Shively, D. H., eds. Personality in Japanese history. 1970. C218
DeVos, G. and Wagatsuma, H. Japan's invisible race. 1966. C219
Dore, R. P. Education in Tokugawa, Japan. 1965. C220
Fukui, H. Party in power. 1970. C221
Han, S. The failure of democracy in South Korea. 1974. C222
Harootunian, H. D. Toward restoration. 1970. C223
Hellmann, D. C. Japanese domestic politics and foreign policy. 1969. C224
Iwata, M. Okubo Toshimichi. 1964. C225
Japanese poetic diaries, tr. by Miner. 1969. C226
Kim, C. I. E. and H. K. Korea and the politics of imperialism. 1968. C227
Lee, C. The politics of Korean nationalism. 1963. C228
Miller, F. O. Minobe Tatsukichi. 1965. C229
Miner, E. R. Japanese poetic diaries. 1969. C230
Mitchell, R. H. The Korean

minority in Japan. 1967. C231
Nakane, C. Japanese society. 1970. C232
Ogata, S. N. Defiance in Manchuria. 1964. C233
Rohlen, T. P. For harmony and strength. 1974. C234
Rutt, R. The Bamboo Grove. 1971. C235
Scalapino, R. A. The Japanese Communist movement, 1920-1966, tr. by Ozaki. 1967. C236
Scalapino, R. A. and Lee, C. S. Communism in China. 2 v. 1972. C237
Scheiner, I. Christian converts & social protest in Meiji Japan. C238
Smethurst, R. J. A social bases for prewar Japanese militarism. 1974. C239
Tokyo Keizai Kenkyu Senta. Postwar economic growth in Japan. 1966. C240
Yamamura, K. Economic policy in postwar Japan. 1967. C241

CALIFORNIA. UNIVERSITY. INSTITUTE OF BUSINESS AND ECONOMIC RESEARCH. PUBLICATIONS.

Akademiia nauk USSR. A history of Russian economic thought, tr. by Dmytryshyn and Pierce. 1964. C242
Alhadeff, D. A. Competition and controls in banking. 1968. C243
____. Monopoly and competition in banking. 1954. C244
Bain, J. S. The economics of the Pacific Coast petroleum industry. 3 pts. 1944-47. C245
Bain, J. S. and Moore, F. T. Literature and... price policy and related topics, 1933-1947. 1947. C246
Baldwin, R. E. Economic development and export growth. 1966. C247
Boutell, W. S. Auditing with the computer. 1965. C248
Brady, R. A. Crisis in Britain. 1950. C249
____. Organization, automation, and society. 1961. C250
Bucklin, L. P. A theory of distribution channel structure. 1966. C251
Bucklin, L. P. and Carman, J. M. The design of consumer research panels. 1967. C252
Carman, J. M. The application of social class in market segmentation. 1965. C253
____ and others. Studies in the demand for consumer household equipment. 1965. C254
Cassady, R. and Jones, W. L. Changing competitive structure in the wholesale grocery trade. 1949. C255
____ and ____. The nature of competition in gasoline distribution at the retail level. 1951. C256
Chase, S. B. Asset prices in economic analysis. 1963. C257
Cho, Y. S. Disguised unemployment in underdeveloped areas. 1963. C258
Collins, N. R. and Preston, L. E. Concentration and price-cost margins in manufacturing industries. 1968. C259
Conant, M. Antitrust in the motion picture industry. 1960. C260
____. Railroad mergers and abandonments. 1964. C261
Conard, J. W. An introduction to the theory of interest. 1959. C262
Crum, W. L. The age structure of the corporate system. 1953. C263
Daggett, S. and Carter, J. P. The structure of transcontinental railroad rates. 1947. C264
Dorfman, R. Application of linear programming to the theory of the firm. 1951. C265
Doyle, L. A. Inter-economy comparisons. 1965. C266
Fellner, W. J. Monetary policies and full employment. 1946. C267
____. A treatise on war inflation. 1942. C268
Fitch, L. C. Taxing municipal bond income. 1950. C269
Gerschenkron, A. Bread and

democracy in Germany. 1944. C270

Gorter, W. and Hildebrand, G. H. The Pacific coast maritime shipping industry. 2 v. 1952-54. C271

Gulick, C. A. and others. History and theories of working class movements. 1955. C272

Hartman, P. T. Collective bargaining & productivity. 1969. C273

Hensley, R. J. Competition, regulation and the public interest in nonlife insurance. 1962. C274

Hirschman, A. O. National power and the structure of foreign trade. 1945. C275

Kidner, F. L. California business cycles. 1946. C276

Kuhn, T. E. Public enterprise economics and transport problems. 1962. C277

LaForce, J. C. The developments in the Spanish textile industry, 1750-1800. 1965. C278

Letiche, J. M., ed. A history of Russian economic thought, tr. by Dmytryshyn and Pierce. 1964. C279

Li, C. The economic development of Communist China. 1959. C280

Luck, M. G. Wartime and postwar earnings. 1948. C281

McKinley, C. Uncle Sam in the Pacific Northwest. 1952. C282

Maisel, S. J. Housebuilding in transition. 1953. C283

Mead, W. J. Competition and oligopsony in the Douglas fir timber industry. 1966. C284

Minsky, H. P., ed. California banking in a growing economy, 1946-1975. 1965. C285

Mosk, S. A. Land tenure problems in the Santa Fe railroad grant area. 1944. C286

Myers, J. G. Consumer image and attitude. 1968. C287

Narver, J. C. Conglomerate mergers and market competition. 1967. C288

Nelson, P. E. and Preston, L. E. Price merchandising in food retailing. 1966. C289

Powell, J. R. The Mexican petroleum industry. 1956. C290

Preston, L. E. and Collins, N. R. Studies in a simulated market. 1966. C291

Reck, D. Government purchasing and competition. 1954. C292

Revzan, D. A. A comprehensive marketing bibliography. 2 pts. 1951. C293

____. The marketing significance of geographical variation in wholesale/retail sales ratios. 1965. C294

____. Perspectives for research in marketing. 1965. C295

Rolph, E. R. The theory of fiscal economics. 1956. C296

Royer lectures: University of California, by Larsson and others. 1967. C297

Scoville, W. C. The persecution of Hugenots and French economic development, 1680-1720. 1960. C298

Staubus, G. J. A theory of accounting to investors. 1961. C299

Stekler, H. O. The structure and performance of the aerospace industry. 1965. C300

Uhr, C. G. Economic doctrines of Knut Wicksell. 1962. C301

Vance, L. L. Scientific method for auditing. 1951. C302

Votaw, D. The six-legged dog. 1964. C303

Walter, J. E. The role of regional security exchanges. 1957. C304

Wendt, P. F. Housing policy. 1962. C305

Weston, J. F. The role of mergers in the growth of large firms. 1953. C306

CALIFORNIA. UNIVERSITY. INSTITUTE OF EAST ASIATIC STUDIES. SOUTH ASIA STUDIES. MODERN INDIA PROJECT. BIBLIOGRAPHICAL STUDY.

1 Wilson, P. A preliminary checklist of the writings of M. N. Ray. 1955. C306a

1 rev. ____. A checklist of the writings of M. N. Ray. 1957. C307
2 ____. Government and politics of India and Pakistan, 1885-1955. 1956. C308

CALIFORNIA. UNIVERSITY. INSTITUTE OF EAST ASIATIC STUDIES. SOUTH ASIA STUDIES. MODERN INDIA PROJECT. MONOGRAPHS.

1 Moore, F. J. and Freydig, C. A. Land tenure legislation in Uttar Pradesh. 1955. C309

CALIFORNIA. UNIVERSITY. INSTITUTE OF INDUSTRIAL RELATIONS. PUBLICATIONS (Univ. of Calif. Pr. unless otherwise noted)

Alhadeff, D. A. Competition and controls in banking. 1968. C310
Belloc, N. Wages in California. 1948. C311
Bendix, R. Work and authority in industry. Wiley. 1958. C312
Berger, B. M. Working-class suburb. 1960. C313
Bernstein, I. Arbitration of wages. 1954. C314
____. The New Deal collective bargaining policy. 1950. C315
Cheit, E. F., ed. The business establishment. Wiley. 1964. C316
Cohen, W. J. Retirement policies under social security. 1957. C317
Foundation for Research on Human Behavior. Modern organization theory, ed. by Haire. Wiley. 1959. C318
Galenson, W., ed. Labor and economic development. Wiley. 1959. C319
____, ed. Labor in developing economics. 1962. C320
____. Trade union democracy in Western Europe. 1961. C321
Garbarino, J. W. Health plans and collective bargaining. 1960. C322
Gordon, M. S. Employment expansion and population growth. 1954. C323
Gorter, W. and Hildebrand, G. H. The Pacific Coast maritime shipping industry, 1930-1948. 2 v. 1952-54. C324
Gulick, C. A. and others, comps. History and theory of working-class movements. 1955. C325
Haire, M., ed. Modern organization theory. Wiley. 1959. C326
Knight, R. E. L. Industrial relations in the San Francisco Bay area, 1900-1918. 1960. C327
Knowles, W. H. Trade union development and industrial relations in the British West Indies. 1959. C328
Kornhauser, W. Scientists in industry, conflict and accomodation. 1962. C329
Leibenstein, H. Economic backwardness and economic growth. Wiley. 1956. C330
Lipset, S. M. and Bendix, R. Social mobility in industrial society. 1959. C331
McEntire, D. The labor force in California. 1952. C332
Perry, L. B. and R. S. A history of the Los Angeles labor movement, 1911-1941. 1963. C333
Phelps, O. W. Discipline and discharge in the unionized firm. 1959. C334
Pierson, F. C. Community wage patterns. 1953. C335
Pinner, F. A. and others. Old age and political behavior. 1959. C336
Reichard, S. K. and others. Aging and personality. 1962. C337
Ross, A. M. Employment policy and labor market. 1965. C338
____. Trade union wage policy. 1948. C339
Ross, A. M. and Hartman, P. T. Changing patterns of industrial conflict. 1960. C340
Steiner, P. O. and Dorfman, R.

The economic status of the aged. 1957. C341
Stimson, G. Rise of the labor movement in Los Angeles. 1955. C342
Vollmer, H. M. Employee rights and the employment relationship. 1960. C343
Warren, E. L. and Bernstein, I. Collective bargaining. 1949. C344
Weintraub, H. Andrew Furuseth. 1959. C345

CALIFORNIA. UNIVERSITY. PUBLICATIONS IN INTERNATIONAL RELATIONS

1:1 Dennis, A. L. P. The Anglo-Japanese alliance. 1923. C346
1:2 Russell, F. M. The international government of the Saar. 1926. C347
1:3 Bellquist, E. C. Some aspects of the recent policy of Sweden. 1929. C348
2 Hobson, A. The International institute of agriculture. 1931. C349
3:1 Kingman, H. L. Effects of Chinese nationalism upon Manchurian railway developments. 1925-1931. C350
3:2 Williams, E. T. Tibet and her neighbors. 1937. C351
3:3 Gyorgy, A. Geopolitics. 1944. C352
4 Cattell, D. T. Communism and the Spanish Civil War. 1955. C353
5 ____. Soviet diplomacy and the Spanish Civil War. 1957. C354

CALIFORNIA. UNIVERSITY. UNIVERSITY AT LOS ANGELES CENTER FOR MEDIEVAL AND RENAISSANCE STUDIES. CONTRIBUTIONS.

1 Matthews, W., ed. Medieval secular literature. 1965. C355
2 Golino, C. L., ed. Galileo reappraised. 1966. C356
3 White, L. T., ed. The transformation of the Roman world. 1966. C357
4 Berger, R., ed. Scientific methods in medieval archaeology. 1970. C358
5 Violence and civil disorder in Italian cities, 1200-1500, ed. by Martines. 1972. C359

CALIFORNIA. UNIVERSITY. UNIVERSITY AT LOS ANGELES. CENTER FOR MEDIEVAL AND RENAISSANCE STUDIES. PUBLICATIONS.

1 Russell, J. B. Dissent and reform in the early Middle Ages. 1965. C360
2 Leonardo's legacy, ed. by O'Malley. 1969. C361
3 Rouse, R. H. and others. Serial bibliographies for medieval studies. 1969. C362
4 Vryonis, S. The decline of Medieval Hellenism in Asia Minor through the fifteenth century. 1971. C363
5 Chodorow, S. Christian political theory & church politics in the mid-twelfth century. 1972. C364
6 Duggan, J. J. The Song of Roland. 1973. C365

CALIFORNIA. UNIVERSITY. UNIVERSITY AT LOS ANGELES. LATIN AMERICAN CENTER. LATIN AMERICAN STUDIES.

1 McCorkle, T. Fajardo's people. 1965. C366
2 Beals, R. L. Community in transition. 1966. C367
3 Aubey, R. T. Nacional Financiera and Mexican industry. 1966. C368
4 Schwerin, K. H. Oil and steel. 1966. C369
5 Karst, K. L. Latin American legal institutions. 1966. C370
6 Violich, F. Community development and the urban planning process in Latin America. 1967. C371
7 Indian Mexico, ed. by Bell. 1967. C372
8 Winnie, W. W. Latin American development. 1967. C373
9 Grebe, M. E. The Chilean

verso. 1967. C374
10 Watson, L. C. The effect of urbanization on socialization practices and personality in Guajiro society. 1968. C375
11 Meighan, C. W. and Foote, L. J. Excavations at Tizapan, El Alto, Jalisco. 1968. C376
12 Wilbert, J., comp. Textos folklóricos de los waraos. 1969. C377
13 Wilkie, J. W. The Bolivian revolution and U.S. aid since 1952. 1969. C378
14 The social anthropology of Latin America, ed. by Goldschmidt and Hoijer. 1970. C379
15 Wilbert, J., comp. Folk literature of the Warao Indians. 1970. C380
16 Congreso Internacional de Literatura Iberoamericana. Homenaje á Ruben Darío. 1970. C381
17 Violich, F. and Astica, J. B. Desarrollo de la comunidad y el proceso de planificación urbana en la América Latina. 1971. C382
18 LaBelle, T. J., comp. Education and development. 1971. C383
19 Sexton, J. D. Education and innovation in a Guatemalan community. 1972. C384
20 Karst, K. L. and others. The evolution of law in the barrios of Carcacas. 1973. C385
21 Woods, C. M. and Graves, T. D. The process of medical change in a highland Guatemalan town. 1973. C386
22 Wilkie, J. W. Elitelore. 1973. C387
23 LaBelle, J. T. and Van Orman, J. R. The new professional in Venezuelan secondary education. 1973. C388
24 Wilbert, J. Yupa folktales. 1974. C389

CALIFORNIA. UNIVERSITY. UNIVERSITY OF CALIFORNIA BIBLIOGRAPHIC GUIDES.

1 Blanchard, J. R. and Ostvold, H. Literature of agricultural research. 1958. C390
Basart, A. P. Serial music. 1961. C391
Coman, E. T. Sources of business information. 1964. C392
Eschelbach, C. J. and Shober, J. L. Aldous Huxley. 1961. C393

CALIFORNIA. UNIVERSITY. UNIVERSITY OF CALIFORNIA PUBLICATIONS. ENGLISH STUDIES.

1 California. University. Department of English. Essays, critical and historical, dedicated to Lily B. Campbell. 1950. C394
2 Mueller, W. B. The anatomy of Robert Burton's England. 1952. C395
3 Stafford, J. The literary criticism of "Young America." 1952. C396
4 Jordan, J. E. Thomas De Quincey, literary critic. 1952. C397
5 Small, H. A. The field of his fame. 1953. C398
6 Lowers, J. K. Mirror for rebels. 1953. C399
7 Hoover, B. B. Samuel Johnson's parliamentary reporting. 1953. C400
8 Shumaker, W. English autobiography. 1954. C401
9 Hafley, J. R. The glass roof; Virginia Woolf as novelist. 1954. C402
10 California. University. Dept. of English. Five Gayley lectures, 1947-1954, by Hart and others. 1954. C403
11 The Image of the work, by Lehman, and others. 1955. C404
12 Meyer, G. D. The scientific lady in England. 1955. C405
13 Stewart, L. D. John Scott of Amwell. 1956. C406
14 Branam, C. G. Eighteenth century adaptations of Shakespearean tragedy. 1956. C407

15 Proctor, M. R. The English university novel. 1957. C408
16 Levy, L. B. Versions of melodrama. 1957. C409
17 Raleigh, J. H. Matthew Arnold and American culture. 1957. C410
18 Wireker, N. Speculum stultorum; ed. by Mozley and Raymo. 1960. C411
19 Paterson, J. The making of The return of the native. 1960. C412
20 Kurth, B. O. Milton and Christian heroism. 1959. C413
21 Spacks, P. A. The varied god. 1959. C414
22 Pizer, D. Hamlin Garland's early work and career. 1960. C415
23 Clemens, S. L. The pattern for Mark Twain's Roughing it, ed. by Rogers. 1961. C416
24 Novak, M. E. Economics and the future of Daniel DeFoe. 1962. C417
25 Heywood, J. A dialogue of proverbs, ed. by Habenicht. 1963. C418
26 Vergilius Maro, P. The Aeneid of Henry Howard, Earl of Surrey, ed. by Ridley. 1963. C419
27 Jones, C. W. The Saint Nicholas liturgy and its literary relationships. 1963. C420
28 Howard, L. The mind of Jonathan Edwards. 1963. C421
29 Patrides, C. A. The phoenix and the ladder. 1964. C422
30 Ridley, F. M. The prioress and the critics. 1965. C423
31 Zirker, M. R. Fielding's social pamphlets. 1966. C424
32 McKenzie, G. The literary character of Walter Pater. 1967. C425
33 Rolle, R. The Contra amatores mundi of Richard Rolle of Hampole, ed. by Theiner. 1968. C426
34 Veeder, W. R. W. B. Yates. 1968. C427
35 Alderson, W. L. and Henderson, A. C. Chaucer and Augustan scholarship. 1970. C428
36 Pomeroy, E. W. The Elizabethean miscellany. 1973. C429

CALIFORNIA. UNIVERSITY. UNIVERSITY OF CALIFORNIA PUBLICATIONS. FOLKLORE STUDIES.

1 Speroni, C. The Italian Wellerism to the end of the seventeenth century. 1953. C430
2 Coloquio de pastores del hijo pródigo. The shepherd's play of the prodigal son, ed. by Barker. 1953. C431
3 Taylor, A. Proverbial comparisons and similes from California. 1954. C432
4 Los pastores. Coloquios de pastores from Jalisco, Mexico, ed. by Robe. 1954. C433
5 Eberhard, W. Minstrel tales from Southeastern Turkey. 1955. C434
6 Hull, V. E. A collection of Irish riddles. 1955. C435
7 Claretus de Solencia. Enigmata, ed. by Peachy. 1957. C436
8 Hansen, T. L. The types of the folktale in Cuba, Puerto Rico, the Dominican Republic, and Spanish South America. 1957. C437
9 Browne, R. B. Popular beliefs and practices from Alabama. 1958. C438
10 Alte newe Zeitung, ed. by Sobel. 1958. C439
11 Woods, B. A. The Devil in dog form. 1959. C440
12 Sutton-Smith, B. The games of New Zealand children. 1959. C441
13 Lessa, W. A. Tales with Ulithi Atoll. 1961. C442
14 Robe, S. L., ed. Hispanic riddles from Panama. 1963. C443
15 Chianis, S., ed. and tr. Folk songs of Manitineia, Greece. 1965. C444
16 Arora, S. L. Proverbial comparisons in Ricardo Palma's Tradiciones

peruanas. 1966. C445
17 Crowley, D. J., ed. I could talk old story good. 1966. C446
18 Fonterose, J. E. The ritual theory of myth. 1966. C447
19 Ward, D. The Divine twins. 1968. C448
20 Robe, S. L., comp. Mexican tales and legends from Los Altos. 1970. C449
21 Long, E. "The maid" and "The hangman." 1971. C450
22 Basgoz, I. and Tietze, A. A corpus of Turkish riddles. 1972. C451
23 Robe, S. L., comp. Mexican tales and legends from Veracruz. 1971. C452
24 ____. Amapa storytellers. 1972. C453
25 Buss, R. J. The Klabautermann of the Northern Seas. 1973. C454
26 Robe, S. L. Index to Mexican folktales. 1974. C455
27 Schwartz, S. P. Poetry and law. 1974. C456
28 Moore, W. B. Molokan and tradition. 1974. C457

CALIFORNIA. UNIVERSITY. UNIVERSITY OF CALIFORNIA PUBLICATIONS IN EAST ASIACTIC PHILOLOGY.

1:1 Boodberg, P. A. UCI: an interim system of transcription for Chinese. 1947. C458
1:2 ____. UCJ: an orthographic system of notation and transcription for Sino-Japanese. 1947. C459
2 Serruys, P. L. M. The Chinese dialects of Han time according to Fang yen. 1959. C460

CALIFORNIA. UNIVERSITY. UNIVERSITY OF CALIFORNIA PUBLICATIONS IN HISTORY.

1:1 McCormac, E. I. Colonial opposition to imperial authority during the French and Indian War. 1911. C461
1:2 Smith, D. E. The viceroy of New Spain. 1913. C462
1:3 Hughes, A. E. The beginning of Spanish settlement in the El Paso district. 1914. C463
2 Marshall, T. M. A history of the western boundary of the Louisiana Purchase, 1819-1891. 1914. C464
3 Bolton, H. E. Texas in the middle eighteenth century. 1915. C465
4:1 Myres, J. L. The influence of anthropology on the course of political science. 1916. C466
4:2 Van Nostrand, J. J. The reorganization of Spain by Augustus. 1916. C467
4:3 Teggart, F. J. Prolegomena to history. 1916. C468
4:4 Putnam, R. California. 1917. C469
5 Priestley, H. I. José de Gálvez. 1916. C470
6 Gittinger, R. The formation of the state of Oklahoma. (1803-1906). 1917. C471
7 Davidson, G. C. The North West company. 1918. C472
8 Chapman, C. E. Catalogue of materials in the Archivo General de Indias for the history of the Pacific coast and the American Southwest. 1919. C473
9 Cunningham, C. H. The audiencia in the Spanish colonies as illustrated by the audencia of Manila, (1583-1800). 1919. C474
10 Brown, E. S. The constitutional history of the Louisiana purchase, 1803-1812. 1920. C475
11 Albright, G. L. Official explorations for Pacific railroads. 1921. C476
12 Williams, M. F. History of the San Francisco Committee of Vigilance of 1851. 1921. C477
13 Binkley, W. C. The expansionist movement in Texas, 1836-1850. 1925. C478
14:1 Van Nostrand, J. J. The imperial domains of Africa Proconsularis. 1925. C479

14:2 Morris, W. A. The early English county court. 1926. C480
14:3 Guttridge, G. H. David Hartley, M. P. 1926. C481
15 Fisher, L. E. Viceregal administration in the Spanish American colonies. 1926. C482
16 Ellison, J. California and the nation, 1850-1869. 1927. C483
17:1 Simpson, L. B. The struggle for Provence, 1593-1596. 1929. C484
17:2 Manley, I. J. Effects of the Germanic invasions of Gaul, 234-284 A. D. 1934. C485
17:3 Ramsey, J. F. Anglo-French relations, 1763-1770. 1939. C486
17:4 Reich, A. M., Sister. The parliamentary abbots to 1470. 1941. C487
18 Leonard, I. A. Don Carlos de Siziienza y Góngora. 1929. C488
19 Simpson, L. B. The encomienda in New Spain. 1929. C489
20 Puryear, V. J. England, Russia and the Straits question. 1844-1856. 1931. C490
21 Wyllys, R. K. The French in Sonora (1850-1854). 1932. C491
22:1 Champion, R. The American correspondence of a Bristol merchant 1766-1776. Letters of Richard Champion, ed. by Guttridge. 1934. C492
23 Thompson, J. W. The dissolution of the Carolingian fisc in the ninth century. 1935. C493
24 Brooks, P. C. Diplomacy and the borderlands. 1939. C494
25 Willis, E. F. Prince Lichnowsky, ambassador of peace. 1942. C495
26 Ogden, A. The California sea otter trade, 1784-1848. 1941. C496
27 Puryear, V. J. France and the Levant from the Burbon restoration to the peace of Kutiah. 1941. C497
28 Guttridge, G. H. English whiggism and the American revolution. 1942. C498
29 Kemble, J. H. The Panama route, 1848-1869. 1943. C499
30 Lantzeff, G. V. Siberia in the seventeenth century. 1943. C500
31 Fisher, R. H. The Russian fur trade, 1550-1700. 1943. C501
32 Mowat, C. L. East Florida as a British province, 1763-1784. 1943. C502
33 Kantorowicz, E. Laudes regiae. 1958. C503
34 Howard, C. N. The British development of West Florida, 1763-1769. 1947. C504
35 Johnston, G. Carolina chronicle, ed. by Klingberg. 1946. C505
36 Clinard, O. J. Japan's influence on American naval power, 1897-1917. 1947. C506
37 Klingberg, F. J., ed. Codrington chronicle. 1949. C507
38 Harvey, R. H. Robert Owen, ed. by Caughey. 1949. C508
39 Brown, T. S. Onesicritus. 1949. C509
40 Murdoch, R. K. The Georgia-Florida frontier, 1793-1796. 1951. C510
41 Galbraith, J. S. The establishment of Canadian diplomatic status at Washington. 1951. C511
42 O'Brien, C. B. Russia under two tsars, 1682-1689. 1952. C512
43 Randall, H. S. The correspondence between Henry Stephens Randall and Hugh Blair Grigsby, 1856-1861, ed. by F. J. and F. W. Klingberg. 1952. C513
44 Guttridge, G. H. The early career of Lord Rockingham, 1730-1765. 1952. C514
45 Shepard, F. W. Price control and the Reign of Terror: France, 1793-1795. 1953. C515
46 Conroy, H. The Japanese frontier in Hawaii, 1868-1898. 1953. C516

47 Lieuwen, E. Petroleum in Venezuela. 1954. C517
48 Greenwalt, E. A. The Point Loma community in California, 1897-1942. 1955. C518
49 Lossky, A. Louis XIV, William III, and the Baltic crisis of 1683. 1954. C519
50 Klingberg, F. W. The Southern Claims Commission. 1955. C520
51 Griffiths, G. William of Hornes, Lord of Héze and the revolution of the Netherlands, 1576-1580. 1954. C521
52 Phelan, J. L. The millennial kingdom of the Franciscans of the New World. 1956. C522
53 LeJau, F. The Carolina chronicle of Dr. Francis LeJau, ed. by Klingberg. 1956. C523
54 Fleming, H. A. Canada's Archtic outlet. 1957. C524
55 Brown, T. S. Timaeus of Tauromenium. 1958. C525
56 Wilson, R. A. Genesis of the Meiji government in Japan, 1868-1871. 1957. C526
57 Ostrander, G. M. The Prohibition movement in California, 1848-1933. 1957. C527
58 Brentano, R. York metropolitan jurisdiction and papal judges delegate, 1279-1296. 1959. C528
59 Smith, D. M. Robert Lansing and American neutrality, 1914-1917. 1958. C529
60 Weber, E. J. The nationalist revival in France, 1905-1914. 1959. C530
61 Hitchcock, W: R. The background of the knights' revolt. 1958. C531
62 Bennett, J. H. Bondsmen and bishops. 1958. C532
63 Van Aken, M. J. Pan-Hispanism. 1959. C533
64 Saloutos, T. Farmer movements in the South, 1865-1933. 1960. C534
65 Addington, H. U. Youthful America. 1960. C535
66 Asher, E. L. The resistance to the maritime classes. 1960. C536
67 Leonard, C. M. Lyon transformed. 1961. C537
68 Africa, T. W. Phylarchus and the Spartan revolution. 1961. C538
69 Burr, R. N. The stillborn Panama congress. 1962. C539
70 Richardson, E. R. The politics of conservation. 1962. C540
71 Daniels, R. The politics of prejudice. 1962. C541
72 Gregory, R. G. Sidney Webb and East Africa. 1962. C542
73 Day, J. and Chambers, M. Aristotle's history of Athenian democracy. 1962. C543
74 O'Brien, C. B. Muscovy and the Ukraine. 1963. C544
75 Wacholder, B. Z. Nicolaus of Damascus. 1962. C545
76 Swain, D. C. Federal conservation policy, 1921-1933. 1963. C546
77 Burr, R. N. By reason or force. 1965. C547
78 Jacobson, D. L. John Dickinson and the revolution in Pennsylvania, 1764-1776. 1965. C548
79 Sonnino, P. Louis XIV's view of the papacy. 1966. C549
80 Machado, M. A. An industry in crisis. 1968. C550
81 Perkins, V. L. Crisis in agriculture. 1969. C551
82 Spyridakis, S. Ptolemaic Itanos and Hellenistic Crete. 1970. C552
83 DeLaix, R. A. Probouleusis at Athens. 1973. C553

CALIFORNIA. UNIVERSITY. UNIVERSITY OF CALIFORNIA PUBLICATIONS IN LIBRARIANSHIP

1:1 Merritt, L. C. The use of subject catalogs in the University of California Library. 1951. C554
2:1 Danton, J. P. United States influence on Norwegian librarianship, 1890-1940. 1957. C555
3 Lomeier, J. A seventeenth-century view of European

libraries, tr. by Montgomery. 1962. C556
4 Held, R. E. Public libraries in California, 1849-1878. 1963. C557
5 Wilson, P. Two kinds of power. 1968. C558
6 Koepp, D. W. Public library government. 1968. C559
7 Harlan, R. D. John Henry Nash. 1970. C560
8 Peterson, K. G. The University of California Library at Berkeley, 1900-1945. 1970. C561
9 Clark, H. A venture in history. 1974. C562/72

CALIFORNIA. UNIVERSITY. UNIVERSITY OF CALIFORNIA PUBLICATIONS IN LINGUISTICS

1:1 Paschall, C. The semasiology of words derived from the Indo-European *nem- . 1943. C573
1:2 Crétien, D. The quantitative method for determining linguistic relationships. 1943. C574
1:3 Kroeber, A. L. Classification of the Yuman languages. 1943. C575
1:4 Malkiel, Y. Development of the Latin suffixes -antia and -entia in the romance languages. 1945. C576
1:5 ____. The derivation of Hispanic fealdad(e), fieldad(e) and Fialdad(e). 1945. C577
1:6 Carmody, F. J. The interrogative system in modern Scottish Gaelic. 1945. C578
1:7 Malkiel, Y. Three Hispanic word studies. 1947. C579
1:8 Carmody, F. J. Manx Gaelic sentence structure in the 1819 Bible and the 1625 Prayer book. 1947. C580
1:9 Malkiel, Y. Hispanic algu(i)en and related formations. 1948. C581
2:1-2 Emeneau, M. B. Kota texts. 2 v. 1944. C582
3:1-2 ____. V. 3, 4. 1946-48. C583
4:1 Beeler, M. S. The Venetic language. 1949. C584
4:2 Chrétien, D. The dialect of the Sierra de Mariveles Negritos. 1951. C585
4:3 Malkiel, Y. The Hispanic suffix -(l)ego. 1951. C586
4:4 Bright, W. Animals of acculturation in the California Indian languages. 1960. C587
5:1 Hoijer, H. An analytical dictionary of the Tinkawa language. 1949. C588
6:1 Haas, M. R. Tuneca texts. 1950. C589
6:2 ____. Tuneca dictionary. 1953. C590
7:1-2 Palmer, P. M. The influence of English on the German vocabulary to 1700. 1950. C591
8 Emeneau, M. B. Studies in Vietnamese (Annamese) grammar. 1951. C592
9 Conklin, H. C. Hanunóo-English vocabulary. 1953. C593
10 Symposium on American Indian Linguistics. Papers from the Symposium on American Indian Linguistics, 1951. 1954. C594
11 Malkiel, Y. Studies in the reconstruction of Hispano-Latin word families. 1954. C595
12 Emeneau, M. B. Kolami. 1955. C596
13 Bright, W. The Karok language. 1957. C597
14 Thomas, L. L. The linguistic theories of N. Ja. Marr. 1957. C598
15 Robins, R. H. The Yurok language grammar. 1958. C599
16 Kroeber, A. L. and Grace, G. W. The Sparkman grammar of Luiseno. 1960. C600
17 Blaisdell, F. W. Preposition-adverbs in Old Icelandic. 1959. C601
18 Leslau, W. A dictionary of Moca. 1959. C602
19 Bull, W. E. Time, tense, and the verb. 1960. C603
20 Robe, S. L. The Spanish of rural Panama. 1960. C604
21 Puhvel, J. Laryngeals and the Indo-European verb.

1960. C605
22 Sapir, E. and Swafesh, M. Yana dictionary. 1960. C606
23 Freeland, L. S. and Broadbent, S. Central Sierra Mikow dictionary. 1960. C607
24 Krishnamurti, B. Telugu verbal bases. 1961. C608
25 Jones, R. B. Karen linguistic studies. 1961. C609
26 Emeneau, M. B. and Burrow, T. Dravidian borrowings from Indo-Aryan. 1962. C610
27 Emeneau, M. B. Brahui and Dravidian comparative grammar. 1962. C611
28 Hüttl-Worth, G. Foreign words in Russian. 1963. C612
29 Summer Institute of Linguistics. Studies in the Athapaskan languages, by Hoijer and others. 1963. C613
30 Barker, M. A. R. Klamath texts. 1963. C614
31 ____. Klamath dictionary. 1963. C615
32 ____. Klamath grammar. 1964. C616
33 Shipley, W. F. Maidu texts and dictionary. 1963. C617
34 Bright, W., ed. Studies in California linguistics. 1964. C618
35 Olmsted, D. L. A history of Palaihnihan phonology. 1964. C619
36 Oswalt, R. L. Kashaya texts. 1964. C620
37 Teeter, K. V. The Wiyot language. 1964. C621
38 Broadbent, S. M. The Southern Sierra Mikow language. 1964. C622
39 Callaghan, C. A. Lake Mikow dictionary. 1965. C623
40 Miller, W. R. Acoma grammar and texts. 1965. C624
41 Shipley, W. F. Maidu grammar. 1964. C625
42 Matteson, E. The Piro (Arawakan) language. 1965. C626
43 Sawyer, J. O. English-Wappo vocabulary. 1965. C627
44 Samarin, W. J. The Gheya language. 1966. C628
45 Olmsted, D. L. Achumawi dictionary. 1966. C629
46 Uldall, H. J. and Shipley, W. Niesenan texts and dictionary. 1966. C630
47 Señán, J. F. de P. The Ventureno confesionario of Jose Señán. 1967. C631
48 Miller, W. R. Uto-Aztecan cognate sets. 1967. C632
49 Shapiro, M. Russian phonetic variants and phonostylistics. 1968. C633
50 Sapir, E. and Hoijer, H. The phonology and morphology of the Navaho language. 1968. C634
51 Bright, W. A Luiseño dictionary. 1968. C635
52 Cooke, J. R. Pronominal reference in Thai, Burmese and Vietnamese. 1968. C636
53 Craddock, J. R. Latin legacy versus substratum residue. 1969. C637
54 Tyler, S. A. Koya. 1969. C638
55 Rand, E. The syntax of Mandarin interrogatives. 1969. C639
56 Foster, M. L. The Tarascan language. 1969. C640
57 Newman, P. A grammar of Tera. 1960. C641
58 Anttila, R. Proto-Indo-European schwebeablaut. 1969. C642
59 Worth, D. S. A dictionary of Western Kamchadal. 1969. C643
60 Callaghan, C. A. Bodega-Mikow dictionary. 1970. C644
61 Kaufman, T. Tzeltal phonology and morphology. 1971. C645
62 Aoki, H. Nez Perce grammar. 1969. C646
63 Georges, E. S. Studies in romance nouns extracted from past participles. 1970. C647
64 Malkiel, Y. Patterns of derivational affixation in the Cabraniego dialect of East-Central Asturian. 1970. C648
65 Studies in American Indian languages, ed. by Sawyer. 1971. C649
66 Langdon, M. A grammar of Diegueño. 1970. C650

67 Schlegel, S. A. Tiruray-English lexicon. 1971. C651
68 Butler, J. L. Latin-inus, -ina, -inus, & -ineus. 1971. C652
69 Bright, E. S. A word geography of California and Nevada. 1971. C653
70 Girard, V. Proto-Takanan phonology. 1971. C654
71 McLendon, S. Proto Pomo. 1974. C655
72 Moshinksy, J. A grammar of Southeastern Pomo. 1974. C656
73 Hoijer, H. Tonkawa texts. 1973. C657
75 Matisoff, J. A. The grammar of Lahu. 1973. C658
76 Lindenfeld, J. Yaqui syntax. 1974. C659
77 Levin, J. F. The Slavic element in the old Prussian Elbing vocabulary. 1974. C660
78 Hoijer, H. A Navaho lexicon. 1974. C661

CALIFORNIA. UNIVERSITY. UNIVERSITY OF CALIFORNIA PUBLICATIONS IN MODERN PHILOLOGY

1:1 Pinger, W. R. R. Der junge Goethe und das Publikum. 1909. C662
1:2 Kurtz, B. P. Studies in the marvelous. 1910. C663
1:3 Weiss, A. Introduction to the philosophy of art. 1910. C664
1:4 Smithson, G. A. The old English Christian epic. 1910. C665
2:1 Winther, F. Wilhelm Busch als dichter, künstler, psychologe und philosoph. 1910. C666
2:2 Cory, H. E. The critics of Edmund Spenser. 1911. C667
2:3 Schevill, R. Some forms of the riddle question and the exercise... 1911. C668
2:4 Herrmann, E. A. Histrionics in the dramas of Franz Grillparzer. 1912. C669
2:5 Cory, H. E. Spenser. 1919. C670
3:1 Wyneken, F. A. Rousseau's Einfluss auf klinger. 1912. C671
3:2 Winther, F. Das gerettete Venedig. 1914. C672
3:3 Richardson, G. F. A neglected aspect of the English romantic revolt. 1915. C673
3:4 Gillesphy, F. L. Layman's Brut. 1916. C674
4:1 Schevill, R. Ovid and the renascence in Spain. 1913. C675
4:2 Chinard, G. Notes sur le voyage de Chateaubriand in Amérique. 1915. C676
4:3 Girard, W. Du transcendantisme consideré essentiellement. 1916. C677
5 Cory, H. E. Edmund Spenser. 1917. C678
6 Schevill, R. The dramatic art of Lope de Vega. 1918. C679
7:1 Cornish, B. Francisco Navarro Villoslada. 1918. C680
7:2 McGuire, E. A study of the writings of Mariano José de Larra. 1918. C681
7:3 Morley, S. G. Studies in Spanish dramatic versification of the siglo de Oro. 1918. C682
7:4 Clark, J. T. Lexicological evolution and conceptual progress. 1918. C683
7:5 Chateaubriand, F. A. R. Les Natchez, ed. by Chinard. 1919. C684
8:1 Bruce, H. L. Voltaire on the English stage. 1918. C685
8:2 Girard, W. Du transcendantalisme considéré sous son aspect social. 1918. C686
8:3 Fay, P. B. The use of tu and vous in Molière. 1920. C687
8:4 Patrick, G. Z. Etude morphologique et syntaxique des vers dans Maristre Pierre Pathelen. 1924. C688
9:1-2 Price, L. M. English-German literary influences. 2 v. 1920. C689
10:1 Pinger, W. R. R. Laurence Sterne and Goethe. 1920. C690

10:2 Bell, C. H. The sister's son in the medieval German epic. 1922. C691
10:3 Reinsch, F. H. Goethe's political interests prior to 1787. 1923. C692
10:4 Whipple, T. K. Martial and the English epigram from Sir Thomas Wyatt to Ben Jonson. 1925. C693
11 The Charles Mills Gayley anniversary papers contributed by former students of Professor Gayley. 1922. C694
12:1 Kleiner, M. Zur entwicklung der futurumschreibung werden mit dem infinitiv. 1925. C695
12:2 Kurtz, B. P. From St. Anthony to St. Guthlac. 1926. C696
12:3 Clement, N. H. The influence of the Arthurian romances on five books of Rabelais. 1926. C697
12:4 Roumiguière, H. Le français dans les relations diplomatiques. 1926. C698
12:5 Wilcox, F. H. Prevost's translations of Richardson's novels. 1927. C699
13:1 Cruz Cano y Olmedilla, R. F. Ocho sainetes inéditos de Ramón de la Cruz. 1925. C700
13:2 Morley, S. G. Spanish ballad problems. 1925. C701
13:3 Spaulding, R. K. History and syntax of the progressive instructions in Spanish. 1926. C702
13:4 Holbrook, R. T. Guillaume Alecis et Pathelin. 1928. C703
14:1 Merlino, C. P. The French studies of Mario Equicola. 1929. C704
14:2 King, H. S. Echoes of the American revolution in German literature. 1929. C705
14:3 Brenner, C. D. L'histoire nationale dans la tragedie française du XVIIIe siècle. 1929. C706
14:4 Rotunda, D. P. A tabulation of early Italian tales. 1930. C707
14:5 Morley, S. G. Lope de Vega's Peregrino lists. 1930. C708
14:6 Simpson, L. P. The sources of Lope de Vega's La prueba de los amigos. 1930. C709
15:1 Wright, L. O. The -ra verb form in Spain. 1932. C710
15:2 Suard, J. B. A. Lettres inédites de Suard à Wilkes. 1932. C711
16:1 Corbato, H. Los misterios del corpus de Valencia. 1932. C712
16:2 La Harpe, J. E. V. de. Le journal des savants et le renommée de Pope en France au XVIIIe siècle. 1933. C713
16:3 Leonard, I. A. Romances of chivalry in the Spanish Indies. 1933. C714
16:4 Carmody, F. J. Le repertoire de l'opera-comique en vaudevilles de 1708 à 1764. 1933. C715
17 Price, M. and L. M. The publication of English literature in Germany in the eighteenth century. 1934. C716
18:1 Gudde, E. G. Social conflicts in medieval German poetry. 1934. C717
18:2 Suard, J. B. A. Correspondence littéraire de Saurd avec le Margrave de Bayreuth. 1934. C718
18:3 Alexius, St. Cans un de Sant Alexis. 1935. C719
18:4 Rowbotham, A. H. The "philosophes" and the propaganda for inoculation of smallpox in eighteenth century France. 1935. C720
18:5 Bunje, E. T. H. A reinterpretation of the expository verses of the Hildebrandslied. 1936. C721
18:6 De Filippis, M. Anecdotes in Manso's "Vita de Tasso." 1936. C722
19 Spencer, F. E. The dramatic works of Luis Velez de Guevara. 1937. C723
20:1 Brenner, C. D. La développement du provoverbe dramatique en France et

sa vagne au XVIIIe siècle. 1937. C724
20:2 Clarke, D. C. Una bibliografia de versificacion española. 1937. C725
20:3 Elsdon, J. H. On the life and work of the Spanish humanist Antonio de Torquemada. 1937. C726
20:4 Holbrook, R. T. X-ray studies of speech articulation. 1937. C727
20:5 De Filippes, M. G. B. Manso's Enciclopedia. 1937. C728
20:6 La Harpe, J. E. V. de. Le journal des savants et l'Angleterre. 1941. C729
21:1 Kany, C. E. The beginnings of the epistolary novel in France, Italy and Spain. 1937. C730
21:2 Torres Ríoseco, A. La novela en la America hispana. 1939. C731
21:3 Kany, C. E. Rounded vowel e in the Spanish diphthong ue. 1940. C732
21:4 Trevisani, F. M. La Cristina. 1941. C733
21:5 Carmody, F. J. An x-ray study of pharyngeal articulation. 1941. C734
21:6 Walpole, R. N. Charlemagne and Roland. 1944. C735
22 Latini, B. Le livres dou Tresor, ed. by Carmody. 1948. C736
23 Schmitz, F. J. Lessing's Stillung in der Entfaltung des individualismus. 1941. C737
24:1 Humiston, C. L. A comparative study of the metrical techniques of Ronsard and Malherde. 1941. C738
24:2 Speroni, C. Proverb and proverbial phrases in Basile's "Pentameron." 1941. C739
24:3 Hand, W. D. A dictionary of words and idioms associated with Judas Iscariot. 1942. C740
24:4 Mulloy, W. J. The German Catholic estimate of Goethe. 1944. C741
25:1 Chrétien, D. Indo-European final -*s in Germanic. 1941. C742
25:2 Ružić, R. H. The aspects of the verb in Serbo-Croatian. 1943. C743
25:3 Selden, E. S. China in German poetry from 1773 to 1833. 1942. C744
25:4 Kirschenbaum, L. Enrique Gaspar and the social drama in Spain. 1944. C745
26:1 Price, L. M. Christian Heinrich Schmid and his translations of English dramas. 1942. C746
26:2 La Harpe, J. E. V. de. L'Abbé Laurent Bordelon et la lutte contre la superstition en France. 1942. C747
26:3 Hull, V. E. and Taylor, A. A collection of Welsh riddles. 1942. C748
26:4 Walpole, R. N. Philip Mouskés and the Pseudo-Turpin Chronicle. 1947. C749
26:5 Edelstein, L. Wieland's "Abderiten" und der deutsche Humanismus. 1950. C750
27:1 Brewer, E. V. The New England interest in Jean Paul Friedrich Richter. 1943. C751
27:2 Price, L. M. The vogue of Marmontel on the German stage. 1944. C752
27:3 Schmitz, F. J. The problem of individualism and the crisis in the lives of Lessing and Hamann. 1944. C753
27:4 Hornburg, L. Poems, ed. by Bell and Gudde. 1945. C754
27:5 Melz, C. T. An evaluation of the earliest German translations of "Don Quixote." 1945. C755
27:6 Wolff, H. M. Heinrich von Kleist als politischer Dichter. 1947. C756
28:1 Templin, E. H. The social approach to literature. 1944. C757
28:2 Goethe, J. C. The correspondence of Johann Caspar Goethe and F. H. Reinsch. 1946. C758
28:3 Mercury, C. "Proverbi vulgari," ed. by Speroni. 1946. C759
28:4 Krause, A. Azorín.

1948. C760
28:5 Nitze, W. A. Perceval and the Holy Grail. 1949. C761
28:6 Olguin, M. Marcelino Menendez Pelayo's theory of art. 1950. C762
28:7 Staaks, W. The theatre of Louis-Benoît Picard. 1952. C763
29-32 Hager, G. Georg Hager, by Bell. 4 v. 1947. C764
33:1 Brenner, C. D. Dramatizations of French short stories in the eighteenth century. 1947. C765
33:2 Leopold of Austria. Li compilacions de la science des estailles, bks. 1-3, ed. by Carmody. 1947. C766
33:3 Eustris, A. A. Racine devants la critique française. 1949. C767
33:4 Bonwit, M. Gustave Flaubert et la principe d'impossibilite. 1950. C768
33:5 Morley, S. G. The pseudonyms and literary disguises of Lope de Vega. 1951. C769
34:1 De Filippis, M. The literary riddle in Italy to the end of the sixteenth century. 1948. C770
34:2 Webber, R. M. Formulistic diction in the Spanish ballad. 1951. C771
34:3 Clarke, D. C. A chronological sketch of Castilian versification... 1952. C772
35:1 Eustis, A. A. Hippolyte Taine and the classical genius. 1951. C773
35:2 Putter, I. Leconte de Lisle and his contemporaries. 1951. C774
35:3 Knodel, A. Jules Renard as critic. 1951. C775
35:4 Jacob, M. Max Jacob and Les Feux de Pares. 1964. C776
36:1 Bell, C. H. The Meistersingerschule at Memmingen and its "Kurtze Entinerffung." 1952. C777
36:2 Bonwit, M. Der liedende Dritte. 1952. C778
36:3 Borden, C. E. The original model for Lessing's "Der junge Gelehrte." 1952. C779
36:4 Brodeur, A. G. The meaning of Snorri's categories. 1952. C780
36:5 Brown, F. A. On education. 1952. C781
36:6 Heller, E. K. Ludwig Hohenwang's "Von der Ritterschaft." 1952. C782
36:7 Jászi, A. O. Rilke's Duineser Elegien und die Einsamkeit. 1952. C783
36:8 Loomis, C. H. The German theater in San Francisco. 1952. C784
36:9 Mileck, J. Hermann Hesse's "Glasperlenspiel." 1952. C785
36:10 Palmer, P. M. German works on America, 1492-1800. 1952. C786
36:11 Puknat, S. B. Religious forms and faith in the Volksbuch. 1952. C787
36:12 Sobel, E. Sebastian Brant, Ovid, and classical allusions in the Narrenschiff." 1952. C788
36:13 Wolff, H. M. Heinrich von Kleist's "Findling." 1952. C789
37 Price, L. M. English literature in Germany. 1953. C790
38:1 Templin, E. H. Money in the plays of Lope de Vega. 1952. C791
38:2 Bonno, G. D. Les relations intellectuelles de Locke avec la France... 1955. C792
38:3 Nitze, W. A. Arthurian names in the Perceval of Chrétien de Troyes. 1955. C793
38:4 Armistead, S. G. A lost version of the Cantar de geste de las mocedades de Rodrigo... 1963. C794
39 Obradović, V. The life and adventures of Dimitrije Obradović. 1953. C795
40:1 De Filippis, M. The literary riddle in Italy in the seventeenth century. 1953. C796
40:2 Sobel, E. The Tristan romance in the Meisterlieder of Hans Sachs. 1968. C797
40:3 Silva Castro, R. Pedro

Antonio González. 1964. C798
40:4 Roertgen, W. F. The Frankfurter gelehrte Anzeigen. 1964. C799
41 Wolff, H. M. Heinrich van Kleist. 1954. C800
42:1 Putter, I. The pessimism of Leconte de Lisle: sources and evaluation. 1954. C801
42:2 ____. ____: the work and the time. 1961. C802
43 Wolff, H. M. Goethe's Novelle "Die Wahlverwandschaften." 1955. C803
44 Price, M. The publication of English humaniora in Germany in the eighteenth century. 1955. C804
45 Nicholls, R. A. Nietzsche in the early works of Thomas Mann. 1955. C805
46 Brandes, G. M. C. Georg Brandes und Arthur Schnitzler. 1956. C806
47 LaHarper, J. E. V. de. Jean-Pierre de Crousaz et le conflit des idées au siècle des lumieres. 1955. C807
48 Dottori, C. de. Il Parnaso, ed. by Golino. 1957. C808
49 Guthke, K. S. Das Leid im werke Gerhart Hauptmanns. 1958. C809
50 Shaw, L. R. Witness of deceit. 1958. C810
51 Mapa mundi. Semeiança del mundo, by Bull and Williams. 1959. C811
52 LeClerc, J. Lettres inedítes de LeClerc à Locke, ed. by Bonne. 1959. C812
53 Andrews, J. R. Juan del Encina. 1959. C813
54 Polt, J. H. R. The writings of Eduardo Mallea. 1959. C814
55:1-2 Morley, S. G. and Tyler, R. W. Los nombres de personages en las comedias de Lope de Vega. 2 v. in 1. 1961. C815
56 Robert, P. R. Jean Giono et les techniques du roman. 1961. C816
57 Spahr, B. L. The archives of the Pegnesischer Blumenorden. 1960. C817
58:1 Monguió, L. Sobre un escritor elogiado por Cervantes. 1960. C818
59 Rubia Barcia, J. A bio-bibliography and iconography of Valle Inclan. 1960. C819
60 Bäuml, F. H. Rhetorical devices and structure in the Ackermann aus Böhmen. 1960. C820
61 Engelsing-Malik, I. "Amor fati" in Zuckmayer's Dramen. 1960. C821
62 Markov, V. The longer poems of Velimir Khlebnikov. 1962. C822
63 Brenner, C. D. The théâtre Italien. 1961. C823
64 Decker, H. W. Pure poetry, 1925-1930. 1962. C824
65 Goll, I. Jean sans Terre, ed. by Carmody. 1962. C825
66 Bowman, F. P. Prosper Mérimée. 1962. C826
67 Hoffmann, C. W. Opposition poetry in Nazi Germany. 1962. C827
68 Kanes, M. Zola's La béte humaine. 1962. C828
69 Ermolaev, H. Soviet literary theories, 1917-1934. 1963. C829
70 Carmody, F. J. The evolution of Apollinaire's Poetics. 1963. C830
71 Jennings, L. B. The ludicrous demon. 1963. C831
72 Weber, R. The Miau manuscript of Benito Perez Galdos. 1964. C832
73 Pedrotti, L. Jozef-Julian Sekowski. 1965. C833
74 The Cancioneiro de Evora, ed. by Askins. 1965. C834
75 Randolph, D. A. Eugenio de Ochoa y el romanticismo español. 1966. C835
76 Spahr, B. L. Anton Ulrich and Aramena. 1966. C836
77 Chapman, A. The Spanish American reception of United States fiction. 1966. C837
78 Ruggerio, M. J. The evolution of the go-between in Spanish literature through the sixteenth century. 1966. C838
79 Knutson, H. C. The ironic game. 1966. C839
80 Englekirk, J. E. and Ramos,

M. M. La narrativa uruguaya. 1967. C840
81 Liber fortunae. The middle French Liber fortunae, ed. by Grigsby. 1967. C841
82 Grune, R. W. The poetic theory of Pierre Reverdy. 1967. C842
83 De Filippis, M. The literary riddle in Italy in the eighteenth century. 1967. C843
84 Cancineiro de corte e de magnates..., ed. by Askins. 1968. C844
85 Basdekis, D. Unamuno and Spanish literature. 1967. C845
86 Putter, I. La dernière illusion de Leconte de Lisle. 1967. C846
87 Taylor, M. C. Gabriela Mistral's religious sensibility. 1968. C847
88 Speroni, C. The aphorisms of Orazio Rinaldi. 1968. C848
89 Greet, A. H. Jacques Prevert's word games. 1968. C849
90 Bertrand, M. L'oeuvre de Jean Prevost. 1968. C850
91 Clarke, D. C. Allegory, decalogue, and deadly sins in La Celestina. 1968. C851
92 Barrette, P. Robert de Blois' Floris et Lyriope. 1968. C852
93 Morris, H. The masked citadel. 1968. C853
94 Wagener, H. Komposition der romane Christian. 1969. C854
95 Polt, J. H. Juan Pablo Forner y Segarra. 1969. C855
96 Griffin, R. Coronation of the poet. 1969. C856
97 Ellis, J. M. Kleist's Prinz Friedrich von Homburg. 1970. C857
98 García, S. Las ideas literarias en España entre 1840 y 1850. 1971. C858
99 Perella, N. J. Night and the sublime in Giacomo Leopardi. 1970. C859
100 Gans, E. L. The discovery of illusion. 1971. C860
101 Johnson, C. B. Matias de los reyes and the craft of fiction. 1972. C861
102 Lindsay, M. Le temps jaune. 1972. C862
103 Faulhaber, C. Latin rhetorical theory in thirteenth and fourteenth Castile. 1972. C863
104 Shideler, R. Voices under the ground. 1973. C864
105 Kunzer, R. G. The Tristan of Gottfried von Strassburg. 1973. C865
106 Linn, R. N. Schiller's Junge Idelisten. 1973. C866
107 Monguio, L. Poesias de don Felipe Pardo y Aliaga. 1973. C867
108 Bonades, A. Corruption, conflict and power in the works and times of Niccolo Machiavelli. 1974. C868
109 Bruno, A. M. Formulaic and non-formulaic style in the Nibelungenlied. 1974. C869

CALIFORNIA. UNIVERSITY. UNIVERSITY OF CALIFORNIA PUBLICATIONS. NEAR EASTERN STUDIES.

1 Leslua, W. Etymological dictionary of Harari. 1963. C870
2 Schramm, G. M. The graphemes of Tiberian Hebrew. 1964. C871
3 Hoenerbach, W. Spanisch-Islamische Urkunden aus der Zeit der Nasriden und Moriscos. 1965. C872
4 Badawy, A. Ancient Egyptian architectural design. 1965. C873
5 Davidson, H. A. The philosophy of Abraham Shalom. 1964. C874
6 Ibn Kammūnah, S. ibn M. Examination of the inquiries into the three faiths, ed. by Perlmann. 1967. C875
7-9 Leslau, W., ed. Ethiopians speak. 3 v. 1967. C876
10 Ruedy, J. Land policy in colony Algeria. 1967. C877
11 Leslau, W. Ethiopians speak. 1968. C878
12 Hetzron, R. The verbal system of Southern Agaw. 1969. C879

13 Monroe, J. T. Hispano-Arabic poetry. 1970. C880
14 Milgrom, J. Studies in Levitical terminology. 1970. C881
15 Monroe, J. T., ed. Risalat at-Tawabic wa z-Aawabic by Abu Amir ibn Shuhaid al-Ashja, i, al-Andalusi. 1971. C882
17 Book of two ways. The ancient Egyptian Book of two ways, ed. by Lesko. 1972. C883

CALIFORNIA. UNIVERSITY. UNIVERSITY OF CALIFORNIA PUBLICATIONS. SLAVIC STUDIES.

1 Lednicki, W. Pushkin's Bronze horseman. 1955. C884

CAMBRIDGE AERONAUTICAL SERIES (Cambridge)

1 Duncan, W. J. The principles of the control and stability of aircraft. 1952. C885
2 Robinson, A. and Laurmann, J. A. Wing theory. 1956. C886
3 Woods, L. C. The theory of subsonic plane flow. 1961. C887

CAMBRIDGE BIOLOGICAL STUDIES

Dalcq, A. M. Form and causality in early development. 1938. C888
Darlington, C. D. The evolution of genetic systems. 1939. C889
Green, D. E. Mechanisms of biological oxidations. 1940. C890
Konorski, J. Conditioned reflexes and neuron organization. 1948. C891
Lerner, I. M. Population genetics and animal improvement. 1950. C892
Rawdon-Smith, A. F. Theories of sensation. 1938. C893
Waddington, C. H. The epigenetics of birds. 1952. C894
____. Organisers & genes. 1940. C895

CAMBRIDGE CLASSICAL STUDIES

Anonymus Londinensis. The medical writings of Anonymus Londinensis, by Jones. 1947. C896
Armstrong, A. H. The architecture of the intelligible universe in the philosophy of Plotinus. 1967. C897
Bailey, D. R. S. Propertiana. 1956. C898
____. Towards a text of Cicero's "Ad Atticum." 1960. C899
Bonner, S. F. The literary treatises of Dionysius of Halicarnassus. 1969. C900
Bramble, J. C. Persius and the programmatic satire. 1974. C901
Bruce, I. A. F. An historical commentary on the "Hellenica Oxyrhnchia." 1967. C902
Crawford, D. J. Kerkeosiris. 1971. C903
Earl, D. C. The political thought of Sallust. 1961. C904
Hodge, A. T. The woodwork of Greek roofs. 1961. C905
Lewis, M. J. T. Temples in Roman Britain. 1966. C906
Moore, J. M. The manuscript tradition of Polybius. 1965. C907
O'Brien, D. Empedocles' cosmic cycle. 1969. C908
Flommer, H. Vitruvius and later Roman building manuals. 1973. C909
Powell, J. E. The history of Herodotus. 1967. C910
Raven, J. E. Pythagoreans and Eleatics. 1948. C911
Runicman, W. G. Plato's later epistemology. 1962. C912
Salway, P. The frontier people of Roman Britain. 1965. C913
Shackleton Bailey, D. R. Towards a text of Cicero's "Ad Atticum." 1960. C914
Shipp, G. P. Studies in the language of Homer. 1972. C915
Skemp, J. B. The theory of motion in Plato's later dialogues. 1942. C916
Talbert, R. J. A. Timoleon and the revival of Greek

Sicily. 1974. C917
Tuckey, T. G. Plato's Charmides. 1951. C918
Warren, P. Minoan stone vases. 1969. C919
Wild, J. P. Textile manufacture in the northern Roman provinces. 1970. C920
Winnington-Ingram, R. P. Modes in ancient Greek music. 1968. C921
Wirszibski, C. Libertas as a political idea at Rome during the late Republic and Early Principate. 1950. C922
Witt, R. E. Albinus and the history of middle Platonism. 1937. C923

CAMBRIDGE GEOGRAPHICAL STUDIES

1 Robson, B. T. Urban analysis. 1969. C924
2 Timms, D. W. G. The urban mosaic. 1971. C925
3 Carson, M. A. and Kirkby, M. J. Hillslope form and process. 1972. C926
4 Chisholm, M. and O'Sullivan, P. Freight flows and spatial aspects of the British economy. 1973. C927
5 Grigg, D. B. The agricultural systems of the world. 1974. C928

CAMBRIDGE LATIN AMERICAN STUDIES (Cambridge)

1 Collier, S. D. W. Ideas and politics of Chilean independence, 1808-1833. 1967. C929
2 Calvert, P. The Mexican Revolution, 1910-1914. 1968. C930
3 Costeloe, M. P. Church wealth in Mexico. 1968. C931
4 Graham, R. Britain and the onset of modernization in Brazil. 1968. C932
5 Klein, H. S. Parties and political change in Bolivia. 1969. C933
6 Bethell, L. Abolition of the Brazilian slave trade. 1969. C934
7 Barkin, D. and King, T. Regional economic development. 1970. C935
8 Furtado, C. The Latin American economy. 1970. C936
9 McGreevey, W. P. Economic history of Colombia, 1845-1939. 1970. C937
10 Brading, D. Miners and merchants in Bourbon, Mexico, 1763-1810. 1970. C938
11 Bazant, J. The disentailment nationalization and sale of church wealth in Mexico. 1970. C939
12 Hamnett, B. R. Politics and trade in Southern Mexico, 1750-1821. 1970. C940
13 Fifer, J. V. Bolivia. 1971. C941
14 Gerhard, P. The historical geography of new Spain. 1971. C942
15 Bakewell, P. J. Silver mining and society in colonial Mexico, Zacayecas. 1971. C943
16 Maxwell, K. R. Conflicts and conspiracies. 1973. C944
17 Martinez-Alier, V. Marriage, class and colour in nineteenth-century Cuba. 1973. C945
18 Halperin-Donghi, T. Politics, economics and society in Argentina in the revolutionary period. 1974. C946

CAMBRIDGE MONOGRAPHS IN EXPERIMENTAL BIOLOGY (Cambridge)

1 Wiggleworth, V. B. The physiology of insect metamorphosis. 1954. C947
2 Beale, G. H. The genetics of Paramecium aurelia. 1954. C948
3 Matthews, G. V. T. Bird navigation. 1955. C949
4 Lees, A. D. The physiology of diapause in anthropods. 1955. C950
5 Edney, E. B. The water relations of terrestrial arthropods. 1957. C951

6 Hawker, L. E. The physiology of reproduction in fungi. 1957. C952
7 Beatty, R. A. Parthenogenesis and polyploidy in mammalian development. 1957. C953
8 Hoyle, G. Comparative physiology of the nervous control of muscular contraction. 1957. C954
9 Pringle, J. W. S. Insect flight. 1957. C955
10 Carlisle, D. B. and Knowles, F. G. W. Endocrine control in crustaceans. 1959. C956
11 Davies, D. D. Intermediary metabolism in plants. 1961. C957
12 Thorpe, W. H. Bird-song. 1961. C958
13 Harker, J. F. The physiology of diurnal rhythms. 1964. C959
14 Treherne, J. E. The neurochemistry of anthropods. 1966. C960
15 Robertson, R. N. Protons, electrons, phosphorylation and active transport. 1968. C961
16 Salt, G. The cellular defence reactions of insects. 1970. C962
17 Crompton, D. W. T. An ecological approach to acanthocephalan physiology. 1970. C963
18 Satchell, G. H. Circulation in fishes. 1971. C964
19 Hills, B. A. Gas transfer in the lungs. 1973. C965

CAMBRIDGE MONOGRAPHS ON MECHANICS AND APPLIED MATHEMATICS (Cambridge)

Batchelor, G. K. The theory of homogeneous turbulence. 1953. C966
____ and Davies, R. M., eds. Surveys in mechanics. 1956. C967
Dungey, J. W. Cosmic electrodynamics. 1958. C968
Friedlander, F. G. Sound pulses. 1958. C969
Greenspan, H. P. The theory of rotating fluids. 1968. C970
Lighthill, M. J. Introduction to Fourier analysis and generalized functions. 1958. C971
Lin, C. The theory of hydrodynamic stability. 1955. C972
Miles, J. W. The potential theory of unsteady supersonic flow. 1959. C973
Munk, W. H. and MacDonald, J. F. The rotation of the earth. 1960. C974
Phillips, O. M. The dynamics of the upper ocean. 1966. C975
Sturrock, P. A. Static and dynamic electron optics. 1955. C976
Synge, J. L. Geometrical mechanics and de Broglie waves. 1954. C977
Townsend, A. A. The structure of turbulent shear flow. 1956. C978
Turner, J. S. Buoyancy effects on fluids. 1972. C979
Ward, G. N. Linearized theory of steady high-speed flow. 1955. C980

CAMBRIDGE MONOGRAPHS ON PHYSICS (Cambridge)

Andrew, E. R. Nuclear magnetic resonance. 1955. C981
Arndt, U. W. and Willis, B. T. M. Single-crystal diffractometry. 1966. C982
Atkins, K. R. Liquid helium. 1959. C983
Bondi, H. Cosmology. 1961. C984
Bowden, F. P. and Yoffe, A. D. Initiation and growth of explosion in liquids and solids. 1952. C985
Broda, E. Advances in radiochemistry and the methods of producing radioelements by neutron irradiation. 1950. C986
Buchdahl, H. A. The concepts of classical thermodynamics. 1966. C987
____. Introduction to Hamiltonian optics. 1971. C988
Burdon, R. S. Surface tension and the spreading of liquids. 1949. C989
Burhop, E. H. S. The Auger

effect and other radiationless transitions. 1952. C990
Christiansen, W. N. and Högbom, J. A. Radiotelescopes. 1969. C991
Cosslett, V. E. and Nixon, W. C. X-ray microscopy. 1961. C992
Croxton, C. A. Liquid state physics. 1973. C993
Devons, S. Excited status of nuclei. 1949. C994
Duckworth, H. E. Mass spectroscopy. 1958. C995
Faber, T. E. Introduction to the theory of liquid metals. 1972. C996
Feather, N. Nuclear stability rules. 1952. C997
Fletcher, N. H. The chemical physics of ice. 1970. C998
Goody, R. M. The physics of the stratosphere. 1954. C999
Grew, G. E. and Ibbs, T. L. Thermal diffusion in gases. 1952. C1000
Hoyle, F. Some recent researches in solar physics. 1949. C1001
Klemperer, O. Electronic optics. 1953. C1002
March, N. H. and others. The many-body problem in quantum mechanics. 1968. C1003
Massey, H. S. Negative ions. 1950. C1004
Mather, K. B. and Swan, P. Nuclear scattering. 1958. C1005
Miller, A. R. The adsorption of gases on solids. 1949. C1006
Moon, P. B. Artificial radioactivity. 1949. C1007
Oatley, C. W. Scanning electron microscope. 1973. C1008
Shoenberg, D. Superconductivity. 1952. C1009
Steel, W. H. Interferometry. 1967. C1010
Stewart, K. H. Ferromagnetic domains. 1954. C1011
Thompson, M. W. Defects and radiation damage in metals. 1968. C1012
Wilkes, M. V. Oscillations of the earth's atmosphere. 1949. C1013
Wilkinson, D. H. Ionization chambers and counters. 1950. C1014
Wilson, J. G. The principles of cloud-chamber technique. 1951. C1015

CAMBRIDGE PAPERS IN SOCIAL ANTHROPOLOGY.

1 Goody, J. R., ed. The developmental cycle in domestic groups. 1958. C1016
2 Leach, E. R., ed. Aspects of caste in south India, Ceylon, and north-west Pakistan. 1960. C1017
3 Fortes, M., ed. Marriage in tribal societies. 1962. C1018
4 Goody, J. Succession to high office. 1966. C1019
5 Leach, E. R., ed. Dialectic in practical religion. 1968. C1020
6 Richards, A. I. and Kuper, A., eds. Councils in action. 1971. C1021
7 Goody, J. R. and Tambiah, S. J. Bridewealth and dowry. 1973. C1022

CAMBRIDGE PAPERS IN SOCIOLOGY (Camb. Univ. Pr.)

1 Ingham, G. K. Size of industrial organization and worker behaviour. 1970. C1023
2 Wedderburn, D. and Crompton, D. Workers' attitudes and technology. 1972. C1024
3 Beynon, H. and Blackburn, R. M. Perceptions of work variations within a factory. 1972. C1025
4 Salaman, G. Community and occupation. 1974. C1026

CAMBRIDGE SOUTH ASIAN STUDIES

1 Gopal, S. British policy in India, 1858-1905. 1966. C1027
2 Palmer, J. A. B. The mutiny outbreak at Meerut in 1857. 1966. C1028
3 Das Gupta, A. Malabar in Asian trade, 1740-1800.

1967. C1029
4 Obeyeskere, G. Land tenure in village Ceylon. 1967. C1030
5 Erdman, H. L. The Swatantra party and Indian conservatism. 1967. C1031
6 Mukherjee, S. N. Sir William Jones. 1967. C1032
7 Majed Khan, A. The transition in Bengal. 1969. C1033
8 Rungta, R. S. The rise of business corporations in India. 1969. C1034
9 Nightingale, P. Trade and empire in Western India, 1784-1806. 1970. C1035
10 Bagchi, A. K. Private investment in India and Pakistan, 1900-1939. 1971. C1036
11 Brown, J. M. Gandhi's rise to power. 1972. C1037
12 Carras, M. C. The dynamics of Indian political factions. 1972. C1038
13 Hardy, P. Muslims of British India. 1972. C1039
14 Johnson, G. Provincial politics and Indian nationalism. 1974. C1040
15 Robinson, M. S. Political structure in a changing Sinhalese village. 1974. C1041
16 Robinson, F. Separatism among Indian Muslims. 1974. C1042

CAMBRIDGE STUDIES IN CRIMINOLOGY (Macmillan)

1 Radzinowicz, L. and Turner, J. W. C., eds. Penal reform in England. 1946. C1043
2 Mental abnormality and crime, by Craig and others. 1944. C1044
3 Barker, F. A. The modern prison system of India. 1944. C1045
4 The Modern approach to criminal law..., by Davies and others. 1945. C1046
5 Glueck, S. and E. After-conduct of discharged offenders. 1945. C1047
6 Barry, J. V. W. and others. An introduction to the criminal law in Australia. 1948. C1048
7 Cambridge. Eng. Univ. Faculty of Law. Dept. of Criminal Science, Detention in remand homes. 1952. C1049
8 Edwards, J. L. J. Mens rea in statutory offences. 1955. C1050
9 Cambridge. Eng. Univ. Faculty of Law. Dept. of Criminal Science. Sexual offences. 1957. C1051
10 ____. The results of probation. 1958. C1052
11 Havard, J. D. J. The detection of secret homicide. 1960. C1053
12 Nyquist, O. Juvenile justice. 1961. C1054
13 Cambridge. Eng. Univ. Institute of Criminology. Attendance centres, by McClintock and others. 1961. C1055
14 ____. Robbery in London, by McClintock and others. 1961. C1056
15 Green, E. Judicial attitude in sentencing. 1961. C1057
16 Cambridge Univ. Institute of Criminology. Offenders as employees. 1962. C1058
17 Collins, P. A. W. Dickens and crime. 1962. C1059
18 Cambridge. Univ. Institute of Criminology. Crimes of violence, ed. by McClintock. 1963. C1060
19 ____. The habitual prisoner. 1963. C1061
20 Hood, R. Borstal re-assessed. 1965. C1062
21 West, D. J. Murder followed by suicide. 1965. C1063
22 McClintock, F. H. and others. Crime in England and Wales. 1968. C1064
23 Cowie, J. and others. Delinquency in girls. 1968. C1065
24 Martin, J. P. The police. 1969. C1066
25 West, D. J. Present conduct and future delinquency. 1969. C1067
26 Mueller, G. O. W. Crime, law and the scholars. 1969. C1068

27 Thomas, D. A. Principles of sentencing. 1970. C1069
29 Paris. Université. Suspended sentence. 1971. C1070
28 Martin, J. P. The social consequences of conviction. 1971. C1071
30 Sparks, R. F. Local prisons. 1971. C1072
31 Hood, R. G. Sentencing the motoring offender. 1972. C1073
32 Bottoms, A. E. Criminals coming of age. 1973. C1074
33 Willett, T. C. Drivers after sentence. 1973. C1075
34 West, D. J. Who becomes delinquent? 1973. C1076

CAMBRIDGE STUDIES IN ECONOMIC HISTORY (Cambridge)

1 Robertson, H. M. Aspects of the rise of economic individualism. 1933. C1077
2 Page, F. M. The estates of Crowland abbey. 1934. C1078
3 Hampson, E. M. The treatment of poverty in Cambridgeshire, 1597-1834. 1934. C1079
4 Merchants of the staple of England. The ordinance book of the merchants of the staple, ed. by Rich. 1937. C1080
5 Henderson, W. O. The Zollverein. 1959. C1081
6 Hope-Jones, A. Income tax in the Napoleonic wars. 1939. C1082
7 Darby, H. C. The medieval fenland. 1940. C1083
8 ____. The Draining of the Fens. 1956. C1084
9 Wilson, C. M. Anglo-Dutch commerce & finance in the eighteenth century. 1941. C1085
10 Morgan, E. V. The theory and practice of central banking, 1791-1913. 1943. C1086
11 Smith, R. A. L. Canterbury cathedral priory. 1943. C1087
12 Greenberg, M. British trade and the opening of China, 1800-42. 1951. C1088
Bourne, A. J. The influence of England on the French agronomes, 1750-1789. 1953. C1089
Dharma Kumar. Land and caste in South India. 1965. C1090
Drake, M. Population and society in Norway. 1969. C1091
Greenberg, M. British trade and the opening of China, 1800-42. 1970. C1092
Griggs, D. B. The agricultural revolution in South Lincolnshire. 1966. C1093
Hallam, H. E. Settlement and society. 1965. C1094
Holmes, G. A. The estates of the higher nobility in fourteenth century England. 1957. C1095
Kent, H. D. K. War and trade in the northern seas. 1972. C1096
King, E. Peterborough Abbey, 1086-1310. 1973. C1097
Rimmer, W. G. Marshalls of Leeds, flax-spinners, 1788-1886. 1960. C1098
Supple, B. E. Commercial crisis and change in England, 1600-1642. 1959. C1099
Titow, J. Z. Winchester yields. 1972. C1100
Tucker, G. S. L. Progress and profits in British economic thought, 1650-1850. 1960. C1101
Wrigley, E. A. Industrial growth and population change. 1961. C1102
Wright, H. R. C. Free trade and protection in the Netherlands, 1816-30. 1955. C1103

CAMBRIDGE STUDIES IN ENGLISH LEGAL HISTORY (Cambridge)

Bell, H. E. An introduction to the history and records of the Court of Wards & Liveries. 1953. C1104
Bellamy, J. G. The law of treason in England in the later Middle Ages. 1970. C1105
Bolland, W. C. A manual of year book studies. 1925. C1106
Bryson, W. H. The equity side of the Exchequer. 1974. C1107

Cockburn, J. S. A history of English assizes, 1558-1714. 1972. C1108
Dowdell, E. G. A hundred years of Quarter sessions. 1932. C1109
Duncan, G. I. O. The High Court of Delegates. 1970. C1110
Dunham, W. H. Hengham. 1965. C1111
Fleta, Ioannis Seldeni Ad Fletam dissertatio reprinted from the edition of 1647, tr. by Ogg. 1925. C1112
Fortescue, J. De laudibus legum Angliae, ed. by Chrimes. 1942. C1113
Hand, G. J. P. English law in Ireland, 1290-1324. 1967. C1114
Helmholz, R. H. Marriage litigation in medieval England. 1974. C1115
Hengham, R. de. Radulphi de Hengham Summae, ed. by Dunham. 1932. C1116
Hill, L. H., ed. The ancient state. 1974. C1117
Hunnisett, R. L. The medieval corner. 1962. C1118
Jackson, R. M. The history of quasi-contrast in English law. 1936. C1119
Jones, G. H. History of the law of charity. 1969. C1120
Nottingham, H. F. 'Manual of Chancery practice' and 'Prolegomena of Chancery and Equity.' 1965. C1121
Plucknett, T. F. T. Early English legal literature. 1958. C1122
____. Statutes and their interpretation in the first half of the 14th century. 1922. C1123
Pound, R. Interpretations of legal history. 1923. C1124
Putnam, B. H. The place in legal history of Sir William Shareshull. 1950. C1125
Robertson, A. J. Anglo-Saxon characters. 1956. C1126
Robson, R. The attorney in eighteenth century England. 1959. C1127
Roxburgh, R. F. The origin of Lincoln's Inn. 1963. C1128
Turner, R. W. The equity of redemption. 1931. C1129
Whitelock, D., ed. and tr. Anglo-Saxon wills. 1930. C1130
Winfield, P. History of conspiracy and abuse of legal practice. 1921. C1131
Wiswall, F. L. Development of English admiralty. 1970. C1132
Yale, D. E. C. Nottingham's treatise. 1966. C1133

CAMBRIDGE STUDIES IN INTERNATIONAL AND COMPARATIVE LAW (Cambridge)

1 Gutteridge, H. C. Comparative law and the conflict of law. 1949. C1134
2 Jones, J. M. Full powers and ratification. 1946. C1135
3 Lauterpacht, H. Recognition in international law. 1947. C1136
4 Street, H. Governmental liability. 1953. C1137
5 O'Connell, D. P. The Law of state succession. 1956. C1138
6 Wortley, B. A. Expropriation in public international law. 1959. C1139
7 O'Connell, D. P. State succession in municipal and international law. 2 v. 1967. C1140
8 Akehurst, M. B. The law governing employment in international organizations. 1967. C1141
9 Markesinis, B. S. The theory and practice of dissolution of parliament. 1973. C1142

CAMBRIDGE STUDIES IN LINGUISTICS

1 Crystal, D. Prosadic systems and intonation in English. 1969. C1143
2 Seuren, P. A. M. Operators and nucleus. 1969. C1144
3 Huddleston, R. D. The sentence in written English. 1971. C1145
4 Anderson, J. M. The grammar of case. 1971. C1146

5 Samuels, M. L. Linguistic evolution. 1972. C1147
6 Matthews, P. H. Infectional morphology. 1972. C1148
7 Brown, G. Phonological rules and dialect variation. 1972. C1149
8 Newton, B. The generative interpretation of dialect. 1972. C1150
9 Dixon, R. M. W. The Dyirbal language of North Queensland. 1972. C1151
10 Derwing, B. L. Transformational grammar as a theory of language acquisition. 1973. C1152
11 Bowerman, M. F. Early syntactic development. 1973. C1153
12 Allen, W. S. Accent and rhythm. 1973. C1154
13 Trudgill, P. The social differentiation of English in Norwich. 1974. C1155
14 Lass, R. and Anderson, J. M. Studies in Old English phonology. 1974. C1156

CAMBRIDGE STUDIES IN MEDIEVAL LIFE AND THOUGHT (Cambridge)

Bennett, H. S. Life on an English manor. 1937. C1157
____. The Pastons and their England. 1922. C1158
Bennett, R. F. The early Dominicans. 1937. C1159
Chadwick, D. Social life in the days of Piers Plowman. 1922. C1160
Coulton, G. G. Five centuries of religion. 4 v. 1923-50. C1161
____. The medieval village. 1925. C1162
____. Scottish abbeys & social life. 1933. C1163
Deanesly, M. The Lollard Bible and other medieval Biblical versions. 1920. C1164
Hartridge, R. A. R. Vicarages in the Middle Ages. 1930. C1165
Owst, G. R. Preaching in medieval England. 1926. C1166
Power, E. E. Medieval English nunneries. 1922. C1167
Snape, R. H. English monastic finances in the later Middle Ages. 1926. C1168
Wood-Legh, K. L. Studies in church life in England under Edward III. 1934. C1169

New series:
1 Miller, E. The abbey & bishopric of Ely. 1951. C1170
2 Finberg, H. P. R. Tavisock Abbey. 1951. C1171
3 Smail, R. C. Crusading warfare, 1097-1193. 1956. C1172
4 Tierney, B. Foundations of the conciliar theory. 1955. C1173
5 Leff, G. Bradwardine and the Pelagians. 1957. C1174
6 Vaughan, R. Matthew Paris. 1958. C1175
7 Brooke, R. B. Early Franciscan government. 1959. C1176
8 Robson, J. A. Wyclif and the Oxford schools. 1961. C1177
9 Wilks, M. The problem of sovereignty in the later Middle Ages. 1963. C1178
10 Constable, G. Monastic tithes, from their origins to the twelfth century. 1964. C1179
11 Morey, A. and Brooke, C. N. L., eds. Gilbert Foliot and his letters. 1965. C1180
12 West, F. J. The justiciarship in England, 1066-1232. 1966. C1181
13 Bowker, M. The secular clergy in the diocese of Lincoln, 1495-1520. 1968. C1182
14 Luscombe, D. E. School of Peter Abelard. 1968. C1183

3d series:
1 Cobban, A. B. The King's Hall within the University of Cambridge in the latter Middle Ages. 1968. C1184
2 Black, A. J. Monarch and community. 1970. C1185
3 Watt, J. A. The church and the two nations in medieval Ireland. 1970. C1186
4 Lineham, P. The Spanish

church and the Papacy in the 13th century. 1971. C1187
5 King, P. D. Law and society in the Visigothic kingdom. 1972. C1188
6 Dobson, R. B. Durham priory. 1973. C1189
7 McGrade, A. S. The political thought of William of Ockham. 1974. C1190

CAMBRIDGE STUDIES IN SOCIAL ANTHROPOLOGY (Cambridge)

1 Abrahams, R. G. The political organization of Unyamwezi. 1967. C1191
2 Tambiah, S. J. Buddhism and the spirit cult in Northeast Thailand. 1970. C1192
3 Kuper, A. Kalahari village politics. 1970. C1193
4 Strathern, A. The rope of Majangir. 1971. C1194
5 Stauder, J. The Majangir ecology and society of a Southwest Ethiopian people. 1971. C1195
6 Bunnag, J. Buddhist monk. Buddhist layman. 1973. C1196
7 Goody, E. N. Contexts of kinship. 1973. C1197
8 Oppong, C. Marriage among a matrilineal elite. 1974. C1198
9 Carter, A. T. Elite politics in rural India. 1973. C1199
10 Maher, V. Women and property in Morocco. 1974. C1200

CAMBRIDGE STUDIES IN THE HISTORY AND THEORY OF POLITICS

Akimov, V. On the dilemmas of Russian Marxism, ed. by Frankel. 1968. C1201
Avineri, S. Hegel's theory of the modern state. 1972. C1202
____. The social and political thought of Karl Marx. 1968. C1203
Barnard, J. G. Herder on social and political culture. 1973. C1204
Charvet, J. The social problem in the philosophy of Rousseau. 1974. C1205
Cowling, M. 1867. 1967. C1206
____. The impact of labour, 1920-1924. 1971. C1207
Franklin, J. H. Jean Bodin and the rise of absolute theory. 1973. C1208
Hegel, G. W. F. Lectures on the philosophy of world history, ed. by Forbes and Nisbet. 1973. C1209
Herder, J. G. J. G. Herder on social and political culture. 1969. C1210
Hotman, F. Francogallia, tr. by Salmon. 1972. C1211
Humboldt, W. von. The limit of state action, ed. by Burrow. 1969. C1212
Jones, A. The politics of reform, 1884. 1972. C1213
Kant, I. Kant's political writings, ed. by Reiss, tr. by Nisbet. 1970. C1214
Kelly, G. A. Idealism, politics and history. 1969. C1215
Kossmann, E. H. and Mellink, A. F., eds. Texts concerning the revolt of the Netherlands. 1973. C1216
Leibniz, G. W. The political writings of Leibniz, ed. by Riley. 1972. C1217
Makhnovets, V. P. Vladimir Akimov on the dilemmas of Russian Marxism, ed. by Frabkel. 1969. C1218
Marx, K. Critique of Hegel's Philosophy of right, tr. by Jolin and O'Malley. 1970. C1219
Moyle, W. An essay upon the Constitution of the Roman government, ed. by Robbins. 1969. C1220
Norman, E. R. The conscience of the state in North America. 1968. C1221
Ollman, B. Alienation. 1971. C1222
Robbins, C., ed. Two English Republican tracts: Plato redivivus by Neville and An essay upon the Constitution of the Roman government, by Moyle. 1969. C1223
Salisbury, R. A. T. G. C. Lord Salisbury on politics, ed. by Smith. 1972. C1224

Shklar, J. N. Men and citizens. 1969. C1225
Stephen, J. F. Liberty, equality, fraternity, ed. by White. 1967. C1226
Turgot, A. R. J. Turgot on progress, sociology and economics, ed. by Meek. 1973. C1227
Walzer, M., ed. Regicide and revolution. 1972. C1228

CAMBRIDGE TRACTS IN MATHEMATICS AND MATHEMATICAL PHYSICS (Cambridge)

1 Leathem, J. G. Volume and surface integrals used in physics. 1960. C1229
2 Hardy, G. H. The integration of functions of a single variable. 1916. C1230
3 Bromwich, T. J. I'A. Quadratic forms and their classification by means of invariant factors. 1906. C1231
4 Whitehead, A. N. The axioms of projective geometry. 1906. C1232
5 ____. The axioms of descriptive geometry. 1907. C1233
6 Mathews, G. B. Algebraic equations. 1930. C1234
7 Whittaker, E. T. The theory of optical instruments. 1907. C1235
8 Leathem, J. G. The elementary theory of the symmetrical optical instrument. 1908. C1236
9 Wright, J. E. Invariants of quadratic differential forms. 1908. C1237
10 Bôcher, M. An introduction to the study of integral equations. 1909. C1238
11 Young, W. H. The fundamental theorems of the differential calculus. 1960. C1239
12 Hardy, G. H. Orders of infinity. 1924. C1240
13 Henderson, A. The twenty-seven lines upon the cubic surface. 1911. C1241
14 Wood, P. W. The twisted cubic. 1913. C1242
15 Watson, G. N. Complex integration and Cauchy's theorem. 1914. C1243
16 Dickson, L. E. Linear algebras. 1914. C1244
17 Havelock, T. H. The propagation of disturbances in dispersive media. 1914. C1245
18 Hardy, G. H. and Riesz, M. The general theory of Dirichlet's series. 1915. C1246
19 Macaulay, F. S. The algebraic theory of modular systems. 1916. C1247
20 Fowler, R. H. The elementary differential geometry of plane curves. 1920. C1248
21 Young, L. C. The theory of integration. 1927. C1249
22 Berwick, W. E. H. Integral bases. 1927. C1250
23 Jeffreys, H. Operational methods in mathematical physics. 1931. C1251
24 Veblen, O. Invariants of quadratic differential forms. 1931. C1252
25 Steward, G. C. The symmetrical optical system. 1928. C1253
26 Titchmarsh, E. C. The zetafunction of Riemann. 1930. C1254
27 Rutherford, D. E. Modular invariants. 1932. C1255
28 Carathéodory, C. Conformal representation. 1958. C1256
29 Veblen, O. and Whitehead, J. H. C. The foundations of differential geometry. 1932. C1257
30 Ingham, A. E. The distribution of prime numbers. 1932. C1258
31 Hopf, E. Mathematical problems of radiative equilibrium. 1934. C1259
32 Bailey, W. N. Generalized hypergeometric series. 1935. C1260
33 Whittaker, J. M. Interpolatory function theory. 1935. C1261
34 Telling, H. G. The rational quartic curve in space of three or four

dimensions. 1936. C1262
35 Landau, E. G. H. Über einige neuere fortschritte der additieven zahlentheorie. 1937. C1263
36 Cramér, H. Random variables and probability distributions. 1962. C1264
37 Synge, J. L. Geometrical optics. 1937. C1265
38 Hardy, G. H. and Rogosinski, W. W. Fourier series. 1956. C1266
39 Baker, H. F. Locus with 25920 linear self-transformations. 1946. C1267
40 Burkill, J. C. The Lebesgue integral. 1951. C1268
41 Estermann, T. Introduction to modern prime number theory. 1952. C1269
42 Northcott, D. G. Ideal theory. 1953. C1270
43 Hilton, P. J. An introduction to homotopy theory. 1953. C1271
44 Cartwright, M. L. Integral functions. 1956. C1272
45 Cassels, J. W. S. An introduction to diophantine approximation. 1957. C1273
46 Cohn, P. M. Lie groups. 1957. C1274
47 Eggleston, H. G. Convexity. 1958. C1275
48 Hayman, W. K. Multivalent functions. 1958. C1276
49 Smithies, F. Integral equations. 1958. C1277
50 Busbridge, I. W. The mathematics of radiative transfer. 1960. C1278
51 Watson, G. L. Integral quadratic forms. 1960. C1279
52 Goldberg, R. R. Fourier transforms. 1961. C1280
53 Robertson, A. P. and W. Topological vector spaces. 1964. C1281
54 Rogers, C. A. Packing and covering. 1964. C1282
55 Copson, E. T. Symptotic expansion. 1965. C1283
56 Collingwood, E. and Lohwater, A. J. The theory of cluster sets. 1968. C1284
57 Copson, E. T. Metric spaces. 1968. C1285
58 Wasan, M. T. Stochastic approximation. 1969. C1286
59 Naimpally, S. A. and Warrack, B. D. Proximity spaces. 1971. C1287
60 Room, T. G. and Kirkpatrick, P. B. Miniquaternion geometry. 1971. C1288
61 Tyrrell, J. A. and Semple, J. G. Generalized Clifford parallelism. 1971. C1289
62 Sharpe, D. W. and Vamos, P. Injective modules. 1972. C1290
63 Roussas, G. G. Contiguity of probability measures. 1972. C1291
64 Mahler, K. Introduction to p-Adic numbers and their function. 1972. C1292
65 Alo, R. A. and Shapiro, H. L. Normal topological spaces. 1973. C1293
66 Smart, D. R. Fixed points theorems. 1973. C1294
67 Biggs, N. Algebraic graph theory. 1974. C1295
68 Preston, C. J. Gibbs States on countable sets. 1974. C1296

CAMBRIDGE. UNIVERSITY. DEPT. OF APPLIED ECONOMICS. MONOGRAPHS.

1 Carter, C. F. and others. The measurement of production movements. 1948. C1297
2 Bray, F. S. Social accounts and the business enterprise sector of the national economy. 1949. C1298
3 Stone, R. The role of measurement in economics. 1951. C1299
4 Prais, S. J. and Houthakker, H. S. The analysis of family budgets. 1955. C1300
5 Aitchison, J. and Brown, J. A. C. The lognormal distribution. 1957. C1301
6 Salter, W. E. G. Productivity and technical change. 1960. C1302
7 Cramer, J. S. The ownership of major consumer durables. 1962. C1303
8 Deane, P. and Cole, W. A.

British economic growth, 1688-1959. 1962. C1304
9 Ghosh, D. N. Experiments with input-output models... 1964. C1305
10 Marris, R. and others. The economics of capital utilisation. 1964. C1306
11 Pyatt, F. G. Priority patterns and the demand for household durable goods. 1964. C1307
12 Bain, A. D. The growth of television ownership in the United Kingdom since the war. 1964. C1308
13 Boehm, K. The British patent system. V. 1. 1967. C1309
14 Revell, J. and others. The wealth of nations. 1967. C1310
15 Ghosh, A. Planning, programming and in put-out models. 1968. C1311
16 Bacharach, M. Biproportional matrices and input-output change. 1970. C1312
17 Mitchell, B. R. and Deane, P. Abstract of British historical statistics. 1970. C1313
18 Mitchell, B. R. and Jones, H. G. Second abstract of British historical statistics. 1971. C1314
19 Singh, A. Takeovers. 1971. C1315
20 Ironmonger, D. S. New commodities and consumer behaviour. 1971. C1316
21 Moggridge, D. E. British monetary policy, 1924-1931. 1972. C1317
22 Ghosh, A. Programming and interregional in-put and out-put analysis. 1972. C1318
23 Taylor, C. T. and Silberston, Z. A. The economic impact of the patent system. 1973. C1319
24 Ellman, M. Planning problems in the USSR. 1973. C1320

CAMBRIDGE. UNIVERSITY. DEPT. OF APPLIED ECONOMICS. OCCASIONAL PAPERS.

1 Wedderburn, D. White-collar redundancy. 1964. C1321
2 Cook, P. L. Railroad workshops. 1964. C1322
3 Pratten, C. and Dean, R. M. The economics of large-scale production in British industry. 1965. C1323
4 Wedderburn, D. Redundancy and the railwaymen. 1965. C1324
5 Roth, G. J. Parking space for cars. 1965. C1325
6 Turner, H. A. Wage, trends, wage policies and collective bargaining. 1965. C1326
7 Singh, A. and others. Growth, probability, and valuation. 1967. C1327
8 George, K. D. Productivity in distribution. 1966. C1328
9 Clack, G. Industrial relations in a British car factory. 1967. C1329
10 Burley, H. Growth rate tables. 1966. C1330
11 Perkins, J. O. N. The Sterling area. 1967. C1331
12 Reddaway, W. B. and others. Effects of U. K. direct investment overseas. Interim report. 1967. C1332
13 Slater, L. J. Fortran programs for economists. 1967. C1333
14 Roberts, G. Demarcation rules in shipbuilding and shiprepairing. 1967. C1334
15 Reddaway, W. B. and others. Effects of U. K. direct investment overseas. Final report. 1968. C1335
16 George, K. D. Productivity and capital expenditure in retailing. 1968. C1336
17 Deakin, B. M. and Leisner, T. Productivity in transport. 1969. C1337
18. Atkinson, A. B. Poverty in Britain and reform of social security. 1969. C1338
19 Moggridge, D. E. Return to gold. 1969. C1339
20 Turner, H. A. Is Britain really strike-prone? 1969. C1340
21 Sutherland, A. Monopolies Commission in action. 1969. C1341

22 Whittington, G. Prediction of profitability and other studies of company behaviour. 1970. C1342
23 Faber, M. L. O. and Potter, J. G. Toward economic independence. 1970. C1343
24 Rowthorn, R. and Hymer, S. International big business, 1957-67. 1970. C1344
25 Ellman, M. Soviet planning today. 1970. C1345
26 Ward, M. The role of investment in the development of Fiji. 1971. C1346
27 Liesner, H. H. and Han, S. S. Britain and the common market. 1971. C1347
28 Pratten, C. F. Economies of scale in manufacturing industry. 1971. C1348
29 Fels, L. Modern mathematics and the teacher. 1971. C1349
30 Rhodes, J. and Kan, A. Office dispersal and regional policy. 1971. C1350
31 Moyle, J. J. The pattern of ordinary share ownership, 1957-1970. 1971. C1351
32 Reddaway, W. B. and others. Effects of selective employment tax. 1973. C1352
34 Slater, L. J. More Fortran programs for economists. 1972. C1353
36 Jackson, D. and others. Do trade unions cause inflation? 1972. C1354
37 Deakin, B. M. and Seward, T. Shipping conferences. 1973. C1355
38 Ward, T. S. The distribution of consumer goods. 1973. C1356
40 Cripps, T. F. and Tarling, R. J. Growth on advanced capitalist economics, 1950-1970. 1973. C1357
41 Paine, S. Exporting workers. 1974. C1358
42 Cockerill, A. and Silberston, Z. A. The steel industry. 1974. C1359

CAMBRIDGE. UNIVERSITY. MUSEUM OF ARCHAEOLOGY AND ETHNOLOGY OCCASIONAL PUBLICATIONS.

1 Bushnell, G. H. S. The archaeology of the Santa Elena Peninsula in south-west Ecuador. 1951. C1360
2 Clark, J. D. The prehistoric cultures of the Horn of Africa. 1954. C1361
3 Mukherjee, R. The ancient inhabitants of Jebel Moya, Sudan. 1955. C1362
4 McBurney, C. B. M. Prehistory and Pleistocene geology in Cyrenaican Libya. 1955. C1363
5 Taylour, W. D. Mycenean pottery in Italy and adjacent areas. 1958. C1364
Talbot, P. A. and Mulhall, H. The physical anthropology of Southern Nigeria. 1962. C1365

CAMBRIDGE. UNIVERSITY. ORIENTAL PUBLICATIONS.

1 Averroës. Commentary on Plato's Republic, ed. by Rosenthal. 1956. C1366
2 Jāmī. Fitzgerald's Salaman and Absal, ed. by Arberry. 1956. C1367
3 Ihara, S. The Japanese family storehouse, tr. by Sargent. 1959. C1368
4 Avesta. Yashts. The Avestan hymn to Mithra, tr. by Gershevitch. 1959. C1369
5 al-Fārābi. Fusūl al-madani, ed. by Dunlap. 1961. C1370
6 Dun Karm, pseud. Dun Karm, poet of Malta, tr. by Arberry. 1961. C1371
7 McEwan, J. R. The political writings of Ogyū Sorai. 1962. C1372
8 Twitchett, D. C. Financial administration under the T'ang dynasty. 1963. C1373
9 Allchin, F. R. Neolithic cattlekeepers of south India. 1963. C1374
10 Blacker, C. The Japanese enlightenment. 1964. C1375

11-12 Loewe, M. Records of Han administration. 1967. C1376
13 McGregor, R. S. Language of Indrajet of Orcha. 1968. C1377
14 Mason, R. H. P. Japan's first general election, 1890. 1968. C1378
15 Mills, D. E. Collection of tales from Uji. 1970. C1379
16-17 Rosenthal, E. I. J. Studia semitica. 2 v. 1970. C1380
18-19 Abramowski, L. and Goodman, A. E. A Nestorian collection of Christological texts. 2 v. 1971. C1381
20 Brock, S. The Syriac version of the Ps. Nonnos mythological Scholia. 1971. C1382
21 Maktari, A. M. A. Water rights and irrigation practices in Lahj. 1971. C1383
22 Baker, J. and Nicolson, E. W., eds. The commentary of Rabbi David Kimhi on Psalms CXX-CL. 1972. C1384

CAMDEN SOCIETY. PUBLICATIONS (Nichols)

1 Bruce, J., ed. Historie of the arrivall of Edward IV in England and the finall recouerye of his kingdomes from Henry VI, ed. by Collier. 1838. C1385
2 Bale, J. Kynge Johan, ed. by Collier. 1838. C1386
3 Wright, T., ed. Alliterative poem on the deposition of King Richard II. 1838. C1387
4 Plumpton correspondence, ed. by Stapleton. 1839. C1388
5 Thoms, W. J., ed. Anecdotes and traditions. 1839. C1389
6 Wright, T., ed. The political songs of England. 1839. C1390
7 Hayward, J. Annals of the first four years of the reign of Queen Elizabeth, ed. by Bruce. 1840. C1391
8 Hunter, J., ed. Ecclesiastical documents... 1840. C1392
9 Norden, J. Speculi Britanniae pars, ed. by Ellis. 1840. C1393
10 Warkworth, J. A chronicle of the first thirteen years of the reign of King Edward the Fourth, ed. by Halliwell-Phillipps. 1839. C1394
11 Kemp, W. Kemp's nine daies wonder..., ed. by Dyce. 1840. C1395
12 Ellesmere, F. E. The Egerton papers, ed. by Collier. 1840. C1396
13 Jocelin de Brakelond. Chronica Jocelini de Brakelonda, ed. by Rokewode. 1840. C1397
14 Croker, T. C., ed. Narratives illustrative of the contests in Ireland in 1641 and 1690. 1841. C1398
15 Rishanger, W. The chronicles of the baron's wars, ed. by Halliwell-Phillipps. 1840. C1399
16 Map, W. The Latin poems commonly attributed to Walter Mapes, ed. by Wright. 1841. C1400
17 Nucius, N. The second book of the travels of Nicander Nucius of Corcyra, ed. by Cramer and Fidler. 1841. C1401
18 Robson, J., ed. Three early English metrical romances. 1842. C1402
19 Dee, J. The private diary of Dr. John Dee, ed. by Halliwell-Phillipps. 1842. C1403
20 Wycliffe, J. An apology for Lollard doctrines, ed. by Todd. 1842. C1404
21 Rutland, J. H. M. Rutland papers, ed. by Jerdan. 1842. C1405
22 Cartwright, T. The diary of Dr. Thomas Cartwright, ed. by Hunter. 1843. C1406
23 Ellis, H., ed. Original letters of eminent literary men of the sixteenth, seventeenth, and eighteenth centuries. 1843. C1407
24 Kyteler, A. A contemporary narrative of the proceedings against Dame Alice

Kyteler, ed. by Wright. 1843. C1408

25 Galfridus Anglicus. Promptorium parvulorum sive clericorum... ed. by Way. V. 1. 1843. C1409

26 Wright, T., ed. Three chapters of letters relating to the suppression of monasteries. 1843. C1410

27 Leicester, R. D. Correspondence of Robert Dudley... ed. by Bruce. 1844. C1411

28 Croniques de London, ed. by Aungier. 1844. C1412

29 Vergilius Maro, P. Three books of Polydore Vergil's English history..., ed. by Ellis. 1844. C1413

30 Halliwell-Phillips, J. O., ed. The Thornton romances. 1844. C1414

31 Verney, R. Verney papers, ed. by Bruce. 1845. C1415

32 Bramston, J. The autobiography of Sir John Bramston, ed. by Braybrooke. 1845. C1416

33 Perth, J. D. Letters from James earl of Perth, ed. by Jerdan. 1845. C1417

34 Fitz-Thedmar, A. De antiquis legibus liber, ed. by Stapleton. 1846. C1418

35 Turpyn, R. The chronicle of Calais, ed. by Nichols. 1846. C1419

36 Vergilius Maro, P. Polydore Vergil's English history..., ed. by Ellis. 1846. C1420

37 A relation, or rather A true account, of the island of England, ed. by Sneyd. 1847. C1421

38 Atthill, W. L., ed. Documents relating to the foundation and antiquities of the collegiate church of Middleham. 1847. C1422

39 The Camden miscellany. V. 1. 1847. C1423

40 Grey de Wilton, A. G. A commentary of the services and charges of William lord Grey of Wilton, ed. by Grey-Egerton. 1847. C1424

41 Yonge, W. Diary written at Colyton and Axminster, Co. Devon, from 1604-1628, ed. by Roberts. 1848. C1425

42 Machin, H. The diary of Henry Machyn..., ed. by Nichols. 1848. C1426

43 Charles, N. The visitation of the county of Huntingdom, ed. by Ellis. 1849. C1427

44 Smith, R. The obituary of Richard Smyth, ed. by Ellis. 1849. C1428

45 Twysden, R. Certaine considerations upon the government of England, ed. by Kemble. 1849. C1429

46 Elizabeth, queen of England. Letters of Queen Elizabeth and King James VI of Scotland, ed. by Bruce. 1849. C1430

47 Chronicon petroburgense, ed. by Stapleton. 1849. C1431

48 The chronicle of Queen Jane, and of two years of Queen Mary, ed. by Nichols. 1850. C1432

49 Tymms, S., ed. Wills and inventories from the registers of the commissary of Bury St. Edmunds and the archdeacon of Sudbury. 1850. C1433

50 Map, W. Gualteri Mapes De nugis curialium distinctions quinque, ed. by Wright. 1850. C1434

51 The pylgrymage of Sir Richard Guylforde to the Holy Land, A.D. 1506, ed. by Ellis. 1851. C1435

52 Guy, H. Moneys received and paid for secret service of Charles II, and James II..., ed. by Akerman. 1851. C1436

53 London. Grey friars. Chronicles of the Grey friars of London, ed. by Nichols. 1852. C1437

54 Same as no. 25. V. 2. 1853. C1438

55 Same as no. 39. V. 2. 1853. C1439

56 Verney family. Letters and papers of the Verney family down to the end of the year 1639, ed. by Bruce. 1853. C1440

57 Ancren riwle. The ancren riwle, ed. by Morton. 1853. C1441

58 Harley, B. (Conway). Letters of the Lady Brilliana Harley, ed. by Lewis. 1854. C1442

59 Kemeseye, J. de. A roll of the household expenses of Richard de Swinfield, ed. by Webb. V. 1. 1854. C1443

60 Gt. Brit. Sovereigns, etc. Grants, etc. from the crown during the reign of Edward the Fifth, ed. by Nichols. 1854. C1444

61 Same as no. 39. V. 3. 1855. C1445

62 Same as no. 59. V. 2. 1855. C1446

63 Charles I, king of Gt. Britain. Charles I in 1646, ed. by Bruce. 1856. C1447

64 Chronicles of England. An English chronicle of the reigns of Richard II, Henry IV, Henry V, and Henry VI written before 1471, ed. by Davies. 1856. C1448

65 Philippus. The Knights hospitalers in England, ed. by Larking. 1857. C1449

66 Rous, J. Diary of John Rous, ed. by Green. 1856. C1450

67 Trevelyan papers, ed. by Collier, Pt. 1. 1857. C1451

68 Davies, R. Journal of the Very Rev. Rowland Davies, ed. by Caulfield. 1857. C1452

69 London. St. Paul's cathedral. The domesday of St. Paul's of the year MCCXXII, ed. by Hale. 1858. C1453

70 Whitelocke, J. Liber famelicus of Sir James Whitelock, ed. by Bruce. 1858. C1454

71 Savile, H. Savile correspondence, ed. by Cooper. 1858. C1455

72 Philippe de Remi. The romance of Blonde of Oxford and Jehan of Dammartin, ed. by Le Roux de Lincy. 1858. C1456

73 Same as no. 39. V. 4. 1859. C1457

74 Symonds, R. Diary of the marches of the royal army during the great civil war, ed. by Long. 1859. C1458

75 Hamilton, W. D., ed. Original papers illustrative of the life and writings of John Milton. 1859. C1459

76 Totnes, G. C. Letters from George lord Carew to Sir Thomas Roe, ed. by Maclean. 1860. C1460

77 Nichols, J. G., ed. Narrative of the days of the reformation, ed. by Foxe. 1859. C1461

78 James I, king of Gt. Britain. Correspondence of King James VI of Scotland with Sir Robert Cecil and others..., ed. by Bruce. 1861. C1462

79 Chamberlain, J. Letters written by John Chamberlain during the reign of Queen Elizabeth, ed. by Williams. 1861. C1463

80 Larking, L. B., ed. Proceedings principally in the county of Kent, in connection with the Parliaments called in 1640...1862. C1464

81 Gt. Brit. Parliament. Parliamentary debates in 1610, ed. by Gardiner. 1862. C1465

82 Cooper, W. D. Lists of foreign Protestants, and aliens, resident in England 1618-1688. 1862. C1466

83 Canterbury, Eng. Wills from Doctors' commons, ed. by Nichols and Bruce. 1863. C1467

84 Same as no. 67. Pt. 2. 1863. C1468

85 The life of Marmaduke Rawdon of York, ed. by Davies. 1863. C1469

86 Monro, C., ed. Letters of Queen Margaret of Anjou and Bishop Beckington and others. 1863. C1470

87 Same as no. 39. V. 5. 1864. C1471

88 Salisbury, R. C. Letters from Sir Robert Cecil and Sir George Carew, ed. by Maclean. 1864. C1472

89 Same as no. 25. V. 3. 1865. C1473
90 Gardiner, S. R., ed. Letters and other documents illustrating the relations between England and Germany at the commencement of the Thirty Years' War. V. 1. 1865. C1474
91 Worcester cathedral. Registrum, ed. by Hale. 1865. C1475
92 Bargrave, J. Pope Alexander the Seventh and the College of cardinals, Robertson. 1867. C1476
93 Crosby, A. J., ed. Accounts and papers relating to Mary queen of Scots, ed. by Crosby and Bruce. 1867. C1477
94 Dingley, T. History from marble. V. 1. 1867. C1478
95 Levens, P. Manipulus vocabulorum, ed. by Wheatley. 1867. C1479
96 Digby, K. Journal of a voyage into the Mediterranean, ed. by Bruce. 1868. C1480
97 Same as no. 94. V. 2. 1868. C1481
98 Same as no. 90. V. 2. 1868. C1482
99 Manningham, J. Diary of John Manningham, ed. by Bruce. 1868. C1483
100 Borough, J. Notes on the treaty carried on at Ripon between King Charles I and the Convenanters of Scotland, A.D. 1640, ed. by Bruce. 1869. C1484
101 Francisco de Jesus. El hecho de los tratados del matrimonio pretendido for the Principe de Gales, ed. by Gardiner. 1869. C1485
102 Ludlow, Eng. Churchwardens' accounts of the town of Ludlow, in Shopshire, from 1540 to the end of the reign of Queen Elizabeth, ed. by Wright. 1869. C1486
103 Gt. Brit. Parliament. Notes on the House of lords..., ed. by Gardiner. 1870. C1487
104 Same as no. 39. V. 6. 1870. C1488
105 Trevelyan papers, ed. by Trevelyan. Pt. 3. 1872. C1489

CAMDEN SOCIETY. PUBLICATIONS. NEW SERIES
(v. 1-55 Nichols, v. 56-62 Royal Hist. Soc.) Camden and Royal Historical Societies amalgamated in 1897. V. 56- pub. by Royal Historical Society.

1 Fortescue, G. M. The Fortescue papers..., ed. by Gardiner. 1871. C1490
2 Shillingford, J. Letters and papers of John Shillingford, ed. by Moore. 1871. C1491
3 St. James's Palace. The old checque book...of the Chapel Royal from 1561 to 1744, ed. by Rimbault. 1872. C1492
4 Bedell, W. A true relation of the life and death of the Right Reverend father in God William Bedell..., ed. by Jones. 1872. C1493
5 Bristol, Eng. The maire of Bristowe is kalendar, ed. by Smith. 1872. C1494
6 Gt. Brit. Parliament, 1625. Debates in the House of commons in 1625, ed. by Gardiner. 1873. C1495
7 Roe, sect. to Colonel John Birch. Military memoirs of Colonel John Birch..., ed. by J. and T. W. Webb. 1873. C1496
8-9 Christie, W. D. Letters addressed from London to Sir Joseph Williamson... 2 v. 1874. C1497
10 Hale, W. H., ed. Account of the executors of Richard, bishop of London 1303. 1874. C1498
11 Wriothesley, C. A chronicle of England during the reigns of the Tudors..., ed. by Hamilton. V. 1. 1875. C1499
12 Masson, D., ed. The quarrel between the Earl of Manchester and Oliver Cromwell. 1875. C1500
13 Halkett, A. The autobiography of Anne lady Halkett, ed. by Nichols. 1875. C1501
14 The Camden miscellany.

V. 7. 1875. C1502
15 Prideaux, H. Letters of Humphrey Prideaux..., ed. by Thompson. 1875. C1503
16 Milton, J. A common-place book of John Milton..., ed. by Horwood. 1876. C1504
17 Gardiner, S. R., ed. The historical collections of a citizen of London in the fifteenth century. 1876. C1505
18 ____. Documents relating to the proceedings against William Prynne, in 1634 and 1637. 1877. C1506
19 Sheppard, J. B., ed. Christ church letters. 1877. C1507
20 Same as no. 11. V. 2. 1877. C1508
21 Harpsfield, N. A treatise on the pretended divorce between Henry VIII and Catherine of Aragon, ed. by Pocock. 1878. C1509
22-23 Thompson, E. M., ed. Correspondence of the family of Hatton. 2 v. 1878. C1510
24 Great Britain Parliament. Notes on the debates in the House of lords..., ed. by Gardiner. 1879. C1511
25 Harris, A. The oeconomy of the Fleete..., ed. by Jessopp. 1879. C1512
26 Simpson, W. S., ed. Documents illustrating the history of S. Paul's Cathedral. 1880. C1513
27 Hamilton, W. H. The Hamilton papers..., ed. by Gardiner. 1880. C1514
28 Gardiner, J. Three fifteenth-century chronicles, ed. by Stowe. 1880. C1515
29 Oxford. Univ. The register of the visitors of the University of Oxford, from A.D. 1647 to A.D. 1658, ed. by Burrows. 1881. C1516
30 Catholicon Anglicum, ed. by Herrtage. 1881. C1517
31 Same as no. 14. V. 8. 1883. C1518
32 Glanville, J. The voyage to Cadiz in 1625, ed. by Grosart. 1883. C1519
33 Harvey, G. Letter-book of Gabriel Harvey, A.D. 1573-1580, ed. by Scott. 1884. C1520
34 Lauderdale, J. M. The Lauderdale papers, ed. by Airy. V. 1. 1884. C1521
35 Leeds, F. G. O. The political memoranda of Francis fifth duke of Leeds, ed. by Browning. 1884. C1522
36 Same as no. 34. V. 2. 1884. C1523
37 Pocock, N., ed. Troubles connected with the prayer book 1549. 1884. C1524
38 Same as no. 34. V. 3. 1885. C1525
39 Gt. Brit. Court of Star Chamber. Reports of cases in the courts of Star chamber and High commission, ed. by Gardinier. 1886. C1526
40 Nicholas, E. The Nicholas papers, ed. by Warner. V. 1. 1886. C1527
41 Battle Abbey. Custumals of Battle Abbey, ed. by Scargill-Bird. 1887. C1528
42 Pococke, R. The travels through England of Dr. Richard Pococke..., ed. by Cartwright. V. 1. 1888. C1529
43 Norwich, Eng. Visitations of the diocese of Norwich, A.D. 1492-1532, ed. by Jessopp. 1888. C1530
44 Same as no. 42. V. 2. 1889. C1531
45 Gardiner, S. R., ed. Documents illustrating the impeachment of the Duke of Buckingham in 1626. 1889. C1532
46 Memoirs relating to Lord Torrington, ed. by Laughton. 1889. C1533
47 Essex, A. C. Selections from the correspondence of Arthur Capel, ed. by Airy. V. 1. 1890. C1534
48 Southwell, cathedral. Visitations and memorials of Southwell minister, ed. by Leach. 1891. C1535
49 Clarke, W. The Clarke papers, ed. by Firth. V. 1. 1891. C1536

50 Same as no. 40. V. 2. 1892. C1537
51 Abingdon abbey. Accounts of the obedientiars of Abingdon Abbey, ed. by Kirk. 1892. C1538
52 Kyngeston, R. Expeditions to Prussia and Holy Land made by Henry IV..., ed. by Smith. 1894. C1539
53 Same as no. 14. V. 9. 1895. C1540
54 Same as no. 49. V. 2. 1894. C1541
55 London. St. Paul's cathedral. Visitations of churches belonging to St. Paul's Cathedral in 1297 and in 1458. 1895. C1542
56 Law, T. G., ed. The archpriest controversy. V. 1. 1896. C1543
57 Same as no. 40. V. 4. 1920. C1544
58 Same as no. 56. V. 2. 1898. C1545
59 Newcastle, T. P-H. A narrative of the changes in the ministry, 1765-1767, ed. by Bateson. 1898. C1546
60 Venables, R. The narrative of General Venables, ed. by Firth. 1900. C1547
61 Same as no. 49. V. 3. 1899. C1548
62 Same as no. 49. V. 4. 1901. C1549

CANADA IN THE ATLANTIC ECONOMY (Univ. of Toronto Pr.)

1 Slater, D. W. World trade and economic growth. 1968. C1550
2 English, H. E. Transatlantic economic community. 1968. C1551
3 Johnson, H. G. and others. Harmonization of national economic policies under free trade. 1968. C1552
4 Trant, G. I. Trade liberalization and Canadian agriculture. 1968. C1553
5 Haviland, W. E. Trade liberalization and the Canadian pulp and paper industry. 1968. C1554
6 Bond, D. E. Trade liberalization and the Canadian furniture industry. 1968. C1555
7 Singer, J. J. Trade liberalization and the Canadian steel industry. 1969. C1556
8 Munro, J. M. Trade liberalization and transportation in international trade. 1969. C1557
9 Shibita, H. Fiscal harmonization under freer trade. 1969. C1558
10 Caves, R. E. and Reuber, G. L. Canadian economic policy and the impact of international capital flows. 1969. C1559
11 Shearer, R. A. and others. Trade liberalization and a regional economy. 1971. C1560
12 Matthews, R. Industrial viability in a free trade economy. 1971. C1561
13 English, H. E. and others. Canada in a wider economic community. 1972. C1562

CANADIAN CENTENARY SERIES (McClelland)

1 Oleson, T. J. Early voyages and northern approaches, 1000-1632. 1964. C1563
2 Trudel, M. The beginnings of New France, 1524-1663, tr. by Claxton. 1973. C1564
3 Eccles, W. J. Canada under Louis XIV. 1964. C1565
5 Stanley, G. F. G. New France, 1744-1760. 1968. C1566
6 Neatby, H. M. Quebec. 1968. C1567
7 Craig, G. M. Upper Canada; the formative years, 1784-1841. 1963. C1568
9 MacNutt, W. S. The Atlantic provinces, 1712-1857. 1965. C1569
10 Careless, J. M. S. The union of the Canadas. 1967. C1570
11 Rich, E. E. The fur trade and the Northwest to 1857.

1967. C1571
12 Morton, W. L. The critical years: the union of British North America, 1857-1873. 1964. C1572
13 Waite, P. B. Canada, 1874-1896. 1971. C1573
16 Zaslow, M. The opening of the Canadian North, 1870-1914. 1971. C1574

CANADIAN CENTENNIAL SERIES (Univ. of Toronto Pr.)

1 Kaye, V. J. Early Ukrainian settlement in Canada, 1895-1900... 1964. C1575
Luchkovich, M. A Ukrainian Canadian in Parliament. 1965. C1576

CANADIAN FRONTIERS OF SETTLEMENT (Macmillian)

1 Mackintosh, W. A. Prairie settlement. 1934. C1577
2 Martin, C. Dominion lands policy. 1939. C1578
Morton, A. S. History of prairie settlement. 1939. C1579
4 Mackintosh, W. A. and others. Economic problems of the prairie provinces. 1935. C1580
5 Murchie, R. W. and others. Agricultural progress on the prairie frontier. 1936. C1581
6 Dawson, C. A. and Murchie, R. W. The settlement of the Peace River country. 1934. C1582
7 Dawson, C. A. Group settlement. 1936. C1583
8 Dawson, C. A. and Younge, E. R. Pioneering in the prairie provinces. 1940. C1584
9 Inness, H. A. Settlement and the mining frontier. 1936. C1585
Lower, A. R. M. Settlement and the forest frontier in eastern Canada. 1936. C1586

CANADIAN GOVERNMENT SERIES (Univ. of Toronto Pr.)

1 Corry, J. A. Democratic government and politics. 1959. C1587
2 Dawson, R. M. The government of Canada. 1957. C1588
3 Gérin-Lajoie, P. Constitutional amendment in Canada. 1950. C1589
4 Ward, N. The Canadian house of Commons. 1950. C1590
5 McKinnon, F. The government of Prince Edward Island. 1951. C1591
6 Crawford, K. G. Canadian municipal government. 1954. C1592
7 Hodgetts, J. E. Pioneer public service. 1956. C1593
8 Beck, J. M. The government of Nova Scotia. 1957. C1594
9 Saywell, J. T. The office of Lieutenant-Governor. 1957. C1595
10 Thorburn, H. G. Politics in New Brunswick. 1961. C1596
11 Ward, N. The public purse. 1962. C1597
12 Dawson, W. F. Procedure in the Canadian House of Commons. 1962. C1598
13 Meisel, J. The Canadian general election of 1957. 1962. C1599
14 Donnelly, M. S. The Government of Manitoba. 1963. C1600
15 Kunz, F. A. The modern Senate of Canada, 1925-1963. 1965. C1601
16 Schindeler, F. F. Responsible government in Ontario. 1969. C1602
17 Noel, S. J. R. Politics in Newfoundland. 1971. C1603

CANADIAN HISTORICAL CONTROVERSIES SERIES (Prentice-Hall)

Burroughs, P. British attitudes toward Canada, 1822-1849. 1971. C1604
Herstein, H. and others. Challenge & survival. 1970. C1605
Neatby, H. M. The Quebec Act. 1972. C1606
Rawlyk, G. A. Revolution

rejected, 1775-1776. 1968. C1607

Zoltvany, Y. F. The government of New France. 1971. C1608

CANADIAN HISTORICAL DOCUMENTS SERIES (Prentice-Hall of Canada, Scarborough, Ont.)

1 Nish, C., tr. and ed. The French régime. 1965. C1609
2 Waite, P. B., ed. Pre-Confederation. 1965. C1610
3 Browne, R. C. and Prang, M. E., eds. Confederation to 1949. 1966. C1611

CANADIAN HISTORICAL READINGS (Univ. of Toronto Pr.)

1 Approaches to Canadian history; essays by Mackintosh and others. 1967. C1612
2 Upper Canadian politics in the 1850's, by Underhill and others. 1967. C1613
3 Confederation; essays by Creighton and others. 1967. C1614
4 Politics of discontent; essays by H. J. Schultz and others. 1967. C1615
5 Constitutionalism and nationalism in Lower Canada, ed. by Cook. 1969. C1616
6 Imperial relations in the age of Laurier, ed. by Berger. 1969. C1617
7 Minorities, schools, and politics, ed. by Brown. 1969. C1618
8 Conscription, ed. by Berger. 1969. C1619

CANADIAN HISTORY SERIES (Doubleday)

1 Costain, T. B. The white and gold. 1954. C1620
2 Rutledge, J. L. Century of conflict. 1956. C1621
3 Raddall, T. H. The path of destiny. 1957. C1622
4 Hardy, W. G. From sea unto sea. 1960. C1623
5 Allen, R. Ordeal by fire. 1961. C1624
6 Fraser, B. The search for identity: Canada, 1945-1967. 1967. C1625

CANADIAN STUDIES IN ECONOMICS (Univ. of Toronto Pr.)

1 Malach, V. W. International cycles and Canada's balance of payments. 1921-33. 1954. C1626
2 Buckley, K. Capital formation in Canada, 1896-1930. 1955. C1627
3 Scott, A. Natural resources. 1955. C1628
4 Main, O. W. The Canadian nickel industry. 1955. C1629
5 Neufeld, E. P. Bank of Canada operations, 1935-54. 1955. C1630
6 Logan, H. A. State intervention and assistance in collective bargaining. 1956. C1631
7 Phillips, W. G. The agricultural implement industry in Canada. 1956. C1632
8 Brecher, I. Monetary and fiscal thought and policy in Canada, 1919-1939. 1957. C1633
9 Blake, G. Customs administration in Canada. 1957. C1634
10 Barber, C. L. Inventories and the business cycle with special reference to Canada. 1958. C1635
11 Safarian, A. E. The Canadian economy in the great depression. 1959. C1636
12 Reuber, G. L. Britain's export trade with Canada. 1960. C1637
13 Wonnacott, P. The Canadian dollar, 1948-1958. 1961. C1638
14 Hartle, D. G. The employment forecast survey. 1962. C1639
15 Kemp, M. C. The demand for Canadian imports, 1926-1955. 1962. C1640
16 Winch, D. M. The economics of highway planning. 1963. C1641
17 Stykolt, S. Economic analysis and combines policy.

1965. C1642
18 Due, J. F. The intercity electric railway industry in Canada. 1966. C1643
19 Lithwick, N. H. Economic growth in Canada. 1966. C1644
20 Triantis, S. G. Cyclical changes in trade balance of countries exporting primary products. 1967. C1645
21 Green, A. G. Regional aspects of Canada's economic growth. 1969. C1646
22 Thompson, R. W. International trade and domestic prosperity. 1970. C1647
23 Smith, L. B. The postwar Canadian housing and residential mortgage markets and the role of government. 1974. C1648

CANADIAN STUDIES IN HISTORY AND GOVERNMENT (Univ. of Toronto Pr.)

1 Moir, J. S. Church and State in Canada West. 1959. C1649
2 Thompson, F. F. The French shore problem in Newfoundland. 1961. C1650
3 Cornell, P. G. The alignment of political groups in Canada, 1841-1867. 1962. C1651
4 Kelsen, R. N. The private member of Parliament and the formation of public policy. 1964. C1652
5 McCabe, J. O. The San Juan boundary question. 1964. C1653
6 Mathews, H. C. The mark of honour. 1965. C1654
7 Gunn, G. E. The political history of Newfoundland. 1966. C1655
8 Wilson, A. Upper Canada's clergy reserves. 1967. C1656
9 Gates, L. T. The land policies of Upper Canada. 1967. C1657
10 Rodney, W. Soldiers of the International. 1968. C1658
11 Dalton, R. C. The Jesuits' Estates question, 1760-1888. 1967. C1659
12 Morrison, D. R. The politics of the Yukon Territory. 1968. C1660
13 Garner, J. The franchise and politics. 1969. C1661
14 Ormsby, W. The emergence of the federal concept in Canada. 1969. C1662

CANADIAN STUDIES IN SOCIOLOGY (Univ. of Toronto Pr.)

1 Zakuta, L. A protest movement becalmed. 1964. C1663
2 Richmond, A. H. Post-war immigrants in Canada. 1967. C1664

CARIBBEAN SERIES (Yale Univ. Pr.)

1 Hall, D. Free Jamaica. 1959. C1665
2 Zayas Alvarado, E. Worker in the cane. 1960. C1666
3 Maunder, W. F. Employment in an underdeveloped area. 1960. C1667
4 Whetten, N. L. Guatemala. 1961. C1668
5 Smith, M. G. Kinship and community in Carricow. 1962. C1669
6 Rouse, I. and Cruxent, J. M. Venezuelan archaeology. 1963. C1670
7 Guerra y Sanchez, R. Sugar and society in the Caribbean. 1964. C1671
8 Goveia, E. V. Slave society in the British Leeward islands at the end of the eighteenth century. 1965. C1672
9 Leyburn, J. G. The Haitian people. 1966. C1673
10 O'Loughlin, C. Economic and political change in the Leeward and Windward Islands. 1968. C1674
11 Hale, C. A. Mexican liberalism in the age of Mora. 1968. C1675
12 Singham, A. W. The hero and the crowd in a colonial polity. 1968. C1676
13 Adamson, A. H. Sugar without slaves. 1972. C1677
14 Wilson, P. J. Crab antics. 1973. C1678

CARNEGIE CORPORATION OF NEW YORK. THE NEGRO IN AMERICAN LIFE (Harper)

Herskovits, M. J. The myth of the Negro past. 1941. C1679
Johnson, C. S. Patterns of Negro segregation. 1943. C1680
Klineberg, O., ed. Characteristics of the American Negro. 1944. C1681
Myrdal, G. An American dilemma. 2 v. 1962. C1682
Sterner, R. M. E. and others. The Negro's share. 1943. C1683

CARNEGIE ENDOWMENT FOR INTERNATIONAL PEACE. DIVISION OF INTERNATIONAL LAW. STUDIES IN THE ADMINISTRATION OF INTERNATIONAL LAW AND ORGANIZATION (Columbia Univ.)

1 Carnegie Endowment for International Peace. The international law of the future. 1944. C1684
2 Hudson, M. O. International tribunals. 1944. C1685
3 Ranshofen-Wertheimer, E. F. The international Secretariat. 1945. C1686
4 Pastuhov, V. D. A guide to the practice of international conferences. 1945. C1687
5 Azcárate y Flórez, P. de. League of Nations and national minorities. 1945. C1688
6 Hill, W. M. The economic and financial organization of the League of Nations. 1946. C1689
7 Renborg, B. A. International drug control. 1947. C1690
8 Hill, W. M. Immunities and privileges of international officials. 1947. C1691
9 Hall, H. D. Mandates, dependencies and trusteeship. 1948. C1692
10 Viner, J. The customs union issue. 1950. C1693
Hall, H. D. The League mandate system and the problem of dependencies. 1945. C1694

CARNEGIE INSTITUTION OF WASHINGTON. PUBLICATIONS.

1 Carnegie institution of Washington. The Carnegie institution of Washington. 1902. C1695
2 ____. Articles of incorporation. 1902. C1696
3 ____. Proceedings of the board of trustees. 1902. C1697
4 Conrad, H. S. The water-lilies. 1905. C1698
5 Burham, S. W. A general catalogue of double stars within 121° of the North pole 1906. C1699
6 Coville, F. V. and MacDougal, D. T. Desert botanical laboratory of the Carnegie institution. 1903. C1700
7 Richards, T. W. and Stull, W. N. New method for determining compressibility. 1903. C1701
8 Farlow, W. G. Bibliographical index of North American fungi. V. 1. 1905. C1702
9 Hill, G. W. The collected mathematical works of George W. Hill. 4 v. 1905-07. C1703
10 Newcomb, S. On the position of the galactic and other principal planes toward which the stars tend to crowd. 1904. C1704
11 ____. A statistical inquiry into the probability of causes of the production of sex in human offspring. 1904. C1705
12 Noguchi, H. The action of snake venom upon cold-blooded animals. 1904. C1706
13 Adams, E. D. The influence of Grenville on Pitt's foreign policy. 1787-98. 1904. C1707
14 Van Tyne, C. H. and Leland, W. G. Guide to the archives of the government of the United States in Washington. 1904. C1708
15 Mottier, D. M. Fecundation in plants. 1904. C1709

16 Jennings, H. S. Contributions to the study of the behavior of lower organisms. 1904. C1710
17 Dorsey, G. A. Traditions of the Arikara. 1904. C1711
18 Morse, A. P. Researches on North American Acridiidae. 1904. C1712
19 Enteman, W. M. Coloration in Polistes. 1904. C1713
20 Duerden, J. E. The coral Siderastrea radians and its postlarval development. 1904. C1714
21 Dorsey, G. A. The mythology of the Wichita. 1904. C1715
22 McLaughlin, A. C. Report on the diplomatic archives of the Department of state, 1789-1840. 1906. C1716
23 Castle, W. E. Heredity of coat characters in guinea-pigs and rabbits. 1905. C1717
24 MacDougal, D. T. and others. Mutants and hybrids of the oenotheras. 1905. C1718
25 Gulick, J. T. Evolution, racial and habitudinal. 1905. C1719
26 Pumpelly, R. and others. Explorations in Turkestan. 1904. C1720
27 Smith, E. F. Bacteria in relation to plant diseases. 3 v. 1905-14. C1721
28 Richards, T. W. and Roger, C. W. A revision of the atomic weights of sodium and chlorine. 1905. C1722
29 Baird, J. W. The color sensitivity of the peripheral retina. 1905. C1723
30 Shull, G. H. Stages in the development of Sium cicutaefolium. 1905. C1724
31 Day, A. L. and others. The isomorphism and thermal properties of feldspars. 1905. C1725
32 Dean, B. Chimaeroid fishes and their development. 1906. C1726
33 Parkhurst, J. A. Researches in stellar photometry during the years 1894 to 1906. 1906. C1727
34 Wieland, G. R. American fossil cycads. 2 v. 1906-16. C1728
35 Coblentz, W. W. Investigations of infra-red spectra. 3 v. 1905-08. C1729
36 Stevens, N. M. Studies in spermatogenesis. 2 v. 1905-06. C1730
37 Harper, R. A. Sexual reproduction and the organization of the nucleus in certain mildews. 1905. C1731
38 Writings on history... 1903. 1905. C1732
39 Handbook of learned societies and institutions: America, ed. by Thompson. 1908. C1733
40 Barus, C. The nucleation of the uncontaminated atmosphere. 1906. C1734
41 Dorsey, G. A. Traditions of the Caddo. 1905. C1735
42 Atwater, W. O. and Benedict, F. G. A respiration calorimeter with applicances for the direct determination of oxygen. 1905. C1736
43 Peters, C. H. F. Heliographic position of sunspots. 1907. C1737
44 Scripture, E. W. Researches in experimental phonetics. 1906. C1738
45 Furness, C. E. Catalogue of stars within two degrees of the North Pole. 1905. C1739
46 Adams, F. D. and Coker, E. G. An investigation into the elastic constants of rocks. 1906. C1740
47 Mayer, A. G. Rhythmical pulsation in Scyphomedusoe. 1906. C1741
48-49 Carnegie institution of Washington. Dept. of genetics. Station for experimental evolution... Papers. 1906. C1742
50 Livingston, B. E. The relation of desert plants to soil moisture and to evaporation. 1906. C1743
51 Stevens, N. M. Studies on the germ cells of aphids. 1906. C1744
52 Davenport, C. B. Inheritance

in poultry. 1906. C1745
53 Müller, W. M. Egypotological researches. 3 v. 1904-20. C1746
54 Carnegie institution of Washington. Research in China. 3 v. 1907-13. C1747
55 Case, E. C. Revision of the Pelycosauria of North America. 1907. C1748
56 Richards, T. W. and Forbes, F. S. Energy changes involved in the dilution of zinc and cadmium amalgams. 1906. C1749
57 Washington, H. S. The Roman comagmatic region. 1906. C1750
58 Pearl, R. and others. Variation and differentiation in Cerato phyllum. 1907. C1751
59 Dorsey, G. A. The Pawnee. 1906. C1752
60 Jones, H. C. and others. Hydrates in aqueous solution. 1907. C1753
61 Richards, T. W. and Behr, G. T. The electromotive force of iron under varying conditions. 1906. C1754
62 Barus, C. Condensation of vapor as induced by nuclei and ions. 1907. C1755
63 Noyes, A. A., ed. The electrical conductivity of aqueous solutions. 1907. C1756
64 Pearl, R. and Clawson, A. B. Variation and correlation in the crayfish. 1907. C1757
65 Same as no. 35. V. 2. 1906. C1758
66 Goss, W. F. M. High steam-pressures in locomotive service. 1907. C1759
67 Banta, A. M. The fauna of Mayfield's Cave. 1907. C1760
68 Morse, A. P. Further researches on North American Acridiidae. 1907. C1761
69 Richards, T. W. and others. Further researches concerning the atomic weights of potassium... 1907. C1762
70 MacCurdy, H. and Castle, W. E. Selection and cross-breeding in relation to the inheritance of coat-pigments and coat-patterns in rats and guinea-pigs. 1907. C1763
71 Uhler, H. S. and Wood, R. W. Atlas of absorption spectra. 1907. C1764
72 Newcomb, S. and Ross, F. E. Investigation of inequalities in the motion of the moon produced by the action of the planets. 1907. C1765
73 Pumpelly, R., ed. Explorations in Turkestan. 2 v. 1908. C1766
74 Arthur, King. The vulgate version of the Arthurian romances, ed. by Sommer. 7 v. 1908-16. C1767
75 Hay, O. P. The fossil turtles of North America. 1908. C1768
76 Richards, T. W. and others. Compressibilities of the elements and their periodic relations. 1907. C1769
77 Benedict, F. G. The influence of inanition of metabolism. 1907. C1770
78 Shaw, J. B. Synopsis of linear associative algebra. 1907. C1771
79 Durand, W. F. Researches on the performance of the screw propeller. 1907. C1772
80 Jones, H. C. and others. Conductivity and viscosity in mixed solvents. 1907. C1773
81 Macdougal, D. T. and others. Mutations, variations, and relationships of the Oenotheras. 1907. C1774
82 Lloyd, F. E. The physiology of stomata. 1908. C1775
83 Pérez, L. M. Guide to the materials for American history in Cuban archives. 1907. C1776
84 Osborne, T. B. The proteins of the wheat kernel. 1907. C1777
85 Hasse, A. R. Index of economic material in documents of the states of the United States. (Cali., Dela., Ill., Ky., Me., Mass., N. H., N. J., N. Y., Ohio, 2 pts., Penna., 3 pts., R. I., Vt.). 1907-22. C1778

86 Ptolemaeus, C. Ptolemy's catalogue of stars, ed. by Peters and Pnobel. 1915. C1779
87 California. State earthquake investigation commission. The California earthquake of April 18, 1906. 2 v. 1908-10. C1780
88 Bjerknes, V. and others. Dynamic meteorology and hydrography. 2 pts. 1910-11. C1781
89 The Old yellow book, ed. by Hodell. 1916. C1782
90 Andrews, C. M. and Davenport, F. G. Guide to the manuscript materials for the history of the United States, to 1783, in the British Museum... 1908. C1783
90a ____. Guide to the materials for American history, to 1783, in the Public Record Office of Great Britain. 2 v. 1912-14. C1784
90b Paullin, C. O. and Paxson, F. L. Guide to the materials in London archives for the history of the United States since 1783. 1914. C1785
91 Shepherd, W. R. Guide to the materials for the history of the United States in Spanish archives. 1907. C1786
92 Van Tyne, C. H. and Leland, W. G. Guide to the archives of the government of the United States in Washington. 1907. C1787
93 Hale, G. E. and Fox, P. The rotation period of the sun as determined from the motions of the calcium flocculi. 1908. C1788
94 Conrad, H. S. The structure and life-history of the hay-scented fern. 1908. C1789
95 Davenport, C. B. Inheritance in canaries. 1908. C1790
96 Barus, C. Condensation of vapor as induced by nuclei and ions. 2 pts. 1908-10. C1791
97 Same as no. 35. V. 3. 5 pts. 1908. C1792
98 Carnegie institution of Washington. Laboratory for plant physiology. Studies at the desert laboratory. 1908. C1793
99 Macdougal. D. T. Botanical features of North American deserts. 1908. C1794
100 Ward, W. H. The seal cylinders of western Asia. 1910. C1795
101 Lutz, F. E. The variation and correlation of certain taxonomic characters of Gryllus. 1908. C1796
102-103 Carnegie institution of Washington. Tortugas laboratory. Papers. V. 1, 2. 1908, 1910. C1797
104 Eigenmann, C. H. Cave vertebrates of America. 1909. C1798
105 Lehmer, D. N. Factor table for the first ten millions. 1956. C1799
106 Chamberlain, R. T. The gases in rocks. 1908. C1800
107 The tidal and other problems by Chamberlain and others. 2 v. 1909. C1801
108 Van Deman, E. B. The Atrium Vestae. 1909. C1802
109 Mayer, A. G. Medusae of the world. 3 v. 1910. C1803
110 Jones, H. C. and Anderson, J. A. The absorption spectra of solutions of certain salts of cobalt... 1909. C1804
111 Noguchi, H. Snake venoms. 1909. C1805
112 Shull, G. H. Bursa bursa-pastoris and Bursa heegeri. 1909. C1806
113 Spalding, V. M. Distribution and movement of desert plants. 1909. C1807
114 Castle, W. E. and others. Studies in inheritance in rabbits. 1909. C1808
115 Carnegie institution of Washington. Dept. of meridian astronomy. Preliminary general catalogue of 6188 stars for the epoch 1900. 1910. C1809
116 Reichert, E. T. and Brown, A. P. The differentiation and specificity of corresponding proteins. 1909. C1810
117 Cannon, W. A. Studies

in heredity as illustrated by the trichomes of species and hybrids of Juglans. 1908. C1811
118 Richards, T. W. and others. Electrochemical investigation of liquid amalgams of thallium... 1909. C1812
119 Perrine, C. D. and others. Determination of the solar parallax from photographs of Eros. 1910. C1813
120 Decker, F. F. The symmetric function tables of the fifteenthic. 1910. C1814
121 Davenport, C. B. Inheritance of characteristics in domestic fowl. 1909. C1815
122 Johnson, R. H. Determinate evolution in the color-pattern of the lady-beetles. 1910. C1816
123 Benedict, F. G. and Carpenter, T. M. Respiration calorimeters for studying the respiratory exchange and energy transformations of man. 1910. C1817
124 Robertson, J. A. List of documents in Spanish Archives relating to the history of the United States. 1910. C1818
125 Richards, T. W. and Willard, H. H. Determinations of atomic weights. 1910. C1819
126 Benedict, F. G. and Thorne, M. C. The metabolism and energy transformations of healthy man during rest. 1910. C1820
127 Goss, W. F. M. Superheated steam in locomotive service. 1910. C1821
128 Fish, C. R. Guide to the materials for American history in Roman and other Italian archives. 1911. C1822
129 Macdougal, D. T. and Cannon, W. A. The conditions of parasitism in plants. 1910. C1823
130 Jones, H. C. and Strong, W. W. A study of the absorption spectra of solutions of certain salts of potassium... 1910. C1824
131 Cannon, W. A. The root habits of desert plants. 1911. C1825
132-133 Same as no. 102. V. 3, 4. 1910-11. C1826
134 Churchill, W. The Polynesian wanderings. 1911. C1827
135 Baxter, G. P. and others. Researches upon the atomic weights of cadmium... 1910. C1828
136 Benedict, F. G. and Joslin, E. P. Metabolism in diabetes mellitus. 1910. C1829
137 Allison, W. H. Inventory of unpublished material for American religious history in Protestant church archives and other repositories. 1910. C1830
138 Adams, W. S. and Lasby, J. B. An investigation of the rotation period of the sun by spectroscopic methods. 1911. C1831
139 Lloyd, F. E. Guayule. 1911. C1832
140 Campbell, D. H. The Eusporangiatae. 1911. C1833
141 Macdougal, D. T. and Spalding, E. S. The water-balance of succulent plants. 1910. C1834
142 Long, J. A. and Mark, E. L. The maturation of the egg of the mouse. 1911. C1835
143 Lutz, F. E. Experiments with Drosophila ampelophila concerning evolution. 1911. C1836
144 Castle, W. E. and Phillips, J. C. On germinal transplantation in vertebrates. 1911. C1837
145 Case, E. C. A revision of the Cotylosauria of North America. 1911. C1838
146 ____. Revision of the Amphibia and Pisces of the permian of North America. 1911. C1839
147 Russell, H. N. Determinations of stellar parallax. 1911. C1840
148 Parker, D. W. Calendar of papers in Washington archives relating to the

territories of the United States. 1911. C1841
149 Barus, C. The production of elliptic interferences in relation to interferometry. 3 pts. 1911. C1842
150 Learned, M. D. Guide to the manuscript materials relating to American history in the German state archives. 1912. C1843
151 Stager, H. W. A Sylow factor table of the first twelve thousand numbers...1916. C1844
152 Nichols, E. L. and Merritt, E. Studies in luminescence. 1912. C1845
153 King, A. S. The influence of a magnetic field upon the spark spectra of iron and titanium. 1912. C1846
154 Churchill, W. Beach-la-mar. 1911. C1847
155 Benedict, F. G. and Slack, E. P. A comparative study of temperature fluctuations in different parts of the human body. 1911. C1848
156 Osborne, T. B. and others. Feed experiments with isolated food-substances. 1911. C1849
157 Day, A. L. and Sosman, R. B. High temperature gas thermometry. 1911. C1850
158 Wright, F. E. The methods of petrographic-microscopic research. 1911. C1851
159 Howard, L. O. and others. The mosquitoes of North and Central America and the West Indies. 4 v. 1912-27. C1852
160 Jones, H. C. and Strong, W. W. The absorption spectra of solutions of comparatively rare salts. 1911. C1853
161 Moulton, F. R. and others. Periodic orbits. 1920. C1854
162 Mayer, A. G. Ctenophores of the Atlantic coast of North America. 1912. C1855
163 Bolton, H. E. Guide to materials for the history of the United States in the principal archives of Mexico. 1913. C1856
164 Coblentz, W. W. A physical study of the firefly. 1912. C1857
165 Lehmer, D. N. List of prime numbers from 1 to 10,006,721. 1914. C1858
166 Benedict, F. G. The composition of the atmosphere. 1912. C1859
167 Benedict, F. G. and Cady, W. G. A bicycle ergometer with an electric brake. 1912. C1860
168 Burham, S. W. Measures of proper motion stars made with 40-inch refractor... 1913. C1861
169 Callaway, M. The infinitive in Anglo-Saxon. 1913. C1862
170 Jones, H. C. and others. The electrical conductivity ...of aqueous solutions of a number of salts and organic acids. 1912. C1863
171 Lancaster, H. C. Pierre Du Ryer. 1912. C1864
172 Parker, D. W. Guide to the materials for United States history in Canadian archives. 1913. C1865
173 Reichert, E. T. The differentiation of specificity of starches in relation to genera, species, etc. 1913. C1866
174 Churchill, W. Easter Island. 1912. C1867
175 Carnegie institution of Washington. Dept. of terrestrial magnetism. Land magnetic observations, by Bauer and others. V. 1, 2, 4 of 175. 1912-27. Ocean magnetic observations, by Bauer and others. V. 3. of 175. 1917. Land magnetic and electric observations, by Fisk and others. V. 6 of 175. 1926. Magnetic results from Watheroo observatory by Fleming and others. 7a-c of v. 175. 1947. Land and ocean magnetic observations, by Wallis, and Green. V. 8 of 175. 1947. Earth-current results at Tucson magnetic observatory, by Rooney. V. 9 of 175. 1946. Magnetic results from Huancayo

observatory by Johnston and others. 10a-c. of 175. 1948-51. Ionospheric research at Huancayo Observatory by Wells and Berkners. V. 11 of 175. Ionospheric research at College, Alaska, by Seaton and others. V. 12 of 175. 1947. Ionospheric research at Watheroo Observatory by Berkner and others. V. 13 of 175. 1912. Cosmic-rays results from Huancayo Observatory, Peru, by Lange and Forbush. V. 14 of 175. 1948. Cosmic results: Huancayo, Peru, Jan. 1946-Dec. 1955, by Lange and Forbush. V. 20 of 175. 1957. Cosmic results: Huancayo, Peru, Jan. 1956-Dec. 1959, by Lange and Forbush. V. 21 of 175. 1961. C1868

176 Benedict, F. G. and Joslin, E. P. A study of metabolism in severe diabetes. 1912. C1869

177 Loeb, L. and others. The venom of Heloderma. 1913. C1870

178 Cannon, W. A. Botanical features of the Algerian Sahara. 1913. C1871

179 Same as no. 48-49. Papers nos. 18, 19. 1913. C1872

180 Jones, H. C. and others. The freezing point... of certain electrolytes in water. 1913. C1873

181 Case, E. C. and others. Permo-Carboniferous vertebrates from New Mexico. 1913. C1874

182-183 Same as no. 102. V. 5, 6. 1914. C1875

184 The Subanu. 1913. C1876

185 Hasse, A. R. Index to United States documents relating to foreign affairs, 1828-1861. 3 pts. 1914-21. C1877

186 Barus, C. The diffusion of gases through liquids and allied experiments. 1913. C1878

187 Benedict, F. G. and Cathcart, E. P. Muscular work. 1913. C1879

188 Davenport, C. B. Heredity of skin color in negro-white crosses. 1913. C1880

189 Osgood, C. G. A concordance to the poems of Edmund Spenser. 1915. C1881

190 Jones, H. C. and Guy, J. S. The absorption spectra of solutions... 1913. C1882

191 Weed, L. H. A reconstruction of nuclear masses in the lower portion of the human brain-stem. 1914. C1883

192 Huntington, E. and others. The climatic factor... 1914. C1884

193 Macdougal, D. T. and others. The Salton Sea. 1914. C1885

194 Shreve, E. B. The daily march of transpiration in a desert perennial. 1914. C1886

195 Castle, W. E. and Phillips, J. C. Piebald rats and selection. 1914. C1887

196 MacDowell, E. C. Size inheritance in rabbits. 1914. C1888

197 Wright, A. H. North American Anura. 1914. C1889

198 Morse, H. N. The osmotic pressure of aqueous solutions. 1914. C1890

199 Shreve, F. A montane rain-forest. 1914. C1891

200 Carnegie institution of Washington. Report upon the present condition and future needs of the science of anthropology. 1913. C1892

201 Benedict, F. G. and Talbot, F. B. The gaseous metabolism of infants. 1914. C1893

202 Cooper, L., comp. A concordance to the works of Horace. 1916. C1894

203 Benedict, F. G. A study of prolonged fasting. 1915. C1895

204 Same as no. 98. 1915. C1896

205 Detlefsen, J. A. Genetic studies on a cavy species cross. 1914. C1897

206 Johnson, D. S. and York, H. H. The relation of plants to tide-levels. 1915. C1898

207 Case, E. C. The Permo-Carboniferous red beds of North America and their vertebrate fauna. 1915. C1899
208 Baldwin, D. L. and others. A concordance to the poems of John Keats. 1917. C1900
209 Richards, H. M. Acidity and gas interchange in cacti. 1915. C1901
210 Jones, H. C. and others. The absorption spectra of solutions as studies by means of the radiomicrometer. 1915. C1902
211-214 Same as no. 102. V. 7-10. 1915-21. C1903
215A Johnson, E. R. and others. History of domestic and foreign commerce of the United States. 1915. C1904
215B Clark, V. S. History of the manufactures in the United States. V. 1. 1607-1860. 1916. C1905
215C Meyer, B. H. and others. History of transportation in the United States before 1860. 1917. C1906
216 Carpenter, T. M. A comparison of methods for determining the respiratory exchange of man. 1915. C1907
217 Shreve, F. The vegetation of a desert mountain range as conditioned by climatic factors. 1915. C1908
218 Stout, A. B. The establishment of varieties in Coleus by the selection of somatic variations. 1915. C1909
219 Morley, S. G. The inscriptions at Copan. 1920. C1910
220 Faust, A. B. Guide to the materials for American history in Swiss and Austrian archives. 1916. C1911
221-227 Carnegie Institution of Washington. Contributions to embryology. V. 1-7. 1915-18. C1912
228 Crampton, H. E. Studies on the variation, distribution, and evolution of the genus Partula: the species inhabiting Tahiti. 1916. C1913
228A ____. The species of the Mariana islands. 1925. C1914
229 Barus, C. Experiments with the displacement interferometer. 1915. C1915
230 Jones, H. C. and others. Conductivities and viscosities in pure and mixed solvents. 1915. C1916
231 Benedict, F. G. and Murschhauser, H. Energy transformations during horizontal walking. 1915. C1917
232 Dodge, R. and Benedict, F. G. Psychological effects of alcohol. 1915. C1918
233 Benedict, F. G. and Talbot, F. B. The physiology of the new-born infant. 1915. C1919
234 Hill, R. R. Descriptive catalogue of the documents relating to the history of the United States in the Papeles Procedentes de Cuba. 1916. C1920
235 Hale, G. E. Ten years' work of a mountain observatory. 1915. C1921
236 Davenport, C. B. The feebly inhibited. 1915. C1922
237 Morgan, T. H. and Bridges, C. B. Sex-linked inheritance in Drosophila. 1916. C1923
238 Moodie, R. L. The coal measures Amphibia of North America. 1916. C1924
239 Golder, F. A. Guide to materials for American history in Russian archives. 2 v. 1917-37. C1925
240 Estabrook, A. H. The Jukes in 1915. 1916. C1926
241 Castle, W. E. and Wright, S. Studies of inheritance in guinea-pigs and rats. 1916. C1927
242 Clements, F. E. Plant succession. 1916. C1928
243 Goodale, H. D. Gonadectomy in relation to the secondary sexual characters of some domestic birds. 1916. C1929
244 Churchill, W. Sissano. 1916. C1930
245 Hedrick, H. B. Interpolation tables. 1918. C1931
246 Carnegie institution of

Washington. Dept. of meridian astronomy. Albany zone catalogues for the epoch 1900. 1918. C1932
247 Barnard, E. E. A photographic atlas of selected regions of the Milky way. 1927. C1933
248 Britton, N. L. and Rose, J. N. The cactaceae. 4 v. 1919-23. C1934
249 Barus, C. Displacement interferometry by the aid of the achromatic fringes. 4 v. 1916-19. C1935
250 Ulugh Beg Ibn Shahrukh. Ulugh Beg's catalogue of stars, ed. by Knobel. 1917. C1936
251-252 Same as no. 102. V. 11, 12. 1917-18. C1937
253 Ivens, W. G. Dictionary and grammar of the language of Sa'a and Ulawa, Solomon Islands. 1918. C1938
254 Davenport, F. G., ed. European treaties bearing on the history of the United States and its dependencies. 4 v. 1917-37. C1939
255 Churchill, W. Club types of nuclear Polynesia. 1917. C1940
256 Dickson, L. E. History of the theory of numbers. 3 v. 1919-23. C1941
257 Whitman, C. O. Posthumous works of Charles O. Whitman. 3 v. 1919. C1942
258 Rowe, L. S. The federal system of the Argentine Republic. 1921. C1943
259 Davenport, C. B. and Scudder, M. T. Naval officers. 1919. C1944
260 Davis, P. B., comp. Studies on solution in its relation to light absorption... 1918. C1945
261 Benedict, F. G. and Carpenter, T. M. Food ingestion and energy transformations. 1918. C1946
262 Boccaccio, G. Lydgate's Fall of princes, ed. by Bergen. 3 pts. 1923-27. C1947
263 Tower, W. L. The mechanism of evolution in Leptinotarsa. 1918. C1948
264 Sturtevant, A. H. An analysis of the effects of selection. 1918. C1949
265 Laughlin, H. H. Duration of the several mitotic stages in the dividing root-tip cells of the common onion. 1919. C1950
266 Miles, W. R. Effect of alcohol on psycho-physiological functions. 1918. C1951
267 Smith, E. F. and Van Haagen, W. K. The atomic weights of boron and fluorine. 1918. C1952
268 Hyde, W. W. Olympic victor monuments and Greek athletic art. 1921. C1953
269 Johnson, D. S. The fruit of Opuntia fulgida. 1918. C1954
270 Reichert, E. T. A biochemic basis for the study of problems of taxonomy. 1919. C1955
271-277 Same as no. 221. V. 8-14. 1918-22. C1956
278 Carnegie instititon of Washington. Contributions to the genetics of Drosophila melanogaster. 1919. C1957
279 Harris, J. A. and Benedict, F. G. A biometric study of basal metabolism in man. 1919. C1958
280 Benedict, F. G. and others. Human vitality and efficiency under prolonged restricted diet. 1919. C1959
281-282 Same as no. 102. V. 13-14. 1919-20. C1960
283 Case, E. C. The environment of vertebrate life in the late Paleozoic in North America. 1919. C1961
284 Livingston, B. E. and Shreve, F. The distribution of vegetation in the United States. 1921. C1962
285 Morgan, T. H. The genetic and the operative evidence relating to secondary sexual characters. 1919. C1963
286 Weaver, J. E. The ecological relations of roots. 1919. C1964
287 Spoehr, H. A. The carbonhydrate economy of

cacti. 1919. C1965
288 Castle, W. E. Studies of heredity in rabbits, rats, and mice. 1919. C1966
289 Douglass, A. E. Climatic cycles and tree-growth. 3 v. 1919-36. C1967
290 Clements, F. E. Plant indicators. 1920. C1968
291 Vaughan, T. W. Contributions to the geology and paleontology of the West Indies. 1919. C1969
292 Weaver, J. E. Root development in the grassland formation. 1920. C1970
293-294 Same as no. 102. V. 15-16. 1920-21. C1971
295 Mohr, O. L. and Cyr, W. A new type of hereditary brachyphalangy in man. 1919. C1972
296 Key, W. M. (Euteman). Heredity and social fitness. 1920. C1973
297 Macdougal, D. T. Hydration and growth. 1920. C1974
298 Nichols, E. L. and others. Fluorescence of the uranyl salts. 1919. C1975
299 Burnett, E. C., ed. Letters of members of the Continental congress. 8 v. 1921-36. C1976
300 Ivens, W. G. Grammar and vocabulary of the Lau language, Solomon Islands. 1921. C1977
301 Sturtevant, A. H. The North American species of Drosophila. 1921. C1978
302 Benedict, F. G. and Talbot, F. B. Metabolism and growth from birth to puberty. 1921. C1979
303 Carpenter, T. M. Tables, factors, and formulas for computing respiratory exchange and biological transformations of energy. 1921. C1980
303A ____. 2d ed. 1924. C1981
303B ____. 3d ed. 1939. C1982
303C ____. 4th ed. 1948. C1983
304 Lowe, E. A. and Rand, E. K. A sixth-century fragment of the letters of Pliny the younger. 1922. C1984
305 Banta, A. M. Selection in Cladocera on the basis of a physiological character. 1921. C1985
306 Carnegie institution of Washington. Contributions to the geology and palaeontology of the West Indies. 1922. C1986
307 Macdougal, D. T. Growth in trees. 1921. C1987
308 Cannon, W. A. Plant habits and habitats in the arid portions of South Australia. 1921. C1988
309 Smith, H. M. Gaseous exchange and physiological requirements for level and grade walking. 1922. C1989
310 Same as no. 249. 1921-25. C1990
311-312 Same as no. 102. V. 17-18. 1922. C1991
313 Hall, H. M. and Long, F. L. Rubber-content of North American plants. 1921. C1992
314 Loftfield, J. V. G. The behavior of stomata. 1921. C1993
315 Clements, F. E. Aeration and air-content: the role of oxygen in root activity. 1921. C1994
316 Weaver, J. E. and others. Development and activities of roots of crop plants. 1922. C1995
317 Hayford, J. F. Effects of winds and of barometric pressures on the Great Lakes. 1922. C1996
318 Wyckoff, R. W. G. The analytical expression of the results of the theory of space-groups. 1930. C1997
319 Cooper, W. S. The broad-sclerophyll vegetation of California. 1922. C1998
320 Castle, W. E. Genetic studies of rabbits and rats. 1922. C1999
321 Case, E. C. New reptiles and stegocephalians from the upper Triassic of western Texas. 1922. C2000
322 Hay, O. P. The Pleistocene of North America and its vertebrated animals

from the states East of the Mississippi. 1923. C2001
322A ____. The Pleistocene of the Middle region of North America and its vertebrated animals. 1924. C2002
322B ____. The Pleistocene of the Western region of North America and its vertebrated animals. 1927. C2003
323 Joslin, E. P. Diabetic metabolism with high and low diets. 1923. C2004
324 Benedict, F. G. and Ritzman, E. G. Undernutrition in steers. 1923. C2005
325 Spoehr, H. A. and McGee, J. M. Studies in plant respiration and photosynthesis. 1923. C2006
326 Hall, H. M. and Clements, F. E. The phylogenetic method in taxonomy. 1923. C2007
327 Bridges, C. B. and Morgan, T. H. The third-chromosome group of mutant characters of Drosophila melanogaster. 1923. C2008
328 Metz, C. W. and others. Genetic studies on Drosophila virilis. 1923. C2009
329 Davenport, C. B. Body-build and its inheritance. 1923. C2010
330 Hackett, C. W., ed. Historical documents relating to New Mexico Nueva Vizcaya, and approaches thereto, to 1773. 3 v. 1923-37. C2011
331 Stock, C. Cenozoic gravigrade edentates of Western North America. 1925. C2012
332 Same as no. 221. V. 15. 1923. C2013
333 Miles, W. R. Alcohol and human efficiency. 1924. C2014
334 James, H. G. The constitutional system of Brazil. 1923. C2015
335 Lothrop, S. K. Tulum. 1924. C2016
336 Clements, F. E. and Long, F. L. Experimental pollination. 1923. C2017
337 Castle, W. E. and others. Contributions to a knowledge of inheritance in mammals. 1926. C2018
338 Gt. Brit. Parliament. Proceedings and debates of the British Parliaments respecting North America, ed. by Stock. 5 v. 1925-41. C2019
339 Perret, F. A. The Vesuvius eruption of 1906. 1924. C2020
340-345 Same as no. 102. V. 19-24. 1924-26. C2021
346 Kellogg, R., ed. Additions to palaeontology of the Pacific Coast and Great Basin regions of North America. 1927. C2022
347 Merriam, J. C. and others. Papers concerning the palaeontology of the Pleistocene of California and Pliocene of Oregon. 1925. C2023
348 Kellogg, R. Additions to the Tertiary history of the pelagic mammals on the Pacific Coast of North America. 1925. C2024
349 Studies on the fossil flora and fauna of the Western United States. 1925. C2025
350 Macdougal, D. T. and Shreve, F. Growth in trees and massive organs in plants. 1924. C2026
351 Howard, W. T. Public health administration and the natural history of disease in Baltimore, Maryland, 1797-1920. 1924. C2027
352 Quaternary climates. 1925. C2028
353 Tatlock, J. S. P. and Kennedy, A. G. A concordance to the complete works of Geoffrey Chaucer and to the Romaunt of the Rose. 1927. C2029
354 Cannon, W. A. General and physiological features of the vegetation of the more arid portions of Southern Africa. 1924. C2030
355 Clements, F. E. and Weaver, J. E. Experimental vegetation. 1924. C2031
356 Clements, F. E. and Goldsmith, G. W. The phytometer method in

ecology. 1924. C2032
357 Jean, F. C. and Weaver, J. E. Root behavior and crop yield under irrigation. 1924. C2033
358 Bidwell, P. W. and Falconer, J. I. History of agriculture in the northern United States, 1620-1860. 1925. C2034
359 Matteson, D. M. List of manuscripts concerning American history preserved in European libraries... 1925. C2035
360 Day, A. L. and Allen, E. T. The volcanic activity and hot springs of Lassen Peak. 1925. C2036
361-363 Same as no. 221. V. 16-18. 1925-26. C2037
364 Corner, G. W. Anatomical texts of the earlier middle ages. 1927. C2038
365 Macdougal, D. T. Reversible variations in volume, pressure and movement of sap in trees. 1925. C2039
366 Woodring, W. P. Miocene mollusks from Bowden, Jamaica. 1925. C2040
367 Jochelson, W. Archaeological investigations in the Aleutian islands. 1925. C2041
368 Cannon, W. A. Physiological features of roots. 1925. C2042
369 Carpenter, T. M. Human metabolism with enemata of alcohol, dextrose, and levulose. 1925. C2043
370 Stuart, G. H. The governmental system of Peru. 1925. C2044
371 Jackson, A. Correspondence of Andrew Jackson, ed. by Bassett. 7 v. 1926-35. C2045
372 Bell, H. C. and others. Guide to British West Indies archive materials. 1926. C2046
373 Macdougal, D. T. The hydrostatic system of trees. 1926. C2047
374 Catterall, H., ed. Judicial cases concerning American slavery and the Negro. 5 v. 1926-37. C2048
375 Case, E. C. Environment of tetrapod life in the late Paleozoic of regions other than North America. 1926. C2049
376 Sarton, G. Introduction to the history of science. 3 v. 1927-48. C2050
377 Benedict, F. G. and Ritzman, E. G. The metabolism of the fasting steer. 1927. C2051
378 Allen, E. T. and Day, A. L. Steam Wells and other thermal activity at "The Geysers," California. 1927. C2052
379 Same as no. 102. V. 25. 1928. C2053
380 Same as no. 221. V. 19. 1927. C2054
381 DuToit, A. L. A geological comparison of South America with South Africa. 1927. C2055
382 Willis, B. Studies in comparative seismology: Earthquake conditions in Chile. 1929. C2056
383 Barus, C. Acoustic experiments with the pin-hole probe and the interferometer u-gage. 1927. C2057
384 Nichols, E. L. and others. Cathodo-luminescence and the luminescence of incandescent solids. 1928. C2058
385 Same as no. 366. Pt. 2. 1928. C2059
386 Carnegie institution of Washington. Dept. of meridian astronomy. San Luis catalogue of 15333 stars for the epoch 1910, by Boss and others. 1928. C2060
387 Dyar, H. G. The mosquitoes of the Americas. 1928. C2061
388 Jochelson, W. Archaeological investigations in Kamchatka. 1928. C2062
389 Hall, H. M. The genus Haplopappus. 1928. C2063
390 Hay, O. P. Second bibliography and catalogue of the fossil Vertebrata of North America. 2 v. 1929-30. C2064

391 Same as no. 102. V. 26. 1929. C2065
392 Leland, W. G., ed. Guide to materials for American history in the libraries and archives of Paris. 2 v. 1932-43. C2066
393 Merriam, J. C. and others. Papers concerning the paleontology of the Cretaceous and later Tertiary of Oregon. 1928. C2067
394 Same as no. 221. V. 20. 1929. C2068
395 Davenport, C. B. and others. Race crossing in Jamaica. 1929. C2069
396 St. John, C. E. and others. Revision of Rowland's Preliminary table of solar spectrum wave-lengths. 1928. C2070
397 Macdougal, D. T. and others. The hydrostatic-pneumatic system of certain trees. 1929. C2071
398 Clements, F. E. and others. Plant competition. 1929. C2072
399 Sturtevant, A. H. and others. Contributions to the genetic Drosophila simulans and Drosophila melanogaster. 1929. C2073
400 Folse, J. A. A new method of eliminating steam flow based upon a new evaporation formula. 1929. C2074
401 Paullin, C. O. Atlas of the historical geography of the United States, ed. by Wright. 1932. C2075
402 Mount Wilson observatory, California. Mount Wilson catalogue of photographic magnitudes in selected areas 1-139. 1930. C2076
403 Carnegie institution of Washington. Contributions to American archaeology. V. 1. 1931. C2077
404 ____. Contributions to palaeontology from Carnegie institution of Washington. 1930. C2078
405 White, D. Flora of the Hermit shale, Grand Canyon, Arizona. 1929. C2079
406 Morris, E. H. and others. The temple of the warriors at Chichen Itzá, Yucatan. 2 v. 1931. C2080
407 Same as no. 221. V. 21. 1930. C2081
408 Goranson, R. W. Thermodynamic relations in multi-component systems. 1930. C2082
409 Donnan, E. Documents illustrative of the history of the slave trade to America. 4 v. 1930-35. C2083
410 Same as no. 228. The species inhabiting Moorea. 1932. C2084
411 McMurrich, J. P. Leonardo da Vinci, the anatomist. 1930. C2085
412 Studies of the Pliocene palaeobotany of California, by Dorf. 1933. C2086
413 Same as no. 102. V. 27. 1931. C2087
414 Same as no. 221. V. 22. 1930. C2088
415 Studies of the pleistocene palaeobotany of California, by Chaney. 1934. C2089
416 Fossil floras of Yellowstone national park and southeastern Oregon by Read and MacGinitie. 1931. C2090
417 Aitken, R. G. New general catalogue of double stars within 120° of the North pole. 1932. C2091
418 Carnegie institution of Washington. Papers concerning the palaeontology of California, Oregon and the northern Great basin province. 1932. C2092
419 ____. Dept. of meridian astronomy. Albany catalogue of 20811 stars for the epoch 1910. 1931. C2093
420 Goldsmith, G. W. and Hafenrichter, A. L. Anthokinetics. 1932. C2094
421 Sturtevant, A. H. and Dobzhansky, T. Contributions to the genetics of certain chromosome anomalies in Drosophila melanogaster. 1931. C2095
422 Merriam, J. C. and Stock, C. The Felidae of Rancho

La Brea. 1932. C2096
423 Van Deman, E. B. The building of the Roman aqueducts. 1934. C2097
424 Thompson, J. E. and others. A preliminary study of the ruins of Cobá, Quintana Roo, Mexico. 1932. C2098
425 Benedict, F. G. The physiology of large reptiles. 1932. C2099
426 Bingham, H. C. Gorillas in a native habitat. 1932. C2100
427 Castle, W. E. and Sawin, P. B. Contributions to the genetics of the domestic rabbit. 1932. C2101
428 Davenport, C. B. The genetical factor in endemic goiter. 1932. C2102
429 Howard, H. Eagles and eaglelike vultures of the Pleistocene of Rancho La Brea. 1932. C2103
430 Gray, L. C. and Thompson, E. K. History of agriculture in the southern United States, to 1860. 1941. C2104
431 Shattuck, G. C. and others. The peninsula of Yucatan. 1933. C2105
432 Jochelson, W. History, ethnology and anthropology of Aleut. 1933. C2106
433 Same as no. 221. V. 23. 1923. C2107
434 Steggerda, M. Anthropometry of adult Maya Indians. 1932. C2108
435 Same as no. 102. V. 28. 1934. C2109
436 Same as no. 403. V. 2. 1934. C2110
437 Morley, S. G. The inscriptions of Petén. 5 v. 1938. C2111
438 Chilam Balam books. The book of Chilam Balam of Chumayel by Roys. 1933. C2112
439 Chaney, R. W. and Sanborn, E. J. The Goshen flora of west central Oregon. 1933. C2113
440 Carnegie institution of Washington. Papers concerning the palaeontology of California, Arizona, and Idaho. 1934. C2114
441 Macdougal, D. T. and Working, E. B. The pneumatic system of plants, especially trees. 1933. C2115
442 Heidel, W. A. The heroic age of science. 1933. C2116
443 Same as no. 221. V. 24. 1933. C2117
444 Lothrop, S. K. Atitlan. 1933. C2118
445 Vickery, H. B. and others. Chemical investigations of the tobacco plant. 1933. C2119
446 Benedict, F. G. and Benedict, C. G. Mental effort in relation to gaseous exchange, heart rate, and mechanics of respiration. 1933. C2120
447 Packard, E. L. and others. Marine mammals. 1934. C2121
448 Redfield, R. and Villa Rojas, A. Chan Kom. 1934. C2122
449 Wieland, G. R. The Cerro Cuadrado petrified forest. 1935. C2123
450 Haasis, F. W. Diametral changes in tree trunks. 1934. C2124
451 Sinnott, E. W. and others. The comparative anatomy of extra-chromosomal types in Datura stramonium. 1934. C2125
452 Same as no. 102. V. 29. 1936. C2126
453 Carnegie institution of Washington. Papers concerning the palaeontology of California, Nevada, and Oregon. 1935. C2127
454 Ruppert, K. The caracol of Chichen Itza, Yucatan, Mexico. 1935. C2128
455 Middle Cenozoic flora of Western North America. 1936. C2129
456 Same as no. 403. V. 3. 1937. C2130
457 Pearse, A. S. and others. The cenotes of Yucatan. 1936. C2131
458 Perret, F. A. The eruption of Mt. Pelée, 1929-1932. 1935. C2132

459 Same as no. 221. V. 25. 1935. C2133
460 Sykes, G. The Colorado delta. 1937. C2134
461 Carnegie institution of Washington. Botany of the Maya area. 1936. C2135
462 Macdougal, D. T. Studies in tree-growth by the dendrographic method. 1936. C2136
463 Hinds, N. E. A. Contributions to Pre-Cambrian geology of western North America. 1936. C2137
464 Dickson, L. E. Researches on Waring's problem. 1935. C2138
465 Eocene flora of western America, by Sanborn and others. 1937. C2139
466 Allen, E. T. and Day, A. L. Hot Springs of the Yellowstone National Park. 1935. C2140
467 Same as no. 102. V. 30. 1936. C2141
468 Carnegie institution of Washington. Dept. of meridian astronomy. General catalogue of 33342 stars for the epoch 1950. 5 v. 1936-37. C2142
469 Antevs, E. Rainfall and tree growth in the Great Basin. 1938. C2143
470 Willis, B. Studies in comparative seismology: East African plateaus and Rift Valleys. 1936. C2144
471 Pollock, H. E. D. Round structures of aboriginal middle America. 1936. C2145
472 Lothrop, S. K. Zaculpa. 1936. C2146
473 Hall, E. R. and others. Studies of tertiary and quarternary mammals of North America. 1936. C2147
474 Benedict, F. G. The physiology of the elephant. 1936. C2148
475 Same as no. 102. V. 31. 1937. C2149
476 Carnegie institution of Washington. Miocene and pliocene floras of Western North America. 1938. C2150
477 Uaxactun, Guatemala. Group E - 1926-1931, by Ricketson. 1937. C2151
478 Lundell, C. L. The vegetation of Petén. 1937. C2152
479 Same as no. 221. V. 26. 1937. C2153
480 Sykes, G. Delta, estuary, and lower portion of the channel of the Colorado River 1933 to 1935. 1937. C2154
481 Grinnell, J. and Linsdale, J. M. Vertebrate animals of Point Lobos reserve, 1934-35. 1936. C2155
482 Kellogg, R. A review of the Archaeoceti. 1936. C2156
483 Same as no. 403. V. 4. 1937. C2157
484 Babcock, E. B. and Stebbins, G. L. The genus Youngia. 1937. C2158
485 Dice, L. R. and Blossom, P. M. Studies of mammalian ecology in southwestern North America. 1937. C2159
486 Glock, W. S. Principles and methods of tree-ring analysis. 1937. C2160
487 Carnegie institution of Washington. Studies on Cenozoic vertebrates of western North America. 1938. C2161
488 Farnam, H. W. Chapters in the history of social legislation in the United States to 1860, ed. by Clark. 1938. C2162
489 Benedict, F. G. and Lee, R. C. Lipogensis in the animal body. 1937. C2163
490 Strain, H. H. Leaf xanthophylls. 1938. C2164
491 Pearse, A. S. and others. Fauna of the caves of Yucatan. 1938. C2165
492 McKee, E. D. The environment and history of the Toroweap and Kaibab formations of northern Arizona and southern Utah. 1938. C2166
493 DeTerra, H. and Paterson, T. T. Studies on the icy age in India and associated human cultures. 1939. C2167

494 Ritzman, E. G. and Benedict, F. G. Nutritional physiology of the adult ruminant. 1938. C2168
495 Gregory, W. K. and others. Fossil anthropoids of the Yale-Cambridge India expedition of 1935. 1938. C2169
496 Same as no. 221. V. 27. 1938. C2170
497 Benedict, F. G. and Lee, R. C. Hibernation and marmot physiology. 1938. C2171
498 Hale, G. E. and Nicholson, S. B. Magnetic observations of sunspots. 1917-24. 1938. C2172
499 Shattuck, G. C. and others. A medical survey of the Republic of Guatemala. 1938. C2173
500 Merriam, J. C. Published papers and addresses. 4 v. 1938. C2174
501 Carnegie institution of Washington. Cooperation in research. 1938. C2175
502 Wauchope, R. Modern Maya houses. 1938. C2176
503 Benedict, F. G. Vital energetics. 1938. C2177
504 Babcock, E. G. and Stebbins, G. L. The American species of Crepis. 1938. C2178
505 Ebtun, Yucatan. The titles of Ebtun, by Roy. 1939. C2179
506 Thompson, J. E. Excavations at San Jose, British Honduras. 1939. C2180
507 Hum, H. H. and Chaney, R. W. A Miocene flora from Shantung Province, China. 1940. C2181
508 Dorf, E. Upper Cretaceous flora of the Rocky mountain region. 1942. C2182
509 Carnegie institution of Washington. Contributions to American anthropology and history. (continues Contributions to American archaeology). V. 5. 1939. C2183
510 Cleven, N. A. N. The political organization of Bolivia. 1940. C2184
511 Chatelain, V. E. The defenses of Spanish Florida, 1565 to 1763. 1941. C2185
512 Perret, F. A. The volcanic-seismic crisis as Montserrat, 1933-37. 1939. C2186
513 Banta, A. M. and others. Studies on the physiology, genetic, and evolution of some Cladocera. 1939. C2187
514 Carnegie institution of Washington. Studies of Cenozoic vertebrates and stratigraphy of western North America. 1940. C2188
515 Flint, A. S. Madison catalogue of 2786 stars for the epoch 1910. 1939. C2189
516 Axelrod, D. I. A Miocene flora from the western border of the Mohave desert. 1939. C2190
517 Same as no. 102. V. 32. 1940. C2191
518 Same as no. 221. V. 28. 1940. C2192
519 Morris, E. H. Archaeological studies in the La Plata district, southwestern Colorado and northwestern New Mexico. 1939. C2193
520 Clausen, J. and others. Experimental studies on the nature of species. 1940. C2194
521 Martin, E. V. and Clements, F. E. Adaptation and origin in the plant world. 1939. C2195
522 Same as no. 461. V. 2. 1940. C2196
523 Same as no. 509. V. 6. 1940. C2197
524 Same as no. 102. V. 33. 1942. C2198
525 Same as no. 221. V. 29. 1941. C2199
526 Daugherty, L. H. The Upper Triassic flora of Arizona. 1941. C2200
527 Gentry, H. S. Rio Mayo plants. 1942. C2201
528 Same as no. 509. V. 7. 1942. C2202
529 Turnage, W. V. and Mallery, T. D. An analysis of rainfall in the Sonoran desert and adjacent territory. 1941. C2203
530 Carnegie institution of

Washington. Studies of Cenozoic vertebrates of western North America and of fossil primates. 1942. C2204

531 Steggerda, M. Maya Indians of Yucatan. 1941. C2205

532 Seares, F. H. and others. Magnitudes and colors of stars North of 80°. 1941. C2206

533 Morris, E. H. and Burgh, R. F. Anasazi basketry. 1941. C2207

534 MacGinitie, H. D. A Middle cocene flora from the central Sierra Nevada. 1941. C2208

535 Same as no. 102. V. 34. 1941. C2209

536-537 Carnegie institution of Washington. Dept. of terrestrial magnetism. Scientific results of cruise VII: Biology. 2 v. 1942. C2210

538 Cressman, L. S. and others. Archaeological researches in the northern Great basin. 1942. C2211

539 Same as no. 102. V. 35. 1942. C2212

540 Williams, H. The geology of Crater lake national park, Oregon. 1942. C2213

541 Same as no. 221. V. 30. 1942. C2214

542 Same as no. 536. V. 3. 1942. C2215

543 Ruppert, K. and Denison, J. H. Archaeological reconnaissance in Campeche, Quintana Roo, and Peten. 1943. C2216

544 Carnegie institution of Washington. Dept. of terrestrial magnetism. Scientific results of cruise VII: Meteorology. V. 1. 1943. C2217

545A, 545B ____. Scientific results of cruise VII: Oceanography. V. 1. pts. 1, 2. 1944. C2218

546 Same as no. 509. V. 8. 1943. C2219

547 Same as no. 544. V. 2. 1943. C2220

548 Roys, R. L. The Indian background of colonial Yucatan. 1943. C2221

549 Perret, F. A. Volcanologic observations. 1950. C2222

550 Martin, E. V. Studies of evaporation and transpiration under controlled conditions. 1943. C2223

551 Carnegie institution of Washington. Fossil vertebrates from western North America and Mexico. 1946. C2224

552 Bridges, C. B. and Brehme, K. S. The mutants of Drosophila melanogaster. 1956. C2225

553 Chaney, R. W. Pliocene floras of California and Oregon. 1944. C2226

554 Dobzhansky, T. and Epling, C. Contributions to the genetics, taxonomy, and ecology of Drosophila pseudoobscura and its relations. 1944. C2227

555 Same as no. 536. V. 4. 1943. C2228

556 Same as no. 545. V. 2. 1944. C2229

557 Same as no. 221. V. 31. 1945. C2230

558 Proskouriakoff, T. An album of Maya architecture. 1946. C2231

559 Villa Rojas, A. The Maya of east central Quintana Roo. 1945. C2232

560 Scholes, F. V. The Maya Chontal Indians of Acalen-Tixchel. 1948. C2233

561 Kidder, A. V. and others. Excavations at Kaminaljuyu, Guatemala. 1946. C2234

562 Carnegie institution of Washington. Dept. of terrestrial magnetism. Scientific results of cruise VII: Chemistry. V. 1. 1944. C2235

563 McKee, E. D. and Resser, C. E. Cambrian history of the Grand canyon region. 1945. C2236

564 Same as no. 520. 1945. C2237

565 Same as no. 536. V. 5. 1944. C2238

566 Clark, H. L. The echinoderm fauna of Australia. 1946. C2239

567 O'Neale, L. M. Textiles of highland Guatemala. 1945. C2240
568 Same as no. 545. V. 3. 1946. C2241
569 Riddle, O. and others. Studies on carbohydrate and fat metabolism with especial reference to the pigeon. 1947. C2242
570 Blake, M. E. Ancient Roman construction in Italy from the prehistoric period to Augustus. 1947. C2243
571 Same as no. 545. V. 4. 1946. C2244
572 Riddle, O. Endocrines and constitution in doves and pigeons. 1947. C2245
573 Shepard, A. O. Plumbate. 1948. C2246
574 Same as no. 509. V. 9. 1948. C2247
575 Same as no. 221. V. 32. 1948. C2248
576 Kidder, A. V. The artifacts of Uaxactun, Guatemala. 1947. C2249
577 Stromsvik, G. Guide book to the ruins of Copan. 1947. C2250
578 Carnegie institution of Washington. Dept. of terrestrial magnetism. Description of the earth's main magnetic field and its secular change. 1947. C2251
579 Babcock, H. D. and Moore, C. E. The solar spectrum. 1947. C2252
580 Carnegie institution of Washington. Dept. of terrestrial magnetism. The geomagnetic field. 1947. C2253
581 Same as no. 520. 1948. C2254
582 Chamberlain, R. S. The conquest and colonization of Yucatan, 1517-1550. 1948. C2255
583 Same as no. 221. V. 33. 1949. C2256
584 Carnegie Institution of Washington. Some Tertiary mammals and birds from North America, by Wilson and others. 1949. C2257
585 Same as no. 509. V. 10. 1949. C2258
586 Spoehr, H. A. and others. Fatty acids and antibacterials from plants. 1949. C2259
587 Barth, T. F. W. Volcanic geology. 1950. C2260
588 Smith, A. L. Uaxactum, Guatemala. 1950. C2261
589 Thompson, J. S. S. Maya hieroglyphic writing. 1950. C2262
590 Axelrod, D. I. Studies in late Tertiary paleobotany. 1950. C2263
591 Shreve, F. Vegetation and flora of the Sonoran Desert. V. 1. 1951. C2264
592 Same as no. 221. V. 34. 1951. C2265
593 Proskouriakoff, T. A. A study of classic Maya sculpture. 1950. C2266
594 Smith, A. L. and Kidder, A. V. Excavation at Nebaj, Guatemala. 1951. C2267
595 Ruppert, K. Chichen Itza. 1952. C2268
596 Same as no. 509. V. 11. 1952. C2269
597 Longyear, J. M. Copan ceramics. 1952. C2270
598 Chamberlain, R. S. The conquest and colonization of Honduras, 1502-1550. 1953. C2271
599 MacGinitie, H. D. Fossil plants of the Florissant beds, Colorado. 1953. C2272
600 Burlew, J. S., ed. Algal culture. 1953. C2273
601 Wilson, R. E. General catalogue of the stellar radial velocities. 1953. C2274
602 Ruppert, K. and others. Bonampak, Chiapas, Mexico. 1955. C2275
603 Same as no. 221. V. 35. 1954. C2276
604 Morris, E. H. and Burgh, R. F. Basket maker II sites near Durango, Colorado. 1954. C2277
605 Godske, C. L. and others. Dynamic meteorology and weather forecasting. 1957. C2278
606 Same as no. 509. V.

12. 1960. C2279

607 Studies of biosynthesis in Escherichia coli by Roberts and others. 1955. C2280

608 Smith, A. L. Archaeological reconnaissance in central Guatemala. 1955. C2281

609 Shepard, A. O. Ceramics for the archaeologist. 1956. C2282

610 Merrill, P. W. Lines of the chemical elements in astronomical spectra. 1956. C2283

611 Same as no. 221. V. 36. 1958. C2284

612 Carnegie Institution of Washington. Dept. of Genetics. Genetic studies with bacteria, by Demerec and others. 1956. C2285

613 Roys, R. L. The political geography of the Yucatan Maya. 1957. C2286

614 Moser, H. The dynamics of bacterial populations maintained in the chemostat. 1958. C2287

615 Same as no. 520. V. 4. 1958. C2288

616 Blake, M. E. Roman construction in Italy from Tiberius through the Flavians. 1959. C2289

617 Carnegie Institution of Washington. Contributions to paleontology. 1959. C2290

618 Sandage, A. The Hubble atlas of galaxies. 1961. C2291

619 Pollock, H. E. D. and others. Mayapan, Yucatan, Mexico. 1962. C2292

620 Forbush, S. E. and Casaverde, M. Equatorial electrojet in Peru. 1961. C2293

621 Same as no. 221. V. 37. 1962. C2294

622 Steinhart, J. S. and Meyer, R. P. Explosion studies of continental structure, University of Wisconsin, 1956-1959. 1961. C2295

623 Nobs, M. A. Experimental studies on species relationships in Ceanothus. 1963. C2296

624 Roberts, R. B., ed. Studies of macromolecular biosynthesis. 1964. C2297

625 Same as no. 221. V. 38. 1966. C2298

626 Howard, R. and others. Atlas of solar magnetic fields. 1968. C2299

627 Lindsley, D. L. and Grell, E. H. Genetic variations of Drosophila Melanogaster. 1968. C2300

628 Hiesey, W. M. and others. Experimental studies on the nature of species. 1971. C2301

629 Garzoli, S. L. An atlas of galactic neutral hydrogen for the region of $270^\circ \leq \ell \leq 310^\circ; -7^\circ \leq b \leq 2^\circ$. 1972. C2302

630 Tuve, M. A. and Lundsager, S. Velocity structures in hydrogen profiles. 1973. C2303

631 O'Rahilly, R. Developmental stages in human embryos. V. 1. 1973. C2304

THE CARNEGIE SERIES IN AMERICAN EDUCATION (McGraw)

Berelson, B. Graduate education in the United States. 1960. C2305

Chall, J. S. Learning to read. 1967. C2306

Clark, B. R. The open door college. 1960. C2307

Cleveland, H. and others. The overseas Americans. 1960. C2308

Cohen, J. W., ed. The superior student in American higher education. 1966. C2309

Conant, J. B. The American high school today. 1959. C2310

____. The education of American teachers. 1963. C2311

____. Shaping American policy. 1964. C2312

Corson, J. J. Governance of colleges and universities. 1960. C2313

Dodds, H. W. and others. The academic president. 1962. C2314

Glenny, L. A. Autonomy of public colleges. 1959. C2315

Henninger, G. R. The technical institute in America. 1959. C2316
Keeton, M. and Hilberry, C. Struggle and promise. 1970. C2317
Kellogg, C. E. and Knapp, D. C. The college of agriculture. 1966. C2318
Kitzhaber, A. R. Themes, theories and therapy. 1963. C2319
McConnell, T. R. A general pattern for an American public higher education. 1962. C2320
MacKenzie, O. and others. Correspondence instruction in the United States. 1968. C2321
Medsker, L. L. The junior college. 1960. C2322
Perkins, D. and others. The education of historians in the United States. 1962. C2323
Pierson, F. C. and others. The education of American businessmen. 1959. C2324
Thomas, R. B. The search for a common learning. 1962. C2325
Weidner, E. W. The world role of universities. 1962. C2326

CARUS MATHEMATICAL MONOGRAPHS (1-8 Open Ct., 9- Wiley)

1 Bliss, G. A. Calculus of variations. 1925. C2327
2 Curtiss, D. R. Analytic functions of a complex variable. 1926. C2328
3 Rietz, H. L. Mathematical statistics. 1927. C2329
4 Young, J. W. Projective geometry. 1930. C2330
5 Smith, D. E. and Ginsburg, J. A history of mathematics in America before 1900. 1934. C2331
6 Jackson, D. Fourier series and orthogonal polynomials. 1941. C2332
7 MacDuffee, C. C. Vectors and matrices. 1943. C2333
8 McCoy, N. H. Rings and ideals. 1948. C2334
9 Pollard, H. S. The theory of algebraic numbers. 1950. C2335
10 Jones, B. W. The arithmetic theory of quadratic forms. 1950. C2336
11 Niven, I. M. Irrational numbers. 1956. C2337
12 Kac, M. Statistical interdependence in probability, analysis and number theory. 1959. C2338
13 Boas, R. P. A primer of real functions. 1960. C2339
14 Ryser, H. J. Combinatorial mathematics. 1963. C2340
15 Herstein, I. N. Noncommutative rings. 1968. C2341
16 Rademacher, H. and Grosswald, E. Dedekind sums. 1972. C2342
17 Davis, P. J. The Schwarz function and its applications. 1974. C2343

CASE STUDIES IN LIBRARY SCIENCE (Shoe String Pr.) (Originally CASE STUDIES IN LIBRARY ADMINISTRATION)

1 Shaffer, K. R. Twenty-five short cases in library personnel administration. 1959. C2344
1 ____. Library personnel administration and supervision. 1968. C2345
2 ____. Twenty-five cases in executive-trustee relationship in public libraries. 1960. C2346
3 ____. The book collection. 1961. C2347
4 Grogan, D. J. Case studies in reference work. 1967. C2348
5 ____. More case studies in reference work. 1972. C2349

CASS LIBRARY OF AFRICAN STUDIES. AFRICANA MODERN LIBRARY (Cass)

1 Garvey, M. Philosophy and opinions of Marcus Garvey compiled by Amy Jacques Garvey. 2 v. 1967. C2350
2 Danquah, J. B. The Akan

doctrine of God. 1968. C2351
3 Sarbah, J. M. Fanti national constitution. 1968. C2352
4 Dust Muhammad. Land of the Pharaohs. 1968. C2353
5 Sarbah, J. M. Fanti Customary laws. 1968. C2354
6 Azikiwe, N. Renascent Africa. 1968. C2355
7 Hill, A. C. and Kilson, M., ed. Apropos of Africa. 1969. C2356
8 Hayford, J. E. C. Collected papers, ed. by Essien-Udoin. 1968. C2357
9 Sibthorpe, A. B. C. The history of Sierra Leone. 1969. C2358
10 Sampson, M. J., ed. West African leadership. 1969. C2359
11 Hayford, J. E. C. Gold coast native institutions. 1969. C2360
12 Horton, J. A. B. Letters on the political conditions of the Gold Coast. 1970. C2361
13 Ayandele, E. A. Holy Johnson. 1970. C2362
14 Blyden, E. W. Black spokesman. 1971. C2363
15 Hayford, J. E. C. The truth about the West African land question. 1971. C2364
16 Ahume, S. R. B. A. The gold coast nation and national consciousness. 1971. C2365
17 Johnson, J. W. D. Towards nationhood in West Africa. 1971. C2366
18 Padmore, G. Africa and world peace. 1972. C2367
19 Blyden, E. W. Selected letters and memoranda, ed. by Lynch. 1974. C2368

CASS LIBRARY OF AFRICAN STUDIES. GENERAL STUDIES (Cass)

1 Henderson, W. O. Studies in German colonial history. 1962. C2369
2 Roberts, S. H. The history of French colonial policy. 1963. C2370
3 Claridge, W. W. A history of the Gold Coast and Ashanti, ed. by Ward. 2 v. 1964. C2371
4 Coupland, R. The British antislavery movement. 1964. C2372
5 Green, M. M. Igbo Village affairs. 1964. C2373
6 Cook, A. N. British enterprise in Nigeria. 1964. C2374
7 Lugard, L. A tropical dependency. 1964. C2375
8 Buell, R. L. The native problem in Africa. 2 v. 1965. C2376
9 Kiewiet, C. W. de. The imperial factor in South Africa. 1965. C2377
10 Geary, W. Nigeria under the British rule. 1965. C2378
11 Temple, O. and C. L. Notes of the tribes. 1965. C2379
12 Trimingham, J. S. Islam in Ethiopia. 1965. C2380
13 ____. Islam in the Sudan. 1965. C2381
14 Lugard, F. D. The dual mandate in British tropical Africa. 1965. C2382
15 Orr, C. The making of northern Nigeria. 1965. C2383
16 Roscoe, J. The Baganda. 1965. C2384
17 Basden, G. T. Niger Ibos. 1966. C2385
18 ____. Among the Ibos of Nigeria. 1966. C2386
19 Donnan, E. Documents illustrative of the history of the slave trade to America. 1966. C2387
20 Vedder, H. South West Africa in early times, tr. by Hall. 1966. C2388
21 Work, M. N. A bibliography of the Negro in Africa and America. 1966. C2389
22 DuBois, W. E. B. Black reconstruction in America. 1966. C2390
23 Eliot, C. The East Africa protectorate. 1968. C2391
24 Dilley, M. R. British policy in Kenya colony. 1966. C2392
25 Gray, J. M. A history of the Gambia. 1966. C2393
26 Hahn, C. H. and others.

The native tribes of South West Africa. 1966. C2394
27 Marwick, B. A. The Swarzi. 1966. C2395
28 Roscoe, J. The northern Bantu. 1966. C2396
29 Stigand, C. H. The land of Zinj. 1966. C2397
30 Davis, J. M., ed. Modern industry and the African. 1967. C2398
31 Talbot, P. A. Life in Southern Nigeria. 1967. C2399
32 Hill, R. A. bibliographical dictionary of the Sudan. 1968. C2400
33 Talbot, P. A. Some Nigerian fertility cults. 1967. C2401
34 ____. Tribes of the Niger Delta. 1967. C2402
35 Hobley, C. W. Bantu beliefs and magic. 1967. C2403
36 Melland, F. H. In witch-bound Africa. 1967. C2404
37 Pearce, F. B. Zanzibar. 1967. C2405
38 Wilson-Haffenden, R. The redmen of Nigeria. 1967. C2406
39 Akpan, N. U. Epitaph to indirect rule. 1967. C2407
40 Whitford, J. Trading life in western and central Africa. 1967. C2408
41 Archer, F. B. The Gambia Colony and protectorate. 1967. C2409
42 MacMichael, H. A. The tribes of northern and central Kordáfon. 1967. C2410
43 Hole, H. M. The making of Rhodesia. 1967. C2411
44 Wingate, F. R. Mahdiism and the Egyptian Sudan. 1968. C2412
45 Hertslet, E. The map of Africa by treaty. 1967. C2413
46 MacMichael, H. A. A history of the Arabs in the Sudan. 2 v. 1967. C2414
47 Palmer, H. R. Sudanese memoirs. 1967. C2415
48 Dennett, R. E. Nigerian studies. 1968. C2416
49 Busia, K. A. The position of the chief in the modern political system of Ashanti. 1968. C2417
50 Schultze, A. The Sultanate of Bornu, tr. by Benton. 1968. C2418
51 Hattersley, C. W. The Baganda at home. 1968. C2419
52 George, C. The rise of British West Africa. 1968. C2420
53 Chessman, R. E. Lake Tana and the Blue Nile. 1968. C2421
54 Hole, H. M. Old Rhodesian days. 1968. C2422
55 Boyes, J. John Boyes, king of the Wa-Kikuyu, ed. by Bulpett. 1968. C2423
56 Stigand, C. H. Equatoria. 1968. C2424
57 Talbot, D. A. Woman's mysteries of a primitive people. 1968. C2425
58 Stayt, H. A. The Bavenda. 1968. C2426
59 Earthy, E. D. Valenge women. 1968. C2427
60 Ross, W. M. Kenya from within. 1968. C2428
61 Delavignette, R. Freedom and authority in French West Africa. 1968. C2429
62 Morel, E. D. Affairs of West Africa. 1968. C2430
63 Routledge, W. S. and K. With a prehistoric people. 1968. C2431
64 Benton, P. A. The languages and peoples of Bornu. 2 v. 1968. C2432
65 Werner, A. Myths and legends of the Hantu. 1968. C2433
66 Lane-Poole, S. A history of Egypt in the Middle Ages. 1968. C2434
67 Leonard, A. G. The lower Niger and its tribes. 1968. C2435
68 Heyworth-Dunne, J. An introduction to the history of education in modern Egypt. 1968. C2436
69 Ingham, E. G. Sierra Leone after a hundred years. 1968. C2437
70 Dennett, R. E. At the back of the black man's mind. 1968. C2438
71 Lugard, L. The rise of

our east African empire. 2 v. 1968. C2439
72 Harris, J. Dawn in darkest Africa. 1968. C2440
73 Morel, E. D. Nigeria. 1968. C2441
74 Tremearne, A. J. N. The ban of the Bori. 1968. C2442
75 Meek, C. K. Land, law and custom in the colonies. 1968. C2443
76 Dundas, C. Kilimanjaro and its peoples. 1968. C2444
77 Massam, J. A. The cliff dwellers of Kenya. 1968. C2445
78 Fuller, F. A vanished dynasty. 1968. C2446
79 Backwell, H. F., ed. The occupation of Hausaland. 1969. C2447
80 Blackman, W. S. The Fellahin of upper Egypt. 1968. C2448
81 Dudley, B. J. Parties and politics in northern Nigeria. 1968. C2449
82 Smith, E. W. The golden stool. 1969. C2450
83 McDermott, P. L. British East Africa. 1969. C2451
84 Hobley, C. W. Kenya from chartered company to crown colony. 1969. C2452
85 Craster, J. E. E. Pemba. 1969. C2453
86 Kirk-Greene, A. H. M. Lugard and the amalgamation of Nigeria. 1968. C2454
87 Bates, O. The eastern Libyans. 1969. C2455
88 Talbot, P. A. Peoples of southern Nigeria. 4 v. 1969. C2456
89 Moore, W. A. History of the Itsekiri, ed. by Lloyd. 1969. C2457
90 Tremearne, A. J. N. Hausa superstitions and customs, ed. by Miskett. 1970. C2458
91 Harley, G. W. Native African medicine. 1970. C2459
92 Ahmed Ibn Fartua. History of the first twelve years of the reign of Mai Idris, ed. by Palmer. 1970. C2460
93 Lugard, F. J. D. Political memoranda, ed. by Kirk-Greene. 1970. C2461
94 Read, M. The Ngoni of Nyasaland. 1970. C2462
95 Huffman, R. Nuer customs and folklore. 1970. C2463
96 Hobley, C. W. Ethnology of A-Kamba and other Eastern African tribes. 1970. C2464
97 Meek, C. K. The northern tribes of Nigeria. 1971. C2465
98 Vandeleur, S. Campaigning on the Upper Nile and Niger. 1974. C2466
99 Nzimiro, F. I. Studies in Ibo political systems. 1972. C2467
100 Cook, A. R. Uganda memories, ed. by Lugard. 1974. C2468
101 Crooks, J. J. A history of the colony of Sierra Leone, Western Africa. 1972. C2469
103 Ita, N. O. Bibliography of Nigeria. 1971. C2470
106 McPhee, A. The economic revolution in British West Africa. 1971. C2471
107 Warren, W. M. and Rubin, N., eds. Dams in Africa. 1968. C2472
108 Graham, C. K. The history of education in Ghana. 1971. C2473
111 Murray, A. V. The school in the bush. 1967. C2474
114 Amsden, A. H. International firms and labour in Kenya. 1971. C2475
115 Bleek, W. H. I. and Lloyd, L. C. Specimens of bushman folklore. 1969. C2476
116 Bryant, A. Zula medicine and medicine man. 1969. C2477
118 King, P. Arms in Africa. 1974. C2478
119 Ekechi, F. K. Missionary enterprise and rivalry in Igboland. 1972. C2479
121 Paul, A. A history of the Beia Tribes of the Sudan. 1971. C2480
122 Macmillan, A., ed. The

red book of West Africa. 1974. C2481
124 Afrifa, A. A. The Ghana coup. 1972. C2482
126 Cameron, D. My Tanganyika service and some Nigeria. 1974. C2483
127 Gazeteers of the northern provinces of Nigeria. 4 v. 1972. C2484
128 Nair, K. K. Politics and society in South Eastern Nigeria, 1841-1906. 1972. C2485
134 Leys, N. Kenya. 1973. C2486
144 Filesi, T. China and Africa in the Middle Ages, tr. by Morison. 1972. C2487
152 Wai, D. M. The Southern Sudan. 1973. C2488

CASS LIBRARY OF AFRICAN STUDIES. MISSIONARY RESEARCHES AND TRAVELS (Cass)

1 Freeman, T. B. Journal of various visits to the kingdom of Ashanti, Aku and Dahomi. 1968. C2489
2 Krapf, J. L. Travels, researches, and missionary labours during and eighteen years' residence in eastern Africa. 1968. C2490
3 Bowen, T. J. Adventures and missionary labours in several countries in the interior of Africa. 1968. C2491
4 Stern, H. A. Wanderings from the Falashas in Abyssinia. 1968. C2492
5 Mackenzie, J. Ten years north of the Orange River. 1968. C2493
6 Young, T. C. Notes on the history of the Tumbuka-Kamanga peoples in the northern province of Nyasaland. 1968. C2494
7 Hepburn, J. D. Twenty years in Khama's country and pioneering among the Batuana of Lake Ngami. 1968. C2495
8 Swann, A. J. Fighting the slave hunters in Central Africa. 1969. C2496
9 Johnston, J. Reality versus romance in South Central Africa. 1969. C2497
10 Arnot, F. S. Garenzanze. 1969. C2498
11 Waddell, H. M. Twenty-nine years in the West Indies and Central Africa, ed. by Jones. 1969. C2499
12 Elmslie, W. A. Among the wild Ngoni, ed. by Nance. 1969. C2500
13 Ashe, R. P. Two kings of Uganda. 1970. C2501
14 Harrison, J. W. A. M. Mackay. 1970. C2502
15 Crowther, S. Journal of an expedition up the Niger and Tshadda rivers. 1970. C2503
16 New, C. Life, wanderings and labours in Eastern Africa. 1971. C2504
17 Fisher, R. Twilight tales of the black Baganda. 1970. C2505
18 Schön, J. F. and Crowther, S. Journals of the Rev. James and Frederick Schön and Mr. Samuel Crowther. 1970. C2506
19 Coillard, F. On the threshold of Central Africa, ed. by Gluckman. 1971. C2507
20 Ashe, R. P. Chronicles of Uganda. 1971. C2508
21 Hore, E. C. Missionary to Tanganyika, 1877-1888, ed. by Wolf. 1971. C2509
23 Thomas, T. M. Eleven years in central South Africa. 1971. C2510

CASS LIBRARY OF AFRICAN STUDIES. SLAVERY SERIES (Cass)

1 Buxton, T. F. The African slave trade and its remedy. 1967. C2511
2 Benezet, A. Some historical account of Guinea. 1968. C2512
3 Cooper, J. The lost continent. 1968. C2513
4 Lloyd, C. The Navy and the slave trade. 1968. C2514
5 Bandinel, J. Some account of the trade in slaves from

Africa as connected with Europe and America. 1968. C2515
6 Sturge, J. and Harvey, T. The West Indies in 1837. 1968. C2516
7 Mackenzie-Grieve, A. The last years of the English slave trade. 1968. C2517
8 Clarkson, T. The history of the rise, progress and accomplishment of the abolition of the African slave-trade by the British Parliament. 1968. C2518
9 ____. An essay on the slavery and commerce of the human species. 1968. C2519
10 Berlioux, E. F. The slave trade in Africa in 1872. 1971. C2520
11 Snelgrave, W. A new account of some parts of Guinea, and the slave trade. 1971. C2521
12 Stephen, G. Anti-slavery recollection in a series of letters addressed to Mrs. Beecher Stowe... 1971. C2522
13 Henson, J. Uncle Tom's story of his life. 1971. C2523
14 Wilberforce, W. An appeal to the religion, justice, and humanity of the inhabitants of the British empire. Also Bridges, G. W. A voice from Jamaica in reply to William Wilberforce. 1972. C2524
15 Abel, A. H. and Klingberg, F. J. A side-light on American relations. 1972. C2525
16 Bickell, R. The West Indies as they are. 1972. C2526

CASS LIBRARY OF AFRICAN STUDIES. SOUTH AFRICAN STUDIES

1 Moodie, D. C. F. The history of the battles and adventures of the British, the Boers, and the Zulus... 2 v. 1968. C2527
2 Newton, A. P. Select documents relating to the unification of South Africa. 2 v. 1968. C2528
3 Stuart, J. A history of the Zulu rebellion, ed. by Marks. 1969. C2529
4 Newton, A. P. Select documents relating to the confiscation of South Africa. 1968. C2530
6 Kadalie, C. My life and the I. C. U. 1970. C2531
10 Brown, J. T. Among the Bantu nomads. 1974. C2532
14 Hellmann, E. Handbook on race relations in South Africa. 1974. C2533
14 Orpen, J. M. Reminiscences of life in South Africa. 2 v. 1969. C2534
20 Theal, G. M. History of South Africa, 1505-1884. 1969. C2535
22 ____. Basutoland Records. 1969. C2536
23 Bird, J. Annals of Natal, 1495-1845. 1972. C2537
24 Cory, G. E. The rise of South Africa. 6 v. 1969. C2538
26 Cowley, C. Kwa-zulu. 1969. C2539
27 Molema, S. M. Montshiwa-Barlong, chief and patriot. 1969. C2540
28 ____. The Bantu past and present. 1969. C2541
29 Stow, G. W. The native races of South Africa. 1969. C2542
30 Taber, E. C. To the Victoria Falls via Matabeleland. 1969. C2543

CASS LIBRARY OF AFRICAN STUDIES. TRAVELS AND NARRATIVES (Cass)

1 Kingsley, M. H. West African studies. 1964. C2544
2 ____. Travels in West Africa. 1965. C2545
3 Barth, H. Travels and discoveries in North and Central Africa. 1965. C2546
4 Coolley, W. D. The Negroland of the Arabs examined and explained. 1966. C2547
5 Dupuis, J. Journal of a residence in Ashantee. 1966. C2548
6 Bowdich, T. E. Mission from Cape Coast Castle to Ashantee. 1966. C2549
7 Cruickshank, B. Eighteen

years on the Gold Coast of Africa. 1966. C2550
8 Matthews, J. A voyage to the River Sierra Leone. 1966. C2551
9 Parkyns, M. Life in Abyssinia. 1966. C2552
10 Forbes, F. E. Dahomey and the Dahomans. 1966. C2553
11 Hutchinson, T. J. Narrative of the Niger, Tshadda, and Binue exploration. 1966. C2554
12 Adams, J. Remarks on the country extending from Cape Palmas to the River Congo. 1966. C2555
13 Lyon, G. F. A narrative of travels in northern Africa in the years 1818, 19, and 20. 1966. C2556
14 Baikie, W. B. Narrative of an exploring voyage up to the Rivers Kwora and Binue. 1966. C2557
15 Clapperton, H. Journal of a second expedition into the interior of Africa. 1966. C2558
16 Salt, H. A voyage to Abyssinia. 1967. C2559
17 Freeman, R. A. Travels and life in Ashanti and Jaman. 1967. C2560
18 Speke, J. H. What led to the discovery of the source of the Nile. 1967. C2561
19 Bosman, W. A new and accurate description of the coast of Guinea. 1967. C2562
20 Meredith, H. An account of the Gold Coast of Africa. 1967. C2563
21 Lander, R. Records of Captain Clapperton's last expedition to Africa. 2 v. 1967. C2564
22 Smith, W. A new voyage to Guinea. 1967. C2565
23 Tuckey, J. K. Narratives of an expedition to explore the River Zaire. 1967. C2566
24 Major, R. H. The life of Prince Henry of Portugal. 1967. C2567
25 Jackson, J. G. An account of Timbuctoo and Housa. 1967. C2568
26 Macaulay, K. The colony of Sierra Leone vindicated from the misrepresentation of Mr. MacQueen of Glasgow. 1968. C2569
27 Mollien, G. Travels in the interior of Africa to the sources of the Senegal and Gambia. 1967. C2570
28 Hutchinson, T. J. Ten years' wanderings among the Ethiopians. 1967. C2571
29 Dalzel, A. The history of Dahomey. 1967. C2572
30 Falconbridge, A. M. Narrative of two voyages to the River Sierra Leone. 1967. C2573
31 Elton, J. F. Travels and researches among the lakes and mountains of Eastern and Central Africa. 1968. C2574
32 Norris, R. Memoirs of the reign of Bossa Ahadee. 1968. C2575
33 Mason, G. H. Life with the Zulus of Natal. 1968. C2576
34 Isenberg, C. W. and Krapf, J. L. Journals detailing their proceedings in the Kingdom of Shoa. 1968. C2577
35 Allen, W. A narrative of the expedition sent to Her Majesty's government to the River Niger. 2 v. 1968. C2578
36 Caillié, E. Travels through Central Africa to Timbuctoo. 2 v. 1968. C2579
37 Höhnel, L. von. Discovery of Lakes Rudolf and Stefanie. 2 v. 1968. C2580
38 Gregory, J. W. The Great Rift Valley. 1968. C2581
39 Sulivan, G. L. Dhow Chasing in Zanzibar water and on the east coast of Africa. 1968. C2582
40 Brackenbury, H. The Ashanti War. 2 v. 1968. C2583
41 Thomson, J. Through Masai land. 1968. C2584
42 Jackson, J. G. An account of the empire of Morocco. 1968. C2585

43 Monteiro, J. J. Angalo and the River Congo. 2 v. 1968. C2586
44 Corry, J. Observations upon the windward coast of Africa... 1968. C2587
45 Melville, E. H. A residence at Sierra Leone described from a journal kept on the spot. 1968. C2588
46 Thomson, J. To the central African lakes and back. 2 v. 1968. C2589
47 Astley, T. A new collection of voyages and travels. 1968. C2590
48 Bindloss, H. In the Niger country. 1968. C2591
49 Duncan, J. Travels in western Africa in 1845 and 1847. 2 v. 1968. C2592
50 Pearce, N. The life and adventures of Nathaniel Pearce. 2 v. 1968. C2593
51 Frobenius, L. The voice of Africa. 2 v. 1969. C2594
52 Winterbottom, T. An account of the native Africans in the neighbourhood of Sierra Leone. 2 v. 1969. C2595
53 McQueen, J. A geographical survey of Africa. 1968. C2596
54 Major, R. H. The discoveries of Prince Henry the Navigator. 1968. C2597
55 Atkins, J. A voyage to Guinea, Brazil, and the West Indies. 1968. C2598
56 Ludolphus, J. A new history of Ethiopia. 1968. C2599
57 Huntley, H. V. Seven years' service on the slave coast of Western Africa. 2 v. 1969. C2600
58 Robertson, G. A. Notes on Africa. 1968. C2601
59 McLeod, J. A voyage to Africa... 1968. C2602
60 Crow, H. Memoirs. 1969. C2603
61 Richardson, J. Narrative of a mission to Central Africa performed in the years 1850-1851, ed. by Abu Boahen. 2 v. 1969. C2604
62 ___. Travels in the great desert of Sahara in 1845-1846, ed. by Abu Boahen. 1969. C2605
63 Hutchinson, T. J. Impressions of Western Africa... 1969. C2606
64 Hawkins, J. A history of a voyage to the coast of Africa... 1970. C2607
65 Blanc, H. A narrative of captivity in Abyssinia. 1970. C2608
66 Pigafetta, F. A report of the kingdom of Congo. 1970. C2609
67 McLeod, L. Travels in Eastern Africa. 2 v. 1971. C2610
68 Laird, M. and Oldfield, R. A. K. Narrative of an expedition into the interior of Africa by River Niger in the steam-vessels Quorra and Alburkah in 1832, 1833 and 1834. 2 v. 1971. C2611
69 Ingham, E. G. Sierra Leone. 1968. C2612

CASS LIBRARY OF INDUSTRIAL CLASSICS

(1) unnumbered. Baines, E. History of the cotton manufacture in Great Britain. 1967. C2613
2 Gaskell, P. Artisans and machinery. 1967. C2614
3 Ure, A. The philosophy of manufactures. 1967. C2615
4 Wing, C. Evils of the factory system. 1967. C2616
5 Scrivenor, H. History of the iron trade. 1967. C2617
6 Warden, A. J. The linen trade. 1967. C2618
7 British Assn. for Advancement of Science. Birmingham and Midland hardware district, ed. by Timmins. 1967. C2619
9 James, J. History of the worsted manufacture in England... 1968. C2620
10 Dodd, W. The factory system illustrated in a series of letters to the Right Hon. Lord Ashley. 1968. C2621
11 Ellison, T. The cotton trade of Great Britain. 1968. C2622

12 Taylor, W. C. Notes of a tour in the manufacturing districts of Lancashire. 1968. C2623
13 Head, G. A home tour through the manufacturing districts of England in the summer of 1835. 1968. C2624
14 Bischoff, J. A comprehensive history of the woollen and worsted manufactures and the natural and commercial history of sheep... 1968. C2625
15 Holland, J. The history and description of fossil fuel, the collieries, and coal trade of Great Britain. 1968. C2626
16 Guest, R. A compensious history of the cotton manufacture. 1968. C2627
17 Lloyd, G. I. H. The cutlery trades. 1968. C2628
18 Prentice, A. History of the anti-corn law league. 2 v. 1968. C2629
19 Kohl, J. G. England and Wales. 1968. C2630
20 Mann, J. A. The cotton trade of Great Britain. 1968. C2631
21 Fell, A. The early iron industry of Furness and Districts. 1968. C2632
22 Watts, J. The facts of the cotton empire. 1968. C2633
23 Leifchild, J. R. Our coal and our coalpits. 1968. C2634
24 ____. Cornwall. 1968. C2635
25 Fielden, J. The curse of the factory system. 1969. C2636
27 Arnold, R. A. The history of the cotton famine. 1974. C2637
28 Faucher, L. Manchester in 1844. 1969. C2638

CASS LIBRARY OF RAILWAY CLASSICS

1 Williams, F. S. Our iron roads. 1968. C2639
2 Head, F. B. Stokers and pokers. 1968. C2640
3 Booth, H. An account of the Liverpool and Manchester Railway. 1969. C2641
4 Curr, J. The coal viewer and engine builder's practical companion. 1970. C2642

CASS LIBRARY OF SCIENCE CLASSICS

1 Moivre, A. de. The doctrine of chances. 1967. C2643
2 Voltaire, F. M. A. de. The elements of Sir Isaac Newton's philosophy. 1967. C2644
3 Goethe, J. W. von. Theory of colours, tr. by Eastlake. 1967. C2645
4 Cavendish, H. The electrical researches of the Honourable Henry Cavendish, ed. by Maxwell. 1967. C2646
5 Whewell, W. The philosophy of the inductive sciences. 2 v. 1967. C2647
6 Babbage, C. The ninth Bridgewater treatise. 1967. C2648
7 Whewell, W. History of the inductive sciences. 3 v. 1967. C2649
8 Hooke, R. Philosophical experiments and observations. 1968. C2650
9 Kirwan, R. An essay on Phlogiston, and the constitution of acids. 1968. C2651
10 Huygens, C. The celestial world discover'd. 1968. C2652
11 Wilkins, J. The mathematical and philosophical works of the Right Rev. John Wilkins. 1970. C2653
12 Newton, I. Correspondence of Sir Isaac Newton and Professor Cotes. 1969. C2654
13 Bergman, T. A dissertation on elective attractions. 1970. C2655
15 Lavoisier, A. Essays, physical and chemical, tr. by Henry. 1970. C2656
16 Barrow, I. The usefulness of mathematical learning explained and demonstrated. 1973. C2657

CASS LIBRARY OF WEST INDIES STUDIES (Cass)

1 Bridges, G. W. The annals of Jamaica. 2 v. 1968. C2658
2 Trollope, A. The West Indies and the Spanish Main. 1968. C2659
3 Sewell, W. The ordeal of free labour in the West Indies. 1969. C2660
4 Southey, T. Chronological history of the West Indies. 1968. C2661
5 Dallas, R. C. The history of the Maroons. 1968. C2662
6 Pitman, F. W. The development of the British West Indies. 1967. C2663
7 Crouse, N. M. The French struggle for the West Indies. 1967. C2664
8 Labat, J. B. Memoirs, tr. by Eaden. 1969. C2665
9 Breen, G. W. The annals of Jamaica. 2 v. 1968. C2666
10 Schomburgk, R. H. A description of British Guiana. 1969. C2667
11 Ligon, R. A true and exact history of the Island of Barbados. 1969. C2668
12 Long, E. The history of Jamaica, ed. by Metcalf. 1969. C2669
13 Joseph, E. L. History of Trinidad. 1970. C2670
14 Caldecott, A. The church in the West Indies. 1970. C2671
15 Salmon, C. S. The Caribbean confederation. 1970. C2672
16 Penson, L. M. The colonial agents of the British West Indies. 1971. C2673
17 Gardner, W. J. A history of Jamaica. 1971. C2674
18 Young, W. An account of the Black Charaibs in the Island of St. Vincent... 1971. C2675
19 Schomburgk, R. H. The history of Barbados. 1971. C2676
20 Fraser, L. M. History of Trinidad from 1781 to 1839. 1971. C2677
21 Coke, T. A history of the West Indies. 3 v. 1971. C2678
22 Davy, J. The West Indies before and since slave emancipation. 1971. C2679
23 Shepard, C. An historical account of the island of St. Vincent. 1971. C2680
24 Pares, R. War and trade in the West Indies. 1971. C2681
25 Ragatz, L. J. The fall of the planter class in the British Caribbean, 1763-1833. 1971. C2682
26 Poyer, J. The history of Barbados from the first discovery of the island in the year 1605 til the accession of Lord Seaforth. 1971. C2683
27 Atwood, T. The history of the island of Dominicana. 1971. C2684
28 Woodcock, H. I. A history of Tobago. 1971. C2685

CATHOLIC RECORD SOCIETY. MONOGRAPHS

1 Williams, J. A. Catholic recusancy in Wiltshire, 1660-1791. 1968. C2686
2 Aveling, J. C. H. Catholic recusancy in the city of York, 1558-1791. 1970. C2687

CATHOLIC RECORD SOCIETY. PUBLICATIONS (Dawson)

1-4 Catholic Record Society. Miscellanea. V. 1-4. 1904-07. C2688
5 ____. Unpublished documents relating to the English martyrs, 1584-1603, ed. by Pollen. 1908. C2689
6-7 Same as nos. 1-4. V. 5, 6. 1908-09. C2690
8 Paris. Convent des filles anglaises. The diary of Blue Nuns... at Paris, 1658-1810. Ed. by Gillow and Trappes-Lomax. 1910. C2691
9 Same as nos. 1-4. V. 7. 1911. C2692
10 Knox, T. F. Douay diaries. Third diary, 1598-1637. 1911. C2693
11 ____. ____. Fourth diary. 1641-1647. 1912. C2694

12 Catholic Record Society. Obituaries. 1913. C2695
13-14 Same as nos. 1-4. V. 7, 8. 1914-15. C2696
15-16 Lancashire, Eng. Registers. 2 v. 1916-17. C2697
17 Same as nos. 1-4. V. 10. 1918. C2698
18 Recusants Exchequer Roll, 1592-93. 1919. C2699
19 Same as nos. 1-4. V. 11. 1920. C2700
20 Same as nos. 15-16. V. 3. 1921. C2701
21 Same as no. 5. 1557-95. Ed. by Pollen and MacMahon. 1922. C2702
22 Same as nos. 1-4. V. 12. 1923. C2703
23 Same as nos. 15-16. V. 4. 1924. C2704
24 Trappes-Lomax, R. Registers of English Franciscan Nuns. 1925. C2705
25 Catholic Record Society. Dominicana. 1926. C2706
26-27 Same as nos. 1-4. V. 13-14. 1927-28. C2707
28 Same as no. 10. Seventh diary, 1715-78. Ed. by Burton and Nolan. 1929. C2708
29 Madrid. English College. Records of the English College at Madrid, 1611-1767, ed. by Henson. 1930. C2709
30 Valladolid. English College. Registers of the English College at Valladolid, 1589-1862. 1931. C2710
31 Same as nos. 15-16. V. 5. 1932. C2711
32 Same as nos. 1-4. V. 15. 1935. C2712
33 McCann, J. and Connolly, H., eds. English Benedictine papers. 1934. C2713
34 London Session papers, ed. by Bowler. 1935. C2714
35 Same as nos. 1-4. V. 16. 1936. C2715
36 Same as nos. 15-16. V. 6. 1937. C2716
37 Rome. English College. The Liber Ruber of the English College, Rome. Nomina alumnorum, 1579-1630. Ed. by Kelly and others. 1939. C2717
38 Registers of the Catholic chapels Royal and of the Portuguese Embassy Chapel, 1662-1829. Ed. by Weale. 1940. C2718
39 Parsons, R. Letters and memorials of Father Robert Parsons, ed. by Hicks. 1942. C2719
40 Same as no. 37. 1961-1783. 1944. C2720
41 Fitzherbert, T. Letters of Thomas Fitzherbert, 1608-10, ed. by Hicks. 1946. C2721
42-44 Hampshire, Eng. Hampshire registers, ed. by Scantlebury. 3 v. 1948-51. C2722
45-46 Harpsfield, N. Archdeacon Harpsfield's Canterbury Visitations. 2 v. 1949-50. C2723
47-48 Warner's history of English persecution of Catholics and the Presbyterian plot. 2 v. 1951-53. C2724
49 Same as nos. 42-44. V. 4. 1955. C2725
50 Mawhood, W. The Mawhood diary, ed. by Reynolds. 1956. C2726
51 England. Wisbech Castle. The Wisbech stirs, 1595-98. 1957. C2727
52 Verstegan, R. Letters and despatches of Richard Verstegab, 1550-1640. 1959. C2728
53 Same as nos. 1-4. V. 17. 1960. C2729
54-55 Rome. English College. The responsa scholarum. 2 v. 1960-62. C2730
56 Same as nos. 1-4. V. 18. 1964. C2731
57 Same as no. 18. 1593-94. C2732
58 Letters of Allen and Barrett, 1572-1598..., with forty-five letters of Richard Barrett. 1966. C2733
59 Wight. New port. New port and Cowes registers. 1967. C2734
60 Recusant documents from the Ellesmere manuscripts.

1968. C2735
61 Same as no. 18. 1594-1596. 1970. C2736
62 Sabran, L. The letter book of Lewis Sabran, ed. by Holt. 1971. C2737
63 Harris, P. R., ed. Douai College documents, 1639-1794. 1972. C2738
64 Loomie, A. J., ed. Spain and the Jacobean Catholics, 1603-12. 1974. C2739

CATHOLIC UNIVERSITY OF AMERICA. ANTHROPOLOGICAL SERIES.

1 Koppert, V. A. Contributions to Clayoquot ethnology. 1930. C2740
2 Cooper, J. M. The northern Algonquian supreme being. 1934. C2741
3 ____. Notes on the ethnology of the Otchipwe of the Lake of the woods and of Rainy lake. 1936. C2742
4 Ward, E. Marriage among the Yoruba. 1936. C2743
5 Cooper, J. M. Snares, deadfalls, and other traps of the northern Algonquians and northern Athapaskans. 1938. C2744
6 Ward, E. Yoruba husband-wife code. 1936. C2745
7 Flannery, R. An analysis of coastal Algonquian culture. 1938. C2746
8 Nimendajú, C. Apinayé. 1938. C2747
9 Jenkins, W. H. Notes on the hunting economy of the Abitibi Indians. 1939. C2748
10 Cooper, J. M. Temporal sequence and the marginal cultures. 1941. C2749
11 Sullivan, R. J. The Ten'a food quest. 1942. C2750
12 Coleman, Bernard, Sister. Decorative designs of the Ojibwa of northern Minnesota. 1947. C2751
13 Van der Eerden, Mary Lucia, Sister. Maternity in a Spanish-American community of New Mexico. 1948. C2752
14 Desmond, G. R. Gambling among the Yakima. 1952. C2753
15 Flannery, R. The Gros Ventres of Montana. V. 1. 1953. C2754
16 Cooper, J. M. The Gros Ventres of Montana. V. 2. 1957. C2755
17 Haile, B. Property concepts of the Navaho Indians. 1954. C2756
18 Sano, C. Changing values of the Japanese family. 1958. C2757
19 McGee, J. T. Cultural stability and changes among the Montagnais Indians of the Lake Melville region of Labrador. 1962. C2758

CATHOLIC UNIVERSITY OF AMERICA. PATRISTIC STUDIES.

1 Jacks, L. V. St. Basil and Greek literature. 1922. C2759
2 Campbell, J. M. The influence of the second Sophistic on the style of the sermons of St. Basil the Great. 1922. C2760
3 Parsons, Wilfrid, Sister. A study of the vocabulary and rhetoric of the letters of St. Augustine. 1923. C2761
4 Colbert, Mary Columkille, Sister. The syntax of the "De Civitate Dei" of St. Augustine. 1923. C2762
5 Ameringer, T. E. The stylistic influence of the second Sophistic on the Panegryical sermons of St. John Chrysostom. 1921. C2763
6 Barry, Inviolata, Sister. St. Augustine the orator. A study of the rhetorical qualities of St. Augustine's "Sermons ad Populum." 1924. C2764
7 Reynolds, G. The Clausulae in the "De Civitate Dei" of St. Augustine. 1924. C2765
8 Augustinus, Aurelius, St.

S. Aurelii Augustini Liber De Catechizandis Rudibus, tr. by Christopher. 1926. C2766
9 Ambrosius, St. Sancti Ambrosii Oratio de obitu Theodosli, tr. by Mannix. 1926. C2767
10 Barry, Mary Finbar, Sister. The vocabulary of the moral-ascetical works of St. Ambrose. 1926. C2768
11 Dickinson, F. W. A. The use of the optative mood in the works of St. John Chrysostom. 1926. C2769
12 Adams, Miriam Annunciata, Sister. The Latinity of the letters of St. Ambrose. 1927. C2770
13 Way, Agnes Clare, Sister. The language and style of the letters of St. Basil. 1927. C2771
14 Arts, Mary Raphael, Sister. The syntax of the Confessions of St. Augustine. 1927. C2772
15 Ambrosius, St. S. Ambrosii De Nabuthae, tr. by McGuire. 1927. C2773
16 Paulinus Mediolanensis. Vita S. Ambrosii, mediolanensis episcopi, a Paulino eius notario ad beatum Augustinum conscripta, tr. by Kaniecka. 1928. C2774
17 Gregorius, St. Bp. of Nyssa. Encomium of Saint Gregory, Bishop of Nyssa, on his Brother Saint Basil, Archbishop of Cappadocian Caesarea, tr. by Stein. 1928. C2775
18 Dinneen, Lucilla, Sister. Titles of address in Christian Greek epistolography to 527 A.D. 1929. C2776
19 Ambrosius, St. S. Ambrosii de Helia et leiunio, tr. by Buck. 1929. C2777
20 Martin, Marie Antoinette, Sister. The use of indirect discourse in the works of St. Ambrose. 1930. C2778
21 O'Brien, Mary Bridget, Sister. Titles of address in Christian Latin epistolography to 543 A.D. 1930. C2779
22 Burns, Mary Albania, Sister. Saint John Chrysostom's homilies on the statutes. 1930. C2780
23 Augustine, Aurelius, St. De doctorina christiana, liber quartus, tr. by Sullivan. 1930. C2781
24 Madden, Mary Daniel, Sister. The pagan divinities and their worships as depicted in the works of St. Augustine exclusive of the City of God. 1930. C2782
25 Murphy, Margaret Gertrude, Sister. St. Basil and monasticism. 1930. C2783
26 Hoey, G. W. P. The use of the optative mood in the work of St. Gregory of Nyssa. 1930. C2784
27 Dwyer, W. F. The vocabulary of Hegi sippus. 1931. C2785
28 Getty, Marie Madeline of Jesus, Sister. Life of the North Africans as revelated in the sermons of St. Augustine. 1930. C2786
29 Diederich, Mary Dorothea, Sister. Vergil in the works of St. Ambrose. 1931. C2787
30 Springer, Mary Theresa of the Cross, Sister. Nature-imagery in the works of St. Ambrose. 1931. C2788
31 Hrdlicka, C. L. A study of the late Latin vocabulary and of the prepositions and demonstrative pronouns in the Confessions of St. Augustine. 1931. C2789
32 Dunn, Mary Borromeo, Sister. The style of the letters of St. Gregory the Great. 1931. C2790
33 Holman, Mary John, Sister. Nature-imagery in the works of St. Augustine. 1931. C2791
34 Cyprianus, St. De habita virginum, tr. by Keenan. 1932. C2792
35 Ambrosius, St. De Tobia, tr. by Zucker. 1933. C2793
36 Cyprianus, St. De mortalitate, tr. by Hannan. 1933. C2794
37 Sullivan, D. D. The life of the North Africans as revealed in the works of Saint Cyprian. 1932. C2795

38 Buttell, Mary Frances, Sister. The rhetoric of St. Hilary of Poitiers. 1933. C2796
39 Mahoney, Albertus, Brother. Vergil in the works of Prudentius. 1934. C2797
40 Delaney, Mary Rosella, Sister. A study of the clausulae in the works of St. Ambrose. 1940. C2798
41 Brown, Mary Vincentia, Sister. The syntax of the prepositions in the works of St. Hilary. 1934. C2799
42 Bogan, Mary Inez, Sister. The vocabulary and style of the soliloquies and dialogues of St. Augustine. 1935. C2800
43 McCormick, J. P. A study of the nominal syntax and of indirect discourse in Hegesippus. 1935. C2801
44 Mahoney, Catherine of Siena, Sister. The rare and late Latin nouns, adjectives, and adverbs in St. Augustine's De Civitate Dei. 1935. C2802
45 Kennan, Mary Emily, Sister. The life and times of St. Augustine as revealed in his letters. 1935. C2803
46 Paluszak, A. B. The subjunctive in the letters of St. Augustine. 1935. C2804
47 Kinnavey, R. J. The vocabulary of St. Hilary of Poitiers as contained in commentarius in Mattheaum, Liber I ad Constantium and De Trinitate. 1947. C2805
48 Mann, Mary Emmanuel, Sister. The clausulae of St. Hilary of Poitiers. 1936. C2806
49 Phillips, L. T. The subordinate temporal, causal, and adversative clauses in the works of St. Ambrose. 1937. C2807
50 Fives, D. C. The use of the optative mood in the works of Theodoret, bishop of Cyrus. 1937. C2808
51 Herron, Margaret Clare, Sister. A study of the clausulae in the writings of St. Jerome. 1937. C2809
52 Muldowney, Mary Sarah, Sister. Word-order in the works of St. Augustine. 1937. C2810
53 Schieman, Mary Bernard, Sister. The rare and late verbs in St. Augustines' De civitate Dei. 1938. C2811
54 Gimborn, D. T. The syntax of the simple cases in St. Hilary of Poitiers. 1938. C2812
55 Prendergast, Agnes Cecile, Sister. The Latinity of the De vita contemplativa of Gulianus Pomerius. 1938. C2813
56 Gillis, J. H. The coordinating particles in Saints Hilary, Jerome, Ambrose, and Augustine. 1938. C2814
57 Fox, Margaret Mary, Sister. The life and times of St. Basil the Great as revealed in his works. 1939. C2815
58 Ambrosius, St. Sancti Ambrosii liber De consolatione Valentiniani, tr. by Kelly. 1940. C2816
59 Halliwell, W. J. The style of Pope St. Leo the Great. 1939. C2817
60 Hritzu, J. N. The style of the letters of St. Jerome. 1939. C2818
61 Wilkins, M. Word-order in selected sermons of the fifth and sixth centuries. 1940. C2819
62 Carroll, Mary Borromeo, Sister. The clausulae in the Confessions of St. Augustine. 1940. C2820
63 Pando, J. C. The life and times of Synesius of Cyrene as revealed in his works. 1940. C2821
64 Nugent, Rosamond, Sister. Portrait of the consecrated woman in Greek Christian literature of the first four centuries. 1941. C2822
65 Murphy, M. G. Nature allusions in the work of Clement of Alexandria. 1930. C2823
66 Ewald, Marie Liguori, Sister. Ovid in the Contra orationem Symmachi of

Prudentius. 1942. C2824
67 Mueller, Mary Magdeleine, Sister. The vocabulary of Pope St. Leo the Great. 1943. C2825
68 Henry, Rose de Lima, Sister. The late Greek optative and its use in the writings of Gregory Nazianzen. 1943. C2826
69 Eaton, A. (Hawkins). The influence of Ovid on Claudian. 1943. C2827
70 Kelly, Jamesetta, Sister. Life and times as revealed in the writings of St. Jerome exclusive of his letters. 1944. C2828
71 Maat, W. A. A rhetorical study of St. John Chrysostom's De sacerdotio. 1944. C2829
72 Augustinus, Aurelius, St. De beata vita, tr. by Brown. 1944. C2830
73 Wagner, Monica, Sister. Rufinus, the translator. 1944. C2831
74 Orientius, St. Orientii Commonitorium, tr. by Tobin. 1945. C2832
75 Ball, Mary Tarcisia, Sister. Nature and the vocabulary of nature in the works of Saint Cyprian. 1946. C2833
76 Sherlock, R. B. The syntax of the nominal forms of the verb, exclusive of the participle, in St. Hilary. 1947. C2834
77 Brennan, Mary Josephine, Sister. A study of the clausulae in the sermons of St. Augustine. 1947. C2835
78 Dressler, H. The usage of 'Ασκέω and its cognates in Greek documents to 100 A. D. 1947. C2836
79 Goggin, Thomas Aquinas, Sister. The times of St. Gregory of Nyssa as reflected in the Letters and the Contra Eunomium. 1948. C2837
80 Baney, Margaret Mary, Sister. Some reflections of life in North Africa in the writings of Tertullian. 1948. C2838
81 Wilde, R. The testament of the Jews in the Greek Christian writers of the first three centuries. 1949. C2839
82 Ellspermann, G. The attitude of the early Christian Latin writers toward pagan literature and learning. 1949. C2840
83 Beyenka, Mary Melchior, Sister. Consolation in Saint Augustine. 1950. C2841
84 Augustinus, Aurelius, St. De fide rerum quae non videntun, tr. by McDonald. 1950. C2842
85 Augustinus, Aurelius, St. De utilitate ieunii, tr. by Rugg. 1950. C2843
86 Marshall, R. T. Studies in the political and socio-religious terminology of the De civitate Dei. 1952. C2844
87 Young, J. J. Studies of the style of the De vocatione omnium gentium ascribed to Prosper of Aquitaine. 1952. C2845
88 Augustinus, Aurelius, St. De natura boni, tr. by Moon. 1955. C2846
89 ____. De excidio urbis Romae sermo, tr. by O'Reilly. 1955. C2847
90 ____. De haeresibus of St. Augustine, ed. by Müller. 1956. C2848
91 ____. De dono perserverantiae, tr. by Lesousky. 1956. C2849
92 Cyprianus, St. De bono patientiae, tr. by Conway. 1957. C2850
93 Gokey, F. X. The terminology for the devil and evil spirits in the Apostolic Fathers. 1961. C2851
94 Cyprianus, St. De opere et Eleemosynis, ed. by Rebenack. 1962. C2852
95 Prosper, Tiro, Aquitanus, St. Carmen de ingratis S. Prosperi Aquitani, tr. by Huegelmeyer. 1963. C2853
96 Rufini presbyteri Liber de fide, tr. by Miller. 1964. C2854
97 Epistula ad Demetriadem de vera humilitate, tr. by Krabbe. 1965. C2855
98 McHugh, M. P. The Carmen de providentia dei

attributed to Prosper of Aquitaine, tr. by McHugh. 1964. C2856
99 Conroy, M. C. Imagery in the Sermones of Maximus, Bishop of Turin. 1965. C2857

CATHOLIC UNIVERSITY OF AMERICA. PHILOSOPHICAL STUDIES.

1 Lucas, G. Agnosticism and religion--an analysis of Spencer's religion of the unknowable. 1895. C2858
2 O'Connor, M. J. Responsibility to moral life. 1903. C2859
3 Schumacher, M. The knowableness of God. 1905. C2860
4 Dubray, C. A. The theory of psychical dispositions. 1905. C2861
5 Hagerty, C. The problems of evil. 1911. C2862
6 Cunningham, W. F. The basis of realism. 1915. C2863
7 Knapke, O. F. The scholastic theory of the species sensibilis. 1915. C2864
8 Smith, H. I. Classification of desires in St. Thomas and in modern sociology. 1915. C2865
9 Michel, V. G. The critical principles of Orestes A. Brownson. 1918. C2866
10 Murphy, E. F. St. Thomas' political doctrine and democracy. 1921. C2867
11 O'Connor, W. P. The concept of the human soul... 1921. C2868
12 Rolbiecki, J. J. The political philosophy of Dante Alighieri. 1922. C2869
13 Bender, J. E. The relation between moral qualities and intelligence according to St. Thomas. 1924. C2870
14 Brennan, E. The theory of abnormal cognitive processes. 1925. C2871
15 McKeough, M. J. The meaning of the rationes seminales in St. Augustine. 1926. C2872
16 Callahan, J. L. A theory of esthetics according to the principles of St. Thomas Aquinas. 1927. C2873
17 Mullane, D. T. Aristotelianism in Thomas Aquinas. 1929. C2874
18 Ward, L. R. Philosophy of value. 1930. C2875
19 Bauer, J. M. Modern notions of faith. 1930. C2876
20 Hart, C. A. The Thomistic concept of mental faculties. 1930. C2877
21 McMahon, F. E. The humanism of Irving Babbitt. 1931. C2878
22 O'Leary, C. J. The substantial composition of man according to St. Bonaventure. 1931. C2879
23 Coady, Mary Anastasia, Sister. The phantasm according to the teaching of St. Thomas. 1932. C2880
24 Talbot, E. F. Knowledge and object. 1932. C2881
25 Ryan, J. K. Modern war and basic ethics. 1933. C2882
26 Killeen, Mary Vincent, Sister. Man in the new humanism. 1934. C2883
27 McAuliffe, Agnes Teresa, Sister. Some modern nonintellectual approaches to God. 1934. C2884
28 Marling, J. The order of nature in the philosophy of St. Thomas Aquinas. 1934. C2885
29 Reilly, G. C. The psychology of St. Albert the Great... 1934. C2886
30 Cronin, J. F. Cardinal Newman: his theory of knowledge. 1935. C2887
31 Casey, J. T. The primacy of metaphysics. 1936. C2888
32 Lucks, H. A. The philosophy of Athenagoras. 1936. C2889
33 Slavin, R. J. The philosophical basis for individual differences according to St. Thomas Aquinas. 1936. C2890
34 Rooney, M. T. Lawlessness law, and sanction. 1937. C2891
35 Ragusa, T. J. The substance theory of mind and

contemporary functionalism. 1937. C2892
36 O'Donnell, C. M. The psychology of St. Bonaventure and St. Thomas Aquinas. 1937. C2893
37 Linehan, J. C. The rational nature of man. 1937. C2894
38 McFadden, C. J. The metaphysical foundations of dialectical materialism. 1938. C2895
39 Wolfe, Mary Joan of Arc, Sister. The problem of solidarism in St. Thomas. 1938. C2896
40 Gerrity, Benignus, Brother. St. Thomas' doctrine of substantial form and the relations between this doctrine and certain problems and movements of contemporary philosophy. 1937. C2897
41 Miron, C. H. The problem of altruism in the philosophy of Saint Thomas. 1939. C2898
42 McAllister, J. B. The letters of St. Thomas Aquinas, de occultis operibus naturae. 1939. C2899
43 Hoban, J. H. The Thomistic concept of person and some of its social implications. 1939. C2900
44 O'Connor, E. M. Potentiality and energy. 1939. C2901
45 Cahill, Mary Camilla, Sister. The absolute and the relative in St. Thomas and in modern philosophy. 1939. C2902
46 O'Brien, Mary Consilia, Sister. The antecedents of being. 1939. C2903
47 Friel, G. Q. Punishment in the philosophy of St. Thomas Aquinas, and among some primitive peoples. 1939. C2904
48 McDonald, W. J. The social value of property according to St. Thomas Aquinas. 1939. C2905
49 Killeen, S. M. The philosophy of labor in St. Thomas. 1939. C2906
50 Ostheimer, A. L. The family. 1939. C2907
51 Sullivan, J. B. An examination of the first principles in thought and being. 1939. C2908
52 Dady, M. Rachel, Sister. The theory of knowledge of Saint Bonaventure. 1939. C2909
53 Kreilkamp, K. The metaphysical foundations of Thomistic jurisprudence. 1939. C2910
54 Tallon, H. J. The concept of self in British and American idealism. 1939. C2911
55 Sleva, V. E. The separated soul in the philosophy of St. Thomas Aquinas. 1940. C2912
56 Meehan, F. X. Efficient causality in Aristotle and in St. Thomas. 1940. C2913
57 Richey, Francis Augustine, Sister. Character control of wealth according to St. Thomas Aquinas. 1940. C2914
58 Mullen, Mary Dominicia, Sister. Essence and operation in thomistic and in modern philosophy. 1941. C2915
59 Brennan, Rose Emmanuella, Sister. The intellectual virtues according to the philosophy of St. Thomas Aquinas. 1941. C2916
60 LeClair, Mary St. Ida, Sister. Utopias and the philosophy of St. Thomas Aquinas. 1941. C2917
61 Ledvina, J. P. A philosophy and psychology of sensation... according to St. Thomas Aquinas. 1941. C2918
62 Udell, Mary Gonzaga, Sister. A theory of criticism of fiction in its moral aspects according to Thomistic principles. 1941. C2919
63 Dougherty, G. V. The moral basis of social order according to St. Thomas. 1941. C2920
64 Harvey, R. J. The metaphysical relation between person and liberty and its application to historical liberalism and totalitarianism. 1942. C2921
65 Joubert, G. Qualities of

citizenship in St. Thomas. 1941. C2922

66 Kinney, Cyril Edwin, Sister. A critique of the philosophy of George Santayana in the light of Thomistic principles. 1942. C2923

67 Shircel, C. L. The univocity of the concept of being in the philosophy of John Duns Scotus. 1942. C2924

68 Ferguson, Jane Frances, Sister. The philosophy of equality in the philosophy of St. Thomas Aquinas. 1943. C2925

69 Hayes, Mary Dolores, Sister. Various group mind theories viewed in the light of Thomistic principles. 1942. C2926

70 Benkert, G. F. The Thomistic conception of an international society. 1942. C2927

71 Penta, C. D. Hope and society. 1942. C2928

72 Ferree, W. The act of social justice. 1942. C2929

73 Fox, J. F. A Thomistic analysis of social order. 1943. C2930

74 Maguire, J. J. The philosophy of modern revolution. 1943. C2931

75 Bennett, O. The nature of demonstrative proof according to the principles of Aristotle and St. Thomas Aquinas. 1943. C2932

76 McSweeney, A. J. The social role of truth according to St. Thomas Aquinas. 1943. C2933

77 Reardon, J. J. Selfishness and the social order. 1943. C2934

78 Fisher, L. Social leadership according to Thomistic principles. 1943. C2935

79 Kerins, J. F. The social role of self-control. 1943. C2936

80 Pousson, L. B. The totalitarian philosophy of education. 1944. C2937

81 O'Toole, C. J. The philosophical theory of creation in the writing of St. Augustine. 1944. C2938

82 Vargas, A. Psychology and philosophy of teaching according to traditional philosophy and modern trends. 1944. C2939

83 Duffy, J. A. A philosophy of poetry based on Thomistic principles. 1944. C2940

84 Gustafson, G. J. The theory of natural appetency in the philosophy of Saint Thomas Aquinas. 1944. C2941

85 Speltz, G. H. The importance of rural life according to the philosophy of St. Thomas Aquinas. 1944. C2942

86 Horrigan, A. F. Metaphysics as a principle of order in the university curriculum. 1944. C2943

87 Kleinz, J. P. The theory of knowledge of Hugh of St. Victor. 1944. C2944

88 Scheu, Marina, Sister. The categories of being in Aristotle and St. Thomas. 1944. C2945

89 Collins, J. D. The Thomistic philosophy of the angels. 1944. C2946

90 Grajewski, M. J. The formal distinction of Duns Scotus. 1944. C2947

91 Duzy, Erminius Stanislaus, Brother. Philosophy of social change according to the principles of St. Thomas. 1944. C2948

92 Hughes, Mary Cosmas, Sister. The intelligibility of the universe in the philosophy of St. Thomas Aquinas. 1946. C2949

93 De Benedictis, M. M. The social thought of St. Bonaventure. 1946. C2950

94 Foley, L. A. A critique of the philosophy of being of Alfred North Whitehead in the light of Thomistic philosophy. 1946. C2951

95 Buckley, G. M. The nature and unity of metaphysics. 1946. C2952

96 Wolter, A. B. The transcendentals and their function in the metaphysics of Duns Scotus. 1946. C2953

97 Smith, V. E. The philosophical frontiers of physics. 1947. C2954
98 Smith, Enid, Sister. The goodness of being in Thomistic philosophy and its contemporary significance. 1947. C2955
99 Sattler, H. V. A philosophy of submission. 1948. C2956
100 Tyrrell, F. M. The role of assent in judgment. 1948. C2957
101 Mohan, R. P. A Thomistic philosophy of civilization and culture. 1948. C2958
102 DeCoursey, Mary Edwin, Sister. The theory of evil in the metaphysics of St. Thomas and its contemporary significance. 1948. C2959
103 Schumacher, L. S. The philosophy of the equitable distribution of wealth. 1949. C2960
104 De la Vega, F. J. Social progress and happiness in the philosophy of St. Thomas Aquinas and contemporary American sociology. 1949. C2961
105 Rzadkiewicz, A. L. The philosophical bases of human liberty according to St. Thomas Aquinas. 1949. C2962
106 Alluntis, F. The problem of expropriation. 1949. C2963
107 Sheppard, V. T. Religion and the concept of democracy. 1949. C2964
108 Porreco, R. E. The place of economics in the philosophical hierarchy. 1949. C2965
109 Buehler, W. J. The role of prudence in education. 1950. C2966
110 Giguere, R. J. The social value of public worship according to Thomistic principles. 1950. C2967
111 Guzikowski, M. E. A philosophy of liberalism in the light of Thomistic principles. (microcards). 1950. C2968
112 McQuade, F. P. A philosophical interpretation of the contemporary crisis of western civilization. 1950. C2969
113 Cronan, E. P. The dignity of a human person. 1950. C2970
114 Hunt, B. B. The nature and significance of the one that follows being in philosophy of St. Thomas Aquinas. 1950. C2971
115 Naughton, E. R. Freedom in education. 1950. C2972
116 Benard, E. D. The problem of belief in the writings of John Henry Newman, William James, and St. Thomas Aquinas. 1950. C2973
117 Franz, E. Q. The Thomistic doctrine on the possible intellect. 1950. C2974
118 Kane, Ann Virginia, Sister. The role of quality in philosophy of St. Thomas Aquinas. 1950. C2975
119 Delehant, Mary Dunstan, Sister. The role of quality in philosophy of St. Thomas Aquinas. 1950. C2976
120 Brennan, M. A., Sister. The origin of the rational soul according to St. Thomas. 1950. C2977
121 Rosenberg, J. R. The principle of individuation; comparative study in St. Thomas, Scotus and Suarez. 1950. C2978
122 Bode, R. R. The philosophy of courage. 1950. C2979
123 Fontaine, R. C. Subsistent accident in the philosophy of St. Thomas and in his predecessors. 1950. C2980
124 Laky, J. J. A study of George Berkeley's philosophy in the light of the philosophy of St. Thomas Aquinas. 1950. C2981
125 Schneider, M. Max Scheler's phenomenological philosophy of values. 1951. C2982
126 Cangemi, D. The Thomistic concept of the vis cogitativa. 1951. C2983
127 Savaria, Madeleine Gabrielle, Sister. Etienne Gilson's concept of the nature and scope of philosophy. 1951. C2984
128 Bagen, J. J. The

brotherhood of man according to St. Thomas Aquinas. 1951. C2985

129 Hogan, J. E. The virtue of prudence in the social philosophy of St. Thomas. 1951. C2986

130 Niemeyer, Mary Fredericus, Sister. The one and the many in the social order according to St. Thomas Aquinas. 1951. C2987

131 Moran, L. P. Permanence and process, a philosophical investigation into the foundations of the law of energy conservation. 1951. C2988

132 Maloney, W. T. Individualism: extreme and moderate. 1951. C2989

133 Dougherty, K. F. The subject, object and method of the philosophy of nature according to Thomas Aquinas. 1951. C2990

134 Noonan, J. T. Banking and the early scholastic analysis of usury. 1951. C2991

135 Wagstaffe, Mary Joseph, Sister. The Thomistic philosophy of culture and the virtue of art. 1951. (Microcard). C2992

136 Weiswurm, A. A. The nature of human knowledge according to St. Gregory of Nyssa. 1952. C2993

137 Dechert, C. R. Thomas More and society. 1952 (Microcard). C2994

138 O'Brien, J. F. The concept of nature in philosophy and physics. 1952 (Microcard). C2995

139 Slattery, K. F. The Thomistic concept of the virtue of temperance and its relations to the emotions. 1952 (Microcard). C2996

140 Harkenrider, E. W. The relation of the virtue of justice to personality. 1952 (Microcard). C2997

141 Breen, J. S. Religion and secularism in the light of Thomistic thought. 1952 (Microcard). C2998

142 Harrington, J. P. J. The contemporary philosophy of security in the light of the scholastic theory of divine providence. 1952 (Microcard). C2999

143 Scheuer, M. J. Philosophy of man in Communism. 1952 (Microcard). C3000

144 Lynam, G. J. The good political ruler according to St. Thomas. 1953. C3001

145 O'Connor, J. J. Philosophical aspects of communication. 1953. C3002

146 Petritz, M. M. The philosophy of anger and the virtues. 1953. C3003

147 Anderson, Mary Evangeline, Sister. The human body in the philosophy of St. Thomas Aquinas. 1953. C3004

148 Reutemann, C. The Thomistic concept of pleasure, as compared with hedonistic and rigoristic philosophies. 1953. C3005

149 Keating, J. The function of the philosopher in American pragmatism. 1953. C3006

150 Simec, Sophie M., Sister. Philosophical basis of human dignity and change in Thomistic and American non-Thomistic philosophy. 1953. C3007

151 Horrigan, Anita, Sister. Moral standards and social organization. 1953. C3008

152 Nolan, P. St. Thomas and the unconscious mind. 1953. C3009

153 Frederickson, O. P. The psychology of ownership. 1954. C3010

154 Coggin, W. A. The role of the will in personality development. 1954. C3011

155 Feld, N. The persistence of realism in the modern scientific interpretation of nature. 1954. C3012

156 Toon, M. The philosophy of sex according to St. Thomas. 1954. C3013

157 Fleckenstein, N. J. A critique of John Dewey's

theory of nature and the knowledge of reality in the light of the principles of Thomism. 1954. C3014
158 Warther, M. A. The transcendental notion of supposit. 1954. C3015
159 Bonansea, B. M. The theory of knowledge of Tommaso Campanella, exposition and critique. 1954. C3016
160 Ramirez, A. Unconscious drives and human freedom in Freud's psychoanalysis. 1955. C3017
161 Doherty, J. J. The concept of man in Communist philosophy. 1955. C3018
162 Myers, J. R. Social distance according to St. Thomas Aquinas. 1955. C3019
163 Burroughs, J. A. Prudence integrating the moral virtues according to St. Thomas Aquinas. 1955. C3020
164 Inagaki, B. R. The constitution of Japan and the natural law. 1955. C3021
165 Masiello, R. The intuition of being according to the metaphysics of St. Thomas Aquinas. 1955. C3022
166 Paparella, B. A. Sociality and sociability, a philosophy of sociability according to St. Thomas Aquinas. 1955. C3023
167 Summers, J. A. St. Thomas and the universal. 1955. C3024
168 McCall, R. E. Reality of substance. 1956. C3025
169 Wheeler, Mary Cecilia, Sister. Philosophy and the Summa theologica of St. Thomas Aquinas. 1956. C3026
170 Sheehan, R. J. The philosophy of happiness according to St. Thomas Aquinas. 1956. C3027
171 O'Hara, M. Kevin, Sister. The connotations of wisdom according to St. Thomas Aquinas. 1956. C3028
172 Foley, M. Thomas Aquinas, Sister. Authority and personality according to St. Thomas Aquinas. 1956. C3029
173 O'Shea, R. S. Truth of being through knowledge by connaturality. 1956. C3030
174 Elbert, E. J. A Thomistic study of the psychology of human character. 1956. C3031
175 Tamme, Anne Mary, Sister. A critique of John Dewey's theory of fine arts in the light of the principles of Thomism. 1956. C3032
176 Heath, T. R. Aristotelian influence in Thomistic wisdom. 1956. C3033
177 Zamoyta, Casimir Stanislaus, Brother. The Unity of man. 1956. C3034
178 Majchrzak, C. J. A brief history of Bonaventurianism. 1957. C3035
179 Kane, W. J. The philosophy of relation in the metaphysics of St. Thomas. 1958. C3036
180 McLean, G. F. Man's knowledge of God according to Paul Tillich. 1958. C3037
181 Gallagher, T. The contemporary status of the notion of existence and its limitation in Thomistic metaphysics. 1958. C3038
182 Mann, J. A. Existential import and the Aristotelian syllogistic. 1958. C3039
183 Conlan, F. A. A critique of the philosophy of religion of Henry Nelson Wieman in the light of Thomistic principles. 1958. C3040
184 Lyons, L. F. Material and formal causality in the philosophy of Aristotle and St. Thomas. 1958. C3041
185 Twomey, J. E. The general notion of the transcendentals in the metaphysics of St. Thomas Aquinas. 1958. C3042
186 Daly, Jeanne Joseph, Sister. The metaphysical foundations of free will. 1958. C3043
187 Case, E. M. A critique of the formative thought underlying Francis Suarez's concept of being. 1959. C3044

188 Aspell, P. J. Thomistic critique of transsubjectivity in recent American realism. 1959. C3045
189 Kinzel, M. M., Sister. The metaphysical basis of certain principles of religious life in the light of certain Thomistic principles. 1959. C3046
190 Putnam, C. C. Beauty in the Pseudo-Denis. 1960. C3047
191 Scholdenbrand, Mary Aloysius, Sister. Phenomenologies of freedom. 1960. C3048
192 Nugent, J. B. The fundamental theistic argument in the metaphysical doctrine of Saint Thomas. 1961. C3049
193 Burt, D. X. The state and religious toleration. 1960. C3050
194 Cunningham, M. A. Certitude and the philosophy of science. 1960. C3051
195 Preston, R. A. Casuality and the Thomistic theory of knowledge. 1960. C3052
196 Fitts, M. P. John Locke's theory of meaning. 1960. C3053
197 Dougherty, J. P. Recent American naturalism. 1960. C3054
198 Quinn, J. M. The doctrine of time in St. Thomas. 1960. C3055
199 DiNardo, R. A. The unity of the human person. 1961. C3056
231 Kearns, T. J. Continuity in Galileo Galilee's new science. 1967. C3057

Philosophical Studies. Abstract Series.
The number in parenthesis refers to the number in the Philosophical Studies series. 1(144), 2(145), 3(146), 4(147), 5(148), 6(149), 7(151), 8(152), 9(153), 10(154), 11(155), 12(156), 13(158), 14(159), 15(160), 16(161), 17(162), 18(163), 19(164), 20(165), 21(166), 22(167), 23(173), 24(176), 25(170), 26(171), 27(172), 28(177), 29(174), 30(179), 31(180), 32(181), 33(182), 34(183), 35(184), 36(185), 37(186), 38(187), 39(188), 40(189), 41(191), 42(192), 43(193), 44(194), 45(195), 46(196), 47(197), 48(198), 49(199).

CATHOLIC UNIVERSITY OF AMERICA. STUDIES IN CHRISTIAN ANTIQUITY

1 Rush, A. C. Death and burial in Christian antiquity. 1941. C3058
2 Reine, F. J. The eucharistic doctrine and liturgy of the mystalogical catecheses of Theodore of Mopsuestia. 1942. C3059
3 Schneweis, E. Angels and demons according to Lactantius. 1944. C3060
4 Micka, E. F. The problem of divine anger in Arnobius and Lactantius. 1943. C3061
5 Plumpe, J. C. Mater ecclesia. 1943. C3062
6 Geoghegen, A. T. The attitude towards labor in early Christianity and ancient culture. 1945. C3063
7 Reilly, G. F. Imperium and sacredotium according to St. Basil the Great. 1945. C3064
8 Duncan, E. J. Baptism in the Demonstrations of Aphraates. 1945. C3065
9 Hummel, E. L. The concept of martyrdom according to St. Cyprian of Carthage. 1946. C3066
10 Emmenegger, J. E. The functions of faith and reason in the theology of Saint Hilary of Poitiers. 1948. C3067
11 Dooley, W. J. Marriage according to St. Ambrose. 1948. C3068
12 Malone, E. E. The monk and the martyrs. 1950. C3069
13 DeClerq, V. C. Ossius of Cordova. 1954. C3070
14 Burghardt, W. J. The image of God in man. 1957. C3071
15 Finn, T. M. The liturgy of Baptismal instructions of St. John Chrysostom. 1967. C3072

16 Dewart, J. M. Theology of grace of Theodore of Mopsuestia. 1972. C3073
17 Riley, H. M. Christian initiation. 1972. C3074
18 Daly, D. J. Christian sacrifice. 1972. C3075
19 Krosnicki, T. A. Ancient patterns in modern prayer. 1972. C3076

CATHOLIC UNIVERSITY OF AMERICA. STUDIES IN LIBRARY SCIENCE.

1 Fry, B. M. and Kortendick, J. J., eds. Library organization and management of technical reports literature. 1953. C3077
2 Kapsner, O. L. A manual of cataloging practice for Catholic author and title series. 1953. C3078
3 Kortendick, J. J. The library in the Catholic theological seminary in the United States. 1963. C3079

CATHOLIC UNIVERSITY OF AMERICA. STUDIES IN MEDIAEVAL HISTORY. NEW SERIES.

1 McKenna, S. Paganism and pagan survivals in Spain up to the fall of the Visigothic kingdom. 1938. C3080
2 Lynch, C. H. Saint Braulio. 1938. C3081
3 Mullins, Patrick Jerome, Sister. The spiritual life according to Saint Isidore of Seville. 1940. C3082
4 Braegelmann, Athanasius, Sister. The life and writings of Saint Ildefonsus of Toledo. 1942. C3083
5 Sage, C. M. Paul Albar of Cordoba. 1943. C3084
6 Murphy, F. X. Rufinus of Aquileia. 1945. C3085
7 Valerius, St. The Vita sancti Fructuosi, tr. by Nock. 1946. C3086
8 Paulus Diaconus Emeritensis. The Vitas sactorum patrum emeretensium. 1946. C3087
9 Carroll, M. Thomas Aquinas, Sister. The venerable Bede. 1946. C3088
10 Blum, O. J. St. Peter Damian. 1947. C3089
11 Valerius, St. Valerio of Bierzo, tr. by Aherne. 1949. C3090
12 Biggs, A. D. Diego Gelmírez. 1949. C3091
13 Smith, J. J. Attitude of John Pecham toward monastic houses under jurisdiction. 1951. C3092
14 O'Malley, E. A. Tello and Theotonio. 1954. C3093
15 Trame, R. H. Rodrigo Sánchez de Arevalo. 1958. C3094
16 Caesarius, St. The rule for nuns of St. Caesarius of Arles, ed. by McCarthy. 1960. C3095
17 Colbert, E. P. The Martyrs of Cordoba. 1962. C3096
18 Van Zijl, T. P. Gerard Groote. 1963. C3097

CATHOLIC UNIVERSITY OF AMERICA. STUDIES IN SACRED THEOLOGY.

1 Dublanchy, E. De Axiomate extra ecclesium nulla salus. 1895. C3098
2 Lucas, G. J. Agnosticism and religion. 1895. C3099
3 Fox, J. J. Religion and morality. 1899. C3100
4 Aiken, C. F. The Dhamma of Gotama the Buddha and the Gospel of Jesus Christ. 1900. C3101
5 Healy, P. J. The Valerian persecution. 1903. C3102
6 O'Connor, M. J. Responsibility and the moral life. 1903. C3103
7 Melody, J. W. Physical basis of marriage. 1903. C3104
8 Weber, N. A. A history of simony in the Christian church from the beginning to the death of Charlemagne. 1909. C3105
9 Ryan, J. A. A living wage.

1906. C3106
10 Petrivits, J. J. C. Theology of the cultus of the Sacred Heart. 1917. C3107
11 Lilzencrantz, J. Spiritism and religion. 1918. C3108
12 Number not assigned.
13 Maroney, T. B. The idea of personality. 1919. C3109
14 Mathis, M. A. The Pauline pistisupostosis. 1920. C3110
15 Motry, H. L. The concept of mortal sin in early Christianity. 1920. C3111
16 Villapando, A. De Clavium potestatis existentia atque natura. 1921. C3112
17 Ohleyer, J. L. The Pauline formulae "Induere Christum." 1921. C3113
18 Bellwald, A. M. Christian science and the Catholic faith. 1922. C3114
19 Temple, P. J. The boyhood consciousness of Christ. 1922. C3115
20 Cuneo, B. H. The Lord's command to baptize. 1923. C3116
21 Mollaun, R. A. St. Paul's concept of Hilasterion according to the Romans III, 25. 1923. C3117
22 Coan, A. J. The rule of faith in the ecclesiastical writings of the first two centuries. 1924. C3118
23 Shaughnessy, G. Catholic growth in the United States, 1790-1920. 1925. C3119
24 Rager, J. C. Political philosophy of Blessed Cardinal Bellarmine. 1926. C3120
25 Costa, A. M. Christ's one sacrifice in its three-fold mede. 1927. C3121
26 Koncevicius, J. B. Russia's attitude toward union with Rome. 1927. C3122
26a Stegman, B. A. Christ, the man from heaven. 1927. C3123
27 Powers, G. C. Nationalism at the Council of Constance, 1414-18. 1927. C3124
28 Hemelt, T. M. Final moral values in sociology. 1929. C3125
29 Gilligan, F. J. The morality of the color line. 1929. C3126
30 Flynn, V. S. The norm of normality. 1928. C3127
31 Barron, J. T. The idea of the absolute in modern British philosophy. 1929. C3128
32 Ziegler, A. K. Church and state in Visigothic Spain. 1930. C3129
33 Costello, C. J. St. Augustine's doctrine on the inspiration and canonicity of scripture. 1930. C3130
34 Dirksen, A. H. The New Testament concept of Metanoia. 1932. C3131
35 Rohling, J. H. The blood of Christ in Christian Latin literature before the year 1000. 1932. C3132
36 Scheper, J. B. Justitia Dei and justification (Romans, I, 17) in early Latin literature. 1932. C3133
37 Scheu, L. E. Die "Weltelemente" beim Apostel Paulus. 1933. C3134
38 Baskfield, G. T. The idea of God in British and American personal idealism. 1933. C3135
39 Gallagher, D. M. Pringle-Pattison's idea of God. 1933. C3136
40 Flores, V. E. Constitutio politica Mexicana cum Catholica theologia comparata. 1934. C3137
41 Kavanagh, W. A. Lay participation in Christ's priesthood. 1935. C3138
42 Kramer, H. G. The indirect voluntary, or Voluntarium in cause. 1935. C3139
43 Ament, E. P. Industrial recovery legislation in the light of Catholic principles. 1936. C3140
44 Callahan, J. D. The Catholic attitude toward a familial minimum wage. 1936. C3141
45 McGowan, J. P. Pierre d'Ailly and the Council of Constance. 1936. C3142

46 McLarney, J. J. The theism of Edgar Sheffield Brightman. 1936. C3143
47 Dowd, E. F. A conspectus of modern Catholic thought on the essence of the eucharistic sacrifice. 1937. C3144
48 Steinbicker, C. R. Poor-relief in the sixteenth century. 1947. C3145
49 Siegman, E. F. The false prophets of the Old Testament. 1939. C3146
50 Gallagher, J. J. Church and state in Germany under Otto the Great (936-973). 1938. C3147
51 Lyons, D. B. The concept of eternal life in the gospel according to Saint John. 1938. C3148
52 McGlinchey, J. M. The teaching of Amen-em-ope and the book of Proverbs. 1939. C3149
53 Redding, J. P. The influence of St. Augustine on the doctrine of the II council of Orange concerning original sin. 1939. C3150
54 Skehan, P. W. The literary relationship between the book of wisdom and the protocanonical wisdom books of the Old Testament. 1938. C3151
55 Knapke, P. J. Frederick Barbarossa's conflict with the papacy. 1939. C3152
56 Paul, J. M. The Catholic attitude toward "production for use and not for profit." 1939. C3153
57 Díaz, P. De resistentia tyrannid. 1941. C3154
58 Bertke, S. The possibility of invincible ignorance of the natural law. (1941). C3155
59 McMahon, J. J. The divine union in the Subida del Monte Carmelo and the Noche oscura of St. John of the Cross. 1941. C3156
60 Regan, R. E. The moral principles governing professional secrecy with an inquiry into some of the more important professional secrets. 1941. C3157
61 Shanley, A. J. Angels and demons according to Lactantius. 1944. C3158
62 Rosswog, B. L. The introduction to the words "true and sincere" into the present day's explanation of God's salvific will. 1943. C3159
63 Dowd, C. M. The visible sanctity of the church as a note and a motive of credibility. 1941. C3160
64 Roedel, F. F. The scientific character of theology. 1942. C3161
65 Welsh, A. J. The scholastic teaching concerning the specific distinction of sins in the lights of current moral theology. 1942. C3162
66 Berwanger, G. J. The morality of the pleasure motive. 1942. C3163
67 Donovan, V. J. Sixtus of Siena and the science of biblical introduction. 1942. C3164
68 Koren, H. De inspiratione Sacrae scripturae secundum doctriam Cornelii a Lapide. 1942. C3165
69 Griese, O. N. The morality of periodic continence. 1942. C3166
70 Kelly, V. J. The negative part of the precept of Sunday and feastday observance. 1942. C3167
71 Lallou, W. J. The "Quam oblationem" of the Roman Canon. 1943. C3168
72 Naber, H. D. The meditation of Mary according to St. Bernard. 1942. C3169
73 Scanlon, J. E. The Blessed Virgin Mary. 1942. C3170
74 Wolfer, S. J. The prayer of Christ according to the teaching of St. Thomas Aquinas. 1942. C3171
75 Bancroft, J. Communication in religious worship with non-Catholics. 1942. C3172
76 O'Brien, R. F. The absolution of recidivists in

the sacrament of penance. 1943. C3173
77 Tensing, R. H. Extra-sacramental justification. 1944. C3174
78 Poirier, L. Les sept églises ou le premier septénaire prophétique de l'Apocalypse. 1943. C3175
79 Hanus, F. Church and state in Silesia under Frederick II (1740-86). 1944. C3176
80 Sirvaitis, C. P. Casti Connubii Monita de Iuribus et officiis patrisfamilias. 1943. C3177
81 Published as 43 in Series 2.
82 Cadden, J. P. The historiography of the American Catholic church. 1943. C3178
83 Duffy, W. The tribal-historical theory of the origin of the Hebrew people. 1944. C3179
83A Lehane, J. B. The morality of American civil legislation concerning eugenical sterilization. 1944. C3180
84 Crowe, M. T. Specific virtue regulating the payment of taxes. 1944. C3181
85 Foley, T. D. The doctrine of the Catholic church in the theology of John Driedo of Louvain. 1946. C3182
86 Cunningham, B. J. The morality of organic transplantation. 1944. C3183
87 Bierberg, R. P. Conversa me, Domine, Psalm 16. 1945. C3184
88 Grabka, G. M. Cardinalis Hosii doctrine de corpore Christi mystico. 1945. C3185
88A Laurent, L. Quebec et l'Eglise aux Etats-Unis sous Mgr. Briand et Mgr. Blessis. 1945. C3186
89 Galus, W. J. The universality of the kingdom of God in the gospels of the Acts of the Apostles. 1945. C3187
90 Wild, J. C. The divinity of Christ in conservative British Protestanism of the present time. 1943. C3188
91 Carney, E. J. The doctrine of St. Augustine on sanctity. 1945. C3189
92 Coerver, R. F. The quality of facility in the moral virtues. 1946. C3190
93 Pansini, F. D. Our first gospel. 1946. C3191
94 Denzer, G. A. The parables of the Kingdom. 1946. C3192
95 Otterbein, A. J. The diaconate according to the apostolic tradition of Hippolytus and derived documents. 1945. C3193
96 Halas, R. B. Judas Iscariot. 1946. C3194
97 Hesburgh, T. M. The relation of the sacramental characters of baptism and confirmation in the lay apostolate. 1945. C3195
98 Number not assigned.
99 Louis, C. J. The theology of Psalm VIII. 1946. C3196
99A Hennessy, A. P. The victory of Christ over Satan... 1946. C3197
100 Pater, T. G. Miraculous abstinence. 1946. C3198
101 Rea, J. E. The common priesthood of the members of the mystical body. 1947. C3199

Never published: 6, 7, 23, 40, 64, 66, 67, 72, 73, 74.

Second series:

1 De Martini, R. The rights of nations to expand by conquest. 1947. C3200
2 Zdrodowski, F. J. The concept of heresy according to Cardinal Hosius. 1947. C3201
3 Bourke, M. M. A study of the metaphor of the olive tree in Romane XI. 1947. C3202
4 Sheedy, C. E. The Eucharistic controversy of the eleventh century against the background of pre-scholastic theology. 1947. C3203
5 May, E. E. Ecce Agnus Dei! 1947. C3204
6 Spitzig, J. A. Sacramental penance in the twelfth

and thirteenth centuries. 1947. C3205
7 Everett, L. P. The nature of sacramental grace. 1948. C3206
8 Gaspar, J. W. Social ideas in the Wisdom literature of the Old Testament. 1947. C3207
9 Stepanich, M. F. The Christology of Zeno of Verona. 1948. C3208
10 Brown, B. A. The numerical distinction of sins according to the Franciscan school of the seventeenth and eighteenth centuries. 1948. C3209
11 O'Brien, V. P. The measure of responsibility in persons influenced by emotion. 1948. C3210
12 Murphy, R. E. A study of Psalm 72. 1948. C3211
13 Booth, G. J. The Offertory rite in the Ordo romanus primus. 1948. C3212
14 Kominiak, B. The theophanies of the Old Testament in the writings of St. Justin. 1948. C3213
15 Glover, W. K. Artificial insemination among human beings. 1948. C3214
16 Dorszynski, J. A. Catholic teaching about the morality of falsehood. 1948. C3215
17 Riley, L. J. The history, nature and use of EPIKEIA in moral theology. 1948. C3216
18 Falanga, A. J. Charity and form of the virtues according to Saint Thomas. 1948. C3217
19 Reilly, B. M. The Elizabethan Puritan's conception of the nature and destiny of fallen man. 1948. C3218
20 Rohr, L. F. The use of the Sacred Scripture in the sermons of St. Anthony of Padua. 1948. C3219
21 Walsh, E. A. The priesthood in the writings of the French school: Berulle, De Condren, Olier. 1949. C3220
22 Sullivan, J. V. Catholic teaching on the morality of euthanasia. 1949. C3221
23 O'Doherty, M. K. The scholastic teaching on the sacrament of Confirmation. 1949. C3222
24 Heidt, W. G. Angelology of the Old Testament. 1949. C3223
25 Figueroa, G. The church and the synagogue in Saint Ambrose. 1949. C3224
26 De Salvo, R. The dogmatic theology on the intention of the minister in the confection of the sacraments. 1949. C3225
27 Costello, J. A. Moral obligation of fraternal correction. 1949. C3226
28 King, W. J. Moral aspects of dishonesty in public office. 1949. C3227
29 Benson, A. The spirit of God in the didactic books of the Old Testament. 1949. C3228
30 Echle, H. A. The terminology of the sacrament of regeneration according to Clement of Alexandria. 1949. C3229
31 Porter, F. L'institution catéchistique au Canada français. 1949. C3230
32 Doherty, J. F. Moral problems of interracial marriage. 1949. C3231
33 Kryger, H. S. The doctrine of the effects of Extreme Unction in its historical development. 1949. C3232
34 Farrell, B. J. Orestes Brownson's approach to the problem of God. 1950. C3233
35 Sharkey, N. Saint Gregory the Great's concept of papal power. 1950. C3234
36 Dolan, G. E. The distinction between the episcopate and the presbyterate according to the Thomistic opinion. 1950. C3235
37 Hsiang, P. S. The Catholic missions in China during the Middle Ages. 1950. C3236
38 Castelot, J. J. Anointing in the Old Testament. 1950. C3237
39 Murphy, W. R. Various concepts of the essence of

original sin current in the twelfth century. 1950. C3238
40 Lyons, J. P. The essential structure of marriage. 1950. C3239
41 Moore, K. B. The moral principles governing the sin of detraction... 1950. C3240
42 Veszelovzsky, A. De concelebratione eucharistica. 1950. C3241
43 Carney, F. W. The purposes of Christian marriage. 1950. C3242
44 Buescher, G. N. The eucharistic teaching of William Ockham. 1950. C3243
45 Bedard, W. M. The symbolism of the baptismal font in early Christian thought. 1950. C3244
46 Dukehart, C. H. State of perfection and the secular priest. 1949. C3245
47 Augustinus, Aurelius, St. De fide et operibus, tr. by Lombardo. 1950. C3246
48 Balducelli, R. Il concerto teologica de carita attraverso le Maggiori interpretazioni patristiche e medievali di 1 ad Cor. XIII. 1950. C3247
49 Ildephonsus, St. Liber de cognitione baptismi, tr. by Billy. 1951. C3248
50 Baur, P. M. The theology of Saint John Damascene's De fide orthodoxa. 1951. C3249
51 Micek, A. A. The apologetics of Martin John Spalding. 1951. C3250
52 Schmidt, F. M. The resurrection of the body according to Tertullian. 1951. C3251
53 Joannes a Sancto Joanne. Tractus de Spiritu Sancto Joannis a Sancto Ioanne. 1951. C3252
54 Kramer, C. Fear and hope according to Saint Alphonsus Ligouri. 1951. C3253
55 Harvey, J. F. Moral theology of the Confessions of St. Augustine. 1951. C3254
56 Medeiros, H. The De Mysteriis and De sacramentis of St. Ambrose. 1951. C3255
57 Williams, G. C. The nature of the Eucharistic accidents. 1951. C3256
58 Hill, W. F. The fruits of the Sacrifice of the Mass. 1951. C3257
59 Nugent, V. J. The concept of charity in the writings of St. Gregory the Great. 1952 (Microcard). C3258
60 Porcel, O. M. La doctrina monastica de San Gregorio Magno y la "Regula monachorum." 1952. C3259
61 Bardes, G. F. Catholic moral teaching on the distribution of profits in the modern corporation. 1951. C3260
62 Fuerst, A. An historical study of the doctrine of the omnipresence of God in selected writings between 1220-1270. 1951. C3261
63 Kennedy, G. T. St. Paul's conception of the priesthood of Melchisedech. 1951. C3262
64 Stafford, R. H. The morality of universal military conscription in peacetime. 1952 (Microcard). C3263
65 Kostrzański, F. H. De culpa theologica in problemate restitutionis damni. 1952 (Microcard). C3264
66 Fonash, I. The doctrine of eternal punishment in the writings of St. Gregory the Great. 1952 (Microcard). C3265
67 Bernardi, P. The Divine Christ, a dogmatical approach. 1952 (Microcard). C3266
68 Sabrey, T. W. The person and works of the Holy Spirit according to the theory of Denys Petau, S. J. 1952 (Microcard). C3267
69 Not published.
70 Cranny, T. F. The moral obligation of voting. 1952. C3268
71 Bernard, G. C. The morality of prize-fighting. 1952. C3269
72 Donegan, A. F. St.

Augustine and the Real presence. 1952. C3270
73 O'Brien, J. P. The right of the state to make disease an impediment to marriage. 1952. C3271
74 Cortelyou, W. T. Banking profit. 1953. C3272
75 Némec, L. Episcopal and Vatican reaction to the persecution of the Catholic Church in Czechoslovakia. 1953. C3273
76 Hanahoe, E. F. Catholic ecumenism. 1953. C3274
77 McKeever, P. E. The necessity of confession for the sacrament of penance. 1954. C3275
78 Davis, J. D. The moral obligation of Catholic civil judges. 1954. C3276
79 McAuliffe, M. F. Catholic moral teaching on the nature and object of conjugal love. 1954. C3277
80 Schroeder, F. J. Père Lagrange and Biblical inspiration. 1954. C3278
81 Quinn, J. R. The recognition of the true church according to John Henry Newman. 1954. C3279
82 Crump, F. J. Pneuma in the Gospels. 1954. C3280
83 Dionsyius. Areopagita, the ecclesiastical hierarchy, tr. by Campbell. 1955. C3281
84 Endebrock, D. M. The parental obligation to care for the religious education of children within the home. 1955. C3282
85 Brokhage, J. D. Francis Patrick Kenrick's opinion on slavery. 1955. C3283
86 Van Antwerp, E. I. St. Augustine: The divination of demons and Care for the dead. 1955. C3284
87 Weller, P. T. The Easter sermons of St. Augustine. 1955. C3285
88 Salm, C. L. The problem of positive theology. 1955. C3286
89 Montano, E. J. The sin of the angels; some aspects of the teaching of St. Thomas. 1955. C3287
90 O'Sullivan, J. J. The moral obligation of parents to educate their children for marriage. 1955. C3288
91 Dibble, R. A. John Henry Newman: the concept of infallible doctrinal authority. 1955. C3289
92 Lohkamp, N. The morality of hysterectomy operations. 1956. C3290
93 Kennedy, F. J. Mary's spiritual maternity according to modern writers. 1957. C3291
94 Butler, I. W. The moral problems of the theatre. 1958. C3292
95 McClain, J. P. The doctrine of heaven in the writings of Saint Gregory the Great. 1956. C3293
96 Schmitz, W. J. The new Holy Week ordo. 1956. C3294
97 Nolan, J. G. Jerome and Jovinian. 1956. C3295
98 Prah, J. A. Communication of non-Catholics in Catholic religious rites. 1956. C3296
99 Zimmerman, A. F. Overpopulation. 1957. C3297
100 Hogan, W. F. Augustine Bonnetty and the problem of faith and reason. 1957. C3298
101 Staab, G. J. The dignity of man in modern papal doctrine. 1957. C3299
102 Maguire, W. E. John of Torquemada. 1957. C3300
103 La Roche, R. La divination. 1957. C3301
104 Lind, C. Priestly studies in modern papal teachings. 1958. C3302
105 Wolfer, W. V. The prayer of Christ according to the teachings of St. Thomas Aquinas. 1958. C3303
106 Shinners, J. J. Morality of medical experimentation on living human subjects... 1958. C3304
106A Kaiser, F. J. The concept of conscience according to John Henry

Newman. 1958. C3305
107 Murphy, J. F. The moral obligation of the individual to participate in Catholic action. 1958. C3306
108 Maguire, A. A. Blood and water. 1958. C3307
109 O'Brien, J. J. The remission of venial sin. 1958. C3308
110 Wahl, J. A. The exclusion of women from holy orders. 1959. C3309
111 Gelinas, J. P. La restauration du thomiste sous Leon XIII et les philosophies nouvelles. 1959. C3310
112 Boland, P. The concept of discretio spirituum in John Gerson's "De probatione Spirituum... 1959. C3311
113 Nienaltowski, H. R. Johann Adam Mohler's Theory of doctrinal development. 1959. C3312
114 Colavechio, X. G. Erroneous conscience and obligations. 1961. C3313
115 King, J. J. The necessity of the church for salvation in selected theological writings of the past century. 1960. C3314
116 Sullivan, C. S. The formulation of the Tridentine doctrine on merit. 1959. C3315
117 Not published.
118 Dinger, C. M. Moral rearmament. 1961. C3316
119 Sharrock, D. J. The theological defense of papal power by St. Alphonsus de Ligouri. 1961. C3317
120 Keating, C. J. The effect of original sin in the scholastic tradition from St. Thomas Aquinas to William Ockham. 1959. C3318
121 Ziegler, J. H. The obligation of the confessor to instruct pentitents. 1959. C3319
121A Bonano, S. The concept of substance and the development of eucharistic theology to the thirteenth century. 1960. C3320
122 Goñi, P. La resurrección de la carne segun San Augustin. 1961. C3321
123A DeMarco, A. A. The church of Rome and the problem of vernacular versus the liturgical language. 1960. C3322
124A O'Donnell, C. M. St. Cyprian on the Lord's prayer. 1960. C3323
125 Regan, A. Dies dominica and dies solis. 1961. C3324
126 Gormley, W. J. Medical hypnosis. 1961. C3325
127 O'Donnell, J. M. The canons of the First Council of Arles, 314 A.D. 1961. C3326
134 Heaney, S. P. The development of the sacramentality of marriage, from Anselm of Laon to Thomas Aquinas. 1963. C3327
136 Riegert, B. M. The obligation of following a religious vocation. 1962. C3328
154 Schafer, A. The position and function of man in the created world according to St. Bonaventure. 1965. C3329
161 Gerke, L. F. Christian marriage a permanent sacrament. 1965. C3330
181 Hunt, W. C. Intuition. 1967. C3331

CATHOLIC UNIVERSITY OF AMERICA. STUDIES IN SOCIOLOGY. ABSTRACT SERIES.

1 Bedard, M. M. Marriage and family relations in current fiction. 1950. C3332
2 Mundy, P. The Negro boy worker in Washington, D.C. 1951. C3333
3 Sirvaitis, C. P. Religious folkways in Lithuania and their conservation among the Lithuanian immigrants in the United States. 1952. C3334
4 Kenrick, M. A. The relationship of housing to tuberculosis in Muscogee County, Georgia. 1957. C3335
5 Smith, M. E. Patterns of interpersonal preferences in a nursing school class. 1952. C3336
6 Fosselman, D. H.

Transitions in the development of a downtown parish. 1952. C3337

7 Zahn, G. C. A descriptive study of the social backgrounds of conscientious objectors in civilian public service during World War II. 1955. C3338

8 Kamerdze, P. A study of the major sociological aspects of truancy within selected census tracts of Washington, D. C. 1955. C3339

9 Dunn, H. E. The self-ideal of selected married Catholics. 1956. C3340

10 O'Rourke, W. An evaluation of the Scanlon plan in the light of Catholic school social principles. 1956. C3341

11 Potvin, R. H. An analysis of labor-management satisfaction within the enterprise councils of Belgian industry. 1958. C3342

12 Burns, M. S. A comparative study of social factors in religious vocations... 1957. C3343

13 Amen, A. Informal groups and institutional adjustment in a Catholic home for the aging. 1959. C3344

14 Madden, M. L. A. Role definitions of Catholic sister educators and expectation of students, their parents and teaching sisters in selected areas of the United States. 1960. C3345

15 Crowley, D. M. The role of the nurse in the bedside care of patients in a general hospital. 1961. C3346

16 Douglas, A. M. A study of social factors which affect career choice in psychiatric nursing. 1961. C3347

17 Paynich, M. L. The therapeutic role of the visiting nurse. 1961. C3348

CAUSES OF INDUSTRIAL PEACE UNDER COLLECTIVE BARGAINING. CASE STUDIES (National Planning Assn.)

1 National planning assn. Committee on the causes of industrial peace under collective bargaining. Crown Zellerbach corporation and the Pacific Coast pulp and paper industry, by Kerr and Randall. 1948. C3349

2 ____. The Libbey-Owen-Ford Glass company and the Federation of Glass, Ceramic and Silica Sand Workers of America, by Harbison and Carr. 1948. C3350

3 ____. Dewey and Almy Chemical Company and the International Chemical workers of America by McGregor and Scanlon. 1948. C3351

4 ____. Hickey-Freeman Company and Amalgamated Clothing Workers of America, by Straus. 1949. C3352

5 ____. Sharon Steel corporation and United Steelworkers of America, by Miller. 1949. C3353

6 ____. Lockheed Aircraft Corporation and International Association of Machinists, by Kerr and Halverson. 1949. C3354

7 ____. Nashua Gummed and Coated Paper Company and seven AFL unions, by Myers and Shultz. 1950. C3355

8 ____. Marathon Corporation and seven labor unions, by Fleming and Witte. 1950. C3356

9 ____. Minnequa Plant of Colorado Fuel and Iron Corporation and two locals of United Steelworkers of America, by Zinke. 1951. C3357

10 ____. Lapointe Machine Tool Company and United Steelworkers of America, by Shultz and Crisara. 1952. C3358

11 ____. American Velvet Company and Textile Workers Union of America, by Paul. 1953. C3359

12 ____. Atlantic Steel Company and United Steelworkers of America, by Gilman and Sweeney. 1953. C3360

13 ____. Working harmony:

a summary of collective bargaining relationships in 18 companies, by Harbison and Coleman. 1953. C3361

14 ___. Fundamentals of labor peace: a final report. 1953. C3362

Golden, S. C. and Parker, V. D., eds. Causes of industrial peace under collective bargaining. 1955. C3363

Publication discontinued.

CAXTON SOCIETY. PUBLICATIONS.

Alan. Alani prioris cantuariensis postea abbatis tewkesberiensis scripta quae extant... 1846. C3364

Anglo-Saxon chronicle. Chronicon Algliae Petriburgense, ed. by Giles. 1845. C3365

Anstruther, R., ed. Epistolae Herberti de Losingra. 1846. C3366

Gaimar, G. Gaimar, Havelok at Herward. The Anglo-Norman metrical chronicle of Geoffrey Gaimar, ed. by Wright. 1850. C3367

Geoffrey. Galfredi Monumentensis Historia Britonum, ed. by Giles. 1844. C3368

Giles, J. A., ed. Anecdota Bedae, Lanfranci, et aliorum. 1851. C3369

___. La revolte du conte de Warwick contre le roi Edward IV. 1849. C3370

___. Scriptores rerum gestarum Willelmi Conquestoris. 1845. C3371

Grosseteste, R. R. Grossetete Carmina anglo-normannica, ed. by Cooke. 1852. C3372

Gualterus. Walteri abbatis dervensis epistolae, ed. by Messiter. 1850. C3373

Henry. Chronicon Henriri de Silegrave, ed. by Hook. 1849. C3374

Heyln, P. Memorial of Bishop Waynflete, ed. by Bloxam. 1851. C3375

Ralph, Radulfi Niger Chronica, ed. by Anstruther. 1851. C3376

THE CENSUS MONOGRAPH SERIES (Wiley)

Bancroft, G. The American labor force. 1958. C3377

Bernert, E. H. America's children. 1958. C3378

Beyer, G. H. and Rose, J. H. Farm housing. 1957. C3379

Duncan, O. D. and Reiss, A. J. Social characteristics of urban and rural communities. 1950. 1956. C3380

Glick, P. C. American families. 1957. C3381

Grabill, W. H. and others. The fertility of American women. 1958. C3382

Hutchinson, E. P. Immigrants and their children, 1850-1950. 1956. C3383

Mighell, R. L. American agriculture. 1955. C3384

Miller, H. P. Income of the American people. 1955. C3385

Ratcliff, R. U. and others. Residential finance. 1950. C3386

Sheldon, H. D. The older population of the United States. 1958. C3387

Taeuber, C. and I. B. The changing population of the United States. 1958. C3388

Winnick, L. and Shilling, N. American housing and its use. 1957. C3389

THE CENTERS OF CIVILIZATION SERIES (Univ. of Okla. Pr.)

1 Robinson, C. A. Athens in the age of Pericles. 1959. C3390

2 Arberry, A. J. Shiraz. 1960. C3391

3 Downey, G. Constantinople in the age of Justinian. 1960. C3392

4 Le Tourneau, R. Fez in the age of the Marinides, tr. by Clement. 1961. C3393

5 Rowell, H. T. Rome in the Augustan Age. 1962. C3394

6 Downey, G. Antioche in the age of Theodosius the

Great. 1962. C3395
7 Kain, R. M. Dublin in the age of William Butler Yeats and Joyce. 1962. C3396
8 Downey, G. Gaza in the early sixth century. 1963. C3397
9 Lewis, B. Istanbul and the civilization of the Ottoman Empire. 1963. C3398
10 Sullivan, R. E. Aix-la-Chapelle in the age of Charlemagne. 1963. C3399
11 Riefstahl, E. Thebes in the time of Amunhotep III. 1964. C3400
12 Ziadeh, N. A. Damascus under the Mamluks. 1964. C3401
13 Wagenknecht, E. C. Chicago. 1964. C3402
14 Voyce, A., ed. Moscow and the roots of Russian culture. 1964. C3403
15 Ruggiers, P. G. Florence in the age of Dante. 1964. C3404
16 Wiet, G. Cairo. 1964. C3405
17 Young, D. Edinburgh in the age of Sir Walter Scott. 1965. C3406
18 Frye, R. N. Bukhara. 1965. C3407
19 Whitehill, W. M. Boston in the age of John Fitzgerald Kennedy. 1966. C3408
20 May, A. J. Vienna in the age of Franz Josef. 1966. C3409
21 Murray, J. J. Amsterdam in the age of Rembrandt. 1967. C3410
22 Cole, W. Kyoto in the Momoyama period. 1967. C3411
23 Bell, A. D. London in the age of Dickens. 1967. C3412
24 Pedley, J. G. Sardis in the age of Croesus. 1968. C3413
25 Robinson, W. W. Los Angeles. 1968. C3414
26 Rogers, G. C. Charleston in the age of the Pinckneys. 1968. C3415
27 Murray, J. J. Antwerp in the age of Plantin and Brueghel. 1969. C3416
28 Wiet, G. Baghdad. 1970. C3417
29 Tyler, W. R. Dijon and the Valois dukes of Burgundy. 1971. C3418
30 Krekic, B. Dubrovnik in the 14th and 15th centuries. 1972. C3419
31 Myers, A. R. London in the age of Chaucer, 1972. C3420
32 Hargreaves-Mawdsley, W. N. Oxford in the age of John Locke. 1973. C3421
33 Mitchell, B. Rome in the High Renaissance. 1973. C3422

CENTRAL ASIATIC STUDIES (Mouton)

1 Loewenthal, R., comp. The Turkic languages and literatures of central Asia. 1957. C3423
2 Jahn, K. Geschichte der Ilhane abaga bis Gaihatu. 1958. C3424
3 Serruys, H. Genealogical tables of the descendants of Dayan-qan. 1958. C3425
4 Schurmann, H. F. The Mongols of Afghanistan. 1962. C3426
5 Chu, W. The Moslem rebellion in North-west China. 1966. C3427
6 Lopatin, I. A. The cult of the dead among the natives of the Amur Basin. 1960. C3428
7 Ssanang Ssetsen, C. Poetical passages in the Erdeni-yin Tobči, ed. by Krueger. 1961. C3429
8 Dabbs, J. A. History of the discovery and exploration of Chinese Turkestan. 1963. C3430
9 Samolin, W. East Turkistan to the twelfth century. 1964. C3431
10 Rashīd al-Dīn Tabīb. Rashīd al-Dīn's history of India. 1965. C3432

CENTRAL ISSUES IN PHILOSOPHY (Prentice-Hall)

Bedau, H. A., comp. Justice and equality. 1971. C3433
Brody, B. A., comp. Moral rules and particular circumstances. 1970. C3434

Dworkin, G., comp. Determinism, free will and moral responsibility. 1970. C3435
Gauthier, D. P., ed. Morality and rational self-interest. 1970. C3436
Grandy, R. E., ed. Theories and observation in science. 1973. C3437
Landesman, C., ed. The foundations of knowledge. 1970. C3438
Lehrer, A. and K. Theory of meaning. 1970. C3439
Levensky, M., comp. Human factual knowledge. 1971. C3440
Mavrodes, G. I., ed. The rationality of belief in God. 1970. C3441
Rosenthal, D. M., comp. Materialism and the mind-body problem. 1971. C3442
Sleigh, R. C., ed. Necessary truth. 1972. C3443

CHAMPLAIN SOCIETY. TORONTO. HUDSON'S BAY COMPANY (13- Univ. of Toronto Pr.)

1 Simpson, G. Journal of occurrences in the Athabasca department by George Simpson, 1820 and 1821, ed. by Rich. 1938. C3444
2 Robertson, C. Colin Robertson's Correspondence book, September 1817 to September 1822, ed. by Rich and Fleming. 1939. C3445
3 Rupert's land. Northern dept. Council. Minutes of council of the Northern department of Rupert land, 1821-31, ed. by Fleming. 1940. C3446
4 McLoughlin, J. The letters of John McLoughlin from Fort Vancouver to the governor and committee, ed. by Rich. 1st ser. 1825-38. 1941. C3447
5 Hudson's Bay Company. Minutes. 1671-74. 1942. C3448
6 Same as no. 4. 2d series. 1839-44. C3449
7 Same as no. 4. 3d series. 1844-46. 1944. C3450
8-9 Same as no. 5. 1679-82, 1682-84. C3451
10 Simpson, G. Part of dispatch from George Simpson, ed. by Rich. 1947. C3452
11 Hudson's Bay Company. Copybook of letters outward &c, begins 29th May, 1680 ends 5 July, 1687, ed. by Rich. 1948. C3453
12 Isham, J. James Isham's observations on Hudson Bay, 1743, ed. by Rich and Johnson. 1949. C3454
13 Ogden, P. S. Peter Skene Ogden's Snake Country journals, 1824-25 and 1825-26, ed. by Rich and Johnson. 1950. C3455
14-15 Hudson's Bay Company. Cumberland House journals and Inland journal, 1775-82, ed. by Rich and Johnson. 2 v. 1951-52. C3456
16 Rae, J. Correspondence with Hudson's Bay Company on the Arctic exploration, 1844-1855, ed. by Rich and Johnson. 1953. C3457
17 Hudson's Bay Company. Moose Fort journals 1783-85, ed. by Rich and Johnson. 1954. C3458
18 Black, S. A journal of a voyage from Rocky Mountain portage in Peace River to the sources of Finlay's Branch and north west ward in summer 1824, ed. by Rich and Johnson. 1955. C3459
19 Colvile, E. London correspondence inward, 1849-1852. 1956. C3460
20 Hudson's Bay Company. Hudson's Bay copy booke of letters, commissions, instructions outward, 1688-1698, ed. by Rich and Johnson. 1957. C3461
21-22 Rich, E. E. The history of the Hudson's Bay Company. V. 1. 1670-1763. V. 2. 1763-1870. 1958-59. C3462
23 Ogden, P. S. Snake country journal, 1826-27, ed. by Davies and Johnson. 1961. C3463
24 Davies, K. G. and Johnson, A. M., eds. Northern

Quebec and Labrador journal and correspondence, 1819-35. 1963. C3464

25 ____. Letters from Hudson Bay, 1703-40. 1965. C3465

26 Johnson, A. M., ed. Saskatchewan journals and correspondence: Edmonton House, 1795-1800, Chesterfield House, 1800-1802. 1967. C3466

27 Graham, A. Andrew Graham's observations on Hudson's Bay, 1767-91, ed. by Williams. 1969. C3467

28 Ogden, P. S. Snake Country journals, ed. by Williams. 1971. C3468

29 Simpson, G. London correspondence inward, from Sir George Simpson, ed. by Williams. 1973. C3469

CHAMPLAIN SOCIETY. TORONTO. PUBLICATIONS.

1 Lescarbot, M. The history of new France, tr. by Grant. V. 1. 1907. C3470

2 Denys, N. The description and natural history of the coasts of North America (Acadia), tr. by Ganong. 1908. C3471

3 Munro, W. B. Documents relating to the seignioral tenure in Canada, 1598-1854. 1908. C3472

4 Wood, W. C. H., ed. The logs of the conquest of Canada. 1909. C3473

5 LeClercq, C. New relation of Gaspesia, tr. by Ganong. 1910. C3474

6 Hearne, S. A journey from Prince of Wales's Fort in Hudson Bay to the Northern Ocean, in the years 1769, 1770, 1771, and 1772, ed. by Tyrrell. 1911. C3475

7 Same as no. 1. V. 2. C3476

8-10 Knox, J. An historical journal of the campaigns in North America, for the years 1757, 1758, 1759, and 1760, ed. by Doughty. 3 v. 1914-16. C3477

11 Same as no. 1. V. 3. 1914. C3478

12 Thompson, D. David Thompson's narrative of his explorations in western America, 1784-1812, ed. by Tyrrell. 1914. C3479

13-15, 17 Wood, W. C. H., ed. Select British documents of the Canadian War of 1812. 3 v. in 4. 1920-28. C3480

16 La Vérendrye, P. G. de V. Journals and letters of Pierre Gaultier de Varennes de la Vérendrye and his sons, ed. by Burpee. 1927. C3481

18 Tyrrell, J. B., ed. Documents relating to the early history of Hudson Bay. 1931. C3482

19 McLean, J. John McLean's notes of a twenty-five year's service in the Hudson's Bay territory, ed. by Wallace. 1932. C3483

20 Diéreville. Relation of the voyage to Port Royal in Acadia or New France. 1933. C3484

21 Hearne, S. Journals of Samuel Hearne and Philip Turnor... 1774-1792, ed. by Tyrrell. 1934. C3485

22 Wallace, W. S., ed. Documents relating to the North west company. 1934. C3486

23 Campbell, P. Travels in the interior inhabited parts of North America, 1791 and 1792, ed. by Langton. 1937. C3487

24 Hargrave, J. The Hargrave correspondence, 1821-1843, ed. by Glazebrook. 1938. C3488

25 Sagard-Théodat, G. The long voyage to the country of the Hurons, ed. by Wrong. 1939. C3489

26 Colnett, J. The journal of Captain James Colnett aboard the Argonout from April 26, 1789 to Nov. 3, 1791, ed. by Howay. 1940. C3490

27 Talman, J. J., ed. Loyalist narratives from Upper Canada. 1946. C3491

28 Hargrave, L. (Mactavish).

Letters of Letitia Hargrave, ed. by Macleod. 1947. C3492
29 Perkins, S. The diary of Simeon Perkins, 1766-1780, ed. by Innis. V. 1. 1948. C3493
30-31 Du Creux, F. The history of Canada, tr. by Robinson, ed. by Conacher. 2 v. 1951-52. C3494
32 Graham, G. S., ed. Walker's expedition to Quebec, 1711. 1953. C3495
33 Dufferin and Ava, F. T. H. Dufferin-Carnarvon correspondence, 1874-1878, ed. by Kiewiet and Underhill. 1955. C3496
34 Begg, A. Red River journal and other documents relating to the Red River resistence of 1869-70, ed. by Morton. 1956. C3497
35 Selkirk, T. D. Lord Selkirk's diary, 1803-1804, ed. by White. 1958. C3498
36 Same as no. 29. V. 2. 1780-1789, ed. by Harvey. 1959. C3499
37 Stacey, C. P., ed. Records of the Nile Voyageurs, 1884-1885. 1959. C3500
38 Aberdeen and Temair, I. M. G. The Canadian journal of Lady Aberdeen, 1893-1898, ed. by Saywell. 1960. C3501
39 Same as no. 29. V. 3. 1790-1796, ed. by Fergusson. 1960. C3502
40 Thompson, D. Narrative, 1784-1812, ed. by Glover. 1962. C3503
41-42 Smith, W. The diary and letters of Chief Justice William Smith, 1784-1793, ed. by Upton. 2 v. 1963-65. C3504
43 Same as no. 29. V. 4. 1968. C3505
44 Spry, I. M., comp. The papers of the Palliser expedition, 1857-1860. 1968. C3506
45 Franchere, G. Journal of a voyage on the northwest coast of North America during the years 1811, 1812, 1813 and 1814. 1969. C3507
46 Norton, J. The journal of Major John Norton, 1816, ed. by Klinck and Talman. 1970. C3508
47 Morton, D. and Roy, E. H., eds. Telegrams of the North-West campaign, 1885. 1972. C3509

CHAMPLAIN SOCIETY. TORONTO. PUBLICATIONS. ONTARIO SERIES (Univ. of Toronto Pr.)

1 Guillet, E. C., ed. The Valley of the Trent. 1957. C3510
2 Preston, R. A., comp. and tr. Royal Fort Frontenac, ed. by Lamontagne. 1958. C3511
3 ____, ed. Kingston before the War of 1812. 1959. C3512
4 Lajeunesse, E. J., ed. The Windsor border region. 1960. C3513
5 Firth, E. G., ed. The town of York, 1793-1815. 1962. C3514
6 Murray, F. B., ed. Muskoka and Haliburton, 1615-1875. 1963. C3515
7 Johnston, C. M., ed. The valley of the Six Nations. 1964. C3516
8 Same as no. 5. V. 2. 1966. C3517
9 Arthur, M. E., comp. Thunder Bay District, 1821-1892. 1972. C3518

THE CHARLES ELIOT NORTON LECTURES (Harvard Univ. Pr.)

1926-27 Murray, G. The classical tradition in poetry. 1927. C3519
1927-28 Maclagan, E. R. D. Italian sculpture of the renaissance. 1935. C3520
1929-30 Garrod, H. W. Poetry and the criticism of life. 1931. C3521
1930-31 Hind, A. M. Rembrandt. 1932. C3522
1932-33 Eliot, T. S. The use of poetry and the use of criticism. 1933. C3523
1933-34 Binyon, L. The spirit

of man in Asian art. 1935. C3524
1937-38 Tinker, C. B. Painter and poet. 1938. C3525
1938-39 Giedion, S. Space, time and architecture. 1962. C3526
1939-40 Stravinskiĭ, I. F. Poétique musicale. 1945. C3527
1940-41 Henriques-Ureña, P. Literary currents in Hispanic America. 1945. C3528
1947-48 Panofsky, E. Early Netherlandish painting. 2 v. 1954. C3529
1948-49 Bowra, C. M. The romantic imagination. 1949. C3530
1949-50 Hindemith, P. A composer's world. 1952. C3531
1951-52 Copland, A. Music and imagination. 1952. C3532
1952-53 Cummings, E. E. I; six non-lectures. 1953. C3533
1953-54 Read, H. E. Icon and idea. 1955. C3534
1955-56 Muir, E. The estate of poetry. 1962. C3535
1956-57 Shahn, B. The shape of content. 1957. C3536
1957-58 Guillén, J. Language and poetry. 1961. C3537
1958-59 Chávez, C. Musical thought. 1961. C3538
1961-62 Nervi, P. L. Aesthetics and technology in building, tr. by Einaudi. 1965. C3539
1962-63 Schrade, L. Tragedy in the art of music. 1964. C3540
1964-65 Day-Lewis, C. The lyric impulse. 1965. C3541
1968-69 Sessions, R. Questions about music. 1970. C3542
1969-70 Trilling, L. Sincerity & authenticity. 1972. C3543
1970-71 Paz, O. Children of the Mire. 1974. C3544

CHAUCER SOCIETY. PUBLICATIONS (Chaucer Society, Kegan Paul, Distributed by Oxford)

First Series:
Boethius. Chaucer's 'Boece' Englisht from "Anicii Manlii Severini Boethii Philosophiae consolationis libri quinque," ed. by Furnivall. 1886. (75) C3545
____. Chaucer's "Boece" Englisht from Boethius's "De consolatione philosophia," ed. by Morris. 1886. (76) C3546

Chaucer, G. Autotypes of Chaucer's manuscripts. 4 pts. 1876-86. (48, 56, 62, 74) C3547
____. The Cambridge ms. (University library, Gg. 4. 27) of Chaucer's Canterbury tales, ed. by Furnivall. 8 parts. 1868-79. (4, 10, 17, 28, 33, 40, 52, 66) C3548
____. The Cambridge ms. Dd. 4. 24. of Chaucer's Canterbury tales, ed. by Furnivall. 2 pts. 1901-02. (95, 96) C3549
____. Chaucer's Troylus and Cryseyde compared with Boccaccio's Filostrato, tr. by Rossetti. 2 pts. 1873, 1883. (44, 65) C3550
____. The Corpus ms. (Corpus Christi coll., Oxford) of Chaucer's Canterbury tales, ed. by Furnivall. 7 parts. 1868-79. (5, 11, 18, 34, 41, 53, 67) C3551
____. The Ellesmere ms. of Chaucer's Canterbury tales, ed. by Furnivall. 8 parts. 1868-79. (2, 8, 16, 26, 32, 38, 50, 70) C3552
____. The Harleian ms. 7334 of Chaucer's Canterbury tales, ed. by Furnivall. 1885. (73) C3553
____. The Hengwrt ms. of Chaucer's Canterbury tales, ed. by Furnivall. 6 parts. 1868-79. (3, 9, 27, 39, 51, 71) C3554
____. The Lansdowne ms. of Chaucer's Canterbury tales, ed. by Furnivall. 7 parts. 1867-79. (7, 13, 20, 36, 43, 55, 69) C3555
____. The manuscripts of Chaucer's Troilus, ed. by Root. 1914 for 1911. (98) C3556
____. More odd texts of

Chaucer's Minor poems, ed. by Furnivall. The compleynte to Pite, Anelida and Arcite, Truth, Lack of Stedfastness, Fortune, Purse. 1886. (77) C3557

____. Notes and corrections for the 8 v. edition. (47) C3558

____. Odd texts of Chaucer's minor poems, ed. by Furnivall. Pt. 1. Parlament of foules, Legende of good women, Balade of Pite, The chroncycle made by Chaucer. 1871. (23). Pt. 2. An A B C, House of Fame, The legend of Good Women, The dethe of Blaunche the Duchess, Complaint to Pity, Parlament of Foules, Truth, Envoy to Scogan, Purse, Two odd bits of Chaucer's Troilus. 1880. C3559

____. A one-text print of Chaucer's minor poems, ed. by Furnivall. Pt. 1. The Dethe of Blaunche the Duchesse, Compleynte to Pite, Parliament of Foules, The Complynt of Mars, The A B C. 1871. (24). Pt. 2. The Mother of God, Anelida and Arcite, The former age, Adam Scrivener, House of Fame, Legend of Good Women, Truth, Compleynt of Venus, Envoy to Scogan, Marriage, Gentilesse, Proverbs, Lack of Stedfastness, Fortune, Chaucer to his Empty Purse. 1880. (61) C3560

____. A one-text print of Chaucer's Troilus and Criseyde from the Campsall ms. of Mr. Bacon Frank, ed. by Furnivall. 1888. (79) C3561

____. A parallel-text edition of Chaucer's minor poems, ed. by Furnivall. Pt. 1. The dethe of Blaunche the Duchesse. The Compleynte to Pite, Parlement of Foules, The Complynte of Mars. 1871. (21). Pt. 2. The A B C, the Mother of God, Anelida and Arcite, The former age, Adam Scrivener, The house of Fame, 1878. (57). Pt. 3. The Legend of Good Women, Truth, The Compleynte of Venus, Envoy to Scogan, Marriage, Gentilesse, Proverbs, Lack of Stedfastness, Fortune, Chaucer to His Empty Purse. 1879. (58) C3562

____. A parallel-text print of Chaucer's Troilus and Criseyde from the Campsall ms. of Mr. Bacon Frank, ed. by Furnivall. 2 pts. 1881, 1882. (63, 64) C3563

____. The Petworth ms. of Chaucer's Canterbury tales, ed. by Furnivall. 7 parts. 1868-79. (6, 12, 19, 35, 42, 54,68) C3564

____. A six-text print of Chaucer's Canterbury tales (from the Ellesmere, Hengwrt 154, Cambridge univ. Gf, 4.27, Corpus Christi coll., Petworth, Lansdowne 851), ed. by Furnivall. 8 v. I. Prologue Knight's tale. 1868. (1) II. Miller's, Reeve's, Cook's Tales, Spuriour tale of Gamelyn. 1870. (14). III. Man of Law's, Shipman's, Prioress's tales, Tales of Sir Thopas. 1871. (15). IV. Tale of Melibeus, Monk's, Nun's, Priest's, Doctor's, Pardoner's, Wife of Bath's, Friar's, Summoner's tales. 1872. (25). V. Clerk's and Merchant's tales. 1873. (30). VI. Squire's and Franklin's tales. 1874. (31). VII. Second Nun's, Canon's Yeoman's, Maniciple's tales, Blank-Parson Link. 1875. (37). VIII. Parson's tale, Mr. Cromie's corrections to the rhyme index. 1877. (49). IX. Index. 1911 for 1884. (72) C3565

____. Specimen extracts from the nine known unprinted mss. of Chaucer's "Troilus" and from Caxton's and Thynne's first editions, ed. by Furnivall. 1914 for 1896. (89) C3566

____. Specimens of all the accessible unprinted manuscripts of the Canterbury tales. 9 pts. Pt. 1. From seven mss. 1890. (81). Pt. 2. From ten mss. 1892. (85). Pt. 3. From six mss. 1893. (86). Pt. 4. From seventeen mss. 1897. (90). Pt. 5. The Doctor-Pardoner link and Pardoner's Prologue and Tale. 1896. (91). Pts. 6-7. The Clerk's tale and head-link. 1897-98. (92, 93). Pt. 8. The Pardoner's Prolog and tale. 1900. (94). Pt. 9. Introduction to Parts IV and VII. 1902. (97) C3567

____. A supplementary parallel-text edition of Chaucer's minor poems, ed. by Furnivall. Pt. 1. The Parliament of Foules, An A B C, Anelida and Arcite, The Legend of Good Women, The Complaint of Mars, Truth, The Compleynt of Venus, Gentilesse, Lack of Stedfastness, Fortune. 1871. 1880. (22, 59) C3568

____. Three more parallel texts of Chaucer's Troilus and Criseyde from mis. no. 61 in Corpus Christi college, ed. by Furnivall. 2 pts. 1894, 1895. (87, 88) C3569

____. A treatise on the astrolabe, ed. by Skeat. 1872. (29) C3570

Corson, H., comp. Index of proper names and subjects to Chaucer's Canterbury tales, ed. by Skeat. 1884. (72) C3571

Cromie, H., comp. Ryme-index to the Ellsmere manuscript of Chaucer's Canterbury tales. 1875. (45, 46, 47) C3572

Marshall, I. and Porter, L. Ryme-index to the manuscript text of Chaucer's minor poems. 1887. (78) C3573

____. 1889. (80) C3574

Roman de la Rose. English. The Romaunt o the Rose. A reprint of the first printed edition by William Thynne, 1532. 1911 for 1890. (82) C3575

____. The Romaunt of the Rose from the unique Glasgow ms., ed. by Kaluza. 1891. (83) C3576

Root, R. K. The textual tradition of Troilus. 1916 for 1912. (99) C3577

Skeat, W. W. Rime-index. 1892 for 1891. (84) C3578

Second Series (Chaucer Society)

Albertano de Brescia. Albertani Brixiensis Liber consolationis et consilii, ed. by Sundby. 1873. (8) C3579

Beryn. The tale of Beryn, ed. by Furnivall and Stone. 1887. (17, 24) C3580

Braithwait, R. Richard Braithwait's Comments in 1665 upon Chaucer's Tales of the Miller and the Wife of Bath, ed. by Spurgeon. 1901. (33) C3581

Brown, C. F. A study of the Miracle of Our Lady told by Chaucer's Prioress. 1910 for 1906. (45) C3582

Chaucer Soc. Essays on Chaucer. Pt. 1. 1868. (2). Pt. 2. 1874. (9). Pt. 3. 1876. (16). Pt. 4. 1878. (18). Pt. 5. 1884. (19). Pt. 6. 1892. (29) C3583

Ellis, A. J. On early English pronunciation. 5 pts. 1870-1889. (1, 4, 5, 11, 25) C3584

Furnivall, F. J., ed. Analogues of Chaucer's Canterbury pilgrimage. 1903. (36) C3585

____. Originals and analogues of some of Chaucer's Canterbury tales, Pt. I. 1872. (7). Pt. 2. 1875. (10). Pt. 3. 1876. (15). Pt. 4. 1886. (20). Pt. 5. 1887. (22) C3586

____. Trial-forewords to my "Parallel text edition of Chaucer's minor poems." 1871. (6) C3587

Hoccleve, T. A new ploughman's tale, ed. by Beatty. 1902. (34) C3588

Kenyon, J. S. The syntax of the infinitive in Chaucer. 1909 for 1905. (44) C3589

Kittredge, G. L. The date of Chaucer's Troilus and other

Chaucer matters. 1909 for 1905. (42) C3590

____. Observations on the language of Chaucer's Troilus. 1891. (28) C3591

Koch, J. The chronology of Chaucer's writing. 1890. (27) C3592

____. A detailed comparison of the 8 mss. of Chaucer's Canterbury Tales. 1913 for 1907. (47) C3593

____. Pardoner's prologue and tale. 1902. (35) C3594

Lane, J. John Lane's continuation of Chaucer's Squire's Tale, ed. by Furnivall. 1890. (23, 26) C3595

____. Life-records of Chaucer, 4 pt. 1875-1900. (12, 14, 21, 32) C3596

Littlehales, H. Some notes on the road from London to Canterbury in the Middle Ages. 1898. (30) C3597

Lydgate, J. Siege of Thebes, ed. by Erdman. 1911 for 1906. (46) C3598

Skeat, W. W. The eight-text edition of The Canterbury Tales: Skeat. 1909 for 1905. (43) C3599

____. Evolution of the Canterbury tales. 1907 for 1903. (38) C3600

Spielmann, M. H. The portraits of Chaucer. 1900. (31) C3601

Spurgeon, C. F. E. Five hundred years of Chaucer criticism and allusion, 1357-1900. Pt. 1. 1914 for 1908. (48). Pt. 2. 1918 for 1909-10. (49, 50). Pt. 3. 1921 for 1913. (52). Pt. 4. 1922 for 1914. (53). Pt. 5. 1922 for 1915. (54). Pt. 6. 1924 for 1917. (55, 56) C3602

Sypherd, W. O. Studies in Chaucer's Hous of Fame. 1907 for 1904. (39) C3603

Tatlock, J. S. P. The development and chronology of Chaucer's works. 1907. (37) C3604

____. Harleian manuscript 7334 and the revision of the Canterbury tales. 1909 for 1904. (41) C3605

____. The scene of the Franklin's tale revisted. 1914 for 1911. (51) C3606

Thynne, F. Animadversions uppon Speght's first edition of Chaucer's Workes. 1876. (13) C3607

Young, K. The origin and development of the story of Troilus and Criseyde. 1908 for 1904. (40) C3608

CHEMICAL ANALYSIS (Interscience)

1 Jacobs, M. B. The analytical chemistry of industrial poisons, hazards and solvents. 1949. C3609

2 Strain, H. M. Chromatographic absorption analysis. 1945. C3610

3 Sandell, E. B. Colorimetric determination of traces of metals. 1959. C3611

4 Flagg, J. F. Organic reagents used in gravimetric and volumetric analysis. 1948. C3612

5 Mitchell, J. and Smith, D. M. Aquametry. 1948. C3613

6 Gunther, F. A. and Blinn, R. C. Analysis of insecticides and acaricides. 1955. C3614

7 Jacobs, M. B. and Scheflan, L. Chemical analysis of industrial solvents. 1953. C3615

8 Boltz, D. F., ed. Colorimetric determinations of nonmetals. 1958. C3616

9 Codell, M. Analytical chemistry of titanium metals and compounds. 1959. C3617

10 Jacobs, M. B. The chemical analysis of air pollutants. 1960. C3618

11 Birks, L. S. X-ray spectrochemical analysis. 1959. C3619

12 Rosen, M. J. and Goldsmith, H. A. Systematic analysis of surface-active agents. 1960. C3620

13 Breyer, B. and Bauer, H. H. Alternating current polarography and tensammetry. 1963. C3621

14 Herrmann, R. and Alkemade, C. T. J. Chemical analysis by flame, tr. by Gilbert. 1963. C3622
15 Ashworth, M. R. F. Titrimetric organic analysis. V. 1. 1964. C3623
16 Ringbom, A. J. Complexation in analytical chemistry. 1963. C3624
17 Birks, L. S. Electron probe microanalysis. 1963. C3625
18 Perrin, D. D. Organic complex reagents. 1964. C3626
19 Wendlandt, W. W. Thermal method of analysis. 1964. C3627
20 Stock, J. T. Amperometric titrations. 1965. C3628
21 Wendlandt, W. W. and Hecht, H. G. Reflective spectroscopy. 1966. C3629
22 Jacobs, M. B. The analytical toxicology of industrial inorganic poisons. 1967. C3630
23 Walton, A. G. The formation and properties of precipitates. 1967. C3631
24 Marx, H. B. and Rechnitz, G. A. Kinetics in analytical chemistry. 1968. C3632
25 Slavin, W. Atomic absorption spectroscopy. 1968. C3633
26 Tsutsui, M., ed. Characterization of organometallic compounds. V. 1. 1969. C3634
27 Maxwell, J. A. Rock and mineral analysis. 1968. C3635
28 Streuli, C. A. and Averill, P. The analytical chemistry of nitrogen and its compounds. 2 v. 1970. C3636
29 Karchmer, J. H., ed. The analytical chemistry of sulfur and its compounds. V. 1. 1969. C3637
30 Tölg, G. Ultramicro elemental analysis. 1970. C3638
31 Sawicki, E. Photometric organic analysis. 1970. C3639
32 Weiss, F. T. Selected methods of organic analysis. 1970. C3640
33 Perrin, D. D. Masking and demasking of chemical reactions. 1970. C3641
34 Soete, D. de and others. Neutron activation analysis. 1972. C3642
35 Tobin, M. C. Laser Raman spectroscopy. 1971. C3643
36 Slavin, M. Emission spectrochemical analysis. 1971. C3644
37 Analytical chemistry of phosphorus compounds, ed. by Halmann. 1972. C3645
38 Winefordner, J. D. and others. Luminescence spectrometry in analytical chemistry. 1972. C3646
39 Nargolwalla, S. S. Activation analysis with beutron generators. 1973. C3647
40 Melnick, L. M. and others. Determination of gaseous elements in metals. 1974. C3648
41 Smith, L. A., ed. Analysis of silicones. 1974. C3649

CHEMICAL PROCESS MONOGRAPH
(Noyes Development Corp.)

1 Symposium on Caustic Production Technique. Caustic soda production technique. 1962. C3650
2 Symposium on Ethyl Alcohol Production Technique. Ethyl alcohol production technique. 1964. C3651
3 Noyes, R. Ammonia and synthesis gas. 1964. C3652
4 Pratt, C. J. and Noyes, R. Nitrogen fertilizer chemical processes. 1965. C3653
5 Rickles, R. N. Exotic metals. 1965. C3654
6 Sitting, M. Acetic acid and anhydride. 1965. C3655
7 ____. Linear alpha olefins and biodegradable detergents. 1965. C3656
8 ____. Chemicals from ethylene. 1965. C3657
9 ____. Chemicals from propylene. 1965. C3658
10 Rickles, R. N. Pollution control. 1965. C3659
11 Oshima, M. Wood chemistry process engineering aspects. 1965. C3660
12 Sitting, M. Acetylene. 1965. C3661
13 ____. Acrylic acid and

esters. 1965. C3662
14 ____. Acrylontrile. 1965. C3663
15 Noyes, R. Potash and potassium fertilizers. 1965. C3664
16 Sitting, M. Aromatics. 1966. C3665
17 ____. Chemicals from aromatics. 1966. C3666
18 ____. Dibasic acids and anhydrides. 1966. C3667
19 ____. Chemicals from C_4 hydrocarbons. 1966. C3668
20 ____. Organometallics. 1966. C3669
21 ____. Caprolactam and higher lactams. 1966. C3670
22 ____. Fluorinated hydrocarbons and polymers. 1966. C3671
23 ____. Oxo process and products. 1966. C3672
24 ____. Vinyl monomers and polymers. 1966. C3673
25 Alexander, A. Man made fiber processing. 1966. C3674
26 Noyes, R. Ammonia and synthesis gas. 1967. C3675

CHEMICAL PROCESS REVIEW
(Noyes Development Corp.)

1 Sitting, M. Synthetic fibers from petroleum. 1967. C3676
2 ____. Polyolefin processes. 1967. C3677
3 ____. Stereo-rubber and other elastomer processes, 1967. 1967. C3678
4 ____. Industrial gases and manufacture and applications. 1964. C3679
5 ____. Pesticide production processes. 1967. C3680
6 ____. Plastic films from petroleum raw materials. 1967. C3681
7 ____. Catalysts and catalytic processes. 1967. C3682
8 ____. Combine hydrocarbons and nitrogen for profit. 1967. C3683
9 Noyes, R. Phosphoric acid by the wet process. 1967. C3684
10 Sitting, M. Combine hydrocarbons, and halogens for profit. 1968. C3685
11 ____. Combine hydrocarbons and oxygen for profit. 1968. C3686
12 ____. Olefins. 1968. C3687
13 Powell, R. Urea process technology. 1968. C3688
14 Mantell, C. L. Electro-organic chemical processing. 1968. C3689
15 Powell, R. Controlled release fertilizers. 1968. C3690
16 Sitting, M. Diolefins. 1968. C3691
17 ____. Aromatics manufacture and derivatives. 1968. C3692
18 Powell, R. Titanium dioxide and titanium tetrachloride. 1968. C3693
19 Sitting, M. Paraffins and cycloparaffins. 1968. C3694
20 Powell, R. Hydrogen peroxide manufacture. 1968. C3695
21 ____. Carbon black technology. 1968. C3696
22 Sitting, M. Acetylene processes and products. 1968. C3697
23 ____. Alcohols, polyols, and phenols. 1968. C3698
24 ____. Air pollution control processes and equipment. 1968. C3699
25 Powell, R. Monosodium glutamate and glutamic acid. 1968. C3700
26 Sitting, M. Polyacetal resins, aldehydes and ketones. 1968. C3701
27 ____. Practical detergent manufacture. 1968. C3702
28 Powell, R. Hydrazene manufacturing processes. 1968. C3703
29 Sitting, M. Synthetic leather from petroleum. 1969. C3704
30 Powell, R. Nitric acid technology. 1969. C3705
31 Sitting, M. Amines, nitriles & isocyanatis. 1969. C3706
32 ____. Water pollution control and solid wastes disposal. 1969. C3707
33 Powell, R. Chlorine and caustic soda manufacture. 1969. C3708
34 Ranney, M. W. Alkali

metal phosphates. 1969. C3709
35 ____. Ammonium phosphates. 1969. C3710
36 Albertson, B. Photochemical processes. 1969. C3711
37 Noyes, R. Citric acid production processes. 1969. C3712
38 Rubel, T. Fibrinolytic enzyme manufacture. 1969. C3713
39 ____. Vitamine E manufacture. 1969. C3714
40 Noyes, R. Vitamin B12 manufacture. 1969. C3715
41 Whiting, R. Radiation chemical processing. 1969. C3716
42 Meltzer, Y. L. Phatalocyanine technology. 1970. C3717
43 Idson, D. B. Antiobesity drug manufacture. 1970. C3718
44 Placek, C. Ion exchange resins. 1970. C3719
45 Gutcho, M. Synthetic perfumery material. 1970. C3720
46 Placek, C. ABS resin manufacture. 1970. C3721
47 Johnson, K. Polycarbonates. 1970. C3722
48 McDonald, M. Spandex manufacture. 1970. C3723
49 Ranney, M. W. Ethylene propyline-diene rubbers. 1970. C3724
50 Placek, C. Polysulfuric manufacture. 1970. C3725
51 ____. Multicomponent fibers. 1971. C3726
52 Sitting, M. Agricultural chemical manufacture, 1971. 1971. C3727
53 Stecher, P. G. Trimellitic anhydride and pyromelltic dianhydride. 1971. C3728
54 Ranney, M. W. Polyimide manufacture. 1971. C3729
55 Sitting, M. Sulfuric acid manufacture and effluent control. 1971. C3730
56 ____. Polyester fiber manufacture. 1971. C3731
57 Goldman, G. K. Liquid fuel from coal, 1972. 1972. C3732
58 Weiss, S. Hydrofluoric acid manufacture, 1972. 1972. C3733
59 Ranney, M. W. Synthetic lubricants, 1972. 1972. C3734
60 Rubel, T. G. Antifoaming and defoaming agents, 1972. 1972. C3735
61 Sitting, M. Polyamide fiber manufacture, 1972. 1972. C3736
62 ____. Acrylic and vinyl fibers, 1972. 1972. C3737
63 Ranney, M. W. Isocyanates manufacture. 1972. C3738
64 Meltzer, Y. Water soluble polymers. 1972. C3739
65 McDermott, J. Liquified natural gas technology. 1972. C3740
66 Sitting, M. Catalyst manufacture. 1972. C3741

CHEMICAL SOCIETY. LONDON. SPECIAL PUBLICATIONS.

1 Chemical Society, London. The kinetics and mechanism of inorganic reactions in the solution..., by Sutton and Chatt. 1954. C3742
2 ____. Peptide chemistry, by Hey. 1955. C3743
3 ____. Recent work on naturally occurring nitrogen heterocyclic compounds, ed. by Schofield, 1955. C3744
4 ____. Recent advances in the chemistry of colouring matters, ed. by Braude. 1956. C3745
5 ____. Antibiotics and mould metabolites, by Johnson and others. 1956. C3746
6-7 Bjerrum, J. and others. Stability constants of metalion complexes. 2 v. 1957-58. C3747
8 Chemical Society, London. Phosphoric esters and related compounds, by Kenner and Brown. 1957. C3748
9 ____. Reactions of free radicals in the gas phase, by Sugden and others. 1957. C3749
10 ____. Recent aspects of the inorganic chemistry of nitrogen, by Maddock and Sharpe. 1957. C3750
11 Tables of interatomic distances and configuration in molecules and ions, by Bowen and others. 1958. C3751
12 Chemical Society, London.

Developments in aromatic chemistry. 1958. C3752
13 Int'l. Conference on co-ordination Chemistry. Lectures delivered and abstracts of papers submitted. 1959. C3753
14 Chemical Society, London. Handbook for Chemical Society authors. 1960. C3754
15 ____. Inorganic polymers. 1961. C3755
16 ____. The transition state. 1962. C3756
17 ____. Stability constants of metalion complexes. 1964. C3757
18 Same as no. 11. V. 2. 1965. C3758
19 Organic reaction mechanisms. 1965. C3759
20 Chemical Society Symposium on Relaxation Methods in Relation to Molecular Structure. Molecular relaxation processes. 1966. C3760
21 International Symposium on Aromaticity. Aromaticity. 1966. C3761
22 International Symposium on the Alkali Metals. Alkali Metals. 1966. C3762
23 International Symposium on the Solution Properties of Natural Polymers. Solution properties of natural polymers. 1968. C3763
24 Essays on free-radical chemistry. 1970. C3764
25 Same as no. 17. Supp. no. 1. 1971. C3765

CHEMISTRY OF FUNCTIONAL GROUPS (Wiley)

Feuer, H. The chemistry of the nitro and nitroso group. 2 v. 1969-70. C3766/76
Patai, S., ed. Chemistry of acyl halides. 1972. C3777
____. The chemistry of alkenes. 2 v. 1964-70. C3778
____. The chemistry of carbon Halogen bond. 2 v. 1974. C3779
____. Chemistry of carbon nitrogen double bonds. 1970. C3780
____. The chemistry of ether linkage. 1967. C3781
____. The chemistry of hydroxyl group. 2 v. 1971. C3782
____. The chemistry of the amino group. 1968. C3783
____. Chemistry of the azido group. 1971. C3784
____. The chemistry of the carboxylic acids and esters. 1970. C3785
____. The chemistry of the carbonyl group. 1966. C3786
____. The chemistry of the quinonoid compound. 2 v. 1974. C3787
____. The chemistry of the Thiol group. 1974. C3788
Rappoport, D. The chemistry of cyano group. 1970. C3789
Zabicky, J. Chemistry of amides. 1970. C3790

CHEMISTRY OF HETEROCYCLIC COMPOUNDS (Interscience)

1 Mann, F. G. The heterocyclic derivatives of phosphorus, arsenic, antimony, bismuth and silicon. 1950. C3791
2 Allen, C. F. H. and others. Six-membered heterocyclic nitrogen compounds with four condensed rings. 1958. C3792
3 Hartough, H. D. and others. Thiophene and its derivatives. 1952. C3793
4 Bambas, L. L. Five-membered heterocyclic compounds with nitrogen and sulfur or nitrogen, sulfur and oxygen (except thiazole). 1952. C3794
5 Simpson, J. C. E. Condensed pyridazine and pyrazine rings (cinnolines, phthalazines and quinoxalines). 1953. C3795
6 Hofmann, K. Imidazole and its derivatives. V. 1. 1953. C3796
7 Hartough, H. D. and others. Compounds with condensed thiophene rings. 1954. C3797
8 Sumpter, W. C. and Miller, F. M. Heterocyclic compounds with indole and

carbazole systems. 1954. C3798
9 Acheson, R. M. Acridines. 1956. C3799
10 Erickson, J. G. and others. The 1, 2, 3- and 1, 2, 4-triazines, tetrazines and pentazines. 1956. C3800
11 Swan, G. A. and Felton, D. G. I. Phenazines. 1957. C3801
12 Allen, C. F. H. The six-membered heterocyclic nitrogen compounds with three condensed rings. 1958. C3802
13 Smolin, E. M. and Rapoport, L. -s- Triazines and derivatives. 1959. C3803
14 Pyridine and its derivatives, ed. by Klingsberg. 4 v. 1960-62. C3804
15 Mosby, W. L. Heterocyclic systems with bridgehead nitrogen atoms. 3 v. 1961. C3805
16 Brown, D. J. The pyrimidines. 1962. C3806
17 Wiley, R. H., ed. Five- and six-membered compounds with nitrogen and oxygen. 1962. C3807
18 Hamer, F. M. The cyanine dyes and related compounds. 1964. C3808
19 Fanta, P. E. and others. Three-and-four-membered rings. 2 v. 1964. C3809
20 Wiley, R. H. and P. Pyrazolones, pyrazolidones, and derivatives. 1964. C3810
21 Breslow, D. S. and Skolnik, H. Multi-sulfur and sulfur and oxygen five-and-six-membered heterocycles. 2 v. 1966. C3811
22 Wiley, R. H., ed. Pyrazolones, pyrazolidones, pyrazolidenis, indazoles, and condensed rings. 1967. C3812
23 Mustafa, A. Furopyrans and Furopyrones. 1967. C3813
24 Fused pyrimides, ed. by Brown. 4 pts. 1967. C3814
25 Indoles, ed. by Houlihan. 1972. C3815
26 Rosowsky, A., ed. Seven membered heterocyclic compounds containing oxygen and sulfur. 1972. C3816
27 Castle, R. N., ed. Condensed pyridazines including cinnolines and phtholazines. 1973. C3817
28 ____. Pyridazines. 1973. C3818
29 Mustafa, A. Benzofurans. 1974. C3819

CHEMISTRY OF NATURAL PRODUCTS (Holden-Day)

1 Ourisson, G. and others. Tetracyclic triterpenes. 1964. C3820
2 Asselineau, J. The bacterial lipids. 1967. C3821
3 Posternak, T. The cyclitols. 1965. C3822
4 Sorm, F. and Dolejs, L. Guaianolides and germacranolides. 1966. C3823
5 Privat de Garilhe, M. Enzymes in nucleic acid research. 1967. C3824
6 Nicolaus, R. A. Melanins. 1968. C3825

THE CHEMISTRY OF NATURAL PRODUCTS (Interscience)

1 Bentley, K. W. The alkaloids. 1957. C3826
2 Mayo, P. de Mono- and sesquiterpenoids. 1959. C3827
3 ____. The higher terpenoids. 1959. C3828
4 Bentley, K. W. The natural pigments. 1960. C3829
5 Dyke, S. F. The carbohydrates. 1960. C3830
6 ____. The chemistry of vitamins. 1965. C3831
7 Same as no. 1. 1966. C3832

CHETHAM SOCIETY. REMAINS, HISTORICAL AND LITERARY, CONNECTED WITH THE PALATINE COUNTIES OF LANCASTER AND CHESTER (Chetham Soc.)

1 Brereton, W. Travels in Holland, the United Provinces, England, Scotland, and Ireland, 1634-35. 1944. C3833
2 Ormerod, G. Tracts relating to military proceedings in Lancashire during the

Great Civil War. 1944. C3834
3 Davies, R. Chester's triumph in honor of her Prince, ed. by Corser. 1844. C3835
4 Martindale, A. The life of Adam Martindale written by himself, ed. by Parkinson. 1845. C3836
5 Hibbert-Ware, S. Lancashire memorials of the rebellion, 1715. 1845. C3836
6 Potts, T. Pott's Discovery of witches in the county of Lancaster. 1845. C3837
7 James, R. Iter lancastrense, ed. by Corser. 1845. C3838
8 Gastrell, F. Notitia cestriensis, ed. by Raines. V. 1. 1845. C3839
9 Heywood, T., ed. The Norris papers. 1846. C3840
10-11 Whalley abbey. The coucher book, ed. by Hulton. V. 1-2. 1846. C3841
12 Moore, H. E. The Moore rental, ed. by Heywood. 1847. C3842
13 Worthington, J. The diary and correspondance of Dr. John Worthington, ed. by Crossley and Christie. V. 1. 1847. C3843
14 Assheton, N. The Journal of Nicholas Assheton, ed. by Raines. 1848. C3844
15 Bradshaw, H. The Holy lyfe and history of Saynt Werburge, ed. by Hawkins. 1848. C3845
16 Same as no. 10. V. 2. C3846
17 Legh, P. Warrington in MCCCCLXV. 1849. C3847
18 Newcome, H. The diary of Rev. Henry Newcome, ed. by Heywood. 1849. C3848
19 Same as no. 8. V. 2. C3849
20 Same as no. 10. V. 4. C3850
21-22 Same as no. 8. V. 3-4. 1850. C3851
23 Robinson, R. A golden Mirrour, ed. by Corser. 1851. C3852
24 Chetham miscellanies, ed. by Langton. V. 1. 1851. C3853
25 Allen, W. Cardinal Allen's defence of Sir William Stanley's surrender of Deventer, ed. by Heywood. 1852. C3854
26-27 Newcome, H. The autobiography of Henry Newcome, ed. by Parkinson. 1852. C3855
28 The Jacobite trials at Manchester in 1694, ed. by Beaumont. 1853. C3856
29 Heywood, T. The earls of Derby and the verse writers and poets of the sixteenth and seventeenth centuries. 1853. C3857
30 Evesham abbey. Documents relating to the Priory of Penwortham, ed. by Hulton. 1853. C3858
31 The Derby household books, ed. by Raines. 1853. C3859
32 Byrom, J. The private journals and literary remains of John Byrom, ed. by Parkinson. V. 1. 1854. C3860
33 Chester, Eng. Lancashire and Cheshire wills and inventories from the ecclesiastical court, Chester, ed. by Piccope. V. 1. 1855. C3861
34 Same as no. 32. V. 2. 1854. C3862
35 Shuttleworth family. The house and farm accounts of the Shuttleworths of Gawthorpe Hall, ed. by Harland. V. 1. 1854. C3863
36 Same as no. 13. V. 2. C3864
37 Same as no. 24. V. 2. 1855-56. C3865
38 French, G. J., ed. Bibliographical notices of the church libraries of Turton and Gorton bequeathed by Humphrey Chetham. 1855. C3866
39 Ffarington, S. M. The Farington papers. 1856. C3867
40 Same as no. 32. V. 3. 1856. C3868
41 Same as no. 35. V. 2. C3869
42 Booker, J. A history of the ancient chapels of Didsbury and Chorlton. 1857. C3870
43 Same as no. 35.

V. 3. C3871
44 Same as no. 32. V. 4. C3872
45 Wilson, T. Miscellanies, ed. by Raines. 1857. C3873
46 Same as no. 35. V. 4. C3874
47 Booker, J. A history of the ancient chapel of Birch. 1859. C3875
48 Chetham library. A catalogue of the collection of tracts for and against Popery, ed. by Jones. V. 1. 1859. C3876
49-50 Harland, J., ed. The Lancashire lieutenancy under the Tudors and Stuarts. 2 v. 1859. C3877
51 Same as no. 33. V. 2. C3878
52 Corser, T. Collectanea anglopoetica. V. 1. 1860. C3879
53 Harland, J., ed. Manecestre. V. 1. 1861. C3880
54 Same as no. 33. V. 3. C3881
55 Same as no. 52. V. 2. 1861. C3882
56 Same as no. 53. V. 2. C3883
57 Same as no. 24. V. 3. 1862. C3884
58 Same as no. 53. V. 3. 1862. C3885
59-60 Raines, F. R. A history of the chantries within the county palatine of Lancaster. 2 v. 1862. C3886
61 Abbott, R. Abbott's journal, ed. by Goss. 1862. C3887
62 Robinson, E. Discourse of the war in Lancashire. 1863. C3888
63 Manchester, England. Court leet. A volume of the court Leet records of the manor of Manchester in the sixteenth century. V. 1. 1863. C3889
64 Same as no. 48. V. 2. 1859. C3890
65 Same as no. 63. V. 2. 1863. C3891
66-67 Raines, F. R. The Stanley papers. Pt. 3. V. 1. 1867. C3892
68 Hartland, H. Collectanea relating to Manchester. V. 1. 1866. C3893
69 Manchester, England. Grammar school. The admission register of the Manchester School, ed. by Smith. V. 1. 1867. C3894
70 Same as no. 66. V. 3. 1867. C3895
71 Same as no. 55. V. 3. 1867. C3896
72 Same as no. 68. V. 2. 1867. C3897
73 Same as no. 69. V. 2. C3898
74 Harland, J., ed. Three Lancashire documents of the fourteenth and fifteenth centuries. 1868. C3899
75 Gt. Brit. College of arms. Lancashire funeral certificates, ed. by King. 1868. C3900
76 Heywood, R. Observations and instructions divine and morall, ed. by Crossley. 1869. C3901
77 Same as no. 52. V. 4. 1867. C3902
78-80 Leycester, P. Tracts written in the controversy respecting the legitimacy of America, ed. by Beaumont. 3 v. 1869. C3903
81 Flower, W. The visitation of the county Palatine of Lancaster in the year 1567, ed. by Raines. 1870. C3904
82 St. George, R. The visitation of the county Palatine of Lancaster in the year 1613, ed. by Raines. 1871. C3905
83 Same as no. 24. V. 4. 1872. C3906
84-85 Dugdale, W. The visitation of the county Palatine of Lancaster, ed. by Raines. V. 1-2. 1872. C3907
86-87 Beaumont, W., ed. Annals of the Lords of Warrington for the first five centuries after the conquest. 2 v. 1872. C3908
88 Same as no. 84. V. 3. 1873. C3909
89-90 Dr. Farmer Chetham M. S., ed. by Grosart. 2 v. 1873. C3910
91 Same as no. 52. V. 5. 1873. C3911
92 Fishwick, H. The history of the parish of Kirkham. 1874. C3912

93-94 Same as no. 69. V. 3. 1867. C3913
95 Towneley, C. and Dodsworth, R. Abstracts of inquisitions post mortem. V. 1. 1875. C3914
96 Same as no. 24. V. 5. 1875. C3915
97 Renaud, F. Contributions towards a history of the ancient parish of Prestbury in Cheshire. 1876. C3916
98 Benolt, T. The visitation of Lancashire and a part of Cheshire. V. 1. 1876. C3917
99 Same as no. 95. V. 2. 1876. C3918
100-102 Same as no. 52. V. 6-8. 1877-78. C3919
103 Same as no. 24. V. 6. 1878. C3920
104-105 Fishwick, H. The history of the parish of Garstang. 1891. C3921
106 Same as no. 52. V. 9. 1879. C3922
107 Gt. Brit. Comm. on seizure. Inventories of goods in the churches and chapels in Lancashire, ed. by Bailey. V. 1. 1879. C3923
108 Same as no. 52. V. 10. 1880. C3924
109 Walworth, N. Correspondence of Nathan Walworth and Peter Seddon of Outwood, ed. by Fletcher. 1880. C3925
110 Same as no. 98. V. 2. 1876. C3926
111 Same as no. 52. V. 11. 1883. C3927
112 Lincoln, H. de L. Two "compoti" of the Lancashire and Cheshire manors of Henry de Lacy, ed. by Lyons. 1884. C3928
113 Same as no. 107. V. 2. 1885. C3929
114 Same as no. 13. V. 3. 1886. C3930
Index to v. 1-114. 2 v. 1893. C3931

New Series:
1-2 Raines, F. R. The vicars of Rochdale, ed. by Howorth. 2 v. 1883. C3932
3 Chester, Eng. Lancashire and Cheshire wills and inventories of Chester, ed. by Earwaker. 1884. C3933
4 Vaux, T. G. A Catechisme; ed. by Law. 1885. C3934
5-6 Raines, F. R. The rectors of Manchester, ed. by Bailey. 2 v. 1885. C3935
7 Christie, R. C. The old church and school libraries of Lancashire, ed. by Christie. 1885. C3936
8 Fishwick, H. The history of the parish of Poulton-le-Fylde. 1885. C3937
9 Furness abbey. The Coucher book of Furness Abbey, ed. by Atkinson. 1:1. 1886. C3938
10 Fishwick, H. The history of the parish of Bispham. 1891. C3939
11 Same as no. 9. V. 1:2. 1886. C3940
12 Blundell, W. The Crosby records, ed. by Gibson. 1889. C3941
13 Chrstie, R. C. A bibliography of the works written and edited by Dr. Worthington. 1888. C3942
14 Same as no. 9. V. 1:3. 1885. C3943
15-18 Bridgeman, G. T. O. The history of the church & manor of Wigan. 4 v. 1888-90. C3944
19 Derby, E. S. Correspondence of Edward, third earl of Derby, ed. by Toller. 1890. C3945
20 Manchester, England. The minutes of the Manchester Presbyterian classis, 1646-60, ed. by Shaw. V. 1. 1890. C3946
21 Raines, F. R. The fellows of the Collegiate church of Manchester, ed. by Renaud. V. 1. 1891. C3947
22 Same as no. 20. V. 2. 1890. C3948
23 Same as no. 21. V. 2. 1891. C3949
24 Same as no. 20. V. 3. 1890. C3950
25 Fishwick, H. The history of the parish of St. Michaels-on-Wyre. 1891. C3951

26 Roper, W. O., ed. Materials for the history of the church of Lancaster. V. 1. 1892. C3952
27 Glynne, S. Notes on the churches of Lancashire, ed. by Atkinson. 1893. C3953
28 Chester, Eng. Lancashire and Cheshire wills and inventories of Chester, 1572 to 1696, ed. by Earwaker. 1894. C3954
29-30 Byrom, J. The poems of John Byrom, ed. by Ward. 3 v. 1912. C3955
31 Same as no. 26. V. 2. 1892. C3956
32 Glynne, S. Notes on churches of Cheshire, ed. by Atkinson. 1894. C3957
33 Jollie, T. The note book of the Rev. Thomas Holly, ed. by Fishwick, 1894. C3958
34-35 Same as no. 29. V. 3-4. 1912. C3959
36 Bury classis. (Presbyterian). Minutes of the Bury Presbyterian classis, 1647-57, ed. by Shaw. V. 1. 1897. C3960
37 Chester, England, Lancashire and Cheshire wills and inventories, ed. by Rylands. 1898-1900. C3961
38-40 Farrer, W., ed. The chartulary of Cokersand Abbey. V. 1-3. 1899. C3962
41 Same as no. 36. V. 2. 1897. C3963
42 Crofton, H. T. A history of the ancient chapel of Stretford. V. 1. 1899. C3964
43 Same as no. 38. V. 4. C3965
44 Act book of the ecclesiastical court of Whalley, ed. by Cooke. 1903. C3966
45 Same as no. 42. V. 2. C3967
46 Salford, England (Lancashire). The portmote of court leet records of Salford, 1597-1669, ed. by Mandley. V. 1. 1904. C3968
47 Chetham miscellanies. V. 1. 1901-02. C3969
48 Same as no. 46. V. 2. 1904. C3970
49-50 Raines, F. R. and Sutton, C. W. Life of Humphrey Chetham. 2 v. 1903. C3971
51 Same as no. 42. V. 3. 1903. C3972
52-55 Crofton, H. T. A history of Newton chapelry in the parish of Manchester. 4 v. 1904-05. C3973
56-57 Same as no. 38. V. 5-6. C3974
58-59 Same as no. 28. V. 3-4. C3975
60 Fishwick, H. The history of the parish of Lytham. 1907. C3976
61-62 Roper, W. O. Materials for the history of Lancaster. 2 v. 1907. C3977
63 Same as no. 47. V. 2. 1909. C3978
64 Same as no. 38. V. 7. C3979
65 Atkinson, J. C., ed. Tracts relating to the civil war in Cheshire, 1641-59. 1909. C3980
66-68 Blackburn, England. Grammar school. The records of the Blackburn grammar school, ed. by Stocks. 3 v. 1909. C3981
69 Halliwell, England. The township books of Halliwell, ed. by Sparke. 1910. C3982
70 Same as no. 29. V. 5. 1912. C3983
71 Fishwick, H., ed. The survey of the manor of Rochdale, 1626. 1910. C3984
72 Weld, J. A history of Leagram. 1913. C3985
73 Same as no. 47. V. 3. 1909. C3986
74 Same as no. 9. 2:1. C3987
75 Domesday book. The Domesday survey of Cheshire, ed. by Tait. 1914. C3988
76 Same as no. 9. 2:2. C3989
77 Lancashire, England. Court of quarter session, ed. by Tait. V. 1. 1590-1606. 1920. C3990
78 Same as no. 74. V. 2, pt. 3. C3991
79 Chester abbey. The chartulary or register of St. Werburgh Abbey, Chester, ed. by Tait.

V. 1. C3992
80 Same as no. 47. V. 4. 1921. C3993
81 Ekwall, E., ed. The place names of Lancashire. 1922. C3994
82 Same as no. 79. V. 2. C3995
83 Gt. Brit. Exchequer. Taxation in Salford hundred, 1524-1802, ed. by Tait. 1922. C3996
84 Cheshire, Eng. Chester county court rolls 1259-97, ed. by Stewart-Brown. 1923. C3997
85 Trappes-Lomax, R. A history of the township and manor of Clayton-le-Moors. 1926. C3998
86 Tupling, G. H. The economic history of Rossendale. 1927. C3999
87 Gt. Brit. Curia regis. Plea rolls of the county Palatine of Lancaster, ed. by Parker. 1928. C4000
88 Hewitt, H. J. Medieval Cheshire. 1929. C4001
89 Brockbank, T. The diary and letter book of Rev. T. Brockbank, ed. by Trappes-Lomax. 1930. C4002
90 Same as no. 47. V. 5. 1930-31. C4003
91 Lancashire, England. Lancashire deeds, ed. by Parker. 1931. C4004
92 Stokes, C. W. Queen Mary's grammar school. 1931. C4005
93 Hornyold-Strickland, H. Biographical sketches of the members of Parliament of Lancashire, 1290-1550. 1935. C4006
94 Same as no. 47. V. 6. 1935. C4007
95 Chippindall, W. H. History of the township of Ireby. 1935. C4008
96 Roskell, J. S. The knights of the shire of the county Palatine of Lancaster, 1377-1460. 1937. C4009
97 Heywood, O. Oliver Heywood's life of John Angier of Denton together with Angier's diary, ed. by Axon. 1937. C4010
98 Cantle, A. The pleas of quo warranto for the county of Lancaster. 1938. C4011
99 Chippindall, W. H. A history of Whittington. 1938. C4012
100 Tait, J. The Chetham society. 1939. C4013
101 Whitaker, H. A descriptive list of the printed maps of Lancashire, 1577-1900. 1938. C4014
102 Chippindall, W. H. A sixteenth century survey and year's account of the estates of Hornby Castle Lancashire. 1939. C4015
103 Walker, F. Historical geography of Southwest Lancashire before the Industrial revolution. 1939. C4016
104 Chippindall, W. H. A history of the parish of Tunstall. 1935. C4017
105 Vernon, W. A middlewich chartulary, ed. by Varley. V. 1. 1936. C4018
106 Whitaker, H. A descriptive list of the maps of Cheshire, 1577-1900. 1938. C4019
107 McLachlan, H. Warrington academy. 1943. C4020
108 Vernon, W. and Tait, J. A Middlewich chartulary, ed. by Varley and Tait. 1939. C4021
109 Same as no. 47. V. 8. 1944-45. C4022
110 Leatherbarrow, J. S. The Lancashire Elizabethean recusants. 1947. C4023

Third Series:

1 Great Britain. Court of the King's Bench. South Lancashire in the reign of Edward II, ed. by Tupling. 1949. C4024
2 Chester. Eng. Courts. Selected roles of the Chester city courts, late thirteenth and fourteenth centuries, by Hopkins. 1950. C4025
3 Willan, T. S. The navigation of the river Weaver in the eighteenth century. 1951. C4026
4 Woodcock, T. Haslingden: a topographical history. 1952. C4027

5 Leycester, P. Charges to the Grand Jury at Quarter Sessions, 1660-1677, ed. by Halcrow. 1953. C4028
6 Gt. Brit. Customs Establishment. Customs letter-books of the port of Liverpool, 1711-1813, ed. by Jarvis. 1954. C4029
7 Jones, D. The church in Chester, 1300-1540. 1957. C4030
8 Winstanley, D. A schoolmaster's notebook, ed. by E. and T. Kelly. 1957. C4031
9 Highet, T. P. The early history of the Davenports of Davenport. 1960. C4032
10 Davies, C. S. (Spencer) The agricultural history of Cheshire, 1750-1850. 1960. C4033
11 Jordan, W. K. The social institutions of Lancashire. 1962. C4034
12 Collier, F. The family economy of the working classes in the cotton industry, 1784-1833. 1964. C4035
13 Robson, D. Some aspects of education in Cheshire. 1966. C4036
14 Stout, W. The autobiography of William Stout of Lancaster, ed. by Marshall. 1967. C4037
15 Craig, R. and Jarvis, R. Liverpool registry of merchant ships. 1967. C4038
16 Kay, R. The Diary of Richard Kay, ed. by Brockbank and Kenworthy. 1968. C4039
17 Haigh, C. The last days of the Lancashire monasteries and the pilgrimage of grace. 1969. C4040
18 Burscough Priory. An edition of the cartulary of Burscough Priory, ed. by Webb. 1970. C4041
19 Wark, K. R. Elizabethan recusancy in Cheshire. 1971. C4042
20 Lowe, N. The Lancashire textile industry in the sixteenth century. 1972. C4043
21 Bankes family. The early records of the Bankes family at Winstanley, ed. by Bankes and Kerridge. 1973. C4044

THE CHICAGO HISTORY OF AMERICAN CIVILIZATION (Univ. of Chicago Pr.)

Agar, H. The price of power. 1957. C4045
Bremmer, R. H. American philanthrophy. 1960. C4046
Coles, H. L. The War of 1812. 1965. C4047
Condit, C. W. American building. 1968. C4048
Cunliffe, M. The Nation takes shape. 1959. C4049
Dorson, R. M. American folklore. 1959. C4050
Ellis, J. T. American Catholicism. 1956. C4051
Franklin, J. H. Reconstruction: after the Civil War. 1961. C4052
Fuller, W. E. The American mail. 1972. C4053
Glazer, N. American Judaism. 1957. C4054
Graeber, N. A. The troubled Union, 1837-65. 1957. C4055/6
Hagan, W. T. American Indians. 1961. C4057
Hays, S. P. The response to industrialism, 1885-1914. 1957. C4058
Hudson, W. S. American Protestantism. 1961. C4059
Jones, M. A. American immigration. 1960. C4060
Leuchtenburg, W. E. The perils of prosperity, 1914-32. 1958. C4061
McCloskey, R. G. The American Supreme Court. 1960. C4062
Morgan, E. S. The birth of the Republic: 1763-89. 1956. C4063
Peckham, H. H. The colonial wars, 1689-1762. 1964. C4064
____. The War for Independence. 1958. C4065
Pelling, H. American labor. 1960. C4066
Perkins, D. The new age of Franklin Roosevelt: 1932-45. 1956. C4067
Rae, J. B. The American automobile. 1965. C4068
Roland, C. P. The Confederacy. 1960. C4069

Sablosky, I. American music. 1969. C4070
Singletary, O. A. The Mexican War. 1960. C4071
Smith, E. B. The death of slavery. 1967. C4072
Stover, J. F. American railroads. 1961. C4073
Weisberger, B. P. The American newspaperman. 1961. C4074

CHICAGO. UNIVERSITY. CENTER FOR MIDDLE EASTERN STUDIES. PUBLICATIONS

1 Conference on the Beginnings of Modernization in the Middle East in the Nineteenth Century. Beginnings of modernization in the Middle East, ed. by Polk and Chambers. 1968. C4075
2 Kuran, A. The mosque in early Ottoman architecture. 1968. C4076
3 El Mallakh, R. Economic development and regional cooperation: Kuwait. 1968. C4077
4 Baer, G. Studies in the social history of modern Egypt. 1969. C4078
5 Coulson, N. J. Conflicts and tensions in Islamic jurisprudence. 1969. C4079
6 Stetkevych, J. The modern Arabic literary language. 1970. C4080
7 Amuzegar, J. and Fekrat, M. A. Iran. 1971. C4081
8 Issawi, C. P., comp. The economic history of Iran, 1800-1914. 1971. C4082
9 Ardalan, N. and Bakhtiar, L. The sense of unity. 1973. C4083

CHICAGO. UNIVERSITY. CHARLES R. WALGREEN FOUNDATION FOR THE STUDY OF AMERICAN INSTITUTIONS. LECTURES (Univ. of Chic. Pr. unless otherwise noted)

1940-41 Craven, A. O. Democracy in American life. 1941. C4084
Hutchison, W. T., ed. Democracy and American unity. 1941. C4085
1941-42 Knox, J., ed. Religion and the present crisis. 1942. C4086
Perry, C. M., ed. The philosophy of American democracy. 1943. C4087
1942-43 Ogburn, W. F., ed. American society in wartime. 1943. C4088
Taliaferro, W. H., ed. Medicine and the war. 1944. C4089
1944 Butler, P. Books and libraries in wartime. 1945. C4090
Huszar, G. B. de, ed. New perspectives on peace. 1944. C4091
1947 Brownlow, L. The President and the Presidency. 1949. C4092
1948 Biddle, F. The world's best hope. 1948. C4093
Orton, W. A. The economic role of the state. 1948. C4094
Voegelin, E. The new science of politics. 1952. C4095
1949 Strauss, L. Natural right and history. 1953. C4096
1950 Potter, D. M. People of plenty. 1954. C4097
1951 Douglas, P. H. Economy in the national government. 1952. C4098
1952 Boorstein, D. J. The genius of American politics. 1953. C4099
Hallowell, J. H. The moral foundation of democracy. 1954. C4100
Meade, J. E. Problems of economic union. 1953. C4101
1953 Horn, R. A. Groups and the Constitution. Stanford Univ. 1956. C4102
Hutchins, R. M. The university of Utopia. 1953. C4103
1954 Randall, H. M. A foreign economic policy for the United States. 1954. C4104
1954 Simpson, A. Puritanism in old and New England. 1955. C4105
1955 Ellis, J. T. American Catholicism. 1956. C4106

1956 Rossiter, C. L. The American Presidency. Harcourt. 1956. C4107
Arendt, H. The human condition. 1958. C4108
Clapp, G. R. The TVA: an approach to the development of a region. 1955. C4109
Dahl, R. A. A preface to democratic theory. 1956. C4110
Edwards, N., ed. Education in a democracy. 1941. C4111
Glazer, N. American Judaism. 1957. C4112
Keenan, G. F. American diplomacy, 1900-1950. 1951. C4113
Kerwin, J. G., ed. Civil-military relationships in American life. 1948. C4114
Lowenstein, K. Political power and the governmental process. 1957. C4115
Maritain, J. Man and the state. 1951. C4116
Merriam, C. E. What is democracy? 1941. C4117
Nef, J. U. The United States and civilization. 1942. C4118
Puttkammer, E. W., ed. War and the law. 1944. C4119
Simon, Y. Philosophy of democratic government. 1951. C4120
Swisher, C. G. The growth of constitutional power in the United States. 1946. C4121
White, L. D., ed. Civil service in wartime. 1945. C4122
Wright, C. W., ed. Economic problems of the war and its aftermath. 1942. C4123
Wright, H. R., ed. Social service in wartime. 1944. C4124

CHICAGO. UNIVERSITY. COMMITTEE ON PUBLICATIONS IN BIOLOGY AND MEDICINE. PUBLICATIONS.

Abramson, D. I. Vascular responses in the extremities of man. 1944. C4125
Aggeler, P. and Lucia, S. P. Hemorrhagic disorders. 1949. C4126
Alexander, F. and Ross, H., eds. Dynamic psychiatry. 1952. C4127
Allen, J. G. Physiology and treatment of peptic ulcer. 1959. C4128
Andrewartha, H. G. and Birch, L. C. The distribution and abundance of animals. 1954. C4129
Aurelianus, C. On acute disease, ed. by Drabkin. 1950. C4130
Babkin, B. P. Pavlov. 1949. C4131
Bayer, L. and Bayley, N. Growth diagnosis. 1959. C4132
Berengario, J. Short introduction to anatomy, tr. by Lind. 1959. C4133
Binger, C. More about psychiatry. 1949. C4134
Blake, E. R. Birds of Mexico, a guide for field identification. 1953. C4135
Bloomfield, A. L. A bibliography of internal medicine. 1958. C4136
Bonin, G. von. The evolution of the human brain. 1963. C4137
Brunschwig, A. Radical surgery in advanced abdominal cancer. 1947. C4138
Clark, W. E. L. G. The fossil evidence for human evolution. 1955. C4139
Conference on dynamics of proliferating tissues, Dynamics of proliferating tissues, ed. by Price. 1959. C4140
Conference on environmental influences on prenatal development. Environmental influences, ed. by Mintz. 1959. C4141
Conference on immunology and development. Immunology and development, ed. by Edds. 1959. C4142
Conference on physiology of insect development. Physiology of insect development, ed. by Campbell. 1959. C4143
Dack, G. M. Food poisoning. 1949. C4144
D'Amour, F. E. Basic physiology. 1961. C4145
____ and Blood, F. R. Manual

for laboratory work in mammalian physiology. 1948. C4146
Davenport, H. W. ABC of acid-base chemistry. 1950. C4147
Du Shane, G. P. Supplemental drawings for embryology. 1955. C4148
Evans, E. A. Biochemical studies of bacterial viruses. 1952. C4149
____. Biological action of the vitamins. 1942. C4150
Field, H. E. and Taylor, M. E. Atlas of cat anatomy. 1950. C4151
Finney, D. J. Experimental design and its statistical basis. 1955. C4152
Frazier, C. N. and Li, H-C. Racial variations on immunity to syphilis. 1948. C4153
French, T. M. Integration of behavior. 3 v. 1952-58. C4154
Fromm-Reichmann, F. Principles of intensive psychotherapy. 1950. C4155
____. Psychoanalysis and psychotherapy, ed. by Bullard. 1959. C4156
Gerard, R. W., ed. and others. Food for life. 1952. C4157
Gomori, G. Microscopic histochemistry. 1952. C4158
Halstead, W. C. Brain and intelligence. 1947. C4159
Hamburger, V. A manual of experimental embryology. 1960. C4160
Herrick, C. J. The brain of the Tiger Salamander. 1948. C4161
____. George Ellett Coghill. 1949. C4162
Hill, L. B. Psychotherapeutic intervention in schizophrenia. 1955. C4163
Horner, H. H. Dental education today. 1947. C4164
Howell, A. B. Speed in animals. 1944. C4165
Huff, A. A manual of medical parasitology. 1943. C4166
Hummer, A. P. Weed seedlings. 1951. C4167
International conference on development, growth, and generation of the nervous system. Genetic neurology. 1950. C4168
International symposium on cytodifferentiation, Brown university. Cytodifferentation, ed. by Rudnick. 1958. C4169
Katz, L. N. and Johnson, V. E. Elements of electrocardiographic interpretation. 1944. C4170
Kobrak, H. G. Middle ear. 1959. C4171
Li, C. Population genetics. 1955. C4172
Lillie, R. S. General biology and physiology of organism. 1945. C4173
Lockwood, D. P. Ugo Benzi. 1951. C4174
McIntyre, J. G. Curare. 1947. C4175
McLean, L. C. and Urist, M. R. Bone; an introduction to the physiology of skeletal tissue. 1961. C4176
Masserman, J. H. Behavior and neurosis. 1943. C4177
Mitchell, J. W. and Marth, P. C. Growth regulators for garden, field, and orchard. 1947. C4178
Moulder, J. W. The biochemistry of intracellular parasitism. 1962. C4179
Neel, J. V. and Schull, W. J. Human heredity. 1955. C4180
Neuman, W. F. and M. W. Chemical dynamics of bone mineral. 1958. C4181
Olson, E. C. and Miller, R. L. Morphological integration. 1958. C4182
Paul, J. R. Clinical epidemiology. 1958. C4183
Potter, E. L. and Adair, F. L. Fetal and neonatal death. 1949. C4184
Rashevsky, N. Mathematical biology of social behavior. 1951. C4185
____. Mathematical biophysics. 1948. C4186
Romer, A. S. Vertebrate paleontology. 1945. C4187
Rothman, S. Physiology and biochemistry of the skin. 1954. C4188
Schafer, P. N. Pathology in general surgery. 1950. C4189

Schindler, R. Gastroscopy. 1950. C4190
Smith, L. D. S. Introduction to the pathogenic anaerobes. 1955. C4191
Soskin, S. and Levine, R. Carbohydrate metabolism. 1952. C4192
Symposium on embryonic nutrition. Embryonic nutrition, ed. by Rudnick. 1958. C4193
Symposium on endocrines in development. Endocrines in development, ed. by Watterson. 1959. C4194
Symposium on mitogenesis. Mitogenesis, ed. by Ducoff and Ehret. 1959. C4195
Symposium on regeneration in vertebrates. Regeneration in vertebrates, ed. by Thornton. 1959. C4196
Symposium on the respiratory enzymes and the biological action of vitamins. Biological action of the vitamins. 1942. C4197
Symposium on wound healing and tissue repair. Wound healing and tissue repair, ed. by Patterson. 1959. C4198
Taliaferro, W. H., ed. Medicine and the war. 1944. C4199
Templeton, F. E. X-ray examination of the stomach. 1944. C4200
Thurstone, L. L. Multiple factor analysis. 1947. C4201
Tiffany, L. H. The algae of Illinois. 1953. C4202
Turner, D. Handbook of diet therapy. 1952. C4203
Van Liere, E. J. Anoxia. 1942. C4204
Weidenreich, F. Apes, giants and man. 1946. C4205
Weiss, P., ed. Genetic neurology. 1950. C4206

CHICAGO. UNIVERSITY. COMMITTEE ON PUBLICATIONS IN THE PHYSICAL SCIENCES. PUBLICATIONS.

Ackerman, E. A. Japan's natural resources and their relation to Japan's economic future. 1953. C4207
Albert, A. A. Fundamental concepts of higher algebra. 1956. C4208
Baldwin, R. B. The face of the moon. 1949. C4209
Battan, L. J. Radar meteorology. 1959. C4210
Brown, H. S., ed. and others. A bibliography on meteorites. 1953. C4211
Byers, H. R. Thunderstorm electricity. 1953. C4212
Chandrasekhar, S. Plasma physics. 1960. C4213
Eitel, W. The physical chemistry of silicates. 1954. C4214
Ercker, L. Treatise on ores and assaying. 1951. C4215
Greenstein, J. L., ed. Stellar atmospheres. 1961. C4216
Hiltner, W. A., ed. Astronomical techniques. 1962. C4217
Kuiper, G. P., ed. Atmospheres of the earth and planets. 1952. C4218
____. The solar system. 3 v. 1953-61. C4219
____ and Middlehurst, B. M., eds. Telescopes. 1961. C4220
Libby, W. F. Radiocarbon dating. 1955. C4221
Middlehurst, B. M. and Kuiper, G. P., eds. The moon, meteorites and comets. 1963. C4222
National Research Council. Structure and properties of solids surfaces, ed. by Gomer and Smith. 1953. C4223
Orear, J. Nuclear physics. 1950. C4224
Priestley, C. H. B. Turbulent transfer in the lower atmosphere. 1959. C4225
Ramberg, H. The origin of metamorphic and metasomatic rocks. 1952. C4226
Rankama, K. and Sahama, T. G. Geochemistry. 1950. C4227
Saucier, W. J. Principles of meteorological analysis. 1955. C4228
Smith, D. P. Hydrogen in metals. 1948. C4229

Strand, K. A., ed. Basic astronomical data. 1963. C4230
Van Biesbroeck, G. Measurement of double stars. 1954. C4231
Weinberg, A. M. and Wigner, E. P. The physical theory of neutron chain reactors. 1958. C4232
Zener, C. M. Elasticity and anelasticity of metals. 1948. C4233

CHICAGO. UNIVERSITY. ECONOMIC RESEARCH CENTER. STUDIES IN ECONOMICS.

1 Friedman, M., ed. Studies in the quantity theory of money. 1956. C4234
2 Becker, G. S. The economics of discrimination. 1957. C4235
Cain, C. G. Married women in the labor force. 1966. C4236
Haavelmo, T. A study in the theory of investment. 1960. C4237
Harberger, A. C. and others, eds. The demand for durable goods. 1960. C4238
Lewis, H. G. Unionism and relative wages in the United States. 1963. C4239
Meigs, J. A. Free reserves and the money supply. 1962. C4240
Meiselman, D. Varieties of monetary experience. 1970. C4241
Morrison, G. R. Liquidity preferences of commercial banks. 1966. C4242
Pesek, B. P. Gross national product of Czechoslovakia in monetary and real terms. 1965. C4243

CHICAGO. UNIVERSITY. GRADUATE LIBRARY SCHOOL. LIBRARY CONFERENCE.

1936 Chicago. University. Graduate library school. Library Institute. Library trends. 1937. C4244
1937 ____. The role of the library in adult education, ed. by Wilson. 1937. C4245
1938 ____. Current issues on library administration, ed. by Joeckel. 1939. C4246
1939 ____. The practice of book selection, ed. by Wilson. 1940. C4247
1940 ____. The acquisition and cataloging of books, ed. by Randall. 1941. C4248
1941 ____. Print, radio and film in a democracy, ed. by Waples. 1942. C4249
1942 ____. The reference function of the library, ed. by Butler. 1943. C4250
1943 ____. The library in the community, ed. by Carnovsky. 1944. C4251
1944 ____. Library extension, problems and solutions, ed. by Joeckel. 1946. C4252
1945 ____. Personnel administration in libraries, ed. by Martin. 1946. C4253
1946 ____. Library buildings for library service, ed. by Fussler. 1947. C4254
1947 ____. Youth, communication and libraries, ed. by Henne. 1949. C4255
1948 ____. Education for librarianship, ed. by Berelson. 1949. C4256
1949 Asheim, L., ed. A forum on the Public Library Inquiry. 1950. C4257
1950 Shera, J. H., ed. Bibliographic organization. 1951. C4258
1951 Butler, P. Scholars, librarians, and booksellers at mid-century. 1953. C4259
1952 Egan, M., ed. The communication of specialized information. 1954. C4260
1953 Carnovsky, L., ed. International aspects of librarianship. 1954. C4261
1954 Fussler, H. H. The function of the library in the modern college. 1954. C4262
1955 Asheim, L., ed. The future of the book. 1955. C4263
1956 Chicago. University. Graduate library school. Library Conference. Toward a better cataloging code.

1956. C4264
1957 Asheim, L., ed. New directions in public library development. 1957. C4265
1958 Winger, H. W., ed. Iron curtains and scholarship. 1958. C4266
1959 Fenwick, S. I., ed. New definitions of school-library service. 1960. C4267
1960 Asheim, L. Persistent issues in American librarianship. 1961. C4268
1961 Ennis, P. H. and Winger, H. W., eds. Seven questions about the profession of librarianship. 1962. C4269
1962 Chicago. University. Graduate library school. The medium-sized public library, ed. by Carnovsky and Winger. 1963. C4270
1963 ____. Library catalogs, ed. by Strout. 1964. C4271
1964 ____. The intellectual foundations of library education, ed. by Swanson. 1965. C4272
1965 ____. Area studies and the library, ed. by Tsien and Winger. 1966. C4273
1966 ____. A critical approach to children's literature, ed. by Fenwick. 1967. C4274
1967 ____. The public library in the urban setting, ed. by Carnovsky. 1968. C4275
1968 ____. Library networks, ed. by Carnovsky. 1969. C4276
1969 Winger, H. W. and Smith, R. D., eds. Deterioration and preservation of library material. 1970. C4277
1970 Swanson, D. R. and Bookstein, A., eds. Operations research. 1972. C4278
1973 Fussler, H. H., ed. Management education. 1974. C4279

CHICAGO. UNIVERSITY. INDUSTRIAL RELATIONS CENTER LIBRARY. SIGNIFICANT SOURCES IN MANAGEMENT, ORGANIZATIONS AND INDUSTRIAL RELATIONS.

1 Golden, O., comp. Executive development. 1954. C4280
2 Webber, I. L., comp. Aging and retirement. 1954. C4281
3 Arlen, E., comp. Industrial research and the professional employee. 1955. C4282
4 Meier, D. W., comp. Foreign trade unions: a bibliographical review. 1955. C4283
5 Golden, O., comp. Training techniques: a bibliographical review. 1956. C4284

CHICAGO. UNIVERSITY. LABORATORY SCHOOL. PUBLICATIONS.

1 Colburn, E. A library for the intermediate grades. 1930. C4285
2 Todd, J. M. Drawing in the elementary school. 1931. C4286
3 Parker, B. M. An introductory course in science in the intermediate grades. 1931. C4287
4 Shepherd, E. E. and others. English instruction in the University high school. 1933. C4288
5 Chicago University. Laboratory schools. Dept. of physical education and health. Physical education and health of school children. 1936. C4289
6 Gray, W. S. and Holmes, E. Development of meaning vocabularies in reading. 1938. C4290
7 Chicago University. Laboratory schools. Science instruction in elementary and high school grades. 1939. C4291
8 Chicago. University. School of education. University high school. Dept. of mathematics. Mathematics instruction in the University high school. 1940. C4292
9 Anderson, H. A. Instruction in English in the University high school. 1941. C4293
10 Colburn, E. Books and

library reading for pupils of the intermediate grades. 1942. C4294

CHICAGO. UNIVERSITY. MODERN PHILOLOGY MONOGRAPHS.

Cross, T. P. Lancelot and Guenevere. 1930. C4295
Hazard, P. and others. Etudes critiques sur Manon Lescaut. 1929. C4296
Perlesvaus. Le haut livre du Graal, ed. by Nitze and Jenkins. 2 v. 1932-37. C4297
Pietsch, K. Spanish Grail fragments. 2 v. 1924-25. C4298
Plomer, H. R. The life and correspondence of Lodowick Bryskett. 1927. C4299
Stevens, D. H. Milton papers. 1927. C4300
Tristan de Leonis, ed. by Northrup. 1928. C4301
Wilkins, E. H. The University of Chicago manuscript of the Genealogia deorum gentilium of Baccaccio. 1927. C4302

CHICAGO. UNIVERSITY. NORMAN WAIT HARRIS MEMORIAL FOUNDATION LECTURES.

1924 Chirol, V. The Occident and the Orient. 1924. C4303
1924 Kraus, H. Germany in transition. 1924. C4304
1924 Visscher, C. de. The stabilization of Europe. 1924. C4305
1925 Woodhead, H. G. W. and others. Occidental interpretations of the Far-Eastern problem. 1926. C4306
1926 Soyeshima, M. and Kuo, P. W. Oriental interpretations of the Far-Eastern problem. 1925. C4307
1926 Saenz, M. and Priestley, H. I. Some Mexican problems. 1926. C4308
1926 Vasconcelos, J. and Gamio, M. Aspects of Mexican civilization. 1926. C4309
1927 Great Britain and the Dominions, by Hurst and others. 1927. C4310
1928 Cassel, G. and others. Foreign investments. 1928. C4311
1929 Gini, C. and others. Population. 1930. C4312
1930 Wright, Q., ed. Interpretations of American foreign policy. 1930. C4313
1931 ____. Unemployment as a world problem. 1931. C4314
1932 ____. Gold and monetary stabilization. 1932. C3415
1933 ____. Public opinion and world-politics. 1933. C3416
1934 An American foreign policy toward international stabilization. 1934. C3417
1935 Harper, S. N., ed. The Soviet union and world-problems. 1935. C4318
1936 Wright, Q., ed. Neutrality and collective security. 1936. C4319
1937 Colby, C. C., ed. Geographic aspects of international relations. 1938. C4320
1938 Rappard, W. E. The crisis of democracy. 1938. C4321
1939 Laves, W. H. C., ed. International security. 1939. C4322
1940 ____. The foundations of a more stable world order. 1941. C4323
1941 ____. Inter-American solidarity. 1941. C4324
1942 Ireland, P. W., ed. The Near East. 1942. C4325
1943 MacNair, H. F. Voices from unoccupied China. 1943. C4326
1944 Schultz, T. W., ed. Food for the world. 1945. C4327
1945 Morgenthau, H. J., ed. Peace, security & the United Nations. 1946. C4328
1946 Wright, Q., ed. A foreign policy for the United States. 1947. C4329
1947 Chicago Univ. The world community, by Wirth and others. 1947. C4330
1948 Ogburn, W. F., ed. Technology and international

relations. 1948. C4331
1949 Talbot, P., ed. South Asia in the world to-day. 1950. C4332
1950 Morgenthau, H. J. Germany and the future of Europe. 1951. C4333
1951 Hoselitz, B. F., ed. The progress of undeveloped areas. 1952. C4334
1953 Stillman, C. W., ed. Africa in the modern world. 1955. C4335
1954 Chicago. University. Norman Wait Harris Memorial Foundation. Population and world politics, ed. by Hauser. Free Pr., 1958. C4336
1956 Wright, Q., ed. United States foreign policy and the United Nations. Amer. Assn. for the United Nations. 1957. C4337

CHICAGO. UNIVERSITY. ORIENTAL INSTITUTE. PUBLICATIONS.

1 Breasted, J. H. Oriental forerunners of Byzantine painting. 1924. C4338
2 Sennacherib. The annals of Sennacherio, ed. by Luckenbill. 1924. C4339
3-4 The Edwin Smith surgical papyrus, ed. by Breasted. 2 v. 1930. C4340
5 Olsten, H. H. von der. Explorations in central Antolia. 1929. C4341
6-7 The Alishar hüyük, ed. by Osten and Schmidt. 2 v. 1930-32. C4342
8 Chicago. University. Oriental Institute. Epigraphic and architectural survey. Medinet Habu. Earlier historical records of Ramses III. 1930. C4343
9 ____. Later historical records of Ramses III. 1932. C4344
10 Sandford, S. and Arkell, W. J. The Paleolithic man and the Nile-Faiyum divide. 1930. C4345
11 Chiera, E. Sumerian lexical texts from the Temple School of Nippur. 1929. C4346
12 Bible, O. T. Proverbs. The proverbs of Solomon in Sahidic Coptic according to the Chicago manuscript, ed. by Worrell. 1931. C4347
13 Bar Hebraeus. Barhebraeus' scholia on the Old Testament, ed. by Sprengling and Graham. 1931. C4348
14 Luckenbill, D. D. Inscriptions from Adab. 1930. C4349
15 Chiera, E. Sumerian epics and myths. 1934. C4350
16 ____. Sumerian texts of varied contents. 1934. C4351
17 Sandford, K. S. and Arkell, W. J. Paleolithic man and the Nile Valley in Nubia and upper Egypt. 1933. C4352
18 Sandford, K. S. Paleolithic man and the Nile Valley in upper and middle Egypt. 1934. C4353
19-20 Same as no. 6-7. Ed. by Schmidt. 2 v. 1932-33. C4354
21 Chicago. University. Oriental Institute. Epigraphic and architectural survey. The excavation of Medinet Habu. V. 1. 1934. C4355
22 Newell, E. T. Ancient Oriental seals in the collection of Mr. Edward T. Newell. 1934. C4356
23 Same as no. 8. The calendar... Rameses II. 1934. C4357
24 Jacobsen, T. and Lloyd, S. Sennacherib's aqueduct at Jerwan. 1935. C4358
25 Chicago. University. Oriental Institute. Epigraphic survey. Reliefs and inscriptions at Karnak. V. 1. 1936. C4359
26 May, H. G. Material remains of the Megiddo cult. 1935. C4360
27 Gelb, I. J. Inscriptions from Alishar and vicinity. 1935. C4361
28-30 Same as no. 6-7. Ed. by Osten. 3 v. 1937. C4362
31 Chicago. University. Oriental Institute. Sakkarah expedition. The mastaba of Mereruka. V. 1. 1938. C4363

32 Lamon, P. S. The Megiddo water system. 1935. C4364
33 Guy, P. L. O. Megiddo tombs. 1938. C4365
34 Coffin texts (Egyptian). The Egyptian coffin texts, 1-75, ed. by Buck. 1935. C4366
35 Chicago. University. Oriental Institute. Epigraphic survey. Rameses III's temple within the great inclosure of Amon. 1936. C4367
36 Chicago. University. Oriental Institute. Medinet Habu. Graffiti facsimiles. 1937. C4368
37 Brett, A. (Baldwin). Ancient oriental seals in the collection of Mrs. Agnes Baldwin Brett. 1936. C4369
38 Chicago. University. Oriental Institute. Excavations in the palace and a city gate, by Loud and others. 1936. C4370
39 ____. The Sakkarah expedition. 1938. C4371
40 ____. The citadel and the town. 1938. C4372
41 Same as no. 21. V. 2. The temples of the eighteenth dynasty. 1939. C4373
42 Lamon, R. S. and Shipton, G. M. Megiddo. 1939. C4374
43 Frankfort, H. and others. The Gimilsin temple and the palace of the rulers at Tell Asmar. 1940. C4375
44 Frankfort, H. Sculpture at the third millennium B. C. from Tell Asmar and Khafājah. 1939. C4376
45 Gelb, I. J., ed. Hittite hieroglyphic monuments. 1939. C4377
46 Sandford, K. S. and Arkell, W. J. Paleolithic man and the Nile Valley in lower Egypt. 1939. C4378
47 Moore, A. Ancient oriental cylinder and other seals. 1940. C4379
48 Braidwood, R. J. Mounds in the plain of Antioch. 1937. C4380
49 Same as no. 34. V. 2. Texts of spell 76-163. 1938. C4381
50 Abbott, N. The rise of the North Arabic script and its Kur'ānic development. 1939. C4382
51 Same as no. 8. V. 4. 1940. C4383
52 Loud, G. The Megiddo ivories. 1939. C4384
53 Delougaz, P. The temple oval at Khafājah. 1940.
54-55 Same as no. 21. The mortuary temple of Rameses III. 2 v. 1941-51. C4386
56 Nelson, H. H. Key plans showing locations of Theban temple decorations. 1941. C4387
57 Gelb, I. J. Nuzi personal names. 1943. C4388
58 Delougaz, P. and Lloyd, S. Pre-Sargonid temples in the Diyala region. 1942. C4389
59 Landsdorff, A. and McCown, D. E. Tall-i-Bakun A, season of 1932. 1942. C4390
60 Frankfort, H. More sculpture from the Diyala region. 1943. C4391
61 Braidwood, R. J. and L. S. Excavations in the Plain of Antioch. 1952. C4392
62 Chicago. University. Megiddo expedition. The Megiddo expedition. 1948. C4393
63 Delougaz, P. Pottery from the Diyala region. 1952. C4394
64 Coffin texts (Egyptian). Texts of spells 164-267, ed. by Buck. 1947. C4395
65 Cameron, G. G. Persepolis treasury tablets. 1948. C4396
66 Same as no. 21. Post-Ramessid remains. 1952. C4397
67 Coffin texts (Egyptian). Texts of spells 268-354, ed. by Buck. 1951. C4398
68-69 Schmidt, E. R. Persepolis. 2 v. 1952-56. C4399
70 Schmidt, E. F. Persepolis III. 1970. C4400
71 Stefanski, E., ed. Coptic ostraca from Medinet Habu.

1953. C4401
72 Frankfort, H. Stratified cylinder seals from the Diyala region. 1955. C4402
73 Same as no. 34. 355-470, ed. by Buck and Gardiner. 1954. C4403
74 Same as no. 25. V. 3. 1954. C4404
75 Abbott, N. Studies in Arabic literary Papyri. 1956. C4405
76 ____. Qur'anic commentary and tradition. V. 2. 1967. C4406
77 ____. Language and literature studies in Arabic Papyri. V. 3. 1970. C4407
78 McCown, D. E. Nipper. V. 1. 1967. C4408
79 McEwan, C. W. and others. Soundings at Tell Fakhariyah. 1958. C4409
80 Lichtheim, M. Demotic ostraca from Medinet Habu. 1957. C4410
81 Same as no. 34. 472-786, ed. by Buck. 1957. C4411
82 Book of the Dead. The Egyptian book of the Dead, ed. by Allen. 1960. C4412
83-84 Same as no. 8. V. 5-6. 1961-62. C4413
85 Delougaz, P. A Byzantine Church at Khirbat-al-Karah. 1959. C4414
86 Seele, K. C. The tomb of Tjanefer at Thebes. 1959. C4415
87 Same as no. 34. 787-1185, ed. by Buck. 1961. C4416
88 Delougaz, P. and others. Private homes and graves in the Dujala region. 1967. C4417
90 Kraeling, C. H. Ptolemais, city of the Libyan Pentapolis. 1962. C4418
91 Bowman, R. A. Aramaic ritual texts from Persepolis. 1971. C4419
92 Hallock, R. T. Persepolis fortification tablets. 1969. C4420
93 Same as no. 8. V. 7. 1964. C4421
94 Same as no. 8. V. 8. 1970. C4422
95 Haines, R. C. Excavations in the Plain of Antioch. 1971. C4423
99 Biggs, R. D. Inscriptions from Tell Abu Salābīkh. 1974. C4424

CHICAGO UNIVERSITY. PUBLICATIONS IN ANTHROPOLOGY.

Archaeological series:

Bennett, J. W. Archaeological explorations in Jo Daviess county, Illinois. 1945. C4425
Cole, F. C. and others. Rediscovering Illinois. 1937. C4426

Ethnological series:

Bennett, W. C. and Zingg, R. M. The Tarahumara. 1935. C4427
Embree, J. Suye mura. 1939. C4428
Giffen, M. M. The role of men and women in Eskimo culture. 1930. C4429
Goodwin, G. The social organization of the western Apache. 1942. C4430
LaFarge, O. Santa Eulalia. 1947. C4431
Miner, H. M. St. Denis. 1939. C4432
Opler, M. E. An Apache lifeway. 1941. C4433
Parsons, E. W. (Clews) Mitla. 1936. C4434
____. Peguche. 1945. C4435
____. Pueblo Indian religion. 1939. C4436
Redfield, R. Tepoztlán. 1930. C4437
Spicer, E. H. Pascua. 1940. C4438
Spier, L. Yuman tribes of the Gila river. 1933. C4439
Wisdom, C. The Chorti Indians of Guatemala. 1940. C4440

Linguistic series:

Haile, B. Navaho sacrificial figurines. 1947. C4441
____. Origin legends of the Navaho Flintway. 1943. C4442
Hoijer, H. Chircahua and Mescalero. Apache texts. 1938. C4443
Jacobs, M. The content and style of an oral literature. 1959. C4444

Li, F-K. Mattole. 1930. C4445
Physical anthropology:
Krogman, W. M. A bibliography of human morphology. 1941. C4446
Social anthropological series:
Barton, R. F. The Kalignas, ed. by Eggan. 1949. C4447
Bowers, A. W. Mandan social and ceremonial organization. 1950. C4449
Redfield, R. A village that chose progress. 1950. C4450
____. The folk culture of Yucatan. 1941. C4451
Social anthropology of North American Indian tribes, ed. by Eggan. 1937. C4452

CHICAGO. UNIVERSITY. SCIENCE SERIES.

Albert, A. A. Modern higher algebra. 1937. C4453
Blichfeldt, H. F. Finite collineation groups. 1917. C4454
Chamberlain, C. J. The living cycads. 1919. C4455
Chamberlin, T. C. The origin of the earth. 1916. C4456
____. The two solar families. 1928. C4457
Child, C. M. Individuality in organisms. 1915. C4458
____. The origin and development of the nervous system. 1921. C4459
Coulter, J. M. The evolution of sex in plants. 1914. C4460
Dickson, L. E. Algebras and their arithmetics. 1923. C4461
____. Studies in the theory of numbers. 1930. C4462
Heisenberg, W. The physical principles of the quantum theory. 1950. C4463
Jones, D. F. Selective fertilization. 1928. C4464
Jordan, E. O. Food poisoning. 1917. C4465
____. Food poisoning and foodborne infection. 1931. C4466
Lane, E. P. Projective differential geometry of curves and surfaces. 1932. C4467
Lillie, F. R. Problems of fertilization. 1919. C4468
Lillie, R. S. Protoplasmic action and nervous action. 1932. C4469
Michelson, A. A. Studies in optics. 1927. C4470
Millikan, R. A. The electron. 1924. C4471
____. Electron (+ and -). 1935. C4472
Moodie, R. L. The antiquity of disease. 1923. C4473
Newman, H. H. Biology of twins. 1917. C4474
____. The physiology of twinning. 1923. C4475
Rashevsky, N. Advances and applications of mathematical biology. 1940. C4476
Tashiro, S. A. A chemical sign of life. 1917. C4477
Thurstone, L. L. The vectors of mind. 1935. C4478
Weatherwax, P. The story of the maize plant. 1923. C4479

CHICAGO. UNIVERSITY. SOCIAL SCIENCE STUDIES.

1, 4, 7 have series title: Studies in social science.
1 Merriam, C. E. and Gosnell, H. F. Non-voting. 1924. C4480
2 Downing, E. R. Teaching science in the schools. 1925. C4481
3 Goode, J. P. The geographic background of Chicago. 1926. C4482
4 Gosnell, H. F. Getting out the vote. 1927. C4483
5 Fryxell, F. M. The physiography of the region of Chicago. 1927. C4484
6 A directory of associations of citizens of Chicago interested in civic welfare. 1927. C4485
7 Jeter, H. R. Trends of population in the region of Chicago. 1927. C4486
8 Houghtelling, L. The income and standard of living unskilled laborers in Chicago. 1927. C4487
9 White, L. D. The city manager. 1927. C4488
10 Beyle, H. C. Governmental reporting in Chicago.

1928. C4489
11 Johnson, C. O. Carter Henry Harrison I. 1928. C4490
12 Palmer, V. M. Field studies in sociology. 1928. C4491
13 Beckner, E. R. A history of labor legislation in Illinois. 1929. C4492
14 White, L. D., ed. Further contributions to the prestige value of public employment. 1932. C4493
15 Duddy, E. A. Agriculture in the Chicago region. 1929. C4494
16 Staley, E. History of the Illinois state federation of labor. 1930. C4495
17 Smith, T. V. and White, L. D., eds. Chicago, an experiment in social science research. 1929. C4496
18 White, L. D., ed. The new social science. 1930. C4497
19 Gosnell, H. F. Why England votes. 1930. C4498
20 Steadman, R. F. Public health organization in the Chicago region. 1930. C4499
21 Brown, E. C. Book and job printing in Chicago. 1931. C4500
22 Monroe, D. Chicago families. 1932. C4501
23 Lepawsky, A. The judicial system of metropolitan Chicago. 1932. C4502
24 White, L. D. Further contributions to the prestige value of public employment. 1932. C4503
25 ____. Whitley councils in the British civil service. 1933. C4504
26 Merriam, C. E. and others. The government of the metropolitan region of Chicago. 1933. C4505
27 Christenson, C. L. Collective bargaining in Chicago. 1933. C4506
28 Edwards, N. The courts and the public schools. 1933. C4507
29 Kellogg, R. M. United States unemployment service. 1933. C4508
30 White, M. R. Water supply organization in the Chicago region. 1934. C4509
31 Lepawsky, A. Home rule for metropolitan Chicago. 1935. C4510
32 Gosnell, H. F. Negro politicians. 1935. C4511
33 Palyi, M. The Chicago credit market. 1937. C4512
34 Gosnell, H. F. Machine politics--Chicago model. 1937. C4513
35 Cavan, R. (Shonle). The family and the depression. 1938. C4514
36 Schultz, H. The theory and measurement of demand. 1938. C4515
37 Vieg, J. A. The government of education in metropolitan Chicago. 1939. C4516
38 Leland, S. E., ed. State-local fiscal relations in Illinois. 1941. C4517
39 Walker, R. A. The planning function in urban government. 1950. C4518
40 Jones, V. Metropolitan government. 1942. C4519

CHICAGO. UNIVERSITY. STUDIES IN THE MAKING OF CITIZENS.

1 Harper, S. N. Civic training in Soviet schools. 1929. C4520
2 Gaus, J. M. Great Britain. 1929. C4521
3 Jászi, O. The dissolution of the Habsburg monarch. 1929. C4522
4 Weber, E. A. The Duk-Duks. 1929. C4523
5 Schneider, H. W. and Clough, S. B. Making fascists. 1929. C4524
6 Brooks, R. C. Civic training in Switzerland. 1930. C4525
7 Kosok, P. Modern Germany. 1933. C4526
8 Merriam, C. E. The making of citizens. 1931. C4527
9 Pierce, B. L. Civic attitudes in American school textbooks. 1930. C4528

CHICAGO. UNIVERSITY. THE UNIVERSITY OF CHICAGO STUDIES IN LIBRARY SCIENCE.

Butler, P. An introduction to library science. 1933. C4529
____. The origin of printing in Europe. 1966. C4530
Chicago. University. Graduate library school. The core of education for librarianship. 1954. C4531
Ch'ien, T. Written on bamboo and silk. 1962. C4532
Condit, L. A pamphlet about pamphlets. 1939. C4533
Fussler, H. H., ed. Management education. 1974. C4534
____. Photographic reproduction for libraries. 1942. C4535
____. Research libraries and technology. 1973. C4536
Fussler, H. and Simon, J. Patterns in the use of books in large research libraries. 1969. C4537
Gleason, E. V. A. The southern Negro and the public library. 1941. C4538
Gray, W. S. and Leary, B. E. What makes a book readable. 1935. C4539
Hanson, J. C. M. A comparative study of cataloging rules. 1939. C4540
Haygood, W. C. Who uses the public library? 1938. C4541
Joeckel, C. B. The government of the American public library. 1939. C4542
____. A metropolitan library in action. 1940. C4543
Merritt, L. C. The United States government as publisher. 1943. C4544
Miles, A. and Martin, L. Public administration and the library. 1941. C4545
Posner, E. American state archives. 1964. C4546
Randall, W. M. Principles of college library administration. 1941. C4547
Shera, J. H., ed. Foundations of the public library. 1949. C4548
Spencer, G. The Chicago public library. 1943. C4549
Stanford, E. B. Library extension under the WPA. 1944. C4550
Thompson, J. W. The medieval libraries. 1939. C4551
Waples, D. Investigating library problems. 1939. C4552
____. National libraries and foreign scholarship. 1936. C4553
____. People and print. 1938. C4554
Waples, D. and Carnovsky, L. Libraries and readers in the state of New York. 1939. C4555
Waples, D. and others. What reading does to people. 1940. C4556
Wilson, L. R. The geography of reading. 1938. C4557
Wilson, L. R. and Tauber, M. F. The University library. 1960. C4558
Wilson, L. R. and Wight, E. A. County library service in the South. 1935. C4559
Includes also nos. C4244-79

CHICAGO. UNIVERSITY. YERKES OBSERVATORY. ASTROPHYSICAL MONOGRAPHS.

Bok, B. J. The distribution of the stars in space. 1937. C4560
Chandrasekhar, S. The introduction to the study of stellar structure. 1939. C4561
____. Principles of stellar dynamics. 1942. C4562
Merrill, P. W. Spectra of long-period variable stars. 1940. C4563
Russell, H. N. and Moore, C. E. The masses of the stars. 1940. C4564

THE CHILTERN LIBRARY (Lehmann)

1 Apuleius, L. The golden ass, ed. by Macneice. 1946. C4565
2 Shelley, P. B. Shelley in Italy, ed. by Lehmann. 1947. C4566
3 Morris, W. On art and

socialism, ed. by Jackson. 1947. C4567
4 LeFanu, S. In a glass darkly, ed. by Pritchett. 1947. C4568
5 James, H. Roderick Hudson, ed. by Swan. 1947. C4569
6 Gaskell, E. C. (Stevenson). Mary Barton, ed. by Cooper. 1947. C4570
7 ____. Cranford and Cousin Phillis, ed. by Jenkins. 1947. C4571
8 Byron, G. G. N. D. Don Juan, ed. by Quennell. 1949. C4572
9 James, H. What Maisie knew, ed. by Swan. 1947. C4573
10 ____. The spoils of Poynton, ed. by Swan. 1947. C4574
11 DeQuincey, T. Recollections of the Lake poets, ed. by Seckville-West. 1948. C4575
12 Gaskell, E. C. (Stevenson). The life of Charlotte Brontë, ed. by Lane. 1947. C4576
13 Beaconsfield, B. D. Coningsby, ed. by Allen. 1948. C4577
14 James, H. The lesson of the Master, ed. by Swan. 1948. C4578
15 Poe, E. A. The tell-tale heart, ed. by Sansom. 1948. C4579
16 Heath-Stubbs, J. F. A. and Wright, D., comps. The forsaken garden. 1950. C4580
17 Congreve, W. Comedies, ed. by Marshall. 1948. C4581
18 Gaskell, E. C. (Stevenson). Wives and daughters, ed. by Lehmann. 1948. C4582
19 Melville, H. The confidence-man, ed. by Fuller. 1947. C4583
20 James, H. Ten short stories, ed. by Swan. 1948. C4584
21 Baroque muse, ed. by Wedgewood. 1949. C4585
22 Gogol, N. V. Tales of good and evil, ed. by Magarshack. 1949. C4586
23 James, H. The American, ed. by Swan. 1949. C4587
24 Blake, W. A selection from William Blake, ed. by Sitwell. 1951. C4588
25 Apperley, C. J. (Nimrod, pseud.). The life of a sportsman, ed. by Moore. 1948. C4589
26 Kinglake, A. W. Eothen, ed. by Newby. 1949. C4590
27 Sterne, L. Life and opinions of Tristram Shandy, ed. by Quennell. 1948. C4591
28 Whymper, E. Travels among the Great Andes of the Equator, ed. by Smythe. 1949. C4592
29 Leslie, C. R. The life of John Constable, ed. by Nicolson. 1949. C4593
30 Smollett, T. Travels through France and Italy, ed. by Sitwell. 1949. C4594
31 James, H. The Princess Casamassima, ed. by Swan. 1950. C4595
32 ____. Washington Square, ed. by Dobree. 1949. C4596
33 Johnson, S. The conversations of Dr. Johnson, ed. by Postgate. 1949. C4597
34 Melville, H. Billy Budd, ed. by Warner. 1951. C4598
35 Dickens, C. The mystery of Edwin Drood, ed. by Innes. 1950. C4599
36 Dostoevskii, F. M. A gentle creature, ed. by Magarshack. 1950. C4600
37 James, H. The Europeans. 1952. C4601
38 ____. The Bostonians. 1952. C4602
39 Melville, H. White jacket. 1952. C4603

CHINA RESEARCH MONOGRAPHS (Univ. of California Pr.)

1 Townsend, J. R. The revolutionization of Chinese youth. 1967. C4604
2 Baum, R. and Teiwes, F. C. Ssu-ch'ing. 1968. C4605
3 Rinden, R. The Red flag waves. 1968. C4606
4 Mehnert, K. Peking and the New Left. 1969. C4607
5 Yu, G. T. China and Tanzania. 1970. C4608
6 Barrett, D. D. Dixie Mission. 1970. C4609
7 Service, J. S. The American papers. 1971. C4610

8 Lovelace, D. D. China and "people's war" in Thailand, 1964-1969. 1971. C4611
9 Porter, J. Tsêng Kuo-han's private bureaucracy. 1972. C4612
10 Waller, D. J. The Kiangsi Soviet Republic. 1973. C4613
11 Bisson, T. A. Yenan in June 1937. 1973. C4614

CHINESE DYNASTIC HISTORIES. TRANSLATIONS (Univ. of Cali. Pr.)

1 Frankel, H. H., ed. Biographies of Meng Hao-jan. 1952. C4615
2 Chin shu. Biography of Ku K'ai-chih, ed. by Ch'en. 1961. C4616
3 Ling-hu, T. Biography of Su Ch'o, tr. by Goodrich. 1961. C4617
4 Chin shu. Account of the Tü-yü-hün in the history of the Chin dynasty, tr. by Carroll. 1953. C4618
5 Ou-yang, H. Biography of Huang Ch'ao, tr. by Levy. 1955. C4619
6 Ling-hu, T. Accounts of Western nations in the history of the Northern Chou Dynasty, ed. by Miller. 1959. C4620
7 Fang, H. Biography of Lu Kuang, tr. by Mather. 1959. C4621
8 Chiu T'ang shu. Biography of An Lu-shan, tr. by Levy. 1960. C4622
9 Ling-hu, T. Biography of Yü-wen Hu, tr. by Dien. 1962. C4623
10 Chien, F. The chronicles of Fu Chien, tr. by Rogers. 1968. C4624

Supplement:
1 Frankel, H. H., comp. Catalogue of translations from the Chinese dynastic histories for the period 220-960. 1957. C4625

CHRISTIAN FAITH SERIES (Doubleday)

Broomall, W. The Holy Spirit. 1963. C4626
Cherbonnier, E. L. Hardness of heart. 1955. C4627
Elmen, P. The restoration of meaning to contemporary life. 1958. C4628
Farrer, A. M. Love almighty and ills unlimited. 1961. C4629
Gilkey, L. B. Maker of heaven and earth. 1959. C4630
Hutchison, J. A. The two cities. 1957. C4631
Jenkins, D. T. The strangeness of the church. 1955. C4632
Kevan, E. F. Salvation. 1963. C4633
Miller, A. The renewal of man. 1954. C4634
____. The man in the mirror. 1958. C4635
Perry, E. The gospel in dispute. 1958. C4636
Pike, J. A. Doing the truth. 1955. C4637
Wolf, W. J. Man's knowledge of God. 1955. C4638
Wright, G. E. and Fuller, R. H. The book of the acts of God. 1957. C4639

THE CHRONICLES OF AMERICA (Yale Univ. Pr.)

1 Huntington, E. The red man's continent. 1921. C4640
2 Richman, I. B. The Spanish conquerors. 1921. C4641
3 Wood, W. C. H. Elizabethean seadogs. 1921. C4642
4 Munro, W. B. Crusaders of New France. 1921. C4643
5 Johnston, M. Pioneers of the old South. 1920. C4644
6 Andrews, C. M. The fathers of New England. 1919. C4645
7 Goodwin, M. (Wilder). Dutch and English on the Hudson. 1920. C4646
8 Fisher, S. G. The Quaker colonies. 1921. C4647
9 Andrews, C. M. Colonial folkways. 1919. C4648
10 Wrong, G. M. The conquest of New France. 1921. C4649
11 Becker, C. L. The eve of the revolution. 1921. C4650

12 Wrong, G. M. Washington and his comrades in arms. 1921. C4651
13 Farrand, M. The fathers of the Constitution. 1921. C4652
14 Ford, H. J. Washington and his colleagues. 1921. C4653
15 Johnson, A. Jefferson and his colleagues. 1921. C4654
16 Corwin, E. S. John Marshall and the Constitution. 1919. C4655
17 Paine, R. D. The fight for a free sea. 1920. C4656
18 Skinner, C. L. Pioneers of the old Southwest. 1919. C4657
19 Ogg, F. A. The Old Northwest. 1921. C4658
20 ____. The reign of Andrew Jackson. 1919. C4659
21 Hulbert, A. B. The paths of inland commerce. 1920. C4660
22 Skinner, C. L. Adventurers of Oregon. 1921. C4661
23 Bolton, H. E. The Spanish borderlands. 1921. C4662
24 Stephenson, N. W. Texas and the Mexican war. 1921. C4663
25 White, S. E. The forty-niners. 1918. C4664
26 Hough, E. The passing of the frontier. 1918. C4665
27 Dodd, W. E. The cotton kingdom. 1919. C4666
28 Macy, J. The anti-slavery crusade. 1921. C4667
29 Stephenson, N. W. Abraham Lincoln and the union. 1921. C4668
30 ____. The day of the confederacy. 1919. C4669
31 Wood, W. C. H. Captains of the civil war. 1921. C4670
32 Fleming, W. L. The sequel of Appomattox. 1921. C4671
33 Slosson, E. E. The American spirit in education. 1921. C4672
34 Perry, B. The American spirit in literature. 1921. C4673
35 Orth, S. P. Our foreigners. 1921. C4674
36 Paine, R. D. The old merchant marine. 1921. C4675
37 Thompson, H. The age of invention. 1921. C4676
38 Moody, J. The railroad builders. 1921. C4677
39 Hendrick, B. J. The age of big business. 1921. C4678
40 Orth, S. P. The armies of labor. 1921. C4679
41 Moody, J. The masters of capital. 1921. C4680
42 Thompson, H. The new South. 1919. C4681
43 Orth, S. P. The boss and the machine. 1921. C4682
44 Ford, H. J. The Cleveland era. 1919. C4683
45 Buck, S. J. The agrarian crusade. 1921. C4684
46 Fish, C. R. The path of empire. 1920. C4685
47 Howland, H. J. Theodore Roosevelt and his times. 1921. C4686
48 Seymour, C. Woodrow Wilson and the world war. 1921. C4687
49 Skelton, O. D. The Canadian dominion. 1919. C4688
50 Shepherd, W. R. The Hispanic nations of the New world. 1921. C4689
51 Faulkner, H. U. From Versailles to the New Deal. 1950. C4690
52 Brogan, D. W. The era of Franklin D. Roosevelt. 1950. C4691
53 Janeway, E. The struggle for survival. 1951. C4692
54 Pratt, F. War for the world. 1950. C4693
55 Nevins, A. The United States in a chaotic world. 1950. C4694
56 ____. The New Deal and world affairs. 1950. C4695
Suppl. vol. Gabriel, R. H. The Yale course of home study. 1924. C4696

CHRONICLES OF CANADA (Glasgow)

Published 1935
1 Leacock, S. B. The dawn of Canadian history. C4697
2 ____. The mariner of St. Malo. C4698
3 Colby, C. W. The founder

of New France. C4699
4 Marquis, T. G. The Jesuit missions. C4700
5 Munro, W. B. The seigneurs of old Canada. C4701
6 Chapais, T. The great intendant. C4702
7 Colby, C. W. The fighting governor. C4703
8 Wood, W. C. H. The great fortress. C4704
9 Doughty, A. G. The Acadian exiles. C4705
10 Wood, W. C. H. The passing of New France. C4706
11 ____. The winning of Canada. C4707
12 ____. The father of British Canada. C4708
13 Wallace, W. S. The United Empire loyalists. C4709
14 Wood, W. C. H. The war with the United States. C4710
15 Marquis, T. G. The war chief of the Ottawas. C4711
16 Wood, L. A. The war chief of the Six nations. C4712
17 Raymond, E. T. Tecumseh. C4713
18 Laut, A. C. The 'Adventurers of England' on Hudson Bay. C4714
19 Burpee, L. J. Pathfinders of the great plains. C4715
20 Leacock, S. B. Adventurers of the far North. C4716
21 Wood, L. A. The Red River Colony. C4717
22 Laut, A. C. Pioneers of the Pacific coast. C4718
23 ____. The Cariboo trail. C4719
24 Wallace, W. S. The Family Compact. C4720
25 De Cellas, A. D. The 'Patriotes' of '37. C4721
26 Grant, W. L. The tribune of Nova Scotia. C4722
27 MacMechan, A. M. The winning of popular government. C4723
28 Colquhoun, A. H. U. The fathers of Confederation. C4724
29 Pope, J. The day of Sir John Macdonald. C4725
30 Skelton, O. D. The day of Sir Wilfrid Laurier. C4726
31 Wood, W. C. H. All afloat. C4727
32 Skelton, O. D. The railway builders. C4728

CINCINNATI. UNIVERSITY. CHARLES PHELPS TAFT MEMORIAL FUND (Princeton Univ. Press unless otherwise stated)

Anderson, O. E. Refrigeration in America. 1953. C4729
Angel, J. L. The human remains. 1951. C4730
Bennett, E. L. The Pylos tablets. 1951. C4731
Birkhoff, G. Hydrodynamics. 1950. C4732
Brant, S. The ship of fools, ed. by Zeydel. Columbia. 1944. C4733
Chase, I. W. U. Horace Walpole. 1943. C4734
Cipolla, C. Money prices and civilization in the Mediterranean world, 5th to the 17th century. 1956. C4735
Egle, W. P. Economic stabilization. 1952. C4736
Ford, C. H. Dickens and his readers. 1955. C4737
Gottfried von Strassburg. Tristan and Isolde, ed. by Zeydel. 1949. C4738
Groves, H. M. Trouble spot in taxation. 1948. C4739
Hack, R. K. God in Greek Philosophy to the time of Socrates. 1931. C4740
Henig, H. The brotherhood of railway clerks. 1937. C4741
Kreider, P. V. Repetition in Shakespeare's plays. 1941. C4742
Krouse, F. M. Milton's Samson and the Christian tradition. 1949. C4743
Marni, A. Allegory in the French heroic poem of the seventeenth century. 1936. C4744
Massinger, P. The bondman, ed. by Spencer. 1932. C4745
Merkel, G., ed. Romanticism and the art of translation. 1956. C4746
Shafer, R., ed. Seventeenth century studies. 2 v. 1933-37. C4747

Staebler, W. The liberal mind of John Morley. 1943. C4748
Univ. of Cincinnati. Excavations at Troy, ed. by Blegen and others. 4 v. 1950-58. C4749
Weinberg, J. R. Nicolaus of Autrecourt. 1948. C4750
Wheeler, C. F. Classical mythology in the plays, masques, and poems of Ben Jonson. 1938. C4751
Wolfram von Eschenbach. The Parzival of Wolfram von Eschenbach, ed. by Zeydel. Univ. of North Carolina. 1951. C4752
Zeydel, E. H. Ludwig Tieck. 1935. C4753
____. Ludwig Tieck and England. 1931. C4754

CIVIL WAR CENTENNIAL SERIES (Indiana Univ. Pr.)

Alexander, E. P. Military memoirs of a Confederate. 1962. C4755
Connolly, J. A. Three years in the Army of the Cumberland, ed. by Angle. 1959. C4756
Cooke, J. E. Wearing of the gray, ed. by Stern. 1959. C4757
Dawson, S. (Morgan). Confederate girl's diary. 1960. C4758
Duke, B. W. A history of Morgan's Cavalry, ed. by Holland. 1960. C4759
Early, J. A. War memoirs, ed. by Vandiver. 1960. C4760
Eggleston, G. C. A Rebel's recollections, ed. by Donald. 1959. C4761
Ferri Pisani, C. Prince Napoleon in America, 1861. 1959. C4762
Fuller, J. F. C. The generalship of Ulysses S. Grant. 1958. C4763
____. Grant & Lee. 1957. C4764
Galwey, T. F. The valiant hours, ed. by Nye. 1961. C4765
Hanna, A. J. Flight into oblivion. 1959. C4766
Hood, J. B. Advance and retreat, ed. by Current. 1959. C4767
Johnston, J. E. Narrative of military operations. 1959. C4768
Laugel, A. The United States during the Civil War. 1961. C4769
Livermore, T. L. Numbers & losses in the Civil War in America, 1861-1865. 1957. C4770
Longstreet, J. From Manassas to Appomattox, ed. by Robertson. 1960. C4771
McClellan, H. B. I rode with Jeb Stuart, ed. by Davis. 1958. C4772
Mosby, J. S. Memoirs, ed. by Russell. 1959. C4773
Porter, H. Campaigning with Grant, ed. Temple. 1961. C4774
Semmes, R. The Confederate raider Alabama, ed. by Stern. 1962. C4775
Sherman, W. T. Memoirs of General William T. Sherman by himself, ed. by Hart. 2 v. in 1. 1957. C4776
Stackpole, E. J. Sheridan in the Shenandoah. 1961. C4777
Stern, P. V. D., ed. Prologue to Sumter. 1961. C4778
____. Soldier life in the Union and Confederate Armies. 1961. C4779
Taylor, W. H. Four years with General Lee. 1962. C4780
Upson, T. F. With Sherman to the sea, ed. by Winther. 1958. C4781

THE CIVILIZATION OF THE AMERICAN INDIAN (Univ. of Okla. Pr.)

1 Thomas, A. B., ed. Forgotten frontiers. 1932. C4782
2 Foreman, G. Indian removal. 1953. C4783
3 Mathews, J. J. Wah'kon-tah. 1932. C4784
4 Foreman, G. Advancing the frontier, 1830-1860. 1933. C4785
5 Seger, J. H. Early days among the Cheyenne and Arapahoe Indians, ed. by Vestal. 1934. C4786
6 Debo, A. The rise and

fall of the Choctaw republic. 1961. C4787
7 Vestal, S., comp. New sources of Indian history, 1850-1891. 1934. C4788
8 Foreman, G. The Five civilized tribes. 1934. C4789
9 Thomas, A. B. After Coronado. 1935. C4790
10 Speck, F. G. Naskapi. 1935. C4791
11 Eastman, E. (Goodale). Pratt. 1935. C4792
12 Bass, A. L. (Bierbower). Cherokee messenger. 1936. C4793
13 Alford, T. W. Civilization, as told to Florence Drake. 1936. C4794
14 Foreman, G. Indians & pioneers. 1936. C4795
15 Hyde, G. E. Red Cloud's folks. 1937. C4796
16 Foreman, G. Sequoyah. 1938. C4797
17 Wardell, M. L. A political history of the Cherokee nation, 1838-1907. 1938. C4798
18 Caughey, J. W. McGillivray of the Creeks. 1938. C4799
19 Dale, E. E. and Litton, G. L., eds. Cherokee cavaliers. 1939. C4800
20 Gabriel, R. H. Elias Boudinot, Cherokee & his America. 1941. C4801
21 Llewellyn, K. N. and Hoebel, E. A. The Cheyenne way. 1941. C4802
22 Debo, A. The road to disappearance. 1941. C4803
23 LaFarge, O., ed. The changing Indian. 1942. C4804
24 Foreman, C. T. Indians abroad, 1493-1938. 1943. C4805
25 Adair, J. The Navajo and Pueblo silversmiths. 1944. C4806
26 Marriott, A. L. The ten grandmothers. 1945. C4807
27 ____. María. 1948. C4808
28 Dale, E. E. Indians of the Southwest. 1949. C4809
29 Popol vuh. Popol vuh; the sacred book of the ancient Quiché Maya, ed. by Goetz and Morley. 1951. C4810
30 O'Kane, W. C. Sun in the sky. 1950. C4811
31 Stubbs, S. A. Bird's eye view of the pueblos. 1950. C4812
32 Turner, K. C. Red men calling on the Great White Father. 1951. C4813
33 Wright, M. H. A guide to the Indian tribes of Oklahoma. 1951. C4814
34 Wallace, E. and Hoebel, E. A. The Comanches. 1952. C4815
35 O'Kane, W. C. The Hopis. 1953. C4816
36 Black Elk, Oglala Indian. The sacred pipe... ed. by Brown. 1953. C4817
37 Annals of the Cakchiquels. The annals of the Cakchiquels, tr. by Recinos and Goetz. 1953. C4818
38 Cotterill, R. S. The southern Indians. 1954. C4819
39 Thompson, J. E. The rise and fall of Maya civilization. 1954. C4820
40 Emmitt, R. The last war trail. 1954. C4821
41 Roe, F. G. The Indian and the horse. 1955. C4822
42 Haines, F. The Nez Percés. 1955. C4823
43 Underhill, R. M. The Navajos. 1956. C4824
44 Grinnell, G. B. The fighting Cheyennes. 1956. C4825
45 Hyde, G. E. A Sioux chronicle. 1956. C4826
46 Vestal, S. Sitting Bull. 1957. C4827
47 McReynolds, E. C. The Seminoles. 1957. C4828
48 Hagan, W. T. The Sac and Fox Indians. 1958. C4829
49 Ewers, J. C. The Blackfeet. 1958. C4830
50 Caso, A. The Aztecs, tr. by Dunham. 1958. C4831
51 Sonnichsen, C. L. The Mescalero Apaches. 1958. C4832
52 Murray, K. A. The Modocs and their war. 1959. C4833
53 Cieza de Léon, P. de. The Incas of Pedro de Cieza de Leon, tr. by Onis.

1959. C4834
54 Hyde, G. E. Indians of the High Plains. 1959. C4835
55 Catlin, G. Episodes from Life among the Indians and Last rambles, ed. by Ross. 1959. C4836
56 Thompson, J. E. S. Maya hieroglyphic writing. 1960. C4837
57 Hyde, G. E. Spotted Tail's folk. 1961. C4838
58 Writers' program. Montana. The Assiniboines, ed. by Kennedy. 1961. C4839
59 Denig, E. T. Five Indian tribes of the upper Missouri, ed. by Ewers. 1961. C4840
60 Mathews, J. J. The Osages. 1961. C4841
61 Young, M. E. Redskins, ruffleshirts and rednecks. 1961. C4842
62 Thompson, J. E. S. A catalog of Maya hieroglyphics. 1962. C4843
63 Mayhall, M. P. The Kiowas. 1962. C4844
64 Hyde, G. E. Indians of the Woodlands. 1962. C4845
65 Woodward, G. S. The Cherokees. 1963. C4846
66 Berthrong, D. J. The Southern Cheyennes. 1963. C4847
67 León-Portilla, M. Aztec thought and culture, tr. by Davis. 1963. C4848
68 Allen, T. D., pseud. Navahos have five fingers. 1963. C4849
69 Brundage, B. C. Empire of the Inca. 1963. C4850
70 Gibson, A. M. The Kickapoos. 1963. C4851
71 Tyler, H. A. Pueblo gods and myths. 1964. C4852
72 Hassrick, R. B. and others. The Sioux. 1964. C4853
73 Newcomb, F. (Johnson). Hosteen Klah. 1964. C4854
74 Trenholm, V. C. and Carley, M. The Shoshonis. 1964. C4855
75 Cohoe, W. A Cheyenne sketchbook, with commentary by Hoebel and Peterson. 1964. C4856
76 Forbes, J. D. Warriors of the Colorado. 1965. C4857
77 Ritual of the Bacabs, tr. and ed. by Roys. 1965. C4858
78 Fisher, L. E. The last Inca revolt, 1780-1783. 1965. C4859
79 Osborne, L. de Jongh. Indian crafts of Guatemala and El Salvador. 1965. C4860
80 Ruby, R. H. and Brown, J. A. Half-Sun on the Columbia. 1965. C4861
81 Kilpatrick, J. F. and A. G., ed. and tr. The shadows of Sequoyah. 1965. C4862
82 Clark, E. F. Indian legends from the Northern Rockies. 1966. C4863
83 Brophy, W. A. and Aberle, S. D. The Indian. 1966. C4864
84 Hilger, M. I. and Mondloch, M. A. Huenun Namku. 1966. C4865
85 Spores, R. The Mixtec kings and their people. 1966. C4866
86 Corkran, D. H. The Creek frontier, 1540-1783. 1967. C4867
87 Chilam Balam Books. The Book of Chilam Balam of Chumayel, tr. by Roys. 1967. C4868
88 Brundage, B. C. Lords of Cuzco. 1967. C4869
89 Ewers, J. C. Indian life on the Upper Missouri. 1968. C4870
90 Moorhead, M. L. Apache frontier. 1968. C4871
91 Scholes, F. V. and others. Maya Chontal Indians of Acalan Indians of Acalan-Tichel. 1968. C4872
92 Leon-Portilla, M. Pre-Columbian literatures of Mexico, tr. by Lobanov. 1968. C4873
93 Woodward, G. S. Pocahontas. 1968. C4874
94 Hotz, G. Eighteenth-century skin paintings, tr. by Malthaner. 1969. C4875
95 Vogel, V. J. American

Indian medicine. 1969. C4876
96 Vaudrin, W. Tanaina tales from Alaska. 1969. C4877
97 Nammack, G. C. The Iroquois land frontier in the colonial period. 1969. C4878
98 The chronicles of Michoacan, tr. by Craine and Reindorp. 1969. C4879
99 Thompson, J. E. S. Maya history and religion. 1969. C4880
100 Powell, P. J. Sweet medicine. 2 v. 1969. C4881
101 Petersen, K. D. Plains Indian art from Fort Marion. 1970. C4882
102 Durán, D. Book of the gods and rites and The ancient calendar. 1971. C4883
103 Anson, B. The Miami Indians. 1970. C4884
104 Ruby, R. H. and Brown, A. J. The Spokane Indians. 1970. C4885
105 Trenholm, V. C. The Arapahoes, our people. 1970. C4886
106 Debo, A. A history of the Indians of the United States. 1970. C4887
107 Grey, H. Tales from the Mohaves. 1971. C4888
108 Beckham, S. J. Requiem for a people. 1971. C4889
109 Gibson, A. M. The Chickasaws. 1971. C4890
110 Venderwerth, W. C. Indian oratory. 1971. C4891
111 Anderson, J. A., ed. The Sioux of the Rosebud, by Hamilton. 1971. C4892
112 Harrod, H. L. Mission among the Blackfeet. 1971. C4893
113 Clarke, M. W. Chief Bowles and the Texas Cherokees. 1971. C4894
114 Unrau, W. E. The Kansa Indians. 1971. C4895
115 Forbes, J. D. Apache, Navaho, and Spaniard. 1971. C4896
116 Baird, W. D. Peter Pitchlynn. 1972. C4897
117 Jiménez, L. Life and death in Milpa Alta, tr. by Horcasitas. 1972. C4898
118 Roys, R. L. The Indian background of colonial Yucatan. 1972. C4899
119 Hamilton, C. Cry of the thunderbird. 1972. C4900
120 Ruby, R. H. and Brown, J. A. The Cayuse Indians. 1972. C4901
121 Schultz, G. A. An Indian Canaan. 1972. C4902
122 Dempsey, H. A. Crowfoot. 1972. C4903
123 Otis, D. S. The Dawes act and the allotment of Indian lands, ed. by Prucha. 1973. C4904
124 Smith, M. E. Picture writing from ancient southern Mexico. 1973. C4905
125 Thrapp, D. L. Victorio and the Mimbres Apaches. 1974. C4906
126 Rogers, J. Red world and white. 1974. C4907
127 Schultz, J. W. Why gone those times? 1974. C4908
128 Hyde, G. E. The Pawnee Indians. 1974. C4909
129 Olsen, F. On the trail of the Arawaks. 1974. C4910
130 Fahey, J. The flathead Indians. 1974. C4911
131 Andrews, G. F. Maya cities. 1974. C4912
132 Morrow, M. Indian rawhide. 1974. C4913

CLAREMONT COLLEGES. CLAREMONT LECTURES.

1940 Pound, R. Contemporary juristic theory. 1940. C4914
1941 Corwin, E. S. Constitutional revolution, ltd. 1941. C4915
1942 Shepardson, W. H. The interests of the United States as a world power. 1942. C4916
1943 Lattimore, O. America and Asia. 1943. C4917
1944 Herring, H. America and the Americas. 1944. C4918
1946 Fisher, H. H. America and Russia in the world

community. 1946. C4919
1946 Smith, T. V. Atomic power and moral faith. 1946. C4920
1947 Jessup, P. C. The international problem of governing mankind. 1947. C4921
1948 Crowther, G. The economic reconstruction of Europe. 1948. C4922
1949 Brandt, K. Germany, key to peace in Europe. 1949. C4923
1950 Baldwin, H. W. Power and politics. 1950. C4924
1951 Simmons, F. L. Mobilization and inflation. 1951. C4925
No lecture given 1952-54.
1955 Mason, E. S. Promoting economic development: the United States and Southern Asia. Castle Pr. 1955. C4926
1956 Wriston, H. M. Diplomacy and democracy. Harper. 1956. C4927
1957 Crowther, G. The wealth and poverty of nations. 1957. C4928
1958 Storey, R. G. Professional leadership. 1958. C4929
1960 Rabi, I. I. My life and times as a physicist. 1960. C4930
1961 Rusk, D. The role of the foundation in American life. 1961. C4931
1962 Keezer, D. M. Are we slaves of some defunct economist? 1963. C4932
1964 Canham, E. D. The American position in the world. 1965. C4933
1967 Pollard, W. G. Man on a spaceship. 1967. C4934
1967 Watson, A. The nature and problems of the third world. 1968. C4935
1969 Roberts, W. O. A view of century 21. 1969. C4936
1973 Sphilhaus, A. F. Harmony of man's industry and living space. 1973. C4937
1974 Linowitz, S. M. This troubled urban world. 1974. C4938

CLASICOS CASTELLANOS
(Espana-Calpe)

1 Teresa, St. Las moradas, ed. by Thomas. 1916. C4939
2 Téllez, G. Tirso de Molina. V. 1. 1932. C4940
3 Garcilaso de la Vega. Obras. 1932. C4941
4 Cervantes Saavedra, M. de. El ingenioso hidalgo don Quijote de la Mancha. V. 1. 1913. C4942
5 Quedevo y Villegas, F. G. de. Vida del Buscón. 1960. C4943
6 Same as no. 4. V. 2. 1961. C4944
7 Torres y Villarroel, D. de. Vida. 1912. C4945
8 Same as no. 4. V. 3. 1962. C4946
9 Rivas, A. P. de S. R. de Madrid R. de B. Romances. V. 1. 1911. C4947
10 Same as no. 4. V. 4. 1962. C4948
11 Avila, J. de. Epištolario espiritual, ed. by Garcia de Diego. 1912. C4949
12 Same as no. 9. V. 2. 1912. C4950
13 Same as no. 4. V. 5. C4951
14 Rujz, J. Libro de buen amor. V. 1. 1946. C4952
15 Castro y Bellvis, G. de. Las mocedades del Cid, ed. by Julia Martinez. 1962. C4953
16 Same as no. 4. V. 6. C4954
17 Same as no. 14. V. 2. 1946. C4955
18 Santillana, I. L. de Mendoza. Canciones y decires. 1942. C4956
19 Same as no. 4. V. 7. 1962. C4957
20 Rojas, F. de. La Celestina, ed. by Cejador y Franco. V. 1. 1941. C4958
21 Villegas, E. M. de. Eróticas ó amatorias, ed. by Alonso Cortés. 1913. C4959
22 Same as no. 4. V. 8. 1922. C4960
23 Same as no. 20. V. 2. 1945. C4961

24 El Cid Campeador. Poema de mio Cid, ed. by Menéndez dez Pidal. 1960. C4962
25 Lazarillo de Tormes. La vida de Lazarillo de Tormes y de sus fortunas y adversidades. 1941. C4963
26 Herrera, F. de. Poesia. 1914. C4964
27 Cervantes Saavedra, M. de. Novelas ejemplares. V. 1. 1943. C4965
28 León, L. P. de. De los nombres de Cristo. V. 1. 1914. C4966
29 Guevara, A. de. Menosprecio de corte y alabanza aldea, ed. by Martinez de Burgos. 1915. C4967
30 Nieremberg, J. E. Epištolario, ed. by Alonso Cortés. 1915. C4968
31 Quevedo y Villegas, F. G. de. Los sueños, ed. by Cejador y Franca. V. 1. 1961. C4969
32 Morto y Cavana, A. Teatro, ed. by Cortes. 1916. C4970
33 Same as no. 28. V. 2. C4971
34 Same as no. 31. V. 2. 1949. C4972
35 Rojas Zorrilla, F. de. Teatro. 1931. C4973
36 Same as no. 27. V. 2. 1962. C4974
37 Ruiz de Alarcón y Mendoza, J. Teatro, ed. by Reyes. 1918. C4975
38 Vélez de Guevara y Dueñas, L. El diablo cojuelo, ed. by Rodriguez Marin. 1941. C4976
39 Vega Carpio, L. F. de. Comedias. V. 1. 1931. C4977
40 Campoamor y Compoosorio, R. M. de las M. de. Poesías, ed. by Rivas Cherif. 1921. C4978
41 Same as no. 28. V. 3. 1921. C4979
42 Castillo Solorzano, A. de. La garduña de Sevilla y anzvelo de las bolsas, ed. by Ruiz Morcuende. 1942. C4980
43 Espinel, V. Vida de Marcos de Obregón, ed. by Gili y Gaya. V. 1. 1940. C4981
44 Gonzalo de Berceo. Berceo, ed. by Solalinde. V. 1. 1922. C4982
45 Larra, M. J. de. Larra, ed. by Lomba y Pedraja. V. 1. 1929. C4983
46 Saavedra Fajardo, D. de. República literaria, ed. by García de Diego. 1942. C4984
47 Espronceda, J. de. Obras poéticas, ed. by Moreno Villa. V. 1. 1923. C4985
48 Feijóo y Montenegro, B. J. Teatro critico universal, ed. by Millares Carlos. V. 1. 1923. C4986
49 Pulgar, H. del. Claros varones de Castila, ed. by Dominguez Bordona. 1923. C4987
50 Same as no. 47. V. 2. 1923. C4988
51 Same as no. 43. V. 2. 1940. C4989
52 Same as no. 45. V. 2. 1929. C4990
53 Same as no. 48. V. 2. 1924. C4991
54 Moncada, F. de. Expedición de los catalanes y aragoneses contra turcos y griegos, ed. by Gili y Gaya. 1941. C4992
55 Juan de la Cruz, St. El cántico espiritual, ed. by Martinez de Burgos. 1944. C4993
56 Quevedo y Villegas, F. G. de. Obras satíricas y festivas, ed. by Salaverría. 1924. C4994
57 Salas Barbadillo, A. J. de. La peregrinación sabia, ed. by Icaza. 1941. C4995
58 Moratín, L. F. de. Teatro, ed. by Ruiz Morcuende. V. 1. 1924. C4996
59 Rueda, L. de. Teatro, ed. by Moreno Villa. 1924. C4997
60 Cueva, J. de la. El inflamador, ed. by Icaza. 1924. C4998
61 Pérez de Guzman, F. Generaciones y semblanzas, ed. by Dominguez Bordona. 1924. C4999
62 Menéndez Pidal, R.

Rodrigo. V. 1. 1925. C5000
63 Zorilla y Moral, J. Poesías, ed. by Alonson Cortés. 1925. C5001
64 Meléndez Valdes, J. Poesías, ed. by Salinas. 1925. C5002
65 Garcia Gutiérrez, A. Venganza catalana, ed. by Lomba. 1941. C5003
66 Forner, J. B. P. Exequias de la lengua castellana, ed. by Salinz y Rodriques. 1925. C5004
67 Same as no. 48. V. 3. 1925. C5005
68 Vega Carpio, L. F. de. Poesías líricas, ed. by Montesinos. V. 1. 1925. C5006
69 Calderón de la Barca, P. Autos sacramentales, ed. by Valbuena Prat. V. 1. 1925. C5007
70 Mira de Amescua, A. Teatro. V. 1. 1926. C5008
71 Same as no. 62. V. 2. C5009
72 Castillejo, C. de. Obra. V. 1. 1926. C5010
73 Alemán, M. Guzman de Alfarache, ed. by Gili y Gaya. V. 1. 1942. C5011
74 Same as no. 69. V. 2. 1927. C5012
75 Same as no. 68. V. 2. 1927. C5013
76 Saavedra, Fajardo, D. de. Idea de un principe politico cristiano representada en cien empresas, ed. by Garcia de Diego. V. 1. 1927. C5014
77 Same as no. 45. V. 3. C5015
78 Quintana, M. J. Poesias, ed. by Alonso Cortés. 1927. C5016
79 Same as no. 72. V. 2. C5017
80 Valera y Alcalá Galiano, J. Pepita Jiminéz, ed. by Azana. 1927. C5018
81 Same as no. 76. V. 2. C5019
82 Same as no. 70. V. 2. C5020
83 Same as no. 73. V. 2. C5021
84 Same as no. 62. V. 3. C5022
85 Feijóo y Montenzero, B. J. Cartas eruditas, ed. by Millares Carlo. 1928. C5023
86 Valdés, J. de. Diálogo de la lengua, ed. by Montesinos. 1928. C5024
87 Same as no. 76. V. 3. C5025
88 Same as no. 72. V. 3. C5026
89 Valdés, A. de. Diálogo de las cosas occuridas en Roma, ed. by Montesinos. 1956. C5027
90 Same as no. 73. V. 3. 1961. C5028
91 Same as no. 72. V. 4. C5029
92 Bretón de los Herreros, M. Teatro, ed. by Alonso Cortés. 1943. C5030
93 Same as no. 73. V. 4. C5031
94 Manrique, J. Cancionero, ed. by Cortina Aravena. 1929. C5032
95 Arolas, J. Poesías del P. Arolos, ed. by Lomba y Pedraja. 1928. C5033
96 Valdés, A. de. Diálogo de Mercurio y Carón, ed. by Montesinos. 1929. C5034
97 Luis de Granada. Guia de pecadores, ed. by Martinez de Burgos. 1929. C5035
98 Teresa, St. Camino de perfección, ed. by Aguado. V. 1. 1929. C5036
99 Pulgar, H. del. Letras, ed. by Dominguez Bordona. 1929. C5037
100 Same as no. 98. V. 2. 1930. C5038
101 Timoneda, J. de. El patrañuelo, ed. by Ruiz Morcuende. 1930. C5039
102 Same as no. 76. V. 4. 1927. C5040
103 Cascales, F. de. Cartas filológicas, ed. by García Soriano. V. 1. 1961. C5041
104-105 Malón de Chaide, P. La conversion de la Magdalena, ed. by Garcia. 2 v. 1930. C5042
106 Calderón de la Barca, P. Comedias religiosas. V. 1. 1930. C5043
107 Martinez de la Rosa, F. Obras dramaticas, ed. by Sarrailh. 1947. C5044
108-109 La vida de Estebanilo Gonzalez. 2 v. 1934. C5045
110-111 Jovellanos, G. M. de. Obras escogidas, ed. by Rio. 2 v. 1935. C5046

112 Cadalso, A. Cartas marruecas. 1935. C5047
113 Hartzenbusch, J. E. Los amantes de Teruel, ed. by Gil Albocete. 1935. C5048
114 Same as no. 73. V. 5. C5049
115-116 Teresa, St. Libro de la fundaciones de Santa Teresa de Jêsus, ed. by Aguado. 2 v. 1940. C5050
117-118 Same as no. 103. V. 2, 3. C5051
119 Mena, Juan de. El laberinto de Fortuna, ed. by Blecua. 1943. C5052
120-121 Lozano, C. Historias y leyendas, ed. by Entrambasaguas. 2 v. 1943. C5053
122 Arteaga, E. La belleza ideal, ed. by Batllori. 1943. C5054
123 Vâzquez, D. Sermones, ed. by Olmedo. 1943. C5055
124 Torre, F. de. Poesías, ed. by Zamora Vicente. 1944. C5056
125 Cervantes Saavedra, M. de. Entremeses. 1945. C5057
126 Terrones del Caño, F. Instruccion de predicadores. 1946. C5058
127 Montemayor, J. de. Los siete libros de la Diana, ed. by Lôpez Estrada. 1962. C5059
128 Poema de Fernân Gonçalez. Poema de Fernân Golzalez, ed. by Zamora Vicente. 1946. C5060
129 Same as no. 110. V. 3. C5061
130 Same as no. 104. V. 3. C5062
131 Têllez, G. Comedias. V. 1. 1947. C5063
132 Vêlez de Guevara, y Dueñas, L. Reinar despuês de morir, y El diablo estâ en cantillana, ed. by Muñoz Cortês. 1948. C5064
133 San Pedro, D. de. Obras, ed. by Gili y Gaya. 1950. C5065
134 Martinez de Toledo, A. Vidas de San Ildefonso y San Isidoro, ed. by Madoz. 1952. C5066
135 Polo, G. G. Diana enamorada, ed. by Ferreres. 1953. C5067
136 Iriarte y Oropesa, T. de. Poesía, ed. by Navarro Gonzalez. 1953. C5068
137 Calderôn de la Barca, P. Comedias de capa y espada, ed. by Valbuena Briones. V. 1. 1962. C5069
138 ____. La vida es sueño..., ed. by Cortina Aravena. 1955. C5070
139 Fernândez de Heredia, J. Obras, ed. by Ferreres. 1955. C5071
140 Menêndez y Pelayo, M. Discursos, ed. by Maria de Cossio. 1956. C5072
141-2 Calderôn de la Barca, P. Dramas de honor, ed. by Valbuena Briones. 1956. C5073
143 Aldana, F. de. Poesías, ed. by Rivers. 1957. C5074
144-5 Pereda, M. de. Pedro Sânchez. 2 v. 1958. C5075
146 Ruiz de Alarcôn y Mendoza, J. Teatro, ed. by Millares Carlo. 1960. C5076
147 ____. Los pechos privilegiados y Ganar amigos, ed. by Millares Carlo. 1960. C5077
148 Isla, J. F. de. Fray Gerundio de Campazas. 2 v. 1960-62. C5078
152 Cadalso, J. Noches lûgubres, ed. by Glendinning. 1961. C5079
153 Rojas Zorrilla, F. de. Morir pensando matar y La vida en el ataud, ed. by MacCurdy. 1961. C5080
154-155 Cervantes Saavedra, M. de. La Galatea, ed. by Avalle-Acre. 2 v. 1961. C5081
156 Vicente, G. Obras dramâticas castellanas, ed. by Hart. 1962. C5082
157 Vega Carpio, L. F. de. El villando en su Rincôn, ed. by Vicente. 1963. C5083
158 Becquer, G. A. Rimas, ed. by Diaz. 1963. C5084
159 Vega Carpio, L. F. de. Peribanoz y el comendador de Ocaña, ed. by Vicente. 1964. C5085
160 Querol, V. W. Poesias, ed. by Guarner. 1965. C5086
161 Torres y Villarroel, D. de.

Visiones y visitas de Torres con don Francisco de Quevedo por la Corte. 1966. C5087
162 López de Yanguas, F. Obras dramáticas. 1968. C5088
163 Mendoza, I. de. Cancionero, ed. by Rodriguez-Puértolas. 1969. C5089
164 Ferrán, A. Obras completas, ed. by Díaz. 1970. C5090
165-67 Gracián, B. El criticón, ed. by Calderón. 3 v. 1971. C5091
168 Forner, J. P. Los gramaticos, ed. by Pedraja. 1971. C5092
169 Zavaleta, J. de. Evores celebrados, ed. by Hersberg. 1972. C5093
170 Rufo, J. Las seiscientas apotegmas y otras obras en verso, ed. by Blecua. 1972. C5094
171 Same as no. 70. V. 3. 1971. C5095
172 Mayans y Siscar, G. Vida de Miguel de Cervantes Saavedra. 1972. C5096
173 Leonardo y Argensola, L. Rimas, ed. by Blecua. 1972. C5097
174-6 Avellaneda, A. F. de. Don Quixote de la Mancha, ed. by Riquer. 1972. C5098
177-8 Alarcón, P. A., ed. El escandalo, ed. by Baquero Goyanes. 1973. C5099
179 Hartzenbusch, J. E. Fábulas, ed. by Navas-Ruiz. 1973. C5100
180 Valle-Inclán, R. del. Luces de bohemia, ed. by Zamora Vincente. 1973. C5101
181 Rueda, L. de. Los enganos. 1974. C5102
182-183 Jaúregui, J. de. Obras, ed. by Ferrer de Alba. 2 v. 1973. C5103
184-186 Leonard y Argensola, L. Rimas. Prologo de Blecua. 2 v. 1974. C5104

CLASSIC AMERICAN HISTORIANS SERIES (Univ. of Chicago Pr.)

Adams, H. History of the United States of America during the administration of Jefferson and Madison, abr. by Samuels. 1967. C5105
Bancroft, G. The history of the United States of America from the discovery of the continent, ed. by Nye. 1966. C5106
Nicolay, J. G. and Hay, J. Abraham Lincoln, ed. by Angle. 1966. C5107
Prescott, W. H. The history of the conquest of Mexico, ed. by Gardiner. 1966. C5108
Rhodes, J. F. History of the United States from the Compromise of 1850, ed. by Nevins. 1966. C5109
Tyler, M. C. A history of American literature, 1607-1783, ed. by Jones. 1967. C5110

CLASSIC EUROPEAN HISTORIANS SERIES (Univ. of Chicago Pr.)

Acton, J. E. E. D. A. Essays in the liberal interpretation of history, ed. by McNeill. 1968. C5111
Carlyle, T. Frederick the Great. 1969. C5112
Croce, B. History of the kingdom of Naples. 1970. C5113
Engels, F. The German revolutions, ed. by Krieger. 1967. C5114
Gregorovius, F. Rome and medieval culture. 1971. C5115
Guizot, F. Historical essays and lectures, ed. by Mellon. 1972. C5116
Halperin, S. W., ed. Essays in modern European historiography. 1970. C5117
Herder, J. G. von. Reflections on the philosophy of history of mankind. 1968. C5118
Kehr, E. Battleship building and party politics in Germany, 1894-1901. 1973. C5119
Michelet, J. History of the French Revolution, ed. by Wright. 1967. C5120
Mommsen, T. The provinces of the Roman Empire, ed. by Broughton. 1968. C5121
Robertson, W. The progress

of society in Europe. 1972. C5122

Taine, H. A. The origins of contemporary France. 1974. C5123

CLASSICA BOTANICA AMERICANA (Hafner)

1 Marshall, E. Arbustum Americanum, ed. by Ewan. 2 v. 1967. C5124
2 Pursh, F. Flora Americae Septentrionalis, ed. by Ewan. 2 v. 1967. C5125
3 Michaux, A. Flora Boreali-Americana, ed. by Ewan. 2 v. 1967. C5126
4 Torrey, J. and Gray, A. Flora of North America, ed. by Ewan. 2 v. 1967. C5127
5 Robin, C. C. Florula ludoviciana, ed. by Ewan. 1967. C5128
6 Elliott, S. Sketch of the botany of South Carolina and Georgia, ed. by Ewan. 2 v. 1968. C5129
7 Nuttall, T. Genera of North American plants. 2 v. 1968. C5130

Supplements
1 Darlington, W. Memorials of Marshall and Bartram, ed. by Ewan. 1967. C5131
2 ____. Reliquiae Baldwinianae, ed. by Ewan. 1968. C5132

CLASSICS IN ANTHROPOLOGY (Univ. of Chicago Pr.)

Boas, F. Kwakiutl ethnology, ed. by Codere. 1966. C5133
Hocart, A. M. Kings and councillors, ed. by Needham. 1970. C5134
Lowrie, R. H. Culture and ethnology. 1966. C5135
McLennan, J. F. Primitive marriage. 1970. C5136
Mooney, J. The ghost-dance religion and the Sioux outbreak of 1890. 1965. C5137
Morgan, L. H. Houses and houselife of the American aborigines. 1965. C5138
Prichard, J. C. Researches into the physical history of man. 1973. C5139
Radin, P. The method and theory of technology. 1966. C5140
Spencer, H. The evolution of society, ed. by Carneiro. 1967. C5141
Tylor, E. B. Researches into the early history of mankind and the development of civilization. 1964. C5142
Wake, C. S. The development of marriage and kinship, ed. by Needham. 1967. C5143

CLASSICS IN EDUCATION (Teachers College, Columbia U.)

1 Mann, H. The republic and the school, ed. by Cremin. 1957. C5144
2 Grattan, C. H., ed. American ideas about adult education. 1959. C5145
3 Davey, J. Dewey on education, ed. by Dworkin. 1959. C5146
4 Fellman, E., ed. The Supreme Court and education. 1960. C5147
5 Scanlon, D. G., ed. International education. 1960. C5148
6 Jefferson, T. Crusade against ignorance. 1961. C5149
7 Hu, C., ed. Chinese education under communism. 1962. C5150
8 Eliot, C. W. Charles W. Eliot and popular education, ed. by Krug. 1961. C5151
9 Lee, G. C., ed. Crusade against ignorance. 1961. C5152
10 Rousseau, J. J. Emile, tr. by Boyd. 1962. C5153
11 ____. Minor educational writings, tr. by Boyd. 1962. C5154
12 Thorndike, E. L. Psychology and the science of education, ed. by Joncich. 1962. C5155
13 The New England primer, ed. by Ford. 1962. C5156
14 Franklin, B. Benjamin Franklin on education, ed. by Best. 1962. C5157
15 Crane, T. R., ed. The colleges and the public, 1787-1862. 1963. C5158
16 Scanlon, D. G., ed.

Traditions of African education. 1964. C5159
17 Webster, N. American spelling book, ed. by Commager. 1962. C5160
18 Woodward, W. H. Vittorino de Feltre and the humanist educators, ed. by Rice. 1963. C5161
19 ____. Desiderius Erasmus concerning the aim and method of education, ed. by Thompson. 1964. C5162
20 Locke, J. John Locke on education, ed. by Gay. 1964. C5163
21 McCluskey, N. G., ed. Catholic education in America. 1964. C5164
22 Sizer, T. R., ed. The age of the academies. 1964. C5165
23 Hall, G. S. Health, growth, and heredity, ed. by Strickland and Burgess. 1965. C5166
24 Borrowman, M. L., ed. Teacher education in America. 1965. C5167
25 Cross, B. M., ed. The educated woman in America. 1965. C5168
26 Emerson, R. W. Emerson on education, ed. by Jones. 1966. C5169
27 Carlton, F. T. Economic influences upon educational progress in the United States, 1820-1850, ed. by Cremin. 1965. C5170
28 Quintilianus, M. F. Quintilian on education, ed. by Smail. 1966. C5171
29 Gwynn, A. O. Roman education from Cicero to Quintilian. 1966. C5172
30 Spencer, H. Herbert Spencer on education, ed. by Kazamias. 1966. C5173
31 Locke, J. Of the conduct of the understanding, ed. by Garforth. 1966. C5174
32 Woodward, W. H. Studies in education during the age of the renaissance. 1967. C5175
33 Comenius, J. A. John Amos Comenius on education, ed. by Piaget. 1967. C5176
34 Caspari, F. Humanism and social order in Tudor England. 1968. C5177
35 Vives, J. L. Introduction to wisdom, ed. by Tobriner. 1968. C5178
36 Nettleship, R. L. The theory of education in the Republic of Plato. 1968. C5179
37 Harrison, J. F. C., comp. Utopianism and education. 1968. C5180
38 Freeman, K. J., comp. Schools of Hellas. 1969. C5181
39 Jarrett, J. L., ed. The educational theories of the Sophists. 1969. C5182
40 Elyot, T. The book named the Governor, ed. by Major. 1970. C5183
41 Gartner, L. P., ed. Jewish education in the United States. 1970. C5184
42 Barnard, H. School architecture, ed. by McClintock. 1970. C5185
43 Mill, J. S. John Stuart Mill on education, ed. by Garforth. 1971. C5186
44 DeMolen, R. L. Richard Mulcaster's positions. 1972. C5187
45 Adamson, J. W. Pioneers of modern education in the seventeenth century. 1971. C5188
46 Sloan, D., comp. The great awakening and American education. 1973. C5189
47 Kaestle, C. F., comp. John Lancaster and the monitorial school movement. 1973. C5190
48 Lazerson, M. and Grubb, W. N., eds. American education and vocationalism. 1974. C5191
49 Kay-Shuttleworth, J. Sir James Kay-Shuttleworth on popular education, ed. by Tholfsen. 1974. C5192

CLASSICS IN MATHEMATICS EDUCATION (Nat'l. Council of Teachers of Mathematics)

1 Loomis, E. S. The Pythagorean proposition. 1970. C5193
2 Smith, D. E. Number stories

of long ago. 1971. C5194
3 Yates, R. C. The trisection problem. 1971. C5195

THE CLASSICS OF INTERNATIONAL LAW (Oxford)

1 Zouche, R. Iuris et iudicii fecialis, sive, iuris inter gentes, et quaestinoum de eodem explicatio, ed. by Holland. 2 v. 1911. C5196
2 Ayala, B. Ayalae De jureet officiis bellicis et disciplina militari, ed. by Westlake. 2 v. 1912. C5197
3 Grotius, H. De jure belli ac pacis, tr. by Kelsey. 2 v. 1913-25. C5198
4 Vattel, E. de. Le droit des gens, tr. by Fenwick. 3 v. 1916. C5199
5 Rachel, S. Samuelis Rachelii De jure naturae et gentium dissertationes, ed. by Bar. 2 v. 1916. C5200
6 Textor, J. W. Joh. Wolfgangi Textoris, Synopsis juris gentium, ed. by Bar. 1916. C5201
7 de Vittoria, F. Reflectiones, de indis et de iure belli, ed. by Nys. 1917. C5202
8 Legnano, G. da. Tractatus de bello, de respresaliis et de duello, ed. by Holland. 1917. C5203
9 Gentili, A. Alberici Gentilis, Hispanicae advocationis. libri dvo, ed. by Abbott. 2 v. 1921. C5204
10 Pufendorf, S. von. De officio hominis et civis juxta legem naturalem libri duo. 2 v. 1927. C5205
11 Byjkershoek, C. von. De dominio Maris dissertatio, ed. by Scott. 1923. C5206
12 Gentili, A. De legationibvs libri tres. 2 v. 1924. C5207
13 Wolff, C. von. Jus gentium methodo scientifica petraracta-tum. 2 v. 1934. C5208
14 Byjkershoek, C. von. Quaestionum juris publici libri duo. 2 v. 1930. C5209
15 Pufendorf, S. Elementorum jurisprudentiae universalis libri duo. 2 v. 1931. C5210
16 Gentili, A. De juri belli libri tres. 2 v. 1933. C5211
17 Pufendorf, S. De jure naturae of gentium libri, tr. by Oldfather. 2 v. 1934. C5212
18 Belli, P. De re militari et bello tractatus. 2 v. 1936. C5213
19 Wheaton, H. Elements of international law, ed. by Wilson. 1936. C5214
20 Suárez, F. Selections from three works of Francisco Suarez. 2 v. 1944. C5215
21 Byjkershoek, C. van. De foro legatorum, tr. by Laing. 1946. C5216
22 Grotius, H. De juri praedae commentarius. 2 v. 1950. C5217
Scott, J. B. Spanish origins of international law. 2 v. 1933. C5218

LES CLASSIQUES FRANÇAIS DU MOYEN AGE (Champion)

1 La chastelaine de Vergi. La chastelaine de Vergi, ed. by Raynaud. 1912. C5219
2 Villon, F. Oeuvres, ed. by Longnon. 1923. C5220
3 Courtois d'Arras. Courtois d'Arras, ed. by Faral. 1922. C5221
4 Alexis St. Legends. La vie de Saint Alexis, ed. by Paris. 1933. C5222
5 Le garçon et l'aveugle. Le garçon et l'aveugle, ed. by Roques. 1911. C5223
6 Adam de la Halle. Le jeu de la feuillee, ed. by Langlois. 1923. C5224
7 Muset, C. Les chansons de Colin Muset, ed. by Bêdier. 1919. C5225
8 Huon le Roi de Cambrai. Huon le Roi, le vair palefroi, ed. by Langfors. 1927. C5226
9 Guillaume IX, duke of Aquitaine. Les chansons de Guillaume IX duc d'Aquitaine, ed. by Jeanroy. 1913. C5227
10 Philippe, of Novara. Mêmoires, ed. by Kohler. 1913. C5228

11 Peire, V. de. Les poêsies de Peire Vidal, ed. by Anglade. 1913. C5229
12 Bêroul. Le roman de Tristan, ed. by Muret. 1947. C5230
13 Huon le Roi de Cambrai. Oeuvres, ed. by Langfors. V. 1. 1913. C5231
14 Gormont et Isembart. Gormont et Isembart, fragment de chanson de geste du XIIe siècle, ed. by Bayot. 1921. C5232
15 Jaufrê Rudel. Les chansons de Jaufrê Rudel, ed. by Jeanroy. 1924. C5233
16 Jeanroy, A. Bibliographie sommaire des chansonniers provencaux. 1916. C5234
17 Bertran de Marseille. La vie de sainte Enimie, ed. by Brunel. 1916. C5235
18 Jeanroy, A. Bibliographie sommaire des chansonniers français du moyen âge. 1918. C5236
19 Aspremont (Chanson de geste) La chanson d'Aspremont, ed. by Brandin. V. 1. 1919. C5237
20 Gautier d'Aupais. Gautier d'Aupais, poème courtois du XIIIe siècle, ed. by Faral. 1919. C5238
21 Foulet, L., ed. Petite syntaxe de l'ancien français. 1919. C5239
22 Couronnement de Louis. Le Couronnement de Louis, ed. by Langlois. 1920. C5240
23 Jeanroy, A. and Langfors, A., eds. Chansons satiriques et bachiques du XIIIe siècle. 1921. C5241
24 Bêthune, Conon de. Les chansons de Conon de Bêthune, ed. by Wallenskold. 1921. C5242
25 Same as no. 19. V. 2. 1920. C5243
26 Pyriamus et Tisbê, ed. by Boer. 1921. C5244
27 Cercamon. Les poêsis de Cercamon, ed. by Jeanroy. 1922. C5245
28 Gerbert de Montreuil. La continuation de Perceval, ed. by Williams. 1922. C5246
29 Benoît le Sainte More. Le Roman de Troie en prose, ed. by Constans et Faral. 1922. C5247
30 Passion du Palatinus (Mystery) La passion du Palatinus, ed. by Frank. 1922. C5248
31 Jean, Le Teinturier d'Arras. Mariage des sept arts. Le mariage des sept arts, par Jehan le Teinturier d'Arras, ed. by Langfors. 1922. C5249
32 Chartier, A. Le quadrilogue invectif, ed. by Droz. 1923. C5250
33 La queste del saint graal. La queste del saint graal, ed. by Pauphilet. 1923. C5251
34 Charles d'Orléans. Poêsies, ed. by Champion. V. 1. 1923. C5252
35 Pathelin. Maistre Pierre Pathelin, ed. by Holbrook. 1924. C5253
36 Adam de la Halle. Adam le Bossu, trouvère artesien du XIIIe siècle: Le Jeu de Robin et Marion suivi du Jeu du Pèlerin, ed. by Langlois. 1924. C5254
37 Jean Renart. Galeran de Bretagne, ed. by Foulet. 1925. C5255
38 Renaut de Beaujeu. Le bel inconnu, ed. by Williams. 1929. C5256
39 Jeanroy, A., ed. Jongleurs et troubadours gascons des XIIe et XIIIe siècles. 1923. C5257
40 Robert de Clari. La conquête de Constantinople, ed. by Bauer. 1924. C5258
41 Aucassin et Nicolette, ed. by Roques. 1936. C5259
42 Guilheim de Cabesting. Les chansons de Guillem de Cabestanh, ed. by Langfors. 1925. C5260
43 Sarrasin, J. P. Lettres françaises du XIIIe siècle: Jean Sarrasin, Lettre à Nicolas Arrode, ed. by Foulet. 1924. C5261
44 Enêas (Romance). Eneas, ed. by Salverda de Grave. V. 1. 1925. C5262
45 Foy d'Agen, Saint, Legend.

La chanson de Saint Foi d'Agen, ed. by Thomas. 1925. C5263
46 Jausbert de Puycibot. Les poêsies de Jausbert da Puycibot, trobadour du XIIIe siècle. 1924. C5264
47 Morawski, J. , ed. Proverbes français anterieurs au XVe siècle. 1925. C5265
48 Bodel, J. Jean Bodel, trouvère artêsien du XIIIe siècle: Le jeu de Saint Nicolas, ed. by Jeanroy. 1925. C5266
49 Rutebeuf. Le miracle de Thêophile, ed. by Frank. 1925. C5267
50 Same as no. 28. V. 2. 1926. C5268
51 Amadas et Idoine. Amades et Ydoine, ed. by Reinhard. 1926. C5269
52 Histoire d'outre mer. La fille du Comte de Ponthieu, ed. by Brunel. 1926. C5270
53 Perdignon. Les chansons de Perdigon, ed. by Chaytor. 1926. C5271
54 Siège de Barbastre. Le siège de Barbastre, ed. by Perrier. 1926. C5272
55 Chrêtien de Troyes. Guillaume d'Angleterre, ed. by Wilmotte. 1927. C5273
56 Same as no. 34. V. 2. 1927. C5274
57 Robert de Boron. Le roman del'estoire dou Graal, ed. by Nitze. 1927. C5275
58 Eustachius, Saint, Legend. La vie de saint Eustache, ed. by 1928. C5276
59 Guiot de Dijon. Les chansons attributees à Guiot de Dijon et Jocelin, ed. by Nissen. 1928. C5277
60 Eustachius, Saint, Legend. La vie de saint Eustache en prose, ed. by Murray. 1929. C5278
61 Bernart Marti. Les poêsie de Bernart Marti, ed. by Hoepffner. 1929. C5279
62 Same as no. 44. V. 2. 1929. C5280
63 Fulk Fitz-Warine (Romance). Rouke Fitz Warin, ed. by Brandin. 1930. C5281
64 Livre de la passion. Le livre de la Passion, ed. by Frank. 1930. C5282
65 Les estampies françaises, ed. by Streng Renkonen. 1930. C5283
66 Charroi de Nîmes. Le charroi de Nîmes, ed. by Perrier. 1931. C5284
67 Maillart, J. Le roman du comte d'Anjou, ed. by Roques. 1931. C5285
68 Sancta Agnes. Le jeu de sainte Agnès, ed. by Jeanroy. 1931. C5286
69 Rêsurrection du Sauveur. La rêsurrection du Sauveur, ed. by Wright. 1931. C5287
70 Guillaume de saint Pathus. Les miracles de saint Louis, ed. by Fay. 1931. C5288
71 Wace. La vie de sainte Marguerite, ed. by Francis. 1932. C5289
72 Trois aveugles de Compiègne. Cortebarbe: les trois aveugles de compiègne, ed. by Gougenheim. 1932. C5290
73 Gêrold, T. La musique au moyen âge. 1932. C5291
74-75 Guy of Warwick. Gui de Warewic, ed. by Ewart. 2 v. 1932-33. C5292
76 Atre pêrilleux. L'atre pêrilleux, ed. by Woledge. 1936. C5293
77 Guernes de Pont-Sainte-Maxence. La vie de saint Thomas Becket, ed. by Walberg. 1936. C5294
78-79 Roman de Renart. Le roman de renart, ed. by Roques. 2 v. 1948-50. C5295
80 Chretien de Troyes. Romans, ed. by Roques. 2 v. 1952-4. C5296
81 Same as no. 78. V. 3. 1955. C5297
82 Chevalier au barisel. Le Chevalier au barisel, ed. by Lecoy. 1955. C5298
83 Roland à Saragosse. Roland à Saragossa, ed. by Roques. 1956. C5299
84 Same as no. 80. V. 2. 1957. C5300
85 Same as no. 78. V. 4. 1956. C5301
86 Same as no. 80. V. 3.

1958. C5302
87 Marie de France. Les Lais de Marie de France, ed. by Lods. 1959. C5303
88 Same as no. 78. V. 5. 1960. C5304
89 Same as no. 80. V. 4. 1961. C5305
90 Same as no. 78. V. 6. C5306
91 Guillaume de Dole. Le Roman de la Rose ou de Guillaume de Dole, ed. by Lecoy. 1962. C5307
92 Roman de la Rose. Le Roman de la Rose by de Lorris and de Meun. V. 1. 1965. C5308
93 Marie de France. Les lais de Marie de France. 1971. C5309
95 Same as no. 92. V. 2. 1967. C5310
98 Same as no. 92. V. 3. 1969. C5311
99 Adam. Le Jeu, ed. by Noomen. 1971. C5312
100 Same as no. 80. V. 2. 1972. C5313

CLINICAL APPROACHES TO PROBLEMS OF CHILDHOOD (Science and Behavior Books)

1 Berlin, I. N. and Szurek, S. A., eds. Learning and its disorders. 1965. C5314
2 Szurek, S. A. and Berlin, I. N., comps. Training in therapeutic work with children. 1967. C5315
3 ____, eds. Psychomatic disorders and mental retardation in children. 1968. C5316
4 ____. The antisocial child. 1969. C5317
5 Szurek, S. A. and others, comps. In-patient care for the psychotic child. 1971. C5318

CLIO (Presses Universitaires de France)

I Les peuples de l'Orient méditerranéen.
1. Delaporte, L. J. Le proche Orient asiatique. 1948. C5319
2. Drioton, E. and Vandier, J. La Egypte. 1946. C5320
II Cohen, R. La Grèce et l'hellénisation du monde antique. 1948. C5321
III Piganiol, A. Histoire de Rome. 1949. C5322
IV Calmette, J. L. A. Le monde féodol. 1951. C5323
V ____. L'elaboration du monde moderne. 1949. C5324
VI Sée, H. E. and Rebillon, A. Le XVIe siècle. 1950. C5325
VII Préclin, E. and Tapié, V. L.
1 Le XVIIe siècle, monarchies centralisées, 1610-1715. 1949. C5326
2 Le XVIIIe siècle. 2 v. 1952. C5327
VIII Villat, L. La révolution et l'Empire, 1789-1815. 2 v. 1947. C5328
IX L'epoque contemporaine. 1815-1919.
1. Villat, L. Restaurations et Révolutions, 1815-1871. 1949. C5329
2. Renouvin, P. and others. La paix armée et la grande guerre, 1870-1919. 1947. C5330
X Histoire de l'Art.
1. Lavedan, P. Antiquité. 1949. C5331
2. ____. Moyen âge et temps moderns. 1950. C5332
3. Rébillon, A. Les temps modernes. 1937. C5333
XI Textes et documents d'histoire.
2. Calmette, J. L. A. Le moyen âge. 1937. C5334
4. Préclin, E. and Renouvin, P. Temps moderne. 1936-37. C5335
XII Atlas historique by Delaporte and others. 2 v. 1936-37. C5336
XIII Delorme, J. Chronologie des civilisations. 1956. C5337

THE COLE LECTURES 1894-1905 M. E. Church Pub. House Nashville, Tenn.; 1906-23, Revell; 1926- (Abingdon-Cokesbury unless otherwise specified)

1894 Wilson, A. W. The witnesses to Christ. 1894. C5338
1900 Granberg, J. C. Experience. 1901. C5339
1903 Hendrix, E. R. The religion of the incarnation. 1903. C5340
1904 Chapman, J. The Christian character. 1910. C5341
1905 Hall, C. C. The universal elements of the Christian religion. 1905. C5342
1906 Smith, F. H. Christ and science. 1906. C5343
1907 Watson, J. God's message to the human soul. 1907. C5344
1908 Jackson, G. The fact of conversion. 1908. C5345
1909 Bishop, C. M. Jesus the worker. 1910. C5346
1910 McDowell, W. F. In the school of Christ. 1910. C5347
1911 Speer, R. E. Some great leaders in the world movement. 1911. C5348
1912 Faunce, W. H. P. What does Christianity mean? 1912. C5349
1913 Ross, G. A. J. The God we trust. 1913. C5350
1914 McConnell, F. J. Personal Christianity... 1914. C5351
1915 Lambuth, W. R. Winning the world for Christ. 1915. C5352
1916 Workman, H. B. The foundation of modern religion. 1916. C5353
1917 MacDonald, J. A. The North American idea. 1917. C5354
1918 Jefferson, C. E. Old truths and new facts. 1918. C5355
1919 Hough, L. H. The productive beliefs. 1919. C5356
1920 King, H. C. A new mind for the new age. 1920. C5357
1921 Kelman, J. The foundations of faith. 1921. C5358
1922 Fosdick, H. E. Christianity and progress. 1922. C5359
1923 Williams, C. D. The gospel of fellowship. 1923. C5360
1924 Cadman, S. P. Imagination and religion. Macmillan. 1926. C5361
1925 Mouzon, E. D. B. The program of Jesus. 1925. C5362
1926 Woelfkin, C. Expanding horizons. 1927. C5363
1927 Gilkey, C. W. Present day dilemmas in religion. 1928. C5364
1928 Hughes, E. H. Christianity and success. 1928. C5365
1929 Ellwood, C. E. Man's social destiny. 1930. C5366
1930 Kirk, H. E. The spirit of Protestantism. 1930. C5367
1931 Mott, J. R. The present day summons to the world mission of Christianity. 1931. C5368
1932 Butterfield, K. L. The Christian enterprise among rural people. 1932. C5369
1933 Coffin, H. S. What men are asking. 1933. C5370
1934 Mathews, S. Creative Christianity. 1934. C5371
1935 Kern, R. B. The basic reliefs of Jesus. 1935. C5372
1936 Jones, R. M. Some problems of life. 1936. C5373
1937 Fisher, F. B. The man that changed the world. 1937. C5374
1938 Atkins, G. G. Christianity and the creative quests. 1939. C5375
1939 Beaven, A. W. Remaking life. 1940. C5376
1940 Aubrey, E. E. Man's search for himself. 1940. C5377
1941 Buttrick, G. A. Prayer. 1942. C5378
1942 Brightman, E. S. The spiritual life. 1942. C5379
1943 Grant, F. C. The earliest gospel. 1943. C5380
1944 Mims, E. Great writers as interpreters of religion. 1945. C5381
1945 Scherer, P. E. The flight of freedom. Harper, 1948. C5382
1946 Lee, U. Render unto the people. 1947. C5383
1947 Smart, W. A. Still the Bible speaks. 1948. C5384
1948 Weigle, L. A. The English New Testament. 1940. C5385
1949 Ferré, N. F. S.

Christianity and society. Harper. 1950. C5386
1950 Sorokin, P. A. Social philosophies of an age crisis. Beacon pr., 1950. C5387
1951 Bultmann, R. K. Jesus Christ and the modern interpretation of the New Testament (not published). C5388
1954 Micklem, N. Ultimate questions. 1955. C5389
1955 Murray, A. V. Natural religion and Christian theology. Harper. 1956. C5390
1958 Tillich, P. Theology of culture. Oxford. 1958. C5391
1962 Colwell, E. C. Jesus and the Gospel. 1963. C5392

COLECCION DE ESCRITORES MEXICANOS (Editorial Porrúa)

1 Juan Inés de la Cruz. Poesías liricas. 1950. C5393
2 Sigüenza y Góngora, C. de. Obras históricas. 1944. C5394
3 Altamirano, I. M. Clemencia. 1944. C5395
4 Ramírez, J. F. Vida de fray Toribio de Motolinía. 1944. C5396
5 Othón, M. J. Poemas rústicos. 1944. C5397
6 Delgado, R. Los parientes ricos. 1944. C5398
7-10 Clavijero, F. J. Historia antigua de México. 4 v. 1945. C5399
11 López-Portillo y Rojas, J. La parcela. 1945. C5400
12 Diaz Mirón, S. Poesías completas. 1947. C5401
13-17 Payno, M. Los bandidos de Rio Frío. 5 v. 1945. C5402
18-19 Riva Palacio, V. Monja y casada, virgen y mártir. 1945. C5403
20-21 ____. Martín Garatuza. 2 v. 1945. C5404
22-23 Reyes, A. Simpatías y diferencias. 2 v. 1945. C5405
24 González Peña, C. La chiquilla. 1946. C5406
25-26 Riva Palacio, V. Los piratas del golfo. 2 v. 1946. C5407
27 Urbina, L. G. La vida literaria de Mexico... 1946. C5408
28-29 ____. Poesías completas. 2 v. 1949. C5409
30-32 Robles, A. de. Diario de sucesos notables (1665-1703). 1946. C5410
33-34 Riva Palacio, V. Memorias de un impostor. 2 v. 1946. C5411
35 Urbina, L. G. Cuentos vividos y Cronicas soñadas. 1946. C5412
36 Sierra, J. Cuentos románticos. 1946. C5413
37-38 Mier Noriega y Guerra, J. S. T. de. Memorias, ed. by Leal. 2 v. 1946. C5414
39 Cuéllar, J. T., de. Ensalada de pollos y Baile y cochino. 1946. C5415
40 González Martinez, E. Preludios. Lirismos. Silentier. Los senderos ocultos. 1946. C5416
41-44 García Icazbalceta, J. Don fray Juan de Zumárraga. 4 v. 1947. C5417
45 Cuéllar, J. T., de. Historia de Chucho el ninfo y La noche buena. 1947. C5418
46-48 Roa Bárcena, J. M. Recuerdos de la invasión norteamericana (1846-48). 3 v. 1947. C5419
49 Delgado, R. Angelina. 1947. C5420
50 Rabasa, E. La bolay La gran cuencia. 1948. C5421
51 ____. El cuarto poder y Moneda falsa. 1948. C5422
52-54 Altamirano, I. M. La literatura nacional; revistas, ensayos, biografias, y prólogos, ed. by Martinez. 3 v. 1949. C5423
55 Acuña, M. Obra de Manuel Acuña, ed. by Martinez. 1949. C5424
56-58 Fernandez de Lizardi, J. J. El periquillo sarniento, ed. by Spell. 3 v. 1949. C5425
59-61 Mora, J. M. L. Mexico y sus revoluciones, ed. by Yañez. 3 v. 1950. C5426
62 Castera, P. Carmen, memorias de un corazón, ed. by González Peña. 1950. C5427

63 Nervo, A. Fuegos fatuos y Pimientos dulces, ed. by Guerrero. 1951. C5428
64-65 Guijo, G. M. de. Diario, 1648-1664, ed. by Terreros. 2 v. 1952. C5429
66-67 Gutiérrez Nájera, M. Poesias completas, ed. by Guerrero. 2 v. 1953. C5430
68 López Velarde, R. Poesías completas y el minutero, ed. by Castro Leal. 1953. C5431
69 Delgado, R. Cuentos y notas. 1953. C5432
70 Castro Leal, A., ed. Las cien mejores poesías líricas mexicanas. 1953. C5433
71 Salado Alvarez, V. Cuentos y narraciones. 1953. C5434
72 Yañez, A. Al filo del agua. 1955. C5435
73 Gorostiza, M. E., ed. Teatro selecto, ed. by María Campos. 1957. C5436
74-75 González de Eslava, F. Los coloquios espirituales y sacramentales, ed. by Rojas Garcidueñas. 2 v. 1958. C5437
76 Campo, A. del. Ocios apuntes y la rumba. 1958. C5438
77 ____. Cosas vistas y Cartones. 1958. C5439
78 Calderón, F. Dramas y poesías. 1959. C5440
79-80 Sierra, J. La hija del Judio, ed. by O'Reilly. 2 v. 1959. C5441
81 Fernandez de Lizardi, J. J. Don Catrin de la Fachenda, y Noche tristes y día alegre. 1959. C5442
82 Icaza, F. A. de. Lope de Vega. 1962. C5443
83 Almazán, P. Un Hereje y un musulman, ed. by Castro Leal. 1962. C5444
84 Novo, S. Antologia, ed. by Leal. 1966. C5445
85 Magdaleno, M. Cabello de elote, ed. by Gringoire. 1966. C5446
86-87 Torres Bodet, J. Obra poetica, ed. by Solana. 2 v. 1967. C5447
88 Rodriquez Galvan, I. Poesia y teatro, ed. by Leal. 1972. C5448

COLECCION DE LIBROS RAROS O CURIOSOS QUE TRATAN DE AMERICA (Suarez)

1 Xerez, F. de. Verdadera relación de la conquista del Perú. 1891. C5449
2 Acuña, C. de. Nuevo descubrimiento del gran rio de las Amazonas. 1895. C5450
3-4 Rocha, D. A. Tratado único y singular del origen de los indios del Perú, Mejico, Santa Fe y Chile. 1891. C5451
5-6 Colón, H. Historia del Almirnate don Cristóbal Colon. 2 v. 1932. C5452
7 Ruiz Blanco, M. Conversión en Piritú (Columbia) de Indios Cumanagotos y Palenques. 1892. C5453
8-9 Vargas Machuca, B. de. Milicia y descripción de las Indias. 1892. C5454
10 Palafox y Mendoza, J. de. Virtudes del Indio. 1893. C5455
11 Tres tratados de America (siglo XVIII). 1894. C5456
12-13 Fernández, J. P. Relación historial de la misiones Indios Chiqutos. 1897. C5457
14-15 Roman y Zamora, J. República de Indias, idolatrias y gobierno en Mejico y Perú antes de la conquista. 2 v. 1897. C5458
16-19 Jarque, F. Ruíz Montoya en Indias (1608-1652). 4 v. 1900. C5459
20 Sigüenza y Gongora, C. de. Infortunios de Alonso Ramirez. Relación de la America Septentrional. 1902. C5460
21 Cisneros, J. L. de. Descripción exacta de la provincia de Benezuela. 1928. C5461
22 Serrando y Sanz, M., ed. Relaciónes históricas de la misiones de padres capuchinos de Venezuela. 1928. C5462

COLECCION DE LIBROS Y DOCUMENTOS REFERENTES A LA HISTORIA DE AMERICA (Suarez)

1 Figueroa, F. de. Relación

de las misiones de la Compañia de Jesus en el pais de los Maynas. 1904. C5463
2-4 Gutiérrez de Santa Clara, P. Historia de las guerras civiles del Perú, 1544-1548. V. 1, 2. 1904. V. 3. 1905. C5464
5-6 Núñez Cabeza de Vaca, A. Relación de los naufragios y comentarios. 2 v. 1906. C5465
7 Hernández, P. El extrañamiento de los Jesuítas del Rio de la Plata y de las misiones del Paraguay por decreto de Carlos III. 1908. C5466
8 Espino, F. Relaciones historicas y geográficas de América Central. 1908. C5467
9 Zurita, A. de. Historia de la Nueva España. V. 1. 1909. C5468
10 Same as no. 2. V. 4. 1910. C5469
11-13 Charlevoix, P. F. J. de. Historia del Paraguay. V. 1. 1910. V. 2. 1912. V. 3. 1913. C5470
14 Serrano y Sanz, M. , ed. Cedulario de las provincias de Santa Marta y Cartagena de Indias. V. 1. 1913. C5471
15-16 Same as no. 11. V. 4. 1913. V. 5. 1915. C5472
17 Mexía de Ovando, P. La Ovandina. V. 1. 1915. C5473
18 Same as no. 11. V. 6. 1916. C5474
19 Muriel D. Historia del Paraguay desde 1747 hasta 1767, tr. by Hernandez. V. 1. 1918. C5475
20-21 Same as no. 2. V. 5. 1925. V. 6. 1929. C5476
22 Foucher, J. Itinerario del misionero en América. 1960. C5477

COLECCION HISTORIA Y FILOSOFIA DE LA CIENCIA (Espasa-Calpe)

Serie Menor:
Babini, J. Origen y naturaleza de la ciencia. 1947. C5478
Becquerel, H. El descubrimiento de la radio-actividad. C5479
Berkeley, G. Teoria de la vision. C5480
Bernard, C. El metodo experimental y otras paginas filosoficas. C5481
Bonola, R. Geometrias no Euclidianas. 1945. C5482
Broglie, L. Sabios y descubridores. 1950. C5483
Cournot, A. A. Tratado del encadenamiento de las ideas fundamentales en las ciencias y en la historia. C5484
Descartes, R. La geometria. C5485
Enríquez, F. Para la historia de la logica. C5486
____. Problemas de la ciencia. C5487
____. Problemas de la logica. C5488
Gibson, C. E. La historia del barco. 1954. C5489
Grassman, H. G. Teoria de la extension. C5490
Hadamard, R. Psicologia de la invencion en el campo matematico. C5491
Hainard, R. Naturaleza y otras mecanismo. C5492
Humboldt, A. freiher von. Oceano, atmosfera y geomagnetismo. C5493
LaCarriere, J. Hereodoto y el descubrimiento de la Tierra. 1974. C5494
Lain Entralgo, P. Vida y obra de Guillermo Harvey. C5495
Laplace, P. S. marquis de. Ensayo filosofico sobre las posibilidades. C5496
Le Chantelier, H. Ciencia e industria. C5497
Le Dantec, F. Ciencia y conciencia. C5498
Lespieau, R. La molecula quimica. C5499
Lobel, J. D. Historia suscinta de la medicina mundial. C5500
Mach, E. Conocimiento y error. C5501
Mieli, A. La ciencia del Renacimiento. 1952. C5502
____. La eclosión del Renacimiento. 1951. C5503
____. La época medieval. 1946. C5504
____. Panorama general de historia de la ciencia. 7 v.

1945. C5505
___. La teoria atomica. C5506
Papp, D. Filosofia de las leyes naturales. C5507
___ and Babini, J. La ciencia del Remacimento; astronomia, fisica, biologia. 1952. C5508
___. La cienca del Remacimento; las ciencas exactes en el siglo XVII. 1954. C5509
___. El siglo del iluminismo. 1955. C5510
Papp, D. and Prelat, C. E. Historia de los principios fundamentales de la Quimica. C5511
Plá, C. Velocidad de la luz y relatividad. 1947. C5512
Prêlat, C. E. Epistemologia de la química. 1947. C5513
___. Epistemologia de las ciencias fisicas. C5514
Sarton, G. La vida de la ciencia. 1950. C5515
Schurman, P. F. Lux y calor. C5516
Seneca, L. A. Los ocho libros de cuestiones naturales. C5517
Spengler, O. Heraclito. C5518
Tannery, J. Ciencia y filosofia. C5519
Uexküll, J. J. baron von. Ideas para una concepcion biologica del mundo. C5520
Vailati, J. Contribucion a la historia de la mecanica. C5521
Serie Mayor:
Aesch, A. G. von. El romanticismo alemân y las ciencias naturales. C5522
Alejandro, J. M. En la hora crepuscular de Europe. 1958. C5523
Dilthey, G. Introduccion a las ciencias del espiritu. C5524
Gibson, C. Historia del barco. C5525
Gode Von Aesch, A. El romanticismo aleman y las ciencias naturales. 1965. C5526
Heidel, W. A. La edad heroica de la ciencia. C5527
Hogben, L. T. ¿Que de la materia viva? C5528
Jevons, W. S. Los principos de la ciencia. C5529
Lacombe, P. La historia considerada como ciencia. C5530
Larroque, E. El hombre y la revolucion cientifica. 1973. C5531
Lucretius Carus, T. De la naturaleza de las cosas. C5532
Mach, E. Desarrollo historico-critico de la mecanica. C5533
Nordenskiold, N. A. E. Evolucion historica de la ciencias biologicas. C5534
Papp, D. Historia de la fisica. C5535
Partington, J. R. Historia de la quimica. C5536
Pearson, E. S. Pearson, creador de la estadistica aplicada. C5537
Perrin, E. S. Los principios de la quimica-fisica. C5538
Rey Pastor, J. and Babini, J. Historia de las matemâtica. 1952. C5539
Santalo Sors, L. Historia de la aeronâutica. 1946. C5540
Russell, B. R. Los principios de la matematica. 1967. C5541
Singer, C. J. Historia de la biologia. C5542
Spengler, O. La decadencia de occidente. 2 v. 1949. C5543

COLGATE UNIVERSITY. HAMILTON, NEW YORK. AREA STUDIES. LATIN AMERICAN SEMINAR REPORTS. 1949.

1 Suslow, L. A. Aspects of social reforms in Guatemala, 1944-49. 1949. C5544
2 Bush, A. C. Organized labor in Guatemala, 1944-1949. 1950. C5545

COLLECTANEA BIBLICA LATINA (Libreria Editrice Vaticana)

1 Bible. O. T. Psalms. Liber Psalmorum, ed. by Amelli. 1912. C5546
2 Codex Rehdigeranus, ed. by Vogels. 1913. C5547
3 Codex Vercellenis, ed. by Gasquet. 1914. C5548
4 Capelle, D. P. Le texte du Psautier latin en Afrique. 1913. C5549
5 Les fragments de Freising, ed. by Bruyne. 1921. C5550
6 Quentin, D. H. Memoire sur

l'établissement du texte de la Vulgate. 1922. C5551
7 Catholic Church. Liturgy and ritual. Le lectionnaire de Luxeuil, by Salmon. V. 1. 1944. C5552
8 Weber, R., ed. Les anciennes versions latines du deuxième livre des Paralipomenès. 1945. C5553
9 Same as no. 7. V. 2. 1953. C5554
10 Weber, R., ed. Le Psautier romain et les anciens Psautiers latins. 1953. C5555
11 Sainte-Marie, D. H. de. S. Hieronymi psalterium iuxta Hebraeos. 1954. C5556
12 Salmon, D. P. Les tituli psalmorum des manuscrits. 1959. C5557
13 Richesses et deficiences des anciens Psautiers latins, by Salmon and others. 1959. C5558
14 Merlo, F. Il salterio di Rufino, ed. by Gribomont. 1972. C5559

COLLECTANEA URBANA (Istituto di Studia Romani)

1 Pietrangeli, C. Scavi e scoperte di antichità, sotto il pontificato di Pio VI. 1958. C5560
2 Battaglia, R. La Cattedra berniniana di S. Pietro. 1943. C5561
3 Canaletti Gaudenti, A. La politica agraria ed annonaria dello Stato Pontificio da Benedetto XIV a Pio VII. 1947. C5562
4 Gasbarri, C. and Giuntella, V. E. Due diari inediti della repubblica Romana del 1798-1799. 1958. C5563
5-7 Huetter, L. Iscrizioni della citta di Roma dal 1871 al 1920. 3 v. 1959-62. C5564
8 Guasti, C. Roma, aprile 1869, ed. by Vian. 1970. C5565

COLLECTION ARTISANALE, COMMERCIALE ET INDUSTRIELLE (Baude)

1 Buisseret, E. Initiation mathématique aux affaires. 1950. C5566
2 ____. Traité de comptabilité pratique. 1952. C5567
3 Baude, J. Principes de droit appliqué aux affaires. 1953. C5568
4-5 Spreutels, M. Technologie et analyse des principaux produits commerçables. 2 v. 1953. C5569
8 Hamaide, R. Code du commerçant et du chef d'entreprise. 1953. C5570
9 Bourgeois, L. Economie des entreprises privées. 1953. C5571
10 Laloire, M. Cours de vente et de publicité. 1953. C5572
11 Belgium. Laws, statutes, etc. Code abrégé de sécurité sociale en Belgium, ed. by Waleffe. 1954. C5573
12 Finit, J. and Simons, M. Cours de commerce et de technique commerciale. 1955. C5574
13 Mottoulle, M. J. Pratique de la grammaire. 1953. C5575
14 ____. Pratique du style et de la correspondance commerciale. 1956. C5576
16 Coppens, E. and Laloire, M. Compatibilités spéciales. 1956. C5577
18 Dauville, M. Initiation aux affaires. 1953. C5578
20 Laloire, M. Savoir-vivre et morale des affaires. 1956. C5579
21 Leener, G. de. Ordre, methode et organisation. 1954. C5580

COLLECTION "BIEN ECRIRE ET BIEN PARLER" (Baude)

1 Soreil, A. Entretiens sur l'art d'écrire. 1946. C5581
2 Dykmans, L. Initiation pratique au métier d'écrire. 2 v. 1947. C5582
3 Grevisse, M. Code de l'orthographe française. 1948. C5583
4 Masson, A. Pour enrichir son vocabulaire. 1949. C5584
5 Desonay, F. L'art d'écrire une lettre. 1945. C5585

6 Hanse, J. Dictionnaire des difficultés grammaticales et lexicologiques. 1949. C5586
7 Surlemont, J. La lettre commerciale. 1948. C5587
8 Desonay, F. Le rapport. 1949. C5588
9 Sion, G. La conversation française. 1948. C5589
10 Jans, A. Un arte de lire. 1950. C5590
11 Hougardy, M. La parole en public. 1951. C5591
12 Kammans, L. P. La prononciation française d'aujourd'hui. 1956. C5592
13 Brun, J. and others. L'art de composer et de rédiger. 1957. C5593
14 Brun, J. and Doppagne, A. La ponctuation et l'art d'écrire. 1956. C5594

COLLECTION CIVILISATION ET CHRISTIANISME (Delachaux)

Berdîaev, N. A. Au seuil de la nouvelle époque. 1947. C5595
____. De l'ésprit bourgeois. 1949. C5596
____. Royaume de l'ésprit et royaume de César. 1951. C5597
____. Vérité et révélation. 1954. C5598
Cullmann, O. Dieu et César. 1955. C5599
Davies, J. G. La vie quotidienne aux temps de l'église ancienne. 1956. C5600
Kierkegaard, S. A. Discour chrêtiens. 1952. C5601
Lieb, F. La Russie évolue. 1946. C5602
Porret, E. Hôtes d'un presbytère. 1953. C5603

COLLECTION CULTURE EUROPEENE (Les Belles-Lettres)

Cultures nationales. Grand-Bretagne:
1 Thompson, P. D. L'humour britannique. 1947. C5604
Echanges intraeueuropeens:
1 Schoell, F. L. Leo Ferrero et la France. 1945. C5605
2 Bronarski, A. L'Italie et la Pologne au cours dés siècles. 1945. C5606
3 ____. Chopin et l'Italie. 1947. C5607
4 Embiricos, A. Les étapes de Jean Moréas. 1948. C5608
France:
1 Michelet, J. Le peuple. 1945. C5609
Grèce:
1 Baud-Bovy, S. Poésie de la Grèce moderne. 1946. C5610
Pologne:
1 Schoell, F. L. Patrimoine. 1944. C5611
2-3 Bronarski, L. Etudes sur Chopin. 2 v. 1944-46. C5612
U. S. S. R.:
1 Dostoevskii, F. M. La Russie face à l'Occident, tr. by Chédel. 1945. C5613

COLLECTION D'ACTUALITES PEDAGOGIQUES ET PSYCHOLOGIQUES (Delachaux)

Aebli, H. Didactique psychologique. 1951. C5614
Anderson, H. Les cliniques psychologiques pour l'enfance aux Etats-Unis et l'oeuvre de William Healy. C5615
Audmars, M. and Lafendel, L. La maison des petits de l'institut J. J. Rousseau. 1956. C5616
Bally, C. La crise du français. C5617
Bang, V. L'évolution de l'écriture de l'enfant à l'adulte. 1959. C5618
Baudouin, C. L'âme enfantine et la psychanalyse. 2 v. 1954. 1951. C5619
____. Suggestion et auto suggestion. 1951. C5620
____. Tolstoï educateur, tr. by Biroukof. 1921. C5621
Beizmann, C. Le Rorschach chez l'enfant de 3 à 10 ans. 1961. C5622
____. Le Rorschach de l'enfant à l'adulte. 1974. C5623
Beth, E. W. and others. L'enseignement des mathématiques. 1955. C5624
Biedma, C. J. and d'Alfonso, P. G. Le langage du dessin. 1954. C5625

Björksten, E. Exercises jeux pour petits et grands, tr. by Jentzer. 1949. C5626
____. Gymnastique fêminine, tr. by Jentzer. C5627
Boehm, L. Les tendances nouvelles de l'éducation prêscolaire aux Etats-Unis. 1952. C5628
Boehme, M. La deterioration dans la demence senile. 1974. C5629
Borel-Maissony, S. Langage oral et écrit. 2 v. 1959-60. C5630
Boschetti, A. M. L'école sereine. 1951. C5631
Boven, W. La science du caractère. 1931. C5632
Bovet, P. Les examens de recrues dans l'armée suisse. 1935. C5633
____. La gènie de Baden-Powell. C5634
____. L'instinct combatif. 1961. C5635
____. Le sentiment religieux et la psychologie de l'enfant. 1951. C5636
____. Vignt ans de vie a l'Institut J. J. Rousseau. 1932. C5637
Burstin, J. L'évolution psychosociale de l'enfant de 10 à 13 ans. 1959. C5638
Bussmann, E. Le transfert dans l'intelligence pratique chez l'enfant. 1946. C5639
Claparède, E. L'école sur mesure. 1953. C5640
____. L'éducation fonctionnelle. 1958. C5641
____. Psychologie de l'enfant et pédagogie expérimentale. 2 v. 1951-52. C5642
Cohen, J. Psychologie du risque et de jeu. 1956. C5643
____. Risque et jeu. 1957. C5644
Cousinet, R. L'education nouvelle. 1951. C5645
Decroly, O. and Hamaïde, A. Le calcul et le mesure au premier degré de l'école Decroly. C5646
Decroly, O. and Monchamp, M. L'initiation à l'activité intellectuelle et motrice par les jeux éducatifs. 1933. C5647
Descoeudres, A. Le développement de l'enfant de à Sept. ans. 1957. C5648
____. L'éducation des enfants arriérés. 1948. C5649
____. L'éducation des enfants anormaux. 1922. C5650
Dewey, J. L'école et l'enfant. 1961. C5651
Diel, P. Principes de l'education et de la reeducation. 1961. C5652
Dottrens, R. L'amelioration des programmes scolaire. 1957. C5653
____. Education et démocratie. 1946. C5654
____. L'éducation nouvelle en Autriche. 1927. C5655
____. L'enseignement de l'écriture. 1936. C5655a
____. L'enseignement individualisé. 1953. C5656
____. Nos enfants et nons. 1954. C5657
____. Nos enfants à l'école. 1954. C5658
____. Le problème de l'inspection et l'éducation nouvelle. 1931. C5659
____. Le progrès à l'école. 1936. C5660
Dottrens, R. and Marcairaz, E. L'apprentissage de la lecture par la méthode globale. 1951. C5661
Douriez-Pinol, M. La construction de l'Espace. 1974. C5662
Dubal, G. Moi et les autres. 1960. C5663
Dubosson, J. Exercices perceptifs et sensori-moteurs. 1957. C5664
____. Exercices sinsoriels. 1956. C5665
____. Le fichier ortholexique. 1962. C5666
____. Propos pedagogiques images. 1960. C5667
____. Le problème de l'orientation scolaire. 1957. C5668
Elslander, J. F. L'enfant libérée. 1948. C5669
Les enfants nerveux, by Béno and others. 1946. C5670
L'espirit international et l'enseignement de l'histoire. 1922. C5671
Erikson, E. H. Enfance et société. 1959. C5672
Eysenck, G. Us et abus de le

psychologie. 1956. C5673
Ferrière, A. L'Amérique latine adopte l'école active. 1931. C5674
____. L'autonomie des écoliers dans les communautes d'enfants. 1950. C5675
____. L'école active. 1947. C5676
____. Nos enfants et l'avenir du pays. 1942. C5677
Fischer, H. Méthodes statistiques en psychologie et en pedagogie. 1955. C5678
Foerster, F. W. L'école et le caractère. 1945. C5679
Freinet, C. Les dits de Mathieu. 1959. C5680
____. L'education du travail. 1960. C5681
Gattegno, C. Introduction à la psychologie de l'affectivité et à l'éducation à l'amour. 1952. C5682
Gobineau, H. de. Génétique de l'écriture et étude de la personalité. 1954. C5683
Godin, P. Manuel d'anthropologie pédagogique. 1919. C5684
Guisenaire, G. and Gattegno, C. Les nombres en couleur. 1955. C5685
Gunning, J. W. L. Jan Ligthart. 1923. C5686
Guyot, M. Tableau graphologique des differens types d'écritures et des tendances caeacterielles qu'ils revelent. 1954. C5687
Haesler, W. Les enfants de la Grand-Route. 1955. C5688
Hamaide, A. La méthode Decroly. 1956. C5689
Huguenin, E. La coéducation des sexes. 1929. C5690
____. Les tribuneau pour enfants. 1935. C5691
Hygiène mentale des enfants et adolescents. 1943. C5692
Inhelder, B. Le diagnostic du raisonnement chez les débiles mentaux. 1962. C5693
Isaacs, S. Les premieres annessade l'enfant. 1955. C5694
Jacobi, J. Complexe, archétype, symbole. 1961. C5695
____. La psychologie de C-G. Jung. 1950. C5696
Jentzer, K. Jeux de plein air et d'intérieur. 1959. C5697
Johannot, L. Le raisonnement mathématique de l'adolescent. 1947. C5698
Jouhy, E. and Shentoub, V. L'évolution de la mentalité de l'enfant pendant la guerre. 1949. C5699
Kacyznska, M. Succès scolaire et intelligence. C5700
Kevorkian, B. L'Emile de Rousseau et l'Emile des écoles normales. 1948. C5701
Klages, L. Expression du caractère dans l'écriture. 1953. C5702
____. Les principes de la caractérologie. 1949. C5703
Kostyleff, N. La réflexologie et les essais d'une psychologie structurale. 1947. C5704
Kramer, C. La frustration. 1959. C5705
Krishnamurti, J. De l'éducation. 1959. C5706
LeGrand, L. Pour une pédagogie de l'étonnement. 1960. C5707
____. La psychologie appliquée à l'éducation intellectuelle. 1961. C5708
Lombardo-Radice, G. Les petits Fabre de Portomaggiore. 1929. C5709
Loosli-Usteri, M. Les enfants difficiles et leur milieu familial. 1935. C5710
Lustenberger, W. Le travail scolaire par groupes. 1953. C5711
Margot, M. L'école opérante. 1960. C5712
Meylan, L. Les humanités et la personne. 1939. C5713
Muller, J. L'enfant psychotique et son adaptation familiale et sociale. 1974. C5714
Muller, L. Recherches sur la compréhension des nombres algebriques. 1956. C5715
____. Recherches sur la compréhension des régles algébriques chez l'enfant. 1954. C5716
Muresanu, C. L'éducation de l'adolescent par la composition libre. 1930. C5717
Nielson, R. F. Le développement de la sociabilité chez

l'enfant. 1951. C5718
Odier, C. L'angoisse et la pensée, magique. 2 v. 1948-49. C5719
____. L'homme esclave de son infériorité. V. 1. 1950. C5720
____. Le rôle des fonctions du noi dans l'evolution psychique. 1950-54. C5721
Ostrovsky, E. L'influence masculine et l'enfant d'âge préscolaire. 1959. C5722
Petre-Lazar, C. L'anthropométrie et les exercices scholaires. 1931. C5723
Piaget, J. La construction du réel chez l'enfant. 1950. C5724
____. La formation du symbole chez l'enfant. 1959. C5725
____. Le jugement et le raisonnement chez l'enfant. 1956. C5726
____. Le langage et la pensée chez l'enfant. 1956. C5727
____. La naissance de l'intelligence chez l'enfant. 1959. C5728
Piaget, J. and Inhelder, B. Le développement des quantités chez l'enfant. 1941. C5729
____. La genese des structures logiques elementaires. 1959. C5730
Piaget, J. and Szeminska, A. La genèse du nombre chez l'enfant. 1950. C5731
Rambert, M. La vie affective et morale de l'enfant. 1949. C5732
Regard, N. Dans une petite école. 1922. C5733
Rey, A. Arriération mentale et premiers exercises éducatifs. 1953. C5734
____. Etude des insuffisances psychologiques. 2 v. 1961. C5735
____. Monographies de psychologie clinique. 1952. C5736
Reymond-Rivier, R. Choix sociométriques et motivations. 1961. C5737
Rochedieu, E. La personnalité et la vie religieuse chez l'adolescent. 1961. C5738
Roller, S. La conjugaison française. 1954. C5739
Roy, F. van. L'enfant infirme, son handicap, son drame, sa guerison. 1954. C5740
Schmid, J. R. Le maître-camarade et la pédagogie libertaire. 1936. C5741
Segers, J. E. La psychologie de l'enfant normal et anormal d'après le O. Decroly. 1948. C5742
Stauffer, E. La méthode relationnelle en psychologie et sociologie selon Léopold von Wiese. 1950. C5743
Stern, E. Le test d'aperception thématique de Murray. 1950. C5744
Tramer, M. Problèmes et détresses d'écoliers. 1953. C5745
Tschumi, R. Theorie de la culture. 1974. C5746
Volpicelli, L. L'école sovietique. 1954. C5747
____. L'évolution de la pedagogie sovietique. 1954. C5748
Walter, W. G. Le cerveau vivant. 1954. C5749
Walther, L. Orientation professionele et carrière libérales. 1936. C5750
Wittwer, J. Les fonctions grammaticales chez l'enfant. 1959. C5751
Zazzo, R. Manuel pour l'examen psychologique de l'enfant. 1959. C5752

COLLECTION DE BIBLIOGRAPHIE CLASSIQUE (Les Belles Lettres)

L'Année philologique. V. 1. 1928- C5753
Collinet, P. Bibliographie des travaux de droit romain en langue française. 1930. C5754
Cousin, J. Bibliographie de la langue latine, 1880-1948. 1951. C5755
Herescu, N. I. Bibliographie de la littérature latine. 1943. C5756
Lamborino, S. Bibliographie de l'antiquité classique, 1896-1914. 2 v. 1951-53. C5757
Marouzeau, J. Dix années de bibliographie classique, bibliographie critiques, et analytique de l'antiquité grécolatine pour la periode, 1914-1924. 2 v.. 1927-28. C5758

COLLECTION D'ETUDES ECONOMIQUES (Librarie genérale de droit et de jurisprudence)

1 Baudin, L. La réforme du crédit. 1938. C5759
2 Leduc, G. La raison contre l'autarcie. 1938. C5760
3 Perroux, F. Syndicalisme et capitalisme. 1938. C5761
4 Vigreux, P-B. De la monnaie à l'economie en France (1933-38). 1938. C5762
5 Aglion, R. Le contrôle des changes. 1939. C5763
6 Fargeaud, P. Le problème de l'embauchage et du licenciement de la main-d'óeuvre. 1939. C5764
7 Piatier, A. L'économie de guerre. 1939. C5765
8 Baudin, L. Le mécanisme des prix. 1939. C5766
9 Rosier, C. La fiscalité française devant l'opinion publique. 1939. C5767
10 Baudin, L. Le corporatisme. 1942. C5768
11 ____. L'économie dirigée à la lumière de l'expérience americaine. 1941. C5769
12 Jolly, P. Le clearing n'est pas mort. 1944. C5770
13 Mallet, R. Le retour à la terre. 1942. C5771
14 Saint-Germes, J. Bourse et banque, nouvelle réglementation du marche financier. 1942. C5772
15 Goblet, Y. M. La formation des régions. 1942. C5773
16 Baudin, P. and L. La consommation dirigée en France en matiére d'alimentation. 1942. C5774
17 Lhomme, J. Capitalisme et économie dirigée dans la France contemporaine. 1943. C5775
18 Marchal, A. L'action ouvrière et la transformation du régime capitaliste. 1943. C5776
19 Lescure, J. Guerre et crises économiques face au chômage. 1944. C5777
20 Gonnard, R. Le propriété dans la doctrine et dans l'histoire. 1943. C5778
21 Lescure, J. Guerre et crises économiques face au chômage. 1944. C5779
22 Valarché, J. L'universalisme. 1945. C5780
23 Guillorit, R. La réglementation des bourses de valeurs en France depuis juin, 1940. 1946. C5781
24 James, E. Les comités d'enterprises. 1945. C5782
25 Lescoiffier, F. L'économie de grand espace. 1946. C5783
26 Déroulede, R. La nouveau statut du fermage et du métayage. 1947. C5784
27 Doucy, A. La sécurité sociale en Belgique. 1947. C5785
28 Reynaud, P. G. Economie politique et psychologie expérimentale. 1946. C5786
29 Dubergé, J. La controle des prix en France. 1947. C5787
30 Rouge, M. F. La géonomie. 1947. C5788
31 Allix, E. Etudes choises d'économie politique et de finance. 1948. C5789
32 Wolff, S. Les Etats-Unis; première puissance économique mondiale. 1950. C5790
33 Mérigot, J. G. and Coulbois, P. Le franc, 1938-1950. 1950. C5791
34 Pasquier, A. Les doctrines sociales en France. 1950. C5792
35 Rouge, M. F. Introduction à un urbanisme expérimental. 1951. C5793
36 Vigreux, P. B. Les droits des actionnaires dans les sociétés anonymes. 1953. C5794
37 Les Transports en France et dans le monde, et le tourisme internationale, by Tissier and others. 1954. C5795
38 Visine, L'économie française face au Marché commun. 1959. C5796
39 Massot, J. Les banques et l'investissement en allemagne accidentale. 1960. C5797
40 Pasquier, A. L'economie du Portugal. 1961. C5798

COLLECTION D'ETUDES LATINES (Les Belles Lettres)

Serie scientifique:
1 Marouzeau, J. La linguistique et l'enseignement du Latin. 1924. C5799
2 Groot, A. W. de. La prose mêtrique des anciens. 1926. C5800
3 Faider, P. Rêpertoire des index et lexiques d'auteurs latins. 1926. C5801
4 Guillemin, A. M. Pline et la vie littêraire de son temps. 1929. C5802
5 Nicolau, M. G. L'origine du cursus rythmique et les dêbuts de l'accent d'intensitê en latin. 1930. C5803
6 Fretê, A. Essai sur la structure dramatique des comedies de Plaute. 1930. C5804
7 Guillemin, A. N. L'originalite de Virgile. 1931. C5805
8 Faider, P. Rêpertoire des êditions de scolies et commentaires d'auteurs latins. 1931. C5806
9 Perrochat, P. Recherches sur la valeur et l'emploi de l'infintif subordonnê latin. 1932. C5807
10 ____. L'utilisation artistique d'une formed expression esquissee. 1932. C5808
11 Gagê, J. Recherches sur les Jeux sêculaires. 1934. C5809
12 Marouzeau, J. Traitê de stylistique appliquêe au latin. 1935. C5810
13 Guillemin, A. M. Le public et la vie littêraire à Rome. 1938. C5811
14 Marouzeau, J. L'ordre des mots dans la phrase latine. 2 v. 1922-38. C5812
15 Perrochat, P. Pêtrone, le festin de Trimalcion. 1939. C5813
16 Cordier, A. Etudes sur le vocabulaire êpique dans l' "Enêide." 1939. C5814
17 Finaert, J. L'êvolution litteraire de saint Augustin. 1939. C5815
18 ____. Saint Augustine rhêteur. 1939. C5816
19 Andrieu, J. Etude critique sur les sigles de personnages et les rubiques de scène dans les anciennes êditions de Têrence. 1941. C5817
20 Loyen, A. Sidoine Apollinaire et l'esprit prêcieux en Gaule, aux derniers jours de l'empire. 1943. C5818
21 LeBonniec, H. Bibliographie de l'histoire naturelle de Pline l'ancien. 1946. C5819
22 Magdelain, A. Auctoritas principis. 1947. C5820
23 Perrochat, P. Les modèles grecs de Salluste. 1949. C5821
24 Same as no. 14. V. 3. 1950. C5822
25 Perret, J. Recherches sur le texte de la "Germanie." 1951. C5823
26 Chouet, M. Les lettres de Salluste à Cesar. 1952. C5824
27 Stern, H. Date et destinataire de l'histoire Auguste. 1953. C5825
28 Rambaud, M. Cicêron et l'histoire romaine. 1953. C5826
29 Andrieu, J. Le dialogue antique. 1954. C5827
30 Nougaret, L. Analyse verbale comparêe du De Signis et des Bucoliques. 1966. C5828

Serie pedagogique:
1 Marouzeau, J. Le pronunciation du latin. 1943. C5829
2 ____. Le traduction du latin. 1943. C5830
3 Damas, P. La pronunciation française du latin depuis le XVIe siècle. 1934. C5831
4 Marouzeau, J. Introduction au latin. 1941. C5832
5 Cousin, J. Evolution et structure de la langue latine. 1944. C5833
6 Marouzeau, J. L'ordre des mots en latin. 1949. C5834
7 ____. Du Latin au français. 1957. C5835

COLLECTION DE LOGIQUE MATHEMATIQUE (Univ. of Louvain Pr.)

1 Beth, E. W. Les fondements logiques des mathêmatiques. 1955. C5836
2 Curry, H. B. Leçons de

logique algêbrique. 1952. C5837
3 Frêchet, M. Pages choisies d'analyse gênêrale. 1953. C5838
4 Wang, H. and MacNaughton, R. Les systèmes axiomatiques de la thêorie des ensembles. 1953. C5839
5 Paris. Univ. Centre d'études de logique symbolique. Applications scientifiques de logique mathêmatique. 1954. C5840
6 Dequoy, N. Axiomatique intuitionniste sans nêgation de la gêomêtrie projective. 1955. C5841
7 Rosser, J. B. Deux equisses de logique. 1956. C5842
8 Robinson, A. Thêorie mêtamathêmatique des idêaux. 1955. C5843
9 Heyting, A. Les fondements des mathêmatiques. 1956. C5844
10 Beth, E. W. L'existence en mathêmatique. 1956. C5845
11 Henkin, L. La structure algêbrique des thêories mathêmatiques. 1956. C5846
12 Beth, M. E. W. La crise de la raison el la logique. 1957. C5847
13 Dubarle, R. P. Initiation à la logique. 1957. C5848
14 Freudenthal, H. Logique mathêmatique appliquêe. 1958. C5849
15 Gazalê, M. J. Les structure de commutation àm valeurs et les calculatrices numeriques. 1959. C5850
16 Tarski, A. Introduction à la logique. 1960. C5851
17 Grzegorczyk, A. Fonctions rêcursives. 1961. C5852
18 Porte, J. Recherches sur la theorie gênêrale des systèmes formels et sur les systèmes connectifs. 1965. C5853
19 Colloquium on the Foundations of Mathematics. Colloque sur les fondements des mathêmatiques et machines mathêmatiques, et leurs applications, ed. by Kolmár. 1965. C5854
20 Mooij, J. J. A. La philosophie de mathêmatiques de Henri Poincarê. 1966. C5855
21 Diego, A. Sur les algèbres de Hilbert. 1966. C5856
22 Dekker, J. C. Les factions combinatoires et les Isols. 1966. C5857
23-24 Fraïssê, R. Cours de logique mathêmatique. 2 v. 1969-71. C5858
Serie B:
1 Gillis, P. P. and others. Thêorie des probabilitês. 1952. C5859
2 Ladrière, J. Les limitations internes des formalismes. 1957. C5860
3 Dopp, J. Logiques construites par une mêthode de deduction naturelle. 1962. C5861
4 Feys, R. Modal logics, ed. by Dopp. 1964. C5862

COLLECTION DE MONOGRAPHIES SUR LA THEORIE DES FONCTIONS (Gauthier-Villars)

Baire, R. Leçons sur les fonctions discontinues. 1930. C5863
Bernstein, H. Leçons sur les progrès rêcents de la thêorie des series de Dirichlet. 1933. C5864
____. Leçons sur les propriêtês extrêmales et la meilleure approximation des fonctions analytiques d'une variable rêelle. 1926. C5865
Blumenthal, O. Principes de la thêorie des fonctions entières d'ordre infini. 1910. C5866
Bôcher, M. Leçons sur les mêthodes de Sturm dans la thêorie des êquations diffêrentielles linêaires et leurs dêveloppements modernes. 1917. C5867
Bonnesen, T. Les problèmes des isopêrimètres et des isêpiphanes. 1929. C5868
Borel, E. F. E. J. Leçons sur la thêorie de la croissance. 1910. C5869
____. Leçons sur la thêorie des fonctions. 1950. C5870
____. Leçons sur les fonctions de variables rêelles et les developpements en sêries de polynomes. 1928. C5871
____. Leçons sur les fonctions

entières. 1900. C5872
____. Leçons sur les fonctions méromorphes. 1917. C5873
____. Leçons sur les fonctions monogènes uniformes d'une variable complexe. 1917. C5874
____. Leçons sur les séries à termes postifs... 1902. C5875
____. Leçons sur les séries divergentes. 1928. C5876
____. Méthodes et problèmes de la théorie des fonctions. 1922. C5877
____. Les nombres inaccessibles. 1951. C5878
Boutroux, P. Leçons sur les fonctions définies par les équations différentielles de premier ordre. 1908. C5879
Carleman, T. Les fonctions quasi analytiques. 1926. C5880
Denjoy, A. Leçons sur le calcul des coefficients d'une série trigonométrique. 4 v. 1941-49. C5881
Dienes, P. Leçons sur les singularités des fonctions analytiques. 1913. C5882
Fréchet, M. Les espaces abstraits et leur théorie considérée comme introduction à l'analyse génerale. 1928. C5883
Giraud, G. Leçons sur les fonctions automorphes. 1910. C5884
Gunther, N. M. La théorie du potentiel et ses applications aux problèmes fondamentaux de la physique mathématique. 1934. C5885
Julia, G. Leçons sur les fonctions uniformes à point singulier essentiel isolé. 1923. C5886
La Vallée Poussin, C. L. de. Intégrales de Lebesgue, fonctions d'ensemble. 1950. C5887
____. Leçons sur l'approximation des fonctions d'une variable réelle. 1952. C5888
Lebesgue, H. L. Leçons sur l'intégration et la recherche des fonctions primitives. 1950. C5889
Lefschetz, S. L'analysis situs et la géométrie algébrique. 1950. C5890
Lévy, P. Leçons d'analyse fonctionnelle professée au College de France. 1922. C5891
____. Problèmes concrets d'analyse fonctionnelle. 1951. C5892
Lindelöf, E. L. Le calcul des résidus et ses applications à la théorie des fonctions. 1952. C5893
Luzin, N. N. Leçons sur les ensembles analytiques et leurs applications. 1930. C5894
Mandelbrojt, S. Séries adhérentes; regularisation des suites applications. 1952. C5895
____. Séries de Fourier et classes quasi-analytiques de fonctions. 1935. C5896
Michel, A. D. Le calcul différential dans les espaces de Banach. 1958- C5897
Montel, P. Leçons sur les familes normales de fonctions analytiques et leurs applications. 1952. C5898
____. Leçons sur les fonctions univalentes ou multivalentes. 1933. C5899
____. Leçons sur les récurrences et leurs applications, ed. by Dufresnoy and Lefebvre. 1957. C5900
____. Leçons sur les séries de polynomes à une variable complexe. 1910. C5901
Nevanlinna, R. H. Le théorème de Picard-Borel et la theorie des fonctions méromorphes. 1929. C5902
Nörlund, N. E. Leçons sur les séries d'interpolation. 1926. C5903
____. Leçons sur les équations linéaires aux différences finies. 1929. C5904
Riesz, F. Les systèmes d'equations linéaires à une infinite d'inconnues. 1952. C5905
Sierpinski, W. Leçons sur les nombres transfinis. 1950. C5906
Stoïlow, S. Leçons sur les principes topologiques de la théorie des fonctions analytiques. 1956. C5907
Volterra, V. and Peres, J. Théorie générale des fonctionelles. 1936. C5908
Volterra, V. Leçons sur la

composition et les fonctions permutables. 1924. C5909
____. Leçons sur les équations intégrales et les équations intégro-différentielles. 1952. C5910
____. Leçons sur les fonctions de lignes. 1952. C5911
____. Théorie générale des fonctionnelles. V. 1. 1936. C5912
Volterra, V. and Hostinsky, B. Opérations infinitésimales linéaires. 1938. C5913
Whittaker, J. M. Sur les séries de bases de polynomes quelconques. 1949. C5914
Zoretti, L. Leçons sur le prolongement analytique. 1911. C5915

COLLECTION DE PHILOLOGIE CLASSIQUE (Klincksieck)

1 Chantraine, P. Grammaire homérique, phonetique et morphologie. 1942. C5916
2 Humbert, J. Syntaxe grecque. 1960. C5917
3 Lejeune, M. Traité de phonétique grecque. 1946. C5918
4 Chantraine, P. Grammaire homérique, syntaxe. 1946. C5919

COLLECTION DU CENTENAIRE DE LA REVOLUTION DE 1848 (Presses Universitaires de France)

Angrand, P. Etienne Cabet et la République de 1848. 1948. C5920
Armand Felix. Les fouriéristes et les luttes révolutionnaires de 1848 à 1851. 1948. C5921
Bastid, P. L'avènement du suffrage universel. 1948. C5922
Bruhat, J. Les journées de février. 1948. C5923
Carnot, P. Hippolyte Carnot et le Ministère de l'instruction publique de la IIe Republique (24 février-5 juillet 1848). 1948. C5924
Cassou, J. La quarante-huitard. 1948. C5925
Chaunu, P. Eugène Sue et la seconde République. 1948. C5926
Cornu, A. Karl Marx et la Révolution de 1848. 1948. C5927
Cuvillier, A. P.-J.-B. Buchez et les origines du socialisme chrétien. 1948. C5928
Dolléans, E. Proudhon et la Révolution de 1848. 1948. C5929
Duveau, G. Raspail. 1948. C5930
Godart, J. A Lyon, en 1848. 1948. C5931
Guillemin, H. Lamartine en 1848. 1948. C5932
Martin, G. L'abolition de l'esclavage (27 avril 1848). 1948. C5933
Molinier, S. Blanqui. 1948. C5934
Monnerville, G. Commération du centenaire de l'abolition de l'esclavage. 1948. C5935
Pommier, J. J. M. Les écrivains devant la Révolution de 1848. 1948. C5936
Rémond, R. Lammennais et la démocratie. 1948. C5937
Schmidt, C. Des Alteliers nationaux aux barricades de juin. 1948. C5938
Schnerb, R. Ledru-Rollin. 1948. C5939
Tersen, E. Le gouvernement provisoire et l'Europe (25 février-12 mai 1848). 1948. C5940
Thomas, E. Les femmes de 1848. 1948. C5941
Vidalenc, J. Louis Blanc (1811-1882). 1948. C5942

COLLECTION HISTORIQUE (Aubier unless otherwise specified)

Aulneau, J. Les grandes dames du Palais-Royal (1635-1870). Denoël. 1943. C5943
Batiffol, L. La vie intime d'une reine de France au XVIIe siècle-Marie de Medicis. Calmann-Levy. 1931. C5944
Baumgardt, R. Magellan. Denoël. 1943. C5945
Berard, J. L'expansion grecque et la colonisation. 1959. C5946
Bourde, G. Urbanisation et immigration en Amerique latine, Buenos Aires. 1972. C5947
Boutruche, R. Seigneurie et

feodalité. 2 v. 1958-70. C5948
Butel, P. Les negociants bordelais. 1973. C5949
Demougeot, E. La formation de l'Europe et les invasions barbares. 1969. C5950
Dollinger, P. La Hanse, XIIe-XVIIe siècles. 1964. C5951
Duby, G. L'économie rurale et la vie des campagnes dans l'occident médiéval. 1962. C5952
Ferro, M. La Revolution de 1917. V. 1. 1967. C5953
Folz, R. L'idée imperiale et les empires dans l'Occident médiéval. 1943. C5954
Franck, L. R. Historie économique et sociale des Etats-Unis de 1919 à 1949. 1950. C5955
Grimal, P. Le siècle des Scipions. 1952. C5956
LaFuye, M. de. Louis XVI. Denoël, 1943. C5957
Lanctôt, G. Montréal sous Maisonneuve, 1642-1665. 1966. C5958
Lasteyrie du Saillant, R. C. Etude sur les comtes et vicomtes de Limoges antérieurs à l'an 1000. Franck. 1874. C5959
Levrons, J. Louis le bien-aimé. 1965. C5960
Lopez, R. L. La révolution commerciale dans l'Europe médiévale. 1973. C5961
Mommsen, T. Etude sur Pline le Jeune. Franck. 1873. C5962
Pacaut, M. La théocratie l'Eglise et le pouvoir au moyen âge. 1957. C5963
Pellegrin, A. Histoire de la Tunisie depuis les origines jusqu'à nos jours. Peyronnet, 1938. C5964
Rémond, R. La droite en France de 1815 à nos jours. 1954. C5965
____. La droite en France de la Iere restauration Mai 1968. 1968. C5966
Robiou de La Tréhonnais, F. M. L. J. Itinéraire des dix-mille. Franck, 1873. C5967
____. Questions homériques. Viewag, 1876. C5968
Roux, J. P. La Turque. Payot. 1953. C5969
Sylvain, C. Histoire de Saint Charles Boromée. 3 v. Société de Saint Augustin. 1884. C5970
Tracou, J. Le maréchal aux liens. Bonne. 1948. C5971
Vermeil, E. L'Allemagne contemporaine, sociale, politique et culturelle, 1890-1950. 2 v. 1953. C5972

COLLECTION L'ACTUALITE PROTESTANTE (Delachaux)

Barth, K. Les allemands et nous. 1945. C5973
____. Les communautés chrétiennes dans la tourmente. 1943. C5974
____. Connaître Dieu et le servir. 1945. C5975
____. Guérison des allemands? 1945. C5976
____. La proclamation de l'evangile. 1961. C5977
Bonhoeffer, D. De la vie communautaire, tr. by Ryser. 1955. C5978
____. Le prix de la grâce. 1962. C5979
Breuil, R. La puissance d'Elie. 1945. C5980
Brémond, A. Edifier l'Eglise. 1945. C5981
Brendel, T. Abolition du christianisme? 1943. C5982
Brunner, E. and others. L'ordre de Dieu. 1946. C5983
Hoffmann, J. G. H. La réforme en Suède. 1532-1572. 1945. C5984
Leenhardt, H. Le mariage chrétien. 1946. C5985
Lewis, C. S. Être ou ne pas être. 1948. C5986
____. Le grand divorce. 1947. C5987
____. Tactique du Diable. 1947. C5988
Mauris, E. and others. L'Eglise parmi nous. 1947. C5989
Niemoeller, M. De la culpabilité allemande. 1946. C5990
Nusslé, H. Dialogue l'islam. 1949. C5991
____. Impressions du Proche-Orient. 1949. C5992

Pury, R. de. Présence de l'éternité. 1946. C5993
Ragaz, L. Le message révolutionnaire. 1945. C5994
Roullet, Y. Lettres, ed. by Maury. 1947. C5995

COLLECTION L'ACTUALITE PROTESTANTE; SERIE BIBLIQUE (Delachaux)

Aeschimann, A. Le prophete Jemerie. 1959. C5996
Balscheit, B. L'alliance de grâce. 1947. C5997
Debard, L. La Bible au foyer. 1956. C5998
Deluz, G. La sagesse de Dieu. 1959. C5999
Diëtrich, S. de. Le dessein de Dieu. 1951. C6000
____. L'heure de l'offrande. 1952. C6001
____. Le renouveau biblique. 1949. C6002
Gollwitzer, H. La joie de Dieu. 1957. C6003
Hoskyns, E. and Davey, F. N. L'enigme du Nouveau Testament. 1949. C6004
Hunter, M. Un Seigneur, une Eglise un Salut. 1950. C6005
Martin-Achard, R. Approche de l'Ancien Testament. 1962. C6006
Pidoux, G. Entre le portique et l'autel. 1959. C6007
Thurneysen, E. La foi et les oeuvres. 1959. C6008
Vischer, W. L'Ancien Testament. 2 v. 1949-51. C6009

COLLECTION "LA PRATIQUE DU BIEN ECRIRE" (Baude)

1 Desonay, F. Exercises pratiques sur l'art d'écrire une lettre. 1946. C6010
2 Verdeyen, P. Code de la secrétaire-sténodactylographe et du correspondant. 1948. C6011
2 ____. 2 v. 1951-54. C6012

COLLECTION PAIDEÏA (Presses Universitaires de France)

Amado, G. Les enfants difficiles. 1955. C6013
Beley, A. P. L. L'enfant instable. 1959. C6014
Berge, A. L'éducation sexuelle chez l'enfant. 1952. C6015
Bergeron, M. Psychologie du premier âge. 1951. C6016
Chassagny, C. L'apprentissage de la lecture chez l'enfant. 1954. C6017
Crêmieux, A. Les difficultés alimentaires de l'enfant. 1954. C6018
Dauphin, A. Hygiène prênatale. 1952. C6019
Debré, R. and Doumic, A. Le sommeil de l'enfant avant trois ans. 1959. C6020
Durand, G. L'adolescent et les sports. 1958. C6021
Fau, R. Les groupes d'enfants et d'adolescents. 1952. C6022
Heuyer, G. Introduction à la psychiatrie infantile. 1952. C6023
Isambert, A. L'éducation des parents. 1960. C6024
Joubrel, H. Le scoutisme dans l'éducation et la reéducation des jeunes. 1951. C6025
Kohler, C. Les déficiences intellectuelles chez l'enfant. 1954. C6026
Koupernik, C. and Soulé, M. Développement psycho-moteur du premier âge. 1954. C6027
Lang, J. L. L'enfance inadaptée. 1962. C6028
Launay, C. L'hygiène mentale de l'écolier. 1959. C6029
Lebovici, S. Les tics chez l'enfant. 1951. C6030
Lemay, M. Les groupes de jeunes inadaptés. 1961. C6031
Le Moal, P. L'enfant excité et déprimé. 1953. C6032
Medici, A. L'ecole et l'enfant. 1955. C6033
Michaux, L. L'enfant pervers. 1952. C6034
Néron, G. L'enfant vagabond. 1952. C6035
Porot, M. L'enfant et les relations familiales. 1959. C6036
Robin, G. Les difficultés scolaires chez l'enfant et leur traitement. 1953. C6037
Rouart, J. Psychopathologie de la puberté et de l'adolescence.

1954. C6038
Rousselet, J. L'adolescent en apprentissage. 1961. C6039
Sutter, J. M. Le mensonge chez l'enfant. 1956. C6040
Widlöcher, D. Le psychodrame chez l'enfant. 1962. C6041

COLLEZIONE DI FILOSOFIA (Taylor)

1 Abbagnano, N. Introduzione all'esistenzialismo. 1947. C6042
2 ____. Filosifia, religione scienza. 1947. C6043
3 Chiodi, P. L'esistenzialismo di Heidegger. 1955. C6044
4 Abbagnano, N. Esistenzialismo positivo. 1948. C6045
5 Vedaldi, A. Essere gli altri. 1948. C6046
6 Scarpelli, U. Esistenzialismo e marxismo. 1960. C6047
7 Paci, E. Il nulla e il problema dell'uomo. 1950. C6048
8 Pareyson, L. Esistenza e persona. 1960. C6049
9 Vedaldi, A. Struttura della proprieta. 1951. C6050
10 Chiodi, P. L'ultimo Heidegger. 1960. C6051
11 Romanell, P. Verso un naturalismo critico. 1953. C6052
12 Paci, E. Tempo e relazione. 1954. C6053
13 Cairola, G. Scritti. 1954. C6054
14 Pedroli, G. La fenomenologia di Husserl. 1958. C6055
15 Invrea, D. Il saggetto esistence. 1960. C6056
16 Vedaldi, A. Dire il tempo. 1960. C6057

COLONIAL HISTORY SERIES (Dawson)

Assn. for Promoting the Discovery of the Interior Parts of Africa. Proceedings. 2 v. 1967. C6058
Austin, H. H. With Macdonald in Uganda. 1904. 1973. C6059
Bannister, S. Humane policy. 1968. C6060
Barnard, R. N. Three years in the Mozambique channel, 1848. 1969. C6061
Beaver, P. African memoranda. 1968. C6062
Beecham, J. Ashantee and the Gold Coast, ed. by Metcalfe. 1968. C6063
Beeckman, D. Voyage to and from the Island of Borneo in the East Indies. 1973. C6064
Beer, G. L. African questions at the Paris Peace Conference, ed. by Gray. 1968. C6065
Belcher, E. R. N. Narrative of a voyage round the world, performed in H. M. S. Sulphur. 2 v. 1970. C6066
____. Narrative of the voyage of H. M. S. Samarang. 2 v. 1970. C6067
Bell, S. S. Colonial administration of Great Britain. 1968. C6068
Bridge, H. Journal of an African crusier, ed. by Hawthorne. 1968. C6069
Buxton, T. F. The African slave trade and its remedy, ed. by Metcalfe. 1968. C6070
Campbell, J. A concise history of the Spanish American war. 1972. C6071
Churchward, W. B. My consolate in Samoa. 1971. C6072
Colomb, P. H. Slave catching in the Indian Ocean. 1968. C6073
Crowther, S. A. and Taylor, J. C. The gospel on the banks of the Niger. 1968. C6074
Cugoano, O. Thoughts and sentiments on the evil and wicked traffic of the slavery and commerce of the human species. 1969. C6075
Cumpston, I. M. Indians overseas in British territories. 1969. C6076
Devereux, W. C. A cruise in the Gorgon. 1968. C6077
Ellis, W. Polynesian researches. 1967. C6078
Equiano, O. Narrative of the life of Olaidah Equiano. 2 v. 1969. C6079
Erskine, J. E. Journal of a cruise among the islands of the West Pacific. 1967. C6080
Evatt, H. V. Rum rebellion.

1968. C6081
Fitzgerald, W. W. A. Travels in the coastlands of British East Africa... 1970. C6082
Foote, A. H. Africa and the American flag. 1970. C6083
Forbes, F. E. Six month's service in the African blockade. 1969. C6084
Gt. Brit. Board of Education. Special reports on educational subjects, V. 12, 13, 14. 3 v. 1968. C6085
Gt. Brit. Parliament. Substance of the debtors on a resolution for abolishing the slave trade... June 1806... 1968. C6086
____. Substance of the debate in the House of Commons on the 15th of May, 1823... 1968. C6087
Helms, L. V. Pioneering in the Far East. 1969. C6088
Higgins, H. B. A new province for law & order. 1968. C6089
Jackson, F. Early days in East Africa. 1969. C6090
Jobson, R. The golden trade. 1968. C6091
Macdonald, D. Africana. 2 v. 1969. C6092
MacDonald, J. R. L. Soldiering and surveying in British East Africa. 1973. C6093
Marais, J. S. The colonization of New Zealand. 1968. C6094
Markham, A. H. The Cruise of the Rosario. 1970. C6095
Martin, R. M. History of the colonies of the British Empire. 1967. C6096
Mendez Pinto, F. M. The voyages and adventures of Fernando Mendez. 1970. C6097
Mills, R. C. The colonisation of Australia. 1968. C6098
New, C. W. Lord Durham. 1968. C6099
Palmer, G. Kidnapping in the South Seas. 1971. C6100
Phillippo, J. M. Jamaica, past and present. 1969. C6101
Pinto, F. M. Voyages and adventures of a Portuguese. 1969. C6102
Pritchard, W. T. Polynesian reminiscences. 1968. C6103
Roebock, J. A. The colonies of England. 1968. C6104
Royal Empire Society. Subject catalogue. 4 v. 1967. C6105
Ruschenberger, W. S. W. Narrative of a voyage round the world. 2 v. 1970. C6106
Sampson, M. J. Gold dust men of affairs. 1969. C6107
Sancho, I. Letters of the late Ignatius Sancho, ed. by Jekyll. 1968. C6108
Savigny, J. B. H. and Corrêard, A. Narrative of a voyage to Senegal in 1816. 1968. C6109
Seemann, B. Viti. 1973. C6110
Stavorinus, J. S. Voyages to the East Indies. 3 v. 1969. C6111
Stevenson, R. L. A footnote to history. 1967. C6112
Stokes, A. A view of the constitution of the British Colonies in North America and the West Indies. 1969. C6113
Sturge, G. L. and Harvey, T. The West Indies in 1837. 1968. C6114
Sullivan, G. L. Dhow chasing in Zanzibar waters and on the eastern coast of Africa. 1967. C6115
Thompson, G. Palm land. 1969. C6116
Thomson, B. H. The diversions of a prime minister. 1968. C6117
____. The Fijians. 1968. C6118
Trollope, A. Australia and New Zealand. 2 v. 1968. C6119
____. North America. 2 v. 1968. C6120
____. South Africa. 2 v. 1968. C6121
____. The West Indies and the Spanish Main. 1968. C6122
Wakefield, E. J. The founders of Canterbury, 1868. 1973. C6123
Webster, W. H. B. Narrative of a voyage to the Southern Atlantic Ocean. 2 v. 1970. C6124
Welman, C. W. The native states of the Gold Coast. 1969. C6125
Wilson, T. B. Narrative of a voyage around the world. 1968. C6126

Woodard, D. The narrative of Captain Woodard. 1969. C6127

COLONIES ET EMPIRE (Presses Universitaires de France)

I. Etudes coloniales.
1 Julien, C. A., ed. Les techniciens de la colonisation. 1946. C6128
2 Mathis, C. J. B. M. J. L'oeuvres des pastoriens en Afrique noire. 1946. C6129
3 Gourou, P. Les pays tropicaux. 1948. C6130
4 Martin, G. Histoire de l'esclavage dans les colonies françaises. 1948. C6131
5 Les politiques d'expansion impérialiste, by Julien and others. 1949. C6132
6 Bonnault, C. de. Histoire du Canada français. 1950. C6133
7 Gandhi, M. K. Expériences de vérité, ou, Autobiographie. 1950. C6134
8 Halperin, V. Lord Milner et l'évolution de l'impérialisme britannique. 1950. C6135
9 Brunschwig, H. L'expansion allemande outre-mer du XVe siècle a nos jours. 1957. C6136
II. Les classiques de la colonisation.
1 Julien, C. A., ed. Les Français en Amérique pendant le première moitie du XVIe siècle. 1946. C6137
5 Champlain, S. de. Les voyages de Samuel Champlain, ed. by Deschamps. 1951. C6138
8 Raynal, F. L'anticolonialisme au XVIIIe siècle., 1951. C6139
10 Bugeaud de la Piconnerie, T. R. Par l'épée et par la charrue. 1948. C6140
11 Schoelcher, V. Esclavage et colonisation, ed. by Tersen. 1948. C6141
13 Galliéni, J. M. Galliene pacificatéur. 1949. C6142
16 Pavie, A. A la conquête des coeurs. 1947. C6143
III. Histoire de l'expansion et de la colonisation françaises.
1 Julien, C. A. Les voyages de decouverte et les premiers establissements XVe-XVIe siècles. 1948. C6144
IV. Géographie de l'union française.
1 Despois, J. L'Afrique blanche française. 2 v. 1949-53. C6145
3 Roqequain, C. Madegascar et les bis dispersees de l'Union française. 1958. C6146
V. Art et litteraire
1 Senghor, L. S., ed. Anthologie de la nouvelle poésie nègre et malgache de langue française. 1948. C6147
2 Urbain-Faublée, M. L'art malgache. 1963. C6148
VI. Peuples et civilisations d'autre mer.
1-2 Leroi-Gourhan, A. and others. Ethnologie de l'Union française. 1953. C6149
3 Le Gentil, G. Decouverte du monde. 1954. C6150
4 Toussaint, A. Histoire de l'Ocean Indien. 1961. C6151

COLSTON RESEARCH SOCIETY. BRISTOL, ENGLAND; COLSTON PAPERS

1 Colston Research Assn. Cosmic radiation. Interscience, 1949. C6152
2 Symposium on Engineering Structures. Engineering structures. 1949. C6153
3 Symposium on Principles and Methods of Colonial Administration. Principles and methods of colonial administration. 1950. C6154
4 James, D. G., ed. The universities and the theatre. Allen. 1950. C6155
5 Suprarenal cortex. Academic. 1952. C6156
6 Colston Research Society. Insecticides and colonial agricultural development. 1953. C6157
7 Symposium on Recent Developments in Cell Physiology. Proceedings of the seventh symposium of the Colston Research Society. 1954. C6158
8 Symposium on the Neurohypophysis. The neurohypophysis, ed. by Heller. 1956. C6159

9 Symposium on Observation and Interpretation. University of Bristol. Observation and Interpretation, ed. by Körner and Pryce. 1957. C6160
10 Colston Research Society. The structure and properties of porous materials, ed. by Everett and Stone. 1958. C6161
11 ____. Hypersonic flow, ed. by Collar and Tinker. 1960. C6162
12 ____. Metaphor and symbol, ed. by Knights and Cottle. 1960. C6163
13 ____. Animal health and production, ed. by Grunsell and Wright. 1962. C6164
14 ____. Music in education, ed. by Grant. 1963. C6165
15 ____. Reality and creative vision in German lyrical poetry, ed. by Closs. 1963. C6166
16 ____. Econometric analysis for national economic planning, ed. by Hart and others. 1964. C6167
17 ____. Submarine geology and geophysics, ed. by Whittard and Bradshaw. 1965. C6168
18 ____. The fungus spore, ed. by Madelin. 1966. C6169
19 ____. The liver, ed. by Read. 1968. C6170
20 Taylor, W., ed. Towards a policy for the education of teachers. 1969. C6171
21 Communication and energy in changing urban environments, ed. by Jones. 1971. C6172
22 Regional forecasting, ed. by Chisholm. 1971. C6173
23 Marine archaeology, ed. by Blackman. 1973. C6174
24 Symposium of the Colston Research Society. Bone, certain aspects of neoplasia, ed. by Price and Ross. 1974. C6175

COLUMBIA PAPYRI. GREEK SERIES (Columbia Univ. Pr.)

1 Westermann, W. L., ed. Upon slavery in Ptolemaic Egypt. 1929. C6176
2 Westermann, W. L. and Keyes, C. W., eds. Tax lists and transportation receipts from Theadelphia. 1932. C6177
3-4 Westermann, W. L. and Hasenoehrl, E. S. Zenon papyri. 2 v. 1934-40. C6178
5 Day, J. and Keyes, C. W., eds. Tax documents from Theadelphia. 1956. C6179

COLUMBIA SLAVIC STUDIES

Brown, G. W. and D. B. A guide to Soviet Russian translations of American literature. 1954. C6180
Current digest of the Soviet press. The Soviet linguistic controversy, tr. by Murra and others. 1951. C6181
Domar, R. A., ed. Six short stories. 1951. C6182
Fredro, A. The major comedies of Alexander Fredro, tr. by Segel. 1969. C6183
Gorchakov, N. A. The theatre in Soviet Russia, tr. by Lehrman. 1957. C6184
Gor'kiĭ, M. Letters of Gorky and Andrew, 1899-1912, ed. by Yershov. 1958. C6185
Gregg, R. A. Fedor Tiutchev. 1965. C6186
Harkins, W. E. Karl Căpek. 1962. C6187
____, ed. Anthology of Czech literature. 1953. C6188
____. Bibliography of Slavic folk literature. 1953. C6189
____. Bibliography of Slavic philology. 1951. C6190
____. The Russia folk epos in Czech literature, 1800-1900. 1951. C6191
Harkins, W. E. and Hnykovâ, M. A modern Czech grammar. 1953. C6192
Harkins, W. E. and Simončič, K. Czech and Slovak literature. 1950. C6193
Jakobson, R. Slavic languages. 1955. C6194
Karamzin, N. M. Letters of a Russian traveler, 1789-1790, tr. by Jonas. 1957. C6195
Kridl, M., ed. Adam Mickiewicz, 1951. C6196
____. An anthology of Polish literature. 1957. C6197
____. A survey of Polish

literature and culture, tr. by Scherer-Virski. 1956. C6198
Manning, C. A., ed. Anthology of eighteenth century Russian literature. V. 1. 1951. C6199
Menges, K. H. Introduction to Old Church Slavic. 1953. C6200
Preobrazhenskii, A. G. Etymological dictionary of the Russian language. 1951. C6201
Pushkin, A. S. Boris Godunov, tr. by Barbour. 1953. C6202
Seduro, V. Dostoevski in Russian literary criticism, 1846-1956. 1957. C6203
Shevelov, G. Y. A prehistory of Slavic. 1965. C6204
Shevelov, I. and Holling, F. A reader in the history of the eastern Slavic languages. 1958. C6205
Stender-Peterson, A. and Congrat-Butlar, S., eds. Anthology of old Russian literature. 1954. C6206
Stilman, L. Graded readings in Russian history. 1960. C6207
____. Readings in Russian history. 1950. C6208
____. Russian alphabet and phonetics. 1952. C6209
____. Russian verbs of motion. 1951. C6210
Trubetskoi, N. S. The common Slavic element in Russian culture. 1949. C6211
Turgenev, I. S. Rudin, ed. by Stilman. 1955. C6212
Wolkonsky, C. A. and Poltoratzky, M. A. Handbook of Russian roots. 1961. C6213
Zen'kovskiĭ, V. V. A history of Russian philosophy. 1953. 2 v. C6214

COLUMBIA STUDIES IN THE SOCIAL SCIENCES.
Preceded by Columbia University. Studies in History, Economics and Public Law.

597 Challener, R. D. The French theory of the nation in arms, 1866-1939. 1952. C6215
580 Cole, C. C. The social ideas of the northern evangelists, 1826-1860. 1954. C6216
581 Shaw, F. The history of New York City Legislation. 1954. C6217
582 Rawley, J. A. Edwin D. Morgan, 1811-1833; merchant in politics. 1955. C6218
583 T'an, Ch'un-lin. The Boxer catastrophe. 1955. C6219
584 Borden, M. The Federalism of James A. Bayard. 1954. C6220
585 Bellush, B. Franklin D. Roosevelt as Governor of New York. 1952. C6221
586 Fusfeld, D. R. The economic thought of Franklin D. Roosevelt and the origins of the New Deal. 1954. C6222
587 Lecht, L. A. Experience under railway labor legislation. 1954. C6223
588 Eisenstadt, A. S. Charles McLean Andrews. 1956. C6224
589 Chapman, J. W. Rousseau-totalitarian or liberal? 1956. C6225
590 Oberholzer, E. Delinquent saints. 1955. C6226
591 Riesenberg, P. N. Inalienability of sovereignty in medieval political thought. 1956. C6227
592 Kluback, W. Wilhelm Dilthey's philosophy of history. 1956. C6228
593 Fuchs, V. R. The economics of the fur industry. 1957. C6229
594 Spitzer, A. B. The revolutionary theories of Louis Auguste Blanqui. 1957. C6230
595 Roche, J. F. Joseph Reed. 1954. C6231
596 Quimby, R. S. The background of Napoleonic warfare. 1957. C6232
597 Ankori, Z. Karaites in Byzantium. 1958. C6233
598 Link, R. G. English theories of economic fluctuations. 1815-1848. 1958. C6234
599 Harmon, E. M. Commodity reserve currency. 1959. C6235
600 Macaulay, H. H. Fringe benefits and their Federal tax treatment. 1957. C6236
601 Grant, C. S. Democracy

in the Connecticut frontier town of Kent. 1961. C6237
602 Hooley, R. W. Financing the natural gas industry. 1958. C6238
603 Freedeman, C. E. The Conseil d'Etat in modern France. 1961. C6239
604 Betts, R. F. Assimilation and association in French colonial theory, 1890-1914. 1961. C6240
605 Rothbard, M. N. The panic of 1898. 1962. C6241
606 Embree, A. T. Charles Grant and British rule in India. 1962. C6242
607 Weston, C. C. English constitutional theory and the House of Lords, 1556-1832. 1965. C6243
608 Leiman, M. M. Jacob N. Cardozo. 1966. C6244

COLUMBIA UNIVERSITY. BUREAU OF APPLIED SOCIAL RESEARCH. PUBLICATIONS.

Cantril, H. and others. The invasion from Mars. Princeton Univ. Pr. 1940. C6245
Columbia University. Bureau of applied social research. The people look at radio. Oxford. 1946. C6246
____. Radio listening in America. Prentice-Hall. 1948. C6247
____. Communications research 1948-49. Harper. 1949. C6248
Davis, K. Human society. Macmillan. 1949. C6249
____. The population of India and Pakistan. Princeton Univ. Pr. 1951. C6250
Davis, K. and others. Modern American society. Rinehart. 1949. C6251
Kracauer, S. and Berkman, P. L. Satellite mentality. Praeger. 1956. C6252
Lazarsfeld, P. F. Radio and the printed page. Duell. 1940. C6253
Lazarsfeld, P. F. and others. The people's choice. Columbia. 1947. C6254
Lazarsfeld, P. F. and Stanton, F. N., eds. Radio research, 1941. Duell. 1941. C6255
____. Radio research, 1942-43. Duell. 1944. C6256
McPhee, W. N. Formal theories of mass behavior. Free Pr. 1963. C6257
Merton, R. K., ed. Continuities in social research. Free Pr. 1950. C6258
____. Social theory and social structure. Free Pr. 1957. C6259
Merton, R. K. and others. Mass persuasion. Harper. 1946. C6260
____, eds. The student-physician. 1957. C6261
Mills, C. W. and others. The Puerto Rican journey. Harper. 1950. C6262
Zeisel, H. Say it with figures. Harper. 1950. C6263

COLUMBIA UNIVERSITY CONTRIBUTIONS TO ANTHROPOLOGY.

1 Frachtenberg, L. F. Coos texts. 1913. C6264
2 Boas, F. Kwakiutl tales. Pt. 1. 1935. C6265
3 ____. Contributions to the ethnology of the Kwakiutl. 1925. C6266
4 Frachtenberg, L. F. Lower Umpqua texts. 1914. C6267
5 Boas, F. Bella Bella texts. 1928. C6268
6 ____. Materials for the study of inheritance in man. 1928. C6269
7 Reichard, G. A. Social life of the Navajo Indians. 1928. C6270
8 Bunzel, R. L. The Pueblo potter. 1929. C6271
9 Mead, M. An inquiry into the question of cultural stability in Polynesia. 1928. C6272
10 Boas, F. The religion of the Kwakiutl Indians. 1930. C6273
11 Herskovits, M. J. The anthropometry of the American Negro. 1930. C6274
12 Andrade, M. J. Quileute texts. 1931. C6275
13 Brenner, A. The influence of technique on the decorative

style in the domestic pottery of Culhuacan. 1931. C6276
14 Fortune, R. F. Omaha secret societies. 1932. C6277
15 Mead, M. The changing culture of an Indian tribe. 1932. C6278
16 Lesser, A. The Pawnee ghost dance hand game. 1933. C6279
17 Stern, B. J. The Lummi Indians of northwest Washington. 1934. C6280
18 Reichard, G. A. Melanesian design. 2 v. 1933. C6281
19 Jacobs, M., ed. Northwest Sahaptin texts. 2 pts. 1934-37. C6282
20 Boas, F. Geographical names of the Kwakiutl Indians. 1934. C6283
21 Benedict, R. Zuni mythology. 2 v. 1935. C6284
22 Kagwa, A. The customs of the Baganda. 1934. C6285
23 Stephen, A. M. Hopi journal of Alexander M. Stephen, ed. by Parsons. 2 v. 1934. C6286
24 Speck, F. G. Catawba texts. 1934. C6287
25 Phinney, A., ed. Nez Percê texts. 1934. C6288
26 Same as no. 2. New series. 1935-43. C6289
27 Herskovits, M. J. and F. Suriname folk-lore. 1936. C6290
28 Whitman, W. The Oto. 1937. C6291
29 Landes, R. Ojibwa sociology. 1937. C6292
30 Underhill, R. M. Social organization of the Papago Indians. 1939. C6293
31 Landes, R. The Ojibwa woman. 1939. C6294
32 Smith, M. W. The Puyallup-Nisqually. 1940. C6295
33 Underhill, R. M. Papago Indian religion. 1946. C6296
34 Whitman, W. The Pueblo Indians of San Ildefonso. 1947. C6297
35 Wagley, C. and Galvao, E. The Tenetehara Indians of Brazil. 1949. C6298
36 Smith, M. W., ed. Indians of the urban Northwest. 1949. C6299
37 Harris, M. Town and country in Brazil. 1956. C6300

COLUMBIA UNIVERSITY. EAST ASIAN INSTITUTE STUDIES

1 Wilbur, C. M. Chinese sources on the history of the Chinese Communist movement. 1950. C6301
2 Shirato, J. Japanese sources in the history of the Chinese Communist movement. 1953. C6302
3 Lane, J. E., ed. Researches in the social sciences on China. 1957. C6303
4 ____. Researches in the social sciences on Japan. V. 1. 1957. C6304
5 Kai, M. and Yampolsky, P. B. Political chronology of Japan, 1885-1957. 1957. C6305
6 Same as no. 4. V. 2. 1959. C6306
7 Ch'en, K. The communist movement in China, ed. by Wilbur. 1960. C6307
Barnett, A. D. Cadres, bureaucracy, and political power in Communist China. Princeton Univ. Pr., 1967. C6308
Borg, D., ed. Pearl Harbor as history. 1973. C6309
Chou, S. The Chinese inflation, 1937-1949. 1963. C6310
Chu, C. Reformer in modern China: Chang Chien, 1853-1926. 1965. C6311
Clubb, O. E. China & Russia. 1971. C6312
Curtis, G. L. Election campaigning. 1971. C6313
Gordon, L. H. D., ed. Taiwan. 1970. C6314
Gurtov, M. The first Vietnam crisis. 1967. C6315
Harrison, J. P. The Communist and Chinese peasant rebellions. 1968. C6316
Ho, P. The ladder of success in Imperial China. 1962. C6317
Hsiao, K. H. Money and monetary policy in Communist China. 1971. C6318
Hsiung, J. C. Law and policy in China's foreign relations.

1972. C6319
Morley, J. W. Japan's foreign policy, 1868-1941. 1974. C6320
Nakamura, J. I. Agricultural production and the economic development of Japan. Princeton Univ. Pr., 1966. C6321
Okamoto, S. The Japanese oligarchy and the Russo-Japanese war. 1970. C6322
Passin, H. Society and education in Japan. 1965. C6323
Ryan, M. G. Japan's first modern novel, tr. by Grayer. 1967. C6324
Suh, D. The Korean Communist movement, 1918-1948. Princeton Univ. Pr., 1967. C6325
____, ed. Documents of Korean Communism. Princeton Univ. Pr., 1970. C6326
Taira, K. Economic development and the labor market in Japan. 1970. C6327
Thayer, N. B. How the Conservatives rule Japan. 1969. C6328
Thurston, D. R. Teachers and politics in Japan. 1973. C6329
Varley, H. P. Imperial restoration in medieval Japan. 1971. C6330
____. Japanese culture. 1973. C6331
Watt, J. R. The district magistrate in late imperial China. 1972. C6332
Webb, H. The Japanese imperial institution in the Tokugawa period. 1968. C6333
____. Research in Japanese sources. 1965. C6334
Weinstein, M. E. Japan's postwar defense policy. 1971. C6335

COLUMBIA UNIVERSITY. PROGRAM ON EAST CENTRAL EUROPE. EAST CENTRAL EUROPEAN STUDIES.

Alton, T. P. and others. Czechoslovak national income and product 1947-1948 and 1955-1956. 1962. C6336
____. Polish national income and product in 1954, 1955 and 1956. 1965. C6337
____. Hungarian national income and product in 1955. 1963. C6338
Budurowycz, B. B. Polish-Soviet relations, 1932-1939. 1963. C6339
Fischer-Galati, S. A. Twentieth century Rumania. 1970. C6340
Hoptner, J. B. Yugoslavia in crisis, 1934-1941. 1962. C6341
Jackson, G. D. Comintern and peasant in East Europe, 1919-1930. 1966. C6342
Kaplan, H. H. The first partition of Pland. 1962. C6343
Kiraly, B. K. Hungary in the late eighteenth century. 1969. C6344
Korbonski, A. Politics of socialist agriculture in Poland, 1945-1960. 1965. C6345
Mastny, V. The Czechs under Nazi rule. 1970. C6346
Oren, A. Bulgarian communism. 1971. C6347
Rothschild, J. The Communist party of Bulgaria. 1959. C6348
____. Pilsudski's Coup d'Etat. 1966. C6349
Shoup, P. Communism and the Yugoslav national question. 1968. C6350

COLUMBIA UNIVERSITY. PUBLICATIONS IN NEAR AND MIDDLE EAST STUDIES (Mouton)

Series A.

1 Qureshi, Ishtiaq Husian. The Muslim community of the Indo-Pakistan subcontinent. 1962. C6351
2 Jeffery, A., ed. A reader on Islam. 1962. C6352
3 Köprülü, F. Demokrasi yolunda. 1964. C6353
4 Spain, J. W. The Pathan borderland. 1963. C6354
5 Allworth, E. Uzbek literary politics. 1964. C6355
6 Garsoian, N. G. The Paulician heresy. 1968. C6356
7 Reychman, J. and Zajaczkowski, A. Handbook of Ottoman-Turkish diplomatics. 1968. C6357
8 Szyliowicz, J. S. Political change in rural Turkey. 1966. C6358
9 Bonebakker, S. A. Some

early definitions of the Tawriya and Safadī's Fadd al-Xitām an-at-Tawriya wa-'l-Istixdām. 1966. C6359
10 Yar-Shater, E. Tati dialect studies. V. 1. 1968. C6360
11 Smith, J. M. The history of the Sarbadar Dynasty, 1336-1381 A.D. 1968. C6361
12 Shaw, S. J. The budget of Ottman Egypt 1005-1006/1596-1597. 1968. C6362
13 Quatrains of Nesimi fourteenth century Turkic Hurufi, ed. by Burrill. 1972. C6363
14 Gerow, E. A glossary of Indian figures of speech. 1974. C6364
15 Hirsch, C. Income distribution in Turkish agriculture. 1973. C6365
16 Gerow, E. A glossary of Indian figures of speech. 1971. C6366

Series B
1 Nêmeth, J. Turkish grammar. 1962. C6367
2 ____. Turkish reader for beginners. 1966. C6368
3 Yar-Shater, A. A grammar of southern Tati dialects. 1969. C6369

COLUMBIA UNIVERSITY. RUSSIAN INSTITUTE. STUDIES.

Alton, T. P. Polish post-war economy. 1954. C6370
Armstrong, J. A. Ukrainian nationalism, 1939-1945. 1962. C6371
Avrich, P. Kronstadt. 1970. C6372
____. The Russian anarchists. 1967. C6373
Bergson, A. Soviet national income and product in 1937. 1953. C6374
Brown, E. J. Mayakovsky. 1973. C6375
____. The proletarian episode in Russian literature, 1928-1932. 1953. C6376
Columbia Univ. Russian Institute. Russian diplomacy and Eastern Europe, 1914-1917. 1963. C6377
DeGeorge, R. T. Soviet ethics and morality. 1969. C6378
Dyck, H. L. Weimar Germany and Soviet Russia. 1966. C6379
Ehre, M. Oblomov and his creator. 1973. C6380
Fisher, R. T. Pattern for Soviet youth. 1959. C6381
Friedberg, M. Russian classics in Soviet jackets. 1962. C6382
Goodman, E. R. The Soviet design for a world state. 1960. C6383
Graham, L. R. The Soviet Academy of Sciences and the Communist Party. 1927-1932. 1967. C6384
Granick, D. Management of the industrial firm in the USSR. 1954. C6385
Grimsted, P. K. Archives and manuscript repositories in the USSR, Moscow and Leningrad. 1972. C6386
Hammond, T. T. Lenin on trade unions and the revolution, 1893-1917. 1954. C6387
Hazard, J. N. Settling disputes in Soviet society. 1960. C6388
Joravsky, D. Soviet Marxism and natural science, 1917-1932. 1961. C6389
Lang, D. M. The last years of the Georgian monarchy, 1658-1832. 1957. C6390
Luckyj, G. S. N. Literary policies in the Soviet Ukraine. 1917-1934. 1956. C6391
McKenzie, K. E. Comintern and world revolution, 1928-1943. 1964. C6392
McLane, C. B. Soviet policy and the Chinese Communists, 1931-1946. 1958. C6393
Maguire, R. A. Red virgin soil. 1968. C6394
Marcuse, H. Soviet Marxism. 1958. C6395
Morley, J. W. The Japanese thrust into Siberia, 1918. 1957. C6396
Noah, H. J. Financing Soviet schools. 1966. C6397
Park, A. G. Bolshevism in Turkestan, 1917-1927. 1957. C6398
Petrovich, M. B. The emergence of Russian Panslavism, 1856-1870. 1956. C6399
Radkey, O. H. The agrarian

foes of bolshevism. 1958. C6400
____. The sickle under the hammer. 1963. C6401
Rieber, A. J. Stalin and the French Communist Party, 1941-1947. 1962. C6402
Rigby, T. H. Communist party membership in the U.S.S.R. 1968. C6403
Rosenberg, W. G. Liberals in the Russian Revolution. 1974. C6404
Senn, A. E. The emergence of modern Lithuania. 1959. C6405
Simmons, E. J. Through the glass of Soviet literature. 1953. C6406
Soviet politics and society in the 1970's, ed. by Morton and Tökes. 1974. C6407
Suny, R. G. The Baku Commune, 1917-1918. 1972. C6408
Thompson, J. M. Russia, Bolshevism and the Versailles peace. 1966. C6409
Von Laue, T. H. Sergi Witte and the industrialization of Russia. 1963. C6410
Whiting, A. S. Soviet policies in China, 1917-1924. 1954. C6411
Zimmerman, W. Soviet perspectives on international relations. 1968. C6412

COLUMBIA UNIVERSITY. STUDIES IN ART, HISTORY AND ARCHAEOLOGY (Random)

1 Wittkower, R. Architectural principles in the age of humanism. 1965. C6413
2 Sette, C. City planning according to artistic principles, tr. by G. R. and C. C. Collins. 1965. C6414
3 Collins, G. R. and C. C. Camillo Sitte and the birth of modern city planning. 1965. C6415
4 Johnson, J. R. The radiance of Chartres. 1965. C6416
5 Peisch, M. L. The Chicago school of architecture. 1964. C6417

COLUMBIA UNIVERSITY STUDIES IN COMPARATIVE LITERATURE.

Chase, L. N. The English heroic play. 1903. C6418
Conant, M. P. The oriental tale in England in the eighteenth century. 1908. C6419
Einstein, L. The Italian Renaissance in England. 1902. C6420
Hall, H. M. Idylls of fishermen. 1912. C6421
Harrison, J. S. Platonism in English poetry in the 16th and 17th centuries. 1903. C6422
Krans, H. S. Irish life in Irish fiction. 1903. C6423
Miles, D. H. The influence of Molière on restoration comedy. 1910. C6424
Upham, A. H. The French influence in English literature from the accession of Elizabeth to the restoration. 1908. C6425
Whicher, G. F. The life and romance of Mrs. Eliza Haywood. 1915. C6426
Wolff, S. L. The Greek romance in Elizabethan prose fiction. 1912. C6427
Merged with Columbia University. Studies in English to form Columbia University. Studies in English and Comparative Literature.

COLUMBIA UNIVERSITY. STUDIES IN ECONOMICS

1 Kenan, P. B. and Lawrence, R., eds. The open economy. 1968. C6428
2 Dewey, D. The theory of imperfect competition. 1969. C6429
3 Shilling, N. Excise taxation of monopoly. 1969. C6430
4 Meyer, R. H. Bankers' diplomacy. 1970. C6431
5 Lancaster, K. Consumer demand. 1971. C6432
6 Whitcomb, D. K. Externalities and welfare. 1962. C6433
7 Findlay, R. International trade and development theory. 1973. C6434

COLUMBIA UNIVERSITY STUDIES IN ENGLISH.

1 Greenslet, F. John Glanville. 1900. C6435
2 Erskine, J. The Elizabethan lyric. 1903. C6436
3 Mustard, W. P. Classical echoes in Tennyson. 1904. C6437
Series 2:
1:1 Leonard, W. E. C. Byron and Byronism in America. 1907. C6438
2:1 Ball, M. Sir Walter Scott as a critic of literature. 1907. C6439
2:2 Loshe, L. D. The early American novel. 1907. C6440
2:3 Goddard, H. C. Studies in New England transcendentalism. 1908. C6441
3:1 Bates, E. S. A study of Shelley's drama The Cenci. 1908. C6442
3:2 Tucker, S. M. Verse-satire in England before the renaissance. 1908. C6443
3:3 Zeitlin, J. The accusative with infinitive. 1908. C6444
4:1 Gildersleeve, V. C. Government regulation of Elizabethan drama. 1908. C6445
5 Wood, A. I. P. The stage history of Shakespeare's King Richard the Third. 1909. C6446
6 Albright, V. E. The Shaksperian stage. 1909. C6447
7 Miller, B. Leigh Hunt's relations with Byron, Shelley and Keats. 1910. C6448
8 Roe, F. W. Thomas Carlyle as a critic of literature. 1910. C6449
9 Wright, E. H. The authorship of Timon of Athens. 1910. C6450
10 Ristine, F. H. English tragicomedy. 1910. C6451
11 Morgan, C. E. The rise of the novel of manners. 1911. C6452
12 Paul, H. G. John Dennis. 1911. C6453
13 Taylor, R. The potential prophecy in England. 1911. C6454
14 Patterson, F. A. The middle English penitential lyric. 1911. C6455
15 Arnold, M. L. The soliloquies of Shakespeare. 1911. C6456
16 Mosher, J. A. The exemplum in the early religious and didactic literature of England. 1911. C6457
17 Hunt, M. L. Thomas Dekker. 1911. C6458
18 James I, king of Great Britain. New poems by James I of England, ed. by Westcott. 1911. C6459
19 Bradsher, E. L. Mathew Carey. 1912. C6460
Merged with Columbia University Studies in Comparative Literature to form Columbia University. Studies in English and Comparative Literature.

COLUMBIA UNIVERSITY STUDIES IN ENGLISH AND COMPARATIVE LITERATURE (Preceded by COLUMBIA UNIVERSITY STUDIES IN ENGLISH, V. 1-3, Series 2, V. 1-22; and COLUMBIA UNIVERSITY. STUDIES IN COMPARATIVE LITERATURE, V. 1-13. Numbering for these was supplied after publication. Numbering for COLUMBIA UNIVERSITY. STUDIES IN ENGLISH AND COMPARATIVE LITERATURE begins with no. 116. There were 70 unnumbered titles published before no. 116.)

Amos, F. A. Early theories of translations. 1920. C6461
Babenroth, A. C. English childhood. 1922. C6462
Barnes, H. F. Charles Fenno Hoffman. 1930. C6463
Barrow, S. F. The medieval society romances. 1924. C6464
Beaty, J. O. John Esten Cooke, Virginian. 1922. C6465
Bentley, H. W. A dictionary of Spanish terms in English. 1932. C6466
Bolwell, R. G. W. The life and works of John Heywood. 1921. C6467
Brewster, D. Aaron Hill. 1913. C6468
Brown, E. G. Milton's blindness. 1934. C6469

Bryant, M. M. English in the law courts. 1930. C6470
Camp, C. W. The artisan in Elizabethan literature. 1924. C6471
Cargill, O. Drama and liturgy. 1930. C6472
Chittick, V. L. O. Thomas Chandler Haliburton. 1924. C6473
Christy, A. The Orient in American transcendentalism. 1932. C6474
Clark, D. L. Rhetoric and poetry in the renaissance. 1922. C6475
Clark, R. B. William Gifford. 1930. C6476
Cohen, H. L. The ballade. 1915. C6477
Cook, E. C. Literary influence in colonial newspapers, 1704-1750. 1912. C6478
Crum, R. B. Scientific thought in poetry. 1931. C6479
Erskine, J. The Elizabethan lyric. 1931. C6480
Everett, C. W. The education of Meremy Bentham. 1931. C6481
Ewen, F. The prestige of Schiller in England, 1788-1859. 1932. C6482
Fansler, D. S. Chaucer and the Roman de la Rose. 1914. C6483
Ferguson, J. D. American literature in Spain. 1916. C6484
Fisher, L. A. The mystic vision in the Grail legend and in the Divine comedy. 1917. C6485
Forsythe, R. S. The relations of Shirley's plays to the Elizabethan drama. 1914. C6486
Foster, F. M. K. English translations from the Greek. 1918. C6487
Freeburg, V. O. Disguise plots in Elizabethan drama. 1915. C6488
Fuess, C. M. Lord Byron as a satirist in verse. 1912. C6489
Gaines, F. P. The southern plantation. 1924. C6490
Gignilliat, G. W. The author of Sanford and Merton. 1932. C6491
Goldmark, R. (Ingersoll) Studies in the influence of the classics of English literature. 1918. C6492
Gray, C. H. Theatrical criticism in London to 1795. 1931. C6493
Haller, W. The early life of Robert Southey, 1774-1803. 1917. C6494
Herold, A. L. James Kirke Paulding. 1926. C6495
Higginson, J. J. Spenser's Shepherd's calendar in relation to contemporary affairs. 1912. C6496
Hoffman, H. L. An odyssey of the soul. 1933. C6497
Hooker, R. Hooker's Ecclesiastical polity, book VIII, ed. by Houk. 1931. C6498
Howe, S. Wilhelm Meister and his English kinsmen. 1930. C6499
Jones, R. F. Lewis Theobald. 1919. C6500
Jordan, J. C. Robert Greene. 1915. C6501
Latham, M. W. The Elizabethan fairies. 1930. C6502
Lockwood, H. D. Tools and the man. 1927. C6503
Loggins, V. The Negro author. 1931. C6504
Loshe, L. D. Early American novel. 1930. C6505
Lyon, J. H. H. A study of The newe Metamorphosis written by J. M., gent., 1600. 1919. C6506
Mesick, J. L. The English traveller in America, 1785-1835. 1922. C6507
Mitchell, J. P. St. Jean de Crèvecoeur. 1916. C6508
Mohl, R. The three estates in medieval and renaissance literature. 1933. C6509
Neff, E. E. Carlyle and Mill. 1924. C6510
Nitchie, E. Vergil and the English poets. 1919. C6511
Patterson, W. M. The rhythm of prose. 1917. C6512
Phillips, W. C. Dickens, Reade, and Collins. 1919. C6513
Powell, C. L. English domestic relations, 1487-1653. 1917. C6514
Reed, A. L. The background of Gray's Elegy. 1924. C6515
Rusk, R. L. The literature of

the middle western frontier. 2 v. 1925. C6516
Sickels, E. M. The gloomy egoist. 1932. C6517
Smith, F. M. Mary Astell. 1916. C6518
Smith, R. M. Froissart and the English chronicle play. 1915. C6519
Smith, W. The commedia dell' arte. 1912. C6520
Steeves, R. H. Learned societies and English literary scholarship in Great Britain and the United States. 1913. C6521
Swain, B. Fools and folly during the middle ages and the renaissance. 1932. C6522
Tandy, J. R. Crackerbox philosophers in American humor and satire. 1925. C6523
Thomas, E. W. Christiana Georgiana Rossetti. 1931. C6524
Tindall, W. Y. John Bunyan. 1934. C6525
Watson, H. F. The sailor in English fiction and drama, 1550-1800. 1931. C6526
Wells, H. W. Poetic imagery. 1924. C6527
Republished as: Poetic imagery illustrated from Elizabethean literature. Russell. 1951. C6528
Williams, B. C., ed. Gnomic poetry in Anglo-Saxon. 1914. C6529
Wright, L. M. The literary life of the early Friends, 1650-1725. 1932. C6530
Yarborough, M. C. John Horne Tooke. 1926. C6531
116 Marshall, R. Italy in English literature, 1755-1815. 1934. C6532
117 Thrall, M. M. H. Rebellious Fraser's. 1934. C6533
118 Nesbitt, G. L. Benthamite reviewing. 1934. C6534
119 Tindall, W. Y. John Bunyan. 1934. C6535
120 Page, E. R. George Colman. 1935. C6536
121 Durling, D. L. Georgic tradition in English poetry. 1935. C6537
122 Bartlett, A. C. The larger rhetorical patterns in Anglo-Saxon poetry. 1935. C6538
123 Rosa, M. W. The silver-fork school. 1936. C6539
124 Mohrenschildt, D. S. von. Russia in the intellectual life of eighteenth-century France. 1936. C6540
125 Langdale, A. B. Phineas Fletcher. 1937. C6541
126 Coffin, C. M. John Donne and the new philosophy. 1937. C6542
127 Richards, E. A. Hudibras in the burlesque tradition. 1937. C6543
128 Dobbie, E. V. K. The manuscripts of Caedmon's hymn and Bede's Death song. 1937. C6544
129 Crane, W. G. Wit and rhetoric in the renaissance. 1937. C6545
130 Gagey, E. M. Ballad opera. 1937. C6546
131 Rathborne, I. E. The meaning of Spenser's fairyland. 1937. C6547
132 Hopper, V. F. Medieval number symbolism. 1938. C6548
133 John, L. C. The Elizabethan sonnet sequence. 1938. C6549
134 Hooker, K. W. The fortunes of Victor Hugo in England. 1938. C6550
135 Riedel, F. C. Crime and punishment in the Old French romances. 1938. C6551
136 Fuller, T. Thomas Fuller's The holy state and the profane state, ed. by Walten. 1938. C6552
137 Merriam, H. G. Edward Moxon. 1939. C6553
138 Anderson, C. R. Melville in the south seas. 1939. C6554
139 Nelson, W. John Skelton, laureate. 1939. C6555
140 Nobbe, G. The North Briton. 1939. C6556
141 Newstead, H. H. Bran the Blessed in Arthurian romance. 1939. C6557
142 Mack, E. C. Public schools and British opinion, 1780-1860. 1939. C6558
143 Barker, R. H. Mr Cibber

of Drury Lane. 1939. C6559
144 Eves, C. K. Matthew Prior. 1939. C6560
145 Valency, M. J. The tragedies of Herod & Mariamne. 1940. C6561
146 Rudman, H. W. Italian nationalism and English letters. 1940. C6562
147 Weber, K. Lucius Cary. 1940. C6563
148 Tolles, W. Tom Taylor and the Victorian drama. 1940. C6564
149 Phillips, J. E. The state in Shakespeare's Greek and Roman plays. 1940. C6565
150 Shuster, G. N. The English ode from Milton to Keats. 1940. C6566
151 Jonas, L. The divine science. 1940. C6567
152 Gove, P. B. The imaginary voyage in prose fiction. 1941. C6568
153 Irwin, W. R. The making of Jonathan Wild. 1941. C6569
154 Bevington, M. M. The Saturday review, 1855-1869. 1941. C6570
155 Quinlan, M. J. Victorian prelude. 1941. C6571
156 O'Connor, M. C., Sister. The Art of dying well. 1942. C6572
157 Jones, L. C. The clubs of the Gregorian rakes. 1942. C6573
158 Izard, T. C. George Whetstone. 1942. C6574
159 Adams, H. H. English domestic, or homiletic tragedy, 1575 to 1642. 1943. C6575
160 Everson, I. G. George Henry Calvert. 1944. C6576
161 Raesly, E. L. Portrait of New Netherlands. 1945. C6577
162 Johnston, G. B. Ben Jonson. 1945. C6578
163 Harlan, A. Owen Meredith. 1946. C6579
164 Stevenson, D. L. The love-game comedy. 1946. C6580
165 Miriam Joseph, Sister. Shakespeare's use of the arts of language. 1947. C6581
166 Patchell, M. F. C. Palmerin romances in Elizabethan prose fiction. 1947. C6582
167 Hyde, M. M. (Crapo) Playwriting for Elizabethean, 1600-1605. 1949. C6583
168 Schoenbaum, S. Middleton's tragedies. 1955. C6584

COLUMBIA UNIVERSITY. STUDIES IN HISTORY, ECONOMICS AND PUBLIC LAW.

1 Wilcox, W. F. The divorce problem. 1897. C6585
2 Goss, J. D. A history of tariff administration in the United States. 1897. C6586
3 Black, G. A. History of municipal land ownership on Manhattan Island. 1891. C6587
4 Douglas, C. H. J. The financial history of Massachusetts to the American Revolution. 1912. C6588
5 Hourwich, I. A. The economics of the Russian village. 1892. C6589
6 Dunscomb, S. W. Bankruptcy. 1893. C6590
7 Rosewater, V. Special assessments. 1893. C6591
8 Bishop, C. F. History of elections in the American colonies. 1893. C6592
9 Beer, G. L. The commercial policy of England toward the American colonies. 1893. C6593
10 Ripley, W. Z. The financial history of Virginia, 1609-1776. 1893. C6594
11 West, M. The inheritance tax. 1908. C6595
12 Wood, F. A. History of taxation in Vermont. 1894. C6596
13 Walker, F. Double taxation in the United States. 1896. C6597
14 Bondy, W. The separation of governmental powers. 1896. C6598
15 Wilcox, D. F. Municipal government in Michigan and Ohio. 1896. C6599
16 Shepherd, W. R. History of proprietary government in

Pennsylvania. 1896. C6600
17 Cushing, H. A. History of the transition from provincial to commonwealth government in Massachusetts. 1896. C6601
18 Emery, H. C. Speculation on the stock and produce exchanges of the United States. 1896. C6602
19 Chadsey, C. E. The struggle between President Johnson and Congress over reconstruction. 1896. C6603
20 Webster, W. C. Recent centralizing tendencies in state educational administration. 1897. C6604
21 Stark, F. R. The abolition of privateering and the declaration of Paris. 1897. C6605
22 Whitten, R. H. Public administration in Massachusetts. 1898. C6606
23 Maltbie, M. R. English local government of to-day. 1897. C6607
24 Crook, J. W. German wage theories. 1898. C6608
25 Fairlie, J. A. The centralization of administration in New York state. 1898. C6609
26 Hall, F. S. Sympathetic strikes and sympathetic lockouts. 1898. C6610
27 Bates, F. G. Rhode Island and the formation of the union. 1898. C6611
28 Sites, C. M. L. Centralized administration of liquor laws in the American commonwealths. 1899. C6612
29 Weber, A. F. The growth of cities in the nineteenth century. 1899. C6613
30 Burke, W. M. History and functions of central labor unions. 1899. C6614
31 Proper, E. E. Colonial immigration laws. 1900. C6615
32 Glasson, W. H. History of military pension legislation in the United States. 1900. C6616
33 Merriam, C. E. History of the theory of sovereignty since Rousseau. 1900. C6617
34 Loeb, I. The legal property relations of married parties. 1900. C6618
35 Sciscó, L. D. Political nativism in New York state. 1901. C6619
36 Woolley, E. C. The reconstruction of Georgia. 1901. C6620
37 Flick, A. C. Loyalism in New York during the American revolution. 1901. C6621
38 Willett, A. H. The economic theory of risk and insurance. 1901. C6622
39 Duggan, S. P. H. The eastern question. 1902. C6623
40 Hall, A. C. Crime in its relations to social progress. 1902. C6624
41 Kinosita, Y. The past and present of Japanese commerce. 1902. C6625
42 Willett, M. The employment of women in the clothing trade. 1902. C6626
43 Orth, S. P. The centralization of administration in Ohio. 1903. C6627
44 Rawles, W. A. Centralization tendencies in the administration of Indiana. 1903. C6628
45 Weston, S. F. Principles of justice in taxation. 1903. C6629
46 Bowman, H. M. The administration of Iowa. 1903. C6630
47 Shepherd, R. P. Turgot and the six edicts. 1903. C6631
48 Ford, G. S. Hanover and Prussia, 1795-1803. 1903. C6632
49 Clark, W. E. Josiah Tucker, economist. 1903. C6633
50 Whitaker, A. C. History and criticism of the labor theory of value in English political economy. 1904. C6634
51 Groat, G. G. Trade unions and the law in New York. 1905. C6635
52 Beard, C. A. The office of justice of the peace in England. 1904. C6636
53 Thomas, D. Y. A history of military government in newly acquired territory of the United States. 1904. C6637

54 Crandall, S. B. Treaties, their making and enforcement. 1904. C6638
55 Jones, T. J. The sociology of a New York city block. 1904. C6639
56 Stangeland, C. E. Pre-Malthusian doctrines of population. 1904. C6640
57 Capen, E. W. The historical development of the poor law of Connecticut. 1905. C6641
58 Banks, E. M. The economics of land tenure in Georgia. 1905. C6642
59 McKeag, E. C. Mistake in contract. 1905. C6643
60 Mussey, H. R. Combination in the mining industry. 1905. C6644
61 Kramer, S. The English craft gilds and the government. 1905. C6645
62 Thorndike, L. The place of magic in the intellectual history of Europe. 1905. C6646
63 Boyd, W. K. The ecclesiastical edicts of the Theodosian code. 1905. C6647
64 Hishida, S. G. The international position of Japan as a great power. 1905. C6648
65 Pond, O. L. Municipal control of public utilities. 1906. C6649
66 Agger, E. E. The budget in the American commonwealths. 1907. C6650
67 Williamson, C. C. The finances of Cleveland. 1907. C6651
68 Gilbert, J. H. Trade and currency in early Oregon. 1907. C6652
69 Smith, P. Luther's table talk. 1907. C6653
70 Jacobstein, M. The tobacco industry in the United States. 1907. C6654
71 Tenney, A. A. Social democracy and population. 1907. C6655
72 Brisco, N. A. The economic policy of Robert Walpole. 1907. C6656
73 Berglund, A. The United States steel corporation. 1907. C6657
74 Friedman, H. G. The taxation of corporations in Massachusetts. 1907. C6658
75 McBain, H. L. De Witt Clinton and the origin of the spoils system in New York. 1907. C6659
76 Miller, E. I. The legislature of the province of Virginia. 1907. C6660
77 Underwood, J. H. The distribution of ownership. 1907. C6661
78 MacLear, A. B. Early New England towns. 1908. C6662
79 Fry, W. H. New Hampshire as a royal province. 1908. C6663
80 Tanner, E. P. The province of New Jersey, 1664-1738. 1908. C6664
81 Weld, L. D. H. Private freight cars and American railways. 1908. C6665
82 Chaddock, R. E. Ohio before 1850. 1908. C6666
83 Arner, G. B. L. Consanguineous marriages in the American population. 1908. C6667
84 Hankins, F. H. Adolphe Quetelet as statistician. 1908. C6668
85 Putnam, B. H. The enforcement of the statutes of labourers during the first decade after the black death. 1908. C6669
86 Whitin, E. S. Factory legislation in Maine. 1908. C6670
87 Davis, M. M. Psychological interpretations of society. 1909. C6671
88 Hayes, C. H. J. An introduction to the sources relating to the Germanic invasions. 1909. C6672
89 Gephart, W. F. Transportation and industrial development in the Middle West. 1909. C6673
90 Schapiro, J. S. Social reform and the reformation. 1909. C6674
91 Parsons, P. A. Responsibility for crime. 1909. C6675

92 Haines, C. G. The conflict over judicial powers in the United States to 1870. 1909. C6676
93 Woolston, H. B. A study of the population of Manhattanville. 1909. C6677
94 Lichtenberger, J. P. Divorce. 1909. C6678
95 Ramsdell, C. W. Reconstruction in Texas. 1910. C6679
96 Lingley, C. R. The transition in Virginia from colony to commonwealth. 1910. C6680
97 Clark, J. M. Standards of reasonableness in local freight discrimination. 1910. C6681
98 Hilkey, C. J. Legal development in colonial Massachusetts. 1910. C6682
99 Odum, H. W. Social and mental traits of the Negro. 1910. C6683
100 Hill, R. T. The public domain and democracy. 1910. C6684
101 Coker, F. W. Organismic theories of the state. 1910. C6685
102 Murray, W. S. The making of the Balkan states. 1910. C6686
103 Brummer, S. D. Political history of New York state during the period of the civil war. 1911. C6687
104 Yen, H. L. A survey of constitutional development in China. 1911. C6688
105 Porter, G. H. Ohio politics during the civil war period. 1911. C6689
106 Reed, A. Z. The territorial basis of government under the state constitutions. 1911. C6690
107 Fisher, E. J. New Jersey as a royal province, 1738 to 1776. 1911. C6691
108 Groat, G. G. Attitude of American courts in labor cases. 1911. C6692
109 Pratt, E. E. Industrial causes of congestion of population in New York City. 1911. C6693
110 Chapin, F. S. Education and the mores, a sociological essay. 1911. C6694
111 Bonham, M. L. The British consuls in the confederacy. 1911. C6695
112-113 Chen Huan-Chang. The economic principles of Confucius and his school. 2 v. 1911. C6696
114 Lowenthal, E. The Ricardian socialists. 1911. C6697
115 Jenkins, H. D. Ibrahim Pasha. 1911. C6698
116 Lorwin, L. L. The labor movement in France. 1912. C6699
____. Syndicalism in France. 1914. C6700
117 Sims, N. L. A Hoosier village. 1912. C6701
118 Dilla, H. M. The politics of Michigan, 1865-1878. 1912. C6702
119 Blakey, R. G. The United States beet-sugar industry and the tariff. 1912. C6703
120 Brehaut, E. An encyclopedist of the dark age. 1912. C6704
121 Ogburn, W. F. Progress and uniformity in child-legislation. 1912. C6705
122 Hall, W. P. British Radicalism, 1791-1797. 1912. C6706
123 Kuhn, A. K. A comparative study of the law of corporations. 1912. C6707
124 Haynes, G. E. The Negro at work in New York city. 1912. C6708
125 Tsu, Y. Y. The spirit of Chinese philanthropy. 1912. C6709
126 Koo, V. K. W. The status of aliens in China. 1912. C6710
127 Blakey, L. S. The sale of liquor in the South. 1912. C6711
128 Vineberg, S. Provincial and local taxation in Canada. 1912. C6712
129 Streightoff, F. H. The distribution of incomes in the United States. 1912. C6713
130 Wood, F. A. The finances

of Vermont. 1913. C6714
131 Davis, W. W. The Civil war and reconstruction in Florida. 1913. C6715
132 Lien, A. J. Privileges and immunities of citizens of the United States. 1913. C6716
133 Moore, B. F. The Supreme Court and unconstitutional legislation. 1913. C6717
134 Lauber, A. W. Indian slavery in colonial times within the present limits of the United States. 1913. C6718
135 Stebbins, H. A. A political history of the state of New York, 1865-1869. 1913. C6719
136 Canfield, L. H. The early persecutions of the Christians. 1913. C6720
137 Osborne, A. A. Speculation of the New York stock exchange. 1913. C6721
138 Knauth, O. W. The policy of the United States towards industrial monopoly. 1914. C6722
139 Moses, R. The civil service of Great Britain. 1914. C6723
140 Sowers, D. C. The financial history of New York state from 1789 to 1912. 1914. C6724
141 Hamilton, J. G. de R. Reconstruction in North Carolina. 1914. C6725
142 Yalman, A. E. The development of modern Turkey as measured by its press. 1914. C6726
143 Chen, S-K. The system of taxation in China in the Tsing dynasty, 1644-1911. 1914. C6727
144 Wei, W. P. The currency problem in China. 1914. C6728
145 Joseph, S. Jewish immigration to the United States from 1881 to 1910. 1914. C6729
146 Coleman, C. B. Constantine the Great and Christianity. 1914. C6730
147 Huttman, M. A. The establishment of Christianity and the proscription of paganism. 1914. C6731
148 Robbins, E. C. Railway conductors. 1914. C6732
149 Ma, Y. C. The finances of the city of New York. 1914. C6733
150 Kendrick, B. B. The journal of the Joint committee of fifteen on reconstruction, 39th Congress, 1865-1867. 1914. C6734
151 Gehlke, C. E. Emile Durkheim's contributions to sociological theory. 1915. C6735
152 Watarai, T. Nationalization of railways in Japan. 1915. C6736
153 Thompson, W. S. Population. 1915. C6737
154 Thompson, C. M. Reconstruction in Georgia. 1915. C6738
155 Russell, E. B. The review of American colonial legislation by the King in council. 1915. C6739
156 Cahall, R. D. B. The Sovereign council of New France. 1915. C6740
157 Drury, H. B. Scientific management; a history and criticism. 1918. C6741
158 Goebel, J. The recognition policy of the United States. 1915. C6742
159 Hsu, M. C. Railway problems in China. 1915. C6743
160 Clements, P. H. The Boxer rebellion. 1915. C6744
161 Hecker, J. F. Russian sociology. 1915. C6745
162 Ferguson, M. State regulation of railroads in the South. 1916. C6746
163 Aḥmand ign Yaḥyā, al-Baldā-durī. The origins of the Islamic state. V. 1. 1916. C6747
163a Ibid. V. 2. 1924. C6748
164 McFall, R. J. Railway monopoly and rate regulation. 1916. C6749
165 Wiest, E. The butter industry in the United States. 1916. C6750
166 Aghňides, N. P. Mohammedan theories of finance. 1916. C6751
167 Surrey, N. M. (Miller) The commerce of Louisiana

during the French régime. 1916. C6752
168 Clarke, E. L. American men of letters, their nature and nurture. 1916. C6753
169 Chu, C. The tariff problem in China. 1916. C6754
170 Adams, A. B. Marketing perishable farm products. 1916. C6755
171 Rosenblatt, F. F. The Chartist movement in its social and economic aspects. 1916. C6756
172 Slosson, P. W. The decline of the Chartist movement. 1916. C6757
173 Faulkner, H. U. Chartism and the churches; a study in democracy. 1916. C6758
174 Riddell, W. A. The rise of ecclesiastical control in Quebec. 1916. C6759
175 Ware, E. E. Political opinion in Massachusetts during the civil war and reconstruction. 1916. C6760
176 Hoagland, H. E. Collective bargaining in the lithographic industry. 1917. C6761
177 Peterson, A. E. New York as an eighteenth century municipality prior to 1731. 1917. C6762
178 Edwards, G. W. New York as an eighteenth century municipality, 1731-1776. 1917. C6763
179 Boyce, W. S. Economic and social history of Chowan county, North Carolina, 1880-1915. 1917. C6764
180 Newcomer, M. Separation of state and local revenues in the United States. 1917. C6765
181 Zollman, C. F. G. American civil church law. 1917. C6766
182 Schlesinger, A. M. The colonial merchants and the American revolution. 1918. C6767
183 Mills, F. C. Contemporary theories of unemployment and unemployment relief. 1917. C6768
184 Curtis, E. N. The French assembly of 1848 and American constitutional doctrines. 1918. C6769
185 Hale, R. L. Valuation and rate-making. 1918. C6770
186 Bradley, H. The enclosures in England. 1918. C6771
187 Huang, H. L. The land tax in China. 1918. C6772
188 Leffingwell, G. W. Social and private life at Rome in the time of Plautus and Terence. 1918. C6773
189 Northcott, C. H. Australian social development. 1918. C6774
190 Florence, P. S. Use of factory statistics in the investigation of industrial fatigue. 1918. C6775
191 Stauffer, V. New England and the Bavarian Illuminati. 1918. C6776
192 Murchinson, C. T. Resale price maintenance. 1919. C6777
193 Brissenden, P. F. The I. W. W. 2d ed. 1920. C6778
194 Flippin, P. S. The royal government in Virginia, 1624-1775. 1919. C6779
195 Caldwell, W. E. Hellenic conceptions of peace. 1919. C6780
196 Higby, C. P. The religious policy of the Bavarian government during the Napoleonic period. 1919. C6781
197 Huang, F-H. Public debts in China. 1919. C6782
198 Fox, D. R. The decline of aristocracy in the politics of New York. 1919. C6783
199 See, C. S. The foreign trade of China. 1919. C6784
200 Carman, H. J. The street surface railway franchises of New York City. 1919. C6785
201 Arent, L. Electric franchises in New York City. 1919. C6786
202 Hutchinson, E. J. Women's wages. 1919. C6787
203 Thomas, H. C. The return of the Democratic party to power in 1884. 1919. C6788

204 Parker, W. The Paris Bourse and French finance. 1920. C6789
205 Klein, P. Prison methods in New York state. 1920. C6790
206 Weld, W. E. India's demand for transportation. 1920. C6791
207 Gillespie, J. E. The influence of oversea expansion on England to 1700. 1920. C6792
208 Ayusawa, I. F. International labor legislation. 1920. C6793
209 Wood, G. A. William Shirley, governor of Massachusetts, 1741-1756. 1920. C6794
210 Park, J. H. The English reform bill of 1867. 1920. C6795
211 Martin, C. E. The policy of the United States as regards intervention. 1921. C6796
212 Prince, S. H. Catastrophe and social change. 1920. C6797
213 Drachsler, J. Intermarriage in New York city. 1921. C6798
214 Miner, C. E. The ratification of the federal Constitution by the state of New York. 1921. C6799
215 Bonbright, J. C. Railroad capitalization. 1920. C6800
216 Douglas, P. H. American apprenticeship and industrial education. 1921. C6801
217 Bell, J. C. Opening a highway to the Pacific, 1838-1846. 1921. C6802
218 Morris, H. L. Parliamentary franchise reform in England from 1885 to 1918. 1921. C6803
219 Scrugham, M. The peaceable Americans of 1860-1861. 1921. C6804
220 Iwasaki, U. The working forces in Japanese politics. 1921. C6805
221 Goldberg, J. A. Social aspects of the treatment of the insane. 1921. C6806
222 Wright, J. M. The free Negro in Maryland, 1634-1860. 1921. C6807
223 Townsend, M. E. Origins of modern German colonialism, 1871-1885. 1921. C6808
224 Odate, G. Japan's financial relations with the United States. 1922. C6809
225 Lee, M. P. Economic history of China. 1921. C6810
226 Li, C. S. Central and social finance in China. 1922. C6811
227 Raymond, D. (Neill). British policy and opinion during the Franco-Prussian war. 1921. C6812
228 Alzona, E. Some French contemporary opinions of the Russian revolution of 1905. 1921. C6813
229 Comstock, A. P. State taxation of personal incomes. 1921. C6814
230 Mueller, H. R. The Whig party in Pennsylvania. 1922. C6815
231 Tucker, D. S. The evolution of people's banks. 1922. C6816
232 Cable, J. R. The Bank of the state of Missouri. 1923. C6817
233 Lawson, L. A. The relation of British policy to the declaration of the Monroe doctrine. 1922. C6818
234 Calman, A. R. Ledru-Rollin and the second French republic. 1922. C6819
235 Arnett, A. M. The Populist movement in Georgia. 1922. C6820
236 Dunaway, W. F. History of the James river and Kanawha company. 1922. C6821
237 Chamberlain, J. P. The regime of the international rivers. 1923. C6822
238 Washburne, G. A. Imperial control of the administration of justice in the thirteen American colonies. 1923. C6823
239 Tsiang, T. F. Labor and empire. 1923. C6824
240 Reyes, J. S. Legislative history of America's economic policy toward the Philippines. 1923. C6825
241 Taft, D. R. Two Portuguese communities in New England. 1923. C6826

242 Oakley, T. P. English penitential discipline and Anglo-Saxon law in their joint influence. 1923. C6827
243 Schulter, W. C. The pre-war business cycle, 1907 to 1914. 1923. C6828
244 Robinson, L. R. Foreign credit facilities in the United Kingdom. 1923. C6829
245 Staples, T. S. Reconstruction in Arkansas, 1862-1874. 1923. C6830
246 Hinrichs, A. F. The United mine workers of America. 1923. C6831
247 Lanfear, V. W. Business fluctuations and the American labor movement, 1915-1922. 1924. C6832
248 Nichols, R. F. The Democratic machine, 1850-1854. 1923. C6833
249 Berman, E. Labor disputes and the President of the United States. 1924. C6834
250 Collins, R. W. Catholicism and the second French republic, 1848-1852. 1923. C6835
251 Wertheimer, M. S. The Pan-German league, 1890-1914. 1924. C6836
252 Shultz, W. J. The humane movement in the United States, 1910-1922. 1924. C6837
253 Rice, S. A. Farmers and workers in American politics. 1924. C6838
254 Tostlebe, A. S. The Bank of North Dakota. 1924. C6839
255 McClure, W. M. A new American commercial policy as evidenced by section 317 of the Tariff act of 1922. 1924. C6840
256 Waterman, W. R. Frances Wright. 1924. C6841
257 Wilkinson, W. J. Tory democracy. 1925. C6842
258 Gulick, C. A. Labor policy of the United States steel corporation. 1924. C6843
259 Baker, E. (Faulkner). Protective labor legislation. 1925. C6844
260 Clausing, R. The Roman colonate. 1925. C6845
261 Hasek, C. W. The introduction of Adam Smith's doctrines into Germany. 1925. C6846
262 Zimmerman, J. F. Impressment of American seaman. 1925. C6847
263 Liu, S. S. Extraterritoriality. 1925. C6848
264 Douglas, D. S. (Wolff). Guillaume de Greef. 1925. C6849
265 McConnell, W. J. Social cleavages in Texas. 1925. C6850
266 Clarkson, J. D. Labour and nationalism in Ireland. 1925. C6851
267 Gazley, J. G. American opinion of German unification, 1848-1871. 1926. C6852
268 Fernández, L. H. The Philippine republic. 1926. C6853
269 Larson, H. M. The wheat market and the farmer in Minnesota, 1858-1900. 1926. C6854
270 Gulley, E. E. Joseph Chamberlain and English social politics. 1926. C6855
271 Ko, T. T. Governmental methods of adjusting labor disputes in North America and Australia. 1926. C6856
272 Chiao, W-H. Devolution in Great Britain. 1926. C6857
273 Macdonald, H. G. Canadian public opinion on the American civil war. 1926. C6858
274 Kerwin, F. G. Federal water power legislation. 1926. C6859
275 Gooden, O. T. Missouri and North Arkansas railroad strike. 1926. C6860
276 Hinkhouse, F. J. The preliminaries of the American revolution. 1926. C6861
277 Reed, R. Negro illegitimacy in New York city. 1926. C6862
278 Stewart, B. M. Canadian labor laws and the treaty. 1926. C6863
279 Grady, H. F. British war finance. 1927. C6864
280 Artman, C. E. Food

costs and city consumers. 1926. C6865
281 Stewart, I. Consular privileges and immunities. 1926. C6866
282 Shaw, K. W. Democracy and finance in China. 1926. C6867
283 Coombs, W. The wages of unskilled labor in manufacturing industries in the United States. 1926. C6868
284 Patton, F. L. Diminishing returns in agriculture. 1926. C6869
285 Takizawa, M. The penetration of money economy in Japan. 1927. C6870
286 Raymond, I. W. The teaching of the early church on the use of wine and strong drinks. 1927. C6871
287 Stern, B. J. Social factors in medical progress. 1927. C6872
288 Thompson, D. F. Professional solidarity among teachers of England. 1927. C6873
289 Comer, J. P. Legislative functions of national administrative authorities. 1927. C6874
290 McCown, A. C. The congressional conferences committee. 1927. C6875
291 Potwin, M. A. Cotton mill people of the Piedmont. 1927. C6876
292 Achinstein, A. Buying power of labor and post-war cycles. 1927. C6877
293 Brebner, J. B. New England's outpost. 1927. C6878
294 Yu, T-C. The interpretations of treaties. 1927. C6879
295 Reynolds, G. G. The distribution of power to regulate interstate carriers. 1928. C6880
296 Bradwin, E. W. The bunkhouseman. 1928. C6881
297 Ch'iu, C-W. The speaker of the House of Representatives since 1896. 1928. C6882
298 Tuan, M-L. Simonde de Sismondi as an economist. 1927. C6883
299 Furuya, S. Y. Japan's foreign exchange and her balance of international payment. 1928. C6884
300 Meneely, A. H. The War department, 1861. 1928. C6885
301 Harada, S. Labor conditions in Japan. 1928. C6886
302 Kraus, M. Intercolonial aspects of American culture on the eve of the revolution. 1928. C6887
303 Hasbrouck, A. Foreign legionnaires in the liberation of Spanish South America. 1928. C6888
304 Wallace, S. C. State administrative supervision over cities. 1928. C6889
305 VanDeusen, J. G. Economic basis of disunion in South Carolina. 1928. C6890
306 Michels, R. K. Cartels, combines and trusts in post-war Germany. 1928. C6891
307 Eberling, E. J. Congressional investigations. 1928. C6892
308 Burgess, J. S. The guilds of Peking. 1928. C6893
309 Matsushita, S. The economic effects of public debts. 1929. C6894
310 Abel, T. F. Systematic sociology in Germany. 1929. C6895
311 Truxal, A. G. Outdoor recreation legislation and its effectiveness. 1929. C6896
312 Waugh, F. V. Quality as a determinate of vegetable prices. 1929. C6897
313 Carey, R. L. Daniel Webster as an economist. 1929. C6898
314 Matsushita, S. Japan in the League of nations. 1929. C6899
315 Galitzi, C. A. A study of assimilation among the Roumanians in the United States. 1929. C6900
316 Morris, R. B. Studies in the history of American law. 1930. C6901
317 Schmidt, G. P. Old time college president. 1930. C6902
318 Haider, C. Capital and labor under fascism.

1930. C6903
319 Morgan, C. E. The origin and history of the New York employing printers' association. 1930. C6904
320 Morris, V. P. Oregon's experience with minimum wage legislation. 1930. C6905
321 Messenger, R. E. Ethical teachings in the Latin hymn of medieval England. 1930. C6906
322 Paustian, P. W. Canal irrigation in the Punjab. 1930. C6907
323 Frank, A. D. The development of the federal program... 1930. C6908
324 Langsam, W. C. The Napoleonic wars and German nationalism in Austria. 1930. C6909
325 Wagner, D. O. The Church of England and social reform since 1854. 1930. C6910
326 Hunt, E. M. American precedents in Australia federation. 1930. C6911
327 Reed, L. S. The labor philosophy of Samuel Gompers. 1930. C6912
328 Lehmann, W. C. Adam Ferguson and the beginnings of modern sociology. 1930. C6913
329 Kennedy, L. V. The Negro peasant turns cityward. 1930. C6914
330 Phelps, C. The Anglo-American peace movement in the mid-nineteenth century. 1930. C6915
331 Wye manor, England. A survey of the manor of Wye, ed. by Muhlfeld. 1933. C6916
332 Woodward, J. L. Foreign news in American morning papers. 1930. C6917
333 Spengler, E. H. Land values in New York in relation to transit facilities. 1930. C6918
334 Reynolds, B. Proponents of limited monarchy in sixteenth century France. 1931. C6919
335 Cheng, S. C-Y. Schemes for the federation of the British empire. 1931. C6920
336 Megaro, G. Vittorio Alfieri. 1930. C6921
337 Love, R. A. Federal financing. 1931. C6922
338 Hansome, M. World workers' educational movements. 1931. C6923
339 Lee, U. The historical backgrounds of early Methodist enthusiasm. 1931. C6924
340 Clark, K. International communications. 1931. C6925
341 Ergang, R. R. Herder and the foundation of German nationalism. 1931. C6926
342 Lewis, E. E. The mobility of the Negro. 1931. C6927
343 Bowen, E. An hypothesis of population growth. 1931. C6928
344 Gilpatrick, D. H. Jeffersonian democracy in North Carolina, 1789-1816. 1931. C6929
345 Goldberg, R. (Webster). Occupational diseases in relation to compensation and health insurance. 1931. C6930
346 McCordock, R. S. British Far Eastern policy, 1894-1900. 1931. C6931
347 Jones, T. C. Clearings and collections. 1931. C6932
348 Hallberg, C. W. The Suez canal. 1931. C6933
349 Shupp, P. F. European powers and the Near Eastern question, 1806-1807. 1931. C6934
350 Thomas, C. M. American neutrality in 1793. 1931. C6935
351 Clark, J. P. (Clark). Deportation of aliens from the United States to Europe. 1931. C6936
352 Waterman, W. C. Prostitution and its repression in New York City, 1900-1931. 1932. C6937
353 Boyd, M. C. Alabama in the fifties. 1931. C6938
354 Hardy, E. R. The large estates of Byzantine Egypt. 1931. C6939
355 Hutchinson, R. G. State-administered locally-shared

taxes. 1931. C6940
356 Cowden, D. J. Measures of exports of the United States. 1931. C6941
357 Barck, O. T. New York city during the war for independence. 1931. C6942
358 Chacko, C. J. The International joint commission between the United States and Canada. 1932. C6943
359 Meyer, L. W. The life and times of Colonel Richard M. Johnson of Kentucky. 1932. C6944
360 Cahen, A. Statistical analysis of American divorce. 1932. C6945
361 Gambs, J. S. The decline of the I. W. W. 1932. C6946
362 Van Deusen, G. G. Sieyes. 1932. C6947
363 Trenholme, L. (Irby). The ratification of the federal Constitution in North Carolina. 1932. C6948
364 Shorr, P. Science and superstition in the eighteenth century. 1932. C6949
365 Lokke, C. L. France and the colonial question. 1932. C6950
366 Neprash, J. A. The Brookhart campaigns in Iowa. 1932. C6951
367 Duncan, J. S. Public and private operation of railways in Brazil. 1932. C6952
368 Kiser, C. V. Sea islands to city. 1932. C6953
369 Kimball, E. P. Sociology and education. 1932. C6954
370 Masters, R. D. International law in national courts. 1932. C6955
371 Sutch, W. B. Price fixing in New Zealand. 1932. C6956
372 Norton, T. L. Trade-union policies in the Massachusetts shoe industry. 1932. C6957
373 Mansfield, H. C. The lake cargo coal rate controversy. 1932. C6958
374 Withers, W. The retirement of national debts. 1932. C6959
375 Barzun, J. The French race. 1932. C6960
376 Lowrie, S. H. Culture conflict in Texas. 1932. C6961
377 Kayser, E. L. The grand social enterprise. 1932. C6962
378 Martin, B. Desertion of the Alabama troops from the Confederate army. 1932. C6963
379 Warburton, C. A. The economic results of prohibition. 1932. C6964
380 Cahill, M. C. Shorter hours. 1932. C6965
381 Cox, R. Competition in the American tobacco industry, 1911-32. 1933. C6966
382 Moss, W. Political parties in the Irish free state. 1933. C6967
383 Engelbrecht, H. C. Johann Gottlieb Fichte. 1933. C6968
384 Janowsky, O. I. The Jews and minority groups. 1933. C6969
385 Mullett, C. F. Fundamental law and the American revolution. 1933. C6970
386 Falnes, O. J. National romanticism in Norway. 1933. C6971
387 Walsh, H. H. The Concordat of 1801. 1933. C6972
388 Tobin, H. J. The termination of multipartite treaties. 1933. C6973
389 Chang, I. The interpretations of treaties by judicial tribunals. 1933. C6974
390 Peardon, T. P. The transition in English historical writing, 1760-1830. 1933. C6975
391 Souter, R. W. Prolegomena to relativity economics. 1933. C6976
392 Coleman, C. H. The election of 1868. 1933. C6977
393 French, P. H. The automobile compensation plan. 1933. C6978
394 Chên, C. Parliamentary opinion of delegated legislation. 1933. C6979
395 Dunkman, W. E. Qualitative credit control. 1933. C6980

396 Wang, C. Dissolution of the British Parliament, 1832-1931. 1934. C6981
397 Morais, H. M. Deism in eighteenth century America. 1934. C6982
398 Pinson, K. S. Pietism as a factor in the rise of German nationalism. 1934. C6983
399 Wood, M. M. The stranger. 1934. C6984
400 Whitney, C. Experiments in credit control. 1934. C6985
401 Bloch, H. A. The concept of changing loyalities. 1934. C6986
402 Collier, K. B. Cosmogonies of our fathers. 1934. C6987
403 Wisan, J. E. The Cuban crisis as reflected in the New York press (1895-1898). 1934. C6988
404 Harrington, V. D. The New York merchant on the eve of the revolution. 1935. C6989
405 Benson, M. S. Women in eighteenth century America. 1935. C6990
406 Coleman, J. K. State administration in South Carolina. 1935. C6991
407 Wirthwein, W. G. Britain and the Balkan crisis, 1875-1878. 1935. C6992
408 Libby, M. (Sherwood). The attitude of Voltaire to magic and the sciences. 1935. C6993
409 Swayzee, C. O. Contempt of court in labor injunction cases. 1935. C6994
410 McKee, S. Labor in colonial New York, 1664-1776. 1935. C6995
411 Connery, R. H. Governmental problems in wild life conservation. 1935. C6996
412 Bremer, C. D. American bank failures. 1935. C6997
413 Pundt, A. G. Arndt and the nationalist awakening in Germany. 1935. C6998
414 Kepner, C. D. Social aspects of the banana industry. 1936. C6999
415 Bussing, I. Public utility regulations and the so-called sliding scale. 1936. C7000
416 Ray, Mary Augustina, Sister. American opinion of Roman Catholicism in the eighteenth century. 1936. C7001
417 Shafer, H. B. The American medical profession 1783 to 1850. 1936. C7002
418 Woodward, F. M. The town proprietors in Vermont. 1936. C7003
419 Allen, E. J. The second United order among the Mormons. 1936. C7004
420 Franklin, C. L. The Negro labor unionist of New York. 1936. C7005
421 Reynolds, G. M. Machine politics in New Orleans, 1897-1926. 1936. C7006
422 Raphael, L. A. (Childs). The Cape-to-Cairo dream. 1936. C7007
423 Mack, R. (Prince). Controlling retailers. 1936. C7008
424 Anderson, S. A. Viking enterprise. 1936. C7009
425 Chang, D. British methods of industrial peace. 1936. C7010
426 Vondracek, F. J. The foreign policy of Czechoslovakia. 1937. C7011
427 Pabst, W. R. Butter and oleomargarine. 1937. C7012
428 Gambrell, M. L. Ministerial training in eighteenth century New England. 1937. C7013
429 Griffin, C. C. The United States and the disruption of the Spanish empire, 1810-1822. 1937. C7014
430 The Liverpool tractate, ed. by Strateman. 1937. C7015
431 Brady, J. H. Rome and the Neopolitan revolution of 1820-1821. 1937. C7016
432 Jewett, F. E. A financial history of Maine. 1937. C7017
433 Field, G. L. The syndical and corporative institutions of Italian Fascism. 1938. C7018

434 Campbell, E. G. The reorganization of the American railroad system, 1893-1900. 1938. C7019
435 Havlik, H. F. Service charges in gas and electric rates. 1938. C7020
436 Northrop, M. B. Control policies of the Reichsbank, 1924-1933. 1938. C7021
437 Eagan, J. M. Maximilien Robespierre. 1938. C7022
438 Robison, G. Revelliere-Lepeaux, citizen director, 1753-1824. 1938. C7023
439 East, R. A. Business enterprise in the American revolutionary era. 1938. C7024
440 McKean, D. D. Pressure on the Legislature of New Jersey. 1938. C7025
441 Manross, W. W. The Episcopal church in the United States, 1800-1840. 1938. C7026
442 Pomerantz, S. I. New York: an American city, 1783-1803. 1938. C7027
443 Saulnier, R. J. Contemporary monetary theory. 1938. C7028
444 Miller, H. S. Price control in fascist Italy. 1938. C7029
445 Alpert, H. Emile Durkheim and his sociology. 1939. C7030
446 Bloss, E. Labor legislation in Czechoslovakia. 1938. C7031
447 Freidman, J. A. The impeachment of Governor William Sulzer. 1939. C7032
448 Weintraub, R. (Goldstein). Government corporations and state law. 1939. C7033
449 Reid, I. D. The Negro immigrant. 1939. C7034
450 Reynolds, M. T. Interdepartmental committees in the national administration. 1939. C7035
451 Griffin, J. I. Strikes. 1939. C7036
452 Williams, E. A. Federal aid for relief. 1939. C7037
453 Abramovitz, M. An approach to a price theory for a changing economy. 1939. C7038
454 Cockroft, G. A. The public life of George Chalmers. 1939. C7039
455 Buthman, W. C. The rise of integral nationalism in France. 1939. C7040
456 Scudi, A. (Turner). The Sacheverell affair. 1939. C7041
457 Silvanie, H. Responsibility of states for acts of unsuccessful insurgent governments. 1939. C7042
458 Yoshpe, H. B. The disposition of Loyalist estates in the southern district of the state of New York. 1939. C7043
459 Williams, J. K. Grant-in-aids under the Public works administration. 1939. C7044
460 Strickland, R. C. Religion and the state in Georgia in the eighteenth century. 1939. C7045
461 Strong, D. F. Austria (October 1918 to March 1919). 1939. C7046
462 Jennings, Marietta, Sister. A pioneer merchant of St. Louis, 1810-1820. 1939. C7047
463 (Not published).
464 Wood, B. Peaceful change and the colonial problem. 1940. C7048
465 McGeary, M. M. The developments in congressional investigative power. 1940. C7049
466 Spector, M. M. (Mitchell). The American department of the British government, 1768-1782. 1940. C7050
467 Fisher, T. R. Industrial disputes and federal legislation. 1940. C7051
468 Bard, E. W. The Port of New York authority. 1942. C7052
469 Mark, I. Agrarian conflicts in colonial New York, 1711-1775. 1940. C7053
470 Hechler, K. W. Insurgency. 1940. C7054
471 McAvoy, T. T. The Catholic Church in Indiana, 1780-1834. 1940. C7055
472 Gaffey, J. D. The productivity of labor in the

rubber tire manufacturing industry. 1940. C7056
473 McCully, B. T. English education and the origins of Indian nationalism. 1940. C7057
474 Rodgers, E. (Cooperrider). Discussion of holidays in the later middle ages. 1940. C7058
475 Trinkaus, C. E. Adversity's nobleman. 1940. C7059
476 Glasser, C. Wage differentials. 1940. C7060
477 Campbell, P. C. Consumer representation in the new deal. 1940. C7061
478 Schroll, Mary Alfred, Sister. Benedictine monasticism as reflected in the Warnefrid-Hildemar commentaries on the rule. 1941. C7062
479 Crothers, G. D. The German elections of 1907. 1941. C7063
480 Emery, R. W. Heresy and inquisition in Narbonne. 1941. C7064
481 Turner, H. H. Case studies of consumers' cooperatives. 1941. C7065
482 Setton, K. M. Christian attitude towards the emperor in the fourth century. 1941. C7066
483 Clagett, M. Giovanni Marliani and late medieval physics. 1941. C7067
484 Rath, R. J. The fall of the Napoleonic kingdom of Italy (1814). 1941. C7068
485 Salera, V. Exchange control and the Argentine market. 1941. C7069
486 Acomb, E. M. The French laic laws, 1879-1889. 1941. C7070
487 Tims, R. W. Germanizing Prussian Poland. 1941. C7071
488 Curtis, W. R. The Lambeth conferences. 1942. C7072
489 Boone, G. The women's trade union leagues in Great Britain and the United States of America. 1942. C7073
490 Chaconas, S. G. Adamantios Korais. 1942. C7074
491 Hayden, S. S. The international protection of wild life. 1942. C7075
492 Robb, J. H. The Primrose league 1883-1906. 1942. C7076
493 Westphal, A. C. F. The House committee on foreign affairs. 1942. C7077
494 Greene, L. J. The Negro in colonial New England. 1620-1776. 1942. C7078
495 Sheedy, A. T. Bartolus on social conditions in the fourteenth century. 1942. C7079
496 Lombardi, J. Labor's voice in the cabinet. 1942. C7080
497 Post, A. Popular freethought in America, 1825-1850. 1943. C7081
498 Witmer, H. E. The property qualifications for members of Parliament. 1943. C7082
499 Crawford, M. M. Student folkways and spending at Indiana University. 1940-1941. 1943. C7083
500 Hurwitz, H. L. Theodore Roosevelt and labor in New York state. 1880-1900. 1943. C7084
501 Aptheker, H. American Negro slave revolts. 1943. C7085
502 Berger, M. The British traveller in America, 1836-1860. 1943. C7086
503 Macmillan, M. (Burham). The war governors in the American revolution. 1943. C7087
504 Warren, S. American freethought, 1860-1914. 1943. C7088
505 Levitats, I. The Jewish community in Russia, 1772-1844. 1943. C7089
506 Golob, E. O. The Méline tariff. 1943. C7090
507 Wolfbein, S. L. The decline of a cotton textile city. 1944. C7091
508 Rice, M. (Hooke). American Catholic opinion in the slavery controversy. 1944. C7092
509 Beik, P. H. A judgment of the old régime. 1944. C7093

510 Hellman, C. D. The comet of 1577. 1944. C7094
511 Ekirch, A. A. The idea of progress in America (1815-1860). 1944. C7095
512 Syrett, H. C. The city of Brooklyn, 1865-1898. 1944. C7096
513 Kennedy, V. D. Union policy and incentive wage methods. 1945. C7097
514 Gillim, M. H. The incidence of excess profits taxation. 1945. C7098
515 Robinson, M. (Russell). An introduction to the papers of the New York prize court, 1861-1865. 1945. C7099
516 Grossman, J. P. William Sylvis, pioneer of American labor. 1945. C7100
517 Doukas, K. A. The French railroads and the state... 1945. C7101
518 Ahearn, D. J. The wages of farm and factory laborers, 1914-1944. 1945. C7102
519 Müller, C. (Feldman). Light metals monopoly. 1946. C7103
520 Shanahan, W. O. Prussian military reforms, 1786-1813. 1945. C7104
521 Wyckoff, V. The public works wage rate and some of its economic effects. 1946. C7105
522 Leonard, W. N. Railroad consolidation under the Transportation act of 1920. 1946. C7106
523 Chamberlain, L. H. The President, Congress and legislation. 1946. C7107
524 Thompson, D. G. B. Ruggles of New York. 1946. C7108
525 Shapiro, E. Credit union development in Wisconsin. 1947. C7109
526 Porter, A. O. County government in Virginia (1607-1904). 1947. C7110
527 MacKay, K. C. The progressive movement of 1924. 1947. C7111
528 Ware, E. K. A constitutional history of Georgia. 1947. C7112
529 Belcher, W. W. Economic rivalry between St. Louis and Chicago, 1850-1880. 1947. C7113
530 Fowler, G. B. Intellectual interests of Engelbert of Admont. 1947. C7114
531 Chamberlin, W. C. Economic development of Iceland through World War II. 1947. C7115
532 Nelson, M. V. A study of judicial review in Virginia, 1789-1928. 1947. C7116
533 Schargo, N. N. History in the Encyclopédie. 1947. C7117
534 Reder, M. W. Studies in the theory of welfare economics. 1947. C7118
535 Millington, H. American diplomacy and the War of the Pacific. 1948. C7119
536 Pleasants, S. A. Fernando Wood of New York. 1948. C7120
537 Rauch, B. American interest in Cuba, 1848-1855. 1948. C7121
538 Inquisition. Inquisition at Albi, 1299-1300: Davis. 1948. C7122
539 Lent, G. E. The impact of the undistributed profits tax, 1936-1937. 1948. C7123
540 Saveth, E. N. American historians and European immigrants. 1948. C7124
541 Campbell, R. F. The history of basic metals price control in World War II. 1948. C7125
542 Leiter, R. D. The foreman in industrial relations. 1948. C7126
543 Graber, D. A. The development of the law belligerent occupation. 1948. C7127
544 Link, E. (Murr). The emancipation of the Austrian peasant. 1949. C7128
545 Hartmann, E. G. The movement to Americanize the immigrant. 1948. C7129
546 Hurwitz, S. J. State intervention in Great Britain. 1949. C7130

547 Williams, E. The animating pursuits of speculation. 1949. C7131
548 Dillon, D. R. The New York triumvirate. 1949. C7132
549 Holleran, M. P. Church state relations in Guatemala. 1949. C7133
550 Ulmer, M. J. The economic theory of cost of living index numbers. 1949. C7134
551 Gold, B. Wartime economic planning in agriculture. 1949. C7135
552 Garraty, J. A. Silas Wright. 1949. C7136
553 Sievers, A. M. Has market capitalism collapsed? 1949. C7137
554 Greig, G. B. Seasonal fluctuations in employment in the women's clothing industry in New York. 1949. C7138
555 Wendell, M. Relations between federal and state courts. 1949. C7139
556 Merlin, S. D. The theory of fluctuation contemporary economic thought. 1949. C7140
557 Berlau, A. J. The German Social Democratic Party, 1914-1921. 1949. C7141
558 Straus, H. A. The attitude of the Congress of Vienna toward nationalism in Germany, Italy, and Poland. 1949. C7142
559 Jenks, W. A. The Austrian electoral reform of 1907. 1950. C7143
560 Edelstein, D. S. Joel Munsell. 1950. C7144
561 Cowan, L. G. France and the Saar, 1680-1948. 1950. C7145
562 Gordon, D. C. The Australian frontier in New Guinea, 1870-1885. 1951. C7146
563 Gibson, F. E. The attitude of the New York Irish toward state and national affairs, 1884-1892. 1951. C7147
564 White, M. I. Personal income tax reduction in a business contraction. 1951. C7148
565 Brown, B. E. American conservatives. 1951. C7149
566 Tirrell, S. R. German agrarian politics after Bismarck's fall. 1951. C7150
567 Ausuble, H. Historians and their craft. 1950. C7151
568 Haller, W. The Puritan frontier: town-planning in New England colonial development, 1630-1660. 1951. C7152
569 Wolfe, M. The French franc between the wars, 1919-1939. 1951. C7153
570 Noether, E. P. Seeds of Italian nationalism, 1700-1815. 1951. C7154
571 Davis, J. A. Regional organization of the Social Security Administration; a case study. 1950. C7155
572 Shulim, J. I. Old Dominion and Napoleon Bonaparte. 1952. C7156
573 Scott, J. A. Republican ideas and the liberal tradition in France 1870-1914. 1951. C7157
574 Smith, F. A. Judicial review of legislation in New York, 1906-1938. 1952. C7158
575 Bauer, E. K. Commentaries on the Constitution, 1790-1860. 1952. C7159
576 Bigelow, D. N. William Conant Church & The Army and Navy journal. 1952. C7160
577 Elbow, M. H. French corporative theory, 1789-1848. 1953. C7161
578 Lander, B. Towards an understanding of juvenile delinquency. 1954. C7162

After this number the title of the series changed to Studies in Social Science. Numbering continues in the new series with no. 579.

COLUMBIA UNIVERSITY STUDIES IN INTERNATIONAL ORGANIZATION

1 Jessup, P. C. and Tauberfeld, H. J. Controls for outer space and the Antarctic analogy. 1959. C7163
2 Rosner, G. The United Nations Emergency force.

1963. C7164
3 Mangone, G. J., ed. U.N. administration of economic and social programs. 1966. C7165
4 Gordenker, L. The UN Secretary-General and the maintenance of peace. 1967. C7166
5 Sharp, W. R. The United Nations Economics and Social Council. 1969. C7167
6 Castandea, J. Legal effects of United Nations resolutions. 1970. C7168
7 Zacher, M. W. Dag Hammarskjold's United Nations. 1970. C7169
8 Kay, D. A. The new nations in the United Nations. 1970. C7170

COLUMBIA UNIVERSITY. STUDIES IN LIBRARY SCIENCE.

1 Schneider, G. Theory and history of bibliography. 1934. C7171
2 Haines, H. E. Living with books. 1951. C7172
3 Fargo, L. F. Preparation for school library work. 1936. C7173
4 Reece, E. J. The curriculum in library schools. 1936. C7174
5 Hamlin, T. F. Some European architectural libraries. 1939. C7175
6 Haines, H. E. What's in a novel. 1942. C7176
7 Tauber, M. F. and others, eds. Technical services in libraries. 1953. C7177
8 Wilson, L. R. The university library. 1956. C7178
9 Columbia University. The Columbia University Libraries, ed. by Tauber. 1957. C7179
10 Symposium on Information storage and Retrieval Theory Systems, and Devices. Storage and retrieval theory, systems and devices. 1958. C7180
11 Ruggles, M. J. and Mostecky, V. Russian and East European publications in the libraries of the United States. 1960. C7181
12 Danton, J. P. Book selection and collections. 1963. C7182
13 Williamson, W. L. William Frederick Poole and the modern library movement. 1963. C7183
14 Schellenberg, T. R. The management of archives. 1965. C7184
15 Tauber, M. F. Louis Round Wilson. 1967. C7185
16 Conference on Library Surveys. Library surveys, ed. by Tauber and Stephens. 1967. C7186
No. 7 published as Studies in Library Service.

COLUMBIA UNIVERSITY. STUDIES IN MUSICOLOGY.

1 Nef, K. An outline of the history of music. 1957. C7187
2 Brennecke, E. John Milton the elder and his music. 1938. C7188
3 Pratt, W. S. The music of the French Psalter of 1562. 1939. C7189
4 Upton, W. T. Anthony Philip Heinrich. 1939. C7190
5 Johnson, H. E. Musical interludes in Boston. 1943. C7191
6 Lowinsky, E. E. Secret chromatic art in the Netherlands motet. 1946. C7192
7 Bartók, B. and Lord, A. B., eds. Serbo-Crotian folk songs. 1951. C7193

COLUMBIA UNIVERSITY. TEACHERS COLLEGE. CONTRIBUTIONS TO EDUCATION.

1 Meriam, J. L. Normal school education and efficiency in teaching. 1905. C7194
2 Cubberley, E. P. School funds and their appropriation. 1905. C7195
3 Suzzallo, H. The rise of local school supervision in Massachusetts. 1906. C7196
4 Mac Vannel, J. A. The educational theories of

Herbart and Froebel. 1905. C7197
5 Strayer, G. D. City school expenditures. 1905. C7198
6 Elliott, E. E. Some fiscal aspects of public education in American cities. 1906. C7199
7 Farrington, F. E. The public primary school system of France. 1906. C7200
8 Jackson, L. L. The educational significance of sixteenth century arithmetic. 1906. C7201
9 Lodge, G. The vocabulary of high school Latin. 1909. C7202
10 Snow, L. F. The college curriculum in the United States. 1907. C7203
11 Abelson, P. The seven liberal arts. 1906. C7204
12 Snedden, D. S. Administration and educational work of American juvenile reform schools. 1907. C7205
13 Williams, A. T. The concept of equality in the writings of Rousseau, Bentham, and Kant. 1907. C7206
14 Cole, P. R. Herbart and Froebel. 1907. C7207
15 Coleman, H. T. J. Public education in upper Canada. 1907. C7208
16 Coursault, J. H. The learning process. 1907. C7209
17 Updegraff, H. The origin of the moving school in Massachusetts. 1908. C7210
18 Earhart, L. B. Systematic study in the elementary schools. 1908. C7211
19 Stone, C. W. Arithmetical abilities and some factors determining them. 1908. C7212
20 Haney, J. D. Lessing's Education of the human race. 1908. C7213
21 Erasmus, D. Ciceronianus. 1908. C7214
22 Stowe, A. R. M. English grammar schools in the reign of Queen Elizabeth. 1908. C7215
23 Stamper, A. W. A history of the teaching of elementary geometry. 1906. C7216
24 Snyder, E. R. The legal status of rural high schools in the United States. 1909. C7217
25 Jackson, G. L. The development of school support in colonial Massachusetts. 1909. C7218
26 Betts, G. H. The distribution and functions of mental imagery. 1909. C7219
27 Cole, P. R. Later Roman education. 1909. C7220
28 Bard, H. E. The city school district statutory provisions for organizational and fiscal affairs. 1909. C7221
29 Nicholson, A. M. The concept standard. 1910. C7222
30 Haney, J. D. Registration of city school children. 1910. C7223
31 Kandel, I. L. The training of elementary school teachers in Germany. 1910. C7224
32 Staniford, P. The training of teachers in England and Wales. 1910. C7225
33 Goodsell, W. The conflict of naturalism and humanism. 1910. C7226
34 Lomer, G. R. The concept of method. 1910. C7227
35 Scott, I. Controversies over the imitation of Cicero as a model for style. 1910. C7228
36 Alexander, C. Some present aspects of the work of teachers' voluntary association in the United States. 1910. C7229
37 Bonser, F. G. The reasoning ability of children in the fourth, fifth, and sixth school grades. 1910. C7230
38 Rabenort, W. L. Spinoza as educator. 1911. C7231
39 Robison, C. H. Agricultural instruction in the public schools of the United States. 1911. C7232
40 Blan, L. B. A special study of the incidence of retardation. 1911. C7233
41 Coffman, L. D. The social composition of the teaching population. 1911. C7234
42 Keyes, C. H. Progress

through the grades of city schools. 1911. C7235
43 Jessup, W. A. The social factors affecting special supervision in the public schools of the United States. 1911. C7236
44 Fitzpatrick, E. A. The educational views and influence of De Witt Clinton. 1911. C7237
45 Inglis, A. J. The rise of the high school in Massachusetts. 1911. C7238
46 Leland, A. P. The educational theory and practice of T. H. Green. 1911. C7239
47 Van Denburg, J. K. Causes of the elimination of students in public secondary schools of New York City. 1911. C7240
48 Stevens, R. The question as a measure of efficiency in instruction. 1912. C7241
49 Brown, S. W. The secularization of American education as shown by state legislation. 1912. C7242
50 Henderson, J. L. Admission to college by certificate. 1912. C7243
51 Burnham, E. Two types of rural schools. 1912. C7244
52 Robbins, C. L. Teachers in Germany in the sixteenth century. 1912. C7245
53 Simpson, B. R. Correlation of mental abilities. 1912. C7246
54 Arai, T. Mental fatigue. 1912. C7247
55 Holland, E. C. The Pennsylvania state normal school and public school system. 1912. C7248
56 Kemp, W. W. The support of schools in colonial New York by the Society for the Propagation of the Gospel. 1913. C7249
57 McConaughy, J. L. The school drama. 1913. C7250
58 Kirby, T. J. Practice in the case of school children. 1913. C7251
59 Buckingham, B. R. Spelling ability. 1913. C7252
60 Knight, E. W. The influence of reconstruction on education in the South. 1913. C7253
61 Miller, J. C. Rural schools in Canada. 1913. C7254
62 Hutchinson, J. H. School costs and school accounting. 1914. C7255
63 Chapman, J. C. Individual differences in ability and improvement. 1914. C7256
64 Kuo, P. W. The Chinese system of public education. 1914. C7257
65 Davidson, P. E. The recapitulation theory and human infancy. 1914. C7258
66 Kelly, F. J. Teachers' marks. 1914. C7259
67 Horn, E. Distribution of opportunity for participation among the various pupils in class-room recitations. 1915. C7260
68 Bronner, A. F. A comparative study of the intelligence of delinquent girls. 1914. C7261
69 Hollingworth, L. Functional periodicity. 1914. C7262
70 Hedges, A. C. Wage worth of school training. 1915. C7263
71 Kelley, T. L. Educational guidance. 1914. C7264
72 Elliott, C. H. Variation in the achievement of pupils. 1914. C7265
73 Barranco, M. Mexico. 1915. C7266
74 Prosser, C. A. A study of the Boston mechanic arts high school. 1915. C7267
75 McDonald, R. A. F. Adjustment of school organization to various population groups. 1915. C7268
76 Mead, C. D. The relations of general intelligence to certain mental and physical traits. 1916. C7269
77 Trabue, M. R. Completion-test language scales. 1916. C7270
78 Thorndike, E. L. and others. Ventilation in relation to mental work. 1916. C7271
79 McCall, W. A. Correlation of some psychological and educational measurements. 1916. C7272
80 Woody, C. Measurements

of some achievements in arithmetic. 1916. C7273
81 Reigart, J. F. The Lancasterian system of instruction in the schools of New York City. 1916. C7274
82 Smith, H. L. A survey of a public school system, Bloomington, Indiana. 1917. C7275
83 Stone, C. W. Standardized reasoning tests in arithmetic and how to utilize them. 1921. C7276
84 Theisen, W. W. The city superintendent and the board of education. 1917. C7277
85 Seybolt, R. E. Apprenticeship & apprenticeship education in colonial New England & New York. 1917. C7278
86 Eaton, T. H. A study of organization and method of the course of study in agriculture in secondary schools. 1917. C7279
87 Heckert, J. W. The organization of instruction materials with special relation to the elementary school curriculum. 1917. C7280
88 Hollingworth, W. C. A. The psychology of special disability in spelling. 1918. C7281
89 Rogers, A. L. Experimental tests of mathematical ability and their prognostic value. 1918. C7282
90 Hotz, H. G. First year algebra scales. 1918. C7283
91 Mead, A. R. The development of free schools in the United States as illustrated by Connecticut and Michigan. 1918. C7284
92 Kruse, P. J. The overlapping of attainments in certain sixth, seventh, and eighth grades. 1918. C7285
93 Maddox, W. A. The free school idea in Virginia before the Civil war. 1918. C7286
94 Noble, S. G. Forty years of public schools in Mississippi. 1918. C7287
95 Steacy, F. W. The interrelations of mental abilities. 1919. C7288
96 Engelhardt, N. L. A school building program for cities. 1918. C7289
97 Cummins, R. A. Improvement and the distribution of practice. 1919. C7290
98 Buckner, C. A. Educational diagnosis of individual pupils. 1919. C7291
99 Fretwell, E. K. A study in educational prognosis. 1919. C7292
100 Wilson, G. M. A survey of the social and business usage of arithmetic. 1919. C7293
101 Van Wagenen, M. J. Historical information and judgment in pupils in the elementary schools. 1919. C7294
102 O'Brien, F. P. The high school failures. 1919. C7295
103 Murdoch, K. The measurement of certain elements of hand sewing. 1919. C7296
104 Lewis, I. B. The education of girls in China. 1919. C7297
105 Woody, T. Early Quaker education in Pennsylvania. 1920. C7298
106 Trueman, G. J. School funds in the Province of Quebec. 1920. C7299
107 Jordan, A. M. Children's interests in reading. 1921. C7300
108 Reavis, G. H. Factors controlling attendance in rural schools. 1921. C7301
109 Berkson, I. B. Theories of Americanization. 1920. C7302
110 Crane, A. G. Education for the disabled in war and industry. 1921. C7303
111 Frost, N. A comparative study of achievement in country and town schools. 1921. C7304
112 Voelker, P. F. The function of ideals and attitudes in social education. 1921. C7305
113 Dunn, F. W. Interest factors in primary reading material. 1921. C7306
114 Hosic, J. F. Empirical studies in reading. 1921. C7307

115 Toops, H. A. Trade tests in education. 1921. C7308
116 Brooks, F. D. Change in mental traits with age determined by annual re-tests. 1921. C7309
117 Rosenberger, N. B. The place of the elementary calculus in the senior high-school mathematics. 1921. C7310
118 Taylor, H. C. The educational significance of the early federal land ordinances. 1922. C7311
119 Norman, J. W. A comparison of tendencies in secondary education in England and the United States. 1922. C7312
120 Knight, F. B. Qualities related to success in teaching. 1922. C7313
121 Gambrill, B. L. College achievement and vocational efficiency. 1922. C7314
122 Moxcey, M. E. Some qualities associated with success in the Christian ministry. 1922. C7315
123 Nordgaard, M. A. A historical survey of algebraic methods of approximating the roots of numerical higher equations up to the year 1819. 1922. C7316
124 Race, H. V. Improvability. 1922. C7317
125 Franzen, R. H. The accomplishment ratio. 1922. C7318
126 Liu, H. C. Non-verbal intelligence tests for use in China. 1922. C7319
127 Chu, J. P. Chinese students in America. 1922. C7320
128 Russell, C. The improvement of city elementary school teacher in service. 1922. C7321
129 Gates, A. I. The psychology of reading and spelling. 1922. C7322
130 Stenquist, J. L. Measurements of mechanical ability. 1921. C7323
131 Coy, G. L. The interests, abilities and achievements of a special class for gifted children. 1923. C7324
132 Symonds, P. M. Special disability in algebra. 1923. C7325
133 Osuna, J. J. Education in Porto Rico. 1923. C7326
134 Taylor, G. A. The inventory of the minds of individuals of six and seven years mental age. 1923. C7327
135 Allen, W. S. A study in Latin prognosis. 1923. C7328
136 Toops, H. A. Tests for vocational guidance of children thirteen to sixteen. 1923. C7329
137 Chang, P. Education for modernization in China. 1923. C7330
138 Wells, G. F. Parish education in colonial Virginia. 1923. C7331
139 Cunningham, B. V. The prognostic value of a primary group test. 1923. C7332
140 Somers, G. T. Pedagogical prognosis. 1923. C7333
141 Crow, C. S. Evaluation of English literature in the high school. 1924. C7334
142 Humphreys, H. C. The factors operating in the location of state normal schools. 1923. C7335
143 Graves, K. B. The influence of specialized training on tests of general intelligence. 1924. C7336
144 Clem, O. M. Detailed factors in Latin prognosis. 1924. C7337
145 Clark, H. F. The cost of government and the support of education. 1924. C7338
146 Touton, F. C. Solving geometric originals. 1924. C7339
147 Mossman, L. C. Changing conceptions relative to the planning of lessons. 1924. C7340
148 Ruggles, A. M. A diagnostic test of aptitude for clerical office work. 1924. C7341
149 Powers, S. R. A diagnostic study of the subject matter of high school

chemistry. 1924. C7342
150 Mort, P. R. The measurement of educational need. 1924. C7343
151 Moore, C. B. Civic education. 1924. C7344
152 Vincent, L. A study of intelligence test elements. 1924. C7345
153 Henzlik, F. E. Rights and liabilities of public school boards under capital outlay contracts. 1924. C7346
154 Bere, M. A comparative study of the mental capacity of children of foreign parentage. 1924. C7347
155 Carrothers, G. E. The physical efficiency of teachers. 1924. C7348
156 Teagarden, F. M. A study of the upper limits of the development of intelligence. 1924. C7349
157 McLure, J. N. The ventilation of school buildings. 1924. C7350
158 Hanson, W. L. The costs of compulsory attendance service in the state of New York. 1924. C7351
159 Packer, P. C. Housing of high school programs. 1924. C7352
160 Andrus, R. A tentative inventory of habits of children from two to four years of age. 1924. C7353
161 Brinkley, S. G. Values of new type examinations in the high school. 1924. C7354
162 Bailor, E. M. Content and form in tests of intelligence. 1924. C7355
163 Curtis, F. D. Some values derived from extensive reading of general science. 1924. C7356
164 Stolz, L. H. (Meek). A study of learning and retention in young children. 1925. C7357
165 Hamilton, F. R. Fiscal support of state teachers colleges. 1924. C7358
166 Ross, C. C. The relation between grade school record and high school achievement. 1925. C7359
167 Reeves, C. E. An analysis of janitor service in elementary schools. 1925. C7360
168 Melchior, W. T. Insuring public school property. 1925. C7361
169 Hall-Quest, A. L. Professional secondary education in teachers colleges. 1925. C7362
170 Wylie, A. T. The opposites test. 1925. C7363
171 Engelhardt, F. Forecasting school population. 1925. C7364
172 Noffsinger, J. S. A program for higher education in the Church of the brethren. 1925. C7365
173 Rogers, F. R. Physical capacity tests in the administration of physical education. 1925. C7366
174 Vanuxem, M. Education of feeble-minded women. 1925. C7367
175 Crabbs, L. M. Measuring efficiency in supervision and teaching. 1925. C7368
176 Watson, G. B. The measurement of fair-mindedness. 1925. C7369
177 Bruner, H. B. The Junior high school at work. 1925. C7370
178 Cook, J. H. A study of the mill schools of North Carolina. 1925. C7371
179 Perry, W. M. A study in the psychology of learning in geometry. 1925. C7372
180 Lentz, T. F. An experimental method for the discovery and development of tests of character. 1925. C7373
181 Singleton, G. G. State responsibility for the support of education in Georgia. 1925. C7374
182 Larson, E. L. One-room and consolidated schools of Connecticut. 1925. C7375
183 Dearborn, N. H. The Oswego movement in American education. 1925. C7376
184 Morrison, F. W.

Equalization of the financial burden of education among counties in North Carolina. 1925. C7377
185 Hunsicker, L. M. A study of the relationship between rate and ability. 1925. C7378
186 Hildreth, G. H. The resemblance of siblings in intelligence and achievement. 1925. C7379
187 Woodring, M. N. A study of the quality of English in Latin translations. 1925. C7380
188 Rosen, E. K. A comparison of the intellectual and educational status of neurotic and normal children in public schools. 1925. C7381
189 Irion, T. W. H. Comprehension difficulties of ninth grade students in the study of literature. 1925. C7382
190 Daily, B. W. The ability of high school pupils to select essential data in solving problems. 1925. C7383
191 Carpenter, W. W. Certain phases of the administration of high school chemistry. 1925. C7384
192 Meltzer, H. Children's social concepts. 1925. C7385
193 Reeder, E. H. A method of directing children's study of geography. 1925. C7386
194 Mosher, R. M. A study of the group method of measurement of sight-singing. 1925. C7387
195 Flanders, J. K. Legislative control of the elementary curriculum. 1925. C7388
196 Flemming, C. (White). A detailed analysis of achievement in the high school. 1925. C7389
197 Smith, H. P. The business administration of a city school system. 1926. C7390
198 Klyver, F. H. The supervision of student-teachers in religious education. 1925. C7391
199 Finley, C. W. Biology in secondary schools and the training of biology teachers. 1926. C7392
200 Emmons, F. E. City school attendance service. 1926. C7393
201 Curoe, P. R. V. Educational attitudes and policies of organized labor in the United States. 1926. C7394
202 Pryor, H. C. Graded units in student-teaching. 1926. C7395
203 Jones, V. A. Effect of age and experience on tests of intelligence. 1926. C7396
204 Noonan, M. E. Influence of summer vacation on the abilities of fifth and sixth grade children. 1926. C7397
205 Wagenhorst, L. H. The administration and cost of high school interscholastic athletics. 1926. C7398
206 Orleans, J. S. A study of the nature of difficulty. 1926. C7399
207 Bartlett, L. W. State control of private incorporated institutions of higher education as defined in decisions of the U. S. Supreme Court. 1926. C7400
208 Loomis, A. K. The techniques of estimating school equipment costs. 1926. C7401
209 Helseth, I. O. Children's thinking. 1926. C7402
210 Grossman, M. The philosophy of the Helvetius. 1926. C7403
211 Schwesinger, G. C. The social-ethical significance of vocabulary. 1926. C7404
212 Ayer, A. M. Some difficulties in elementary school history. 1926. C7405
213 Olsen, H. C. The works of boards of education. 1926. C7406
214 Hertzberg, O. E. A comparative study of different methods used in teaching beginners to write. 1926. C7407
215 Job, L. B. Business management of institutional homes for children. 1926. C7408
216 Woodyard, E. The effect of time upon varability. 1926. C7409
217 Saxman, E. J. Students' use in leisure time of activities learned in physical

education in state teachers college. 1926. C7410
218 Tilton, J. W. The relation between association and the higher mental processes. 1926. C7411
219 Day, M. S. Scheubel as an algebraist. 1926. C7412
220 Brown, A. W. The unevenness of the abilities of dull and bright children. 1926. C7413
221 McHale, K. Comparative psychology and hygiene of the overweight child. 1926. C7414
222 Strang, R. M. Subject matter in health education. 1926. C7415
223 Kennon, L. H. V. Tests of literary vocabulary for teachers of English. 1926. C7416
224 Lerrigo, M. O. Health problem sources. 1926. C7417
225 Weidemann, C. C. How to construct the true-false examination. 1926. C7418
226 Not published.
227 Jones, W. B. Job analysis and curriculum construction in the metal trades industry. 1926. C7419
228 Taylor, R. D. Principles of school supply management. 1926. C7420
229 Blanekship, A. S. The accessibility of rural schoolhouses in Texas. 1926. C7421
230 Willing, M. H. Valid diagnosis in high school composition. 1926. C7422
231 Totah, K. A. The contribution of the Arabs to education. 1926. C7423
232 Stroh, M. M. Literature for grades 7-9. 1926. C7424
233 Hill, C. M. A decade of progress in teacher training. 1927. C7425
234 Granrud, J. E. The organization and objectives of state teachers' associations. 1926. C7426
235 Arent, E. The relation of the state of private education in Norway. 1926. C7427
236 Rufi, J. The small high school. 1926. C7428
237 Butterweck, J. S. The problem of teaching high school pupils how to study. 1926. C7429
238 Ford, W. S. Some administrative problems of the high school cafeteria. 1926. C7430
239 Neumann, G. B. A study of international attitudes of high school students. 1926. C7431
240 Schwartz, H. M. Improvement in the maintenance of public school buildings. 1926. C7432
241 Mathews, C. O. The grade placement of curriculum materials in the social studies. 1926. C7433
242 Shaw, F. L. State public reports. 1926. C7434
243 Steele, R. M. A study of teacher training in Vermont. 1926. C7435
244 McMullen, L. B. The service load in teacher training institutions of the United States. 1927. C7436
245 Carroll, R. P. An experimental study of comprehension in reading. 1927. C7437
246 Anderson, E. W. The teacher contract and other legal phases of teacher status. 1927. C7438
247 Smith, J. M. The training of high school teachers in Louisiana. 1927. C7439
248 Walters, F. C. A statistical study of certain aspects of the time factor in intelligence. 1927. C7440
249 Quance, F. M. Part-time types of elementary schools in New York city. 1926. C7441
250 Hamilton, O. T. The courts and the curriculum. 1927. C7442
251 Sanford, V. The history and significance of certain standard problems in algebra. 1927. C7443
252 Spence, R. B. The improvement of college marking systems. 1927. C7444
253 Johnson, G. B. Organization of the required physical

education for women in state universities. 1927. C7445
254 Thompson, H. An experimental study of the beginning reading of deaf-mutes. 1927. C7446
255 Nesmith, M. E. An objective determination of stories and poems for the primary grades. 1927. C7447
256 Stuart, H. The training of modern foreign language teachers... 1927. C7448
257 Massó, G. Education in Utopias. 1927. C7449
258 Hypes, J. L. Social participation in a rural New England town. 1927. C7450
259 Cunningham, K. S. The measurement of early levels of intelligence. 1927. C7451
260 Waring, E. M. The relation between early language habits and early habits of conduct control. 1927. C7452
261 Smith, M. Education and the integration of behavior. 1927. C7453
262 Bender, J. F. The functions of courts in enforcing school attendance laws. 1927. C7454
263 Benedict, M. J. The God of the Old Testament in relation to war. 1927. C7455
264 Morphet, E. L. The measurement and interpretation of school building utilization. 1927. C7456
265 Koos, F. H. State participation in public school library service. 1927. C7457
266 Myers, A. F. A teacher-training program for Ohio. 1927. C7458
267 Landis, B. Y. Professional codes. 1927. C7459
268 Elliott, R. The organization of professional training in physical education in state universities. 1927. C7460
269 Carr, J. W. Factors affecting distribution of trained teachers among rural white elementary schools of North Carolina. 1927. C7461
270 Morehart, G. C. The legal status of city school boards. 1927. C7462
271 Irvin, O. W. State budget control of state institutions of higher education. 1928. C7463
272 Reynolds, O. E. The social and economic status of college students. 1927. C7464
273 Abelson, H. H. The improvement of intelligence testing. 1927. C7465
274 Dyer, W. P. Activities of the elementary school principal for the improvement of instruction. 1927. C7466
275 Coryell, N. G. An evaluation of extensive and intensive teaching of literature. 1927. C7467
276 Craig, G. S. Certain techniques used in developing a course of study in science for the Horace Mann elementary school. 1927. C7468
277 Jacobs, C. L. The relation of the teacher's education to her effectiveness. 1928. C7469
278 Borgeson, F. C. The administration of elementary and secondary education in Sweden. 1927. C7470
279 Todd, W. H. What citizens know about their schools. 1927. C7471
280 Garrison, N. L. Status and work of the training supervisor. 1927. C7472
281 Hockett, J. A. A determination of the major problems of American life. 1927. C7473
282 Thomas, M. W. Public school plumbing equipment. 1928. C7474
283 Laws, G. Parent-child relationships. 1927. C7475
284 Duvall, S. M. The Methodist Episcopal church and education up to 1869. 1928. C7476
285 Linton, C. A study of some problems arising in the admission of students as candidates for professional degrees in education. 1927. C7477
286 Jewett, I. A. English in state teachers colleges.

1927. C7478
287 Van de Voort, A. M. The teaching of science in normal schools and teachers colleges. 1927. C7479
288 Reynolds, M. M. Negativism of pre-school children. 1928. C7480
289 Burns, R. L. Measurement of the need for transporting pupils. 1927. C7481
290 Reed, M. M. An investigation of practices in first grade admission and promotion. 1927. C7482
291 Snedden, D. A. A study in disguised intelligence tests. 1927. C7483
292 Wilson, F. T. Learning of bright and dull children. 1928. C7484
293 Griffin, O. B. The evolution of the Connecticut state school system. 1928. C7485
294 Harper, M. H. Social beliefs and attitudes of American educators. 1927. C7486
295 Brubacher, J. S. The judicial power of the New York state commissioner of education. 1927. C7487
296 Uhrbrock, R. S. An analysis of the Downey will-temperament tests. 1928. C7488
297 Ziegler, F. F. School attendance as a factor in school progress. 1928. C7489
298 Ho, C. J. Personnel studies of scientists in the United States. 1928. C7490
299 Tidwell, C. J. State control of textbooks. 1928. C7491
300 Elsbree, W. S. Teacher turnover in the cities and villages of New York State. 1928. C7492
301 Holloway, W. J. Participation in curriculum making as a means of supervision of rural schools. 1928. C7493
302 Hollingshead, A. D. An evaluation of the use of certain educational and mental measurements for purposes of classification. 1928. C7494
303 Horton, R. E. Measurable outcomes of individual laboratory work in high school chemistry. 1928. C7495
304 Allen, I. M. The teacher's contractual status as revealed by an analysis of American court decisions. 1928. C7496
305 Young, D. S. Control of available public school income. 1928. C7497
306 Fisher, J. E. Democracy and mission education in Korea. 1928. C7498
307 Meader, J. L. Normal school education in Connecticut. 1928. C7499
308 Neulen, L. N. State aid for educational projects in the public schools. 1928. C7500
309 Linscheid, A. In-service improvement of the state teachers college faculty. 1928. C7501
310 Slay, R. J. The development of the teaching of agriculture in Mississippi. 1928. C7502
311 Meadows, L. R. A study of the teaching of English composition in teachers colleges of the United States. 1928. C7503
312 Huber, M. (Blanton). The influence of intelligence upon children's reading interests. 1928. C7504
313 Schaaf, W. L. A course for teachers of junior high school mathematics. 1928. C7505
314 McDowell, E. V. Educational and emotional adjustments of stuttering children. 1928. C7506
315 Mahan, T. J. An analysis of the characteristics of citizenship. 1928. C7507
316 Zirbes, L. Comparative studies of current practice in reading. 1928. C7508
317 Meader, E. B. Teaching speech in the elementary school. 1928. C7509
318 Dyer, A. I. The administration of home economics in city schools. 1928. C7510
319 Sturtevant, S. M. and Strang, R. M. A personnel

study of deans of women in teachers colleges and normal schools. 1928. C7511

320 Harry, D. P. Cost of living of teachers in the state of New York. 1928. C7512

321 Keys, N. The improvement of measurement through cumulative testing. 1928. C7513

322 Hsia, J-C. A study of the sociability of elementary school children. 1928. C7514

323 Alpert, A. The solving of problem-situations by preschool children. 1928. C7515

324 Everett, J. P. The fundamental skills of algebra. 1928. C7516

325 Brownell, C. L. A scale for measuring the antero-posterior posture of ninth grade boys. 1928. C7517

326 Jones, J. L. A personnel study of women deans in college and universities. 1928. C7518

327 Boardman, C. W. Professional tests as measures of teaching efficiency in high school. 1928. C7519

328 Bamesberger, V. C. An appraisal of a social studies course. 1928. C7520

329 Cocking, W. D. Administrative procedures in curriculum making in public schools. 1928. C7521

330 Johns, R. L. State and local administration of school transportation. 1928. C7522

331 Acheson, E. L. The construction of junior church school curricula. 1929. C7523

332 Bain, W. E. An analytical study of teaching in nursery school, kindergarten and first grade. 1928. C7524

333 Mann, C. H. How schools use their time. 1928. C7525

334 Coale, W. B. The professional needs of teachers of English. 1928. C7526

335 Beechel, E. E. A citizenship program for elementary schools. 1928. C7527

336 Chadbourne, A. H. The beginnings of education in Maine. 1928. C7528

337 Reals, W. H. A study of the summer high school. 1928. C7529

338 Chen, H. S. The comparative coachability of certain types of intelligence tests. 1928. C7530

339 Scott, H. A. Personnel study of directors of physical education for men in colleges and universities. 1929. C7531

340 Bowden, A. O. Consumers use of arithmetic. 1929. C7532

341 Chappelear, C. S. Health subject matter in natural sciences. 1929. C7533

342 Morris, W. H. Personal traits and success in teaching. 1929. C7534

343 Morris, J. T. Considerations in establishing a junior college. 1929. C7535

344 Laton, A. D. The psychology of learning applied to health education through biology. 1929. C7536

345 Dyde, W. F. Public secondary education in Canada. 1929. C7537

346 McGuffey, V. Differences in the activities of teachers in rural one-teacher schools and of grade teachers in cities. 1929. C7538

347 Rosenlof, G. W. Library facilities in teacher-training institutions. 1929. C7539

348 Gauger, M. E. The modifiability of response to taste stimuli in the preschool child. 1929. C7540

349 Soper, W. W. Legal limitations on the rights and powers of school boards with respect to taxation. 1929. C7541

350 Branegan, G. A. Home economics teacher training under the Smith-Hughes act, 1917-1927. 1929. C7542

351 O'Shea, H. E. A study of the effect of the interest of a passage of learned vocabulary. 1930. C7543

352 Smith, C. A. Some relationships existing in school

expenditure among Florida counties. 1929. C7544
353 Alexander, U. S. Special legislation affecting public schools. 1929. C7545
354 Weekes, B. E. The influence of meaning on children's choices of poetry. 1929. C7546
355 Farley, B. M. What to tell the people about the public schools. 1929. C7547
356 Tilson, M. A. Problems of preschool children. 1929. C7548
357 Sayers, E. V. Educational issues and unity of experience. 1929. C7549
358 Caswell, H. L. City school surveys. 1929. C7550
359 Wheat, H. G. The relative merits of conventional and imaginative types of problems in arithmetic. 1929. C7551
360 Haefner, R. The educational significance of left-handedness. 1929. C7552
361 Schwegler, R. A. A study of introvert-extrovert responses to certain test situations. 1929. C7553
362 Speer, R. K. Measurement of appreciation in poetry, prose, and art, and studies in appreciation. 1929. C7554
363 Tink, E. L. Certain phases of county educational organization. 1929. C7555
364 McAllister, J. E. The training of Negro teachers in Louisiana. 1929. C7556
365 Judy-Bond, H. E. Trends and needs in home management. 1929. C7557
366 Val Alstyne, D. The environment of three-year-old children. 1929. C7558
367 Scott, A. (White). A comparative study of responses of children of certain nationalities on... tests. 1929. C7559
368 Halsey, H. R. Borrowing money for the public schools. 1929. C7560
369 Oktavec, F. L. The professional education of special men teachers of physical education in Prussia. 1929. C7561
370 Vaughan, W. E. Articulation in English between the high school and college. 1929. C7562
371 Baldwin, J. W. The social studies laboratory. 1929. C7563
372 Leonard, J. P. The use of practice exercises in the teaching of capitalization and punctuation. 1930. C7564
373 Schachtman, J. Elements of English related to the judgment of poetry in grade eleven. 1929. C7565
374 Buckton, L. V. College and university bands. 1929. C7566
375 Moffett, M. The social background and activities of teachers college students. 1929. C7567
376 Cottrell, D. P. Instruction and instructional facilities in the colleges of the United Lutheran church in America. 1929. C7568
377 Le Sourd, H. M. The university work of the United Lutheran church in America. 1929. C7569
378 Limbert, P. M. Denominational policies in the support and supervision of higher education. 1929. C7570
379 Schott, C. P. Physical education in the colleges of the United Lutheran church in America. 1929. C7571
380 Van Wagensen, B. (Clark). Extra-curricular activities in the colleges of the United Lutheran church in America. 1929. C7572
381 Marine, E. L. The effect of familiarity with the examiner upon Stanford-Binet test performance. 1929. C7573
382 Newcomb, T. M. The consistency of certain extrovert-introvert behavior patterns of 51 problem boys. 1929. C7574
383 Siceloff, M. (McAdory). The construction and validation of an art test. 1929. C7575
384 Maller, J. B. Cooperation

and competition. 1929. C7576
385 Omar Khayyām. The algebra of Omar Khayyām, ed. by Kaser. 1929. C7577
386 McCormick, C. The teaching of general mathematics in the secondary schools of the U. S. 1929. C7578
387 Linn, H. H. Safeguarding school funds. 1929. C7579
388 Yakel, R. The legal control of the administration of public school expenditures. 1929. C7580
389 Upshall, C. C. Day schools vs institutions for the deaf. 1929. C7581
390 Sharp, L. B. Education and the summer camp. 1930. C7582
391 Bishop, E. A. The development of a state school system. 1930. C7583
392 McGinnis, W. C. School administrative and supervisory organizations in cities of 20,000 to 50,000 population. 1929. C7584
393 Sturtevant, S. M. and Strang, R. M. A personnel study of deans of girls in high schools. 1929. C7585
394 Field, H. A. Extensive individual reading versus class reading. 1930. C7586
395 Broady, K. O. School provision for individual differences. 1930. C7587
396 Garretson, O. K. Relationships between expressed preferences and curricular abilities of ninth grade boys. 1930. C7588
397 Billig, F. G. A technique for developing content for a professional course in science for teachers in elementary schools. 1930. C7589
398 Shang, C. I. A method of selecting foreign stories for the American elementary schools. 1929. C7590
399 Bellingrath, G. G. Qualities associated with leadership in the extra-curricular activities of the high school. 1930. C7591
400 Baird, D. O. A study of biology notebook work in New York state. 1930. C7592
401 Allen, C. M. Some effects produced in an individual by knowledge of his own intellectual level. 1930. C7593
402 Jameson, E. D. Physical education for the preparation of general elementary school teachers. 1930. C7594
403 Congdon, A. R. Training in high-school mathematics essential for success in certain college subjects. 1930. C7595
404 Newlun, C. O. Teaching children to summarize in fifth grade history. 1930. C7596
405 Powell, J. J. A study of problem material in high school algebra. 1929. C7597
406 Rubado, C. A. Problems of the city school superintendent in the field of arithmetic. 1930. C7598
407 Oberteuffer, D. Personal hygiene for college students. 1930. C7599
408 Sharman, J. R. Physical education facilities for the public accredited high schools of Alabama. 1930. C7600
409 Blom, E. C. Radio and electric power supply equipment for schools. 1930. C7601
410 MacLean, A. H. The idea of God in Protestant religious education. 1930. C7602
411 Barton, W. A. Outlining as a study procedure. 1930. C7603
412 Rankin, M. Trends in educational occupations. 1930. C7604
413 Morris, L. L. The single salary schedule. 1930. C7605
414 Jenkins, L. M. A comparative study of motor achievements of children of five, six, and seven years of age. 1930. C7606
415 Knode, J. C. Orienting the student in college. 1930. C7607
416 Macdonald, M. E. The

significance of various kinds of preparation for the city-elementary school principalship in Pennsylvania. 1930. C7608

417 Hwang, P. Errors and improvement in rating English composition by means of a composition scale. 1930. C7609

418 Robinson, C. L. Psychology and preparation of the teacher of the elementary school. 1930. C7610

419 Hayes, W. J. Some factors influencing participation in voluntary school group activities. 1930. C7611

420 Krieger, L. B. M. Prediction of success in professional courses for teachers. 1930. C7612

421 Smith, M. M. The equipment of the school theater. 1930. C7613

422 Cooper, H. An accounting of progress and attendance of rural school children in Delaware. 1930. C7614

423 Hilleboe, G. L. Finding and teaching atypical children. 1930. C7615

424 Lamson, E. E. A study of young gifted children in senior high school. 1930. C7616

425 Chandler, P. G. Some methods of teaching in six representative state teachers colleges of the United States. 1930. C7617

426 Deputy, E. C. Predicting first-grade reading achievement. 1930. C7618

427 Nichols, C. A. Moral education among the North American Indians. 1930. C7619

428 Smith, H. A. Economy in public school fire insurance. 1930. C7620

429 Shaffer, L. F. Children's interpretation of cartoons. 1930. C7621

430 Leonard, E. (Andruss). Concerning our girls and what they tell us. 1930. C7622

431 Nuttall, L. J. Progress in adjusting differences of amount of educational opportunity offered under the county systems of Maryland and Utah. 1930. C7623

432 Stover, W. S. Alumni stimulation by the American college president. 1930. C7624

433 Hartley, H. (Willey). Tests of the interpretative reading of poetry for teachers of English. 1930. C7625

434 Brogan, W. The work of placement officers in teacher training institutions. 1930. C7626

435 Rivlin, H. N. Functional grammar. 1930. C7627

436 Thompson, R. S. The effectiveness of modern spelling instruction. 1930. C7628

437 Gray, H. A. Some factors in the undergraduate careers of young college students. 1930. C7629

438 Lorge, I. Influence of regularly interpolated time intervals upon subsequent learning. 1930. C7630

439 Carroll, H. A. Generalization of bright and dull children. 1930. C7631

440 Kiely, M. Comparison of students of teachers college and students of liberal-arts colleges. 1931. C7632

441 McGowan, E. A. A comparative study of detergents. 1930. C7633

442 Betzner, J. Content and form of original compositions dictated by children from five to eight years of age. 1930. C7634

443 McNeil, M. A comparative study of entrance to teacher-training institutions. 1930. C7635

444 King, L. H. Mental and interest tests. 1931. C7636

445 Shoemaker, L. (Meier). Natural science education in the German elementary school. 1930. C7637

446 Walker, E. A study of the Traité des indivisibles of Gilles Persone de Roberval. 1932. C7638

447 Phillips, V. Evidence of

the need of education for efficient purchasing. 1931. C7639
448 Shaw, R. W. Some aspects of self-insight. 1931. C7640
449 Rutledge, S. A. The development of guiding principles for the administration of teachers colleges and normal schools. 1931. C7641
450 Boillin, M. L. Determination of the interrelations, between various anthropometric measurements of college women. 1930. C7642
451 Bushnell, P. P. An analytical contrast of oral with written English. 1930. C7643
452 Keliher, A. V. A critical study of homogeneous grouping. 1931. C7644
453 Smith, J. H. Legal limitations on bonds and taxation for public school buildings. 1930. C7645
454 Goldberger, A. M. Variability in continuation school populations. 1931. C7646
455 Brunstetter, M. R. Business management in schools systems of different size. 1931. C7647
456 Ketler, F. C. Reserve funds in public school finance. 1931. C7648
457 Burr, M. Y. A study of homogeneous grouping... 1931. C7649
458 Rogers, C. R. Measuring personality adjustment in children nine to thirteen years of age. 1931. C7650
459 Leighton, F. H. A basis for building a course in economics of the home. 1931. C7651
460 Stratemeyer, F. B. The effective use of curriculum materials. 1931. C7652
461 Lepley, R. Dependability in philosophy of education. 1931. C7653
462 Matzen, J. M. State constitutional provisions for education. 1931. C7654
463 Kilander, H. F. Science education in the secondary schools of Sweden. 1931. C7655
464 Grossnickle, F. E. Capital outlay in relation to a state's minimum educational program. 1931. C7656
465 Weeks, H. F. Factors influencing the choice of courses by students in certain liberal arts colleges. 1931. C7657
466 Zyve, C. An experimental study of spelling methods. 1931. C7658
467 Saller, R. C. Happiness self-estimates of young men. 1931. C7659
468 Tyler, H. T. The bearing of certain personality factors other than intelligence on academic success. 1931. C7660
469 Collmann, R. D. The psychogalvanic reactions of exceptional and normal school children. 1931. C7661
470 Witty, P. A. A study of deviates in versatility and sociability of play interest. 1931. C7662
471 Clark, Z. R. The recognition of merit in superintendents' reports to the public. 1931. C7663
472 Sartorius, I. (Craig). Generalization in spelling. 1931. C7664
473 Elliott, A. E. Paraguay. 1931. C7665
474 Proctor, A. M. Safeguarding the school board's purchase of architects' working drawings. 1931. C7666
475 Schleier, L. M. Problems in the training of certain special-class teachers. 1931. C7667
476 Fitch, H. N. An analysis of the supervisory activities and techniques of the elementary school training supervisor. 1931. C7668
477 Bomar, W. M. The education of homemakers for community activities. 1931. C7669
478 Bathurst, E. G. A teachers college follow-up service. 1931. C7670
479 Harner, N. C. Factors

related to Sunday school growth and decline in the eastern synod of the Reformed church in the U. S. 1931. C7671
480 Class, E. Prescription and election in elementary-school teachers curricula in state teachers colleges. 1931. C7672
481 Street, R. F. A gestalt completion test. 1931. C7673
482 Seidlin, J. A critical study of the teaching of elementary college mathematics. 1931. C7674
483 Neulen, L. N. Problem solving in arithmetic. 1931. C7675
484 Caliver, A. A personnel study of Negro college students. 1931. C7676
485 Pope, R. V. Factors affecting the elimination of women students from selected coeducational colleges of liberal arts. 1931. C7677
486 Shipley, G. T. An evaluation of guided study and small-group discussion in a normal school. 1931. C7678
487 Baugher, J. I. Organization and administration of practice-teaching in privately endowed colleges of liberal arts. 1931. C7679
488 Marshall, E. M. Evaluation of types of student-teaching. 1932. C7680
489 Magee, H. J. Unit costs of salaries in teachers college and normal schools. 1931. C7681
490 Gunther, T. C. Manipulative participation in the study of elementary industrial arts. 1931. C7682
491 Hager, W. E. The quest for vocational adjustment in the profession of education. 1931. C7683
492 Byrne, L. Check list materials for public school building specifications. 1931. C7684
493 Stephens, J. M. The influence of different stimuli upon preceding bonds. 1931. C7685
494 Coleman, J. H. Written composition interests of junior and senior high school pupils. 1931. C7686
495 Hahn, J. L. A critical evaluation of a supervisory program in kindergarten-primary grades. 1931. C7687
496 Essex, D. L. Bonding versus pay-as-you-go in the financing of school buildings. 1931. C7688
497 Connor, R. The scholastic behavior of a selected group of undergraduate home economic students. 1931. C7689
498 Wheat, L. B. Free associations to common words. 1931. C7690
499 Madden, R. The school status of the hard of hearing child. 1931. C7691
500 Pangburn, J. M. The evolution of the American teachers college. 1932. C7692
501 Nelson, G. E. The introductory biological sciences in the traditional liberal arts college. 1931. C7693
502 Brodshaug, M. Buildings and equipment for home economics in secondary schools. 1931. C7694
503 Kûrani, H. A. Selecting the college student in America. 1931. C7695
504 Drake, C. A. A study of an interest test and an affectivity test in forecasting freshman success in college. 1931. C7696
505 Barthelmess, H. M. The validity of intelligence test elements. 1931. C7697
506 Hyde, M. W. Standards for publicity programs in state supported colleges and universities. 1931. C7698
507 Grote, C. Housing and living conditions of women students in the Western Illinois state teachers college at Macomb. 1931. C7699
508 Schmidt, A. W. The development of a state's minimum educational program. 1931. C7700
509 Langford, H. D. Educational service. 1931. C7701
510 Bennett, A. A

comparative study of subnormal children in the elementary grades. 1932. C7702
511 Young, E. B. A study of the curricula of seven selected women's colleges of the southern states. 1931. C7703
512 McLees, M. H. A study of the elementary teaching personnel of Hunterdon... N. J. 1932. C7704
513 Seele, E. S. The organization and activities of the National education association. 1932. C7705
514 Long, J. A. Motor abilities of deaf children. 1932. C7706
515 Davis, E. C. Methods and techniques used in surveying health and physical education in city schools. 1932. C7707
516 Mellinger, B. E. Children's interests in pictures. 1932. C7708
517 King, L. M. Learning and applying spelling rules in grades three to eight. 1932. C7709
518 Bowles, R. P. The operation and effect of a single salary schedule. 1932. C7710
519 Spencer, P. R. A state minimum teachers' salary schedule. 1932. C7711
520 Park, M. G. Training in objective educational measurements for elementary school teachers. 1932. C7712
521 Lochhead, J. The education of young children in England. 1932. C7713
522 Van Houten, L. H. Length of service of Pennsylvania high school teachers. 1932. C7714
523 Jacobsen, E. W. Educational opportunities provided for post-graduate students in public high schools. 1932. C7715
524 MacNeel, J. R. Admission of students as candidates for master's degree. 1932. C7716
525 Bond, E. A. The professional treatment of the subject matter of arithmetic. 1934. C7717
526 Holmstedt, R. W. A study of the effects of the teacher tenure law in New Jersey. 1932. C7718
527 Woodward, L. E. Relations of religious training and life patterns to the adult religious life. 1932. C7719
528 Peterson, F. E. Philosophies of education current in the preparation of teachers of the U. S. 1933. C7720
529 Long, H. M. Public secondary education for Negroes in North Carolina. 1932. C7721
530 Elbin, P. N. The improvement of college worship. 1932. C7722
531 Biddle, W. W. Propaganda and education. 1932. C7723
532 Zubin, J. Some effects of incentives. 1932. C7724
533 Chauncey, M. R. The educational and occupational preferences of college seniors. 1932. C7725
534 Schmidt, G. A. Vocational education in agriculture in federally-aided secondary schools. 1932. C7726
535 Durost, W. N. Children's collecting activity related to social factors. 1932. C7727
536 Townsend, M. E. The administration of student personnel services in teaching-training institutions of the United States. 1932. C7728
537 Crustsinger, G. M. Survey study of teacher training in Texas. 1932. C7729
538 Flowers, J. G. Content of student-teaching courses designed for the training of secondary teachers in state teachers colleges. 1932. C7730
539 Frawley, H. M. Certain procedures of studying poetry in the fifth grade. 1932. C7731
540 Bildersee, A. State scholarship students at Hunter college of the city of New York. 1932. C7732
541 Hughes, W. L. The

administration of health and physical education for men in colleges and universities. 1932. C7733

542 Waller, J. F. Outside demands and pressures on the public schools. 1932. C7734

543 Tewksbury, D. G. The founding of American colleges and universities before the Civil war. 1932. C7735

544 Featherstone, W. B. The curriculum of the special class. 1932. C7736

545 Welles, H. H. The measurement of certain aspects of personality among hard of hearing adults. 1932. C7737

546 Daniel, R. P. A psychological study of delinquent and non-delinquent Negro boys. 1932. C7738

547 Lawler, E. S. A technique for comparing the amount of new aid required for state equalization programs. 1932. C7739

548 Lacey, J. M. Social studies concepts of children in the first three grades. 1932. C7740

549 Bradley, A. D. A geometry of repeating design and geometry of design for high schools. 1933. C7741

550 Stratton, D. C. Problems of students in a graduate school of education. 1933. C7742

551 Pannell, H. C. The preparation and work of Alabama high school teachers. 1933. C7743

552 Young, L. P. The administration of merit-type teachers' salary schedules. 1933. C7744

553 Clemensen, J. (Williams). Study outlines in physics. 1933. C7745

554 Wilson, G. H. The religious and educational philosophy of the Young women's Christian association. 1933. C7746

555 Kolstad, A. A study of opinions of some international problems. 1933. C7747

556 Lee, D. M. (Potter). The importance of reading for achieving in grades four, five, and six. 1933. C7748

557 Whitcraft, L. H. Some influences of the requirements and examinations of the College entrance examination board on mathematics in secondary schools in the United States. 1933. C7749

558 Dransfield, J. E. Administration of enrichment to superior children in a typical classroom. 1933. C7750

559 Brown, M. A. Leadership among high school pupils. 1933. C7751

560 Dienst, C. F. The administration of endowments. 1933. C7752

561 Sparling, E. J. Do college students choose vocations wisely? 1933. C7753

562 Wrightstone, J. W. Stimulation of educational undertakings. 1933. C7754

563 Dinin, S. Judaism in a changing civilization. 1933. C7755

564 Kuhlmann, W. D. Teacher absence and leave regulations. 1933. C7756

565 Arnspiger, V. C. Measuring the effectiveness of sound pictures as teaching aids. 1933. C7757

566 Kasuya, Y. Comparative study of the secondary education of girls in England, Germany and the United States. 1933. C7758

567 Findley, W. G. Specialization of verbal facility at the college entrance level. 1933. C7759

568 Portenier, L. G. Pupils of low mentality in high school. 1933. C7760

569 Brown, R. Mathematical difficulties of students of educational statistics. 1933. C7761

570 Lindsay, J. A. Annual and semiannual promotion. 1933. C7762

571 Sperle, D. H. The case method technique in professional training. 1933. C7763

572 Fagerstrom, W. H. Mathematical facts and processes prerequisite to the study of calculus. 1933. C7764
573 Powell, O. E. Educational returns at varying expenditure levels. 1933. C7765
574 Blake, W. H. A preliminary study of the interpretation of bodily expression. 1933. C7766
575 Peterson, A. G. The training of elementary and secondary teachers in Sweden. 1933. C7767
576 Bryan, H. M. Some problems in the provision of professional education for college teachers. 1933. C7768
577 Beach, F. F. The custody of school funds. 1933. C7769
578 Boney, C. de. W. A study of library reading in the primary grades. 1933. C7770
579 Cyr, F. W. Responsibility for rural-school administration. 1933. C7771
580 Thorndike, E. L. An experimental study of rewards. 1933. C7772
581 Sahlstrom, J. W. Some code controls of school building construction in American cities. 1933. C7773
582 Ladd, M. R. The relation of social, economic and personal characteristics to reading ability. 1933. C7774
583 Moore, M. (Whiteside). A study of young high school graduates. 1933. C7775
584 Bennett, T. G. A health program for the children of a county. 1933. C7776
585 McKane, K. A comparison of the intelligence of deaf and hearing children. 1933. C7777
586 Clark, L. V. A study of the relationship between the the vocational home economics teacher training curricula of... women's colleges and expected responsibilities of beginning teachers. 1933. C7778
587 French, W. Promotional plans in the high school. 1933. C7779
588 West, P. A study of ability grouping in the elementary school. 1933. C7780
589 Spencer, M. E. Health education for teachers. 1933. C7781
590 Tuckman, J. The influence of varying amounts of punishment on mental connections. 1933. C7782
591 Pearman, W. I. Support of state educational programs by dedication of specific revenues and by general revenue appropriations. 1933. C7783
592 Morrison, R. H. Internal administrative organization in teachers colleges. 1933. C7784
593 Long, F. M. Desireable physical facilities for an activity program. 1933. C7785
594 Carley, V. A. Student aid in the secondary schools of the United States. 1933. C7786
595 Cherrington, B. M. Methods of education in international attitudes. 1934. C7787
596 Sauvain, W. H. A study of the opinions of certain professional and non-professional groups regarding homogeneous or ability grouping. 1934. C7788
597 Kinder, J. S. The internal administration of the liberal arts college. 1934. C7789
598 Adams, F. (Greene). The initiation of an activity program into a public school. 1934. C7790
599 Weis, E. H. F. The music preparation of elementary teachers in state teachers colleges. 1934. C7791
600 Stewart, W. H. A comparative study of the concentration and regular plans of organization in the senior high school. 1934. C7792
601 Holbeck, E. S. An analysis of the activities and potentialities for achievement of the parent-teacher association. 1934. C7793

602 Clarke, H. The professional training of the hospital dietitian. 1934. C7794
603 Peters, D. W. The status of the married woman teacher. 1934. C7795
604 Gooch, W. I. Junior high school costs. 1934. C7796
605 Clark, F. G. The control of state-supported teacher-training programs for Negroes. 1934. C7797
606 Deyoe, G. P. Certain trends in curriculum practices and policies in state normal schools and teachers colleges. 1934. C7798
607 Chassell, C. F. The relation between morality and intellect. 1934. C7799
608 Partridge, E. D. Leadership among adolescent boys. 1934. C7800
609 Holmes, D. O. W. The evolution of the Negro college. 1934. C7801
610 Unzicker, C. E. An experimental study of the effect of the use of the typewriter on beginning reading. 1934. C7802
611 Davis, H. M. The use of state high school examinations as an instrument for judging the work of teachers. 1934. C7803
612 Cheney, R. E. Equipment specifications for high schools. 1934. C7804
613 Scott, C. W. Indefinite teacher tenure. 1934. C7805
614 Nash, W. L. A study of the stated aims and purposes of the departments of military science... in the land-grant colleges of the U. S. 1934. C7806
615 Baldwin, C. C. Organization and administration of substitute-teaching service in city-school systems. 1934. C7807
616 Merriam, T. W. The relations between scholastic achievement in a school of social work and six factors in students' background. 1934. C7808
617 Westfall, L. H. A study of verbal accompaniments to educational motion pictures. 1934. C7809
618 Strayer, G. D. Centralizing tendencies in the administration of public education. 1934. C7810
619 LaFollette, C. (Tipton). A study of the problems of 652 gainfully employed married women homemakers. 1934. C7811
620 Brenner, B. Effect of immediate and delayed praise and blame upon learning and recall. 1934. C7812
621 Smith, M. The relationship between item validity and test validity. 1934. C7813
622 Jones, H. A. The administration of health and physical education in New York state. 1934. C7814
623 Hoffman, M. N. H. The measurement of bilingual background. 1934. C7815
624 Misner, F. M. Extra costs and incidental costs in the erection of school buildings. 1934. C7816
625 Bair, F. H. The social understandings of the superintendents of schools. 1934. C7817
626 Davis, W. R. The development and present status of Negro education in east Texas. 1934. C7818
627 Sanford, D. S. Inter-institutional agreements in higher education. 1934. C7819
628 Little, H. A. Potential economics in the reorganization of local school attendance units. 1934. C7820
629 Nardi, N. Zionism and education in Palestine. 1934. C7821
630 Dilley, F. B. Teacher certification in Ohio and a proposed plan of reconstruction. 1935. C7822
631 Wyland, R. O. Scouting in the schools. 1934. C7823
632 Ward, M. S. Philosophies of administration current in the deanship of the liberal arts college. 1934. C7824
633 Haupt, G. W. An

experimental application of a philosophy of science teaching in an elementary school. 1935. C7825
634 Franzblau, A. N. Religious belief and character among Jewish adolescents. 1934. C7826
635 Dorgan, E. J. Luther Halsey Gulick. 1934. C7827
636 Ruef, D. Health education in senior high schools. 1934. C7828
637 Campbell, R. G. State supervision and regulation of budgetary procedure in public school systems. 1935. C7829
638 Watson, A. E. Experimental studies in the psychology and pedagogy of spelling. 1935. C7830
639 Threlkeid, H. Educational and vocational plans of college seniors... in forty-five Pennsylvania colleges. 1935. C7831
640 Symington, T. A. Religious liberals and conservatives. 1935. C7832
641 Morrisett, L. N. Letters of recommendation. 1935. C7833
642 Bernard, T. B. Secondary education under different types of district organization. 1935. C7834
643 Fitz-Simons, M. J. Some parent-child relationships. 1935. C7835
644 Jencke, G. E. A study of précis writing as composition technique. 1935. C7836
645 Euler, H. L. County unification in Kansas. 1935. C7837
646 Stacy, W. H. Integration of adult education. 1935. C7838
647 Wade, J. T. A measurement of the secondary school as a part of the pupil's environment. 1935. C7839
648 Doyle, Mary Peter, Sister. A study of play selection in women's colleges. 1935. C7840
649 Briscoe, A. O. The size of the local unit for administration and supervision of public schools. 1935. C7841
650 Rock, R. T. The influence upon learning of the qualitative variation of after-effects. 1935. C7842
651 Myers, T. R. Intra-family relationships and pupil adjustment. 1935. C7843
652 Simpson, M. Parent preferences of young children. 1935. C7844
653 O'Dell, D. The history of journalism education in the United States. 1935. C7845
654 Elliff, M. Some relationships between supply and demand for newly trained teachers. 1935. C7846
655 Strebel, R. F. The nature of the supervision of student-teaching in universities using cooperating public high schools. 1935. C7847
656 Fendrick, P. Visual characteristics of poor readers. 1935. C7848
657 Bond, G. L. The auditory and speech characteristics of poor readers. 1935. C7849
658 Dodge, A. F. Occupational ability patterns. 1935. C7850
659 Quayle, M. S. A study of some aspects of satisfaction in the vocation of stenography. 1935. C7851
660 Yeager, T. C. An analysis of certain traits of selected high school seniors interested in teaching. 1935. C7852
661 Preston, E. C. Principles and statutory provisions relating to... welfare services of the public schools. 1935. C7853
662 Holy, R. A. The relationship of city planning to school plant planning. 1935. C7854
663 Smith, G. B. Purposes and conditions affecting the nature and extent of participation of adults in courses in the Home study department of Columbia University. 1935. C7855
664 Linder, R. G. An evaluation of the courses in education of a state teachers college by teachers in service. 1935. C7856

665 Jones, L. M. A factorial analysis of ability in fundamental motor skills. 1935. C7857
666 Rinsland, H. D. Analysis of completion sentences and arithmetical problems as items for intelligence tests. 1935. C7858
667 Jones, G. Extra-curricular activities in relation to the curriculum. 1935. C7859
668 Campbell, N. M. The elementary school teacher's treatment of classroom behavior problems. 1935. C7860
669 Chisholm, L. L. The economic ability of the states to finance public schools. 1936. C7861
670 Stombaugh, R. M. A survey of the movements cumulating in industrial arts education in secondary schools. 1936. C7862
671 Shopshire, O. E. The teaching of history in English schools. 1936. C7863
672 Robinson, A. E. The professional education of elementary teachers in the field of arithmetic. 1936. C7864
673 Burton, H. (Kolshorn). The re-establishment of the Indians in their pueblo life through the revival of their traditional crafts. 1936. C7865
674 Sobel, F. (Selkin). Teachers' marks and objective tests as indices of school adjustment. 1936. C7866
675 Hays, E. College entrance requirements in English. 1936. C7867
676 Odenweller, A. L. Predicting the quality of teaching. 1936. C7868
677 Leverton, G. H. The production of later nineteenth century American drama. 1936. C7869
678 Lyon, R. M. The basis for constructing curricular materials in adult education for Carolina cotton mill workers. 1936. C7870
679 Rogers, M. P. A state's supervision of its elementary schools. 1936. C7871
680 Rodgers, E. G. An experimental investigation of the teaching of team games. 1936. C7872
681 Munkres, A. Personality studies of six-year-old children in classroom situations. 1936. C7873
682 Duggan, A. S. A comparative study of undergraduate women majors and nonmajors in physical education with respect to certain personal traits. 1936. C7874
683 Griffey, C. H. The history of local school control in the state of New York. 1936. C7875
684 Williamson, O. J. Provisions for general theory courses in the professional education of teachers. 1936. C7876
685 Kramer, M. E. Dramatic tournaments in the secondary schools. 1936. C7877
686 Garinger, E. H. The administration of discipline in the high school. 1936. C7878
687 Brunschwig, L. A study of some personality aspects of deaf children. 1936. C7879
688 Forlano, G. School learning, with various methods of practice and rewards. 1936. C7880
689 Kent, D. C. A study of the results of planning for home economics education in the Southern states. 1936. C7881
690 Hartill, R. M. Homogeneous grouping as a policy in the elementary schools of N. Y. city. 1936. C7882
691 Akridge, G. H. Pupil progress policies and practices. 1937. C7883
692 Henderson, E. L. The organization and administration of student teaching in state teachers colleges. 1937. C7884
693 Davis, B. F. A study of shorthand teaching. 1936. C7885
694 Oberholtzer, E. E. An integrated curriculum in

practice. 1937. C7886
695 Bayliss, W. B. An evaluation of a plan for character education. 1937. C7887
696 Lyon, M. The selection of books for adult study groups. 1937. C7888
697 Habbe, S. Personality adjustments of adolescent boys with impaired hearing. 1936. C7889
698 Cornell, F. G. Measure of tax-paying ability of local school administrative units. 1936. C7890
699 Pritchard, M. C. The mechanical ability of subnormal boys. 1937. C7891
700 Matthews, M. T. Experience-worlds of mountain people. 1937. C7892
701 McEachern, E. A survey and evaluation of the education of school music teachers in the United States. 1937. C7893
702 Manske, A. J. The reflection of teachers attitudes in the attitudes of their pupils. 1936. C7894
703 Wilkins, E. G. Public school tax management in Texas. 1937. C7895
704 Smith, M. R. Student aid. 1937. C7896
705 Kirkendall, L. A. Factors related to the changes in school adjustment of high school pupils. 1937. C7897
706 Hellmich, E. W. The mathematics in certain elementary social studies in secondary schools and colleges. 1937. C7898
707 Lazar, M. Reading interests, activities, and opportunities of bright, average and dull children. 1937. C7899
708 Bryan, R. C. Pupil rating of secondary school teachers. 1937. C7900
709 Gilson, M. (Stewart). Developing a high school chemistry course adapted to the differentiated needs of boys and girls. 1937. C7901
710 Bason, C. H. Study of the homeland and civilization in the elementary schools of Germany. 1937. C7902
711 Mooney, E. S. An analysis of the supervision of student teaching. 1937. C7903
712 Arsenian, S. Bilingualism and mental development. 1937. C7904
713 McCullough, A. M. A critical analysis of the fuel management program for schools. 1937. C7905
714 Brown, H. A. Certain basic teacher-education policies and their development and significance in a selected state. 1937. C7906
715 Gemmill, A. M. An experimental study at New York state teachers college... to determine a science program for... elementary... teachers. 1937. C7907
716 Nordly, G. L. The administration of intramural athletics for men in colleges and universities. 1937. C7908
717 Kuder, M. S. Trends of professional arts college. 1937. C7909
718 Oberholtzer, K. E. American agricultural problems in the social studies. 1937. C7910
719 DiNapoli, P. J. Homework in the New York City elementary schools. 1937. C7911
720 Tucker, L. E. A study of problem pupils. 1937. C7912
721 Wallenstein, N. Character and personality of children from broken homes. 1937. C7913
722 Pugmire, D. R. The administration of personnel in correctional institutions in New York state. 1937. C7914
723 Nelson, E. M. An analysis of content of student-teaching courses for education of elementary teachers in state teachers colleges. 1937. C7915
724 Bennett, L. J. Secretarial assistance in teachers colleges and normal schools. 1937. C7916

725 Efron, A. The teaching of physical sciences in the secondary schools of the United States, France, and Soviet Russia. 1937. C7917
726 Eisner, H. The classroom teacher's estimation of intelligence and industry of high school students. 1937. C7918
727 Russell, D. H. Characteristics of good and poor spellers. 1937. C7919
728 West, J. Y. A technique for appraising certain observable behavior of children in science in elementary schools. 1937. C7920
729 Milligan, N. G. Relationship of the professed philosophy to the suggested educational experiences. 1937. C7921
730 Vance, C. S. The Girl reserve movement of the Young women's Christian association. 1937. C7922
731 Dambach, J. I. Physical education in Germany. 1937. C7923
732 Henderson, H. R. A curriculum study in a mountain district. 1937. C7924
733 Howard, G. W. A measurement of achievement in motor skills of college men in the game situation of basketball. 1937. C7925
734 Stratemeyer, C. G. Supervision in German elementary education, 1918-1933. 1938. C7926
735 Walke, N. S. Traits characteristic of men majoring in physical education at the Pennsylvania state college. 1937. C7927
736 Christianson, H. M. Bodily rhythmic movements of young children in relation to rhythm in music. 1938. C7928
737 Riddle, J. I. The six-year rural high school. 1937. C7929
738 Johnson, J. T. The relative merits of three methods of subtraction. 1938. C7930
739 Patty, W. L. A study of mechanism in education. 1938. C7931
740 Coulbourn, J. Selection of teachers in large city school systems. 1938. C7932
741 Haggerty, H. R. Certain factors in the professional education of women teachers of physical education. 1938. C7933
742 O'Connor, Z. C. The runaway boy in the correction school. 1938. C7934
743 Gellermann, W. The American legion as educator. 1938. C7935
744 Spieseke, A. W. The first textbooks in American history. 1938. C7936
745 Strickland, R. G. A study of the possibilities of graphs as a means of instruction in the first four grades of the elementary school. 1938. C7937
746 Cole, M. I. Cooperation between the faculty of the campus elementary training school and the other departments of teachers colleges and normal schools. 1938. C7938
747 Pickett, H. C. An analysis of proofs and solutions of exercises used in plain geometry tests. 1938. C7939
748 Simpson, R. H. A study of those who influence and of those who are influenced in a discussion. 1938. C7940
749 Varty, J. W. Manuscript writing and spelling achievement. 1938. C7941
750 Moor, A. P. The library-museum of music and dance. 1938. C7942
751 Stanton, M. B. Mechanical ability of deaf children. 1938. C7943
752 Pluggé, D. E. History of Greek play production in American colleges and universities from 1881 to 1936. 1938. C7944
753 Holt, A. D. The struggle for a state system of public schools in Tennessee, 1903-1936. 1938. C7945
754 Murray, Teresa Gertrude, Sister. Vocational guidance in Catholic secondary schools.

1938. C7946
755 Bennett, C. C. An inquiry into the genesis of poor reading. 1938. C7947
756 Wagner, E. (Bond). Reading and ninth grade achievement. 1938. C7948
757 Kuhn, E. G. The pronunciation of vowel sounds. 1938. C7949
758 Kangley, L. Poetry preferences in the junior high school. 1938. C7950
759 Davies, J. E. Fundamentals of housing study. 1938. C7951
760 Lombardi, M. (Maher). The inter-trait rating technique. 1938. C7952
761 Atyeo, H. C. The excursion as a teaching technique. 1939. C7953
762 Herber, H. T. The influence of Public works administration on school building construction in New York state, 1933-1936. 1938. C7954
763 Thiele, C. L. The contributions of generalization to the learning of the additional facts. 1938. C7955
764 Tansil, R. C. The contributions of cumulative personnel records to a teacher-education program. 1939. C7956
765 Williams, J. P. Social adjustment in Methodism. 1938. C7957
766 Blair, G. M. Mentally superior and inferior children in junior and senior high school. 1938. C7958
767 Holmes, L. H. A history of the position of dean of women in a selected group of co-educational colleges and universities in the U. S. 1939. C7959
768 Butterfield, O. M. Love problems of adolescence. 1939. C7960
769 Mallory, V. S. The relative difficulty of certain topics in mathematics for slow-moving ninth grade pupils. 1939. C7961
770 Rearick, E. C. Dances of the Hungarians. 1939. C7962
771 Bailey, F. L. A planned supply of teachers for Vermont. 1939. C7963
772 Bingham, N. E. Teaching nutrition in biology classes. 1939. C7964
773 Tape, H. A. Factors affecting turnover of teachers of the one-room rural schools of Michigan. 1939. C7965
774 Beall, E. The relation of various anthropometric measurements of selected college women to success in physical activities. 1939. C7966
775 Wheelwright, L. F. An experimental study of the perceptibility and spacing of musical symbols. 1939. C7967
776 Hansburg, H. An experimental study of the effect of the use of the print shop in the improvement of spelling, reading, and visual perception. 1939. C7968
777 Timmons, W. M. Decisions and attitudes as outcomes of the discussions of a social problem. 1939. C7969
778 Fraser, J. A. Outcomes of a study excursion. 1939. C7970
779 Allard, L. E. A study of the leisure activities of certain elementary school teachers of Long Island. 1939. C7971
780 Nestrick, W. V. Constructional activities of adult males. 1939. C7972
781 Tyler, I. K. Spelling as a secondary learning. 1939. C7973
782 Pyle, T. P. The teacher's dependency load. 1939. C7974
783 Patton, L. K. The purposes of church-related colleges. 1940. C7975
784 Davis, H. Personnel administration in three non-teaching services of the public schools. 1939. C7976
785 Knott, W. D. The influence of tax-leeway on educational adaptability. 1939. C7977
786 Gore, G. W. In-service professional improvement of

Negro public school teachers in Tennessee. 1940. C7978
787 Sturtevant, S. M. and others. Trends in student personnel work as represented in the positions of the deans of women and deans of girls... 1940. C7979
788 Simmons, R. (McKnight). A study of a group of children of exceptionally high intelligence quotients in situations... 1940. C7980
789 Cillié, F. S. Centralization or decentralization? 1940. C7981
790 Bateman, E. A. Development of the county-unit school district in Utah. 1940. C7982
791 Sullivan, J. C. A study of the social attitudes and information on public problems of women teachers in secondary schools. 1940. C7983
792 Conklin, A. M. Failure of highly intelligent pupils. 1940. C7984
793 Mason, C. D. Adaptation of instruction to individual differences in the preparation of teachers in normal schools and teachers colleges. 1940. C7985
794 Sprague, H. A. A decade of progress in the preparation of secondary school teachers. 1940. C7986
795 Goetsch, H. B. Parental income and college opportunities. 1940. C7987
796 Kennan, R. B. The private correspondence school enrollee. 1940. C7988
797 Bond, A. D. An experience in the teaching of genetics. 1940. C7989
798 Boyd, E. N. A diagnostic study of students' difficulties in general mathematics in first year college work. 1940. C7990
799 Gentry, J. R. Immediate effects of interpolated rest periods on learning and performance. 1940. C7991
800 Benz, M. G. Family counseling service in a university community. 1940. C7992
801 Farnsworth, P. T. Adaptation processes in public school systems. 1940. C7993
802 Dunklin, H. T. The prevention of failure in first grade reading by means of adjusted instruction. 1940. C7994
803 Goggans, S. Units of work and centers of interest in the organization of the elementary school curriculum. 1940. C7995
804 Richardson, J. W. Problems of articulation between the units of secondary education. 1940. C7996
805 Shuster, C. N. A study of the problems in teaching the slide rule. 1940. C7997
806 Hinton, E. M. An analytical study of the qualities of style and rhetoric found in English compositions. 1940. C7998
807 Armacost, G. H. High school principals' annual reports. 1940. C7999
808 Sattgast, C. R. The administration of college and university endowments. 1940. C8000
809 Anderson, J. P. A study of the relationships between certain aspects of parental behavior and attitudes and the behavior of junior high school pupils. 1940. C8001
810 Tucker, C. A study of mothers' practices and children's activities in a cooperative nursery school. 1940. C8002
811 Gans, R. A study of critical reading comprehension in the intermediate grades. 1940. C8003
812 Cunningham, H. A. Material facilities needed in the training of intermediate grade teachers in science. 1940. C8004
813 Bond, E. A. Tenth-grade abilities and achievements. 1940. C8005
814 Justman, J. Theories of secondary education in the United States. 1940. C8006
815 Wright, M. M. (Thompson). The education of

Negroes in New Jersey. 1941. C8007
816 Harris, R. M. Teachers' social knowledge and its relation to pupil's responses. 1941. C8008
817 Ebey, G. W. Adaptability among the elementary school of an American city. 1940. C8009
818 Burpee, R. H. Seven quickly administered tests of physical capacity and their use in detecting physical incapacity for motor activity. 1940. C8010
819 Jenkins, D. R. Growth and decline of agricultural villages. 1940. C8011
820 Alexander, W. M. State leadership in improving instruction. 1940. C8012
821 Goldstein, H. Reading and listening comprehension at various controlled rates. 1940. C8013
822 Colson, E. M. The analysis of the specific references to Negroes in selected curricula for the education of teachers. 1940. C8014
823 Morgan, R. Arbitration in the men's clothing industry in New York city. 1940. C8015
824 Cain, M. (Clough). The historical development of state normal schools for white teachers in Maryland. 1941. C8016
825 Reid, C. F. Education in the territories and outlying possessions of the United States. 1941. C8017
826 Nicholson, E. Education and the Boy scout movement in America. 1941. C8018
827 Howard, H. Mathematics teachers' views on certain issues in the teaching of mathematics. 1941. C8019
828 Poe, A. C. School liability for injuries to pupils. 1941. C8020
829 Saylor, J. G. Factors associated with participation in cooperative programs of curriculum development. 1941. C8021
830 Price, L. Creative group work on the campus. 1941. C8022
831 Goldfarb, W. An investigation of reaction time in older adults... 1941. C8023
832 Fine, B. College publicity in the United States. 1941. C8024
833 Todd, J. E. Social norms and the behavior of college students. 1941. C8025
834 Chatterton, R. H. Methods of lesson observing by preservice student-teachers. 1941. C8026
835 Falk, H. A. Corporal punishment. 1941. C8027
836 Willmott, J. N. High school boys electing industrial arts. 1941. C8028
837 Spadino, E. J. Writing and laterality characteristics of stuttering children. 1941. C8029
838 Rope, F. T. Opinion conflict and school support. 1941. C8030
839 Luecke, E. L. Factors related to children's participation in certain types of home activities. 1941. C8031
840 Kilgore, W. A. Identification of ability to apply principles of physics. 1941. C8032
841 Zeller, D. The relative importance of factors of interest in reading materials for junior high school pupils. 1941. C8033
842 Bormann, H. H. Unit costs of school building. 1941. C8034
843 Glaser, E. M. An experiment in the development of critical thinking. 1941. C8035
844 Davis, E. W. A functional pattern technique for classification of jobs. 1942. C8036
845 Long, C. D. School-leaving youth and employment. 1941. C8037
846 Williams, E. I. F. The actual and potential use of laboratory schools in state normal schools and teachers colleges. 1942. C8038
847 Thorndike, E. L. The teaching of English suffixes.

1941. C8039
848 Doane, D. C. The needs of youth. 1941. C8040
849 Lancaster, J. H. The use of the library by student teachers. 1941. C8041
850 McKim, M. G. The reading of verbal material in ninth grade algebra. 1941. C8042
851 Stratford, W. D. Some restrictions and limitations to the free interstate movement of teachers. 1942. C8043
852 Alford, H. D. Procedure for school district reorganization. 1942. C8044
853 Barden, J. G. A suggested program of teacher training for mission schools among the Batetela. 1941. C8045
854 Gavian, R. M. (Wood). Education for economic competence in grades I to VI. 1942. C8046
855 Wren, H. A. Vocational aspiration levels of adults. 1942. C8047
856 Drummond, L. W. Youth and instruction in marriage and family living. 1942. C8048
857 Laleger, G. E. Vocational interests of high school girls... 1942. C8049
858 Rorer, J. A. Principles of democratic supervision. 1942. C8050
859 Ogilvie, M. Terminology and definitions of speech defects. 1942. C8051
860 Watkins, J. G. Objective measurement of instrumental performance. 1942. C8052
861 Conant, M. E. (Martin). The construction of a diagnostic reading test...1942. C8053
862 Daniel, W. G. The reading interests and need of Negro college freshmen regarding social science materials. 1942. C8054
863 Perry, K. F. An experiment with a diversified art program. 1942. C8055
864 Waters, E. A. A study of the application of an educational theory to science instruction. 1942. C8056
865 Coleman, R. The development of informal geometry. 1942. C8057
866 Tait, J. W. Some aspects of the effect of the dominant American culture upon children of Italian-born parents. 1942. C8058
867 Clayton, A. S. Emergent mind and education. 1943. C8059
868 Brewer, W. L. Factors affecting student achievement and change in a physical science survey course. 1942. C8060
869 Rowe, C. E. The writing of infrequently used words in shorthand. 1943. C8061
870 Salley, R. E. Some factors affecting the supply of and demand for pre-school teachers in New York city. 1943. C8062
871 Hayes, M. L. A study of the classroom disturbances of eighth grade boys and girls. 1943. C8063
872 Hyatt, A. V. The place of oral reading in the social program. 1943. C8064
873 Osborne, A. E. The relationship between certain psychological tests and shorthand achievement. 1943. C8065
874 Mathias, W. D. Ideas of God and conduct. 1943. C8066
875 Machover, S. Cultural and racial variations in patterns of intellect. 1943. C8067
876 Cobb, L. S. A study of the functions of physical education in higher education. 1943. C8068
877 Harrell, R. F. Effect of added thiamine on learning. 1943. C8069
878 Cason, E. M. (Boeker). Mechanical methods for increasing the speed of reading. 1943. C8070
879 Howard, F. T. Complexity of mental processes in science testing. 1943. C8071
880 De Marco, R. R. The Italianization of African natives. 1943. C8072
881 Bergen, C. M. Some

sources of children's science information. 1943. C8073
882 Budge, A. A study of chord frequencies... 1943. C8074
883 McNally, H. J. The readability of certain type sizes and forms in sight-saving classes. 1943. C8075
884 Bénézet, L. T. General education in the progressive college. 1943. C8076
885 Christy, V. A. Evaluation of choral music. 1943. C8077
886 Norberg, K. D. American democracy and secondary education. 1943. C8078
887 Smith, F. T. An experiment in modifying attitudes toward the Negro. 1943. C8079
888 Berry, J. R. Current conceptions of democracy. 1943. C8080
889 Kaplan, A. A. Socio-economic circumstances and adult participation in certain cultural and educational activities. 1943. C8081
890 Snyder, H. E. Educational in-breeding. 1943. C8082
891 Hamalianen, A. E. Appraisal of anecdotal records. 1943. C8083
892 McIntosh, J. B. Learning by exposure to wrong forms in grammar and spelling. 1944. C8084
893 Brown, K. E. General mathematics in American colleges. 1943. C8085
894 Newell, C. A. Class size and adaptability. 1943. C8086
895 Benne, K. D. A conception of authority. 1943. C8087
896 Urban, J. Behavior changes resulting from a study of communicable diseases. 1943. C8088
897 Flesch, R. F. Marks of readable style. 1943. C8089
898 Offner, H. L. Administrative procedures for changing curriculum patterns for selected state teachers colleges. 1944. C8090
899 Potter, D. Debating in the colonial chartered colleges. 1944. C8091
900 Wightwick, M. I. Vocational interest patterns. 1945. C8092
901 Everote, W. P. Agricultural science to serve youth. 1944. C8093
902 Rondileau, A. Education for installment buying. 1944. C8094
903 Potter, T. M. An analysis of the work of general clerical employees. 1944. C8095
904 Abernathy, A. A study of expenditures and services in physical education. 1944. C8096
905 Burns, S. Harmonic skills used by selected high school choral leaders. 1945. C8097
906 Rankin, M. Children's interests in library books of fiction. 1945. C8098
907 Todd, L. P. Wartime relations of the federal government and the public schools, 1917-1918. 1945. C8099
908 Zeitlin, J. Disciples of the wise. 1945. C8100
909 Wesman, A. G. A study of transfer of training from high school subjects to intelligence. 1945. C8101
910 Vincent, W. S. Emerging patterns of public school practice. 1945. C8102
911 French, J. Trends in employment and earnings for 19 graduating classes of a teachers college. 1945. C8103
912 Silverman, S. S. Clothing and appearance. 1945. C8104
913 Mackie, R. P. Crippled children in American education, 1939-1942. 1945. C8105
914 Friedman, B. B. Foundations of the measurement of values. 1946. C8106
915 Ferguson, M. The service load of a staff nurse in one official public health agent. 1945. C8107
916 Brumbaugh, S. B. Democratic experience and education in the National league of women voters. 1946. C8108
917 Westover, F. L. Controlled eye movements versus practice exercises in

reading. 1946. C8109
918 Hartley, R. E. Sociality in preadolescent boys. 1946. C8110
919 Kitay, P. M. Radicalism and conservatism toward conventional religion. 1947. C8111
920 McMurry, D. Herbartain contributions to history instruction in American elementary schools. 1947. C8112
921 Mase, D. J. Etiology of articulatory speech defects. 1946. C8113
922 Boeker, M. (Draper). The status of the beginning calculus students in pre-calculus college mathematics. 1947. C8114
923 Vergara, A. M. (Dwyer). A critical study of a group of college women's responses to poetry. 1946. C8115
924 Kaback, G. R. Vocational personalities. 1946. C8116
925 Sutherland, E. One-step problem patterns and their relation to problem solving in arithmetic. 1947. C8117
926 Oakes, M. E. Children's explanation of natural phenomena. 1948. C8118
927 Zaki, A-el-H. A study of child welfare in a rural New York county. 1947. C8119
928 Harrell, R. F. Further effects of added thiamin on learning and other processes. 1947. C8120
929 McLure, W. P. The effect of population sparsity on school costs. 1947. C8121
930 Johnson, G. Some ethical implications of a naturalistic philosophy of education. 1947. C8122
931 Hill, K. E. Children's contributions in science discussions. 1947. C8123
932 Sterner, A. P. Radio, motion picture, and reading interests. 1947. C8124
933 Kushner, R. (Estrin). The relationship between content of an adult intelligence test and intelligence test score as a function of age. 1947. C8125
934 Christiansen, N. W. The relation of supervision and other factors to certain phases of musical achievement in the rural schools of Utah. 1948. C8126
935 Smith, A. W. Participation in organizations. 1948. C8127
936 Rossignol, L. J. The relationship among hearing acuity speech production, and reading performance in grades 1A, 1B, and 2A. 1948. C8128
937 Escalona, S. K. An application of the level of aspiration experiment to the study of personality. 1948. C8129
938 McManus, R. L. (Metcalfe). The effect of experience on nursing achievement. 1948. C8130
939 Potter, M. C. Perception of symbol orientation and early reading success. 1949. C8131
940 Dorman, H. G. Toward understanding Islam. 1948. C8132
941 Tinkelman, S. Difficulty prediction of test items. 1948. C8133
942 Low, T. L. The educational philosophy and practice of art museums in the United States. 1948. C8134
943 Cohen, R. N. The financial control of education in the consolidated city of New York. 1948. C8135
944 Wollner, M. H. B. Childrens' voluntary reading as an expression of individuality. 1949. C8136
945 Rudolf, K. B. The effect of reading instruction in achievement in eighth grade social studies. 1949. C8137
946 Bavly, S. Family food consumption in Palestine. 1949. C8138
947 Gillaspie, B. V. Consumer questions and their significance. 1949. C8139
948 Watson, J. M. The education of school music teachers for community music leadership. 1949. C8140

949 Epstein, B. Immediate and retention effects of interpolated rest periods on learning performance. 1949. C8141
950 Ives, O. L. A critique of teachers' ratings of high school boys... 1949. C8142
951 Fuller, K. G. An experimental study of two methods of long division. 1949. C8143
952 Mossin, A. C. Spelling performance and contentment in relation to school background. 1949. C8144
953 Mitchell, M. A. The relationship of reading to the social acceptability of sixth grade children. 1949. C8145
954 Almy, M. C. Children's experiences prior to first grade success in beginning reading. 1949. C8146
955 Lampkin, R. H. Variability in recognizing scientific inquiry. 1949. C8147
956 Wilson, P. (Park). College women who express futility. 1950. C8148
957 Lee, G. C. The struggle for federal aid, first phase. 1949. C8149
958 Wilson, M. K. A study of the achievement of college students in beginning courses in food preparation and serving and related factors. 1949. C8150
959 Sarhan, E-D. A-M. Interests and culture. 1950. C8151
960 Goff, R. M. Problems and emotional difficulties of Negro children... 1950. C8152
961 Gordon, P. The availability of contemporary American music for performing groups in high schools and colleges. 1950. C8153
962 Doppelt, J. E. The organization of mental abilities in the age range 13 to 17. 1950. C8154
963 Roach, H. P. History of speech education at Columbia college, 1754-1940. 1950. C8155
964 Frizzle, A. L. A study of some of the influences of Regents requirements and examinations in French. 1950. C8156
965 Hyde, F. (Salls). Protestant leadership education schools. 1950. C8157
966 Goldberg, S. Army training of illiterates in World War II. 1951. C8158
967 Koth, Y. S. E. Science and science education in Egyptian society. 1951. C8159
968 Jennings, M. V. The development of the modern problems course in the senior high school. 1950. C8160
969 Lightfoot, G. F. Personality characteristics of bright and dull children. 1951. C8161
970 Korner, I. N. Experimental investigation of some aspects of the problem of repression. 1950. C8162
971 Kaho, E. E. Analysis of the study of music literature in selected American colleges. 1951. C8163
972 Not published.
973 Radwan, A. F. A. Old and new forces in Egyptian education. 1951. C8164
974 Magruder, E. C. A historical study of the educational agencies of the Southern Baptist Convention, 1845-1945. 1951. C8165

COLUMBIA UNIVERSITY. TEACHERS COLLEGE. HORACE MANN-LINCOLN INSTITUTE OF SCHOOL EXPERIMENTATION. PUBLICATIONS.

Almy, M. C. Ways of studying children. 1959. C8166
____ and others. Young children's thinking. 1960. C8167
Corey, S. M. Action research to improve school practices. 1953. C8168
____ and others. Teachers prepare for discussion group leadership. 1953. C8169
Counts, G. S. Education and American civilization. 1952. C8170
Cunningham, R. and others. Understanding group behavior

of boys and girls. 1951. C8171
Del Solar, C. Parent and teachers view the child. 1949. C8172
Durkin, D. Children who read early. 1966. C8173
8mm sound film and education conf. Proceedings. 1962. C8174
Flapan, D. Children's understanding of social interaction. 1968. C8175
Foshay, A. W. and others. Children's social values. 1954. C8176
Goldberg, M. L. Research and the talented. 1965. C8177
____ and others. The effect of ability grouping. 1966. C8178
Herbert, J. and Swayze, J. Wireless observation. 1964. C8179
Jersild, A. T. In search of self. 1952. C8180
____. When teachers face themselves. 1955. C8181
Jersild, A. T. and others. Child development and the curriculum. 1946. C8182
____. The influence of psychotherapy on the teacher's life and work. 1962. C8183
____. Joys and problems of child rearing. 1949. C8184
____ and Lazar, E. A. The meaning of psychotherapy in the teacher's life and work. 1962. C8185
____ and Tasch, R. Children's interests and what they suggest for education. 1949. C8186
Lawler, M. R. Curriculum consultants at work. 1958. C8187
Lindsey, M. and others. Improving laboratory experiences in teacher education. 1959. C8188
Mackenzie, G. N. and Corey, S. M. Instructional leadership. 1954. C8189
Miel, A. and others. Cooperative procedures in learning. 1952. C8190
Miles, M. B. Learning to work in groups. 1959. C8191
____, ed. Innovation in education. 1964. C8192
Passow, A. H. and others. Planning for talented youth. 1955. C8193
____. Training curriculum leaders for cooperative research. 1955. C8194
The professional is educator; ed. by Foshay. 1970. C8195
Raph, J. B. and others. Bright underachievers. 1966. C8196
Shumsky, A. The action research way of learning. 1958. C8197
Stratemeyer, F. B. Developing a curriculum for modern living. 1957. C8198
____ and others. Guides to a curriculum for modern living. 1952. C8199
Super, D. E. and Bachrach, P. B. Scientific careers and vocational development theory. 1957. C8200
Tannenbaum, A. J. Adolescent attitudes toward academic brilliance. 1962. C8201

COLUMBIA UNIVERSITY. TEACHERS COLLEGE. INSTITUTE OF ADMINISTRATIVE RESEARCH. STUDY.

1 Pierce, T. M. Controllable community characteristics related to the quality of education. 1947. C8202
2 Westby, C. O. Local autonomy for school communities in cities. 1947. C8203
3 Metropolitan school study council. Public action for powerful schools. 1949. C8204
4 Woollatt, L. H. The cost quality relationship on the growing edge. 1949. C8205
5 Skogsberg, A. H. Administrative operational patterns. 1950. C8206
6 Cocking, W. The regional introduction of educational practices in urban school systems of the United States. 1951. C8207
7 Berthold, C. A. Administrative concern for individual differences. 1951. C8208
8 Barrington, T. M. The introduction of selected educational practices into teachers colleges and their laboratory schools. 1953. C8209

9 Polley, J. W. and others. Community action for education. 1953. C8210
10 Fletcher, W. G. Sociological background for community improvement. 1955. C8211
11 Ross, D. H. and McKenna, B. Class size. 1955. C8212
12 Mort, P. R. and Furno, O. F. Theory and synthesis of a sequential simplex. 1960. C8213
13 Swanson, A. D. Effective administrative strategy. 1961. C8214

COLUMBIA UNIVERSITY. TEACHERS COLLEGE. INSTITUTE OF HIGHER EDUCATION. PUBLICATION.

Aldridge, G. J. Liberal education and social work. 1965. C8215
Brick, M. and McGrath, E. J. Innovation in liberal arts colleges. 1969. C8216
Dressel, P. L. and Lorimer, M. F. Attitudes of liberal arts faculty members toward liberal and professional education. 1960. C8217
Gould, J. W. The academic deanship. 1964. C8218
Holstein, E. J. and McGrath, E. J. Liberal education and engineering. 1960. C8219
Hungate, T. L. and McGrath, E. J. A new trimester three-year degree program. 1963. C8220
Kephart, W. M. and others. Liberal education and business. 1963. C8221
Lee, J. A. and Dressel, P. L. Liberal education and home economics. 1963. C8222
McGrath, E. J. Are liberal arts colleges becoming professional schools? 1958. C8223
____. The graduate school and the decline of liberal education. 1959. C8224
____. Memo to a college faculty member. 1961. C8225
____. The predominately Negro colleges and universities in transition. 1965. C8226
____. The quantity and quality of college teachers. 1961. C8227
____, ed. Cooperative long-range planning in liberal arts college. 1964. C8228
____. The liberal arts college and the emergent caste system. 1966. C8229
____. The liberal arts college's responsibility for the individual student. 1966. C8230
____. Universal higher education. 1966. C8231
____ and Johnson, J. T. The changing mission of home economics. 1968. C8232
____ and Meeth, R., eds. Cooperative long range planning in liberal arts colleges. 1964. C8233
____ and Russell, C. H. Are school teachers illiberally educated? 1961. C8234
Meeth, L. R., ed. Selected issues in higher education. 1965. C8235
New prospects for the small liberal arts college, ed. by Letter. 1968. C8236
Newcomer, J. and others. Liberal education and pharmacy. 1960. C8237
Rudy, S. W. The evolving liberal arts curriculum. 1960. C8238
Russell, C. H. Liberal education and nursing. 1959. C8239
Selected issues in college administration, ed. by McGrath. 1967. C8240
Simons, W. E. Liberal education in the service academies. 1965. C8241
The time has come today, ed. by Letter. 1970. C8242
Vaccaro, L. C. and Covert, J. T., eds. Student freedom in American higher education. 1969. C8243
Wager, W. and McGrath, E. J. Liberal education and music. 1962. C8244
Williams, A. R. General education in higher education. 1968. C8245

COMMISSION ON FINANCING HIGHER EDUCATION. STAFF TECHNICAL PAPERS (Columbia Univ. Pr.)

Allen, H. K. State public finance and state institutions of higher education in the United States. 1952. C8246
Association of American Universities Commission on financing higher education. Nature and needs of higher education. 1952. C8247
____. The staff report of the commission on financing higher education by Millet and others. 1952. C8248
Axt, R. G. The Federal government and financing higher education. 1952. C8249
Campbell, W. V. Current operating expenditures and income of higher education in the United States. 1952. C8250
Dodds, H. W. and others. Government assistance to universities in Great Britain. 1952. C8251
Hofstadter, R. and Hardy, C. D. The development and scope of higher education in the United States. 1955. C8252
Hollinshead, B. S. Who should go to college. 1952. C8253
Millet, J. D., ed. An atlas of higher education in the United States. 1952. C8254
____. Financing higher education in the United States. 1952. C8255
Ostheimer, R. H. A statistical analysis of the organization of higher education in the United States, 1948-49. 1951. C8256
____. Student charges and financing higher education. 1953. C8257

COMMITTEE FOR ECONOMIC DEVELOPMENT. RESEARCH STUDY (McGraw)

Abbott, C. C. Financing business during the transition. 1946. C8258
Clark, J. M. Demobilization of wartime economic controls. 1944. C8259
Colean, M. L. and Newcomb, R. Stabilizing construction. 1952. C8260
Committee for economic development. Jobs and markets. 1946. C8261
Goldenweiser, E. A. American monetary policy. 1951. C8262
____. Monetary management. 1949. C8263
Groves, H. M. Postwar taxation and economic progress. 1946. C8264
____. Production, jobs, and taxes. 1944. C8265
Hoover, C. B. International trade and domestic employment. 1945. C8266
Kaplan, A. D. H. The liquidation of war production. 1944. C8267
____. Small business. 1948. C8268
Lasswell, H. D. National security and individual freedom. 1950. C8269
____. World politics faces economics. 1945. C8270
Lester, R. A. Providing for unemployed workers in the transition. 1945. C8271
Mason, E. S. Controlling world trade. 1946. C8272-82
Moulton, E. L. New Mexico's future. 1945. C8283
Schultz, T. W. Agriculture in an unstable economy. 1945. C8284
Smithies, A. The budgetary process in the United States. 1955. C8285

COMMUNICATION ARTS BOOKS (Hastings)

Art Directors Club of New York. Symbology, ed. by Whitney. 1960. C8286
The anatomy of a television commercial, ed. by Diamant. 1970. C8287
Baddeley, W. H. The technique of documentary film production. 1962. C8288
Begley, M. Auditioning for

____. The technique of television production. 1961. C8337
Niggli, A., ed. International poster annual. V. 13. 1967. C8338
Nisbett, A. The technique of the sound studio. 1962. C8339
Oringel, R. S. Audio control handbook for radio and television broadcasting. 1963. C8340
Quaal, W. L. and Martin, L. A. Broadcast management. 1968. C8341
Radio programming in action, ed. by Taylor. 1967. C8342
Reisz, K., comp. The technique of film editing. 1966. C8343
Roe, Y. The television dilemma... 1962. C8344
____, ed. Television station management. 1964. C8345
Ross, R. J. Color film for color television. 1970. C8346
Rotha, P. Documentary film. 1963. C8347
____, ed. Television in the making. 1956. C8348
Settel, I., ed. Top TV shows of the year, 1954-1955. 1955. C8349
Shepard, H. C. and Meyer, L. Posing for a camera. 1960. C8350
Small, W. J. To kill a messenger. 1970. C8351
Souton, M. R. The technique of the motion picture camera. 1967. C8352
Steinberg, C. S. The communicative arts. 1970. C8353
____, ed. Mass media and communication. 1966. C8354
Stroebel, L. D. View camera techniques. 1967. C8355
Swallow, N. Factual television. 1966. C8356
Television station ownership, ed. by Cherington and others. 1971. C8357
Tyrrell, R. The work of the television journalist. 1972. C8358
Visual Communications Conf. Creativity, ed. by Smith. 1959. C8359
____. Visual communications, ed. by Baker. 1961. C8360
____. Symbology, ed. by Whitney. 1960. C8361
Vysot͡skii, M. Z. Wide screen cinema and stereophonic sound, tr. by York. 1971. C8362
Wade, R. J. Staging TV programs and commercials. 1954. C8363
Wainwright, C. A. Television commercials. 1970. C8364
____. The television copywriter. 1966. C8365
Wolseley, R. E. The changing magazine. 1973. C8366
Young, F. and Petzold, P. The work of the motion picture cameraman. 1972. C8367

COMMUNISM IN AMERICAN LIFE.

Aaron, D. Writers on the left. Harcourt, 1961. C8368
Draper, T. American Communism and Soviet Russia. Viking, 1960. C8369
____. The roots of American communism. Viking, 1957. C8370
Glazer, N. The social basis of American Communism. Harcourt, 1961. C8371
Iversen, R. W. The Communists & the schools. Harcourt, 1959. C8372
Latham, E. The Communist controversy in Washington. 1966. C8373
Meyer, F. S. The moulding of Communists. Harcourt, 1961. C8374
Record, W. Race and radicalism. Cornell Univ. Pr. 1964. C8375
Rossiter, C. Marxism. Harcourt, 1960. C8376
Roy, R. L. Communism and the churches. Harcourt, 1960. C8377
Shannon, D. A. The decline of American Communism. Harcourt, 1959. C8378

COMPARATIVE ETHNOLOGICAL STUDIES (Gumperts)

1 Nordenskiöld, E., friherre. An ethno-geographical analysis of the material culture of two Indian tribes in the Gran Chaco, tr. by Fuhrken. 1919. C8379
2 ____. The changes in the material culture of two Indian tribes under the influence of new surroundings. 1920. C8380
3 ____. The ethnography of South-America seen from Mojos in Bolivia. 1924. C8381
4 ____. The copper and bronze ages in South America, tr. by Fuhrken. 1921. C8382
5 ____. Deductions suggested by the geographical distribution of some post-Columbian words used by the Indians of S. America, tr. by Fuhrken. 1922. C8383
6 ____. The secret of the Peruvian quipus, tr. by Fuhrken. 2 pts. 1922. C8384
7 ____. Picture-writings and other documents, tr. by Leijer. 2 pts. 1928-30. C8385
8 ____. Modifications in Indian culture through invention and loans, tr. by Leijer. 1930. C8386
9 ____. Origin of the Indian civilization in South America. Santesson, C. G., An arrow poison with cardiac effect from the New World. Wassén, H., The ancient Peruvian Abacus. 1931. C8387
10 ____. An historical and ethnological survey of the Cuna Indians, ed. by Wassén. 1938. C8388

COMPARATIVE LIBRARY STUDIES (Shoe String Pr.)

Balnaves, J. Australian libraries. 1966. C8389
Campbell, H. C. Canadian libraries. 1969. C8390
Ferguson, J. Libraries in France. 1971. C8391
Libraries in the USSR, ed. by Francis. 1971. C8392
Simsova, S., ed. Lenin Krupskaia and libraries, tr. by Peacock and Prescott. 1968. C8393
____. Nicholas Rubakin and bibliopsychology, tr. by Mackee and Peacock. 1968. C8394
____ and Mackee, M., eds. A handbook of comparative librarianship. 1970. C8395
Taylor, L. E. South African libraries. 1967. C8396

COMPARATIVE STUDIES IN CULTURES AND CIVILIZATIONS (Univ. of Chicago Pr.)

1 Wright, A. F., ed. Studies in Chinese thought. 1953. C8397
2 Von Grunebaum, G. E., ed. Studies in Islamic cultural history. 1954. C8398
3 Hoijer, H., ed. Language in culture. 1954. C8399
4 Von Grunebaum, G. E., ed. Islam. 1955. C8400
5 Redfield, R., ed. The little community. 1955. C8401
6 Marriott, M., ed. Village India; studies in the little community. 1955. C8402
7 Von Grunebaum, G. E., ed. Unity and variety in Muslim civilization. 1955. C8403
8 Fairbanks, J. K., ed. Chinese thought and institutions. 1957. C8404

CONCEPTS IN WESTERN THOUGHT SERIES (Praeger)

Bird, O. A. The idea of justice. 1967. C8405
Hazo, R. G. The idea of love. 1967. C8406
McGill, V. J. The idea of happiness. 1967. C8407
Van Doren, C. L. The idea of progress. 1967. C8408

CONCILIUM THEOLOGY IN THE AGE OF RENEWAL (1-50 Paulist; 51- Seabury)

1 Church and mankind. 1965. C8409

2 The church and the liturgy. 1965. C8410
3 The pastoral mission of the church. 1965. C8411
4 The church and ecumenism. 1965. C8412
5 Moral problems and Christian personalism. 1965. C8413
6 The church and the world. 1965. C8414
7 Historical problems of church renewal. 1965. C8415
8 Pastoral reform in church government. 1965. C8416
9 Spirituality in church and word. 1965. C8417
10 The human reality of Sacred Scripture. 1965. C8418
11 Who is Jesus of Nazareth? 1966. C8419
12 The church worships. 1966. C8420
13 Rethinking the church's mission. 1966. C8421
14 Do we know the others? 1966. C8422
15 War, poverty, freedom. 1966. C8423
16 Is God dead? 1966. C8424
17 Historical investigations. 1966. C8425
18 Religious freedom, canon law, ed. by Edelby and Urresti. 1966. C8426
19 Spirituality in the secular city. 1966. C8427
20 The dynamism of Biblical tradition. 1967. C8428
21 Man as man & believer, ed. by Schillebeeckx and Williams. 1967. C8429
22 Adult baptism and the catechumenate. 1967. C8430
23 Rahner, K. The pastoral approach to atheism, tr. by Westow. 1967. C8431
24 The sacraments. 1967. C8432
25 Understanding the signs of the times, ed. by Bockle. 1967. C8433
26 The evolving world and theology, ed. by Metz. 1967. C8434
27 Progress and decline in the history of church renewal, ed. by Aubert. 1967. C8435
28 Postconciliar thoughts, ed. by Edelby and others. 1967. C8436
29 Opportunities for belief and behavior, ed. by Duquoc. 1967. C8437
30 How does the Christian confront the Old Testament?, ed. by Benoit. 1968. C8438
31 Schillebeeckx, E. C. F. A. The sacraments in general. 1968. C8439
32 Reforming the rights of death, ed. by Wagner. 1968. C8440
33 The renewal of preaching, by Rahner. 1968. C8441
34 Küng, H., ed. Apostolic succession. 1968. C8442
35 The social message of the gospels, ed. by Böckle. 1968. C8443
36 Faith and the world of politics, ed. by Metz. 1968. C8444
37 Prophets in the church, ed. by Aubert. 1968. C8445
38 The sacraments in theology and canon law, ed. by Edelby and others. 1968. C8446
39 The gift of joy, ed. by Duquoc. 1968. C8447
40 The breaking of bread, ed. by Benoit and others. 1969. C8448
41 The problem of eschatology, ed. by Schillebeeckx and Willems. 1969. C8449
42 The crisis of liturgical reform. 1969. C8450
43 The identity of the priest, ed. by Rahner. 1969. C8451
44 The future of ecumenism, ed. by Küng. 1969. C8452
45 Dilemmas of tomorrow's world, ed. by Böckle and Bumer. 1969. C8453
46 The development of fundamental theology, ed. by Metz. 1969. C8454
47 Sacralization and secularization, ed. by Aubert. 1969. C8455
48 The future of canon law, ed. by Edelby and others. 1969. C8456
49 Secularization and spirituality, ed. by Duquoc. 1969. C8457
50 The presence of God, ed. by Benoît and others.

1969. C8458
51 Dogma and pluralism, ed. by Schillebeeckx. 1970. C8459
52 Prayer and community, ed. by Schmidt. 1970. C8460
53 Catechetics for the future, ed. by Müller. 1970. C8461
54 Post-ecumenical Christianity, ed. by Küng. 1970. C8462
55 The future of marriage as an institution, ed. by Böckle. 1970. C8463
56 Moral evil under challenge, ed. by Metz. 1970. C8464
57 Church history in future perspective, ed. by Aubert. 1970. C8465
58 Structures of the church, ed. by Urresti. 1970. C8466
59 Dimensions of spirituality, ed. by Duquoc. 1970. C8467
60 Immorality and resurrection, ed. by Benoît and Murphy. 1970. C8468
61 Sacramental reconciliation, ed. by Schillebeeckx. 1971. C8469
62 Liturgy in transition, ed. by Schmidt. 1971. C8470
63 Democratization of the church, ed. by Müller. 1971. C8471
64 Papal ministry in the church, ed. by Küng. 1971. C8472
65 The manipulated man, ed. by Böckle. 1971. C8473
66 Perspectives of a political ecclesiology, ed. by Metz. 1971. C8474
67 History: self understanding of the church, ed. by Aubert. 1971. C8475
68 Contestation in the church, ed. by Urresti. 1971. C8476
69 The concrete Christian life, ed. by Duquoc. 1971. C8477
70 Theology, exegesis and proclamation, ed. by Benoît and Murphy. 1971. C8478
71 The unifying role of the bishop, ed. by Schillebeeckx. 1972. C8479
72 Liturgy self expression of the church, ed. by Schmidt. 1972. C8480
73 Müller, A. and Greinacher, N., comps. On-going reform of the church. 1972. C8481
74 The plurality of ministries, ed. by Küng and Kasper. 1972. C8482
75 Man in a new society, ed. by Bockle. 1972. C8483
76 New questions on God, ed. by Matz. 1972. C8484
77 Election and consensus in the church, ed. by Alberigo and Weiler. 1972. C8485
78 Bassett, W. W. and Huizing, P., eds. Celibacy in the church. 1972. C8486
79 Duquoc, C. and Geffre, C., eds. The prayer life. 1972. C8487
80 Office and ministry in the church, ed. by Iersel and Murphy. 1972. C8488
81 The persistence of religion, ed. by Greeley and Baum. 1972. C8489
82 Liturgical experience of faith, ed. by Schmidt and Power. 1973. C8490
83 Schillebeeckx, E. C. F. A. Truth and certainty. 1973. C8491
84 Müller, A. and Greinacher, N., eds. Political commitment and Christian community. 1973. C8492
85 The crisis of religious language, ed. by Metz and Jossua. 1973. C8493
86 Humanism and Christianity, ed. by Géffre. 1973. C8494
87 Bassett, W. and Huizing, P. The future of Christian marriage. 1973. C8495
88 Kung, H. and Kasper, W., eds. Polarization in the church. 1973. C8496
89 Duquoc, C. and Floristan, C., eds. Spiritual revivals. 1973. C8497
90 Bockle, F. and Pohler, J. M., eds. Power and the word of God. 1974. C8498
91 Baum, G. and Greeley, A., eds. The church as institution. 1974. C8499
92 Schmidt, H. and Power, D., eds. Politics and liturgy. 1974. C8500
93 Schillebeeckx, E. C. F. A. and Van Lersel, B. Jesus Christ and human freedom. 1974. C8501

94 Müller, A. and Greinacher, N., eds. The experience of dying. 1974. C8502
95 Metz, J. B. and Jossua, F. P. Theology of joy. 1974. C8503
96 Geffre, C. and Gutierrez, G., eds. The mystical and political dimension of the Christian faith. 1974. C8504

Sections:
Dogma: 1, 11, 21, 31, 41, 51, 61, 71, 81.
Liturgy: 2, 12, 22, 32, 42, 52, 62, 72.
Pastoral theology: 3, 13, 23, 33, 43, 53, 63, 73.
Ecumenical theology: 4, 14, 24, 34, 44, 54, 64, 74.
Moral theology: 5, 15, 25, 35, 45, 55, 65, 75.
Fundamental theology: 6, 16, 26, 36, 46, 56, 66, 76.
Church history: 7, 17, 27, 37, 47, 57, 67, 77.
Canon law: 8, 18, 28, 38, 48, 58, 68, 78.
Spirituality: 9, 19, 29, 39, 49, 59, 69, 79.
Scripture: 10, 20, 30, 40, 50, 60, 70, 80.

CONFEDERATE CENTENNIAL STUDIES (Confederate)

1 Coulter, E. M. Lost generation. 1956. C8505
2 Monaghan, J. Swamp Fox of the Confederacy. 1956. C8506
3 Silver, J. W. Confederate morale and church propaganda. 1957. C8507
4 Hoole, W. S. Vizetelly covers the Confederacy. 1957. C8508
5 Nichols, J. L. Confederate engineers. 1957. C8509
6 Anderson, J. Q. A Texan surgeon in the C. S. A. 1957. C8510
7 Jordan, W. T. Rebels in the making. 1958. C8511
8 Yates, R. E. The Confederacy and Zeb Vance. 1958. C8512
9 Scheibert, J. Seven months in the Rebel states during the North American war, 1863, tr. by Hayes, ed. by Hoole. 1958. C8513
10 Montgomery, H. Howell Cobb's Confederate career. 1959. C8514
11 Hunnicutt, J. L. Reconstruction in west Alabama, ed. by Hoole. 1959. C8515
12 Jones, M. S. and Mallard, M. J. Yankees a coming, ed. by Monroe. 1959. C8516
13 Hesseltine, W. B. Lincoln's plan of reconstruction. 1959. C8517
14 Mann, A. D. "My ever dearest friend," ed. by Moore. 1960. C8518
15 Hanna, A. J. and K. A. Confederate exiles in Venezuela. 1960. C8519
16 Hoole, W. S. Alabama Tories. 1960. C8520
17 Davis, C. S. Colin J. McRae. 1961. C8521
18 Keene, J. L. The peace convention of 1861. 1961. C8522
19 Jones, W. D. The Confederate rams at Birkenhead. 1961. C8523
20 Harris, W. C. Leroy Pope Walker. 1962. C8524
21 Girard, C. A visit to the Confederate States of America in 1863, tr. and ed. by Hoole. 1962. C8525
22 White, W. W. The Confederate veteran. 1962. C8526
23 Pecquet du Bellet, P. The diplomacy of the Confederate Cabinet of Richmond and its agents abroad, ed. by Hoole. 1963. C8527
24 Graves, H. L. A Confederate marine: a sketch of Henry Lea Graves, ed. by Harwell. 1963. C8528
25 Walker, G. F. (Gholson). Private journal, 1862-1865, ed. by Henderson. 1963. C8529
26 Hoole, W. S. Lawley covers the Confederacy. 1964. C8530
27 Summersell, C. G. The cruise of C. SS. Sumter. 1965. C8531

Series discontinued.

CONFERENCE ON RESEARCH IN INCOME AND WEALTH. STUDIES IN INCOME AND WEALTH (Nat'l. Bureau of Economic Research)

1 Conference on research in income and wealth. Studies in income and wealth. Eight papers on concepts and measurement of national income. 1937. C8532
2 ____. Six papers on wealth measurement... 1938. C8533
3 ____. Seven papers on income size distribution... 1939. C8534
4 Barger, H. Outlay and income in the United States, 1921-1938. 1942. C8535
5 Same as no. 1. Income size and distribution in the United States. Pt. 1. 1943. C8536
6 Same as no. 1. Seven papers on government product... 1943. C8537
7 Mendershausen, H. Changes in income distribution during the great depression. 1946. C8538
8 Same as no. 1. Eleven papers primarily concerned with estimates of national income... 1946. C8539
9 Hanna, F. A. and others. Analysis of Wisconsin income. 1948. C8540
10 Same as no. 1. Eight papers on standardizing basic concepts of national bookkeeping by American, British, and Canadian statisticians. 1947. C8541
11 Same as no. 1. Six papers on the industrial distribution of manpower... 1949. C8542
12 Same as no. 1. Thirteen papers on national wealth. 1950. C8543
13 Same as no. 1. Ten papers on size distribution of income. 1951. C8544
14 Same as no. 1. The second volume on wealth. 1951. C8545
15 Same as no. 1. Eight papers on size distribution of income. 1952. C8546
16 ____. Long-range economic projection. 1954. C8547
17 ____. Short-term economic forecasting. 1955. C8548
18 ____. Input-output analysis. 1955. C8549
19 ____. Problems of capital formation. 1956. C8550
20 ____. Problems in the international comparison of economic accounts. 1957. C8551
21 ____. Regional income. 1957. C8552
22 ____. An appraisal of the 1950 census income data. 1958. C8553
23 ____. An appraisal of the 1950 census income data. 1958. C8554
24 ____. Trends in the American economy in the nineteenth century. 1960. C8555
25 ____. Output, input, and productivity measurement. 1961. C8556
26 ____. The flow-of-funds approach to social accounting. 1962. C8557
27 Conference on the Behavior of Income Shares. The behavior of income shares. 1964. C8558
28 Conference on Models of Income Determination. Models of income determination. 1964. C8559
29 Measuring the nation's wealth. Materials developed by the Wealth Inventory Planning Study. Govt. Printing Off., 1964. C8560
30 Conference on Research in Income and Wealth. Output, employment, and productivity in the United States after 1800. 1966. C8561
31 The theory and empirical analysis of production, ed. by Brown. 1967. C8562
32 Conference on Research in Income and Wealth. The industrial composition of income and product, ed. by Kendrick. 1968. C8563
33 ____. Six papers on the size distribution of wealth and income, ed. by Soltow. 1969. C8564
34 Fuchs, V. R. Production and productivity in the service

industries. 1969. C8565
35 Conference on Education and Income. Education, income, and human capital, ed. by Hansen. 1970. C8566
36 Conference on Ecometric Models of Cyclical Behavior. Ecometric models of cyclical behavior, ed. by Heckman. 2 v. 1972. C8567
37 Conference on Research in Income and Wealth. Uses of international prices and output data, ed. by Daly. 1972. C8568
38 Conference on the Measurement of Economic and Social Performance, ed. by Moss. 1973. C8569

CONGRESSIONAL LEADERSHIP SERIES (Acropolis Books)

1 Warden, R. D. Metcalf of Montana. 1965. C8570
2 Wilson, A. E. Liberal leader in the House: Frank Thompson, Jr. 1968. C8571
3 Penney, A. C. The golden voice of the Senate. 1968. C8572
4 Phillips, W. G. Yarborough of Texas. 1969. C8573

CONNAISSANCE DES LETTRES (Hatier-Boivin) (1-28 published as Le Livre de l'Etudiant.)

29 Lebègue, R. Ronsard. 1950. C8574
30 Mesnard, J. Pascal. 1951. C8575
31 Caraccio, A. Stendhal. 1951. C8576
32 Saulnier, V. L. Du Bellay. 1951. C8577
33 Perret, J. Virgile. 1952. C8578
34 Castex, P. G. Vigny. 1952. C8579
35 Barrère, J. B. Hugo, l'homme et l'oeuvre. 1952. C8580
36 Adam, A. Verlaine. 1953. C8580a
37 Michaud, G. Mallarmé. 1953. C8580b
38 Salomon, P. George Sand. 1953. C8580c
40 Flottes, P. Leconte de Lisle. 1954. C8580d
41 Ruff, M. A. Baudelaire. 1955. C8580e
42 Fabre, J. André Chénier. 1955. C8580f
43 LeGentil, P. La chanson de Roland. 1955. C8580g
44 Roddier, H. L'abbé Prevost. 1955. C8580h
45 Alquié, F. Descartes. 1956. C8580i
46 Moreau, P. Chateaubriand. 1956. C8580j
47 Pomeau, R. Beaumarchais. 1956. C8580k
48 Cellier, L. Gérard de Nerval. 1956. C8580l
49 Bossuat, R. Le roman de Renard. 1957. C8580m
50 Frappier, J. Chrétien de Troyes. 1957. C8580n
51 Renucci, P. Dante. 1958. C8580o
52 Couton, G. Corneille. 1958. C8580p
53 Perret, J. Horace. 1959. C8580q
54 Regard, M. Sainte-Beuve. 1959. C8580r
55 Guyon, B. Péguy. 1960. C8580s
56 Reboul, P. Laforgue. 1960. C8580t
57 Robichez, J. Romain Rolland. 1961. C8581
59 LeGentil, P. Villon. 1967. C8582
60 Ruff, M. A. Rimbaud. 1968. C8583
61 Digeon, C. Flaubert. 1970. C8584
62 Lebégue, R. Le théâtre comeque en France. 1972. C8585

CONNECTICUT COLLEGE FOR WOMEN. NEW LONDON, CONNECTICUT. COLLEGE MONOGRAPH.

1 Smyser, H. M. and Magoun, F. P., trs. Survivals in old Norwegian of medieval English, French and German literature. 1941. C8586
2 Minar, E. L., Jr. Early Pythagorean politics in theory and practice. 1942. C8587

3 Destler, C. M. American radicalism, 1865-1901: essays and documents. 1946. C8588
4 Magoun, F. P., tr. Walter of Aquitaine, tr. by Magoun and Smyser. 1950. C8589
5 Fussell, P. Theory of prosody in eighteenth-century England. 1954. C8590
6 Haines, G. German influence upon English education and science, 1800-1866. 1957. C8591
7 Kolb, G. L. Juan del Valle y Caviedes. 1959. C8592
8 Baldwin, W. Beware the cat..., ed. by Holden. 1963. C8593
9 Haines, G. Essays on German influence upon English education and science, 1859-1919. 1969. C8594

CONTEMPORARY AMERICAN HISTORY SERIES (Columbia Univ. Pr.)

1 Wittner, L. S. Rebels against war. 1969. C8595
2 Ross, D. R. B. Preparing for Ulysses. 1969. C8596
Gaddis, J. L. The United States and the origins of the cold war, 1941-1947. 1972. C8597
Hamby, A. L. Beyond the New Deal. 1973. C8598
Herring, G. C. Aids to Russia, 1941-1946. 1973. C8599

CONTEMPORARY CIVILIZATION SERIES (Holt)

Adloff, R. West Africa. 1964. C8600
Christopher, J. B. Lebanon. 1966. C8601
Dean, V. (Micheles) and Harootunian, H. D. West and non-West. 1963. C8602
Hammer, E. J. Vietnam, yesterday and today. 1966. C8603
Kuhn, D. and F. The Philippines, yesterday and today. 1966. C8604
Langer, P. F. Japan, yesterday and today. 1966. C8605
Silvert, K. H. Chile, yesterday and today. 1965. C8606
Stevens, G. G. Egypt, yesterday and today. 1963. C8607
Wilber, D. N. Pakistan, yesterday and today. 1964. C8608

CONTEMPORARY COMMUNITY HEALTH SERIES (Univ. of Pittsburgh Pr.)

Altman, I. Methodology in evaluating the quality of medical care. 1970. C8609
Child care work with emotionally disturbed children, by Foster and others. 1971. C8610
Crocetti, G. M. and others. Contemporary attitudes towards mental illness. 1973. C8611
Cussler, M. and Gordon, E. W. Dentists, patients, and auxiliaries. 1968. C8612
Elmer, E. Children in jeopardy. 1967. C8613
Fry, H. G. and others. Education and manpower for community health. 1967. C8614
Greenblatt, M. and others. Dynamics of institutional change. 1971. C8615
Heck, E. T. and others. A guide to mental health services. 1973. C8616
Keller, D. S. A psychiatric record manual for the hospital. 1970. C8617
Long-term childhood illness, by Sultz and others. 1972. C8618
Mattinson, J. Marriage and mental handicap. 1971. C8619
McMichael, J. K. Handicap. 1971. C8620
Mencher, S. British private medical practice and the national health service. 1968. C8621
Mott, B. J. F. Anatomy of a coordinating council. 1968. C8622
Prothero, R. M. Migrants and malaria in Africa. 1968. C8623
Racism and mental health, by

Willie and others. 1973. C8624
Weiner, L. and others. Home treatment. 1969. C8625

CONTEMPORARY LATIN AMERICAN CLASSICS (Southern Illinois Univ. Pr.)

1 Icaza, J. The villagers (Huasipungo), tr. by Dulsey. 1964. C8626
2 Martí, J. Martí on the U. S. A., tr. by Baralt. 1966. C8627
3 Anderson Imbert, E. The other side of the mirror (El grimorio), tr. by Reade. 1966. C8628
4 Aguilera Malta, D. Manuela, la caballeresa del sol, tr. by Jones. 1967. C8629
5 Valdelomar, A. Our children of the sun, tr. by Thompson. 1968. C8630
6 Canfield, D. L. East meets West, ed. by Davis. 1968. C8631
Benítez, F. The poisoned water, tr. by Ellsworth. 1973. C8632
Jones, W. K., tr. Men and angels. 1970. C8633
Usigli, R. Two plays by Rodolfo Usigli, tr. by Bledsoe. 1971. C8634

CONTEMPORARY PERSPECTIVES IN PHILOSOPHY SERIES (Prentice-Hall)

Anderson, A. Minds and machines. 1964. C8635
Canfield, J. Purpose in nature. 1966. C8636
Chappell, V. C., ed. Ordinary language. 1964. C8637
Pike, N., ed. God and evil. 1964. C8638
Pitcher, G., ed. Truth. 1964. C8639
Tomas, V., ed. Creativity in the arts. 1964. C8640

CONTEMPORARY PHILOSOPHY (Cornell Univ. Pr.)

Baier, K. The moral point of view. 1958. C8641
Barker, S. F. Induction and hypothesis. 1957. C8642
Chisholm, R. M. Perceiving. 1957. C8643
Geach, P. T. Reference and generality. 1962. C8644
Hintikka, K. J. J. Knowledge and belief. 1962. C8645
Martin, C. B. Religious belief. 1959. C8646
Plantinga, A. God and other minds. 1967. C8647
Shoemaker, S. Self-knowledge and self-identity. 1963. C8648
Steiner, M. Mathematical knowledge. 1974. C8649
Vendler, Z. Res cogitans. 1972. C8650
Wertheimer, R. The significance of sense. 1972. C8651
Wright, G. H. von. Explanation and understanding. 1971. C8652

CONTEMPORARY SOVIET UNION SERIES: INSTITUTIONS AND POLICIES (Praeger)

Conquest, R., ed. Agricultural workers in the U. S. S. R. 1968. C8653
____. Industrial workers in the U. S. S. R. 1967. C8654
____. Justice and the legal systems in the USSR. 1968. C8655
____. The politics of ideas in the U. S. S. R. 1967. C8656
____. Religion in the U. S. S. R. 1968. C8657
____. Soviet nationalities policy in practice. 1967. C8658
____. The Soviet police system. 1967. C8659
____. The Soviet policy system. 1968. C8660

CONTEMPORARY THEOLOGY SERIES

Curtis, C. J. and Rousseau, R. W., eds. Contemporary Protestant thought. Bruce, 1970. C8661
Elert, W. The Lord's Supper today, tr. by Bertram. Concordia Pub. House, 1973. C8662
Hamann, F. P. Unity and

fellowship and ecumenicity. Concordia Pub. House, 1973. C8663

Kehoe, K., comp. The theology of God sources. Bruce, 1971. C8664

Klotz, J. W. A Christian view of abortion. Concordia Pub. House, 1973. C8665

Maier, W. A. Form criticism reexamined. Concordia Pub. House, 1973. C8666

Poetsch, H. L. Marxism and Christianity, ed. by Schmiege. Concordia Pub. House, 1973. C8667

Preus, J. A. O. It is written. Concordia Pub. House, 1971. C8668

Scaer, D. P. The Apostolic scriptures. Concordia Pub. House, 1971. C8669

_____. The Lutheran World Federation. Concordia Pub. House, 1971. C8670

Scharlemann, M. H. The ethics of revolution. Concordia Pub. House, 1971. C8671

Scott, W. A., comp. Sources of Protestant theology. Bruce, 1971. C8672

Tapia, R. J., comp. The theology of Christ. Bruce, 1971. C8673

CONTRIBUTI ALLA BIBLIOTECA BIBLIOGRAFICA ITALICA (Sansoni)

1 Ascarelli, F. La tipografia cinquecentina italiana. 1953. C8674

2 Angeleri, C. Bibliografia le stampe popolari a carattere profano secoli XVI e XVII conservati nelle Biblioteca nazionale centrale di Firenze. 1953. C8675

3 Parenti, M. Rarità bibliografische dell'Ottocento. V. 1. 1953. C8676

4 Manferrari, U. Dizionario universale delle opere melodrammatiche. V. 1. 1954. C8677

5 Nicolini, S. Bibliografia degli antichi cataloghi a stampa di biblioteche italiane, secoli XVII-XVIII. 1954. C8678

6 Milano, A. Biblioteca historica italo-judaica. 1954. C8679

7 Righini, B. I periodici fiorentini (1597-1950). V. 1. 1955. C8680

8 Same as no. 4. V. 2. 1955. C8681

9 Same as no. 7. V. 2. 1955. C8682

10 Same as no. 4. V. 3. 1955. C8683

11 Leonetti, F. Carducci e i suoi contemporanei. 1955. C8684

12 Fucilla, J. G. Saggistica litteraria italiana. 1956. C8685

13 Same as no. 3. V. 2. 1956. C8686

14 Borroni, F. Le carte Rajna della Biblioteca marucelliana. 1956. C8687

15 Rocco di Torrepadula, G. Biblioteca galileiana raccolta dal principe Giampaolo Rocco di Torrepadula. 1957. C8688

16 Same as no. 3. V. 3. 1957. C8689

17 Scuricini Greco, M. L. Miniature riccardiane. 1958. C8690

18 Ciferri, R. and Redaelli, P. Bibliographia mycopathologica. V. 1. 1958. C8691

19 Same as no. 3. V. 4. 1959. C8692

20 Same as no. 18. V. 2. 1959. C8693

21 Falqui, E. Bibliografia e iconografia del futurismo. 1959. C8694

22 Same as no. 3. V. 5. 1960. C8695

23 Semarano, G., ed. Omaggio a Marino Parenti. 1960. C8696

24-25 Same as no. 3. V. 6-7. 1964. C8697

26 _____. Supplemento to V. 6, 1954-63. 1964. C8698

27 Same as no. 3. V. 8. 1964. C8699

CONTRIBUTIONS IN AFRO-AMERICAN AND AFRICAN STUDIES (Greenwood Pr.)

1 Boulware, M. H. The oratory of Negro leaders. 1969. C8700
2 Canter, M., comp. Black labor in America. 1969. C8701
3 Reardon, W. R. and Pawley, T. D., eds. The Black teacher and the dramatic arts. 1970. C8702
4 Refugees south to the Saraha, ed. by Brooks and El-Ayouty. 1970. C8703
5 Weisbord, R. G. Bittersweet encounter. 1970. C8704
6 Fowler, A. L. The Black infantry in the West. 1971. C8705
7 Lombardi, J. V. The decline and abolition of Negro slavery in Venezuela. 1971. C8706
8 Perry, M. A bio-bibliography of Countée P. Cullen. 1971. C8707
9 Necheles, R. F. The Abbe Grégoire. 1971. C8708
10 Walton, H. The political philosophy of Martin Luther King, Jr. 1971. C8709
11 Rawick, G. P. The American slave. 19 v. 1972. C8710
12 Nigeria, ed. by Okpaku. 1972. C8711
13 Thompson, D. C. Private black colleges at the crossroads. 1973. C8712
14 Weisbord, R. G. Ebony kinship. 1973. C8713
16 Harris, M. A. A Negro history of Manhattan. 1968. C8714

CONTRIBUTIONS TO ECONOMIC ANALYSIS (North Holland)

1 Tinbergen, J. On the theory of economic policy. 1952. C8715
2 Zimmerman, L. J. The propensity to monopolize. 1952. C8716
3 Haavelmo, T. A study in the theory of economic evolution. 1954. C8717
4 Koyck, L. M. Distributed lags and investment analysis. 1954. C8718
5 Goris, H. Price-determining factors in American tobacco markets. 1954. C8719
6 Tinbergen, J. Centralization and decentralization in economic policy. 1954. C8720
7 Theil, H. Linear aggregation of economic relations. 1954. C8721
8 Mendershausen, H. Two postwar recoveries of the German economy. 1955. C8722
9 Klein, L. R. and Goldberger, A. S. An econometric model of the United States, 1929-1952. 1955. C8723
10 Tinbergen, J. Economic policy. 1956. C8724
11 Diab, M. A. The United States capital position and the structure of its foreign trade. 1956. C8725
12 Narasimham, N. V. A. A short term planning model for India. 1956. C8726
13 Chow, G. C. Demand for automobiles in the United States. 1957. C8727
14 Lefeber, L. Allocation in space. 1958. C8728
15 Theil, H. and others. Economic forecasts and policy. 1958. C8729
16 Bjerve, P. J. Planning in Norway, 1947-1956. 1959. C8730
17 Rand Corporation. Time series analysis of interindustry demands, by Arrow and Hoffenberg. 1959. C8731
18 Chakravarty, S. The logic of investment planning. 1959. C8732
19 Goldberger, A. S. Impact multipliers and dynamic properties of the Klein-Goldberger model. 1959. C8733
20 Qayum, A. Theory and policy of accounting prices. 1960. C8734
21 Johansen, L. A multi-sectoral study of economic growth. 1960. C8735
22 Eizenga, W. Demographic factors and savings.

1961. C8736
23 Hansen, B. Foreign trade credits and exchange reserves. 1961. C8737
24 Wonnacott, R. J. Canadian-American dependence. 1961. C8738
25 David, M. H. Family composition and consumption. 1962. C8739
26 Fisher, F. M. A priori information and time series analysis. 1962. C8740
27 Fisher, F. M. and Kaysen, C. A study in econometrics. 1962. C8741
28 Michaely, M. Concentration in international trade. 1962. C8742
29 Marglin, S. A. Approaches to dynamic investment planning. 1963. C8743
30 Day, R. H. Recursive programming and production response. 1963. C8744
31 Minhas, B. S. An international comparison of factor costs and factor use. 1963. C8745
32 Kuh, E. Capital stock growth. 1963. C8746
33 Pitchford, J. D. A study of cost and demand inflation. 1963. C8747
34 Correa, H. The economics of human resources. 1963. C8748
35 Boon, G. K. Economic choice of human and physical factors in production. 1964. C8749
36 Wold, H. O. A., ed. Econometric model building. 1964. C8750
37 Schipper, L. Consumer discretionary behavior. 1964. C8751
38 Friedlaender, A. F. The interstate highway system. 1965. C8752
39 Ghosh, A. Efficiency in location and interregional flows. 1965. C8753
40 Oury, B. A production model for wheat and food grains in France, 1946-61. 1966. C8754
41 Dean, E. R. The supply response of African farmers. 1966. C8755
42 Linnemann, H. An econometric study of international trade flows. 1966. C8756
43 Goldfeld, S. M. Commercial bank behavior and economic activity. 1966. C8757
44 Pavlopoulos, P. A statistical model for the Greek economy, 1949-1959. 1966. C8758
45 Kornai, J. Mathematical planning of structural decisions, tr. by Hatvany and Morvay. 1967. C8759
46 Blaestra, P. The demand for natural gas in the United States. 1967. C8760
47 Balopoulos, E. Fiscal models of the United Kingdom economy. 1967. C8761
48 Bradley, P. G. The economics of crude petroleum production. 1967. C8762
49 Childs, G. L. Unfilled orders and inventories. 1967. C8763
50 Jong, F. J., ed. Dimensional analysis for economists. 1967. C8764
51 Feldstein, M. S. Economic analysis for health service efficiency. 1967. C8765
52 Moriguchi, C. Business cycles and manufactures' short-term production decisions. 1967. C8766
53 Galatin, M. Economics of scale and technological change in thermal power generation. 1968. C8767
54 Delahanty, G. E. Nonproduction workers in U. S. manufacturing. 1968. C8768
55 Behrman, J. R. Supply response in underdeveloped agriculture. 1969. C8769
56 Branson, W. H. Financial capital in the U. S. balance of payments. 1969. C8770
57 Praag, B. M. S. van. Individual welfare functions and consumer behavior. 1968. C8771
58 Katz, J. M. Production functions. 1969. C8772
59 Fair, R. C. The short-run demand for workers and

hours. 1969. C8773
60 Prachowny, M. F. J. A structural model of the U. S. balance of power. 1969. C8774
61 Kemp, M. C. A contribution to the general equilibrium theory of preferential trading. 1969. C8775
62 Belsley, D. A. Industry production behavior. 1970. C8776
63 Inagaski, M. Optimal economic growth. 1970. C8777
64 Ginsburg, A. L. American and British regional export determinants. 1970. C8778
65 Lee, T. C. and others. Estimating the parameters of the Markov probability model from aggregate time series data. 1970. C8779
66 Sereck-Hanssen, J. Optimal patterns of location. 1970. C8780
67 Cline, W. R. Economic consequences of a land reform in Brazil. 1970. C8781
68 Clark, P. B. Planning import substitution. 1970. C8782
69 Westphal, L. E. Planning investments with economics of scale. 1971. C8783
70 Olsen, E. H. International trade theory and regional income differences. 1971. C8784
71 Frontiers of quantitative economics, ed. by Intriligator. 1971. C8785
72 Griliches, Z. and Ringstad, V. Economics of scale and the form of the production function. 1971. C8786
73 Takayama, T. and Judge, G. G. Spatial and temporal price and allocation models. 1971. C8787
74 Philips, L. and others. Effects of industrial concentration. 1971. C8788
75 Johansen, L. Production functions. 1972. C8789
76 Evans, H. D. A general equilibrium analysis of protection. 1972. C8790
77 Goldfeld, S. M. and Quandt, R. E. Nonlinear methods in econometrics. 1972. C8791
78 Ball, R. J. The international linkage of national economic models. 1973. C8792
79 Somermeyer, W. H. and Bannink, R. A consumption-savings model and its applications. 1972. C8793
80 Schmalenesee, R. The economics of advertising. 1972. C8794
81 Pindyck, R. S. Optimal planning for economic stabilization. 1973. C8795
82 Judge, G. G. and Takayama, T. Studies in economic planning over space and time. 1973. C8796
83 Eckaus, R. S. and Rosenstein-Rodan, P. N. Analysis of development problems. 1973. C8797
84 Corbo Lioi, V. Inflation in developing countries. 1974. C8798
85 Pitchford, J. D. Population in economic growth. 1974. C8799
86 Fienberg, S. E. and Zellner, A. Studies in Bayesian econometrics and statistics. 1974. C8800
87 Intriligator, M. D. and Kendrick, D. A. Frontiers of quantitative economics. V. 2. 1974. C8801

CONTRIBUTIONS TO LIBRARY LITERATURE SERIES (Shoe String Pr.)

1 Marshall, J. D. and others, eds. Books, libraries, librarians. 1955. C8802
2 ____, ed. Of, by, and for librarians. 1960. C8803
3 ____. An American library history reader. 1961. C8804
4 Trinker, C. L., ed. Better libraries make better schools. 1962. C8805
5 Rowland, A. R., ed. Reference services. 1964. C8806
6 Olding, R. K., ed. Readings in library cataloging. 1966. C8807
7 Tennessee. University. Library. The library in the university, ed. by Jesse. 1967. C8808
8 Rowland, A. R., ed. The catalog and cataloging.

1969. C8809
9 Trinkner, C. L., ed. Teaching for better use of libraries. 1970. C8810
10 Marshall, J. D., ed. Of, by and for libraries. 1973. C8811

CONTROVERSIES IN POLITICAL SCIENCE SERIES (Lieber-Atherton)

Avineri, S., ed. Marx. 1971. C8812
Bachrach, P., ed. Political elites in a democracy. 1971. C8813
Bandura, A. Psychological modeling. 1972. C8814
Barkun, M. Law and the social problem. 1971. C8815
Berkowitz, L., ed. The roots of aggression. 1969. C8816
Bienen, H. The military and modernization. 1971. C8817
Bondurant, J. V. and Fisher, M. W., eds. Conflict. 1971. C8818
Buss, A. H. and E., eds. Theories of schizophrenia. 1968. C8819
Champlin, J. R., ed. Power. 1971. C8820
Chinoy, E., ed. The urban future. 1971. C8821
Connolly, W. E., ed. The bias of pluralism. 1969. C8822
Ellig, R., ed. National health care. 1971. C8823
Eulau, H., ed. Behavioralism in political science. 1968. C8824
____. Political behavior. 1968. C8825
Goode, E., ed. Marijuana. 1969. C8826
Greenberg, E. S., ed. Political socialization. 1971. C8827
Grey, A., ed. Class and personality in society. 1968. C8828
Grey, A. G., ed. Man, woman and marriage. 1971. C8829
Hoffman, R. L., ed. Anarchism. 1971. C8830
Jacobson, H. K., ed. The shaping of foreign policy. 1969. C8831
Kateb, G., ed. Utopia. 1971. C8832
Kaufman, W. Hegel's political philosophy. 1971. C8833
Levine, M. Motivation in humor. 1971. C8834
Loewenberg, G., ed. Modern parliaments. 1971. C8835
McCafferty, J. A. Capital punishment. 1970. C8836
McLaren, I. A. Natural regulation of animal populations. 1971. C8837
Pitkin, H., ed. Representation. 1969. C8838
Rejai, M., ed. Decline of ideology? 1971. C8839
Schmeidler, G., ed. Extrasensory perception. 1968. C8840
Suedfeld, P. and Koslin, B. L. Alternatives in attitude theory. 1971. C8841
Williams, G. C., ed. Group selection. 1971. C8842

COOPER MONOGRAPHS ON ENGLISH AND AMERICAN LANGUAGE AND LITERATURE (Francke)

1 Schnyder, H. Die wiederbelebung des mittelalters im humoristischen abbild. 1956. C8843
2 Gerstner-Hirzel, A. The economy of action and word in Shakespeare's plays. 1957. C8844
3 Holder-Barrell, A. The development of imagery and its functional significance in Henry James' novels. 1959. C8845
4 Nagy, N. C. de. The poetry of Ezra Pound. 1968. C8846
5 Chaucer, G. A seventeenth century modernization of the first three books of Chaucer's "Troilus and Criseyden," ed. by Wright. 1960. C8847
6 Schnyder, S. Sir Gawain and the Green Knight. 1961. C8848
7 Staehelin-Wackernagel, A. The Puritan settler in the American novel before the Civil War. 1961. C8849

8 Hägin, H. The epic hero and the decline of heroic poetry. 1964. C8850
9 Schmid, H. The dramatic criticism of William Archer. 1964. C8851
10 Hasler, J. Switzerland in the life and works of Henry James. 1966. C8852
11 Nagy, N. C. de. Ezra Pound's poetic and literary tradition. 1966. C8853
12 Meier, E. Realism and reality. 1967. C8854
13 Dedio, A. Das dramatische werk von Lady Gregory. 1967. C8855
14 Nagy, N. C. de. Michael Drayton's "England's Heroical Epistle." 1968. C8856
15 Scheibler, R. The love plays of Eugene O'Neill. 1970. C8857
16 Bothe, D. Direkte und indirekte transkription. 1971. C8858
17 Fricker, F. Ben Jonson's plays in performance and the Jacobean theatres. 1972. C8859
18 Engler, B. Rudolf Alexander Schröders Ubersetzungen von Shakespeare's dramen. 1973. C8860
19 Elmer, W. The terminology of fishing. 1973. C8861
20 Glauser, B. The Scottish-English linguistic border. 1974. C8862
21 Hasler, J. Shakespeare's theatrical notation. 1974. C8863

CORNELL INTERNATIONAL INDUSTRIAL AND LABOR RELATIONS. REPORTS.

1 Neufeld, M. F. Labor unions and national politics in Italian industrial plants. 1954. C8864
2 Windmuller, J. P. American labor and the international labor movement. 1954. C8865
3 Ornati, O. A. Jobs and workers in India. 1955. C8866
4 Sturmthal, A. F., ed. Contemporary collective bargaining in seven countries. 1957. C8867
5 Neufeld, M. F. Italy. 1961. C8868
6 ____. Poor countries and authoritarian rule. 1965. C8869
7 Morris, J. O. Elites, intellectuals, and consensus. 1966. C8870
8 Gregory, P. Industrial wages in Chile. 1967. C8871

CORNELL REPRINTS IN URBAN STUDIES.

Artle, R. The structure of the Stockholm economy. 1965. C8872
Olmstead, F. L. Landscape into cityscape, ed. by Fein. 1968. C8873
Weber, A. F. The growth of cities in the nineteenth century. 1963. C8874

CORNELL STUDIES IN ATHROPOLOGY.

Barclay, H. B. Buurri al Lamaab. 1964. C8875
Doughty, P. L. and M. F. Huaylas. 1968. C8876
Fraser, T. M. Rusembilan. 1960. C8877
Hughes, C. C. and J. M. An Eskimo village in the modern world. 1960. C8878
Sasaki, T. T. Fruitland, New Mexico. 1960. C8879
Stein, W. W. Hualcan. 1961. C8880
Weingrod, A. Reluctant pioneers. 1966. C8881

CORNELL STUDIES IN CIVIL LIBERTY.

Barrett, E. L. The Tenney committee. 1951. C8882
Bontecou, E. The Federal loyalty-security program. 1953. C8883
Byse, C. and Joughin, G. L. Tenure in American higher education. 1959. C8884
Carr, R. K. Federal protection of civil rights. 1947. C8885
____. The House Committee on Un-American activities, 1945-50. 1952. C8886
Chamberlain, L. H. Loyalty and legislative action. 1951. C8887

Countryman, V. Un-American activities in the state of Washington. 1951. C8888
Cushman, R. E. Civil liberties in the United States. 1956. C8889
Edgerton, H. W. Freedom in the balance, ed. by Bontecou. 1960. C8890
Gellhorn, W. Security, loyalty, and science. 1950. C8891
____, ed. The states and subversion. 1952. C8892
Konvitz, M. R. The alien and the Asiatic in American law. 1946. C8893
____. Aspects of liberty. 1958. C8894
____, ed. Bill of rights reader. 1960. C8895
____. Civil rights in immigration. 1953. C8896
____. Fundamental liberties of a free people. 1957. C8897
____, ed. First amendment freedoms. 1963. C8898
Longaker, R. P. The Presidency and the individual liberties. 1961. C8899
Record, W. Race and radicalism. 1964. C8900
Rosenbloom, D. H. Federal service and the Constitution. 1969. C8901
Sibley, M. Q. and Jacob, P. E. Conscription of conscience. 1952. C8902
Sigler, J. A. Double jeopardy. 1969. C8903
Smith, J. M. Freedom's fetters. 1956. C8904
Wiecek, W. M. The guarantee change of the U. S. Constitution. 1972. C8905

CORNELL STUDIES IN ENGLISH (1-17 printed by Yale Univ. Pr. 17- printed by Cornell Univ. Pr. 1- distributed by Cornell Univ. Pr.)

1 Northup, C. S., comp. A bibliography of Thomas Gray. 1917. C8906
2 Thayer, M. R. The influence of Horace on the chief English poets of the nineteenth century. 1916. C8907
3 Gt. Brit. Office of the revels. The dramatic records of Sir Henry Marbert... ed. by Adams. 1917. C8908
4 Gilbert, A. H. A geographical dictionary of Milton. 1919. C8909
5 Crane, T. F. Italian social customs of the sixteenth century and their influence on the literatures of Europe. 1920. C8910
6 Bradley, J. F., and Adams, J. Q. The Jonson allusion-book. 1922. C8911
7 Wordsworth, W. The Ecclesiastical sonnets of William Wordsworth, ed. by Potts. 1922. C8912
8 Langdon, I. Milton's theory of poetry and fine art. 1924. C8913
9 Northup, C. S., comp. A register of bibliographies of the English language and literature. 1925. C8914
10 Steele, M. S. Plays and masques at court during the reigns of Elizabeth, James and Charles. 1926. C8915
11 Cooper, L., and Gudeman, A. A bibliography of the Poetics of Aristotle. 1928. C8916
12 Milton, J. Milton on education, ed. by Ainsworth. 1928. C8917
13 Nungezer, E. A dictionary of actors and other persons associated with the public representation of plays in England before 1642. 1929. C8918
14 Sanders, G. D. Elizabeth Gaskell. 1929. C8919
15 Milton, J. The Latin poems of John Milton, ed. by Mackellar. 1930. C8920
16 Pico della Mirandola, G. F. On the imagination, ed. by Caplan. 1930. C8921
17 Herrick, M. T. The Poetics of Aristotle in England. 1930. C8922
18 The Wits: or, Sport upon sport, ed. by Elson. 1932. C8923
19 Sibley, G. M., comp. The

lost plays and masques, 1500-1642. 1933. C8924
20 Kent, E. E. Goldsmith and his booksellers. 1933. C8925
21 Wordsworth, W. and Reed, H. Wordsworth & Reed, ed. by Broughton. 1933. C8926
22 Bissell, F. O. Fielding's theory of the novel. 1933. C8927
23 Hutton, J. The Greek anthology in Italy to the year 1800. 1935. C8928
24 Blodgett, H. W. Walt Whitman in England. 1934. C8929
25 Baldwin, S. E. Charles Kingsley. 1934. C8930
26 Tenney, E. A. Thomas Lodge. 1935. C8931
27 Colerdige, S. (Coleridge). Sara Coleridge and Henry Reed, ed. by Broughton. 1937. C8932
28 Ryan, A. M. A map of Old English monasteries and related ecclesiastical foundations, A. D. 400-1066. 1939. C8933
29 Wordsworth, W. The white doe of Rylstone, ed. by Comparetti. 1940. C8934
30 French, W. H. Essays on King Horn. 1940. C8935
31 Cooper, L. Methods and aims in the study of literature. 1940. C8936
32 Wordsworth, W. Some letters of the Wordsworth family, ed. by Broughton. 1942. C8937
33 Cooper, L. Experiments in education. 1943. C8938
34 Ross, M. M. Milton's royalism. 1943. C8939
35 Samuel, I. Plato and Milton. 1947. C8940
36 Hoppe, H. R. The bad quarto of Romeo and Juliet. 1948. C8941
37 Sale, W. M. Samuel Richardson. 1950. C8942
38 Chapman, C. O. An index of names in Pearl, Purity, Patience and Gawain. 1951. C8943
39 Broughton, L. N. and others. Robert Browning: a bibliography, 1830-1950. 1953. C8944
40 Adams, H. Blake and Yeats. 1955. C8945
41 Novarr, D. The making of Walton's Lives. 1958. C8946
42 The Vitellius Psalter, ed. by Rosier. 1962. C8947
43 Traherne, T. Christian ethicks, ed. by Marks. 1968. C8948

CORNELL STUDIES IN INDUSTRIAL AND LABOR RELATIONS.

1 Adams, L. P. Wartime manpower mobilization. 1951. C8949
2 McKelvey, J. T. AFL attitudes toward production, 1900-1932. 1952. C8950
3 Tolles, N. A. and Raimon, R. L. Sources of wage information. 1952. C8951
4 Seidenberg, J. The labor injunction in New York City. 1953. C8952
5 Jensen, V. H. Nonferrous metals industry unionism. 1954. C8953
6 Blumen, I. and others. The industrial mobility of labor as a probability process. 1955. C8954
7 Christie, R. A. Empire in wood. 1956. C8955
8 Adams, L. P. and Aronson, R. L. Workers and industrial change. 1957. C8956
9 Landsberger, H. A. Hawthorne revisited. 1958. C8957
10 Morris, J. O. Conflict within the AFL. 1958. C8958
11 Cook, A. H. Union democracy. 1963. C8959
12 Hanslowe, K. L. Procedures and policies of the New York State Labor Relations Board. 1964. C8960
13 Cook, D. Fringe benefits. 1964. C8961
14 Doherty, R. E. Teaching industrial relations in high school. 1965. C8962
15 Hildebrand, G. H. and Liu, T. Manufacturing production functions in the United States, 1957. 1965. C8963
16 Adams, L. P. The public employment service in transition, 1933-1968. 1969. C8964

17 Carpenter, J. T. Competition and collective bargaining in the middle trades, 1910-1967. 1972. C8965

CORNELL STUDIES IN PHILOSOPHY (1-7 Macmillan, 8- Longman, distributed by Cornell Univ. Pr.)

1 Robins, E. P. Some problems of Lotze's theory of knowledge, ed. by Creighton. 1900. C8966
2 Griswold, H. D. Brahman. 1900. C8967
3 Dolson, G. N. The philosophy of Friedrich Nietzsche. 1901. C8968
4 Moore, V. F. The ethical aspect of Lotze's metaphysics. 1901. C8969
5 Truman, N. E. Maine de Biran's philosophy of will. 1904. C8970
6 Crawford, A. W. The philosophy of F. H. Jacobi. 1905. C8971
7 Talbot, E. B. The fundamental principle of Fichte's philosophy. 1906. C8972
8 Cunningham, G. W. Thought and reality in Hegel's system. 1910. C8973
9 Tsanoff, R. A. Schopenhauer's criticism of Kant's theory of experience. 1911. C8974
10 Townsend, H. G. The principle of individuality in the philosophy of Thomas Hill Green. 1914. C8975
11 Howard, D. T. John Dewey's logical theory. 1918. C8976
12 Swabey, M. T. (Collins). Some modern conceptions of natural law. 1920. C8977
13 Morrow, G. R. The ethical and economic theories of Adam Smith. 1923. C8978
14 Whitchurch, I. G. The philosophical bases of asceticism in the Platonic writings and in the pre-Platonic tradition. 1923. C8979
15 Hawes, R. P. The logic of contemporary English realism. 1923. C8980
16 Crawford, L. S. The philosophy of Emile Boutroux as representative of French idealism in the nineteenth century. 1924. C8981
17 Smart, H. R. The philosophical presuppositions of mathematical logic. 1925. C8982

CORNELL UNIVERSITY. CORNELL PUBLICATIONS IN THE HISTORY OF SCIENCE

Adelmann, H. B. Marcello Malpighi and the evolution of embryology. 5 v. 1966. C8983
Fabricius, H. The embryological treatises. 2 v. 1966. C8984
Galenus, C. Galen on the usefulness of the parts of the body, ed. by May. 2 v. 1968. C8985
Temkin, O. Galenism. 1973. C8986

CORNELL UNIVERSITY. CORNELL ROMANCE STUDIES.

1 Liber de miraculis sanctae Dei genitricis mariae, ed. by Crane. 1925. C8987
2 Hall, R. A., ed. Descriptive Italian grammar. V. 2. 1948. C8988
3 Tyard, P. de. The universe of Pontus de Tyard, ed. by Lapp. 1950. C8989

CORNELL UNIVERSITY. HOUSING RESEARCH CENTER RESEARCH PUBLICATIONS.

1 Adams, L. P. Mackesey, T. W. Commuting patterns of industrial workers. 1955. C8990
2 Beyer, G. H. and Partner, J. W. Marketing handbook for prefabricated housing industry. 1955. C8991
3 ____ and others. Houses are for people. 1955. C8992

CORNELL UNIVERSITY. MESSENGER LECTURES IN THE EVOLUTION OF CIVILIZATION (Cornell Univ. Pr. unless otherwise specified)

1926-27 Grierson, H. J. C. Cross currents in English literature of the XVIIth century. 1929. C8993
1928-29 Thorndike, E. L. Human learning. 1931. C8994
1931 Morgan, T. H. The scientific basis of evolution. 1932. C8995
1934 Eddington, A. S. New pathways in science. 1935. C8996
1938-39 McIlwain, C. H. Constitutionalism. Macmillan, 1940. C8997
1940-41 Pottle, F. A. The idiom of poetry. 1941. C8998
1940-41 Sigerist, H. E. Civilization and disease. 1944. C8999
1941-42 Rockefeller institute for medical research, N. Y. Virus diseases, by Rivers and others. 1943. C9000
1942-43 Peyre, H. Writers and their critics. 1944. C9001
1944-45 Bush, D. Paradise Lost in our time. 1945. C9002
1945-46 Muller, H. J. and others. Genetics, medicine and man. 1947. C9003
1946-47 Slichter, S. H. The challenge of industrial relations. 1947. C9004
1947-48 Jones, H. M. The theory of American literature. 1948. C9005
1947-48 Menninger, W. C. Psychiatry. 1948. C9006
1950-51 Clausen, J. C. Stages in the evolution of plant species. 1951. C9007
1950-51 DuVigneaud, V. A trail of research in sulfur chemistry and metabolism and related fields. 1952. C9008
1952 Krutch, J. W. "Modernism" in modern drama. 1953. C9009
1955 Mason, A. T. Security through freedom. 1955. C9010
1956 Kirkland, E. C. Dream and thought in the business community. 1956. C9011
1957 Guthrie, W. K. C. In the beginning... 1957. C9012
1957 Kroeber, A. L. Style and civilizations. 1957. C9013
1958 Wigglesworth, V. B. The control of growth and form. 1959. C9014
1964 Feynman, R. P. The character of physical law. 1965. C9015
1967 Romilly, J. de. Time in Greek tragedy. 1968. C9016

CORNELL UNIVERSITY. MODERN INDONESIA PROJECT. MONOGRAPH SERIES

Abdullah, T. Schools and politics. 1971. C9017
Anderson, B. R. O. Mythology and the tolerance of Javanese. 1965. C9018
Djajadiningrat, I. N. The beginnings of the Indonesian-Dutch negotiations and the Hoge Veluwe talks. 1958. C9019
Federspiel, H. M. Persatuan Islam. 1970. C9020
Feith, H. The Wilopo Cabinet, 1952-1953. 1958. C9021
Goethals, P. R. Aspects of local government in a Sumbawan village. 1961. C9022
Koentjaraningrat. Some social-anthropological observations of gotong rojong practices in two villages of central Java, tr. by Holt. 1961. C9023
Lev, D. S. The transition to guided democracy. 1966. C9024
Mackie, J. A. C. Problems of the Indonesian inflation. 1967. C9025
Moertono, S. State and statecraft in old Java. 1968. C9026
Nitisastro, W. and Ismael, J. E. The government, economy, and taxes of a central Javanese village, tr. by Ward. 1959. C9027
Smail, J. R. W. Bandung in the early revolution, 1945-1946. 1964. C9028

Soemardjen, S. The dynamics of community development in rural Central and West Java. 1963. C9029

Tedjasukmana, I. The political character of the Indonesian trade union movement. 1958. C9030

Willmott, D. E. The national status of the Chinese in Indonesia, 1900-1958. 1961. C9031

CORNELL UNIVERSITY. STUDIES IN CLASSICAL PHILOLOGY (Andrew, Ginn, Macmillan publishers, distributed by Cornell Univ. Pr.)

1 Hale, W. G. The CUM-constructions. 2 v. 1887-89. C9032
2 Wheeler, B. I. Analogy and the scope of its application in language. 1887. C9033
3 Walton, A. The cult of Asklepios. 1894. C9034
4 Botsford, G. W. The development of the Athenian constitution. 1893. C9035
5 Van Cleef, F. L. Index Antiphontevs composvit. 1895. C9036
6 Elmer, H. C. Studies in Latin moods and tenses. 1898. C9037
7 Ferguson, W. C. The Athenian secretaries. 1898. C9038
8 Bates, F. O. The five post-Kleisthenean tribes. 1898. C9039
9 Bennett, C. E. Critique of some recent subjunctive theories. 1898. C9040
10 Ferguson, W. S. The Athenian archons of the third and second centuries before Christ. 1899. C9041
11 Lander, M. K. and Kellogg, M. F. Index in Xenophontis Memorabilia. 1900. C9042
12 Fairbanks, A. A study of the Greek paean. 1900. C9043
13 Durham, C. L. The subjunctive clauses in Plautus, not including indirect questions. 1901. C9044
14 Babcock, C. L. A study in case rivalry. 1901. C9045
15 Neville, K. P. R. The case-construction after the comparative in Latin. 1901. C9046
16 Newton, H. C. The epigraphical evidence for the reigns of Vespasian and Titus. 1901. C9047
17 Powell, B. Erichtonius and the three daughters of Cecrops. 1906. C9048
18 Lane, M. C. Index to the fragments of the Greek elegiac and iambic poets. 1908. C9049
19 Jones, H. L. The poetic plural of Greek tragedy in the light of Homeric usage. 1910. C9050
20 Cowles, F. H. Gaius Verres. 1917. C9051
21 Mountford, J. F., ed. Quotations from classical authors in medieval Latin glossaries. 1925. C9052
22 Isocrates. De pace and Philippus, ed. by Laistner. 1927. C9053
23 Mountford, J. F. and Schultz, J. T. Index rerum et nominum in scholiis servii et Aelii Donati tractatorum. 1930. C9054
24 Caplan, H. Mediaeval artes praedicandi: a hand-list. 1934. C9055
25 ____. Mediaeval artes praedicandi: a supplementary handlist. 1936. C9056
26 Starr, C. G. The Roman imperial navy, 31 B. C. - A. D. 324. 1941. C9057
27 Solmsen, F. Plato's theology. 1942. C9058
28 Hutton, J. The Greek anthology in France and in the Latin writers of the Netherlands to the year 1800. 1946. C9059
29 Hansen, E. V. The Attalids of Pergamon. 1947. C9060
30 Solmsen, F. Hesiod and Aeschylus. 1949. C9061
31 Kirkwood, G. M. A study of Sophoclean drama. 1958. C9062
32 Wallach, L. Alcuin and Charlemagne. 1959. C9063
33 Solmsen, F. Aristotle's

system of the physical world. 1960. C9064
34 Wiesen, D. S. St. Jerome as a satirist. 1964. C9065
35 North, H. Sophrosyne. 1966. C9066
36 Hansen, E. V. The Attalids of Pergamon. 2d ed. 1971. C9067
37 Kirkwood, G. M. Early Greek monody. 1973. C9068
38 Kirkwood, G. M., ed. Poetry and poetics from ancient Greece to the Renaissance. 1974. C9069

CORONADO CUARTO CENTENNIAL PUBLICATIONS, 1540-1940.

1 Bolton, H. E. Coronado on the Turquoise Trail. 1949. C9070
2 Hammond, G. P. and Rey, A., eds. Narratives of the Coronado expedition, 1540-1542. 1940. C9071
3 Hammond, G. P. and Rey, A. The rediscovery of New Mexico, 1580-1594. 1967. C9072
4 Benavides, A. de. Fray Alonso de Benavides' revised Memorial of 1634. 1945. C9073
5-6 Hammond, G. P. and Rey, A. Don Juan de Oñate. 2 v. 1953. C9074
8-9 Hackett, C. W., ed. Revolt of the Pueblo Indians of New Mexico and Otermin's attempted reconquest, 1680-1682. 2 v. 1942. C9075
10 Vargas Zapata y Luzán Ponze de León D. de. First expedition of Vargas into New Mexico. 1692. 1940. C9076
11 Thomas, A. B. The Plains Indians and New Mexico, 1751-1778. 1940. C9077
12 Pfefferkorn, I. Sonora. 1949. C9078
7 not published.

CORONADO CUARTO CENTENNIAL PUBLICATIONS, 1540-1940. BANDELIER - MORGAN SERIES.

Bandelier, A. F. A. and Morgan, L. H. Pioneers in American anthropology, ed. by White. 2 v. 1940. C9079

CORPUS GENERAL DES PHILOSOPHES FRANÇAIS. AUTEURS MODERNES (Presses Universitaires de France)

3 Bodin, J. Oeuvres philosophiques, ed. by Mesnard. V. 1. 1952. C9080
33 Condillac, E. B., de. Oeuvres philosophiques, ed. by LeRoy. 3 v. 1947-51. C9081
41, 1 Buffon, G. L. L. de. Oeuvres philosophiques, ed. by Piveteau and Bruneau. 1954. C9082
44 Cabanis, P. J. G. Oeuvres philosophiques, ed. by Lehec and Cazeneuvé. 2 v. 1956- C9083

CORPUS OF MEDIAEVAL SCIENTIFIC TEXTS (Univ. of Chicago Pr.)

1 Rufinus. The herbal of Rufinus, ed. by Thorndike and Benjamin. 1946. C9084
2 Thorndike, L., ed. and trans. The Sphere of Sacrobosco and its commentators. 1949. C9085
3 Thorndike, L., ed. Latin treatises on comets between 1238 and 1368 A.D. 1950. C9086

THE CORPUS OF ROMAN LAW (Corpus juris Romani)

1 Codex Theodosianus. The Theodosian code and novels, ed. and tr. by Pharr. Princeton Univ. Pr., 1952. C9087
2 Rome. Laws, Statutes, etc. Ancient Roman statues, ed. by Johnson. Univ. of Texas Pr., 1961. C9088

CORPUS SCRIPTORUM CHRISTIANORUM ORIENTALIUM (CSCO)

1-6 Chronica minora, ed. by Guidi and others. 6 v. 1903-05. C9089
7-8 Brooks, E. W., ed. and tr. Vitae vivorum apud Monophysitas celebrerrimorim, ed. by Brooks. 2 v. 1907. C9090
9-10 Philoxenus, Bp. Philoxeni Mabbugensis tractus tres de trinitate et incarnations. 2 v. 1907. C9091
11-12 Isho'yabh. Iso'yabh Patriarche III Liber epistularum, ed. by Duval. 2 v. 1904-05. C9092
13-14 Dionysius bar Salibi. Expositio liturgiae, ed. by Labourt. 2 v. 1903. C9093
15-16 ____. Commentarii in evangelia, ed. by Sedláček and Chabot. V. 1. 2 pts. 1906. C9094
17 British museum. Documenta ad origines monophysitarum illustrandas, ed. by Chabot. V. 1. 1908. C9095
18-19 Littmann, E. Philosophi abessini. 2 v. 1904. C9096
20-21 Zenāhū la-negūs Sarda Dengel. Historia regis Sarsa Dengel, ed. by Conti Rossini. 2 v. 1907. C9097
22-25 Zenāhū la negūs A'laf Sagad. Annales Iohannis I, Iyāsu I, Bakāffā, ed. by Guidi. 4 v. 1903-05. C9098
26-27 Gadla Yārēd. Vitae sanctorum antiquiorum Gadev Yārēd, seu Acta Sancti Yārēd, ed. by Conti Rossini. 2 v. 1904. C9099
28-29 Gadla Basalota Mika'el. Vitae sanctorum indigenarum, seu Acta Sancti Basalota Mikā'ēl..., ed. by Conti Rossini. 2 v. 1905. C9100
30-31 Gadla Aron. Vitae sanctorum indigenarum, seu Acta Sancti Aaronis..., ed. by Turaiev. 2 v. 1908. C9101
32 Gadla Ewostātēwos. Vitae sanctorum indigenarum, ed. by Turaiev. 1906. C9102
33-34 Gadla Marqorewos. Vitae sanctorum indigenarum, ed. by Conti Rossini. 2 v. 19094. C9103
35-36 Gadla Ferē-Mikā'el. Vitae sanctorum indigenarum, ed. by Turaiev. 2 v. 1905. C9104
37-38 Esteves Pereira, F. M., ed. Acta martyrum. 2 v. 1907. C9105
39-40 Chaîne, M., ed. Apocrypha de B. Maria Virgine. 2 v. 1909. C9106
41-42 Leipoldt, I. and Crum, W. Sinuthii archimandritae vita et opera omnia, ed. by Leipoldt and Crum. V. 1, 3. 1906-08. C9107
43-44 Balestri, I. and Hyvernat, H. Acta martyrum. 2 v. 1907-08. C9108
45-46 Butrus ibn al-Muhadhdhib. Petrus ibn Rahib: Chronicon orientale, ed. by Cheikho. 2 v. 1903. C9109
47-49 Coptic church. Synaxarium Alexandrinun, ed. by Forget. V. 1, 3 pts. 1905-06. C9110
50-51 Eutychius. Annales. 2 v. 1906-09. C9111
52 Severus ibn al Mukaffa' Auba. Historia patriarcharum Alexandrinorum, ed. by Seybold. V. 1. 1904. C9112
53 Dionysius bar Salibi. In Apocalypsim, Actus et Epistulas catholicas, ed. by Sedlaček. V. 1. 1904. C9113
54 Book of Axum. Documenta ad illustrandam historiam, ed. by Conti Rossini. V. 1. 1909. C9114
55 Theodorus bar Kōnī. Liber scholiorum. V. 1. 1910. C9115
56-57 Gadla Abuna Abakerazūn. Vitae sanctorum indigenarum, ed. by Conti Rossini. 2 v. 1910. C9116
58 Same as no. 54. V. 2. 1910. C9117
59 Same as no. 52. V. 2. 1910. C9118
60 Same as no. 53. V. 2.

1910. C9119
61 Târîka zi'ahōmū lanegūśna'-Iyāsū walaneguśna'Iyo'as. Annales regum Isāyu II et Iyo'ās, ed. by Guidi. V. 1. 1910. C9120
62-63 Elias bar Shināya. Opus chronologicum, ed. by Brooks, tr. by Chabot. 2 v. in 4. 1910. C9121
64 Gīwargīs. Anonymi auctoris Expositio officiorum ecclesiae, Georgio Arbelensi vulgo adscripta, ed. by Connolly. V. 1. 1911. C9122
65 Agapius, Bp. Agapius Episcopus Mabbugensis, historia universalis, ed. by Cheikho. 1912. C9123
66 Same as no. 61. V. 2. 1912. C9124
67 Same as nos. 47-49. V. 2. 1912. C9125
68 Gadla'Emna Walatta Pētros. Vitae sanctorum indigenarum, ed. by Jaeger. 1912. C9126
69 Same as no. 55. V. 2. 1912. C9127
70 Cyrillus, St. S. Cyrilli Alexandrini Commentarii in Lucam, ed. by Chabot. 1912. C9128
71-72 Same as no. 64. V. 2-3. 1913. C9129
73 Same as nos. 41-42. V. 4. 1913. C9130
74-75 Timotheus, I. Epistulae, ed. by Braun. V. 1. 1914-1915. C9131
76 Same as no. 64. V. 2. C9132
77 Same as nos. 15-16. V. 1. Pt. 2. 1915. C9133
78 Same as nos. 47-49. V. 1. 1922. C9134
79-80 Bābai, the elder. Liber de unione. Ed. by Vaschalde. 2 v. 1915. C9135
81-82 Anonymi auctoris Chronicon ad annum Christi 1234 pertinens. Ed. by Chabot and Barsaum. 2 v. 1920, 1916. C9136
83-84 Zacharias, rhetor. Historia ecclesiastica Zachariae rhetori vulgo adscripta. Ed. by Brooks and Chabot. 2 v. 1919-1921. C9137
85 Same as nos. 15-16. V. 1. Pt. 2. 1922. C9138
86 Same as nos. 43-44. V. 2. 1924. C9139
87-88 Same as nos. 83-84. 2 v. 1924. C9140
89 Vita Sancti Pachomii. S. Pachomii vita Bohairice scripta, ed. by Lefort. V. 1. 1925. C9141
90 Same as nos. 47-49. V. 2. 1926. C9142
91 Incerti auctoris Chronicon anonymum Pseudo-Dionsyianum vulgo dictum. Ed. by Chabot. V. 1. 1927. C9143
92 Iacobi Edesseni Hexaemeron seu in opus creationis libri septem by Chabot. V. 1. 1928. C9144
93-94 Severus Sozoplitanus. Liber contra impium Grammaticum, ed. by Lebon. V. 1. 1929. C9145
95 Same as nos. 15-16. V. 2. Pt. 1. 1931. C9146
96 Same as no. 42. Ed. by Wiesmann. V. 3. 1931. C9147
97 Same as no. 92. Ed. by Vaschalde. V. 2. 1932. C9148
98 Same as nos. 15-16. V. 2. Pt. 1. 1933. C9149
99-100 Lefort, L. T. S. Pachomii vitae sahidice scriptae. 2 v. 1933-34. C9150
101-102 Same as nos. 93-94. V. 2. 1933. C9151
103 Same as no. 17. V. 2. 1933. C9152
104 Same as no. 91. V. 2. 1933. C9153
105-106 Joannes, Bp. Historiae ecclesiasticae pars tertia, ed. by Brooks. 2 v. 1952. C9154
107 Same as no. 89. V. 2. 1936. C9155
108 Same as nos. 41-42. 1936. C9156
109 Same as nos. 81-82. 1937. C9157
110 Jacob of Serug. Iacobi Sarugensis epistulae quotquot supersunt. 1937. C9158
111-112 Same as nos. 93-94. 1 v. 1938. C9159

115-116 Theodorus, Bp. Commentarius in Evangelium Iohannis Apostoli. Ed. by Vosté. 2 v. 1940. C9160
117-118 Athanasius, St. S. Antonii vitae versio Sahadica. Ed. by Garitte. 2 v. 1949. C9161
119-120 Severus Sozopolitanus. Severi Antiocheni Orationes ad Nephalium, ed. by Lebon. 2 v. 1949. C9162
121 Same as no. 91. 1949. C9163
122-123 Catholic church. Liturgiae Ibericae antiquiores. Ed. by Tarchnisvili. 2 v. 1950. C9164
124 Lefort, L. T. Concordance du Nouveau Testament sahidique. V. 1:1. 1950. C9165
125 Same as nos. 43-44. 1950. C9166
126 Īšhō-dadh. Commentaire d'Iso'dad de Merv sur l'Ancien Testament. I. Gènese. V. 1. 1950. C9167
127 Honigmann, E. Evêques et évêchés monophysites d'Asie antérieur au VIe siècle. 1951. C9168
128 Vööbus, A. Studies in the history of the Gospel text in Syriac. 1951. C9169
129 Wiesmann, H. Sinuthii vita bohairice. 1951. C9170
130-131 Habib ibn Khidma, A. R. Die Scriften des Jakobiten Habib ibn Hidma, Abu Ra'ita. Ed. by Graf. 2 v. 1951. C9171
132 LaNarratio de rebus Armeniae, ed. by Garitte. 1952. C9172
133-134 Severus Sozopolitanus. Sévère d'Antioch; le Philalèthe. Ed. by Hespel. 2 v. 1952. C9173
135-136 Apostolic Fathers. Les Pères apostoliques en copte. Ed. by Lefort. 2 v. 1952. C9174
137 Ephraem, St. Commentaire de l'Evangile concordant, ed. by Leloir. V. 1. 1953. C9175
138-139 George, St. Miracularum S. Georgii Megalo-martyris collectio altera, ed. by Arras. 2 v. in 1. 1953. C9176
140 Cyrillus, St. S. Cyrilli Alexandrini Commentarii in Lucam. 1953. C9177
141-142 Reyndets, B. Lexique comparé du texte grec et des versions latine. 2 v. 1954. C9178
143-144 Gregorius. Typicon. Ed. by Tarchnišvile. 2 v. 1954. C9179
145 Same as no. 137. V. 2. 1954. C9180
146 Honigmann, E. Le couvent de Barsauma et le Patriarcat jacobite d'Antoiche et de Syrie. 1954. C9181
147 Graf, G. Verzeichnis arabischer kirchlicher Termini. 1954. C9182
148-149 Antonius, St. Lettres de S. Antone, ed. by Garitte. 2 v. in 1. 1955. C9183
150-151 Athanasius, St. Lettres festales et pastorales en copte, ed. by Lefort. 2 v. in 1. 1955. C9184
152-153 Ephraem, St. In Genesim et in Exodum commentarii, ed. by Tonneau. 2 v. in 1. 1955. C9185
154-155 ____. Hymnen de fide, ed. by Beck. 2 v. 1955. C9186
156 Same as no. 126. V. 2. 1955. C9187
157-158 Besa, Abbot. Letters and sermons, ed. by Kuhn. 2 v. 1956. C9188
159-160 Pachomius, St. Oeuvres de S. Pachôme et de ses disciples, ed. by Lefort. 2 v. 1956. C9189
161-162 Abu al-Faraj'Abd Allah ibn al Tayyib. Fiqh an-nasrānīya, "Das Reclet der Christenheit," ed. by Hoenerbach and Spies. 2 v. 1956. C9190
163-164 Krestos Samra. Atti di Krestos Samra. Ed. by Cerulli. 2 v. 1956. C9191
165 Garitte, G. Catalogue des manuscrits géorgiens littéraires du Mont Sinaï. 1956. C9192
166 Monumenta Iberica antiquora..., ed. by Molitor. 1956. C9193

167-168 Same as nos. 161-162. 2 v. 1957. C9194
169-170 Ephraem, St. Hymnen contra haereses, ed. by Beck. 2 v. 1957. C9195
171-172 Simeon, St. Vies géogiennes de S. Syméon Stylite l'ancien et de S. Ephrem, ed. by Garitte. 2 v. in 1. 1957. C9196
173 Same as no. 124. V. 1:2. C9197
174-175 Ephraem, St. Hymnen de paradiso und Contra Julianum, ed. by Beck. 2 v. in 1. 1957. C9198
176 Ishō-dadh. Commentaite d'Iso'dad de Merv sur l'Ancien Testament. II. Exode Deuteronome, ed. by van den Eynde. V. 1. 1958. C9199
177-178 Bible. Papyrus Bodmer III; Evangile de Jean et Genèse I-IV, 2 en bohaïrique, ed. by Kaiser. 2 v. in 1. 1958. C9200
179 Same as no. 176. V. 2. 1958. C9201
180 Ephraem St. L'Evangile d'Ephrem d'apres les oeuvres éditées, ed. by Leloir. 1958. C9202
181-182 Actes de Filmona. Ed. by Allotte de la Fuÿe. 2 v. in 1. 1958. C9203
183 Same as no. 124. V. 2:1. C9204
184 Vööbus, A. History of asceticism in the Syrian Orient. V. 1. 1958. C9205
185 Same as no. 124. V. 2:2. 1959. C9206
186-187 Ephraem, St. Hymnen de nativitate, ed. by Beck. 2 v. 1959. C9207
188-189 Armenian Church. Le grand lectionnaire de l'Eglise de Jerusalem, ed. by Tarchnišvili. 2 v. 1959. C9208
190-191 Paris. Bibliothèque Nationale. Atti di Giulio di Aqfahs, ed. by Cerulli. 2 v. in 1. 1959. C9209
192-193 Eutychius, Patriarch. The book of the demonstration (Kitab-al-Burhan). 1960. C9210
194-195 Bible. Manuscripts. Papyrus Bodmer VI, ed. by Kasser. 2 v. in 1. 1960. C9211
197 Same as no. 184. V. 2. 1960. C9212
198-199 Ephraem, St. Hymnen de ecclesia. Ed. by Beck, 1960. C9213
200-201 Sahdona, Bp. Oeuvres spirituelles, ed. by Halleux. 2 v. 1960. C9214
202-203 La prise de Jerusalem. La prise de Jerusalem par les Parses en. 614, ed. by Garitte. 1960. C9215
204-205 Grand (Le) lectionnaire de l'Eglise de Jerusalem, ed. by Tarchnischvili. V. 2. 1960. C9216
206-207 Pseudo-Shenoute. Pseudo-Shenoute on Christian behaviour, ed. by Kuhn. 1960. C9217
208 Helena, Aethiopum regina. Helenae Aethiopum reginae quae ferunther preces et carmina, ed. by van der Oudenrijn. V. 1. 1960. C9218
209 Eutychius, Patriarch. The book of the demonstration. Pt. 2., ed. by Cachia. 1961. C9219
210 ____. Part 2, ed. by Watt. 1961. C9220
211 Same as no. 208. V. 2. 1960. C9221
212-213 Ephraem, St. Sermones de fide, ed. by Beck. 2 v. 1961. C9222
214-215 Same as nos. 200-201. 1961. C9223
216-217 Dawit' Alawkay. The penitential of David of Ganjak, ed. by Dowsett. 1965. C9224
218-219 Ephraem, St. Carmina nisibena, ed. by Beck. 2 v. 1961. C9225
220 ____. Doctrines et méthodes de S. Ephrem d'apres son Commentaire de l'Evangile concordant, by Leloir. 1961. C9226
221-222 Zará Ya'qob. Das Mashafa Milād... und Mashafa Sellāsē, ed. by Wendt. 2 v. in 1. 1962. C9227
223-224 Ephraem Syrus, St.

Hymnen de virgintate, ed. by Beck. 2 v. in 1. 1962. C9228
225-226 Coptic Church. Die Bucher der Einsetzung der Erzengel Michael und Gabriel, ed. by Muller. 1962. C9229
227 Leloir, L. Le temoignage d'Ephrem sur le Diatessaron. 1962. C9230
228 Molitar, J. Glossarium Ibericum in quattor Evangelia et Actus Apostolorum antiquiores versions etiam textus Chanmeti et Haemetri completens. 1962. C9231
229-230 Same as no. 126. V. 2, 3. 1963. C9232
231-232 Philoxène de Mabbox. Lettre aux moines de Senoun, ed. by de Halleux. 2 v. 1963. C9233
233-234 Elī. Mēmrā sur S. Mār Philoxène de Mabbog, ed. by de Halleux. 2 v. in 1. 1963. C9234
235-236 Same as nos. 221-222. 2 v. in 1. 1963. C9235
237 V. 2. 1963. C9236
238-239 Collectio monastica, ed. by Arras. 2 v. in 1. 1963. C9237
240-241 Same as nos. 218-219. 1963. C9238
242 Abramowski, L. Untersuchungen zum Liber Heraclides des Nestorius. 1963. C9239
243 Same as no. 166. V. 4. 1963. C9240
244 Severus Sozopolitanus. La polemique antijulianeste, ed. by Hespel. V. 1. 1964. C9241
246-247 Ephrem, S. Des heiligen Ephraem des Syres Hymnen De Ieiunio, ed. by Beck. 1964. C9242
248-249 ____. Des heiligen Ephraem des Syrer Paschahymnen, ed. by Beck. 2 v. in 1. 1964. C9243
250 ____. Zaia Ya'qob Il libro della luce del Negus Zara Yā'qob (Mashafa Berhān) ed. by Ricci. V. 1. 1964. C9244
251 Il libro della Luce del Negus Zar'a Ya'gob, ed. by Rossini and Ricci. 1965. C9245
252-255 Same as nos. 200-201. 4 v. 1965. C9246
256 Molitar, J. Synopsis latina Evangeliorum ibericorum antiquissimorum secundum Matthaeum, ed. by Molitor. 1965. C9247
257-258 Athanasius, St. Athanasiuna syriaeca, ed. by Thomson. 2 v. 1965. C9248
259-260 Iyasus, Mo'a. Actes de Iyasus Mo'a, ed. by Kur. 1965. C9249
261-262 Same as V. 250. V. 2, 3. 1965. C9250
263-264 Hippolytus, St. Itaites d'Hippolyte sur David et Goliath, ed. by Garitte. 2 v. 1965. C9251
265 Same as no. 228. V. 5. 1965. C9252
266 Vööbus, A. History of the school of Nisibis. 1965. C9253
267 Blau, Y. A grammar of Christian Arabic. V. 1. 1968. C9254
268-269 Kuhn, K. H. A panegyric on John the Baptist. 2 v. 1966. C9255
270-271 Ephraem Syrus, St. Des heiligen Ephraem des Syrers Sermo de Domino Nostro, ed. by Beck. 2 v. 1966. C9256
272-273 Athanasius, St. Athanasiana syriaca. 2 v. 1967. C9257
274-275 Ibn at-Taiyib. Ibn at-Taiyib, ed. by Sanders. 2 v. 1967. C9258
276 Same as no. 267. V. 2. 1967. C9259
277-278 Arras, V. Patericon aethiopice. 2 v. 1967. C9260
279 Same as no. 267. V. 3. 1967. C9261
280 Same as no. 228. V. 6. 1967. C9262
281-282 Bible. N.T. Die ötheopische Ubersetzung der Johannes-Apokalpse, ed. by Hofmann. 1967. C9263
283-284 Bible. N.T. Citations du Nouveau Testament dans l'ancienne tradition arménienne, ed. by Leloir. 2 v. 1967. C9264

285-286 Garitte, G. Version georgienne de la vie de Sainte Marthe. 2 v. 1968. C9265
287-288 Kur, S., ed. Actes de Samuel de Dabra Wagag. 2 v. 1968. C9266
289-290 Draguet, R. Les cinq recensions de l'Ascéticon syriaque d'Abba Isaie. 2 v. 1968. C9267
291-292 Egan, G. A., ed. Saint Ephrem. 2 v. 1968. C9268
293-294 Same as no. 289-290. 2 v. 1968. C9269
295-296 Same as nos. 93-94. 1968. C9270
297 Same as no. 281. 1969. C9271
298-299 Cerulli, E. Les vies ethiopiennes de Saint Alexis l'homme de Dieu. 2 v. 1969. C9272
300 Blum, G. G. Rabbula von Edessa. 1969. C9273
301-302 Same as no. 93-94. 1969. C9274
303-304 Same as no. 126. V. 3-4. 1969. C9275
305-306 Same as no. 155. V. 10-11. 1969. C9276
307 Vööbus, A. Syrische kanonessammlungen. 1970. C9277
308-309 Sader, J. Le de oblatione de Jean de Dara. 2 v. 1970. C9278
310 Fiey, J. M. Jalons pour une histoire de l'Eglise en Iraq. 1970. C9279
311-312 Same as nos. 154-155. 2 v. 1970. C9280
313-314 Drescher, J. The Coptic (Sahidic) version of kingdoms. 2 v. 1970. C9281
315 Kerschensteiner, J. Der altsyrische Paulustext. 1970. C9282
316 Ricci, L. Vita di Walatta pietros. 1970. C9283
317 Same as no. 307. V. 2. 1970. C9284
318-319 Same as no. 133. V. 3, 4. 1971. C9285
320-321 Same as nos. 154-155. 1972. C9286
322-323 Beck, E. Des heiligen Ephraem des Syrers hymnen auf Abraham Kidunaya and Julianos Saba. 2 v. 1972. C9287
324-325 Same as nos. 257-258. 1972. C9288
326-327 Draguet, R. Commentaire du livre d'Abbe Isaie par Dadiso Qatraya. 1972. C9289
328-329 Van den Eynde, C. Commentaire d'Iso'dad de Merv sur l'ancien Testament. 2 v. 1972. C9290
330-331 Kur, S. Actes de Marha Krestos. 2 v. 1972. C9291
332-333 Schneider, M. Actes de Za-Yohannes de Kébrān. 2 v. 1972. C9292
334-335 Same as nos. 218-219. V. 4. 1973. C9293
336-337 Pushaka de Ketaba de-Aba Isha'ya. Commentaire anonyme du livre d'abba Isaie, ed. by Draguet. 2 v. 1973. C9294
338-339 Hayman, A. P. The disputation of Sergius the stylite against a Jew. 2 v. 1973. C9295
340-341 Garitte, G. Expugnationis hierosolymae. 2 v. 1973. C9296
342-343 Arras, V. De transitu Mariae apocrypha aethiopice. 2 v. 1973. C9297
344-345 Vööbus, A. Handschriftliche überlieferung der Mēmrē-dichtung des Ja'qob von Serüg. 2 v. 1973. C9298
346 Gero, S. Byzantine iconoclasm during the reign of Leo III. 1973. C9299
347-348 Same as no. 340-341. 2 v. 1974. C9300
349-350 Orlandi, T. Constantini episcopi urbis siout economia in Athanasium duo. 2 v. 1974. C9301
351-352 Same as nos. 257-258. 2 v. 1974. C9302
353 Leloir, A. Paterica armeniaca a P. P. mechitaristis edita nune latine reddita. V. 1. 1974. C9303
354 Same as nos. 81-82. V. 2. 1974. C9304
355-356 Macomber, W. F. Six explanations of the

liturgical feasts. 2 v. 1974. C9305

357-358 Frank, R. M. The oldest Arabic translation of the wisdom of Jesus Ben Sirach. 2 v. 1974. C9306

V. 1-125 (1903-50) carried J. B. Chabot's scheme consisting of an abbreviation indicating language followed by a Roman numeral according to content, e.g. History, Theology, etc. Indicated here is current sub-series with whole numbering given in parentheses.

Scriptores Aetheopici: 1-23 (18-40), 24(54), 25-27(56-58), 28(61), 29(66), 30(68), 31-32(138-39), 33-34(163-64), 35-36(181-82), 37-38(190-91), 39(208), 40(211), 41-42(221-22), 43-44(235-36), 45-46(238-39), 47-48(250-51), 49-52(259-62), 53-54(277-78), 55-56(281-82), 57-58(287-88), 59-60(298-99), 61(316), 62-65(330-33), 66-67(342-43), 68-69(351-52)

Scriptores Arabici: 1-8(45-52), 9(59), 10(65), 11(67), 12(78), 13(90), 14-15(130-31), 16-17(161-62), 18-19(167-68), 20-21(192-93), 22-23(209-10), 24-25(274-75), 26-27(340-41), 28-29(347-48), 30-31(357-58)

Scriptores Armeniaci: 1(137), 2(145), 3-4(216-17), 5-6(291-92)

Scriptores Coptici: 1-4(41-44), 5(73), 7(89), 8(96), 9-10(99-100), 11-12(107-8), 13-14(117-18), 15(125), 16(129), 17-18(135-36), 19-20(150-51), 21-24(157-60), 25-26(177-78), 27-28(194-95), 29-30(206-7), 31-32(225-26), 33-34(268-69), 35-36(313-14), 37-38(349-50)

Scriptores Iberici: 1-2(122-23), 3-4(143-44), 5-6(148-49), 7-8(171-72), 9-10(188-89), 11-14(202-5), 15-16(263-64), 17-18(285-86)

Scriptores Syriaci: 1-17(1-17), 18(53), 19(55), 20(60), 21-25(62-64), 26-29(69-72), 30-33(74-77), 34-42(79-88), 43-47(97-98), 50-55(101-6), 56-63(109-16), 64-66(119-21), 67(126), 68-69(133-34), 70(140), 71-75(152-56), 76-77(169-70), 78-80(174-6), 81(179), 82-83(186-87), 84-87(198-201), 88-91(212-15), 92-93(218-19), 94-95(223-24), 96-101(229-34), 102-3(240-41), 104-9(244-49), 110-3(252-55), 114-15(257-58), 116-19(289-90), 122-25(293-96), 126-31(301-6), 132-33(308-9), 134-35(311-12), 136-47(318-29), 148-53(334-39), 154-56(354-55)

Subsidia: 1(124), 2-3(127-28), 4(132), 5-6(141-42), 7-8(146-47), 9-10(165-66), 11(173), 12(180), 13-15(183-85), 16-17(196-97), 18(220), 19-20(227-28), 21(237), 22-23(243), 24(256), 25-27(265-67), 28(276), 29-30(279-80), 31-32(283-84), 33(297), 34(300), 35(307), 36(310), 37(315), 38(317), 39-41(344-46)

CORPUS SCRIPTORIUM ECCLESIASTICORUM LATINORUM (1-15, Geroldi, 16- Hölder)

1 Severus, S. Sculpicii Severi libri qui supersunt, ed. by Halm. 1866. C9307

2 Minucius Felix, M. M. Minucii Felicis Octavius, ed. by Halm. 1867. C9308

3 Cyprianus, St. S. Thasci Caecili Cypriani Opera omnia, ed. by Hartel. 3 v. 1868-71. C9309

4 Arnobius Afer. Arnobii Adversvs nationes libri VII, ed. by Reifferscheid. 1875. C9310

5 Orosius, P. Pavli Orosii Historiarvm adversvm paganos libri VII, ed. by Zangemeister. 1882. C9311

6 Ennodius, M. F., St. Magni Felicis Ennodii Opera omnia, ed. by Hartel. 1882. C9312

7 Victor, St. Victoris episcopi vitensis Historia persecutionis africanae provinciae, ed. by Petschenig. 1881. C9313

8 Salvianus. Salvinai

presbyteri Massiliensis Opera omnia, ed. by Pauly. 1883. C9314
9:1 Eugippius. Evgippii Excerpta ex operibus S. Avgvstini, ed. by Knöll. 1885. C9315
9:2 ___. Evgippii Vita Sancti Severini, ed. by Knoll. 1886. C9316
10 Sedulius. Sedvlii Opera omnia, ed. by Huemer. 1885. C9317
11 Claudianus Mamertus. Clavdiani Mamerti Opera, ed. by Engelbrecht. 1885. C9318
12 Augustinus, Aurelius, St. S. Avreli Avgvstini Hipponensis episcopi Liber qvi appellatvr Specvlvm..., ed. by Weihrich. 1887. C9319
13 Cassianus, J. Iohannis Cassiani Conlationes XXIII, ed. by Petschenig. 1886. C9320
14 Lucifer, bp. Lvciferi Calaritani Opvscvla, ed. by Hartel. 1886. C9321
15 Commodianus. Commodiani Carmina, ed. by Dombart. 1887. C9322
16 Poetae christiani minores, ed. by Petschenig and others. 1888. C9323
17 Cassianus, J. Iohannis Cassiani De instivtis coenobiorvm et de octo principalivm vitiorvm remediis libri XII, ed. by Petschenig. 1888. C9324
18 Priscillianus, bp. of Avila. Priscilliani qvae svpersvnt, ed. by Schepss. 1889. C9325
19 Lactanivs, L. C. F. L. Caeli Firmiani Lactanti Opera omnia, ed. by Brandt and Lavbmann. V. 1. 1890. C9326
20 Tertullianus, Q. S. F. Qvinti Septimi Florentis Tertvlliani Opera, ed. by Reifferscheid. V. 1. 1890. C9327
21 Faustus, St. Favsti Reiensis Praeter sermones psevdoevsebianos opera, ed. by Engelbrecht. 1891. C9328
22 Hilarius, St. S. Hilarii episcopi Pictaviensis Tractatvs svper Psalmos, ed. by Zingerle. 1891. C9329
23 Cyprianus Gallus. Cypriani Galli poetae Heptatevchos, ed. by Peiper. 1881. C9330
24 Juvencus, C. V. A. Gai Vetti Aqvilini Ivvenci Evangeliorvm libri qvattvor, ed. by Hvemer. 1891. C9331
25:1 Augustinus, Aurelius, St. Sancti Avreli Avgvstini De vtilitate credendi, ed. by Zycha. 1891. C9332
25:2 ___. Sancti Avreli Avgvstini Contra Felicem, ed. by Zycha. 1892. C9333
26 Optatus, St. S. Optati Milevitani libri VII, ed. by Ziwsa. 1893. C9334
27 Same as no. 19. V. 2-3 in 1. 1897. C9335
28:1 Augustinus, Aurelius, St. Sancti Avreli Avgvstini De Genesi ad litteram libri dvodecim, ed. by Zycha. 1894. C9336
28:2 ___. Sancti Avreli Avgvstini Qvaestionvm in Heptatevchvm libri VII, ed. by Zycha. 1895. C9337
29 Paulinus, St. Sancti Pontii Meropii Pavlini Nolani Epistvlae, ed. by Hartel. 1894. C9338
30 ___. Sancti Pontii Meropii Pavlini Nolani Carmina, ed. by Hartel. 1894. C9339
31 Eucherius, St. Sancti Evcherii Lvgdvnensis Formvlae spiritalis intelligentiae, ed. by Wotke. 1894. C9340
32 Ambrosius, St. Sancti Ambrosii Opera, ed. by Schenkl and others. V. 1. 1897. C9341
33 Augustinus, Aurelius, St. Sancti Avreli Avgvstini Confessionvm libri tredecim, ed. by Knoll. 1896. C9342
34 ___. S. Avreli Avgvstini Hipponiensis episcopi Epistvlae, ed. by Goldbacher. 5 v. in 4. V. 1. 1895. C9343
35 Epistvlae imperatorvm pontificvm aliorvm inde ab a. CCCLXVII vsqve ad a. DLIII datae Avellana qvae dicitvr collectio, ed.

by Günther. 2 v. 1895-98. C9344
36 Augustinus, Aurelius, St. Sancti Avreli Avgvstini Retractationvm libri dvo, ed. by Knöll. 1902. C9345
37 Josephus, F. Flavii Iosephi Opera ex versione latina antiqva, ed. by Boysen. 1898. C9346
38 Philastrius, St. Sancti Filastrii episcopi Brixensis Diversarvm hereson liber, ed. by Marx. 1989. C9347
39 Geyer, P., ed. Itinera hierosolymitana sacevli III-VIII. 1898. C9348
40 Augustinus, Aurelius, St. Sancti Avrelii Avgvstini episcopi De civitate Dei libri XXII, ed. by Hoffmann. 2 v. 1899-1900. C9349
41 ____. Sancti Avreli Avgvstini De fide et symbolo, ed. by Zycha. 1900. C9350
42 ____. Sancti Avreli Avgvstini De perfectione ivstitiae hominis..., ed. by Zycha. 1902. C9351
43 ____. Sancti Avreli Avgvstini De consensv evangelistarvm libri qvattvor, ed. by Weihrich. 1904. C9352
44 Same as no. 34. V. 2. C9353
45 Scriptores ecclesiastici minores saecvlorvm IV. V. VI., ed. by Bratke. 1904. C9354
46 Rufinus, T. Tyrannii Rvfini Orationvm Gregorii Nazianzeni novem interpretatio, ed. by Engelbrecht. 1910. C9355
47 Same as no. 20. V. 3. 1906. C9356
48 Boethius. Anicii Manlii Severini Boethii In Isagogen Porphyrii commenta, ed. by Brandt. 1906. C9357
49 Victorinus, St. Victorini episcopi Petavionensis Opera, ed. by Haussleiter. 1916. C9358
50 Augustinus, Aurelius, St. Psevdo-Avgvstini Qvaestiones Veteris et Novi Testamenti CXXVII, ed. by Souter. 1908. C9359
51-53 ____. Sancti Avreli Avgvstini Scripta contra donastistas. 3 v. 1908-10. C9360
54-56 Hieronymus, St. Sancti Evsbeii Hieronymi Epistvlae, ed. by Hilberg. 3 v. 1910-18. C9361
57-58 Same as no. 34. V. 3, 4. 1911-23. C9362
59 Hieronymus, St. Sancti Evsebii Hieronymi In Hieremiam prophetam libri six, ed. by Reiter. 1913. C9363
57-58 Same as no. 34. V. 3-4. 1911-23. C9364
60 Augustinus, Aurelius, St. Sancti Avreli Avgvstini De peccatorvm meritis et remissione et de baptismo parvvlorum ad Marcellinvm libri tres..., ed. by Vrba and Zycha. 1913. C9365
61 Prudentia Clemens, A. Avrelii Prvdentii Clementis Carmina, ed. by Bergman. 1926. C9366
62 Same as no. 32. V. 2. C9367
63 Augustinus, Aurelius, St. Sancti Avreli Avgvstini Contra academicos libri tres..., ed. by Knöll. 1922. C9368
64 Same as no. 32. V. 3. C9369
65 Hilarius, St. S. Hilarii episcopi Pictaviensis Opera, ed. by Feder. 1916. C9370
66 Josephus, F. Hegesippi qvi dicitvr historiae libri V, ed. by Vssani. 1932. C9371
67 Boethius. Ancii Manlii Severini Boethii Philosophiae consolationis libri qvinque, ed. by Weinberger and Hauler. 1934. C9372
68 Gaudentius, St. Tractus, ed. by Glueck. 1936. C9373
69-70 Tertullianus, Q. S. F. Qvinti Septimi Florentis Tertvliani Apologeticvm. 2 v. 1939-42. C9374
71 Cassiodorus Senator, F. M. A. Cassiodorvs, historia ecclesiastica tripartita, ed. by Jacob and Hanslik. 1952. C9375
72 Arator. Arator, De actibvs apostolorvm, ed. by McKinlay. 1951. C9376

73 Same as no. 32. V. 4. C9377
74 Augustinus, Aurelius, St. De libero arbitrio libri tres, ed. by Green. 1956. C9378
75 Benedictus, St. Regvla Benedicti, ed. by Hanslick. 1960. C9379
76 Same as no. 20. V. 4. 1957. C9380
77 Augustinus, Aurelius, St. De magistro liber unus, ed. by Weigel. 1959. C9381
78-79 Same as no. 32. V. 8-9. 1962. C9382
80 Augustinus, Aurelius, St. De doctrina christiana, ed. by Green. 1963. C9383
81 Ambrosiaster. Ambrosiastri que dicitur Commentarius in Epistulas Paulinas, ed. by Vogels. 3 v. 1966. C9384
82 Same as no. 32. Ed. by Faller. V. 10. 1968. C9385
83 Victorinus, C. M. Opera, ed. by Henry and Hadot. V. 1. 1971. C9386
84 Same as no. 80. V. 2. 1971. C9387

COUNCIL ON FOREIGN RELATIONS. STUDIES IN AMERICAN FOREIGN RELATIONS.

1 Feuerlein, W. and Hannan, E. Dollars in Latin America. 1941. C9388
2 Diebold, W. New directions in our trade policy. 1941. C9389
3 Lissitzyn, O. J. International air transport and national policy. 1942. C9390
4 The United States in a multinational economy, by Viner and others. 1945. C9391
5 Price, H. and Schorske, C. E. The problem of Germany. 1947. C9392

COURS DE PHILOSOPHIE (Hachette)

1 Burloud, A. Psychologie. 1948. C9393
2 Mouy, P. Logique et philosophie de sciences. 1944. C9394
3 Bridoux, A. Morale. 1945. C9395

COWLES COMMISION FOR RESEARCH IN ECONOMICS (1-9 Principia Pr., 10-11 Wiley, 12- Yale Univ. Pr.)

1 Roos, C. F. Dynamic economics. 1934. C9396
2 ____. NRA economic planning. 1937. C9397
3 Cowles Commission for Research in Economics. Common-stock indexes, 1871-1937. 1939. C9398
4 Leavens, D. H. Silver money. 1939. C9399
5 Tintner, G. The variate difference method. 1940. C9400
6 Davis, H. T. The analysis of economic time series. 1941. C9401
7 Mosak, J. L. General equilibrium theory in international trade. 1944. C9402
8 Lange, O. R. Price flexibility and employment. 1944. C9403
9 Katona, G. Price control and business. 1945. C9404
10 Koopmans, T., ed. Statistical inferences in dynamic economic models. 1950. C9405
11 Klein, L. R. Economic fluctuations in the United States, 1921-1941. 1950. C9406
12 Arrow, K. J. Social choice and individual values. 1951. C9407
13 Cowles Commission for Research in Economics. Activity analysis of production and allocation proceedings of a conference, ed. by Koopmans. 1951. C9408
14 Hood, W. C. and Koopmans, T. C., eds. Studies in econometric method. 1953. C9409
15 Hildreth, C. and Jarrett, F. G. A statistical study of livestock production and marketing. 1955. C9410
16 Markowitz, H. M. Portfolio selection. 1959. C9411
17 Debreu, G. Theory of value. 1959. C9412

18 Manne, A. S. and Markowitz, H. M., eds. Studies in process analysis. 1963. C9413
19 Lester, D. D. and Tobin, J., eds. Risk aversion and portfolio choice. 1967. C9414
20 ____ and others, eds. Studies of portfolio behavior. 1967. C9415
21 ____ and Tobin, J., eds. Financial markets and economic activity. 1967. C9416
22 Marschak, J. and Radner, R. Economic theory of teams. 1972. C9417
23 Rothenberg, T. J. Efficient estimation with A Priori information. 1973. C9418
24 Scarf, H. The computation of economic equilibria. 1973. C9419

CREDO PERSPECTIVE SERIES (Simon)

Buber, M. A believing humanism. 1967. C9420
Joannes XXIII, Pope. An invitation to hope, tr. by Clancy. 1967. C9421
Sinnott, E. W. The bridge of life. 1966. C9422
Sweeney, J. J. Vision and image. 1968. C9423
Tillich, P. My search for absolutes. 1967. C9424

CRITICAL ESSAYS IN MODERN LITERATURE (Univ. of Pittsburgh Pr.)

Bergonzi, B. The situation of the novel. 1970. C9425
Brignano, R. C. Richard Wright. 1970. C9426
Calder, J. Chronicles of conscience. 1969. C9427
DeFalco, J. The hero in Hemingway's short stories. 1963. C9428
Draper, J. W. Stratford to Dogberry. 1961. C9429
Hoffmann, C. G. Joyce Cary. 1965. C9430
Maud, R. Entrances to Dylan Thomas' poetry. 1963. C9431
Mooney, H. J. James Gould Cozzens. 1963. C9432
Morris, R. K. The novels of Russell Powell. 1968. C9433
Pratt, A. Dylan Thomas' early prose. 1970. C9434
Pritchard, R. E. D. H. Lawrence. 1971. C9435
Seib, K. James Agee. 1968. C9436
Woodruff, S. C. The short stories of Ambrose Bierce. 1964. C9437

CRITICAL ISSUES IN PSYCHOLOGY (Macmillan)

Breland, K. and M. Animal behavior. 1966. C9438
Ellis, H. C. The transfer of learning. 1965. C9439
Fowler, H. Curiosity and exploratory behavior. 1965. C9440
Lawson, P. R. Frustration. 1965. C9441
Leibowitz, H. W. Visual perception. 1965. C9442
Mensh, I. N. Clinical psychology. 1966. C9443
Moss, C. S. Hypnosis in perspective. 1965. C9444
Ray, W. S. The experimental psychology of original thinking. 1967. C9445
Webb, W. B. Sleep. 1968. C9446

CRITICAL PERIODS OF HISTORY (Lippincott)

Brody, D. Labor in crisis. 1965. C9447
Brown, T. N. Irish-American nationalism, 1870-1890. 1966. C9448
Current, R. N. Lincoln and the first shot. 1963. C9449
Glad, P. W. McKinley, Bryan and the people. 1964. C9450
Holtman, R. B. The Napoleonic revolution. 1967. C9451
Kirby, J. T. Darkness at the dawning. 1972. C9452
Lafore, L. The end of glory. 1969. C9453
____. The long fuse. 1965. C9454
McCraw, T. K. TVA and the

power fight, 1933-1939. 1971. C9455
Polenberg, R. War and society. 1972. C9456
Rawley, J. A. Race and politics. 1969. C9457
Remini, R. V. The election of Andrew Jackson. 1963. C9458
Von Laue, T. H. Why Lenin? Why Stalin? 1964. C9459

CRITICAL STUDIES IN ART HISTORY (Thames)

Branner, R. Chartres Cathedral. 1969. C9460
Martin, J. R. Rubens. 1969. C9461
Seymour, C. Michelangelo. 1972. C9462
Stubblebine, J. H. Giotto. 1969. C9463

CROSSCURRENTS IN WORLD HISTORY (Dial)

Bowra, C. M. Perichan Athens. 1971. C9464
Hill, C. God's Englishman: Oliver Cromwell and the English Revolution. 1970. C9465
MacMullen, R. Constantine. 1969. C9466
Robertson, D. W. Abelard and Heloise. 1972. C9467
Strayer, J. R. The Albigensian Crusades. 1971. C9468

CROSSCURRENTS: MODERN CRITIQUES (Southern Illinois Univ. Pr.)

Aldington, R. Richard Aldington, ed. by Kershaw. 1970. C9469
____. Soft answer. 1967. C9470
Allentuck, M., ed. The achievement of Isaac Bashevis Singer. 1969. C9471
Becker, L. F. Henry de Montherlant. 1970. C9472
Belkind, A., comp. Dos Passos. 1971. C9473
Bertocci, A. P. From symbolism to Baudelaire. 1964. C9474
Bloom, E. A. and L. D. Willa Cather's gift of sympathy. 1962. C9475
Borello, A. H. G. Wells. 1972. C9476
Bowen, Z. Padraic Colum. 1970. C9477
Boyle, K. Plagued by the nightingale. 1966. C9478
____. Year before last. 1969. C9479
Brophy, J. D. Edith Sitwell. 1968. C9480
Browning, P. M. Flannery O'Connor. 1974. C9481
Burchard, R. C. John Updike. 1971. C9482
Burne, G. S. Remy de Gourmont. 1963. C9483-4
Cargill, O. Toward a pluralistic criticism. 1965. C9485
Cowley, M., ed. After the genteel tradition. 1964. C9486
Denommé, R. T. French Parnassian poets. 1972. C9487
____. Ninteenth-century French romantic poets. 1969. C9488
Dick, B. F. The Hellenism of Mary Renault. 1972. C9489
Enck, J. J. Wallace Stevens. 1964. C9490
Evans, O. Anaïs Nin, ed. by Moore. 1968. C9491
Fitzgerald, Z. Save me a waltz, ed. by Moore. 1968. C9492
Fowlie, W. The French critic. 1968. C9493
Freedman, M. American drama in social context. 1971. C9494
Freeman, M. The moral impulse. 1967. C9495
French, W. The social novel at the end of an era. 1966. C9496
Friedman, N. E. E. Cummings. 1964. C9497
Gibson, D. B. The fiction of Stephen Crane. 1968. C9498
Glicksberg, C. J. The tragic vision in twentieth-century literature. 1963. C9499
Gomme, A. Attitudes to criticism. 1966. C9500
Grebstein, S. N. Hemingway's craft. 1973. C9501
Haney, W. Modern fiction. 1971. C9502

Hillegas, M. R., ed. Shadows of imagination. 1969. C9503
Hoffman, F. J. The art of Southern fiction. 1967. C9504
____. Samuel Beckett. 1962. C9505
Hogan, R. The independence of Elmer Rice. 1965. C9506
Holbrook, D. Dylan Thomas and poetic dissociation. 1964. C9507
Hollis, J. R. Harold Pinter. 1970. C9508
Holloway, J. Joseph Holloway's Abbey theatre, ed. by Hogan and O'Neill. 1967. C9509
Hoyt, C. A. Minor British novelists. 1967. C9510
Karl, F. R. C. P. Snow. 1963. C9511
Kaufmann, D. L. Norman Mailer. 1969. C9512
Kelvin, N. E. M. Forster. 1967. C9513
Kessler, J. F., ed. American poems. 1964. C9514
Kraft, J. The early tales of Henry James. 1970. C9515
Kriegel, L. Edmund Wilson. 1971. C9516
Lawrence, D. H. Boy in the bush. 1971. C9517
____. The white peacock. 1966. C9518
Lehan, R. D. A dangerous crossing. 1973. C9519
____. F. Scott Fitzgerald and the craft of fiction. 1966. C9520
Lindenberger, H. S. Georg Büchner. 1964. C9521
Lutwack, L. Heroic fiction. 1971. C9522
Lyons, C. R. Bertolt Brecht. 1968. C9523
____. Henrik Ibsen. 1972. C9524
Lyons, J. O. The college novel in America. 1962. C9525
McMurray, W. The literary realism of William Dean Howells. 1967. C9526
Madden, D., ed. American dreams, American nightmares. 1970. C9527
____. Proletarian writers of the thirties. 1968. C9528
____. Tough guy writers of the thirties. 1968. C9529
Magalaner, M. The fiction of Katherine Mansfield. 1971. C9530
Malin, I. Jews and Americans. 1965. C9531
____. Nathanael West's novels. 1972. C9532
____. New American Gothic. 1962. C9533
____. Saul Bellow's fiction. 1969. C9534
Malone, M. The plays of Sean O'Casey. 1969. C9535
Mandel, S., ed. Contemporary European novelists. 1968. C9536
____. Group 47. 1973. C9537
____. Rainer Maria Rilke, the poetic instinct. 1965. C9538
Margolies, E. The art of Richard Wright. 1969. C9539
Markovic, V. E. The changing face. 1970. C9540
Mersereau, J. Mikhail Lermontov. 1962. C9541
Minor American novelists, ed. by Hoyt. 1970. C9542
Moore, H. T. Age of the modern and other literary essays. 1971. C9543
____, ed. Contemporary American novelists. 1964. C9544
____. Twentieth-century French literature since World War II. 1966. C9545
____. Twentieth-century French literature to World War II. 1966. C9546
____. The world of Lawrence Durrell. 1962. C9547
____ and Parry, A. Twentieth-century Russian literature. 1974. C9548
Morris, R. K. Continuance and change. 1972. C9549
Murry, J. M. Poets, critics, mystics. 1970. C9550
O'Connor, W. V. The grotesque. 1962. C9551
____. The new university wits and the end of modernism. 1963. C9552
Ostrom, A. The poetic world of William Carlos Williams. 1966. C9553
Pachmuss, T. F. M. Dostoevsky. 1963. C9554
Pacifici, S. The modern Italian novel. 1967. C9555
Paolucci, A. From tension to

tonic. 1972. C9556
____. Pirandello's theatre. 1974. C9557
Pearce, R. Stages of the clown. 1970. C9558
Phillips, R. The confessional poets. 1973. C9559
Pinsker, S. The Schlemiel as metaphor. 1971. C9560
Pizer, D. Realism and naturalism in nineteenth century American literature. 1966. C9561
Prescott, J. Exploring James Joyce. 1964. C9562
Quasimodo, S. The poet and the politician and other essays, tr. by Bergin and Pacifici. 1964. C9563
Raleigh, J. H. The plays of Eugene O'Neill. 1965. C9564
____. Time, place, and idea. 1968. C9565
Ramsey, W., ed. Jules Laforgue. 1969. C9566
Rees, R. George Orwell. 1962. C9567
____. Selections from J. Middleton Murry. 1968. C9568
____. Simone Weil. 1968. C9569
Rosengarten, F. Vasco Pratolini. 1965. C9570
Ross, J. and Freed, D. The existentialism of Alberto Moravia. 1972. C9571
Rowland, M. F. Pasternak's Doctor Zhivago. 1967. C9572
Roy, E. British drama since Shaw. 1972. C9573
____. Christopher Fry. 1968. C9574
Schlueter, P. The novels of Doris Lessing. 1973. C9575
Shahane, V. A. Rudyard Kipling activist and artist. 1973. C9576
Shapiro, C., ed. Contemporary British novelists. 1965. C9577
____. Theodore Dreiser. 1962. C9578
Steene, B. The greatest fire. 1973. C9579
Stewart, L. D. Paul Bowles. 1974. C9580
Stolzfus, B. F. Alain Robbe-Grillet and the French novel. 1964. C9581
____. Gide's eagles. 1968. C9582
Stone, E. A certain morbidness. 1969. C9583
Stromberg, R. N. Arnold J. Toynbee. 1972. C9584
Taylor, L. E. Pastoral and antipastoral patterns in John Updike's fiction. 1971. C9585
Tharpe, J. John Barth. 1974. C9586
____. Nathaniel Hawthorne. 1967. C9587
Thompson, E. T. S. Eliot. 1963. C9588
Tiefenbrun, R. Moment of torment. 1973. C9589
Turner, D. T. In a minor chord. 1971. C9590
Valgemae, M. Accelerated grimace. 1972. C9591
Wasserstrom, W. The legacy of Van Wyck Brooks. 1971. C9592
Wells, H. G. The wealth of Mr. Waddy, ed. by H. Wilson. 1969. C9593
Wells, W. Tycoons and locusts. 1973. C9594
Wickes, G., ed. Henry Miller and the critics. 1963. C9595
Widmer, K. The literary rebel. 1965. C9596
Wolfe, P. Rebecca West. 1971. C9597
Woodbridge, H. E. G. B. Shaw. 1963. C9598

CROSSCURRENTS: MODERN FICTION (Southern Illinois Univ. Pr.)

Aldington, R. Soft answer. 1967. C9599
Boyle, K. Plagued by the nightingale. 1966. C9600
____. Year before last. 1969. C9601
Cantwell, R. The land of plenty. 1971. C9602
Doolittle, H. Palimpsist. 1968. C9603
Fitzgerald, Z. (Sayre). Save me the waltz. 1967. C9604
Kelley, E. S. Weeds. 1972. C9605
Lawrence, D. H. The white peacock. 1966. C9606
____ and Skinner, M. L. The

boy in the bush. 1971. C9607
Shaw, G. B. Cashel Byron's profession. 1968. C9608
Stuart, F. Black list. 1971. C9609
Wells, H. G. Wealth of Mr. Waddy. 1969. C9610

THE CULTURES OF MANKIND (Brazillier)

Brantl, R., ed. Medieval culture. 1966. C9611
Mates, J. and Cantelupe, E., eds. Renaissance culture. 1966. C9612
Peckham, M., ed. Romanticism. 1965. C9613
Phelps, R., ed. Twentieth-century culture. 1965. C9614
Rutman, D. B. The morning of America, 1603-1789. 1971. C9615
Schneider, I., ed. The enlightenment. 1965. C9616
Von Hildebrand, A., ed. Greek culture. 1966. C9617
Weinstein, L., ed. The age of reason. 1965. C9618
Wills, G., ed. Roman culture. 1966. C9619

CURRENT CONCEPTS IN BIOLOGY (Macmillan)

Alexopoulos, C. J. and Bold, H. C. Algae and fungi. 1967. C9620
Battley, E. H. and Phillips, E. A. Basic demonstrations in biology. 1971. C9621
Boughey, A. S. Ecology of populations. 1968. C9622
Bowen, W. R. Experimental cell biology. 1969. C9623
Case, J. Sensory mechanisms. 1966. C9624
Davis, D. E. Integral animal behavior. 1966. C9625
DeBusk, A. G. Molecular genetics. 1968. C9626
Fraser, D. Virus and molecular biology. 1967. C9627
Frye, B. E. Hormonal control in vertebrates. 1967. C9628
Goldsby, R. A. Cells and energy. 1967. C9629
Guthe, K. F. The physiology of cells. 1968. C9630
Hamilton, T. H. Process and pattern in evolution. 1967. C9631
Russell-Hunter, W. D. A biology of lower invertebrates. 1968. C9632
Saunders, J. W. Animal morphogenesis. 1968. C9633
Solbrig, O. T. Evolution and systematics. 1966. C9634
Torrey, J. G. Development in flowering plants. 1967. C9635
Waddington, C. H. Principles of development and differentiations. 1966. C9636

CURRENT CONCEPTS IN BIOLOGY (Macmillan)

Doyle, W. T. The biology of higher cryptograms. 1970. C9637
Lenhoff, E. S. Tools of biology. 1966. C9638
Russell-Hunter, W. D. A biology of higher invertebrates. 1969. C9639
Whittaker, R. H. Communities and ecosystems. 1970. C9640

CURRENT PROBLEMS (Cambridge)

1 Bartlett, F. C. Political propaganda. 1940. C9641
2 Reddaway, W. F. Problems of the Baltic. 1940. C9642
3 Thomson, D. The democratic ideal in France and England. 1940. C9643
4 Guillebaud, C. W. The social policy of Nazi Germany. 1941. C9644
5 Richmond, H. W. British strategy. 1941. C9645
6 Livingstone, R. W. The future in education. 1941. C9646
7 Barker, E. The ideas and ideals of the British Empire. 1941. C9647
8 Winfield, P. H. The foundations & the future of international law. 1941. C9648
9 Brogan, D. W. Politics & law in the United States.

1941. C9649
10 Lennard, R. V. Democracy. 1941. C9650
11 Routh, H. V. The diffusion of English culture outside England. 1941. C9651
12 Macartney, C. A. Problems of the Danube basin. 1942. C9652
13 Hughes, D. W. The public schools and the future. 1942. C9653
14 De Montmorency, G. F. The Indian states and Indian federation. 1942. C9654
15 Humby, S. R. and James, E. J. F. Science and education. 1942. C9655
16 Wood, H. G. Christianity and civilisation. 1943. C9656
17 Livingstone, R. W. Education for a world adrift. 1943. C9657
18 Harris, H. W. The daily press. 1943. C9658
19 Butterfield, H. The Englishman and his history. 1944. C9659
20 Walker, E. A. Colonies. 1944. C9660
21 Harris, H. W. Problems of the peace. 1944. C9661
22 Evennett, H. O. The Catholic schools of England and Wales. 1944. C9662
23 MacCurdy, J. T. Germany, Russia and the future. 1944. C9663
24 Field, G. C. Pacificism and conscientious objection. 1945. C9664
25 Macartney, M. H. H. The rebuilding of Italy. 1945. C9665
26 Orwin, C. S. Problems of the countryside. 1945. C9666
27 Einstein, L. D. Historical change. 1946. C9667
28 Carrington, C. E. An exposition of empire. 1947. C9668
29 Thomson, D. Equality. 1949. C9669
30 Jessup, F. Problems of local government in England and Wales. 1949. C9670
31 Wood, H. G. Religious liberty today. 1949. C9671

CURRENT PROBLEMS IN EDUCATION (Appleton-Century)

Blodgett, H. E. and Warfield, G. J. Understanding mentally retarded children. 1959. C9671a
Britton, E. C. and Winans, J. M. Growing from infancy to adulthood. 1958. C9672
Brueckner, L. J. Improving the arithmetic program. 1957. C9673
Cassidy, R. F. Counseling in the physical education program. 1959. C9674
Darrow, H. F. and Howes, V. M. Approaches to individualized reading. 1960. C9675
Davies, E. A. The elementary school child and his posture patterns. 1958. C9676
DeBernardis, A. The use of instructional materials. 1960. C9677
Griffiths, D. E. Administrative theory. 1959. C9678
O'Rourke, M. A. and Burton, W. H. Workshops for teachers. 1957. C9679
Stewart, L. J. and others. Improving reading in the junior high school. 1957. C9680
Strang, R. M. and Linquist, D. M. The administrator and the improvement of reading. 1960. C9681
Wilt, M. E. Creativity in the elementary school. 1959. C9682
Yauch, W. A. Helping teachers understand principals. 1957. C9683

-D-

DAEDALUS LIBRARY (1964-69 Houghton; 1970- Braziller)

American Academy of Arts and Sciences. Toward the year 2,000, ed. by Bell. 1968. D1

America's changing environment, ed. by Revelle and Landsberg. 1970. D2

Conference on Conditions of World Order. Conditions of world order, ed. by Hoffman. 1968. D3

Daedalus. The Negro American, ed. by Parsons and Clark. 1966. D4

____. The professions in America, ed. by Lynn. 1965. D5

____. Science and culture, ed. by Holton. 1965. D6

The embattled university, ed. by Graubard and Ballotti. 1970. D7

Franklin, J. H., ed. Color and race. 1968. D8

Freund, P. A., ed. Experimentation with human subjects. 1970. D9

Goldston, E. and others, comps. The American business corporation. 1972. D10

Graubard, S. R., ed. A new Europe? 1964. D11

Kagan, J., comp. Creativity and learning. 1967. D12

Lifton, R. J., ed. The woman in America. 1965. D13

Lipset, S. M. and Altbach, P. G., comps. Students in revolt. 1969. D14

McLoughlin, W. G. and Bellah, R. N., eds. Religion in America. 1968. D15

Manuel, F. E., ed. Utopia and utopian thought. 1966. D16

Meyerson, M., ed. The conscience of the city. 1970. D17

Morison, R. S., ed. The contemporary university, U.S.A. 1966. D18

Peyre, H., ed. Fiction in several languages. 1968. D19

Rustow, D. A., ed. Philosophers and kings. 1970. D20

DAILY LIFE SERIES (Macmillan)

Andrieux, M. Daily life in papal Rome in the eighteenth century, tr. by Fitton. 1968. D21

____. Daily life in Venice in the time of Casanova, tr. by Fitton. 1972. D22

Auboyer, J. Daily life in ancient India, tr. by Taylor. 1965. D23

Balandier, G. Daily life in the kingdom of the Kongo. 1968. D24

Baudin, L. Daily life in Peru under the last Incas, tr. by Bradford. 1962. D25

Brion, M. Daily life in Vienna of Mozart and Schubert, tr. by Stewart. 1962. D26

Charles-Picard, G. Daily life in Carthage in the time of Hannibal, tr. by Foster. 1961. D27

Daniel-Rops, H. Daily life in Palestine at the time of Christ. 1962. D28

Descola, J. Daily life in colonial Peru. 1968. D29

Douville, J. and Casanova, J. D. Daily life in early Canada. 1968. D30

Flacelière, R. Daily life in Greece at the time of Pericles, tr. by Green. 1965. D31

Gernet, J. Daily life in China, on the eve of the

Mongol invasion, tr. by Wright. 1962. D32
Heurgon, J. Daily life of the Etruscans, tr. by Kirkup. 1964. D33
Levron, J. Daily life at Versailles in the seventeenth and eighteenth centuries. 1968. D34
Louis Frédéric, pseud. Daily life in Japan at the time of the Samurai, 1185-1603, tr. by Lowe. 1972. D35
Lucas-Dubreton, J. Daily life in Florence in the time of the Medici, tr. by Sells. 1960. D36
Mireaux, E. Daily life in the time of Homer, tr. by Sells. 1959. D37
Robiquet, J. Daily life in France under Napoleon, tr. by Macdonald. 1963. D38
____. Daily life in the French Revolution, tr. by Kirkup. 1964. D39
Soustelle, J. Daily life of the Aztecs, tr. by O'Brian. 1962. D40
Troyat, H. Daily life in Russia in the time of the last tsars, tr. by Barnes. 1962. D41
Vaussard, M. Daily life in eighteenth century Italy, tr. by Heron. 1963. D42
Zumthor, P. Daily life in Rembrandt's Holland, tr. by Taylor. 1963. D43

DALLAS. SOUTHERN METHODIST UNIVERSITY. SOUTHERN METHODIST UNIVERSITY CONTRIBUTIONS IN ANTHROPOLOGY.

1 Wendorf, F., ed. Contributions to the prehistory of Nubia, by Chmielewski and others. 1965. D44
2 Combined Prehistoric Expedition to Egyptian and Sudanese Nubia. The prehistory of Nubia, ed. by Wendorf. 1968. D45
3 Woodall, J. N. Archaeological excavations in the Toledo Bend Reservoir. 1969. D46
4 Lorrain, D. Archaeological excavations in the Fish Creek reservoir. 1969. D47
5 Skinner, S. A. and others. Archaeological investigations at the Sam Kaufman site Red River County, Texas. 1970. D48
6 Gibson, J. L. Archaeological survey at Caddo Lake, Louisiana and Texas. 1970. D49
7 Skinner, S. A. Prehistoric settlement of the DeCordova Bend Reservoir, Central Texas. 1971. D50
8 McCormick, O. F. The archaeological resources in the Lake Monticello area of Titus County, Texas. 1973. D51
9 Mahler, W. F. Botanical survey of the Lake Monticello area. 1973. D52
10 Skinner, S. A. and Humphreys, G. K. The historic and prehistoric archaeological resources of the Squaw Creek reservoir. 1973. D53
11 Anderson, K. and others. Archaeological investigations at Lake Palestine, Texas. 1974. D54
12 Hyatt, R. D. and others. Archaeological research at Cooper Lake. 1974. D55

DALLAS. SOUTHERN METHODIST UNIVERSITY. STUDIES IN JURISPRUDENCE.

1 Harding, A. L., ed. Origins of the natural law tradition, by Wilkins and others. 1954. D56
2 ____. Natural law and natural rights, by Outler and others. 1955. D57
3 ____. Religion, Morality and law, by Fitch and others. 1956. D58
4 ____. The administration of justice in retrospect. 1957. D59
5 ____. Free man versus his government, by Cunenggim and others. 1958. D60
6 Harding, A. L. and others, eds. Fundamental law in criminal prosecutions.

1959. D61
7 Harding, A. L., ed. Responsibility in law and in morals, by Fulton and others. 1960. D62
8 ____. The rule of the law, by Macdonald and others. 1961. D63

DEFORMATION AND FLOW (Interscience)

1 Frey-Wyssling, A., ed. Deformation and flow in biological systems. 1952. D64
2 Green, H. S. The molecular theory of fluids. 1952. D65
3 Barkas, W. W. and others. Mechanical properties of wood and paper, ed. by Meredith. 1953. D66
4 Scott-Blair, G. W., ed. Foodstuffs. 1953. D67
5 Hermans, J. J., ed. Flow properties of disperse systems. 1953. D68
6 Reiners, M., ed. Building materials, their elasticity and inelasticity. 1955. D69
7 Meredith, R., ed. The mechanical properties of textile fibers. 1956. D70

DELHI. UNIVERSITY. SCHOOL OF ECONOMICS MONOGRAPHS.

1 Rao, V. K. R. V. An economic review of refugee rehabilitation in India, a study of Nilokherl Township. 1954. D71
2 Ghosh, A. B. Sales tax in India. 1954. D72
3 Rao, V. K. R. V. An economic review of refugee rehabilitation in India, a study of Faridabad Township. 1955. D73
4 Gopal, M. H. Indian economy since independence. 1955. D74
5 Same as no. 1. A study of Kingsway Camp. 1955. D75
6 Same as no. 1. A study of Rajpura Township. 1955. D76
7 Same as no. 1. A study of Tripuri Township. 1955. D77

DEMOGRAPHIE ET SOCIETES (S. E. V. P. E. N.)

1 Rousseau, R. La population de la Savoie jusqu'en 1861. 1960. D78
2 Lapeyre, H. Géographie de l'Espagne morisque. 1960. D79
3 Goubert, P. Beauvais et le Beauvaisis de 1600 à 1730. 1960. D80
4 Nadal, G. and Giralt, E. La population catalane de 1553 à 1717. 1960. D81
5 Baratier, E. La demographie provençale du XIIIe au XVIe siècle avec chiffres de comparaison pour le XVIIIe siècle. 1961. D82
6 Baehrel, R. Une croissance. 1961. D83
7 Carpentier, E. Une ville devant la peste. 1962. D84
8 Daumard, A. Le bourgeoisie parisienne de 1815 à 1848. 1963. D85
9 Higounet-Nadal, M. Comptes de la taille et les sources de l'histoire demographique de Perigueux. 1965. D86
10 Couturier, M. Recherches sur les structures sociales de Chateaudun. 1967. D87
11 Zinck, A. Azereix. 1968. D88
12 Bennassar, B. Reserches sur les grandes épidémies dans le nord de l'Espagne à la fin du XVIe siècle. 1969. D89
13 Lachiver, M. La population de Meulan du XVIIIe au XIXe siècle. 1969. D90
13 Niccolini, L. Il libro degli affari proprii casa de Lapo di Giovanni Niccolini de'Sirigatti. 1969. D91
14 Arbellot, G. La cartographie statistique automatique appliquée à l'histoire. 1970. D92
16 Lafon, J. Les Epoux bordelais. 1972. D93

DES TROIS MAGES (Delachaux)

1 Visser 't. Hooft, W. A.

Rembrandt et la Bible. 1947. D94
2 Braspart, M. Du Bartas, poète chrétien. 1947. D95
3 Chazel, P. Figures de proue. 1948. D96
4 Barth, K. Images du XVIIe siècle. 1949. D97

DETROIT STUDIES IN MUSIC BIBLIOGRAPHY (Information Coordinators)

1 Nettl, B. Reference materials in ethnomusicology. 1967. D98
2 Paladian, S. Sir Arthur Sullivan. 1961. D99
3 MacArdle, D. W. An index to Beethoven's conversation book. 1962. D100
4 Mixter, K. E. General bibliography for music research. 1962. D101
5 Mattfeld, J. A handbook of American operatic premieres, 1731-1962. 1963. D102
6 Coover, J. B. and Colvig, R. Medieval and Renaissance music on long-playing records. 1964. D103
7 Mangler, J. E. Rhode Island music and musicians, 1733-1850. 1965. D104
8 Blum, F. Jean Sibelius. 1965. D105
9 Hartley, K. R. Bibliography of theses and dissertations in sacred music. 1967. D106
10 Frucjtman, C. S. Checklist to vocal chamber works by Benedetto Marcello. 1967. D107
11 Warner, T. E. An annotated bibliography of woodwind instrumental books, 1600-1830. 1967. D108
12 Hansell, S. H. Works for solo voice of Johann Adolph Hasse, 1699-1783. 1968. D109
13 Stahl, D. A. A selected descography of solo song. 1968. Supp. 1970. D110
14 Epstein, D. J. Music publishing in Chicago before 1871. 1969. D111
15 Spiess, L. B. and Stanford, T. An introduction to certain musical archives. 1969. D112
16 Weichlein, W. J. A checklist of twentieth-century choral music for male voices. 1970. D113
17 Roberts, K. C. A checklist of twentieth-century choral music for male voices. 1970. D114
18 DeSmet, R. Published music for the viola da gamba and other viols. 1971. D115
19 Lee, D. A. The world of Christoph Nichelmann. 1971. D116
20 Gillespie, J. E. The reed trip. 1971. D117
21 Parkinson, J. A. An index to the vocal works of Thomas Augustine Arne and Michael Arne. 1972. D118
22 Krummel, D. W. Bibliotheca Bolduaniana. 1972. D119
23 Krohn, E. C. Music published in the Middle Western States before the Civil War. 1972. D120
24 Stahl, D. A. Selected discography of solo song. 1972. D121
25 Iotti, O. R. Violin and violoncello in duo without accompaniment. 1972. D122
26 Same as no. 6. Suppl. 1962-71. 1973. D123
27 Marks, P. F. Bibliography of literature concerning Yemenite-Jewish music. 1973. D124
28 Gillespie, J. E. Solos for unaccompanied clarinet. 1973. D125
29 Abravanel, C. Claude Debussy. 1974. D126
30 Sollinger, C. String class publications in the United States, 1851-1951. 1974. D127
31 Kenneson, C. Bibliography of cello ensemble music. 1974. D128

DEUTSCHE BEITRÄGE ZUR WIRTSCHAFTS UND GESELLSCHAFTSLEHRE (Fischer)

1 Baxa, J. Geschichte der produktivitätstheorie.

1926. D129
2 Seidler-Schmid, G. Die systemgedanken der sogenanten klassischen volkswirtschaftslehre. 1926. D130
3 Andreae, W. F. Bausteine zu einer universalistischen Steuerlehre. 1927. D131
4 Mayer, G. Die Freihandelslehre in Deutschland. 1927. D132
5 Heinrich, W. Grundlagen einer universalistischen krisenlehre. 1928. D133
6 Sauter, J. Baader und Kant. 1928. D134
7 Below, G. von. Die entstehung soziologie. 1928. D135
8 Arendt, W. Die staats und gesellschaftslehre Alberts des Grossen. 1929. D136
9 Westphalen zu Furstenberg, F. A. Die theoretuschen grundlagen der sozialpolitik. 1931. D137
10 Guttmann, V. Industriepolitik. 1932. D138
11 Ottel, F. Ständische des geldes. 1934. D139
12 Westphalen zu Furstenberg, F. A. Die lohnfrage. 1934. D140
13 Czernin von und zu Chudenitz, P. Die borse. 1937. D141
14 Becher, W. Platon und Fichte. 1937. D142
15 Ottel, F. Bankpolitik. 1937. D143

THE DEVELOPMENT OF WESTERN CIVILIZATION (Cornell Univ. Pr.)

Baldwin, M. W. The medieval church. 1953. D144
Friedrich, C. J. and Blitzer, C. The age of power. 1957. D145
Harbison, E. H. The age of Reformation. 1955. D146
Johnson, J. and Percy, W. The age of recovery. 1970. D147
Katz, S. The decline of Rome and the rise of mediaeval Europe. 1955. D148
Lerner, R. E. The age of adversity. 1968. D149
Manuel, F. E. The age of reason. 1951. D150
Nowell, C. E. The great discoveries and the first colonial empires. 1954. D151
Orlinsky, H. M. Ancient Israel. 1960. D152
Painter, S. Mediaeval society. 1951. D153
____. The rise of the feudal monarchies. 1951. D154
Smith, M. The ancient Greeks. 1960. D155
Starr, C. G. The emergence of Rome as ruler of the Western World. 1953. D156
Sullivan, R. E. Heirs of the Roman Empire. 1960. D157

DEVELOPMENTS IN SEDIMENTOLOGY (Amer. Elsevier)

1 International Sedimentalogical Cong. Deltaic and shallow marine deposits, ed. by Van Straatan. 1964. D158
2 Amstutz, G. C., ed. Sedimentology and ore genesis. 1964. D159
3 Bouma, A. H. and Brouwer, A., eds. Turbidits. 1964. D160
4 Tickell, F. G. The techniques of sedimentary mineralogy. 1965. D161
5 Ingle, J. C. The movement of beach sand. 1966. D162
6 Plas, L. van der. The identification of detrital feldspars. 1966. D163
7 Dzulyński, S. and Walton, E. K. Sedimentary features of Flysch and greywackes. 1965. D164
8 Larsen, G., ed. and Chilingar, G. V. Diagenesis in sediments. 1967. D165
9 Chillinger, G. V. and others, eds. Carbonate rocks. 2 v. 1967. D166
10 Duff, P. M. D. and others. Cyclic sedimentation. 1967. D167
11 Reeves, C. C. Introduction to paleolimnology. 1968. D168
12 Bathurst, R. G. C. Carbonate sediments and their

diagenesis. 1971. D169
13 Manten, A. A. Silurian reefs of Gotland. 1971. D170
14 Glennie, K. W. Desert sedimentary environments. 1970. D171
15 Weaver, C. E. and Pollard, L. D. The chemistry of clay minerals. 1973. D172
16 Rieke, H. H. and Chilingarian, G. V. Compaction of argillaceous sediments. 1973. D173
17 Picard, M. D. and High, L. R. Sedimentary structures of ephemeral streams. 1973. D174

DICKINSON LECTURES IN ACCOUNTING (Harvard Univ. Pr. 1952- Harvard Univ. Div. of Research)

1939-40 May, G. O. and others. The Dickinson lectures in accounting. 1943. D175
1940-41 Staub, W. A. Auditing developments during the present century. 1942. D176
1941 May, G. O. Improvement in financial accounts... The position of the public accountant in relation to business and government in Great Britain, by L. Halsey... Recent and prospective developments in accounting theory, by W. A. Paton. 1943. D177
1941-42 Hatfield, H. R. Surplus and dividends. 1943. D178
1942-43 Heiss, C. A. Accounting in the administration of large business enterprises. 1943. D179
1946-47 Jackson, J. H. The comptroller. 1948. D180
1952-53 Humphreys, H. E. Accounting and the accountant in management. 1953. D181
1953-54 Funston, G. K. Wanted. 1954. D182
1954-55 Perry, D. P. Public accounting practice and accounting education. 1955. D183
Published as articles in the Harvard Business Review:
1947-48 Bailey, G. D. "Problems in reporting corporation income." "Concepts of income." (2 articles)
1948-49 Sanders, T. H. "Depreciation and 1949 price levels." "Two concepts of accounting." (2 articles)
1949-50 Dean, A. H. "Accounting for pensions." (2 articles)
1950-51 Brundage, P. F. "The path of accounting." (2 articles)
1951-52 Greer, H. C. "Prices and costs in a free economy." "Prices and costs under government regulations." (2 articles)

DIJON. UNIVERSITE. PUBLICATIONS. (Société des Belles Lettres)

1 Melanges par mm. Boutaric Connes, Petot, Stouff. 1928. D184
2 A la mémoire d'Emile Roy. 1929. D185
3 Stouff, L. Essai sur Mélusine, roman du XIVe s. par Jean d'Arras. 1930. D186
4 Fizaine, S. La vie politique dans la Côte-d'Or sous Louis XVIII. 1931. D187
5 Jean d'Arra, J. Mélusine, ed. by Stouff. 1932. D188
6 Bouchard, M. L'Academie de Dijon et le premier discours de Rousseau. 1950. D189
7 Folz, R. La souvenir et la légende de Charlemagne dans l'Empire germanique médiéval. 1950. D190
8 Bianquis, G. Etudes sur Goethe. 1951. D191
9 Dijon. Université. Travaux de la Faculté des sciences. 1952. D192
10 Gay, J. L. Les effets pécuniaires du mariage en Nivernais... 1953. D193
11 Bugnon, F. Recherches sur la ramification des ampelidacees. 1953. D194
12 Richard, J. Les ducs de

Bourgoyne et la formation du duché du XIe au XIVe siècle. 1954. D195
13 Lebel, P. Principes et méthodes d'hydroymie française. 1956. D196
14 Drovot, H. Une carrière: François Rude. 1958. D197
15 Laurent, R. Les vignerons de la Côte d'or. 2 v. 1958. D198
16 Actes du colloque sur les influences helleniques en Gaule. 1958. D199
17 Moreau, J. P. Le vie rurale dans le sud-est du Bassin parisien. 1958. D200
18 Rat, P. Les pays crétace's basco-cant-abriques. 1959. D201
19 Oursel, R. La dispute et la grâce. 1959. D202
20 Joffroy, R. L'oppidum de Vix et la civilisation hallstattienne finale dans l'est de la France. 1960. D203
21 Saint-Jacob, P. de. Les paysans de la Bourgoynes du Nord au dernier siècle de l'ancien régime. 1960. D204
22 Ternois, R. Zola et son temps. 1961. D205
23 Humbert, F. Les finances municipales de Dijon, du milieu du XIVe siècle à 1477. 1962. D206
24 Armengand, A. L'opinión publique en France et la crise nationale allemande en 1866. 1962. D207
25 Antoine, A. Antoine, lettres à Pauline, ed. by Pruner. 1962. D208
26 Leguai, A. Les ducs de Bourbon pendant la crise monarchique du XVe siècle. 1962. D209
27 Dijon. Université. Hommage à Maurice Blondel, by Bouchard and others. 1962. D210
28 Saint Jacob, P. de. Documents relatifs à la communauté villageoise en Bourgoyne du milieu du XVIIe siècle à la Révolution. 1962. D211
30 Journées d'étude sur le Contrat social, Dijon. 1962. D212
31 Hommage au Prof. Pierre Etienne-Martin. 1964. D213
32 Saint-Denis, E. de. Essais sur le rire et le sourire des Latins. 1965. D214
33 Balzac, H. de. L'enfant mandit, ed. by Germain. 1965. D215
34 Baretti, G. Poésie inédites ou rares, ed. by Jonard. 1966. D216
35 Malet, A. Le traité theologico-politique de Spinoza et la pensée biblique. 1966. D217
36 Bart, J. Recherches sur l'histoire des successions ab intestat dans le droit du duche de Bourgogne... 1966. D218
37 Treyer, C. Sahara, 1956-1962. 1966. D219
38 Ternois, R. Zola et ses amis italiens, documents inedits. 1967. D220
39 Gadille, R. Le Vignoble de la cote bourguignonne... 1967. D221
40 Kapidzic-Osmanagic, H. Le surréalisme serbe et ses rapports avec le surréalisme français. 1968. D222
41 Fromental, J. La réforme en Bourgogne aux XVIe et XVIIe siècles. 1969. D223
42 Jonard, N. Italo Svevo et la crise de la bourgeosie sur européenne, essai. 1969. D224
43 Suratteau, J. R. Les elections de l'an VI et le "coup d'Etat" du 22 floral. 1971. D225

DOCUMENTARY HISTORY OF AMERICAN LIFE (McGraw)

1 Greene, J. P., ed. Settlements to society, 1584-1763. 1966. D226
2 ____, comp. Colonies to nation, 1763-1789. 1967. D227
3 Johannsen, R. W., ed. Democracy on trial, 1845-1877. 1966. D228
6 Shannon, D. A., ed. Progressivism and postwar disillusionment, 1898-1928.

1966. D229
7 Rollins, A. B., ed. Depression, recovery, and war, 1929-1945. 1966. D230
8 May, E. R., ed. Anxiety and affluence, 1945-1965. 1966. D231

DOCUMENTARY HISTORY OF THE UNITED STATES (Univ. of South Carolina Pr.)

Abrams, R. M., ed. The issues of the Populist and progressive eras. 1969. D232
Buchanan, A. R., ed. The United States and World War II. 1972. D233
Cohen, S., ed. Reform, war, and reaction, 1912-1932. 1972. D234
Cox, L. and J. H., eds. Reconstruction, the Negro and the new South. 1973. D235
Cunningham, N. E., comp. The early Republic, 1789-1828. 1968. D236
Ferrell, R. H., ed. America as a world power. 1971. D237
Ferrell, R. H., comp. Foundations of American diplomacy, 1775-1782. 1968. D238
Garraty, J. A., comp. The transformation of American society, 1870-1890. 1968. D239
Gibson, C., ed. The Spanish tradition in America. 1968. D240
Greene, J. P., ed. Great Britain and the American colonies, 1606-1763. 1970. D241
Handy, R. T., ed. Religion in the American experience. 1972. D242
Hugins, W. E., ed. The reform impulse, 1825-1850. 1972. D243
Land, A. C., ed. Bases of the planting society. 1969. D244
Leuchtenburg, W., ed. The New Deal. 1968. D245
McDonald, F. and E. S., comp. Confederation and constitution, 1781-1789. 1968. D246
Morris, R. B., ed. The American Revolution, 1763-1783. 1971. D247
North, D. C. and Thomas, R. P. The growth of American economy to 1860. 1968. D248
Quinn, D. B., ed. North American discovery. 1971. D249
Remini, R. V., ed. The age of Jackson. 1972. D250
Sosin, J. M., ed. The opening of the West. 1969. D251
Vaughan, A. T., ed. The Puritan tradition in America. 1972. D252
Zoltvany, Y. F., ed. The French tradition in America. 1969. D253

DOCUMENTARY HISTORY OF WESTERN CIVILIZATION (Walker)

Albrecht-Carrie, R. The concert of Europe. 1968. D254
Baldwin, M. W., ed. Christianity through the thirteenth century. 1970. D255
Beik, P. H., ed. The French Revolution. 1971. D256
Black, E. C. British politics in the nineteenth century. 1969. D257
____, ed. Victorian culture and society. 1973. D258
Clough, S. B. and others. The economic history of Europe. 1968. D259
Crocker, L. G., ed. The age of enlightenment. 1969. D260
Curtin, P. D., ed. Imperialism. 1972. D261
Delzell, C. F., ed. Mediterranean Fascism, 1919-1945. 1971. D262
Forster, R. and E., eds. European society in the eighteenth century. 1969. D263
Hall, M., ed. Nature and nature's laws. 1970. D264
Halsted, J. B., ed. Romanticism. 1968. D265
Hamerow, T. S., ed. The age of Bismarck. 1973. D266
Herlihy, D., ed. The history of feudalism. 1971. D267
____. Medieval culture and society. D268

Hillerbrand, H. J., ed. The Protestant Reformation. 1968. D269
Jones, A. H. M. A history of Rome through the fifth century. 2 v. 1968. D270
King, J. C. The first World War. 1973. D271
Macartney, C. A., ed. The evolution of the Hapsburg and Hollenzollern dynasties. 1969. D272
Mack-Smith, D. The making of Italy. 1968. D273
Meyer, H. C. The long generation. 1973. D274
Parry, J. H. The European reconnaissance. 1968. D275
Ranum, O. and P. The Century of Louis XIV. 1972. D276
Rowen, H. H. The Low countries in early modern times. 1973. D277
Salvadori, M., ed. Modern socialism. 1968. D278
Stromberg, R. N., ed. Realism, naturalism, and symbolism. 1968. D279
Symcox, G., ed. War, diplomacy, and imperialism, 1618-1763. 1973. D280
Thomson, D. France. 1968. D281
Wagar, W. W., ed. Science, faith, and man. 1968. D282
Walker, M., ed. Metternich's Europe. 1968. D283

DOCUMENTI E RICERCHE (Taylor)

1 Viano, C. A. La logica di Aristotele. 1955. D284
Abbagnano, N. Possibilità e libertà. 1956. D285
____. Problemi di sociologia. 1959. D286
Chiodi, P. La "Deduzione" nell opera di Kant. 1961. D287
Crescenzo, G. de. Francis Hutcheson e il suo tempo. 1968. D288
Ferrarotti, F. La sociologia come partecipazione. 1961. D289
Locke, J. Scritti editi e inediti sulla tolleranza. 1961. D290
Munitz, M. K. Spazio tempo e creazione. 1959. D291
Peirce, C. S. Caso, amore e logica. 1956. D292
Statera, G. Logica, linguaggio e sociologia. 1967. D293
Studi sulla dialettica, by Abbagnano and others. 1958. D294
Visalberghi, A. Esperienza e valutazione. 1958. D295

DOCUMENTS IN AMERICAN CIVILIZATION (New York Univ. Pr.)

Aaron, D., comp. The strenuous decade. 1970. D296
Bode, C. American life in the 1840's. 1967. D297
Eisinger, C. E., comp. The 1940's. 1969. D298
Rozwenc, E. C., ed. Ideology and power in the age of Jackson. 1964. D299
Sanford, C. L., ed. Quest for America, 1810-1824. 1964. D300
Smith, H. N., ed. Popular culture and industrialism, 1865-1890. 1967. D301
Spiller, R. E., ed. The American literary revolution. 1967. D302
Washburn, W. E., ed. The Indian and the white man. 1964. D303

DOCUMENTS OF MODERN HISTORY (St. Martin's Pr.)

Anderson, M. S., comp. The great power and the Near East, 1744-1923. 1970. D304
Burke, P. The Renaissance sense of the past. 1969. D305
Challener, R. D., comp. From isolation to containment, 1921-1952. 1970. D306
Collins, I., comp. Government and society in France, 1814-1848. 1970. D307
Cumpston, I. M., ed. The growth of the British Commonwealth, 1880-1932. 1973. D308
Dickens, A. G. and Carr, D.

The Reformation in England. 1968. D309
Gash, N., comp. The age of Peel. 1968. D310
Holmes, G. and Speck, W. A. The divided society. 1968. D311
Hurstfield, J., comp. Elizabethan people. 1972. D312
Link, A. S., comp. The diplomacy of world power. 1970. D313
Medlicott, W. N., comp. Bismarck and Europe. 1971. D314
Roberts, M. Sweden as a great power. 1968. D315
Rupp, E. G. and Drewery, B., comp. Martin Luther. 1970. D316
Wright, L. B. and Fowler, E. W. English colonization in North America. 1969. D317

DUGDALE SOCIETY. PUBLICATIONS (Oxford)

1 Stratford-upon-Avon. Minutes and accounts of the corporation of Stratford-upon-Avon and other records, 1553-1566, ed. by Savage. V. 1. 1921. D318
2 Warwickshire, Eng. Abstract of the baliff's accounts of monastic & other estates in the county of Warwick... 1547, ed. by Carter. 1923. D319
3 Same as no. 1. 1566-1577. V. 2. 1924. D320
4 Birmingham, Eng. King Edward's school. The records of the school, ed. by Carter. V. 1. 1924. D321
5 Same as no. 1. 1577-1586. V. 3. 1926. D322
6 Gt. Brit. Exchequer. The lay subsidy roll for Warwickshire of 6 Edward III (1332), tr. and ed. by Carter. 1926. D323
7 Same as no. 4. V. 2. 1928. D324
8 Edgbaston, Eng. (parish). The registers of Edgbaston parish church, 1636-1812, ed. by James. V. 1. 1928. D325
9 Worcester, Eng. (diocese). The register of Walter Reynolds, bishop of Worcester, 1308-1313, ed. by Wilson. 1928. D326
10 Same as no. 1, 1586-1592. V. 4. 1929. D327
11 Gt. Brit. Court of common pleas. Warwickshire feet of fines 1195-1284, comp. by Stokes. V. 1. 1932. D328
12 Same as no. 4. Ed. by Carter and Barnard. V. 3. 1933. D329
13 Coventry, Eng. Guild of the Holy Trinity, St. Mary, St. John the Baptist and St. Katherine. Register, ed. by Harris. 1935. D330
14 Same as no. 8. V. 2. 1936. D331
15 Same as no. 11. Comp. by Drucker. V. 3. 1943. D332
16 Kimball, E. G., ed. Rolls of Warwickshire and Coventry sessions of peace, 1377-1397. 1940. D333
17 Beardwood, A., ed. The Statute merchant roll of Coventry, 1392-1416. 1939. D334
18 Same as no. 15. Comp. by Stokes and Drucker. V. 2. 1940. D335
19 Coventry, Eng. Guild of the Holy Trinity, St. Mary, St. John the Baptist and St. Katherine. Records, ed. by Templeton. 1944. D336
20 Same as no. 4. V. 4. 1948. D337
21 Hilton, R. H., ed. Minister's account of the Warwickshire estates of the Duke of Clarence, 1479-80. 1952. D338
22 Warwickshire, Eng. Ecclesiastical terriors of Warwickshire parishes. V. 1. 1956. D339
23 Greene, J. Correspondence of The Reverend Joseph Greene, ed. by Fox. 1965. D340
24 Stoneleigh Abbey. The Stoneleigh leger book, ed. by Hilton. 1960. D341

25 Same as no. 4. Ed. by Chatwin. V. 5. 1963. D342
26 Warwick, Eng. Ministers' account of the collegiate church of St. Mary's, Warwick, 1432-85, ed. by Styles. 1969. D343
27 Same as no. 22. V. 2. 1971. D344
28 Morgan, P., ed. Warwickshire printers' notices, 1799-1866. 1970. D345

DUKE HISTORICAL PUBLICATIONS (Duke Univ. Pr.)

Addy, G. M. The enlightenment in the University of Salamanca. 1966. D346
Beers, B. F. Vain endeavor. 1962. D347
Blakeley, B. L. The Colonial Office, 1868-1892. 1971. D348
Bumgartner, L. E. José del Valle of Central America. 1963. D349
Cantor, L. A prologue to the protest movement. 1969. D350
Duly, L. C. British land policy at the Cape, 1795-1844. 1968. D351
Durden, R. F. Reconstructions bonds & twentieth-century politics. 1962. D352
Esler, A. The aspiring mind of the Elizabethean younger generation. 1966. D353
Goff, R. D. Confederate supply management. 1968. D354
Hollyday, F. B. M. Bismarck's rival. 1960. D355
Maltby, W. S. The black legend in England. 1971. D356
Nelson, R. R. The Home Office, 1782-1801. 1969. D357
Partin, M. O. Waldeck-Rousseau, Combes and the church, 1899-1905. 1969. D358
Salmond, J. A. The Civilian Conservation Corps, 1933-1942. 1967. D359
Scott, W. E. Alliance against Hitler. 1962. D360
Stark, J. D. Damned uncountryman: William Watts Ball. 1968. D361
Steele, A. R. Flowers for the king. 1964. D362
TePaske, J. The governorship of Spanish Florida, 1700-1763. 1964. D363
Young, C. R. Hubert Walter. 1968. D364

DUKE MONOGRAPHS IN MEDIEVAL AND RENAISSANCE STUDIES

1 Kristeller, P. O. Medieval aspects of Renaissance learning. 1974. D365

DUKE STUDIES IN RELIGION

1 Pannill, H. B. The religious faith of John Fiske. 1957. D366
2 Brown, M. P. The authentic works of Ignatius. 1963. D367

DUKE UNIVERSITY. COMMONWEALTH-STUDIES CENTER. PROGRAM IN COMPARATIVE STUDIES ON SOUTHERN ASIA. MONOGRAPH AND OCCASIONAL PAPERS SERIES

1 Hazelhurst, L. W. Entreprenuership and the merchant caste in a Punjabi city. 1966. D368
2 Barrier, N. G. The Punjab alienation of land bill of 1900. 1966. D369
3 Berry, W. M. Aspects of the Frontier crimes regulation in Pakistan. 1966. D370
4 Wheeler, R. S. Divisional councils in East Pakistan. 1967. D371
5 Symposium on Regions and Regionalism in South Asia. Regions and regionalism in South Asian studies, ed. by Crane. 1967. D372
6 Apte, M. L. and Pattanayak, D. P. An outline of Kumauni grammar. 1967. D373
7 Di Bona, J. E. Change and conflict in an Indian university. 1968. D374
8 Prakesh, V. New towns in India. 1969. D375
9 Crane, R. I. Modernization in India. 1970. D376

10 Symposium on Urban India. Urban India, ed. by Fox. 1970. D377

DUKE UNIVERSITY. COMMONWEALTH STUDIES CENTER. PROGRAM IN COMPARATIVE STUDIES IN SOUTHERN ASIA. PUBLICATION SERIES

1 Braibanti, R. J. D. Research on the bureaucracy of Pakistan. 1966. D378
2 Kearney, R. N. Communalism and language in the politics of Ceylon. 1967. D379
3 Swan, R. O. Munshi Premchand of Lamhi village. 1969. D380

DUKE UNIVERSITY COMMONWEALTH-STUDIES CENTER. PUBLICATIONS.

1 Underhill, F. H. The British Commonwealth. 1956. D381
2 Robertson, H. M. South Africa. 1957. D382
3 Donaldson, A. G. Some comparative aspects of Irish law. 1957. D383
4 Bauer, P. T. Economic analysis and policy in underdeveloped countries. 1957. D384
5 Scarrow, H. A. The higher public service of the Commonwealth of Australia. 1957. D385
6 Oliver, H. M. Economic opinion and policy in Ceylon. 1957. D386
7 Jennings, W. I. Problems of the new commonwealth. 1958. D387
8 Mansergh, N. and others. Commonwealth perspectives. 1958. D388
9 Duke University. Commonwealth-Studies Center. Evolving Canadian federalism, by Lower and others. 1958. D389
10 Silcock, T. H. The commonwealth economy in Southeast Asia. 1959. D390
11 Ratchford, B. U. Public expenditure in Australia. 1959. D391
12 Duke Univ. Commonwealth-Studies Center. The American economic impact on Canada, by Aitken and others. 1959. D392
13 Braibanti, R. J. D. and Spengler, J. J. Tradition, values, and socio-economic development. 1969. D393
14 Duke University. Commonwealth-Studies Center. The growth of Canadian policies in external affairs, by Keenleyside and others. 1960. D394
15 Goodwin, C. D. W. Canadian economic thought. 1961. D395
16 Hoover, C. B., ed. Economic systems of the commonwealth. 1962. D396
17 Tilman, R. O. and others, ed. The Nigerian political scene. 1962. D397
18 Braibanti, R. J. D. and others. Administration and economic development in India, ed. by Braibanti and Spengler. 1963. D398
19 Deener, D. R., ed. Canada-United States treaty relations, by Wilson and others. 1963. D399
20 Piper, D. C. and Cole, T., eds. Post-primary education and political and economic development, by Andrews and others. 1964. D400
21 Tilman, R. O. Bureaucratic transition in Malaya. 1964. D401
22 Newbury, C. W. The West African. 1964. D402
23 Hamilton, W. B., ed. The transfer of institutions, by Lerner and others. 1964. D403
24 Goodwin, C. D. W. Economic inquiry in Australia. 1966. D404
25 Hamilton, W. B. and others, eds. A decade to the Commonwealth, 1955-1964. 1966. D405
26 Braibanti, R. Research on bureaucracy of Pakistan. 1966. D406
27 Wilson, R. R., ed. The international law standard

and commonwealth developments. 1966. D407
28 Braibanti, R., ed. Asian bureaucratic systems emergent from the British imperial tradition. 1966. D408
29 Oreston, R. A. Canada and Imperial Defense. 1967. D409
30 Piper, D. C. The international law of the Great Lakes. 1967. D410
31 Saylor, R. G. The economic system of Sierra Leone. 1968. D411
32 Leach, R. H., ed. Contemporary Canada. 1968. D412
33 Wilson, R. R., ed. International and comparative law of the commonwealth. 1968. D413
34 Smith, J. H. Colonial cadet in Nigeria. 1968. D414
35 Sharwood-Smith, B. Recollections of British Administration in the Cameroons and Northern Nigeria. 1969. D415
36 Braibanti, R. J. D., ed. Political and administrative development. 1969. D416
37 Kubicek, R. V. The administration of imperialism. 1969. D417
38 Wilson, R. R. International law and contemporary commonwealth issues. 1971. D418
39 Ball, M. M. The "Open" Commonwealth. 1971. D419
40 The influence of the United States on Canadian development, ed. by Preston. 1972. D420
41 Johnston, W. R. Sovereignty and protection. 1973. D421
42 Goodwin, C. D. W. The image of Australia. 1974. D422

DUKE UNIVERSITY. SOCIOLOGICAL SERIES (Duke Univ. Pr.)

1 Chugerman, S. Lester F. Ward. 1939. D423
2 Mayer, J. Social science principles in the light of scientific method. 1941. D424
3 Porterfield, A. L. Creative factors in scientific research. 1941. D425
4 Sorokin, P. A. Sociocultural causality, space, time. 1943. D426
5 Yinger, J. M. Religion in the struggle for power. 1961. D427
6 Eister, A. W. Drawing-room conversion. 1950. D428
7 Becker, H. Through values to social interpretation. 1950. D429
8 Patrick, C. H. Alcohol, culture, and society. 1952. D430
9 Burma, J. H. Spanish-speaking groups in the United States. 1954. D431
Gordon, M. M. Social class in American sociology. 1958. D432

DUMBARTON OAKS PAPERS (Harvard Univ. Pr., Augustin Dumbarton Oaks)

1 Dumbarton Oaks inaugural lectures, 1940, by Focillon and others. 1941. D433
2 Peirce, H. and Tyler, R. Three Byzantine works of art. 1941. D434
3 Dumbarton Oaks papers, no. 3, by Kitzinger and others. 1946. D435
4 ____. No. 4, by Vasiliev and others. 1948. D436
5 ____. No. 5, by Grabar and others. 1950. D437
6 ____. No. 6, by Dvornik and others. 1951. D438
7 ____. No. 7, by Ladner and others. 1953. D439
8 ____. No. 8, by Wolff and others. 1954. D440
9-10 ____. Nos. 9-10, by Vasiliev and others. 1957. D441
11 ____. No. 11, by Wolfson and others. 1958. D442
12 ____. No. 12, by Dumbarton Oaks research library. 1959. D443
13 ____. No. 13, by Ostrogorsky and others. 1959. D444
14 ____. No. 14, by Kantorowicz and others. 1960. D445
15 ____. No. 15, by Vermeule and others. 1961. D446

16 ____. No. 16, by Mango and others. 1962. D447
17 ____. No. 17, by Jones and others. 1963. D448
18 ____. No. 18, by Miles and others. 1964. D449
19 ____. No. 19, by Ostrogorsky and others. 1965. D450
20 ____. No. 20, by Weitzmann and others. 1966. D451
21 ____. No. 21, by Teall and others. 1967. D452
22 ____. No. 22, by Forsyth and others. 1969. D453
23, 24 ____. Nos. 23, 24, by Underwood and others. 1969-70. D454
25 ____. No. 25, by Ostrogorsky and others. 1971. D455
26 ____. No. 26, by Mango and others. 1972. D456
27 ____. No. 27. 1973. D457
28 ____. No. 28. 1974. D458

DUMBARTON OAKS STUDIES (Harvard Univ. Pr., Augustin Dumbarton Oaks)

1 Vasiliev, A. A. Justin the First. 1950. D459
2 Hanfmann, G. M. A. The Season sarcophagus in Dumbarton Oaks. 2 v. 1952. D460
3 Photius I, St. The homilies of Photius, tr. by Mango. 1958. D461
4 Dvornik, F. The idea of apostolicity in Byzantium and the legend of the apostle Andrew. 1958. D462
5 Deér, J. The dynastic porphyry tombs of the Norman period in Sicily. 1959. D463
6 Demus, O. The church of San Marco in Venice. 1960. D464
7 Dodd, E. C. Byzantine silver stamps. 1962. D465
8 Mango, C. A. Materials for the study of the mosaics of St. Sophia at Istanbul. 1962. D466
9 Dvornik, F. Early Christian and Byzantine political philosophy. 2 v. 1966. D467
10 Alexander, P. J. The oracle of Baalbek. 1968. D468
11 Nicol, D. M. The Byzantine family of Kantakouzenos. 1968. D469
12 Hendy, M. F. Coinage and money in the Byzantine empire. 1969. D470
13 Evans, D. B. Leontius of Byzantium. 1970. D471

DUQUESNE STUDIES. AFRICAN SERIES.

1 Loogman, A. Swahili grammar and syntax. 1965. D472
2 ____. Swahili readings. 1967. D473
3 Pollock, N. H. Nyasaland and Northern Rhodesia. 1971. D474
4 Johnston, H. A. S. Denham in Bornu. 1973. D475

DUQUESNE STUDIES. PHILOLOGICAL SERIES.

1 Huckabay, C. John Milton. 1960. D476
2 Lydgate, J. A critical edition of John Lydgate's Life of Our Lord, by Lauritis. 1961. D477
3 McNeir, W. F. and Provost, F. Annotated bibliography of Edmund Spenser, 1937-1960. 1962. D478
4 Clarke, D. C. Morphology of fifteenth century Castilian verse. 1964. D479
5 Petit, H. H., ed. Essays and studies in language and literature. 1964. D480
6 Cash, A. H. Sterne's comedy of moral sentiments. 1966. D481
7 Roberts, J. R. A critical anthology of English recusant devotional prose, 1558-1603. 1966. D482
8 Richmond, V. E. B. Laments for the dead in medieval narrative. 1966. D483
9 Wimbledon, R. Wimbledon's serom: Redde rationem villicationis tue, ed. by Knight. 1967. D484
10 Fiore, A. P., ed. The upright heart and pure. 1967. D485
11 Piper, D. G. B. V. A.

Kaverin. 1970. D486
12 Beardsley, T. S. Hispano-classical translations printed between 1482 and 1699. 1970. D487
13 Ives, M. Analogue of harmony. 1970. D488
14 Meyers, W. E. A figure given. 1970. D489
15 Gibbs, M. Wiplichez wibes reht. 1972. D490
16 Graham, I. Schiller. 1974. D491

DUQUESNE STUDIES. PHILOSOPHICAL SERIES.

1 Melsen, A. G. M. van. From atomos to atom, tr. by Koren. 1952. D492
2 ____. The philosophy of nature. 1961. D493
3 Laer, P. H. van. Philosophico-scientific problems. 1953. D494
4 Vio, T. de. The analogy of names, ed. by Bushinski and Koren. 1959. D495
5 Louvain. Université Catholique. Truth and freedom, by ... Raeymaeker and others. 1954. D496
6 Laer, P. H. van and Koren, H. J. Philosophy of science. V. 1. 1956. D497
7 Strasser, S. The soul in metaphysical and empirical psychology. 1957. D498
8 Dondeyne, A. Contemporary European thought and Christian faith, ed. by McMullin and Burnheim. 1958. D499
9 Charlesworth, M. J. Philosophy and linguistic analysis. 1959. D500
10 Kwant, R. C. Philosophy of labor. 1960. D501
11 ____. Encounter, tr. by Adolfs. 1960. D502
12 Luijpen, W. A. M. Existential phenomenology. 1960. D503
13 Melsen, A. G. M. van. Science and technology. 1961. D504
14 Same as no. 6. V. 2. 1962. D505
15 Kwant, R. C. The phenomenological philosophy of Merleau-Ponty. 1963. D506
16 Peters, J. A. J. Metaphysics. 1963. D507
17 Luijpen, W. A. M. Phenomenology and atheism, tr. by Van de Putte. 1964. D508
18 Plattel, M. G. Social philosophy. 1965. D509
19 Melsen, A. G. M. van. Evolution and philosophy. 1965. D510
20 Kwant, R. C. From phrenology to metaphysics. 1966. D511
21 Kockelmans, J. J. Phenomenology and physical science. 1966. D512
22 Luijpen, W. A. M. Phenomenology of natural law, tr. by Koren. 1967. D513
23 Melsen, A. G. M. van. Physical science and ethics. 1967. D514
24 Levinas, E. Totality and infinity. 1969. D515
25 Strasser, S. The idea of dialogal phenomenology. 1969. D516
26 Melsen, A. G. M. van. Science and responsibility, tr. by Koren. 1970. D517
27 Berger, H. Progressive and conservative man, tr. by Koren. 1971. D518
28 Peursen, C. A. van. Phenomenology and analytical philosophy. 1972. D519
29 Plattel, M. G. Utopian and critical thinking. 1972. D520
30 Peursen, C. A. van. Phenomenology and reality, tr. by Koren. 1972. D521
31 Ihde, D. Sense and significance. 1973. D522
32 Sallis, J. Phenomenology and the return to beginnings. 1973. D523
33 ____. Being and logos. 1974. D524

DUQUESNE STUDIES. PSYCHOLOGICAL STUDIES.

1 Strasser, S. Phenomenology and the human sciences. 1963. D525
2 Gurwitsch, A. The field of consciousness. 1964. D526
3 Van Kaam, A. L. Existential foundations of psychology. 1966. D527
4 Kockelmans, J. J. Edmund Husserl's phenomenological psychology, tr. by Jager. 1967. D528
5 Linchoten, J. On the way toward a phenomenological psychology, ed. by Giorgi. 1968. D529
6 Buytendijk, F. J. J. Prolegomena to an anthropological physiology. 1974. D530

DUQUESNE STUDIES. SPIRITAN SERIES.

1 Koren, H. J. The Spiritans. 1958. D531
2 Van Kaam, A. L. A light to the Gentiles. 1959. D532
3 Poullart des Places, C. F. P. Spiritual writings, ed. by Koren. 1959. D533
4 Koren, H. J. Knaves and knights? 1962. D534
5 Libermann, F. M. P. The spiritual letters of the Venerable Francis Libermann, ed. by Van de Putte and Collery. V. 1. 1962. D535
6-8 ____. Same as no. 5. V. 2-4. 1963-65. D536
9 ____. Same as no. 5. V. 5. 1966. D537

DUQUESNE STUDIES. THEOLOGICAL SERIES.

1 Dondeyne, A. Faith and the world. 1963. D538
2 Schoonenberg, P. God's world in the making. 1964. D539
3 Swidler, L. J., ed. Scripture and ecumenism. 1965. D540
4 Pol, W. H. van de. Anglicanism in ecumenical perspective, tr. by Putte. 1965. D541
5 Walgrave, J. H. Person and society. 1965. D542
6 Bilsen, B. van. The changing Church. 1966. D543
7 Heitjke, J. An ecumenical light on the renewal of religious community life. 1967. D544
8 Fries, H. Bultmann-Barth and Catholic theology, tr. by Swidler. 1967. D545
9 Folet, H. A. Ecumenical breakthrough. 1970. D546
10 Leasy, G. Witness to the faith. 1972. D547
11 Schwiy, G. Structuralism and Christianity. 1971. D548
12 Luijpen, W. A. M. Theology as anthropology. 1973. D549

EARLY ENGLISH MANUSCRIPTS IN FACSIMILE (Rosenkilde)

1 Beowulf. The Thorkelin transcripts of Beowulf in facsimile, ed. by Malone. 1951. E1
2 Beda, Venerabilis. The Lenigrad Bede, ed. by Arngart. 1952. E2
3 Orosius, P. The Tollemache Orosius, ed. by Campbell. 1953. E3
4 Anglo-Saxon chronicle. The Peterborough chronicle, ed. by Whitelock. 1954. E4
5 Laece boc. Bald's Leechbock, ed. by Wright. 1955. E5
6 Gregorius I, the Great, St. The regula pastoralis of St. Gregory the Great, ed. by Ker. 1956. E6
7 Ernulf, Bp. Textus Raffensis, ed. by Sawyer. V. 1. 1957. E7
8 Catholic church. Liturgy and ritual. Psalter. The Paris psalter, ed. by Colgrave. 1958. E8
9 Beda Venerabilis. The Moore Beda, ed. by Blair. 1959. E9
10 Blickling homilies. The Blickling homilies, ed. by Willard. 1960. E10
11 Same as no. 7. V. 2. 1962. E11
12 British Museum. The Nowell codex, ed. by Malone. 1963. E12
13 Aelfric. First series of Catholic homilies, ed. by Eliason. 1966. E13
14 Catholic Church. Liturgy and ritual. The Vespasian Psalter, ed. by Wright. 1967. E14
15 Benedictus, St. The reule of St. Benedict, ed. by Farmer. 1968. E15
16 Durham ritual, ed. by Brown and others. 1969. E16
17 Cotton Nero A, ed. by Lyon. 1971. E17
18 The Old English illustrated Hexateuch, ed. by Dodwell and Clemoes. 1974. E18

EARLY ENGLISH TEXT SOCIETY EXTRA SERIES (Trubner, pub. by Oxford after 1916)

Extra series are designated by roman numeral numbering.

1 Guillaume de Palerne. The romance of William of Palerne, ed. by Skeat. 1867. E19
2 Ellis, A. J. On early English pronunciation. Ellis. Pt. 1. 1869. E20
3 Book of curtesye. Caxton's Book of curtesye, ed. by Furnivall. 1868. E21
4 Havelok the Dane. The lay of Havelok the Dane, ed. by Skeat. 1868. E22
5 Boethius. Chaucer's translation of Boethius's "De consolatione philosophiae," ed. by Morris. 1868. E23
6 Beatrix. The romance of the Cheuelere assigne, ed. by Aldenham. 1868. E24
7 Same as no. 2. Pt. 2. 1868. E25
8 Furnivall, F. J., ed. Queene Elizabethes achademy. 1869. E26
9 Viles, E., ed. The fraternitye of vacabondes of John Awdeley. 1869. E27
10 Boorde, A. The fyrst

boke of the introduction of knowledge made by Andrew Borde, ed. by Furnivall. 1870. E28
11 Barbour, J. The Bruce, ed. by White. V. 1. 1870. E29
12 Starkey, T. England in the reign of King Henry the Eighth. Pt. 2. 1871. E30
13 Fish, S. A supplicacyon for the beggers, ed. by Furnivall. 1871. E31
14 Same as no. 2. Pt. 3. 1871. E32
15 Crowley, R. The select works of Robert Crowley, ed. by Cowper. 1872. E33
16 Chaucer, G. A treatise on the astrolabe, ed. by Skeat. 1872. E34
17-18 The complaynt of Scotlande, ed. by Murray. 2 parts. 1872-73. E35
19 The myroure of Oure Ladye, ed. by Blunt. 1873. E36
20 Lovelich, H. The history of the holy grail, ed. by Furnivall. Pt. 1. 1874. E37
21 Same as no. 11. V. 2. 1874. E38
22 Brinkelow, H. Henry Brinklow's Complaynt of Roderyck Mors, ed. by Cowper. 1874. E39
23 Same as no. 2. Pt. 3. 1874. E40
24 Same as no. 20. Pt. 2. 1875. E41
25-26 Guy of Warwick. The romances of Guy of Warwick, ed. by Zupitza. 2 parts. 1875-76. E42
27 Fisher, J. The English works of John Fisher, ed. by Mayor. 1876. E43
28 Same as no. 20. Pt. 3. 1877. E44
29 Same as no. 11. V. 3. 1877. E45
30 Same as no. 20. Pt. 4. 1878. E46
31 Alisaunder. Alexander and Dindimus, ed. by Skeats. 1878. E47
32 Same as no. 12. Pt. 1. 1878. E48
33 Gesta Romanorum. The early English versions of the Gesta Romanorum, ed. by Herrtage. 1879. E49
34 Fierabras. Sir Ferumbras, ed. by Herrtage. 1879. E50
35 Herrtage, S. J. H., ed. "The sege off Melayne" and "The romance of Duke Rowland and Sir Otuell of Spayne." 1880. E51
36-37 Fierabras. The lyf of the noble and Crysten prynce, Charles the Grete, ed. by Hervon. 1881. E52
38 Hausknecht, E., ed. The Romaunce of the Sowdone of Babylone... 1881. E53
39 Herrtage, S. J. H., ed. The taill of Rauf Coilyear. 1882. E54
40 Huon of Bordeaux. The Boke of Duke Huon of Burdeaux, ed. by Lee. Pt. 1. 1882. E55
41 Same as no. 40. Pt. 2. 1885. E56
42 Guy of Warwick. The romance of Guy of Warwick, ed. by Zupitza. Pt. 1. 1883. E57
43 Same as no. 40. Pt. 3. 1887. E58
44-45 Quatre fils Aimon. The four sonnes of Aymon, ed. by Richardson. 2 pts. 1884-85. E59
46 Beuve de Hanstone. The romance of Sir Beues of Hamtoun, ed. by Kölbing. Pt. 1. 1885. E60
47 The wars of Alexander. The wars of Alexander, ed. by Skeat. 1886. E61
48 Same as no. 46. Pt. 2. 1886. E62
49 Same as no. 42. Pt. 2. 1887. E63
50 Same as no. 40. Pt. 4. 1887. E64
51 Torrent of Portyngale. Torrent of Portyngale, ed. by Adams. 1887. E65
52 Bullein, W. A dialogue against the feuer pestilence, ed. by Bullen. 1888. E66
53 Vicary, T. The anatomie of the bodie of man, ed. by Furnivall. 1888. E67

54 Chartier, A. The curial made by maystere Alain Charretier, ed. by Furnivall. 1888. E68
55 Same as no. 11. V. 4. 1889. E69
56 Same as no. 2. Pt. 4. 1889. E70
57 Eneydes. Caxton's Eneydos, 1490, ed. by Culley and Furnivall. 1890. E71
58 Blancandin. Caxton's Blanchardyn and Eglantine, ed. by Kellner. 1890. E72
59 Same as no. 42. Pt. 3. 1891. E73
60 Lydgate, J. Lydgate's Temple of glass, ed. by Schick. 1891. E74
61 Hoccleve, T. Hoccleve's works, ed. by Furnivall. V. 1. 1892. E75
62 Chester plays. The Chester plays, ed. by Deimling. Pt. 1. 1893. E76
63 Imitatio Christi. The earliest English translation of the first three books of the De imitatione Christi, tr. by Atkinson, Richmond, and Ingram. 1893. E77
64 Guilelmus, abp. of Tyre. Godeffroy of Boloyne, ed. by Colvin. 1893. E78
65 Same as no. 46. Pt. 3. 1894. E79
66 Secretum secretorum. Lydgate and Burgh's Secrees of old philisoffres, ed. by Steele. 1894. E80
67 Les trois fils de rois. The king's three sons, ed. by Furnivall. 1895. E81
68 Jean d'Arras. Melusine, ed. by Donald. 1895. E82
69 Lydgate, J. The assembly of gods, ed. by Triggs. 1896. E83
70 Digby plays. The Digby plays, ed. by Furnivall. 1896. E84
71 Towneley plays. The Towneley plays, ed. by England. 1897. E85
72 Same as no. 61. V. 2. 1897. E86
73 Same as no. 61. Ed. by Gollancz. V. 3. 1925. E87
74 Secretum secretorum. Three prose versions of the Secreta secretorum, ed. by Steele. 1898. E88
75 Speculum Gy de Warewyke. Speculum Gy de Warewyke, ed. by Morrill. 1898. E89
76 Ashby, G. George Ashby's poems, ed. by Bateson. 1899. E90
77 Guillaume de Deguilleville. The pilgrimage of the life of man, ed. by Furnivall. Pt. 1. 1899. E91
78 Robinson, T. The life and death of Mary Magdalene, ed. by Sommer. 1899. E92
79 Caxton, W. Dialogues in French and English, ed. by Bradley. 1900. E93
80 Lydgate, J. Lydgate's minor poems, ed. by Glauning. 1900. E94
81-82 Gower, J. The English works of John Gower, Confessio Amantis, ed. by Macaulay. 2 v. 1900-01. E95
83 Same as no. 77. Pt. 2. 1901. E96
84 Lydgate, J. Lydgate's Reson and sensuallyte, ed. by Sieper. Pt. 1. 1901. E97
85 Scott, A. The poems of Alexander Scott, ed. by Donald. 1902. E98
86 William, of Shoreham. The poems of William of Shoreham, ed. by Konrath. 1902. E99
87 Coventry plays. Two Coventry Corpus Christi plays, ed. by Craig. 1957. E100
88 Lemorte Arthur. Le morte Arthur, ed. by Bruce. 1903. E101
89 Same as no. 84. Pt. 2. 1903. E102
90 Littlehales, H., ed. English fragments from Latin medieval service-books. 1903. E103
91 Furnivall, F. J., ed. The Marco plays, ed. by Pollard. 1904. E104
92 Same as no. 77. Pt. 3.

1904. E105
93 Lovelich, H. Merlin, ed. by Kock. Pt. 1. 1940. E106
94 Respublica. Respublica, A. D. 1553, ed. by Magnus. 1905. E107
95 Same as no. 20. Pt. 5. 1905. E108
96 Mirk, J. Mirk's festial, ed. by Erbe. 1905. E109
97 Lydgate, J. Lydgate's Troy book, ed. by Bergen. Pt. 1. 1906. E110
98 Skelton, J. Magnfycence, ed. by Ramsay. 1908. E111
99 Emare. The romance of Emaré, ed. by Rickert. 1908. E112
100 Harrowing of hell. The Middle-English Harrowing of hell and Gospel of Nicodemus, ed. by Hulme. 1907. E113
101 Hill, R. Songs, Carols, and other miscellaneous poems, ed. by Dyboski. 1908. E114
102 Galfridus Anglicus. The Promptorium parvulorum, ed. by Mayhew. 1908. E115
103 Same as no. 97. Pt. 2. 1908. E116
104 Waterhouse, O., ed. The non-cycle mystery plays. 1909. E117
105 Beryn. The tale of Beryn, ed. by Furnivall and Stone. 1909. E118
106 Same as no. 97. Pt. 3. 1910. E119
107 Lydgate, J. The minor poems of John Lydgate, ed. by MacCracken. Pt. 1. 1910. E120
108 Lydgate, J. Lydgate's Siege of Thebes. V. 1. 1911. E121
109 Partonopeus de Blois. The Middle-English versions of Partonope of Blois, ed. by Bödtker. 1912. E122
110 Image du monde. Caxton's Mirrour of the world, ed. by Prior. 1914. E123
111 Lefèvre, R. The history of Jason, ed. by Monro. 1913. E124
112 Same as no. 93. Pt. 2. 1913. E125
113 Salusbury, J. Poems of Sir John Salusbury and Robert Chester, ed. by Brown. 1914. E126
114 Lichfield, Eng. Gild of St. Mary. The Gild of St. Mary, Lichfield, ed. by Furnivall. 1920. E127
115 Same as no. 62. Pt. 2. 1916. E128
116 Bible, N. T. Epistles of Paul. English. The Pauline epistles contained in ms. Parker 32, ed. by Powell. 1916. E129
117 Hall, R. The life of Fisher: Bayne. 1915. E130
118 The earliest arithmetics in English, ed. by Stelle. 1922. E131
119 The owl and the nightingale. The owl and the nightingale, ed. by Grattan and Sykes. 1935. E132
120 Coventry plays. Ludus Coventriae, ed. by Block. 1922. E133
121-4 Boccaccio, G. Lydgate's Fall of princes, ed. by Bergen. 4 v. 1924-27. E134
125 Same as no. 108. V. 2. 1930. E135
126 Same as no. 97. Pt. 4. 1935. E136

EARLY ENGLISH TEXT SOCIETY. ORIGINAL SERIES (Trubner, pub. by Oxford after 1916, 135b pub. by Kegan)

1 Morris, R., ed. Early English alliterative poems. 1864. E137
2 Arthur, ed. by Furnivall. 1864. E138
3 Lauder, W. The extant poetical works of William Lauder, ed. by Hall and Furnivall. 1870. E139
4 Gawain and the Grene knight. Sir Gawayne and the Green knight, ed. by Morris. 1864. E140
5 Hume, A. Of the orthographie and congruitie of the Britain tongue, ed. by

Wheatley. 1865. E141
6 Lancelot. Lancelot of the Laik, ed. by Skeat. 1865. E142
7 Genesis and Exodus. The story of Genesis and Exodus, ed. by Morris. 1865. E143
8 Morte Arthure. Morte Arthure, ed. by Brock. 1865. E144
9 Thynne, F. Chaucer, ed. by Kingsley. 1865. E145
10 Merlin. Merlin, Pt. 1, ed. by Wheatley. 1899. E146
11 Lindsay, D. Sir David Lyndesay's works, ed. by Small, Pt. 1. 1865. E147
12 Adam, of Cobsam. The wright's chaste wife, ed. by Furnivall. 2d ed. 1869. E148
13 Margaret, Saint. Seinte Marherte meiden ant martyr, ed. by Cockayne. 1866. E149
14 Horn, King. King Horn, Floriz and Blaucheflur, the Assumption of Our Lady, ed. by Lumby and McKnight. 1866. E150
15 Furnivall, F. J., ed. Political, religious, and love poems. 1866. E151
16 The book of quinte essence. The book of quinte essence or the fifth being, ed. by Furnivall. 1889. E152
17 Langland, W. Parallel extracts from twenty-nine manuscripts of Piers Plowman, ed. by Skeat. 1866. E153
____. ...from forty-five manuscripts...2d ed. 1886. E154
18 Hali meidenhad. Hali meidenhad, ed. by Cockayne. 1922. E155
19 Same as no. 11. Pt. 2. 1866. E156
20 Rolle, R. English prose treatises of Richard Rolle de Hampole, ed. by Perry. 1921. E157
21 Same as no. 10. Pt. 2. 1899. E158
22 Couldrette, The romans of Partenay..., tr. by Skeat. Rev. ed. 1899. E159
23 Michel, D. Ayenbite of inwyt, ed. by Morris. 1866. E160
24 Furnivall, F. J., ed. Hymns to the Virgin & Christ. 1867. E161
25 ____. The stacions of Rome. 1867. E162
26 Perry, G. G. Religious pieces in prose and verse, ed. by Perry. 1914. E163
27 Levens, P. Manipulus vocabulorum, ed. by Wheatley. 1867. E164
28 Langland, W. The vision of William concerning Piers Plowman, ed. by Skeat. Pt. 1. 1867. E165
29 Morris, R., ed. Old English homilies and homiletic treatises: Morris. Pt. 1. 1868. E166
30 Piers the Plowman's creed. Pierce the Ploughmans crede, ed. by Skeat. 1867. E167
31 Mirk, J. Instructions for parish priests, ed. by Peacock. 1868. E168
32 Furnivall, F. J., ed. The babees book... 1868. E169
33 La Tour-Landry, G. de. The book of the knight of La Tour-Landry, ed. by Wright. 1868. E170
34 Same as no. 29. Pt. 2. 1868. E171
35 Lindsay, D. Sir David Lyndesay's Works, ed. by Hall. Pt. 3. 1868. E172
36 Same as no. 10. Pt. 3. 1899. E173
37 Same as no. 35. Pt. 4. 1869. E174
38 Same as no. 28. Pt. 2. 1869. E175
39 Colonne, G. delle. The "Gest hystoriale" of the destruction of Troy... ed. by Panton and Donaldson. Pt. 1. 1869. E176
40 Smith, J. T., ed. English gilds. 1870. E177
41 Same as no. 3. 1870. E178
42 Bernard de Clairvaux, Saint. Bernardus De cura rei famuliaris with some early Scottish prophecies, &c, ed. by Lumby. 1870. E179
43 Lumby, J. R., ed. Ratis raving, and other moral and religious pieces, in prose and verse. 1870. E180

44 Joseph, of Arimathea. Joseph of Arimathie, ed. by Skeat. 1871. E181
45 Gregorius I, the Great, Saint. King Alfred's West-Saxon version of Gregory's Pastoral care, ed. by the Sweet. Pt. 1. 1871. E182
46 Morris, R., ed. Legends of the holy rood. 1871. E183
47 Lindsay, D. Sir David Lyndesay's Works, ed. by Murray. 1871. E184
48 The times' whistle, ed. by Cowper. 1871. E185
49 Morris, R. An Old English miscellany containing a bestiary..., ed. by Morris. 1872. E186
50 Same as no. 45. Pt. 2. 1872. E187
51 Juliana, Saint. Peliflade of St. Juliana, ed. by Cockayne. 1872. E188
52 Palladius, R. T. A. Palladius On husbondrie, ed. by Lodge. Pt. 1. 1872. E189
53 Morris, R., ed. Old English homilies of the twelfth century, ed. by Morris. 1873. E190
54 Same as no. 28. Pt. 3. 1873. E191
55 Generides Generydes, ed. by Wright. Pt. 1. 1873. E192
56 Same as no. 35. Pt. 2. 1874. E193
57 Cursor mundi. Cursor mundi, ed. by Morris. Pt. 1. 1874. E194
58 Blickling homilies. The Blickling homilies of the tenth century, ed. by Morris. Pt. 1. 1874. E195
59 Same as no. 57. Pt. 2. 1874. E196
60 Bonaventura, Saint. Meditations on the Supper of Our Lord, and the hours of the passion, ed. by Cowper. 1875. E197
61 Thomas, of Erceldoune. The romance and prophecies of Thomas of Erceldoune, ed. by Murray. 1875. E198
62 Same as no. 57. Pt. 3. 1875. E199
63 Same as no. 58. Pt. 2. 1876. E200
64 Thynne, F. Emblemes and epigrames, ed. by Furnivall. 1876. E201
65 Lumby, J. R., ed. Be domes daege, De die judicii. 1876. E202
66 Same as no. 57. Pt. 4. 1876. E203
67 Same as no. 28. Pt. 4. 1877. E204
68 Same as no. 57. Pt. 5. 1877. E205
69 Furnivall, F. J., ed. Adam Davy's 5 dreams about Edward II. 1878. E206
70 Same as no. 55. Pt. 2. 1878. E207
71 The Lay folks mass book, ed. by Simmon. 1879. E208
72 Same as no. 52. Pt. 2. 1879. E209
73 Same as no. 58. Pt. 3. 1880. E210
74 Wycliffe, J. The English works of Wyclif, ed. by Matthew. 1880. E211
75 Catholicon anglicum. Catholicon anglicum, ed. by Herrtage. 1881. E212
76 Aelfric. Aelfric's Lives of saints, ed. by Skeats. Pt. 1. 1881. E213
77 Beowulf. Autotypes of the unique Cotton ms. Vitellius A xv, ed. by Zupitza. 1882. E214
78 Canterbury. The fifty earliest English wills in the Court of probate, London, ed. by Furnivall. 1882. E215
79 Orosius, P. King Alfred's Orosius, ed. by Sweet. 1883. E216
79b Extra Volume. The Epinal glossary. The Epinal glossary, Latin and Old English of the eighth century, ed. by Sweet. 1883. E217
80 Catharina, Saint. The life of Saint Katherine, ed. by Einenkel. 1884. E218
81 Same as no. 28. Pt. 5. 1884. E219
82 Same as no. 76. Pt. 2. 1885. E220
83 Sweet, H., ed. The oldest

English texts. 1885. E221
84 Same as no. 12. Supp. 1886. E222
85 Joannes, of Hildesheim. The three kings of Cologne, ed. by Horstmann. 1886. E223
86 The lives of women saints of our contrie of England, ed. by Horstmann. 1886. E224
87 South English legendary. The early South-English legendary, ed. by Horstmann. 1887. E225
88 Bradshaw, H. The life of Saint Werburge of Chester, ed. by Horstmann. 1887. E226
89 Vices and virtues. Vices and virtues, ed. by Holthausen. Pt. 1. 1888. E227
90 Benedictus, Saint. The rule of S. Benet, ed. by Logeman. 1888. E228
91 Austin, T., ed. Two fifteenth-century cookery-books. 1888. E229
92 Catholic church. Liturgy and ritual. Psalter. Eadwine's Canterbury Psalter, ed. by Harsley. 1889. E230
93 Defensor. Defensor's Liber scintillarum, ed. by Rhodes. 1889. E231
94 Same as no. 76. Pt. 3. 1890. E232
95 Beda Venerabilis. The Old English version of Bede's Ecclesiastical history of the English people, ed. by Miller. Pt. 1. 1890. E233
96 Same as no. 95. Pt. 2. 1891. E234
97 Bible. O. T. Psalms. English. The earliest complete English prose Psalter, ed. by Bülbring. 1891. E235
98 Vernon manuscript. The minor poems of the Vernon ms., ed. by Horstmann. Pt. 1. 1892. E236
99 Same as no. 57. Pt. 4. 1892. E237
100 Capgrave, J. The life of St. Katharine of Alexandria, ed. by Horstmann. 1893. E238
101 Cursor mundi. Cursor mundi, ed. by Hupe. Pt. 5. 1893. E239
102 Lanfranco, of Milan. Lanfrank's "Science of cirurgie," ed. by Fleischhacker. 1894. E240
103 Napier, A. S., ed. History of the holy rood-tree. 1894. E241
104 Exeter book. The Exeter book, ed. by Gollancz and Mackie. 2 v. 1895. E242
105 Catholic church. Liturgy and ritual. Primer. The Prymer, ed. by Littlehales. Pt. 1. 1895. E243
106 Rolle, R. The fire of love, and The Mending of life, ed. by Misyn. 1896. E244
107 Giraldus Cambrensis. The English conquest of Ireland, ed. by Furnivall. 1869. E245
108 Chester, Eng. Child-marriages, divorces, and ratifications, &c. in the diocese of Chester, A. D. 1561-6, ed. by Furnivall. 1897. E246
109 Same as no. 105. Pt. 2. 1897. E247
110 Same as no. 65. Pt. 2:1. 1898. E248
111 Same as no. 65. Pt. 2:2. 1898. E249
112 Merlin. Merlin, ed. by Mead. Pt. 4. 1899. E250
113 Elizabeth, queen of England, tr. Queen Elizabeth's Englishings of Boethius, De consolatine philosophiae, A. D. 1593; Plutarch, De curiositate (1598), Horace, De arte poetica, A. D. 1598, ed. by Pemberton. 1899. E251
114 Same as no. 76. Pt. 4. 1900. E252
115 Jacob's well. Jacob's well, ed. by Brandeis. 1900. E253
116 Martyrologium. An Old English martyrology, ed. by Herzfield. 1900. E254
117 Vernon manuscript. The minor poems of the Vernon ms., ed. by Furnivall. 1919. E255
118 Thoresby, J. The lay folks catechism, ed. by

Simmons. 1901. E256
119 Mannyng, R. Robert of Brunne's "Handlyng synne," ed. by Furnivall. Pt. 1. 1901. E257
120 Benedictus, Saint. Three Middle-English versions of the Rule of St. Benet and two contemporary rituals for the ordination of nuns, ed. by Koch. 1902. E258
121-122 Troy. The Laud Troy book, ed. by Wülfing. 1902-03. E259
123 Same as no. 119. Pt. 1. 1903. E260
124 Kail, J., ed. Twenty-six political and other poems... Pt. 1. 1904. E261
125 London. St. Mary at Hill. The medieval records of a London city church, ed. by Littlehales. Pt. 1. 1904. E262
126 Alphabetum narrationum. An alphabet of tales, ed. by Banks. Pt. 1. 1904. E263
127 Same as no. 126. Pt. 2. 1905. E264
128 Same as no. 125. Pt. 2. 1905. E265
129-30 Godstow nunnery. The English register of Godstow nunnery, ed. by Clark. 2 Pts. 1911, 1906. E266
131 Layamon. The Brut, ed. by Brie. Pt. 1. 1906. E267
132 Metham, J. The works of John Metham, ed. by Craig. 1916. E268
133 Oseney abbey. The English register of Oseney abbey, ed. by Clark. Pt. 1. 1907. E269
134 Coventry. The Coventry leet book, ed. by Harris. Pt. 1. 1907. E270
135 Same as no. 134. Pt. 2. 1907. E271
135b Extra Issue. Manly, J. M. Piers the Plowman and its sequence. 1908. E272
136 Same as no. 131. Pt. 2. 1908. E273
137 Belfour, A. O., ed. Twelfth century homilies in ms. Bodley 343. Pt. 1. 1909. E274
138 Same as no. 134. Pt. 3. 1909. E275
139 Arderne, J. Treatise of fistula in ano, haemorrhoids, and clysters, ed. by Power. 1910. E276
139b-f, Extra Issue. Jusserand, J. A. A. J. The Piers Plowman controversy. 1910. E277
140 Capgrave, J. John Capgrave's lives of St. Augustine and St. Gilbert of Sempringham, ed. by Munro. 1910. E278
141 Erthe upon erthe. The Middle English poem, Erthe upon erthe, ed. by Murray. 1911. E279
142 Same as no. 129. Pt. 3. 1911. E280
143 The prose life of Alexander, ed. by Westlake. 1913. E281
144 Same as no. 133. Pt. 2. 1913. E282
145 Northern Passion. The Northern Passion, ed. by Foster. V. 1. 1913. E283
146 Same as no. 134. Pt. 4. 1913. E284
147 Same as no. 145. V. 2. 1916. E285
148 A Fifteenth-century courtesy book, ed. by Chambers. 1914. E286
149 Lincoln, Eng. Lincoln diocese documents, 1450-1544, ed. by Clark. 1914. E287
150 Chrodegang, Saint. The Old English version of the enlarged rule of Chrodegang together with the Latin original, ed. by Napier. 1916. E288
151 The lanterne of liȝt, ed. by Swinburn. 1917. E289
152 Early English homilies, from the twelfth century ms. Vesp. D. XIV. 1917. E290
153-154 Mandeville, J. Mandeville's travels, ed. by Hamelius. 2 v. 1919-23. E291
155 The Wheatley manuscript, ed. by Day. 1921. E292
156 Pecock, R. The donet,

ed. by Hitchcock. 1921. E293
157 Bible. N. T. Gospels. English. Harmonies. The Pepysian Gospel harmony, ed. by Goates. 1922. E294
158 Meditations on the life and passion of Christ, ed. by D'Evelyn. 1921. E295
159 Same as no. 89. Pt. 2. 1921. E296
160 Aelfric. The Old English version of Heptateuch, ed. by Crawford. 1921. E297
161 Rypins, S., ed. Three old English prose texts in Ms. Cotton Vitellius A XV. 1924. E298
162 Pearl, Cleanness, Patience and Sir Gawain, ed. by Gollancz. 1922. E299
163 London. St. Bartholomew's priory. The book of the foundation of St. Bartholomew's church in London, ed. by Moore. 1923. E300
164 Pecock, R. The folewer to the Donet, ed. by Hitchcock. 1924. E301
165 Middleton, C. The famous histories of Chinon of England, ed. by Mead. 1925. E302
166 Life of Christ. A stanzaic life of Christ, ed. by Foster. 1926. E303
167 Trevisa, J. Dialgous inter militem et clericum, ed. by Perry. 1925. E304
168 Lull, R. The book of the Ordre of chyualry, ed. by Byles. 1926. E305
169 Southern passion. The Southern passion, ed. by Brown. 1927. E306
170 Boethius. De consolatione philosophiae, ed. by Science. 1927. E307
171 Pecock, R. The reule of Crysten religioun, ed. by Greet. 1927. E308
172 Seege of Troye. The seege or batayle of Troye, ed. by Barnicle. 1927. E309
173 Hawes, S. The pastime of pleasure, ed. by Mead. 1927. E310
174 Anne, Saint. The Middle English stanzaic versions of the life of Saint Anne, ed. by Parker. 1928. Corrigenda. 1930. E311
175 Barclay, A. The eclogues of Alexander Barclay, ed. by White. 1928. E312
176 Caxton, W. The prologue and epilogues of William Caxton, ed. by Crotch. 1928. E313
177 Byrhtferth. Byrhtfert's Manual (A. D. 1011), ed. by Crawford. 1929. E314
178 Birgitta, Saint. The revelations of Saint Birgitta, ed. by Cumming. 1929. E315
179 Nevill, W. The castell of pleasure, ed. by Cornelius. 1930. E316
180 More, T., saint. The apologye of Syr Thomas More, ed. by Taft. 1930. E317
181 Dance of death. The dance of death, ed. by Warren. 1931. E318
182 Speculum Christiani. Speculum Christiani, ed. by Holmstedt. 1933. E319
183 Same as no. 145. Supplement. 1930. E320
184 Audelay, J. The poems of John Audelay, ed. by Whiting. 1931. E321
185 Lovelich, H. Merlin, ed. by Kock. Pt. 3. 1932. E322
186 Harpsfield, N. The life and death of Sr Thomas Moore, ed. by Hitchcock. 1932. E323
187 Stanbridge, J. The Vulgaria of John Stanbridge and the Vulgaria of Robert Whittinton, ed. by White. 1932. E324
188 Siege of Jerusalem. The siege of Jerusalem, ed. by Kölbing. 1932. E325
189 Pisan, C. de. The book of fayttes of armes and of chyualrye, ed. by Byles. 1937. E326
190 Evans, J., ed. English mediaeval lapidaries. 1933. E327
191 Seven sages. The seven sages of Rome, ed. by Brunner. 1933. E328

192 Lydgate, J. The minor poems of John Lydgate, ed. by MacCracken. 1910. E329
193 Margaret, Saint. Seinte Marherete Þe meiden ant martyr, ed. by Mack. 1934. E330
194 Same as no. 104. 1934. E331
195 The quatrefoil of love. The quatrefoil of love, ed. by Gollancz. 1935. E332
196 Metrical chronicle of England. An anonymous short English metrical chronicle, ed. by Zettl. 1935. E333
197 Roper, W. The lyfe of Sir Thomas Moore, ed. by Hitchcock. 1935. E334
198 Fierabras. Firumbras and Otuel and Roland, ed. by O'Sullivan. 1935. E335
199 Mum and the sothsegger. Mum and the sothsegger, ed. by Steele. 1936. E336
200 Speculum sacredotale. Speculum sacredotale, ed. by Weatherly. 1936. E337
201 Vegetius Renatus, F. Knyghthode and bataile, ed. by Dyboski and Arend. 1935. E338
202 Gnaphaeus, G. The comedy of Acolastus, ed. by Palsgrave and Carver. 1937. E339
203 Amis et Amiles. Amis and Amiloun, ed. by Leach. 1937. E340
204 Valentin et Orson. Valentine and Orson, ed. by Dickson. 1937. E341
205 Boccaccio, G. Early English versions of the tales of Guiscardo and Ghismonda and Titus and Gisippus from the Decameron, ed. by Wright. 1937. E342
206 Bokenham, O. Legendys of hooly wummen, ed. by Serjeantson. 1938. E343
207 Liber de diversis medicinis. The 'Liber de diversis medicinis,' ed. by Ogden. 1938. E344
208 Anglo-Saxon chronicle. The Parker chronicle and laws, ed. by Flower and Smith. 1941. E345
209 Middle English sermons, ed. by Ross. 1940. E346
210 Gawain and the Grene knight. Sir Gawain and the Green knight, ed. by Gollancz. 1940. E347
211 al-Mubashshir ibn Fatik, A. W. The dicts and sayings of the philosophers, ed. by Bühler. 1941. E348
212 Kempe, M. (Burnham). The book of Margery Kempe, ed. by Meech. 1940. E349
213 Aelfric. Aelfric's De temporibus anni, ed. by Henel. 1942. E350
214 Boccaccio, G. Forty-six lives, ed. by Wright. 1943. E351
215 Charles d'Orléans. The English poems of Charles of Orleans, ed. by Day. V. 1. 1941. E352
216 Ancren riwle. The Latin text of the Ancrene riwle, ed. by D'Evelyn. 1944. E353
217 Laurent. The book of vices and virtues, ed. by Francis. 1942. E354
218 Cloud of unknowing. The cloud of unknowing and the Book of privy counselling, ed. by Hodgson. 1944. E355
219 Ancren riwle. The French text of the Ancrene riwle, ed. by Herbert. 1944. E356
220 Same as no. 215. V. 2. 1946. E357
221 Degrevant. The romance of Sir Degrevant, ed. by Casson. 1949. E358
222 The lyfe of Syr Thomas, ed. by Hitchcock. 1950. E359
223 Tretyse of Love. The tretyse of love, ed. by Fisher. 1951. E360
224 Athelston. At helsten, ed. by Trouce. 1951. E361
225 Ancren riwle. English text of the Ancrene riwle, ed. by Day. 1952. E362
226 Respublica. Respublica, attributed to Udall, reedited by Greg. 1952. E363
227 Alisaunder. Kyng Alisaunder, ed. by Smithers. V. 1. 1952. E364
228 Robert, Saint Robert of Knaresborough. Legend. The

metrical life of St. Robert of Knaresborough, ed. by Bazire. 1953. E365
229 Ancren riwle. The English text of the Ancrene riwle, ed. by Wilson. 1954. E366
230 Barclay, A. The life of St. George, ed. by Nelson. 1955. E367
231 Dionysius Areopagita. Deonise Hid divinite, and other treatises on contemplative prayer related to the Cloud of unknowing, ed. by Hodgson. 1955. E368
232 Ancren riwle. The English text of the Acrene riwle, ed. by Baugh. 1956. E369
233 Diodorus Siculus. The Bibliotheca historica, tr. by Skelton. V. 1. 1956. E370
234 Paris e Viana. English. Paris and Vienne, tr. by Caxton, ed. by Leach. 1957. E371
235-6 South English legendary. The South English legendary, ed. by D'Evelyn and Mill. 2 v. 1956. E372
237 Same as no. 227. V. 2. 1957. E373
238 Robinson, R. Phonetic writings, ed. by Dobson. 1957. E374
239 Same as no. 233. V. 2. 1957. E375
240 Ancren riwle. The French text of the Ancren riwle, ed. from the Trinity College ms. R 147...by Trethewey. 1958. E376
241 Thompson, W. M., ed. Þe wohunge of Ure Lauerd. 1958. E377
242 Catholic church. Liturgy and ritual. Psalter. The Salisbury psalter, ed. by C. and K. Sisam. 1959. E378
243 Cavendish, G. The life and death of Cardinal Wolsey, by Sylvester. 1959. E379
244 Same as no. 235-6. Ed. by Mills. V. 3. 1959. E380
245 Beowulf. Beowulf...British Museum ms. Cotton Vitellius A. XV. 2d ed. Ed. by Aupitza. 1960. E381
246 Parlement of the thre ages. The parlement of thę thre ages, ed. by Offord. 1959. E382
247 Oxford. Univ. Bodleian Library. Facsimilie of Ms. Bodley 34: St. Katherine..., ed. by Ker. 1960. E383
248 Juliana, St. Þe liflade ant te passium of Seinte Iuliene, ed. by d'Ardenne. 1961. E384
249 Ancren riwle. Ancrene wisse, ed. by Tolkien. 1962. E385
250 Laȝamon. Lazamon: Brut, ed. by Brook and Leslie. V. 1. 1963. E386
251 The owl and the nightingale. The owl and the nightingale, ed. by Ker. 1963. E387
252 Ancren riwle. The English text of the Ancrene riwle, ed. by Mack. 1963. E388
253 Mandeville, J. The Bodley version of Mandeville's travels, ed. by Seymour. 1963. E389
254 Ywain and Gawain. Ywain and Gawain, ed. by Friedman and Harrington. 1964. E390
255 British Museum. Facsimile of British Museum MS. Harley 2253, ed. by Ker. 1965. E391
256 Eglamour. Sir Eglamour of Artois, ed. by Richardson. 1965. E392
257 Erasmus, D. The praise of folie, ed. by Miller. 1965. E393
258 Caterina de Siena, St. The orcherd of Syon, ed. by Hodgson and Liegey. V. 1. 1966. E394
259-260 Aelfric, Abbot. Homilies of AElfric, ed. by Pope. 2 v. 1967-68. E395
261 Lybeaus Desconus, ed. by Mills. 1969. E396
262 Eccles, M., ed. The Marco plays. 1969. E397
263 Reynard the Fox. The history of Reynard the Fox, tr. by Coxton, ed. by Blake. 1970. E398

264 Pisan, C. de. The epistle of Thea, tr. by Scope, ed. by Bühler. 1970. E399
265 Guy de Chauliac. The cyrurgie of Guy de Chauliac, ed. by Ogden. 1971. E400
266 Wulfstan II, Abp. Canons of Edgar, ed. by Fowler. 1972. E401
267 Ancrene riwle. The English text of the Ancrene Riwle, ed. by Dobson. 1972. E402
268 Arthour and Merlin. Of Arthour and of Merlin, ed. by Macrae-Gibson. V. 1. 1973. E403
269 The metrical version of Mendeville's travels, ed. by Seymour. 1973. E404
270 Chartier, A. Le traité de l'Esperance, ed. by Blayney. 1974. E405

Suppl. text.
1 Davis, N., comp. Non-cycle and fragments. 1970. E406
2 La Tour Landry, G. de. The book of the knight of the Tower, tr. by Caxton, ed. by Offord. 1971. E407

EARLY ICELANDIC MANUSCRIPTS IN FACSIMILE (Rosenkilde)

1 Sturlunga saga; manuscript no. 122 a fol. in the Arnamgnaean collection, ed. by Benediktsson. 1958. E408
2 Codex Scardensis. Codex Scardensis, ed. by Slay. 1960. E409
3 Skalholtsbok yngsta. The sagas of King Sverrir and King Hakon the Old, ed. by Holm-Olsen. 1961. E410
4 Lives of saints. Lives of saints, Perg. fol. nr. 2, in the Royal Library, Stockholm, ed. by Lindblad. 1963. E411
5 Bergsbók. Bergsbók, ed. by Lindblod. 1963. E412
6 Thomasskina. Thomasskina. Gl. kgl. saml. 1008 fol., in the Royal Library, Copenhagen, ed. by Loth. 1964. E413
7 Karlsson, S., comp. Sagas of Icelandic bishops. 1967. E414
8 Hulda. Sagas of the kings of Norway, 1035-1177, ed. by Louis-Jensen. 1968. E415
9 Skalholtsbok eldri, ed. by Vestergard-Nielsen. 1972. E416
10 Romances. Ed. by Slay. 1972. E417

EAST EUROPEAN FUND. RESEARCH PROGRAM ON THE U. S. S. R. STUDIES (Praeger)

1 Filipov, A. P. Logic and dialetic in the Soviet Union. 1952. E418
2 Krypton, C., pseud. The northern sea route. 1953. E419
3 Slusser, R., ed. Soviet economic policy in postwar Germany. 1953. E420
4 Lawrynenko, J. Ukranian communism and Soviet Russian policy towards the Ukraine. 1953. E421
5 Kazakov, G., pseud. Soviet peat resources. 1954. E422
6 Brzezinski, Z., ed. Political control in the Soviet Army. 1954. E423
7 Bradshaw, M., ed. Soviet theatres, 1917-1941. 1954. E424
8 Sosnovy, T. The housing problem in the Soviet Union, ed. by Goldstein. 1954. E425
9 Majstrenko, I. Borot'bism, tr. by Luckyj and Rubnytsky, ed. by Dornan. 1954. E426
10 Seduro, V. The Byelorussian theatre and drama, ed. by Lehrman. 1955. E427
11 Olkhovsky, A. V. Music under the Soviets. 1955. E428
12 Babitsky, P. The Soviet film industry. 1955. E429
13 Belov, F. The history of a Soviet collective farm. 1955. E430
14 Krypton, C., pseud. The northern sea route and the economy of the Soviet North. 1956. E431
14 Wolin, S. and Slusser, R. M. The Soviet secret police. 1957. E432

16 Black, C. E., ed. Rewriting Russian history. 1956. E433
18 Kline, G. L., ed. Soviet education. 1957. E434
20 Zavalishin, V. Early Soviet writers. 1958. E435

ECOLE FRANÇAISE D'ATHENES. TRAVAUX ET MEMOIRES (Boccard)

1 Mirambel, A. Etude descriptive du parler maniote méridional. 1929. E436
2-3 Deonna, W. Dédale, ou La statue de la Grèce archaique. 2 v. 1930. E437
4 Haspels, C. H. E. Attic black-figured lekythoi. 1936. E438
5 Collart, P. Philippes ville de Macédoine. 1937. E439
6 Reverdin, O. La religion de la cité platonicienne. 1938. E440
7 Deonna, W. La vie privée des Déliens. 1940. E441
8 Stikas, E. L'église byzantine de Christianou en Triphylie. 1951. E442
9 Sokolowski, F., ed. Lois sacrées de l'Asie Mineure. 1955. E443
10 Ghali-Kahil, L. B. Les enlèvements et le retour d'Hélène dans les textes et les documents figurés. 1955. E444
11 Sokolowski, F. Lois sacrées des cités grecques. Supp. 1962. E445
12 Dascalakis, A. Problèmes historiques autour de la bataille des Termopyles. 1962. E446
13 Pelikidis, C. Histoire de l'Ephébie attique des origines à 31 avant J.C. 1962. E447
14 Faure, P. Fonctions des cavernes crétoises. 1964. E448
15 Deonna, W. Le symbolisme de l'oeil. 1965. E449
16 Orlandos, A. Les matériaux de construction et la technique architecturale des anciens Grecs. V. 1. 1966. E450
17 Ducrey, P. Le traitement des prisenniers de guerre dans la Grèce antique des origines à la conquête romaine. 1968. E451
18 Sokolowski, F. Lois sacrées des cités grecques. 1969. E452
19 Same as no. 16. V. 2. 1969. E453

ECOLOGICAL STUDIES SERIES (Springer)

1 Reichle, D. E. Analysis of temperate forest ecosystems. 1970. E454
2 Ellenberg, H. Integrated experimental ecology. 1971. E455
3 The Biology of the Indian Ocean. Ed. by Zeitzschelaid and Gerlach. 1973. E456
4 Physical aspects of soil water and salts in ecosystems, ed. by Hadas. 1973. E457
5 Arid zone irrigation, ed. by Yaron and others. 1973. E458
6 Stern, K. and Roche, L. Genetics of forest ecosystems. 1974. E459
7 Mediterranean-type ecosystems, ed. by DiCastri and Mooney. 1973. E460
8 Phenology and seasonality modeling, ed. by Leith. 1974. E461

ECONOMIC HANDBOOK SERIES (McGraw)

Burns, E. M. Social security and public policy. 1956. E462
Carlson, V. Economic security in the United States. 1962. E463
Coppock, J. D. International economic instability. 1962. E464
Duesenberry, J. S. Business cycles and economic growth. 1958. E465
Hansen, A. H. The American economy. 1957. E465a
____. Economic issues of the 1960's. 1960. E465b
____. A guide to Keynes.

1953. E466

____. Monetary theory and fiscal policy. 1949. E467

Harris, S. E. International and interregional economics. 1957. E468

Henderson, J. M. and Quandt, R. E. Microeconomic theory. 1958. E469

Hoover, E. M. The location of economic activity. 1948. E470

Johnston, J. Statistical cost analysis. 1960. E471

Kindleberger, C. P. Economic development. 1958. E472

Lerner, A. P. Economics of employment. 1951. E473

Mikesell, R. F. United States economic policy and international relations. 1952. E474

Schelling, T. C. National income behavior. 1951. E475

Sweezy, P. M. Socialism. 1949. E476

Taylor, O. A history of economic thought. 1960. E477

Tinbergen, J. and Bos, H. C. Mathematical models of economic growth. 1962. E478

Valavanis, S. Econometrics. 1959. E479

Wright, D. M. Capitalism. 1951. E480

ECONOMICS AND POLITICS OF PUBLIC EDUCATION (Syracuse Univ. Pr.)

1 Bailey, S. K. Schoolmen and politics. 1962. E481

2 Martin, R. C. Government and the suburban school. 1962. E482

3 Munger, F. J. and Fenno, R. F. National politics and federal aid to education. 1962. E483

4 Sufrin, S. C. Issues in federal aid to education. 1962. E484

5 Clark, H. F. Cost and quality in public education. 1963. E485

6 Gortner, R. A. Federal aid to science education. 1963. E486

7 Burkhead, J. State and local taxes for public education. 1963. E487

8 Sufrin, S. C. Administering the National Defense Education Act. 1963. E488

9 Labovitz, I. M. Aid for federally affected public schools. 1963. E489

10 Bloomberg, W. and others. Suburban power structures and public education. 1963. E490

11 Miner, J. Social and economic factors in spending for public education. 1963. E491

12 Wasserman, W. Education and quantity indexes. 1963. E492

EDINBURGH BILINGUAL LIBRARY (Univ. of Texas Pr.)

1 Valery, P. Le cimetiere Marin, ed. by Martin. 1972. E493

2 Racine, J. B. Phèdre, ed. by Knight. 1972. E494

3 Press, A. R., ed. Anthology of troubadour lyric poetry. 1972. E495

4 Pessoa, F. Selected poems, ed. by Rickard. 1972. E496

5 Martin, G. D., ed. Anthology of contemporary French poetry. 1972. E497

6 Bonaventura, pseud. Die nachtwachen des Bonaventura, ed. by Gillespie. 1972. E498

7 Labé, L. Sonnets, ed. by Sharratt, tr. by Martin. 1973. E499-E500

8 Tieck, L. Die gestiefelte Kater, ed. and tr. by Gillespie. 1974. E501

EDINBURGH. UNIVERSITY. EDINBURGH UNIVERSITY PUBLICATIONS: HISTORY, PHILOSOPHY, AND ECONOMICS

1 Vecchio, G. del. Justice. 1952. E502

2 Plant, M. The domestic life of Scotland in the eighteenth century. 1952. E503

3 Donaldson, G. The making of the Scottish Prayer Book of 1637. 1954. E504
4 Ritchie, R. L. G. The Normans in Scotland. 1954. E505
5 Lamont, W. D. The value judgement. 1955. E506
6 Macartney, C. A. October fifteenth. 2 v. 1962. E507
7 Bultmann, R. K. History and eschatology. 1957. E508
8 Hay, D. Europe. 1957. E509
9 Shepperson, G. and Price, T. Independent African. 1958. E510
10 Buchanan, G. The tyrannous reign of Mary Stewart. 1958. E511
11 Ritchie, A. D. Studies in the history and methods of the sciences. 1958. E512
12 Davie, G. E. The democratic intellect. 1961. E513
13 Macartney, C. A. Hungary. 1962. E514
14 Flinn, M. W. Men of iron. 1962. E515
15 Kochan, L. The struggle for Germany, 1914-1945. 1963. E516
16 Richardson, H. G. and Sayles, G. O. The governance of mediaeval England from the conquest to the Magna Carta. 1963. E517
17 Bosworth, C. E. The Ghaznavids. 1963. E518
18 Sanderson, G. N. England, Europe and the Upper Nile, 1882-1899. 1965. E519
19 Rae, T. I. The administration of the Scottish frontier. 1966. E520
20 Richardson, H. and Sayles, G. O. Law and legislation. 1967. E521
21 Ardal Pall Steinthorsson. Passion and value in Hume's Treatise. 1966. E522
22 Jackson, W. T. The enterprising Scot. 1968. E523

EDINBURGH UNIVERSITY. EDINBURGH UNIVERSITY PUBLICATIONS: SCIENCE AND MATHEMATICS TEXTS.

1 Feather, N. An introduction to the physics of mass, length, and time. 1959. E524
2 Clark, W. E. L. G. The antecedents of man. 1959. E525
3 Sillitto, R. M. Non-realistic quantum mechanics. 1960. E526
4 Feather, N. An introduction to the physics of vibrations and waves. 1961. E527
5 Robson, J. D. An introduction to random vibration. 1963. E528
6 Brook, A. J. The living plant. 1964. E529
7 Brown, A. F. C. Statistical physics. 1968. E530
8 Feather, N. Electricity and matter. 1968. E531

EDINBURGH. UNIVERSITY. PUBLICATIONS: LANGUAGE AND LITERATURE.

1 Poulet, G. Etudes sur le temps humain. 1949. E532
2 Legge, M. D. Anglo-Norman in the cloisters. 1950. E533
3 Daniels, M. The French drama of the unspoken. 1953. E534
4 Jackson, K. Language and history in early Britain. 1953. E535
5 Sandmann, M. Subject and predicate. 1954. E536
6 Bell, R. Introduction to the Qur'ān. 1953. E537
7 Butter, P. Shelley's idols of the cave. 1954. E538
8 Chang, H. Allegory and courtesy in Spenser. 1955. E539
9 Rankin, O. S. Jewish religious polemic of early and later centuries. 1956. E540
10 Goethe, J. W. von. Letters from Goethe, tr. by Herzfield and Sym. 1957. E541
11 Catholic Church. The Benedictine Office, ed. by Ure. 1957. E542
12 Daniel, N. Islam and the West. 1960. E543
13 Patterson, D. The Hebrew

novel in Czarist Russia. 1964. E544
14 Knodel, A. Saint-John Perse. 1966. E545
15 Daniel, N. Islam, Europe and Empire. 1966. E546

L'EDUCATION FAMILIALE NOUVELLE (Bloud)

1 Vérine, Mme. Les dix commandements des parents. 1946. E547
2 Berge, A. Les défauts de l'enfant. 1946. E548
3 Lévesque, J. Les conditions d'une bonne croissance de l'enfant. 1947. E549
4 Dublineau, J. Les grandes crises de l'enfance. 1947. E550
5 Pange, P. L. M. (de Broglie). Les clefs du paradis. 1948. E551
6 Réflexions sur la psychanalyse, by Lhermitte and others. 1949. E552
7 Jérome, J. Le scrupule. 1950. E553
8 Fargues, M. La foi des petits enfants. 1950. E554
9 Verine, Mme. L'amour des autres ou l'éducation de la fraternité. 1950. E555

EDUCATION FOR LIVING (Harper)

Andrew, D. C. and Willey, R. D. V. Administration and organization of the guidance program. 1958. E556
Bayles, E. E. The theory and practice of teaching. 1950. E557
Brown, T. J. Student teaching in a secondary school. 1960. E558
Campbell, C. M., ed. Practical applications of democratic administration. 1952. E559
Downie, N. M. and Heath, R. W. Basic statistical methods. 1959. E560
Franzén, C. G. F. Foundations of secondary education. 1955. E561
Gronlund, N. E. Sociometry in the classroom. 1959. E562
Kaplan, L. and Baron, D. Mental hygiene and life. 1952. E563
Krug, E. A. Curriculum planning. 1957. E564
Leese, J. and others. The teacher in curriculum making. 1961. E565
Mathewson, R. H. Guidance policy and practice. 1962. E566
____. A strategy for American education. 1957. E567
Reinhardt, E. American education. 1960. E568
Remmers, H. H. and Gage, N. L. Educational measurement and evaluation. 1955. E569
____ and others. Growth, teaching, and learning. 1957. E570
____. Introduction to educational psychology. 1960. E571
____. A practical introduction to measurement and evaluation. 1965. E572
Rummel, J. F. An introduction to research procedures in education. 1958. E573
Sands, L. B. An introduction to teaching in secondary schools. 1949. E574
Schneideman, R. Democratic education in practice. 1945. E575
Traxler, A. E. Techniques of guidance. 1945. E576
____ and others. Introduction to testing and the use of test results in public schools. 1953. E577
Tuttle, H. S. Dynamic psychology and conduct. 1949. E578
Wallin, J. E. W. Education of mentally handicapped children. 1955. E579
Washton, N. S. Science teaching in the secondary school. 1961. E580
Willey, R. D. V. Guidance in elementary education. 1960. E581
____ and Andrews, D. C. Modern methods and techniques in guidance. 1955. E582
____ and Strong, W. M. Group procedures in guidance. 1957. E583

Yeager, W. A. Administration and the pupil. 1949. E584
____. Administration and the teacher. 1954. E585
____. Administration of the non-instrumental personnel and services. 1959. E586

EDUCATION IN LARGE CITIES SERIES (Syracuse Univ. Pr.)

1 Meranto, P. The politics of federal aid to education in 1965. 1967. E587
2 Burkhead, J. and others. Input and output in large city high schools. 1967. E588
3 Rosenthal, A. Pedagogues and power. 1969. E589
4 Sacks, S. and others. City schools / Suburban schools. 1972. E590

THE EDWARD L. BERNAYS FOUNDATION LECTURES (New York Univ.)

1944 Safeguarding civil liberty today, by Becker and others. 1945. E591
1950 The social responsibility of management, by Chase and others. 1950. E592

ELECTRONICS MATERIALS REVIEWS (Noyes Development Corp.)

1 Sitting, M. Pure chemical elements for semiconductors, 1969. 1969. E593
2 ____. Manufacture of semiconductor compounds, 1969. 1969. E594
3 ____. Semiconductor crystal manufacture. 1969. E595
4 ____. Doping and semiconductor junction formation. 1970. E596
5 ____. Producing films of electronics materials. 1970. E597
6 ____. Electroluminescent materials, 1970. 1970. E598
7 ____. Thermoelectric materials, 1970. 1970. E599
8 ____. Photoconductive materials. 1970. E600
9 ____. Magnetic materials, 1970. 1970. E601
10 ____. Battery materials, by Paul Conrad. 1970. E602
11 ____. Superconducting materials, 1970. 1970. E603
12 ____. Resistor materials, by Paul Conrad. 1971. E604

ELIZABETHAN BIBLIOGRAPHIES (Elizabethan Bibliographies) (Comp. by Samuel Aaron Tannenbaum) Scholars' facsimiles and reprints

1 Christopher Marlowe. 1937. Suppl. 1937. E605
2 Ben Jonson. 1938. Suppl. 1948. E606
3-5 Beaumont & Fletcher, George Chapman, Philip Massinger. 1938, Suppl. Beaumont and Fletcher, 1946. Chapman. 1946. E607
6-7 Thomas Heywood, Thomas Dekker. 1939. E608
8 Robert Greene. 1939, Suppl. 1945. E609
9 Shakspeare's Macbeth. 1939. E610
10 Shakspere's Sonnets. 1940. E611
11 Thomas Lodge. 1940. E612
12 John Lyly. 1940. E613
13 Thomas Middleton. 1940. E614
14 John Marston. 1940. E615
15 George Peele. 1940. E616
16 Shakspere's King Lear. 1940. E617
17 Shakspere's Merchant of Venice. 1941. E618
18 Thomas Kyd. 1941. E619
19 John Webster. 1941. E620
20-21 John Ford & Thomas Nashe. 1941. E621
22 Michael Drayton. 1941. E622
23 Sir Philip Sidney. 1941. E623
24 Michel Eyquem de Montaigne. 1942. E624
25 Samuel Daniel. 1942. E625
26 George Gascoigne. 1942. E626
27 Anthony Mundy. 1942. E627
28 Shakspere's Othello. 1943. E628
29 Shakspere's Troilus &

Cressida. 1943. E629
30-32 Marie Stuart. 1944-46. E630
33 Cyril Tourneur. 1946. E631
34 James Shirley. 1946. E632
35 George Herbert. 1946. E633
36 John Heywood. 1946. E634
37 Roger Ascham. 1946. E635
38 Thomas Randolph. 1947. E636
39 Nicholas Breton. 1947. E637
40 Robert Herrick. 1949. E638
41 Shakespere's Romeo and Juliet. 1950. E639

EMPIRE STATE HISTORICAL PUBLICATIONS SERIES (Friedman)

1 Gabriel, R. H. The evolution of Long Island. 1960. E640
2 Skinner, A. The Indians of Manhattan Island and vicinity. 1961. E641
3 Beauchamp, W. M. A history of the New York Iroquois. 1961. E642
4 Overton, J. M. Long Island story. 1961. E643
5 Thompson, B. F. History of Long Island. 3 v. 1961. E644
6 Tooker, W. W. Indian place names on Long Island and islands adjacent. 1962. E645
7 Converse, H. M. Myths and legends of the New York Iroquois. 1962. E646
8 Abbott, W. C. New York in the American Revolution. 1962. E647
9 Marshall, B. Colonial Hempstead. 1962. E648
10 Jaray, C., comp. The mills of Long Island. 1962. E649
11 Bobbé, D. De Witt Clinton. 1962. E650
12 Donaldson, A. L. A history of the Adirondacks. 2 v. 1963. E651
13 Adams, J. T. Memorials of Old Bridgehampton. 1962. E652
14 ____. History of the town of Southampton. 1962. E653
15 Flint, M. B. Long Island before the Revolution. 1967. E654
16 Earle, A. M. Colonial days in Old New York. 1962. E655
17 Bayles, R. M. Historical and descriptive sketches of Suffolk County 1962. E656
18 Flick, A. C., ed. History of the state of New York. 10 v. in 5. 1962. E657
19 Spaulding, E. W. New York in the critical period, 1783-1789. 1963. E658
20 Swiggett, H. War out of Niagara. 1963. E659
21 Halsey, F. W. The Old New York frontier. 1963. E660
22 Voelbel, M. M. The story of an island. 1963. E661
23 Overton, J. M. Indian life on Long Island. 1963. E662
24 Cornplanter, J. Legends of the Longhouse. 1963. E663
25 Fox, D. R. Yankees and Yorkers. 1963. E664
26 Jackson, B. Stories of old Long Island. 1963. E665
27 Pomerantz, S. L. New York. 1965. E666
28 Spaulding, E. W. His Excellency George Clinton. 1964. E667
29 Hamilton, M. W. The country printer. 1964. E668
30 Smith, R. A tour of four great rivers. 1963. E669
31 Beauchamp, W. M. Iroquois folk lore. 1965. E670
32 Furman, G. The antiquities of Long Island. 1968. E671
33 Mark, I. Agrarian conflicts in colonial New York, 1711-1775. 1965. E672
34 Raesly, E. L. Portrait of New Netherland. 1965. E673
35 Jaray, C., comp. Historic chronicles of New Amsterdam. 1st ser. 1968. E674
36 ____. ____. 2d ser. 1968. E675
37 Ernst, R. Immigrant life in New York City, 1825-1863. 1965. E676
38 McKee, S. Labor in colonial New York, 1664-1776. 1965. E677
39 Barck, O. T. New York City during the war for independence. 1966. E678
40 Eberlein, H. D. Manor houses and historic homes of Long Island and Staten

Island. 1966. E679
41 Perry, C. Underground empire. 1966. E680
42 Clarke, T. W. Emigres in the wilderness. 1967. E681
43 Parker, A. C. The history of the Seneca Indians. 1967. E682
44 New York State Division of Archives. The American Revolution in New York. 1967. E683
45 Janvier, T. A. The Dutch founding of New York. 1967. E684
46 Peterson, A. E. and Edwards, G. W. New York as an eighteenth century municipality. 2 v. 1967. E685
47 Verplanck, W. E. and Collyer, M. W. The sloops of the Hudson. 1968. E686
48 Peel, R. V. The political clubs of New York City. 1968. E687
49 Todd, C. B. In Old New York. 1968. E688
50 Lydekker, J. W. The faithful Mohawks. 1968. E689
51 Nestler, H. The bibliography of New York state communities. 1968. E690
52 Dyson, V. Heather flower. 1968. E691
53 Clarke, T. W. The bloody Mohawk. 1968. E692
54 Wallace, P. A. W. The white roots of peace. 1968. E693
55 Manhattan Co. Manna-hatin. 1968. E694
56 Snyder, C. M. Oswego. 1968. E695
57-58 Chalmers, H. Tales of the Mohawk. 2 v. 1968. E696
59 Sobin, D. P. Dynamics of community change. 1968. E697
60 Singleton, E. Social New York under the Georges, 1714-1776. 2 v. 1969. E698
61 Maurice, A. B. New York in fiction. 1968. E699
62 Ulmann, A. New Yorkers from Stuyvesant to Roosevelt. 1969. E700
63 Innes, J. H. New Amsterdam and its people. 1968. E701
64 Goodwin, M. W. and others, eds. Historic New York. 4 v. 1969. E702
65 Pauli, H. and Ashton, E. B. I lift my lamp. 1969. E703
66 Wilson, R. R. Historic Long Island. 1969. E704
67 Wilstach, P. Hudson River landings. 1969. E705
68 Van der Water, F. F. Lake Champlain and Lake George. 1969. E706
69 Alexander, D. S. A political history of the state of New York. 4 v. 1969. E707
70 Ulmann, A. A landmark history of New York. 1969. E708
71 Murphy, H. C. Anthology of New Netherland. 1969. E709
72 French, J. G. Gazetteer of the state of New York. 1969. E710
73 Pursh, F. Journal of a botanical excursion in the northeastern parts of the state of New York and Pennsylvania during the year 1807, ed. by Beauchamp. 1969. E711
74 Onderdonk, H. Documents and letters intended to illustrate the revolutionary incidents of Queens county. 1969. E712
75 ____. Revolutionary incidents of Suffolk and Kings. 1969. E713
76 Shaw, E. R. Legends of Fire Island and the south side. 1969. E714
77 Stevens, W. O. Discovering Long Island. 1969. E715
78 Dyson, V. The human story of Long Island. 1969. E716
79 ____. Anecdotes and events in Long Island history. 1969. E717
80 Bush, M. H. Revolutionary enigma. 1969. E718
81 Berbrich, J. D. Three voices of Paumanok. 1969. E719
82 Hammon, J. America's first Negro poet, ed. by Ransom. 1968. E720

83 Barber, J. W. and Howe, H. Historical collections of the State of New York. 1970. E721
84 Cochran, T. C. New York in the Confederation. 1970. E722
85 Longstreth, T. M. The Catskills. 1970. E723
86 Morrison, J. H. History of New York shipyards. 1970. E724
87 Pound, A. Lake Ontario. 1970. E725
88 Shepherd, W. R. The story of New Amsterdam. 1970. E726
89 Berbich, J. D., comp. Sounds and sweet airs. 1970. E727
90 Cagney, W. O. The heritage of Long Island, ed. by Barbich. 1970. E728
91 Funnell, B. H. Walt Whitman on Long Island. 1971. E729
92 Marhoefer, B. Witches, whales, petticoats & sails. 1971. E730
93 Canfield, W. W., comp. The legends of the Iroquois. 1971. E731
94 Bolton, R. P. Indian life of long ago in the city of New York. 1971. E732
95 Ruttenber, E. M. History of the Indian tribes of Hudson River. 1971. E733
96 Trelease, A. W. Indian affairs in colonial New York. 1971. E734
97 Schmitt, F. P. Mark well the whale! 1971. E735

ENGLISH BIBLIOGRAPHICAL SOURCES (Gregg)

Series 1: Periodical lists of new publications

1 The monthly catalogue, 1714-17. 1964. E736
2 ____, 1723-1730. 2 v. 1964. E737
3 A register of books, 1728-1732. 1964. E738
4 Bibliotheca annua, 1699-1703. 1964. E739
5 The annual catalogue, 1736-37. 1965. E740
6 Kimber, E., comp. The Gentleman's magazine, 1731-51. 1967. E741
7 The monthly catalogues from 'The London Magazine,' 1732-66. 1967. E742
8 The British Magazine. The lists of books from the British Magazine, 1746-50. 1965. E743

Series 2: Catalogues of books in circulation.

1 Mausnell, A. The catalogue of English printed books, 1955. 1966. E744
2 London, W. William London: a catalogue of the most venible books in England (1657, 1658, 1660). 1965. E745
3 Clavell, R. A catalogue of all the books printed in England since the dreadful fire of London in 1666 to the end of Michaelmas term, 1672. 1965. E746
4 ____. The general catalogue of books printed in England since the dreadful fire of London, 1666 to the end of Trinity Term, 1674. 1965. E747
5 ____. A catalogue of all the books printed in England since the dreadful fire of London, 1666 to the end of Trinity Term, 1680. 1965. E748
6 ____. A catalogue of books printed in England since the dreadful fire of London in 1666 to the end of Michaelmas Term, 1695. 1966. E749

Series 3: Printer's manuals

1 Watson, J. The history of the art of printing. 1965. E750
2 Smith, J. The printer's grammar. 1966. E751
3 Luckombe, P. The history and art of printing. 1965. E752
4 Stower, C. The printer's grammar. 1965. E753
5 Johnson, J. Typographia. V. 1. 1966. E754
6 Hansard, T. C. Typographia. 1966. E755
7 Timperley, C. H. The printer's manual. 1966. E756

8 Savage, W. A dictionary of the art of printing. 1966. E757

ENGLISH DIALECT SOCIETY. PUBLICATIONS.

1 Skeat, W. W., ed. Reprinted glossaries. 1873. E758
2 ____, ed. A bibliographical list of the works that have been published, or are known to exist in ms., illustrative of the various dialects of English. V. 1. 1877. E759
3 Harland, J. A glossary of words used in Swaledale, Yorkshire. 1873. E760
4 Sweet, H. A history of English sounds from the earliest period. 1874. E761
5-6 Same as no. 1. V. 3-4. E762
6 Ray, J. A collection of English words not generally used, ed. by Skeat. 1874. E763
6:2 Paris, W. D. A dictionary of the Sussex dialect and collections of provincialisms in use in the county of Sussex. 1875. E764
7 Elsworthy, F. T. The dialect of west Somerset. 1875. E765
8 Same as no. 2. V. 2. E766
9 Robinson, F. K. A glossary of words used in the neighborhood of Whitby. V. 1. 1876. E767
10 Nodal, J. H. and Milner, G. A glossary of the Lancashire dialect. V. 1. 1875. E768
11 Morris, R. On the survival of early English words in our present dialects. 1876. E769
12 Skeat, W. W., ed. Original glossaries. 1876. E770
13 Same as no. 9. V. 2. 1876. E771
14 Robinson, C. C. A glossary of words pertaining to the dialect of mid-Yorkshire. 1876. E772
15 Peacock, E. A glossary of words used in the wapentakes of Manley and Corringham, Lincolnshire. 1877. E773
16 Ross, F. A glossary of words used in Holderness in the Fast Riding of Yorkshire. 1877. E774
17 Bonaparte, L. L. On the dialects of eleven southern and southwestern counties. 1877. E775
18 Same as no. 2. V. 3. 1877. E776
19 Elsworthy, F. T. An outline of the grammar of the dialect of west Somerset. 1877. E777
20 Dickinson, W. A glossary of words and phrases pertaining to the dialect of Cumberland. V. 1. 1878. E778
21 Tusser, T. Five hundred pointes of good husbandrie. 1878. E779
22 Britten, J. A dictionary of English plant-names. V. 1. 1886. E780
23 Same as no. 1. V. 4. 1879. E781
24 Same as no. 20. V. 2. 1879. E782
25 Specimens of English dialects, ed. by Elsworthy and others. 1879. E783
26 Same as no. 22. V. 2. 1886. E784
27 Courtney, M. A. Glossary of words in use in Cornwall. 1880. E785
28 Patterson, W. H. A glossary of words in use in counties of Antrim and Down... 1880. E786
29 An early English hym to the Virgin, by Furnivall. 1880. E787
30 Britten, J., ed. Old country and farming words. 1880. E788
31 Evans, A. B., ed. Leicestershire words, phrases, and proverbs. 1881. E789
32 Skeat, W. W. Original glossaries. 1881. E790
33 English dialect Society. Report, 1st-17th. 1873-92. E791
34 Turner, W. Names of herbes. 1881. E792
35 Same as no. 10. V. 2. 1882. E793
36 Chamberlain, E. L. A glossary of west Worcestershire words. 1882. E794

37 Fitzherbert, A. The book of husbandry. 1882. E795
38 Friend, H. A glossary of Devonshire plant names. 1882. E796
39 Easther, A. A glossary of the dialect of Almondbury and Huddersfield. 1883. E797
40 Cope, W. H., comp. and ed. A glossary of Hampshire words and phrases. 1883. E798
41 Berners, J. An oldern form of The treatyse of fysshynge wyth an angle attributed to Dame Juliana Barnes. 1883. E799

(Privately ed. and pr. by Thomas Satchell, Pub. by Wm. Satchell, London. Numbered as Society publication)

41 Bailey, N. English dialect words of the eighteenth century as shown in the "Universal etymological dictionary" of Nathaniel Bailey. 1883. E800
42 Lawson, R. Upton-on-Severn words and phrases. 1884. E801
43 Skeat, B. M. A word-list illustrating the correspondence of modern English. 1884. E802
44 Holland, R. A glossary of words used in the county of Chester. V. 1. 1886. E803
45 Same as no. 22. V. 3. 1886. E804
46 Same as no. 44. V. 2. 1886. E805
47 Swainson, C. Provincial names and folk lore of British birds. 1885. E806
48 Hallam, T. Four dialect words. 1885. E807
49 Ellis, A. J. Report on dialectal work from May 1885, to May 1887. 1886. E808
50 Elsworthy, F. T. The west Somerset word-book. 1886. E809
51 Same as no. 44. V. 3. 1886. E810
52 Cole, R. E. G. A glossary of words used in south-west Lincolnshire. 1886. E811
53 Darlington, T. The folk-speech of south Cheshire. 1887. E812
54 Parish, W. D. A dictionary of Kentish dialect and provincialism in use in the county of Kent. 1887. E813
55 Same as no. 49. V. 2. 1887. E814
56 Lowsley, B., comp. A glossary of Berkshire words and phrases. 1888. E815
57 Addy, S. O., ed. A glossary of words used in the neighborhood of Sheffield. 1888. E816
58-59 Peacock, E. A glossary of words used in the wapentakes of Manley and Corringham, Lincolnshire. 1889. E817
60 Ellis, A. J. English dialects. 1890. E818
61 Robertson, J. D. A glossary of dialect & archaic words used in the county of Gloucester. 1890. E819
62 Same as no. 57. Suppl. 1891. E820
63 Bülbring, K. D. Ablaut in the modern dialects of the south of England. 1891. E821
64 Wordsworth, C., comp. Rutland words. 1891. E822
65 Chope, R. P. The dialect of Hartland, Devonshire. 1891. E823
66 Heslop, R. O. Northumberland words. V. 1. 1892. E824
67 Wright, J. A grammar of the dialect of Windhill. 1892. E825
68 Same as no. 66. V. 2. 1893. E826
69 Dartnell, G. E. and Goddard, E. H. A glossary of words used in the county of Wiltshire. 1893. E827
70 Gower, G. W. G. L. A glossary of Surrey words. 1893. E828
71 Same as no. 66. V. 3. 1894. E829
72 Salisbury, J., comp. A glossary of words and phrases used in S. E. Worcestershire. 1893. E830
73 Northall, G. F. Folk-phrases of four counties. 1894. E831
74 Palgrave, F. M. T. A list of words and phrases

in every-day use by the natives of Hetton-le-Hole in the county of Durham. 1896. E832
75 Rye, W. A glossary of words used in East Anglia. 1895. E833
76 Skeat, W. W., ed. Nine specimens of English dialects. 1896. E834
77 Ellwood, T. Lakeland and Iceland. 1895. E835
78 Pegge, S. Two collections of Derbicisms... 1896. E836
79 Northall, G. F. A Warwickshire word-book. 1896. E837
80 Heslop, R. O. A bibliographical list of works illustrative of the dialect of Northumberland. 1896. E838

ENGLISH HISTORICAL SOCIETY, LONDON. PUBLICATIONS.

Beda. Venerabilis Bedae opera historica..., ed. by Stevenson. 2 v. 1841. E839
Chronicque de la traison et mort de Richard Deux roy d'Angleterre... ed. by Williams. 1846. E840
Florence. Florentii Wigorniensis monarchi Chronicon ex chronicis..., ed. by Thorpe. 2 v. 1848-49. E841
Gesta Stephani, regis Anglorum..., ed. by Sewell. 1846. E842
Gildas. Gildas De excidio Britanniae..., ed. by Stevenson. 1838. E843
Hemingford, W. de. Chronicon domini Walteri de Hemingburgh..., ed. by Hamilton. 2 v. 1848-49. E844
Henrici Quinti, Angliae regis..., ed. by Williams. 1850. E845
Kemble, J. M., ed. Codex diplomaticus aevi saxonici. 6 v. 1839-48. E846
Murimuth, A. Adami Murimuthensis Chronica sui temporis..., ed. by Hog. 1846. E847
Nennius. Nenii Historia Britonum ..., ed. by Stevenson. 1838. E848
Richard of Devizes. Chronicon Ricardi Divisiensis de rebus gestis Ricardi Primi regis Angliae, ed. by Stevenson. 1838. E849
Roger of Wendover. Rogeri de Wendover Chronicon, ed. by Coxe. 4 v. 1841-42. E850
Trivet, N. F. Nicholai Triveti, de ordine frat. Praedicatorum Annales sex regum Angliae..., ed. by Hog. 1845. E851
William of Malmesbury. Willelmi Malmesbiriensis monarchi Gesta regum Anglorum, atque Historia novella..., ed. by Hardy. 2 v. 1840. E852
William of Newburgh. Historia rerum anglicarum Willelmi Parvi, ordinis Sancti Augustini canonici regularis in coenobio Beatae Mariae de Newburgh..., ed. by Hamilton. 2 v. 1856. E853

ENGLISH MEN OF LETTERS. This series has been published in various editions. The letter following the date of publication refers to the edition. All editions were published unnumbered except the Harper edition, ed. by Morley. The series number for this edition accompanies the letter.

A. Harper, ed. by Morley.
B. Harper, ed. by Morley (13v. ed. pub. 1894)
C. Harper. Handy edition.
D. Lovell.
E. Macmillan.
F. Macmillan, ed. by Morley.
G. Macmillan. New series. Ed. by Squires.

Ainger, A. Charles Lamb. 1882 (A), 1894 (B9:2), 1887(C), 1919 (E), 1882 (F) E854
____. Crabbe. 1903. (F) E855
Bailey, J. C. Walt Whitman. 1926 (G) E856
Benson, A. C. Edward Fitzgerald. 1879 (A), 1894 (B 1:2), 1887 (C), 1884 (D), 1904 (E) E857
____. Walter Pater. 1906 (E) E858
____. Rossetti. 1904 (E), 1904 (F) E859
Birrell, A. Andrew Marvell.

1905 (E) E860

———. William Hazlitt. 1902 (E) E861

Black, W. Goldsmith. 1879 (A), 1894 (B 11:2), 1887 (C), 1883 (D), 1905 (F) E862

Blunden, E. C. Thomas Hardy. 1941 (G) E863

Bradley, W. A. William Cullen Bryant. 1905 (E) E864

Burdett, O. William Blake. 1926 (G) E865

Chesterton, G. K. Robert Browning. 1903 (E) E866

Church, R. W. Bacon. 1894 (B 6:3), 1895 (F) E867

———. Spenser. 1879 (A), 1894 (B 7:3), 1887 (C), 1884 (D), 1906 (F) E868

Colvin, S. Keats. 1894 (B 13:1), 1887 (F) E869

———. Landor. 1881 (A), 1894 (B 4:3), 1887 (C), 1888 (F) E870

Courthope, W. F. Addison. 1884 (A), 1894 (B 12:2), 1903 (E), 1911 (F) E871

Dobson, A. Fanny Burney. 1903 (F) E872

———. Fielding. 1887 (A), 1894 (B 5:3), 1907 (E) E873

———. Samuel Richardson. 1902 (E) E874

Dowden, E. Southey. 1902 (A), 1894 (B 2:1), 1887 (C), 1884 (D), 1906 (E) E875

Fowler, T. Locke. 1880 (A), 1894 (B 11:1), 1887 (C), 1884 (D), 1906 (E) E876

Freeman, J. Herman Melville. 1926 (G) E877

Froude, J. A. Bunyan. 1880 (A), 1894 (B 6:1), 1887 (C), 1884 (D), 1903 (E) E878

Gosse, E. W. Gray. 1887 (A), 1894 (B 11:3), 1889 (F) E879

———. Sir Thomas Browne. 1905 (F) E880

Gwynn, S. L. Robert Louis Stevenson. 1939 (E), 1939 (G) E881

———. Thomas Moore. 1905 (E), 1905 (F) E882

Harrison, F. John Ruskin. 1902 (F) E883

Higginson, T. W. John Greenleaf Whittier. 1902 (E) E884

Hirst, F. W. Adam Smith. 1904 (E), 1904 (F) E885

Hutton, R. H. Sir Walter Scott. 1879 (A), 1894 (B 7:1), 1887 (C), 1884 (D), 1903 (E) E886

Huxley, T. H. Hume. 1879 (A), 1894 (B 8:3), 1887 (C), 1884 (D), 1902 (E) E887

James, H. Hawthorne. 1907 (A), 1894 (B 13:2), 1887 (C), 1879 (F) E888

Jebb, R. C. Bentley. 1887 (A), 1894 (B:1), 1889 (F) E889

Lawless, E. Maria Edgeworth. 1904 (E) E890

Lyall, A. C. Tennyson. 1902 (E) E891

Macaulay, G. C. James Thomson. 1907 (E) E892

Masson, D. De Quincey. 1894 (B 9:3), 1887 (C), 1902 (F) E893

Minto, W. Defoe. 1879 (A), 1894 (B 2:3), 1887 (C), 1874 (D), 1885 (E) E894

Morison, J. A. C. Gibbons. 1879 (A), 1894 (B 1:2), 1887 (C), 1884 (D), 1904 (E) E895

———. Macaulay. 1883 (A), 1894 (B 5:2), 1887 (C), 1903 (E), 1882 (F) E896

Morley, J. M. Burke. 1879 (A), 1894 (B 5:1), 1887 (C), 1884 (D), 1928 (E), 1904 (F) E897

Myers, F. W. H. Wordsworth. 1881 (A), 1894 (B 10:2), 1887 (C), 1884 (D), 1906 (E) E898

Nichol, J. Byron. 1880 (A), 1894 (B 2:2), 1887 (C), 1884 (D), 1908 (E) E899

———. Thomas Carlyle. 1892 (A), 1894 (B 13:3), 1904 (F) E900

Nicolson, H. G. Swinburne. 1926 (E), 1926 (G) E901

Noyes, A. William Morris. 1908 (E) E902

Oliphant, M. O. (Wilson). Sheridan. 1887 (A), 1894 (B 12:3) E903

Pattison, M. Milton. 1880 (A), 1894 (B 1:1), 1887 (C), 1884 (D), 1911 (F) E904

Paul, H. W. Matthew Arnold. 1902 (E), 1902 (F) E905

Peck, H. T. William Hickling Prescott. 1905 (E) E906

Ponsonby, A. P. Samuel Pepys. 1928 (E), 1928 (G) E907

Priestley, J. B. George Meredith. 1926 (G) E908

____. Thomas Love Peacock. 1927 (E) E909

Raleigh, W. A. Shakespeare. 1907 (E) E910

Russell, G. W. E. Sydney Smith. 1904 (E) E911

Saintsbury, G. E. B. Dryden. 1894 (B 3:1), 1887 (C), 1906 (E) E912

Shairp, J. C. Robert Burns. 1879 (A), 1894 (B 10:3), 1887 (C), 1906 (F) E913

Shanks, E. Edgar Allan Poe. 1937 (G) E914

Smith, G. Cowper. 1880 (A), 1894 (B 4:2), 1880 (C), 1904 (E), 1898 (F) E915

Smith, G. G. Ben Jonson. 1919 (G) E916

Stephen, L. Alexander Pope. 1880 (A), 1894 (B 3:2), 1887 (C), 1884 (D), 1908 (F) E917

____. George Eliot. 1902 (E), 1902 (F) E918

____. Hobbes. 1904 (E) E919

____. Samuel Johnson. 1878 (A), 1894 (B 6:2), 1887 (C), 1884 (D), 1908 (F) E920

____. Swift. 1882 (A), 1894 (B 8:2), 1887 (C), 1882 (F) E921

Stuart, D. M. Christiana Rossetti. 1930 (E) E922

____. Horace Walpole. 1927 (G) E923

Symonds, J. A. Shelley. 1879 (A), 1894 (B 1:3), 1887 (C), 1884 (D), 1902 (F) E924

____. Sir Philip Sidney. 1887 (A), 1894 (B 3:3), 1906 (E), 1902 (F) E925

Traill, H. D. Coleridge. 1844 (A), 1894 (B 10:1), 1906 (F) E926

____. Sterne. 1887 (A), 1894 (B 8:1), 1889 (E) E927

Trollope, A. Thackeray. 1879 (A), 1894 (B 12:1), 1887 (C), 1906 (E) E928

Walpole, H. Anthony Trollope. 1928 (F), 1928 (G) E929

Ward, A. W. Chaucer. 1880 (A), 1894 (B 9:1), 1887 (C), 1884 (D), 1902 (F) E930

____. Dickens. 1887 (A), 1894 (B 7:2), 1906 (E), 1882 (F) E931

Warre Cornish, F. Jane Austen. 1914 (E) E932

Woodberry, G. E. Ralph Waldo Emerson. 1907 (E) E933

ENGLISH MONOGRAPHS (Nat'l. Council of Teachers of English)

1 Leonard, S. A. Current English usage. 1932. E934

2 Lewin, W. Photoplay appreciation in American high schools. 1934. E935

3 Campbell, O. J., comp. The teaching of college English. 1934. E936

4 National council of teachers of English. Curriculum commission. An experience curriculum in English. 1936. E937

5 National council of teachers of English. Committee on correlation. A correlated curriculum. 1936. E938

6 Center, S. S. and Persons, G. L. Teaching high-school students to read. 1937. E939

7 Marckwardt, A. H. and Walcott, F. G. Facts about current English usage. 1938. E940

8 National council of teachers of English. Conducting experiences in English by Broening and others. 1939. E941

9 National council of teachers of English. Committee on international relations. Education for peace. 1940. E942

10 Fries, C. C. American English grammar. 1940. E943

11 Smith, D. V. Evaluating instruction in secondary school English. 1941. E944

12 Child, E. D. and Finch, H. R. Producing school movies. 1941. E945

13 National council of teachers of English. Committee on individual differences.

Pupils are people. 1941. E946
14 Herzberg, M. J., ed. Radio and English teaching. 1941. E947
15 Kennedy, A. G. English usage. 1942. E948
16 Pooley, R. C. Teaching English usage. 1946. E949
17 National council of teachers of English. Committee on Reading at the Secondary School and College Levels. Reading in an age of mass communication, ed. by Gray. 1949. E950
18 Laird, C. G., ed. The world through literature. 1951. E951
Series discontinued.

ENGLISH NOVELISTS.

Ashley, R. Wilkie Collins. Roy. 1952. E952
Blake, G. Barrie and the kailyard school. Roy. 1952. E953
Brooke, J. Ronald Firbank. Roy. 1951. E954
Browne, N. Sheridan Le Fanu. Roy. 1951. E955
Campbell, O. W. Thomas Love Peacock. 1953. E956
Evans, M. George Gissing, 1857-1903. Barker. 1951. E957
Laski, M. Mrs. Ewing, Mrs. Moleworth and Mrs. Hodgson Burnett. Barker. 1950. E958
Speaight, R. George Eliot. 1954. E959
Swan, M. Henry James. Roy. 1952. E960
Symons, J. Charles Dickens. Roy. 1951. E961
West, A. P. D. H. Lawrence. Barker. 1951. E962
Includes also those listed under English Novelists (Denver).

THE ENGLISH NOVELISTS (DENVER) (Swallow)

Allen, W. E. Arnold Bennett. 1949. E963
Armstrong, M. D. George Borrow. 1950. E694
Bentley, P. E. The Brontës. 1947. E695
Brown, B. C. Anthony Trollope. 1950. E966
Cole, G. D. H. Samuel Butler and The way of all flesh. 1947. E967
Cooper, L. U. Robert Louis Stevenson. 1948. E968
Croft-Cooke, R. Rudyard Kipling. 1948. E969
Ffrench, Y. Mrs. Gaskell. 1949. E970
Hawkins, D. Thomas Hardy. 1951. E971
Jenkins, E. Henry Fielding. 1948. E972
Kennedy, M. Jane Austen. 1950. E973
Lytton, E. R. B-L. Bulwer-Lytton. 1948. E974
Newby, P. H. Maria Edgeworth. 1950. E975
Nicholson, N. H. G. Wells. 1950. E976
Pope-Hennessy, Dame U. (Birch). Sir Walter Scott. 1949. E977
Originally published in England by Home and Van Thal.

ENGLISH NOVELISTS (LONDON) (Home)

Laski, M. Mrs. Ewing, Mrs. Moleworth and Mrs. Hodgson Burnett. 1950. E978
West, A. P. D. H. Lawrence. Barker. 1951. E979
Includes also those listed under English Novelists (Denver).

ENGLISH PLACE-NAME SOCIETY, SURVEY OF ENGLISH PLACE-NAMES (Cambridge)

1 Mawer, A. and Stenton, F. M., eds. Introduction to the survey of English place-names. 1924. E980
2 ____. The place-names of Buckinghamshire. 1925. E981
3 ____. The place-names of Bedfordshire & Huntingdonshire. 1926. E982
4 Mawer, A. and others, ed. The place-names of Worcestershire. 1927. E983
5 Smith, A. H., ed. The place-names of North Riding of Yorkshire. 1928. E984

6-7 Mawer, A. and others, eds. The place-names of Sussex. 2 pts. 1929-30. E985
8-9 Gover, J. E. B. and others, eds. The place-names of Devon. 2 pts. 1931-32. E986
10 ____. The place-names of Northamptonshire. 1933. E987
11 ____. The place-names of Surrey. 1934. E988
12 Reaney, P. H., ed. The place-names of Essex. 1935. E989
13 Gover, J. E. B. and others, eds. The place-names of Warwickshire. 1936. E990
14 Smith, A. H., eds. The place-names of the East Riding of Yorkshire and York. 1937. E991
15 Gover, J. E. B. and others, eds. The place-names of Hertfordshire. 1938. E992
16 ____. The place-names of Wiltshire. 1939. E993
17 ____. The place-names of Nottinghamshire. 1940. E994
18 ____. The place-names of Middlesex. 1942. E995
19 Reaney, P. H., ed. The place-names of Cambridgeshire and the Isle of Ely. 1943. E996
20-22 The place-names of Cumberland, by Armstrong and others. 3 v. 1950-53. E997
23-24 Gelling, M. The place-names of Oxfordshire. 1954. E998
25-26 Smith, A. L. English place-name elements. 2 v. 1956. E999
27-29 Cameron, K. The place-names of Derbyshire. 3 v. 1959. E1000
30-37 Smith, A. H. The place-names of the West Riding of Yorkshire. 7 v. 1961-62. E1001
38-41 ____. The place-names of Gloucestershire. 4 v. 1964-65. E1002
42-43 ____. The place-names of Westmorland. 2 v. 1967. E1003
44-48 Dodgson, J. McN., ed. The place-names of Cheshire. 4 pts. 1970-71. E1004
49 Gelling, M. The place-names of Berkshire. V. 1. 1973. E1005

EPOCHEN DER DEUTSCHEN LITERATUR (Metzler)

1 Golther, W. Die deutsche dichtung im mittelalter (800-1500). 1949. E1006
2 t. 1 Stammler, W. Von der Mystik zum Barock 1400-1600. 1950. E1007
T. 2 Hankamer, P. Deutsche gegenreformation und deutsches barock. 1947. E1008
3 t. 1 Schneider, F. J. Die deutsche dichtung der Aufklärungszeit. 1948. E1009
T. 2 Schneider, F. J. Die deutsche Dichtung der Geniezeit. 1952. E1010
4 t. 1 Schultz, F. Klassik und romantik der deutschen. Die Grundlagen der klassischromantischen literatur. 1959. E1011
T. 2 Schultz, F. Klassik und romantik der deutschen. Wesen und form en der klassisch-romantischen literatur. 1959. E1012
5 t. 1 Bieber, H. Der kampf um die tradition, die deutsche dichtung im europäischen geistesleben, 1830-1880. 1928. E1013
T. 2 Martini, F. Deutsche literatur im bürgerlichen realismus, 1848-1898. E1014
6 Naumann, H. Die deutsche dichtung der gegenwart, Vom Naturalismus bis zum Expressionismus. 1933. E1015
7 Ruprecht, E. Literarische manifeste des naturalismus 1880-1892. 1962. E1016

EPOCHS OF AMERICAN HISTORY (Longman)

1 Thwaites, R. G. Colonies. 1915. (later replaced by Jernegan, M. W. The American colonies (1492-1750). 1929. E1017
2 Hart, A. B. Formation of

the Union, 1750-1829. 1937. E1018
3 Wilson, W. Division and reunion. 1926. E1019
4 Bassett, J. S. Expansion and reform. 1926. E1020

ERGEBNISSE DER ANGEWANDTEN MATHEMATIK (Springer) (Continued as SPRINGER TRACTS IN NATURAL PHILOSOPHY)

1 Büchner, H. Die praktische Behandlung von Integral-Gleischungen. 1952. E1021
2 Buchholz, H. Die konfluente hypergeometrische Funktion. 1953. E1022
3 Dorfner, K. R. Dreidimensionale Überschallprobleme der Gasdynamik. 1957. E1023
4 Franz, W. Theorie der Beugung elektromagnetische Wellem. 1957. E1024
5 Kröner, E. Kontinuumstheorie der Versetzungen und Eigenspannungen. 1958. E1025
6 Milne-Thomson, L. M. Plane elastic systems. 1960. E1026
7 Grioli, G. Mathematical theory of elastic equilibrium. 1962. E1027
8 Milne-Thomson, L. M. Antiplane elastic system. 1962. E1028

ERGEBNISSE DER MATHEMATIK UND IHRER GRENZGEBIETE (Springer 1932-35: Chelsea 1936-54) (Springer, 1955-)

1:1 Reidemeister, K. Knotentheorie. 1932. E1029
1:2 Federhofer, K. Graphische kinematik und kindetostatik. 1932. E1030
1:3 Strutt, M. J. O. Lamésche-Mathiensche und verwandte funktionen in physik und technik. 1932. E1031
1:4 Hohenenser, K. Die Methoden zur ängenaherten Lösung von Eigenwert-problemen in der Elastokinetik. 1932. E1032
1:5 Bohr, H. A. Fastperiodische funktionen. 1932. E1033
2:1 Veblen, O. Projektive relativitätstheories. 1933. E1034
2:2 Radó, T. On the problem of Plateau. 1933. E1035
2:3 Kolmogarov, A. N. Grundbegriffe der wahrscheinlich-keitsrechnung. 1933. E1036
2:4 Khīnchīn, A. I. Asymptotische gesetze der Wahrscheinlichkeitsrechnung. 1948. E1037
2:5 MacDuffee, C. D. The theory of matrices. 1933. E1038
3:1 Bonnesen, T. Theorie der konvexen körper. 1934. E1039
3:2 Struik, D. J. Theory of linear connections. 1934. E1040
3:3 Behnke, H. Theorie der Funktionen meherer komplexer Veränderlichen. 1934. E1041
3:4 Heyting, A. Mathematische grundlagenforschung. 1934. E1042
3:5 Zariski, O. Algebraic surfaces. 1948. E1043
4:1 Deuring, M. Algebren. 1935. E1044
4:2 Waerden, B. L. von der. Gruppen von linearen transformationen. 1948. E1045
4:3 Krull, W. Ideal theorie. 1948. E1046
4:4 Koksma, J. F. Diophantische approximationen. 1936. E1047
4:5 Carathéodory, C. Geometrische optik. 1937. E1048
5:1 Radó, T. Subharmonic functions. 1949. E1049
5:2 Hopf, E. Ergodentheorie. 1948. E1050
5:3 Ertel, H. Methoden und probleme der dynamischen meteorologie. 1938. E1051
5:4 Skolem, T. Diophantische gleichunzen. 1950. E1052
5:5 Nagy, B. S. Spektraldarstellung linearer transformationen. 1942. E1053
Neue folge:
1 Bachmann, H. Transfinite Zahlen. 1955. E1054
2 Miranda, C. Equazioni alle derivate parziali di tipo ellittico. 1955. E1055

3 Bierberbach, L. Analytische Fortsetzung. 1955. E1056
4 Samuel, P. Méthodes d'algèbre abstraite en géométrie algébrique. 1955. E1057
5 Dieundonné, J. La géométrie des groupes classiques. 1955. E1058
6 Roth, L. Algebraic threefolds. 1955. E1059
7 Ostmann, H. H. Additive Zahlentheorie. V. 1. 1956. E1060
8 Wittich, H. Neuere untersuchungen über eindeutige analytische funktionen. 1955. E1061
9 Hirzebruch, F. Neue topologische Methoden in der algebraischen Geometrie. 1962. E1062
10 Suzuki, M. Structure of a group and the structure of its lattice of subgroups. 1956. E1063
11 Same as no. 7. V. 2. 1956. E1064
12 Baldassari, M. Algebraic varities. 1956. E1065
13 Segre, B. Some properties of differentiable varities and transformations... 1957. E1066
14 Coxeter, H. S. M. and Moser, W. O. J. Generators and relations for discrete groups. 1957. E1067
15 Zeller, K. Theorie der Limitierungsverfahren. 1958. E1068
16 Cesari, L. Asymptotic behavior and stability problems in ordinary differential equations. 1958. E1069
17 Severi, F. Il teorema di Riemann-Roch per curve, superficie e varietà; questioni collegate. 1958. E1070
18 Jenkins, J. A. Univalent functions and conformal mapping. 1958. E1071
19 Boas, R. P. and Buck, R. C. Polynomial expansions of analytic functions. 1958. E1072
20 Bruck, R. H. A survey of binary systems. 1958. E1073
21 Day, M. M. Normad linear spaces. 1962. E1074
22 Hahn, W. Theorie und Anwendung der direkten Methode von Ljapunov. 1959. E1075
23 Bergman, S. Integral operators in the theory of linear partial differential equations. 1961. E1076
24 Kappos, D. A. Strukturtheorie der Wahrescheinlichkeitsfelder und-räume. 1960. E1077
25 Sikorski, R. Boolean algebras. 1960. E1078
26 Künzi, H. P. Quasikonforme Abbildungen. 1960. E1079
27 Schatten, R. Norm ideals of completely continuous operators. 1960. E1080
28 Noshiro, K. Cluster sets. 1960. E1081
29 Jacobs, K. Neuere Methoden und Ergebnisse der Ergodentheorie. 1960. E1082
30 Beckenbach, L. F. and Bellman, R. Inequalities. 1961. E1083
31 Wolfowitz, J. Coding theorems of information theory. 1961. E1084
32 Constantinescu, C. Ideale Ränder Riemannscher Flachen von Corneliu Constantinescu und Aurel Cornea. 1963. E1085
33 Conner, P. E. and Floyd, E. E. Differentiable periodic maps. 1964. E1086
34 Mumford, D. Geometric invariant theory. 1965. E1087
35 Gabriel, P. and Zisman, M. Categories of fractions and homotopy theory. 1965. E1088
36 Putnam, C. R. Commutation properties of Hilbert space operators. 1966. E1089
37 Neumann, H. Varieties of groups. 1966. E1090
38 Boas, R. P. Integrability theorems for trigonometric transforms. 1967. E1091
39 Szokefalvi-Nagy, B. Spektraldarstellung linearer Transformationes des Hilbertschen Raumes. 1967. E1092
40 Seligman, G. B. Modular

lie algebras. 1967. E1093
41 Deuring, M. Algebren. 1968. E1094
42 Schutte, K. Vollständige systeme modaler und intuitionistischer logik. 1968. E1095
43 Smullyan, R. M. First-order logic. 1968. E1096
44 Dembrowski, P. Finite geometries. 1968. E1097
45 Linnik, Y. V. Ergodic properties of algebraic fields. 1968. E1098
46 Krull, W. Idealtheorie. 1968. E1099
47 Nachbin, L. Topology on spaces of holomorphic mappings. 1968. E1100
48 Ionescu Tulcea, A. and C. Topics in the theory of lifting. 1969. E1101
49 Hayes, C. A. and Pauc, C. Y. Derivation and martingales. 1969. E1102
50 Kahane, J. P. Series de Fourier absolument convergentes. 1970. E1103
51 Behnke, H. and Thellen, P. Theorie der funktionen mehrerer komplexer veränderlichen. 2d ed. 1970. E1104
52 Wilf, H. S. Finite sections of the classical inequalities. 1970. E1105
53 Ramis, J. P. Sous-ensembles analytiques d'une variété banachique complexe. 1970. E1106
54 Buseman, H. Recent synthetic differential geometry. 1970. E1107
55 Walter, W. Differential and integral inequalities, tr. by Rosenblatt and Shampine. 1970. E1108
56 Monna, A. F. Analyse nonarchimedienne. 1970. E1109
57 Alfsen, E. M. Compact convex sets and boundary integrals. 1971. E1110
58 Greco, S. and Salmon, P. Topics in m-adic topologies. 1971. E1111
59 Lopez de Medrano, S. Involutions on manifolds. 1971. E1112
60 Sakai, S. C*-algebras and W*-algebras. 1971. E1113
61 Zariski, O. Algebraic surfaces. Supp. 1971. E1114
62-63 Robinson, D. J. S. Finiteness conditions and generalized soluble groups. 1974. E1115
64 Hakim, M. Topos annelés et schémas relatifs. 1972. E1116
65 Browder, W. Surgery on simply-connected manifolds. 1972. E1117
66 Pieatsch, A. Nuclear locality convex spaces, tr. by Ruckle. 1972. E1118
67 Dellacherie, C. Capacités et processus stochestiques. 1972. E1119
68 Raghunathan, M. S. Discrete subgroups of lie groups. 1972. E1120
69 Rourke, C. P. and Sanderson, B. J. Introduction to piecewise linear topology. 1972. E1121
70 Kobayashi, S. Transformation groups in differential geometry. 1972. E1122
71 Tougeron, J. C. Idéaux de fonctions différentiables. 1972. E1123
72 Gikhman, I. I. and Skorohod, A. V. Stochastic differential equations, tr. by Wickshire. 1972. E1124
73 Milnor, J. W. and Husemoller, D. Symmetric bilinear forms. 1973. E1125
74 Fossum, R. M. The divisor class group of a Krull domain. 1973. E1126
75 Springer, T. A. Jordan algebras and algebraic groups. 1973. E1127
76 Wehrfritz, B. A. F. Infinite linear groups. 1973. E1128
77 Radjavi, H. and Rosenthal, P. Invariant subspaces. 1973. E1129
78 Bognar, J. Indefinite inner product spaces. 1974. E1130
79 Korohod, A. Integration in Hilbert space. 1974. E1131
80 Bonsall, F. F. and Duncan, J. Complete normed algebras. 1973. E1132

81 Crossler, J. N. and Nerode, A. A combinatorial functors. 1974. E1133

ESSAYS IN DIVINITY (Univ. of Chicago Pr.)

1 The history of religions, by Wach and others, ed. by Ketagawa and others. 1967. E1134
2 The impact of the church, by Brun and others, ed. by Brauer. 1968. E1135
3 The dialogue between theology and psychology, ed. by Aden and others, ed. by Homans. 1968. E1136
4 Adversity and grace, by Browning and others, ed. by Scott. 1968. E1137
5 Brauer, J. C., ed. Reinterpretation in American church history, by Beaver and others. 1968. E1138
6 Rylaarsdam, J. C. Transitions in biblical scholarship. 1968. E1139
7 Meland, B. E. Future of empirical theology. 1969. E1140

THE ETHICS AND ECONOMICS OF SOCIETY (Harper)

Boulding, K. E. The organizational revolution. 1953. E1141
Bowen, H. R. Social responsibilities of businessmen. 1953. E1142
Childs, M. W. and Cater, D. Ethics in a business society. 1954. E1143
Christian values and economic life, by Bennett and others. 1954. E1144
Fitch, J. A. Social responsibilities of organized labor. 1957. E1145
Hoyt, E. E. and others. American income and its use. 1954. E1146
Johnson, F. E. and Ackerman, J. E. The church as employer, money raiser, and investor. 1959. E1147
Obenhaus, V. Ethics for an industrial age. 1965. E1148
Schramm, W. L. Responsibility in mass communication. 1969. E1149
Ward, A. D., ed. Goals of economic life. 1953. E1150
____ and others. The American economy-attitudes and opinions. 1955. E1151
Wilcox, W. W. Social responsibility in farm leadership. 1956. E1152

ETHNIC CHRONOLOGY SERIES (Oceana)

1 Dennis, H. C., comp. The American Indian, 1492-1970. 1971. E1153
2 Sloan, I. J., comp. Blacks in America, 1492-1970. 1971. E1154
3 ____. Jews in America, 1621-1970. 1971. E1155
4 LoGatto, A. F., comp. The Italians in America, 1492-1972. 1972. E1156
5 Smit, J. W., comp. The Dutch in America, 1609-1970. 1972. E1157
6 Furer, H. B., comp. The Scandinavians in America, 986-1970. 1972. E1158
7 ____. The British in America, 1578-1970. 1972. E1159
8 Furer, H. B., comp. The Germans in America, 1607-1970. 1973. E1160
9 Renkiewicz, F., comp. The Poles in America, 1608-1972. 1973. E1161
10 Griffin, W. D., comp. The Irish in America, 550-1972. 1973. E1162
11 Cordasco, F., comp. The Puerto Ricans, 1497-1973. 1973. E1163
12 Natella, A. A. The Spanish in America. 1974. E1164
13 Karklis, M. and others. The Latvians in America. 1974. E1165
14 Tung, W. L. The Chinese in America. 1974. E1166
15 Herman, M. The Japanese in America. 1974. E1167

ETRE ET PENSER, CAHIERS DE PHILOSOPHIE (Edition de la Baconnière)

1 L'homme. I. Métaphysique et transcendance. 1943. E1168
2 Muller, M. De Descartes à Marcel Proust. 1943. E1169
3 Segond, J. L. P. Valeurs de la prière. 1943. E1170
4-5 Odier, C. Les deux sources consciente et inconsciente de la vie morale. 1947. E1171
6 Wahl, J. A. Existence humaine et transcendance. 1944. E1172
7 Schaerer, R. Dieu, l'homme et la vie d'après Platon. 1944. E1173
8 Porret, E. La philosophie chrétienne en Russie, Nicolas Berdiaeff. 1944. E1174
9 Lacroix, J. Le sens du dialogue. 1944. E1175
10 Christoff, D. Le temps et les valeurs. 1945. E1176
11 Magny, C-E. Les sandales d'Empédocle, essai sur les limites de la littérature. 1945. E1177
12 Brunschvicg, L. Descartes et Pascal, lecteurs de Montaigne. 1945. E1178
13 Delanglade, J. Signe et symbole. 1946. E1179
14 Hersch, J. L'être et la forme. 1946. E1180
15 Muller, P. De la psychologie à l'anthropologie. 1946. E1181
16 Baudin, E. La philosophie de Pascal. 1946. E1182
17 ____. Pascal et Descartes. 1946. E1183
18 ____. Pascal, les Libertins et les Jansenistes. 1946. E1184
19 ____. Pascal et la casuistique. 1946. E1185
20 Brunschvicg, L. L'esprit européen. 1946. E1186
21 Guillermit, L. Le sens du destin. 1948. E1187
22 Losskiî, N. O. Des conditions de la morale absolue. 1948. E1188
23 Wavre, F. L'imagination du réel. 1948. E1189
24 Burger, J. D. Saint Augustin. 1948. E1190
25 Piguet, J. C. Découverte de la musique. 1948. E1191
26 Mottier, G. Detérminisme et liberté, essai sur les sources métaphysiques du dêbat. 1948. E1192
27 L'homme. Metaphysique et conscience de soi. 1948. E1193
28 Jankélévitch, V. Debussy et le mystère. 1949. E1194
29 Congres des sociétés de philosophie de langue française. La liberté. 1949. E1195
30 Deucalion... cahier publié sous la direction de Jean Wahl. V. 3. Verité et liberté. 1950. E1196
31 Wavre, R. La figure de monde. 1950. E1197
32 Le Problème de la vie par Emile Guyénot et al. 1951. E1198
33-34 Lequier, J. Oeuvres complètes. 1952. E1199
35 Vial, J. De l'être musical. 1952. E1200
36 Same as no. 30. V. 4. Le diurne et la nocturne. 1953. E1201
37 Kelsen, H. Théorie pure du droit, tr. by Thévenaz. 1953. E1202
38 Bollnow, O. F. Les tonalités affectives, tr. by L. and R. Savioz. 1954. E1203
39 Bourjade, J. Principes et caractériologie. 1954. E1204
40 Same as no. 30. V. 5. Etudes hégéliennes. E1205
41-43 Maine de Biran, P. Journal, ed. by Gouhier. 3 v. 1954. E1206
44 Pucelle, J. L'idéalisme en Angleterre de Coleridge à Bradley. 1955. E1207
45 Wust, P. Incertitude et risque, tr. by du Loup. 1957. E1208
46-47 Thévenaz, P. L'homme et sa raison. 2 v. 1956. E1209
48 Same as no. 30. V. 6. Art et le Jeu. 1958. E1210
49 Muller, M. Idées et archetypes de Platon à Elie

des marchés des produits de base. 1959. E1244
29 Gabbay, R. E. A political study of the Arab-Jewish conflict. 1959. E1245
30 Gobineau, J. A. de. Les dépêches diplomatiques du comte de Gobineau en Perse, ed. by Hytier. 1959. E1246
31 Knapp, B. Le système préférentiel et les etats tiers. 1959. E1247
32 Same as no. 26. V. 2. 1960. E1248
33 Albrecht-Carrie, R. France, Europe and the two world wars. 1960. E1249
34 Kassem, B. Decadence et absolutisme dans l'oeuvre de Montesquieu. 1960. E1250
35 Cohen, A. La Société des Nations devant le conflict italo-ethiopien. 1960. E1251
36 Hüsler, A. Contribution à l'étude de l'élaboration de la politique étranagère britannique. 1961. E1252
37 Mawrizki, S. L'industrie lourde en Union soviétique. 1961. E1253
38 Botzaris, N. Visions balkaniques dans la préparation de la révolution grecque, 1789-1821. 1962. E1254
39 Reiser, P. L'organisation régionale interaméricaine des travailleurs de la confédération internationale des syndicats libres de 1951 à 1961. 1962. E1255
40 Rihs, C. Voltaire. 1962. E1256
41 Fontela Montes, E. Commerce extérieur et développement économique. 1962. E1257
42 Ilams, T. M. Dreyfus, diplomatists and the dual alliance. 1962. E1258
43 Ton That Thien. India and South East Asia, 1947-1960. 1963. E1259
44 Farajallah, S. B. Le Groupe afro-asiatique dans le cadre des Nations Unies. 1963. E1260
45 Chatterjee, I. Economic development, payments deficit and payment restriction. 1963. E1261
46 Friedländer, S. Hitler et les Etats-Unis, 1939-1941. 1963. E1262
47 Sosa-Rodrigues, R. Les problèmes structurels des relations économiques internationales de l'Ameriques latine. 1963. E1263
48 Ferron, O. de. Le problème des transports et le Marché Commun. 1965. E1264
49 Fiechter, J. J. Le socialisme français. 1965. E1265
50 Reszler, A. Le National-Socialisme dans le roman contemporain, 1933-1958. 1966. E1266

ETUDES D'HISTOIRE ET DE PHILOSOPHIE RELIGIEUSES. CAHIERS (1922-40 Istra, 1940- Presses universitaires de France)

1 Strohl, H. L'Evolution religieuse de Luther jusqu'en 1515. 1922. E1267
2 Vermeil, E. La pensée religieuse d'Ernest Troeltsche. 1922. E1268
3 Caussé, A. Les "pauvres" d'Israël. 1922. E1269
4 Will, R. La liberté chrétienne. 1922. E1270
5 Hauter, C. Religion et réalité. 1922. E1271
6 Pannier, J. L'Eglise réformée de Paris sous Louis XIII. 1922. E1272
7 Gerold, C. T. La faculté de théologie et le séminaire protestant de Strasbourg. 1923. E1273
8 Causse, A. Israël et la vision de l'humanité. 1923. E1274
9 Strohl, H. L'epanouissement de la pensée religieuse de Luther. 1924. E1275
10 Will, R. Le culte. V. 1. 1924. E1276
11 Pommier, J. Renan et Strasbourg. 1926. E1277
12 Fridrichsen, A. Le miracle, problème du nouveau testament. 1925. E1278
13 Ménégoz, F. Le problème

de la prière. 1932. E1279
14 Causse, A. Les plus vieux chants de la Bible. 1926. E1280
15 Hering, J. Phénoménologie et philosophie religieuse. 1926. E1281
16 Mowindkel, S. Le décalogue. 1927. E1282
17 Hauter, C. Essai sur l'objet religieux. 1928. E1283
18 Bill, A. La morale et la loi dans la philosophie antique. 1928. E1284
19 Causse, A. Les dispersés d'Israël. 1928. E1285
20 Schweizer, J. Le cardinal Louis de Lapalud et son procès. 1929. E1286
21 Same as no. 10. V. 2. 1929. E1287
22 Eppel, R. Le piétisme juif dans les testaments des douze patriarches. 1930. E1288
23 Cullmann, O. Le problème littéraire et historique du roman pseudo-Clémentin. 1930. E1289
24 Ménégoz, F. Réflexions sur le problème de Dieu. 1931. E1290
25 Gérold, T. Les pères de l'égise et la musique. 1931. E1291
26 Coman, J. L'idée de la némésis chez Eschyle. 1951. E1292
27 Wencelius, L. La philosophie de l'art chez les néo-scolastiques français. 1933. E1293
28 Courvoisier, J. La notion d'église chez Bucer. 1933. E1294
29 Same as no. 10. V. 3. 1935. E1295
30 Baldensperger, G. Le tombeau vide. 1935. E1296
31 Monod, V. Dévalorisation de l'homme. 1935. E1297
32 Pannier, J. Les origines de la confession de foi et la discipline des églises réformées de France. 1936. E1298
33 Causse, A. Du groupe ethnique a la communauté religieuse. 1937. E1299
34 Scherding, P. Christophe Blumhardt et son père. 1937. E1300
35 Héring, J. Le royaume de Dieu et sa venue d'apres Jesus et St. Paul. 1937. E1301
36 Cailliet, E. Mysticisme et "mentalité mystique." 1938. E1302
37 Benoît, J. D. Direction spirituelle et protestantisme. 1941. E1303
38 Wendel, F. L'église de Strasbourg, sa constitution et son organisation 1532-1535. 1942. E1304
39 Ménégoz, F. Le Christianisme. 1943. E1305
40 Clavier, H. L'accès au Royaume de Dieu. 1944. E1306
41 Wendel, F. Calvin. 1950. E1307
42 Cullman, O. Les sacrements dans l'Evangile johannique. 1951. E1308
43 Benoît, A. La baptème chrétien au second siècle; la théologie des Pères. 1953. E1309
44 Voeltzel, R. Vraie et fausee église selon les théologiens protestants française du XVIIe siècle. 1956. E1310
45 Strohl, H. Luther jusqu'en 1520. 1962. E1311
46 Shestov, L. Sola fide: Luther et l'église. 1957. E1312
47 Prunet, O. La morale chrétienne d'après les écrits johanniques. 1957. E1313
49 Chevallier, M. L'ésprit et le Messie, dans le bas-judaisme et le Nouveau Testament. 1958. E1314
50 Lys, D. Nephesh. 1959. E1315
51 Burgelin, P. Commentaire du discourse de metaphysique de Leibniz. 1959. E1316
52 Benoît, A. Saint Irénée. 1960. E1317
53 Voetzel, R. Education et révélation. 1960. E1318
54 Boutteir, M. En Christ. 1962. E1319
55 Strohl, H. Luther jusqu'en 1520. 1962. E1320

56 Lys, D. Rûach. 1962. E1321
58 Cyprianus, St. L'oraison dominicale, ed. by Reveilland. 1964. E1322
60 Gounelle, A. L' "Entretien de Pascal avec M. de Sacy." 1966. E1323
61 Prunet, O. La morale de Clement d'Alexandrie et le Nouveau Testament. 1966. E1324
62 Tagawa, K. Miracles et Evangile. 1966. E1325
63 Gabus, J. P. Introduction à la théologie de la culture de Paul Tillich. 1969. E1326

ETUDES DE LITTERATURE ETRANGERE ET COMPAREE (1-24 Boivin; 25- Didier)

1 Merimée, P. Lettres à Fanny Lagdon, ed. by Connes and Trahard. 1938. E1327
2 Portier, L. Antonio Fogazzaro. 1937. E1328
3 Mackay, M. E. Meredith et la France. 1937. E1329
4 Arrighi, P. La vérisme dans le prose narrative italienne. 1937. E1330
5 ____. La poésie vériste en Italie. 1937. E1331
6 Fogazzaro, A. Poésies, tr. by Portier. 1937. E1332
7 Jourda, P. L'exotisme dans la littérature française depuis Chateaubriand. 1938. E1333
8 Taylor, A. C. Carlyle et la pensée latins. 1937. E1334
9 ____. Le président de Brosse et l'Australie. 1938. E1335
10 Michel, V. C. M. Wieland. 1938. E1336
11 Bowe, M. C. François Rio. 1938. E1337
12 Brosses, C. de. Le président de Brosse et ses amis de Genève, ed. by Bezard. 1939. E1338
13 Rouillard, C. D. The Turk in French history, thought and literature 1510-1660. 1941. E1339
14 Simon, J. Herman Melville. 1939. E1340
15 ____. La polynésie dans la littérature. 1939. E1341
16 Lemaître, H. Essai sur le mythe de Psyché dans la litérature français. 1939. E1342
17 Tuzet, H. Voyageurs français en Sicile, 1802-48. 1945. E1343
18 Dédéyan, C. Montaigne chez ses amis anglo-saxons. 1944. E1344
19 ____. Essai sur le journal de voyage de Montaigne. 1944. E1345
20 Gennari, G. Le premier voyage di Mme. de Staël en Italie. 1947. E1346
21 Roddier, H. J.-J. Rousseau en Angleterre au XVIIIe siècle. 1950. E1347
22 UNESCO. General conference. Actes du IV Congres d'histoire litterature. 3 v. 1948. E1348
23 Knight, R. C. Racine et la Grèce. 1950. E1349
24 Greene, E. J. H. T. S. Eliot et la France. 1951. E1350
25 Mouraud, M. Une irlandaise liberale en France sous la restauration: Lady Morgan. 1954. E1351
26 Escarpit, R. L'Angleterre dans l'oeuvre de Madam de Staël. 1954. E1352
27 Dale, E. H. La poésie française en Angleterre, 1850-1890. 1954. E1353
28 Mortier, R. Un précurseur de Madame de Staël: Charles Vanderbourg. 1955. E1354
29 Guyard, M. F. La Grande-Bretagne dans le roman française, 1914-1940. 1954. E1355
30 Boucher, M. La Revolution de 1789 vue par les écrivains allemands, ses contemporains. 1954. E1356
31 Voisine, J.-J. J. Rousseau en Angleterre à l'époque romantique. 1956. E1357
32 Dédéyan, C. Stendhal et les Chroniques italiennes. 1956. E1358
33 Dresch, J. Heine a Paris, d'après sa

correspondance et les tepoignages de ses contemporains. 1956. E1359
34 Congrès National de Littérature Comparee, Bordeaux, 1956. Littérature generale et histoire des idées. 1958. E1360
35 Second Congrès National de Littérature Comparee, 1957. Actes. 1958. E1361
36 Tissier, A. M. de Crac. 1959. E1362
37 Maixner, R. Charles Nodier et l'Illyrie. 1960. E1363
38 Samic', M. Les voyageurs français en Bosnie. 1960. E1364
39 Sicroff, A. A. Les controverses des statuts de "pureté de sang." en Espagne du XVe au XVIe siècle. 1960. E1365
40 Third Congrès National de Littérature Comparee, Dijon, 1959. La France, la Bourgogne, et la Suisse au XVIIIe siècle. 1960. E1366
41 Parreaux, A. The publication of The monk. 1960. E1367
42 Bataillon, M. La Cèlestine selon Fernando de Rojas. 1961. E1368
43 Fourth Congrès National de Littèrature Comparee. Espagne et littèrature. 1962. E1369
44 Jeune, S. De F. T. Graindorge à A. O. Barnabooth les types Américains dans le roman et la theatre français (1861-1917). 1963. E1370
45 Watkin, M. La civilisation française dans les Mabinogion. 1962. E1371
46 Congrès national de littérature comparée. Imprimerie, commerce et littérature. 1965. E1372
47 Bousquet, J. Les thèmes du reve dans la littérature romantique. 1964. E1373
48 Smit, W. A. P. and Brachin, P. Vondel, 1587-1679. 1964. E1374
49 Congrès national de littérature comparée. Littérature savante et littérature populaire. 1964. E1375
50 Connaissance de l'etranger. 1964. E1376
51 Mazon, A. Deux Russes écrivains français. 1964. E1377
52 Ibrovac, M. Claude Fauriel et la fortune européenne des poesies populaires grecque et serbe. 1966. E1378
53 Congrès national de littérature comparée. Moyen âge et littérature comparée. 1967. E1379
54 Cros, E. Portee et Le Gueux. 1967. E1380
55 Munteano, B. Constantes dialectiques en litterature et en histoire. 1967. E1381
56 Corbet, C. L'opinion française face à l'inconnue russe. 1967. E1382
57 Munteano, B. Constantes dialectiques en littérature et en histoire. 1968. E1383
58 Dumont, R. Stefan Zweig et la France. 1967. E1384
59 Cermakian, M. La princesse des Ursins. 1969. E1385
60 Congrès national de littérature comparée. L'italianisme en France au XVIIIe siècle. 1970. E1386
61 Louca, A. Voyageurs et écrivains égyptiens en France au XIXe siècle. 1970. E1387
62 Genuist, A. Le théâtre de Shakespeare dans l'oeuvre de Pierre Le Tourneur. 1971. E1388
63 Munoz, M. B. de. La guerre civile espagnole et la littérature française. 1972. E1389
64 Bromfield, J. C. De Lorenzino de Medicis à Lorenzaccio. 1972. E1390
65 Duvivier, R. Le dynamisme existentiel de Jean de la Croix. 1972. E1391
66 Amblard, M. C. L'OEuvre fantastique de Balzac. 1972. E1392
67 Larbaud, V. Correspondance, 1923-1952 de Valery Larbaud et Alfonso Reyes,

ed. by Patout. 1972. E1393
68 Huvos, K. Cinq mirages américains. 1972. E1394
69 Herr, E. Les origines de l'Espagne romantique. 1974. E1395
70 Monaco, M. Shakespeare on the French stage in the 18th century. 1974. E1396

ETUDES DE PHILOLOGIE ET D'HISTOIRE (Droz)

1 Huguet, E. L'évolution du sens des mots depuis le XVIe siècle. 1967. E1397
2 ____. Mots disparus ou vieillis depuis le XVIe siècle. 1967. E1398
3 Hauben, P. J. Three Spanish heretics and the Reformation. 1967. E1399
4 Screech, M. A. Marot évangelique. 1967. E1400
5 Pommier, J. La mystique de Marcel Proust. 1968. E1401
6 Ashley, L. R. N. Authorship and evidence. 1968. E1402
7 Beer, J. M. A. Villehardouin. 1968. E1403
8 Raitière, A. L'interpretation dramatique selon Dorat et Samson. 1968. E1404
9 Dimaras, C. T. La Grèce au temps des Lumières. 1969. E1405
10 Secret, F. L'ésotérisme de Guy Le Fèvre se La Boderie. 1969. E1406
11 Bakhuizen van den Brink, J. N. Juan de Valdes réformateur en Espagne et en Italie. 1969. E1407
12 Monnier, L. Généve et l'Italie. 1969. E1408
13 Ganoczy, A. La bibliothèque de l'Académie de Calvin. 1969. E1409
14 Gaubil, L. P. Correspondance sur la Chine, ed. by Simon. 1969. E1410
15 Cottrell, R. D. Brantôme. 1970. E1411
16 Secret, F. Bibliographie des manuscrits de Guillaume Postel. 1970. E1412
17 Luppe, R. de. Madame de Staël et J.-B.-A. Suard. 1970. E1413
18 Medlin, W. K. and Patrimelis, C. G. Renaissance influence and religious reforms in Russia. 1970. E1414
19 Balayé, S. Les carnets de voyage de Madame de Staël. E1415
20 Schwartzbach, B. E. Voltaire's Old Testament criticism. 1971. E1416
21 Fraser, T. P. Le Duchat first editor of Rabelais. 1971. E1417
22 Kirness, W. J. Le français de théâtre italien. 1971. E1418
23 Busino, G. Histoire et société en Italie. 1972. E1419
24 Calame, A. Anne de Roc he-Guilhen. 1973. E1420
25 Proust, J., ed. Recherches nouvelles sur quelques écrivains des Lumières. 1972. E1421
26 Dupuy, C. De Thou and the index, ed. by Soman. 1972. E1422
27 Smith, M. Joachim Du Bellay's veiled victim. 1974. E1423

ETUDES DE PHILOLOGIE SLAVE (Almquist & Wiksall)

1 Jacobsson, G. Le nom de temps lěto dans les langues slaves. 1947. E1424
2 Thörnquist, C. Studien über die nordischen Lehnwörter im Russischen. 1948. E1425
3 Nilsson, N. A. Die Apollonius-Erzählung in den slavischen literaturen. 1949. E1426
4 ____. Gogol et Petersbourg. 1954. E1427
5 Wallmén, O. Alte tschechische pflanzennamen und rezepte im botanicon dorstens... 1954. E1428
6 Birnbaum, H. Untersuchungen zu den Zukunftsumschreibungen mit dem infinitiv im altkirchenslavischen. 1958. E1429
7 Nilsson, N. A. Ibsen in

Russland. 1958. E1430
8 Ruke-Dravina, V. Diminutive in lettischen. 1959. E1431
9 Baecklund, A. Personal names in medieval Velikij Novgorod. 1959. E1432
10 Nilsson, N. A. Russian heraldic virši from the 17th century. 1964. E1433
11 Sjöberg, A. Synonymous use of synthetical and analytical reaction in Old Church Slavonic verbs. 1964. E1434
12 Eriksson, G. Le nid prav- dans son champ sémantique. 1967. E1435

ETUDES DE PHILOSOPHIE MEDIEVALE (Vrin)

1 Gilson, E. H. Le thomisme, introduction à la philosophie de saint Thomas D'Aquin. 1944. E1436
____. Le thomisme introduction au système de saint Thomas D'Aquin. 1927. E1437
2 Carton, R. L'expérience physique chez Roger Bacon. 1924. E1438
3 ____. L'expérience mystique de l'illumination intérieure chez Roger Bacon. 1924. E1439
4 Gilson, E. H. La philosophie de saint Bonaventure. 1924. E1440
5 Carton, R. La synthèse doctrinale de Roger Bacon. 1924. E1441
6 Gouhier, H. G. La pensée religieuse de Descartes. 1924. E1442
7 Bertrand-Barraud, D. Les idées philosophiques de Bernardin Ochin, de Sienne. 1924. E1443
8 Bréhier, E. Les idées philosophiques et religieuses de Philon d'Alexandrie. 1925. E1444
9 Bissen, J-M. L'exemplairisme divin selon saint Bonaventure. 1929. E1445
10 Bonnefoy, J. Le Saint-Espirit et ses dons selon Saint Bonaventure. 1929. E1446
11 Gilson, E. H. Introduction a l'étude de saint Augustin. 1943. E1447
12 Lull, R. L'ars compendiose de R. Lulle, ed. by Ottaviano. 1930. E1448
13 Gilson, E. H. Etudes sur le rôle de la pensée médiévale dans la formation du système cartésien. 1930. E1449
14 Forest, A. La structure métaphysique du concret selon saint Thomas d'Aquin. 1931. E1450
15 Davy, M. M., ed. Les sermons universitaires parisiens de 1230-1231; contribution à l'histoire de la prédication médiévale. 1931. E1451
16 Théry, G. Etudes Dionysiennes. Hilduin, tr. de Denys. 1932. E1452
17-18 Glorieux, P. Répertoire des maîtres en théologie de Paris au XIIIe siècle. 2 v. 1933-34. E1453
18 also Gilson, E. H. Etudes su le rôle de la pensée médiévale dans la formation du système cartesien. 1930. E1454
19 Théry, G. Etudes Dionysiennes Hilduin, traducteur de Denys edition de sa traduction. 1937. E1455
20 Gilson, E. H. La théologie mystique de saint Bernard. 1934. E1456
21 Vignaux, P. Luther commentateur des Sentences (Livre I, distinction XVIII). 1935. E1457
22 Guigues du Chastel. Meditationes Gvigonis Prioris Cartvsiae. Le recuil des pensées du b. Guigue, ed. par Wilmart. 1936. E1458
23 Ockham, W. Le Tractatus de principiis theologiae attribué à G. d'Occam, ed. by Beaudry. 1936. E1459
24 ____. Guillelmi de Occam Breviloquium de potestate papae; ed. by Baudry. 1937. E1460
25 Paulus, J. Henri de Gand; essai sur les tendances et sa métaphysique. 1938. E1461

26 Boehm, A. Le "vinculum substantiale" chez Leibniz; ses origines historiques. 1938. E1462
27 Rohmer, J. La finalité morale chez les théologiens de saint Augustin à Duns Scot. 1939. E1463
28 Gilson, E. H. Dante et la philosophie. 1939. E1464
29 Guillaume de Saint-Thierry. Un traité de la vie solitaire. 2 v. 1940. E1465
30 Combes, A. Jean Gerson, commentateur dionysien. 1940. E1466
31 Festugière, A. M. J. La philosophie de l'amour des Marsile Ficin et son influence sur la littérature française au XVIe siècle. 1941. E1467
32 Combes, A. Jean de Montreuil et le chancelier Gerson. 1942. E1468
33 Gilson, E. H. L'esprit de la philosophie mediévale. 1944. E1469
34 Combes, A. Un inédit de saint Anselme? 1944. E1470
35 Vajda, G. Introduction à la pensée juive du Moyen Age. 1947. E1471
36 Sagnard, F. L. M. M. La gnose valentinienne et le témoignage de saint Irénée. 1947. E1472
37 Gardet, L. Introduction à la théologie musulmane; essai de théologie comparée. 1948. E1473
38 Baudry, L., ed. La querelli des futurs continqents (Louvain 1465-1475). 1950. E1474
39 Baudry, L. Guillaume D'Occam, sa vie, ses oeuvres, ses idées sociales et politiques. 1949. E1475
40 Pezard, A. Dante sous la pluie de feu (Enfer, chant XV). 1950. E1476
41 Gardet, L. La pensée religieuse d'Avicenne (Ibn Sīnā). 1951. E1477
42 Gilson, E. H. Jean Duns Scot. 1951. E1478
43 Gaìth, J. La conception de la liberté chez Grégoire de Nysse. 1953. E1479
44 Joannes de Ripa. Conclusions, ed. by Combes. 1957. E1480
45 Chenu, M. D. La theologie au douzième siècle. 1957. E1481
46 Vajda, G. L'amour de Dieu dans la théologie juive du moyen âge. 1957. E1482
47 Jolivet, J. Godescalc d'Orbais et la Trinité. 1958. E1483
48 Lossky, V. Théologie negative et connaissance de Dieu chez Maitre Eckhart. 1960. E1484
49 Vajda, G. Isaac Aibalag, averroiste juif, ed. by D'alGhazali. 1960. E1485
50 Matthaeus de Aesquasparta, Card. Quaestiones disputatae de Anima XIII, ed. by Gondras. 1961. E1486
51 Guillaume de Moerbeke. La version latine inédite du "De fato" d'Alexandre, ed. by Thillet. 1962. E1487
52 D'Alverny, M. T. Alain de Lille. 1963. E1488
53-54 Glorieux, P. Aux origines de la Sorbonne. 2 v. 1964. E1489
55 Laporte, J. La destinée de la nature humaine selon Thomas d'Aquin. 1965. E1490
56 Badawi, A. Le Transmission de la philosophie de la grecque au monde arabe. 1968. E1491
57 Jolivet, J. Arts du langage chez Abélard. 1969. E1492
58 Chatillon, J. Théologie, spiritualité et métaphysique dans l'oeuvre oratoire d'Archard de Saint Victor. 1969. E1493
59 Glorieux, P. La faculté des arts et ses maîtres au XIIIe siècle. 1971. E1494
60 Badawí, A. R. Histoire de philosophie en Islam. 2 v. 1972. E1495
61 Gilson, E. Dante et Béatrice. 1974. E1496

ETUDES DE PSYCHOLOGIE ET DE PHILOSOPHIE (Vrin)

1 Lalo, C. L'art loin de la vie. 1946. E1497
2 Tilquin, A. Le behaviorisme. 1942. E1498
3 Guillaume, P. Introduction à la psychologie. 1946. E1499
4 Piaget, J. Classes, relations et nombres. 1942. E1500
5 Cassirer, E. Descartes. Corneille. Christine de Suède. 1942. E1501
6 Rey Herme, P. Quelques aspects du progrés pédagogique dans la rééducation de la jeunesse délinquante. 1945. E1502
7 Château, J. La réel et l'imaginaire dans le jeu de l'enfant. 1946. E1503
8 ____. Le jeu de l'enfant. 1946. E1504
9 Meyerson, I. Les fonctions psychologiques et les oeuvres. 1948. E1505
10 Viaud, G. Le phototropisme animal. 1948. E1506
11 Michaud, E. Essai sur l'organisation de la connaissance entre 19 et 14 ans. 1949. E1507
12 Malrieu, P. Les émotions et la personalité de l'enfant. 1952. E1508
13 Château, J. Ecole et éducation. 1957. E1509
14 Francis, P. La perception de la musique. 1958. E1510
15 Passeron, R. L'oeuvre picturale et les fonctions de l'apparence. 1962. E1511
16 Vurpillot, E. L'organisation perceptive, son role dans l'évolution des illusions optico-géometriques. 1966. E1512
17 Tran-Thong. Stades et concept de stade de développement de l'enfant dans la psychologie contemporaine... 1967. E1513
18 Snyders, G. Le Goût musical en France aux XVIIe et XVIIIe siècles... 1968. E1514
19 Cohen, J. Les robots humains dans le mythe et la science, ed. by Dambuyant. 1968. E1515
20 Ehrlich, S. Les mecanismes du comportement verbal. 1968. E1516

ETUDES DE THEOLOGIE ET D'HISTOIRE DE LA SPIRITUALITE (Vrin)

1 Gilson, E. H. Théologie et histoire de la spiritualité. 1943. E1517
2 Du Manoir de Juaye, H. Dogme et spiritualité chez saint Cyrille d'Alexandire. 1944. E1518
3 Camelot, T. Foi et gnose, introduction à l'étude de la connaissance mystique chez Clément d'Alexandrie. 1945. E1519
4-5 Combes, A. Essai sur la critique de Ruysbroeck par Gerson. 2 v. 1945-48. E1520
7 Leclerq, J. La spíritualité de Pierre de Celle (1115-1183). 1946. E1521
8 Gerson, J. Six sermons français inédits. 1947. E1522
9 Leclerq, J. Un maître de la vie spirituelle au XIe siècle, Jean de Fecamp. 1946. E1523
10 Petit, F. La spíritualité des prémontrés aux XIIe et XIIIe siècles. 1947. E1524
11 Fidèle de Ros, Fr. Le frère Bernardin de Laredo. 1948. E1525
12 Bouchereaux, S. M. La réforme des carmes en France Jean de Saint-Samson. 1949. E1526
13 Catta, E. La Visitation Sainte-Marie de Nantes, 1630-1792. 1954. E1527
14 Davy, M. M. Théologie et mystique de Guillaume de Saint-Thierry. 1954. E1528
15 Surin, J. J. Poesis spirituelles. 1957. E1529
16 Bossuet, J. B. Elévations sur les mystères, ed. by Dréano. 1962. E1530
17 ____. Meditation sur l'évangile. 1965. E1531
18 Festugierè, A. M. J. George Herbert. 1971. E1532

ETUDES ET COMMENTAIRES
(Klincksieck)

1 Ernout, A. Philologica. 1946. E1533
2 Saint-Denis, E. de. Le vocabulaire des animaux marins en latin classique. 1947. E1534
3 Des Places, E. Le pronom chez Pindare. 1948. E1535
4 Hippocrates. Spurious and doubtful works. L'ancienne médecine, tr. by Festugière. 1948. E1536
5 Redard, G. Les noms grecs en -της, -τις et principalement en -ιτης, -ιτις. 1949. E1537
6 Laroche, E. Histoire de la racine nem-en grec ancien. 1950. E1538
7 André, J. Etude sur les termes de couleur dans la langue latine. 1949. E1539
8 ____. La vie et l'oeuvre de C. Asinius Pollion. 1950. E1540
9 Delebecque, E. Le cheval dans l'Iliade. 1951. E1541
10 ____. Euripide et la guerre du Péloponnèse. 1951. E1542
11 Vian, F. La guerre des géants. 1952. E1543
12 Moulinier, L. Le pur et l'impur dans la pensée et la sensibilité Grecs. 1952. E1544
13 Irigoin, J. Histoire du texte de Pindare. 1952. E1545
14 Martin, E. Essai sur les rhythmes de la chanson grecque antique. 1953. E1546
15 ____. Trois documents du musique grecque. 1953. E1547
16 Irigoin, J. Recherches sur les mètres de la lyrique chorale grecque. 1953. E1548
17 Mugler, C. Deux thèmes de la cosmologie grecque; devenir cyclique et pluralité des mondes. 1953. E1549
18 Ernout, A. Aspects do vocabulaire latin. 1954. E1550
19 Dumézil, G. Rituels indo-européens à Rome. 1954. E1551
20 Defradas, J. Plutarque, le Banquet des 7 sages. 1954. E1552
21 ____. Les thèmes de la propagande delphique. 1954. E1553
22 Martin, J. Histoire du texte des Phénomènes d'Aratos. 1956. E1554
23 André, J. Lexique des termes de botanique en latin. 1956. E1555
24 Chantraine, P. Etudes sur le vocabulaire grec. 1956. E1556
25 Delebecque, E. Essai sur le vie de Xénephon. 1957. E1557
26 Ernout, A. Philologica. V. 2. 1957. E1558
27 LeBonniec, H. Le culte de Cérès à Rome. 1958. E1559
28-29 Mugler, C. Dictionnaire historique de la terminologie géométrique des Grec. 2 v. 1958. E1560
30 Vian, F. Recherches sur les Posthomerica de Quintus de Smyrne. 1959. E1561
31 Gagnepain, J. Les noms grecs en οε et en Ᾱ. 1959. E1562
32 Weil, R. L' "archéologie" de Platon. 1959. E1563
33 Burguière, P. Histoire de l'infinitif en grec. 1959. E1564
34 Vicaire, P. Platon. 1960. E1565
35 Mugler, C. La physique de Platon. 1960. E1566
36 Weil, R. Aristote et l'histoire, essai sur la "Politique." 1960. E1567
37 Perrot, J. Les derives latins en -men et mentum. 1961. E1568
38 Ernout, A. Le dialecte ombrien. 1961. E1569
39 André, J. L'alimentation et la cruisine à Rome. 1961. E1570
40 Malingrey, A. M. Philosophia. 1961. E1571
41 VanBrock, N. Recherches sur le vocabulaire médical di grec ancien. 1961. E1572
42 Guiraud, C. La phrase nominale en grec, d'Homere à Euripide. 1962. E1573
43 Hipponax d'Ephese. Les fragments d'Hipponax, ed.

by Masson. 1962. E1574

44 Michel, A. Le dialogue des orateurs de Tacite et la philosophie de Cicéron. 1962. E1575

45 Pelletier, A. Flavius Josephe, adaptateur de la Lettre d'Aristée. 1962. E1576

46 Mugler, C. Les origines de la science grecque chez Homère. 1963. E1577

47 Monteil, P. La phrase relative en grec ancien, des origines a la fin du Ve siècle. 1963. E1578

48 Vian, F. Les origines de Thèbes. 1963. E1579

49 Guiraud, C. Les verbes signifiant voir en latin. 1963. E1580

50 Hellegouarc'h, J. Le monosyllabe dans l'hexamétre latin. 1963. E1581

51 Des Places, E. Syngeneia. 1963. E1582

52 Bonneau, D. La crue du Nil, divinité égyptienne. 1964. E1583

53 Mugler, C. Dictionnaire historique de la terminologie optique des Grecs. 1964. E1584

54 Monteil, P. Beau et laid en latin. 1964. E1585

55 Meillet, A. Apercu d'une histoire de la langue grecque. 1964. E1586

56 Bossuet, J. B. Platon et Aristote. 1964. E1587

57 Bader, F. Les composés grecs du type de Demiourgos. 1964. E1588

58 Apicius. L'art culinaire. 1965. E1589

59 Same as no. 1. V. 3. 1965. E1590

60 Graz, L. Le feu l'Iliade et l'Odyssée. 1965. E1591

61 Daniel, S. Recherches sur le vocabulaire du culte dans la Septante. 1965. E1592

62 Atallah, W. Adonis dans la litterature et l'art grecs. 1965. E1593

63 Soubiran, J. L'élision dans le poésie latine. 1966. E1594

64 Corlu, A. Recherches sur les mots relatifs à l'idee de prière, d'Homère aux Tragiques. 1966. E1595

65 Sznycer, M. Les Passages puniques en transcription latine dans le Poenulus de Plante. 1967. E1596

66 André, J. Les Mons d'oiseaux en latin... 1967. E1597

67 Masson, E. Recherches sur les plus anciens emprunts sémitiques en grec... 1967. E1598

68 Tuilier, A. Recherches critiques sur la tradition du texte d'Euripide. 1968. E1599

69 Huart, P. Le vocabulaire de l'analyse psychologique dans l'oeuvre de Thucydide. 1968. E1600

70 Moussy, C. Recherches sur τρέφω [i. e. trepho] et les verbes grecs signifiant nourrier. 1969. E1601

71 Mignot, X. Les verbes dénominatifs latins. 1969. E1602

72 Quellet, H. Les dérivés latins en -or. 1969. E1603

73 Plutarches. Le demon de Socrate, ed. by Corlu. 1970. E1604

74 ____. Plutarches en France au XVIe siècle, comp. by Aulotte. 1971. E1605

75 Laroche, E. Catalogue des textes hitties. 1971. E1606

76 Mignot, X. Recherches sur le suffixe - rns, - inros. 1972. E1607

77 Tuilier, A. Etude comparée du texte et des scholies d'Euripides. 1972. E1608

78 Plutarches. Consolation à Apollonios, ed. by Hani. 1972. E1609

79 Melanges de linguistique et de philologie greques offerts à Pierre Chantraine. 1972. E1610

80 Perpillou, J. L. Les substantifs grecs en ευς. 1973. E1611

81 Huart, P. Gnōmē chez Thucydide et ses contemporains. 1973. E1612

82 Baudot, A. Musiciens romains de l'antiquite. 1973. E1613
83 Tiffou, E. Essai sur la pensee morale de Salluste a la lumiere de ses prologues. 1973. E1614
84 Festugiere, A. J. Observations stylistiques sur l'Evangile de Saint Jean. 1974. E1615
85-86 Weber, E. Musique et theatre dans les pays rhenans. 2 v. 1974. E1616
87 Peron, J. Les Images maritimes de Pindare. 1974. E1617

ETUDES ORIENTALES, PUBLIEES PAR L'INSTITUT FRANÇAIS D'ARCHEOLOGIE DE STAMBOUL (Boccard)

1 Saussey, E. Prosateurs turcs contemporains. 1936. E1618
2 Robert, L. Villes d'Asie Mineure. 1936. E1619
3 Koprulu Mehmed, F., ed. Les origines dé l'empire ottoman. 1936. E1620
4 Saussey, E. Litterature populaire turque. 1937. E1621
5 Robert, L. Etudes anatoliennes. 1938. E1622
6 Yaltkaya Serefeddin. La duplication de l'autel. 1943. E1623
7 Jestin, R. La verbe sumérien. V. 1. 1945. E1624
8 Yaltkaya Serefiddin. Correspondance philosophique de Ibn Sab'in avec l'empereur Frederic II de Hohenstaufen. 1945. E1625
9 Same as no. 7. V. 2. 1943. E1626
10 Anadolu. Revue des études d'archéologie et d'histoire en Turguie. V. 1. 1951. E1627
11 Metzger, H. Catalogue des monuments votif du Musée d'Adalia. 1952. E1628
12 Same as no. 10. V. 2. 1951. E1629
13 Same as no. 7. V. 3. 1951. E1630

ETUDES POLITIQUE, ECONOMIQUE ET SOCIALES (Dalloz)

1 Ponteil, F. Histoire générale contemporaine. 1958. E1631
2 Chenot, B. Organisation économique de l'Etat. 1965. E1632
3 Chevalier, L. Démographie générale. 1951. E1633
4 Droz, J. Histoire diplomatique de 1648 à 1919. 1952. E1634
5 Barrère, A. Théorie économique et impulsion keynésienne. 1952. E1635
6 Chevaillier, J. J. Histoire des institutions politiques de la France moderne, 1789-1945. 1958. E1636
7 Duroselle, J. B. Histoire diplomatique de 1919 à nos jours. 1962. E1637
8 Chardonnet, J. Les grandes puissances. V. 1. 1953. E1638
9 Dumont, R. Economie agricole dans le monde. 1954. E1639
10 Ferronnière, J. and Chillaz, E. de. Les operations de banque. 1954. E1640
11 Deschamps, H. J. Peuples et nations d'outre-mer. 1954. E1641
12 Same as no. 8. V. 2. 1955. E1642
13 Chardonnet, J. L'economie française. V. 1. 1958. E1643
14 Barrere, A. Politique financière. 1958. E1644
15 Same as no. 13. V. 2. 1959. E1645
16 Simon, M. Les financement des entreprises. 1961. E1646
17 Rodière, R. Droit maritime, d'après le Précis du doyen Georges Ripert. 1963. E1647
18 Puget, H. Les institutions administratives éntrangères. 1969. E1648
19 Calvez, J. Y. Aspects politiques et sociaux des pays en voie de developpement. 1971. E1649
20 Girardet, R. Problemes contemporains de defense nationale. 1974. E1650
21 `Merle, M. Sociologie des

relations internationales. 1974. E1651

ETUDES SUR L'HISTOIRE, L'ECONOMIE ET LA SOCIOLOGIE DES PAYS SLAVES (Mouton) (1-5 pub. as ETUDES SUR L'ECONOMIE ET SOCIOLOGIE DES PAYS SLAVES)

1 Bobrowski, C. Formation du système Soviétique de planification. 1956. E1652
2 Smith, R. E. F. The origins of farming in Russia. 1959. E1653
3 Greyfié de Bellecombe, L. Les conventions collectives de travail en union Soviétique. 1958. E1654
4 Chambre, H. L'Aménagement du territoire en U. R. S. S. 1959. E1655
5 Pavlowitch, S. K. Anglo-Russian rivalry in Serbia. 1961. E1656
6 Portal, R., ed. Le statut des paysans libérés du servage. 1963. E1657
7 T͡Sereteli, I. G. Vospominan͡ia o Ferral'skoĭ revoliut͡sii. 2 v. 1963. E1658
8 Pascal, P. Avvakum et les débuts du raskol. 1963. E1659
9 Lewin, M. Paysannerie et le pouvair soviétique, 1928-1930. 1966. E1660
10 Kerblay, B. H. Les marches paysans in U. S. S. R. 1968. E1661
11 Buryshkin, P. A. Bibliographie sur la franc-maconnerie in Russie. 1967. E1662
12 Alexander II. The politics of autocracy, ed. by Rieber. 1966. E1663
13 Chaianov, A. O. OEuvres choises de A. V. Cajanov, ed. by Kerblay. 1967. E1664
14 Confino, M. Systèmes agraires et progrès agricole. 1969. E1665
15 Lesure, M. Les sources de l'histoire de Russie aux Archives nationales. 1970. E1666
16 Granjard, H., ed. Quelques lettres d'Ivan Tourguenev à Pauline Viardot. 1974. E1667

EUROPEAN DEMOGRAPHIC MONOGRAPHS (Nijhoff)

1 Stone, K. H. Norway's internal migration to new farms since 1920. 1971. E1668
2 Baučić, I. The effect of emigration from Yugoslavia and the problems of returning emigrant workers. 1972. E1669
3 Beijer, G. Brain drain - Auszug des Geistes - Exode des cerveaux. 1972. E1670
4 Stone, K. H. Northern Finland's post-war colonizing and emigration. 1973. E1671

EUROPEAN FOLKLORE SERIES (Rosenkilde)

1 Bødker, L. and others, eds. European folk tales. 1963. E1672
2 Seemann, E. and others, comps. European folk ballads. 1967. E1673
3 Schmidt, L. Le théâtre populaire Européen. 1972. E1674
4 European anecdotes and jests, ed. by Ranke. 1972. E1675

THE EVOLUTION OF CAPITALISM (Arno)

Allen, Z. The practical tourist. 2 v. in 1. 1972. E1676
Bridge, J. H. The inside history of the Carnegie Steel Company. 1972. E1677
Broderick, J. The economic morals of the Jesuits. 1972. E1678
Burlamaqui, J. J. The principles of natural and politic law, tr. by Nugent. 1972. E1679
Capitalism and Fascism. 1972. E1680
Corey, L. The decline of American capitalism. 1972. E1681
De Witt, J. The true interest and political maxims of the Republic of Holland.

1972. E1682
Dos Passos, J. R. Commercial trusts. 1972. E1683
Fanfani, A. Catholicism, Protestantism and capitalism. 1972. E1684
Gaskell, P. The manufacturing population of England. 1972. E1685
Göhre, P. Three months in a workshop. 1972. E1686
Greeley, H. Essays designed to elucidate the science of political economy. 1972. E1687
Grotius, H. The freedom of the seas. 1972. E1688
Hadley, A. T. Economics. 1972. E1689
Knight, C. Capital and labour. 1972. E1690
Malynes, G. de. England's view in the unmasking of two paradoxes. 1972. E1691
Marquand, H. A. The dynamics of industrial combination. 1972. E1692
Mercantilist views of trade and monopoly. 1972. E1693
Morrison, C. An essay on the relations between labour and capital. 1972. E1694
Nicholson, J. S. The effects of machinery on wages. 1972. E1695
One hundred years' progress of the United States. 1972. E1696
The poetry of industry. 1972. E1697
Pre-capitalist economic thought. 1972. E1698
Prompting prosperity. 1972. E1699
Proudhon, P. J. System of economical contradictions. 1972. E1700
Religious attitudes toward usury. 1972. E1701
Roscher, W. Principles of political economy. 2 v. in 1. 1972. E1702
Scoville, W. C. Revolution in glassmaking. 1972. E1703
Selden, J. Of the dominion. 1972. E1704
Senior, N. W. Industrial efficiency and social economy. 1972. E1705
Spann, O. The history of economics. 1972. E1706
The usury debate after Adam Smith. 1972. E1707
The usury debate in the seventeenth century. 1971. E1708
Varga, E. Twentieth century capitalism. 1972. E1709
Young, A. Arthur Young on industry and economics. 1972. E1710

EXPLORATION SERIES IN EDUCATION (Harper)

Abraham, W. Common sense about gifted children. 1958. E1711
____. A time for teaching. 1964. E1712
Arnstine, D. Philosophy of education. 1967. E1713
Ayer, F. C. Fundamentals of instructional supervision. 1954. E1714
Battle, J. A. and Shannon, R. L. The new idea in education. 1968. E1715
Blount, N. S. and Klausmeier, H. J. Teaching in the secondary school. 1968. E1716
Brown, B. B. The experimental mind in education. 1968. E1717
Burke, A. J. Financing public schools in the United States. 1951. E1718
Burrup, P. E. Modern high school administration. 1962. E1719
____. The teacher and the public school system. 1967. E1720
Cooper, S. and Fitzwater, C. O. County school administration. 1954. E1721
Cramer, R. V. and Domian, O. E. Administration and supervision in the school. 1960. E1722
Davis, D. C. Patterns of primary education. 1963. E1723
Devereux, G. Therapeutic education. 1958. E1724
Duker, S. The public schools and religion. 1966. E1725
Eye, G. G. The new teacher comes to school. 1958. E1726

____ and Netzer, L. A. Supervision of instruction. 1965. E1727
Fantini, M. D. and Weinstein, G. The disadvantaged. 1968. E1728
Faunce, R. C. Secondary school administration. 1955. E1729
Featherstone, E. G. and Culp, D. P. Pupil transportation. 1965. E1730
Foff, A. and Grambs, J. D., eds. Readings in education. 1958. E1731
Frasier, G. W. An introduction to the study of education. 1965. E1732
Getzels, J. W. and others. Educational administration as a social process. 1968. E1733
Gordon, I. J. Human development. 1969. E1734
____. The teacher as a guidance worker. 1956. E1735
Graff, O. B. and Street, C. M. Improving competence in educational administration. 1956. E1736
Green, J. A. Fields of teaching and educational series. 1966. E1737
Grittner, F. M. Teaching foreign languages. 1969. E1738
Hagman, H. L. and Schwartz, A. Administration in profile for school executives. 1965. E1739
Hanna, G. R. and McAllister, M. K. Books, young people and reading guidance. 1960. E1740
Hilliway, T. The American two-year college. 1958. E1741
Howard, C. F. and Dumas, E. Teaching a contemporary mathematics in elementary schools. 1966. E1742
Hughes, J. M. Human relations in educational organization. 1957. E1743
Hunnicutt, C. W. and Iverson, W. J., eds. Research in the three R's. 1958. E1744
Keith, L. G. and others. Contemporary curriculum in the elementary school. 1968. E1745
Klausmeier, H. J. Principles and practices of secondary school teaching. 1953. E1746
____. Teaching in the secondary school. 1958. E1747
____ and Dresden, K. Teaching in the elementary school. 1962. E1748
Knezevich, S. J. Administration of public education. 1962. E1749
____ and Fowkles, J. G. Business management of local school systems. 1960. E1750
Koos, L. V. Junior high school trends. 1955. E1751
Kreitlow, B. W. Rural education. 1954. E1752
Krug, E. A. Salient dates in American education, 1935-1964. 1966. E1753
____. The secondary school curriculum. 1960. E1754
____. The shaping of the American high school. 2 v. 1964-7. E1755
____ and others. Administering curriculum planning. 1956. E1756
Logan, F. M. Growth of art in American schools. 1955. E1757
Loughary, J. W. Man-machine systems in education. 1966. E1758
McCloskey, G. E. Education and public understanding. 1967. E1759
Manning, D. The qualitative elementary school. 1963. E1760
Miller, C. H. Guidance service. 1965. E1761
Miller, R. I., ed. The nongraded school. 1967. E1762
Moore, H. E. and Walters, N. B. Personnel administration in education. 1955. E1763
Muldoon, M. W. Learning to teach. 1956. E1764
Nerbovig, M. H. and Klausmeier, H. J. Teaching in the elementary school. 1969. E1765
Patterson, C. H. Counseling the emotionally disturbed. 1958. E1766
Peterson, L. J. and others. The law and public school

operation. 1969. E1767
Phillips, B. N. and others. Psychology at work in the elementary school classroom. 1960. E1768
Pilgrim, G. R. H. Books, young people and reading guidance. 1968. E1769
Popham, W. J. Educational statistics. 1967. E1770
Ripple, R. E., ed. Readings in learning and human activities. 1971. E1771
Roberts, R. W. Vocational and practical arts education. 1971. E1772
Rothney, J. W. M. and others. Guidance practices and results. 1958. E1773
____. Measurement and guidance. 1959. E1774
Rucker, W. R. Curriculum development in the elementary school. 1960. E1775
Sanders, N. M. Classroom questions. 1966. E1776
Shaplin, J. T. and Olds, H. F. Team teaching. 1964. E1777
Stoff, S. and Schwartzberg, H., eds. The human encounter. 1969. E1778
Sumption, M. R. and Landis, J. L. Planning functional school buildings. 1957. E1779
Sur, W. R. and Schuller, C. F. Music education for teenagers. 1966. E1780
Thurston, L. M. and Roe, W. H. State school administration. 1957. E1781
White, M. A. and Harris, M. W. The school psychologist. 1961. E1782
White, V. Studying the individual pupil. 1958. E1783
Willing, M. H. and others. Schools and democratic society. 1951. E1784
Wittich, W. A. and Schuller, C. F. Audio-visual materials. 1973. E1785

EYEWITNESS ACCOUNTS OF THE AMERICAN REVOLUTION (Arno)

Series I:
Allaire, A. Diary of Lieutenant Anthony Allaire. 1967. E1786
Andre, J. Journal. 1967. E1787
Bangs, I. Journal of Lieutenant Isaac Bangs. 1967. E1788
Boudinot, E. Journal of historical recollections of American events during the revolutionary war. 1967. E1789
Carrington, H. B. Battles of the American Revolution. 1967. E1790
Chadwick, F. E., ed. The Graves papers and other documents... 1967. E1791
Collins, V. L. A brief narrative of the ravages of the British and Hessians at Princeton in 1776-1777. 1969. E1792
de Chastellux, F. J. Travels in North America. 2 v. 1967. E1793
Fanning, N. Fanning's narrative being the memoirs of Nathaniel Fanning..., ed. by Barnes. 1967. E1794
Hawkins, C. The adventures of Christopher Hawkins. 1967. E1795
Heath, W. Memoirs of Major-General William Heath. 1967. E1796
Henry, J. J. Account of Arnold's campaign against Quebec... 1967. E1797
Herbert, C. A relic of the Revolution. 1967. E1798
Jones, C. C., ed. The siege of Savannah, in 1779. 1967. E1799
Jones, T. History of New York during the Revolutionary War. 2 v. 1967. E1800
Lamb, R. An original and authentic journal of occurrences during the late American war. 1968. E1801
MacKenzie, F. Diary... 2 v. 1967. E1802
McRobert, P. A tour through part of the North Provinces of America. 1967. E1803
Martin, J. P. A narrative of some of the adventures, dangers, and sufferings of a Revolutionary soldier. 1967. E1804

Massachusetts Provincial Congress. A narrative of the excursion and ravages of the King's troops... 1967. E1805
Moody, J. Lieut. James Moody's narrative of his exertions and sufferings in the cause of government. 1967. E1806
Moultrie, W. Memoirs of the American Revolution. 1967. E1807
Riedesel, F. Letters and journals relating to the war of the American Revolution. 1969. E1808
Simcoe, J. G. A history of the operations of a partisan corps... 1967. E1809
Smith, J. F. D. A tour of the United States of America... 2 v. 1968. E1810
Tallmadge, B. Memoirs. 1968. E1811
Tarleton, B. A history of the campaigns of 1780 and 1781 in the Southern Provinces of North America. 1968. E1812
Uhledorf, B. A. The siege of Charlestown. 1968. E1813
Von Krafft, J. C. P. Journal of Lt. John Charles Philip Von Kraft. 1968. E1814
Wells, L. S. The journal of a voyage from Charlestown, S. C. 1968. E1815
Series II:
Anbury, T. Travels through the interior parts of America. 2 v. 1969. E1816
Barker, J. The British in Boston. 1969. E1817
Bew, J. (publisher). Minutes of a conspiracy against the liberties in America. 1969. E1818
Biron, A. L. de G. Memoires, tr. by Scott Moncrieff. 1969. E1819
Blanchard, C. The journal of Claude Blanchard, tr. by Duane. 1969. E1820
Burgoyne, J. A state of the expedition from Canada. 1969. E1821
Carroll, C. Journal of Charles Carroll, ed. by Mayer. 1969. E1822
Drayton, J. Memoirs of the American Revolution. 2 v. 1969. E1823
Feltman, W. The journal of Lieutenant William Feltman. 1969. E1824
Graydon, A. Memoirs of his own time, ed. by Littrell. 1969. E1825
Laurens, J. Army correspondence, 1777-1778. 1969. E1826
Lauzun, A. L. de G. de. Memoirs. 1969. E1827
Lee, H. Memoirs of the war in the South. 1969. E1828
Marshall, C. Extracts from the diary of Christopher Marshall, ed. by William Marshall. 1969. E1829
Moore, F., ed. Diary of the American Revolution. 2 v. 1969. E1830
____. Songs and ballads of the American Revolution. 1969. E1831
Morris, M. Private journal of Margaret Morris. 1969. E1832
O'Beirne, T. A candid and impartial narrative of the transactions of the fleet under Lord Howe. 1969. E1833
Parry, H. Court martial of Capt. John Moutray. 1969. E1834
Pontgibaud, C. de. A French volunteer of the War of Independence, tr. by Douglas. 1969. E1835
Riedesel, F. A. Memoirs and letters and journals of Major-General Riedesel, tr. by Stone. 2 v. 1969. E1836
Roberts, L. Memoirs of Captain Lemuel Roberts. 1969. E1837
Robin, A. New travel through North America. 1969. E1838
Rosenthal, Baron. Journal of a volunteer expedition to Sandusky. 1969. E1839
Rowe, J. Letters and diary of John Rowe, ed. by Cunningham. 1969. E1840
Schaukirk, E. G. Diary of Reverend Ewald Gustave

Schaukirk. 1969. E1841
Senter, I. The journal of Isaac Senter. 1969. E1842
Serle, A. The American journal of Ambrose Serle, ed. by Tatum. 1969. E1843
Smith, J. H. Narratives of the death of Major André. 1969. E1844
Smith, W. Historical memoirs of William Smith, ed. by Sabine. 1969. E1845
Stedman, C. The history of the American war. 2 v. 1969. E1846
Thacher, J. Military journal of the American Revolution. 1969. E1847
Townsend, J. The battle of Brandywine. 1969. E1848
Webb, S. Correspondence and journal of Samuel Webb, ed. by Ford. 3 v. 1969. E1849
Wilkinson, E. Letters of Eliza Wilkinson, ed. by Gilman. 1969. E1850
Willett, W. M. A narrative of the military actions of Colonel Marinus Willett. 1969. E1851
Wister, S. Sally Wister's journal, ed. by Myers. 1969. E1852

Series III:

Anderson, E. Personal recollections of Captain Enoch Anderson, ed. by Bellas. 1971. E1853
Angell, I. Diary of Colonel Israel Angell, ed. by Field. 1970. E1854
Baldwin, J. The Revolutionary journal of Col. Jeduthan Baldwin, ed. by T. W. Baldwin. 1971. E1855
Beebe, L. Journal of Dr. Lewis Beebe, ed. by Kirkland. 1971. E1856
Blatchford, J. The narrative of John Blatchford, ed. by Bushnell. 1971. E1857
Brooke, F. J. A family narrative. 1971. E1858
Calef, J., ed. The siege of Penobscot by the rebels. 1971. E1859
Coghlan, M. Memoirs of Mr. Coghlan. 1971. E1860
DeBerniere, H. Gage's instructions: Thomas Gage. 1971. E1861
Denny, E. Military journal of Major Ebenezer Denny. 1971. E1862
Dudley, D. Theatrum majorum, ed. by Gilman. 1971. E1863
Evelyn, W. G. Memoirs and letters of Captain W. Glanville Evelyn, ed. by Scull. 1971. E1864
Fitch, J. The New York diary of Lieutenant Jabez Fitch, ed. by Sabine. 1971. E1865
Freneau, P. Some account of the capture of the ship "Aurora." 1971. E1866
Galloway, G. G. Diary of Grace Growden Galloway, ed. by Werner. 1971. E1867
Gibbes, R. W., ed. Documentary history of the American Revolution. 1971. E1868
Green, E. Diary of Ezra Green, ed. by W. C. Green. 1971. E1869
Harrison, S. A. Memoir of Lieutenant Colonel Tench Tilgham, ed. by Harrison. 1971. E1870
Hulton, A. Letters of a Loyalist lady, Ann Hulton. 1971. E1871
Hunt, G., ed. Fragments of Revolutionary history. 1971. E1872
Jones, J. Letters of Joseph Jones of Virginia, ed. by Ford. 1971. E1873
____. Plain concise practical remarks on the treatment of wounds and fractures. 1971. E1874
Lee, W. Letters of William Lee, ed. by Ford. 1971. E1875
Leggett, A. The narrative of Abraham Leggett, ed. by Bushnell. 1971. E1876
Lincoln, R. The papers of Captain Rufus Lincoln of Wareham, Mass., ed. by J. M. Lincoln. 1971. E1877
McHenry, J. A sidelight on history. 1971. E1878
Mauduit, I. Observations upon the conduct of S-r W-----m

H--r at the White Plains. 1971. E1879
Pausch, G. Journal of Captain Pausch, tr. and ed. by Stone. 1971. E1880
Rathbun, J. Narrative of Jonathan Rathbun. 1971. E1881
Reed, E. D. The life of Esther DeBardt. 1971. E1882
Robertson, A. Archibald Robertson, ed. by Lydenberg. 1971. E1883
Rochambeau, J. B. D. de V. Memoirs of the Marshall Count De Rochambeau, tr. by Wright. 1971. E1884
Smith, W. Historical memoirs from 26 August 1778 to 12 November 1783, ed. by Sabine. 2 v. 1969-1971. E1885
Stuart, J., ed. Memoir of Indian Wars, and other occurrences. 1971. E1886
Weedon, G. Valley Forge orderly book of General George Weedon. 1971. E1887

-F-

FACSIMILE REPRINTS IN THE HISTORY OF SCIENCE (Univ. of Ill. Pr.)

1 Young, J. R. An experimental inquiry into the principles of nutrition, ed. by Rose. 1959. F1
2 Galilei, G. Discourse on bodies in water, tr. by Salusbury. 1960. F2
3 Drake, D. Malaria in the interior valley of North America, ed. by Levine. 1964. F3
4 Lister, M. A. A journey to Paris in the year 1698, ed. by Stearns. 1967. F4

FACSIMILE TEXT SOCIETY. PUBLICATIONS (Columbia Univ. Pr.)

Ser. I: Literature and language
1 Donne, J. Biathanatos, ed. by Hebel. 1930. F5
2 Warton, T. Poems on several occasions. 1930. F6
3 Poems on several occasions, ed. by a gentleman of Virginia; ed. by Rusk. 1930. F7
4 Reeve, C. The progress of romance, and The history of Charoba, ed. by McGill. 1930. F8
5 Franklin, A. A dissertation on liberty and necessity, pleasure and pain, ed. by Wroth. 1930. F9
6 Cooper, J. F. Letter to Gen. Lafayette, ed. by Spiller. 1932. F10
Ward, E. Five travel scripts, commonly attributed to Edward Ward, ed. by Troyer. 1933. F11
8 Byron, G. G. N. B. Fugitive pieces, ed. by Kessel. 1933. F12
9 Poe, E. A. Al Aaraaf, ed. by Mabbott. 1933. F13
Ser. II: History
1 Goodman, C. How superior powers oght to be obeyd, ed. by McIlwain. 1931. F14
Ser. III: Philosophy
1 More, H. Enchiridion ethicum, ed. by Lamprecht. 1930. F15
2 Cudworth, R. A sermon preached before the House of Commons, March 31, 1647. 1930. F16
3 Rust, G. A letter of resolution concerning Origen and the chief of his opinions, ed. by Nicolson. 1933. F17
4 Glanville, J. The vanity of dogmatizing, ed. by Prior. 1931. F18
Ser. V: Economics
1 Mun, T. A discourse of trade, from England unto the East-Indies, 1621. 1930. F19
2 Wheeler, J. A treatise on commerce, ed. by Hotchkiss. 1931. F20
17 Milton, J. The Cambridge manuscript, ed. by Patterson. 1933. F21
18 Bunyan, J. Pilgrim's progress. 1928. F22
19 Milton, J. Areopagitica. 1934. F23
20 Keats, J. Lamia, ed. by Hollingworth and Weekes. 1936. F24
21 ____. Poems, 1817. 1927. F25
22 Omar Khayyām. Rubáiyát, tr. by Fitzgerald. 1934. F26
23 Browne, T. Hydriotaphia.

1927. F27
24 Blake, W. Poetical sketches. 1927. F28
25 Wordsworth, W. Lyrical ballads. 1926. F29
26 Donne, J. The first Aniuersaire. 1934. F30
27 Milton, J. Minor poems, ed. by Lawes. 1934. F31
28 Collins, W. Odes on several descriptive and allegoric subjects. 1927. F32
29 Shelley, P. B. Adonais. 1927. F33
30 Goldsmith, O. Deserted village. 1929. F34
31 Jonson, B. Alchemist. 1927. F35
32 Spenser, E. Amoretti and Epithalamion. 1927. F36
33 Donne, J. J. Juvenilia, ed. by Bennett. 1936. F37
34 Jonson, B. Epigrams, The forest, Underwoods, ed. by Hudson. 1936. F38
35 Poe, E. A. Poems... ed. of 1831. 1936. F39
36 Shakespeare, W. Sonnets. 1936. F40
37 Sidney, P. The defense of Poesie. 1936. F41
38 The power of sympathy, ed. by Ellis. 2 v. 1937. F42
39 The American magazine, ed. by Richardson. 1937. F43
40 Denton, D. A brief description of New York, ed. by Poltsists. 1937. F44
41 The General magazine and historical chronicle, ed. by Franklin. 1938. F45
42 Mather, C. Manuductio ad ministerium, ed. by Holmes. 1938. F46
43 Southern, J. Pandora, ed. by Parks. 1938. F47
44 Defoe's Review, ed. by Secord. 1938. F48
45 Justa Edovardo King, ed. by Mossner. 1939. F49
46 Foster, H. (Webster). The coquette, ed. by Brown. 1939. F50
47 Whitman, W. Leaves of grass, ed. by Furness. 1939. F51
48 Brunt, S. A voyage to Cacklogallinia, ed. by Nicolson. 1940. F52
49 Byles, M. Poems on several occasions, ed. by Carlson. 1940. F53
50 Bright, T. A treatise on melancholie, ed. by Vautrollier. 1940. F54
51 Poe, E. A. Tamberlane, ed. by Mabbott. 1941. F55
52 Irving, W. Letters of Jonathan Oldstyle, ed. by Williams. 1941. F56
53 Donne, J. Ignatius his conclave, ed. by Coffin. 1941. F57
54 The dignity of kingship asserted, ed. by Parker. 1942. F58
55 Peacham, H. The truth of our times, ed. by Cawley. 1942. F59
56 Poe, E. A. The raven, ed. by Mabbott. 1942. F60

FAMILY IN AMERICA (Arno)

Abbott, J. S. C. The mother at home. 1972. F61
Addams, J. A new conscience and an ancient evil. 1972. F62
The aged and the depression, ed. by Rubinow. 1972. F63
Alcott, W. A. The young husband. 1972. F64
____. The young wife. 1972. F65
Amer. Academy of Political and Social Science. The American family in World War II. 1972. F66
American Sociological Society. The family. 1972. F67
Baldwin, B. T. and others. Farm children. 1972. F68
Beebe, G. W. Contraception and fertility in the Southern Appalachians. 1972. F69
Birth control and morality in nineteenth century America. 1972. F70
Brandt, L. Five hundred and seventy-four deserters and their families. Also Baldwin, W. H. Family desertion and non-support laws. 1972. F71
Breckinridge, S. P. The

family and the state. 1972. F72
Calverton, V. F. The bankruptcy of marriage. 1972. F73
Carlier, A. Marriage in the United States. 1972. F74
Child, L. The mother's book. 1972. F75
Child care in rural America. 1972. F76
Child rearing literature of the twentieth century. 1972. F77
The Colonial American family. 1972. F78
Commander, L. K. The American idea. 1972. F79
Davis, K. B. Factors in the sex life of twenty-two hundred women. 1972. F80
Dennis, W. The Hopi child. 1972. F81
Epstein, A. Facing old age. 1972. F82
The family and social service in the 1920's. 1972. F83
Hagood, M. J. Mothers of the South. 1972. F84
Hall, G. S. Senescence. 1972. F85
____. Youth. 1972. F86
Hathway, M. The migratory worker and family life. 1972. F87
Homan, W. J. Children and Quakerism. 1972. F88
Key, E. The century of the child. 1972. F89
Kirchwey, F., ed. Our changing morality. 1972. F90
Kopp, M. E. Birth control in practice. 1972. F91
Lawton, G., ed. New goals for old age. 1972. F92
Lichtenberger, J. P. Divorce. 1972. F93
Lindsey, B. B. and Evans, W. The compassionate marriage. 1972. F94
Lou, H. H. Juvenile courts in the United States. 1972. F95
Monroe, D. Chicago families. 1972. F96
Mowrer, E. R. Family disorganization. 1972. F97
Reed, R. The illegitimate family in New York City. 1972. F98
Robinson, C. H. Seventy birth control clinics. 1972. F99
Watson, J. B. Psychological care of the infant and child. 1972. F100
White House Conf. on Child Health and Protection. The adolescent in the family. 1972. F101
____. The home and the child. 1972. F102
____. The young child in the home. 1972. F103
Young, D., ed. The modern American family. 1972. F104

FAR EAST ECONOMIC SERIES (Bailey)

1 Kenrick, D. M. Price control and its practice in Hong Kong. 1956. F105

THE FAR WEST AND THE ROCKIES HISTORICAL SERIES, 1820-1875 (A. H. Clark)

1 Hafen, L. R. and A. W., eds. Old Spanish Trail. 1954. F106
2 ____. Journals of forty-niners. 1954. F107
3 ____. To the Rockies and Oregon. 1955. F108
4-5 Sage, R. B. Letters and papers, 1836-1847, ed. by L. R. and A. W. Hafen. 1956. F109
6 Bell, J. R. The journal of Captain John R. Bell..., ed. by Fuller and Hafen. 1957. F110
7 Heap, G. H. Central route to the Pacific, ed. by L. R. and A. W. Hafen. 1957. F111
8 Hafen, L. R. and A. W., eds. The Utah expedition, 1857-1858. 1958. F112
9 ____. Relations with the Indians of the Plains, 1857-1861. 1959. F113
10 Jackson, W. H. The diaries of William Henry Jackson, ed. by L. R. and A. W. Hafen. 1959. F114
11 Hafen, L. R. and A. W., eds. Fremont's fourth expedition. 1960. F115
12 ____. Powder River campaigns and Sawyers Expedition

of 1865. 1961. F116
13 ____. Reports from Colorado; the Wildman letters, 1859-1865... 1961. F117
14 Hafen, L. L. and A. W. Handcarts to Zion. 1960. F118
15 ____. General analytical index to the fifteen volume series and supplement to the Journals of the forty-niners, Salt Lake to Los Angeles. 1962. F119

THE FATHERS OF THE CHURCH, A NEW TRANSLATION (Fathers of the Church)

1 Apostolic Fathers. The Apostolic Fathers, tr. by Glimm and others. 1947. F120
2 Augustinus, Aurelius, St. Christian instruction. 1947. F121
3 Salvianus. The writings of Salvian, tr. by O'Sullivan. 1947. F122
4 Augustinus, Aurelius, St. Immortality of the Soul... 1948. F123
5 ____. The happy life... 1948. F124
6 Justinus Martyr, St. Saint Justin Martyr. 1949. F125
7 Nicetas. St. Niceta of Remesiana, tr. by Peebles. 1949. F126
8 Augustinus, Aurelius, St. The city of God. V. 1. 1949. F127
9 Basilius, St. Writings: ascestical works. 1950. F128
10 Tertullianus, Q. S. F. Tertullian, tr. by Arbesmann and others. 1950. F129
11 Augustinus, Aurelius, St. Commentary on the sermon on the mount, tr. by Kavanagh. 1951. F130
12 ____. Letters, (1-82), tr. by Parsons. 1951. F131
13 Basilius, St. Letters, tr. by Way. (1-185), V. 1. 1951. F132
14 Same as no. 7. V. 2. 1952. F133
15 Deferrari, R. J., ed. Early Christian biographies. 1952. F134
16 Augustinus, Aurelius, St. Treatises on various subjects. 1952. F135
17 Petrus Chrysolgus, St. Saint Peter Chrysologus: Selected sermons, by George E. Ganss. 1953. F136
18 Same as no. 12. (83-130), tr. by Parsons. 1953. F137
19 Eusebius Pamphill. Ecclesiastical history, bks. 1-5, tr. by Deferrari. 1953. F138
20 Same as no. 12, (131-164). 1953. F139
21 Augustinus, Aurelius, St. Confessions, tr. by Bourke. 1953. F140
22 Funeral orations of Saint Gregory Nazianzen and Saint Ambrose, tr. by McCauley and others. 1953. F141
23 Clemens, Titus Flavius, Alexandrinus. Christ the educator, tr. by Wood. 1954. F142
24 Same as no. 8. (17-22), tr. by Walsh. 1954. F143
25 Hilarius, St. The Trinity, tr. by McKenna. 1954. F144
26 Ambrosius, St. Letters, tr. by Beyenka. 1954. F145
27 Augustinus, Aurelius, St. Treatise on marriage and other subjects, tr. by Wilcox. 1955. F146
28 Same as no. 13 (186-368). V. 2. 1956. F147
29 Same as no. 19 (6-10). 1956. F148
30 Same as no. 12 (165-203). 1956. F149
31 Caesarius, St. Sermons, tr. by Mueller. V. 1. 1956. F150
32 Same as no. 12 (204-272). 1956. F151
33 Chrysostomus, Joannes, St. Commentary on St. John the apostle the evangelist homilies 1-47, tr. by Goggin. 1957. F152
34 Leo I, the Great, St. Letters, tr. by Hunt. 1957. F153
35 Augustinus, Aurelius, St. Against Julian, tr. by

Schumacher. 1957. F154
36 Cyprianus, St. Treatises, tr. by Defarrari. 1958. F155
37 Joannes of Damascus, St. Writings, tr. by Moore. 1958. F156
38 Augustinus, Aurelius, St. Sermons on the liturgical seasons, tr. by Muldowney. 1959. F157
39 Gregorius I, the Great, St. Dialogues, tr. by Zimmerman. 1959. F158
40 Tertullianus, Q. S. F. Disciplinary, moral and ascetical works, tr. by Arbssmann and others. 1959. F159
41 Same as no. 33. Homilies 48-88. 1960. F160
42 Ambrosius, St. Hexameron, Paradise, Cain and Abel, ed. by Savage. 1961. F161
43 Prudentius Clemens, A. Poems, tr. by Eagen. V. 1. 1962. F162
44 Ambrosius, St. Saint Ambrose: theological and dogmatic works, tr. by Deferrari. 1963. F163
45 Augustinus, Aurelia, St. The Trinity, tr. by McKenna. 1963. F164
46 Basilius, St. Exegetic homilies, tr. by Way. 1963. F165
47 Same as no. 31. V. 2. F166
48 Hieronymus, St. The homilies of Saint Jerome, tr. by Ewald. V. 1. 1964. F167
49 Lactantius, L. C. F. The divine institutes, bks. I-VII, tr. by McDonald. 1964. F168
50 Orosius, P. The seven books of history against the pagans, ed. by Deferrari. 1964. F169
51 Cyprianus, St. Letters (1-81), tr. by Donna. 1964. F170
52 Same as no. 43. V. 2. 1965. F171
53 Hieronymus, St. Saint Jerome, dogmatic and polemical works, tr. by Hritzu. 1965. F172
54 Lactantius, L. C. F. Minor works, tr. by McDonald. 1965. F173
55 Eugippius. The life of Saint Severin, tr. by Biller and Krestan. 1965. F174
56 Augustinus Aurelius, St. The Catholic and Manichaean ways of life, tr. by D. A. and I. J. Gallagher. 1966. F175
57 Same as no. 48. V. 2. 1966. F176
58 Gregory of Nyssa. Ascetical works, tr. by Callahan. 1967. F177
59 Augustinus, Aurelius, St. The teacher, tr. by Russell. 1968. F178
60 Augustinus, Aurelius, St. The retractions, tr. by Bogan. 1968. F179
61 Cyril, St. The works of Saint Cyril of Jerusalem, tr. by McCauley and Stephenson. V. 1. 1969. F180
62-63 Iberian Fathers, tr. by Barlow. 2 v. 1969. F181
64 Same as no. 61. V. 2. 1970. F182
65 Ambrosius, St. Seven exegetical works, tr. by McHugh. 1971. F183
66 Same as no. 31. V. 3. 1974. F184

FATS AND OILS (Interscience)

1 Bailey, A. E. Industrial oil and fat products. 1951. F185
2 Markley, K. S. Fatty acids. 1960. F186
3 Bailey, A. E. Melting and solidification of fats and fatty acids. 1950. F187
4 Bailey, A. E., ed. Cottonseed and cottonseed products. 1948. F188
5 Markley, K. S. Soybeans and soybean products. 2 v. 1950-51. F189

Davidsohn, I. and others. Soap manufacture. 2 v. 1953-56. F190

FERGUSON FOUNDATION AGRICULTURAL ENGINEERING SERIES (Wiley)

Bainer, R. and others. Principles of farm machinery. 1955. F191

Barger, E. L. and others. Tractors and their power units. 1952. F192
Barre, H. J. and Sammet, L. L. Farm structures. 1950. F193
Farrall, A. W. Dairy engineering. 1953. F194
Frevert, R. K. and others. Soil and water conservation engineering. 1955. F195
Henderson, S. M. Agricultural process engineering. 1955. F196
Hienton, T. E. and others. Electricity in agricultural engineering. 1958. F197

THE FIELD OF MUSIC (Rinehart)

1 Goldman, R. F. The concert band. 1946. F198
2 Letz, H. Music for the violin and viola. 1948. F199
3 Kagen, S., comp. Music for the voice. 1949. F200
4 ____. On studying singing. 1950. F201
5 Friskin, J. and Freundlich, I. Music for the piano. 1954. F202
5 Seaman, J., ed. Great orchestral music. 1950. F203
A blank label was inserted in this book stating it is V. 5 of the series. A publisher's letter later said that the statement was an error.

FIELD STUDIES IN THE MODERN CULTURE OF THE SOUTH (Univ. of North Carolina)

1 Rubin, M. Plantation County. 1951. F204
2 Lewis, H. Blackways of Kent. 1955. F205
3 Morland, J. K. Millways of Kent. 1958. F206

FILSON CLUB. PUBLICATIONS.

1 Durrett, R. T. John Filson. 1884. F207
2 Speed, T. The Wilderness road. 1886. F208
3 Perrin, W. H. The pioneer press of Kentucky. 1888. F209
4 Whitsitt, W. H. The life and times of Judge Caleb Wallace. 1888. F210
5 Durrett, R. T. An historical sketch of St. Paul's Church, Louisville, Ky... 1889. F211
6 Brown, J. M. The political beginnings of Kentucky. 1889. F212
7 Filson Club. The centenary of Kentucky... 1892. F213
8 Durrett, R. T. The centenary of Louisville. 1893. F214
9 Speed, T. The political club, Danville, Kentucky. 1894. F215
10 Call, R. E. The life and writings of Rafinesque. 1895. F216
11 Peter, R. and J. The history of Transylvania University. 1896. F217
12 Durrett, R. T. Bryant's Station and the memorial proceedings... 1897. F218
13 Johnston, J. S. First explorations of Kentucky: Doctor Thomas Walker's journal. 1898. F219
14 The Clay family, by Smith. 1899. F220
15 Pirtle, A. The battle of Tippecanoe. 1900. F221
16 Ranck, G. W. Boonesborough. 1901. F222
17 Price, S. W. The old masters of the Bluegrass. 1902. F223
18 Young, B. H. The battle of the Thames. 1903. F224
19 Smith, Z. F. The battle of New Orleans. 1904. F225
20 Peter, R. The history of the Medical department of Transylvania University. 1905. F226
21 Quisenberry, A. C. Lopez's expeditions to Cuba, 1850-1851. 1906. F227
22 Pickett, T. C. The quest for a lost race. 1907. F228
23 Durrett, R. T. Traditions of the earliest visits of foreigners to North America. 1908. F229
24:1 Townsend, J. W. The life of James Francis Leonard. 1909. F230
24:2 Price, S. W. Biographical

sketch of Colonel Joseph Crockett. 1909. F231
25 Young, B. H. The prehistoric men of Kentucky. 1910. F232
26 Verhoeff, M. The Kentucky mountains. 1911. F233
27 Robertson, J. R. Petitions of the early inhabitants of Kentucky to the General Assembly of Virginia, 1769 to 1792. 1914. F234
28 Verhoeff, M. The Kentucky river navigation. 1917. F235
29 Martin, A. E. The anti-slavery movement in Kentucky prior to 1850. 1918. F236
30 Rothert, O. A. The story of a poet: Madison Cawein. 1921. F237
31 Littell, W. Reprints of Littell's Political transactions in and concerning Kentucky, ed. by Bodley. 1922. F238
32 Rothert, O. A. The Filson club and its activities, 1884-1922. 1922. F239
33 Jillson, W. R. The Kentucky land grants. 1925. F240
34 ____. Old Kentucky entries and deeds. 1926. F241
35 Filson, J. Filson's Kentucke. 1929. F242
36 Bodley, T. Our first great west. 1938. F243

THE FIRST AMERICAN FRONTIER (Arno)

Agnew, D. A history of the region of Pennsylvania north of the Ohio and west of the Allegheny River. 1971. F244
Alden, G. H. New governments west of the Alleghenies before 1780. 1971. F245
Barrett, J. A. Evolution of the ordinance of 1787. 1971. F246
Billon, F. L. Annals of St. Louis in its early days under the French and Spanish dominations. 1971. F247
____. Annals of St. Louis in its territorial days from 1804 to 1821. 1971. F248
Bodley, T., ed. Littell's political transactions in and concerning Kentucky. Letter of George Nicholas to his friend in Virginia. Also General Wilkerson's memorial. 1971. F249
Boynton, B. Authentic memoirs of William Augustus Bowles. 1971. F250
Bradley, A. G. The fight with France for North America. 1971. F251
Brannan, J., ed. Official letters of the military and naval officers of the United States. 1971. F252
Brown, J. P. Old frontiers. 1971. F253
Brown, S. R. The Western Gazetteer. 1971. F254
Cist, C. The Cincinnati miscellany. 1971. F255
Claiborne, N. H. Notes on the war in the South. 1971. F256
Clark, D. Proofs of the corruption of Gen. James Wilkinson. 1971. F257
Clark, G. R. Col. George Rogers Clark's sketch of his campaign in the Illinois in 1778-9. 1971. F258
Collins, L. Historical sketches of Kentucky. 1971. F259
Cutler, J. A topographical description of the state of Ohio. 1971. F260
Cutler, J. P. Life and times of Ephraim Cutler. 1972. F261
Darlington, M. C., ed. Fort Pitt and letters from the frontier. 1971. F262
____. History of Col. Henry Boquet and the western frontiers of Pennsylvania. 1971. F263
De Schweinitz, E. The life and times of David Zeisberger. 1971. F264
Dillon, J. B. A history of Indiana. 1971. F265
Eaton, J. H. The life of Andrew Jackson. 1971. F266
English, W. H. Conquest of the country northwest of the River Ohio. 1971. F267
Flint, T. Indian wars of the west. 1971. F268
Forbes, J. Writings of General

John Forbes. 1971. F269
Forman, S. S. Narrative of a journey down the Ohio and Mississippi in 1789-90. 1971. F270
Haywood, J. The Civil and political history of the state of Tennessee. 1971. F271
Heckewelder, J. History, manners, and customs of the Indian nations... 1971. F272
____. A narrative of the mission of the United Brethren among the Delaware and Mohegan Indians. 1971. F273
Hildreth, S. P. Pioneer history. 1971. F274
Houck, L. The boundaries of the Louisiana Purchase. 1971. F275
____. A history of Missouri. 1971. F276
____. The Spanish Regime in Missouri. 1971. F277
Jacob, J. J. A biographical sketch of the life of the late Captain Michael Cresap. 1971. F278
Jones, D. A journal of two visits made to some nations of Indians on the west side of the River Ohio. 1971. F279
Kenton, E. Simon Kenton. 1971. F280
Loudon, A. A selection of some of the most interesting narratives of outrages committed by the Indians... 1971. F281
Lundy's Lane Historical Society. Documents relating to the invasion of Canada and the surrender of Detroit. 1971. F282
Monnette, J. W. History of the discovery and settlement of the Valley of the Mississippi. 1971. F283
Morse, J. The American Gazetteer. 1971. F284
Pickett, A. J. History of Alabama. 1971. F285
Pope, J. A tour through the southern and western territories of the United States of North America. 1971. F286
Putnam, A. W. History of Middle Tennessee. 1971. F287
Ramsey, J. G. M. The annals of Tennessee to the end of the eighteenth century. 1971. F288
Ranck, G. W. Boonesborough. 1971. F289
Robertson, J. R. Petitions of the early inhabitants of Kentucky to the General Assembly of Virginia. 1971. F290
Royce, C. C., comp. Indian land cessions in the United States. 1971. F291
Rupp, I. D. History of Northampton, Lehigh, Monroe, Carbon, and Schuykill counties. 1971. F292
Safford, W. H. The Blennerhassett papers. 1971. F293
St. Clair, A. A narrative of the manner in which the campaign against the Indians, in the year 1791 was conducted. 1971. F294
Sargent, W., ed. A history of an expedition against Fort DuQuesne in 1755. 1971. F295
Severance, F. H. An old frontier of France. 1971. F296
Sipe, C. H. Fort Ligonier and its times. 1971. F297
Stevens, H. N. Lewis Evans. 1971. F298
Timberlake, H. The memoirs of Lieut. Henry Timberlake. 1971. F299
Tome, P. Pioneer life. 1971. F300
Trent, W. Journal of Captain William Trent from Logstown to Pickawillany. 1971. F301
Walton, J. S. Conrad Weiser and the Indian policy of Colonial Pennsylvania. 1971. F302
Withers, A. S. Chronicles of border warfare. 1971. F303

FLETCHER SCHOOL STUDIES IN INTERNATIONAL AFFAIRS (Tufts Univ.)

Cabot, J. M. Toward our common American destiny. 1955. F304
Cole, A. B., ed. Conflict in Indo-China and international repercussions. 1956. F305

Halm, G. N. Economic systems. 1951. F306
____. The economics of money and banking. Irwin. 1956. F307
Imlah, A. H. Economic elements in the Pax Britannica. Harvard. 1958. F308
Kelsen, H. Principles of international law. 1952. F309
Stone, J. Legal controls of international conflict. 1959. F310

FLETCHER SCHOOL STUDIES IN INTERNATIONAL LAW (Rinehart)

Cabot, J. M. Toward our common American destiny. 1955. F311
Cole, A. B., ed. Conflict in Indo-China and international repercussions, ed. by Lande and others. 1956. F312
Halm, G. N. Economic systems. 1951. F313
Hawkins, H. C. Commercial treaties & agreements. 1952. F314
Kelsen, H. Principles on international law. 1952. F315
Stone, J. Legal controls of international conflict. 1959. F316

FLORA NEOTROPICA MONOGRAPHS (Hafner)

1 Cowan, R. S. Swartzia. 1968. F317
2 Cuatrecasas, J. Brunelliaceae. 1970. F318
3-5 Singer, R. Omphalinae-Phaeocollybia-Strobilmycetaceae. 1970. F319
6 Lowy, B. Tremeliales. 1971. F320
7 Berg, C. C. Moraceae, Olmediae, and Brosimeae. 1972. F321
8 Maas, P. J. M. Zingiberaceae Costoideae. 1972. F322
9 Prance, G. T. Chrysobalanceae. 1972. F323
10-11 ____. Dichapetakaceae rhabdodendranceae. 2 v. in 1. 1972. F324
12 Prance, G. T. and da Silva, M. F. Caryocaraceae. 1972. F325
13 Rogers, D. J. and Appan, S. G. Manihot manihotides. 1973. F326
14 Smith, L. B. Bromeliaceae. 1973. F327

FLORIDA STATE UNIVERSITY. TALLAHASSEE. RESEARCH COUNCIL. FLORIDA STATE UNIVERSITY STUDIES

1 Randel, W. and others, eds. Contributions to science. 1950. F328
2 Toumin, L. and others, eds. Studies in social sciences. 1951. F329
3 ____. Studies in modern language and literature. 1951. F330
4 ____. Studies in history and political science. 1951. F331
5 ____. Studies in English and American literature. 1952. F332
6 ____. Studies in literature and philosophy. 1952. F333
7 ____. Papers from the Oceanographic Institute. 1952. F334
8 ____. Papers in natural science and social science. 1952. F335
9 Jordan, W., ed. Developments in education. 1953. F336
10 ____. Essays in the social sciences. 1953. F337
11 ____. Monographs in English and American literature. 1953. F338
12 Shores, L. Challenge to librarianship. 1953. F339
13 Same as no. 1, no. 2. 1954. F340
14 Jordan, W., ed. Studies in history and literature. 1954. F341
15 Florida State University. Education in Florida past and present. 1954. F342
16 Studies in anthropology. 1954. F343
17 Jordan, W. George Washington Campbell of Tennessee. 1955. F344
18 Mamatey, V., ed. Studies

in music history and theory. 1955. F345
19 ____. Studies in English and American literature. 1955. F346
20 Beck, E. R. Verdict on Schacht. 1955. F347
21 Florida State University. Techniques used to improve education. 1955. F348
22 ____. Papers. 1952. F349
23 ____. Woodrow Wilson centennial series. 1956. F350
24 Kurz, H. Tidal marshes of the Gulf and Atlantic coasts of northern Florida... 1957. F351
25 Campbell, D. S. Doak S. Campbell, southern educator. 1957. F352
26 Florida State University. Procedures used to improve education. 1957. F353
27 Jordan, W. T. Ante-bellum Alabama. 1957. F354
28 The Negro in American society, ed. by Preu. 1958. F355
29 Van Stan, I. Problems in Pre-Columbian textile classification. 1958. F356
30 Florida State University. Florida educators. 1959. F357
31 Beck, E. R. Death of a Prussian republic. 1959. F358
32 Int'l. Conf. on the Nuclear Optical Model. Proceedings, ed. by Green and others. 1959. F359
33 Preu, J. A. The dean and the anarchist. 1959. F360
34 Marshall, M. Herbs, hoecakes, and husbandry, ed. by Jordan. 1960. F361
35 Strozier, R. Selected speeches of Robert Strozier. 1960. F362
36 Greenhut, M. L. and Colberg, M. R. Factors in the location of Florida industry. 1962. F363
37 Bach, J. The concerted symphonies, ed. by White. 1963. F364
38 Morris, H. Richard Barnfield Colin's child. 1963. F365
39 Rogers, W. W. Ante-bellum Thomas County. 1963. F366
40 Campbell, D. S. A university in transition. 1964. F367
41 Rogers, W. W. Thomas County during the Civil War. 1964. F368
42 Murphy, C. Thomas Moreley, editions of Italian canzonets and madrigals. 1964. F369
43 Blackwell, G. Selected addresses of Gordon W. Blackwell. 1965. F370
44 Howard, D. D. The battle of Bissaco. 1965. F371
45 Macesich, G. Commercial banking and regional development in the U. S. 1965. F372
46 Richardson, J. M. Negro in the reconstruction of Florida. 1965. F373
47 Tschirgi, H. D. An investigation of performance evaluation in agencies of the Florida merit system. 1966. F374
48 Rush, N. O. Spain's final triumph over Great Britain in the Gulf of Mexico. 1966. F375
49 Miller, K. S. and Gregg, C. M. Mental health and the lower social classes. 1966. F376
50 Beck, E. R. On teaching history in colleges and universities. 1966. F377
51 Jones, J. P. Black Jack, John A. Logan and southern Illinois in the Civil War era. 1966. F378

Ceased publication.

FLORIDA. UNIVERSITY. INSTITUTE OF GERONTOLOGY SERIES.

1 Southern Conf. on Gerontology. Problems of America's aging population, ed. by Smith. 1951. F379
2 ____. Living in the later years, ed. by Smith. 1952. F380
3 ____. Health in the later years, ed. by Maclachian. 1953. F381
4 ____. Economic problems of retirement, ed. by Hurff. 1954. F382

5 ____. Aging and retirement, ed. by Webber. 1955. F383
6 ____. Aging: a current appraisal, ed. by Webber. 1956. F384
7 ____. Service for the aging, ed. by Webber. 1957. F385
8 ____. Organized religion and older people, ed. by Scudder. 1958. F386
9 ____. Society and the health of older people, ed. by Webber. 1959. F387
10 ____. Aging: a regional appraisal, ed. by Osterbind. 1961. F388
11 ____. Aging in a changing society, ed. by Albrecht. 1962. F389
12 ____. Continuing education in the later years, ed. by Dixon. 1963. F390
13 ____. Social changes and aging in the twentieth century, ed. by Alleger. 1964. F391
14 ____. Maintaining high level wellness in older years, ed. by Knowles. 1965. F392
15 ____. Medical care under social security, ed. by Webber. 1966. F393
16 ____. Income in retirement, ed. by Osterbind. 1967. F394
17 ____. Potentialities for later living, ed. by Thomason. 1968. F395
18 ____. Feasible planning for social change, ed. by Osterbind. 1969. F396
19 ____. Health care services for the aged, ed. by Osterbind. 1970. F397
20 ____. New careers for older people, ed. by Osterbind. 1971. F398
21 ____. Independent living for older people. 1972. F399
22 ____. Areawide planning for independent living for older people. 1973. F400
23 ____. Migration, mobility and aging. 1974. F401

FLORIDA. UNIVERSITY. SCHOOL OF INTER-AMERICAN STUDIES. PUBLICATION SERIES ONE.

1 Wilgus, A. C., ed. The Caribbean at mid-century. 1951. F402
2 ____. The Caribbean: peoples, problems and prospects. 1952. F403
3 ____. Caribbean: contemporary trends. 1953. F404
4 ____. Caribbean: its economy. 1954. F405
5 ____. Caribbean: its culture. 1955. F406
6 ____. Caribbean: its political problems. 1956. F407
7 ____. Caribbean: contemporary international relations. 1957. F408
8 ____. Caribbean: British, Dutch, French, United States. 1957. F409
9 ____. Caribbean: natural resources. 1958. F410
10 ____. Caribbean: contemporary education. 1960. F411
11 ____. Caribbean: the Central American area. 1961. F412
12 ____. Caribbean: contemporary Colombia. 1962. F413
13 ____. The Caribbean: Venezuelan development. 1963. F414
14 ____. The Caribbean: Mexico today. 1964. F415
15 ____. The Caribbean: health problems. 1965. F416
16 ____. The Caribbean: current United States relations. 1966. F417
17 ____. The Caribbean: its hemispheric role. 1968. F418

FLORIDA. UNIVERSITY. UNIVERSITY OF FLORIDA STUDIES. BIOLOGICAL SCIENCE SERIES.

1:1 Byers, C. F. A contribution to the knowledge of Florida Odonata. 1930. F419
2:1 Hubbell, T. H. A monographic revision of the Genus Ceuthophilus. 1936. F420
3:1 Carr, A. F. A contribution to the herpetology of Florida. 1940. F421
3:2 Hobbs, H. H. The

crayfishes of Florida. 1942. F422
4:1 Laessle, A. M. The plant communities of the Welaka area. 1942. F423
4:2 Goin, C. J. Studies on the life history of Eleutherodactylus Ricordii Planirostris. 1947. F424
4:3 Pierce, E. L. An annual cycle of the Plankton and chemistry of four aquatic habitats in Northern Florida. 1947. F425
4:4 Berner, L. The mayflies of Florida. 1950. F426
5:1 Young, F. N. The water beetles of Florida. 1954. F427

FOLGER DOCUMENTS OF TUDOR AND STUART CIVILIZATION (Cornell Univ. Pr.)

Ascham, R. The schoolmaster (1570), ed. by Ryan. 1967. F428
Burghley, W. C. The execution of justice in England, by Cecil, ed. by Kingdon. 1965. F429
A discourse of the commonweal of this realm of England, ed. by Dewar. 1969. F430
Eburne, R. A plain pathway to plantations (1624), ed. by Wright. 1962. F431
Edward VI, King of England. Chronicle and political papers, ed. by Jordan. 1966. F432
Fletcher, G. Of the Rus. Commonwealth, ed. by Schmidt. 1966. F433
Harrison, W. The description of England, ed. by Edelen. 1968. F434
Jewel, J. An apology of the Church of England, ed. by Booty. 1963. F435
Knachel, P. A. Eikon Baslike. 1966. F436
Lambarde, W. William Lambarde and local government, ed. by Read. 1962. F437
Lattimer, H. Selected sermons, ed. by Chester. 1968. F438
Nedham, M. The case of the Commonwealth of England, ed. by Knachel. 1969. F439
Peacham, H. The complete gentleman, The truth of our time, and The art of living in London, ed. by Heltzel. 1962. F440
Smythe, J. Certain discourses military, ed. by Hale. 1964. F441
Smythe, T. A discourse of the Commonwealth of this realm of England, ed. by Dewar. 1969. F442
Southwell, R. Two letters and short rules of a good life, ed. by Brown. 1973. F443
Stubbs, J. Gaping Gulf, ed. by Berry. 1968. F444
Thomas, W. The history of Italy (1549), ed. by Parks. 1963. F445
Tuvill, D. Essays, political and moral, ed. by Lievsay. 1971. F446
Williams, R. The actions of the Low Countries, ed. by Davies. 1964. F447
Wotton, H. Elements of architecture. 1968. F448
Wright, L. B., ed. Advice to a son. 1962. F449

FOLGER MONOGRAPHS ON TUDOR AND STUART CIVILIZATION (Univ. of Va. Pr.)

Coleridge, S. T. Coleridge on Shakespeare, ed. by Foakes. 1971. F450
Knachel, P. A. England and Fronde. 1967. F451
Quinn, D. B. The Elizabetheans and the Irish. 1966. F452

FOLGER SHAKESPEARE LIBRARY PUBLICATIONS.

1 Shakespeare, W. Titus Andronicus, the first quarto. 1594, ed. by Adams. 1936. F453
2 ____. The passionate pilgrim, 1599, ed. by Adams. 1939. F454
3 ____. The passionate pilgrim, 1612, ed. by Rollins. 1940. F455
4 Middleton, T. The ghost

of Lucrere, ed. by Adams. 1937. F456

5 Oenone and Paris, by T. H., 1594, ed. by Adams. 1943. F457

6 Middleton, T. Hengist, king of Kent, ed. by Bald. 1938. F458

7 Folger Shakespeare Library. Joseph Quincy Adams memorial studies, ed. by McManawan and others. 1948. F459

Ascham, R. The schoolmaster (1570), ed. by Ryan. 1967. F460

Wright, L. B. Middle-class culture in Elizabethean England. 1958. F461

____. Shakespeare celebrated. 1966. F462

FOLK-LORE SOCIETY. PUBLICATIONS (Glaisher)

2 Henderson, W. Notes on the folklore of the Northern counties of England and the Borders. 1879. F463

4 Aubrey, J. Remaines of Gentilisme and Judaisme. 1881. F464

7 Gregor, W. Notes of the folklore of the North-east of Scotland. 1881. F465

9 Comparetti, D. P. A. Researches respecting the Book of Sinibâd. 1882. F466

12 Black, W. G. Folk-medicine. 1883. F467

13 Jones, W. H. and Kropf, L. L., eds. The folk-tales of the Magyars. 1886. F468

15 Callaway, H. The religious system of the Amazulu. 1884. F469

17 Swainson, C. The folk-lore and provincial names of British birds. 1885. F470

20 Gomme, G. L. The handbook of folklore. 1890. F471

22 Chamberlain, B. H. Aino folklore. 1888. F472

23 Nutt, A. Studies on the legend of the Holy Grail. 1888. F473

25 MacInnes, D. Folk and hero tales. 1890. F474

26 Jacobus de Vitriaco. The exempla, ed. by Crane. 1890. F475

29 Hardy, J., ed. The Denham tracts. V. 1. 1891. F476

31 Cox, M. E. R. Cinderella, three and forty-five variants, ed. by Cox. 1892. F477

33 Saxo Grammaticus. The first nine books of the Danish history, tr. by Elton. 1894. F478

35 Same as no. 29. V. 2. F479

37 County folklore. V. 1. 1895. F480

39 Bower, H. M. The elevation & procession of the Ceri at Gubbio. 1896. F481

41 Dennett, R. E. Notes on the folklore of the Fjort, ed. by Kingsley. 1897. F482

43 Starr, F. Catalogue of a collection of objects illustrating the folk-lore of Mexico. 1898. F483

45 Same as no. 37. V. 2. 1899. F484

47 Maclagan, R. C., comp. The games & diversions of Argyleshire. 1901. F485

49 Same as no. 37. V. 3. 1901. F486

51 Owen, M. A. Folk-lore of the Musquakie Indians of North America and catalogue of Musquakie beadwork and other objects in the collection of the Folklore society. 1904. F487

53 Same as no. 37. V. 4. 1903. F488

55 Jekyll, W. Jamaican song and story. 1907. F489

57 Folklore Society, London. Bibliography of folklore. 3 parts. 1905-07. F490

59 Dames, M. L. Popular poetry of the Baloches. 2 v. in 1. 1907. F491

60 Gerould, G. H. The grateful dead. 1908. F492

63 Same as no. 37. V. 5. 1908. F493

65, 67 Hartland, E. S. Primitive paternity. 2 v. 1909. F494

69 Same as no. 37. V. 6. 1911. F495
71 Same as no. 37. V. 7. 1912. F496
73 Burne, C. S. The handbook of folklore. 1914. F497
75a Gaster, M. Rumanian bird and beast stories. 1915. F498
89 Stephens, T. A. Proverb literature, ed. by Bonser. 1928. F499
97 Wright, A. R. British calendar customs. England. V. 1. 1936. F500
100 Banks, M. M., ed. British calendar customs. Scotland. V. 1. 1937. F501
102 Same as no. 97. V. 2. 1938. F502
104 Same as no. 100. V. 2. 1939. F503
106 Same as no. 97. V. 3. 1940. F504
108 Same as no. 100. V. 3. 1941. F505
110 Paton, C. I. Manx calendar customs. 1940. F506
112 Banks, M. M., ed. British calendar customs: Orkney and Shetland. 1946. F507
114 Tongue, R. L. Somerset folklore. 1965. F508
121 Bonser, W. A bibliography of folklore. 1961. F509
127 Cawte, E. C. and others. English ritual drama. 1968. F510
130 Bonser, W. and Percival, A. Bibliography of Folklore, 1958-1967. 1970. F511

Some publications in this series were issued as the Society's periodical publications. They are:
Folk-lore: 27, 28, 30, 32, 34, 36, 38, 40, 42, 44, 46, 48, 50, 52, 54, 56, 58, 61, 62, 64, 66, 68, 70, 72, 74, 76-88, 90-96, 98, 99, 101, 103, 105, 107, 109, 111, 115-119, 122-6, 128-9, 131-3
Folk-lore journal: 11, 14, 16, 18, 19, 21, 24
Folk-lore record: 1, 3, 5, 6, 8, 10
114 not published.

FOLKTALES OF THE WORLD (Univ. of Chicago Pr.)

Briggs, K. M. and Tongue, R. L., eds. Folktales of England. 1965. F512
Christiansen, R. T., ed. Folktales of Norway, tr. by Iversen. 1964. F513
Dégh, L., ed. Folktales of Hungary, tr. by Halász. 1965. F514
Eberhard, W., ed. Folktales of China. 1965. F515
Massignon, G., ed. Folktales of France, ed. by Hyland. 1968. F516
Megas, G. A., ed. Folktales of Greece, tr. by Coladices. 1970. F517
Noy, D. and Amos, B., eds. Folktales of Israel, tr. by Baharav. 1963. F518
O'Súilleaubháin, S. Folktales of Ireland, tr. by O'Sullivan. 1966. F519
Parades, A., ed. Folktales of Mexico. 1970. F520
Pino-Saavedra, Y., ed. Folktales of Chile, tr. by Gray. 1968. F521
Ranke, K., ed. Folktales of Germany, ed. by Baumann. 1966. F522
Seki, K., ed. Folktales of Japan, tr. by Adams. 1963. F523

FONDATION NATIONALE DES SCIENCES POLITIQUES. CAHIERS (Colin)

1 Etudes de sociologie électorate, par C. Morazé et al. 1947. F524
2 Garavel, J. Les paysans de Morette. 1948. F525
3 Goetz-Girey, R. La pensée syndicale française. 1948. F526
4 La Modernisation des instruments de travail et méthodes dans les administrations publiques, par Puget et al. 1948. F527
5 Cadart, J. Régime électoral et régime parlementaire en Grand-Bretagne.

1948. F528
6 Braibant, G. La planification en Tchécoslovaquie. 1948. F529
7 Dessus, G. Matériaux pour une géographie volontaire de l'industrie française. 1949. F530
8 Les Fondement de la politique extérieure des Etats Unis, par Allix et al. 1949. F531
9 Siegfried, A. Géographie électorale de l'Ardèche sous la IIIe République. 1949. F532
10 Guiot, P. Thurins, démogéographique d'une commune rurale de l'ouest lyonnais. 1949. F533
11 Nef, J. U. La route de la guerre totale. 1949. F534
12 Etudes sur la banlieue de Paris, essais méthodologiques. 1950. F535
13 Etudes politiques anglo-saxonnes. 1950. F536
14 Léger, C. La démocratie industrielle et les comités d'entreprise en Suède. 1950. F537
15 Brochier, H. Finances publiques et redistribution des revenus. 1950. F538
16 Duverger, M. et al. L'influence des systèmes électoraux sur la vie politique. 1950. F539
17 Bettelheim, C. and Frere, S. Auxerre en 1950. 1950. F540
18 Crosa, E. et al., eds. La constitution italienne de 1948. 1950. F541
19 Les "Sciences de la politique" aux Etats-Unis, par Arrow et al. 1951. F542
20 Etudes economiques allemandes. 1951. F543
21 Boulouis, J. Essai sur la politique des subventions administratives. 1951. F544
22 Waline, P. Les syndicats aux Etats-Unis. 1951. F545
23 Latreille, A. and Siegfried, A. Les forces religieuses et la vie politique: Catholicisme et Protestantisme. 1951. F546
24 Martin, J. P. Les finances de guerre du Canada. 1951. F547
25 Simon, P. H. Témoins de l'homme: La condition humaine dans la littérature française du XXe siècle. 1951. F548
26 Goguel-Nyegaard, F. and Dupeux, G. Sociologie électorale. 1951. F549
27 Goguel-Nyegaard, F. Géographie des elections françaises de 1870 à 1951. 1951. F550
28 Monbeig, P. Pionniers et planteurs de São Paulo. 1952. F551
29 Barnérias, J. S. L'équilibre économique international. 1952. F552
30 Vincenot, Y. Le service de santé en Grande-Bretagne. 1952. F553
31 Pelloux, R. and others, eds. Libéralisme, traditionnalisme, décentralisation. 1952. F554
32 International Geographical Union. L'amenagement de l'espace, par Gottman et al. 1952. F555
33 Gaudemet, P. M. Le civil service britannique. 1952. F556
34 Rist, M. La Federal Reserve et les difficultés monétaires d'après la guerre. 1945-50. 1952. F557
35 Ramus, A. Vie paysanne et technique agricole. 1952. F558
36 Ducros, B. L'action des grands marchés financiers sur l'équilibre monétaire. 1952. F559
37 Cambiaire, A. de. L'autoconsommation agricole en France. 1952. F560
38 Lavau, G. E. Partis politiques et réalités sociales. 1953. F561
39 Chardonnet, J. Les grands types de complexes industriels. 1953. F562
40 Mendras, H. Etudes de sociologie rurale: Novis & Virgin. 1953. F563
41 Brussels. Institut des relations internationales. La Communauté européene du Charbon et de l'acier.

1953. F564
42 Seurin, J. L. La structure interne des partis politiques américains. 1953. F565
43 Bernard, P. Economie et sociologie de la Seine-et-Marne, 1850-1950. 1953. F566
44 Lambert, J. Le Brésil. 1953. F567
45 Gouhier, J. Le Mans aux milieu du XXe siècle. 1953. F568
46 Bernard, J. R. Le système "utility." 1953. F569
47 Mabileau, A. Le Parti libéral dans la système constitutionnel britannique. 1953. F570
48 Calvez, J. Y. Droit international et souveraineté en U. R. S. S. 1953. F571
49 Postel, C. L'Aéroport de Paris. 1953. F572
50 Naissance du nouvelles démocraties. Deux rapports, by Bailey. 1953. F573
51 Morazé, C. Les trois âges du Brésil. 1954. F574
52 Hoffmann, S. Organisations internationales et pouvoirs politiques des états. 1954. F575
53 Duplessis, G. Les mariages en France. 1954. F576
54 Lidderdale, D. W. S. Le Parlement français. 1954. F577
55 Association française de service politique. La politique étrangère et ses fondements. 1954. F578
56 Naville, P. La vie de travail et ses problèmes. 1954. F579
57 Grosser, A., ed. Administration et politique en Allemagne occidentale. 1954. F580
58 Duroselle, J. B. and others. Les relations germano-soviétique de 1933 à 1939. F581
59 Langrod, J. S. La science et l'enseignement de l'administration publique aux Etats-Unis. 1954. F582
60 Goguel-Nyegaard, F., ed. Nouvelles études de sociologie électorale. 1954. F583
61 Jeanneney, J. M. Les commerces de détail en Europe occidentale. 1954. F584
62 Gouault, J. Comment la France est devenue républicaine, les elections à l'Assemblée nationale 1870-1875. 1954. F585
63 Chardonnet, J. La sidérurgie française. 1954. F586
64 Simon, P. H. L'esprit et l'histoire. 1954. F587
65 Perrot, M. La monnaie et l'opinion publique en France et en Angleterre, de 1924 à 1936. 1955. F588
66 Chapman, B. L'administration locale en France. 1955. F589
67 Balandier, G. Sociologie des Brazzavilles noires. 1955. F590
68 Mathiot, A. La régime politique britannique. 1955. F591
69 Labasse, J. Les capitaux et la region, étude géographique. 1955. F592
70 Rézette, R. Les partis politique marocains. 1955. F593
71 Clément, P. and Xydias, N. Vienne sur le Rhône. 1955. F594
72 Dogan, M. and Narbonne, J. Les Françaises face à la politique. 1955. F595
73 Campion, G. F. M. C. and Lidderdale, D. W. S. La procédure parlementaire en Europe. 1955. F596
74 Association française de science politique. Partis politiques et classes sociales. 1955. F597
75 Fohlen, C. Une affaire de famille au XIXe siècle: Méquillet-Nablot. 1955. F598
76 Galant, H. C. Histoire politique de la sécurité social française, 1945-1952. 1955. F599
77 Bobrowski, C. La Yougoslavie socialiste. 1956. F600
78 Grosser, A., ed. Les relations internationales de l'Allemagne occidentale. 1956. F601
79 Moraze, C. Les Français de la République. 1956. F602
80 La Querelle de la C. E. D.,

ed. by Aron and Lerner. 1956. F603
81 Hoffmann, S. and others. Le mouvement Poujade. 1956. F604
82 Association française de science politique. Les élections du 2 janvier 1956, ed. by Duverger and others. 1957. F605
83 Moussa, P. Les chances économiques de la communauté franco-africaine. 1957. F606
84 Sailly, J. de. La zone sterling. 1957. F607
85 Duroselle, J. B., ed. Les frontieres européennes de l'U. R. S. S. 1917-1941. 1957. F608
86 Morice, J. La demande d'automobiles en France. 1957. F609
87 Jeanneney, J. M. Tableaux statistiques relatifs à l'économie française et l'économie mondiale. 1957. F610
88 Malissen, J. Investissement et financement. 1957. F611
89 France. Laws, statutes, etc. Textes de droit économique et social français, 1789-1957, by Jeanneney and Perrot. 1957. F612
90 Bouissou, M. La Chambre des lords au XXe siècle (1911-1949). 1957. F613
91 Bouvier, C. La collectivisation de l'agriculture en U. R. S. S. 1958. F614
92 Kayser, J. and others, eds. La presse de province sous la Troisième République. 1958. F615
93 Boyon, J. Naissance d'un état africain: le Ghana... 1958. F616
94 Association française de science politique. Les paysans et la politique dans la France contemporaines, ed. by Fauvet and Mendras. 1958. F617
95 Meynaud, J. Les groupes de pression en France. 1958. F618
96 Long, R. Les élections legislatives dans la Côte-d-Or depuis 1870. 1958. F619
97 Conac, G. La fonction publique aux Etats-Unis. 1958. F620
98 Lasserre, G. Libreville. 1958. F621
99 Dupeux, G. Le front populaire et les élections de 1936. 1959. F622
100 Meynaud, J. Introduction à la science politique. 1959. F623
101 Gendarme, R. L'économie de l'Algérie... 1959. F624
102 Chardonnet, J. Metropoles économiques... 1959. F625
103 Simon, P. H. Théâtre et destin. 1959. F626
104 Meyriat, J., ed. La Calabre... by Seronde and others. 1960. F627
105 Ferraton, H. Syndicalisme ouvrier et social-démocratie en Norvége. 1960. F628
106 Fall, B. B. La Viet-Minh. 1960. F629
107 Cotteret, J. M. and others. Lois électorales et inégalités de représentation en France, 1936-1960. 1960. F630
108 Lassale, J. P. La Cour suprême et le problème communiste aux Etats-Unis. 1960. F631
109 Association française de science politique. L'établissement de la Cinquième Republique. 1960. F632
110 Babeau, A. Les conseils ouvriers en Poloyne. 1960. F633
111 Aymard, P. La banque et l'état. 1960. F634
112 Moscovici, S. Reconversion industrielle et changements sociaux. 1961. F635
113 Olivesi, A. and Roncayolo, M. Géographie électorale des Bouches-du-Rhone. 1961. F636
114 Saint Marc, P. La France dans la C. E. C. A. 1961. F637
115 Barral, P. Le départment de l'Isère sous la IIIe République, histoire sociale

et politique. 1962. F638
116-117 Rémond, R. Les Etats-Unis devant l'opinion française pendant la première moitie du XIXe siècle. 2 v. 1962. F639
118 Meynaud, J. Nouvelles études sur les groupes de pression en France. 1962. F640
119 Centre d'Etude de la Vie Politique Française. Le référendum de 8 janvier 1961, ed. by Goguel. 1962. F641
120 Association française de science politique. La dépolitisation. 1962. F642
121 Centre d'Etudes des Relations Internationales. Les nouveaux Etats dans les relations internationales. 1962. F643
122 Kayser, J. Le quotidien français. 1963. F644
123 Girardet, R., ed. La crise militaire française, 1945-1962, by Bouju and others. 1964. F645
124 Goguel-Nyegaard, F., ed. Le referendum du 8 avril 1962. 1963. F646
125 Chasseriaud, J. P. Le parti démocrate chretien en Italie. 1965. F647
126 Duroselle, J. B. and Meyriat, J. La communauté internationale face aux jeunes Etats. 1964. F648
127 Blondel, J. La société politique britannique. 1964. F649
128 Masnata, F. Le Parti socialiste et la tradition démocratique en Suisse. 1963. F650
129 Prost, A. La C. G. T. à l'époque du front populaire, 1934-1939. 1964. F651
130 Rémond, R., ed. Forces religieuses et attitudes politiques dans la France contemporaine. 1965. F652
131 Duroselle, J. B. and Meyriat, J., eds. Politiques nationales envers les jeunes Etats. 1964. F653
132 Charnay, J. P. Les scrutins politiques en France de 1815 à 1962. 1964. F654
133 Szokolóczy-Syllaba, J. Les organisations professionelles françaises et le Marché commun. 1965. F655
134 Adam, G. La C. F. T. C. 1940-1958. 1964. F656
135 Grenoble. Université. Administration traditionnelle et planification régionale. 1964. F657
136 Hermet, G. Le problème meridional de l'Espagne. 1965. F658
137 Adam, G. Atlas des élections sociales en France. 1964. F659
138 Centre de recherche et d'information socio-politiques. La décision politique en Belgique, by Meyn and others. 1965. F660
139 Gournay, B. Introduction à la science administrative. 1966. F661
140 Colloque sur la planification comme processus de décision. La planification comme processus de décision. 1965. F662
141 Carrere d'Encausse, H. Réforme et révolution chez les Musulmans de l'Empire russe. 1966. F663
142 Centre d'etude de la vie politique française. La referendum d'Octobre et les élections de Novembre 1962. 1965. F664
143 Michelat, G. and Thomas, J. P. Dimensions du nationalisme. 1966. F665
144 Mayeur, F. L'Aube, étude d'un journal d'opinion. 1966. F666
145 Soulie, G. and Champenois, L. Le Royaume d'-Arabie saoudite face à l'Islam révolutionnaire. 1966. F667
146 Centre d'étude de la vie politique française. Régime interne et politique extérieure dans les pays d'Asie. 1966. F668
147 Hackett, J. and A. M. L'économie britannique. 1966. F669
148 Marie, C. L'évolution du comportement politique dans une ville en expansion.

1966. F670
149 Bourricaud, F. Pouvir et société dans le Pérou contemporain. 1967. F671
150 Benhamou-Hirtz, A. Les relations collectives dans la sideurgie américaine. 1967. F672
151 Merle, M. and others. Les Eglises chretiennes et de décolonisation. 1967. F673
152 Lombard, J. Autorités traditionnelles et pouvoirs européens en Afrique noire. 1967. F674
153 Charlot, J. L'Union pour la Nouvelle Republique. 1967. F675
154 Ziebura, G. Léon Blum et le parti socialiste, tr. by Duplex. 1967. F676
155 Colloque sur "Leon Blum, chef de gouvernment." Leon Blum. 1967. F677
156 Fistié, P. L'evolution de la Thailande contemporaine. 1967. F678
157 Tudesq, A. J. Les Conseillers generaux en France au temps de Guizot. 1967. F679
158 Chardonnet, J. Métropoles économiques, deuxième série. 1968. F680
159 Goguel, F. Géographie des elections françaises sous la III et la IVe République. 1970. F681
160 Vincent, G. Les Professeurs du second degré. 1967. F682
161 Mabileau, A. Décolonisation et régimes politiques en Afrique noire. 1967. F682a
162 Lancelot, A. L'Obstentionnesme électoral' en France. 1968. F683
163 Roig, C. La Socialisation politique des enfants. 1968. F684
164 Barral, P. Les Agrariens français de Méline à Pisani. 1968. F685
165 Etienne, J. M. Naissance et évolution du mouvement rexiste jusqu'à la guerre. 1968. F686
166 Semidei, M. Les Etats-Unis et la revolution cubaine. 1968. F687
167 Kessler, M. C. Le Conseil d'état. 1968. F688
168 Waline, P. Cinquante ans de rapports entre patrons et auvriers en Allemagne. V. 1. 1968. F689
169 Centre d'étude de la vie politique française. L'élection presidentielle de Décembre 1965. 1970. F690
170 ____. Les élections législatives de mars 1967. 1970. F691
171 Tabelau des partis politiques en Amérique du sud. 1969. F692
172 Medard, J. F. Communauté locale et organisation communautaire aux Etats-Unis. 1969. F693
173 Dreyfus, F. G. La vie politique en Alsace, 1919-1936. 1969. F694
174 Huet, P. and DeSailly, J. Politique économique de la Grande-Bretagne depuis 1945. 1969. F695
175 Le communisme en France. 1969. F696
176 Tradition et changement en Toscane, ed. by Meyriat. 1971. F697
177 Mossuz, J. André Malraux et le gaullesme. 1970. F698
178 Same as no. 168. V. 2. 1971. F699
179 Vincent, G. Les lycéens, contribution à l'étude du milieu scolaire. 1971. F700
180 Daniel, J. Guerre et cinéma. 1972. F701
181 Bonnet, S. Sociologie politique et religieuse de la Lorraine. 1972. F702
182 Sternhell, Z. Maurice Berres et la nationalisme française. 1972. F703
183 Grosser, A. L'explication politique. 1972. F704
184 Travernier, Y. L'univers politique des paysans dans la France contemporaine. 1972. F705
185 Charlot, M. La "democratie" à l'anglaise les campagnes électorales en

Grande-Bretagne depuis 1931. 1972. F706
186 Leruez, J. Planification et politique en Grande-Bretagne. 1972. F707
187 Le Clère, B. Les préfets du second Empire. 1973. F708
188 Madelin, H. Pétrole et politique en Mediterranee occidentale. 1973. F709
189 Dupart, G. Révolution et autogestion rurale en Algerie. 1973. F710
190 Sfez, L. Critique de la décision. 1974. F711
191 Gilhodes, P. Politique et violence. 1974. F712
192 Vatin, J. C. L'Algérie politique. 1974. F713
193 Ruhl, L. La politique militaire de le Vème République. 1974. F714

FOOD, AGRICULTURE, AND WORLD WAR II (Stanford Univ. Pr.)

1 Wickizer, V. D. Coffee, tea and cocoa. 1951. F715
2 Brandt, K. and others. Germany's agricultural and food policies in World War II. V. 2. 1953. F716
3 Johnston, B. F. and others. Japanese food management in World War II. 1953. F717
4 Knight, H. Food administration in India, 1939-47. 1954. F718
5 Tinley, J. M. South African food and agriculture in World War II. 1954. F719
6 Crawford, J. G. and others. Wartime agriculture in Australia and New Zealand, 1939-50. 1954. F720
7 Hammond, R. J. Food and agriculture in Britain, 1939-45. 1954. F721
8 Zagorov, S. D. and others. The agricultural economy of the Danubian countries, 1935-45. 1955. F722
9 Lamer, M. The world fertilizer economy. 1957. F723
10 Lloyd, E. M. H. Food and inflation in the Middle East, 1940-45. 1956. F724
11 Roll, E. The Combined Food Board. 1956. F725
12 Timoshenko, V. P. and Swerling, B. C. The world's sugar. 1958. F726
Britnell, G. E. and Fowke, V. C. Canadian agriculture in war and peace, 1935-50. 1962. F727

FOOD PROCESSING REVIEW (Noyes Development Corp.)

1 Noyes, R. Freeze drying of foods and biologicals. 1968. F728
2 ____. Dehydration processes. 1969. F729
3 ____. Protein food supplements. 1969. F730
4 Lachmann, A. Snacks and fried products. 1969. F731
5 Bernarcyk, N. Edible oils and fats, 1969. 1969. F732
6 Gutterson, M. Confectionary products. 1969. F733
7 Gutcho, S. Alcoholic malt beverage, 1969. 1969. F734
8 Pintauro, N. Soluble coffee manufacturing processes, 1969. 1969. F735
9 Gutterson, M. Baked goods production processes, 1969. 1969. F736
10 Gutcho, M. Animal feeds, 1970. 1970. F737
11 Pintauro, N. Soluble tea production processes. 1970. F738
12 Karmas, E. Fresh meat processing. 1970. F739
13 Daniels, R. Modern breakfast cereal processing. 1970. F740
14 Karmas, E. Meat product manufacture. 1970. F741
15 Gutterson, M. Fruit juice technology, 1970. 1970. F742
16 Daniels, R. Rice and bulgar quick-cooking processes. 1970. F743
17 Wilcox, G. Eggs, cheese and yogurt processing. 1971. F744
18 ____. Milk, cheese and butter technology. 1971. F745
19 Gutterson, M. Vegetable processing. 1971. F746

20 Weiss, G. Poultry processing. 1971. F747
21 Gutterson, M. Fruit processing. 1971. F748
22 Gillies, M. T. Seafood processing. 1971. F749
23 Wieland, H. Enzymes in food processing and products. 1972. F750
24 Karmas, E. Sausage processing. 1972. F751
25 Pintauro, N. Agglomeration process in food manufacture. 1972. F752
26 Gutterson, M. Food canning techniques, 1972. 1972. F753
27 Wieland, H. Cocoa and chocolate processing, 1972. 1972. F754

FOODS OF THE WORLD (Time-Life)

Bailey, A. The cooking of the British Isles. 1969. F755
Bennett, V. The South Pacific cookbook. 1970. F756
Brown, D. American cooking. 1968. F757
____. American cooking: the Northwest. 1970. F758
____ and others. American cooking: the melting pot. 1971. F759
____. The cooking of Scandinavia. 1968. F760
Clairborne, C. and Franey, P. Classic French cooking. 1970. F761
Feibelman, P. S. American cooking: creole and Acadian. 1971. F762
____. The cooking of Spain and Portugal. 1969. F763
Field, M. and F. Quintet of cuisines. 1970. F764
Fisher, M. F. The cooking of provincial France. 1968. F765
Hahn, E. The cooking of China. 1968. F766
Hazelton, N. S. The cooking of Germany. 1969. F767
Leonard, J. N. American cooking: the Great West. 1971. F768
____. American cooking: New England. 1970. F769
____. Latin American cooking. 1969. F770
Nickles, H. C. Middle Eastern cooking. 1969. F771
Papashvily, H. and G. The cooking of Russia. 1969. F772
Rama Rau, S. The cooking of India. 1969. F773
Root, W. L. The cooking of Italy. 1969. F774
Steinberg, R. The cooking of Japan. 1969. F775
____. Pacific and Southeast Asia cooking. 1970. F776
Time-Life Books. Kitchen guide. 1968. F777
Van der Post, L. African cooking. 1971. F778
Walter, E. American cooking: Southern style. 1971. F779
Waugh, A. Wines and spirits. 1968. F780
Wechsberg, J. The cooking of Vienna's empire. 1968. F781
Wilson, J. American cooking: the Eastern heartland. 1971. F782
Wolfe, L. The cooking of the Caribbean Islands. 1970. F783

FORBES LECTURES OF THE NEW YORK SCHOOL OF SOCIAL WORK (Columbia Univ. Pr.)

Hewes, A. The contribution of economics to social work. 1930. F784
MacIver, R. M. The contribution of sociology to social work. 1931. F785
Niebuhr, R. The contribution of religion to social work. 1932. F786

THE FOREIGN POLICY RESEARCH INSTITUTE SERIES (Praeger)

1 Whitaker, A. P. Argentine upheaval. 1956. F787
2 Niemeyer, G. and Reshetar, J. S. An inquiry into Soviet mentality. 1956. F788
3 Strausz-Hupé, R. and others, eds. American-Asian tensions. 1956. F789

4 Meissner, B. The Communist Party of the Soviet Union, ed. by Reshetar. 1956. F790
5 Strauss-Hupé, R. and Hazard, H. W., eds. The idea of colonialism. 1958. F791
6 Qubain, F. I. The reconstruction of Iraq, 1950-1957. 1958. F792
7 Schneider, R. M. Communism in Guatemala. 1958. F793
8 Wheelock, K. Nasser's new Egypt. 1960. F794
9 Reshetar, J. S. A concise history of the Communist Party of the Soviet Union. 1960. F795
10 Leng, S. C. Sun Yat-sen and communism. 1960. F796

FORWOOD LECTURES

1933 Webb, C. C. J. Religion and theism. Allen. 1934. F797
1934 Dawson, C. H. Mediaeval religion. Sheed. 1934. F798
1935 Stocks, J. L. Time, cause and eternity. Macmillan. 1938. F799
1945 Laird, J. On human freedom. Allen. 1947. F800
1952 Bell, H. I. Cults and creeds in Graeco-Roman Egypt. Liverpool Univ. Pr. 1953. F801
1956 Arberry, A. J. Revolution and reason in Islam. Macmillan. 1957. F802
1960 MacMurray, J. Religion, art and science. Liverpool Univ. Pr. 1961. F803
1964 Brandon, S. G. F. History, time and deity. Manchester Univ. Pr. 1965. F804

FOUNDATION FOR FOREIGN AFFAIRS SERIES (Regnery)

1 Rippy, J. F. Globe and hemisphere. 1958. F805
2 Peeters, P. Massive retaliation. 1959. F806
3 Kulski, W. W. Peaceful coexistence. 1959. F807
4 Szaz, Z. M. Germany's eastern frontiers. 1960. F808
5 McGovern, W. M. Strategic intelligence and the shape of tomorrow. 1961. F809
6 Rothfels, H. The German opposition to Hitler. 1962. F810
7 Collier, D. S. and Glaser, K., eds. Berlin and the future of eastern Europe. 1963. F811
8 Dallin, D. J. From purge to co-existence... 1964. F812
9 Collier, D. S. and Glaser, K., eds. Western integration and the future of Eastern Europe. 1964. F813
10 Collier, D. S. and Glaser, K. Western policy and Eastern Europe. 1964. F814
11 Avtorkhanov, A. Western policy and Eastern Europe. 1966. F815
12 Elements of change in Eastern Europe, ed. by Collier and Glaser. 1968. F816
13 The conditions of peace in Europe, ed. by Collier and Glaser. 1969. F817
14 Petrov, V. A study in diplomacy. 1971. F818

FOUNDATIONS IN EDUCATION (McGraw)

Brown, L. M. General philosophy in education. 1966. F819
Brubacher, J. S. A history of the problems of education. 1966. F820
____. Modern philosophies of education. 1962. F821
Cook, L. A. and E. F. A sociological approach to education. 1960. F822
Cox, P. W. L. and Mercer, B. E. Education in a democracy. 1961. F823
DeYoung, C. A. and Wynn, R. American education. 1964. F824
Dorros, S. Teaching as a profession. 1968. F825
Good, C. V. Dictionary of education. 1959. F826
Meyer, A. E. An educational history of the Western World. 1965. F827

Richey, R. W. Planning for teaching. 1963. F828
Thut, I. N. and Adams, D. Educational patterns in contemporary societies. 1964. F829
Wiggin, G. A. Education and nationalism. 1962. F830
Wynn, R. Careers in education. 1960. F831

FOUNDATIONS OF EARTH SCIENCE SERIES (Prentice-Hall)

Bloom, A. L. The surface of the earth. 1969. F832
Clark, S. The structure of the earth. 1971. F833
Eichler, D. L. Geologic time. 1968. F834
Ernst, W. G. Earth materials. 1969. F835
Goody, R. and Walker, J. Atmospheres. 1972. F836
Laporte, L. F. Ancient environments. 1968. F837
McAlester, A. L. The history of life. 1968. F838
Skinner, B. J. Earth resources. 1969. F839
____ and Turekian, K. K. Man and the ocean. 1973. F840
Turekian, K. K. Oceans. 1968. F841

FOUNDATIONS OF MODERN BIOLOGY SERIES (Prentice-Hall)

Ambramoff, P. and Thomas, R. Investigations of cells and organisms. 1968. F842
Barry, J. Molecular biology. 1964. F843
Bates, M. Man in nature. 1964. F844
Bold, H. C. The giant kingdom. 1964. F845
Bonner, D. M. and Mills, S. E. Heredity. 1964. F846
Brewer, J. and others. Experimental techniques in biochemistry. 1974. F847
Buffaloe, M. Animal and plant diversity. 1968. F848
Dethier, V. G. and Stellar, E. Animal behavior. 1964. F849
Galston, A. W. The green plant. 1968. F850
____. The life of the green plant. 1964. F851
Hanson, E. D. Animal diversity. 1964. F852
McElroy, W. D. Cell physiology and biochemistry. 1964. F853
____ and others. Foundations of biology. 1968. F854
____ and Swanson, C. P. Modern cell biology. 1968. F855
Macey, R. Human physiology. 1968. F856
Schmidt-Nielson, K. Animal physiology. 1964. F857
Sussman, M. Developmental biology. 1973. F858
____. Growth and development. 1964. F859
Swanson, C. P. The cell. 1964. F860
Wallace, B. and Srb, A. M. Adaptation. 1964. F861
White, E. H. Chemical background for the biological sciences. 1964. F862

FOUNDATIONS OF MODERN ORGANIC CHEMISTRY SERIES (Prentice-Hall)

Allinger, N. L. and J. Structure of organic molecules. 1965. F863
Barker, R. Organic chemistry of biological compounds. 1972. F864
Bates, R. and Schaefer, J. Research techniques in organic chemistry. 1971. F865
DePuy, C. and Chapman, O. Molecular reactions and photochemistry. 1971. F866
Dyer, J. Applications of adsorption spectroscopy of organic compounds. 1965. F867
____. Organic spectral problems. 1972. F868
Gutsche, C. D. Chemistry of carbonyl compounds. 1967. F869
Henderson, R. and others. Problems in organic chemistry. 1968. F870
Ireland, R. Organic synthesis. 1969. F871

Pryor, W. Introduction to free radical chemistry. 1966. F872
Rinehart, K. Oxidation and reduction of organic compounds. 1972. F873
Saunders, W. Ionic aliphatic reactions. 1966. F874
Stewart, R. Investigation of organic reactions. 1966. F875
Stille, J. Industrial organic chemistry. 1968. F876
Stock, L. Aromatic substitution reactions. 1968. F877
Trahanovsky, W. Functional groups in organic compounds. 1971. F878
Traynham, J. Organic nomenclature. 1969. F879

FOUNDATIONS OF MODERN POLITICAL SCIENCE (Prentice-Hall)

Black, C. L. Perspectives in constitutional law. 1963. F880
Dahl, R. A. Modern political analysis. 1963. F881
____ and Neubauer, D. E., eds. Readings in modern political analysis. 1968. F882
Deutsch, K. W. The analysis of international relations. 1969. F883
Frohock, F. M. Normative political theory. 1974. F884
Gertzog, I. Readings on state and local government. 1970. F885
Greenstein, F. I. The American party system. 1963. F886
Kaufman, H. Politics and policies in State and local governments. 1963. F887
Lane, R. E. and Sears, D. O. Public opinion. 1964. F888
Lindbloom, C. E. The policy-making process. 1968. F889
Polsby, N. W. Congress and the Presidency. 1964. F890
Rosenbaum, N. Readings on the international political systems. 1970. F891
Tufte, E. Data analyses for politics and policy. 1974. F892
Watkins, F. M. The area of ideology. 1964. F893
Wolfinger, R. E., ed. Readings in American political behavior. 1966. F894
Wootton, G. Interest-groups. 1970. F895
Young, O. R. Systems of political science. 1968. F896

FRANCE. INSTITUT NATIONAL D'ETUDES DEMOGRAPHIQUES, PARIS. ET DOCUMENTS. CAHIERS (Presses Univ. de France)

1 France. Institut national d'études démographiques. Les travaux du Haut Comité consultatif de la population et de la famille en 1945. 1946. F897
2 ____. Documents sur l'immigration. 1947. F898
3 ____. Désirs des français en matière d'habitation urbaine. 1947. F899
4 ____. Une possibilité d'immigration italienne en France. 1947. F900
5 Daric, J. L'activité professionelle des femmes en France. 1947. F901
6 Chevalier, L. Le problème démographique nord-africain. 1947. F902
7 Daric, J. Vieillissement de la population et prolongation de la vie active. 1948. F903
8 France. Institut national d'études démographiques. Dépeuplement rural et peuplement rationnel. 1949. F904
9 ____. Cinq enquêtes sociales. 1950. F905
10 Chevalier, L. La formation de la population parisienne au XIXe siècle. 1950. F906
11 Sutter, J. L'eugénique. 1950. F907
12 Bourgeois-Pichat, J. Mesure de la fécondité des populations. 1950. F908
13 France. Institut national d'études démographiques. Le niveau intellectuel des enfants d'âge scholaire. 1950. F909
14 George, P. Introduction à

l'étude géographique de la population du monde. 1951. F910
15 Chevalier, L. Madagascar. 1952. F911
16 Henry, L. Fecondité des mariages. 1952. F912
17 Bénard, J. and others. Vues sur l'économie de la population de la France jusqu'en 1970. 1953. F913
18 Prigent, R., ed. Renouveau des idées sur la famille. 1954. F914
19 Girard, A. and Stoezel, J. Français et imigrées. 2 v. 1953. F915
21 France. Institut national d'études démographiques. Economie et population. V. 1. Spengler, J. J. Economie et population. 1954. F916
22 Henripin, J. La population canadienne au début du XVIIIe siècle. 1954. F917
23 Same as no. 13. V. 2. 1954. F918
24 France. Institut national d'études démographiques. Les Algeriens en France. 1955. F919
25 Pouthas, C. H. La population française pendant la première moitié du XIXe siècle. 1956. F920
26 Henry, L. Ancienne familles genevoises; études démographique: XVIe-XXe siècle. 1956. F921
27 Balandier, G., ed. Le "tiers monde." 1956. F922
28 Same as no. 21. V. 2. 1956. F923
29 Ledermann, S. Alcohol, alcoholisme, alcoholisation. V. 1. 1956. F924
30 France. Institut national d'études démographiques. Région Languedoc-Roussillon. 1957. F925
31 ____. Migrations professionnelles. 1957. F926
32 Okazaki, A. Histoire du Japon. 1958. F927
33 Gautier, E. La population du Crulai paroisse normande. 1958. F928
34 George, P. Questions de géographie de la population. 1959. F929
35 La prévention des naissance dans la famille... by Bergues and others. 1960. F930
36 Gérard, A. and others. Facturs sociaux et culturels de la mortalité infantile. 1960. F931
37 Vincent, P. Recherches sur la fecondité biologique. 1961. F932
38 Girard, A. La réussite sociale en France. 1961. F933
39 Balandier, G. Le Tiers-monde. 1961. F934
40 Lipinski, E. De Copernic à Stanislas Lesczczynski. 1962. F935
41 Same as no. 29. V. 2. 1963. F936
42 Guélaud-Leridon, F. Le travail des femmes en France. 1964. F937
43 Pourcher, G., ed. Le peuplement de Paris. 1964. F938
44 Girard, A. Le choix du conjoint. 1964. F939
45 Valmary, P. Familles paysannes au XVIIIe siècle en Bas Quercy. 1965. F940
46 Sutter, J. L'Atteinte des incisives latérales supérieures. 1966. F941
47 Malecot, G. Probabilitiés et hérédité. 1966. F942
48 Guéland-Leridon, F. Recherches sur la condition féminine dans la société d'aujourd hui. 1967. F943
49 Clerc, P. Grands ensembles, banlieves nouvelles, enquete démographique et psycho-sociologique... 1967. F944
50 Bandot, J. Conditions de vie et d'emploi des jeunes travailleurs... 1968. F945
51 Hugues, P. and Peslier, M. Les Professions en France. 1969. F946
52 Conditions de vie et besoins des personnes âgées en France. V. 1. 1969. F947
53 Ledermann, S. Nouvelles

tables-types de moralité. 1969. F948

54 France. Institute national d'études démographiques. Enquête nationale sur le niveau intellectual des enfants d'âge scolaire, by Clerc and Bendetto. 1969. F949

55 Charbonneau, H. Tourouvre-au-Perche aux XVIIe et XVIIIe siècle. 1970. F950

56 Leridon, H. and others. Fécondite et famille en Martinique. 1970. F951

57 Lévy, C. Les jeunes handicape's mentaux. 1970. F952

58 Courgeau, D. Les champs migratoires in France. 1970. F953

59 Merlin, P. L'exode rural. 1971. F954

60 Génétique et populations; hommage à Jean Sutter. 1971. F955

61 France. Institut National d'études démographiques. Les agriculteurs âges. 1972. F956

62 La Luxation congénitale de la hanche, by Sutter. 1972. F957

63 Vallin, J. La moralité par génération en France depuis 1899. 1973. F958

64 Same as no. 54. V. 2. 1973. F959

65 Léridon, H. Aspects biométriques de la fécondité humaine. 1973. F960

FRANKLIN LECTURES IN THE SCIENCES AND HUMANITIES (Univ. of Ala. Pr.)

1 Fuller, R. B. and others. Approaching the benign environment. 1970. F961

2 The shape of likelihood, by Eisley and others. 1971. F962

3 Our secular cathedrals, by Richardson and others. 1973. F963

FRIBOURG. UNIVERSITE. INSTITUT DES SCIENCES ECONOMIQUES ET SOCIALE. VEROFFENTLICHUNGEN (Univ. of Fribourg Pr.)

1 Valarché, J. La mobilité des ruraux dans une société libre. 1954. F964

2 Optiz, H. J. Der verwaltungsbegriff in der betriebswirtschaftslehre. 1955. F965

3 Bökelmann, M. Die reserveteile im anlageintensiven industriebetrieb. 1955. F966

4 Fleck, F. Untersuchungen zur ökonomischen theorie vom technischen fortschritt. 1958. F967

5 Wittmann, W. Die agrarpreisbildung. 1960. F968

6 Ollmann, F. J. Berufsnachwuchserziehung als sozialpolitische aufgabe. 1960. F969

7 Ith, H. Das diskonthaus in den USA. 1961. F970

8 Geisser, H. O. Marktforschung in der schweizerischen produktionsgüterindustrie. 1961. F971

9 Reutter, J. E. F. Der finanzhaushalt der kantone. 1962. F972

10 Morard, N. Fonctionnement et perspectives de la communauté europeenne du charbon et de l'acier. 1962. F973

11 Gauard, G. Nouvelles énergies et structures économiques. 1962. F974

12 Bunter, A. Die industriellen unternehmungen von P. Theodosius Florentini. 1962. F975

13 Cabernard, P. Die angordnungen als mittel der betruebswirtschaftlichen und der militärischen organisation. 1963. F976

14 Valarché, J. Recherches sur la modernisation agrocile au languedoc et en Vénétie. 1963. F977

15 Eppler, R. Das problem der steuerinzidenz bei gewinnsteuern. 1965. F978

16 Comby, B. Les relations entre le mobilité de travail et l'amenagement du territoire dans l'Europe de l'aprèsguerre. 1966. F979

17 Kümin, A. Das Selbstbedienungswarenhaus in den USA und seine entwicklung in Europe. 1967. F980
18 Pang, M. T. Les communes populaires rurales en Chine. 1967. F981
19 Comte, B. Développement rural et cooperation agricole en Afrique tropicale. 1968. F982
20 Commission nationale suisse de l'UNESCO. Exode rural et depeuplement de la montagne en suisse. 1966. F983
21 Casetti, G. Die kategorie des sozialen wandels. 1970. F984
22 Ratti, R. I traffici internazionali di transito e la regione di Chiasso. 1971. F985
23 Herkens, E. Das Investitiones und wertproblem in der sowjetwirtschaft. 1972. F986
24 Mattei, A. La demande dynamique. 1971. F987
25 Conus, H. L'entreprise innovatrice et sa croissance par l'investissement. 1972. F988
26 Deiss, J. La theorie pure les termes de l'echange international. 1972. F989
27 Dafflon, B. R. Les effets macro-économiques de la dette publique. 1973. F990
28 Pasquier, R. L'animation agricole. 1973. F991
29 Lucchini, R. Sociologie du fascisme. 1973. F992
30 Comby, B. La planification régionale dans les pays andins. 1973. F993
31 Pang, T. L'aide alimentaire. 1974. F994

FRONTIER MILITARY SERIES
(A. H. Clark)

1 Hunt, A. The Army of the Pacific. 1951. F995
2 ____. Major General James Henry Carleton, 1814-1873. 1958. F996
3 Heyman, M. L. Prudent soldier. 1959. F997
4 Grivas, T. Military governments in California, 1846-1850. 1963. F998
5 Richardson, R. N. The frontier of northwest Texas, 1846 to 1876. 1963. F999
6 Wood, R. G. Stephen Harriman Long. 1966. F1000
7 Smith, C. C. Emilio Kosterlitzky. 1970. F1001
8 Upton, R., comp. Fort Custer on the Big Horn, 1877-1898. 1973. F1002
9 Thompson, P. Peter Thompson's Narrative of the Battle of the Little Big Horn. 1974. F1003
10 Davidson, H. K. Black Jack Davidson. 1974. F1004

FRONTIERS IN CHEMISTRY
(Interscience)

1 Burk, R. E. and Grummitt, O. J., eds. The chemistry of large molecules. 1943. F1005
2 ____. The chemical background for enzyme research. 1943. F1006
3 ____. Advances in nuclear chemistry and theoretical organic chemistry. 1945. F1007
4 ____. Major instruments of science and their application to chemistry. 1945. F1008
5 ____. Chemical architecture. 1948. F1009
6 ____. High molecular weight organic compounds. 1949. F1010
7 ____. Recent advances in analytical chemistry. 1949. F1011
8 ____. Frontiers in colloid chemistry. 1950. F1012

FRONTIERS IN CHEMISTRY
(Benjamin)

Bak, T. A. Contributions to the theory of chemical kinetics. 1963. F1013
Ballhausen, C. J. and Gray, H. B. Molecular orbital theory. 1964. F1014
Bartlett, P. D. Nonclassical ions. 1965. F1015
Bernheim, R. Optical pumping. 1965. F1016

Bersolm, M. and Baird, J. C. An introduction to electron paramagnetic resonance. 1966. F1017
Bruice, T. C. Biorganic mechanics. V. 1. 1966. F1018
Craig, D. P. and Walmsley, S. H. Excitons in molecular crystals. 1968. F1019
Eaton, G. and Lipscomb, W. N. Nuclear magnetic resonance studies of boron hydrides and related compounds. 1969. F1020
Hamilton, W. C. and Ibers, J. A. Hydrogen bonding of solids. 1968. F1021
Hill, T. L. Thermodynamics of small systems. 2 v. 1963-64. F1022
Khalatnikov, I. M. Introduction to the theory of superfluidity. 1965. F1023
Langford, C. H. and Gray, H. B. Ligand substitution processes. 1965. F1024
Parr, R. G. The quantum theory of molecular electronic structure. 1963. F1025
Richards, J. H. and Hendrickson, J. B. The biosynthesis of steroids, terpenes, and acetogenins. 1964. F1026
Sheppard, W. A. and Sharts, C. M. Organic fluorine chemistry. 1969. F1027
Stewart, R. Oxidation mechanisms. 1964. F1028
Turro, N. J. Molecular photochemistry. 1965. F1029
Wilberg, K. B. Computer programming for chemists. 1965. F1030

FRONTIERS IN PHYSICS: A LECTURE NOTE AND REPRINT SERIES (Benjamin)

Adler, S. L. and Dashen, R. F. Current algebras and applications to particle physics. 1968. F1031
Anderson, P. W. Concepts in solids. 1963. F1032
Barger, V. D. and Cline, D. B. Phenomenological theories of high energy scattering. 1969. F1033
Bloembergen, N. Nonlinear optics. 1965. F1034
____. Nuclear magnetic relaxation. 1961. F1035
Bogolubov, N. N. and others. Introduction to axiomatic quantum field theory. 1973. F1036
Brout, R. H. Phase transitions. 1965. F1037
Caianiello, E. R. Combinatorics and renormalization in quantum field theory. 1973. F1038
Chew, G. F. S-matrix theory of strong interactions. 1961. F1039
Chouquard, P. The anharmonic crystal. 1967. F1040
Davidson, R. C. Theory of nonneutral plasmas. 1974. F1041
Feynman, R. P. Photon-Hadron interactions. 1972. F1042
____. Quantum electrodynamics. 1961. F1043
____. The theory of fundamental processes. 1961. F1044
____. Statistical mechanics. 1972. F1045
Field, G. B. and others. The Redshift controversy. 1974. F1046
Frauenfelder, H. The Mössbauer effect. 1962. F1047
Frautschi, S. C. Regge poles and S-matrix theory. 1963. F1048
Frisch, H. L. and others. The equilibrium theory of classical fluids. 1964. F1049
Gell-Mann, M. and Ne'eman, Y., eds. The eightfold way. 1964. F1050
Gennes, P. G. Superconductivity of metals and alloys, tr. by Pincus. F1051
Harrison, W. A. Pseudopotentials in the theory of metal. 1966. F1052
Hofstadter, R., ed. Electron scattering and nuclear and nucleon structure. 1963. F1053
Horn, D. Hadron physics at very high energies. 1973. F1054

Hove, L. and others. Problems in quantum theory of many-particle systems. 1961. F1055
Ichimaru, S. Basic principles of plasma physics. 1973. F1056
Jacob, M. and Chew, G. F. Strong-interaction physics. 1964. F1057
Kadonoff, L. Quantum statistical mechanics. 1962. F1058
Khalatnikov, I. M. An introduction to the theory of superfluidity, tr. by Hohenberg. 1965. F1059
Kokkedee, J. J. J. The Quark model. 1969. F1060
Lane, A. M. Nuclear theory. 1963. F1061
Loucks, T. L. Augmented plane wave method. 1967. F1062
Migdal, A. B. Nuclear theory, tr. by Leggett. 1968. F1063
____ and Krainov, V. Approximation methods in quantum mechanics. 1969. F1064
Ne'eman, Y. Algebraic theory of particle physics. 1967. F1065
Nozières, P. Theory of interacting Fermi systems, tr. by Hone. 1964. F1066
Omnès, R. and Froissart, M. Mandelstran theory and Regge poles. 1964. F1067
Pake, G. Paramagnetic resonance. 1962. F1068
Pake, G. E. and Estle, T. L. The physical principles of electron paramagnetic resonance. 1972. F1069
Pine, D. The many-body problem. 1961. F1070
Sagdeev, R. Z. and Galeev, A. A. Non-linear plasma theory, ed. by O'Neill and Book. 1969. F1071
Schreiffer, J. R. Theory of superconductivity. 1964. F1072
Schwinger, J. and Kohler, R. Quantum kinematics and dynamics. 1970. F1073
Squires, E. J. Complex angular moments and particle physics. 1963. F1074
Van Hove, L. and others. Problems in quantum theory of many-particle systems. 1961. F1075

FRONTIERS OF BIOLOGY (North-Holland)

1 Gauze, G. F. Microbial models of cancer cells. 1966. F1076
2 Finter, N. B., ed. Interferons. 1966. F1077
3 Lush, I. E. The biochemical genetics of vertebrates except man. 1966. F1078
4 Turk, J. L. Delayed hypersensitivity. 1967. F1079
5 Court-Brown, W. M. Human population cytogenetics. 1967. F1080
6 Cleaver, J. E. Thymidine metabolism and cell kinetics. 1967. F1081
7 Weiss, L. The cell periphery, metastasis and other contact phenomena. 1967. F1082
8 Friendenberg, R. M. The electrostatics of biological cell membranes. 1967. F1083
9 Bull, L. B. and others. The pyrrolizidine alkaloids. 1968. F1084
10 Balis, M. E. Antagonists and nucelic acids. 1968. F1085
11 Nelson, D. S. Macrophages and immunity. 1969. F1086
12 Yčas, M. The biological code. 1969. F1087
13 Blakley, R. L. The biochemistry of folic acid and related pteridines. 1969. F1088
14 Dingle, J. T. and Fell, H. B., eds. Lysosomes in biology and pathology. 2 v. 1969. F1089
15 Lima-de-Faria, A., ed. Handbook of molecular cytology. 1969. F1090
16 Lengerova, A. Immunogenetics of tissue transplantation. 1969. F1091
17 Bartels, H. Prenatal respiration. 1970. F1092
18 Brambell, F. W. R. The transmission of passive immunity from mother to young. 1972. F1093
19 Harris, H. The principles

of human biochemical genetics. 1970. F1094
20 Solomon, J. B. Foetal and neonatal immunology. 1971. F1095
21 Antonini, E. and Brunori, M. Hemoglobin and myoglobin in their reaction with ligands. 1971. F1096
22 Fjerdingstad, E. J., ed. Chemical transfer of learned information. 1971. F1097
23 Ponnamperuma, C., ed. Exobiology. 1972. F1098
24 Metcalf, D. and Moore, M. A. S. Haempoietic cells. 1971. F1099
25 Borek, F., ed. Immunogenicity. 1972. F1100
26 Aldridge, W. N. and Reiner, F. Enzyme inhibitors as substrates. 1972. F1101
27 Bosch, L., ed. The mechanism of protein synthesis and its regulation. 1972. F1102
28 Stanworth, D. Immediate hypersensitivity. 1973. F1103
29 Same as no. 14. V. 3. 1972. F1104
30 Bligh, J. Temperature regulations in mammals and other vertebrates. 1973. F1105
31 Gibbs, A. J., ed. Viruses and invertebrates. 1973. F1106
32 Birch, M. C. Pheromenes. 1974. F1107

THE FUTURE MAKERS (Heineman)

Cross, W. John Diebold. 1965. F1108
____. Samuel S. Stratton. 1964. F1109
Gonzalez, A. F. Eugene H. Nickerson. 1964. F1110
Hymoff, E. Stig von Bayer. 1965. F1111

-G-

GABRIEL RICHARD LECTURES. 1950 (Bruce)

1950 Hoffman, R. J. S. The spirit of politics and the future of freedom. 1950. G1
1951 Neill, T. P. Religion and culture. 1952. G2
1952 Shuster, G. N. Cultural cooperation and the peace. 1953. G3
1953 LaDrière, J. C. Directions in contemporary criticism and literary scholarship. 1955. G4
1954 Kerr, W. Criticism and censorship. 1954. G5
1955 Pegis, A. C. Christian philosophy and intellectual freedom. 1960. G6
1961 Ellis, J. T. John Lancaster Spalding. 1961. G7

GENERAL CHEMISTRY MONOGRAPH SERIES (Benjamin)

Barrow, G. M. The structure of molecules. 1963. G8
Basolo, F. and Johnson, R. C. Coordination and chemistry. 1964. G9
Choppin, G. R. Nuclei and radioactivity. 1964. G10
Gray, H. B. Electrons and chemical bonding. 1964. G11
Herz, W. The shape of carbon compounds. 1963. G12
Hochstrasser, R. M. Behavior of electrons in atoms. 1964. G13
Johnson, R. C. Introductive descriptive chemistry. 1966. G14
King, E. L. How chemical reactions occur. 1963. G15
Larsen, E. M. Transitional elements. 1965. G16
Light, R. J. A brief introduction to biochemistry. 1968. G17
Mahan, B. H. Elementary chemical thermodynamics. 1963. G18
Moore, W. J. Seven solid states. 1967. G19

GENERAL ELECTRIC SERIES (Wiley)

Alger, P. L. The nature of polyphase induction machines. 1951. G20
Bewley, L. V. Traveling waves of transmission systems. 1951. G21
Bloomquist, W. C. and others. Capacitors for industry. 1950. G22
Blume, F. L. and others. Transformer engineering. 1951. G23
Chestnut, H. and Mayer, R. W. Servomechanisms and regulating system design. 2 v. 1959. G24
Clarke, E. Circuit analysis of A-C power systems. 2 v. 1943-50. G25
Concordia, C. Synchronous machines. 1951. G26
Crary, S. B. Power system stability. 2 v. 1945-47. G27
Healy, W. L. and Rau, A. H. Simplified drafting practice. 1953. G28
Heumann, G. W. Magnetic control of industrial motors. 1954. G29
Hix, C. F. and Alley, R. P. Physical laws and effects. 1958. G30

Kaufmann, R. H. and Finison, H. J. D-C power systems for aircraft. 1952. G31
Keller, E. G. Mathematics of modern engineering. 2 v. 1942. G32
Kinnard, I. F., ed. Applied electrical measurements. 1956. G33
Kirchmayer, L. K. Economic control of interconnected systems. 1959. G34
____. Economic operation of power systems. 1958. G35
Kron, G. Equivalent circuits of electric machinery. 1951. G36
____. A short course in tensor analysis for electrical engineers. 1942. G37
____. Tensor analysis of new works. 1939. G38
Lewis, W. W. The protection of transmission systems against lightning. 1950. G39
McCracken, D. D. Digital computers programming. 1957. G40
Mason, C. R. The art and science of protective relaying. 1956. G41
Newman, L. E. Modern turbines. 1944. G42
Peterson, H. A. Transients in power systems. 1951. G43
Ramo, S. and Whinnery, L. R. Fields and waves in modern radio. 1944. G44
Rothe, F. S. An introduction to power system analysis. 1953. G45
Shoults, D. R. and Rife, C. J. Electric motors in industry. 1942. G46
Shriner, R. I. and Fuson, R. C. Systematic identification of organic compounds. 1948. G47
Smith, C. W. Aircraft gas turbines. 1956. G48
Storm, H. F. Magnetic amplifiers. 1955. G49
Young, J. F. Materials and processes. 1954. G50

GENEVA. GRADUATE INSTITUTE OF INTERNATIONAL STUDIES. ETUDES ET TRAVAUX (Drox)

1 Moussa, F. Le service diplomatique des états arabes. 1960. G51
2 Vanek, J. The balance of payments... 1962. G52
3 Bremond, J. La coordination énérgetique en Europe ...1961. G53
4 Johnson, H. G. and Kenen, P. R. Trade and development. 1965. G54
5 Knitel, H. G. Les délégations du Comite international de la Croix-Rouge. 1967. G55
6 Allais, M. L'économique en tant que science. 1968. G56
7 ____. Economics as a science. 1968. G57
8 Frei, D. Dimensionen neutraler politik. 1969. G58
9 L'Hullier, J. Les organizations internationales de coopération économique e le commerce exterieur des pays en voie de développement. 1970. G59
10 Lecourt, R. Le juge devant le Marché Commun. 1970. G60
11 L'union monetaire en Europe, by Swobda and others. 1972. G61
12 Vigne, J. Le rôle des intérêts économiques dans l'évolution du droit de la mer. 1972. G62
13 Les résolutions dans la formation du droit international du développement. 1972. G63
14 Les organismes non gouvernementaux en suisse. 1973. G64

GENEVA. GRADUATE INSTITUTE OF INTERNATIONAL STUDIES. PUBLICATIONS. (25-Droz)

1 Rolin, H. A. La politique de la Belgique dans la Société de nations. Lundig. 1931. G65
2 Munch, P. La politique de Danemark dans la Société des nations. Kundig. 1931. G66
3 Manning, C. A. W. The

policies of the British dominions in the League of Nations. Oxford. 1932. G67

4 Berdahl, C. A. The policy of the United States with respect to the League of Nations. Kundig. 1932. G68

5 Hötzsch, O. Le caractère et la situation internationale de l'union des soviets. Kundig. 1932. G69

6 Steed, H. W. The antecedents of postwar Europe. Oxford. 1932. G70

7 Jackh, E. Die politik Deutschlands im Völkerbund. Kundig. 1932. G71

8 Hötzsch, O. La politique extérieure de l'allemagne de 1871 à 1914. Kundig. 1933. G72

9 Leener, G. de. La politique commerciale de la Belgique. Sirey. 1934. G73

10 Porri, V. La politique commerciale de l'Italie. Sirey. 1934. G74

11 Lauterpacht, H. The development of international law by the Permanent court of international justice. Longmans. 1934. G75

12 Röpke, W. German commercial policy. Longmans. 1934. G76

13 Landry, A. La politique commerciale de la France. Sirey. 1934. G77

14 Wright, Q. The causes of war and the conditions of peace. Longmans. 1935. G78

15 Rougier, L. A. P. Les mystiques politiques contemporaines et leurs incidences internationales. Sirey. 1935. G79

16 Scelle, G. Théorie juridique de la révision des traités. Sirey. 1936. G80

17 Lambert, J. La vengeance privee et les fondements du droit international justice. Sirey. 1936. G81

18 Hayek, F. A. von. Monetary nationalism and international stability. Longmans. 1939. G82

19 Nathan, R. Le Rôle international des grands marches financiers. Sirey. 1938. G83

20 Gelderen, J. J. von. The recent development of economic foreign policy in the Netherlands East Indies. 1939. G84

21 Martin, V. La vie internationale dans la Grèce des cités. Sirey. 1940. G85

22 Kaeckenbeeck, G. S. F. C. De la guerre à la paix. Naville. 1940. G86

23 Rappard, W. E. Cinq siècles de sécurité collective. Sirey. 1945. G87

24 Schitzer, A. F. De la diversite et de l'unification du droit. Verlag für Recht und Gesellschaft. 1946. G88

25 Schoell, F. L. Les tensions raciales dans l'Union sud-africaine et leurs incidences internationales. 1956. G89

26 Chardonnet, J. Une oeuvre nécessaire. 1956. G90

27 Zehnder, A. Politique extérieure et politique du commerce extérieure. 1957. G91

28 Halle, L. J. Guerre nucléaire et paix nucléaire. 1958. G92

29 Gonard, S. La recherche opérationelle et la décision. 1958. G93

30 Woodhouse, C. M. Britain and the Middle East. 1959. G94

31 L'Huillier, J. A. La cooperation economique internationale. 1959. G95

32 Röpke, W. L'economie mondiale aux XIXe et XXe siècle. 1959. G96

33 Molnár, M. and L. Imre Nagy. 1959. G97

34 Etienne, G. De Caboul à Pékin. 1959. G98

35 Heilperin, M. A. Studies in economic nationalism. 1960. G99

36 Aspaturian, V. V. The Union Republics in Soviet diplomacy. 1960. G100

38 Hague. Permanent Court of International Justice. Répertoire des décisions et

des documents de la procédure écrite et orale de la Cour permente de justice internationale..., ed. by Guggenheim. V. 1. 1961. G101

39 Freymond, J., ed. La Première Internationale. 2 v. 1962. G102

40 Cahier, P. Le droit diplomatique contemporain. 1962. G103

41 Siotis, J. Essai sur le Secrétariat international. 1963. G104

42 Molnar, M. La déclin de la Première Internationale. 1963. G105

43 Paris. Peace Conference, 1919. Proceedings, tr. by Whitton. 1964. G106

44 Freymond, J. Etudes de documents sur la première internationale en Suisse. 1964. G107

45 Contributions à l'histoire du Comintern, ed. by Freymond. 1965. G108

46 Inflation et ordre monetaire international, by Rueff and others. 1967. G109

47 Same as no. 38. V. 2. 1967. G110

48 Same as no. 39. V. 3. 1968. G111

49 Collart, Y. Le parti socialiste suisse et l'Internationale, 1914-1915. 1969. G112

50 Beguin, P. Les entreprises conjointes internationales dans les pays en voies de developpement. 1972. G113

51 Same as no. 38. V. 3. 1972. G114

GEOLOGICAL SOCIETY OF AMERICA. MEMOIR.

1 Schuchert, C. Stratigraphy of western Newfoundland. 1934. G115

2 Reudemann, R. Paleozoic plankton of North America. 1934. G116

3 Veatch, A. C. Evolution of the Congo basin. 1935. G117

4 Anderson, R. van V. Geology in the coastal Atlas of western Algeria. 1936. G118

5 Balk, R. Structural behavior of igneous rocks. 1937. G119

6 Knopf, E. F. (Bliss) and Ingerson, E. Structural petrology. 1938. G120

7 Buddington, A. F. Adirondack igneous rocks and their metamorphism. 1939. G121

8 Emmons, R. C. The universal stage. 1943. G122

9 Vaughan, T. W. American Old and Middle Tertiary larger Foraminifera and corals. 1945. G123

10 Clark, B. L. Radiolaria from the Kreyenhagen formation near Los Banos, California. 1945. G124

11 Gardner, J. A. Mollusca of the Tertiary formations of northeastern Mexico. 1945. G125

12 Howell, B. F. Revision of the upper Cambrian faunas of New Jersey. 1945. G126

13 Wanless, H. R. Pennsylvanian geology of a part of the southern Appalachian coal field. 1946. G127

14 Stainbrook, M. A. Brachiopoda of the Independence shale of Iowa. 1945. G128

15 Kerr, P. F. Tungsten mineralization in the United States. 1946. G129

16 Clark, B. L. Eocene faunas from the department of Bolivar, Colombia. 1946. G130

17 Thompson, M. L. Permian fusulinids of California. 1946. G131

18 Cloos, E. Lineation. 1946. G132

19 Reudemann, R. Graptolites of North America. 1947. G133

20 Durham, J. W. Corals from the Gulf of California and the north Pacific coast of America. 1947. G134

21 Jaggar, T. A. Origin and development of craters. 1947. G135

22 Washburn, A. L. Reconnaissance geology of portions

of Victoria Island and adjacent regions, Arctic Canada. 1947. G136

23 Miller, A. K. Tertiary nautiloids of the Americas. 1947. G137

24 Pike, W. S. Intertonguing marine and nonmarine Upper Cretaceous deposits of New Mexico, Arizona, and southwestern Colorado. 1947. G138

25 Edinger, T. Evolution of the horse brain. 1948. G139

26 Branson, C. C. Bibliographic index of Permian invertebrates. 1948. G140

27 Worzel, J. L. Propagation of sound in the ocean. 1948. G141

28 Geological Society of America. Origin of granite. 1948. G142

29 Larsen, E. S. Batholith and associated rocks of Corona, Elsinore, and San Luis Rey quadrangles, Southern California. 1948. G143

30 Turner, F. J. Mineralogical and structural evolution of the metamorphic rocks. 1948. G144

31 Beal, C. H. Reconnaissance of the geology and oil possibilities of Baja California, Mexico. 1948. G145

32 Renz, H. H. Stratigraphy and fauna of the Agua Salada group, State of Falcón, Venezuela. 1948. G146

33 Geology and origin of South Park, Colorado. 1949. G147

34 Teichert, C. Permian crinoid Calceolispongia. 1949. G148

35 Weaver, C. E. Geology of the coast ranges immediately north of the San Francisco Bay region, California. 1949. G149

36 Newell, N. D. Geology of the Lake Titicaca region, Peru and Bolivia. 1949. G150

37 Camp, C. L. Bibliography of fossil vertebrates, 1939-43. 1949. G151

38 Stoyanow, A. Lower Cretaceous stratigraphy in southeastern Arizona. 1949. G152

39 Geological Society of America. Sedimentary facies in geologic history. 1949. G153

40 Stumm, E. C. Revision of the families and genera of the Devonian tetracorals. 1949. G154

41 Miller, A. K. American Permian nautiloids. 1949. G155

42 Wang, Y. Maquoketa Brachiopoda of Iowa. 1949. G156

43 1940 E. W. Scripps cruise to the Gulf of California. 1950. G157

44 Bassler, R. S. Faunal lists and descriptions of Paleozoic corals. 1950. G158

45 Bastian, E. S. Interpretation of ore textures. 1950. G159

46 Phleger, F. B. Ecology of Foraminfera. 2 pts. 1951. G160

47 Interpretation of aeromagnetic maps. 1951. G161

48 Kay, M. North American geosynclines. 1951. G162

49 Bucher, W. H. Geologic structure and orogenic history of Venezuela. 1952. G163

50 Goldman, M. I. Deformation, metamorphism, and mineralization in gypsum-anhydrite cap rock, Sulphur Salt Dome, Louisiana. 1952. G164

51 La Motte, R. S. Catalogue of the Cenozoic plants of North America through 1950. 1952. G165

52 Emmons, R. C. Selected petrogenic relationships of plagioclase. 1953. G166

53 Petrunkevitch, A. I. Paleozoic and Mesozoic Archnida of Europe. 1953. G167

54 LeRoy, L. W. Biostratigraphy of the Magfi section, Egypt. 1953. G168

55 Cooper, B. N. Trilobites from the lower Champlainian formation of the Appalachian Valley. 1953. G169

56 Williams, A. North American and European stropheodontids. 1953. G170

57 Camp, C. L. and others. Bibliography of fossil

vertebrates, 1944-1948. 1953. G171
58 Newell, N. D. Upper Paleozoic of Peru. 1953. G172
59 Whittington, H. B. Silicified Middle Ordovician trilobites. 1953. G173
60 Donnay, J. D. H. and others. Crystal data. 1954. G174
61 McKee, E. D. Stratigraphy and history of Moenkopi formation of Triassic age. 1954. G175
62 Miller, A. K. and others. Ordovician cephalopod fauna of Baffin Island. 1954. G176
63 Wanless, H. R. and others. Paleozoic and Mesozoic rocks of Gros Ventre... 1955. G177
64 Hamilton, E. L. Sunken islands of the Mid-Pacific mountains. 1956. G178
65 Jenks, W. F., ed. Handbook of South American geology. 1956. G179
66 Hanzawa, S. Cenozoic Foraminfera of Micronesia. 1957. G180
67 National Research Council. Committee on a Treatise. Treatise on marine ecology and paleoecology, ed. by Ladd. 2 v. 1957. G181
68 Sando, W. J. Beekmantown group, Lower Ordovician of Maryland. 1957. G182
69 Galloway, J. J. and Kaska, H. V. Genus Pentremites and its species. 1957. G183
70 Elias, M. K. and Condra, G. E. Fenestella from the Permian of west Texas. 1957. G184
71 Anderson, F. M. Upper Cretaceous of the Pacific coast. 1958. G185
72 Cooper, W. S. Coastal sand dunes of Oregon and Washington. 1958. G186
73 Fyfe, W. S. and others. Metamorphic reactions and metamorphic facies. 1958. G187
74 Tuttle, O. F. and Bowen, N. L. Origin of granite in the light of experimental studies in the system... 1958. G188
75 Ridge, J. D. Selected bibliographies of hydrothermal and magmatic mineral deposits. 1958. G189
76 Palmer, K. V. W. Type specimens of marine mollusca described by P. P. Carpenter from the West Coast. 1958. G190
77 Wisser, E. H. Relation of ore deposition to doming in the North American cordillers. 1960. G191
78 LaRocque, A. Molluscan faunas of the Flagstaff formation of central Utah. 1960. G192
79 Symposium on Rock Deformation. Rock deformation, a symposium, ed. by Griggs and Handin. 1960. G193
80 Hess, H. H. Stillwater igneous complex, Montana, a quantitative mineralogical study. 1960. G194
81 Muir-Wood, H. M. and Cooper, G. A. Morphology, classification and life habits of the Productoidea. 1960. G195
82 Becker, H. F. Oligocene plants from the Upper Ruby River Basin, southwestern Montana. 1961. G196
83 Perkins, B. F. Biostratigraphic studies in the Comanche. 1961. G197
84 Camp, C. L. and Allison, H. J. Bibliography of fossil vertebrates, 1949-1953. 1961. G198
85 Berry, L. G. and Thompson, R. M. X-ray power data for ore minerals. 1962. G199
86 Kraft, J. Morphologic and systematic relationships of some middle Ordovician Ostracoda. 1962. G200
87 Romer, A. S. and others. Bibliography of fossil vertebrates, exclusive of North America, 1509-1927. 1962. G201
88 Ross, C. A. Standard Wolfcampian series (Permian), Glass Mountains, Texas. 1963. G202

THE GEORGE FISHER BAKER NON-RESIDENT LECTURESHIP IN CHEMISTRY AT CORNELL UNIVERSITY (1-10 McGraw; 11- Cornell Univ. Pr.)

boron and silicon. 1933. G267
13 Desch, C. H. The chemistry of solids. 1934. G268
14 Hahn, O. Applied radiochemistry. 1936. G269
15 Bragg, W. L. Atomic structure of minerals. 1937. G270
16 Gortner, R. A. Selected topics in colloid chemistry. 1937. G271
17 Daniels, F. Chemical kinetics. 1938. G272
18 Pauling, L. C. The nature of chemical bond and the structure of molecules and crystals. 1960. G273
19 Ingold, C. K. Structure and mechanism in organic chemistry. 1953. G274
20 Robertson, J. M. Organic crystals and molecules. 1953. G275
21 Flory, P. J. Principles of polymer chemistry. 1953. G276
22 Iler, R. K. The colloid chemistry of silica and silicates. 1955. G277
23 Bell, R. P. The proton in chemistry. 1973. G278
23 Brown, H. C. Boranes in organic chemistry. 1972. G279
Herzberg, G. The spectra and structures of simple free radicals. 1971. G280

GEORGE PEABODY COLLEGE FOR TEACHERS. CONTRIBUTIONS TO EDUCATION.

1 Roemer, J. Function of secondary education. 1920. G281
2 Sharp, L. A. The present status of rural teachers in the South. 1920. G282
3 Judd, C. D. The summer school as an agency for training of teachers in the United States. 1921. G283
4 Webb, H. A. General science instruction in the grades. 1921. G284
5 Storm, A. V. How the land-grant colleges are preparing special teachers of agriculture. 1921. G285
6 Phelps, S. J. The administration of county high schools in the South. 1920. G286
7 Shreve, F. A comparative study of directed and undirected teaching. 1922. G287
8 Garrison, W. D. Variation in achievement and ability within the grades. 1922. G288
9 Mallory, J. N. A study of the relation of some physical defects to achievement in the elementary school. 1922. G289
10 Ivy, H. M. What is the relation of academic preparation... of rural teachers in Mississippi to their pay? 1922. G290
11 Weaver, C. P. The hermit in English literature. 1924. G291
12 Zeigel, W. H. The relation to extra-mural study to residence enrollment and scholastic standing. 1924. G292
13 Meadows, T. B. Status of agricultural projects in the South. 1924. G293
14 Hillman, J. E. Some aspects of science in the elementary schools. 1924. G294
15 Sherrod, C. C. The administration of state teacher colleges through faculty committees. 1925. G295
16 Bourne, W. R. A method of evaluating secondary school units. 1925. G296
17 Donovan, H. L. A state's elementary teacher-training problem. 1925. G297
18 Grant, J. R. State's teacher-training problems. 1925. G298
19 Grise, F. C. Content and method in high-school Latin from the viewpoint of pupils and of teachers. 1925. G299
20 Robertson, M. S. Oral problem solving in the elementary school. 1925. G300
21 Crabb, A. L. A study in the nomenclature and mechanics employed in catalogue presentations of courses in education. 1926. G301
22 Leiper, M. A. A diagnostic study of errors made by college freshmen in their

written composition. 1926. G302
23 Sisk, T. K. The interrelations of speed in simple and complex responses. 1926. G303
24 Collier, C. B. The dean of the state teachers college. 1926. G304
25 Falls, J. D. Job analysis of state high school supervisor in the United States. 1926. G305
26 ReBarker, H. A study of the simple integral processes of arithmetic. 1926. G306
27 Napier, T. H. Trends in the curricula for training teachers. 1926. G307
28 Meadows, J. C. The functions of a state university. 1927. G308
29 Parkinson, B. L. The professional preparation and certification of white elementary secondary public school teachers in South Carolina. 1926. G309
30 Collins, E. A. Classification of chartered schools in Missouri. 1926. G310
31 Dawson, H. A. Standards of expenditures for... city school costs. 1927. G311
32 Smith, N. A. The Latin element in Shakespeare and the Bible. 2 v. 1929. G312
33 Mitchell, M. R. A critical evaluation of the type study plan as an organizing principle for texts in American history. 1926. G313
34 Shankle, G. E. Poetry of American farm life. 1926. G314
35 Garris, E. W. The organization and administration of a state program in agricultural education. 1926. G315
36 Barnett, A. Organized community activities of agriculture teachers. 1926. G316
37 McClure, C. H. Opposition in Missouri to Thomas Hart Benton. 1927. G317
38 Golightly, T. J. The present status of the teaching of morals in the public high schools. 1926. G318
39 Terrell, R. F. A study of early journalistic writings of Henry W. Grady. 1927. G319
40 Patrick, W. A comparison of residence and extension teaching. 1927. G320
41 Manchester, P. T. Bibliography and critique of the Spanish translations from the poetry of the United States. 1927. G321
42 Robinson, J. R. Instructional records. 1927. G322
43 Cuff, N. B. The relation of overlearning to retention. 1927. G323
44 Garrison, K. C. An analytic study of rational learning. 1928. G324
45 Baker, E. W. The development of elementary English language textbooks in the United States. 1929. G325
46 Hedrick, C. E. Social and economic aspects of slavery in the transmontane prior to 1850. 1927. G326
47 Jarrett, R. P. Status of courses in psychology. 1928. G327
48 Adams, C. L. A study of variability and grade progress. 1927. G328
49 Beck, E. C. A study of the conference and nonconference methods of teaching freshmen. 1928. G329
50 Lowrey, R. G. The English sentence in literature and in freshmen college composition. 1928. G330
51 Boynton, P. L. A study of the relationship between the intelligence and moral judgments of college students. 1929. G331
52 Turner, H. L. Tentative standards for the distribution of expenditure in county school systems in the South. 1929. G332
53 Hounchell, P. The training of junior high school teachers. 1929. G333
54 Ivins, L. S. Training teachers of vocational agriculture in service. 1929. G334
55 Johnson, Z. T. The political policies of Howell

Cobb. 1929. G335
56 Wood, C. R. Does "personality" have a definite and consistent use in education? 1929. G336
57 Dodd, J. H. A history of production of the iron and steel industry. 1928. G337
58 Brantley, R. L. Georgia journalism of the civil war period. 1929. G338
59 Robinson, R. R. Two centuries of change in the content of school readers. 1930. G339
60 Waller, J. C. Tenure and transiency of teachers in Kentucky. 1929. G340
61 Mitchell, B. F. A study of a systematic method of teaching. 1929. G341
62 White, R. H. Development of the Tennessee state education organization, 1796-1929. 1929. G342
63 Krusé, S. A. A critical analysis of principles of teaching... 1929. G343
64 Eason, J. L. A diagnostic study of technical incorrectness in the writing of graduates... 1929. G344
65 Bedwell, R. L. Improvement of reading in the public schools. 1929. G345
66 Southall, M. K. Direct agencies of supervision as used by general elementary supervisors. 1929. G346
67 Altstetter, M. L. The elementary training school building. 1930. G347
68 Jennings, J. Rules and regulations concerning employed personnel of city schools. 1929. G348
69 Vaughan, A. W. State teacher college curricula for the development of teachers of English. 1929. G349
70 Campbell, D. S. A critical study of the stated purposes of the junior college. 1930. G350
71 Anthony, R. E. Anachronisms in Vergil's Aeneid. 1930. G351
72 Roller, B. Children in American poetry, 1610-1900. 1930. G352
73 Cooke, D. H. The white superintendent and the Negro schools in North Carolina. 1930. G353
74 Lewis, C. D. Rural intelligence in relation to rural population. 1929. G354
75 Edds, J. H. The measurement of verbal and nonverbal abilities. 1930. G355
76 Gwinn, C. W. An experimental study of college classroom teaching. 1930. G356
77 Lee, H. The relation of the state superintendent of education to the educational achievement and educational progress of the state. 1930. G357
78 Gillentine, F. M. A controlled experiment in fifth grade reading. 1930. G358
79 Rhodes, M. C. History of taxation in Mississippi, (1798-1929). 1931. G359
80 Turner, A. L. A study of the contents of Sewanee review. 1931. G360
81 Poret, G. C. The contributions of William Harold Payne to public education. 1930. G361
82 Ryle, W. H. Missouri. 1931. G362
83 Irby, N. M. A program for the equalization of educational opportunities in... Arkansas. 1930. G363
84 Herndon, T. C. A study of benzaldehyde electrode. 1930. G364
85 Taff, N. O. History of state revenue and taxation in Kentucky. 1931. G365
86 Cook, H. M. The training of state teachers college faculties. 1931. G366
87 Stretch, L. B. The relation of problem solving ability in arithmetic... 1931. G367
88 Kennamer, L. C. Geography of the Callahan divide. 1932. G368
89 Thomason, R. F. The Priapea and Ovid. 1931. G369
90 Jones, H. L. A study of the fitness of the high school

teachers of Tennessee. 1931. G370

91 Orr, M. L. The state supported colleges for women. 1930. G371

92 Craig, V. Y. A study of the sources from which rural teachers in service seek... aid in teaching... 1931. G372

93 Foote, I. P. Tenure of high school teachers. 1931. G373

94 Ford, F. A. Ratio of achievement to ability as found among fifth grade pupils. 1931. G374

95 Greene, J. E. The relative reliability and validity of Rational learning tests... 1932. G375

96 Hinson, M. R. Equations for predicting senior high school teachers' salaries in Florida. 1931. G376

97 Scarborough, R. The opposition to slavery in Georgia prior to 1860. 1933. G377

98 Egan, E. P. The effect of fore-exercises on test reliability. 1932. G378

99 Smith, T. E. The rise of teacher training in Kentucky. 1932. G379

100 Leavell, U. W. Philanthropy in negro education. 1930. G380

101 Yarbrough, W. H. Economic aspects of slavery... 1932. G381

102 Jones, W. C. A comparative study of certain phases of the status of graduates... in the teaching profession. 1931. G382

103 Frey, A. L. The swan-knight legend. 1931. G383

104 McGinnis, H. J. The state teachers college president. 1932. G384

105 Ellis, E. An evaluation of state programs of secondary education. 1932. G385

106 Loomis, B. W. The educational influence of Richards Edwards. 1932. G386

107 Freeman, C. P. Ecology of the cedar glade vegetation near Nashville, Tennessee. 1933. G387

108 Jordan, F. The social composition of the secondary schools of the southern states. 1933. G388

109 Magill, A. C. The calcium antagonism in soil and oak wood. 1933. G389

110 Mallory, A. E. The significance of plane geometry as a college entrance requirement. 1932. G390

111 Matthews, J. C. The contributions of Joseph Baldwin to public education. 1932. G391

112 Bruner, C. V. An abstract of the religious instruction of the slaves in the antebellum South. 1933. G392

113 George, J. B. The influence of court decisions in shaping school policies in Mississippi. 1932. G393

114 Taylor, H. An interpretation of the early administration of the Peabody education fund. 1933. G394

115 Shuler, C. E. The professional treatment of freshmen mathematics in teachers colleges. 1933. G395

116 Dickenson, H. F. Primary and secondary discriminative reactions. 1933. G396

117 Rowland, W. T. Aims of public education in the United States. 1933. G397

118 Hyatt, O. W. The development of secondary education in Alabama prior to 1920. G398

119 Carleton, R. K. The personal equation in chemical analysis. 1934. G399

120 Smith, C. W. Concha Espina and her women characters. 1933. G400

121 McGuire, S. H. Trends in principles and practices of equalization of educational opportunity. 1934. G401

122 Perry, R. D. Prediction equations for success in college mathematics. 1934. G402

123 Hicks, F. R. The mental health of teachers. 1934. G403

124 Bandy, W. T., comp.

Baudelaire judged by his contemporaries. 1933. G404
125 Brewton, J. E. The functions of state education association journals. 1933. G405
126 McCarrell, F. The development of teacher training school. 1934. G406
127 Puntney, A. T. Robert Browning as a dramatist. 1934. G407
128 Pruett, H. School plant requirements for standardized elementary and accredited high schools. 1934. G408
129 Goulding, R. L. The development of teacher training in Florida. 1934. G409
130 Enlow, E. R. A statistical slide rule. 1934. G410
131 Glover, G. G. Immediate pre-civil war compromise efforts. 1934. G411
132 Riley, S. B. The life and works of Albert Pike to 1860. 1934. G412
133 Coe, R. L. Predicting first-year high-school success in a country school system. 1934. G413
134 Shores, L. Origins of the American college library, 1638-1800. 1934. G414
135 Reeves, S. N. Tests of quality for school equipment and supplies. 1934. G415
136 Geiger, A. J. The six-year high school. 1934. G416
137 Moore, E. W. Difficulties recognized by elementary teachers... 1934. G417
138 Witherington, A. M. Legal trends of in-service training of public school teachers. 1934. G418
139 Young, A. L. The comparative efficiency of varied and constant methods in sensori-motor learning. 1934. G419
140 Smith, E. M. A study of failures in the Chattanooga junior high schools. 1934. G420
141 Belcher, G. L. The public school debt of Kentucky. 1934. G421
142 Kenney, C. E. The type and control of public elementary school units in the United States. 1934. G422
143 Lacy, H. M. French lyric poetry in English and American translations. 1934. G423
144 Hounchell, S. The principal literary magazines of the Ohio valley to 1840. 1934. G424
145 Rawlins, G. M. The distribution of calcium and iron in black oak trees. 1934. G425
146 Glazner, J. F. The geography of the great Appalachian valley of Alabama. 1934. G426
147 Wright, M. H. Mary Virginia Hawes Terhune. 1934. G427
148 Simmons, I. F. The private chartered educational institutions of Tennessee. 1934. G428
149 Kirtley, J. A. The attitude of the church toward labor's industrial problems. 1932. G429
150 Haynes, H. C. Relation of teacher intelligence... to types of questions. 1935. G430
151 Dilla, G. P. French and English mutual analyses. 1935. G431
152 Wise, J. H. An evaluation of extra-curricular activities in large southern high schools. 1933. G432
153 Partin, R. L. The secession movement in Tennessee. 1935. G433
154 Browne, W. A. The Llano estacado. 1935. G434
155 Floyd, H. H. Individual differences in gustation. 1935. G435
156 Folk, E. E. W. W. Holden, political journalist. 1934. G436
157 Smith, C. C. An evaluation of a supervisory program in a city school system. 1933. G437
158 Saucier, E. M. Charles Gayarre. 1933. G438
159 Cruze, W. W. Maturation and learning in chicks.

1934. G439
160 Jaggers, C. H. The superstitions in junior high school pupils. 1935. G440
161 Phillips, W. S. An analysis of certain characteristics of active and prospective teachers. 1935. G441
162 Carter, R. L. School centralization and pupil transportation... 1935. G442
163 Boyd, H. L. English grammar in American schools from 1850 to 1890. 1935. G443
164 Moore, J. E. A comparative study of delinquent and dependent boys. 1935. G444
165 Dittes, F. L. The biological availability of cystine found in soybean cheese. 1935. G445
166 Adams, H. Thaddeus H. Caraway in the U. S. Senate. 1935. G446
167 Smith, B. R. The ability of Kentucky to finance public education. 1932. G447
168 Armstrong, N. B. Teacher-accounting record forms for large cities. 1935. G448
169 Flanagan, B. A history of state banking in North Carolina to 1866. 1935. G449
170 Stroop, J. R. Studies of interference in serial verbal reaction. 1935. G450
171 Schug, H. L. Latin sources of Berceo's Sacrificio de la misa. 1936. G451
172 Ritchie, W. The public career of Cassius M. Clay. 1934. G452
173 Meyer, A. M. A history of the Southern association of colleges and secondary schools. 1943. G453
174 Cook, E. M. An analysis of the methods used in solving a rational learning problem. 1936. G454
175 Ray, J. J. The generalized ability of dull, bright, and superior students. 1936. G455
176 Austin, J. G. The trends of the county school superintendency in Alabama, 1890-1930. 1936. G456
177 Blair, R. V. Phases of the modern theory of conics and their professional treatment. 1935. G457
178 Long, J. K. Trends in the equalization of educational opportunity in North Carolina. 1936. G458
179 Elrod, L. H. Teacher supply, training, and demand in Tennessee as related to certification. 1934. G459
180 Cuff, R. P. A study of the classical mythology in Hawthorne's writings. 1936. G460
181 Bounous, J. D. The Waldensian patois of Pramol. 1936. G461
182 Rochedieu, C. A. Contribution to the study of Jean Jacques Rousseau. 1934. G462
183 Cline, R. The life and work of Seaman A. Knapp. 1936. G463
184 Allen, C. H. Legal principles governing practice teaching in state teachers colleges... 1937. G464
185 Winfrey, M. E. A personality study of college girls. 1936. G465
186 Judd, R. D. The educational contributions of Horace Holley. 1936. G466
187 Burkett, E. M. A study of American dictionaries of the English language before 1861. 1936. G467
188 Hill, R. R. The relation of teacher preparation to pupil achievement. 1936. G468
189 Hoskins, A. B. The effectiveness of the part and the whole methods of study. 1936. G469
190 Keso, E. E. The senatorial career of Robert Latham Owen. 1937. G470
191 Meyer, A. M. An ecological study of cedar glade invertebrates near Nashville, Tennessee. 1937. G471
192 Hait, K. B. An analytical study of the generalizing ability of college students. 1936. G472
193 Silvey, C. T. A study of

personal reactions to the solmization methods of teaching music reading. 1937. G473
194 Anderson, H. W. Trends in causes of teacher dismissal as shown by American court decisions. 1937. G474
195 Brinson, L. B. A study of the life and works of Richard Malcolm Johnston. 1937. G475
196 Cordrey, W. A. Some significant applications of mathematics to the physical sciences. 1937. G476
197 Farris, T. N. Severance taxation in Louisiana. 1937. G477
198 Barker, E. P. The contribution of Methodism to education in Kentucky. 1937. G478
199 Colvert, C. C. A critical analysis of the public junior college curriculum. 1937. G479
200 Shearer, A. E. Procedures in curriculum revision programs of selected states. 1937. G480
201 Christy, O. B. The development of the teaching of general biology in the secondary schools. 1936. G481
202 Willey, W. M. The supply and demand of secondary school teachers in Kentucky. 1937. G482
203 Fountain, A. M. A study of courses in technical writing. 1938. G483
204 Pummill, L. E. The function of mathematics in adult education. 1938. G484
205 Rooker, H. G. The stage history of the portrayal of Shakespeare's Hamlet. 1932. G485
206 Rankin, F. S. The religious attitudes of college students. 1938. G486
207 Atkinson, C. Education by radio in American schools. 1938. G487
208 Vaugham, W. H. Robert Jefferson Breckenridge as an educational administrator. 1937. G488
209 Link, S. G. Matthew Arnold's "sweetness and light" in America, 1848-1938. 1938. G489
210 Reynolds, C. W. The development of generalized science courses in state teachers colleges. 1938. G490
211 Wickiser, R. L. The development of a public education policy in Illinois. 1938. G491
212 Wright, J. T. C. The function of mathematics in a state education program. 1938. G492
213 Van Cleve, C. F. The teaching of Shakespearean plays in American secondary schools. 1937. G493
214 Shane, M. L. France in letters of Prosper Mérimee, 1826-70. 1938. G494
215 Burgess, H. O. Vacation plans for staff members of large city school systems. 1938. G495
216 Ferrell, D. T. Relation between current expenditures and certain measures of educational efficiency in Kentucky. 1936. G496
217 Cooke, J. V. The integrated method vs. a formal method in teaching arithmetic. 1938. G497
218 Boyer, W. H. Blind alley length as a selective factor in maze learning. 1937. G498
219 Easom, P. H. Public school legislation in Mississippi, 1860 to 1930. 1937. G499
220 Cornette, J. P. A history of the Western Kentucky state teachers college. 1938. G500
221 Wade, B. M. The development of secondary education in Tennessee. 1938. G501
222 O'Quinn, R. L. An evaluation of the results of grouping superior calculus students. 1938. G502
223 Gilmore, C. H. Distribution among state agencies of the control of public education. 1938. G503
224 Stout, C. L. Trends of methods contents, and beliefs in geography textbooks,

1784-1895. 1937. G504

225 Robert, E. B. The administration of the Peabody education fund from 1880 to 1905. 1936. G505

226 Reynolds, T. H. Economic aspects of the Monroe doctrine. 1938. G506

227 Spellings, W. W. The nine-foot waterways of the South. 1936. G507

228 Fort, M. K. The relationship between pupils' responses and certain other factors. 1936. G508

229 Reid, J. W. The problem of droughts in Arkansas agriculture. 1939. G509

230 Altstetter, M. (Fink). Elementary education in America as shown by professional books, 1829-1899. 1938. G510

231 Windrow, J. E. The life and works of John Berrien Lindsley. 1937. G511

232 Yates, O. W. The Sunday school board of the Southern Baptist convention. 1938. G512

233 Farrar, J. The development of public secondary education in Louisiana, 1876-1908. 1939. G513

234 Ayre, H. G. An analytical study of individual differences in plane geometry. 1937. G514

235 Cartwright, B. A. Four decades of development of psychology in state teachers colleges. 1938. G515

236 Miller, L. C. The Shenandoah valley in Virginia. 1939. G516

237 Evans, H. B. History of the organization and administration of Cumberland Presbyterian colleges. 1939. G517

238 Hall, E. E. The geography of the interior low plateau and associated lowlands of southern Illinois. 1939. G518

239 Ferguson, W. C. Instructional problems of generalized science in the senior high school. 1939. G519

240 Hodgson, J. A comparison of three Tennessee urban centers. 1939. G520

241 Bradford, A. L. The direction of educational dramatics in the high school. 1939. G521

242 Lawton, S. M. The religious life of South Carolina coastal and sea island Negroes. 1939. G522

243 Scott, P. C. A comparative study of achievement in college freshmen mathematics. 1939. G523

244 Hunter, H. R. The development of the public secondary schools of Atlanta, Georgia. 1939. G524

245 Jenkins, F. C. The development of the public, white high school in Mississippi. 1939. G525

246 McGehee, W. A study of retarded children in the elementary school. 1939. G526

247 Hunter, L. Some important biological problems of the southeastern region. 1939. G527

248 Cathcart, M. E. The historical development of the teaching of biology in the Carolinas. 1939. G528

249 Hankins, C. F. Extended leave for public school teachers in large city school systems. 1939. G529

250 Fraley, L. M. A comparison of the general athletic ability of white and Negro men of college age. 1939. G530

251 Willis, L. J. A comparative study of the reading achievements of white and Negro children. 1939. G531

252 Hollister, P. L. Development of the teaching of introductory biology in American colleges. 1939. G532

253 Waffle, E. M. Eben Sperry Stearns. 1940. G533

254 Hunt, R. L. A study of factors influencing the public-school curriculum of Kentucky. 1937. G534

255 McCuiston, F. Graduate instruction for Negroes in the United States. 1939. G535

256 Bigelow, R. G. A critical appraisal of a state secondary

school program. 1939. G536
257 Frick, T. A. Slope vegetation near Nashville, Tennessee. 1939. G537
258 Ray, A. B. College experiences recommended for the training of elementary teachers. 1940. G538
259 Armstrong, L. E. The relation of certain factors to children's behavior characteristics. 1940. G539
260 Rackley, J. R. The relationship of the study of history to student attitudes. 1940. G540
261 Thomasson, C. W. A study of the interests of junior high school pupils. 1940. G541
262 Collinson, L. Chronological acceleration and retardation at junior high school levels. 1940. G542
263 Moon, R. C. Certain factors influencing relative difficulty of grouped fundamental arithmetic combinations. 1940. G543
264 Coleman, H. A. The relationship of socio-economic status to the performance of junior high school students. 1940. G544
265 Owens, M. R. The development of white secondary schools in Arkansas. 1940. G545
266 Lewis, W. D. A study of superior children in the elementary school. 1940. G546
267 Woodruff, N. H. Mathematics used in biology. 1940. G547
268 Alexander, P. W. John Eaton. 1940. G548
269 Beauchamp, R. O. Relation of science achievement to certain academic and social factors. 1940. G549
270 Behrens, M. S. An evaluation of reading readiness. 1940. G550
271 Caillouette, W. J. Quantitative studies in the poetry of Francis Thompson. 1940. G551
272 Flack, H. W. Totalitarianism and physical education. 1940. G552
273 Glover, T. H. Development of the biological sciences in teachers colleges of the middle West. 1940. G553
274 Holden, B. S. A study of some characteristics of pupils participating in student government. 1940. G554
275 McClimans, J. W. Functional units of instruction in senior mathematics. 1940. G555
276 McClurkin, W. D. Refunding Arkansas school bonds. 1940. G556
277 Mayes, V. W. A critical study of the needs and interests of youth. 1940. G557
278 Moorman, R. H. Some educational implications of Descartes' synthesis of mathematics and philosophy. 1940. G558
279 Sachs, H. J. The teaching of vocabulary. 1940. G559
280 Brouillette, J. W. The third phase of the Peabody education fund. 1940. G560
281 Kinzer, J. R. A study of the educational philosophy of William Torrey Harris. 1940. G561
282 Gager, W. A. Terminal business mathematics in the junior college. 1940. G562
283 Measamer, M. B. Factors associated with success and failure in learning the social studies. 1940. G563
284 Bingham, H. J. The relation of certain social attitudes to school achievement. 1940. G564
285 Bickley, A. W. Intelligence diagnostics of certain animal learning adapted to human subjects. 1939. G565
286 Emmons, S. R. Difficulties encountered by teachers in trying to develop a curriculum for the secondary school. 1941. G566
287 Gerber, J. N. Trends of relative emphasis on science and social studies in accredited secondary schools of Tennessee, 1930...1940. 1941. G567
288 Hamlin, C. H. Conflicting

forces in North Carolina education. 1941. G568
289 Martin, R. L. The Sequatchie valley, Tennessee. 1941. G569
290 Wang, J. D. A study of certain factors associated with children's play interests. 1941. G570
291 Deer, G. H. Factors associated with extreme retardation and acceleration in reading. 1939. G571
292 Brewington, A. W. A survey of speech education in the American junior college. 1941. G572
293 Boles, L. L. Relative significance of certain science topics for Florida children. 1941. G573
294 Moncreiff, R. A study of factors relating to problematic behavior in elementary school children. 1939. G574
295 McBride, O. The teaching of English in the Southern ante bellum academy. 1941. G575
296 Allen, J. The diary of Randal William McGavock, 1852-1862. 1941. G576
297 Bentley, I. Texas literary and educational magazines. 1941. G577
298 Cox, W. C. A study of English prepositions. 1941. G578
299 Dabney, O. B. Judicial interpretation of authority of common school boards in Kentucky. 1941. G579
300 Giles, F. P. Development of art courses in Southern association state teachers colleges. 1941. G580
301 Morris, J. W. The agglomerated settlements of the greater Seminole area. 1941. G581
302 Moyers, R. A. A history of education in New Mexico. 1941. G582
303 Schaff, W. R. Equalization as a factor in the scholastic qualifications of elementary-school teachers in Tennessee. 1941. G583
304 Smith, M. L. The teaching of biography in school and college. 1941. G584
305 Stone, M. L. An analysis of the total faculty workshop technique. 1941. G585
306 Sudduth, S. B. Study and appraisal of health education in Alabama secondary schools. 1941. G586
307 Russell, J. L. The problem of special assessments against school property. 1941. G587
308 Adams, R. H. Stratification, diural and seasonal migration of the animals in a deciduous forest. 1941. G588
309 Young, F. M. An analysis of certain variables in a developmental study of language. 1941. G589
310 Portré-Bobinski, G. French civilization and culture in Natchitoches. 1941. G590
311 Hruza, T. An investigation of some factors in the appreciation of poetry. 1941. G591
312 Mecham, G. P. A study of emotional instability of teachers and their pupils. 1940. G592
313 Jones, H. C. Plant ecology of the Berry schools property, Floyd county, Georgia. 1941. G593
314 Michelson, D. D. The contribution of William F. Phelps to public education. 1940. G594
315 Karnes, H. T. Professional preparation of teachers of secondary mathematics. 1940. G595
316 Obenchain, I. R. A study of certain differences in four year high school boys and girls. 1940. G596
317 Baldwin, E. B. An analysis of the white high school social studies teachers of Tennessee for 1939-40. 1942. G597
318 Barbee, J. D. The relationship between teacher training and experience and pupil success in social studies. 1942. G598

319 Fite, D. H. A study of subsistence farming in seven middle Tennessee schools. 1942. G599
320 Kennedy, T. H. Cultural effects of isolation on a homogeneous rural area. 1942. G600
321 McLellan, E. A. Composite of good practices in white public elementary and secondary schools of Louisiana. 1942. G601
322 Owen, M. C. The education of distinguished Southerners, as revealed in biographies. 1942. G602
323 Picklesimer, P. W. The new bright tobacco belt of North Carolina. 1942. G603
324 Sheley, C. F. The role of the fable in present day French education. 1942. G604
325 Denney, C. C. Diagnostic indices of the socio-economic backgrounds of school children. 1942. G605
326 Kauffman, H. M. A history of the music educators national conference. 1942. G606
327 McMahon, O. K. A study of fifth grade children to read various types of material. 1942. G607
328 Peck, R. C. Jabez Lamar Monroe Curry. 1942. G608
329 Randolph, V. R. An historical study of certification laws in Illinois. 1942. G609
330 Spikes, L. E. Evaluating an informal program of public school education. 1942. G610
331 Tyler, T. H. How free is a free school. 1942. G611
332 Gray, S. W. The relation of individual variability to intelligence and emotional stability. 1941. G612
333 Cowen, Z. Selected literature and activities for children of the middle grades. 1941. G613
334 Meadows, J. L. Effectiveness of distributed and massed learning for children of varying intelligence. 1941. G614
335 Guy, G. M. The relationship between academic success and five extra-scholastic factors. 1941. G615
336 Epstein, L. J. An attitudinal study of delinquent and dependent boys. 1941. G616
337 Gee, J. G. Guidance in the public secondary schools of the Southern association. 1933. G617
338 Carruth, J. E. Relationship between achievement and cost, attendance and preparation of teachers. 1934. G618
340 Boyce, E. M. Inter-institutional cooperation in higher education in the South. 1943. G619
341 Dotson, J. A. Socio-economic background and changing education in Harlan county, Kentucky. 1943. G620
342 Graham, W. W. Mathematics as a tool in engineering theory and practice. 1943. G621
343 Johnston, R. W. Legal aspects of insuring public school property. 1943. G622
344 Pottle, R. R. Intonation problems in school bands. 1943. G623
345 Roberts, J. B. Inbreeding practiced in appointing college and university teachers and administrators. 1943. G624
346 Todd, L. O. Meeting the needs of junior college students. 1943. G625
347 Fawcett, V. E. English grammar in American public schools from 1890 to 1940. 1943. G626
348 Hasslock, C. W. A critical study of home economics curricula in four-year colleges. 1943. G627
349 Lee, E. F. Material on Tennessee education published in Tennessee magazines. 1943. G628
350 Lee, R. C. Portrayal of the college in modern American novels, 1932-42. 1943. G629
351 McCune, E. H. Socio-economic analysis of municipal

junior college students in Oklahoma. 1943. G630
352 Marcum, D. M. Fundamental experience concepts and primary basal reading materials. 1943. G631
353 Minor, L. P. Certain factors influencing children to leave the elementary school. 1943. G632
354 Olson, C. M. Educational implications of what Levy county children like and do. 1943. G633
355 Tallant, J. G. Political readjustment in Tennessee, 1869-70. 1943. G634
356 Walker, F. T. William Peterfield Trent. 1943. G635
357 Young, M. N. History of the organization and development of Church of Christ colleges. 1943. G636
358 Malone, J. M. The relation of the Alabama state testing program to achievement in college. 1941. G637
359 Crow, O. F. The control of the University of South Carolina, 1801-1926. 1931. G638
361 Ayers, A. R. Three administrative problems relative to air-age education. 1944. G639
362 Haggard, E. M. Syllable-stress in French words as used by Chaucer and Spenser. 1944. G640
363 Hepler, J. C. The educational content of some national literary periodicals, 1850-1900. 3 v. 1944. G641
364 Huebner, M. S. A study of reading interests and preferences in educational objectives. 1944. G642
365 Spaulding, K. C. Rabun Gap-Nacoochee school. 1944. G643
366 Robbins, F. Geography of west Tennessee. 1930. G644
367 Neil, R. J. The development of the competition-festival in music education. 1944. G645
368 Robson, J. B. Thirty years of growth of secondary education in Louisiana, 1908-38. 1944. G646
369 Best, C. J. Vocal and instrumental music rooms and equipment in secondary schools. 1945. G647
370 Kelley, M. M. Trends in an evolving program of supervision in Virginia. 1945. G648
371 Minsky, H. S. Ernest Bloch and his music. 1945. G649
372 Hammond, W. R. Economic history of transportation on Ouachita-Black river of north west Louisiana. 1945. G650
373 Stark, G. W. Beginnings of teacher training in Mississippi. 1945. G651
374 Dalton, W. T. The treatment of rural life in elementary school reading textbooks. 1945. G652
375 Hudson, R. L. The sermon as teaching with special emphasis on motivation. 1945. G653
376 Wiant, B. M. The character and function of music in Chinese culture. 1946. G654
377 Rucker, E. The chemical content of biology textbooks and reference books. 1944. G655
378 Holladay, A. M. A program of vocational-chemical education in Tennessee. 1946. G656
379 Mason, R. L. The life of the people of Cannon county, Tennessee. 1946. G657
380 Jones, J. P. A history and appreciation course of our own American music. 1946. G658
381 Brown, C. F. Lateral dominance and reading in the elementary school. 1946. G659
382 Comfort, R. O. The training of town and country ministers in the United States. 1946. G660
383 Eyler, C. M. Techniques of political propaganda in English drama, 1700-50. 1946. G661
384 Knobbs, P. B. D. The

development of the separate system of education in Missouri. 1946. G662
385 McCallum, W. J. Motion pictures and film-strips in selected secondary schools. 1946. G663
386 Moore, W. E. Mark Twain's techniques of humor. 1946. G664
387 White, J. B. A study of the teachers in the small rural schools of South Carolina... 1946. G665
388 Cobb, J. E. A study of functional reading. 1948. G666
389 Hogarth, C. P. Policy making in colleges related to the Methodist Church. 1949. G667
390 Hurst, H. Illinois State Normal University and the public school movement. 1948. G668
392 Funderburk, R. S. The history of conservation education in the United States. 1948. G669
394 Kidd, K. P. Objectives of mathematical training in the public junior college. 1948. G670
395 McCharen, W. K. Selected community school programs in the South. 1948. G671
396 Mattox, F. W. The teaching of religion in the public schools. 1948. G672
397 Pickard, W. L. Evolution of algebra as a secondary school subject. 1948. G673
398 Reed, D. H. The history of teachers colleges in New Mexico. 1948. G674
399 Suderman, D. H. The music program of church-controlled liberal arts colleges in Kansas. 1948. G675
400 Wiser, J. E. Chemistry usage by books and teachers in home economics courses. 1949. G676
401 Dark, H. J. The life and work of Herbert Ellsworth Slaught. 1948. G677
402 Layton, W. I. The analysis of certification requirements for teachers of mathematics. 1949. G678
403 Simms, C. W. The present legal status of the public junior college. 1948. G679
404 Baird, J. O. The life and works of Charles Edgar Little. 1949. G680
405 Beasley, W. The life and educational contributions of James D. Porter. 1950. G681
406 Bulber, F. G. Teacher activities of the vocal school music program. 1949. G682
407 Jobe, E. B. Curriculum development in Mississippi public white high schools, 1900-45. 1950. G683
408 Little, T. C. Administration of school supply purchase in Kentucky. 1949. G684
409 McFaddin, G. The development of state-authorized supervision of rural elementary white schools in Alabama. 1949. G685
410 Mason, W. S. The people of Florida as portrayed in American fiction. 1949. G686
411 Richardson, J. M. The contributions of John William Abercrombie to public education. 1949. G687
412 Garrison, H. E. Lay education commissions in the Southern states. 1952. G688
413 Kegley, T. M. Peabody scholarships. 1877-99. 1950. G689
414 Martin, T. K. The administration of instruction in Southern Baptist colleges and universities. 1949. G690
415 Banks, J. H. Critical thinking in college freshman mathematics. 1949. G691
418 Jaggers, W. G. The Southern states work-conference. 1949. G692
419 Moorer, S. H. State supervision in Florida. 1949. G693
420 Poppen, H. A. A factor-analysis study of prognastic tests in algebra. 1951. G694
421 Shepherd, F. M. English written usage in selected high schools in India and America. 1951. G695

422 Garvey, Albertus Magnus, Sister. A vocabulary and concept study of recent primary readers. 1951. G696
423 Staton, T. F. Relation of selected factors to individual prestige achieved in seminars. 1950. G697
424 Styza, C. J. A critical analysis of oral English in southern secondary schools. 1948. G698
426 Doggett, J. M. English periodicals (1704-14) and their reflection of social life. 1950. G699
427 Bryant, H. C. Criteria for teacher certification. 1950. G700
428 Clark, J. R. Indoor facilities for physical education activities in the senior high school grades. 1950. G701
429 Dickinson, H. E. The origin and development of the aim of family life education in American secondary schools. 1950. G702
430 Gillard, K. I. Michigan as recorded in its writings. 1950. G703
339, 360, 391, 393, 416, 417, 425 not published.
Ceased being published in book form after 430. 431--available in typed manuscript form only.

GEORGIA. UNIVERSITY. UNIVERSITY OF GEORGIA. MONOGRAPHS.

1 Brown, C. S. Repetition in Zola's novels. 1952. G704
2 Hart, J. F. The British moorlands. 1955. G705
3 Jones, W. D. Lord Aberdeen and the Americas. 1958. G706
4 McPherson, R. G. Theory of higher education in nineteenth century England. 1959. G707
5 Smith, H. R. Democracy and the public interest. 1960. G708
6 Vinson, J. C. Referendum for isolation. 1961. G709
7 Parks, E. W. William Gilmore Simms as literary critic. 1961. G710
8 Beaumont, C. A. Swift's classical rhetoric. 1961. G711
9 Jones, R. E. The alienated hero in modern French drama. 1962. G712
10 Lott, R. E. The structure and style of Azorin's El caballero inactual. 1963. G713
11 Montgomery, H. Johnny Cobb, Confederate aristocrat. 1964. G714
12 Blackstone, W. T. Francis Hutcheson and contemporary ethical theory. 1965. G715
13 Blaine, R. M. Thomas Holcroft and the revolutionary novel. 1965. G716
14 Beaumont, C. A. Swift's use of the Bible. 1965. G717
15 Cunningham, H. Field medical services at the Battle of Manassas. 1966. G718
16 Harrison, R. Samuel Beckett's "Murphy." 1967. G719
17 Leibniz, G. W. General investigations concerning the analysis of concepts and truths, ed. by O'Briant. 1968. G720
18 Hudson, C. M. The Catawba Nation. 1970. G721

GERMANISTISCHE ARBEITSHEFTE (Niemeyer)

1 Werner, O. Einführung in die strukturelle Beschreibung des Deutschen. V. 1. 1970. G722
2 Hundsnurscher, F. Neuere methoden der semantik. 1970. G723
3 Herrlitz, W. Historische phonologie des Deutschen. V. 1. 1970. G724
4 Naumann, B. Wortbildung in der deutschen gegenwartssprache. 1972. G725
5 Bühler, H. and others. Linguistik I, by Bühler and others. 1971. G726
6 Heringer, H. J. Generative grammatik und formale logik. 1972. G727
7 Cluver, A. D. de V.

Merkmalsgrammatik der deutschen sprache. 1972. G728
8-9 Lenders, W. Einführung in die linguistische datenverarbeitung I. 2 v. 1971. G729
10 Same as no. 1. V. 2. 1972. G730
11 Weber, H. Methoden der syntax. 1972. G731
12 Fritz, G. Bedeutungswandel im deutschen. 1972. G732
13 Same as no. 3. V. 2. 1973. G733
14 Ramge, H. Spracherwerb. 1973. G734
15 Ammon, U. Probleme der soziolinguistik. 1973. G735
16 Burger, H. and Jaksche, H. Idiomatik des deutschen. 1974. G736
17 Oomen, U. Linguistische grundlagen poetischer texte. 1974. G737
Ergänzungsreihe:
1 Abraham, W. Terminologie zur neueren linguistik. 1974. G738

GERMANY. VERKEHRSWISSENSCHAFTLICHEN FORSCHUNGSRATS. VERKEHRSWISSENSCHAFTLICHE ABHANDLUNGEN (Fischer)

1 Haemmerle, H. Zur wirtschaftlichen und rechtlichen organisation der deutschen seehäfen. 1936. G739
2 Wiedenfeld, K. Die monopoltendenz des kapitals im spiegel der verkehrsmittel. 1937. G740
3 Helander, S. Nationale verkehrsplanung. 1937. G741
4 Berlin. Deutsches institut für wirtschaftsforschung. Stand und aussichten des gewerblichen gütenfernverkehrs mit lastkraftwagen. 1937. G742
5 Napp-Zinn, A. F. Binnenschiffahrtspolitik der Niederlande. 1938. G743
6 Schulz-Kiesow, P. Die Verflechtung von See-und Binnenschiffahrt. V. 1. Der seeverkehr der deutschen binnenhafen. 1938. G744
7 Berlin. Deutsches institut für wirtschaftsforschung. Haltungskosten von personenkraftfahrzuegen. 1938. G745
8 ____. Der werkverkehr mit lastkraftwagen. 1939. G746
9 ____. Der wettbewerb in der seeschiffahrt. 1940. G747
10 Neesen, I. F. Gestaltung und wirstshaftlichkeit der landwasser- und luftfahrzeuge. V. 1. Der einfluss der geschwindigkeit auf die gestaltung und wirtschaftlichkeit der land- , wasser- und luftfahrzeuge. 1940. G748
11 Boesser, W. Die fernsprechtarife der welt und ihre grundlagen. 1940. G749
12 Schulz-Kiesow, P. Die durchgehenden eisenbahnseefrachttarife. 1941. G750
13 Blum, C. Strassenbahn und Omnibus in Stadtinnern. 1942. G751

GESCHICHTE DER VÖLKER UND STAATEN (Oldenbourg)

Andersson, I. Schwedische Geschichte, von den Aufängen bis zur Gegenwart. 1950. G752
Ballersteros y Beretta, A. Geschichte Spaniens. 1943. G753
Benedikt, H. , ed. Geschichte der republik österreich, by Goldinger and others. 1954. G754
Brandt, A. von. Schwedische geschichte. 1950. G755
Brandt, C. and others. Der kommunismus in China. 1952. G756
Brockelmann, C. Geschichte der islamischen Völker und staaten. 1943. G757
Dahms, H. G. Geschichte der Vereingten Staaten von Amerika. 1953. G758
Disselhof, H. D. Geschichte der altamerikanischen Kulturen. 1953. G759
Franzel, E. Geschichte unserer zeit, 1870-1950. 1952. G760
Hintrager, O. Geschichte von Südafrika. 1952. G761

Hölze, E. Russland und Amerika. 1953. G762
Jaochimsen, P. Die reformation als epoche der deutschen geschichte. 1951. G763
Kirby, E. S. Einführung in die wirtschafts - und sozialgeschichte Chinas. G764
Ritter, G. Staatskunts und kreigshandwerk. V. 1. 1954. G765
Seignobos, C. Geschichte der franzosischen nation. 1947. G766
Stadmüller, G. Geschichte Südosteuropas. 1950. G767
Stieve, F. Geschichte des deutschen Volkes. 1943. G768
Treue, W. Illustrierte kulturgeschichte des Altags. 1952. G769
Trevelyan, G. M. Geschichte Englands. 1949. G770
Volkmann, H. Kleopatra. 1953. G771
Wartburg, W. von. Geschichte der Schweiz. 1950. G772
Wilken, U. Griechische Geschichte im Rahmen der Altertumsgeschichte. 1951. G773
Wittram, R. Baltische Geschichte. 1954. G774

GIFFORD LECTURES.

1888 Müller, F. M. Natural religion. Longmans. 1889. G775
1890 Stirling, J. H. Philosophy and theology. T. &T. Clark. 1890. G776
1890-91, 1891-92 Caird, E. The evolution of religion. 2 v. Macmillan. 1893. G777
1891 Müller, F. M. Anthropological religion. Longmans. 1903. G778
1891, 1893 Stokes, G. G. Natural theology. 2 v. Black. 1891-93. G779
1892 Müller, F. M. Theosophy. Longmans. 1893. G780
1892-93 1895-96 Caird, J. The fundamental ideas of Christianity. MacLehose. 1904. G781
1894 Pfleiderer, O. Philosophy of theism. 1st ser. Scribner. 1895. G782
1894-95 Fraser, A. C. Philosophy of theism. 1st ser. Scribner. 1895. G783
1895-96 ____ ____ 2d ser. Blackwood. 1896. G784
1896-98 Ward, J. Naturalism and agnosticism. Macmillan. 1899. G785
1897 Bruce, A. B. The provential order of the world. Scribner. 1897. G786
1897-99 Theile, C. P. Elements of the science of religion. 2 v. Blackwood. 1897-99. G787
1898 Bruce, A. B. The moral order of the world in ancient and modern thought. Hodder. 1899. G788
1898-1900 Royce, J. The world and the individual. Longmans. 1917. G789
1900-01, 1901-02 Caird, E. The evolution of theology in the Greek philosophers. 2 v. MacLehose. 1904. G790
1901-02 James, W. The varieties of religious experience. Macmillan. 1901. G791
1902 Sayce, A. H. The religions of ancient Egypt and Babylonia. T. &T. Clark. 1902. G792
1902-04 Haldane, R. B. The pathway to reality. Dutton. 1926. G793
1904-05 Gwatkin, H. M. The knowledge of God and its historical development. 2 v. T. &T. Clark. 1906. G794
1904-06 Adam, J. The religious teachers of Greece. T. &T. Clark. 1908. G795
1907 Bradley, A. C. Ideals of religion. Macmillan. 1940. G796
1907-08 Driesch, H. The science and philosophy of the organism. 2 v. Macmillan. 1908. G797
1907-10 Ward, J. The realism of ends. Cambridge. 1920. G798
1909-10 Fowler, W. W. The religious experiences of the Roman people. Macmillan. 1922. G799
1910-12 Watson, J. The interpretation of religious experience. 2 v. MacLehose. 1912. G800

1911 Bosanquet, B. The principles of individuality and value. Macmillan. 1912. G801

1911-12 Frazer, J. G. The belief in immortality and the worship of the dead. 2 v. Macmillan. 1913-24. G802

1912 Bosanquet, B. The value and destiny of the individual. Macmillan. 1913. G803

1912-13 Seth Pringle-Patterson, A. The idea of God in the light of recent philosophy. Oxford. 1920. G804

1914 Balfour, A. J. B. Theism and humanism. Doran. 1915. G805

1914-15 Sorley, W. R. Moral values and the idea of God. Cambridge Univ. Pr. 1918. G806

1915-16 Ramsay, W. N. Asianic elements in Greek civilisation. Yale. 1928. G807

1915-16 Thomson, J. A. The system of animate nature. 2 v. Holt. 1920. G808

1916-18 Alexander, S. Space, time, and deity. 2 v. Macmillan. 1927. G809

1917-18 Inge, W. R. The philosophy of Plotinus. Longman. 1948. G810

1918-19 Webb, C. C. J. God and personality. 1st course. Macmillan. 1918. G811

1918-19 ____. Divine personality and human life. 2d course. Macmillan. 1920. G812

1920 Farnell, L. R. Greek hero cults and ideas of immortality. Oxford. 1921. G813

1920 Royce, J. The world and the individual. Macmillan. 1920. G814

1920-21 Jones, H. A faith that enquires. Macmillan. 1922. G815

1921-22 Hobson, E. W. The domain of natural science. Cambridge Univ. Pr. 1923. G816

1922 Morgan, C. L. Emergent evolution. Williams. 1923. G817

1922 Seth Pringle-Patterson, A. The idea of immortality. Oxford. 1923. G818

1922-23 Balfour, A. J. B. Theism and thought. Doran. 1924. G819

1923 Morgan, C. L. Life, mind and spirit. Holt. 1925. G820

1923 Seth Pringle Patterson, A. Studies in the philosophy of religion. Oxford. 1930. G821

1924-25 Farnell, L. R. The attributes of God. Oxford. 1925. G822

1924-25 Frazer, J. G. The worship of nature. Macmillan. 1926. G823

1924-25 Paterson, W. P. The nature of religion. Hodder. 1926. G824

1924-26 Mitchell, W. The place of minds in the world. Macmillan. 1933. G825

1926-28 Taylor, A. E. The faith of a moralist. 2 v. Macmillan. 1930. G826

1927 Eddington, A. S. The nature of the physical world. Macmillan. 1929. G827

1927-28 Haldane, J. S. The sciences and philosophy. Doubleday. 1929. G828

1927-28 Whitehead, A. N. Process and reality. Macmillan. 1957. G829

1927-29 Barnes, E. W. Scientific theory and religion. Macmillan. 1933. G830

1929 Dewey, J. The quest for certitude. Minton. 1929. G831

1929-30 Gore, C. Philosophy of the good life. Longman. 1934. G832

1931 Soderblom, N. The living God. Oxford. 1933. G833

1931-32 Gilson, E. H. The spirit of medieval philosophy. Sheed. 1950. G834

1931-32 Marett, R. R. Faith, hope and charity in primitive religion. Oxford. 1932. G835

1932-33 ____. Sacraments of simple folks. Oxford. 1933. G836

1933 Bevan, E. B. Holy images. Macmillan.

1940. G837
1933-34 ____. Symbolism and belief. Macmillan. 1941. G838
1933-34 Temple, W. Nature, man and God. Macmillan. 1935. G839
1935-36 Henson, R. H. Christian morality. Oxford. 1936. G840
1935-36 Ross, W. D. Foundations of ethics. Oxford. 1951. G841
1935-37 Dixon, W. M. The human situation. Longmans. 1937. G842
1936 Jaeger, W. W. The theology of the early Greek philosophers. Oxford. 1937. G843
1936-37 Dixon, W. The human situation. Longman. 1937. G844
1937-38 Barth, K. The knowledge of God and the service of God. Scribner. 1939. G845
1937-38 Sherrington, C. S. Man on his nature. Cambridge. 1952. G846
1939 Bidez, J. Eos; ou, Platon et l'Orient. Académie royale de Belgique. 1945. G847
1939 Laird, J. Theism and cosmology. Allen. 1940. G848
1939 Niebuhr, R. The nature and destiny of man. 2 v. Scribner. 1941. G849
1939-40 Kroner, R. The primacy of faith. Macmillan. 1943. G850
1940 Laird, J. Mind and diety. Philosophical library. 1941. G851
1947 Dawson, C. Religion and culture. Sheed. 1948. G852
1947-48 Brunner, H. E. Christianity and civilization. 2 v. Scribner. 1948-49. G853
1948-49 Dawson, C. Religion and the rise of Western civilization. Sheed. 1950. G854
1948-49 MacBeath, A. Experiments in living. Macmillan. 1952. G855
1949-50 Marcel, G. The mystery of being. 2 v. Regnery. 1951. G856
1950 Farmer, H. H. Revelation and religion. Harper. 1954. G857
1951 Raven, C. E. Natural religion and Christian theology. 1st ser. Cambridge. 1953. G858
1951 ____. Natural religion and Christian theology. 2d. ser. Cambridge. 1953. G859
1952-53 Toynbee, A. J. An historian's approach to religion. Oxford. 1956. G860
1953-54 Macmurray, J. The form of the personal. 2 v. Harper. 1958. G861
1955 Bultmann, R. K. The presence of eternity. Harper. 1957. G862
(Also published as: History and eschatology. Harper. 1957) G863
1955-57 Hodgson, L. For faith and freedom. 2 v. Scribner. 1956-57. G864
1957 Farrer, A. The freedom of the will. Macmillan. 1958. G865
Tillich, P. J. Systematic theology. 2 v. Univ. of Chicago Pr. 1951-57. G866
1959-60 Weizsäcker, C. F. van. The relevance of science. Harper. 1964. G867
1961-62 Baillie, J. The sense of the presence of God. Scribner. 1962. G868
1964-65 Findlay, J. N. The discipline of the cave. Humanities. 1966. G869
1964-65 Hardy, A. C. The divine flame. 1966. G870
1965-66 Findlay, J. N. The transcendence of the cave. Humanities. 1968. G871
1966-68 Lewis, H. D. The elusive mind. Humanities. 1969. G872
1967-69 Zaehner, R. C. Concordance discord. Oxford. 1972. G873
1969-70 Leeuwen, A. T. van. Critique Heaven. Lutterworth. 1972. G874
1970-71 Mascall, E. L. The openness of being. Westminster Pr. 1971. G875
1971-73 Kenny, A. and others. The phenomenon of mind. 2 parts. 1972-73. G876

GLASGOW. UNIVERSITY. DEPT. OF SOCIAL AND ECONOMIC RESEARCH. SOCIAL AND ECONOMIC STUDIES (Cambridge)

1 Collier, A. The crofting problem. 1953. G877
2 Glasgow. University. The Scottish economy, ed. by Cairncross. 1954. G878
3 Fay, C. R. Adam Smith and the Scotland of his day. 1956. G879
4 Miller, J. John Miller of Glasgow, 1735-1801, his life and thought and his contributions to sociological analysis, by Lehmann. 1960. G880
5 Robertson, D. J. Factory wage structures and national agreements. 1960. G881
6 Parkinson, J. R. The economics of shipbuilding in the United Kingdom. 1960. G882
7 Paterson, T. T. Glasgow limited. 1960. G883

New series:
1 McCrone, G. The economics of subsidising agriculture. 1962. G884
2 Meek, R. L. The economics of physiocracy. 1963. G885
3 Hart, P. E. Studies in profit, business saving and investment in the United Kingdom, 1920-1962. V. 1. 1965. G886
4 McCrone, G. Scotland's economic progress, 1951-1960. 1965. G887
5 Reid, G. L., ed. Fringe benefits, labour costs and social security. 1965. G888
6 Gaskin, M. The Scottish banks. 1965. G889
7 Hunter, A. Competition and the law. 1966. G890
8 Brown, C. V. The Nigerian banking system. 1966. G891
9 MacBean, A. I. Export instability and economic development. 1967. G892
10 Checkland, S. G. The mines of Tharsis. 1967. G893
11 Macfie, A. L. The individual in society. 1967. G894
12 Aldcroft, D. H., ed. The development of British industry and foreign competition. 1968. G895
13 Same as no. 3. V. 2. 1968. G896
14 Richardson, H. W. and Aldcroft, D. H. Building in the British economy between the wars. 1968. G897
15 McCrone, G. Regional policy in Britain. 1969. G898
16 Cullingworth, J. B. and Orr, S. C. Regional and urban studies. 1969. G899
17 Sumner, G. Planning local authority service for the elderly. 1969. G900
18 Hunter, L. C. Labour problems of technological change. 1970. G901
19 Allen, K. and MacLennan, M. C. Regional problems and policies in Italy and France. 1970. G902
20 Johnson, K. M. and Garnett, H. C. The economics of containerisation. 1971. G903
21 Campbell, T. D. Adam Smith's science of morals. 1971. G904
22 Labour markets under different employment conditions, by Mackey and others. 1971. G905

GLASGOW. UNIVERSITY. DEPT. OF SOCIAL AND ECONOMIC RESEARCH. SOCIAL AND ECONOMIC STUDIES. OCCASIONAL PAPERS (Oliver & Boyd)

1 Cramond, R. D. Allocation of council houses. 1964. G906
2 Grieve, R. and Robertson, D. J. The city and the region. 1964. G907
3 Wilson, T. Policies for regional development. 1964. G908
4 Stewart, J. M. W. A pricing system for roads. 1965. G909
5 Cameron, G. C. and Clark, B. D. Industrial movement and the regional problem. 1966. G910

6 Cameron, G. C. and Reid, G. L. Scottish economic planning and the attraction of industry. 1966. G911
7 Jephcott, P. Time of one's own. 1967. G912
8 Cullingworth, J. B. A profile of Glasgow housing, 1965. 1968. G913
9 Hart, T. The comprehensive development area. 1968. G914
10 Regional policy in E. F. T. A., prepared by Allen and Hermansen. 1968. G915
11 Cameron, H. M. Student accomodation. 1969. G916
12 Hollingsworth, T. H. Migration. 1970. G917
13 Jephcott, A. P. and Robinson, H. Homes in high flats. 1971. G918
14 Cameron, G. and Wingo, L. Cities, regions and public policies. 1973. G919

GLASGOW. UNIVERSITY. DEPT. OF SOCIAL AND ECONOMIC RESEARCH. SOCIAL AND ECONOMIC RESEARCH. SOCIAL AND ECONOMIC STUDIES. RESEARCH PAPERS.

1 Cramond, R. D. Housing policy in Scotland. 1966. G920
2 Musil, J. Housing needs and policy in Great Britain and Czechoslovakia. 1966. G921
3 Murray, G. J. Voluntary organizations and social welfare. 1969. G922
4 Sleeman, J. Voluntary services in seven hospitals in Scotland. 1969. G923

GODKIN LECTURES, HARVARD UNIVERSITY (Harvard Univ. Pr. unless otherwise noted)

1909 Sedgwick, A. G. The democratic mistake. 1960. G924
1920 Storey, M. Problems of to-day. Houghton. 1920. G925
1924-25 Luce, R. Congress. 1926. G926
1926-27 Hibben, J. G. Self-legislated obligations. 1927. G927
1932-33 Seasongood, M. Local government in the United States. 1933. G928
1934 Lippmann, W. The method of freedom. Macmillan. 1934. G929
1935 Douglas, L. W. The liberal tradition. VanNostrand. 1935. G930
1937-38 Baldwin, R. N. Civil liberties and industrial conflict. 1938. G931
1938 Myrdal, G. Population. 1940. G932
1939 Moses, R. Theory and practice in politics. 1939. G933
1941 Merriam, C. E. On the agenda of democracy. 1941. G934
1944-45 Copland, D. B. The road to high employment. 1945. G935
1949 Flanders, R. E. The American century. 1950. G936
1950 Clay, L. D. B. Germany and the fight for freedom. 1950. G937
1951 Douglas, P. H. Ethics in government. 1952. G938
1953 McCloy, J. J. The challenge to American foreign policy. 1953. G939
1955 Jackson, R. H. The Supreme Court in the American system of government. 1955. G940
1955 O'Brian, J. L. National security and individual freedom. 1955. G941
1956 Bowles, C. American politics in a revolutionary world. 1956. G942
1957 Gaitskell, H. T. N. The challenge of coexistence. 1957. G943
1958 Conant, J. B. Germany and freedom. 1958. G944
1960 Snow, C. P. Science and government. 1961. G945
1962 Rockefeller, N. A. The future of federalism. 1962. G946
1963 Kerr, C. The uses of the university. 1963. G947
1964 Ashby, E. African universities and Western tradition. 1964. G948

1965 Weaver, R. C. Dilemmas of urban America. 1965. G949
1966 Heller, W. W. New dimensions of political thought. 1966. G950
1967 Heath, E. Old world, new horizons. 1970. G951
1968 Bundy, M. The strength of government. 1968. G952
1970 Crossman, R. H. S. The myth of cabinet government. 1971. G953

GÖTTINGER BAUSTEINE ZUR GESCHICHTSWISSENSCHAFT (Musterschmidt)

1 Höcker, W. Der gesandte bunsen als Vermittler zwischen Deutschland und England. 1951. G954
2 Quirin, K. H. Herrschaft und Gemeinde nach mittelalterlichen Quelien des 12-18 Jahrhunderts. 1952. G955
3-4 Bussmann, W. Treitsche, Sein Welt- und Geschichtsbild. 1952. G956
5 Haaf, R. ten. Deutschordensstaat und Deutschordensballeien. 1954. G957
6 Ruffmann, K. H. Das Russlandbild im England Shakespeares. 1952. G958
7 Vogelsand, T. Die Frau als Herrscherin im hohen Mittelalter, Studien zur "consors regni" Formel. 1954. G959
8 Ritscher, H. Fontane, Seine politische Gedankenwelt vergriffen. 1953. G960
9 Schussler, W. Die Daily-Telegraph-Affare, Furst Bulow, Kaiser Wilhelm und die Krise des Zweiten Reiches 1908. 1908. G961
10-11 Murawski, K. E. Zwischen Tannenberg und Thorn... 2 v. 1953. G962
12 Thielen, G. Die Kultur am Hofe Herzog Albrechts von Preussen. 1953. G963
13-14 Mengel, I. Elisabeth von Braunschweig-Lüneburg und Albrecht von Preussen... 1954. G964
15 Thiele, E. T. Das Gesandtschaftswesen in Preussen im 16 Jahrhundert. 1954. G965
16 Terveen, F. Gesamtstaat und Retablissement... 1954. G966
17 Dockhorn, K. Deutscher Geist und angelsachsische Geistesgeschichte. 1954. G967
18 Treue, W. Der Krimkrieg und die Entstehung der modernen flotten. 1954. G968
19 Hinrichs, K. Ranke und die Geschichtstheologie der Goethezeit. 1954. G969
20 Muralt, L. von. Bismarcks verantwortlichkeit. 1955. G970
21 Hubatsch, W. Die Ara Tirpitz, Studien zur deutschen Marinepolitik 1890-1918. 1955. G971
22 Groote, W. von. Die Entstehung des Nationalbewusstseins in Nordwestdeutschland 1790-1830. 1955. G972
23 Forstreuter, K. Preussen und Russland von den Anfangen des Deutschen Ordens bis zu Peter dem Grossen. 1955. G973
24 Easum, C. V. Prinz Heinrich von Preussen. 1958. G974
25 Heidegger, H. Die deutsche Sozialdemokratie und der nationale Staat 1870-1920... 1956. G975
26 Wucher, A. Theodor Mommsen, Geschichtsschreibung. 1956. G976
27 Brauer-Gramm, H. Der Landvogt Peter von Hagenbach. 1957. G977
28 Steglich, W. Bündnissicherung oder Verstandigungsfrieden. 1958. G978
29 Wischofer, H. Die ostpreussischen Stände im letzten Jahrhundert vor dem Regierungsantritt des Grossen Kurfürsten. 1958. G979
30 Hauser, O. Deutschland und der englisch-russische Gegensatz, 1900-1914. 1958. G980
31 Klempt, A. Die Sackularisierung der 'universal-historischen Affassung. 1960. G981

32 Eisenbart, L. Kleiderordnung der deutschen Städte von der Mitte des 14. bis zum Ende des 16 Jahrunderts. 1962. G982
33 Fesefeldt, W. Englische Staatstheorie des 13 Jahrhunderts, Henry de Bracton und sein Werk. 1962. G983
34 Reichel, W. Studien zur Wandlung von Max Lehmanns preussisch-deutschen Geschichtsbild. 1963. G984
35 Grolle, J. Langesgechichte in der Zeit der deutschen Spätanfklärung. 1963. G985
36 Scheel, W. Das "Berliner Politische Wochenblatt" und die politische und soziale Revolution in Frankreich und England. 1964. G986
37 Boockmann, H. Laurentius Blumenau. 1965. G987
38 Genschel, H. Die Verdrängung der Juden aus der Wirtschaft im Dritten Reich. 1966. G988
39 Schlingensiepen-Poggen, A. Das Sozialethos der lutherischen Aufklärungstehologie am Vorabend der industriellen Revolution. 1967. G989
40 Hünigen, G. Nikolaj Pavlovic Ignat'ev und die russische Balkanpolitik, 1875-1878. 1968. G990
41 Nolte, H. H. Religiose toleranz in Russland, 1600-1725. 1970. G991
42 Bitsch, H. Das Erzstift Lyon zwischen Frankreich und dem reich in Hohen Mittelalter. 1971. G992
43 Behnen, M. Das Preussische wochenblatt (1851-1861). 1971. G993
44 Stein, P. Die neuroientierung der osterreichisch-ungarischen aussenpolitik, 1895-1897. 1972. G994

GOKHALE INSTITUTE OF POLITICS AND ECONOMICS. MONOGRAPH SERIES (Asia Pub. House)

1 Padki, M. B. and others. Utilization of local resources. 1967. G995
2 Koti, R. K. Capacity utilisation and factors affecting it in certain Indian industries, 1966-67. 1967. G996
3 Kulkarni, M. G. Problems of tribal development. 1968. G997
4 Muranjan, S. W. Study of the high yielding varieties programme in a district in Maharashtra. 1968. G998
5 Rajapurohit, A. R. Study of the high yielding varieties programme in a district in Maharashtra. 1968. G999
6 Prasad, B. The Indian Cotton Mills Federation. 1968. G1000
7 Sapre, S. G. A study of tractor cultivation in Shahada. 1969. G1001
9 Koti, R. K. Utilisation of industrial capacity in India, 1967-68. 1968. G1002
10 Gajarajam, C. S. Planned rehabilitation and economic change. 1970. G1003
11 Kulkarni, M. G. Problems of development in a backward area. 1971. G1004
13 Danekar, V. M. and Pethe, V. P. A survey of famine conditions in the affected regions of Maharashtra and Mysore. 1972. G1005
16 Mulla, G. R. Disposal of government waste lands for cultivation in Poona District, Maharashtra. 1972. G1006

GOKHALE INSTITUTE OF POLITICS AND ECONOMICS. PUBLICATIONS. (Asia Pub. House)

1 Gadgil, D. R. The salaries of public officials in India. 1931. G1007
2 ____. Imperial preference for India. 1932. G1008
3 Gadgil, D. R. and V. R. A survey of the marketing of fruit in Poona. 1933. G1009
4 ____. A survey of motorbus transportation in six districts of the Bombay presidency. 1935. G1010

5 Joshi, N. M. Urban handicrafts of the Bombay Deccan. 1936. G1011
6 Sivaswamy, K. G. Legislative protection and relief of agriculturist debtors in India. 1939. G1012
7 Gadgil, D. R. A survey of farm business in Wai taluka. 1940. G1013
8 Sovani, N. V. The population problem in India. 1942. G1014
9 Gadgil, D. R. Regulation of wages and other problems of industrial labour in India. 1945. G1015
10 ____. War and Indian economy policy. 1944. G1016
11 Ghurye, G. S. The aborigines-"so called"- and their future. 1943. G1017
12 Gadgil, D. R. Poona. V. 1. 1945. G1018
13 ____. Federating India. 1945. G1019
14 Kakade, R. G. A socio-economic survey of weaving communities in Sholapur. 1947. G1020
15 Gadgil, D. R. The Federal problem in India. 1947. G1021
16 Joski, T. M. Bombay finance (1921-1946). 1947. G1022
17 Gadgil, D. R. Economic effects of irrigation. 1948. G1023
18 Sovani, N. V. The social survey of Kolhapur City. V. 1. 1948. G1024
19 Gadgil, D. R. Some observations on the draft constitution. 1948. G1025
20 India. Commodity Prices Board. Reports, ed. by Sovani. 1948. G1026
21 Sovani, N. V. Post-war inflation in India. 1949. G1027
22 ____. Planning of post-war economic development in India. 1951. G1028
23-24 Same as no. 18. V. 3-4. 1951-52. G1029
25 Same as no. 12. V. 2. 1952. G1030
26 Dandekar, V. M. Report on the Poona schedules of the National Sample Survey, 1950-51. 1953. G1031
27 ____ and K. Survey of fertility and morality in Poona district. 1953. G1032
28 Raman Rao, A. V. Structure and working of village panchayats. 1954. G1033
29 Dandekar, V. M. Second report on the Poona schedules of the National Sample Survey, 1950-51. 1954. G1034
30 Gadgil, D. R. Economic policy and development. 1955. G1035
31 Sovani, N. V. and Dandekar, K. Fertility survey of Nasik, Kolaba and Salara (North) districts. 1955. G1036
32 Gadgil, D. R. and Dandekar, V. M. Primary education in Satara District. 1955. G1037
33 Dandekar, V. M. Use of food surpluses for economic development. 1956. G1038
34 Sovani, N. V. Poona. 1956. G1039
35 Dandekar, A. M. and Khudanpur, G. J. Working of Bombay Tenancy Act. 1957. G1040
36 Patvardhan, V. S. Food control in Bombay Province, 1939-1949. 1958. G1041
37 Danekar, K. Demographic survey of six-rural communities. 1959. G1042
38 Sovani, N. V. and Rath, N. Economics of a multiple-purpose river dam. 1960. G1043
39 Gadgil, D. R. Planning and economic policy in India. 1962. G1044
40 Agrawal, G. D. and Khudanpur, G. P. Methods & practice of farm accounts. 1961. G1045
41 Balakrishnan, G. Financing small scale industries in India, 1950-1952. 1961. G1046
42 Brahme, S. Distribution and consumption of cloth in Poona. 1962. G1047
43 Kamat, A. R. and Deshmukh, A. G. Wastage in college education. 1963. G1048
44 Lambert, R. D. Workers,

factories and social changes in India. 1963. G1049
45 Mukerji, K. Levels of economic activity and public expenditures in India. 1965. G1050
46 Gadgil, D. R. Sholapur City. 1965. G1051
47 Patvardhan, V. S. British agricultural marketing. 1965. G1052
48 Rath, N. and Patvardhan, V. S. Impact of assistance under P. L. 480 on Indian economy. 1966. G1053
49 Dandekar, K. Communication in family planning. 1966. G1054
50 Namjoshi, M. V. Chambers of commerce in India. 1966. G1055
51 Brahme, S. Deluge in Poona. 1967. G1056
52 Kamat, A. R. Two studies in education. 1969. G1057
53 Karve, D. G. Cooperation. 1968. G1058
54 Gadgil, D. R. Human rights in a multinational society. 1969. G1059
55 ____. The making of man. 1969. G1060
56 Kamat, A. R. Progress of education in rural Maharashtra. 1970. G1061
57 Rath, V. Index of Indian economic journals, 1961-1965. 1971. G1062
59 Gadgil, D. R. Planning and economic policy in India. 1972. G1063

GOTHENBURG STUDIES IN ENGLISH (Almqvist & Wiksell)

1 Rudskoger, A. Fair, foul, nice, proper; a contribution to the study of polysemy. 1962. G1064
2 Ellegård, A. The auxiliary do. 1953. G1065
3 Karlberg, G. The English interrogative pronouns. 1954. G1066
4 Behre, F. Meditative-polemic should in modern English that-clauses. 1955. G1067
5 Ohlander, U. A Middle English metrical paraphrase of the Old Testament. 2 v. 1955. G1068
6 Barber, C. L. The idea of honour in the English drama, 1591-1700. 1957. G1069
7 Stubelius, S. Airship, aeroplane, aircraft; study in the history of terms for aircraft in English. 1958. G1070
8 Ellegård, A. Darwin and the general reader. 1958. G1071
9 Stubelius, S. Balloon, flying-machine, helicopter, further studies in the history of terms for aircraft in English. 1960. G1072
10 Behre, F. Papers on English vocabulary and syntax. 1961. G1073
11 Same as no. 5. V. 3. 1961. G1074
12 Olsson, Y. On the syntax of the English verb with special references to have a look and similar complex structures. 1961. G1075
13 Ellegård, A. A statistical method for determining authorship. 1962. G1076
14 Barber, C. L. and others. Contributions to English syntax and philology. 1962. G1077
15 Ellegård, A. English, Latin, and morphemic analyses. 1963. G1078
16 Same as no. 5. V. 4. 1963. G1079
17 Frykman, E. W. E. Aytoun, pioneer professor of English at Edinburgh. 1963. G1080
18 ____. "Bitter knowledge" and "unconquerable hope." 1966. G1081
19 Behre, F. Studies in Agatha Christie's writings. 1967. G1082
20 Svartnik, J. The Evans statement. 1968. G1083
21 Ljung, M. English denominal adjectives. 1970. G1084
22 Kjellmer, G. Context and meaning. 1971. G1085
23 Mannheimer, A. The generations in Meredith. 1972. G1086
24 Ohlander, U. A middle

English rhetoric. 1972. G1087
25 Melander, I. The poetry of Sylvia Plath. 1972. G1088
26 Von Elek, C. Teaching foreign language grammar. 1972. G1089

GOVERNMENT CONTROL OF THE ECONOMIC ORDER (Univ. of Minnesota Pr.)

1 Lippincott, B. E., ed. Government control of the economic order. 1935. G1090
2 ___. On the economic theory of socialism. 1938. G1091/2

GOVERNMENT IN THE MODERN WORLD (Macmillan)

Alker, H. R. Mathematics and politics. 1965. G1093
Fried, R. C. Comparative political institutions. 1966. G1094
Goldman, R. M. The Democratic Party in American politics. 1966. G1095
Hargrove, E. C. Presidential leadership. 1966. G1096
Holtzman, A. Interest groups and lobbying. 1966. G1097
Jones, C. O. The Republican Party in American politics. 1965. G1098
Krislov, S. The Supreme Court in the political process. 1965. G1099
Levine, E. L. An introduction to American government. 1968. G1100
Lockard, D. Toward equal opportunity. 1968. G1101
McClelland, C. A. Theory and the international system. 1966. G1102
McLellan, D. S. The cold war in transition. 1966. G1103
Nelson, J. M. Aid, influence, and foreign policy. 1968. G1104
Redford, E. S. The role of government in the American economy. 1966. G1105
Russett, B. M. Trends in world politics. 1965. G1106
Tarr, D. W. American strategy in the nuclear age. 1966. G1107

THE GOVERNMENTS OF MODERN EUROPE (Van Nostrand)

Arneson, B. A. The democratic monarchies of Scandinavia. 1949. G1108
Harper, S. N. The government of the Soviet Union. 1949. G1109
Pollock, J. K. The government of greater Germany. 1938. G1110
Rappard, W. E. The government of Switzerland. 1936. G1111
Sharp, W. R. The government of the French republic. 3 v. in 1. 1938. G1112

GREAT AGES OF MAN (Silver Burdett)

Blitzer, C. Age of kings. 1967. G1113
Bowra, C. M. Classical Greece. 1965. G1114
Burchell, S. C. Age of progress. 1966. G1115
Casson, L. Ancient Egypt. 1965. G1116
Colton, J. Twentieth century. 1968. G1117
Davidson, B. African kingdoms. 1966. G1118
Fremantle, A. (Jackson). Age of faith. 1965. G1119
Gay, P. Age of enlightenment. 1966. G1120
Hadas, M. Imperial Rome. 1965. G1121
Hale, J. R. Age of exploration. 1966. G1122
___. The Renaissance. 1965. G1123
Kramer, S. N. Cradle of civilization. 1967. G1124
Lafore, L. The age of political revolution. 1966. G1125
Leonard, J. N. Ancient America. 1967. G1126
___. Early Japan. 1968. G1127
Muller, H. J. The age of social revolution. 1966. G1128
Osborne, J. The Old South. 1970. G1129
Peyre, H. The age of reason. 1966. G1130
Schafer, E. H. Ancient China.

1970. G1131
Schulberg, L. and others. Historic India. 1968. G1132
Sherrard, P. Byzantium. 1966. G1133
Simon, E. The Reformation. 1966. G1134
Simons, G. Barbarian Europe. 1968. G1135
Stewart, D. Early Islam. 1967. G1136
Wallace, R. The rise of Russia. 1967. G1137

THE GREAT AGES OF WESTERN PHILOSOPHY (Houghton)

1 Fremantle, A. The age of belief. 1955. G1138
2 Santillana, G. de. The age of adventure. 1956. G1139
3 Hampshire, S., ed. The age of reason. 1956. G1140
4 Berlin, I., ed. The age of enlightenment. 1956. G1141
5 Aiken, H. D., ed. The age of ideology. 1956. G1142
6 White, M. G., ed. The age of analysis. 1955. G1143

THE GREAT AGES OF WORLD ARCHITECTURE (Brazillier)

Alex, W. Japanese architecture. 1963. G1144
Branner, R. Gothic architecture. 1961. G1145
Brown, F. E. Roman architecture. G1146
Hoag, J. D. Western Islamic architecture. 1963. G1147
Lowry, B. Renaissance architecture. 1962. G1148
MacDonald, W. L. Early Christian and Byzantine architecture. 1962. G1149
Millon, H. A. Baroque and rococo architecture. 1961. G1150
Robertson, D. Pre-Columbian architecture. 1963. G1151
Saalman, H. Medieval architecture, European architecture, 600-1200. 1962. G1152
Scranton, R. L. Greek architecture. 1962. G1153
Scully, V. J. Modern architecture. 1961. G1154
Wu, N. I. Chinese and Indian architecture. 1963. G1155

GREAT AMERICAN ARTIST SERIES (Brazillier)

Goodrich, L. Albert P. Ryder. 1959. G1156
____. Winslow Homer. 1959. G1157
Goossen, E. C. Stuart Davis. 1959. G1158
Hess, T. B. Willem de Kooning. 1959. G1159
O'Hara, F. Jackson Pollock. 1959. G1160
Porter, F. Thomas Eakins. 1959. G1161

GREAT ART AND ARTISTS OF THE WORLD (Watts)

Bowness, A., ed. Impressionists and post-impressionists. 1965. G1162
Garlick, K., ed. British and North American art to 1900. 1965. G1163
Hammacher, A. M. and Vandenbrande, R. H. Flemish and Dutch art. 1965. G1164
Laclotte, M., ed. French art from 1350 to 1850. 1965. G1165
Monteverdi, M., ed. Italian art to 1850. 1965. G1166
Myers, B. S. How to look at art. 1965. G1167
Origins of Western art, by Strong and others. 1965. G1168
Sullivan, M. Chinese and Japanese art. 1965. G1169
Sylvester, D., ed. Modern art. 1965. G1170
Vey, H. and Salas, X. de. German and Spanish art to 1900. 1965. G1171

GREAT BATTLES OF HISTORY (Lippincott)

Asprey, R. B. The first battle of the Marne. 1962. G1172
Blumenson, M. Anzio. 1963. G1173
Craig, G. A. The Battle of Königgrätz. 1964. G1174

Davis, B. The Cowpens-Guilford Courthouse campaign. 1962. G1175
Dayan, M. Diary of the Sinai Company. 1966. G1176
Dierks, J. C. A leap to arms. 1970. G1177
Duggan, M. Trenton. 1966. G1178
Falls, B. B. Hell is a very small place. 1967. G1179
Falls, C. B. Armageddon: 1918. 1964. G1180
____. The Battle of Caporetto. 1965. G1181
____. Caporetto, 1917. 1966. G1182
Furneaux, R. The Zulu War. 1963. G1183
Gibbs, P. The Battle of the Alma. 1963. G1184
Griffith, S. B. The battle for Guadalcanal. 1963. G1185
Hargreaves, R. Red sun rising. 1962. G1186
Heinl, R. D. Victory at high tide. 1968. G1187
Lavender, D. S. Climax at Buena Vista. 1966. G1188
MacDonald, C. B. The Battle of the Huertgen Forest. 1963. G1189
Majdalany, F. The Battle of El Alamein. 1965. G1190
Miers, E. S. The last campaign. 1972. G1191
Muller, C. G. The darkest day: 1814. 1963. G1192
Parrish, T. D. The Bulge. 1966. G1193
Sandoz, M. The Battle of Little Bighorn. 1966. G1194
West, W. O. Gettysburg. 1966. G1195

GREAT BRITAIN. COLONIAL OFFICE. COLONIAL RESEARCH PUBLICATIONS (H. M. Stationery Office)

1 Bauer, P. T. Report on a visit to the rubber growing small-holdings of Malaya. 1948. G1196
2 Denbenham, F. Report on the water resources of the Bechuanaland Protectorate... 1948. G1197
3 Northcott, C. H., ed. African labour efficiency survey. 1949. G1198
4 Murray, S. S. Report on tobacco. 1949. G1199
5 Oxley, T. A. Grain storage in East and Central Africa. 1950. G1200
6 Tooth, G. Studies in mental illness in the Gold Coast. 1950. G1201
7 Longley, E. O. Contagious caprine pleuro-pneumonia. 1951. G1202
8 Pollitt, H. W. W. Colonial road problems. 1950. G1203
9 Watson, J. S. The rat problem in Cyprus. 1951. G1204
10 Uvarov, B. P. Locust research and control, 1929-1950. 1951. G1205
11 Hunt, K. E. Statistics for colonial agriculture. 1952. G1206
12 Gt. Brit. Colonial office. Insect infestation of stored food products in Nigeria. 1952. G1207
13 Dowson, E. M. and Sheppard, V. L. O. Land registration. 1956. G1208
14 Kaberry, P. M. Women of the grassfields. 1952. G1209
15 Wells, A. F. Friendly societies in the West Indies. 1953. G1210
16 Anderson, J. N. D. Islamic law in Africa. 1955. G1211
17 Pollitt, H. W. W. Colonial road problems. 1954. G1212
18 Williams, F. H. P. Report on roads and road problems in South East Asia and the Caribbean. 1957. G1213
19 King, F. H. H. Money in British East Asia. 1957. G1214
20 Eastop, V. F. Study of the Aphididae of East Africa. 1957. G1215
21 Salmond, K. F. A report on investigations into grain storage problems in Nyasaland Protectorate. 1957. G1216

22 Hunt, K. E. Colonial agricultural statistics. 1957. G1217
23 Allan, J. A. The grasses of Barbados. 1957. G1218
24 Gt. Brit. British Honduras Land Use Survey. Lands in British Honduras, by Wright and others, ed. by Rommey. 1959. G1219
25 Brooks, A. C. Study of the Thomson's gazelle Gazella thomsonii Gunther in Tanganyika. 1961. G1220

GREAT BRITAIN. COLONIAL OFFICE. COLONIAL RESEARCH STUDIES (H. M. Stationery Office)

1 Leach, E. R. Social science research in Sarawak. 1950. G1221
2 Acworth, A. W. Buildings of architectural or historic interest in the British West Indies. 1951. G1222
3 Mayer, P. Two studies in applied anthropology in Kenya. 1951. G1223
4 Huntingford, G. W. B. Nandi work and culture. 1950. G1224
5 Mair, L. P. Native administration in central Nyasaland. 1952. G1225
6 Gt. Brit. Colonial office. An annotated bibliography on land tenure in the British and British protected territories... 1952. G1226
7 Epstein, A. L. The administration of justice and the urban African. 1953. G1227
8 Haswell, M. R. Economics of agriculture in a Savannah village. 1953. G1228
9 Morris, H. S. Report on a Melanau sago producing community in Sarawak. 1953. G1229
10 Greaves, I. Colonial monetary conditions. 1953. G1230
11 Prest, A. R. The national income in Nigeria, 1950-51. 1953. G1231
12 Holme, R. V. and Sherwood, E. G. P. The fertilizer requirements of the Kenya highlands. 1954. G1232
13 Sheddick, V. G. J. Land tenure in Basutoland. 1954. G1233
14 Geddes, W. R. The Land Dayaks of Sarawak. 1954. G1234
15 Bohannan, P. Tiv farm and settlement. 1954. G1235
16 Smith, M. G. The economy of Hausa communities of Zaria. 1955. G1236
17 Wright, F. C. African consumers in Nyasaland and Tanganyika. 1955. G1237
18 Freeman, J. D. Iban agriculture. 1955. G1238
19 Goody, J. R. The social organisation of the LoWiili. 1956. G1239
20 Freedman, M. Chinese family and marriage in Singapore. 1957. G1240
21 Hall, D. W. and others. Underground storage of grain. 1956. G1241
22 Meek, C. K. Land tenure and land administration in Nigeria and the Cameroons. 1957. G1242
23 Prest, A. R. A fiscal survey of the British Caribbean. 1957. G1243
24 Moser, C. A. The measurement of levels of living with special reference to Jamaica. 1957. G1244
25 Ridley, M. W. and Percy, R. The exploitation of sea birds in Seychelles. 1958. G1245
26 Peacock, A. T. and Dosser, D. G. M. The national income of Tanganyika, 1952-54. 1958. G1246
27 Walker, G. J. Traffic and transport in Nigeria. 1959. G1247
28 Prevett, P. F. An investigation into the storage problems of rice in Sierra Leone. 1959. G1248
29 Lang, D. M. Soils of Malta and Gozo. 1962. G1249
30 Girling, F. K. The Acholi of Uganda. 1960. G1250
31 Nye, J. W. B. The insect pests of graminaceous crops in East Africa. 1960. G1251

32 Hawkins, E. K. Roads and road transport in our underdeveloped country. 1962. G1252
33 Middleton, J. Land tenure in Zanzibar. 1961. G1253
34 Benedict, B. Indians in a plural society. 1961. G1254
35 Carter, H. N. Notes on the tonal system of Northern Rhodesian plateau Tonga. 1962. G1255

GREAT BRITAIN. PUBLIC RECORD OFFICE. RERUM BRITANNICARUM MEDII AEVI SCRIPTORES.

1 Capgrave, J. The chronicles of England, ed. by Hingeston. 1858. G1256
2 Abingdon Abbey. Chronicon monasterii de Abingdon, ed. by Stevenson. 2 v. 1858. G1257
3 Luard, H. R. Lives of Edward the Confessor. 1858. G1258
4 Monumenta franciscana. 2 v. 1858-1882. G1259
5 Netter, T. Fasciculi Zizaniorum magistri Johannis Wycliff cum tritico, ed. by Shirley. 1858. G1260
6 Boece, H. The buik of the croniclis of Scotland, ed. by Turnbull. 1858. G1261
7 Capgrave, J. Johannis Capgrave libri de illustribus Henricis, ed. by Hingeston. 1858. G1262
7a ____. The book of the illustrious Henries, tr. by Hingeston. 1858. G1263
8 Thomas, of Elmham. Historia Monasterii S. Augustini Cantauriensis, ed. by Hardwick. 1858. G1264
9 Eulogium (historiarum sive temporis) Chronicon ab orbe condito usque ad annum Domini MCCCLXVI, ed. by Haydon. 3 v. 1858-63. G1265
10 Gairdner, J., ed. Historia regis Henrici Septimi, a Bernardo Anderea Tholosati conscripta. 1858. G1266
11 Cole, C. A., ed. Memorials of Henry the Fifth, king of England. 1858. G1267
12 London. Corporation. Munimenta Gildhallae Londoniensis; Liber albus, liber custumarum et liber Hern, ed. by Riley. 3 v. 1859-1862. G1268
13 Johannes de Oxenedes. Chronica Johannis de Oxenedes, ed. by Ellis. 1859. G1269
14 Wright, T. Political poems and songs, relating to English history, ed. by Wright. 2 v. 1859-1861. G1270
15 Bacon, R. Fr. Rogeri Bacon Opera quaedam hactenus inedita, ed. by Brewer. 1859. G1271
16 Bartholomaeus de Cotton. Bartholomaei de Cotton, monachi norwicensis, historia anglicana, ed. by Luard. 1859. G1272
17 Brut y tywysogion. Brut y Tywysogion; or, The chronicle of the princes, ed. by Ithel. 1860. G1273
18 Hingeston-Randolph, F. C., ed. Royal and historical letters during the reign of Henry the Fourth. 1960. G1274
19 Peacock, R. The repressor of over much blaming of the clergy, ed. by Babington. 2 v. 1860. G1275
20 Annales Cambriae, ed. by Williams. 1860. G1276
21 Giraldus Cambrensis. Giraldi Cambrensis opera, ed. by Brewer. 8 v. 1861-1891. G1277
22 Stevenson, J., ed. Letters and papers illustrative of the wars of the English in France during the reign of Henry the Sixth. 2 v. 1861-1864. G1278
23 Anglo-Saxon Chronicle. The Anglo-Saxon Chronicle, ed. by Thorpe. 2 v. 1861. G1279
24 Gairdner, J., ed. Letters and papers illustrative of the reigns of Richard III and Henry VII. 2 v. 1861-1863. G1280
25 Grosseteste, R. Roberti

Grosseteste episcopi quondam lincolniensis epistolae, ed. by Luard. 1861. G1281

26 Hardy, T. D. Descriptive catalogues of material relating to the history of Great Britain and Ireland, to the end of the reign of Henry VII. 3 v. 1862-1871. G1282

27 Shirley, W. W., ed. Royal and other historical letters illustrative of the reign of Henry III. 2 v. 1862-1866. G1283

28 Chronica of the Monastery of St. Albans.
pt. 1 Walsingham, T. Thomas Walsingham, quondam monachi S. Albani historia anglican, ed. by Riley. 1863-1864. G1284
pt. 2 Rishanger, W. Willelmi Rishanger, quondam anonymorum chronica et annales, regnantibus Henrico Tertio et Edwardo Primo, ed. by Riley. 1865. G1285
pt. 3 Trokelowe, J. Johannis de Trokelowe, et Henrici de Blaneforde monachorum S. Albani, necnon quorundam anonymorum Chronica et annales regnantibus Henrico Tertio, Edwardo Primo, Edwardo Secundo, Ricardo Secundo et Henrico Quarto, ed. by Riley. 1866. G1286
pt. 4 Walsingham, T. Gesta abbatum monasterii Sancti Albani, ed. by Riley. 1867-1869. G1287
pt. 5 Amundesham, J. Annales monasterii S. Albani a Johanne Amundesham, monacho ut videtur, conscripti, ed. by Riley. 1870-1871. G1288
pt. 6 St. Alban's Abbey. Registra quorundam abbatum monasterii S. Albani qui saeculo XV floruere, ed. by Riley. 1872-1873. G1289
pt. 7 Walsingham, T. Ypodigma neustriae a Thomas Walsingham, quondam monacho monasterii S. Albani conscriptum, ed. by Riley. 1876. G1290

29 Evesham abbey. Chronicon abbatiae de Evesham ad annum 1418, ed. by Macray. 1863. G1291

30 Richard of Cirencester. Ricardi de Cirencestria. Speculum historale de gestis regum Angliae, ed. by Mayor. 2 v. 1863-1869. G1292

31 Gt. Brit. Yearbooks 1272-1307. Yearbooks of the reign of Edward the First, ed. by Horwood. 5 v. 1863-79. Yearbooks of Edward Third, ed. by Pike. 15 v. 1883-1911. G1293

32 Stevenson, J., ed. Narratives of the expulsion of the English from Normandy MCCCXLIX-MCCCCL. 1863. G1294

33 Gloucester cathedral. Historia et cartularium monasterii Sancti Petri Gloucestriae, ed. by Hart. 3 v. 1863-1867. G1295

34 Neckam, A. Alexandri Neckam. De naturis rerum libri duo, ed. by Wright. 1863. G1296

35 Cockayne, T. O., ed. Leechdoms, wortcunning and starcraft of early England. 3 v. 1864-1866. G1297

36 Luard, H. R., ed. Annales monastici. 5 v. 1864-1869. G1298

37 Adam of Eynsham. Magna vita S. Hugonis, episcopi Lincolniensis, ed. by Dimock. 1864. G1299

38 Stubbs, W. bp. of Oxford, ed. Chronicles and memorials of the reign of Richard I. 2 v. 1864-1865. G1300

39 Wavrin, J. de. Recueil des croniques et anchiennes istories de la Grant Bretaigne, ed. by Hardy. 5 v. 1864-1891. G1301

40 ____. A collection of the chronicles and ancient histories of Great Britain, tr. by Hardy. 3 v. 1864-1891. G1302

41 Higden, R. Polychronicon Ranulphi Hidgen monachi Destrensis, ed. by Lumby. 9 v. 1865-1888. G1303

42 Le livere de reis de

Britaniae e Le livere de reis de Engleterre, ed. by Glover. 1865. G1304

43 Thomas of Burton. Chronica monasterii de Melsa, a fundatione usque ad annum 1396, ed. by Bond. 3 v. 1866-1868. G1305

44 Paris, M. Matthaei Parisiensis, monachi Sancti Albani, Historia Anglorum, sive ut vulgo dicitur, Historia minor, ed. by Madden. 3 v. 1866-1869. G1306

45 Hyde abbey. Liber monasterii de Hyda, ed. by Edwards. 1866. G1307

46 Chronicon Scotorum. Chronicum Scotorum, ed. by Hennessy. 1866. G1308

47 Peter, of Langtoft. The chronicle of Pierre Langtoft in French verse, ed. by Wright. 2 v. 1866-1868. G1309

48 Cogadh Gaedhel re Gallaibh. The war of the Gaedhil with the Gaill, ed. by Todd. 1867. G1310

49 Gesta regis Henrici Secundi Benedicti abbatis, ed. by Stubbs. 2 v. 1867. G1311

50 Oxford. University. Munimenta academica, ed. by Anstey. 1868. G1312

51 Hoveden, Roger of. Chronica magestri Rogeri de Hovedene, ed. by Stubbs. 4 v. 1868-1871. G1313

52 William of Malmesbury. Willelmi Malmasbiryensis monachi De gestis pontificum Anglorum libri quinque, ed. by Hamilton. 1870. G1314

53 Gilbert, J. T., ed. Historic and municipal documents of Ireland, A. D. 1172-1320. 1870. G1315

54 Annals of Loch Cé, ed. by Hennessy. 2 v. 1871. G1316

55 Black book of the Admiralty. Monumenta juridica, ed. by Twiss. 4 v. 1871-1876. G1317

56 Beckington, T. Memorials of the reign of Henry VI, ed. by Williams. 2 v. 1872. G1318

57 Paris, M. Matthaei Parisiensis, monachi Sancti Albani, Chronica majora, ed. by Laurd. 7 v. 1872-83. G1319

58 Walter of Coventry. Memoriale fratris Walteri de Coventria, ed. by Stubbs. 2 v. 1872-73. G1320

59 Wright, T., ed. The Anglo-Latin satirical poets and epigrammatists of the twelfth century. 2 v. 1872. G1321

60 Campbell, W., ed. Materials for a history of the reign of Henry VII. 2 v. 1873-77. G1322

61 Raine, J., ed. Historical papers and letters from the northern registers. 1873. G1323

62 Durham, Eng. (Diocese). Registrum Palatinum dunelemense, ed. by Hardy. 4 v. 1873-78. G1324

63 Stubbs, W., ed. Memorials of Saint Dunstan, archbishop of Canterbury. 1874. G1325

64 Chronicon Angliae ab anno domini 1328 usque ad annum 1388, ed. by Thompson. 1874. G1326

65 Thómas saga erkibiskups, ed. by Magnússon. 2 v. 1875-83. G1327

66 Ralph of Coggeshell. Radulphi de Coggeshell Chronicon anglicanorum, ed. by Stevenson. 1875. G1328

67 Robertson, J. C., ed. Materials for the history of Thomas Becket. 7 v. 1875-1885. G1329

68 Diceto, Ralph de. Radulfi de Diceto decani Lundoniensis opera historica, ed. by Stubbs. 2 v. 1876. G1330

69 Gt. Brit. Privy Council. A roll of the proceedings of the king's council in Ireland for a portion of the sixteenth year of the reign of Richard the Second, ed. by Graves. 1877. G1331

70 Bracton, H. de. Henrici de Bracton De legibus et consuetudinibus Angliae, ed. by Twiss. 6 v. 1878-1883. G1332

71 Raine, J., ed. The

historians of the church of York and its archbishops. 3 v. 1879-94. G1333

72 Malmesbury abbey. Registrum malmesburiense, ed. by Brewer. 2 v. 1879-80. G1334

73 Gervase of Canterbury. The historical works of Gervase of Canterbury, ed. by Stubbs. 2 v. 1870-80. G1335

74 Henry of Huntington. Henrici archidiaconi huntendunensis historia anglorum, ed. by Arnold. 1879. G1336

75 Simeon of Durham. Symeonis monachi opera omnia, ed. by Thomas. 2 v. 1882-1885. G1337

76 Stubbs, W., ed. Chronicles of the reigns of Edward I and Edward II. 2 v. 1882-83. G1338

77 Peckham, J. Registrum epistolorum fratris Johannis Peckham, archieposcopi cantuariensis, ed. by Martin. 3 v. 1882-85. G1339

78 Salisbury, Eng. (Diocese). Vetus registrum sarisberiense alias dictum Registrum S, Osmundi Episcopi, ed. by Jones. 2 v. 1883-84. G1340

79 Ramsey abbey. Cartularium monasterii de Rameseia, ed. by Hart. 3 v. 1884-1893. G1341

80 Dublin. St. Mary's Abbey. Chartularies of St. Mary's abbey, Dublin, ed. by Gilbert. 2 v. 1884. G1342

81 Eadmer. Eadmeri Historia novorum in Anglia, ed. by Rule. 1884. G1343

82 Howlett, R., ed. Chronicles of the reigns of Stephen, Henry II and Richard I. 4 v. 1884-1889. G1344

83 Ramsey abbey. Chronicon abbatiae rameseiensis, ed. by Macray. 1886. G1345

84 Roger of Wendover. Rogeri de Wendover libri qui dicitur Flores historiarum, ed. by Hewlett. 3 v. 1886-89. G1346

85 Canterbury, England. Christ Church Priory. Literae cantauarienses, ed. by Sheppard. 3 v. 1887-89. G1347

86 Robert, of Gloucester. The metrical chronicle of Robert of Gloucester, ed. by Wright. 2 v. 1887. G1348

87 Mannyng, R. The story of England, ed. by Furnwall. 2 v. 1887. G1349

88 Icelandic sagas...4 v. 1887-94. G1350

89 Stokes, W. The tripartite life of Patrick. 2 v. 1887. G1351

90 William of Malmesbury. Willelmi Malmesbieiensis monachi De gestis regum anglicorum, libri quinque, ed. by Stubbs. 1887-1889. G1352

91 Gaimer, G. Lestoire des Engles solum la translacion Maistre Geffrei Gaimar, ed. by Hardy. 2 v. 1888-1889. G1353

92 Knighton, H. Chronicon Henrici Knighton, ed. by Lumbly. 2 v. 1889-95. G1354

93 Murimuth, A. Adae Murimuth Continuatio chronicorum, ed. by Thompson. 1889. G1355

94 Dublin. Abbey of St. Thomas the Martyr. Register of the abbey of St. Thomas, Dublin, ed. by Gilbert. 1889. G1356

95 Matthew of Westminster. Flores historiarum, ed. by Luard. 3 v. 1890. G1357

96 Arnold, T., ed. Memorials of St. Edmund's Abbey. 3 v. 1890-1896. G1358

97 Salisbury, Eng. (Diocese). Charters and documents illustrating the history of the cathedral, city, and diocese of Salisbury, ed. by Rich. 1891. G1359

98 Gt. Brit. Parliament. Records of the Parliament, ed. by Maitland. 1893. G1360

99 Gt. Brit. Exchequer. The Red book of the Exchequer, ed. by Hall. 3 v. 1896. G1361

GREAT DRAUGHTSMEN SERIES (Brazillier)

Bonnier, H. Rembrandt, tr. by Benedict. 1970. G1362
Cotté, S. Claude Lorrain, tr. by Sebba. 1971. G1363
Hoetink, H. Durer, tr. by Lindsay. 1971. G1364
Huyghe, R. Watteau, tr. by Bray. 1970. G1365
Delacroix, tr. by Michelman. 1971. G1366
Waldemar-George, pseud. Rouault, tr. by Lindsay. 1971. G1367

GREAT EXPLORERS SERIES (Delacorte)

Carpenter, R., ed. Beyond the pillars of Heracles. 1968. G1368
Hanson, E. P., ed. South from the Spanish Main. 1967. G1369
Lattimore, O. and E., eds. Silk, spices and empire. 1968. G1370
Wright, L. B., comp. The moving frontier. 1972. G1371
____. West and by North. 1971. G1372

THE GREAT HISTORIES (Twayne)

1 Gibbon, E. The decline and fall of the Roman Empire, ed. by Trevor-Roper. 1963. G1373
2 Thucydides. The Peloponnesian wars, tr. by Jowett. 1963. G1374
3 Herodotus. History of the Greek and Persian War, tr. by Rawlinson, ed. by Forrest. 1963. G1375
4 Voltaire, F. M. A. de. The age of Louis XIV, tr. by Brumfit. 1963. G1376
5 Adams, H. The education of Henry Adams, ed. by Saveth. 1963. G1377
6 Guicciardi, F. History of Italy and History of Florence, tr. by Grayson, ed. by Hale. 1964. G1378
7 Tacitus, C. The annals and histories, tr. by Church and Brodribb, ed. by Lloyd-Jones. 1965. G1379
8 Josephus. The Jewish wars. 1966. G1380
9 Prescott, W. H. The conquest of Mexico, ed. by Howell. 1966. G1381
10 Polybius. The histories, tr. by Chambers, ed. by Badian. 1967. G1382
11 Machiavelli, N. The history of Florence and other selections, ed. by Gilmore. 1968. G1383
12 Procopius of Caesarea. History of the wars, tr. by Cameron. 1969. G1384

GREAT LIVES (Macmillan)

1 Drinkwater, J. Shakespeare. 1956. G1385
2 Ponsonby, A. P. Queen Victoria. 1933. G1386
3 Turner, W. J. Wagner. 1933. G1387
4 Dobree, B. John Wesley. 1933. G1388
5 Steegmann, J. Sir Joshua Reynolds. 1933. G1389
6 Lockhart, J. G. Cecil Rhodes. 1933. G1390
7 Birrell, F. Gladstone. 1933. G1391
8 Fremantle, A. (Jackson). George Eliot. 1933. G1392
9 Willis, I. C. The Brontës. 1933. G1393
10 Hayward, J. Charles II. 1933. G1394
11 Darwin, B. R. M. Dickens. 1933. G1395
12 Pryce-Jones, A. Beethoven. 1948. G1396
13 Symons, A. J. A. H. M. Stanley. 1933. G1397
14 Clutton-Brock, A. Blake. 1933. G1398
15 Darlington, W. A. Sheridan. 1933. G1399
16 Carswell, C. (MacFarlane). Robert Burns. 1933. G1400
17 Wortham, H. E. Edward VII. 1933. G1401
18 Ellis, G. U. Thackeray. 1933. G1402
19 Brooks, G. Napoleon III. 1933. G1403
20 Campbell, G. A. Strindberg.

1933. G1404
21 Tunstall, W. C. B. Nelson. 1933. G1405
22 Maine, B. Chopin. 1933. G1406
23 Abraham, G. E. H. Nietzsche. 1933. G1407
24 Charteris, J. Haig. 1933. G1408
25 Meynell, E. H. (Moorhouse). Bach. 1947. G1409
26 Macaulay, R. Milton. 1934. G1410
27 Hingston, R. W. G. Darwin. 1934. G1411
28 Quennell, P. Byron. 1934. G1412
29 Burra, P. Van Gogh. 1934. G1413
30 Rawlence, G. Jane Austen. 1934. G1414
31 Williams, O. Charles Lamb. 1934. G1415
32 Evans, B. I. Keats. 1934. G1416
33 Weekley, M. William Morris. 1934. G1417
34 MacBride, E. W. Huxley. 1934. G1418
35 Darwin, B. R. M. W. G. Grace. 1934. G1419
36 Dark, S. Newman. 1934. G1420
37 Pearce, G. R. Dumas père. 1934. G1421
38 Lammond, D. Carlyle. 1934. G1422
39 Bailey, R. Shelley. 1934. G1423
40 Martin, T. Faraday. 1934. G1424
41 Talbot, J. E. Mozart. 1949. G1425
42 Dent, E. J. Handel. 1934. G1426
43 Scudder, E. S. Garibaldi. 1934. G1427
44 Bowen, I. Corben. 1935. G1428
45 Allen, B. M. Gordon. 1935. G1429
46 Bell, D. Drake. 1935. G1430
47 Abraham, G. E. H. Tolstoy. 1935. G1431
48 Brogan, D. W. Abraham Lincoln. 1935. G1432
49 Gould, R. T. Captain Cook. 1935. G1433
50 Roberts, S. C. Doctor Johnson. 1935. G1434
51 Misnumbered 52.
52 Lenanton, C. M. A. Prince Charles Edward. 1935. G1435
Sampson, A. Wolsey. 1935. G1436
53 Malcolm-Smith, E. F. Palmerston. 1935. G1437
54 Ketton-Cremer, R. W. Thomas Gray. 1935. G1438
55 Petrie, C. A. William Pitt. 1935. G1439
56 Elwin, M. DeQuincey. 1935. G1440
57 Fyfe, H. H. Keir Hardie. 1935. G1441
58 Lammond, D. Florence Nightingale. 1935. G1442
59 Ross Williamson, H. King James I. 1936. G1443
60 Pollock, F. Spinoza. 1935. G1444
61 Somervell, D. C. Livingstone. 1936. G1445
62 Hayward, F. H. Alfred the Great. 1935. G1446
63 Burra, P. Wordsworth. 1936. G1447
64 Crow, G. H. Ruskin. 1936. G1448
65 Beeley, H. Disraeli. 1936. G1449
66 Pearce, G. R. John Knox. 1936. G1450
67 Cruttwell, C. R. M. F. Wellington. 1936. G1451
68 Dark, S. Manning. 1936. G1452
69 Abraham, G. E. H. Dostoevsky. 1936. G1453
70 McCallum, R. B. Asquith. 1936. G1454
71 Williams, C. H. Queen Elizabeth. 1936. G1455
72 Campbell, G. A. Mary, Queen of Scots. 1936. G1456
73 Dunbar, G. Clive. 1936. G1457
74 Boase, T. S. R. St. Francis of Assisi. 1936. G1458
75 Clark, G. K. Peel. 1936. G1459
76 Pakenham, P. King Charles I. 1936. G1460
77 Hill, R. Liszt. 1941. G1461

78 Webb, G. Wren. 1937. G1462
79 Smith, J. A. R. L. Stevenson. 1937. G1463
80 Sprigge, C. J. S. Karl Marx. 1938. G1464
81 Ashley, M. P. Marlborough. 1956. G1465
82 Wedgworth, C. V. Oliver Cromwell. 1939. G1466
83 Butterfield, H. Napoleon. 1939. G1467
84 Richards, V. T. E. Lawrence. 1939. G1468
85 Hill, R. Brahms. 1941. G1469
86 Petrie, C. A. Joseph Chamberlain. 1940. G1470
87 Morrow, I. F. D. Bismarck. 1943. G1471
89 Myers, R. H. Debussy. 1948. G1472
90 Abraham, G. E. H. Tchaikovsky. 1949. G1473
91 ____. Rimsky-Korsakov. 1949. G1474
92 Horton, J. Grieg. 1950. G1475

GREAT LIVES IN BRIEF (Knopf)

Almedingen, M. E. St. Francis of Assisi. 1967. G1476
Burlingame, R. Henry Ford. 1955. G1477
Chidsey, D. B. Elizabeth I. 1955. G1478
Duggan, A. L. Julius Caesar. 1955. G1479
Flexner, J. T. Gilbert Stuart. 1955. G1480
Garraty, J. A. Woodrow Wilson. 1956. G1481
Godden, R. Hans Christian Andersen. 1954. G1482
Guérard, A. Napoleon I. 1956. G1483
____. Napoleon III. 1955. G1484
Holbrook, S. H. James J. Hill. 1955. G1485
Mack Smith, D. Garibaldi. 1956. G1486
Maurois, A. Alexandre Dumas. 1954. G1487
Miers, E. S. Robert E. Lee. 1956. G1488
Moore, R. E. Charles Darwin. 1954. G1489
Sheean, V. Mahatma Gandhi. 1954. G1490
Vallery-Radot, P. Louis Pasteur. 1958. G1491

GREAT LIVES OBSERVED (Prentice-Hall)

Anderson, H., ed. Jesus. 1967. G1492
Ashley, M., ed. Cromwell. 1969. G1493
Borden, M., ed. George Washington. 1969. G1494
____ and P., eds. The American Tory. 1972. G1495
Braeman, J., ed. Wilson. 1972. G1496
Cantor, M., ed. Hamilton. 1970. G1497
Ch'en, J., ed. Mao. 1969. G1498
Churchill, W. L. S. Churchill, ed. by Gilbert. 1967. G1499
Coit, M. L., ed. John C. Calhoun. 1969. G1500
Cronon, E., ed. Marcus Garvey. 1973. G1501
Foner, E., ed. Nat Turner. 1971. G1502
Frederickson, G. M., comp. William Lloyd Garrison. 1968. G1503
Gilbert, M., ed. Lloyd George. 1968. G1504
Graham, H. D., ed. Huey Long. 1969. G1505
Grantham, D., ed. Theodore Roosevelt. 1971. G1506
Hitler, ed. by Stein. 1968. G1507
Hollyday, F. B. M., ed. Bismarck. 1970. G1508
Hutt, M., ed. Napoleon. 1972. G1509
Koch, A., ed. Jefferson. 1971. G1510
Kutler, S. I., ed. John Marshall. 1972. G1511
Lenin, V. I. Lenin, ed. by Silverman. 1972. G1512
Levine, J. M., ed. Elizabeth I. 1969. G1513
Mack Smith, D., ed. Garibaldi. 1969. G1514
Matusow, A. J., ed. Joseph R. McCarthy. 1970. G1515
Maxwell, R. S., ed. LaFollette. 1969. G1516
Nash, G. D., ed. Franklin

Delano Roosevelt. 1967. G1517
Oliva, L. J., ed. Catherine the Great. 1971. G1518
____. Peter the Great. 1970. G1519
Quarles, B., com. Frederick Douglass. 1968. G1520
Radosh, R., ed. Debs. 1972. G1521
Rae, J. B., ed. Henry Ford. 1969. G1522
Rigby, T. H., ed. Stalin. 1966. G1523
Roider, K., ed. Maria Theresa. 1973. G1524
Rudé, G., ed. Robespierre. 1967. G1525
Rule, J. C., ed. Louis XIV. 1974. G1526
Smith, I. H., ed. Trotsky. 1973. G1527
Snyder, L. L., ed. Frederick the Great. 1971. G1528
Starobin, R. S., ed. Denmark Vesey. 1970. G1529
Stein, G. H., ed. Hitler. 1968. G1530
Stern, G. E., ed. Gompers. 1971. G1531
Thornbrough, E., ed. Black Reconstructionists. 1972. G1532
Thornbrough, E. L., ed. Booker T. Washington. 1969. G1533
Tuttle, W. M., ed. W. E. B. DuBois. 1973. G1534
Tyson, G., ed. Toussaint L'Ouverture. 1972. G1535
Warch, R., ed. John Brown. 1973. G1536
Wittner, L., ed. MacArthur. 1971. G1537

GREAT MUSEUMS OF THE WORLD (NEW YORK) (Newsweek)

Brera, Milan. Text by Ciordi and others. 1970. G1538
British Museum, London. Text by Caleca and others. 1967. G1539
Egyptian Museum, Cairo. Text by Donadoni and others. 1969. G1540
Louvre, Paris. Text by Regoli and others. 1967. G1541
Madrid. Museo Nacional de Pintura y Escultura. Prado, Madrid. Text by Pallucchini. 1968. G1542
Museum of Fine Arts, Boston. Text by Cavallo and others. 1969. G1543
National Gallery, London. Text by Dalli Regoli. 1969. G1544
National Gallery, Washington. Text by Gandolfo and others. 1968. G1545
National Museum, Tokyo. Text by Giuganimo and Tamburello. 1968. G1546
National Museum of Anthropology, Mexico City. Text by Ragghianti and Collabi. 1970. G1547
Picture Gallery of the Art History Museum, Vienna. Text by Faggin and others. 1970. G1548
Pinakothek, Munich. Text by Salvini. 1969. G1549
Rijkmuseum, Amsterdam. Text by Faggin and others. 1969. G1549a
Uffizi, Florence. Text by Regali and others. 1968. G1549b
Vatican museums: Rome. Text by Regol and others. 1968. G1549c

GREAT PULPIT MASTERS (Revell)

1 Moody, D. L. Dwight L. Moody, ed. by Erdman. 1949. G1550
2 Spurgeon, C. H. Charles H. Spurgeon, ed. by Blackwood. 1949. G1551
3 Torrey, R. A. R. A. Torrey, ed. by Culbertson. 1950. G1552
4 Jones, S. P. Sam Jones, ed. by Holt. 1950. G1553
5 Jowett, J. H. J. H. Jowett, ed. by Homrighausen. 1950. G1554
6 Meyer, F. B. F. B. Meyer, ed. by Lee. 1950. G1555
7 Poling, D. A. Daniel A. Poling, ed. by Talmage. 1951. G1556
8 Gordon, A. J. A. J. Gordon, ed. by Wood. 1951. G1557

GREAT RELIGIOUS FESTIVALS SERIES (Schuman)

1 Count, E. W. 4,000 years of Christmas. 1948. G1558
2 Gaster, T. H. Passover. 1949. G1559
3 Linton, R. and A. S. We gather together. 1949. G1560
4 Watts, A. W. Easter. 1950. G1561
5 Linton, R. and A. S. Halloween through twenty centuries. 1950. G1562
6 Gaster, T. H. Purim and Hanukkah in custom and tradition. 1950. G1563
Eberhard, W. Chinese festivals. 1952. G1564
Monks, J. L. Great Catholic festivals. 1951. G1565
Seidenspinner, C. A. Great Protestant festivals. 1952. G1566

GREAT WEST AND INDIAN SERIES (Westernlore)

1 Bailey, P. D. Sam Brannan and the California Mormons. 1953. G1567
2 ____. Walkara, Hawk of the Mountains. 1954. G1568
3 Backus, C. K. The King of Beaver Island. 1955. G1569
4 Woodward, A. Feud on the Colorado. 1955. G1570
5 Walters, M. H. Early days and Indian ways. 1956. G1571
6 Benedict, K. A journey through New Mexico's First Judicial District in 1864, ed. by Wallace. 1956. G1572
7 Sweeny, T. W. Journal, 1849-1853, ed. by Woodward. 1956. G1573
8 Mitchell, A. R. Jim Savage and the Tulareño Indians. 1957. G1574
9 Schiel, J. H. W. The land between. 1957. G1575
10 Bailey, P. D. Wovoka. 1957. G1576
11 Shinn, C. H. Graphic description of Pacific coast outlaws. 1958. G1577
12 Bigelow, J. On the bloody trail of Geronimo. 1958. G1578
13 Kerby, R. L. The Confederate invasion of New Mexico and Arizona. 1958. G1579
14 Doctor, J. E. Shotguns on Sunday. 1958. G1580
15 Evans, M. Long John Dunn of Taos. 1959. G1581
16 Ward, H. Prairie schooner lady. 1959. G1582
17 Craig, R. S. The fighting parson. 1959. G1583
18 James, H. C. The Cahuilla. Indians. 1959. G1584
19 Jones, D. W. Forty years among Indians. 1960. G1585
20 Whipple, A. W. The Whipple report. 1961. G1586
21 Forrest, E. R. The snake dance of the Hopi Indians. 1961. G1587
22 Utley, R. M. Custer and the great controversy. 1962. G1588
23 Wright, W. Washoe rambles. 1962. G1589
24 Gray, A. B. Survey of a route on the 32nd parallel for the Texas Western Railroad, 1854, ed. by Bailey. 1963. G1590
25 Walker, J. G. The Navajo reconnaissance, 1859. 1964. G1591
26 Bailey, L. R. The long walk, a history of Navajo wars, 1846-68. 1964. G1592
27 Bennett, K. Kaibah. 1964. G1593
28 Templeton, S. W. The lame captain. 1965. G1594
29 Baker, P. (Biddlecome). The Wild Bunch at Robbers Roost. 1965. G1595
30 Parkhill, F. The blazed trail of Antoine Leroux. 1965. G1596
31 Older, F. George Heart, California pioneer, ed. by Wilkie. 1966. G1597
32 Bailey, L. R. Indian slave trade in the Southwest. 1966. G1598
33 Paine, L. Texas Ben Thompson. 1966. G1599
34 Amarel, A. A. Will James. 1967. G1600
35 Faulk, O. B. Too far

north, too far south. 1967. G1601
36 Terrell, J. U. Estevanico the Black. 1968. G1602
37 Schellie, D. Vast domain of blood. 1968. G1603
38 Horka-Follick, L. Los Hermanos pentinentes. 1969. G1604
39 Paige, H. W. Songs of the Teton Sioux. 1969. G1605
40 Bird, T. Tell them they lie. 1971. G1606
41 Stout, J. A. The liberators. 1973. G1607
42 Love, F. Mining camps and ghost towns. 1973. G1608
43 Robinson, J. M. West from Fort Pierre. 1974. G1609

THE GROTIUS SOCIETY. LONDON. PUBLICATIONS (Longmans)

1 Kaekenbeeck, G. S. F. C. International rivers. 1918. G1610
2 Roosegaarde Bisschop, W. The Saar controversy. 1924. G1611
3 Nathan, M. The renascence of international law. 1945. G1612
4 Knight, W. S. M., ed. The life and works of Hugo Grotius. 1925. G1613
5 Colombos, C. J. A treatise on the law of prize. 1949. G1614

DIE GRUNDLEHREN DER MATHEMATISCHEN WISSENSCHAFTEN IN EINZELDARSTELLUNGEN (Springer)

1 Blaschke, W. Vorlesungen über differentialgeometrie und geometrische Grundlagen von Einstein's Relativitätstheorie. V. 1. 1945. G1615
2 Knopp, K. Theorie und anwendung der unendlichen reihen. 1964. G1616
3 Hurwitz, A. Vorlesungen über allgemeine funktionentheorie und elliptische funktionen. 1929. G1617
4 Madelung, E. and Boehle, K. Die mathematischen hilfsmittel des physikers. 1964. G1618
5 Speiser, A. Die theorie der gruppen von endlicher ordnung. 1946. G1619
6 Bierberbach, L. Theorie der differentialgleichungen. 1744. G1620
7 Same as no. 1. V. 2. 1946. G1621
8 Kerékjartó, B. von. Vorlesungen über topologie. V. 1. 1923. G1622
9 Frankel, A. A. Einleitung in die Mengenlehre. 1946. G1623
10 Schouten, J. A. Ricci-calculus. 1954. G1624
11 Runge, C. D. and König, H. Vorlesungen über numerisches Rechnen. 1924. G1625
12 Courant, R. and Hilbert, D. Methoden der mathematischen physik. V. 1. 1931. G1626
13 Nörlund, N. E. Vorlesungen über differenzenrichnung. 1924. G1627
14 Steinitz, E. Vorlesungen über die theorie der Polyeder. 1934. G1628
15-16 Klein, F. von. Elementarmathematik vom hoheren standpunkte. 2 v. 1968. G1629
17 Whittaker, E. T. Analytische dynamik der punkter und starren körper. 1924. G1630
18 Eddington, A. S. Relativitatstheorie in mathematischer behandlung. V. 1. 1925. G1631
19-20 Polya, G. and Szegö, G. Aufgaben und lehrsatze und lehrsatze und der analysis. 2 v. 1925. G1632
21 Schoenflies, A. M. Einführung in die analytische geometrie der Ebene und der Raumes. 1931. G1633
22 Klein, F. Vorlesungen über höhere geometrie. 1926. G1634
23 Pasch, M. Vorlesungen über neuere geometrie. 1945. G1635
24-25 Klein, F. Vorlesungen über die Entwicklung der

mathematik im 19. Jahrhundert. 2 v. 1926-27. G1636
26 ___. Vorlesungen über nichteuklidische geometrie. 1928. G1637
27 Hilbert, D. and Ackermann, W. Grundzüge der theoretischen logik. 1967. G1638
28 Levi-Civita, T. Der absolute differentialkalkul und seine aumendungen in geometrie und physik. 1928. G1639
29 Same as no. 1. V. 3. 1929. G1640
30 Lichtenstein, L. Grundlagen der hydromechanik von Leon Lichtenstein. 1968. G1641
31 Kellogg, O. D. Foundations of potential theory. 1929. G1642
32 Reidemeister, K. Vorlesungen über grundlagen der geometrie. 1968. G1643
33-34 Waerden, B. L. van der. Moderne algebre. 2 v. 1964. G1644
35 Herzberger, M. Strahlenoptik. 1931. G1645
36 Waerden, B. L. van der. Die gruppentheoretische methode in der quantenmechanik. 1932. G1646
37 Hilbert, D. and Cohn-Vossen, S. Anschauliche geometrie. 1944. G1647
38 Von Neumann, J. Mathematische grundlagen der quantenmechanik. 1943. G1648
39 Klein, F. Vorlesungen über die hypergeometrische funktion gehalten an der Universitat Gottingen im wintersemester 1893/94. 1933. G1649
40 Hilbert, D. and Bernays, P. Grundlagen der mathematik. V. 1. 1968. G1650
41 Steinitz, E. Vorlesungen über die theorie der polyeder, unter einschluss der elemente der topologie. 1934. G1651
42 Juel, C. Vorlesungen über projektive geometrie mit besonderer berucksichtegung der v. Staudtschen imaginärtheorie. 1945. G1652
43 Neugebauer, O. Vorlesungen über geschichte mathematischen wissenschaften. V. 1. 1934. G1653
44 Nielsen, J. Vorlesungen über elementare mechanik, ed. by Fenchel. 1935. G1654
45 Aleksandrov, P. S. Topologie. 1935. G1655
46 Nevanlinna, R. H. Eindeutige analytische funktionen. 1953. G1656
47 Doetsch, G. Theorie und anwendung der Laplace-transformation. 1937. G1657
48 Same as no. 12. V. 2. 1937. G1658
49 Blaschke, W. and Bol, G. Geometrie der gewebe. 1938. G1659
50 Same as no. 40. V. 2. 1939. G1660
51 Waerden, B. L. van der. Einführung in die algebraische geometrie. 1939. G1661
52 Magnus, W. and Obergettinger, F. Soni. 1966. G1662
53 Flugge, S. and Marschall, H. Rechenmethoden der quantentheorie dargestellt in aufgaben und Lösungen. V. 1. 1952. G1663
54 Doetsch, G. Tabellan zur Laplace-Transformation und Anleitung zum Gebrauch. 1947. G1664
55 Obergettingen, F. and Magnus, W. Anwendung der elliptischen funktionen in physik und technik. 1949. G1665
56 Toeplitz, O. Die entwicklung der infinitesimalrechnung. V. 1. 1949. G1666
57 Hamel, G. Theoretische mechanik. 1949. G1667
58 Blaschke, W. Einführung in die differentialgeometrie. 1950. G1668
59 Hasse, H. Vorlesungen über zahlentheorie. 1964. G1669
60 Collatz, L. The numerical treatment of differential equations, tr. by Williams. 1960. G1670
61 Maak, W. Fastperiodische funktionen. 1967. G1671
62 Sauer, R. Anfangswertprobleme bei partiellen

differentialgleischungen. 1958. G1672
63 Eichler, M. Quadratische formen und orthogonale gruppen. 1952. G1673
64 Nevanlinna, R. H. Uniformisierung. 1953. G1674
65 Fejes Tóth, L. Lagerungen in der ebene, auf der Kugel und im Raum. 1953. G1675
66 Bieberbach, L. Theorie der gewohnlichen differentialgleichungen. 1965. G1676
67 Byrd, P. F. and Friedman, M. D. Handbook of elliptic integrals for engineers and physicists. 1954. G1677
68 Aumann, G. Reelle funktionen. 1954. G1678
69 Schmidt, H. Mathematische gesetze der logik I. 1960. G1679/99
70 Ludwig, G. Die grundlagen der quantenmechanik. 1954. G1700
71 Meixner, J. and Schäfke, F. W. Mathieusche funktionen und sphäroidfunktionen mit anwendungen auf physikalische und technische probleme. 1954. G1701
72 Nöbeling, G. Grundlagen der analytischen topologie. 1954. G1702
73 Hermes, H. Einführung in die verbanstheorie. 1955. G1703
74 Boerner, H. Darstellungen von Gruppen. 1955. G1704
75 Radó, T. and Reichekderfer, P. V. Continuous transformations in analysis. 1955. G1705
76 Tricomi, F. G. Vorlesungen über orthogonalreihen. 1955. G1706
77 Behnke, H. and Sommer, F. Theorie der analytischen funktionen einer komplexen veranderlichen. 1965. G1707
78 Lorenzen, P. Einführung in der operative logik und mathematik. 1968. G1708
79 Saxer, W. Versicherungsmathematik. V. 1. 1955. G1709
80 Pickert, G. Projektive ebenen. 1955. G1710
81 Schneider, T. Einführung in die transzendenten zahlen. 1957. G1711
82 Specht, W. Gruppentheorie. 1956. G1712
83 Bieberbach, L. Einführung in die theorie der differentialgleichungen im reellen gebiet. 1956. G1713
84 Conforto, F. Abelsche funktionen und algebraische geometrie. 1956. G1714
85 Siegel, C. L. Vorlesungen über Himmelsmechanik. 1956. G1715
86 Richter, H. Wahrschleinlichkeitstheorie. 1966. G1716
87 Waerden, B. L. van der. Mathematische statistik. 1965. G1717
88 Müller, C. Grundprobleme der mathematischen theorie elektromagnetischer schwingungen. 1957. G1718
89 Pfluger, A. Theorie der riemannschen flächen. 1957. G1719
90 Oberhettinger, F. Tabellen zur Fourier transformation. 1957. G1720
91 Prachar, K. Primzahlverteilung. 1957. G1721
92 Rehbock, F. Darstellende geometrie. 1964. G1722
93 Hadwiger, H. Vorlesungen über inhalt, oberflache und isoperimetrie. 1957. G1723
94 Funk, P. Variationsrechnung und ihre anwendung in physik und technik. 1962. G1724
95 Maeda, F. Kontinuierliche geometrien. 1958. G1725
96 Bachmann, F. Aufbau der geometrie aus dem spiegelungsbegriff. 1959. G1726
97 Greub, W. Linear algebra. 1967. G1727
98 Same as no. 79. V. 2. 1958. G1728
99 Cassels, J. W. S. An introduction to the geometry of numbers. 1959. G1729
100 Koppenfels, W. G. M. von and Stallmann, F. Praxis der konformen abbildung. 1959. G1730
101 Rund, H. The differential

geometry of Finsler spaces. 1959. G1731
102 Nevanlinna, F. and R. Absolute analysis. 1959. G1732
103 Schutte, K. Beweistheorie. 1960. G1733
104 Chung, K. L. Markov chains with stationary transition probabilities. 1967. G1734
105 Rinow, W. Die innere geometrie der metrischen räume. G1735
106 Scholz, H. and Hasenjäger, G. Grundzüge der mathematischen logik. 1961. G1736
107 Köthe, G. Topologische lineare räume I. 1960. G1737
108 Dynkin, E. B. Die grundlagen der theorie der markoffschen prozesse. 1961. G1738
109 Hermes, H. Aufzählbarkeit, entscheidbarkeit, berechenbarkeit. 1961. G1739
110 Dinghas, A. Vorlesungen über funktionentheorie. 1961. G1740
111 Lions, J. L. Equations différentielles opérationnelles et problemes aux limites. 1961. G1741
112 Morgenstern, D. Vorlesungen über theoretische mechanik. 1961. G1742
113 Meschkowski, H. Hilbertsche räume mit kernfunktion. 1962. G1743
114 MacLane, S. Homology. 1963. G1744
115 Hewitt, E. Abstract harmonic analysis. V. 1. 1963. G1745
116 Hörmander, L. Linear partial differential operators. 1964. G1746
117 O'Meara, O. T. Introduction to quadratic forms. 1963. G1747
118 Schäfke, F. W. Einführung in die theorie der speziellen funktionen der mathematischen physik. 1963. G1748
119 Harris, T. E. The theory of branching processes. 1963. G1749
120 Collatz, L. Funktionanalysis und numerische mathematik. 1964. G1750
121-122 Dynkin, L. Markov processes. 2 v. 1965. G1751
123 Yosida, K. Functional analysis. 1968. G1752
124 Morgenstern, D. Einführung in die wahrscheinlichkeitsrechnung und mathematische statistik. 1965. G1753
125 Itô, K. and McKean, H. P. Diffusion and their sample paths. 1965. G1754
126 Lehto, O. Quasikonforme abbildungen. 1965. G1755
127 Hermes, H. Enumerability, decidability, computability. 1965. G1756
128 Braun, H. Jordan-algebren. 1965. G1757
129 Nikodym, O. M. The mathematical apparatus for quantum-theories. 1966. G1758
130 Morrey, C. B. Multiple integrals in the calculus of variations. 1966. G1759
131 Hirzebruch, F. Topological methods in algebraic geometry. 1966. G1760
132 Kato, T. Perturbation theory for linear operators. 1966. G1761
133 Haupt, O. Geometrische ordnungen. 1967. G1762
134 Huppert, B. Endliche Gruppen. V. 1. 1967. G1763
135 Rutishauser, H. Description of Algol. 1967. G1764
136 Greub, W. H. Multilinear algebra. 1967. G1765
137 Bauer, F. L. and others, eds. Handbook for automatic computation. V. 1. 1967. G1766
138 Hahn, W. Stability of motion, tr. by Baartz. 1967. G1767
139-142 Mathematische hilfsmittel des ingenieurs, ed. by Sauer and Szabó. 4 v. 1967-68. G1768
143 Schur, I. Vorlesungen über invariantentheorie. 1968. G1769
144 Weil, A. Basic number theory. 1967. G1770/1
145 Butzer, P. L. and Bernes, H. Semi-groups of operators and approximation. 1967. G1772

146 Trèves, F. Locally convex spaces and linear partial differential equations. 1967. G1773
147 Lamotke, K. Semisimpliz algebraische topologie. 1968. G1774
148 Chandrasekharan, K. Introduction to analytic number theory. 1968. G1775
149 Sario, L. Capacity functions. 1969. G1776
150 Iosifescu, M. and Theodorescu, R. Random processes and learning. 1969. G1777
151 Mandl, P. Analytical treatment of one-dimensional Markov processes. 1968. G1778
152 Hewitt, E. and Ross, K. A. Abstract harmonic analysis II. 1969. G1779
153 Federer, H. Geometric measure theory. 1969. G1780
154 Singer, I. Bases in Banach spaces. 1969. G1781
155 Müller, C. Foundations of the mathematical theory of electromagnetic waves, tr. by Higgins. 1969. G1782
156 Van der Waerden, B. L. Mathematical statistics, tr. by Thompson and Sherman. 1969. G1783
157 Prohorov, Y. V. P. and Rozanov, J. A. R. Probability theory. 1969. G1784
158 Constantinescu, C. and Cornea, A. Potential theory on harmonic spaces. 1972. G1785
159 Köthe, G. Topological vector space I, tr. by Garling. 1969. G1786
161 Bhat, U. N. Stability theory of dynamical systems. 1969. G1787
162 Nevanlinna, R. Analytic functions, tr. by Emig. 1969. G1788
163 Stoer, J. and Witzgall, C. Convexity and optimization in finite dimensions. V. 1. 1969. G1789
164 Sario, L. and Nakai, M. Classification theory of Riemann surfaces. 1969. G1790
165 Mitrinovic, D. S. and Vasic, P. M. Analytic inequalities. 1970. G1791
166 Grothendieck, A. and Dieudonné, J. A. Eléments de géométric algébrique. V. 1. 1971. G1792
167 Chandrasekharan, K. Arithmetical functions. 1970. G1793
168 Palamodov, V. P. Linear differential operators with constant coefficients, tr. by Brown. 1970. G1794
169 Rademacher, H. Topics in analytic number theory, ed. by Newman. 1972. G1795
170 Lions, J. L. Optimal control of systems governed by partial differential equations, tr. by Mitter. 1971. G1796
171 Singer, I. Best approximation in normed linear spaces by elements of linear subspaces, tr. by Georgescu. 1970. G1797
172 Buhlmann, H. Mathematical methods in risk theory. 1971. G1798
173 Maeda, F. and S. Theory of symmetric lattices. 1972. G1799
174 Stiefel, E. L. and Scheifele, G. Linear and regular celestial mechanics. 1971. G1800
175 Larsen, R. An introduction to the theory of multipliers. 1971. G1801
176 Grauet, H. and Remmert, R. Analytische stellenalgebren. 1971. G1802
177-178 Flügge, S. Practical quantum mechanics. 2 v. 1971. G1803
179 Giraud, J. Chomologie von abélienne. 1971. G1804
180 Landkof, N. S. Foundations of modern potential theory. 1972. G1805
181-183 Lions, J. L. and Magenes, E. Non-homogeneous boundary value problems and applications, tr. by Kenneth. 3 v. 1972. G1806
184 Rosenblatt, M. Markov processes. 1971. G1807
185 Rubinowicz, W. Sommerfeldsche Polynommethode. 1972. G1808

186 Wilkinson, J. H. and Reinsch, C. Linear algebra. 1971. G1809
187 Siegel, C. L. and Moser, J. K. Lectures on celestial mechanics, tr. by Kalme. 1971. G1810
188-189 Warner, G. Harmonic analysis on semi-simple Lie groups. 2 v. 1972. G1811
190-1 Faith, C. C. Algebra. 2 v. 1973. G1812
192 Mal'cev, A. I. Algebraic systems. 1972. G1813
193 Polya, G. and Szegö, G. Problems and theorems in analysis, tr. by Aeppli. V. 1. 1972. G1814
194 Igusa, J. Theta functions. 1972. G1815
195 Berberun, S. K. Baer *-rings. 1972. G1816
196 Athreya, K. B. and Ney, P. E. Branching processes. 1972. G1817
197 Benz, W. Vorlesungen über geometrie der algebren. 1973. G1818
198 Gaal, S. A. Linear analysis and representation theory. 1973. G1819
200 Dold, A. Lectures on algebraic topology. 1972. G1820
202 Schmetterer, L. Introduction to mathematical statistics. 1974. G1821
203 Schoeneberg, B. Elliptic modular functions. 1974. G1822
204 Popov, V. M. Hyperstability of control systems, tr. by Georgescu. 1973. G1823
206 André, M. Homologie des algebres commutatives. 1974. G1824
207 Donoghue, W. F. Monotone matrix functions and analytic continuation. 1974. G1825
209 Ringel, G. Map color theorem. 1974. G1826

GRUNDRISS DER PHILOSOPHISCHEN WISSENSCHAFTEN (Mohr)

Cassirer, E. Die philosophie der aufklärung. 1932. G1827
Joël, K. Geschichte der antiken philosophie. 1921. G1828
Kroner, R. Von Kant bis Hegel. 2 v. 1921-24. G1829
Windelband, W. Einleitung in die philosophie. 1923. G1830

GUIDE BIBLIOGRAFICHE (Fondazione Leonardo per la cultural italiana, distributed by Hoepli)

Series I:
1 Almagià, R. La geografia. 1919. G1831
2 Levi, C. Il teatro. 1919. G1832
3 Béguinot, A. La botanica. 1920. G1833
4 Tonelli, L. La critica. 1920. G1834
5 Piccioni, L. Il giornalismo. 1920. G1835
6 Bilancioni, G. La storia della medicina. 1920. G1836
7 Ussani, V. Lingua e lettere latine. 1921. G1837
8-9 Egidi, P. La storia medioevale. 1922. G1838
10 Solmi, A. La storia del dritto italiano. 1922. G1839
11-12 Fumagalli, G. La bibliografia. 1923. G1840
13 Francisci, P. de. Il diritto romano. 1923. G1841
14-15 Russo, L. I narratori. 1923. G1842
16 Baglioni, S. La filiologia. 1923. G1843
17-18 Piovano, G. A. Gli studi di greco. 1924. G1844
19 Gabrieli, G. Italia judaica. 1924. G1845
20-21 Bruers, A. V. Gioberti. 1924. G1846
22 Bustico, G. Il teatro musicale italiano. 1924. G1847
23-24 Lemmi, F. Il risorgimento. 1926. G1848
25-27 Forcella, R. D'Annunzio. 1863-83. 2 v. 1926. G1849
28-30 Miniati, P. F. D. Guerrazzi. 1927. G1850
31-36 Scolari, F. Alessandro Volta. 1927. G1851
37-39 Forcella, R. D'Annunzio, 1884-85. 2 v. 1928. G1852
40-42 Neri, F. Gli studi

franco-italiani nel primo quarto del sec. XX. 1928. G1853
43-44 Facchinetti, V. San Francesco d'Assisi. 1928. G1854
Series II:
1 Evola, N. D. Origini e dottrina del fascismo. 1935. G1855
2 Forcella, R. D'Annunzio. 1886. 1936. G1856
3 Marcelleti, M. Bibliografia delle sanzioni. 1937. G1857
4 Same as no. 2. (series II). 1887. 1937. G1858
5 Mattei, R. de. La storia delle dottrine politiche. 1938. G1859
6 Parenti, M. Bibliografia mussoliniana. V. 1. 1940. G1860
7-8 Mambelli, G. Gli studi virgiliani nel secolo XX. 1940. G1861
Series III:
1 Gradilone, A. Bibliografia sindicale corporativa, 1923-40. 1942. G1862

GUIDE BIBLIOGRAFICHE ITALIANE (Agenzie generale italiana del libro)

Caporali, R. Storia della musica e critica musicale, 1921-35. 1935. G1863
Gabrieli, G. Bibliografia degli studi orientalistici in Italia, 1912-34. 1935. G1864
Gazzetti, F. Lo stato fascista, 1921-35. 1935. G1865
Gorresio, V. Paesi e problemi africani. 1937. G1866
Grassi Mola, E. Scienza delle costruzione. 1938. G1867
Lama, E. Corporativismo, 1921-35. 1935. G1868
Neppi, A. Arti figurative, 1921-35. 1935. G1869

HAKLUYT SOCIETY. PUBLICATIONS.

1st Series:

1 Hawkins, R. The observations of Sir Richard Hawkins, Knt., ed. by Bethune. 1847. H1

2 Colombo, C. Select letters of Christopher Columbus, ed. by Major. 1848. H2

3 Raleigh, W. The discovery of... Guiana, ed. by Schomburgk. 1848. H3

4 Maynarde, T. Sir Francis Drake, his voyage, 1595, ed. by Cooley. 1894. H4

5 Rundull, T., ed. Narratives of voyages toward the Northwest. 1849. H5

6 Strachey, W. The historie of travaile into Virginia Britannia, ed. by Major. 1849. H6

7 Hakluyt, R., comp. Divers voyages touching the discovery of America... ed. by Jones. 1850. H7

8 Rundall, T., ed. Memorials of the empire of Japan. 1851. H8

9 The discovery and conquest of Terra Florida by Don Ferdinando de Soto..., ed. by Rye. 1851. H9

10 Herberstein, S. von. Notes upon Russia, ed. by Major. 2 v. 1851-52. H10

11 Coats, W. The Geography of Hudson's Bay, ed. by Barrow. 1852. H11

12 Same as no. 10. V. 2. 1852. H12

13 Veer, G. de. A true description of three voyages by the northeast, ed. by Beke. 1863. H13

14-15 González de Mendoza, J. The history of the great and mighty kingdom of China, ed. by Staunton. 2 v. 1853-54. H14

16 Same as no. 4. V. 2. 1855. H15

17 Orléans, P. J. d'. The history of the two Tartar conquerors of China, ed. by Ellesmere. 1855. H16

18 White, A., ed. A collection of documents on Spitzbergen and Greenland. 1855. H17

19 Middleton, H. The voyage of Sir Henry Middleton to Bantam and the Maluco Islands, ed. by Corney. 1856. H18

20 Bond, E. A., ed. Russia at the close of the sixteenth century. 1856. H19

21 Benzoni, G. History of the New world, ed. by Smyth. 1857. H20

22 Major, R. H., ed. India in the fifteenth century. 1857. H21

23 Champlain, S. de. Narrative of a voyage to the West Indies and Mexico, ed. by Shaw. 1859. H22

24 Markham, C. R. Expeditions into the valley of the Amazons, 1539-1540, 1639, ed. by Markham. 1859. H23

25 Major, R. H., ed. Early voyages to Terra Australis. 1859. H24

25 Suppl. Extracts from a letter addressed to Sir Henry Ellis "On the discovery of Australia by the Portuguese in 1601." 1861. H25

26 González de Clavijo, R. Narrative of the embassy of Ruy González de Clavijo to the court of Timour, ed.

by Markham. 1859. H26
27 Asher, G. M., ed. Henry Hudson the Navigator, 1607-13. 1860. H27
28 Simon, P. The expedition of Pedro de Ursua & Lope de Aguirre, ed. by Markham. 1861. H28
29 Enriquez de Guzman, A. The life and acts of Don Alonzo Enriquez de Guzman, ed. by Markham. 1862. H29
30 Galvão, A. The discoveries of the world, ed. by Bethune. 1862. H30
31 Jordanus Catalani, bp. of Columbum. Mirabilia descripta. The wonders of the East, ed. by Yule. 1863. H31
32 Varthema, L. de. The travels of Ludovico di Varthema..., ed. by Badger. 1863. H32
33 Cieza de Léon, P. de. The travels of Pedro de Cieza de Leon, A. D. 1532-50, ed. by Markham. 1864. H33
34 Andagoya, A. P. de. Narrative of the Proceedings of Pedrarias Davila, ed. by Markham. 1865. H34
35 Barbosa, D. A description of the coasts of East Africa and Malabar, ed. by Stanley. 1866. H35
36-37 Yule, H., ed. Cathay and the Way Thither. 2 v. 1866. H36
38 Best, G. The three voyages of Sir Martin Frobisher, ed. by Best. 1867. H37
39 Morga, A. de. The Philippine Islands, ed. by Stanley. 1868. H38
40 Cortés, H. The fifth letter of Hernan Cortes, tr. by Gayangos. 1868. H39
41 Garcilaso de la Vega, el Inca. The royal commentaries of the Yncas, ed. by Markham. V. 1. 1869. H40
42 Corrêa, G. The three voyages of Vasco da Gama, ed. by Stanley. 1869. H41
43 Same as no. 2. 2d ed. 1870. H42
44 Salil-Ibn-Ruzaik. History of the imâms and seyyids of Omân, ed. by Badger. 1871. H43
45 Same as no. 41. V. 2. 1871. H44
46 Bontier, P. The Canarian, ed. by Major. 1871. H45
47 Markham, C. R., tr. Reports on the discovery of Peru. 1872. H46
48 Markham, C. R. Narratives of the rites and laws of the Yncas, ed. by Markham. 1872. H47
49a Barbaro, G. Travels to Tana and Persia, tr. by Thomas. 1873. H48
49b Grey, C., tr. A narrative of Italian travels in Persia..., ed. by Grey. 1873. H49
50 Zeno, N. The voyages of the Venetian brothers, Nicolò and Antonio Zeno, ed. by Major. 1873. H50
51 Staden, H. The captivity of Hans Stade of Hesse in 1547-55, ed. by Burton. 1874. H51
52 Stanley, H. E. J. S. The first voyage round the world by Magellan. 1518-21. 1874. H52
53 Albuquerque, A. de. The commentaries of the Great Alfonso Dalboquerque, ed. by Birch. V. 1. 1875. H53
54 Veer, G. de. The three voyages of William Barents to the Arctic Regions, in 1594, 1595, and 1596, ed. by Beynen. 1876. H54
55 Same as no. 53. V. 2. 1875. H55
56 Markham, C. R., ed. The voyage of Sir James Lancaster, Knt, to the East Indies. 1877. H56
57 Same as no. 1. 2d ed. 1877. H57
58 Schiltberger, J. The bondage and travels of Johann Schiltberger, ed. by Bruun. 1879. H58
59 Davys, J. The voyages and works of John Davis, the Navigator, ed. by Markham. 1880. H59
60-61 Acosta, J. de. The natural & moral history of the

Indies, ed. by Markham. 2 v. 1880. H60
62 Same as no. 53. V. 2. 1880. H61
63 Markham, C. R., ed. The voyages of William Baffin, 1612-1622. 1881. H62
64 Alvares, F. Narrative of the Portuguese embassy to Abyssinia, ed. by Stanley. 1881. H63
65 The Histoyre of the Bermudaes or Summer islands, ed. by Lefroy. 1881. H64
66-67 Cocks, R. The diary of Richard Cocks, ed. by Thompson. 2 v. 1883. H65
68 Same as no. 33. V. 2. 1883. H66
69 Same as no. 53. V. 4. 1883. H67
70-71 Linschoten, J. H. van. The voyage of John Huyghen van Linschoten to the East Indies, ed. by Burnell. 2 v. 1885. H68
72-73 Morgan, E. D., ed. Early voyages and travels to Russia and Persia. 2 v. 1886. H69
74-75 Hedges, W. The diary of William Hedges, Esq., ed. by Yule. 2 v. 1887-88. H70
76-77 Pyrard, F. The voyages of François Pyrard of Laval, ed. by Gray and Bell. 2 v. 1887-90. H71
78 Same as no. 74. V. 3. 1879. H72
79 Hues, R. Tractatus de Globis, et eorum Usu, ed. by Markham. 1889. H73
79:2 Sailing directions for the circumnavigation of England, ed. by Morgan. 1889. H74
80 Same as no. 76. V. 2. 1889. H75
81 Dominguez, H. E. D. L. L., ed. The conquest of the river Plate, 1535-1555. 1889. H76
82-83 Leguat, F. The voyage of François Leguat of Bresse, 1690-98, ed. by Oliver. 2 v. 1891. H77
84-85 Valle, P. della. The travels of Pietro della Valle in India, ed. by Grey. 2 v. 1892. H78
86 Colombo, C. The journal of Christopher Columbus, ed. by Markham. 1893. H79
87 Bent, J. B., ed. Early voyages and travels in the Levant. 1893. H80
88-89 Christy, M., ed. The voyages of Captain Luke Foxe, of Hull, and Captain Thomas James of Bristol. 2 v. 1893. H81
90 Vespucci, A. The letters of Americo Vespucci, ed. by Markham. 1894. H82
91 Sarmiento de Gamboa, P. Narratives of the voyages of Pedro Sarmiento de Gambóa to the Straits of Magellan, 1579-80. 1894. H83
92-94 Leo Africanus, J. The history and description of Africa, ed. by Brown. 3 v. 1896. H84
95 Eannes de Azurara, G. The chronicle of the discovery and conquest of Guinea, ed. by Beazley and Prestage. V. 1. 1896. H85
96-97 Gosch, C. C. A., ed. Danish Arctic expeditions, 1605-1620. 2 v. 1896-97. H86
98 Cosmas, I. The topographia Christian of Cosmas, ed. by McCrindle. 1897. H87
99 ____. A journal of the first voyage of Vasco da Gama, 1497-1499, ed. by Ravenstein. 1898. H88
100 Same as no. 95. V. 2. 1899. H89

2d Series:
1-2 Roe, T. The embassy of Sir Thomas Roe to the court of the Great Mogul, 1615-19, ed. by Foster. 2 v. 1899. H90
3 Warner, G. F., ed. The voyage of Robert Dudley to the West Indies and Guiana in 1594-1595. 1899. H91
4 Ruysbroek, W. van. The journeys of William de Rubruquis...and John de Plano Carpino, ed. by Rockhill. 1900. H92

5 Saris, J. The voyage of Captain John Saris to Japan, in 1613, ed. by Satow. 1900. H93

6 Battell, A. The strange adventures of Andrew Battell of Leigh, in Angola..., ed. by Ravenstein. 1901. H94

7-8 Amherst, W. A. T-A. and Thomson, B., eds. The discovery of the Solomon Islands in 1568. 2 v. 1901. H95

9 Teixeira, P. The travels of Pedro Teixeira, with his "King of Rarmuz" and extracts from his "King of Persia," tr. by Sinclair. 1902. H96

10 Castanhoso, M. de. The Portuguese expedition to Abyssinia in 1541-43, ed. by Whiteway. 1920. H97

11 Conway, W. M., ed. Early Dutch and English voyages to Spitzbergen in the seventeenth century. 1902. H98

12 Bowrey, T., ed. A geographical account of the countries round the bay of Bengal. 1905. H99

13 Corney, B. G., ed. The voyage of Captain Don Felipe González. 1908. H100

14-15 Queiros, P. F. de. The voyages of Pedro Fernández de Quiros, 1595 to 1606, ed. by Markham. 2 v. 1904. H101

16 Jourdain, J. The journal of John Jourdain, 1608-1617, ed. by Foster. 1905. H102

17 Mundy, P. The Travels in Europe and Asia, 1608-1617, ed. by Temple. V. 1. 1907. H103

18 Spilbergen, J. van. East and West Indian mirror, tr. by Villiers. 1906. H104

19-20 Fryer, J. A new account of East India and Persia, ed. by Crooke. 2 v. 1909-12. H105

21 Espinosa, A. de. The Guanches of Tenerife, the holy image of Our Lady of Candelaria, ed. by Markham. 1907. H106

22 Sarmiento de Gamboa, P. History of the Incas, ed. by Markham. 1907. H107

22 Suppl. A. A narrative of the vice-regal embassy to Vilcabamba, 1571...by de Oviedo, ed. by Markham. 1907. H108

23-25 Diaz del Castillo, B. The true history of the conquest of New Spain, ed. by Maudslay. 3 v. 1908-16. H109

26-27 Storm van's Gravesande, L. Rise of British Guiana, ed. by Harris and Villiers. 2 v. 1911. H110

28 Markham, C. R. Early Spanish voyages to the strait of Magellan, tr. and ed. by Markham. 1911. H111

29 Libro del conoscimento. Book of knowledge..., ed. by Markham. 1912. H112

30 Same as no. 23. V. 4. 1912. H113

31 Cieza de Léon, P. de. The war of Quito, ed. by Markham. 1913. H114

32 Corney, B. G., ed. The quest and occupation of Tahiti. V. 1. 1913. H115

33 Same as no. 36, ser. 1. New. ed. V. 1. 1913. H116

34 Nuttall, Z., ed. New light on Drake. 1914. H117

35 Same as no. 17. V. 2. 1914. H118

36 Same as no. 32. V. 2. 1914. H119

37-38 Same as no. 36, ser. 1. New ed. V. 3, 1. 1914-15. H120

39 Same as no. 19-20. V. 3. 1915. H121

40 Same as no. 23-25. V. 5. 1916. H122

41 Same as no. 36, ser. 1. New ed. V. 4. 1916. H123

42 Cieza de Léon, P. de. The war of Chupas, ed. by Markham. 1913. H124

43 Same as no. 32. V. 2. 1918. H125

44 Barbosa, D. The book of Duarte Barbosa, ed. by Dames. V. 1. 1918. H126

45-46 Same as no. 17. V. 3. 2 pts. 1919. H127

47 Muntaner, R. The chronicle of Muntaner, ed. by

Goodenough. V. 1. 1920. H128
48 Montesinos, F. Memorias antiguas historiales del Peru, ed. by Means. 1920. H129
49 Same as no. 44. V. 2. 1921. H130
50 Same as no. 47. V. 2. 1921. H131
51 Fritz, S. Journal of the travels and labours of Father Samuel Fritz, ed. by Edmundson. 1922. H132
52 Lockerby, W. Journal of William Lockerby, sandalwood trader in the Fijian islands during the year 1808-1809, ed. by Thurn and Wharton. 1925. H133
53 Olafsson, J. The life of the Icelander, Jon Olafsson, ed. by Phillipotts. V. 1. 1923. H134
54 Cieza de Léon, P. de. Civil wars in Peru, ed. by Markham. 1923. H135
55 Same as no. 17. V. 4. 1924. H136
56 Harlow, V. T., ed. Colonising expeditions to the West Indies and Guiana, 1623-1667. 1925. H137
57 Mortoft, F. Francis Mortoft: his book, ed. by Letts. 1925. H138
58 Bowrey, T. Papers of Thomas Bowrey, 1669-1713, ed. by Temple. Pt. 1. 1927. H139
59 Manrique, S. Travels of Sebastien Manrique, 1629-1643, ed. by Luard. V. 1. 1927. H140
60 Harcourt, R. A relation to the voyage to Guiana, 1613, ed. by Harris. 1928. H141
61 Same as no. 59. V. 2. 1927. H142
62 Spain. Archivo general de Indias, Seville. Spanish documents concerning English voyages to the Caribbean, 1527-1568, ed. by Wright. 1929. H143
63 Carruthers, D., ed. The desert route to India. 1929. H144
64 Prado y Tovar, D. de. New light on the discovery of Australia, ed. by Stevens. 1930. H145
65 Colombo, C. Voyages of Columbus, ed. by Jane. V. 1. 1929. H146
66 Moreland, W. H., ed. Relations of Golconda in the early seventeenth century. 1931. H147
67 Sanderson, J. The travels of John Sanderson in the Levant, 1584-1602, ed. by Foster. 1931. H148
68 Same as no. 53. V. 2. 1932. H149
69 Barlow, R. A brief summe of geographie, ed. by Taylor. 1931. H150
70 Same as no. 65. V. 2. 1932. H151
71 Spain. Archivo general de Indias, Seville. Documents concerning English voyages to the Spanish Main, 1569-1580, ed. by Wright. 1932. H152
72 Burnell, J. Bombay in the days of Queen Anne, ed. by Cotton and Anstey. 1933. H153
73 Wafer, L. A new voyage and description of the Isthmus of America, ed. by Joyce. 1934. H154
74 Floris, P. Peter Floris, his voyage to the East Indies, ed. by Moreland. 1934. H155
75 Foster, W. The voyage of Thomas Best to the East Indies, 1612-14. 1934. H156
76-77 Hakluyt, H. R. The original writings & correspondence of the two Richard Hakluyts, ed. by Taylor. 2 v. 1935. H157
78 Same as no. 17. V. 5. 1936. H158
79 Pacheco Pereira, D. Esmeraldo de Situ Orbis, ed. by Kimble. 1936. H159
80 Crone, G. R., ed. and tr. The voyages of Cadamosto. 1937. H160
81 Greenlee, W. B., ed. The voyage of Pedro Alvarez Cabral to Brazil and India. 1937. H161

82 Foster, W., ed. The voyages of Nicholas Downton to the East Indies, 1614-15. 1938. H162

83-84 Quinn, D. B., ed. The voyages and colonising enterprises of Sir Humphrey Gilbert. 2 v. 1940. H163

85 Foster, W., ed. The voyage of Sir James Lancaster to Brazil and the East Indies, 1591-1603. 1940. H164

86-87 Blake, J. W., ed. Europeans in West Africa, 1450-1560. 2 v. 1940. H165

88 Middleton, H. The voyage of Sir Henry Middleton to the Moluccas, 1604-06, ed. by Foster. 1943. H166

89-90 Pires, T. The Suma Oriental of Tomé Pires and The book of Francisco Rodrigues, ed. by Cortesão. 2 v. 1944. H167

91-92 Bellingshausen, F. G. von. The voyage of Captain Bellingshausen to the Antarctic seas, 1819-21, ed. by Debenham. 2 v. 1945. H168

93 Hakluyt Society. Richard Hakluyt & his successors, ed. by Lynam. 1946. H169

94 Harff, A. R. von. The pilgrimage of Arnold von Harff, Knight, ed. by Letts. 1946. H170

95-97 Carré, A. The travels of the Abbe Carré, ed. by Fawcett. 3 v. 1947-48. H171

98 Robertson, G. The discovery of Tahiti, ed. by Carrington. 1948. H172

99 Spain. Archivio General de Indias, Seville. Further English voyages to Spanish America, 1583-1594, ed. by Wright. 1951. H173

100 Pitts, J. The Red sea and adjacent countries at the close of the seventeenth century, ed. by Foster. 1949. H174

101-102 Mandeville, Sir J. Travels, tr. by Letta. 1953. H175

103 Strachey, W. The historie of travell into Virginia Britania (1612), ed. by Wright and Freund. 1953. H176

104-105 Quinn, D. B., ed. The Roanoke voyages, 1584-1590, ed. by Quinn. 2 v. 1955. H177

106 Boxer, C. R. South China in the sixteenth century. 1953. H178

107 Beckingham, C. F. Some records of Ethiopia, 1593-1646, tr. by Beckingham and Huntingsford. 1954. H179

108 Letts, M. H. I., ed. and tr. The travels of Leo of Rozmital through Germany, Flanders, England... 1957. H180

109 Crawford, O. G. S., ed. Ethiopian itineraries, circa 1400-1524... 1958. H181

110 Ibn Batuta. Travels, A. D., 1325-1354; tr... from the Arabic text, ed. by Defrémery and Sanguinetti, by Gibbs. V. 1. 1958. H182

111 Andrews, K. R., ed. English privateering voyages to the West Indies. 1959. H183

112 Gomes de Brito, B. The tragic history of the sea, ed. by Boxer. 1959. H184

113 Taylor, E. G. R. The troublesome voyage of Captain Edward Fenton, 1582-1583. 1959. H185

114-115 Alvares, F. The Prester John of the Indies, ed. by Beckingham and Huntingford. 2 v. 1961. H186

116 Davies, J. The history of the Tahitian Mission, 1799-1830, ed. by Newbury. 1961. H187

117 Same as no. 110. V. 2. 1962. H188

118-119 Navarrete, D. The travels and controversies of Friar Domingo Navarrete, ed. by Cummins. 2 v. 1962. H189

120 Williamson, J. A. The Cabot voyages and Bristol discovery under Henry VII. 1962. H190

121 Bourne, W. A regiment for the sea, and other writings on navigation, ed. by

Taylor. 1963. H191
122 Byron, J. Byron's journal of his circumnavigation, 1764-1766, ed. by Gallagher. 1964. H192
123 Bovill, E. W., ed. Missions to the Niger. V. 1. 1964. H193
124-125 Carteret, P. Carteret's voyage round the world, 1766-1769, ed. by Wallis. 2 v. 1965. H194
126-127 Kelly, C., ed. La Australia Del Espiritu Santo. 1964. H195
128-130 Same as no. 123. V. 2-4. 1966. H196
131 Bishop, C. The journal and letters of Captain Charles Bishop on the north-west coast of America, ed. by Roe. 1967. H197
132 Gomes de Brito, B. Further selections from the tragic history of the sea, tr. by Boxer. 1968. H198
133-135 Leichhardt, L. The letters of F. W. Ludwig Leichhardt, tr. by Aurousseau. 3 v. 1968. H199
136-137 Barbour, P. L., ed. The Jamestown voyages under the First Charter, 1606-1609. 2 v. 1968. H200
138-139 Allen, W. E. D., ed. Russian embassies to the Gregorian kings, 1589-1605. 2 v. 1970. H201
140 Morga, A. de. Sucesos de las Islas Filipinas, tr. by Cummins. 1971. H202
141 Same as 110. V. 2. 1971. H203
142 Andrews, K. R., ed. The last voyage of Drake and Hawkins. 1972. H204
143 Peard, G. George Peard's journal of the voyage of H. M. S. Blossom to the Pacific, ed. by Gough. 1972. H205
144-5 Quinn, D. B., ed. The Hakluyt handbook. 2 v. 1973-4. H206
Extra Series:
1-12 Hakluyt, R. The principal navigations, voyages, traffiques, and discoveries of the English nation. 12 v. 1903-05. H207
13 ____. The texts and versions of John de Plano Carpino and William de Rubruquis, ed. by Beazley. 1903. H208
14-33 Purchas, S. Hakluytus posthumus, or Purchas, his pilgrimes. 20 v. 1905-07. H209
34-36 Cook, J. The Journals on his voyages of discovery, ed. by Beaglehole. 3 v. 1955-68. H210
38 Colomba, C. The journal of Christopher Columbus, tr. by Jane, rev. by Vigneras. 1960. H211
39 Hakluyt, R. The principal navigations, voiages and discoveries of the English nation. (1589 imprint) Ed. by Quinn and Skelton. 2 v. 1965. H212
40 Jephson, A. J. M. The diary of A. J. Mountenay Jephson, ed. by Middleton and M. D. Jephson. 1968. H213
41 Mackenzie, A. The journals and letters of Sir Alexander Mackenzie, ed. by Lamb. 1972. H214
42 Ma Huan. Ying-Ya Sheng-lan, ed. by Mills. 1970. H215

HALE FOUNDATION LECTURE SERIES (Scribner unless otherwise noted)

1908-9 Lutkin, P. C. Church hymns and church music. Young Churchmen. 1910. H216
1910 Wordsworth, J. The national church of Sweden. Young Churchmen. 1911. H217
1914 Mitchell, A. Biographical studies in Scottish church history. Young Churchmen. 1914. H218
1915 Mercer, S. A. B. The Ethiopic liturgy. Mowbray. 1915. H219
1922 Gavin, F. Some aspects of contemporary Greek

orthodox thought. Morehouse. 1923. H220
1927-28 Grant, F. C. New horizons of the Christian faith. Morehouse. 1928. H221
1929-30 Easton, B. S. Christ in the Gospels. 1930. H222
1932 Oliver, J. R. Psychiatry and mental health. 1932. H223
1933 Peck, W. G. The social implications of the Oxford movement. 1933. H224
1935 Douglas, C. W. Church music in history and practice. 1962. H225
1937 Tucker, H. St. G. The history of the Episcopal church in Japan. 1938. H226
1938 James, F. Personalities of the Old Testament. 1939. H227
1943 Chorley, E. C. Men and movements in the American Episcopal church. 1946. H228
1947 Vidler, A. R. Witness to the light. 1948. H229
1950 Hodgson, L. The doctrine of the atonement. 1951. H230
1951 Yerkes, R. K. Sacrifice in Greek and Roman religions and early Judaism. 1952. H231
1953 Dawley, P. M. John Whitgift and the English Reformation. 1954. H232

HANDBOOKS OF AMERICAN LITERATURE (Hendricks)

Allen, G. W. Walt Whitman handbook. 1946. H233
Carpenter, F. I. Emerson handbook. 1953. H234
Hayford, H. Melville handbook. 1959. H235
Long, E. H. Mark Twain handbook. 1956. H236

HANDBOOKS OF AMERICAN NATURAL HISTORY (Comstock)

Bishop, S. C. Handbook of salamanders. 1943. H237
Bousfield, E. L. Shallow-water gammaridean Amphipoda of New England. 1973. H238
Carr, A. F. Handbook of turtles. 1952. H239
Comstock, A. (Botsford). Handbook of nature-study. 1939. H240
Comstock, J. H. The spider book. 1940. H241
Hamilton, W. J. The mammals of eastern United States. 1943. H242
Johnsgard, P. A. Handbook of water-fowl behavior. 1965. H243
Matheson, R. Handbook of the mosquitoes of North America. 1944. H244
Muenscher, W. C. Aquatic plants of the United States. 1944. H245
Smith, H. B. Handbook of lizards. 1946. H246
Wright, A. (Allen) and A. H. Handbook of frogs and toads. 1949. H247
Wright, A. H. Handbook of snakes of the United States and Canada. 2 v. 1957. H248

HARLEIAN SOCIETY. PUBLICATIONS.

1 Cook, R. The visitation of London in the year 1568, ed. by Howard and Armytage. 1869. H249
2 Camden, W. The visitation of the county of Leicester in the year 1619, ed. by Fetherston. 1870. H250
3 ____. The visitation of the county of Rutland in the year 1618-19, ed. by Armytage. 1870. H251
4 Flower, W. The visitations of the county of Nottingham in the years 1569 and 1614..., ed. by Marshall. 1871. H252
5 Harvey, W. The visitations of the county of Oxford taken in the years 1566...1634..., ed. by Turner. 1871. H253
6 Saint-George, H. The visitation of the county of Devon in the year 1620, ed. by Colby. 1872. H254
7 Saint-George, R. The visitation of the county of Cumberland in the year 1615, ed. by Fetherston. 1872. H255

8 Le Neve, P. Le Neve's pedigrees of the knights, ed. by Marshall. 1873. H256
9 Saint-George, H. The visitation of the county of Cornwall in the year 1620, ed. by Vivian and Droke. 1874. H257
10 Chester, J. L., ed. The marriage, baptismal, and burial registers of the collegiate church, or, Abbey of St. Peter, Westminster. 1876. H258/9
11 Saint-George, H. The visitation of the county of Somerset in the year 1623, ed. by Colby. 1876. H260
12 Camden, W. The visitation of the county of Warwick in the year 1619..., ed. by Fetherston. 1877. H261
13-14 Metcalfe, W. C., ed. The visitations of Essex by Hawley, 1552... 2 v. 1878-79. H262
15 Saint-George, H. The visitation of London... 1633, 1634 and 1635, ed. by Howard and Chester. V. 1. 1880. H263
16 Flower, W. The visitation of Yorkshire in the years 1563 and 1564, ed. by Norcliffe. 1881. H264
17 Same as no. 15. V. 2. 1883. H265
18 Glover, R. The visitation of Cheshire in the year 1580, ed. by Rylands. 1882. H266
19 Harvey, W. The visitation of Bedfordshire... 1566, 1582 and 1634, ed. by Blaydes. 1884. H267
20 Saint-George, H. The visitation of the county of Dorset..., ed. by Rylands. 1885. Addenda. 1888. H268
21 Chitting, H. The visitation of the county of Gloucester..., ed. by Maclean and Heane. 1885. H269
22 Cook, R. The visitations of Hertfordshire... 1572... 1634, ed. by Metcalfe. 1886. H270
23 Chester, J. L. Allegations for marriage licences issued by the dean and chapter of Westminster, 1558 to 1699, ed. by Armytage. 1886. H271
24 Canterbury, Eng. Allegations for marriage licenses issued from the Faculty office of the Archbishop of Canterbury at London, 1543 to 1869 extracted by Chester, ed. by Armytage. 1886. H272
25 ____. Allegations for marriage licenses issued by the Bishop of London, ed. by Armytage. V. 1. 1520-1610. 1887. H273
26 ____. ____. V. 2. 1611-1828. 1887. H274
27 Phillimore, W. P. W., ed. The visitation of the county of Worcester... 1569. 1888. H275
28-29 Treswell, R. The visitation of Shopshire, taken in the year 1623..., ed. by Grazebrook. 2 v. 1889. H276
30 Canterbury, Eng. Allegations for marriage licenses issued by the Vicar-General of the Archbishop of Canterbury, ed. by Armytage. 1677-1687. 1890. H277
31 ____. ____. 1687-1694. 1890. H278
32 Harvey, W. The visitacion of Norfolk..., ed. by Rye. 1891. H279
33 Same as no. 30. 1660 to 1668. 1892. H280
34 Same as no. 30. 1669 to 1679. 1892. H281
35-36 Moens, W. J. C. Hampshire allegations for marriage licenses granted by the Bishop of Winchester 1689 to 1837. 2 v. 1893. H282
37-40 Hunter, J. Familae minorium, ed. by Clay. 4 v. 1894-96. H283
41 Saint-George, H. The visitation of Cambridge made in a [1575]..., ed. by Clay. 1897. H284
42 Philipot, J. The visitation of Kent... 1619-1621, ed. by Hovenden. 1898. H285
43 Benolt, T. The visitations of the county of Surrey made and taken in the years

1530...1572...1623..., ed. by Bannerman. 1899. H286

44-49 Musgave, W. Obituary prior to 1800 as for as relates England, Scotland and Ireland, ed. by Armytage. 6 v. 1899-1901. H287

50-52 Maddison, A. R., ed. Lincolnshire pedigrees. 3 v. 1902-04. H288

53 Benolt, T. The visitations of the county of Sussex, made and taken in the years 1530... and 1633-4, ed. by Bannerman. 1905. H289

54 Bysshe, E. A visitation of the county of Kent...(1663-1668)..., ed. by Armytage. 1906. H290

55 Same as nos. 50-52. Index. 1906. H291

56-57 Rylands, W. H., ed. The four visitations of Berkshire made and taken by Thomas Benolt..., ed. by Rylands. 2 v. 1907-08. H292

58 Philipot, J. The visitation of the county of Buckingham made in 1634 by James Philipot..., ed. by Rylands. 1909. H293

59 Saint-George, R. Pedigrees made at the visitation of Cheshire, 1613, ed. by Armytage and Rylands. 1909. H294

60 Armytage, G. J., ed. A visitation of the county of Surrey. 1910. H295

61 Bysshe, E. A visitation of the county of Suffolk..., ed. by Rylands. 1910. H296

62 May, T. The visitation of the county of Warwick..., ed. by Rylands. 1911. H297

63 Dugdale, W. Staffordshire pedigrees, ed. by Armytage and Rylands. 1912. H298

64 Benolt, T. Pedigrees from the visitation of Hampshire..., ed. by Rylands. 1913. H299

65 Mundy, R., comp. Middlesex pedigrees, ed. by Armytage. 1914. H300

66 Foster, J. Grantees of arms, in docquets and patents to the end of the seventeenth century, ed. by Rylands. 1915. H301

67-68 ____. Grantees of arms... 1687 and 1898, ed. by Rylands. 2 v. 1916. H302

69-72 Sudbury, Eng. Allegations for marriage licenses in the archdeaconry of Sudbury, ed. by W. B. and G. G. B. Bannerman. 1684-1754, 1755-1781, 1782-1814, 1815-1839. 4 v. 1918-21. H303

73 Burghill, F. The visitation of the county of Rutland... 1681..., ed. by Rylands. 1922. H304

74 Benolt, T. The visitations of Kent (1530-1), ed. by Bannerman. V. 1. 1923. H305

75 ____. V. 2. 1574 and 1592. 1924. H306

76-77 Littledale, W. A., ed. A collection of miscellaneous grants... 2 v. 1925-26. H307

78-79 Gt. Brit. Court of chancery. An index of persons named in early chancery proceedings, Richard II (1385) to Edward II (1467). 2 v. 1927-28. H308

80-84 Moor, C., comp. Knights of Edward I. 5 v. 1929-32. H309

85-86 Bysshe, E. The visitation of Norfolk, ed. by Clarke and Campling. 2 v. 1933-34. H310

87 Saint-George, H. The visitation of the county of Northampton in the year 1681, ed. by Longden. 1935. H311

88 Hunter, J. Hunter's pedigrees, ed. by Walker. 1936. H312

89 Bysshe, E. The visitation of Sussex..., ed. by Clarke. 1937. H313

90 Butler, A. T., ed. The visitation of Worcestershire. 1938. H314

91 Campling, A. East Anglican pedigrees. V. 1. 1939. H315

92 Whitmore, J. B. and Hughes Clarke, A. W. London visitation pedigrees, 1664. 1940. H316

93 Adams, A. Cheshire visitation pedigrees, 1663.

1941. H317
94-96 Walker, J. W., ed. Yorkshire pedigrees. 3 v. 1942-44. H318
97 Same as no. 91. V. 2. 1945. H319
98 Lawrance, H. Heraldry from military monuments before 1350 in England and Wales. 1946. H320
99 Whitmore, J. B. A genealogical guide. V. 1. 1947. H321
100 Wagner, A. R. A catalogue of English mediaeval roll of arms. 1950. H322
101-2 Same as no. 99. V. 2-3. 1949-50. H323
103 Loyd, L. C. The origins of some Anglo-Norman families, ed. by Clay and Douglas. 1951. H324
104 Same as no. 99. V. 4. 1953. H325
105-6 Saint-George, H. and Lennard, S. Wiltshire visitation pedigrees, 1623, ed. by Squibb. 1954. H326
107 Gt. Brit. Court of Chivalry. Report of the heraldic cases in the Court of Chivalry, 1623-1723, ed. by Squibb. 1956. H327
108 Elmhirt, E. M. Merchant's marks. 1959. H328
109-10 Cooke, R. Visitation of London, 1568 with additional pedigrees 1569-90..., ed. by Stanford and Rawlins. 1963. H329
111-12 London, H. S. The life of William Bruges. 1970. H330
113-14 Rolls of Arms, Henry III. 1967. H331
115-16 Steer, F. W. A catalogue of the Earl Marshal's papers at Arundel Castle, ed. by Steer. 1964. H332

HARLEIAN SOCIETY. PUBLICATIONS. REGISTERS.

1 London. St. Peter, Cornhill. A register of all christninges, burialles & weddinges within the parish of St. Peeters upon Cornhill, ed. by Gower. 1877. H33
2 Canterbury cathedral. The register booke of christninges, marriages, and burialls within the precincts of the cathedrall and metropoliticall church of Christe of Canterburie, ed. by Hovenden. 1878. H334
3 London, St. Dionis. The reiester booke of Saynte De'nis Backchurch parishe... 1538, ed. by Chester. 1878. H335
4 Same as no. 1. V. 2. 1879. H336
5 London. St. Mary Aldermary (Parish). The parish registers of St. Mary's Aldermary, London... 1558 to 1754, ed. by Chester. 1880. H337
6 London, St. Thomas the Apostle (Parish). The parish registers of St. Thomas the Apostle, London... 1558 to 1754, ed. by Chester. 1881. H338
7 London. St. Michael (Parish). The parish register of St. Michael, Cornhill, London, containing the mariages, baptisms, and burials from 1546 to 1754, ed. by Chester. 1882. H339
8 London. St. Antholin (Parish). The parish register of St. Antholin, Budge Row, London... from 1538 to 1754..., ed. by Chester. 1883. H340
9-10 London. St. James (Parish). A true register of all christenings, marriages... 1551, ed. by Hovenden. 2 v. 1884-85. H341
11 Westminster, Eng. St. George (Parish). The register book of marriages belonging to the parish of St. George..., ed. by Chapman. V. 1. 1725-1787. 1886. H342
12 Stourton, Eng. The registers of Stourton county Wilts from 1570 to 1800, ed. by Ellis. 1887. H343
13 Same as no. 9-10. V. 3. 1887. H344
14 Same as no. 11. V. 2.

1788-1809. 1888. H345
15 Armytage, G. J., ed. Register of baptisms and marriages, 1889. H346
16 Kensington, Eng. Parish register of Kensington Co., Middlesex, from A.D. 1539 to A.D. 1675, ed. by McNamara and Story-Maskelyne. 1890. H347
17 Same as nos. 9-10. V. 4. 1891. H348
18 Charterhouse. The registers and monumental inscriptions of Charterhouse chapel, ed. by Collins. 1892. H349
19-20 Same as nos. 9-10. V. 5-6. 1893-4. H350
21 London. Christ's church, Newgate. The register of Christ church, Newgate, 1538-1754, ed. by Littledale. 1895. H351
22 Same as no. 11. V. 2. 1810-1828. 1896. H352
23 Durham cathedral. The baptismal, marriage, and burial registers of the Cathedral church of Christ and Blessed Mary the virgin at Durham, 1609-1896, ed. by Armytage. 1897. H353
24 Same as no. 11. V. 4. 1824-1837. 1897. H354
25 Westminster, Eng. St. Martin in the fields (Parish). A register of the baptisms, marriages, and burials in the parish of St. Martin in the Fields..., ed. by Mason. V. 1. 1550-1619. 1898. H355
26 London. St. Paul's cathedral. The registers of St. Paul's Cathedral..., ed. by Clay. 1899. H356
27-28 Bath, Eng. Abbey church of SS. Peter and Paul. The registers of the Abbey church of SS. Peter and Paul, Bath, ed. by Jewers. 2 v. 1900-01. H357
29-30 London. St. Vedast church. The register of St. Vedast... London. 2 v. 1902-03. H358
31 London, St. Helen (Parish). The registers of St. Helen's Bishopgate, London, ed. by Bannerman. 1904. H359
32 London. St. Martin Outwich (Parish). The registers of St. Martin Outwich, London, ed. by Bannerman. 1905. H360
33-37 London. St. Paul's church. The register of St. Paul's church... London, ed. by Hunt. 5 v. 1906-09. H361
38-41 London. St. Benêt, (Parish). The registers of St. Benêt and St. Peter, Paul's wharf, London, ed. by Littledale. 4 v. 1909-12. H362
42 London. St. Mildred. The register of St. Mildred, London, ed. by Bannerman. 1912. H363
43 London. All Hallows, Bread Street (Parish). The register of All Hallows, Bread Street..., ed. by Bannerman. 1913. H364
44-45 London. St. Mary le Bow (Parish). The registers of St. Mary le Bowe, Cheapshire..., ed. by Bannerman. 2 v. 1914-15. H365
46 London. St. Olave (Parish). The registers of St. Olave... London, 1563-1700, ed. by Bannerman. 1916. H366
47-48 London. St. Marylebone (Parish). The registers of marriages of St. Mary le Bone, 1668-1812 and of Oxford Chapel... 1736-1754, ed. by Bannerman. 2 v. 1917-18. H367
49-50 London. St. Stephen's. The register of St. Stephen's ...London, ed. by Bannerman. 2 v. 1919-20. H368
51-57 Same as nos. 47-48. V. 3-7. 1921-27. H369
58 London. St. Mary Mounthaw. The register of St. Mary Mounthaw, 1568-1649. 1928. H370
59-60 London. St. Mary Somerset (Parish). The register of St. Mary Somerset, London, ed. by Bannerman. 2 v. 1929-30. H371
61-62 London. St. Mary the

Virgin (Parish). The registers of St. Mary the Virgin..., ed. by Bannerman. 2 v. 1931. H372

63 London. St. Matthew (Parish). The register of St. Matthew...1538-1812, ed. by Bannerman. 1933. H373

64 Westminster, England. St. Margaret. Register of St. Margaret's...1660-75, ed. by Tanner. 1935. H374

65 Same as nos. 61-62. V. 3. 1935. H375

66 Same as no. 25. V. 2. 1619-1636. 1936. H376

67-68 London. St. Clement (Parish). The register of St. Clement, Eastcheap and St. Martin Orgar, ed. by Clarke. 2 v. 1937-38. H377

69 London. St. Dunstan in the East (Church). The register of St. Dunstan in the East, London, ed. by Clarke. V. 1. 1939. H378

70-71 London. St. Lawrence Jewry (Church). The register of St. Lawrence Jewry, London, ed. by Clarke. 2 v. 1940-41. H379

72-73 London. St. Mary Magdalen church. The registers of St. Mary Magdalen, ed. by Clarke. 2 v. 1942-43. H380

74 Same as nos. 72-73. V. 3. 1944 (V. 3 has title: The register of St. Michael Brassishaw, London). H381

75-81 London. Royal Hospital. The registers of St. Katharine by the Tower, London, ed. by Clarke. 7 v. 1945-53. H382

82-83 London. Classical Presbyteries. Fourth Classis. The register book of the Fourth classis in the province of London, 1646-59. 2 v. 1953. H383

84-87 London. St. Dunstan in the East. The registers of St. Dunstan in the East, London, 1653-1766. V. 2, 3. 1955-58. H384

88 St. Margaret's Church. Westminster. The registers of St. Margaret's, Westminster. 1968. H385

HART, SCHAFFNER & MARX PRIZE ESSAYS (Houghton)

1 Howard, E. D. The cause and extent of the recent industrial progress of Germany. 1907. H386

2 Lauck, W. J. The causes of the panic of 1893. 1907. H387

3 Person, H. S. Industrial education. 1907. H388

4 Merritt, A. N. Federal regulation of railway rates. 1906. H389

5 Dunmore, W. T. Ship subsidies. 1907. H390

6 Skelton, O. D. Socialism. 1911. H391

7 Campbell, G. L. Industrial accidents and their compensation. 1911. H392

8 Streightoff, F. H. The standard of living among the industrial people of America. 1911. H393

9 Clapp, E. J. The navigable Rhine. 1911. H394

10 Robinson, L. N. History and organization of criminal statistics in the United States. 1911. H395

11 Anderson, B. M. Social value. 1911. H396

12 Strombeck, J. F. Freight classification. 1912. H397

13 Moulton, H. G. Waterways versus railways. 1912. H398

14 Brace, H. H. The value of organized speculation. 1913. H399

15 Leake, A. H. Industrial education. 1913. H400

16 Smith, H. E. The United States federal income tax history from 1861 to 1871. 1914. H401

17 Watkins, G. P. Welfare as an economic quantity. 1915. H402

18 Suffern, A. E. Conciliation and arbitration in the coal industry of America. 1915. H403

19 Donald, W. J. A. The Canadian iron and steel

industry. 1915. H404
20 Dunbar, D. E. The tin-plate industry. 1915. H405
21 Leake, A. H. The means and methods of agricultural education. 1915. H406
22 Scheftel, Y. The taxation of land value. 1916. H407
23 Vanderblue, H. B. Railroad valuation. 1917. H408
24 MacGibbon, D. A. Railway rates and the Canadian railway commission. 1917. H409
25 Nourse, E. G. The Chicago produce market. 1918. H410
26 Stockett, J. N. The arbitral determination of railway wages. 1918. H411
27 Lincoln, E. E. The results of municipal electric lighting in Massachusetts. 1918. H412
28 Hartman, H. H. Fair value. 1920. H413
29 Dozier, H. D. A history of the Atlantic coast line railroad. 1920. H414
30 Furniss, E. S. The position of the laborer in a system of nationalism. 1920. H415
31 Knight, F. H. Risk, uncertainty and profit. 1921. H416
32 Robb, T. B. The guaranty of bank deposits. 1921. H417
33 Carroll, M. R. Labor and politics. 1923. H418
34 Morgan, C. S. Regulation and the management of public utilities. 1923. H419
35 Kyrk, H. A theory of consumption. 1923. H420
36 Ely, O. Railway rates and cost of service. 1924. H421
37 Ware, N. The industrial worker: 1840-1860. 1924. H422
38 Morley, F. Unemployment relief in Great Britain. 1924. H423
39 Ryan, F. W. Usury and usury laws. 1924. H424
40 Stehman, J. W. The financial history of the American telephone and telegraph company. 1925. H425
41 Stocking, G. W. The oil industry and the competitive system. 1925. H426
42 Shultz, W. J. The taxation of inheritance. 1926. H427
43 Schwulst, E. B. Extension of bank credit. 1927. H428
44 Seltzer, L. H. A financial history of the American automobile industry. 1928. H429
45 Leland, S. E. The classified property tax in the United States. 1928. H430
46 Kuhlmann, C. B. The development of the flour-milling industry. 1929. H431
46 (i.e. 47) Kuznets, S. S. Secular movements in production and prices. 1930. H432
48 Ware, C. F. The early New England manufacture. 1931. H433
49 Helderman, L. C. National and state banks. 1931. H434
50 Southard, F. A. American industry in Europe. 1931. H435
51 Smith, N. L. The fair rate of return in public utility. 1932. H436
52 Herbst, A. The negro in the slaughtering and meatpacking industry in Chicago. 1932. H437
53 Hohman, H. F. The development of social insurance and minimum wage legislature in Great Britain. 1933. H438

HARVARD BOOKS IN BIOLOGY.

1 Dunn, L. C. Heredity and evolution in human population. 1959. H439
2 Lindauer, M. Communication among social bees. 1961. H440
3 Burnet, F. M. The integrity of the body. 1962. H441
4 Roeder, K. D. Nerve cells and insect behavior. 1963. H442
5 Phaff, H. J. and others. The life of yeasts. 1966. H443
6 Weygoldt, P. The biology of pseudoscorpions. 1969. H444
7 Marshall, N. B. Explorations in the life of fishes.

1971. H445

HARVARD BOOKS ON ASTRONOMY

Aller, L. H. Atoms, stars, and nebulae. 1971. H446
Bok, B. J. and P. F. The milky way. 1957. H447
Menzel, D. H. Our sun. 1959. H448
Miczaika, G. R. P. and Sinton, W. M. Tools of the astronomer. 1961. H449
Payne-Gaposchkin, C. H. Stars in the making. 1952. H450
Shapley, H. Galaxies. 1961. H451
Sobolev, V. V. Moving envelops of stars, tr. by Gaposchkin. 1960. H452
Watson, F. G. Between the planets. 1956. H453
Whipple, F. L. Earth, moon, and planets. 1968. H454

HARVARD BULLETINS IN EDUCATION (1-3 published as Harvard-Newton bulletins)

1 Learned, W. S. A school system as an education laboratory. 1914. H455
2 Ballou, F. W. Scales for the measurement of English composition. 1914. H456
3 Wright, F. W. Bridging the gap: the transfer class. 1915. H457
4 Brewer, J. M. and Kelly, R. W. A selected critical bibliography of vocational guidance. 1917. H458
5 A descriptive bibliography of measurement in elementary subjects, by Holmes and others. 1917. H459
6 Davis, R. Business practice in elementary schools. 1917. H460
7 Irwin, R. B. Sight-saving classes in the public schools. 1920. H461
8 Price, R. R. The financial support of the university of Michigan. 1923. H462
9 Gerry, H. L. A test of high-school chemistry. 1924. H463
10 Brewer, J. M. and others. Mental measurement in education and vocational guidance. 1924. H464
11 Gove, F. S. Religious education on public school time. 1926. H465
12 Nichols, F. G. A new conception of office practice. 1927. H466
13 Kellermann, F. The effect of the world war on European education. 1928. H467
14 Dudley, L. L. The location of city school plants. 1929. H468
15 Cabot, S. P. Secondary education in Germany. 1930. H469
16 Smith, F. C. Curriculum problems in industrial education. 1930. H470
17 Waterman, F. Studies and tests on Vergil's Aeneid. 1930. H471
18 Marshall, M. V. Education as a social force. 1931. H472
19 Seyfert, W. C. School size and school efficiency. 1937. H473
20 Dearborn, W. F. and Rothney, J. W. M. Scholastic, economic and social backgrounds of unemployed youth. 1938. H474
21 Foster, C. R. Editorial treatment of education in the American press. 1938. H475
22 Deemer, W. L. An empirical study of the relative merits of Gregg shorthand and Script shorthand. 1944. H476

HARVARD CITY PLANNING STUDIES.

1 Hubbard, H. V. and others. Airports. 1930. H477
2 Ford, G. B. Building height, bulk, and form. 1931. H478
3 Whitten, R. H. and Adams, T. Neighborhoods of small homes. 1931. H479
4 Bartholomew, H. Urban land uses. 1932. H480
5 Comey, A. C. Transition zoning. 1933. H481
6 Adams, T. The design of

residential areas. 1934. H482
7 Bassett, E. M. Model laws for planning cities, counties, and states. 1935. H483
8 Black, R. V. N. Building lines and reservations for future streets. 1935. H484
9 Malcher, F. The steadyflow traffic system. 1935. H485
10 Hubbard, T. (Kimball) and McNamara, K. Manual of information on city planning and zoning. 1923. Supp.: Bibliography of planning, 1928-1935. 1936. H486
11 Nolen, J. and Hubbard, H. V. Parkways and land values. 1937. H487
12 Walker, M. L. Urban blight and slums. 1938. H488
13 Bettman, A. City and regional planning papers. 1946. H489
14 Branch, M. C. Aerial photography in urban planning and research. 1948. H490
15 Bartholomew, H. Land uses in American cities. 1955. H491
16 Rodwin, L. The British new town's policy. 1956. H492
17 Branch, M. C. City planning and aerial information. 1971. H493
18 Shillaber, C. A library classification for city and regional planning. 1973. H494

HARVARD DOCUMENTS IN THE HISTORY OF EDUCATION.

1 Peirce, C. and Lamson, M. The first state normal school in America, ed. by Norton. 1926. H495
2 Seybolt, R. F. The private schools of colonial Boston, 1635-1775. 1935. H496
3 Ulich, R. A sequence of educational influences. 1935. H497

HARVARD EAST ASIAN MONOGRAPH SERIES

1 Liang, F. The single-whip method (I-t'iao-pien fa) of taxation in China, tr. by Wang-Yü-ch'unan. 1956. H498
2 Hinton, H. C. The grain tribute system of China, 1845-1911. 1956. H499
3 Carlson, E. C. The Kaiping mines (1877-1912). 1957. H500
4 Chao, K. Agrarian policies of mainland China. 1957. H501
5 Snow, E. Random notes on Red China (1936-1945). 1957. H502
6 Beal, E. G. The origin of likin, 1853-1864. 1958. H503
7 Chao, K. Economic planning and organization in mainland China. 2 v. 1959-60. H504
8 Fairbank, J. K., comp. Ch'ing documents. 2 v. 1965. H505
9 Yin, H. and Y. Economic statistics in mainland China, 1949-1957. 1960. H506
10 Franke, W. The reform and abolition of the traditional Chinese examination system. 1961. H507
11 Feuerwerker, A. and Cheng, S. Chinese Communist studies of modern Chinese history. 1961. H508
12 Stanley, C. J. Late Ch'ing finance. 1961. H509
13 Meng, S. M. The Tsungli Yamen. 1962. H510
14 Teng, S. Historiography of the Taiping rebellion. 1962. H511
15 Liu, C. Controversies in modern Chinese intellectual history. 1964. H512
16 Rhoads, E. J. M. and others. The Chinese Red Army, 1927-1963. 1964. H513
17 Nathan, A. J. A history of the China international famine relief commission. 1965. H514
18 King, F. H. H. and Clarke, P. A research guide to China-coast newspapers, 1822-1911. 1965. H515
19 Joffe, E. Party and army. 1965. H516
20 Tsukahira, T. G. Feudal control in Tokugawa Japan. 1966. H517
21 Liu, K., ed. American

missionaries in China. 1966. H518
22 Moseley, G. A Sino-Soviet cultural frontier. 1966. H519
23 Nathan, C. F. Plague prevention and politics in Manchuria, 1910-1931. 1967. H520
24 Bennett, A. A. John Fryer. 1967. H521
25 Friedman, D. J. The road from isolation. 1968. H522
26 LeFevour, E. Western enterprise in late Ch'ing China. 1967. H523
27 Neuhauser, C. Third world politics. 1968. H524
28 Sun, K. C. The economic development of Manchuria in the first half of the twentieth century. 1968. H525
29 Burki, S. J. A study of Chinese Communes. 1969. H526
30 Vincent, J. C. The extraterritorial system in China. 1969. H527
31 Chi, M. S. The Chinese question during the first World War. 1969. H528
32 Phillips, C. J. Protestant America and the pagan world. 1969. H529
33 Pusey, J. R. Wu Han. 1970. H530
34 Cheng, Y. Postal communication in China and its modernization. 1970. H531
35 Blumenthal, T. Saving in postwar Japan. 1970. H532
36 Frost, P. The Bakumatsu currency crisis. 1970. H533
37 Lockwood, S. C. Augustine Heard and Company, 1858-1962. 1971. H534
38 Campbell, R. R. James Duncan Campbell. 1970. H535
39 Cohen, J. A., ed. The dynamics of China's foreign relations. 1970. H536
40 Akimova, V. V. Two years in revolutionary China, 1925-1927, tr. by Levine. 1971. H537
41 Medzini, M. French policy in Japan during the closing years of the Tokugawa regime. 1971. H538
42 The cultural revolution in the provinces. 1971. H539
43 Forsythe, S. A. An American missionary community in China. 1971. H540
44 Reflections on the May fourth movement, ed. by Schwartz. 1972. H541
45 Choe, C. Y. The rule of the Taewŏn'gun. 1972. H542
46 Hall, W. P. J. A bibliographical guide to Japanese research on the Chinese economy, 1958-1970. 1972. H543
47 Gerson, J. J. Horatio Nelson Lay and Sino-British relations, 1854-1864. 1972. H544
48 Bohr, P. R. Famine in China and the missionary. 1972. H545
49 Wilkinson, E. The history of imperial China. 1973. H546
50 Dean, B. China and Great Britain. 1973. H547
51 Carlson, E. C. The Foochow missionaries. 1973. H548
52 Wang, Y. An estimate of the landtax collection in China 1753 and 1908. 1973. H549
55 Vohra, R. Lao She and the Chinese Revolution. 1974. H550

HARVARD EAST ASIAN SERIES (1-10 published as HARVARD EAST ASIAN STUDIES.)

11 Cohen, P. A. China and Christianity. 1963. H551
12 Young, A. N. China and the helping hand, 1937-1945. 1963. H552
13 Chou, T. Research guide to the May fourth movement. 1963. H553
14 Borg, D. The United States and the Far Eastern crisis of 1933-1938. 1964. H554
15 Banno, M. China and the West, 1858-1861. 1964. H555
16 Schwartz, B. I. In search of wealth and power. 1964. H556
17 Hirschmeier, J. The origins of entrepreneurship in

Meiji Japan. 1964. H557
18 Chang, H. Commissioner Lin and the Opium War. 1964. H558
19 King, F. H. H. Money and monetary policy in China, 1845-1895. 1965. H559
20 Young, A. N. China's wartime finance and inflation, 1937-1945. 1965. H560
21 How, C. Foreign investment and economic development in China, 1840-1937. 1965. H561
22 Iriye, A. After imperialism. 1965. H562
23 Akita, G. Foundations of constitutional government in modern Japan, 1868-1900. 1967. H563
24 Pittau, J. Political thought in early Meiji Japan. 1967. H564
25 Rawlinson, J. L. China's struggle for naval development. 1967. H565
26 Welch, H. The practice of Chinese Buddhism, 1900-1950. V. 1. 1967. H566
27 Meisner, M. J. Li Ta-chao and the origins of Chinese Marxism. 1967. H567
28 Lang, O. Pa Chin and his writings. 1967. H568
29 Goldman, M. Literary dissent in Communist China. 1967. H569
30 Totman, C. D. Politics in Tokugawa Bakufu, 1600-1843. 1967. H570
31 Najita, T. Hara Kei in the politics of compromise. 1967. H571
32 The Chinese world order, ed. by Fairbank. 1968. H572
33 Welch, J. J. The Buddhist revival in China. 1968. H573
34 Croizier, R. E. Traditional medicine in modern China. 1968. H574
35 Duus, P. Party rivalry and political change in Taisho Japan. 1968. H575
36 Young, M. B. The rhetoric of empire. 1968. H576
37 Wilson, G. M. Radical nationalist in Japan. 1969. H577
38 Thomson, J. C. While China faced West. 1969. H578
39 Arima, T. The failure of freedom. 1969. H579
40 Hay, S. N. Asian ideas of east and west. 1969. H580
41 Vogel, E. F. Canton under Communism. 1969. H581
42 Furth, C. Ting Wen-chiang. 1970. H582
43 Lee, R. H. G. The Manchurian frontier in Ch'ing history. 1970. H583
44 Matsumoto, S. Motoori Norinaga, 1730-1801. 1970. H584
45 Hao, Y. The comprador in nineteenth century China. 1970. H585
46 Grieder, J. B. Hu Shih and the Chinese renaissance. 1970. H586
47 Myers, R. H. The Chinese peasant economy. 1970. H587
48 Minear, R. H. Japanese tradition and western law. 1970. H588
49 Kuhn, P. A. Rebellion and its enemies in late Imperial China. 1970. H589
50 Rankin, M. B. Early Chinese revolutionaries. 1971. H590
51 Wu, S. H. L. Communication and imperial control in China. 1970. H591
52 Woodside, A. B. Vietnam and the Chinese model. 1971. H592
53 Adshead, S. A. M. The modernization of the Chinese salt administration. 1970. H593
54 Ayers, W. Chang Chih-Tung and educational reform in China. 1971. H594
55 Roy, D. T. Kuo Mo-Jo. 1970. H595
56 Garrett, S. S. Social reformers in urban China. 1971. H596
57 Klein, D. W. and Clark, A. B. Biographic dictionary of Chinese Communism. 1971. H597
58 Schrecker, J. E. Imperialism and Chinese nationalism. 1971. H598
59 Kahn, H. L. Monarchy in the emperor's eyes. 1971. H599

60 Hackett, R. F. Yamagata Aritomo in the rise of modern Japan. 1971. H600
61 Mancall, M. Russia and China. 1971. H601
62 Selden, M. The Yenan way in revolutionary China. 1971. H602
63 Loewen, J. W. The Mississippi Chinese. 1971. H603
64 Chang, H. Liang Ch'i - ch'ao and intellectual transition in China, 1890-1917. 1971. H604
65 Brandt, V. S. R. A Korean village. 1971. H605
66 Rawski, E. S. Agricultural change and the peasant economy of South China. 1972. H606
67 Bunker, G. E. The peace conspiracy. 1971. H607
68 Hall, I. P. Mori Arinori. 1973. H608
69 Welch, H. Buddhism under Mao. 1972. H609
70 Smith, H. Japan's first student radicals. 1972. H610
71 Lee, L. O. The romantic generation of modern Chinese writers. 1973. H611
72 Elison, G. Deus destroyed. 1974. H612
73 Wang, Y. C. Land taxation in China. 1974. H613
74 Kierman, F. A. and Fairbank, J. K., eds. Chinese ways in warfare. 1973. H614
75 Wills, J. E. Pepper, guns, and parleys. 1974. H615
76 Yamamura, K. A study of Samurai income and entrepreneurship. 1974. H616

HARVARD EAST ASIAN STUDIES.

1 Feuerwerker, A. China's early industrialization. 1958. H617
2 Liang, C. Intellectual trends in the Ch'ing period, tr. by Hsü. 1959. H618
3 Liu, J. T. Reform in Sung China. 1959. H619
4 Ho, P. Studies on the population of China, 1368-1953. 1959. H620
5 Hsü, C. China's entrance into the family of nations. 1960. H621
6 Chow, T. The May fourth movement. 1960. H622
7 Ch'ing administrative terms, ed. by Sun. 1961. H623
8 Liu, K-C. Anglo American steamship rivalry in China, 1862-1874. 1962. H624
9 Ch'u, T. Local government in China under the Ch'ing. 1962. H625
10 Communist China, 1955-1959. Foreword by Bowie and Fairbanks. 1962. H626

Continued as the Harvard East Asian Series.

HARVARD ECONOMIC STUDIES.

1 Price, W. H. The English patents of monopoly. 1913. H627
2 Wolfe, A. B. The lodging house problem in Boston. 1906. H628
3 Lewis, G. R. The stannaries, a study of the English tin miner. 1908. H629
4 Daggett, S. Railroad reorganization. 1908. H630
5 Wright, C. W. Wool-growing and the tariff. 1910. H631
6 Holcombe, A. N. Public ownership of telephones on the continent of Europe. 1911. H632
7 Hemmeon, J. C. The history of the British post office. 1912. H633
8 Copeland, M. T. The cotton manufacturing industry of the United States. 1912. H634
9 Usher, A. P. The history of the grain trade in France, 1400-1710. 1913. H635
10 Dewing, A. S. Corporate promotions and reorganizations. 1914. H636
11 Jones, E. The anthracite coal combination in the United States. 1914. H637
12 Taussig, F. W. Some aspects of the tariff question. 1931. H638
13 Gras, N. S. B. The evolution of the English corn market, from the twelfth to the eighteenth century.

1351-1500. 1936. H677
52 Hunt, B. C. The development of the business corporation in England, 1800-1867. 1936. H678
53 Harris, S. E. Exchange depreciation. 1936. H679
54 Cassels, J. M. A study of fluid milk prices. 1937. H680
55 Hoover, E. M., Jr. Location theory and the shoe and leather industries. 1937. H681
56 Maxwell, J. A. Federal subsidies to the provincial governments in Canada. 1937. H682
57 Oakes, E. E. Studies in Massachusetts town finance. 1937. H683
58 Wallace, D. H. Market control in the aluminum industry. 1937. H684
59 Abbott, C. C. The New York bond market, 1920-1930. 1937. H685
60 Greef, A. O. The commercial paper house in the United States. 1938. H686
61 Roberts, C. The Middlesex canal, 1793-1860. 1938. H687
62 Welk, W. G. Fascist economic policy. 1938. H688
63 Sweezy, P. M. Monopoly and competition in the English coal trade. 1550-1850. 1938. H689
64 Wood, E. English theories of central banking control, 1819-1858. 1939. H690
65 Bullock, C. J. Politics, finance, and consequences. 1939. H691
66 Poole, K. E. German financial policies, 1932-1939. 1939. H692
67 Triffin, R. Monopolistic competition and general equilibrium theory. 1940. H693
68 Guthrie, J. A. The newsprint paper industry. 1941. H694
69 Ellis, H. S. Exchange control in central Europe. 1941. H695
70 Cole, A. H. and Williamson, H. F. The American carpet manufacture. 1941. H696
71 Hutchins, J. G. B. The American maritime industries and public policy, 1789-1914. 1941. H697
72 Wright, D. M. The creation of purchasing power. 1942. H698
73 Frickey, E. Economic fluctuations in the United States. 1942. H699
74 Berry, T. S. Western prices before 1861. 1943. H700
75 Usher, A. P. The early history of deposit banking in Mediterranean Europe. 1943. H701
76 Bergson, A. The structure of soviet wages. 1944. H702
77 Roberts, W. A. State taxation of metallic deposits. 1944. H703
78 Burgin, M. The economic aspects of Argentine federalism, 1820-1852. 1946. H704
79 Maxwell, J. A. The fiscal impact of federalism in the United States. 1946. H705
80 Samuelson, P. A. Foundations of economic analysis. 1947. H706
81 Hamilton, E. J. War and prices in Spain, 1651-1800. 1947. H707
82 Frickey, E. Production in the United States, 1860-1914. 1947. H708
83 Morgan, T. Hawaii, a century of economic change, 1778-1876. 1948. H709
84 Duerr, W. A. The economic problems of forestry in the Appalachian Region. 1949. H710
85 Chang, P. Agriculture and industrialization. 1949. H711
86 Davis, P. The development of the American glass industry. 1949. H712
87 Duesenberry, J. S. Income, saving, and the theory of consumer behavior. 1949. H713
88 Wallich, H. C. Monetary problems of an export economy, the Cuban experience, 1914-1947. 1950. H714
89 Mighell, R. L. and Black, J. D. Interregional

competition in agriculture. 1951. H715
90 Keyes, L. S. Federal control of entry into air transportation. 1951. H716
91 Bressler, R. G. City milk distribution. 1952. H717
92 Malenbaum, W. The world wheat economy, 1885-1939. 1953. H718
93 Sanderson, F. H. Methods of crop forecasting. 1954. H719
94 White, D. J. The New England fishing industry. 1954. H720
95 Heckscher, E. F. An economic history of Sweden, tr. by Ohlin. 1954. H721
96 Taylor, O. H. Economics and liberalism. 1955. H722
97 Davies, M. (Gay). The enforcement of English apprenticeship. 1956. H723
98 Manne, A. S. Scheduling of petroleum refinery operations. 1956. H724
99 Kaysen, C. United States v. United Shoe Machinery Corporation. 1956. H725
100 Mason, E. S. Economic concentration and the monopoly problem. 1957. H726
101 Hargreaves, M. W. M. Dry farming in the northern Great Plains, 1900-1925. 1956. H727
102 Meyer, J. R. and Kuh, E. The investment decision. 1957. H728
103 Henderson, J. M. The efficiency of the coal industry. 1958. H729
104 Eckstein, O. Water-resources development. 1958. H730
105 Haberler, G. Prosperity and depression. 1958. H731
106 Bourneuf, A. Norway, the planned revival. 1958. H732
107 Meyer, J. R. and others. The economics of competition in the transportation industries. 1959. H733
108 Stovel, J. A. Canada in the world economy. 1959. H734
109 Klein, B. H. Germany's economic preparations for war. 1959. H735
110 Lippitt, V. G. Determinants of consumer demand for house furnishings and equipment. 1959. H736
111 Black, J. D., ed. Economics for agriculture. 1959. H737
112 Cave, R. E. and Holton, R. H. The Canadian economy. 1959. H738
113 Adelman, M. A. A & P. 1959. H739
114 Tun, T. Theory of markets. 1960. H740
115 Caves, R. E. Trade and economic structure. 1960. H741
116 Kenen, P. B. British monetary policy and the balance of payments, 1951-1957. 1960. H742
117 Smith, V. L. Investment and production. 1961. H743
118 Nurkse, R. Equilibrium and growth in the world economy, ed. by Haberler and Stern. 1961. H744
119 Sylos Labini, P. Oligopoly and technical progress, tr. by Henderson. 1962. H745
120 Caves, R. E. Air transport and its regulators. 1962. H746
121 Travis, W. P. The theory of trade and protection. 1964. H747
122 Moyer, R. Competition in the midwestern coal industry. 1964. H748
123 Vanek, J. General equilibrium of international discrimination. 1965. H749
124 Olson, M. The logic of collective bargaining. 1965. H750
125 McGuire, M. C. Secrecy and the arms race. 1965. H751
126 Houthakker, H. S. and Taylor, L. D. Consumer demand in the United States. 1929-1970. 1965. H752
127 Fishlow, A. American railroads and the transformation of the antebellum economy. 1966. H753
128 Perkins, D. H. Market

control and planning in Communist China. 1966. H754
129 Wonnacott, R. J. Free trade between the United States and Canada. 1967. H755
130 Officer, L. H. An econometric model of Canada under the fluctuating exchange rate. 1968. H756
131 McGouldrick, P. F. New England textiles in the nineteenth century. 1968. H757
132 Goodhart, C. A. E. The New York money market and finance of trade. 1969. H758
133 Bowles, S. Planning educational systems for economic growth. 1969. H759
134 MacEwan, A. Development alternatives in Pakistan. 1971. H760
135 Caves, R. E. and Reuber, G. L. Capital transfers and economic policy. 1971. H761
136 Chenery, H. B., ed. Studies in development planning. 1971. H762
137 Repetto, R. C. Time in India's development programmes. 1971. H763
138 Spooner, F. C. The international economy and monetary movement in France, 1493-1725. 1972. H764
139 Solow, B. L. The land question and the Irish economy, 1870-1903. 1971. H765
140 Metzler, L. A. Collected papers. 1973. H766
141 Ofer, G. The service sector in Soviet economic growth. 1973. H767
142 McCloskey, D. N. Economic maturity and entrepreneurial decline. 1973. H768
143 Spence, A. Market signaling. 1974. H769

HARVARD ENGLISH STUDIES

1 The interpretation of narrative, ed. by Bloomfield. 1970. H770
2 Twentieth-century literature, ed. by Brower. 1971. H771
3 Levin, H., ed. Veins of humor. 1972. H772
4 Uses of literature, ed. by Engel. 1973. H773
5 Benson, L. D., ed. The learned and the lewed. 1974. H774

HARVARD GERMANIC STUDIES.

1 Haywood, B. Novales. 1959. H775
2 Paff, W. J. The geographical and ethnic names of bidriks saga. 1959. H776
3 Schwarz, E. Hofmannsthal und Calderon. 1962. H777
4 Simon, E. Neidhart von Reuental. 1966. H778

HARVARD HISTORICAL MONOGRAPHS.

1 Ferguson, W. S. Athenian tribal cycles in the Hellenistic age. 1932. H779
2 Teignmouth, J. S. The private record of an Indian governor-generalship. 1933. H780
3 Hedges, J. B. The federal railway land subsidy policy of Canada. 1934. H781
4 Mosely, P. E. Russian diplomacy and the opening of the Eastern question in 1838 and 1839. 1934. H782
5 Hanke, L. The first social experiments in America. 1935. H783
6 Squires, J. D. British propaganda at home and in the United States, 1914-1917. 1935. H784
7 Scott, F. D. Bernadotte and the fall of Napoleon. 1935. H785
8 Greer, D. The incidence of the terror during the French Revolution. 1935. H786
9 Brinton, C. C. French revolutionary legislation on illegitimacy, 1789-1804. 1936. H787
10 Gleason, S. E. An ecclesiastical barony of the Middle Ages, the bishopric of Bayeux, 1066-1204. 1936. H788
11 Gardner, C. S. Chinese traditional historiography.

1938. H789
12 Strayer, J. R. and Taylor, C. H. Studies in early French taxation. 1939. H790
13 Newhall, R. A. Muster and review, a problem of English military administration, 1420-1440. 1940. H791
14 Morison, S. E. Portuguese voyages to America in the fifteenth century. 1940. H792
15 Gilmore, M. P. Argument from Roman law in political thought, 1200-1600. 1941. H793
16 Whitaker, A. P. The Huancavelica mercury mine. 1941. H794
17 Miller, B. The Palace school of Muhammad the Conqueror. 1941. H795
18 Boyd, C. E. A Cistercian nunery in mediaeval Italy, the story of Rifreddo in Saluzzo, 1220-1300. 1943. H796
19 Odegaard, C. E. Vassi and fideles in the Carolingian empire. 1945. H797
20 Keeney, B. C. Judgment by peers. 1949. H798
21 Radkey, O. H. The election to the Russian Constituent Assembly of 1917. 1950. H799
22 Dennett, D. C. Conversion and the poll tax in early Islam. 1950. H800
23 Merk, F. Albert Gallatin and the Oregon problem. 1950. H801
24 Greer, D. M. The incidence of the emigration during the French Revolution. 1951. H802
25 Wright, L. E. Alterations of the words of Jesus, as quoted in the literature of the second century. 1952. H803
26 Levenson, J. R. Liang Ch'i-ch'ao and the mind of modern China. 1953. H804
27 Jansen, M. B. The Japanese and Sun Yet-Sen. 1954. H805
28 Walcott, R. English politics in the early eighteenth century. 1956. H806
29 Noland, A. The founding of the French Socialist party, 1893-1905. 1956. H807
30 Graubard, S. R. British Labour and the Russian Revolution, 1917-1924. 1956. H808
31 Koehl, R. L. RKFDV. 1957. H809
32 Crosby, G. R. Disarmament and peace in British politics, 1914-1919. 1957. H810
33 Bouwsma, W. J. Concordia mundi. 1957. H811
34 Rosenberg, H. Bureaucracy, aristocracy and autocracy. 1958. H812
35 MacCaffrey, W. Exeter, 1540-1640. 1958. H813
36 Vyverberg, H. Historical pessimism in the French Enlightenment. 1958. H814
37 Rice, E. F. The Renaissance idea of wisdom. 1958. H815
38 Eisenstein, E. L. The first professional revolutionist. 1959. H816
39 Page, S. W. The formation of the Baltic States. 1959. H817
40 Hays, S. P. Conservation and the gospel of efficiency. 1959. H818
41 Wade, R. C. The urban frontier. 1959. H819
42 Wright, H. M. New Zealand, 1769-1840. 1959. H820
43 Fischer-Galati, S. A. Ottoman imperialism and German Protestantism, 1521-1555. 1959. H821
44 King, J. C. Foch versus Clemenceau. 1960. H822
45 Brody, D. Steelworkers in America. 1960. H823
46 Leiby, J. Carroll Wright and labor reform. 1960. H824
47 Craig, A. M. Chōshu in the Meiji restoration. 1961. H825
48 Berman, M. John Fiske. 1961. H826
49 Southgate, W. M. John Jewel and the problem of doctrinal authority. 1962. H827
50 Bennett, E. W. Germany and the diplomacy of the financial crisis, 1931. 1962. H828

51 Perry, T. W. Public opinion, propaganda, and politics in eighteenth-century England. 1962. H829
52 MacMullen, R. Soldier and civilian in the later Roman Empire. 1963. H830
53 Gray, C. M. Copyhold, equity, and the common law. 1963. H831
54 Black, E. C. The association. 1963. H832
55 Drescher, S. Tocqueville and England. 1964. H833
56 Walker, M. Germany and the emigration, 1816-1885. 1964. H834
57 Lukashevich, S. Ivan Aksakov, 1823-1886. 1965. H835
58 Raack, R. C. The fall of Stein. 1965. H836
59 Wood, C. T. The French apanages and the Capetian monarchy, 1224-1328. 1966. H837
60 Holt, L. J. Congressional insurgents and the party system, 1909-1916. 1967. H838
61 Hitchins, K. The Rumanian national movement in Transylvania, 1780-1849. 1969. H839
62 Greenberg, L. M. Sisters of liberty. 1971. H840
63 Spitzer, A. B. Old hatreds and young hopes. 1971. H841
64 Hughes, J. M. To the Maginot Line. 1971. H842
65 Molho, A. Florentine public finances in the early Renaissance, 1400-1433. 1971. H843
66 Dawson, P. Provincial magistrates and revolutionary politics in France, 1789-1795. 1972. H844
67 Callahan, R. The East India Company and army reform, 1783-1798. 1972. H845
68 James, F. G. Ireland in the Empire. 1973. H846

HARVARD HISTORICAL MONOGRAPHS (Ginn)

1 Mason, E. C. The veto power. 1891. H847
2 Hart, A. B. Introduction to the study of federal government. 1891. H848

HARVARD HISTORICAL STUDIES.

1 Dubois, W. E. B. The suppression of the African slave trade to the United States of America, 1638-1870. 1896. H849
2 Harding, S. B. The contest over the ratification of the Federal constitution in the state of Massachusetts. 1896. H850
3 Houston, D. F. A critical study of nullification in South Carolina. 1896. H851
4 Dallinger, F. W. Nominations for elective office in the United States. 1903. H852
5 Gross, C. A bibliography of British municipal history. 1897. H853
6 Smith, T. C. The Liberty and Free soil parties in the Northwest. 1897. H854
7 Greene, E. B. The provincial governor in the English colonies of North America. 1898. H855
8 Lapsley, G. T. The county palatine of Durham. 1900. H856
9 Cross, A. L. The Anglican episcopate and the American colonies. 1902. H857
10 Hatch, L. C. The administration of the American revolutionary army. 1904. H858
11 Fish, C. R. The civil service and the patronage. 1905. H859
12 Duniway, C. A. The development of freedom of the press in Massachusetts. 1906. H860
13 Munro, W. B. The seignorial system in Canada. 1907. H861
14 Morris, W. A. The frankpledge system. 1910. H862
15 Kimball, E. The public life of Joseph Dudley. 1911. H863
16 Carolina Maria, consort of Ferdinand I. Mémoire de Marie Caroline..., ed. by Johnston. 1912. H864
17 Barrington, W. W. B. The Barrington-Bernard correspondence, ed. by Channing

and Coolidge. 1912. H865
18 Lybyer, A. H. The government of the Ottoman empire in the time of Suleiman the Magnificent. 1913. H866
19 Buck, S. J. The Granger movement. 1913. H867
20 Hemmeon, M. de W. Burgage tenure in mediaeval England. 1914. H868
21 New York (Colony). An abridgement of the Indian affairs contained in four-folio volumes, ed. by McIlwain. 1915. H869
22 Gray, H. L. English field systems. 1915. H870
23 Lord, R. H. The second partition of Poland. 1915. H871
24 Haskins, C. H. Norman institutions. 1918. H872
25 David, C. W. Robert Curthose. 1920. H873
26 Fuller, J. V. Bismarck's diplomacy at its zenith. 1922. H874
27 Haskins, C. H. Studies in the history of mediaeval science. 1927. H875
28 Lord, R. H. The origins of the war of 1870. 1924. H876
29 Perkins, D. The Monroe doctrine, 1823-26. 1932. H877
30 Langer, W. L. The Franco-Russian alliance, 1890-94. 1929. H878
31 Simpson, G. Fur trade and empire, ed. by Merk. 1931. H879
32 Steefel, L. D. The Schleswig-Holstein question. 1932. H880
33 Vander Velde, L. G. The Presbyterian churches and the federal Union, 1861-69. 1932. H881
34 Gray, H. L. The influence of the Commons on early legislation. 1932. H882
35 McKay, D. C. The National workshops. 1933. H883
36 Clark, C. W. Franz Joseph and Bismarck. 1934. H884
37 Hussey, R. D. The Caracas company, 1728-1784. 1934. H885
38 Lee, D. E. Great Britain and the Cyprus convention policy of 1878. 1934. H886
39 Doolin, P. R. The Fronde. 1935. H887
40 Wilson, A. M. French foreign policy during the administration of Cardinal Fleury, 1726-1743. 1936. H888
41 Deutsch, H. C. The genesis of Napoleonic imperialism. 1938. H889
42 Helmreich, E. C. The diplomacy of the Balkan wars, 1912-13. 1938. H890
43 Imlah, A. H. Lord Ellenborough. 1939. H891
44 Scramuzza, V. M. The Emperor Claudius. 1940. H892
45 Leopold, R. W. Robert Dale Owen. 1940. H893
46 Graham, G. S. Sea power and British North America, 1783-1820. 1941. H894
47 Church, W. F. Constitutional thought in sixteenth-century France. 1941. H895
48 Hexter, J. H. The reign of King Pym. 1941. H896
49 Rupp, G. H. A wavering friendship. 1941. H897
50 Handlin, O. Boston's immigrants, 1790-1865. 1941. H898
51 Bailey, F. E. British policy and the Turkish reform movement. 1942. H899
52 Sirich, J. B. The revolutionary committees in the departments of France. 1943. H900
53 Schwarz, H. F. The Imperial privy council in the seventeenth century. 1943. H901
54 Abell, A. I. The urban impact on American protestantism. 1943. H902
55 Furber, H. John Company at work. 1948. H903
56 Howe, W. The Mining Guild of New Spain and its Tribunal General. 1949. H904
57 Gleason, J. H. The genesis of Russophobia in Great Britain. 1950. H905
58 Gillispie, C. C. Genesis and geology. 1951. H906
59 Humphrey, R. D. Georges Sorel. 1951. H907

60 Waite, R. G. L. Vanguard of nazism. 1952. H908
61 Riasanovsky, N. V. Russian and the West in the teaching of the Slavophiles. 1952. H909
62-63 Fairbank, J. K. Trade and diplomacy on the China coast. 2 v. 1953. H910
64 Ford, F. L. Robe and sword. 1953. H911
65 Schorske, C. E. German social democracy, 1905-1917. 1955. H912
66 Davies, W. E. Patriotism on parade. 1955. H913
67 Schwartz, H. Samuel Gridley Howe, 1801-1876. 1956. H914
68 Lyon, B. D. From fief to indenture. 1957. H915
69 Stein, S. J. Vassouras. 1957. H916
70 McGann, T. F. Argentina, the United States, and the Inter-American system, 1880-1914. 1957. H917
71 May, E. R. The World War and American isolation. 1959. H918
72 Blake, J. B. Public health in the town of Boston, 1630-1822. 1959. H919
73 Labaree, B. W. Patriots and partisans. 1962. H920
74 Sedgwick, A. C. The ralliement in French politics, 1890-1898. 1965. H921
75 Pottinger, E. A. Napoleon III and the German crisis. 1966. H922
76 Goffart, W. The Le Mans forgeries. 1966. H923
77 Resnick, D. P. The white terror and the political reaction after Waterloo. 1966. H924
78 Peter the Venerable. Letters, ed. by Constable. 2 v. 1967. H925
79 Eastman, L. E. Throne and mandarians. 1967. H926
80 Matusow, A. J. Farm policies and politics in the Truman years. 1967. H927
81 Bankwitz, P. C. F. Maxime Weygand and civil-military relations in modern France. 1968. H928
82 Wilcox, D. J. The development of Florentine humanistic historiography in the fifteenth century. 1969. H929
83 Padberg, J. W. Colleges in controversy. 1969. H930
84 Brewslow, M. A. A mirror of England. 1970. H931
85 Higonnet, P. L. R. Pont-de-Montvert. 1971. H932
86 Halpern, P. G. The Mediterranean naval situation. 1970. H933
87 Ruigh, R. E. The Parliament of 1624. 1971. H934
88 Laiou, A. E. Constantinople and the Latins. 1972. H935
89 Nugent, D. Ecumenism in the age of the Reformation. 1974. H936
90 McCaughey, R. A. Josiah Quincy. 1974. H937

HARVARD KEATS MEMORIAL STUDIES.

1 Rollins, H. E. Keats' reputation in America to 1848. 1946. H938

HARVARD LEGAL STUDIES.

Haar, C. M. Land planning law in a free society. 1951. H939

HARVARD MIDDLE EASTERN MONOGRAPHS.

1 Asfour, E. Y. Syria. 1959. H940
2 Upton, J. M. The history of modern Iran. 1960. H941
3 Harrell, R. S. A linguistic analysis of Egyptian radio Arabic. 1960. H942
4 Beling, W. A. Pan-Arabism and labor. 1960. H943
5 Langley, K. M. The industrialization of Iraq. 1961. H944
6 Fuller, A. H. Buarij. 1961. H945
7 Cezzar, A. Ottoman Egypt in the eighteenth century. 1962. H946
8 Prothero, E. T. Child rearing in Lebanon. 1961. H947

9 Gordon, D. C. North Africa's French legacy, 1954-1962. 1962. H948
10 Blanc, H. Communal dialects in Baghdad. 1964. H949
11 Husayn Afandi. Ottoman Egypt in the age of the French Revolution, ed. by Shaw. 1964. H950
12 Stewart, C. F. The economy of Morocco, 1912-1962. 1964. H951
13 Kanovsky, E. The economy of the Israeli kibbutz. 1966. H952
14 Yamak, L. Z. The Syrian Social Nationalist Party. 1966. H953
15 Gendzier, I. L. The practical visions of Ya'qub Sanu'. 1966. H954
16 al-Tunisi, K. al-D. The surest path, ed. by Brown. 1967. H955
17 Robinson, R. D. High-level manpower in economic development. 1967. H956
18 Halstead, J. P. Rebirth of a nation. 1968. H957
19 Gordon, D. C. Women of Algeria. 1968. H958
20 Williams, J. R. The youth of Haouch el Harimi. 1968. H959
21 Altoma, S. J. The problem of diglossia in Arabic. 1969. H960
22 Klausner, C. L. The Seljuk Vezirate. 1973. H961

HARVARD MIDDLE EASTERN STUDIES.

1 Finnie, D. H. Desert enterprise. 1958. H962
2 Meyer, A. J. Middle Eastern capitalism. 1959. H963
3 Halpern, B. The idea of the Jewish state. 1961. H964
4 Rivlin, H. A. B. The agricultural policy of Muhammed 'Alī in Egypt. 1961. H965
5 Safran, N. Egypt in search of political community. 1961. H966
6 Meyer, A. J. and Vassiliou, S. G. The economy of Cyprus. 1962. H967
7 Sā'igh, Y. A. Entrepreneurs of Lebanon. 1962. H968
8 Polk, W. R. The opening of South Lebanon, 1788-1840. 1963. H969
9 Robinson, R. D. The First Turkish Republic. 1963. H970
10 Sanjian, A. K. The Armenian communities in Syria under Ottoman dominion. 1965. H971
11 Lapidus, I. M. Muslim cities in the later Middle Ages. 1966. H972
12 Gulick, J. Tripoli. 1967. H973
13 Finnie, D. H. Pioneers East. 1967. H974
14 Fernea, R. A. Shaykh and Effendi. 1969. H975
15 Shaw, S. J. Between old and new. 1971. H976
16 Bulliet, R. W. The patricians of Nishapur. 1972. H977

HARVARD MONOGRAPHS IN APPLIED SCIENCE.

1 Le Corbeiller, P. Matrix analysis of electric networks. 1950. H978
2 Leet, L. D. Earth waves. 1950. H979
3 Westergaard, H. M. Theory of electricity and plasticity. 1952. H980
4 Garrett, C. G. B. Magnetic cooling. 1954. H981
5 Hunt, F. V. Electroacoustics. 1954. H982
6 Pearson, C. E. Theoretical elasticity. 1959. H983
7 King, R. W. P. and Wu, T. The scattering and diffraction of waves. 1959. H984
8 Oettinger, A. G. Automatic language translation. 1960. H985
9 Gomer, R. Field emission and field ionization. 1961. H986

HARVARD MONOGRAPHS IN THE HISTORY OF SCIENCE

Dannenfeldt, K. H. Leonhard Rauwolf. 1968. H987

Descartes, R. Treatise on man, tr. by Hall. 1972. H988
Elkana, Y. Discussion of the conservation of energy. 1974. H989
Kennedy, E. S. and Pingree, D. The astrological history of Māshā Allāh. 1970. H990
Leicester, H. M. Development of biochemical concepts from ancient to modern times. 1974. H991
Sivin, M. Chinese alchemy: preliminary studies. 1968. H992
Swazey, J. P. Reflexes and motor integration. 1969. H993
Thackray, A. Atoms and powers. 1970. H994
____. John Dalton. 1972. H995

HARVARD ORIENTAL SERIES.

1 Arya-Sūra. The Jātaka-mālā, ed. by Kern. 1914. H996
2 Kapila. The Sāmkhya-pravacana-bhāsya, ed. by Garbe. 1895. H997
3 Warren, H. C. Buddhism in translations. 1922. H998
4 Raja-sekhara. Raja-cekhara's Karpūra-mañjarī, ed. by Konow. 1901. H999
5-6 Saunaka. The Bṛhad-devata attributed to Saunaka, ed. by Macdonell. 2 v. 1904. H1000
7-8 Vedas. Atharvaveda. The Atharva-veda Samhitā, tr. by Whitney. 1905. H1001
9 Sūdraka. The little clay cart, tr. by Ryder. 1905. H1002
10 Bloomfield, M. A Vedic concordance. 1906. H1003
11 Pañchatantra. The Panchatantra, ed. by Hertel. 1908. H1004
12 Hertel, J. The Panchatantra-text of Purnabhadra. 1912. H1005
13 Pañchatantra. The Panchatantra-text of Purnabhadra, ed. by Hertel. 1912. H1006
14 ____. The Panchatantra, ed. by Hertel. 1915. H1007
15 Bhāravi. Bharavi's poem, Kiratarjuniya, tr. by Cappeller. 1912. H1008
16 Kālidāsa. Kalidasa's Sakuntala, ed. by Pischel. 1922. H1009
17 Patañjali. The Yoga system of Patañjali, tr. by Woods. 1914. H1010
18-19 Veda. Yajurveda-Taittirīya-samhitā. The Veda of the Black Yajus school, tr. by Keith. 2 v. 1914. H1011
20 Vedas. Rigveda. Selections. Rig-veda repetitions ...with critical discussion by Bloomfield. 2 v. 1916. H1012
21 Bhavabhūti. Rama's later history, tr. by Belvalkar. 1915. H1013
24 Same as no. 20. V. 2. 1916. H1014
25 Aitareyabrāhmana. Rigveda Brahmanas, tr. by Keith. 1920. H1015
26-27 Vikrama-carita. Vikrama's adventures, tr. by Edgerton. 2 v. 1926. H1016
28-30 Dhammapadattakathā. Buddhist legends, tr. by Burlingame. 3 v. 1921. H1017
31-32 Keith, A. B. The religion and philosophy of the Veda and Upanishads. 2 v. 1925. H1018
33-36 Vedas. Rigveda German. Der Rig-Veda aus dem Sanskrit in Deutsche übers und mit einem laufenden Kommentar versehen von Geldner. 4 v. 1952-57. H1019
37 Suttanipāta. Buddha's teachings, ed. by Chalmers. 1932. H1020
38-39 Mahābhārata. Bhagavadgitā. The Bhagavad-gitā, ed. by Edgerton. 2 v. 1944-52. H1021
40 Ingalls, D. H. H. Materials for the study of Navya-Nyāya logic. 1951. H1022
41 Buddhaghosa. Visuddimagga of Buddhaghosâcariya, ed. by Warren. 1950. H1023
42 Vidyākara, comp. The Subhāsitaratnakosa, ed. by Kosambi and Gokdale. 1957. H1024
43 Sankarācārya. The

Saundaryalahari, ed. by Brown. 1958. H1025
44 Vidyākara, comp. An anthology of Sanskrit court poetry: Vidyākara's Subhāsitaratnakosa, tr. by Ingalls. 1965. H1026
45 Frye, R. N., ed. The histories of Nishopur. 1965. H1027
46 Matilal, B. K. The Navya-Nyāya doctrine of negotiation. 1968. H1028
47 Dignāga. Dignaga, on perception, tr. by Hattori. 1968. H1029
22, 23 not published.

HARVARD POLITIC STUDIES.

Beer, S. H. The city of reason. 1949. H1030
Benson, G. C. S. The administration of the civil service in Massachusetts. 1935. H1031
Bischoff, R. F. Nazi conquest through German culture. 1942. H1032
Brecht, A. and Glaser, C. The art and technique of administration in German ministries. 1940. H1033
Cherington, C. R. The regulation of railroad abandonments. 1948. H1034
Claude, I. L. National minorities. 1955. H1035
Derthick, M. The National Guard in politics. 1965. H1036
Eckstein, H. The English health service. 1958. H1037
Einaudi, M. The physiocratic doctrine of judicial control. 1938. H1038
Elliott, W. E. Y. The rise of guardian democracy. 1974. H1039
Elsbree, H. L. Interstate transmission of electric power. 1931. H1040
Fainsod, M. International socialism and the world war. 1935. H1041
Fenno, R. F. The President's Cabinet. 1959. H1042
Garceau, O. The political life of the American medical association. 1941. H1043
Godine, M. R. The labor problem in the public service. 1951. H1044
Goodsell, C. T. Administration of a revolution. 1965. H1045
Hanson, D. W. From kingdom to commonwealth. 1970. H1046
Herring, E. P. Federal commissioners. 1936. H1047
Johnson, G. G. The Treasury and monetary policy, 1933-38. 1939. H1048
Kramnick, I. Bolingsbroke and his circle. 1968. H1049
Lakoff, S. A. Equality in political philosophy. 1964. H1050
Larkin, J. D. The President's control of the tariff. 1936. H1051
Maass, A. A. Muddy waters, the Army Engineers and the Nation's rivers. 1951. H1052
McCloskey, R. G. American conservatism in the age of enterprise. 1951. H1053
Maddox, W. P. Foreign relations in British Labour politics. 1934. H1054
Mayhew, D. R. Party loyalty among congressmen. 1966. H1055
Nichols, J. A. Germany after Bismarck. 1958. H1056
Palamountain, J. C. The politics of distribution. 1955. H1057
Safran, N. Egypt in search of political community. 1961. H1058
Sigmund, P. E. Nicholas of Cusa and medieval political thought. 1963. H1059
Sly, J. F. Town government in Massachusetts, 1620-1930. 1930. H1060
Smith, B. L. R. The Rand Corporation. 1966. H1061
Somers, H. M. Presidential agency: the OWMR. 1950. H1061a
Spiro, H. J. The politics of German codetermination. 1958. H1062
Thurston, J. Government proprietary corporations in the English-speaking countries. 1937. H1063
Ulam, A. B. Philosophical foundations of English socialism. 1951. H1064

Watkins, F. M. The failure of constitutional emergency powers under the German republic. 1939. H1065
Wild, P. S. Sanctions and treaty enforcement. 1934. H1066
Wright, B. F. American interpretations of natural law. 1931. H1067

HARVARD PUBLICATIONS IN MUSIC

1 Holborne, A. The complete works of Anthony Holborne, ed. by Kanazawa. V. 1. 1967. H1068
2 Sammartini, G. B. The symphonies of G. B. Sammartini, ed. by Churgin. V. 1. 1968. H1069
3-4 Francesco Canova da Milano. The lute music of Francesco Canova da Milano, 1497-1543, ed. by Ness. 2 v. 1970. H1070
5 Same as no. 1. V. 2. 1972. H1071
6 Scarlatti, O. The operas of Alessandro Scarlatti, ed. by Grout. 1972. H1072

HARVARD SEMITIC MONOGRAPHS

1 Shenkel, J. D. Chronology and recensional development in the Greek text of kings. 1968. H1073
2 Purvis, J. D. The Samaritan Pentateuch and the origin of the Samaritan sect. 1968. H1074
3 O'Connell, K. G. The Theodotionic revision of the Book of Exodus. 1972. H1075
4 Clifford, R. J. The cosmic mountain in Canaan and the Old Testament. 1972. H1076
5 Miller, P. D. The divine warrior in early Israel. 1973. H1077
6 Janzen, J. G. Studies in the text of Jeremiah. 1973. H1078

HARVARD SEMITIC SERIES

1-2 Reisner, G. A. Harvard excavations at Samaria. 2 v. 1924. H1079
3-4 Harvard Univ. Sumerian tablets in the Harvard Semitic Museum. 2 v. 1915. H1080
5 Harvard Univ. Excavations at Nuzi conducted by the Semitic Museum and the Fogg Art Museum. V. 1. 1929. H1081
6 Wolfson, H. A. Crescas' critique of Aristotle. 1929. H1082
7 Never published.
8 Pappus. The commentary of Pappus on book x, y of Euclid's Elements, by Junge and Thomson. 1930. H1083
9-10 Same as no. 5. V. 2, 3. 1932-33. H1084
11 Belkin, S. Philo and the oral law. 1940. H1085
12 Epstein, L. M. Marriage laws in the Bible and the Talmud. 1942. H1086
13-16 Same as no. 5. V. 4-7. 1942-58. H1087
17 Mantel, H. Studies in the history of the Sandhedrin. 1961. H1088
18 Twersky, I. Rabad of Posquiéres. 1962. H1089
19 Same as no. 5. V. 8. 1962. H1090
20 Peckham, J. B. The development of the late Phoenician scripts. 1968. H1091
21 Jacobsen, T. Toward the image of Tammuz and other essays on Mesopotamian history and culture, ed. by Moran. 1970. H1092

HARVARD SERIES OF LEGAL BIBLIOGRAPHIES.

1 Calhoun, G. and Delamere, C. A working bibliography of Greek law. 1927. H1093
2 Keitt, L. An annotated bibliography of bibliographies of statutory materials of the United States. 1934. H1094
3 Setaro, F. C. A bibliography of the writings of Roscoe Pound. 1942. H1095

HARVARD SOCIOLOGICAL STUDIES

1 Carver, T. N. The essential

factors of social evolution. 1935. H1096
2 Sorokin, P. A. and Berger, C. Q. Time-budgets of human behavior. 1939. H1097
3 Timasheff, N. S. An introduction to the sociology of law. 1939. H1098
4 Firey, W. I. Land use in central Boston. 1947. H1099

HARVARD STUDIES IN ADMINISTRATIVE LAW.

1 Patterson, E. W. The insurance commissioner in the United States. 1927. H1100
2 Dickinson, J. Administrative justice and the supremacy of law in the United States. 1927. H1101
3 Stephens, H. M. Administrative tribunals and the rules of evidence. 1933. H1102
4 Willis, J. The parliamentary powers of English government departments. 1933. H1103
5 McFarland, C. Judicial control of the Federal trade commission and the Interstate commerce commission. 1933. H1104
6 Jaffe, L. J. Judicial aspects of foreign relations. 1933. H1105

HARVARD STUDIES IN AMERICAN-EAST ASIAN RELATIONS

1 May, E. R. and Thomson, J. C. American-East Asian relations. 1970. H1106
2 Iriye, A. Pacific estrangement. 1972. H1107
3 Gulick, E. V. Peter Parker and the opening of China. 1973. H1108
4 Stanley, P. W. A nation in the making. 1974. H1109
5 Pelz, S. E. Race to Pearl Harbor. 1974. H1110

HARVARD STUDIES IN BUSINESS HISTORY

1 Porter, K. W. John Jacob Astor. 1931. H1111
2 Larson, H. M. Jay Cooke. 1936. H1112
3 Porter, K. W., ed. The Jacksons and the Lees. 1937. H1113
4 Gras, N. S. B. The Massachusetts First National Bank of Boston, 1784-1934. 1937. H1114
5 Hower, R. M. The history of an advertising agency: N. W. Ayer & Son at work. 1949. H1115
6 Stalson, J. O. Marketing life insurance. 1942. H1116
7 Hower, R. M. History of Macy's of New York. 1943. H1117
8 Gibb, G. S. The whitesmiths of Taunton: a history of Reed & Barton. 1943. H1118
9 Popple, C. S. Development of two bank groups in the central Northwest. 1944. H1119
10 Baxter, W. T. The House of Hancock: business in Boston, 1724-1775. 1945. H1120
11 Moore, C. W. Timing a century: history of the Waltham Watch Company. 1945. H1121
12 Larson, H. M. Guide to business history: materials for the study of American business history and suggestions for their use. 1948. H1122
13 Knowlton, E. H. (Puffer). Pepperell's progress: history of a cotton textile company. 1948. H1123
14 Hidy, R. W. The House of Baring in American trade and finance: English merchant bankers at work, 1763-1861. 1949. H1124
15 Navin, T. R. The Whitin Machine Works since 1831. 1950. H1125
16 Gibb, G. S. The Saco-Lowell Shops: textile machinery building in New England, 1813-1949. 1950. H1126
17 Ewing, J. S. and Norton, N. P. Broadlooms and businessmen. 1954. H1127
18 Tooker, E. Nathan Trotter,

Philadelphia merchant, 1787-1853. 1955. H1128
19 White, G. T. A history of the Massachusetts Hospital Life Insurance Company. 1955. H1129
20 Parish, W. J. The Charles Infield Company. 1961. H1130
21 De Roover, R. A. The rise and decline of the Medici Bank, 1397-1494. 1963. H1131
22 Davison, R. A. Isaac Hicks. 1964. H1132
23 Johnson, A. M. and Supple, B. E. Boston capitalists and western railroads. 1967. H1133
24 Johnson, A. M. Petroleum pipelines and public policy. 1967. H1134
25 Carosso, V. P. Investment banking in America. 1970. H1135
26 Seaburg, C. and Paterson, S. Merchant prince of Boston, Colonel T. H. Perkins, 1764-1854. 1971. H1136
27 Wilkins, M. The maturing of multinational enterprise. 1974. H1137

HARVARD STUDIES IN COMPARATIVE LITERATURE

1 Santayana, G. Three philosophical poets. 1910. H1138
2 Schofield, W. H. Chivalry in English literature. 1912. H1139
3 Campbell, O. J. The comedies of Holberg. 1914. H1140
4 Post, C. R. Medieval Spanish allegory. 1915. H1141
5 Schofield, W. H. Mythical bards and The life of William Wallace. 1920. H1142
6 Leach, H. G. Angevin Britain and Scandinavia. 1921. H1143
7 Shannon, E. F. Chaucer and the Roman poets. 1929. H1144
8 Millican, C. B. Spencer and the Table Round. 1932. H1145
9 Eger and Grime. Eger and Grime, ed. by Caldwell. 1933. H1146
10 Spargo, J. W. Virgil the necromancer. 1934. H1147
11 Whiting, B. J. Chaucer's use of proverbs. 1934. H1148
12 Simmons, E. J. English literature and culture in Russia, (1553-1840). 1935. H1149
13 Baldensperger, F., ed. D'Edmond Spenser à Alan Seeger: cent petits poèmes anglais traduits en vers français. 1938. H1150
14 Whiting, B. J. Proverbs in the earlier English drama with illustrations from contemporary French plays. 1938. H1151
15 McPeek, J. A. S. Catullus in strange and distant Britain. 1939. H1152
16 Clark, A. F. B. Jean Racine. 1939. H1153
17 Le Blanc, J. B. Un voyageur-philosophie au XVIIIe siècle, ed. by Cassidy. 1941. H1154
18 Greenough, C. N. A bibliography of the Theophrastan characters in English. 1947. H1155
19 Atkins, S. P. The Testament of Werther in poetry and drama. 1949. H1156
20 Levin, H. T., ed. Perspectives of criticism. 1950. H1157
21 Bowman, H. E. Vissarion Belinski, 1811-1848. 1954. H1158
22 Levin, H. Contexts of criticism. 1957. H1159
23 Brower, R. A., ed. On translation. 1958. H1160
24 Lord, A. B. The singer of tales. 1960. H1161
25 Kaiser, W. J. Praisers of folly: Erasmus, Rabelais, Shakespeare. 1963. H1162
26 Alter, R. Rogue's progress. 1964. H1163
27 Fanger, D. L. Dostoevsky and romantic realism. 1965. H1164
28 Andersson, T. M. The Icelandic family saga. 1966. H1165
29 Segal, E. Roman laughter. 1968. H1166
30 Merivale, P. Pan the goat-god. 1969. H1167
31 Quinones, R. J. The Renaissance discovery of time. 1972. H1168
32 Levin, H. Grounds for comparison. 1972. H1169

HARVARD STUDIES IN EAST ASIAN LAW

1 Law in Imperial China, ed. by Bodde and Morris. 1967. H1170
2 Cohen, J. A. The criminal process in the People's Republic of China, 1949-1963. 1968. H1171
3 Johnston, D. M. and Chiu, H., eds. Agreements of the People's Republic of China. 1968. H1172
4 Cohen, J. A., ed. Contemporary Chinese law. 1970. H1173
5 Chiu, H. The People's Republic of China and the law of treaties. 1972. H1174
6 Cohen, J. A. and Chiu, H., eds. People's China and international law. 1973. H1175
7 Metzger, T. A. The internal organization of Ch'ing bureaucracy. 1973. H1176

HARVARD STUDIES IN EDUCATION

1 Learned, W. S. The oberlehrer. 1914. H1177
2 Ballou, F. W. The appointment of teachers in cities. 1915. H1178
3 Harvard Univ. The teaching of economics in Harvard University. 1917. H1179
4 Dewey, G. Relativ frequency of English speech sounds. 1923. H1180
5 Hopkins, L. T. The intelligence of continuation-school children in Massachusetts. 1924. H1181
6 Price, R. R. The financial support of state universities. 1924. H1182
7 Wentworth, M. M. Individual differences in the intelligence of school children. 1926. H1183
8 Maverick, L. A. The vocational guidance of college students. 1926. H1184
9 Spaulding, F. T. The small junior high school. 1927. H1185
10 Davis, G. P. What shall the public schools do for the feeble-minded? 1927. (book suppressed). H1186
10 Weill, B. C. The behavior of young children of the same family. 1928. H1187
11 Stephens, S. D. Individual instruction in English composition. 1928. H1188
12 Robbins, P. An approach to composition through psychology. 1929. H1189
13 Bragdon, H. D. Counseling the college student. 1929. H1190
14 Prescott, D. A. Education and international relations. 1930. H1191
15 St. John, C. W. Educational achievement in relation to intelligence. 1930. H1192
16 Honeywell, R. J. The educational work of Thomas Jefferson. 1931. H1193
17 College entrance examination board. Examining the examination in English, by Thomas and others. 1931. H1194
18 Beatley, B. Achievement in the junior high school. 1932. H1195
19 Merry, R. V. Problems in the education of visually handicapped children. 1933. H1196
20 Rulon, P. J. The sound motion picture in science teaching. 1933. H1197
21 Wilson, H. E. The fusion of social studies in junior high schools. 1933. H1198
22 Dudley, L. L. The school and the community. 1933. H1199
23 Nichols, F. G. and Wissmann, S. W. The personal secretary. 1934. H1200
24 Smallwood, M. L. An historical study of examinations and grading systems in early American universities. 1935. H1201
25 Holmes, P. A tercentenary history of the Boston Public Latin school, 1635-1935. 1935. H1202
26 Kelley, T. L. Essential traits of mental life. 1935. H1203
27 Robbins, P. Incentives to

composition. 1936. H1204
28 Deemer, W. L. and Rulon, P. J. An experimental comparison of two shorthand systems. 1942. H1205
29 Elwell, C. E. Influence of the enlightenment on the Catholic theory of religious education in France. 1944. H1206
30 Knapp, R. H. American regionalism and social education. 1947. H1207

HARVARD STUDIES IN ENGLISH

1 Dodd, W. G. Courtly love in Chaucer and Gower. 1913. H1208
2 Mackenzie, W. R. The English moralities from the point of view of allegory. 1914. H1209
3 Bernbaum, E. The drama of sensibility. 1915. H1210
4 Perry, H. T. E. The first duchess of Newcastle and her husband as figures in literary history. 1918. H1211
5 Souers, P. W. The matchless Orinda. 1931. H1212
6 Bond, R. P. English burlesque poetry, 1700-1750. 1932. H1213
7 Allen, R. J. The clubs of Augustan London. 1933. H1214
8 Judge, C. B. Elizabethean book-pirates. 1934. H1215
9 D'Urfey, T. The songs of Thomas D'Urfey, ed. by Day. 1933. H1216
10 Eccles, M. Christopher Marlowe in London. 1934. H1217
11 Green, C. C. The neo-classic theory of tragedy in England during the eighteenth century. 1934. H1218
12 White, H. O. Plagiarism and imitation during the English renaissance. 1935. H1219
13 Sperry, W. L. Wordsworth's anti-climax. 1935. H1220
14 Myrick, K. O. Sir Philip Sidney as a literary craftsman. 1935. H1221
15 Borgman, A. S. The life and death of William Mountfort. 1935. H1222
16 Beattie, L. M. John Arbuthnot, mathematician and satirist. 1935. H1223
17 Noyes, R. G. Ben Jonson on the English stage. 1935. H1224
18 Bush, D. Mythology and the romantic tradition in English poetry. 1937. H1225
19 Houghton, W. E. The formation of Thomas Fuller's Holy and profane states. 1938. H1226
20 Wilson, E. C. England's Eliza. 1939. H1227
21 Boyce, B. Tom Brown of facetious memory, Grub Street in the age of Dryden. 1939. H1228

HARVARD STUDIES IN INTERNATIONAL LAW

1 Ladas, S. P. The international protection of trade marks, by the American republics. 1929. H1229
2 ____. The international protection of industrial property. 1930. H1230
____. The international protection of literary and artistic property. 2 v. 1938. H1231

HARVARD STUDIES IN JURISPRUDENCE

1 Huston, C. A. The enforcement of decrees in equity. 1915. H1232
2 Henderson, G. C. The position of foreign corporations in American constitutional law. 1918. H1233
3 Dickinson, E. D. The equality of states in international law. 1920. H1234
4 Haines, C. G. The revival of natural law concepts. 1930. H1235
5 Ehrlich, E. Fundamental principles of the sociology of law, tr. by Moll. 1936. H1236

HARVARD STUDIES IN MONOPOLY AND COMPETITION

1 Crum, W. L. Corporate size and earning power. 1939. H1237
2 Reynolds, L. G. The control of competition in Canada. 1940. H1238
3 Miller, J. P. Unfair competition. 1941. H1239
4 Sweezy, M. B. (Yaple). The structure of the Nazi economy. 1941. H1240
5 Brems, H. Product equilibrium under monopolistic competition. 1951. H1241

HARVARD STUDIES IN ROMANCE LANGUAGES

1 Giacomo da Lentini. The poetry of Giacomo da Lentino, ed. by Langley. 1915. H1242
2 Hawkins, R. L. Maistre Charles Fontaine. 1916. H1243
3 Potter, M. A. Four essays. 1917. H1244
4 Wright, C. H. C. French classicism. 1920. H1245
5 Allard, L. La comédie de moeurs en France au dix-neuvième siècle. V. 1. 1923. H1246
6 Grant, E. M. French poetry and modern industry, 1830-1870. 1927. H1247
7 Hawkins, R. L. Madame de Staël and the United States. 1930. H1248
8 Gliglois. Gliglois, a French Arthurian romance of the thirteenth century, ed. by Livingston. 1932. H1249
9 Hawkins, R. L., comp. Newly discovered French letters ... 1933. H1250
10 Gregersen, H. Ibsen and Spain. 1936. H1251
11 Hawkins, R. L. Auguste Comte and the United States. 1936. H1252
12 Kilgour, R. L. The decline of chivalry as shown in French literature of the late middle ages. 1937. H1253
13 Agnes, St. The Old French lives of Saint Agnes and other vernacular versions of the middle ages, ed. by Denomy. 1938. H1254
14 Hawkins, R. L. Positivism in the United States, (1853-1861). 1938. H1255
15 Torrielli, A. J. Italian opinion on America as revealed by Italian travellers, 1850-1900. 1941. H1256
16 Keating, L. C. Studies on the literary salon in France, 1550-1615. 1941. H1257
17 Harvey, H. G. The theatre of the Basoche. 1941. H1258
18 Clements, R. J. Critical theory and practice of the Pléiade. 1942. H1259
19 Shaw, E. P. Jacques Cazotte. 1942. H1260
20 Domingo de Guzmán, St. The life of Saint Dominic in Old French verse, ed. by Manning. 1944. H1261
21 Grant, E. M. The career of Victor Hugo. 1945. H1262
22 Camões, L. de. Os Lusiadas, ed. by Ford. 1946. H1263
23 Pelmont, R. A. Paul Valéry et les beaux-arts. 1949. H1264
24 Livingston, C. H. Le jongleur Gautier Le Leu. 1951. H1265
25 Hippocrates. Les amorphismes Ypocras de Martin de Saint-Gilles, 1362-1365, ed. by Lafeuille. 1954. H1266
26 Rogers, F. M. The travels of the Infante Dom Pedro of Portugal. 1961. H1267
27 Shroder, M. Z. Icarus. 1961. H1268
28 Cota, S. Memorias, ed. by Keniston. 1964. H1269
29 Casa, F. P. The dramatic craftsmanship of Moreto. 1966. H1270
30 Hafter, M. Z. Gracian and perfection. 1966. H1271
31 Fernández de Figueroa, M. A Spaniard in the Portuguese Indies, by McKenna. 1967. H1272
32 Lipschutz, I. H. Spanish painting and the French romantics. 1972. H1273

HARVARD STUDIES IN TECHNOLOGY AND SOCIETY

Carter, A. P. Structural change in the American economy. 1970. H1274
The corporate economy, ed. by Marris. 1971. H1275
Human aspects of biomedical innovations, ed. by Mendelsohn. 1971. H1276
Mesthene, E. G. Technological change. 1970. H1277
Oettinger, A. G. and Marks, S. Run, computer, run. 1971. H1278
Rosenbloom, R. S. and Marris, R., eds. Social innovations in the city. 1969. H1279
Westin, A. F., ed. Information technology in a democracy. 1972. H1280

HARVARD STUDIES IN THE CONFLICT OF LAWS

1 Harding, A. L. Double taxation of property and income. 1933. H1281
2 Read, H. E. Recognition and enforcement of foreign judgments in the common law units of the British commonwealths. 1938. H1282
3 Nékám, A. The personality conception of the legal entity. 1938. H1283
4 Robertson, A. H. Characterization in the conflict of laws. 1940. H1284
5 Cook, W. W. The logical and legal bases of the conflict of laws. 1942. H1285

HARVARD STUDIES IN URBAN HISTORY

Frisch, M. H. Town into city. 1972. H1286
Hammond, M. and Bartson, L. J. The city in the ancient world. 1972. H1287
Pred, A. R. Urban growth and the circulation of information. 1973. H1288
Scott, J. W. The glassworkers of Carmaux. 1974. H1289

HARVARD THEOLOGICAL STUDIES

1 Torrey, C. C. The composition and date of Acts. 1916. H1290
2 Hatch, W. H. P. The Pauline idea of faith in its relation to Jewish and Hellenistic religion. 1917. H1291
3 Arnold, W. R. Ephod and Ark. 1917. H1292
4 Edmunds, C. C. and Hatch, W. H. P. The Gospel manuscripts of the General theological seminary. 1918. H1293
5 Macarius, St. Macarii anecdota, ed. by Marriott. 1918. H1294
6 Cadbury, H. J. The style and literary method of Luke. 2 v. 1919-20. H1295
7 Bacon, B. W. Is Mark a Roman gospel? 1919. H1296
8 Emerton, E. The Defensor pacts of Marsiglio of Padua. 1920. H1297
9 An answer to John Robinson of Leyden, by a Puritan friend, ed. by Burrage. 1920. H1298
10 Coynbeare, F. C. Russian dissenters. 1921. H1299
11 Athos (Monasteries) Vatopedia. Catalogue of the Greek manuscripts in the library of the monastery of Vatopedi on Mt. Athos. 1924. H1300
12 Athos (Monasteries) Laura. Catalogue of the Greek manuscripts in the library of the Laura on Mt. Athos, by Spyridon, and Sophronios Eustratiades. 1925. H1301
13 Smith, P. A key to the Colloquies of Erasmus. 1927. H1302
14 Ropes, J. H. The singular problem of the epistle to the Galatians. 1929. H1303
15 Serapion, St. Against the Manichees, ed. by Casey. 1931. H1304
16 Servetus, M. The two treatises of Servetus on the Trinity, tr. by Wilbur. 1932. H1305
17 Lake, K. and New, S., eds.

Six collations of New Testament manuscripts. 1932. H1306
18 Williams, G. H. The Norman anonymous of 1100 A. D. 1951. H1307
19 Cranz, F. E. An essay on the development of Luther's thought on justice, law and society. 1959. H1308
20 Sundberg, A. C. The Old Testament of the early church. 1964. H1309
21 Dow, S. and Healey, R. F. A sacred calender of Eleusis. 1965. H1310
22 Albright, W. F. The Proto-Sinaitic inscriptions and their decipherment. 1966. H1311
23 Yizhar, M. Bibliography of Hebrew publications on the Dead Sea scrolls, 1948-1964. 1967. H1312
24 Yamauchi, E. M. Gnostic ethics and Mandaean origins. 1970. H1313
25 Worthley, H. F. An inventory of the records of the particular (Congregational) churches of Massachusetts gathered, 1620-1805. 1970. H1314
26 Nickelburg, G. Resurrection, immorality, and eternal life in intertestamental Judaism. 1972. H1315
27 Preus, J. S. Carlstadt's Ordinaciones and Luther's liberty. 1974. H1316

HARVARD UNIVERSITY. CENTER FOR INTERNATIONAL AFFAIRS. STUDY (Harvard Univ. Pr. unless otherwise stated)

1 Brzezinski, Z. K. The Soviet bloc, unity and conflict. 1960. H1317
2 Vali, F. A. Rift and revolt in Hungary. 1961. H1318
3 Meyer, A. J. and Vassiliou, S. G. The economy of Cyprus. 1962. H1319
4 Sā-igh, Y. A. Entrepreneurs of Lebanon. 1962. H1320
Galula, D. Counter insurgency warfare. Prager. 1964. H1321 (Also published as: Counter insurgency warfare and practice. Pall Mall. 1964.)
Gordon, L. and Grommers, E. L. United States manufacturing investment in Brazil. 1962. H1322
In search of France, by Hoffmann and others. 1963. H1323
Kissinger, H. A. The Necessity for choice. Harper. 1961. H1324
Schelling, T. C. and Halperin, M. H. Strategy and arms control. Twentieth Century Fund. 1961. H1325

HARVARD UNIVERSITY. CENTER FOR THE STUDY OF THE HISTORY OF LIBERTY IN AMERICA. PUBLICATIONS.

Arieli, Y. Individualism and nationalism in American ideology. 1964. H1326
Aronson, S. H. Status and kinship in the higher civil service. 1964. H1327
Barth, G. Bitter strength. 1964. H1328
Brown, R. M. The South Carolina Regulators. 1963. H1329
Bushman, R. L. From Puritan to Yankee. 1967. H1330
Calhoun, D. H. Professional lives in America. 1965. H1331
Goodman, P. The Democratic-Republicans of Massachusetts. 1964. H1332
Handlin, O. and M. F. The dimensions of liberty. 1961. H1333
____, eds. The popular sources of political authority. 1966. H1334
James, S. V. A people among peoples. 1963. H1335
Keller, M. The life insurance enterprise, 1885-1910. 1963. H1336
Lane, R. Policing the city. 1967. H1337
Levy, L. W. Jefferson and civil liberties. 1963. H1338
Lubove, R. The professional altruist. 1965. H1339
____. The struggle for social security, 1900-1935. 1968. H1340
McLoughlin, W. G. New England

dissent. 2 v. 1971. H1341
Preston, W. Aliens and dissenters. 1963. H1342
Rothman, D. J. Politics and power. 1966. H1343
Salsbury, S. The State, the investor, and the railroad. 1967. H1344

HARVARD UNIVERSITY. COMPUTATION LABORATORY. ANNALS.

1 Harvard university. Computation Laboratory. A manual of operation for the automatic sequence controlled calculator. 1946. H1345
2 ____. Tables of the modified Hankel functions of order one-third and of their derivatives. 1945. H1346
3-14 ____. Tables of the Bessel functions of the first kind of orders. 12 v. 1947-51. H1347
16 Symposium on Large-Scale Digital Calculating Machinery, Harvard University, 1947 Proceedings of a Symposium on Large-Scale Digital Calculating Machinery. V. 1. 1948. H1348
17 Harvard university. Computation Laboratory. Tables for the design of missiles. 1948. H1349
18-19 ____. Tables of generalized sine-and cosine-integral functions. 2 v. 1949. H1350
20 ____. Tables of inverse hyperbolic functions. 1949. H1351
21 ____. Tables of the generalized exponential-integral functions. 1949. H1352
22 ____. Tables of the function $\frac{\sin \phi}{\phi}$ and of its first eleven derivatives. 1949. H1353
23 ____. Tables of the error function and of its first twenty derivatives. 1952. H1354
24 ____. Description of a relay calculator. 1949. H1355
25 ____. Description of a magnetic drum calculator. 1952. H1356
26 Same as no. 16. V. 2. 1951. H1357
27 Harvard university. Computation Laboratory. Synthesis of electronic computing and control circuits. 1951. H1358
29-30 International symposium on the Theory of Switching, Harvard University. Proceedings. 2 v. 1959. H1359
31 Symposium on digital computers and their application, 1961. Proceedings. 1962. H1360
35 Harvard University. Computation Laboratory. Tables of the cumulative binomial probability distribution. 1955. H1361
40 Harvard University. Computation Laboratory. Tables of the function arc sin z. 1956. H1362
41 Cohen, J. E. A model of simple competition. 1966. H1363

Nos. 15, 28, 32-34, 36-39 not yet published.

HARVARD UNIVERSITY. MONOGRAPHS IN MEDICINE AND PUBLIC HEALTH.

1 Salter, W. T. The endocrine function of iodine. 1940. H1364
2 Drinker, C. K. and Yoffey, J. M. Lymphatics, lymph and lymphoid tissue. 1941. H1365
3 Schoenheimer, R. The dynamic state of body constituents. 1942. H1366
4 Cobb, S. Borderlands of psychiatry. 1943. H1367
5 Puffer, R. R. Familial susceptibility to tuberculosis. 1944. H1368
6 Dubos, R. J. The bacterial cell... 1945. H1369
7 Drinker, C. K. Pulmonary edema and inflammation. 1945. H1370
8 Burnet, F. M. Virus as organism. 1945. H1371
9 Psychiatric research, by Drinker and others. 1947. H1372

10 Altschule, M. D. Physiology in diseases of the heart and lungs. 1954. H1373
11 Monroe, R. T. Diseases in old age. 1951. H1374
12 Stanbury, J. B. and others. Endemic goiter. 1954. H1375
13 Dubos, R. J. Biochemical determinants of microbial diseases. 1954. H1376

HARVARD UNIVERSITY. PHI BETA KAPPA PRIZE ESSAYS.

1934 Owen, W. A study in highway economics. 1934. H1377
1935 Haskins, G. L. The statute of York and the interest of the Commons. 1935. H1378
1936 Paul, R. W. The abrogation of the gentlemen's agreement. 1936. H1379
1937 Szathmary, A. The aesthetic theory of Bergson. 1937. H1380
1938 Moore, J. A. Sophocles and Aretè. 1938. H1381
1939 Greenhood, E. R. A detailed proof of the chi-square test of goodness of fit. 1940. H1382
1940 Dulles, A. Princeps Concordiae. 1941. H1383
1949 Gray, C. Hugh Latimer and the sixteenth century. 1950. H1384
1950 Bellah, R. N. Apache kinship system. 1952. H1385

HARVARD UNIVERSITY. RESEARCH CENTER IN ENTREPRENEURIAL HISTORY. STUDIES IN ENTREPRENEURIAL HISTORY.

Aitken, H. G. J. The Welland Canal Company: a study in Canadian enterprise. 1954. H1386
Bailyn, B. The New England merchants in the seventeenth century. 1955. H1387
Chandler, A. D. Henry Varnum Poor. 1956. H1388
Cochran, T. C. Railroad leaders, 1845-1890. 1953. H1389
Dales, J. H. Hydroelectricity and industrial development in Quebec, 1898-1940. 1957. H1390
Diamond, S. O. The reputation of the American businessman. 1955. H1391
Harvard University Research Center in Entrepreneurial History. Changes and the entrepreneur. 1949. H1392
Landes, D. S. Bankers and pashas. 1958. H1393
Miller, W., ed. Men in business. 1952. H1394
Nadworny, N. J. Scientific management and the unions, 1900-1932. 1955. H1395
Passer, H. C. The electrical manufacturers, 1875-1900. 1953. H1396
Stein, S. J. The Brazilian cotton manufacture. 1957. H1397

HARVARD UNIVERSITY. RUSSIAN RESEARCH CENTER. RUSSIAN RESEARCH CENTER STUDIES.

1 Inkeles, A. Public opinion in Soviet Russia. 1950. H1398
2 Moore, B. Soviet politics. 1950. H1399
3 Berman, H. J. Justice in Russia. 1950. H1400
4 Schwartz, B. I. Chinese communism and the rise of Mao. 1951. H1401
5 Ulam, A. B. Titoism and the Cominform. 1952. H1402
6 Brandt, C. and others, eds. A documentary history of Chinese Communism. 1952. H1403
7 Bauer, R. A. The new man in Soviet psychology. 1952. H1404
8 Fischer, G. Soviet opposition to Stalin. 1952. H1405
9 Shimkin, D. B. Minerals, a key to Soviet power. 1953. H1406
10 Konstantinovsky, B. A. Soviet law in action, ed. by Berman. 1953. H1407
11 Fainsod, M. How Russia is ruled. 1953. H1408
12 Moore, B. Terror and progress USSR. 1954. H1409
13 Pipes, R. The formation of

the Soviet Union. 1954. H1410
14 Meyer, A. G. Marxism. 1954. H1411
15 Hodgman, D. R. Soviet industrial production, 1928-1951. 1954. H1412
16 Holzman, F. D. Soviet taxation. 1955. H1413
17 Berman, H. J. and Kerner, M. Soviet military law and administration. 1955. H1414
18 ____, eds. and trs. Documents on Soviet military law & administration. 1955. H1415
19 Haimson, L. H. The Russian Marxists & the origins of bolshevism. 1955. H1416
20 Brzezinski, Z. The permanent purge. 1956. H1417
21 Vakar, N. P. Belorussia. 1956. H1418
22 ____. A bibliographical guide to Belorussia. 1956. H1419
23 Wolff, R. L. The Balkans in our time. 1956. H1420
24 Bauer, R. A. and others. How the Soviet system works. 1956. H1421
25 Clark, M. G. The economics of Soviet steel. 1956. H1422
26 Meyer, A. G. Leninism. 1957. H1423
27 Berliner, J. S. Factory and manager in the USSR. 1957. H1424
28 Hunter, H. Soviet transportation policy. 1957. H1425
29 Field, M. G. Doctor and patient in Soviet Russia. 1957. H1426
30 Fischer, G. Russian liberalism from gentry to intelligentsia. 1958. H1427
31 Brandt, C. Stalin's failure in China, 1924-1927. 1958. H1428
32 Dziewanowski, M. K. The Communist Party of Poland. 1959. H1429
33 Karamzin, N. M. Memoir on ancient and modern Russia, tr. by Pipes. 1959. H1430
34 ____. Russian text, ed. by Pipes. 1959. H1431
35 Inkeles, A. and others. The Soviet citizen. 1959. H1432
36 Zenkovsky, S. A. Pan-Turkism and Islam in Russia. 1959. H1433
37 Brzezinski, Z. K. The Soviet bloc, unity and conflict. 1960. H1434
38 Rogger, H. National consciousness in eighteenth-century Russia. 1960. H1435
39 Malia, M. Alexander Herzen and the birth of Russian socialism, 1812-1855. 1961. H1436
40 Daniels, R. V. The conscience of the revolution. 1960. H1437
41 Erlich, A. The Soviet industrialization debate, 1924-1928. 1960. H1438
42 Monas, S. The Third Section. 1961. H1439
43 Mendel, A. P. Dilemmas of progress in tsarist Russia. 1961. H1440
44 Swarze, H. Political control of literature in the USSR, 1946-1959. 1962. H1441
45 Campbell, R. W. Accounting in Soviet planning and management. 1963. H1442
46 Pipes, R. Social democracy and the St. Petersburg labor movement, 1885-1897. 1963. H1443
47 Ulam, A. B. The new face of Soviet totalitarianism. 1963. H1444
48 Shulman, M. D. Stalin's foreign policy reappraised. 1963. H1445
49 Kassof, A. H. The Soviet youth program. 1965. H1446
50 Russia. Soviet criminal law and procedure, by Berman, tr. by Berman and Spindler. 1966. H1447
51 Bromke, A. Poland's politics. 1966. H1448
52 Azrael, J. R. Managerial power and Soviet politics. 1966. H1449
53 McMaster, R. E. Danilevsky. 1967. H1450
54 Becker, S. Russia's protectorates in Central Asia. 1968. H1451
55 Pipes, R., ed. Revolutionary Russia. 1968. H1452

56 Geiger, H. K. The family in Soviet Russia. 1968. H1453
57 Inkeles, A. Social change in Soviet Russia. 1968. H1454
58 Hough, J. F. The Soviet perfects. 1969. H1455
59 Wandycz, P. S. Soviet-Polish relations. 1969. H1456
60 Miller, R. F. One hundred thousand tractors. 1970. H1457
61 Joravsky, D. The Lysenko affair. 1970. H1458
62 Fireside, H. Icon and swastika. 1971. H1459
63 Volin, L. A century of Russian agriculture. 1971. H1460
64 Pipes, R. Struve. 1970. H1461
65 Gerstein, L. Nikolai Strakhov. 1971. H1462
66 Keenan, E. L. The Kurbskii-Groznyi apocrypha. 1971. H1463
67 Woehrlin, W. F. Chernyshevskii. 1971. H1464
68 Gleason, A. European and Muscovite. 1971. H1465
69 Boss, V. Newton and Russia. 1972. H1466
70 Ascher, A. Pavel Axelrod and the development of Menshevism. 1972. H1467
71 Ofer, G. The service sector in Soviet economic growth. 1973. H1468
72 Sinel, A. The classroom and the chancellery. 1973. H1469
73 Holzman, F. D. Foreign trade under central planning. 1974. H1470

HARVARD UNIVERSITY. SEMINARS IN THE HISTORY OF IDEAS

1 Boas, G. Vox Populi. 1969. H1471

HARVARD UNIVERSITY SERIES ON COMPETITION IN AMERICAN INDUSTRY.

1 Markham, J. W. Competition in the rayon industry. 1952. H1472
2 Cookenboo, L. Crude oil pipe lines and competition in the oil industry. 1955. H1473
3 Bain, J. S. Barriers to the new competition. 1956. H1474
4 Loescher, S. M. Imperfect collusion in the cement industry. 1959. H1475
5 McKie, J. W. Tin cans and tin plates. 1959. H1476
6 Peck, M. J. Competition in the aluminum industry. 1961. H1477
7 Kaysen, C. Antitrust policy. 1959. H1478

HARVARD YENCHING INSTITUTE. MONOGRAPH SERIES

1 Herrmann, A. Historical and commercial atlas of China. 1935. H1479
2 Ecke, G. The twin pagodas of Zayton. 1972. H1480
3-4 Clark, E., ed. Two Lamaistic pantheons. 2 v. 1949. H1481
5-6 Dye, D. S. A grammar of Chinese lattice. 1949. H1482
7 Janse, O. R. T. Archaeological research in Indo-China. V. 1. 1947. H1483
8-9 Rock, J. F. C. The ancient Na'khi Kingdom of Southwest China. 1947. H1484
10 Same as no. 7. V. 2. 1951. H1485
11 Han, Y. Han shih wai chuan. 1952. H1486
12 Yang, L. Money and credit in China. 1952. H1487
13 Kracke, E. A. Civil service in early Sung China, 960-1067. 1953. H1488
14 Hall, J. W. Tanuma Okitsugu, 1719-1788. 1955. H1489
15 Chikamatsu, M. The love suicide at Amijima, ed. by Shively. 1953. H1490
16 Pina, R. C. Song synadty musical sources and their interpretations. 1967. H1491
17 Yoshikawa, K. An introduction to Sung poetry. 1967. H1492
18 Nakayama, S. A history of Japanese astronomy. 1969. H1493
19 Izumi, S. The Izumi Shikibu diary, tr. by Cranston. 1969. H1494

20 Keikai, comp. Miraculous stories from the Japanese Buddhist tradition, tr. by Nakamura. 1973. H1495
21 Hanan, P. The Chinese short story. 1973. H1496

HARVARD-YENCHING INSTITUTE. SCRIPTA MONGOLICA

1 Altan Tobči, ed. by Cleaves. 1952. H1497
2 Sayand Secen. Erdeni Tobči. 4 pts. 1956. H1498
3 Ras. pungsuy. Bolor Erike. 5 pts. 1959. H1499
4 Manual of Mongolian astrology and divination, ed. by Cleaves. 1969. H1500

HARVARD-YENCHING INSTITUTE. STUDIES (Harvard Univ. Pr.)

1 Fairbank, J. K. and Liu, K. Modern China. 1950. H1501
2 Têng, S. and Biggerstaff, K., comp. An annotated bibliography of selected Chinese reference works. 1950. H1502
3 Hightower, J. R. Topics in Chinese literature. 1953. H1503
4 Yang, L. Topics in Chinese history. 1950. H1504
5 Lehmann, W. P. and Faust, L. Grammar of formal written Japanese. 1951. H1505
6 Ssú-ma, K. The Chronicle of the three Kingdoms (220-265), ed. by Baxter. V. 1. 1952. H1506
7 Han, Yü Poetische werke, tr. by von Zach, ed. by Hightower. 1952. H1507
8 Tu, F. Gedichte, tr. by Zach, ed. by Hightower. 1952. H1508
9 Wang, I. Official relations between China and Japan, 1368-1549. 1953. H1509
10 Irvin, R. G. The evolution of a Chinese novel: Shui-hu-chaun. 1953. H1510
11 Bodman, N. C. A linguistic study of the Shih ming. 1954. H1511
12 Buck, F. H. Comparative study of postpositions in Mongolian dialects and the written language. 1955. H1512
13 Han, Y. The veritable records of the T'ang emperor Shun-tsung. 1955. H1513
14 Bishop, J. L. The colloquial short story in China. 1956. H1514
15 Baxter, G. W. Index to the imperial register of tz'u prosody, Ch'in-ting tz'u-p'n. 1956. H1515
16 Sung, L. Economic structure, of the Yüan dynasty, tr. by Schurmann. 1956. H1516
17 Raghunātha Siromani. The Padārthatattvanirūpanam of Raghunātha Siromani, ed. and tr. by Potter. 1957. H1517
18 Hsiao, T., ed. Die chinesische Anthologie, ed. by Fang. 2 v. 1958. H1518
19 Fairbank, J. K. and Têng, S. Ch'ing administration. 1960. H1519
20 Yang, L. Studies in Chinese institutional history. 1961. H1520
21 Bishop, J. L. Studies in Chinese literature. 1961. H1521
22 Feng, H. The Chinese kinship system. 1948. H1522
23 Bishop, J. L., ed. Studies of governmental institutions in Chinese history. 1968. H1523
24 Yang, L. S. Excursions in sinology. 1968. H1524
25 Haedong Kosŭng Chŏn. Lives of eminent Korean monks, tr. by Lee. 1969. H1525
26 Fairbank, J. K. and others. Japanese studies of modern China. 1971. H1526
27 Bush, S. The Chinese literation painting. 1971. H1527
28 Fairbanks, W. Adventures in retrieval. 1972. H1528
29 Reischauer, E. O. and Yamagiwa, J. K. Translations from early Japanese literature. 1972. H1529

HASKELL LECTURES. OBERLIN COLLEGE, OBERLIN, OHIO.

1911-12 Loofs, F. What is the truth about Jesus Christ. Scribner. 1913. H1530

1912-13 Jastrow, M. Hebrew and Babylonian traditions. Scribner. 1914. H1531
1913-14 Rashdall, H. Conscience and Christ. Duckworth. 1916. H1532
1918-19 Lake, L. Landmarks in the history of early Christianity. Macmillan. 1920. H1533
1919-20 Mackintoch, H. R. The originality of the Christian message. Scribner. 1920. H1534
1923-24 Jones, R. M. Fundamental ends of life. Macmillan. 1924. H1535
1924-25 Otto, R. West-östliche mystik. Klotz. 1926. H1536
Otto, R. Mysticism east and west. Macmillan. 1932. H1537
1925-26 Glaver, T. R. Influence of Christ in the ancient world. Yale. 1929. H1538
1928-29 Deissmann, G. The New Testament in the light of modern research. Doran. 1929. H1539
1929-30 Montgomery, J. A. Arabia & the Bible. Univ. of Penna. 1934. H1540
1933-34 Meek, T. J. Hebrew origins. Harper. 1936. H1541
1936-37 Cash, W. W. Christianity and Islam. Harper. 1937. H1542
1939 Cave, S. Hinduism or Christianity? 1939. H1543
1939-40 Grant, F. C. The gospel of the kingdom. Macmillan. 1940. H1544
1948-49 Wright, G. E. The Old Testament against its environment. SCM Pr. 1950. H1545
1950-51 Johnson, A. R. Sacral kingdom in Ancient Israel. Univ. of Wales. 1955. H1546
1956 Simon, M. St. Stephen and the Hellenists in the primitive church. Longmans. 1958. H1547
1956-57 Cross, F. M. The ancient library of Qumrân and modern Biblical studies. Doubleday. 1958. H1548

HEIDELBERG SCIENCE LIBRARY (Springer)

1 Bünning, E. The physiological clock. 1967. H1549
2 Ziswiler, V. Extinct and vanishing animals. 1967. H1550
3 Kitaigorodskiy, A. I. Order and disorder in the world of atoms, tr. by Scripta Technica. 1967. H1551
4 Zähner, H. and Maas, W. K. Biology of antibiotics. 1972. H1552
5-6 Unsöld, A. The new cosmos. 1969. H1553
7 Born, N. Physics in my generation. 1969. H1554
8 Von Brücke, F. T. and others. The pharmacology of psychotherapeutic drugs, tr. by Siggs. 1969. H1555
9 Lembeck, F. and Sewing, K. F. Pharmacological facts and figures, tr. by Heller and Ferguson. 1969. H1556
10 Fuhrmann, W. and Vogel, F. Genetic counseling, tr. by Kurth. 1969. H1557
11 Botvinnik, M. M. Computers, chess and long-range planning. 1970. H1558
12 Dertinger, H. and Jung, H. Molecular radiation biology, tr. by Hüber and Gresham. 1970. H1559
13 Eccles, J. C. Facing reality. 1970. H1560
14 Thenius, E. Fossils and the life of the past. 1972. H1561
16 Roederer, J. G. Introduction to the physics and psychophysics of music. 1973. H1562
17 Mandelkern, L. An introduction to macromolecules. 1972. H1563
18 Wallach, D. F. H. The plasma membrane. 1972. H1564
19 Brachet, J. Introduction to molecular embryology. 1974. H1565

HEIDELBERGER ABHANDLUNGEN ZUR PHILOSOPHIE UND IHRE GESCHICHTE (Mohr)

1 Rickert, H. Das eine, die einheit und die eins. 1924. H1566
2 Glockner, H. Der begriff in Hegels philosophie. 1924. H1567
3 Hoffmann, E. Die sprache und die archaische logik. 1925. H1568
4 Ralfs, G. Das irrationale im begriff. 1925. H1569
5 Oppenheimer, H. Die logik der soziologischen begriffsbildung mit besonderer beruecksichtigung von Max Weber. 1925. H1570
6 Zocher, R. Die objektive geltungslogik und der immanenzgedanke. 1926. H1571
7 Pflaum, H. Die idee der liebe in ihrem Wandel vom Mittelalter zur Renaissance. 1926. H1572
8 Herrigel, E. Urstoff und urform. 1926. H1573
9 Zepf, M. Augustins Confessiones. 1926. H1574
10 Lang, W. Das traumbuch des synesius von Kyrene. 1926. H1575
11 Wolf, E. Grotius, Pufendorf, Thomasius. Drei Kapitel zur Gestaltgeschichte der Rechtswissenschaft. 1927. H1576
12 Stein, A. Pestalozzi und die Kantische philosophie. 1927. H1577
13 Theodorakopulos, J. Platons dialektik des seins. 1927. H1578
14 Emrich, H. Goethe's intuition. 1928. H1579
15 Stegemann, V. Augustins Gottesstaat. 1928. H1580
16 Christmann, F. Biologische kausalität. 1928. H1581
17 Meifort, J. Der Platonismus bei Clemens Alexandrinus. 1928. H1582
18 Nebel, G. Plotins kategorien der intelligiblen welt. 1929. H1583
19 Kristeller, P. O. Der begriff der seele in der ethik des Plotin. 1929. H1584
20 Böhm, F. J. Die logik der aesthetik. 1930. H1585
21 Kreis, F. Phaenomenologie und kritizismus. 1930. H1586
22 Schilling, H. Das ethos der mesotes. 1930. H1587
23 Ralfs, G. Sinn und sein im gegenstande der erkenntnis. 1931. H1588
24 Cassirer, H. Aristoteles' schrift "Von der Seele." 1932. H1589
25 Böhm, F. J. Ontologie der geschichte. 1933. H1590
26 Falkenheim, H. Goethe und Hegel. 1934. H1591
27 Cramer, W. Das problem der reinen anschauung. 1937. H1592
28 Rickert, H. Unmittelbarkeit und sinndeutung. 1939. H1593
29 Wundt, M. Die deutsche schulmetaphysik des 17. jahrhunderts. 1939. H1594
30 Ackermann, O. Kant im urteil Nietzsches. 1939. H1595
31 Scholz, K. Fröbels erziehungslehre. 1940. H1596
32 Wundt, M. Die deutsche schulphilosophie im zeitalter der aufklärung. 1945. H1597

HENRY E. HUNTINGTON LIBRARY AND ART GALLERY, SAN MARINO, CALIF. HUNTINGTON LIBRARY LISTS.

1 Henry E. Huntington Library and Art gallery. Check list of American laws, charters and constitutions of the 17th and 18th centuries..., comp. by Waters. 1936. H1598
2 ____. Sporting books in the Huntington library, comp. by Wright. 1937. H1599
3 ____. Incunabula in the Huntington library, comp. by Mead. 1937. H1600
4 ____. Catalogue of the Larpent plays in the Huntington library, comp. by MacMillan. 1939. H1601
5 ____. American manuscript collections in the Huntington library for the history of the

seventeenth and eighteenth centuries, comp. by Cuthbert. 1941. H1602

6 ____. Catalogue of music in the Huntington Library printed before 1801, comp. by Backus. 1949. H1603

HENRY E. HUNTINGTON LIBRARY AND ART GALLERY, SAN MARINO, CALIF. HUNTINGTON LIBRARY PUBLICATIONS.

Adams, J. The spur of fame, ed. by Shutz and Adair. 1966. H1604
Anderson, W. M. An American Maximilian's Mexico, 1865-1866, ed. by Ruiz. 1959. H1605
____. The Rocky Mountain journals, ed. by Morgan and Harris. 1967. H1606
Ashley, R. Of honour, ed. by Heltzel. 1947. H1607
Austin, J. C., ed. Fields of the Atlantic monthly. 1953. H1608
Baker, M. I. and C. H. C. The life and circumstances of James Brydges. 1949. H1609
Bale, J. King Johan, ed. by Adams. 1969. H1610
Baur, J. E. The health seekers of southern California, 1870-1900. 1959. H1611
Billington, R. A. Genesis of the frontier thesis. 1971. H1612
____, ed. and Whitehill, W. M. "Dear Lady." 1970. H1613
Billington, R. A., ed. The reinterpretation of early American history. 1966. H1614
Bingham, E. R. Charles F. Lummis. 1955. H1615
Bliss, A. and Carey, S. Camellias. 1971. H1616
Boyd, B. Chaucer and the medieval book. 1973. H1617
Boyd, B. M., ed. The Middle English miracles of the Virgin. 1964. H1618
Breton, N. and others. The ardor of amorous devices, 1957, ed. by Rollins. 1936. H1619
____. Britton's bowre of delight, 1591, ed. by Rollins. 1933. H1620
Buchanan, A. R. David S. Terry of California. 1956. H1621
Byrd, A. An essay upon the government of the English plantations on the continent of America, ed. by Wright. 1945. H1622
Campbell, L. B. Shakespeare's "Histories." 1947. H1623
Campbell, O. J. Comicall satyre and Shakespeare's Troilus and Cressida. 1938. H1624
Carter, R. Letters of Robert Carter, 1720-1727, ed. by Wright. 1940. H1625
Cheyne, G. The letters of Dr. George Cheyne to the Countess of Huntington, ed. by Mullett. 1940. H1626
Claypoole, J. C. Letter book, ed. by Balderston. 1967. H1627
Cleland, R. G. The cattle on a thousand hills. 1951. H1628
____. The Irvine Ranch. 1962. H1629
____. The placed Sespe. 1940. H1630
Cleland, R. G. and Putnam, F. B. Isais W. Hellman and the Farmers and Merchant Bank. 1965. H1631
Clemens, S. L. Mark Twain to Mrs. Fairbanks. 1949. H1632
Crosby, E. O. Memoirs of Elisha Oscar Crosby, ed. by Barker. 1945. H1633
Cuthbert, N. B., ed. Lincoln and the Baltimore Plot, 1861. 1949. H1634
Davies, G. Essays on the later Stuarts. 1958. H1635
____. The restoration of Charles II. 1955. H1636
DePorte, M. V. Nightmares and hobby horses. 1974. H1637
Dickey, F. M. Not wisely but too well. 1957. H1638
A discourse upon the exposicion and understandinge of statutes with Sir Thomas Egerton's additions, ed. by Thorne. 1942. H1639
Dumke, G. S. The boom of the eighties in Southern California.

1963. H1640
Elton, W. R. King Lear and the gods. 1965. H1641
Evans, G. W. B. Mexican gold trail, ed. by Dumke. 1945. H1642
Flaxman, J. Drawings by John Flaxman in the Huntington collection, ed. by Wark. 1970. H1643
Foote, M. H. A Victorian gentlewoman in the Far West, ed. by Paul. 1972. H1644
Ford, W. A. Thirty explosive years in Los Angeles County. 1961. H1645
Foster, A. J. Jeffersonian America, ed. by Davis. 1954. H1646
Franklin, B. Autobiography, ed. by Farrand. 1964. H1647
____. Memoires, ed. by Farrand. 1949. H1648
Garland, H. Diaries, ed. by Pizer. 1968. H1649
Geiger, M. Franciscan missionaries in Hispanic California, 1769-1848. 1969. H1650
Goldsmith, O. The grumbler, ed. by Wood. 1931. H1651
Hamilton, A. C. The early Shakespeare. 1967. H1652
Heninger, S. K. Touches of sweet harmony. 1974. H1653
Henry E. Huntington Library and Art Gallery. Catalogue of the William Blake drawings and paintings in the Huntington Library. 1957. H1654
____. Early British drawings in the Huntington Collection, ed. by Work. 1969. H1655
____. French decorative art in the Huntington collection. 1961. H1656
____. The Huntington Art collection, comp. by Wark. 1970. H1657
____. Sculpture in the Huntington collection, ed. by Marks. 1959. H1658
____. Ten centuries of manuscripts in the Huntington Library, by Schulz and others. 1962. H1659
Hine, R. V. California's Utopian colonies. 1953. H1660
Hubble, E. P. The nature of science and other lectures. 1954. H1661
Hunter, R. Quebec to Caroline in 1785-1786, ed. by Wright and Tinling. 1943. H1662
Hutton, W. R. California, 1847-1852, ed. by Waters. 1942. H1663
____. Glances at California, 1847-1853, ed. by Waters. 1942. H1664
Janssens, V. E. A. The life and adventures in California of Don Agustin Janssens, 1834-1856, ed. by Ellison and Price. 1953. H1665
Johnson, F. R. Astronomical thought in renaissance England. 1937. H1666
Kirker, H. California's architectural frontier. 1960. H1667
Kocher, P. H. Science and religion in Elizabethan England. 1953. H1668
Larkin, T. O. First and last consul. 1962. H1669
Larson, G. O. The "Americanization" of Utah for statehood. 1971. H1670
Lavender, D. The story of Cyprus Mines Corporation. 1962. H1671
Lee, J. D. A Mormon Chronicle, ed. by Cleland and Brooks. 2 v. 1955. H1672
Lee, R. E. "To Markie," ed. by Craven. 1933. H1673
Levy, F. J. Tudor historical thought. 1967. H1674
Longinos Martinez, J. California in 1792, tr. by Simpson. 1938. H1675
McEwen, G. D. The oracle of the coffee house. 1972. H1676
Mariken van Nimmegen. Mary of Nimmegen, ed. by Ayres and Barnouw. 1932. H1677
Massachusetts. Laws and statutes. The laws and liberties of Massachusetts, ed. by Farrand. 1929. H1678
Mayhew, G. P. Rage or raillery, ed. by Davis. 1967. H1679
Megquier, M. J. Apron full of gold. 1949. H1680
Mirrour for magistrates, ed. by Campbell. 1938. H1681

Mirrour for magistrates. Parts added to the Mirror for magistrates, ed. by Campbell. 1946. H1682
Moffett, T. Nobilis, tr. by Heltzel and Hudson. 1940. H1683
Oliver, P. Origin and progress of the American Rebellion, ed. by Adair and Schutz. 1961. H1684
Ormsby, W. L. The Butterfield Overland Mail, ed. by Wright and Bynum. 1942. H1685
Osbun, A. G. To California and the South Seas, ed. by Kemble. 1966. H1686
Oswalt, W. H. Mission of Change in Alaska. 1963. H1687
Pain, P. Daily meditations, ed. by Howard. 1936. H1688
Peterson, D. L. Time, tide, and tempest. 1973. H1689
Plutarchus. Quyete of mynde, tr. by Wyat. 1931. H1690
Pomfret, J. E. The Henry E. Huntington Library and Art Gallery from its beginning to 1969. 1969. H1691
Reed, E. B. Christmas carols printed in the sixteenth century. 1932. H1692
Reynolds, J. Discourses on art, ed. by Wark. 1959. H1693
Rolle, A. F. An American in California. 1956. H1694
Rose, L. J. L. J. Rose of Sunny Slope, 1827-1879. 1959. H1695
Rowlandson, T. Drawings for a tour in a post chaise, ed. by Wark. 1963. H1696
____. Drawings for "The English Dance of Death," ed. by Wark. 1966. H1697
Ruiz, R. E. Mexico. 1963. H1698
Serle, A. The American journal of Ambrose Serle, secretary to Lord Howe, 1776-1778, ed. by Tatum. 1940. H1699
Shakespeare, W. Hamlet. The first quarto, 1603. 1931. H1700
____. Hamlet. The second quarto, 1604, ed. by Campbell. 1938. H1701
Smith, H. Shakespeare's romances. 1972. H1702
Spalding, W. A. William Andrew Spalding, ed. by Hine. 1961. H1703
Steadman, J. M. The lamb and the elephant. 1974. H1704
Stewart, S. The expanded voice. 1970. H1705
Swan, H. Music in the Southwest, 1825-1950. 1952. H1706
Taylor, B. The unpublished letters of Bayard Taylor in the Huntington Library, ed. by Schutz. 1937. H1707
Thorpe, J. Principles of textual criticism. 1972. H1708
Turner, F. J. Frederick Jackson Turner's legacy. 1965. H1709
Vorspan, M. and Gartner, L. P. History of the Jews of Los Angeles. 1970. H1710
Walker, F. Jack London and the Klondike. 1966. H1711
Wark, R. R. Drawings from the Turner Shakespeare. 1973. H1712
____. Meet the ladies. 1972. H1713
____. Rowlandson's drawings for a tour in a post chaise. 1963. H1714
____. Ten British pictures. 1971. H1715
Washington, G. Washington's map of Mount Vernon. 1932. H1716
Whitaker, V. K. The mirror up to nature. 1965. H1717
____. Shakespeare's use of learning. 1953. H1718
White, G. T. Scientists in conflict. 1968. H1719
Wilkins, J. F. An artist on the Overland Trail, ed. by McDernott. 1968. H1720
Williams, D. A. David C. Broderick. 1969. H1721
Wilson, B. D. The Indians of southern California in 1852, ed. by Coughey. 1952. H1722
Wright, L. B. The first gentlemen of Virginia. 1940. H1723
____. Middle-class culture in Elizabethean England. 1935. H1724
Wright, L. H. American fiction, 1744-1850. 1948. H1725
____. ____, 1851-1875.

1957. H1726
____. ____, 1876-1900. 1966. H1727

HEPSA ELY SILLIMAN MEMORIAL LECTURES (Yale University Pr. unless otherwise stated)

1904 Thomson, J. J. Electricity and matter. Scribner. 1904. H1728
1906 Nernst, W. Experimental and theoretical applications of thermodynamics to chemistry. 1907. H1729
1910 Campbell, W. W. Stellar motions. 1913. H1730
1911 Verworn, M. Irritability. 1913. H1731
1913 Problems of American geology, by Rice and others. 1915. H1732
1916 Haldane, J. S. Organism and environment as illustrated by the physiology of breathing. 1918. H1733
1918 A Century of science in America, by Dana and others. 1918. H1734
1920 Hadamard, J. S. Lectures on Crouchy's problem in linear partial differential equations. 1923. H1735
1922 Krogh, A. The anatomy and physiology of capillaries. 1929. H1736
1928 Henderson, L. J. Blood. 1928. H1737
1932 Richardson, O. W. Molecular hydrogen and its spectrum. 1934. H1738
1934 Daly, R. A. The changing world of the ice age. 1934. H1739
1935 Hubble, E. P. The realm of the nebulae. 1936. H1740
1937 Watson, D. S. Paleontology and modern biology. 1951. H1741
1939 Goldschmitt, R. B. The material basis of evolution. 1940. H1742
1947 Science in progress. V. 6. Ed. by Baitsell. 1949. H1743
1949 Baitsell, G. A., ed. The centennial of the Sheffield Scientific School. 1950. H1744
1950 Fermi, E. Elementary particles. 1951. H1745
1951 Urey, H. C. The planets. 1952. H1746
Arrhenius, S. A. Theories of solutions. 1912. H1747
Bateson, W. Problems of genetics. 1913. H1748
Chibnall, A. C. Protein metabolism in the plant. 1939. H1749
Cumont, F. V. M. After life in Roman paganism. 1959. H1750
Dobzhansky, T. Mankind evolving. 1962. H1751
Granit, R. Receptors and sensory perception. 1955. H1752
Haldane, J. S. and Priestley, J. G. Respiration. 1935. H1753
Iddings, J. P. The problem of volcanism. 1914. H1754
Lewis, G. N. The anatomy of science. 1926. H1755
Morgan, T. H. The theory of the gene. 1928. H1756
Osler, W. The evolution of modern medicine. 1921. H1757
Petterson, H. The ocean floor. 1954. H1758
Rutherford, E. R. Radioactive transformations. 1906. H1759
Seaborg, G. T. The transuranium elements. 1958. H1760
Sherrington, C. E. The integrative action of the nervous system. 1948. H1761
Spemann, H. Embryonic development and induction. 1938. H1762
Spence, K. Behavior theory and conditioning. 1956. H1763
Von Neumann, J. The computer and the brain. 1958. H1764
Wieland, H. On the mechanism of oxidation. 1932. H1765

HERITAGE OF SOCIOLOGY (Univ. of Chicago Pr.)

Abrams, P. Origins of British sociology. 1969. H1766
Bellah, R. N., ed. Emile Durkheim on morality and society. 1973. H1767
Blackwell, J. E. and Janowitz, M. Black sociologists.

1974. H1768
Booth, C. Charles Booth on the city. 1967. H1769
Cottrell, L. S. and others, eds. Ernest W. Burgess on community, family and delinquency. 1973. H1770
Edwards, L. P. The natural history of revolution. 1970. H1771
Faris, R. E. L. Chicago sociology. 1970. H1772
Frazier, E. F. E. Franklin Frazier on race relations, ed. by Edwards. 1968. H1773
Geiger, T. Theodor Geiger on social order and mass society. 1969. H1774
Henderson, L. J. Henderson on the social system. 1970. H1775
MacIver, R. M. Robert M. MacIver on community society and power, ed. by Bramson. 1970. H1776
McKenzie, R. D. Roderick D. McKenzie on human ecology, ed. by Hawley. 1958. H1777
Masaryk, T. G. Suicide and the meaning of civilization. 1970. H1778
Mead, G. H. George Herbert Mead on social psychology, ed. by Strauss. 1968. H1779
Ogburn, W. F. William F. Ogburn on culture and social change, ed. by Duncan. 1964. H1780
Park, R. E. The crowd and the public and other essays, ed. by Elsner. 1972. H1781
____. Introduction to science of sociology. 1969. H1782
____. Robert E. Park on social control and collective behavior, ed. by Turner. 1967. H1783
Park, R. E. and others. The city. 1967. H1784
Schneider, L., ed. The Scottish moralists on human nature and society. 1967. H1785
Schutz, A. Alfred Schutz on phenomenology and social relations. 1970. H1786
Short, J. F. The social fabric of the metropolis. 1970. H1787
Simmel, G. George Simmel on individuality and social forms, ed. by Levine. 1971. H1788
Smelser, N. J., ed. Karl Marx on society and social change. 1973. H1789
Spencer, H. Herbert Spencer on social evolution, ed. by Peel. 1972. H1790
Sutherland, E. H. On analyzing crime, ed. by Schuessler. 1973. H1791
Tarde, G. Gabriel Tarde on communication and social influence. 1969. H1792
Thomas, W. I. W. I. Thomas on social organization and social personality, ed. by Janowitz. 1966. H1793
Toennies, F. Ferdinand Toennies on pure, applied and empirical sociology. 1970. H1794
Waller, W. W. William W. Waller on the family, education, and war. 1970. H1795
Weber, M. On charisma and institution building, ed. by Eisenstadt. 1969. H1796
Wirth, L. Louis Wirth on cities and social life, ed. by Reiss. 1964. H1797
Znaniecki, F. Florian Znaniecki on humanistic sociology, ed. by Bierstedt. 1969. H1798

HESPERIA: SCHRIFTEN ZUR GERMANISCHEN PHILOLOGIE (Johns Hopkins Univ. Pr.)

1 Collitz, H. Das schwache präteritum und seine vorgeschichte. 1912. H1799
2 Burchinal, M. C. Hans Sachs and Goethe. 1912. H1800
3 Riemer, G. C. L. Wörterbuch und reimverzeichnis zu dem Armen Heinrich Hartmann's von Aue. 1912. H1801
4 Morgan, B. Q. Nature in middle high German lyrics. 1914. H1802
5 Rhyne, O. P. Mixed preterites in German. 1915. H1803
6 Rudwin, M. L. Der Teufel in den deutschen geistlichen spielen der mittelalters und der reformationalszeit. 1915. H1804
7 Price, L. M. The attitude

of Gustav Freytag and Julian Schmidt toward English literature (1848-1862). 1915. H1805

8 Sehrt, E. H. Zur geschichte der Westgermanischen konjunktion und. 1916. H1806

9 Blankenagel, J. C. The attitude of Heinrich von Kleist toward the problem of life. 1917. H1807

10 Schaffer, A. George Rudolf Weckerlin, the embodiment of a transitional stage in German metrics. 1918. H1808

11 McCobb, A. L. The double preterit form gie-gienc, lie-liez, vie-vienc in middle high German. 1936. H1809

12 Silz, W. Heinrich V. Kleist's conception of the tragic. 1923. H1810

13 Kroesch, S. Germanic words for deceive. 1923. H1811

14 Sehrt, E. H. Vollstañdiges wortenbuch zum Heliand und zur altsachsichen. 1966. H1812

15 French, W. Mediaeval civilization as illustrated by the Fastnachtspiele of Hans Sachs. 1925. H1813

16 Liptzin, S. The weavers in German literature. 1926. H1814

17 Harn, E. M. Wieland's Neuer Amandis. 1928. H1815

18 Goodloe, J. F. Nomina agentis-auf-el im neubochdeutschen. 1929. H1816

19 Schneiders, M. Die einheimischen nicht komponierten schwachen verben der janklasse im altnordischen. 1938. H1817

20 Bang, C. K. Maske und gesicht in den werken Conrad Ferdinand Meyers. 1940. H1818

21 Runge, E. A. Primitivism and related ideas in sturm und drang literature. 1946. H1819

22 Michael, W. F. Die geistlichen prozessionsspiele in deutschland. 1947. H1820

HIBBERT LECTURES (Macmillan unless otherwise specified)

1878 Muller, F. M. Lectures on the origin and growth of religion as illustrated in the religions of India. Longmans. 1878. H1821

1879 Renouf, P. L. Lectures on the origin and growth of religion as illustrated by the religion of ancient Egypt. Scribner. 1880. H1822

1880 Renan, E. Lectures on the influence of the institutions, thought and culture of Rome, on Christianity and the development of the Catholic Church. Williams. 1898. H1823

1881 Davids, T. W. R. Lectures on the origin and growth of religion as illustrated by some points in the history of Indian Buddhism. Putnam. 1882. H1824

1882 Kuenen, A. National religions and universal religions. Scribner. 1882. H1825

1883 Beard, C. The reformation of the sixteenth century in its relation to modern thought and knowledge. Williams. 1903. H1826

1884 Reville, A. Lectures... by the native religions of Mexico and Peru. Williams. 1884. H1827
Also published as: The native religions of Mexico and Peru. Scribner. 1884. H1828

1885 Pfeiderer, O. Lectures on the influence of the apostle Paul on the development of Christianity. Williams. 1885. H1829
Also published as: The influence of the apostle Paul on the development of Christianity. Scribner. 1885. H1830

1886 Rhys, J. Lectures on the origin and growth of religion as illustrated by Celtic heathendom. Williams. 1898. H1831

1887 Sayce, A. H. Lectures ...of the ancient Babylonians. Williams. 1888. H1832

1888 Hatch, E. The influence of Greek ideas and usages upon the Christian church.

Williams. 1891. H1833
1891 Goblet d'Alviella, E. F. Lectures on the origin and growth of the conception of God as illustrated by anthropology and history. Williams. 1892. H1834
1892 Montefiore, C. J. G. Lectures on origin and growth of religion as illustrated by the religion of the ancient Hebrews. Williams. 1897. H1835
1893 Upton, C. B. Lectures on the bases of religious belief. Williams. 1909. H1836
1894 Drummond, J. Via, veritas vita. Williams. 1895. H1837
1907 Beard, C. The reformation of the sixteenth century. Constable. 1907. H1838
1909 James, W. A pluralistic universe. Longmans. 1909. H1839
1911 Farnell, L. R. The higher aspects of Greek religion. Scribner. 1912. H1840
1912 Moulton, J. H. Early Zoroastrianism. Williams. 1913. H1841
1913 Margoliouth, D. S. The early development of Mohammendanism. Scribner. 1914. H1842
1914 Giles, H. A. Confucianism. Scribner. 1915. H1843
1916 Carpenter, J. E. Theism in modern India. Williams. 1921. H1844
1916 LaVallee Poussin, L. de. The way of Nirvana. Cambridge. 1917. H1845
1916 Wicksteed, P. H. The reactions between dogma and philosophy... Williams. 1920. H1846
1921 Moffatt, J. The approach to the New Testament. Hodder. 1921. H1847
1922 Jacks, L. P. Religious perplexities. Hodder. 1923. H1848
1923 Adler, F. The reconstruction of the spiritual ideal. Appleton. 1924. H1849
1923 Jacks, L. P. A living universe. Harper. 1924. H1850
1924 ____. The challenge of life. Harper. 1925. H1851
1926 Farnell, L. R. The higher aspects of Greek religion. Constable. 1926. H1852
1927 Sperry, W. L. The paradox of religion. 1927. H1853
1929 Rādhākrishnan. Idealist's view of life. 1932. H1854
1930 Tagore, R. The religion of man. 1931. H1855
1931 Hicks, G. D. The philosophical bases of theism. 1937. H1856
1932 Conway, R. S. Ancient Italy and modern religion. 1933. H1857
1933 Jacks, L. P. The revolt against mechanism. 1934. H1858
1937 Murray, G. Liberality and civilization. 1938. H1859
1938 Hocking, W. E. Living religions and a world of faith. 1940. H1860
1946 Major, H. D. A. Civilisation and religious values. 1948. H1861
1953 Samuel, H. L. S. A century's changes of outlook. Cambridge. 1953. H1862
1957 Murray, A. V. The state and the church in a free society. Cambridge. 1958. H1863
1959 Willey, B. Darwin and Butler. Harcourt. 1960. H1864
1963 Nuttall, G. F. and others. The beginnings of nonconformity. J. Clarke. 1964. H1865
1965 Hilliard, F. H. and others. Christianity in education. Allen & Unwin. 1966. H1866

HIGH POLYMERS (Wiley - Interscience)

1 Carothers, W. H. Collected papers by Wallace Hume Carothers on high polymeric substances, ed. by Mark and Whitby. 1940. H1867
2 Mark, H. and Tobolsky, A. V. Physical chemistry of high polymeric systems. 1950. H1868

3 Burnett, G. M. Mechanism of polymer reactions. 1954. H1869
4 Meyer, K. H. Natural and synthetic high polymers. 1950. H1870
5 Ott, E. and others, eds. Cellulose and cellulose derivatives. 2nd ed. 3 v. 1954-55. H1871
6 Alfrey, T. Mechanical behavior of high polymers. 1948. H1872
7 Carswell, T. S. Phenoplasts. 1947. H1873
8 Alfrey, T. and others. Copolymerization. 1952. H1874
9 Bovey, F. A. and others. Emulsion polymerization. 1955. H1875
10 Schildkneckt, C. E., ed. Polymer processes. 1956. H1876
11 Raff, R. A. V. and Allison, J. B. Polyethylene. 1956. H1877
12 Kline, G. M. Analytical chemistry of polymers. 3 v. 1959-62. H1878
13 Gaylord, N. G., ed. Polyethers. 3 v. 1962. H1879
14 Not yet published.
15 Chapiro, A. Radiation chemistry of polymeric systems. 1962. H1880
16 Saunders, J. H. Polyurethanes. 1962. H1881
17 Vol'kenstein, M. V. Configurational statistics of polymeric chains, tr. by S. N. and M. J. Timasheff. 1963. H1882
18 Ham, G. E., ed. Copolymerization. 1964. H1883
19 Fettes, E. M., ed. Chemical reactions of polymers. 1964. H1884
20 Raff, R. A. V. and Doak, K. W., eds. Crystalline olefin polymers. V. 1. 1964. H1885
21 Morawetz, H. Macromolecules in solution. 1965. H1886
22 Birshstein, T. and Ptitsyn, O. Conformation of macromolecules. 1966. H1887
23 Kennedy, J. P. and Tornqvist, E. G. M., ed. Polymer chemistry of synthetic elastomers. Pt. 1. 1968. H1888
24 Leonard, E. C., ed. Vinyl monomers. Pt. 1. 1969. H1889
25 Fluoroplymers, ed. by Wall. 1972. H1890
26 Frisch, K. C., ed. Cyclic monomers. 1972. H1891
27 Stille, J. K. and Campbell, T. W., eds. Condensation monomers. 1972. H1892
28 Schildknecht, C. E. Allyl compounds and their polymers. 1972. H1893

HIGH SPEED AERO-DYNAMICS AND JET PROPULSION (Princeton)

1 Rossini, F. D., ed. Thermodynamics and physics of matter. 1955. H1894
2 Lewis, B. and others, eds. Combustion processes. 1956. H1895
3 Emmons, H. W., ed. Fundamentals of gas dynamics. 1958. H1896
4 Moore, F. K., ed. Theory of laminar flows. 1962. H1897
5 Lin, C., ed. Turbulent flows and heat transfer. 1959. H1898
6 Sears, W. R., ed. General theory of high speed aerodynamics. 1954. H1899
7 Donovan, A. F. and Lawrence, H. R. Aerodynamic components of aircraft at high speeds. 1957. H1900
8 High speed problems of aircraft and experimental methods, ed. by Donovan and others. 1961. H1901
9 Physical measurements in gas dynamics and combustion. Pt. 1, ed. by Ladenburg. Pt. 2, by Lewis and others. 1954. H1902
10 Hawthorne, W. R., ed. Aerodynamics of turbines and compressors. 1964. H1903
11 Hawthorne, W. R. and Olson, W. T., eds. Design and performance of gas turbine power plants. 1960. H1904

12 Lancaster, O. E., ed. Jet propulsion engines. 1959. H1905

HISPANIC FOUNDATION BIBLIOGRAPHICAL SERIES (U.S. Library of Congress)

1 Granier, J. A. Latin American belles-lettres in English translation. 1943. H1906
2 U.S. Library of Congress. Hispanic Foundation. A provisional bibliography of United States books translated into Portuguese. 1957. H1907
3 ___. A provisional bibliography of United States books translated into Spanish. 1957. H1908
4 Gardiner, C. H. William Hickling Prescott. 1959. H1909
5 Okinshevich, L. and Gorokhoff, C. J., comp. Latin America in Soviet writings, 1954-1958. 1959. H1910
6 U.S. Library of Congress. Works by Miguel de Cervantes Saavedra in the Library of Congress, ed. by Aguilera. 1960. H1911
7 Besso, H. V. Ladino books in the Library of Congress. 1963. H1912
8 U.S. Library of Congress. Hispanic Foundation. Spanish and Portuguese traditions of United States books, 1955-1962. 1963. H1913
9 Andrews, D. H. Latin America, ed. by Hillmon. 1964. H1914
10 U.S. Library of Congress. Hispanic Foundation. National directory of Latin Americanists. 1966. H1915
11 Dorn, G. M., comp. Latin America. 1967. H1916
12 Same as 10. 2d ed. 1971. H1917
13 Dorn, G. M., comp. Latin America, Spain and Portugal. 1971. H1918

HISTOIRE DE L'EGLISE DEPUIS LES ORIGINES JUSQU'A NOS JOURS (Bloud)

1 Lebreton, J. and Zeiller, J. L'église primitive. 1946. H1919
2 ___. De la fin 2e siècle à la paix constantinienne. 1948. H1920
3 Palanque, J. R. and others. De la paix constantinienne à la mort de Théodose. 1945. H1921
4 Labriolle, P. C. de and others. De la mort de Théodose à l'élection de Grégoire le Grand. 1945. H1922
5 Bréhier, L. and Aigrain, R. Grégoire le Grand, les états barbares et la conquête arabe (590-757). 1947. H1923
6 Amann, E. L'époque carolingienne. 1947. H1924
7 ___ and Dumas, A. L'église au pouvoir des laïques (888-1057). 1943. H1925
8 Fliche, A. La réforme grégorienne et la reconquête chrétienne (1057-1123). 1946. H1926
9 Fliche, A. and others. Du premier Concile du Latran à l'avènement d'Innocent III (1123-1198). 1944. H1927
10 ___. La chrétienté romaine (1198-1274). 1950. H1928
11 Arquillier, H. X. and others. La centralisation pontificale et les tendances nationales. 1969. H1929
12 Le Bras, G. Les institutions ecclésiastiques de la chrétienté médiévale. 1958. H1930
13 Forest, A. and others. Le mouvement doctrinal du XIe au XIVe siècle. 1951. H1931
14 Delaruelle, E. and others. L'Eglise au temps du grand schisme et de la crise conciliaire (1378-1449). 2 v. 1962-64. H1932
15 Aubenas, R. and Ricard, R. L'Eglise et la Renaissance (1449-1517). 1951. H1933
16 Moreáu, E. de and others. La crise religieuse du XVIe siècle. 1950. H1934
17 Cristiani, L. Le Eglise à l'epoque du Concile de Trente. 1948. H1935
18 Willaert, L. La restauration

catholique, 1563-1648. V. 1. 1960. H1936
19 Préclin, E. and Jarry, E. Les luttes politiques et doctrinales aux XVIIe et XVIIIe siècles. 2 v. 1955-56. H1937
20 Leflon, J. La crise révolutionnaire, 1789-1846. 1949. H1938
21 Aubert, R. Le pontificat de Pie IX (1846-1878). 1952. H1939
22 Bruley, E. L'Eglise à fin du XIXe siècle et au debut du XXe. 1974. H1940

HISTOIRE DES IDEES ET CRITIQUE LITTERAIRE (Droz)

1 Dyson, R. M. Les sensations et la sensibilité chez Francis Jammes. 1954. H1941
2 Hampton, J. Nicolas-Antoine Boulanger et la science de son temps. 1955. H1942
3 Duckworth, C. A study of Léon Bopp. 1955. H1943
4 Cornuz, J. Jules Michelot. 1955. H1944
5 Bell, D. M. Etude sur le Songe du vieil pèlerin de P. de Mézières. 1955. H1945
6 Ceitac, J. Voltaire et l'affaire des natifs. 1956. H1946
7 Zayed, G. Lettres inédites de Verlaine à Cazals. 1957. H1947
8 Collet, G. P. George Moore et la France. 1957. H1948
9 Croniczer, E. Quelques antécédents de à la recherche du temps perdu. 1957. H1949
10 Martini, M. Une reine du Second Empire: Marie Laetitia Bonaparte-Wyse. 1957. H1950
11 Healey, F. F. Rousseau et Napoléon. 1957. H1951
12 Temmer, M. J. Time in Rousseau and Kant. 1958. H1952
13 Bourgeois, A. La vie de Rene Boylesve. 1958. H1953
14 Brody, J. Boileau and Longinus. 1958. H1954
15 Buckler, W. E. Matthew Arnold's Books. 1958. H1955
16 Freudmann, F. R. The memoirs of Madame de La Guette. 1958. H1956
17 Rudhardt, J. Notions fondamentales de la pensée religieuse et actes constitutifs du culte dans la Grèce classique. 1958. H1957
18 Waldinger, R. Voltaire and reform in the light of the French Revolution. 1959. H1958
19 Jensen, C. A. E. L'évolution du romantisme. 1959. H1959
20 Healey, F. G. The literary culture of Napoleon. 1959. H1960
21 Brachfield, G. I. André Gide and the Communist temptation. 1959. H1961
22 Scales, D. Alphonse Karr. 1959. H1962
23 Robinson, R. E. William Hazlitt's Life of Napoleon Bonaparte. 1959. H1963
24 Perkins, M. L. The moral and political philosophy of the Abbe Pierre. 1959. H1964
25 Zagona, H. G. The legend of Salome and the principle of art for art's sake. 1959. H1965
26 Porter, L. C. La fatrasie et la fatras. 1960. H1966
27 Freudmann, F. R. L'etonnant Gourville. 1960. H1967
28 Testuz, M. Les idées religieuses du Livre des jubilés. 1960. H1968
29 Teichmann, E. La fortune de E. T. A. Hoffmann en France. 1961. H1969
30 Duval, E. L. Téodor de Wyzewa. 1961. H1970
31 Dentan, M. Humour et création littéraire dans l'oeuvre de Kafka. 1961. H1971
32 Barko, I. L'esthétique littéraire de Charles Maurras. 1961. H1972
33 Sutton, H. The life and work of Juan Richepin. 1961. H1973
34 Monty, J. La critique littéraire de Melchoir Grimm. 1961. H1974
35 Gourier, F. Etude des oeuvres poétiques de Saint-Amant. 1961. H1975

36 Robert, D. Genève et les église réformées de France. 1961. H1976
37 ____. Textes et documents relatifs à l'histoire des églises réformées en France. 1962. H1977
38 Myers, R. L. The dramatic theories of Elie-Catherine Fréron. 1962. H1978
39 Kuhn, R. The return to reality. 1962. H1979
40 Kolbert, J. Edmond Jaloux et sa critique littéraire. 1962. H1980
41 Calin, W. C. The old French epic of revolt. 1962. H1981
42 Bell, D. M. L'idéal éthique de la royauté en France au moyen âge. 1962. H1982
43 Braunstein, E. François de Curel et le théâtre d'idées. 1962. H1983
44 Jasenas, E. Marceline Desbordes-Valmore devant la critique. 1962. H1984
45 Guiragossian, D. Voltaire's Faceties. 1963. H1985
46 Denommé, R. T. The naturalism of Gustave Geffroy. 1963. H1986
47 Kanes, M. L'Atelier de Zola. 1963. H1987
48 Bergens, A. Raymond Queneau. 1963. H1988
49 Hogue, H. H. S. Of changes in B. Constant's Books on religion... 1964. H1989
50 Harding, F. J. W. Matthew Arnold. 1964. H1990
51 Brooks, R. A. Voltaire and Leibniz. 1964. H1991
52 Maurocordato, A. Anglo-American influences in Paul Claudel. 1964. H1992
53 Trousson, R. Le thème de Promethee dans la litterature europeenne. 2 v. 1964. H1993
54 Stone, J. A. Sophocles and Racine. 1964. H1994
55 May, G. De Jean-Jacques Rousseau à Madame Roland. 1964. H1995
56 Bailey, H. P. Hamlet in France. 1964. H1996
57 Soulier, J. P. Lautréamont. 1964. H1997
58 Rogers, B. G. Proust's narrative techniques. 1965. H1998
59 Seylaz, J. L. Les liaisons dangereuses et la création romanesque chez Laclos. 1965. H1999
60 Cornelius, P. Languages in seventeenth and early eighteenth-century imaginary voyages. 1965. H2000
61 Colby, A. M. The portrait in twelfth century French literature. 1965. H2001
62 Allart, H. Nouvelles lettres à Sainte-Beuve. 1965. H2002
63 Muller, M. Les voix narratives dans la Recherches du temps perdu. 1965. H2003
64 Autret, J. Ruskin and the French before Marcel Proust. 1966. H2004
65 Deguise, P. Benjamin Constant méconnu: Le Livre de la religion. 1966. H2005
66 Weinshenker, A. B. Falconet. 1966. H2006
67 Gindine, Y. Aragon prosateur surréaliste. 1966. H2007
68 Schwartz, J. Diderot and Montaigne. 1966. H2008
69 Alter, J. La vision du monde d'Alain Robbe-Grillet. 1966. H2009
70 Nicod, M. Du réalisme à la réalitè. 1966. H2010
71 Sholad, B. Charlemagne in Spain. 1966. H2011
72 Browder, C. André Breton. 1967. H2012
73 Sareil, J. Seeai sur Candide. 1967. H2013
74 May, G. Diderot et Baudelaire. 1973. H2014
75 Lanius, E. W. Cyrano de Bergerac and the universe of the imagination. 1967. H2015
76 Tricaud, M. L. Le baroque dans le theatre de Paul Claudel. 1967. H2016
77 Hardee, A. M. Jean de Lannel and the preclassical French novel. 1967. H2017
78 Gochberg, H. S. Stage of dreams. 1967. H2018
79 Goodrich, N. L. Charles de Orléans. 1967. H2019

80 Hytier, J. Questions de littérature. 1967. H2020
81 Dulait, S. Inventaire raisonné des autographes de Molière. 1967. H2021
82 Rogers, B. G. The novels and stories of Barbey d'Aurevilly. 1967. H2022
83 Brady, P. L'oeuvre de Emile Zola. 1968. H2023
84 Holdheim, W. W. Theory and practice of the novel. 1968. H2024
85 Putter, I. Le dernière illusion de Leconte de Lisle. 1968. H2025
86 Marmier, X. Journal, ed. by Kaye. 2 v. 1968. H2026
87 Haidu, P. Aesthetic distance in Chrétien de Troyes. 1968. H2027
88 Dassonville, M. Ronsard. 1968. H2028
89 Prince, G. J. Métaphysique et technique dans l'oeuvre romanesque de Sartre. 1968. H2029
90 Paxton, N. The development of Mallarmé's Prose style. 1968. H2030
91 Lausanne. Benjamin Constant, ed. by Cordey and Seylaz. 1968. H2031
92 Giraud, Y. F. A. La fable de Daphné. 1968. H2032
93 Meylan, J. P. La revue de Genève. 1968. H2033
94 Perkins, J. A. The concept of the self in the French enlightenment. 1969. H2034
95 Mortier, R. Clartés et ombres du siècle des Lumières. 1969. H2035
96 Nesselroth, P. W. Lautréamont's imagery. 1969. H2036
97 Besser, G. R. Balzac's concept of genius. 1969. H2037
98 Spencer, M. C. The art of criticism of Théophile Gautier. 1969. H2038
99 Bonard, O. Peinture et création litteraire chez Balzac. 1970. H2039
100 Chateaubriand, ed. by Switzer. 1970. H2040
101 Trembley, G. Marcel Schwab, faussaire de la nature. 1970. H2041
102 Sareil, J. Les tencin. 1970. H2042
103 Alter, J. V. L'esprit antibourgeois sous l'ancien régime. 1970. H2043
104 Conlon, P. M. Prelude au siècle des lumieres en France. V. 1. 1970. H2044
105 Fellows, O. From Voltaire to La nouvelle critique. 1970. H2045
106 Brady, V. P. Love in the theatre of Marivoux. 1970. H2046
107 Fenelon, F. Oeuvres-plus-que-completes, ed. by Halperin. 2 v. 1970. H2047
108 Cutler, M. G. Evocations of the eighteenth century in French poetry. 1970. H2048
109 Alcover, M. La pensee philosophique et scientifique de Cyrano de Bergerac. 1970. H2049
110 Thompson, C. W. Victor Hugo and the graphic arts. 1970. H2050
111 Dassonville, M. Ronsard. 1970. H2051
112 Hyde, J. K. Benjamin Fondane. 1971. H2052
113 Andlau, B. d'. La jeunesse de Madame de Stael. 1971. H2053
114 Kaye, E. Xavier Forneret dit (L'homme noir). 1971. H2054
115 Same as no. 104. V. 2. H2055
116 Somville, L. Devanciers du surrealisme. 1971. H2056
117 Van Delft, L. La Bruyère moraliste. 1971. H2057
118 The persistent voice. Essays on Hellenism in French literature... in honor of Henri M. Peyre. 1971. H2058
119 Laurie, H. C. Two studies in Chretien de Troyes. 1972. H2059
120 Mattei, M. Lettres de Marie Mattei à Théophile Gautier, ed. by Kaye. 1972. H2060
121 Same as no. 104. V. 3. 1972. H2061
122 Gruber, A. C. Les

grandes fetes et leurs décors à l'époque de Louis XVI. 1972. H2062
123 Haidu, P. Lion-quede coupée. 1972. H2063
124 Zakarian, R. H. Zola's Germinal. 1972. H2064
125 Masson, A. Le décor de bibliothèques. 1972. H2065
126 Girdlestone, C. La tragédie en musique, considérée comme genre littéraire. 1972. H2066
127 Kogel, R. Pierre Charron. 1972. H2067
128 Simons, M. A. Amitié et passion, Rousseau et Sauttersheim. 1972. H2068
129 Smithson, R. N. The evolution of the historical method of Augustin Thierry. 1973. H2069
130 Turbet-Delof, G. L'Afrique barbaresque dans la littérature française. 1973. H2070
131 Same as no. 104. V. 4. 1973. H2071
132 Schub, L. R. Léon-Paul Fargue. 1973. H2072
133 Estaunié, E. Souvenirs. 1973. H2073
134 Bowman, F. Le Christ romantique. 1973. H2074
135 Gautier, T. Voyage pittoresque en Algérie. 1973. H2075
136 Harding, F. J. W. Jean-Marie Guyau. 1973. H2076
137 Pfohl, R. Racine's Iphigénie. 1974. H2077
138 Turbet-Delof, G. La presse periodique française et l'Afrique barbaresque au XVIIe siècle. 1973. H2078
139 Conlon, P. M. Prélude au siècle des lumières en France. 1974. H2079
140 Essays on Diderot and the enlightenment in honor of Otis Fellows, ed. by Pappas. 1974. H2080
141 Grimsley, R. From Montesquieu to Laclos. 1974. H2081
142 Croquette, B. De Montaigne à Pascal. 1974. H2082
143 Lowrie, J. O. The violent mystique. 1974. H2083
144 Mortier, R. La poetique des ruines en France. 1974. H2084
145 Kelly, T. E. Le haut livre du graal, perlesvaus. 1974. H2085

HISTOIRE DES RELATIONS INTERNATIONALES (Hachette)

1 Ganshof, F. L. Le Moyen Age. 1953. H2086
2-3 Zeller, G. Les temps modernes. 2 v. 1953-55. H2087
4 Fugier, A. La Révolution française et l'Empire napoléonien. 1954. H2088
5-6 Renouvin, P. Le XIXe [i. e. dix neuvième] siècle. 2 v. 1954-55. H2089
7-8 ___. Les crises du XXe siècle. 2 v. 1957-59. H2090

HISTOIRE DU MONDE (Boccard)

1 Cavaignac, E. Prolégomènes. 1922. H2091
2 ___. Le monde méditerranéen... 1929. H2092
3 La Vallée-Poussin, L. de. Indo-Européens et Indo-Iranians. 1924. H2093
4 Maspero, H. La Chine antique. 1927. H2094
5:1 Cavaignac, E. La paix romaine. 1928. H2095
5:2 Zeiller, J. L'empire romain et l'église. 1928. H2096
6:1 La Vallée-Poussin, L. de. L'Inde au temps des Mauryas et des barbares Grecs, Scythes, Parthes et Yuetchi. 1930. H2097
6:2 ___. Dynasties et histoire de l'Inde depuis Kanishka jusqu-aux invasions musulmanes. 1935. H2098
7:1 Gaudefroy-Demombynes, M. and Platonov, S. F. Le monde musulman et byzantin jusqu-aux croisades. 1931. H2099
7:2 Fliche, A. La chrétienté medievale, 395-1254. 1929. H2100
8:1 Prasad, I. L'Inde du VIIe au XVIe siècle. 1930. H2101

8:2 Coedes, G. Les états hindouisés d'Indochine et d'Indonésie. 1948. H2102
8:3 Grousset, R. L'empire mongol. 1941. H2103
8:4 Platonov, S. F. La Russie moscovite. 1932. H2104
9 Langlois, C. L'Amérique pré-colombienne et la conquête européenne. 1928. H2105
10 Linden, H. Van der. L'hégémonie européenne. 1936. H2106
11 Cavaignac, E. Introduction: Politique mondiale (1492-1575). 1934. H2107
12 Vaucher, P. Le monde anglo-saxon au XIXe siècle. 1926. H2108
12 bis. Vermeil, E. L'empire allemand, 1871-1900. 1926. H2109
13:1 Rocheblave, S. Les arts plastique de 1500 à 1815. 1928. H1210
13:2 Chevaillier, L. La musique. 1928. H2111
13:3 Pérès, J. Les sciences exactes. 1930. H2112
13:4 Metzger, H. La chimie. 1930. H2113
13:5 Ambard, L. La biologie. 1930. H2114

HISTOIRE DU TRAVAIL ET DE LA VIE ECONOMIQUE (Aubier)

Antony, H. Economie et prospective. 1973. H2115
Baudin, L. Le crédit. 1934. H2116
Bourgin, G. L'Etat corporatif en Italie. 1935. H2117
Coyle, D. C. Le système politique de Etats-Unis. 1960. H2118
Laroque, P. Les rapports entre patrons et ouvriers. 1938. H2119
Lascaux, R. The crise et problème monétaire. 1935. H2120
Lefranc, G. Les expériences syndicales en France de 1939 à 1950. 1950. H2121
____. Les expériences syndicales internationales des origines à nos jours. 1952. H2122
____. Grèves d'hier et d'aujourd'hui. 1973. H2123
____. Histoire des doctrines sociales dans l'Europe contemporaine. 1957. H2124
____. Jaurès et le socialisme des intellectuels. 1972. H2125
Montreuil, J. Histoire du mouvement ouvrier en France. 1946. H2126
Mosse, R. Economie et législation industrielles. 1940. H2127
Philip, A. La gauche, mythes et réalités. 1972. H2128
____. Histoire des faits économiques et sociaux de 1800 à nos jours. 1961. H2129
____. May 1968 et la foi démocratique. 1965. H2130
____. Trade unionisme et syndicalisme. 1936. H2131
Renaudeau, F. Le parti travailliste de Grande-Bretagne, 1900-45. 1946. H2132
Rosier, C. L'impôt; qu'est-ce que l'impôt? 1936. H2133

HISTOIRE GENERALE (Presses universitaires de France)

1. Histoire ancienne.
1 Moret, A. Histoire de l'Orient.
  1 Préhistoire. 1950. H2134
  2 IIe et Ier millénaires. 1941. H2135
2 Histoire de la Grece.
  1-3 Glotz, G. and Cohen, R. Des origines aux guerres médiques. 1949. H2136
  2 La Grèce au Ve siècle. 1949. H2137
  3 La Grèce au IVe siècle. 1947. H2138
  4 Glotz, G. and others. Alexandre et l'hellénisation du monde antique.
    1 Alexandre et le démembrement de son empire. 1945. H2139
3 Histoire romaine.
  1 Pais, E. Des origines à l'achièvement de la conquête. 1940. H2140
  2 Bloch, J. and others.

La république romaine.
2 v. 1940-43. H2141
3 Carcopino, J. César.
1950. H2142
3 Homo, L. Le haut-empire. 1941. H2143
4:1 Besnier, M. L'Empire romain de l'avènement des Sévères au Concile de Nicée. 1945. H2144
4:2 Piganiol, A. L'empire chrétien, 325-395. 1947. H2145
4 Histoire du moyen âge.
1 Lot, F. Les destinées de l'Empire en occident de 395 à 888. 2 v. 1947. H2146
2 Fliche, A. L'Europe occidentale de 888 à 1125. 1941. H2147
3 Diehl, C. Le monde oriental de 395 à 1081. 1936. H2148
4:1 Jordan, E. L'Allemagne et l'Italie aux XIIe et XIIIe. 1939. H2149
4:2 Petit-Dutaillis, C. and Guinard, P. L'essor des états d'Occident. 1944. H2150
6:1 Fawtier, R. Pt. 1. L'Europe occidentale de 1270 à 1380. Pt. 2. L'Europe occidentale de 1270 à 1328. 1940. H2151
6:2 Coville, A. L'Europe occidentale de 1270 à 1380. L'Europe occidentale de 1328 à 1380. 1941. H2152
7:1-2 Calmette, J. and Déprez, E. L'Europe occidentale de la fin du XIVe siècle aux guerres d'Italie.
1 La France et l'Angleterre en conflict. 1937. H2153
2 Les premières grandes puissances. 1929. H2154
8 Pirenne, H. and others. La civilisation occidenttale au moyen âge. 1944. H2155
9 Diehl, C. and others. L'Europe orientale de 1081 à 1453. 1945. H2156
10:1 Grousset, R. L'Asie orientale des origines au XVe siècle.
1 Les empires. 1941. H2157
2 Les institutiones. 1941. H2158
5 Not published.

HISTOIRE SOCIALISTE (1789-1900) (Ruoff)

1 Jaures, J. L. La Constituante. (1789-1791). 1901. H2159
2 ____. La Législative (1791-1792). 1904? H2160
3-4 ____. La Convention. 2 v. 1904? H2161
5 Deville, G. P. Thermidor & directoire (1794-1799). 1904. H2162
6 Brousse, P. Consulate & empire (1799-1815). 1905. H2163
7 Viviani, R. La restauration (1814-1830). 1906. H2164
8 Fournière, E. La règne de Louis Philippe (1830-1848). 1906. H2165
9 Renard, G. F. La république de 1848 (1848-1852). 1907. H2166
10 Thomas, A. Le second empire (1852-1870). 1907. H2167
11 Jaures, J. L. La guerre franco-allemande (1870-1871). 1908. H2168
12 Labusquiere, J. La troisième république (1871-1900). 1908. H2169
Index Thomas, A. A. Table analytique alphabétique. 1908. H2170

HISTORIC OKLAHOMA SERIES (Univ. of Okla. Pr.)

1 Foreman, G. Fort Gibson. 1943. H2171
2 ____. Down the Texas trail. 1936. H2172
3 Forbes, G. Guthrie. 1938. H2173
4 Kaho, N. The Will Rogers country. 1941. H2174
5 Debo, A. Tulsa. 1943. H2175
6 Foreman, G. Muskogee. 1943. H2176

HISTORICAL AND CULTURAL DICTIONARIES OF ASIA (Scarecrow)

1 Riley, C. H. Historical and cultural dictionary of Saudi Arabia. 1972. H2177
2 Hedrick, B. C. and A. K. Historical and cultural dictionary of Nepal. 1972. H2178
3 Maury, E. G. Historical and cultural dictionary of the Philippines. 1973. H2179
4 Maring, J. M. and E. G. Historical and cultural dictionary of Burma. 1973. H2180

HISTORICAL PROBLEMS: STUDIES AND DOCUMENTS (Barnes and Noble)

1 Norman, E. R. Anti-Catholicism in Victorian England. 1968. H2181
2 Simon, W. M. Germany in the age of Bismarck. 1968. H2182
3 Marshall, P. J. Problems of empire. 1968. H2183
4 Titow, J. Z. English rural society, 1200-1350. 1969. H2184
5 O'Neill, W. L. The woman movement. 1969. H2185
6 Kerridge, E. Agrarian problems of the sixteenth century and after. 1969. H2186
7 Shennan, J. H. Government and society in France. 1969. H2187
8 Cross, C. The Royal supremacy in the Elizabethan Church. 1969. H2188
9 McKelvey, B. The city in American history. 1969. H2189
10 Wolffe, B. P. Crown lands 1461 to 1536. 1970. H2190
11 Beales, D. The risorgimento and the unification of Italy. 1971. H2191
12 Morgan, K. O. The age of Lloyd George. 1971. H2192
13 Jones, W. J. Politics and the Bench. 1971. H2193
14 Youings, J. A. The dissolution of the monasteries. 1971. H2194
15 Hill, B. H. Medieval monarchy in action. 1972. H2195
16 Ault, W. O. Open-field farming in medieval England. 1972. H2196
17 ____. ____: a study of village by-laws. 1972. H2197
18 Drummond, I. M. British economic policy and the empire. 1972. H2198
19 Brown, R. A. Origins of English feudalism. 1973. H2199
20 Glover, R. A. Britain at Bay. 1973. H2200
21 Levine, M. Tudor dynastic problems, 1460-1571. 1973. H2201
22 Roseveare, H. The Treasury, 1660-1870. 1973. H2202
23 Hurwitz, E. F. Politics and public conscience. 1973. H2203

HISTORICAL RECORDS SURVEY. AMERICAN IMPRINTS INVENTORY Nos. 21, 22, 28-30, 33-35, 37, 46-51 not published

1 Historical records survey. A preliminary check list of Missouri imprints, 1808-1850. Survey, 1734 New York Ave., N.Y. 1937. H2204
2 Martin, M. R. Check list of Minnesota imprints, 1849-1865. Survey, 950 Michigan Ave., Evanston, Ill. 1938. H2205
3 Historical records survey. A check list of Arizona imprints, 1860-1890. Survey, 950 Michigan Ave., Evanston, Ill. 1938. H2206
4 Historical records survey. A check list of Chicago ante-fire imprints, 1851-1871. Survey, 950 Michigan Ave., Evanston, Ill. 1938. H2207
5 McMurtie, D. C. Check list of Kentucky imprints, 1787-1810. Survey, 9th and Broadway, Louisville, Ky. 1939. H2208
6 McMurtie, D. C. and Allen, A. H. Check list of Kentucky imprints, 1811-20. Survey, 9th and Broadway, Louisville, Ky. 1939. H2209

7 Historical records survey. A check list of Nevada imprints, 1859-1890. Survey, 950 Michigan Ave., Evanston, Ill. 1939. H2210

8 Historical records survey. Alabama. Check list of Alabama imprints, 1807-1840. Survey, 2104 1/2 2d Ave., N. Birmingham, Ala. 1939. H2211

9 Morsch, L. M. Check list of New Jersey imprints, 1784-1800. Survey, 34th and Frisby Sts., Baltimore, Maryland. 1939. H2212

10 Historical records survey. Check list of Kansas imprints, 1854-1876. Survey, 812 Kansas Ave., Topeka, Kans. 1939. H2213

11 Chicago Historical Society, Library. A check list of the Kellogg collection of "patent inside" newspapers of 1876. Survey, 950 Michigan Ave., Evanston, Ill. 1939. H2214

12 McMurtie, D. C. A check list of the imprints of Sag Harbor, L. I., 1791-1820. Survey, 950 Michigan Ave., Evanston, Ill. 1939. H2215

13 Historical records survey. A check list of the Idaho imprints, 1839-90. Survey, 950 Michigan Ave., Evanston, Ill. 1940. H2216

14 ____. A check list of West Virginia imprints, 1791-1830. Survey, 950 Michigan Ave., Evanston, Ill. 1940. H2217

15 ____. A check list of Iowa imprints, 1838-1860. Survey, 950 Michigan Ave., Evanston, Ill. 1940. H2218

16 ____. List of Tennessee imprints, 1793-1840 in Tennessee libraries. Survey, Nashville, Tenn. 1941. H2219

17 Historical records survey. Ohio. A check list of Ohio imprints, 1796-1820. Ohio State Museum, Columbus, Ohio. 1941. H2220

18 Historical records survey. Illinois. A check list of Wyoming imprints, 1866-1890. Survey, 950 Michigan Ave., Evanston, Ill. 1941. H2221

19 Foote, L. B. Bibliography of the official publications of Louisiana, 1803-1934. Survey, Louisiana State Univ. Baton Rouge, La. 1942. H2222

20 Historical records survey. Tennessee. Check list of Tennessee imprints, 1841-1850. Survey, Nashville, Tenn. 1941. H2223

23-24 Historical records survey. Wisconsin. A check list of Wisconsin imprints, 1833-49, 1850-54. 2 v. Survey, Madison, Wis. 1942. H2224

25 Historical records survey. Illinois. Check list of New Mexico imprints and publications, 1784-1876. Survey, New Mexico. 1942. H2225

26-27 Historical records survey. Nebraska. A check list of Nebraska non-documentary imprints, 1847-76. Division of community service programs, W. P. A., Lincoln, Neb. 1942. H2226

31 Historical records survey. California. A check list of California non-documentary imprints, 1833-55. W. P. A., Los Angeles, Calif. 1942. H2227

32 Historical records survey. Illinois. A check list of Tennessee imprints, 1793-1840. Survey, 950 Michigan Ave., Evanston, Ill. 1942. H2228

36 Historical records survey. Illinois. A check list of Utica imprints, 1799-1840. Survey, 950 Michigan Ave., Evanston, Ill. 1942. H2229

38 Historical records survey. Kentucky. Supplementary check list of Kentucky imprints, 1788-1820. 1942 (Misnumbered 25) H2230

39 Historical records survey. Arkansas. A check list of Arkansas imprints, 1821-76. Survey, Little Rock, Ark. 1942. H2231

40 American imprints inventory project. Massachusetts. A

check list of Massachusetts imprints, 1801. V. 1. 1942. H2232
41-42 Historical records survey. A check list of Wisconsin imprints, 1855-59, 1859-63. 2 v. 1942. H2233
44 Historical records survey. Washington (State). A check list of Washington imprints, 1853-76. Survey, Seattle, Wash. 1942. H2234
45 Same as no. 40. 1802. V. 2. 1942. H2235
52 Historical records survey. Michigan. Preliminary check list of Michigan imprints, 1796-1850. Survey, Detroit, Mich. 1942. H2236

HISTORIES OF THE AMERICAN FRONTIER (Holt)

Bannon, J. F. The Spanish Borderlands frontier. 1970. H2237
Billington, R. A. America's frontier heritage. 1966. H2238
Eccles, W. J. The Canadian frontier, 1534-1760. 1969. H2239
Fite, G. C. The farmer's frontier, 1865-1900. 1966. H2240
Horsman, R. The frontier in the formative years. 1970. H2241
Leach, D. E. The northern colonial frontier, 1607-1763. 1966. H2242
Paul, R. W. Mining frontiers of the Far West, 1848-1880. 1963. H2243
Sosin, J. M. The Revolutionary frontier, 1763-1783. 1967. 1963. H2244
Winther, O. O. The transportation frontier, 1763-83. 1964. H2245

HISTORY OF AMERICAN FOREIGN POLICY (Macmillan)

Dulles, F. R. Prelude to world power. 1965. H2246

A HISTORY OF AMERICAN LIFE (Macmillan)

1 Priestley, H. I. The coming of the white man, 1492-1848. 1929. H2247
2 Wertenbaker, T. J. The first Americans, 1607-1690. 1927. H2248
3 Adams, J. T. Provincial society, 1690-1763. 1927. H2249
4 Greene, E. B. The revolutionary generation, 1763-1790. 1943. H2250
5 Krout, J. A. The completion of independence, 1790-1830. 1944. H2251
6 Fish, C. R. The rise of the common man. 1929. H2252
7 Cole, A. C. The irrepressible conflict, 1850-1865. 1934. H2253
8 Nevins, A. The emergence of modern America, 1865-1878. 1927. H2254
9 Tarbell, I. M. The nationalizing of business, 1878-1898. 1936. H2255
10 Schlesinger, A. M. The rise of the city, 1878-1898. 1933. H2256
11 Faulkner, H. U. The quest for social justice, 1898-1914. 1931. H2257
12 Slosson, P. W. The great crusade and after, 1914-1928. 1931. H2258
13 Wecter, D. The age of the great depression, 1929-1941. 1948. H2259

HISTORY OF CIVILIZATION (Knopf unless otherwise stated)

Christianity and the Middle Ages:
Boissonnade, P. Life and work in medieval Europe (fifth to the fifteenth centuries), tr. by Powers. 1927. H2260
Guignebert, C. A. H. Jesus, tr. by Hooke. 1935. H2261
Labriolle, P. C. de. History and literature of Christianity from Tertullian to Boethius, tr. by Wilson. 1924. H2262
Newton, A. P., ed. Travel and travellers of the middle ages. 1926. H2263
Petit-Dutaillis, C. E. The feudal monarchy in France

and England from the tenth to thirteenth century, tr. by Hunt. 1949. H2264

Early Empire:

Guignebert, C. A. H. The Jewish world in the time of Jesus, tr. by Hooke. 1939. H2265

Lods, A. Israel, from its beginnings to the middle of the eighth century, tr. by Hooke. 1932. H2266

____. The prophets and the rise of Judaism, tr. by Hooke. Trench. 1937. H2267

Moret, A. The Nile and Egyptian civilization, tr. by Dobie. 1928. H2268

Historical Ethnology:

Bendann, E. Death customs. 1930. H2269

Buxton, L. H. D. The peoples of Asia. 1925. H2270

Fox, C. E. The threshold of the Pacific, tr. by Smith. 1924. H2271

Karsten, R. The civilization of the South American Indians. 1926. H2272

Macleod, W. C. The American Indian frontier. 1928. H2273

Middle Ages to Modern:

Cartellieri, O. The Court of Burgandy, tr. by Letts. 1929. H2274

Lewis, E. Medieval political philosophy. 2 v. 1954. H2275

Prestage, E., ed. Chivalry. 1928. H2276

Modern History:

George, M. D. London life in the XVIIIth century. 1925. H2277

LeFevre, L. Liberty and restraint. 1931. H2278

Reichwein, A. China and Europe in the eighteenth century, tr. by Powell. 1925. H2279

Renard, G. F. and Weulerse, G. Life and work in modern Europe (fifteenth to eighteenth centuries), tr. by Clark. 1929. H2280

Pre-History and Antiquity:

Burn, A. R. Minoans, Philistines and Greeks, B.C. 1400-900. 1930. H2281

____. The world of Hesiod. Trench. 1936. H2282

Burns, A. R. Money and monetary policy in early times. 1927. H2283

Chapot, V. The Roman world, tr. by Parker. 1928. H2284

Childe, V. G. The Aryans. 1926. H2285

____. The dawn of European civilization. Trubner. 1957. H2286

Declareuil, J. Rome the law giver, tr. by Parker. 1927. H2287

Delaporte, L. J. Mesopotamia, tr. by Childe. 1925. H2288

Febvre, L. P. V. A geographical introduction to history. 1925. H2289

Ghurye, G. S. Caste and race in India. Trench. 1932. H2290

Glotz, G. The AEgean civilization, tr. by Dobie and Riley. 1925. H2291

____. Ancient Greece at work, tr. by Dobie. 1926. H2292

____. The Greek city and its institutions, tr. by Mallinson. 1929. H2293

Granet, M. Chinese civilization, tr. by Innes and Brailsford. 1930. H2294

Grenier, A. The Roman spirit in religion, thought, and art. 1926. H2295

Homo, L. P. Primitive Italy and the beginnings of Roman imperialism, tr. by Childe. 1927. H2296

____. Roman political institutions from city to state, tr. by Dobie. 1929. H2297

Huart, C. I. Ancient Persia and Iranian civilization. 1927. H2298

Hubert, H. The rise of the Celts, tr. by Dobie. 1934. H2299

____. The greatness and decline of the Celts. 1934. H2300

Jardé, A. F. V. The formation of the Greek people, tr. by Roble. 1926. H2301

Jouguet, P. Macedonian imperialism and the Hellenization of the East, tr. by Dobie. 1928. H2302

Lot, F. The end of the ancient

world, tr. by Leon. 1931. H2303
Louis, P. Ancient Rome at work. 1927. H2304
Mackenzie, D. A. The migration of symbols and their relations to belief and customs. 1926. H2305
Masson-Oursel, P. and others. Ancient India and Indian civilization, tr. by Collum. 1934. H2306
Moret, A. and Davy, G. From tribe to empire, tr. by Childe. 1926. H2307
____. The Nile and Egyptian civilization, tr. by Dobie. 1927. H2308
Morgan, J. J. M. de. Prehistoric man, tr. by Paxton. 1934. H2309
Parker, E. H. A thousand years of the Tartars. 1926. H2310
Perrier, E. The earth before history, tr. by Radin and Collum. 1934. H2311
Pittard, E. Race and history, tr. by Collum. 1926. H2312
Reich, E. Graeco-Roman institutions. 1890. H2313
Renard, G. F. Life and work in prehistoric times, tr. by Clark. 1929. H2314
Ridder, A. H. P. de and Deonna, W. Art in Greece, tr. by Collum. 1927. H2315
Rivers, W. H. R. Social organization, ed. by Perry. 1924. H2316
Robin, L. Greek thought and the origins of the scientific spirit, ed. by Dobie. 1928. H2317
Robinson, D. M. Short history of Greece. 1936. H2318
Sidhanta, N. K. K. The heroic age of India. 1930. H2319
Thomas, E. J. The history of Buddhist thought. 1933. H2320
____. The life of Buddha as legend and history. 1927. H2321
Toutain, J. The economic life of the ancient world, tr. by Dobie. 1930. H2322
Vendryes, J. Language, tr. by Radin. 1931. H2323
Subject histories:
Cumston, C. G. An introduction to the history of medicine. 1926. H2324
Gray, C. The history of music. 1935. H2325
Summers, M. The geography of witchcraft. 1927. H2326
____. The history of witchcraft and demonology. 1926. H2327

THE HISTORY OF CIVILIZATION SERIES (Praeger)

Ashley, M. P. The golden century: Europe, 1598-1715. 1969. H2328
Bowra, C. M. The Greek experience. 1969. H2329
Burney, C. A. and Lang, D. A. The peoples of the hills. 1972. H2330
Clissord, S. Bernardo O'Higgins and the independence of Chile. 1969. H2331
Erickson, A. B. and Havram, M. J. England, prehistory to the present. 1968. H2332
Frye, R. N. The heritage of Persia. 1969. H2333
Grant, M. The world of Rome. 1969. H2334
Hatton, R. Europe in the age of Louis XIV, ed. by Barraclough. 1969. H2335
Heer, F. The Holy Roman Empire, tr. by Sondheimer. 1969. H2336
Hobsbawm, E. J. The age of Revolution. 1969. H2337
Mansergh, N. The commonwealth experience. 1969. H2338
Montet, P. Eternal Egypt. 1969. H2339
Moscati, S. The world of the Phoenicians, tr. by Hamilton. 1969. H2340
Parry, J. H. The age of reconnaissance; discovery. 1969. H2341
Pudney, J. Suez, De Lessep's canal. 1969. H2342
Rudé, G. F. E. Europe in the eighteenth century. 1972. H2343
Vatikiotis, P. J. The modern history of Egypte. 1969. H2344
Vogt, J. The decline of Rome. 1969. H2345

A HISTORY OF ENGLAND (Methuen)

1 Oman, C. W. C. England before the Norman Conquest. 1910. H2346
2 Davis, H. W. C. England under the Norman and Angevin, 1066-1272. 1958. H2347
3 Vickers, K. H. England in the later middle ages. 1960. H2348
4 Innes, A. D. England under the Tudors. 1911. H2349
5 Trevelyan, G. M. England under the Stuarts. 1925. H2350
6 Robertson, C. G. England under the Hanoverians. 1911. H2351
7 Marriott, J. A. R. England since Waterloo. 1954. H2352
8 ____. Modern England, 1885-1932. 1948. H2353
____. ____, 1885-1955. 1960. H2354

HISTORY OF EUROPE SERIES (Harper)

Droz, J. Europe between revolutions, 1815-1848. 1968. H2355
Elliott, J. H. Europe divided, 1559-1598. 1969. H2356
Elton, G. R. Reformation Europe, 1517-1599. 1966. H2357
Hale, J. R. Renaissance Europe. 1972. H2358
Ogg, D. Europe of the ancien regimé, 1715-1783. 1966. H2359
Rudé, G. Revolutionary Europe, 1783-1815. 1966. H2360
Stoye, J. Europe unfolding, 1648-1688. 1970. H2361
Wiskemann, E. Europe of the dictators, 1919-1945. 1966. H2362

HISTORY OF EUROPEAN CIVILIZATION (Harcourt)

Aston, M. The fifteenth century. 1968. H2363
Barraclough, G. The medieval papacy. 1968. H2364
Bautier, R. H. The economic development of medieval Europe. 1971. H2365
Behrens, C. B. A. The ancien régime. 1967. H2366
Brooke, C. N. L. The twelfth century Renaissance. 1969. H2367
Brown, P. The world of late antiquity. 1971. H2368
Chambers, D. S. The imperial age of Venice, 1380-1580. 1970. H2369
Coles, P. The Ottoman impact on Europe. 1968. H2370
Crouzet, M. The European Renaissance since 1945, tr. by Baron. 1971. H2371
Dickens, A. G. The Counter Reformation. 1969. H2372
____. Reformation and society in sixteenth century Europe. 1968. H2373
Eastern and Western Europe in the Middle Ages, ed. by Graus and others. 1970. H2374
Ferguson, J. The heritage of Hellenism. 1973. H2375
Gollwitzer, H. Europe in the age of imperialism. 1969. H2376
Haley, K. H. D. The Dutch in the seventeenth century. 1972. H2377
Hampson, N. The first European revolution, 1776-1815. 1969. H2378
Henderson, W. O. The industrialization of Europe, 1780-1914. 1969. H2379
Hatton, R. M. Europe in the age of Louis XIV. 1970. H2380
Hoetzsch, O. The evolution of Russia. 1967. H2381
Jackson, G. The making of Medieval Spain. 1972. H2382
Littman, R. J. The Greek experiment. 1974. H2383
Mosse, W. E. Liberal Europe. 1974. H2384
Nettl, J. P. The Soviet achievement. 1968. H2385
Pollard, S. European economic integration. 1974. H2386
Silberschmidt, M. The United States and Europe, tr. by Brawnjohn. 1972. H2387
Smith, A. G. R. Science and society in the sixteenth and seventeenth centuries.

1973. H2388
Talmon, J. L. Romanticism and revolt. 1967. H2389
Taylor, A. J. P. From Sarajeno to Postdam. 1967. H2390
Trevor-Roper, H. R. The rise of Christian Europe. 1968. H2391
Vryonis, S. Byzantium and Europe. 1967. H2392
Wangermann, E. The Austrian achievement. 1973. H2393
Wittram, R. Russia and Europe. 1973. H2394

HISTORY OF HUMAN SOCIETY (Knopf)

Alden, J. R. Pioneer America. 1966. H2395
Andrewes, A. The Greeks. 1967. H2396
Boxer, C. R. The Dutch seaborne empire, 1600-1800. 1965. H2397
____. The Portuguese seaborne Empire, 1415-1825. 1969. H2398
Clark, J. G. and Piggott, S. Prehistoric societies. 1965. H2399
Dudley, D. R. The Romans, 850 B.C.-A.D. 337. 1970. H2400
Parry, J. H. The Spanish seaborne empire. 1966. H2401
Piggott, S. and Clark, J. G. Prehistoric societies. 1965. H2402

THE HISTORY OF IDEAS SERIES (Princeton Univ. Pr.)

1 Cassirer, E. Rousseau, Kant, Goethe. 1945. H2403
2 Nicolson, M. H. Newton demands the muse. 1946. H2404
3 Nelson, B. The idea of usury. 1949. H2405
4 Bodde, D. and G. S. Tolstoy and China. 1950. H2406
5 Hexter, J. H. More's Utopia. 1952. H2407
6 Vartanian, A. Diderot and Descartes. 1953. H2408

HISTORY OF MEDICINE SERIES (1-35 Hafner; 36- Scarecrow)

2 Fracastoro, G. Hieronymi Fracastorii De contagione et contagiosis morbis et eorum curatione, tr. by Wright. Putnam. 1930. H2409
4 Doe, J. A bibliography of the works of Ambroise Paré. Univ. of Chicago Pr. 1937. H2410
5 Halsey, R. H. How the President, Thomas Jefferson, and Doctor Benjamin Waterhouse established vaccination... Univ. of Chicago Pr. 1936. H2411
6 Ornstein, M. The role of scientific societies in the seventeenth century. Univ. of Chicago Pr. 1938. H2412
7 Ramazzini, B. De morbis artificum Bernardini Ramazzini diatriba, tr. by Wright. Univ. of Chicago Pr. 1940. H2413
8 Van Ingen, P. The New York Academy of Medicine. Columbia Univ. Pr. 1949. H2414
9 Gilbert, J. B. A bibliography of articles on the history of American medicine. New York Academy of Medicine. 1951. H2415
10 Lancisi, G. M. De aneurysmatibus, opus posthumum, ed. by Wright. Macmillan. 1952. H2416
11 Lambert, S. W. and others. Three Visalian essays to accompany the Icones anatomicae of 1934. Macmillan. 1952. H2417
12 Borgognoni, T. The surgery of Theodoric, tr. by Campbell and Colton. 2 v. Appleton. 1959-60. H2418
13 Morgagri, G. B. The seats and causes of diseases investigated by anatomy. 3 v. Hafner. 1960. H2419
14 Pinel, P. A treatise on insanity, tr. by Davis. Hafner. 1962. H2420
15 Rush, B. Medical inquiries and observations upon the

diseases of the mind. Hafner. 1962. H2421
16 Corvisart des Marets, J. N. An essay on the organic diseases and lesions of the heart and great vessels, tr. by Gates. Hafner. H2422
17 Laennec, R. T. H. A treatise on the diseases of the chest, tr. by Forbes. Hafner. 1962. H2423
18 Hederden, W. Commentaries on the history and cure of diseases. 1962. H2424
19 Charcot, J. M. Lectures in the diseases of the nervous system, tr. by Sigerson. Hafner. 1962. H2425
20 Bowditch, H. I. The young stethoscopist. Hafner. 1964. H2426
21 Burns, A. Observations on some of the most frequent and important diseases of the heart. 1964. H2427
22 Hales, S. Statical essays. Hafner. 1964. H2428
23 Ramazzini, B. Diseases of workers, tr. by Wright. Hafner. 1964. H2429
24 Woodward, J. J. Outlines of the chief camp diseases of the United States armies. Hafner. 1964. H2430
25 Esquirol, J. E. D. Mental maladies, ed. by Saussure. Hafner. 1965. H2431
26 Griesinger, W. Mental pathology and therapeutics, ed. by Ackerknecht. Hafner. 1965. H2432
27 Garrison, F. H. Contributions to the history of medicine. 1966. H2433
28 Puschmann, T. A. A historical education, ed. by Ackerknecht. Hafner. 1966. H2434
29 Clossy, S. Observations on some of the diseases of the parts of the human body. 1966. H2435
30 Bick, E. M. Source book of orthopaedics. 1968. H2436
31 Bucknill, J. C. and Tuke, D. H. A manual of psychological medicine. 1968. H2437
32 John of Mirfield. Surgery. 1968. H2438
33 Kraepelin, E. Lectures on clinical psychiatry. Hafner. 1968. H2439
34 Meynert, T. Psychiatry. V. 1. 1968. H2440
35 Ray, I. Mental hygiene. 1968. H2441
36 Smith, S. The city that was. 1973. H2442
37 Virchow, R. L. K. Postmortem examinations, ed. by Putschar. 1973. H2443
38 New York (City). The marihuana problem in the city of New York, ed. by Wallace. 1973. H2444
39 Duclaux, E. Pasteur, ed. by Dubos. 1973. H2445
40 Walker, A. Documents and dates of modern discoveries in the nervous system, ed. by Cranefield. 1973. H2446
42 Ober, W. B., ed. Great men of Guy's. 1973. H2447
43 ____. The resurrectionists. 1974. H2448

HISTORY OF MUSIC (Stuttman)

1 Burkhalter, A. L. Ancient and Oriental music, ed. by Goldron. 1966. H2449
2 ____. Byzantine and medieval music, by Goldron. 1968. H2450
3 ____. Minstrels and masters, by Goldron. 1968. H2451
4 ____. Music of the Renaissance, by Goldron. 1968. H2452

HISTORY OF RELIGION SERIES (Holt)

Davies, J. G. The early Christian church. 1965. H2453
Iurville-Petre, E. O. G. Myths and religion of the North. 1964. H2454
McKenzie, J. L. The Roman Catholic Church. 1969. H2455
Marty, M. E. Protestantism. 1972. H2456
Pre-Columbian American religions, by Krickeberg and others. 1969. H2457
Rahman, F. Islam. 1967. H2458

Smith, D. H. Chinese religions. 1968. H2459
Widengren, G. Mani and manichaeism, tr. by Kessler. 1965. H2460

HISTORY OF SCIENCE LIBRARY (Amer. Elsevier)

Alton, E. J. The vortex theory of planetary motions. 1972. H2461
Davies, G. L. The earth in decay. 1970. H2462
Debus, A. G. The English paracelsians. 1965. H2463
____. Science and education in the 17th century. 1970. H2464
Gasman, D. The scientific origins of national socialism. 1971. H2465
Hales, S. Vegetable staticks. 1970. H2466
Hero, of Alexandria. The pneumatics of Hero of Alexandria, tr. by Greenwood, ed. by Woodcroft. 1971. H2467
Hoffmann, F. Fundamenta medicinae. 1971. H2468
Hoskin, M. A. William Herschel and the construction of the heavens. 1963. H2469
King, L. S. The road to medical enlightenment, 1650-1695. 1970. H2470
Middleton, W. E. K. A history of the theory of rain. 1965. H2471
Multhauf, R. P. The origins of chemistry. 1967. H2472
Nye, M. J. Molecular reality. 1972. H2473
Rudwick, M. J. S. The meaning of fossils. 1972. H2474
Sabra, A. I. Theories of light. 1969. H2475
Scott, W. L. The conflict between atomism and conservation theory. 1960. H2476
Talbot, C. H. Medicine in medieval England. 1969. H2477
Westfall, R. S. Force in Newton's physics. 1971. H2478
Whitteridge, G. William Harvey and the circulation of the blood. 1971. H2479
Wolf, A. and others. A history of science, technology, and philosophy in the 16th and 17th centuries. 1950. H2480
____. A history of science, technology and philosophy in the eighteenth century. 1952. H2481
Wright, T. An original theory of new hypothesis of the universe. 1971. H2482

HISTORY OF THE SECOND WORLD WAR (H. M. Stationer's Office)

United Kingdom Civil Series: Introductory.
Great Britain. Central Statistical Office. Statistical digest of the war. 1951. H2483
Hancock, W. K. and Gowing, M. M. British war economy. 1949. H2484
Payton-Smith, D. J. Oil. 1971. H2485
Postan, M. M. British war production. 1952. H2486
____ and others. Design and development of weapons. 1964. H2487
Titmuss, R. M. Problems of social policy. 1950. H2488
General Series.
Behren, C. B. A. Merchant shipping and the demands of war. 1955. H2489
Court, W. H. B. Coal. 1951. H2490
Ferguson, S. and Fitzgerald, H. Studies in the social services. 1954. H2491
Hammond, R. J. Food. 3 v. 1951-62. H2492
Hargreaves, E. L. and Gowing, M. M. Civil industry and trade. 1952. H2493
Kohan, C. M. Works and buildings. 1952. H2494
Medlicott, W. M. The economic blockade. 2 v. 1952-59. H2495
Murray, E. A. H. Agriculture. 1955. H2496
O'Brien, T. H. Civil defense. 1954. H2497
Parker, H. M. D. Manpower. 1957. H2498
Savage, C. I. Inland transport. 1957. H2499
Sayers, R. S. Financial policy,

1939-45. 1956. H2500
War Production Series.
Ashworth, W. Contracts and finance. 1953. H2501
Hall, H. D. North American supply. 1955. H2502
____. Studies of oversea supply. 1956. H2503
Hornby, W. Factories and plant. 1958. H2504
Hurstfield, J. The control of raw materials. 1953. H2505
Inman, P. Labour in the munitions industries. 1957. H2506
Scott, J. D. and Hughes, R. The administration of war production. 1956. H2507
United Kingdom Medical Series: Civilian Services.
Dunn, C. L., ed. The emergency medical service. 2 v. 1952-3. H2508
Green, F. H. K. and Couell, G., eds. Medical research. 1953. H2509
MacNatly, A. S. The civilian health and medical services. V. 1. The ministry of health services. V. 2. The colonies. 1953-55. H2510
Clinical Volumes.
Cope, Z., ed. Medicine and pathology. 1952. H2511
____. Surgery. 1953. H2512
Fighting Services: Army.
Crew, F. A. E., ed. The Army Medical Services: Administration. 2 v. 1953-55. H2513
____. The Army Medical Services: campaigns. 3 v. 1956. H2514
Fighting Services: Navy.
Coulter, J. L. S. The Royal Medical Services. 2 v. 1954-56. H2515
Fighting Services: Royal Air Force.
Rexford-Welch, S. C. The Royal Air Forces medical services. 3 v. 1954-58. H2516
United Kingdom Military Services: Campaigns.
Collier, B. The defence of the United Kingdom. 1957. H2517
Derry, T. K. The campaign in Norway. 1952. H2518
Donnison, F. S. V. Civil affairs and military government: central organization and planning. 1966. H2519
Ellis, L. F. Victory in the West, 1944-45. 2 v. 1969. H2520
____. The war in France and Flanders, 1939-40. 1953. H2521
Foot, M. R. D. SOE in France. 1966. H2562
Joslen, H. F. Orders of Battle, 1939-45. 2 v. 1967. H2523
Kirby, S. W. and others. The war against Japan. 4 v. 1957-63. H2524
Playfair, I. S. O. The Mediterranean and Middle East. 4 v. 1954-66. H2525
Roskill, S. W. The war at sea. 3 v. 1954-61. H2526
Webster, C. K. and Frankland, N. The strategic air offensive against Germany, 1939-1945. 4 v. 1961-62. H2527
Woodward, L. British foreign policy in the second World War. 1968. H2528
Civil Affairs and Military Government.
Donnison, F. S. V. British military administration in the Far East, 1943-46. 1935. H2529
____. Civil affairs and military government, north-west Europe, 1944-1946. 1961. H2530
Harris, C. R. S. Allied military administration of Italy, 1943-1945. 1957. H2531
Grand Strategy.
Butler, J. R. M., ed. Grand strategy. V. 2. 1957. V. 6. 1956. 6 v. 1956-63. H2532

A HISTORY OF THE SOUTH (Louisiana State Univ. Pr.)

1 Craven, W. F. The southern colonies in the seventeenth century, 1607-1689. 1949. H2533
3 Alden, J. R. The South in the Revolution, 1763-1789. 1957. H2534
4 Abernathy, T. P. The South

in the new nation, 1789-1819. 1961. H2535
5 Syndor, C. S. The development of Southern sectionalism, 1819-1848. 1948. H2536
6 Craven, A. The growth of Southern nationalism, 1848-1861. 1953. H2537
7 Coulter, E. M. The Confederate States of America, 1861-1865. 1950. H2538
8 ____. The South during reconstruction, 1865-1877. 1947. H2539
9 Woodward, C. V. Origins of the new South, 1877-1913. 1951. H2540
10 Tindall, G. B. The emergence of the new South, 1913-1945. 1967. H2541
2 in preparation.

HISTORY OF WESTERN POLITICAL THOUGHT (Free Pr.)

Harrison, W. Conflict and compromise. 1965. H2542
____, ed. Sources in British political thought, 1593-1900. 1965. H2543
Kagan, D. The great dialogue. 1965. H2544
____, ed. Sources in Greek political thought from Homer to Polybius. 1965. H2545
Kariel, H. S. In search of authority. 1964. H2546
____, ed. Sources in twentieth-century political thought. 1964. H2547

HOGARTH LECTURES ON LITERATURE (LONDON) (Hogarth)

1 Quiller-Couch, A. T. A lecture on lectures. 1927. H2548
2 Lucas, F. L. Tragedy in relation to Aristotle's "Poetics." 1928. H2549
3 Nicoll, A. Studies in Shakespeare. 1928. H2550
4 Nicolson, H. G. The development of English biography. 1928. H2551
5 Grierson, H. J. C. Lyrical poetry from Blake to Hardy. 1928. H2552
____. Lyrical poetry of the nineteenth century. (Amer. ed.) Harcourt. 1929. H2553
6 Muir, E. The structure of the novel. 1928. H2554
7 Read, H. E. Phases of English poetry. 1929. H2555
8 Kellett, E. E. The whirligig of taste. 1929. H2556
9 Blunden, E. C. Nature in English literature. 1929. H2557
10 Wolfe, H. Notes on English verse. 1929. H2558
11 Cole, G. D. H. Politics and literature. 1929. H2559
12 Vines, S. The course of English classicism. 1930. H2560
13 Macleod, N. German lyric poetry. 1930. H2561
14 Macaulay, R. Some religious elements in English literature. 1931. H2562
15 Stewart, J. Poetry in France and England. 1931. H2563
16 Leech, C. John Webster. 1951. H2564
New Series:
1 Sutherland, J. The medium of poetry. 1934. H2565
2 Tillyard, E. M. W. The English Renaissance. 1952. H2566

THE HOLT LIBRARY OF SCIENCE

Ahrendt, M. H. The mathematics of space exploration. 1965. H2567
Beck, S. D. Animal photoperiodism. 1963. H2568
Blough, S. D. Experiments in psychology. 1964. H2569
Boolootian, A. A. and Thomas, J. Marine biology. 1967. H2570
Caidin, M. Flying. 1963. H2571
____. Wings into space. 1964. H2572
Eklund, C. D. and Beckman, J. Antarctica. 1963. H2573
Emme, E. M. A history of space flight. 1965. H2574
Faget, M. Manned space flight. 1965. H2575
Fitzpatrick, F. L. Our animal resources. 1963. H2576
____. Our plant resources.

1964. H2577
Gardner, M. H. Chemistry in the space age. 1965. H2578
Gluck, I. D. Optics. 1964. H2579
Goodwin, H. L. The images of space. 1965. H2580
Hall, R. P. Protozoa. 1964. H2581
Henry, J. P. Biomedical aspects of space flight. 1965. H2582
Hunter, M. W. Thrust in space. 1965. H2583
Hymoff, E. Guidance and control of spacecraft. 1965. H2584
Jaffe, L. Communication in space. 1965. H2585
Kamen, M. D. A tracer experiment. 1964. H2586
King, A. C. and Read, C. B. Pathways to probability. 1963. H2587
Lasker, G. Human evolution. 1963. H2588
Morowitz, H. L. Life and the physical science. 1963. H2589
Naugle, J. E. Unmanned space flight. 1965. H2590
Park, R. A. and Magness, T. Interplanetary navigation. 1963. H2591
Ramsey, W. L. and Burckley, R. A. Modern earth science. 1965. H2592
Rosenberg, J. L. Photosynthesis. 1965. H2593
Schultz, G. Glaciers and the ice age. 1963. H2594
Seifert, H. S. and M. S. Orbital space flight. 1965. H2595
Sigel, M. M. Viruses, cells, and hosts. 1965. H2596
Sollers, A. A. Ours is the earth. 1963. H2597
Stern, P. D. Our space environment. 1965. H2598
Sutton, R. M. The physics of space. 1965. H2599
Thomas, S. Computers. 1965. H2600
____. Satellite tracking facilities. 1963. H2601
Wallace, B. Radiation, genes, and man. 1959. H2602
Widger, W. K. Meteorological satellites. 1965. H2603
Woodburn, J. H. Cancer. 1964. H2604
Yasso, W. Oceanography. 1965. H2605
Young, R. S. Extraterrestrial biology. 1965. H2606

LES HOMMES ET LA TERRE (S. E. V. P. E. N.)

1 Massé, P. Varennes et ses maîtres. 1956. H2607
2 Merle, L. La métairie et l'évolution agraire de la Gatine poitevine de la fin du Moyen Age à la Révolution. 1958. H2608
3 Venard, M. Bourgeois et paysans au XVIIe siècle. 1957. H2609
4 Sclafert, T. Cultures en haute-orivence. 1959. H2610
5 Guerin, I. La vie rurale en Sologne aux XIVe et XVe siècle. 1960. H2611
6 Devèze, M. La vie de la forêt française au XIVe siècle. 2 v. 1961. H2612
7 Fourquin, G. Le domaine royal en Gâtinais après la prisée de 1332. 1963. H2613
8 Vigier, P. Essai sur le répartition de la propriété foncière... 1964. H2614
9 Salomon, N. La campagne de nouvelle-Castille à la fin du XVIe siècle. 1965. H2615
10 Higounet, C. La grange de Vaulerent. 1965. H2616
11 Internationale des Historiens de l'Economie. Villages desertes et histoire economique. 1965. H2617
12 Silbert, A. Le Portugal Mediterraneen à la fin de l'ancien regime XVIIIe debut XIXe siècle. 1966. H2618
13 Bourde, A. J. Agronomie et agronomes en France au XVIIIe siècle. 3 v. 1967. H2619

HOOVER INSTITUTION STUDIES (1-24 Stanford Univ. Pr. 25- Hoover Institution Pr.)

1 Duignan, P. and Clendenen, C. The United States and the African slave trade,

1619-1862. 1963. H2620
2 Doolin, D. J., ed. Communist China. 1964. H2621
3 Johnson, C. A. Revolution and the social system. 1964. H2622
4 Fagen, R. R., ed. Cuba. 1964. H2623
5 Clendenen, C. C. and Dulgnan, P. Americans in black Africa up to 1865. 1964. H2624
6 Stevens, G. G. Jordan River partition. 1965. H2625
7 Doolin, D. J. Territorial claims in the Sino-Soviet conflict. 1965. H2626
8 Kilby, P. African enterprise. 1965. H2627
9 Czudnowski, M. M. and Landau, J. M. The Israeli Communist Party and the election of the fifth Knesset. 1965. H2628
10 Mote, M. E. Soviet local and republic elections. 1965. H2629
11 Paige, G. D. The Korean People's Democratic Republic. 1966. H2630
12 Rupen, R. A. The Mongolian People's Republic. 1966. H2631
13 Aspaturian, V. V. The Soviet Union in the world communist system. 1966. H2632
14 Doolin, D. J. and North, R. C. The Chinese People's Republic. 1966. H2633
15 Lenin, V. I. Lenin reader, ed. by Possony. 1966. H2634
16 Lammers, D. N. Explaining Munich. 1966. H2635
17 Clenenden, C. and others. Americans in Africa. 1966. H2636
18 LeVine, V. T. Political leadership in Africa. 1967. H2637
19 De Craemer, W. The emerging physician. 1968. H2638
20 Freeman, R. A. Socialism and private enterprise in equatorial Asia. 1967. H2639
21 Jamgotch, N. Soviet-East European dialogue. 1968. H2640
22 Thomas, J. I. Education for Communism. 1969. H2641
23 Smock, D. I. Trade union conflict. 1969. H2642
24 Alexander, R. J. The Communist party of Venezuela. 1969. H2643
25 Wu, Y. As Peking sees us. 1969. H2644
26 Davidson, A. The Communist party of Australia. 1969. H2645
27 Adams, T. W. AKEL. 1971. H2646
28 Gann, L. Guerrillas in history. 1971. H2647
29 Bovis, H. The Jerusalem question. 1971. H2648
30 Langer, P. F. Communism in Japan. 1972. H2649
31 Hinton, H. C. The bear at the gate. 1971. H2650
32 Váli, F. A. The Turkish straits and NATO. 1972. H2651
33 Harris, G. S. Troubled alliance. 1972. H2652
34 Hsieh, W. Chinese historiography on the revolution of 1911. 1972. H2653
35 Rabushka, A. Race and politics in urban Malaya. 1972. H2654
36 Roberts, P. C. and Stephenson, M. A. Marx theory of exchange. 1972. H2655
37 Scalapino, R. A. Asia and the major powers. 1972. H2656
38 Penniman, H. R. Elections in South Vietnam. 1972. H2657
39 Snetsinger, J. Truman and the creation of Israel. 1972. H2658
40 Freeman, R. A. Tax loopholes. 1973. H2659
41 Rabushka, A. The changing face of Hong Kong. 1973. H2660
42 Demsetz, H. The market concentration doctrine. 1973. H2661
43 Kaplan, M. A. The rationale for NATO. 1973. H2662
44 Emmerson, J. K. Will Japan rearm? 1973. H2663
46 Neilam, E. and Smith, C. R. The future of the China market. 1974. H2664

HORN BOOK PAPERS (Horn Book)

1 Miller, B. E., ed. Newbery medal books, 1922-1955. 1955. H2665
2 Miller, B. E. and Field, E. W. Caldecott medal books, 1938-1957. 1957. H2666

HORNBOOK SERIES (West)

Arant, H. W. Handbook of the law of suretyship and guaranty. 1931. H2667
Atkinson, T. E. Handbook of the law of wills and administration of decedents' estates. 1953. H2668
____. Handbook of the law of wills and other principles of succession. 1953. H2669
Black, H. C. Handbook of American constitutional law. 1927. H2670
____. Handbook on the law and practice of bankruptcy. 1930. H2671
____. Handbook on the law of judicial precedents. 1912. H2672
____. Judicial precedents. 1926. H2673
Bogert, G. G. Handbook of the law of trusts. 1952. H2674
Bowman, M. J. Handbook of elementary law. 1929. H2675
Britton, W. E. Handbook of the law of bills and notes. 1961. H2676
Burby, W. E. Handbook of the law of real property. 1954. H2677
____. Illustrative cases on the law of real property. 1943. H2678
Burdick, W. L. Handbook of the law of real property. 1943. H2679
Calamari, J. D. and Perillo, J. M. The law of contrasts. 1970. H2680
Chapin, H. G. Handbook of the law of torts. 1917. H2681
Childs, F. H. Handbook of suretyship and guaranty. 1907. H2682
Chommie, J. C. The law of Federal income taxation. 1968. H2683
Clark, C. E. and others. Handbook of the law of code pleading. 1947. H2684
Clark, H. H. The law of domestic relations in the United States. 1968. H2685
Clarke, W. L. Handbook of criminal procedure. 1918. H2686
____. Handbook of the law of contracts. 1931. H2687
____. Handbook on criminal law. 1915. H2688
____. Handbook on the law of private corporations. 1916. H2689
Clephane, W. C. Handbook on equity pleading and practice. 1926. H2690
Cooley, R. W. Handbook of the law of municipal corporations. 1914. H2691
____. Illustrative cases on damages. 1935. H2692
Crane, J. A. Handbook on the law of partnership and other incorporated associations. 1952. H2693
Davis, K. C. Administrative law text. 1959. H2694
Dobie, A. M. Handbook of federal jurisdiction and procedures. 1928. H2695
____. Handbook on the law of bailments and carriers. 1914. H2696
____. Illustrative cases on bailments and carriers. 1914. H2697
Dodds, D. R. Handbook on the law of remedies. 1973. H2698
Eaton, J. W. Handbook of equity jurisprudence. 1923. H2699
Epstein, D. G. Teaching materials on debtor-auditor relations. 1973. H2700
Gilmore, E. A. Handbook on the law of partnership. 1911. H2701
Glenn, E. F. Handbook of international law. 1895. H2702
Goodrich, H. F. Handbook of the conflict of laws. 1949. H2703
Hagman, D. C. Urban planning and land development control

law. 1971. H2704
Hale, W. B. Handbook on the law of damages. 1912. H2705
Hemingway, R. W. The law of oil and gas. 1971. H2706
Henn, H. G. Handbook of the law of corporations and other business enterprises. 1961. H2707
Henson, R. D. Handbook on secured transactions under the Uniform commercial code. 1973. H2708
Hughes, R. M. Handbook of admiralty law. 1920. H2709
Huie, W. O. and others. Cases and materials on oil and gas. 1972. H2710
Koffler, J. H. and Rippy, A. Handbook of common law pleading. 1969. H2711
Kragen, A. A. and McNulty, J. K. Cases and materials on Federal income taxation. 1970. H2712
Kripke, H. Consumer credit. 1970. H2713
LaFave, W. R. and Scott, A. W. Handbook on criminal law. 1972. H2714
Law of the poor, by LaFrance and others. 1973. H2715
Lockhart, W. B. and others. Constitutional law. 1970. H2716
Lowndes, C. L. H. and Kramer, R. Federal estate and gift taxes. 1962. H2717
McClintock, H. L. Handbook of the principles of equity. 1948. H2718
McCormick, C. T. Cases and materials on damages. 1935. H2719
____. Handbook on the law of evidence. 1954. H2720
____. Handbook on the law of damages. 1935. H2721
McKelvey, J. J. Handbook of the law of evidence. 1944. H2722
MacLachlan, J. A. Cases and materials on bankruptcy. 1956. H2723
Madden, J. W. Handbook on the law of persons and domestic relations. 1931. H2724
Miller, J. Handbook of criminal law. 1934. H2725
Nordstrom, R. H. Handbook of the law of sales. 1970. H2726
Norton, C. P. Handbook of the law of bills and notes. 1914. H2727
Osborne, G. E. Handbook on the law of mortgages. 1951. H2728
Pease, J. G. The student's summary of the law of contract. 1909. H2729
Prosser, W. L. Handbook of the law of torts. 1955. H2730
Radin, M. Handbook of Anglo-American legal history. 1936. H2731
____. Handbook of Roman law. 1927. H2732
Robinson, G. H. Handbook of admiralty law in the United States. 1939. H2733
Rottschaefer, H. Handbook of American constitutional law. 1939. H2734
Seavey, W. A. Handbook of the law of agency. 1964. H2735
Shipman, B. J. Handbook of common-law pleading. 1923. H2736
Simes, L. M. Handbook on the law of future interests. 1951. H2737
Simpson, L. P. Handbook of the law of contracts. 1954. H2738
____. Handbook on the law of suretyship. 1950. H2739
Smith, W. D. Handbook of elementary law. 1939. H2740
Stevens, R. S. Handbook of the law of private corporations. 1949. H2741
Tiffany, F. B. Handbook of the law of banks and banking. 1912. H2742
____. Handbook of the law of principal and agent. 1924. H2743
____. Handbook of the law of sales. 1908. H2744
Tiffany, W. C. Handbook on the law of persons and domestic relations. 1921. H2745
Vance, W. R. Handbook on the law of insurance. 1951. H2746

insurance in the United States. 1971. H2788

Willett, A. H. The economic theory of risk and insurance. 1951. H2789

HUMAN RELATIONS AREA FILES, INC. COUNTRY SURVEY SERIES.

1 Wilber, D. N. ed. Afghanistan. 1956. H2790
2 Human Relations Area Files, inc. North Borneo, Brunei Sarawak (British Borneo). 1956. H2791
3 Vreeland, H. H., ed. Iran. 1957. H2792
4 Patai, R., ed. Jordan. 1957. H2793
5 Fitzsimmons, T., ed. RSFSR (Russian Soviet Federated Socialist Republic). 1957. H2794
6 Harris, G. L., ed. Egypt. 1957. H2795
7 Steinberg, D. J. Cambodia. 1957. H2796
8 Blanchard, W. Thailand. 1958. H2797

THE HUMANIST BOOKSHELF (Philosophical Lib.)

Lamont, C., ed. Humanism as a philosophy. 1949. H2798

____. The illusion of immortality. 1959. H2799

____. Man answers death. 1952. H2800

____. The philosophy of humanism. 1958. H2801

HUMANITIES AND LANGUAGE SERIES (Boston College Pr.)

Bonn, J. L. Collected speeches. 1947. H2802

____. Life of poetry. 1947. H2803

Farragher, B. P., ed. Humanistic poetry. 1948. H2804

McNulty, P. S. Humanistic readings in English prose. 1947. H2805

HUNDRED YEARS SERIES (Duckworth)

Abraham, G. E. H. A hundred years of music. 1949. H2806

Carter, G. S. A hundred years of evolution. 1958. H2807

Cressy, Y. A hundred years of mechanical engineering. 1937. H2808

Daniel, G. E. A hundred years of archaeology. 1950. H2809

Dawes, B. A hundred years of biology. 1952. H2810

Falls, C. B. A hundred years of war. 1953. H2811

Findlay, A. A hundred years of chemistry. 1948. H2812

Flugel, J. C. A hundred years of psychology. 1951. H2813

Freeman, T. W. A hundred years of geography. 1961. H2814

Jones, G. P. A hundred years of economic development. 1940. H2815

Lloyd, W. E. B. A hundred years of medicine. 1971. H2816

Mitchell, G. D. A hundred years of sociology. 1968. H2817

Newton, A. P. A hundred years of the British empire. 1940. H2818

Northedge, F. S. A hundred years of international relations. 1971. H2819

Passmore, J. D. A hundred years of philosophy. 1957. H2820

Penniman, T. K. A hundred years of anthropology. 1952. H2821

Peterson, A. D. C. A hundred years of education. 1952. H2822

Sherrington, C. E. R. A hundred years of inland transport, 1830-1933. 1934. H2823

Smellie, K. B. A hundred years of English government. 1951. H2824

Vines, S. A hundred years of English literature. 1950. H2825

Waterfield, R. L. A hundred years of astronomy. 1938. H2826

Wilson, W. A hundred years
of physics. 1950. H2827

I MONUMENTI ROMANI (Istituto di Studi Romani)

1 Coloni, A. M. Stadium Domitiani. 1943. I1
2 Pallottino, M. L'Arco degli argentari. 1946. I2
3 Bartoli, A. Curia Senatus. 1962. I3
4 Iacopi, G. L'antro di Tiberio a Sperlonga. 1963. I4
5 Il sepolcro del fornaio M. Virgilio Eurisace a Porta Maggiore, a cura di Rossetto. 1973. I5

IBADAN HISTORY SERIES (Humanities)

Adeleye, R. A. Power and diplomacy in Northern Nigeria, 1804-1906. 1971. I6
Afigbo, A. E. The warrant chiefs. 1972. I7
Ajayi, J. F. A. Christian missions in Nigeria, 1841-1891. 1965. I8
Akintoye, S. A. Revolution and power politics in Yorubaland, 1840-1893. 1971. I9
Anene, J. C. The international boundaries of Nigeria, 1885-1960. 1970. I10
Atanda, J. A. The new Oyo empire. 1973. I11
Ayandele, E. A. The missionary impact on modern Nigeria, 1843-1914. 1967. I12
Cookey, S. J. S. Britain and the Congo question. 1967. I13
Ikime, O. Niger Delta rivalry. 1969. I14
Last, M. The Sokoto Caliphate. 1969. I15
Oloruntimehin, B. O. The Segu Tukulor Empire. 1972. I16
Omer-Cooper, J. D. The Zulu aftermath. 1966. I17
Ryder, A. F. C. Benin and the Europeans, 1485-1894. 1969. I18
Tamuno, T. N. The evaluation of the Nigerian state. 1972. I19

IBERO-AMERICANA (Univ. of Calif. Pr.)

1 Sauer, C. O. and Brand, D. Aztatlán. 1932. I20
2 Beals, R. L. The comparative ethnology of northern Mexico before 1750. 1932. I21
3 Sauer, C. O. The road to Cibola. 1932. I22
4 Taylor, P. S. A Spanish-Mexican peasant community. 1933. I23
5 Sauer, C. O. The distribution of aboriginal tribes and languages in northwestern Mexico. 1934. I24
6 Beals, R. L. The Acaxee. 1933. I25
7 Simpson, L. B. Studies in the administration of the Indians in New Spain. V. 1. 1934. I26
8 Kroeber, A. L. Uto-Aztecan languages of Mexico. 1934. I27
9 Radin, P. An historical legend of the Zapotecs. 1934. I28
10 Sauer, C. O. Aboriginal population of northwestern Mexico. 1935. I29
11 Nomland, G. A. New archaeological sites from the state of Falcón, Venezuela. 1935. I30
12 Cook, S. F. The extent and significance of disease among the Indians of Baja,

52 Ruddle, K. The Yukpa civilization system. 1974. I67

IDEAS AND INSTITUTIONS IN WESTERN CIVILIZATION (Macmillan)

1 Alexander, P. J., ed. The ancient world to 300 A. D. 1963. I68
2 Cantor, N. F., ed. The medieval world, 300-1300. 1963. I69
3 Elton, G. R., ed. Renaissance and Reformation, 1300-1648. 1963. I70
4 Rowen, H. H., ed. From absolutism to revolution, 1648-1848. 1962. I71
5 Kohn, H., ed. The modern world, 1848-present. 1963. I72

ILLINOIS CONTRIBUTIONS TO LIBRARIANSHIP (Univ. of Ill. Pr.)

1 Illinois. Univ. Library school assn. Fifty years of education for librarianship. 1943. I73
2 Metcalf, K. D. and others. The program of instruction in library schools. 1943. I74
3 McDiarmid, E. W. and J. The administration of the American public library. 1943. I75
4 Faye, C. U. Fifteenth century printed books at the University of Illinois. 1949. I76
5 Brough, K. D. Scholar's workshop. 1953. I77
6 Schick, F. L., ed. The future of library service. 1961. I78
7 Holley, E. G. Charles Evans. 1963. I79
8 Downs, R. B. and Jenkins, F. B., eds. Bibliography. 1967. I80

ILLINOIS STATE HISTORICAL LIBRARY. COLLECTIONS.

1 Beckwith, H. W., ed. Documents, papers, materials and publications relating to the Northwest and the state of Illinois. 1903. I81
2 Cahokia, Ill. Cahokia records, 1778-1790, ed. by Alvord. 1907. I82
3 Lincoln, A. The Lincoln-Douglas debate of 1858, ed. by Sparks. 1908. I83
4 Illinois. Governor. The governor's letter-books, ed. by Greene. V. 1. 1909. I84
5 Alvord, C. W., ed. Kaskaskia records, 1778-1790. 1909. I85
6 Scott, F. W. Newspapers and periodicals of Illinois, 1814-1879. 1910. I86
7 Same as no. 4. V. 2. 1840-1853. 1911. I87
8 Clark, G. R. George Rogers Clark papers, 1771-1784, ed. by James. V. 1. 1912. I88
9 Buck, S. J. Travel and description, 1765-1865. 1914. I89
10 Alvord, C. W. and Carter, C. E., eds. The critical period 1763-1765. 1915. I90
11 ____. The new régime, 1765-1767. 1917. I91
12 Pease, T. C. The county archives of the state of Illinois. 1915. I92
13 Verlie, E. J., ed. Illinois constitutions. 1919. I93
14 Cole, A. C., ed. The constitutional debates of 1847. 1919. I94
15 Alvord, C. W., ed. Governor Edward Coles. 1920. I95
16 ____. Trade and politics, 1767-1769. 1921. I96
17 Northwest Terr. The laws of the Northwest Territory, 1788-1800, ed. by Pease. 1925. I97
18 Pease, T. C., ed. Illinois election returns, 1818-1848. 1923. I98
19 Same as no. 8. V. 2. 1926. I99
20 Browning, O. H. The diary of Orville Hickman Browning, ed. by Pease and Randall. V. 1. 1925. I100
21 Indiana (Ter.) Laws, statutes, etc. The laws of the Indiana

Territory, 1801-1809, ed. by Philbrick. 1930. I101
22 Same as no. 2. V. 2. 1933. I102
23 Pease, T. C., ed. The French foundations, 1680-1693. 1934. I103
24 Norton, M. C., ed. Illinois census returns. V. 1. 1935. I104
25 Illinois (Terr.) Laws, statutes, etc. The laws of the Illinois Territory, 1809-1818, ed. by Philbrick. 1950. I105
26 Same as no. 24. V. 2. 1934. I106
27 Pease, T. C., ed. Anglo-French boundary disputes in the West, 1749-1763. 1936. I107
28 Illinois (Ter.) Laws, statutes, etc. Pope's digest, 1815, ed. by Philbrick. V. 1. 1938. I108
29 Pease, T. C. and Jenison, E. Illinois on the eve of the seven years' war, 1747-1755. 1940. I109
30 Same as no. 28. V. 2. 1940. I110
31-32 Monaghan, J., ed. Lincoln bibliography, 1839-1939. 2 v. 1943-45. I111
33 Lincoln, A. Created equal, ed. by Angle. 1958. I112
34 Bogue, M. B. Patterns from the sod. 1959. I113
35 Whitney, E. M., comp. The Black Hawk War, 1831-1832. V. 1, 2:1. 1970-73. I114

The series has the following subseries. The number in parentheses refers to the volume number in the series.

Bibliographical: 1(6), 2(9), 3(12), 4(31), 5(32).
Biographical: 1(15).
British: 1(10), 2(11), 3(16).
Constitutional: 1(13), 2(14).
Executive: 1(4), 2(7).
French: 1(23), 2(27), 3(29).
Land: 1(34).
Law: 1(17), 2(21), 3(28), 4(30), 5(25).
Lincoln: 1(3), 2(20), 3(22).
Statistical: 1(18), 2(24), 3(26).
Virginia: 1(2), 2(5), 3(8), 4(19).

ILLINOIS STATE HISTORICAL SOCIETY. OCCASIONAL PUBLICATIONS.

50 Ayers, J. T. The diary of James T. Ayers, Civil War recruiter. 1947. I115
51 Drury, J. Old Illinois houses. 1948. I116
52 Scamehorn, H. L. Balloons to jets. 1957. I117
53 Allen, J. W. Legends and lore of Southern Illinois. 1964. I118
54 Adams, J. N., comp. Illinois place names. 1968. I119

The Occasional Publications continue the numbering of: Transactions (1-43) and Papers in Illinois History (44-49).

ILLINOIS STUDIES IN ANTHROPOLOGY

1 Faron, L. C. Mapuche social structure. 1961. I120
2 Goldman, I. The Cubeo Indians of the Northwest Amazon. 1963. I121
3 Lehman, F. K. The structure of Chen society. 1963. I122
4 Deetz, J. The dynamics of stylistic change in Arekara ceramics. 1965. I123
5 Alkire, W. H. Lamotrek Atoll and inter-island socioeconomic ties. 1965. I124
6 Nagata, S. Modern transformations of Moenkopi Pueblo. 1969. I125
7 Young, P. D. Ngawbe. 1971. I126
8 Ross, H. M. Baegu. 1973. I127
9 Ballonoff, P. A., ed. Mathematical models of social and cognitive structures. 1974. I128

ILLINOIS UNIVERSITY. ILLINOIS STUDIES IN THE SOCIAL SCIENCES

1:1-2 Bogart, E. L. Financial history of Ohio. 1912. I129
1:3 Upson, L. D. Sources of

municipal revenues in Illinois. 1912. I130
1:4 Reiff, P. F. Friedrich Gentz. 1912. I131
2:1 Moore, J. R. Taxation of corporations in Illinois other than railroads since 1872. 1913. I132
2:2-3 Phillips, P. C. The West in the diplomacy of the American Revolution. 1913. I133
2:4 Dowrie, G. W. The development of banking in Illinois, 1817-63. 1913. I134
3:1-2 Haig, R. M. A history of the general property tax in Illinois. 1914. I135
3:3 Babcock, K. C. The Scandinavian element in the United States. 1914. I136
3:4 Reed, S. M. Church and state in Massachusetts, 1691-1740. 1914. I137
4:1 Thompson, C. M. The Illinois Whigs before 1846. 1915. I138
4:2 Oldfather, W. A. and Canter, H. V. The defeat of Varus and the German frontier policy of Augustus. 1915. I139
4:3-4 Brownson, H. G. The history of the Illinois central railroad to 1870. 1915. I140
5:1 Wright, Q. The enforcement of international law through municipal law in the United States. 1916. I141
5:2 Morehouse, F. M. The life of Jesse W. Fell. 1916. I142
5:3 Stewart, C. L. Land tenure in the United States, with special reference to Illinois. 1916. I143
5:4 Young, L. E. Mine taxation in the United States. 1917. I144
6:1-2 Debel, N. H. The veto power of the governor of Illinois. 1917. I145
6:3 Hoagland, H. E. Wage bargaining on the vessels of the Great Lakes. 1917. I146
6:4 Jones, P. V. B. The household of a Tudor nobleman. 1917. I147
7:1-2 Wang, C. Legislative regulation of railway finance in England. 1918. I148
7:3 Story, R. M. The American municipal executive. 1918. I149
7:4 Stowell, C. J. The Journeymen tailors' union of America. 1919. I150
8:1 Lloyd, J. W. Co-operative and other organized methods of marketing California horticultural products. 1919. I151
8:2 Moore, B. F. The history of cumulative voting and minority representation in Illinois. 1919. I152
8:3-4 Watkins, G. S. Labor problems and labor administration in the United States during the world war. 1920. I153
9:1-2 Berdahl, C. A. War powers of the executive in the United States. 1921. I154
9:3 Dietz, F. C. English government finance, 1485-1558. 1921. I155
9:4 Palm, F. C. The economic policies of Richelieu. 1922. I156
10:1 Dunbar, L. B. The story of monarchial tendencies in the United States, 1776-1801. 1923. I157
10:2 Nelson, M. N. Open price associations. 1923. I158
10:3-4 Miller, E. J. Workmen's representation in industrial government. 1924. I159
11:1-2 Russel, R. R. Economic aspects of southern sectionalism, 1840-61. 1924. I160
11:3-4 Rodkey, F. S. The Turco-Egyptian question in the relations of England, France, and Russia, 1832-41. 1924-25. I161
12:1-2 White, H. Executive influence in determining military policy in the United States. 1925. I162
12:3 Sargent, R. L. The size of the slave population at Athens during the fifth and fourth centuries before Christ.

works administration. 1938. I197
23:4 Heaton, J. W. Mob violence in the late Roman republic, 133-49. B.C. 1939. I198
24:1 Hiller, E. T. Houseboat and river-bottoms people. 1939. I199
24:2 Rafuse, R. W. The extradition of nationals. 1939. I200
24:3 Sandmeyer, E. C. The anti-Chinese movement in California. 1939. I201
24:4 Helms, L. A. The contributions of Lord Overstone to the theory of currency and banking. 1939. I202
25:1-2 Mange, A. E. The Near Eastern policy of Napoleon III. 1940. I203
25:3 Lentz, G. G. The enforcement of the orders of state public service commissions. 1940. I204
25:4 David, W. D. European diplomacy in the Near Eastern question, 1906-09. 1940. I205
26:1 Bonnell, A. T. German control over international economic relations, 1930-40. 1940. I206
26:2 Kendall, W. John Locke and the doctrine of majority rule. 1941. I207
26:3 Caldwell, N. W. The French in the Mississippi Valley, 1750 to 1760. 1941. I208
26:4 Stripling, G. W. F. The Ottoman Turks and the Arabs, 1511-74. 1942. I209
27:1-2 Baldwin, C. D. Economic planning. 1942. I210
27:3 Shay, M. L. The Ottoman empire from 1720 to 1734. 1944. I211
27:4 Weaver, L. H. School consolidation and state aid in Illinois. 1944. I212
28:1 Wachman, M. History of the Social-democratic party of Milwaukee, 1897-1910. 1945. I213
28:2 Garvey, N. F. Financial problems arising from changes in school district boundaries. 1946. I214
28:3 Rohkam, W. and Pratt, O. C. Studies in French administrative law. 1947. I215
28:4 Andrus, O. The Civil war letters of Sergeant Onley Andrus, ed. by Shannon. 1947. I216
29:1-2 Bardolph, R. Agricultural literature and the early Illinois farmer. 1948. I217
29:3 Belting, N. M. Kaskaskia under the French regime. 1948. I218
29:4 Stearns, J. The role of Metternich in undermining Napoleon. 1948. I219
30:1 Fisher, S. N. Foreign relations of Turkey, 1481-1512. 1948. I220
30:2-3 Witney, F. Wartime experiences of the National Labor Relations Board, 1941-45. 1949. I221
30:4 Holland, L. M. The direct primary in Georgia. 1949. I222
31:1 Cremeans, C. D. The reception of Calvanistic thought in England. 1949. I223
31:2 Canterbury, Eng. The metropolitan visitations of William Courteney, ed. by Dahmus. 1950. I224
31:3 Brucker, G. A. Jean-Sylvain Bailly. 1950. I225
31:4 Edelman, J. M. The licensing of radio services in the United States. 1950. I226
32:1 Miller, D. C. Taxes, the public debt, and transfer of income. 1950. I227
32:2 Carlson, T. L. The Illinois Military Tract. 1951. I228
32:3-4 Steiner, G. Y. The Congressional conference committee: Seventieth to Eightieth Congresses. 1951. I229
33:1 Hedlund, E. C. The transportation economics of the soybean processing industry. 1952. I230
33:2-3 Parsons, M. B. The use of licensing power by

ILLINOIS UNIVERSITY. STUDIES IN LANGUAGE AND LITERATURE.

4:1 Whitford, R. C. Madame de Staël's literary reputation in England. 1918. I268
4:2-4 Oldfather, W. A. and others. Index verborum qvae in Senecae fabulis necnon in Octavia praetexta reperiuntur. 3 v. 1918. I269
5:1-2 Keiser, A. The influence of Christianity on the vocabulary of Old English poetry. 1919. I270
5:3 Jones, H. S. V. Spenser's defense of Lord Grey. 1919. I271
5:4 Aesopus. Ysopet-Avionnet, ed. by Oldfather. 1921. I272
6:1 Seris, H. La colección cervantina de la sociedad hispanica de América. 1918. I273
6:2-3 Cicero, M. T. M. Tulli Ciceronis De divinatione, liber primos, ed. by Pease. 1923. I274
6:4 Robinson, R. P. De fragmenti Suetoniani De grammaticis et rhetoribus codicum nexu et fide. 1922. I275
7:1 Howard, R. Sir Robert Howard's comedy, "The Committee," ed. by Thurber. 1921. I276
7:2 Brooks, N. C. The sepulchre of Christ in art and liturgy. 1922. I277
7:3 Flom, G. T. The language of the Konungs Skuggsja. 1922. I278
7:4 Austin, J. C. The significant name in Terence. 1923. I279
8:1 Sutcliffe, E. G. Emerson's theories of literary expression. 1923. I280
8:2-3 Same as no. 6:2. Liber secundus. 1923. I281
8:4 Same as no. 7:3. V. 2. 1924. I282
9:1 Secord, A. W. Studies in the narrative method of Defoe. 1924. I283
9:2 Titchener, J. B. The manuscript-tradition of Plutarch's Aetia graeca and Aetia romana. 1924. I284
9:3 Fracastoro, G. Naugerius, sive de poetica dialogus. 1924. I285
9:4 Lowe, C. G. The manuscript-tradition of pseudo-Plutarch's Vitae secem oratorum. 1924. I286
10:1 Canter, H. V. Rhetorical elements in the tragedies of Seneca. 1925. I287
10:2 Williams, C. A. Oriental affinities of the legend of hairy anchorite. 2 v. 1925. I288
10:3 Geoffrey. The Vita Merlini, ed. by Parry. 1925. I289
10:4 Borgarthings kristinréttr. The Borgarthing law of the Codex tunsbergensis, ed. by Flom. 1926. I290
11:1-2 Hillebrand, H. N. The child actors. 1926. I291
11:3 Hamilton, A. A study of Spanish manners, 1750-1800. 1926. I292
11:4 Same as no. 10:2. V. 2. 1927. I293
12:1 Van Horne, J. El Bernardo of Bernardo de Balbuena. 1927. I294
12:2-3 Bundy, M. W. The theory of imagination in classical and medieval thought. 1927. I295
12:4 Jeffreys, G. The Merope of George Jeffreys as a source of Voltaire's Mérope, by Oliver. 1927. I296
13:1 Gulapingslög hin eldri. Fragment AM 315 E of the Oldger Gulathing law, ed. by Flom. 1928. I297
13:2 Heidler, J. B. The history from 1700 to 1800, of English criticism of prose fiction. 1928. I298
13:3-4 Trowbridge, M. L. Philological studies in ancient glass. 1930. I299
14:1-2 Kelso, R. The doctrine of the English gentleman in the sixteenth century. 1929. I300
14:3 Fletcher, H. F. The use of the Bible in Milton's prose. 1929. I301
14:4 Homíliubók. Codex A M 619 quarto, ed. by Flom. 1929. I302
15:1-2 Kelley, C. P. The

early development of Henry James. 1930. I303
15:3 Valbuena, B. de. La grandeze mexicana de Bernardo de Balbuena, ed. by Van Horne. 1930. I304
15:4 Burris, Q. G. Richard Doddridge Blackmore. 1930. I305
16:1 Fletcher, H. F. Contributions to a Milton bibliography, 1800-1930. 1931. I306
16:2 Jacob, P. E. Remy de Gourmont. 1931. I307
16:3-4 Meres, F. Francis Meres's treatise "Poetrie," ed. by Allen. 1933. I308
17:1-2 Goldman, M. S. Sir Philip Sidney and the Arcadia. 1934. I309
17:3-4 Macbeth, G. John Gibson Lockhart. 1935. I310
18:1-2 Williams, C. A. The German legends of the Hairy Anchorite, ed. by Allen. 1935. I311
18:3-4 Morrow, G. R. Studies in the Platonic Epistles. 1935. I312
19:1-2 Jehle, M. I. Das deutsche kuntsmärchen von der romantic zum naturalismus. 1935. I313
19:3-4 Johnson, W. G. James Thomson's influence on Swedish literature in the eighteenth century. 1936. I314
20:1-2 Diller, A. Race mixture among the Greeks before Alexander. 1937. I315
20:3-4 Gulapingslöghin eldri. The old Norwegian general law of the Gulathing, ed. by Flom. 1937. I316
21:1-2 Roche, A. V. Les idées traditionalistes en France de Rivarol à Charles Maurras. 1937. I317
21:3-4 Ross, F. E. Goethe in modern France. 1937. I318
22:1-2 Hamilton, M. (Neal). Music in eighteenth century Spain. 1937. I319
22:3-4 Wright, W. F. Sensibility in English prose fiction, 1760-1814. 1937. I320
23:1-2 Sūdraka, rajah of Magadha. Mrechkatika, tr. by Oliver. 1938. I321
23:3 Johnson, R. P. Compositiones Variae from Codex 490, Biblioteca capitolare, Lucca, Italy. 1939. I322
23:4 Krenn, E. Der föroyische dichter Páll Nólsoy und sein Vogellied. 1939. I323
24:1-2 Daly, L. W. and Suchier, W. Altercatio Hadriani Augusti et Epicteti Philosophi. 1939. I324
24:3-4 Templeman, W. D. The life and works of William Gilpin. 1939. I325
25:1-2 France, A. H. Briefe and August Hermann Francke, ed. by Geissendoerfer. 1939. I326
25:3 Morrow, G. R. Plato's law of slavery in its relation to Greek law. 1939. I327
25:4 Harris, J. W. John Bale. 1940. I328
26:1 Krenn, E. Die entwicklung der foeroyischen literatur. 1940. I329
26:2 Will, S. F. A bibliography of American studies on the French renaissance, (1500-1600). 1940. I330
26:3-4 Harris, B. Charles Sackville. 1940. I331
27:1 Liddell, M. H. The elements of sound and their relation to language. 1940. I332
27:2 Gettmann, R. A. Turgenev in England and America. 1941. I333
27:3-4 Reginald. The Vita sancti Malchi of Reginald of Canterbury, ed. by Lind. 1942. I334
28:1-2 Lattimore, R. A. Themes in Greek and Latin epitaphs. 1942. I335
28:3-4 The wars of Cyprus, ed. by Brawner. 1942. I336
29:1 Illinois. Univ. Scandinavian studies presented to George T. Flom, ed. by Larsen and Williams. 1942. I337
29:2-3 Moloney, M. F. John Donne. 1944. I338
29:4 Flom, G. T. The morphology of the dialect of Aurland. 1944. I339

30:1 Hammer, C. Goethe's Dichtung und wahrheit. 1945. I340
30:2-3 Stone, R. C. The language of the Latin text of Codex Bezae. 1946. I341
30:4 Harding, D. P. Milton and the renaissance Ovid. 1946. I342
31:1-2 Reiff, P. Die ästhetik der deutschen frührmantik, ed. by Geissendoerfer. 1946. I343
31:3-4 Dunkin, P. S. Post-Aristophanic comedy. 1946. I344
32:1 Herrick, M. T. The fusion of Horatian and Aristotelian literary criticism, 1531-55. 1946. I345
32:2-3 Wasserman, E. R. Elizabethean poetry in the eighteenth century. 1947. I346
32:4 May, G. C. Tragédie cornélienne. 1948. I347
33:1-2 Kolb, P. La Correspondance de Marcel Proust. 1949. I348
33:3-4 Allen, D. C. The legend of Noah. 1949. I349
34:1-2 Herrick, M. T. Comic theory in the sixteenth century. 1950. I350
34:3 Heywood, T. The Rape of Lucrece, ed. by Holaday. 1950. I351
34:4 Smiley, J. R. Diderot's relations with Grimm. 1950. I352
35:1-2 Milton, J. An apology against a pamphlet called A modest confutation of the animadversions upon the remonstrant against Smectymnus. 1951. I353
35:3 Townsend, F. G. Ruskin and the landscape feeling. 1951. I354
35:4 Robbins, E. W. Dramatic characterization in printed commentaries on Terence, 1473-1600. 1951. I355
36:1-2 Turyn, A. Studies in the manuscript tradition of the tragedies of Sophocles. 1952. I356
36:3 Le Sage, L. Jean Giraudoux. 1952. I357
36:4 Beyle, M. H. Henri III, un acte inédit (par) Stendhal. 1952. I358
37:1 Alexius, Saint. Legend. Two old Portuguese versions of the Life of Saint Alexis, ed. by Allen. 1953. I359
37:2 Rehder, H. Johann Nicolaus Meinhard und seine Überstezungen. 1953. I360
37:3 Philippson, E. A. Die Genealogie der Gotter in germanischer Religion, Mythologie und Theologie. 1953. I361
37:4 Hallowell, R. E. Ronsard and the conventional Roman clergy. 1954. I362
38 Kahane, H. R. and Pietrangeli, A. R., eds. Descriptive studies in Spanish grammar. 1954. I363
39 Herrick, M. T. Tragicomedy: its origin and development in Italy, France and England. 1955. I364
40 Roger, R. W. The major satires of Pope. 1955. I365
41 Heywood, J. Works, and miscellaneous short poems, ed. by Milligan. 1956. I366
42 Sherbo, A. Samuel Johnson, editor of Shakespeare. 1956. I367
43 Turyn, A. The Byzantine manuscript tradition of tragedies of Euripides. 1957. I368
44 Nicholas, C. Introduction and notes to Milton's History of Britain. 1957. I369
45 LeSage, L. Marcel Proust and his literary friends. 1958. I370
46 Frey, J. R., ed. Schiller. 1959. I371
47 Beaty, J. Middlemarch from notebook to novel. 1960. I372
48 "A library for younger schollers," comp. by an English scholar-priest about 1655, ed. by DeJordy and Fletcher. 1961. I373
49 Lida de Malkiel, M. R. Two Spanish masterpieces. 1961. I374
50 Harding, D. P. The club of Hercules. 1962. I375

51 Robins, H. F. If this be heresy, a study of Milton and Origen. 1963. I376
52 Watson, T. A humanist's "trew imitation." Thomas Watson's Absalom, tr. by Smith. 1964. I377
53 Bowen, B. C. Les caractéristiques essentielles de la farce française et leur survivance dans les années, 1550-1620. 1964. I378
54 Valdés, M. J. Death in the literature of Unamuno. 1964. I379
55 Reiman, D. H. Shelley's The triumph of life. 1965. I380
56 Kahane, H. R. and others. The Krater and the Grail. 1965. I381
57 DeLey, H. Marcel Proust de le Duc de Saint-Simon. 1966. I382
58 Heller, J. L., ed. Classical studies presented to Ben Edwin Perry. 1968. I383
59 Dessen, C. S. Iumctura Callidus acri. 1968. I384
60 Bucknall, B. J. The religion of art in Proust. 1970. I385
61 Willis, J. A. Latin textual criticism. 1972. I386
62 Bowen, B. C. The age of bluff. 1972. I387
63 Goodin, G. The English novel in the nineteenth century. 1973. I388

ILLUSTRATED GUIDES TO POTTERY AND PORCELAIN (Praeger)

Godden, G. A. Coalport and Coalbrookdale porcelains. 1970. I389
____. The illustrated guide to Lowestaft porcelain. 1969. I390
____. The illustrated guide to Mason's patent ironstone china and related wares. 1971. I391
____. The illustrated guide to Ridgway porcelains. 1972. I392
____. The illustrated guide to Staffordshire salt-glazed stoneware. 1971. I393
Rice, D. G. The illustrated guide to Rockingham pottery and porcelain. 1971. I394
Sandon, H. The illustrated guide to Worcester porcelain, 1751-1793. 1969. I395
Smith, A. The illustrated guide to Liverpool Herculaneum pottery, 1796-1840. 1970. I396

IMMIGRANT HERITAGE OF AMERICA SERIES (Twayne)

Andersen, H. W. The Norwegian-Americans. 1974. I397
Coombs, N. The Black experience in America. 1972. I398
Curran, T. J. Xenophobia and immigration, 1820-1930. 1974. I399
DeJong, G. F. The Dutch in America. 1974. I400
Hauberg, C. A. Puerto Rico and the Puerto Ricans. 1974. I401
Iorizzo, L. J. and Mondello, S. The Italian Americans. 1971. I402
Melendy, H. B. The Oriental Americans. 1972. I403
Miller, S. M. The radical immigrant. 1973. I404
Neidle, C. S. Great immigrants. 1972. I405
____. The new Americans. 1972. I406
O'Grady, J. P. How the Irish became Americans. 1973. I407

INDIANA HISTORICAL COLLECTIONS

1-2 Kettleborough, C., ed. Constitution making in Indiana. 2 v. 1916. I408
3 Indiana Hist. Comm. Indiana as seen by early travelers, ed. by Lindley. 1916. I409
4 Wolford, L. J. The play-party in Indiana. 1916. I410
No no. Indiana Hist. Comm. The Indiana centennial, 1916, ed. by Lindley. 1919. I411
6 ____. Gold star honor roll. 1921. I412
7 Indiana. Governor. Governors messages and letters,

ed. by Esarey, 1800-1811. 1922. I413
8 Greenough, W. S. The war purse of Indiana. 1922. I414
9 Same as no. 7. 1812-1816. 1922. I415
10 Straub, E. F. A sergeant's diary in the World War. 1923. I416
11 Clarke, G. G. George W. Julian. 1923. I417
12 Same as no. 7. 1816-1825. 1924. I418
13 Dufour, P. The Swiss settlement of Switzerland county, Indiana. 1925. I419
14 Goebel, D. (Burne). William Henry Harrison. 1926. I420
15 Griswold, B. J., ed. Fort Wayne. 1927. I421
16 Rauch, J. G. and Armstrong, N. C. A bibliography of the laws of Indiana, 1788-1927. 1928. I422
17 Same as no. 1. V. 3. 1930. I423
18 Rider, H. A. Indiana book of merit. 1932. I424
19 Pence, G. and Armstrong, N. C. Indiana boundaries... 1933. I425
20 Indiana (Ter.) Laws, statutes, etc. The laws of Indiana Territory, 1809-1816, ed. by Ewbank and Riker. 1934. I426
21-22 Robinson, S. Solon Robinson, pioneer and agriculturist; selected writings, ed. by Kellar. 2 v. 1936. I427
23 Gipson, L. H., ed. The Moravian Indian mission on White river, tr. by Stocker and others. 1938. I428
24-26 Tipton, J. The John Tipton papers, comp. and ed. by Blackburn and others. 3 v. 1942. I429
27 Hendrickson, W. B. David Dale Owen. 1943. I430
28 Cummins, C. C. Indiana public opinion and the world war, 1914-1917. 1945. I431
29 Indiana. Governor. Executive proceedings of the state of Indiana, 1816-1836, ed. by Riker. 1947. I432
30 Roll, C. Colonel Dick Thompson. 1948. I433
31 Stampp, K. M. Indiana politics during the Civil war. 1949. I434
32 Indiana (Ter.) General Assembly Journals, 1805-1815, ed. by Thornbrough and Riker. 1950. I435
33 Smith, W. H. Schuyler Colfax. 1952. I436
34 Same as no. 7. 1825-1831. 1954. I437
35 Byrd, C. K. and Peckham, H. H. A bibliography of Indiana imprints, 1804-1853. 1955. I438
36 Thornbrough, G., ed. Readings in Indiana history. 1956. I439
37 Thornbrough, E. L. The Negro in Indiana. 1957. I440
38 Noble, N. Messages and papers relating to the administration of Noah Noble, Governor of Indiana, 1831-1837, ed. by Riker and Thornbrough. 1958. I441
39 Moore, P. A. The Calumet region. 1959. I442
40 Riker, R. L., comp. Indiana election returns, 1816-1851. 1960. I443
41 Indiana. Indiana in the War of the Rebellion. 1960. I444
42 Shumaker, A. W. A history of Indiana literature. 1962. I445
43 Wallace, D. Messages and papers relating to the administration of David Wallace, Governor of Indiana, 1837-1840, ed. by Riker. 1963. I446
44 Bigger, S. Messages and papers relating to the administration of Samuel Bigger, Governor of Indiana, 1840-1843, ed. by Thornbrough. 1964. I447
45 Riddleberger, P. W. George Washington Julian. 1966. I448
46 Poinsatte, C. R. Fort Wayne during the canal era, 1828-1955. 1969. I449
47 McCord, S. S., comp. Travel accounts of Indiana, 1679-1961. 1970. I450

48 Tredway, G. T. Democratic opposition to the Lincoln administration in Indiana. 1973. I451

INDIANA HISTORICAL SOCIETY. PUBLICATIONS.

1:1 Indiana Hist. Soc. Proceedings of the Indiana Historical Society, 1830-1886. 1897. I452
1:2 Dane, M. Letter of Nathan Dane concerning the Ordinance of 1878. Gov. Patrick Henry's secret letter of instruction to George Rogers Clark. 1897. I453
1:3 Wylie, A. The uses of history. 1897. I454
1:4 Dillon, J. B. The national decline of the Miami Indians. 1897. I455
1:5 Bolton, N. Early history of Indianapolis and central Indiana. 1897. I456
1:6 Campbell, J. L. Joseph G. Marshall. 1897. I457
1:7 Denby, C. Judge John Law. 1897. I458
1:8 Cox, E. T. Archaeology. 1897. I459
1:9 Ferris, E. The early settlement of the Miami country. 1897. I460
2:1 Howe, D. W. The laws and courts of Northwest and Indian Territories. 1886. I461
2:2 Coburn, J. and Biddle, H. P. The life and services of John B. Dillon. 1886. I462
2:3 Cooley, T. M. The acquisition of Louisiana. 1887. I463
2:4 Martindale, C. Loughery's defeat and Pigeon Roost massacre. 1888. I464
2:5 Howe, D. W. A descriptive catalogue of the official publications of the territory and state of Indiana from 1800 to 1890. 1890. I465
2:6 Julian, G. W. The rank of Charles Osborn as an anti-slavery pioneer. 1891. I466
2:7 Ridpath, J. C. The man in history. 1893. I467
2:8 Craig, O. J. Ouiatanon. 1893. I468
2:9 Ferguson, C. P. Reminiscences of a journey to Indianapolis in the year 1836. 1893. I469
2:10 Duncan, R. B. "Old settlers." 1894. I470
2:11 Dunn, J. P. Documents relating to the French settlements on the Wabash. 1894. I471
2:12 ____. Slavery petitions and papers. 1894. I472
3:1 English, W. E. A history of early Indianapolis masonry. 1895. I473
3:2 Mallet, E. Sieur de Vincennes. 1897. I474
3:3 Indiana (Territory) Executive journal of Indiana Territory, 1800-1816, ed. by Woollen and others. 1900. I475
3:4 Dunn, J. P. The mission on the Ouabache. 1902. I476
3:5 Sloan, G. W. Fifty years in pharmacy. 1903. I477
3:6 Mills, C. Caleb Mills and the Indiana school system, by Moores. 1905. I478
4:1 Owen, W. Diary of William Owen, ed. by Hiatt. 1906. I479
4:2 Dunn, J. P. The word Hoosier. 1907. I480
Wrigley, S. A. John Finley. 1907. I481
4:3 Webster, H. J. William Henry Harrison's administration of Indiana Territory. 1907. I482
4:4 Howe, D. W. Making a capitol in the wilderness. 1908. I483
4:5 U. S. Census Off. Names of persons enumerated in Marion county, Indiana, at the fifth census, 1830. 1908. I484
4:6 Henry, W. E. Some elements of Indiana's population. 1908. I485
4:7 Browning, E. G. Lockerbie's assessment list of Indianapolis, 1835. 1909. I486
4:8 Woodburn, J. A. The Scotch-Irish Presbyterians in Monroe County, Indiana. 1910. I487

4:9 Holliday, J. H. Indianapolis and the civil war. 1911. I488
5:1 McBride, R. W. Lincoln's body guard. 1911. I489
5:2 Esarey, L. Internal improvements in early Indiana. 1912. I490
5:3 Elliott, J. T. The Sultana disaster. 1913. I491
5:4 Holliday, J. H. An Indian village, New Harmony. 1914. I492
5:5 Major, N. J., ed. The pioneers of Morgan county. 1915. I493
5:6 Smith, C. W. Life and military services of Brevet-Major General Robt. S. Foster. 1915. I494
6:1 Ohio Valley Hist. Assn. Proceedings of the tenth annual meeting, ed. by Lindley. 1917? I495
6:2 Dean, T. Journal..., ed. by J. C. Dean. 1918. I496
6:3 Wilson, G. R. Early Indiana trails and surveys. 1919. I497
6:4 Indiana Hist. Soc. Minutes of the Society, 1886-1918. 1919. I498
7:1 Roy, P. G. Sieur de Vincennes identified. 1918? I499
7:2 Ewbank, L. B. Morgan's raid in Indiana. 1918? I500
7:3 Woollen, W. W. Reminiscences of the early Marion county bar. 1919? I501
7:4 Burns, L. The national road in Indiana. 1919. I502
7:5 Hodges, L. (Fletcher). Early Indianapolis. 1919? I503
7:6 King, W. F. One hundred years in public health in Indiana. 1921. I504
7:7 Hay, H. Fort Wayne in 1790, by Quaife. 1921. I505
7:8 Morris, H. Washington county giants. 1921. I506
7:9 Miller, E. J. The science of Columbus. 1921. I507
7:10 Moores, C. W. Abraham Lincoln, lawyer. 1922. I508
8:1 Wilson, G. R. Judge James Lockhart. 1923. I509
8:2 Dunn, C. and E., tr. Indiana's first war. 1924. I510
8:3 Iglehart, J. E. The environment of Abraham Lincoln in Indiana. 1925. I511
Ehrmann, E. An account of the DeBruler family. 1925. I512
8:4 Knoblock, O. M. Early navigation on the St. Joseph River. 1925. I513
8:5 Schweinitz, L. D. von. The journey of Lewis David von Schweinitz to Goshen, Bartholomew County, in 1831, tr. by Gerber. 1927. I514
8:6 Sheehan, B. M. (Vrooman). The northern boundary of Indiana. 1928. I515
8:7 Snepp, D. W. Evansville's channel of trade and the secession movement. 1850-1865. 1928. I516
8:8 Rabb, K. (Milner). Indiana coverlets and coverlet weavers. 1928. I517
8:9 Burns, L. Life in Old Vincennes. 1929. I518
9 Foulke, W. D. Lucius B. Swift. 1930. I519
10:1 Coleman, C. B., ed. Centennial handbook, Indiana historical society, 1830-1930. 1930. I520
10:2 Greene, E. B. Our pioneer historical societies. 1931. I521
10:3 Murphy, C. B. The political career of Jessie D. Bright. 1931. I522
10:4 Jennings, J. Unedited letters, comp. by Riker. 1932. I523
10:5 Buechner, C. B. The Pokagons. 1933. I524
11:1 Pears, T. C., ed. New Harmony, an adventure in happiness; papers of Thomas and Sarah Pears. 1933. I525
11:2 Hatcher, S. B. A history of Spiceland Academy 1826 to 1921. 1934. I526
11:3 Burns, L. Early architects and builders of Indiana. 1935. I527
11:4 Schramm, J. The Schramm letters, ed. by Vonnegut. 1935. I528
11:5 McMurtie, D. C. Indiana imprints, 1804-1849. 1937. I529

12 Thompson, C. N. Sons of the wilderness: John and William Conner. 1937. I530
13:1 Daniels, W. J. The village at the end of the road. 1938. I531
13:2 McDaniel, E. H. The contribution of the Society of Friends to education in Indiana. 1939. I532
13:3 Winslow, H. L. and Moore, J. R. H. Camp Morton, 1861-1865. 1940. I533
14:1 Petit, B. M. The trail of death, ed. by McKee. 1941. I534
14:2 Macdonald, D. The diaries of Donald Macdonald, 1824-1826, ed. by Snedeker. 1942. I535
14:3 Peat, W. D. Portraits and painters of the governors of Indiana, 1800-1943. 1944. I536
15:1 Knollenberg, B. Pioneer sketches of the Upper Whitewater Valley. 1945. I537
15:2 Wilson, G. R. and Thornbrough, G. The Buffalo trace. 1946. I538
15:3 Maclure, W. Education and reform at New Harmony, ed. by Bestor. 1948. I539
15:4 Lux, L. The Vincennes donation lands. 1949. I540
16:1 Candler, J. A friendly mission, ed. by Thornbrough. 1951. I541
16:2 Johnson, O. A home in the woods, ed. by H. Johnson. 1951. I542
16:3 Smith, D. L., ed. From Greene Ville to Fallen Timbers. 1952. I543
17 Power, R. L. Planting Corn Belt culture. 1953. I544
18:1 Scott, J. The Indiana gazeteer; or, Topographical dictionary. 1954. I545
18:2 Krauskopf, F., ed. and tr. Ouiatanon documents. 1955. I546
18:3 Marshall, L. (Carr). I, alone, remember. 1956. I547
18:4 Rose, E. B. The circle the center of our universe. 1957. I548
19 Harmar, J. Outpost on the Wabash, ed. by Thornbrough. 1957. I549
20:1 Royse, M. A. The Bennet family. 1958. I550
20:2 Wolford, L. J. The play-party in Indiana. 1959. I551
20:3 Sullivan, W. G. English's Opera House. 1960. I552
21 U. S. Bureau of Indian Affairs. Letter book of the Indian Agency at Fort Wayne, 1809-1815, ed. by Thornbrough. 1961. I553
22 Badollet, J. L. The correspondence of John Badollet and Albert Gallatin, 1804-1836, ed. by Thornbrough. 1963. I554
23:1 White, T. To Oregon in 1852, ed. by Winther and Thornbrough. 1964. I555
23:2 Blair, D. Harmonist construction. 1964. I556
23:3 Hartley, W. D. The search for Henry Cross. 1966. I557
23:4 Owen, R. D. To Holland and to New Harmony, ed. by Elliott. 1969. I558
24 Woehrmann, P. At the headwaters of the Maumee. 1971. I559
25:1 Walters, B. L. Furniture makers of Indiana, 1793 to 1850. 1972. I560

INDIANA UNIVERSITY. FOLKLORE INSTITUTE. MONOGRAPH SERIES (1-22 Published as INDIANA UNIVERSITY. INDIANA UNIVERSITY PUBLICATIONS. FOLKLORE SERIES)

1 Brewster, P. G., ed. Ballads and songs of Indiana. 1940. I560a
2 Rotunda, D. P. Motif-index of the Italian novella in prose. 1942. I561
3 Kiefer, E. E. Albert Wesselski and recent folktale theories. 1947. I562
4 Proverbia communia. Proverbia communia; a fifteenth century collection of Dutch proverbs, ed. by Jente. 1947. I563
5 Childers, J. W. Motif index

of the cuentos of Juan Timoneda. 1948. I564
6 Sebeok, T. A., ed. Studies in Cheremis folklore. V. 1. 1952. I565
7 Cross, T. P. Motif-index of early Irish literature. 1952. I566
8 Thompson, S., ed. Four symposia on folklore, 1950. 1953. I567
9 Richmond, W. E., eds. Studies in folklore, in honor of distinguished service professor Stith Thompson. 1957. I568
10 Thompson, S. and Balys, J. The oral tales of India. 1958. I569
11 Sebeok, T. A. and Brewster, P. G. Studies in Cheremis: games. 1958. I570
12 Dorson, R. M., ed. Negro tales from Pine Bluff, Arkansas and Calvin, Michigan. 2 v. 1958. I571
13 Patai, R. and others, eds. Studies in Biblical and Jewish folklore. 1960. I572
14 Nettl, B. Cheremis musical styles. 1960. I573
15 Brunvard, J. H., comp. A dictionary of proverbs and proverbial phrases from books published by Indiana authors before 1890. 1961. I574
16 Dorson, R. M., ed. Folklore research around the world. 1961. I575
17 ____. Studies in Japanese folklore. 1963. I576
18 Simmons, M. E. A bibliography of the romance and related forms in Spanish America. 1963. I577
19 Ives, E. D. Larry Gorman. 1964. I578
20 Baughman, E. A type and motif index of the folktales of England and North America. 1964. I579
21 Kirkland, E. C. A bibliography of South Asian folklore. 1966. I580
22 Munch, P. A. The song tradition of Tristan da Cunha. 1970. I581
23 Eberhard, W. Studies in Chinese folklore and related essays. 1970. I582
24 Randolph, V. Ozark folklore. 1972. I583

INDIANA UNIVERSITY. INDIANA UNIVERSITY PUBLICATIONS. HUMANITIES SERIES.

1 Moore, J. R. Defoe in the pillory and other studies. 1939. I584
2 Judson, A. C. Thomas Watts, archdeacon of Middlesex (and Edmund Spenser). 1939. I585
3 Gottfried, R. B. Geoffrey Fenton's Historie de Guicciardin. 1940. I586
4 Ellis, F. M. (Hankemeier). Hans Sachs studies I. V. 1. 1941. I587
5 Noyes, R. Wordsworth and Jeffrey in controversy. 1941. I588
6 Rey, A. and Solalinde, G. Ensayo de una bibliografía de las leyendas troyanas en la literatura española. 1942. I589
7 Seeber, E. D., ed. Choix de pièces huguenotes, 1685-1756. 1942. I590
8 Mueller, J. H. and Hevner, K. Trends in musical taste. 1942. I591
9 Moore, J. R. Defoe's sources for Robert Drury's journal. 1943. I592
10 Wooley, E. O. Studies in Theodor Storm. 1943. I593
11 Campion, C. M. Oeuvres de Charles-Michel Campion, poète marseillais du dix-huitième siècle, ed. by Seeber and Remak. 1943. I594
12 Mills, L. J. Peter Hausted, playwright, poet and preacher. 1944. I595
13 Henryson, R. A modernization of Robert Henryson's Testament of Cresseid, notes by Stearns. 1945. I596
14 Cook, H. H. Paul Hervieu and French classicism. 1945. I597
15 Hill, J. M., ed. Poesías germanescas. 1945. I598

16 Emerson, R. W. Napoleon; or, The man of the world, notes by Davidson. 1947. I599
17 Bryan, W. L. The measured and the not-yet-measured. 1947. I600
18 Poesse, W. The internal line-structure of thirty autograph plays of Lope de Vega. 1949. I601
19 Hausted, P. Senile odium, ed. and tr. by Mills. 1949. I602
20 Judson, A. C. Notes on the life of Edmund Spenser. 1949. I603
21 Hill, J. M. Voces germanescas, recogidas y ordenadas. 1949. I604
22 Indiana University. Goethe bicentennial studies by members of the faculty of Indiana University, ed. by Meessen. 1950. I605
23 Hausted, P. The rival friends, ed. by Mills. 1951. I606
24 Castigos é documentos del Rey don Sancho IV. Castigos é documentos para bien vivir ordenados por el Rey don Sancho IV, ed. by Rey. 1952. I607
25 MacClintock, L. The age of Pirandello. 1951. I608
26 Whitman and Rolleston, ed. by Frenz. 1951. I609
27 Senilis amor, ed. and tr. by Mills. 1949. I610
28 Ushenko, A. P. Dynamics of art. 1953. I611
29 Brumbaugh, R. S. Plato's mathematical imagination. 1954. I612
30 Stout, S. E. Scribe and critic at work in Pliny's letters. 1954. I613
31 Bembo, P. Gil Asolani, tr. by Gottfried. 1954. I614
32 Champigny, R. Portrait of a symbolist hero. 1954. I615
33 Vega Carpio, L. F. de. El príncipe despeñado, ed. by Hoge. 1954. I616
34 Moody, R. America takes the stage. 1955. I617
35 Sells, A. L. Animal poetry in French & English literature & the Greek tradition. 1955. I618
36 Swift, J. An inquiry into the behavior of the Queen's last ministry, ed. by Ehrenpreis. 1956. I619
37 MacClintock, S. Perversity and error. 1956. I620
38 Simmons, M. E. The Mexican corrido as a source for interpretative study of modern Mexico, 1870-1950. 1957. I621
39 Lloyd, C. The Lloyd-Manning letters, ed. by Beatty. 1957. I622
40 Fuerst, N. Phases of Rilke. 1958. I623
41 Judson, A. C. Sidney's appearance. 1958. I624
42 Champigny, R. Stages on Sartre's way, 1938-52. 1959. I625
43 On the threshold of liberty, tr. by Seeber. 1959. I626
44 Libro de los çient capitulos. El Libro de los cien capítulos, ed. by Rey. 1960. I627
45 Carter, H. H. A dictionary of Middle English musical terms, ed. by Gerhard and others. 1961. I628
46 Lawlis, M. E. Apology for the middle class. 1960. I629
47 Moore, J. R. A checklist of the writings of Daniel Defoe. 1960. I630
48 Martin, T. The instructed vision. 1961. I631
49 Plinius Caecilius Secundas, C. Plinius, epistudae, ed. by Stout. 1962. I632
50 Pappas, J. N. Voltaire & D'Alembert. 1962. I633
51 Hope, Q. M. Saint-Evremond, the honnête homme as critic. 1962. I634
52 Vickery, W. N. The cult of optimism. 1963. I635
53 Barnett, G. L. Charles Lamb: The evolution of Elia. 1964. I636
54 Rabkin, G. Drama and commitment. 1964. I637
55 Mills, L. J. The tragedies of Shakespeare's Anthony and Cleopatra. 1964. I638
56 Shirley, J. The Cardinal,

ed. by Forker. 1964. I639
57 Panuccio dal Bagno. The poetry of Panuccio, ed. by Musa. 1965. I640
58 Shusterman, D. The quest for certitude in E. M. Forster's fiction. 1965. I641
59 Boyle, R. Robert Boyle on natural philosophy, ed. by Hall. 1965. I642
60 Kaufmann, W. Musical notations of the Orient. 1966. I643
61 Smith, D. E. John Bunyan in America. 1966. I644
62 Warner, L. Through his letters, ed. by Bowie. 1966. I645
63 Arnold, M. A study of the poetic temperament in Victorian England. 1966. I646
64 Proffer, C. R. Keys to Lolita. 1968. I647
65 Noyes, R. Wordsworth and the art of landscape. 1968. I648
66 Geduld, H. M. Prince of publishers. 1969. I649
67 Dickason, D. H. William Williams. 1970. I650
68 Austin, A. T. S. Eliot. 1971. I651
69 Chaitin, G. D. The unhappy few. 1972. I652
71 Guido delle Colonne. Historia destructionis troiae, tr. by Meek. 1973. I653
72 Grossmann, R. Ontological reduction. 1973. I654
73 Fisk, M. Nature and necessity. 1974. I655

INDIANA UNIVERSITY. INDIANA UNIVERSITY. PUBLICATIONS. RUSSIAN AND EAST EUROPEAN SERIES. (1-19 published as: Slavic and East European Series)

1 Minn, E. (Kangasmaa). Derivation. 1956. I656
2 Indiana slavic studies. V. 1. 1956. I657
3 Wandycz, P. S. Czechoslovak-Polish confederation, and the Great Powers, 1940-1943. 1956. I658
4 Conference on Resources and Planning in Eastern Europe, Indiana University. Resources and planning in Eastern Europe, ed. by Pounds and Spulber. 1957. I659
5 Pehrson, R. N. The bilateral network of social relations in Könkämä Lapp District. 1957. I660
6 Lundin, C. L. Finland in the Second World War. 1958. I661
7 Vishnîak, M. V. Sovremennye Zapiski. 1957. (Pub. in Russian) I662
8 Newmark, L. Structural grammar of Albanian. 1957. I663
9 American bibliography of Slavic and East European studies... 1956, ed. by Shaw and others. 1957. I664
10 ____. 1957. 1958. I665
11 Pounds, N. J. G. The Upper Silesian industrial region. 1958. I666
12 Byrnes, R. F. Bibliography of American publications on East Central Europe, 1945-1957. 1958. I667
13 Same as no. 2. V. 2. 1958. I668
14 Benes, V. L. and others, eds. The second Soviet-Yugoslav dispute. 1959. I669
15 Byrnes, R. F. The non-western areas in undergraduate education in Indiana. 1959. I670
16 Horecky, P. L. Libraries and bibliographic centers in the Soviet Union. 1959. I671
17 Jelavich, B. (Brightfield). Russia and the Rumanian national cause. 1959. I672
18 Same as no. 9. 1958. 1959. I673
19 Gorokhoff, B. I. Publishing in the U. S. S. R. 1959. I674
20 Yarmolinsky, A. Literature under Communism. 1960. I675
21 Same as no. 9. 1960. 1960. I676
22 Rintala, M. Three generations. 1962. I677
23 Drahomaniv, M. T. Notes

on the Slavic religio-ethical legends, tr. by Count. 1961. I678
24 Pounds, N. J. G., ed. Geographical essays on Eastern Europe. 1961. I679
25 Conference on the Study of the Soviet Economy, Ind. Univ. Study of the Soviet economy. 1961. I680
26 Same as no. 9. 1960. 1962. I681
27 Same as no. 9. 1961. Ed. by Todd and Viederman. 1963. I682
28 Same as no. 2. V. 3. 1963. I683
29 Same as no. 9. 1962. Ed. by Todd and others. 1964. I684
30 Maklakov, V. A. The first State Duma, tr. by Belkin. 1964. I685
31 Horak, S. Poland's international affairs, 1919-1960. 1964. I686
32 Same as no. 9. 1963. Ed. by Todd and others. 1965. I687
33 Kirchner, W. and Whittaker, C. H. Commercial relations between Russia and East European series for 1964. 1966. I688
34 Same as no. 9. 1964. Ed. by Epstein and Whittaker. 1966. I689
35 Wyspianski, S. The return of Odysseus, tr. by Clarke. 1966. I690
36 Same as no. 2. V. 4. 1967. I691
37 Same as no. 9. 1965. 1968. I692
38 Alexander, J. T. The imperial Russian government and Pugachev's revolt. 1968. I693
39 Aboucher, A. Soviet planning and spatial efficiency. 1971. I694
40 Same as no. 9. Ed. by Epstein. 1971. I695
41 Revolution and politics in Russia, ed. by A. and J. Rabinowitch. 1972. I696
42 Epstein, F. T. Germany and the East, ed. by Byrnes. 1974. I697

INDIANA UNIVERSITY. INDIANA UNIVERSITY PUBLICATIONS. SOCIAL SCIENCE SERIES.

1 U. S. Constitution. The constitution of the United States at the end of one hundred fifty years, ed. by Willis. 1939. I698
2 Dean, J. The management counsel profession. 1940. I699
3 Winther, O. O. The trans-Mississippi West, a guide to its periodical literature (1811-1938). 1942. I700
4 Wormuth, F. D. Class struggle. 1946. I701
5 Andressohn, J. C. The ancestry and life of Godfrey of Bouillon. 1947. I702
6 Delivanis, D. J. and Cleveland, W. C. Greek monetary developments, 1939-1948. 1949. I703
7 Winther, O. O. The old Oregon country. 1950. I704
8 Economic theory in review, by Earley and others. 1950. I705
9 Montulé, E. de. Travels in America, 1816-1817, tr. by Seeber. 1951. I706
10 Murray, J. J. Essays in modern European history. 1951. I707
11 Barnhart, J. D. Valley of democracy. 1953. I708
12 Oliver, H. M. A critique of socio-economic goals. 1954. I709
13 Walpole, H. W., baron. An honest diplomat at the Hague, ed. by Murray. 1955. I710
14 Hanssen, H. H. Diary of a dying empire, ed. by Lutz and others. 1955. I711
15 Sutherland, E. H. The Sutherland papers, ed. by Cohen and others. 1956. I712
16 Baxter, M. G. Orville H. Browning. 1957. I713
17 Mooney, C. C. Slavery in Tennessee. 1957. I714
18 Siffin, W. J. The legislative council in the American

states. 1959. I715
19 Winther, O. O. A classified bibliography of the periodical literature of the trans-Mississippi West, 1811-1957. 1961. I716
20 Cavnes, M. The Hoosier community at war. 1961. I717
21 Schweitzer, A. Big business in the Third Reich. 1964. I718
22 Nehrt, C. L. Nuclear power plants in international markets. 1965. I719
23 Friedman, B. The financial role of Indiana in World War II. 1965. I720
24 Christenson, C. L. and Myren, R. A. The Walsh-Healey public contracts act. 1966. I721
25 Stanfield, H. S. The diary of Howard Stillwell Stanfield, ed. by Detzler. 1968. I722
26 Winther, O. O. and Van Orman, R. A. A classified bibliography of the trans-Mississippi West. 1970. I723
27 Merli, F. J. Great Britain and the Confederate Navy. 1970. I724
28 Walker, H. D. Market power and price levels in the ethical drug industry. 1971. I725
29 Antoun, R. T. Arab village. 1972. I726
30 Tittle, C. R. Society of subordinates. 1973. I727

INDIANA. UNIVERSITY. INTERNATIONAL STUDIES.

Bailey, S. D. Voting in the Security Council. 1969. I728
Bowie, T. R. East-West in art. 1966. I729
Byrnes, R. F. Pobedonostsev. 1968. I730
Farnsworth, B. William C. Bullitt and the Soviet Union. 1967. I730a
Gehlen, M. P. The Communist Party of the Soviet Union. 1969. I731
____. The politics of co-existence. 1967. I732
Guback, T. H. The international film industry. 1969. I733
Hansen, N. M. French regional planning. 1968. I734
Heggoy, A. A. Insurgency and countersurgency in Algeria. 1972. I735
Herz, M. F. Beginnings of the cold war. 1966. I736
International communication and the new diplomacy, ed. by Hoffman. 1968. I737
Lewis, B. The Middle East and the West. 1964. I738
Ling, D. L. Tunisia. 1967. I739
Mehlinger, H. D. and Thompson, J. M. Count Witte and the Tsarist government in the 1905 revolution. 1972. I740
Meo, L. M. T. Lebanon. 1965. I741
Perkins, D. The diplomacy of a new age. 1967. I742
Rabinowitch, A. Prelude to revolution. 1968. I743
Sabaliūnas, L. Lithuania in crisis. 1971. I744
Spulber, N., ed. Foundations of Soviet strategy for economic growth. 1964. I745
____. Soviet strategy for economic growth. 1964. I746
Traina, R. American diplomacy and the American Civil War. 1968. I747

INDIANA UNIVERSITY. RESEARCH CENTER IN ANTHROPOLOGY, FOLKLORE, AND LINGUISTICS. PUBLICATIONS.

1 Sapir, E. and Swadesh, M. Native accounts of Nootka ethnography. 1955. I748
2 Minn, E. (Kangasmaa). Derivation. 1956. I749
3 Pehrson, R. N. The bilateral network of social relations in Könkämä Lapp District. 1957. I750
4 Newmark, L. Structural grammar of Albanian. 1957. I751
5 Longacre, R. E. Proto-Mixtecan. 1957. I752
6 Newman, S. S. Zuni dictionary. 1958. I753
7 Albright, R. W. The international phonetic alphabet.

1958. I754

8 Jacobs, M. Clackmas Chinook texts. Pt. 1. 1958. I755

9 Kahane, H. R. and others. The development of the verbal categories in child language. 1958. I756

10 Propp, V. Morphology of the folktale, ed. by Pirkova-Jakobson. 1958. I757

11 Same as no. 8. Pt. 2. 1959. I758

12 Lees, R. B. The grammar of English nominalizations. 1960. I759

13 Ferguson, C. A., ed. Linguistic diversity in South Asia. 1960. I760

14 Language Laboratory Conf. Language teaching today, ed. by Oinas. 1960. I761

15 Inverarity, R. B. Visual files coding index. 1960. I762

16 Yen, I. Y. A grammatical analysis of Syău Jīng. 1960. I763

17 Bunak, V. V. and others, eds. Contemporary racialogy and racism, tr. by Count. 1961. I764

18 Language Laboratory Conf. Materials and techniques for the language laboratory, ed. by Najam. 1962. I765

19 Waterhouse, V. G. The grammatical structure of Oaxaca Chantal. 1962. I766

20 Abramson, A. S. The vowels and tones of standard Thai. 1962. I767

21 Conference on Lexicography. Problems in lexicography, ed. by Householder and Saporta. 1962. I768

22 Joos, M. The five clocks. 1962. I769

23 Loeb, E. M. In feudal Africa. 1963. I770

24 Koutsoudas, A. Verb morphology of modern Greek. 1962. I771

25 Greenberg, J. H. The language of Africa. 1963. I772

26 Driver, H. E. and W. Ethnography and acculturation of the Chichimeca-Jonaz of northeast Mexico. 1963. I773

27 Language Laboratory Conf. Structural drill and the language laboratory, ed. by Gravit and Valdman. 1963. I774

28 Rastorgueva, V. S. A short sketch of Tajek grammar, ed. by Paper. 1963. I775

29 ____. A short sketch of the grammar of Persian, tr. by Hill, ed. by Paper. 1964. I776

30 Postal, P. Constituent structure. 1964. I777

31 Householder, F. W. and others. Reference grammar of literary Dhimotiki. 1964. I778

32 Levin, N. B. The Assiniboine language. 1964. I779

33 Shafeev, D. A. A short grammatical outline of Pashto, tr. and ed. by Paper. 1964. I780

34 Lehiste, I. Acoustical characteristics of selected English consonants. 1964. I781

35 Abaev, V. I. A grammatical sketch of Ossetic. 1964. I782

36 Fishman, J. A. Yiddish in America. 1965. I783

37 Herzog, M. I. The Yiddish language in northern Poland. 1965. I784

38 Noble, G. K. Proto-Arawakan and its descendants. 1965. I785

39 Scott, C. T. Persian and Arabic riddles. 1965. I786

40 Foreign Language Conference. Language learning, ed. by Najam. 1965. I787

41 Bendix, E. H. Componential analysis of general vocabulary. 1966. I788

42 Bowman, E. The minor fragmentary sentences of corpus of spoken English. 1966. I789

43 Burling, R. Proto Lolo-Burmese. 1967. I790

44 Lieberson, S. Explorations in sociolinguistics. 1967. I791

45 Mathiot, M. An approach to the cognitive study of language. 1968. I792

INDIANA. UNIVERSITY. STUDIES IN THE HISTORY AND THEORY OF LINGUISTICS

Baudouin de Courtenay, J. I. N. A Baudouin de Courtenay anthology, ed. by Stankiewicz. 1971. I793
Bloomfield, L. A Leonard Bloomfield anthology, ed. by Hockett. 1970. I794
Crystal, D. and Davy, D. Investigating English style. 1969. I795
DeLaguna, G. M. (Andrus). Speech. 1963. I796
Firth, J. R. Selected papers of J. R. Firth, ed. by Palmer. 1969. I797
Garvin, P. L. and Spolsky, B., eds. Computation in linguistics. 1966. I798
Godel, R., ed. Geneva school reader in linguistics. 1969. I799
Halliday, M. A. K. and others. The linguistic sciences and language teaching. 1964. I800
Haugen, E. Norwegian language in America. 1969. I801
Hymes, D., ed. Studies in the history of linguistics. 1974. I802
Jespersen, O. Mankind, nation and individual from a linguistic point of view. 1964. I803
Kurath, H. Studies in area linguistics. 1972. I804
Leech, G. N. Towards a semantic description of English. 1970. I805
Lehmann, W. P., comp. A reader in nineteenth century historical Indo-European linguistics. 1967. I806
Leopold, W. F. Bibliography of child language. 1972. I807
Linguistic Institute Research Seminar. Computation in linguistics. 1967. I808
McIntosh, A. and Halliday, M. A. K. Patterns and language. 1967. I809
Mackey, W. F. Language teaching analysis. 1967. I810
Malinowski, B. Coral gardens and their magic. 2 v. 1965. I811
Marckwardt, A. H. Linguistics and the teaching of English. 1966. I812
Osgood, C. E. and Sebeok, T. A., eds. Psycholinguistics. 1965. I813
Pedersen, H. The discovery of language, tr. by Spargo. 1962. I814
Quirk, R. Essays on the English language. 1968. I815
Robins, R. H. General linguistics. 1965. I816
____. A short history of linguistics. 1968. I817
Sebeok, T. A., ed. Portraits of linguists. 1966. I818
Stern, G. Meaning and change of meaning. 1964. I819
UCLA Conference on Historical Linguistics in the Perspective of Transformational Theory. Linguistic change and generative theory, ed. by Stockwell and Macaulay. 1972. I820
Vachek, J. The linguistic school of Prague. 1966. I821
____, comp. A Prague school reader in linguistics. 1964. I822

INDIANA UNIVERSITY. URALIC AND ALTAIC SERIES.

1 Indiana University. Committee on Uralic Studies. American studies in Uralic linguistics. 1960. I823
2 Poppe, N. N. Buriat grammar. 1960. I824
3 Hakulinen, L. The structure and development of the Finnish language, tr. by Atkinson. 1961. I825
4 Martin, S. E. Dagur Mongolian grammar, texts and lexicon. 1961. I826
5 Sebeok, T. A. and Ingemann, F. J. An Eastern Cheremis manual. 1961. I827
6 Lees, R. B. The phonology of modern standard Turkish. 1961. I828
7 Krueger, J. R. Chuvash manual. 1961. I829
8 Bosson, J. E. Buriat reader, ed. by Poppe. 1962. I830

9 Zeps, V. J. Latvian and Finnic linguistic convergences. 1962. 1831
10 Poppe, N. Uzbek newspaper reader. 1962. 1832
11 Lotz, J., ed. Hungarian reader. 1962. 1833
12 Harms, R. T. Estonian grammar. 1962. 1834
13 Poppe, N., ed. American studies in Altaic linguistics. 1962. 1835
14 Hajdú, P. The Samoyed peoples and languages. 1963. 1836
15 Austerlitz, R. P. Finnish reader and glossary. 1966. 1837
16 Olmsted, D. L. Korean folklore reader. 1964. 1838
17 Tauli, V. Structural tendencies in Uralic languages. 1963. 1839
18 Sjoberg, A. F. (Connery). Uzbek structural grammar. 1963. 1840
19 Swift, L. B. A reference grammar of modern Turkish 1962. 1841
20 Krader, L. Social organization of the Mongol-Turkic pastoral nomads. 1963. 1842
21 Krueger, J. R. Yakut manual. 1963. 1843
22 Tietze, A. Turkish literary reader. 1963. 1844
23 Permanent Int'l. Altaistic Conf. Aspects of Altaic civilization, ed. by Sinor and Francis. 1963. 1845
24 Street, J. C. Khalkha structure. 1963. 1846
25 Poppe, N. N. Tatar manual. 1963. 1847
26 Krader, L. Peoples of central Asia. 1963. 1848
27 Lehtinen, M. K. T. Basic course in Finnish. 1964. 1849
28 Shnitnikov, B. N. Kazakh-English dictionary. 1966. 1850
29 Austin, W. M. and others. Mongol reader. 1964. 1851
30 Smedt, A. de and Mostaert, A. Le dialecte monguor. 1964. (Microfilm) 1852
31 Oras, A. Estonian literary reader. 1964. 1853
32 Bol'shaîa sovetskaîa entsiklopediîa. The Turkic people, ed. by Krueher. 1963. 1854
33 Hebert, R. J. and Poppe, N. N. Kirghiz manual. 1964. 1855
34 Oinas, F. J. Estonian literary reader. 1964. 1856
35 Böhtlingk, O. von. Über die Sprache der Jakuten. 1964. 1857
36 Poppe, N. Bashkir manual. 1964. 1858
37 Rupen, R. A. Mongols of the twentieth century. 2 v. 1965. 1859
38 Bosson, J. E. Modern Mongolian. 1964. 1860
39 Vuorela, T. The Finno-Ugric peoples, tr. by Atkinson. 1964. 1861
40 Wiedemann, F. J. Syrjanischdeutsches Worterbuch. 1964. 1862
41 Keresztes, K. Morphemic and semantic analysis of the word families: Finnish ete- and Hungarian el- , fore- . 1964. 1863
42 Harms, R. T. Finnish structural sketch. 1964. 1864
43 Riasanovsky, V. A. Fundamental principles of Mongol law. 1965. 1865
44 Ravila, P. Finnish literary reader. 1965. 1866
45 Householder, F. W. and Lofti, M. Basic course in Azerbaijani. 1965. 1867
46 Kalmán, B. Vogul chrestomathy. 1965. 1868
47 Rédei, K. Northern Ostyak chrestomathy. 1965. 1869
48 Riazanovskii, V. A. Customary law of the nomadic tribes of Siberia. 1965. 1870
49 Hasselbrink, G. Alternative analyses of the phonemic system in central south-Lappish. 1965. 1871
50 Décsy, G. Yurak chrestomathy. 1966. 1872
51 Gulya, J. Eastern Ostyak chrestomathy. 1966. 1873
52 Erdely, S. Methods and principles of Hungarian ethnomusicology. 1965. 1874
53 Castrén, M. A. Grammatik

der samojedischen Sprachen. 1966. I875
54 Oinas, F. J. Basic course in Estonian. 1966. I876
55 See no. 11. Vocabulary and notes to Hungarian reader. 1966. I877
56 Popov, A. A. The Nganasan, tr. by Ristinen. 1966. I878
57 Diószegi, V., ed. Popular beliefs and folklore tradition in Siberia. 1968. I879
58 Yüan cah'o pi shih. Studies in the secret history of the Mongols. 1965. I880
59 Raun, O. Basic course in Uzbek. 1969. I881
60 Eckmann, J. Chagatay manual. 1966. I882
61 Pozdneev, A. M. Mongolia and the Mongola, ed. by Krueger. 1971. I883
62 Fishman, J. A. Hungarian language maintenance in the United States. 1966. I884
63 Lotz, J. The Uralic and Altaic Program of the American Council of Learned Societies. 1966. I885
64 Rubel, P. G. The Kalmyk Mongols. 1967. I886
65 Lehiste, I. Constant quantity and phrenological units in Estonian. 1966. I887
66 Keleti szemle. V. 1. 1966. I888
67 Zsilka, J. The system of Hungarian sentence patterns. 1967. I889
68 Ariste, P. A grammar of the Votic language. 1968. I890
69 Tekin, T. A grammar of the Orkhan Turkic. 1968. I891
70 Ashmartin, N. I. Thesaurus linguae Tschuvaschirum. 4 v. 1969. I892
71 Maranda, E. K. Finnish folklore reader and glossary. 1968. I893
72 Ahokas, J. A. A history of Finnish literature. 1973. I894
73 Hangin, J. G. Basic course in Mongolian, ed. by Krueger. 1968. I895
74 Vértes, E. Die ostjaischen Probomina. 1967. I896
75 Szabo, L. Selkup texts. 1967. I897
76 Kiefer, F. On emphasis and word order in Hungarian. 1967. I898
77 Foltiny, S. The Hungarian archaeological collection of the American Museum of Natural History in New York. 1969. I899
78 Budnez, J. A comparative dictionary of Finno-Ugric elements in the Hungarian vocabulary. 1966. I900
79 Radlov, V. V. South-Siberian oral literature. V. 1. 1967. I901
80 Lakó, G. Proto Finno-Ugric sources of the Hungarian phonetic stock. 1968. I902
81 The First Votyak grammar, ed. by Décsy. 1967. I903
82 Vienker, W. Die Farze des finnougrischen substrats in der russischen sprache. 1967. I904
83 Tamás, L. Etymologisch-historisches Wörterbuch der ungarischen Elemente im Rumänischen. 1967. I905
84 Béathy, E. Die Bezeichmengen für Himmelsrichtungen in den finnisch-ugrischen sprachen. 1967. I906
85 Arany, A. L. The phonological system of a Hungarian dialect. 1967. I907
86 Basgöz, I. and Wilson, H. E. Educational problems in Turkey, 1920-1940. 1968. I908
87 Thomsen, V. L. P. On the influence of Germanic languages on Finnic and Lapp. 1969. I909
88 Krueger, J. R. Mongolian epigraphical dictionary in reverse listing. 1967. I910
89 Hangin, J. G. A concise English-Mongolian dictionary. 1969. I911
90 Kurman, G. The development of writen Estonian. 1968. I912
91 Sajnovics, J. Joanne's Sajnovics Demonstratio idioma Ungarorum. 1967. I913

92 Anandadhvaja. A treasury of aphoristic jewels. 1969. I914
93 Stoebke, R. Die verhältniswörter in den ostseefinnischen sprachen. 1968. I915
94 Krueger, J. R., ed. Cheremis-Chuvash lexical relationships. 1968. I916
95 Gyarmathi, S. Affinitas linguae Hungaricae cum linguis Finnicae originis grammaticae demonstrata. 1968. I917
96 Sinor, D. Inner Asia. 1969. I918
97 Magdics, K. Studies in the acoustic characteristics of Hungarian speech sounds. 1969. I919
98 Molnár, A. Nova grammatica ungarica, by Szenciensis. 1970. I920
99 Demko, G. K. The Russian colonization of Kazakhstan, 1896-1916. 1969. I921
100 Krueger, J. R. The Uralic and Altaric series; an analytic index. 1970. I922
101 Redei, K., comp. Permjakisches Wörterverzeichnis aus dem Jahre 1833 auf Grund der Aufzeichnungen F. A. Wolegows. 1968. I923
102 Montgomery, D. C., comp. Mongolian newspaper reader. 1969. I924
103 Erdélyi, I. Selkupisches Wörterverzeichnis Tas-Dialekt. 1970. I925
104 Sa'di. A fourteenth century Turkish translation of Sa'di's Gulistān, ed. by Bodrogligeti. 1970. I926
105 Nemser, W. An experimental study of phonological interference in the English of Hungarians. 1971. I927
106 Sum-pa-mKhan-po. The annals of Kohonor, by Ho-Chin-Yang. 1969. I928
107 Raun, A. Essays in Finno-Ugric and Finnic linguistics. 1971. I929
108 Paulson, I. The old Estonian folk religion, tr. by Kitching and Kõvamees. 1971. I930
109 Rédei, K. Die syrjänischen Lehnwörter im Wogulischen. 1970. I931
110 Veenker, W. Vogul suffixes and pronouns. 1969. I932
111 Shoolbraid, G. M. H. The oral epic of Siberia and Central Asia. 1974. I933
112 Sjogren, A. J. Notes about the congregations in Kemi-Lappmark. 1974. I934
113 Gadā'ī. The Divan of Gadā'ī, by Eckmann. 1971. I935
114 Lie, H. Die Mandscher-Sprachkunde in Korea. 1972. I936
115 Doerfer, G. and others. Khalaj materials. 1971. I937
116 Witsen, N. Khalaj en Oost Tartarye, ed. by Doerfer. 1974. I938
117 Kerek, A. Hungarian metrics. 1971. I939
118 Tietze, A. Advanced Turkish reader. 1973. I940
119 Luthy, M. J. Phonological and lexical aspects of colloquial Finnish. 1973. I941
120 Basgöz, M. I., comp. Turkish folklore reader. 1970. I942
121 Yüan ch'ao pi shih. Index to secret history of the Mongols by De Rachewiltz. 1972. I943
123 Stone, F. A. The rub of cultures in modern Turkey. 1973. I944

INDO-IRANIAN MONOGRAPHS (Mouton)

1 Kathinavastu. A comparative study of the Kathinavastu. 1957. I945
2 Bosch, F. D. K. The golden germ. 1960. I946
3 Novotny, F. Eine durch Miniaturen erläuterte Doctrina mystica aus Srinaga. 1958. I947
4 Ras-chun. Mi la pa'i r Nam thar. 1959. I947a
5 Zide, N. H., ed. Studies in comparative Austroasiatic linguistics. 1966. I948
6 Conze, E. The Prajnāparamitā literature. 1960. I949

7 Róna - Tas, A. Tibeto-Mongolica. 1966. 1950
8 Rje, M. G. Fundamentals of the Buddhist Tantras, ed. by Lessing and Wayman. 1971. 1951
9 Schokker, G. H., ed. The Padataditaka of Syamilaka. V. 1. 1966. 1952

INDUSTRIAL INNOVATION SERIES (Duckworth)

Bowley, M. Innovations in building materials. 1961. 1953
Corlett, W. J. The economic development of detergents. 1958. 1954
Donnithorne, A. G. British rubber manufacturing. 1958. 1955
Hague, D. C. The economics of man-made fibres. 1957. 1956
Sturmey, S. G. The economic development of radio. 1958. 1957
Wray, M. J. The women's outerwear industry. 1957. 1958

INDUSTRIE ET ARTISANAT (Mouton)

1 Bouvier, J. Le mouvement du profit en France au XIXe siècle. 1965. 1959
2 Colloque International Charbon et Sciences Humanies, by Trenard and others. 1966. 1960
3 Vial, J. L'industrialisation de la sidérurgie française. 1967. 1961
4 Endrei, W. L'évolution des techniques du filage et du tissage. 1968. 1962
5 Geremek, B. Le salariat dans la main-d'oeuvre Parisienne au moyen-âge. 1969. 1963
6 Le Bâtiment. 2 v. 1971- 1964
7 Caron, F. Histoire de l'exploitation d'un grand résau. 1973. 1965
8 Gillet, M. Les charbonnage du Nord de la France au XIXe siècle. 1973. 1966

INDUSTRY AND TRADE IN SOME DEVELOPING COUNTRIES (Oxford)

Bergsman, J. Brazil. 1970. 1967
Bhagwati, J. N. and Desai, P. India. 1970. 1968
Hsing, M-H. Taiwan. 1971. 1969
King, T. Mexico. 1970. 1970
Lewis, S. R. Pakistan. 1970. 1971
Little, I. and others. Industry and trade in some developing countries. 1970. 1972
Power, J. H. The Philippines. 1971. 1973

INSTITUT FRANÇAIS D'ARCHEOLOGIE DE STAMBOUL. MEMOIRES (Boccard)

1 Istanbul. Université Kutuphane. Les manuscripts orientaux illustrès de la Bibliothèque de l'université de Stamboul. 1974
2 Chaput, E. Voyages d'études géologiques et géomorphogéniques en Turquie. 1936. 1975
3 Istanbul. Tablettes sumériennes de Suruppak. 1937. 1976
4 Devambez, P. Grand bronzes du Musée de Stamboul. 1937. 1977
5 Delaporte, L. Malatya fouilles de la Mission archeologique française. 1940. 1978
6 Gabriel, A. Châteaux tures du Bosphore. 1945. 1979
7 Le sanctuaire de Sinuri près de Mylasa. V. 1. Roberts, L. Les inscriptions grecques. 1945. 1980

INSTITUT FRANÇAIS DE WASHINGTON, WASHINGTON, D. C. HISTORICAL DOCUMENTS (John Hopkins Pr. unless otherwise indicated)

1 France. Treaties, etc. 1774-1792. The treaties of

1778, ed. by Chinard. 1928. I981
2 Lafayette, M. J. P. Y. R. G. du M., marquis de. Lafayette in Virginia, comp. by Chinard. 1928. I982
3 Kite, E. S., ed. L'Enfant and Washington, 1791-1792. 1929. I983
4 Chinard, G., ed. Houdon in America. 1930. I984
5 Durand, of Dauphinè. Un Français en Virginie, ed. by Chinard. 1932. I985
6 Oliver, P. Iconographie metálique du géneral Lafayette. 1933. I986
7 Nolan, J. B. Lafayette in America. 1934. I987
8 Colbert, E. C. V. Voyage dans l'intérieur des Etats Unis et au Canada, ed. by Chinard. 1935. I988
9 Merle d'Aubigne, G. La vie américaine de Guillaume Merle d'Aubigné, ed. by Chinard. 1935. I989
10 Lapérouse, J. F. de. G. Le voyage de Lapérouse sur les côtes de l'Alaska et de la Californie (1786), ed. by Chinard. 1937. I990
11 Rice, H. C. Barthélemi Tardiveau, a French trader in the West. 1938. I991
12 LaRochefoucauld Linancourt, F. A. F. de. Journal de voyage en Amérique d'un séjour à Philadelphie. 1940. I992

Extra vol.

Baisnée, J. A. France and the establishment of the American Catholic hierarchy. 1934. I993
Childs, F. S. French refugee life in the United States, 1790-1800. 1940. I994
Ditchy, J. K. Les Acadiens louisianais et leur parler. 1932. I995
France, Ministère des affaires étrangères. Despatches and instructions of Conrad Alexander Gérard, 1778-1780, ed. by Meng. 1939. I996
Gottschalk, L. R. Lady-in-waiting, the romance of Lafayette and Aglaé de Hunolstein. 1939. I997
Hume, E. E. La Fayette and the Society of the Cincinnati. 1934. I998
Kite, E. S. Brigadier-General Louis Lebègue Duportail. 1933. I999
McDermott, J. F. Private libraries in Creole Saint Louis. 1938. I1000
Mondésir, E. de. Souvenirs, sur Saint-Suplice pendant la revolution, ed. by Chinard. 1942. I1001
Montmort, R. comte de. Antoine Charles de Houx, tr. by Gough. 1935. I1002
Murphy, E. R. Henry de Tonty. 1941. I1003
Saugrain de Vigne, A. F. L'odyssée américaine d'une familie française, ed. by Selter. 1936. I1004
Scott, J. B. De Grasse à Yorktown. Institut français de Washington. 1931. I1005
Waldo, L. P. The French drama in America in the eighteenth century and its influence on the American drama of that period, 1701-1800. 1942. I1006
Washington, G. Correspondence of George Washington and Comte de Grasse, 1781, Aug. 17-Nov. 4. Govt. Pr. Off. I1007

INSTITUTE FOR ADMINISTRATIVE OFFICERS OF HIGHER INSTITUTIONS. PROCEEDINGS (Univ. of Chicago Pr.)

1 Gray, W. S., ed. The junior college curriculum. 1929. I1008
2 ____. The training of college teachers. 1930. I1009
3 ____. Recent trends in American college education. 1931. I1010
4 ____. Provision for the individual in college education. 1932. I1011
5 ____. Needed readjustments in higher education. 1933. I1012

6 ____. General education. 1934. I1013
7 ____. The academic and professional preparation of secondary school teachers. 1935. I1014
8 ____. Tests and measurements in higher education. 1936. I1015
9 ____. Current issues in higher education. 1937. I1016
10 ____. The preparation and inservice training of college teaching. 1938. I1017
11 Russell, J. D., ed. The outlook for higher education. 1939. I1018
12 ____. Student personnel services in colleges and universities. 1941. I1019
13 ____. New frontiers in collegiate instruction. 1941. I1020
14 ____. Terminal education in higher institutions. 1942. I1021
15 ____. Higher education under war conditions. 1943. I1022
16 ____. Higher education in the post-war period. 1944. I1023
17 ____. Emergent responsible in higher education. 1946. I1024
18 Russell, J. D. Problems of faculty personnel. 1946. I1025
19 Burns, N., ed. The administration of higher institutions under changing conditions. 1947. I1026
20 ____. The community responsibilities of institutions of higher learning. 1948. I1027

INSTITUTE FOR CONSUMER EDUCATION

1 National conference on consumer education, Stephens college. Next steps in consumer education. 1939. I1028
2 ____. Making consumer education effective. Ward Ritchie Pr. 1940. I1029
3 ____. Consumer education for life problems. Artcraft Pr. 1941. I1030

INSTITUTE OF COMMUNITY STUDIES. REPORTS. (Free Pr.)

1 Young, M. and Willmott, P. Family and kinship in East London. Routledge. 1957. I1031
2 Townsend, P. The family life of old people. Free Pr. 1957. I1032
3 Marris, P. Widows and their families. Routledge. 1958. I1033
4 Willmott, P. and Young, M. Family and class in a London suburb. Humanities. 1960. I1034
5 Marris, P. Family and social change in an African city. 1961. I1035
6 Jackson, B. and Marsden, D. Education and the working class. 1962. I1036
7 Mills, E. Living with mental illness. 1962. I1037
8 Willmott, P. The evolution of a community. 1963. I1038
9 Cartwright, A. Human relations and hospital care. 1964. I1039
10 Marris, P. The experience of higher education. 1964. I1040
11 Jackson, B. Streaming. 1964. I1041
12 Young, M. D. Innovation and research in education. 1965. I1042
13 Runciman, W. G. Relative deprivations and social justice. 1966. I1043
14 Willmont, P. Adolescent boys of East London. 1966. I1044
15 Marris, P. and Rein, M. Dilemmas of social reform. 1967. I1045

Cartwright, A. Parents and family planning services. 1970. I1046
____. Patients and their doctors. 1967. I1047
Marris, P. and Somerset, A. African businessmen. 1971. I1048
Mills, R. Young outsiders.

1968. I1049
Runciman, W. G. Relative deprivation and social justice. 1966. I1050
Young, M. and McGeeney, P. Learning begins at home. 1968. I1051
Young, M. and Willmont, P. The symmetrical family. 1957. I1052

INSTITUTE OF EARLY AMERICAN HISTORY AND CULTURE. PUBLICATIONS.

Abbot, W. W. The royal governors of Georgia. 1959. I1053
Adams, H. The Adams-Jefferson letters, ed. by Cappon. 2 v. 1959. I1054
Adair, D. Fame and the founding fathers, ed. by Colbourn. 1974. I1055
Bailyn, B. Education in the forming of American society. 1960. I1056
Battis, E. J. Saints and secretaries. 1962. I1057
Bell, W. J. Early American science. 1955. I1058
Bernhard, W. E. A. Fisher Ames. 1965. I1059
Beverly, R. The history of the present state of Virginia, ed. by Wright. 1947. I1060
Boyd, J. P. and Hemphill, W. E. The murder of George Wythe: two essays. 1955. I1061
Bridenbaugh, C. Peter Harrison, first American architect. 1949. I1062
Bushman, R. L., comp. The Great awakening. 1970. I1063
Charles, J. The origins of the American party system. 1956. I1064
Chastellux, F. J., marquis de. Travels in North America, in the years 1780, 1781 and 1782, tr. by Rice. 2 v. 1963. I1065
Closen, L. von. The revolutionary journal of Baron Ludwig von Closen, tr. and ed. by Acomb. 1959. I1066
Colbourn, H. T. The lamp of experience. 1965. I1067
Cunningham, N. E. The Jeffersonian Republicans. 1958. I1068
____. The Jeffersonian Republicans in power. 1963. I1069
Dunn, R. S. Sugar and slaves. 1972. I1070
Ernst, R. Rufus King. 1968. I1071
Essays on the American Revolution, ed. by Kurtz and Hudson. 1973. I1072
Fenton, W. N. and Butterfield, L. H. American Indian and white relations before 1830. 1956. I1073
Ferguson, E. J. The power of the purse. 1961. I1074
Flaherty, D. H., ed. Essays in the history of early American law. 1969. I1075
Foster, M. S. "Out of small beginnings..." 1962. I1076
Franklin, B. Letters to the press, 1758-1775, ed. by Crane. 1950. I1077
Greene, J. P. The quest for power. 1963. I1078
Gruber, I. D. The Howe brothers and the American Revolution. 1972. I1079
Hall, D. D. The faithful shepherd. 1972. I1080
Hall, M. Benjamin Franklin & Polly Baker. 1960. I1081
Hall, M. G. Edward Randolph and the American colonies. 1960. I1082
____ and others, eds. The glorious revolution in America. 1964. I1083
Hamilton, A. Gentleman's progress; Dr. Alexander Hamilton, 1744, ed. by Bridenbaugh. 1948. I1084
Higginbotham, D. Daniel Morgan. 1961. I1085
Hindle, B. The pursuit of science in Revolutionary America, 1735-1789. 1956. I1086
____. Technology in early America. 1966. I1087
Hood, G. Bonnin and Morris of Philadelphia. 1972. I1088
Jefferson, T. Notes on the State of Virginia, ed. by

Peden. 1955. I1089
Jordan, W. D. White over black. 1968. I1090
Leder, L. H. Robert Livingston...and the politics of New York. 1961. I1091
Main, J. T. The antifederalists. 1962. I1092
____. Political parties before the Constitution. 1971. I1093
Marshall, J. Papers, ed. by Johnson and Cullen. V. 1. 1974. I1094
Morgan, E. S. The gentle Puritan. 1962. I1095
____, ed. Prologue to revolution. 1959. I1096
____ and H. M. The Stamp act crisis. 1953. I1097
Munford, R. The Candidates. 1948. I1098
Old Dominion in the seventeenth century. 1974. I1099
Prince, C. E. New Jersey's Jeffersonian Republicans. 1967. I1100
Quarles, B. The Negro in the American Revolution. 1961. I1101
Riedesel, F. C. L. Baroness von Riedesel and the American Revolution, ed. by Brown and Huth. 1965. I1102
Rutland, R. A. The birth of the Bill of Rights. 1776-1791. 1955. I1103
Rutman, D. B. Winthrop's Boston. 1965. I1104
Schutz, J. A. William Shirley. 1962. I1105
Sirmans, M. E. Colonial South Carolina. 1966. I1106
Smelser, M. The campaign for the Sugar Islands, 1759. 1955. I1107
Smith, A. E. Colonists in bondage. 1947. I1108
Smith, C. P. James Wilson, founding father, 1742-1798. 1956. I1109
Smith, J. M. Freedom's fetters. 1956. I1110
____, ed. Seventeenth-century America. 1959. I1111
Smith, P. H. Loyalists and Redcoats. 1964. I1112
Sydnor, C. S. Gentlemen freeholders. 1952. I1113
Taylor, R. J. Massachusetts, colony to commonwealth. 1961. I1114
Thompson, M. Moses Brown. 1962. I1115
Tolles, F. B. Meeting house and counting house. 1948. I1116
Tucker, L. L. Puritan protagonist. 1962. I1117
Tucker, L. W. William Plumer of New Hampshire, 1759-1850. 1962. I1118
Ubbelholde, C. Vice-admiralty courts and the American revolution. 1960. I1119
Virginia Gazette. Index 1736-1780, comp. by Cappon and Duff. 1950. I1120
Wainwright, N. B. George Croghan. 1959. I1121
Waller, G. M. Samuel Vetch. 1960. I1122
Washburn, W. E. The Governor and the rebel. 1957. I1123
Waters, J. The Otis family in provincial and revolutionary Massachusetts. 1969. I1124
Watlington, P. The Partisan spirit. 1972. I1125
Whitehill, W. M. The arts in early American history. 1965. I1126
Woodmason, C. The Carolina backcountry on the eve of the Revolution, ed. by Hooker. 1953. I1127
Wood, G. S. The creation of the American republic. 1969. I1128
Young, A. F. The Democratic Republicans of New York. 1967. I1129
Zahniser, M. R. Charles Cotesworth Pinckney. 1967. I1130
Zeichner, O. Connecticut's years of controversy. 1949. I1131

INSTITUTE OF ECONOMIC RESEARCH, DHARWAR. PUBLICATIONS (Bhatkal)

1 Kale, B. D. A survey of handicrafts in South Mysore. 1963. I1132

2 Jathar, R. V. Evolution of panchayati raj in India. 1964. I1133
3 Sovani, N. V. The European economic community. 1965. I1134
4 Raine, B. L. Family at the cross roads. 1967. I1135
5 Koteshwar, R. K. Public cooperation in developmental programme. 1964. I1136
6 Jorapur, P. B. Economic overview of Dharwar block. 1964. I1137
7 Kale, B. D. Family planning enquiry in Dharwar Taluka. 1966. I1138
8 ____. Family planning enquiry in rural Shimoga. 1966. I1139
9 Katti, A. P. A study of seasonal in-migrants in Shimoga District. 1966. I1140
10 Koteshwar, R. K. A demographic study of a Malenad village in Mysore State-Kogilgeri. 1968. I1141
11 Katti, A. P., ed. Seminar on demographic aspects of Mysore state. 1968. I1142
12 Jorapur, P. B. A demographic study of Dharwar block. 1968. I1143
13 Kale, B. D. A survey of rural carpentry and blacksmithy in Dharwar district. 1965. I1144
14 ____ and Jorapur, P. B. Demographic report of Mysore State, 1901-61. 1969. I1145
15 Katti, A. P. and Hasalkar, J. B. A study of sterilized males. 1970. I1146
16 Kale, B. D. Family planning resurvey in Dharwar. 1969. I1147
17 Katti, A. P., ed. Seminar on family planning and resource mobilization. 1969. I1148
18 Gurajar, N. W. Indian planning and resource mobilization. 1969. I1149
19 Katti, A. P. and Hasalkar, J. B. History of rural immigrants in Shimoga district. 1971. I1150
20 Katti, A. P. and Koteshwar, R. K. A district town resurveyed. 1971. I1151
21 ____. A study of family planning among high school teachers. 1973. I1152
22 Jorapur, P. B. A demographic study of Shimoga District. 1973. I1153
23 Katti, A. P. and Hasalkar, J. B. Sterilized males in Chitradurga district. 1973. I1154
24 Katti, A. P., ed. Regional seminar on family planning and demographic aspects. 1972. I1155

INSTITUTE OF HISPANIC STUDIES. STUDIES IN HISPANIC LITERATURE (Institue of Hispanic Studies)

1 Peers, E. A. From Cadalco to Ruben Dario. 1940. I1156
2 ____, ed. Studies in golden age poetry and drama. 1946. I1157
3 McClelland, I. L. The origins of the romantic movement in Spain. 1937. I1158
4 Piñeyro y Barry, E. J. N. The romantics of Spain. 1934. I1159

INSTITUTE OF METALS. MONOGRAPH AND REPORT SERIES (Institute of Metals)

1 Hume-Rothery, W. and Raynor, G. V. The structure of metals and alloys. 1962. I1160
2 Haughton, J. L. The constitutional diagrams of alloys: a bibliography. 1956. I1161
3 Hume-Rothery, W. Atomic theory for students of metallurgy. 1960. I1162
4 Raynor, G. V. An introduction to the electron theory of metals. 1947. I1163
5 Institute of Metals. Symposium on internal stresses in metals and alloys. 1948. I1164
6 ____. Symposium on metallurgical aspects of non-ferrous

metal melting and casting of ingots for working. 1949. I1165
7 Ruddle, R. W. The solidification of castings: a review of the literature. 1957. I1166
8 Institute of Metals. Metallurgical applications of the electron microscope. 1950. I1167
9 ____. The hot working of non-ferrous metals and alloys. 1951. I1168
10 Hanstock, R. F. The non-destructive testing of metals. 1951. I1169
11 Lumsden, J. Thermodynamics of alloys. 1952. I1170
12 Institute of Metals. The cold working of non-ferrous metals and alloys. 1952. I1171
13 ____. Properties of metallic surfaces. 1953. I1172
14 ____. Equipment for the thermal treatment of non-ferrous metals and alloys. 1953. I1173
15-17 ____. The control of quality in the production of wrought non-ferrous metals and alloys. 3 v. 1953-55. I1174
18 ____. The mechanism of phase transformations in metals. 1956. I1175
19 Ruddle, R. W. The running and gating of sand castings: a review of the literature. 1956. I1176
20 Institute of Metals. The final forming and shaping of wrought non-ferrous metals. 1956. I1177
21 Masing, G. The foundations of metallography, tr. by Thompson. 1956. I1178
22 Institute of Metals. Metallurgical aspects of the control of quality in non-ferrous castings. 1957. I1179
23 ____. Vacancies and other point defects in metals and alloys. 1958. I1180
24 ____. Advances in inspection techniques as aids to process control in non-ferrous metals production. 1959. I1181
25 Phillips, H. W. L. Annotated equilibrium diagrams of some aluminium alloy systems. 1959. I1182
26 Hume-Rothery, W. Elements of structural metallurgy. 1961. I1183
27 Institute of Metals. Uranium and graphite. 1962. I1184
28 International Conference on the Metallurgy of Beryllium. The metallurgy of beryllium. 1963. I1185
29 Winegard, W. C. An introduction to the solidification of metals. 1964. I1186
30 Nutting, J. and Baker, R. G. The microstructure of metals. 1965. I1187
31 International Conference on Plutonium. Plutonium, ed. by Kay and Waldron. 1967. I1188
32 Thermal and high-strain fatigue. 1967. I1189
33 The Mechanism of phase transformations in crystalline solids. 1969. I1190
34 Copper and its alloys. 1970. I1191
35 The effective and economic use of the special characteristics of aluminium and its alloys. 1972. I1192

INSTITUTE OF PACIFIC RELATIONS. ECONOMIC SURVEY OF THE PACIFIC AREA.

1 Pelzer, K. J. Population and land utilization. 1941. I1193
2 Greene, K. R. C. Transportation, and Phillips, J. D. Foreign trade. 1942. I1194
3 Mitchell, K. L. Industrialization of the western Pacific. 1942. I1195

INSTITUTE OF PACIFIC RELATIONS. I. P. R. INQUIRY SERIES.

Allen, G. C. Japanese industry. 1940. I1196
Barnett, R. W. Economic Shanghai. 1941. I1197
Bisson, T. A. American policy in the Far East, 1931-41.

INSTITUTE OF PACIFIC RELATIONS. INTERNATIONAL RESEARCH SERIES (Institute of Pacific Relations unless otherwise specified)

1942. I1236
Brecher, M. The struggle for Kashmir. Oxford. 1953. I1237
Buck, J. L. Land utilization in China. 3 v. Univ. of Chic. Pr. 1937. I1238
Callis, H. G. Foreign capital in southeast Asia. 1942. I1239
Chen, T. The emigrant communities in South China. 1940. I1240
Christian, J. L. Modern Burma. 1942. I1241
Decker, J. A. Labor problems in the Pacific mandates. Oxford. 1941. I1242
Elsbree, W. H. Japan's role in Southeast Asian national movements. Cambridge. 1953. I1243
Emerson, R. Representative government in Southeast Asia. Harvard. 1955. I1244
Fall, B. B. The Viet-Minh regime. 1954. I1245
Fei, H. China's gentry; essays in rural-urban relations. Univ. of Chicago Pr. 1953. I1246
Furnivall, J. S. Progress and welfare in southeast Asia. 1941. I1247
Gamble, S. D. Ting Hsien: a North China rural community. 1954. I1248
Ganguli, B. N. India's economic relations with the Far East. 1956. I1249
Grad, A. J. Formosa today. 1942. I1250
Gull, E. M. British economic interests in the Far East. 1943. I1251
Hammer, J. The struggle for Indochina. 1954. I1252
Hinder, E. M. Social and industrial problem of Shanghai. 1942. I1253
Holland, W., ed. Asian nationalism and the West. Macmillan. 1953. I1254
Hsia, R. Economic planning in communist China. 1955. I1255
Ingram, J. C. Economic change in Thailand since 1850. Stanford Univ. Pr. 1955. I1256
Institute of Pacific relations. Agrarian China. Univ. of Chic. 1939. I1257
____. Agricultural organization in New Zealand. 1936. I1258
____. An economic survey of the Pacific area... 3 v. 1941-42. I1259
____. Industrial Japan. 1941. I1260
Japan and America today, by Reischauer and others. Stanford. 1953. I1261
Jones, F. C. Japan's new order in East Asia: its rise and fall, 1937-1945. Oxford. 1954. I1262
Kat Angelino, P. de. Some remarks on the wages paid in the Netherlands Indies, tr. by Hamilton. 1936. I1263
Keesing, F. M. South seas in the modern world. 1945. I1264
Landon, K. P. The Chinese in Thailand. Oxford. 1941. I1265
Langer, P. F. and Swearingen, A. R. Japanese communism today. 1953. I1266
Lattimore, O. Inner Asian frontiers of China. 1951. I1267
____. Nationalism and revolution in Mongolia, trans. by Lattimore and Onon. 1955. I1268
Lava, H. C. Levels of living in the Ilocos regions. 1938. I1269
Lee, H. K. Land utilization and rural economy in Korea. 1936. I1270
Lin, W. The future of foreign business and foreign investments in China. 1939. I1271
McFadden, C. H. A bibliography of Pacific area maps. Amer. Council. 1941. I1272
McNaught, C. Canada gets the news. Ryerson. 1940. I1273
Mander, L. A. Some dependent peoples of the South Pacific. Macmillan. 1954. I1274
Masani, M. R. The Communist party of India. Macmillan. 1954. I1275
Mills, L. A. British rule in

eastern Asia. Univ. of Minn. 1942. I1276
Nasu, S. Aspects of Japanese agriculture. 1941. I1277
New Zealand institute of international affairs. Agricultural organization in New Zealand, by Belshaw and others. 1936. I1278
Normano, J. F. The Japanese in South America. 1943. I1279
Pelzer, K. J. Pioneer settlement in the Asiatic tropics. Amer. Council. 1942. I1280
Purcell, V. W. W. S. Malaya: Communist or free. Stanford Univ. Pr. 1954. I1281
Reed, S. W. The making of modern New Guinea. Amer. Philosophical soc. 1943. I1282
Robequain, C. Malaya, Indonesia, Borneo and the Philippines. Longmans. 1954. I1283
Royal Institute of international affairs. Shanghai and Tientsin. 1940. I1284
Runes, I. T. General standards of living and wages of workers in the Philippine sugar industry. 1939. I1285
Scheltama, A. M. P. A. The food consumption of the native inhabitants of Java and Madura, tr. by Hamilton. 1936. I1286
Scott, F. R. and Cassidy, H. M. Labour conditions in the men's clothing industry. 1935. I1287
Shepherd, J. Industry in southeast Asia. 1941. I1288
Smith, S. B. Air transport in the Pacific area. 1941. I1289
Stanner, W. E. H. The South Sea in transition. Australasian Pub. Co. 1953. I1290
Sutherland, I. L. G., ed. The Maori people today. Oxford. 1941. I1291
Thirumalai, S. Post-war agricultural problems and policies in India. 1954. I1292
Thomas, S. B. Government and administration in Communist China. 1955. I1293
Thompson, V. M. Postmortem on Malaya. Macmillan. 1943. I1294
____. Thailand, the new Siam. Macmillan. 1941. I1295
____ and Adloff, R. Minority problems in Southeast Asia. Stanford. 1955. I1296
Uyeda, T. The growth of population and occupational changes in Japan, 1920-1935. 1936. I1297
____. The small industries of Japan. 1936. I1298
____ and Inokuchi, T. Cost of living and real wages in Japan, 1914-1936. 1936. I1299
Wentworth, E. L. C. and Simpich, F. Living standards of Filipino families on an Hawaiian sugar plantation. 1936. I1300
Wint, G. The British in Asia. 1954. I1301
Wright, P. G. Trade and trade barriers in the Pacific. 1935. I1302
Yaniaihara, T. Pacific islands under Japanese mandate. Amer. Council. 1940. I1303
Zinkin, M. Asia and the West. 1953. I1304

INSTITUTE OF PACIFIC RELATIONS. STUDIES OF THE PACIFIC.

1 Institute of Pacific relations. American council. American Far East policy and the Sino-Japanese war. 1938. I1305
2 Brunner, E. de. S. Rural Australia and New Zealand. 1938. I1306
3 Gregory, H. E. and Barnes, K. North Pacific fisheries. 1939. I1307
4 Thompson, L. Fijian frontier. 1940. I1308
5 Royal institute of international affairs. Shanghai and Tientsin. 1940. I1309
6 McFadden, C. H. A bibliography of Pacific area maps. 1941. I1310
7 Wentworth, E. L. C. Filipino plantation workers in Hawaii. 1941. I1311
8 Thompson, L. Guam and its people. 1946. I1312

INSTITUTE OF POLITICS, WILLIAMS COLLEGE. PUBLICATIONS (Pub. by Macmillan 1922, Yale Univ. Pr. 1923-)

Altrincham, E. W. M. G. The greatest experiment in history. 1924. I1313
Aubert, L. The reconstruction of Europe. 1925. I1314
Birkenhead, F. E. S. Approaches to world problems. 1924. I1315
Bolshevism, fascism, and capitalism, by G. S. Counts and others. 1932. I1316
Bonn, M. J. The crisis of European democracy. 1925. I1317
Bryce, J. B. International relations. 1922. I1318
Chirol, V. The reawakening of the Orient... 1925. I1319
Cippico, A. Italy, the central problem of the Mediterranean. 1926. I1320
Cunningham, N. E. Jeffersonian republicans. 1958. I1321
Fujisawa, R. The recent aims and political development of Japan. 1923. I1322
Grigg, E. W. M. The greatest experiment in history. 1924. I1323
Hoetzsch, O. Germany's domestic and foreign policies. 1929. I1324
The Institute of politics at Williamstown, Mass. 1931. I1325
Institute of politics, Williams college. Round-table conferences of the Institute of Politics at its first session, 1921. 1923. I1326
Institute of politics, Williams college. Report of the round tables and general conferences at the eleventh session. 1931. I1327
Institute of politics, Williams college. Report of the round tables and general conferences at the twelfth session. 1932. I1328
Kerr, P. H. and Curtis, L. The prevention of war. 1923. I1329
Kessler, H. K. U. Germany and Europe. 1923. I1330
Korff, S. A. Russia's foreign relations during the last half century. 1922. I1331
Mendelssohn Bartholdy, A. The European situation. 1927. I1332
Meston, J. S. M. Nationhood for India. 1931. I1333
Panaretoff, S. Near Eastern affairs and conditions. 1922. I1334
Percy, E. S. C. Maritime trade in war. 1930. I1335
Pierard, L. Belgian problems since the war. 1929. I1336
Poole, D. C. The conduct of foreign relations under modern democratic conditions. 1924. I1337
Rappard, W. E. International relations as viewed from Geneva. 1925. I1338
____. Uniting Europe. 1930. I1339
Reinhold, P. P. The economic, financial, political state of Germany since the war. 1928. I1340
Sforza, C. Diplomatic Europe since the treaty of Versailles. 1928. I1341
Siegfried, A. France, a study in nationality. 1930. I1342
Simons, W. The evolution of international public law in Europe since Grotius. 1931. I1343
Tawney, R. H. The British labor movement. 1925. I1344
Teleki, P. The evolution of Hungary and its place in European history. 1923. I1345
Tittoni, T. Modern Italy. 1922. I1346
Viallate, A. Economic imperialism and international relations during the last fifty years. 1923. I1347
Washburn, W. E. Governor and the rebel. 1958. I1348
Willert, A. Aspects of British foreign policy. 1928. I1349
Zeballos, E. S. Las conferencias en Williamstown. 1927. I1350

INSTITUTTET FOR SAMMENLIGNENDE KULTURFORSKNING, OSLO (Oslo Inst. sold by Harvard Univ. Pr.)

Series A: Forelesninger.
1 Instituttet for sammenlignende kulturforskning. Four introductory lectures. 1925. I1351
1a ____. Fire innkednings-forelesninger. 1925. I1352
2 Meillet, A. La méthode comparative en linguistique historique. 1925. I1353
3 Vinogradoff, P. Custom and right. 1925. I1354
4 Jespersen, O. Mankind, nation and individual from a linguistic point of view. 1925. I1355
4a ____. Menneskehed, nasjon og individ i sproget. 1925. I1356
5 Shetelig, H. Préhistorie de la Norvège. 1926. I1357
5a ____. Norges forhistorie. 1925. I1358
6 Brøgger, A. W. Kulturgeschichte des norwegischen altertums. 1926. I1359
6a ____. Det norske folk i oldtiden. 1925. I1360
7 Mienhof, C. Die religionen der Afrikaner in ihrem Zusammenhang mit dem wirtschaftsleben. 1926. I1361
8 Karlgren, B. Philology and ancient China. 1926. I1362
9 Olsen, M. B. Farms and fanes of ancient Norway. 1928. I1363
9a ____. AEttegard og helligdom. 1926. I1364
10 Liestøl, K. The origin of the Icelandic family sagas. 1930. I1365
10a ____. Upphavet til den islendske aettesaga. 1929. I1366
11 Dopsch, A. Die altere wirtschafts- und sozialgeschichte der Bauern in den Alpenländern Österreichs. 1930. I1367
12 Nordhagen, R. De senkvartaere klimaveslinger i Nord-Europa og deres betydning for kulturforskningen. 1933. I1368
13 San Nicolò, M. Beitrage zur rechtsgeschichte im bereiche der keilschriftlichen rechtsquellen. 1931. I1369
14-15 Bidrag til bondesamfundets histoire, by Brøgger and others. 2 v. 1933. I1370
16 Shetelig, H. Vikingeminner i Vest-Europa. 1933. I1371
17 Götze, A. Hethiter, Churriter und Assyrer. 1936. I1372
18 Sommerfelt, A. La langue et la société. 1938. I1373
19 Shetelig, H. Classical impulses in Scandinavian art from the migration period to the Viking age. 1949. I1374
20 Childe, V. G. Prehistoric migrations in Europe. 1950. I1375
21 Dyggve, E. History of Salonitan Christianity. 1951. I1376
22 Granet, M. La feodalité chinoise. 1952. I1377
23 L'Orange, H. P. Studies on the iconography of cosmic kingship in the ancient world. 1953. I1378
24 Immink, P. W. A. At the roots of medieval society. 1958. I1379
25 Löfstedt, E. Late Latin. 1959. I1380
26 Instituttet for sammeling kulturforskning. Lapps and Norsemen in olden times. 1967. I1381

Series B: Skrifter.
1 Moe, M. Samlede skrifter. V. 1. 1925. I1382
2 Bodding, P. O., ed. Santal folk tales. V. 1. 1925. I1383
3 Qvigstad, J. K., ed. Lappiske eventyr og saga. V. 1. 1927. I1384
4 Lagercrantz, E. Wörterbuch des südlappischen nach der mundart von Wefsen. 1926. I1385
5 Krohn, K. Die folkloristische arbeitsmethode. 1926. I1386
6 Same as no. 1. V. 2. 1926. I1387
7 Same as no. 2. V. 2.

1927. I1388
8 Boas, F. Primitive art. 1927. I1389
9 Same as no. 1. V. 3. 1927. I1390
10 Same as no. 3. V. 2. 1928. I1391
11 Morgenstierne, G. Indo-Iranian frontier languages. V. 1. 1929. I1392
12 Same as no. 3. V. 3. 1929. I1393
13 Nummedal, A. Stone age finds in Finnmark. 1929. I1394
14 Same as no. 2. V. 3. 1929. I1395
15 Same as no. 3. V. 4. 1929. I1396
16 Lehtisalo, T. Beitrage zur Kenntnis der Renntierzucht bei den Juraksamojeden. 1932. I1397
17 Nielsen, K. H. Lappisk ordbok. 2 v. 1932-34. I1398
18 Schreiner, K. E. Zur osteologie der Lappen. 2 v. 1935. 1931. I1399
18:3 ____. Further note on the craniology of the Lapps. 1945. I1400
19 Bloch, M. L. B. Les caractères originaux de l'histoire rurale française. 1931. I1401
20 Qvigstad, J. K. Lappische heilkunde. 1932. I1402
21 Gjessing, G. Artiske helleristninger i Nord-Norge. V. 1. 1932. I1403
22 L'Orange, H. P. Studien zur geschichte des spätantiken porträts. 1933. I1404
23 Petersen, J. G. T. Gamle gardsanlegg i Rogaland fra forhistorisk tid og middelaider. 1933. I1405
24 Solem, E. T. Lappiske rettsstudier. 1933. I1406
25 Gjessing, R. R. Die Kautokeinolappen. 1934. I1407
26 Engelstad, E. S. Østnorske ristninger og malinger av den artiske gruppe. 1934. I1408
27 Grieg, S. Jernaldershus pa lista. 1934. I1409
28 Qvigstad, J. K. De lappiske stedsnavn i Troms fylke. 1935. I1410
29 Lorimer, D. L. R. The Burushaski language. 3 v. 1938. I1411
30 Gjessing, G. Nordenfjelske ristninger og malinger av den arktiske gruppe. 1936. I1412
31 Petersen, J. G. T. Gamle gardsanlegg i rogaland. 1936. I1413
32 Bøe, J. and Nummedal, A. Le Finnmarkien. 1936. I1414
33 Qvigstad, J. K. De lappiske stedsnavn i Finnmark og Nordland fylker. 1938. I1415
34 Smith, P. L. Kautokeino og Kautokeino-lappense. 1938. I1416
35 Same as no. 11. V. 2. 1938. I1417
36 Schreiner, K. E. Crania norvegica. 2 v. 1939-47. I1418
37 Gjessing, G. Østfolds jordbruksristninger. 1940. I1419
38 Frödin, J. Zentraleuropas alpwirtschaft. 2 v. 1940-41. I1420
39 Gjessing, G. Yngre steinalder i Nord-Norge. 1942. I1421
40 Same as no. 11. V. 3. 1944. I1422
41 Gjessing, G. Traen-funnene. 1943. I1423
42 Qvigstad, J. K. De lappiske appellative stedsnavn. 1944. I1424
43 Bergsland, K. Røros-lappisk grammatikk. 1946. I1425
44 L'Orange, H. P. Apotheosis in ancient portraiture. 1947. I1426
45 Beito, O. T. Norske saeternamm. 1953. I1427
46 Frödin, J. Skagar och myrar i Norra Sverige. V. 1. 1953. I1428
47 Solheim, S. Norsk saetertradisjon. 1952. I1429
48 Reinton, L. Saeterbruket i Noreg. 1957. I1430
49 Same as no. 21. V. 2. 1959. I1431

50 Gansdal, J. The Santal khũts. 1960. I1432
51 Lorimer, D. L. R. Werchikwar English vocabulary. 1962. I1433
52 Vogt, H. Dictionnaire de la langue oubykh. 1963. I1434
53 Marstrander, S. Ostfold's jordbruksristningeri Skjeberg. 1963. I1435
54 Dahl, O. C. Contes malgaches en dialecte sakalava. 1968. I1436
55 Berg, A. Norske gardstun. 1968. I1437
56 Fagereng, E. Une famille de dynasties malgaches. 1971. I1438
57 Vogt, H. Grammaire de la langue géogienne. 1971. I1439

Series C:
1:1 Instituttet for sammenlignende kulturforskning, Oslo. Report on the activities of the Institute for comparative research in human culture in the years 1923-26. 1928. I1440
1:2 Morgenstierne, G. Report on a linguistic mission to Afghanistan. 1926. I1441
1:3 ____. Report of the activities of the Institute for comparative research in human culture in the years 1927-July 1930. I1442
2:1 Bull, E. Vergleichende studien über die kulturverhältnisse des bauerntums. 1930. I1443
2:2 ____. Sammenlignende studier over bondesamfundets kulturforhold. 1929. I1444
2:3 Bjørn, A. Nye boplassfund fra yngre stenalder i Finnmark. 1930. I1445
2:4 Brøgger, A. W. Nord-Norges bosetningshistoire. 1931. I1446
3:1 Morgenstierne, G. Report on a linguistic mission to north-western India. 1932. I1447
3:2 Same as no. 1:3. July 1930-July 1934. 1934. I1448
3:3 Gjessing, G. Fra steinalder til jernalder i Finnmark. 1935. I1449
4:1 Oslo. Instituttet for sammenlignende kulturforskning. Report of the activities of the institute for comparative research in human culture in the years July 1934-July 1939. I1450
4:2 Gjessing, G. and G. Lappedrakten. 1940. I1451
4:3 Schreiner, K. E. Om en trepanert finnmarksskalle fra steinalderen. 1940. I1452
4:4 Vogt, H. Report on the activities of the institute for comparative research in human culture in the years 1939-45. 1946. I1453
5 Institute for Comparative Research in Human Culture. Report, ed. by Vogt. 1956. I1454

INTEGRATION AND COMMUNITY BUILDING IN EASTERN EUROPE (Johns Hopkins Pr.)

Fischer-Galati, S. A. The Socialist Republic of Rumania. 1969. I1455
Hanhardt, A. M. The German Democratic Republic. 1968. I1456
Kovrig, B. The Hungarian People's Republic. 1970. I1457
Morrison, J. F. The Polish People's Republic. 1968. I1458
Oren, N. Revolution administered. 1973. I1459
Pano, N. C. The People's Republic of Albania. 1968. I1460
Suda, Z. The Czechoslovak Socialist Republic. 1969. I1461
Zaninovich, M. G. The development of Socialist Yugoslavia. 1968. I1462

INTER-AMERICAN BIBLIOGRAPHICAL AND LIBRARY ASSOCIATION SERIES (Inter-American Bibl. and Library Ass'n. unless otherwise stated)

Series I:
1 1935-36 Rubio, D. A glossary of technical library and allied terms in Spanish and English. Mimeform Pr.

1936. I1463
2 1936-37 Wilgus, A. C. Histories and historians of Hispanic America. 1936. I1464
3 1937-38 Gosnell, C. F. Spanish personal names. 1938. I1465
4 1938-39 McLean, M. D. El contenido literario de "El Siglo diez y nueve." 1940. I1466
5 1939-40 Boggs, R. S. Bibliography of Latin American folklore. Wilson. 1940. I1467
6 1940-41 Roberts, S. E. José Toribio Medina. 1941. I1468
7 1941-42 Nichols, M. W. The gaucho: cattle hunter, cavalryman, ideal of romance. Duke. 1942. I1469
8 1942-44 Weil, F. J. Argentine riddle. Day. 1944. I1470
9 1944-45 Davis, H. E. Makers of democracy in Latin America. Wilson. 1945. I1471
10 1946-47 ____. Latin American leaders. Wilson. 1949. I1472
11 1949-50 ____. Social science trends in Latin America. Amer. Univ. Press. 1950. I1473
12 1951-52 Topete, J. M. A working bibliography of Latin American literature. 1951. I1474
13 Kantor, H. A bibliography of unpublished doctoral dissertations and master's theses dealing with governments, politics, and international relations of Latin America. 1953. I1475

Series II:
1-5 Inter-American bibliographical and library association. Proceedings. 1938-42. I1476
6 ____. Inter-American library conference. 1946. I1477

Series III:
1 Grismar, R. L. A reference index to twelve thousand Spanish American authors. Wilson. 1939. I1478

INTERAMERICAN LEGAL STUDIES (Oceana)

1 Bayitch, S. A. Guide to interamerican legal studies. 1957. I1479
2 ____. Interamerican law of fisheries. 1958. I1480
3 Mexico: a symposium on law and government. 1958. I1481
4 Alloway, C. C. United States Constitutional law, 1850-1875. 1958. I1482
5 Bayitch, S. A. Aircraft mortgage in the Americas. 1960. I1483
6 ____. Latin America. 1961. I1484
7 Chommie, J. G. and others. El Derecho de los Estados Unidos. 1963. I1485
8 Bayitch, S. A. Latin America and the Caribbean. 1967. I1486

INTERGOVERNMENTAL RELATIONS IN THE U.S. RESEARCH MONOGRAPHS (Univ. of Minnesota)

1 Talbott, F. Intergovernmental relations and the courts. 1950. I1487
2 Gomez, R. A. Intergovernmental relations in highways. 1950. I1488
3 Morlan, R. L. Intergovernmental relations in education. 1950. I1489
4 Wyatt, L. Intergovernmental relations in public health. 1951. I1490
5 Raup, R. Intergovernmental relations in social welfare. 1952. I1491
6 Rourke, F. E. Intergovernmental relations in employment security. 1952. I1492
7 Ylvisaker, P. N. Intergovernmental relations at the grass roots. 1956. I1493
8 Anderson, W. and Durfee, W. D. Intergovernmental fiscal relations. 1956. I1494
9 Weidner, E. W. Intergovernmental relations as seen by public officials. 1960. I1495

10 Anderson, W. Intergovernmental relations in review. 1960. I1496

INTERNATIONAL ASSOCIATION FOR RESEARCH IN INCOME AND WEALTH (Bowes)

International association for research in income and wealth. Bibliography on income and wealth. V. 1. 1937-47, ed. by Creamer. V. 2. 1948-49, ed. by Deane. 1949-50. V. 3. 1950, ed. by Deane. V. 4. 1951, ed. by Deane. V. 5. 1952, ed. by Deane. 1952. V. 6, 1953-54, ed. by Deane. 1958. I1497

1 ____. Income and wealth, by Stone and others. Ser. 1. 1951. I1498

2 Kuznets, S. and Goldsmith, R. W. Income and wealth of the United States. Ser. 2. 1952. I1499

3 International association for research in income and wealth. Income and wealth, by Creamer and others. Ser. 3. 1952. I1500

4 ____. Income and wealth, by Frisch and others. Ser. 4. 1954. I1501

5 ____. Income and wealth, by Jeffreys and others. Ser. 5. 1955. I1502

6 ____. Income and wealth, by Gilbert and others. Ser. 6. 1956. I1503

7 Firestone, O. J. Canada's economic development. 1958. I1504

8 Goldsmith, R. W. and Saunders, C. The measurement of national wealth. 1959. I1505

9 Deane, P., ed. Studies in social and financial accounting. 1961. I1506

10 Same as no. 3. Ed. by Clark and others. Ser. 7. 1962. I1507

THE INTERNATIONAL ASTROPHYSICS SERIES (Wiley)

1 Harang, L. The aurorae. 1951. I1508

2 Porter, J. G. Comets and meteor streams. 1952. I1509

3 Aller, L. H. Gaseous nebulae. 1956. I1510

4 McVittie, G. C. General relativity and cosmology. 1956. I1511

5 Kopal, Z. Close binary systems. 1959. I1512

6 Menzel, D. H. and others. Stellar interiors. 1963. I1513

7 Bray, R. J. and Loughhead, R. E. Sunspots. 1964. I1514

8 ____. The solar granulation. 1967. I1515

9 Wickramasinghe, N. C. Intersellar grains. 1967. I1516

INTERNATIONAL LIBRARY OF NEGRO LIFE AND HISTORY (Arno)

Henderson, E. B. The black athlete. 1969. I1517

Morais, H. M. The history of the Negro in medicine. 1969. I1518

Patterson, L., comp. Anthology of the American Negro in the theatre. 1968. I1519

____. An introduction to Black literature in America... 1970. I1520

____. The Negro in music and art. 1970. I1521

Robinson, W. S. Historical Negro biographies. 1970. I1522

Romero, P. W., comp. I too am American. 1970. I1523

Wesley, C. H. In freedom's footsteps. 1970. I1524

____. Negro Americans in the Civil War. 1970. I1525

____. The quest for equality. 1970. I1526

INTERNATIONAL LIBRARY OF PHILOSOPHY AND SCIENTIFIC METHOD (Humanities)

Allen, R. E. Plato's "Euthyphro" and the earlier theory of forms. 1970. I1527

____, ed. Studies in Plato's metaphysics. 1965. I1528

Armstrong, D. M. A materialist theory of the mind. 1968. I1529
____. Perception and the physical world. 1961. I1530
Bambraugh, R., ed. New essays on Plato and Aristotle. 1965. I1531
Barry, B. Political argument. 1965. I1532
Becker, L. C. On justifying moral judgments. 1973. I1533
Bird, G. Kant's theory of knowledge. 1962. I1534
Bogen, J. Wittgenstein's philosophy of language. 1972. I1535
Brentano, F. C. The foundation and construction of ethics, ed. by Mayer. 1973. I1536
____. The origin of knowledge of right and wrong, ed. by Kraus. 1969. I1537
____. Psychology from an empirical standpoint, ed. by Kraus, tr. by Rancurello and others. 1973. I1538
____. The true and the evident, ed. by Kraus. 1966. I1539
Broad, C. D. Lectures on psychical research. 1962. I1540
Brown, R. and Rollins, C. D., eds. Contemporary philosophy in Australia. 1970. I1541
Buchler, J. Charles Peirce's empiricism. 1966. I1542
Bultmann, R. Faith and understanding, tr. by Smith. 1969. I1543
Crombie, I. N. An examination of Plato's doctrines. 2 v. 1962-63. I1544
Day, J. P. Inductive probability. 1961. I1545
Dennett, D. C. Content and consciousness. 1970. I1546
Dretske, R. M. Seeing and knowing. 1969. I1547
Ducasse, C. J. Truth, knowledge and causation. 1969. I1548
Edel, A. Method in ethical theory. 1963. I1549
Fann, K. T., ed. Symposium on J. L. Austin. 1969. I1550
Findlay, J. N. Plato. 1974. I1551
Flew, A. G. N. Hume's philosophy of belief. 1961. I1552
Fogelin, R. J. Evidence and meaning. 1967. I1553
Franklin, R. L. Freewill and determinism. 1969. I1554
Furley, D. J. and Allen, R. E., eds. Studies in presocratic philosophy. 1970. I1555
Gale, R. M. The language of time. 1968. I1556
Glover, J. Responsibility. 1970. I1557
Goldman, L. The hidden God, tr. by Thody. 1963. I1558
Hamlyn, D. W. Sensation and perception. 1961. I1559
Husserl, E. Logical investigations. 1970. I1560
Kemp, J. Reason, action and morality. 1964. I1561
Körner, S. Experience and theory. 1966. I1562
Lazerowitz, M. Studies in metaphilosophy. 1964. I1563
Linsky, L. Referring. 1967. I1564
MacIntosh, J. J. and Coval, S. C., eds. The business of reason. 1969. I1565
Meiland, J. W. Talking about particulars. 1970. I1566
Merleau-Ponty, M. Phrenology of perception, tr. by Smith. 1962. I1567
Montefiore, A. British analytical philosophy. 1966. I1568
Naess, A. Scepticism. 1969. I1569
Perelman, C. The idea of justice and the problem of argument, tr. by Petrie. 1963. I1570
Ross, A. Directives and norms. 1968. I1571
Schlesinger, G. Methods in the physical sciences. 1963. I1572
Sellars, W. Science, perception, and reality. 1963. I1573
Shwayder, D. S. The stratification of behaviour. 1965. I1574
Skolimowski, H. Polish analytical philosophy. 1967. I1575
Smart, J. J. C. Philosophy and scientific realism.

1963. I1576
Smythies, J. R., ed. Brain and mind, by Kuhlenbeck and others. 1965. I1577
____, ed. Science and the E. S. P. 1967. I1578
Sprigge, T. Facts, words and beliefs. 1970. I1579
Taylor, C. The explanation of behaviour. 1964. I1580
Williams, B., ed. British analytical philosophy. 1966. I1581
Winch, P., ed. Studies in the philosophy of Wittgenstein. 1969. I1582
Wittgenstein, L. Tractus logico-philosophicus, tr. by Pears and McGuinness. 1961. I1583
Wright, G. H. von. Norm and action. 1963. I1584
____. The varieties of goodness. 1963. I1585
Zinkerngal, P. Conditions for description, tr. by Lindum. 1962. I1586

INTERNATIONAL LIBRARY OF PSYCHOLOGY, PHILOSOPHY AND SCIENTIFIC METHOD (Harcourt unless otherwise stated)

Adler, A. Individual psychology. 1932. I1587
____. The practice and theory of individual psychology. 1951. I1588
Adler, M. J. Dialectic. 1927. I1589
Aldrich, C. R. The primitive mind and modern civilization. 1931. I1590
Allen, A. H. B. Pleasure & instinct. 1930. I1591
Alverdes, F. The psychology of animals in relation to human psychology. 1932. I1592
____. Social life in the animal world. 1927. I1593
Anthony, S. The child's discovery of death. 1940. I1594
Anton, J. P. Aristotle's theory of contrariety. Humanities. 1957. I1595/99
Armstrong, D. Perception and the physical world. Humanities. 1961. I1600
Bentham, J. Theory of fictions. 1959. I1601
____. The theory of legislation. 1950. I1602
Bird, G. Kant's theory of knowledge. Humanities. 1962. I1603
Black, M. The nature of mathematics. 1959. I1604
Bogen, J. Wittgenstein's philosophy of language. 1972. I1605
Bogoslovsky, B. B. The technique of controversy. 1941. I1606
Britton, K. Communication. 1939. I1607
Broad, C. D. Ethics and the history of philosophy. 1952. I1608
____. Five types of ethical theory. 1959. I1609
____. Lectures on psychical research. Humanities. 1962. I1610
____. The mind and its place in nature. 1925. I1611
____. Religion, philosophy and physical research. 1953. I1612
____. Scientific thought. 1959. I1613
Buchanan, S. M. The doctrine of signatures. 1938. I1614
____. Possibility. 1927. I1615
Buchler, J. Charles Peirce's empiricism. 1939. I1616
Bühler, K. The mental development of the child. 1930. I1617
____. The mental growth of the child. 1930. I1618
Burrow, N. T. The social basis of consciousness. 1927. I1619
Burtt, E. A. The metaphysical foundations of modern physical science. 1925. I1620
Cairns, H. Law and the social sciences. 1935. I1621
Campion, G. G. and Smith, G. E. The neural basis of thought. 1934. I1622
Carington, W. The measurement of emotion. Routledge. 1922. I1623

Carnap, R. The logical syntax of language. 1927. I1624
Chwistek, L. The limits of science. 1948. I1625
Collins, M. Colour blindness. 1925. I1626
Crawshay-Williams, R. Methods and criteria of reasoning. Humanities. 1957. I1627
Crombie, I. M. An examination of Plato's doctrines. Humanities. 1962. I1628
Day, J. P. Inductive probability. Humanities. 1961. I1629
Dennett, D. C. Content and consciousness. 1969. I1630
Downey, J. E. Creative imagination. 1929. I1631
Eng, H. K. The psychology of children's drawings. 1954. I1632
Flew, A. G. N. Hume's philosophy of belief. Humanities. 1961. I1633
Florence, P. S. The statistical methods in economics and political science. 1929. I1634
Fogelin, R. J. Evidence and meaning. 1967. I1635
Fox, C. Educational psychology. 1950. I1636
____. The mind and its body. 1932. I1637
Franklin, C. Colour and colour theories. 1929. I1638
Franklin, R. L. Freewill and determinism. 1968. I1639
Fritz, C. A. Bertrand Russell's construction of the external world. 1952. I1640
Gale, R. M. The language of time. 1968. I1641
Glover, J. Responsibility. 1970. I1642
Gordon, R. G. The neurotic personality. 1926. I1643
____. Personality. 1927. I1644
Gregory, J. C. The nature of laughter. 1924. I1645
Hader, J. J. and Lindeman, E. C. Dynamic social research. 1933. I1646
Hall, E. W. What is value? 1952. I1647
Hamilton, E. R. The art of interrogation. 1929. I1648
Hamlyn, D. W. Sensation and perception. 1961. I1649
Hartmann, E. von. Philosophy of the unconscious. 1931. I1650
Hawk, S. M. Speech disorder. 1933. I1651
Herzberg, A. The psychology of philosophers. 1929. I1652
Hoop, J. H. van der. Character and the unconscious. 1923. I1653
____. Conscious orientation. 1939. I1654
Hsiao, K. C. Political pluralism. 1927. I1655
Hulme, T. E. Speculations. 1936. I1656
Humphrey, G. The nature of learning in its relation to the living system. 1933. I1657
Jaensch, E. Eidetic imagery and typological methods of investigation. 1930. I1658
Jung, C. G. Contributions to analytical psychology. 1928. I1659
____. Psychological types. 1923. I1660
Kemp, J. Reason, action and morality. 1963. I1661
King, C. D. The psychology of consciousness. 1932. I1662
Kirkpatrick, E. A. Psychology of man in the making. 1932. I1663
____. The science of man in the making. Routledge. 1932. I1664
Koffka, K. The growth of the mind. 1959. I1665
____. Principles of gestalt psychology. 1950. I1666
Köhler, W. The mentality of apes. 1925. I1667
Kretschmer, E. Physique and character. 1951. I1668
____. The psychology of men of genius. 1931. I1669
Laignel-Lavastine, M. Concentric method in the diagnosis of psychoneurotics. 1931. I1670
Lange, F. A. The history of materialism... 1925. I1671
Lazerowitz, M. The structure of metaphysics. Routledge. 1955. I1672
Lean, M. Sense-perception

and matter. 1953. I1673
Leuba, J. H. Psychology of religious mysticism. 1925. I1674
Lewis, M. M. Infant speech. 1951. I1675
Liang Chi-Chao. History of Chinese political thought, during the early Tsin period. 1930. I1676
Liao, W. K. The individual and the community. 1933. I1677
Lodge, R. C. The philosophy of Plato. Routledge. 1956. I1678
____. Plato's theory of art. Humanities. 1953. I1679
____. Plato's theory of education. 1948. I1680
____. Plato's theory of ethics. 1928. I1681
Lorimer, F. Growth of reason. 1929. I1682
MacCurdy, J. T. The psychology of emotion, morbid and normal. 1925. I1683
MacIntosh, J. J. and Coval, S., eds. The business of reason. 1969. I1684
Malinowski, B. Crime and custom in savage society. 1932. I1685
____. Sex and repression in savage society. 1951. I1686
Mannheim, K. Ideology and utopia. 1936. I1687
Markey, J. The symbolic process and its integration in children. 1928. I1688
Marston, W. M. Emotions of normal people. 1928. I1689
____ and others. Integrative psychology. 1931. I1690
Masson-Oursel, P. Comparative philosophy. 1926. I1691
Merleau-Ponty, M. Phenomenology of perception. Humanities. 1962. I1692
Michael, J. and Adler, M. J. Crime, law, and social science. 1933. I1693
Mitchell, T. W. Problems in psychopathology. 1927. I1694
Money-Kyrle, R. E. The development of the sexual impulses. 1932. I1695
Montmasson, J. M. Invention and the unconscious. 1932. I1696
Moore, G. E. Philosophical studies. 1922. I1697
Murphy, G. An historical introduction to modern psychology. 1929. I1698
Nicod, J. Foundations of geometry induction. 1930. I1699
Ogden, C. K. and Richards, I. A. The meaning of meaning. 1956. I1700
Paget, R. A. Human speech. 1930. I1701
Parmenides Eleates. Plato and Parmenides. 1939. I1702
Paulhan, F. The laws of feeling. 1930. I1703
Peirce, C. S. S. Chance, love and logic. 1923. I1704
____. The philosophy of Peirce. 1956. I1705
____. The philosophical writings of Peirce, ed. by Buchler. Routledge. 1956. I1706
Petermann, B. The gestalt theory and the problem of configuration. 1932. I1707
Piaget, The child's conception of geometry. Routledge. 1960. I1708
____. The child's conception of number. 1952. I1709
____. The child's conception of physical causality. 1930. I1710
____. The child's conception of the world. 1929. I1711
____. The language and thought of the child. 1959. I1712
____. The origin of intelligence in the child. Routledge. 1953. I1713
____. The psychology of intelligence. 1950. I1714
____ and others. Judgment and reasoning in the child. 1928. I1715
____. The moral judgment of the child. 1932. I1716
____ and Inhelder, B. The child's conception of space. Routledge. 1956. I1717
Piéron, H. Principles of experimental psychology. 1929. I1718

____. Thought and the brain. 1927. I1719
Plato. Phaedo, tr. by Bluck. Routledge. 1955. I1720
____. Plato and Parmenidas. Parmenides' Way of truth and Plato's Parmenides, tr. by Cornford. Kegan, Paul Trench. 1939. I1721
____. Plato's cosmology, tr. by Cornford. 1937. I1722
____. Plato's theory of knowledge. 1946. I1723
Pole, W. The philosophy of music. 1924. I1724
____. Problems of personality. 1925. I1725
Rabaud, E. How animals find their way about. 1928. I1726
Ramsey, F. P. The foundations of mathematics. 1931. I1727
Rank, O. The trauma of birth. 1929. I1728
Révész, G. The psychology of a musical prodigy. 1925. I1729
Richards, I. A. Mencius on the mind. 1932. I1730
____. Principles of literary criticism. 1924. I1731
Rignano, E. Biological memory. 1926. I1732
____. The nature of life. 1930. I1733
____. The psychology of reasoning. 1924. I1734
Ritchie, A. D. Scientific method. 1923. I1735
Rivers, W. H. R. Conflict and dream. 1923. I1736
____. Medicine, magic and religion. 1924. I1737
____. Psychology and ethnology. 1926. I1738
____. Psychology and politics. 1923. I1739
Roback, A. A. The psychology of character. 1952. I1740
Rohde, E. Psyche. 1925. I1741
Russell, B. A. The analysis of matter. 1927. I1742
Sanctis, S. de. Religious conversion. 1927. I1743
Schoen, M., ed. The effects of music. 1927. I1744
Sinclair, W. A. The conditions of knowing. 1951. I1745
Smart, N. Reasons and faiths. 1958. I1746
Smith, A. Wealth of nations. 1922. I1747
Smith, W. W. Measurement of emotion. 1922. I1748
Smythies, J. R. Analysis of perception. 1956. I1749
Stephen, K. The misuse of mind. 1922. I1750
Stinchfield, S. M. Speech disorders. 1933. I1751
Sturt, M. The psychology of time. 1925. I1752
Taba, H. The dynamics of education. 1933. I1753
Thalbitzer, S. Emotion and insanity. 1926. I1754
Thurstone, L. L. The nature of intelligence. 1924. I1755
Tischner, R. E. Telepathy and clairvoyance. 1925. I1756
Uexküll, J. J. Theoretical biology. 1926. I1757
Vaihinger, H. The psychology of as if. 1924. I1758
Vossler, K. The spirit of language in education. 1932. I1759
Weinberg, J. R. An examination of logical positivism. 1936. I1760
Westermarck, E. A. Ethical relativity. 1932. I1761
Wheeler, W. M. The social insects. 1928. I1762
Willemse, W. A. Constitution-types in delinquency. 1932. I1763
Winch, P., ed. Studies in the philosophy of Wittgenstein. 1969. I1764
Wittgenstein, L. Tractatus logico-philosophicus, tr. by Pears and McGuinness. 1962. I1765
Woodger, J. H. Biological principles. 1929. I1766
Wright, G. H. von. Explanation and understanding. 1971. I1767
____. Logical studies. Humanities. 1957. I1768
____. A treatise on induction and probability. 1952. I1769
Wyatt, H. G. The psychology of intelligence and will. 1930. I1770

Zeller, E. Outline of the history of Greek philosophy. 1929. I1771
Zinkernagel, P. Conditions of description. Humanities. 1962. I1772
Znosko-Borovsky, E. A. Middle game in chess. 1922. I1773
Zuckermann, S. The social life of monkeys and apes. 1932. I1774

INTERNATIONAL LIBRARY OF SOCIOLOGY AND SOCIAL RECONSTRUCTION (Routledge unless otherwise specified)

Ajzensted, S. N. The absorption of immigrants. 1954. I1775
Ammar, H. M. Growing up in an Egyptian village. 1954. I1776
Ancel, M. Social defence, tr. by Wilson. 1965. I1777
Anderson, N. Work and leisure. 1961. I1778
Andrezejewski, S. Military organization and society. 1954. I1779
Argyle, M. Religious behavior. Free Pr. 1958. I1780
Ashdown, M. and Brown, S. C. Social service and mental health. 1953. I1781
Ashworth, W. The genesis of modern British town planning. 1954. I1782
Association for Planning and Regional Reconstruction. The social background of a plan, ed. by Glass. 1948. I1783
Bagley, C. The social psychology of the epileptic child. 1971. I1784
Banks, J. A. Prosperity and parenthood. 1954. I1785
Banks, O. Parity and prestige in English secondary education. 1955. I1786
Barbu, Z. Democracy and dictatorship. 1956. I1787
____. Problems of historical psychology. 1960. I1788
Barnsley, J. H. The social reality of ethics. 1972. I1789
Basch, A. The Danube basin and the German economic sphere. 1943. I1790
Bastide, R. The sociology of mental disorder. 1972. I1791
Becker, H. German youth. 1946. I1792
Beljame, A. Men of letters and the English public in the eighteenth century. 1948. I1793
Bell, C. Middle class families. 1969. I1794
Belov, F. The history of a soviet collective farm. 1956. I1795
Belshaw, C. The conditions of social performance. 1970. I1796
Benney, M. and others. How people vote. 1956. I1797
Bentwick, J. Education in Israel. 1970. I1798
Blackburn, J. M. The framework of human behaviour. 1947. I1799
____. Psychology and the social pattern. 1945. I1800
Blyth, W. A. L. English primary education. 1972. I1801
Bonné, A. The economic development of the Middle East. 1945. I1802
____. State and economics in the Middle East. 1955. I1803
____. Studies in economic development. 1960. I1804
Bracey, H. E. English rural life. 1959. I1805
Bramstedt, E. K. Dictatorship and political police. Oxford. 1945. I1806
Brandel-Syrier, M. Reeftown elite. 1971. I1807
Brown, R. Explanation in service science. 1963. I1808
Bruford, W. H. Chekhov and his Russia. 1948. I1809
Burton, H. M. The education of the countryman. 1944. I1810
Burton, L. Vulnerable children. 1968. I1811
Cain, M. E. Society and the policeman's role. 1972. I1812
Carlebach, J. Caring for children in trouble. 1970. I1813
Chambers, R. J. H. Settlement

schemes in tropical Africa. 1969. I1814
Chapman, D. The home and social status. 1955. I1815
Cloward, R. A. and Ohlin, L. E. Delinquency and opportunity. 1961. I1816
Cohen, A. K. Delinquent boys. 1956. I1817
Cole, G. D. H. Studies in class structure. 1955. I1818
Collier, K. G. The social purposes of education. Humanities. 1959. I1819
Connell, W. F. The educational thought and influence of Matthew Arnold. 1950. I1820
Coontz, S. H. Population theories and economic interpretation. 1957. I1821
Coser, L. A. The functions of social conflict. 1956. I1822
Crick, B. The American science of politics. 1959. I1823
Crook, D. and I. Revolution in a Chinese village. 1959. I1824
Crook, I. and D. The first years of Yangyi Commune. 1966. I1825
Cullingworth, J. B. Housing needs and planning policy. 1961. I1826
Cumming, I. Helvetius. 1955. I1827
Dale, R. R. From school to university. 1954. I1828
____ and Griffith, S. Down stream. 1965. I1829
Degras, H. E. How people vote. 1956. I1830
Dent, H. C. Education in transition. 1944. I1831
DeRidder, J. C. The personality of the urban African in South Africa. 1961. I1832
Dickie-Clark, H. F. The marginal situation. 1966. I1833
Dickinson, R. E. City and region. 1964. I1834
____. City, region and regionalism. 1947. I1835
____. The city region in Western Europe. 1967. I1836
____. The regions of Germany. 1945. I1837
____. The west European city. 1951. I1838
Diesing, P. Patterns of discovery in the social sciences. 1972. I1839
Dollard, J. and others. Frustration and aggression. 1944. I1840
Dore, R. P. City life in Japan. 1958. I1841
____. Education in Tokugawa Japan. 1971. I1842
Douglas, D. Transitional economic systems. 1953. I1843
Douglas, J. E., ed. Understanding everyday life. 1971. I1844
Downes, D. M. The delinquent solution. 1966. I1845
Dube, S. C. Indian village. 1955. I1846
____. India's changing villages. 1958. I1847
Dunlop, A. B. and McCabe, S. Young men in detention centres. 1965. I1848
Durkheim, E. Professional ethics and civil morals, tr. by Brookfield. Free Pr. 1958. I1849
____. Socialism and Saint-Simon, ed. by Gouldner, tr. by Stattler. 1959. I1850
____. Suicide. 1952. I1851
Edmonds, E. L. The school inspector. 1962. I1852
Egerton, R. Legal aid. 1945. I1853
Eisenstadt, S. N. The absorption of immigrants. Free Pr. 1955. I1854
____. From generation to generation. Free Pr. 1955. I1855
Eldridge, J. E. T. Industrial disputes. 1969. I1856
Embree, J. F. A Japanese village. 1946. I1857
Eppel, E. M. and M. Adolescents and morality. 1966. I1858
Evans, K. M. Sociometry and education. 1962. I1859
Fei, H. Peasant life in China. 1943. I1860
____ and Chang, T. Earthbound China. 1949. I1861
Firth, R. W. Malay fishermen. 1946. I1862

Fleming, C. M. Adolescence. 1948. I1863
____. The social psychology of education. 1960. I1864
____, ed. Studies in the social psychology of adolescence. Humanities. 1959. I1865
Folsom, J. K. Family and democratic society. 1949. I1866
Ford, J. Social class and the comprehensive school. 1970. I1867
Forder, A., ed. Penelope Hall's social services in England and Wales. 1969. I1868
Foster, P. J. Education and the social change in Ghana. 1970. I1869
Fox, L. M. The English prison and Borstal systems. 1952. I1870
Fraser, W. R. Education and society in modern France. 1963. I1871
Friedländer, K. The psychoanalytical approach to juvenile delinquency. 1947. I1872
Fromm, E. The fear of freedom. 1942. I1873
____. The sane society. 1956. I1874
Gavron, H. The captive wife. 1966. I1875
George, V. Foster care. 1970. I1876
____ and Wilding, P. Motherless families. 1972. I1877
George, V. N. Social security. 1969. I1878
Gibson, Q. B. The logic of social enquiry. Humanities. 1960. I1879
Glaser, B. and Strauss, A. L. Status passage. 1971. I1880
Glass, D. V., ed. Social mobility in Britain. 1954. I1881
Glass, R. D. (Lazarus). Social background of a plan. 1948. I1882
Glueck, S. and E. T. Family environment and delinquency. 1962. I1883
Goetschius, G. W. Working with community groups. 1969. I1884
____. Working with unattached youth. 1967. I1885
Goldschmidt, W. R. Understanding human society. 1959. I1886
Gouldner, A. W. Patterns of industrial bureaucracy. 1955. I1887
____. Wildcat strike. 1955. I1888
Grace, G. R. Role conflict and the teacher. 1972. I1889
Grygier, T. Oppression. 1954. I1890
Gulliver, P. H. The family herds. 1955. I1891
____. Social control in an African society. 1969. I1892
Gurvitch, G. D. Sociology of law. 1947. I1893
Gutkind, E. A. Creative demobilisation. 2 v. 1944. I1894
____. Revolution of environment. 1946. I1895
Hall, M. P. The church in social work. 1965. I1896
____. The social services of modern England. 1960. I1897
Hallowell, J. H. The decline of liberalism as an ideology. 1946. I1898
Halmos, P. Solitude and privacy. 1952. I1899
____. Towards a measure of man. 1957. I1900
Hans, N. A. Comparative education. 1949. I1901
____. New Trends in education in the eighteenth century. 1951. I1902
Hargreaves, D. H. Interpersonal relations and education. 1972. I1903
____. Social relations in a secondary school. 1967. I1904
Haswell, M. R. Economics of development in village India. 1967. I1905
Hertz, F. O. Nationality in history and politics. 1944. I1906
Hetzler, S. A. Applied measures for promoting technological growth. 1970. I1907
____. Technological growth and social change. 1969. I1908
Heywood, J. S. Children in care. Humanities. 1959. I1909

____. An introduction to teaching casework skills. 1964. I1910

Hodges, H. A. The philosophy of Wilhelm Dilthey. 1952. I1911

____. William Dilthey. 1944. I1912

Hoenig, J. and Hamilton, M. W. The desegregation of the mentally ill. 1969. I1913

Hogbin, H. I. P. Transformation scene. 1951. I1914

Hollitscher, W. Sigmund Freud. 1947. I1915

Hollowell, P. G. The lorry driver. 1968. I1916

Holmes, B. Problems in education. 1965. I1917

Homan, G. C. The human group. 1951. I1918

____. Sentiments & activities. 1962. I1919

____. Social behaviour. 1962. I1920

Hsü, F. L. K. Religion, science and human crises. 1952. I1921

____. Under the ancestors' shadow. 1949. I1922

Hughes, E. C. French Canada in transition. 1946. I1923

Huizinga, J. Homó ludens. 1949. I1924

Humphreys, A. J. New Dubliners. 1966. I1925

Hutt, W. H. Plan for reconstruction. 1943. I1926

Infield, H. F. Cooperative communities at work. 1947. I1927

____. Cooperative living in Palestine. 1946. I1928

Isaac, J. Economics of migration. 1947. I1929

Isajiw, W. W. Causation and functionalism in sociology. 1968. I1930

Ishwaran, K. Shivapur. 1968. I1931

____. Tradition and economy in village India. 1966. I1932

Jacks, M. L. Total education. 1946. I1933

Jackson, B. Working class community. 1968. I1934

Jarvie, I. C. Concepts and society. 1972. I1935

____. Revolution in anthropology. 1971. I1936

____. Towards a sociology of the cinema. 1971. I1937

____ and Agassi, J., eds. Hong-Kong. 1969. I1938

Jefferys, M. Mobility in the labour market. 1954. I1939

Jennings, H. Societies in the making. 1962. I1940

Johnson, H. M. Sociology. 1961. I1941

Jones, G. N. Planned organizational change. 1968. I1942

Jones, K. Lunacy, law and conscience, 1744-1845. 1955. I1943

____. Mental health and social policy. 1960. I1944

____ and Sidebotham, R. Mental hospitals at work. 1962. I1945

Kastell, J. Casework in child care. 1962. I1946

Kelsall, R. K. Higher civil servants. 1955. I1947

Kelsen, H. Society and nature. 1946. I1948

Kerr, M. The people of Ship Street. 1958. I1949

King, R. Values and involvement in a grammar school. 1970. I1950

King, R. D. and others. Patterns of residential care. 1971. I1951

Klein, J. Samples from English culture. 2 v. 1964. I1952

____. The study of groups. 1956. I1953

Klein, V. Britain's married women workers. 1965. I1954

____. The feminine character. 1946. I1955

____ and Myrdal, A. Woman's two roles. 1956. I1956

Knight, F. H. and Merriam, T. W. The economic order and religion. 1948. I1957

Köhler, W. Mentality of apes. 1948. I1958

Kohn-Bramstedt, E. Dictatorship and political police. 1945. I1959

König, R. The community. 1970. I1960

Kornhauser, W. The politics of mass society. 1960. I1961

Laidler, H. W. History of socialism. 1969. I1962
____. Social economic movements. 1949. I1963
Lasswell, H. D. An analysis of political behaviour. 1948. I1964
____ and Kaplan, A. Power and society. 1952. I1965
Lawton, D. Social class, language and education. 1968. I1966
Leigh, J. Young people and leisure. 1971. I1967
Levy, A. B. Private corporations and their control. 2 v. 1950. I1968
Levy, H. Retail trade associations. 1942. I1969
____. The shops of Britain. 1948. I1970
Liepmann, K. K. Apprenticeship. 1960. I1971
____. The journey to work. 1944. I1972
Lin, Y. The golden wing. 1948. I1973
Linton, R. The cultural background of personality. 1947. I1974
Little, K. L. The Mende of Sierra Leone. 1951. I1975
____. Negroes in Britain. 1948. I1976
Littlejohn, J. Westrigg. 1963. I1977
Lopez-Rey, M. Crime. 1970. I1978
Lowie, R. H. Social organization. 1950. I1979
McWhinnie, A. M. Adopted children. 1967. I1980
Mann, P. H. An approach to urban sociology. 1965. I1981
Mannheim, H. Comparative criminology. 2 v. 1965. I1982
____. Criminal justice and social reconstruction. 1946. I1983
____. Group problems in crime and punishment. 1955. I1984
____. Juvenile delinquency in English middletown. 1948. I1985
Mannheim, K. Diagnosis of our times. 1944. I1986
____. Essays on sociology and social psychology. 1953. I1987
____. Essays on the sociology of culture. 1956. I1988
____. Essays on the sociology of knowledge. 1952. I1989
____. Freedom, power and democratic planning. 1951. I1990
____. Systematic sociology. 1957. I1991
____ and Stewart, W. A. C. An introduction to the sociology of education. 1962. I1992
Mansur, F. Process of independence. 1962. I1993
Marsh, D. C. The changing social structure of England and Wales, 1871-1951. Humanities. 1958. I1994
Martin, A. W. O. von. Sociology of the renaissance. 1944. I1995
Martin, D. A. Pacificism. 1970. I1996
Martindale, D. A. The nature and types of sociological theory. 1961. I1997
Maunier, R. The sociology of colonies. 2 v. 1949. I1998
Maus, H. A. A short history of sociology. 1962. I1999
Mayer, A. C. Caste and kinship in central India. 1960. I2000
____. Peasants in the Pacific. 1961. I2001
Mayer, J. P. Political thought in France. 1961. I2002
Mayo, E. The social problems of an industrial civilization. 1949. I2003
Meek, D. L., ed. and tr. Soviet youth. 1957. I2004
Mess, H. A. Voluntary social service since 1918. 1948. I2005
Mey, H. Field-theory. 1972. I2006
Miller, N. E. and Dollard, J. Social learning and imitation. 1950. I2007
Millerson, G. The qualifying associations. 1964. I2008
Misch, G. A history of autobiography in antiquity. 2 v. 1950. I2009
Morris, M. Voluntary work in the welfare state. 1970. I2010

Morris, P. Put away. 1969. I2011
Morris, R. N. The sixth form and college entrance. 1969. I2012
____ and Mogey, J. The sociology of housing. 1965. I2013
Morris, T. The criminal area. 1958. I2014
____ and others. Pentonville. 1963. I2015
Mouzelis, N. P. Organisation and bureaucracy. 1967. I2016
Mulkay, M. J. Functionalism, exchange and theoretical strategy. 1971. I2017
Myrdal, A. (Reimer). Nation and family. 1945. I2018
____. Women's two roles. 1956. I2019
Myrdal, G. The political elements in the development of economic theory. 1953. I2020
____. Value in social theory. 1958. I2021
Nelson, G. K. Spiritualism and society. 1969. I2022
Nokes, P. The professional task in welfare practice. 1968. I2023
Ogburn, W. F. and Nimkoff, M. F. A handbook of sociology. 1960. I2024
Orlans, H. Stevenage. 1952. I2025
Ortega y Gasset, J. Mission of the university. 1946. I2026
Osborne, H. Indians of the Andes: Aymaras and Quechuas. 1952. I2027
Ottaway, A. K. C. Education and society. 1962. I2028
____. Learning through experience. 1966. I2029
Parsons, T. and others. Family, socialization and interaction processes. 1956. I2030
Parsons, T. and Smelser, N. J. Economy and society. 1957. I2031
Patterson, S. Colour and culture in South Africa. 1953. I2032
Peers, R. Adult education. 1958. I2033
Polanyi, M. The logic of liberty. 1951. I2034
Pritchard, D. G. Education and the handicapped, 1760-1960. 1963. I2035
Reissman, L. Class in American society. 1960. I2036
Remmling, G. W., ed. Towards the sociology of knowledge. 1970. I2037
Renner, K. The institutions of private law and their social functions. 1949. I2038
Rex, J. Key problems of sociological theory. 1962. I2039
Richardson, H. J. Adolescent girls in approved schools. 1969. I2040
Richmond, O. H. Colour prejudice in Britain. 1956. I2041
Ridder, J. C. de. The personality of the urban African in South Africa. 1970. I2042
Roche, M. Phenomenology. 1971. I2043
Rooff, M. Voluntary societies and social policy. Humanities. 1957. I2044
Rose, A. M. and others. Human behavior and social processes. 1962. I2045
____. Mental health and mental disorder. 1956. I2046
Rosser, C. and Harris, C. The family and social change. 1965. I2047
Rust, F. Dance in society. 1969. I2048
Sahay, A. Sociological analysis. 1972. I2049
Samuel, R. and Thomas, R. H. Education and society in modern Germany. 1949. I2050
Schenk, H. G. A. V. The aftermath of the Napoleonic wars. 1947. I2051
Saville, J. Rural depopulation in England and Wales, 1851-1951. 1957. I2052
Schlesinger, R. Central European democracy and its background. 1953. I2053
____. Changing attitudes in Soviet Russia. 2 v. 1949-56. I2054
____. Federalism in central and eastern Europe. 1945. I2055
____. Marx. 1950. I2056
____. Soviet legal theory. 1951. I2057

Schücking, L. L. The sociology of literary tastes. 1944. I2058
Shenfield, B. E. Social policies for old age. 1957. I2059
Silbermann, A. The sociology of music, tr. by Stewart. 1963. I2060
Simon, B., ed. Educational psychology in the Soviet Union, tr. by Ellis and others. 1957. I2061
Sklair, L. The sociology of progress. 1970. I2062
Smelser, N. J. Social change in the industrial revolution. 1959. I2063
____. Theory of collective behavior. 1962. I2064
Smith, R. T. The Negro family in British Guiana. 1956. I2065
Smythies, J. R. Analysis of perception. 1956. I2066
Spencer, J. C. Crime and the Services. 1954. I2067
Spinley, B. M. The deprived and the privileged. 1953. I2068
Stark, W. America. 1947. I2069
____. The fundamental forms of social thought. 1962. I2070
____. The history of economics in relation to social development. 1944. I2071
____. The ideal foundations of economic thought. 1943. I2072
____. Montesquieu, pioneer of the sociology of knowledge. 1960. I2073
____. The sociology of knowledge. 1958. I2074
Stark, W. The sociology of religion. 5 v. 1966-72. I2075
Stephenson, G. M. The development of conscience. 1964. I2076
Stimson, C. Education after school. 1948. I2077
Stratta, E. The education of borstal boys. 1970. I2078
Thomson, D. and others. Patterns of peacemaking. 1948. I2079
Timms, N. Psychiatric social work in Great Britain. 1970. I2080
____. Social casework. 1964. I2081
Tönnies, F. Community and association. 1955. I2082
Trasler, G. The explanation of criminality. 1962. I2083
____. In place of parents. 1960. I2084
Trouton, R. Peasant renaissance in Yugoslavia. 1952. I2085
Urry, J. Reference groups and the theory of revolution. 1970. I2086
Verney, D. V. In place of political systems. 1959. I2087
Wach, J. Sociology of religion. 1944. I2088
Warner, W. L. and others. Who shall be educated? 1946. I2089
Watt, W. M. Islam and the integration of society. 1961. I2090
Weber, A. Farewell to European history. 1947. I2091
Weber, M. From Max Weber. 1948. I2092
Williams, G. (Rosenblum). The price of social security. 1944. I2093
____. Recruitment to skilled trades. Humanities. 1957. I2094
Williams, W. M. The country craftsman. 1958. I2095
____. The sociology of an English village: Gosforth. 1956. I2096
Wittlin, A. S. The museum. 1949. I2097
Wolfstein, M. Disaster. 1957. I2098
Wootton, G. Workers, unions and the state. 1966. I2099
Yale university. Institute of human relations. Frustration and aggression. 1944. I2100
Yang, M. A Chinese village. 1948. I2101
Young, A. F. Industrial injuries insurance. 1964. I2102
____. Social services in British industry. 1969. I2103
____ and Ashton, E. T. British social work in the nineteenth century. 1956. I2104
Young, K. Handbook of social psychology. 1944. I2105
____. Personality and problems

of adjustment. 1947. I2106
Zeller, E. Outlines of history of Greek philosophy. 1948. I2107
Zinkenagel, P. Conditions for description, tr. by Lindum. 1962. I2108

INTERNATIONAL MONOGRAPHS AND TEXTS IN PHYSICS AND ASTRONOMY (Previously published as Interscience Monographs in Physics and Astronomy)

1 Cohen, E. R. and others. The fundamental constants of physics. 1957. I2109
2 Dienes, G. J. and Vineyard, G. H. Radiation effects in solids. 1957. I2110
3 Bogoli͡ubov, N. N. and Shirkov, D. V. Introduction to the theory of quantized fields, tr. by Volkoff. 1959. I2111
4 Marion, J. B. and Fowler, J. L., eds. Fast neutron physics. V. 1. 1960. I2112
5 Ritson, D. M. Techniques of high energy physics. 1960. I2113
6 Thomas, R. N. and Athay, R. G. Physics of the solar chromosphere. 1961. I2114
7 Aller, L. H. Abundance of the elements. 1961. I2115
8 Parker, E. N. Interplanetary dynamical processes. 1963. I2116
9 Longmire, C. L. Elementary plasma physics. 1963. I2117
10 Brout, R. H. and Carruthers, P. Lectures on the many-election problems. 1963. I2118
11 Akhiezer, A. I. and Beresteͭskiĭ, V. B. Quantum electrodynamics, tr. by Volkoff. 1965. I2119
12 Lumley, J. L. and Panofsky, H. A. The structure of atmospheric turbulence. 1964. I2120
13 Heidenreich, R. D. Fundamentals of transmission electron microscopy. 1964. I2121
14 Rickayzen, G. The theory of superconductivity. 1965. I2122
15 Seegar, R. J. and Temple, G., eds. Research frontiers in fluid dynamics. 1965. I2123
16 Wu, C. and Moszkowski, S. A. Beta decay. 1966. I2124
17 Steffan, K. G. High energy beam optics. 1965. I2125
18 Agranovich, V. M. and Ginzburg, V. L. Spatial dispersion in crystal optics and the theory of excitons. 1966. I2126
19 Migdal, A. B. Theory of finite Fermi systems, tr. by Chomet. 1967. I2127
20 Moisiwitsch, B. L. Variational principles. 1966. I2128
21 Shklovskiĭ, I. S. Supernovae. 1968. I2129
22 Hayakawa, S. Cosmic ray physics. 1969. I2130
24 Marshak, R. E. and others. Theory of weak interactions in particle physics. 1969. I2131
25 Austern, N. Direct nuclear reaction. 1970. I2132
26 Emch, G. G. Algebraic methods in statistical mechanics and Quantum field theory. 1972. I2133
27 Jones, W. and March, N. H. Theoretical solid state physics. 1973. I2134

INTERNATIONAL MONOGRAPHS ON RADIO (Oxford)

Barlow, H. E. M. and Brown, J. Radio surface waves. 1962. I2135
Moullin, E. B. Radio aerials. 1949. I2136
Pawsey, J. L. and Bracewell, R. N. Radio astronomy. 1955. I2137
Störmer, C. The polar aurora. 1955. I2138
Watson, W. H. The physical principles of wave guide transmission and antenna systems. 1947. I2139

INTERNATIONAL PROPAGANDA AND COMMUNICATION (Arno)

Bruntz, G. G. Allied propaganda and the collapse of the German empire in 1918. 1972. I2140
Childs, H. L., ed. Propaganda and dictatorship. 1972. I2141
____ and Whitton, J. B., eds. Propaganda by short wave. 1972. I2142
Codding, G. A. The International Telecommunication Union. 1972. I2143
Commission on Freedom of the Press. Peoples speaking to peoples, by White and Leigh. 1972. I2144
Creel, G. How we advertised America. 1972. I2145
De Mendelssohn, P. Japan's political warfare. 1972. I2146
Desmond, R. W. The press and world affairs. 1972. I2147
Farago, L., ed. German psychological warfare. 1972. I2148
Francis-Williams, E. F. W. Transmitting world news. 1972. I2149
Hadamovsky, E. Propaganda and national power. 1972. I2150
Huth, A. La radio diffusion puissance mondiale. 1972. I2151
International Press Institute. The flow of news. 1972. I2152
____. Surveys, no. 1-6. 1972. I2153
International Propaganda/Communications. Selections. 1972. I2154
Lavine, H. and Wechsler, J. War propaganda and the United States. 1972. I2155
Lerner, D., ed. Propaganda in war and crisis. 1972. I2156
Linebarger, P. Psychological warfare. 1972. I2157
Lockhart, R. H. B. Comes the reckoning. 1972. I2158
Macmahon, A. W. Memorandum on the postwar information program of the United States. 1972. I2159
Nafziger, R. O., comp. International news and the press. 1972. I2160
Read, J. M. Atrocity propaganda. 1972. I2161
Riegel, O. W. Mobilizing for chaos. 1972. I2162
Rogerson, S. Propaganda in the next war. 1972. I2163
Summers, R. E., ed. American's weapons on psychological warfare. 1972. I2164
Terrou, F. and Solai, L. Legislation for press. 1972. I2165
Thomson, C. A. Overseas information service of the United States government. 1972. I2166
Tribolet, L. B. The international aspects of electrical communications in the Pacific area. 1972. I2167
UNESCO. Press film radio. V. 1-5. 1972. I2168
____. Television. 1972. I2169
Wright, Q., ed. Public opinion and world-politics. 1972. I2170

INTERNATIONAL PSYCHO-ANALYTICAL LIBRARY (44-Int. Univ. Pr.)

1 Putnam, J. J. Addresses on psycho-analysis. Clarke. 1951. I2171
2 Ferenczi, S. Psycho-analysis and the war neuroses. Stechert. 1921. I2172
3 Flügel, J. C. The psychoanalytic study of the family Hogarth. 1931. I2173
4 Freud, S. Beyond the pleasure principle. Ballou. 1922. I2174
5 Jones, E. Essays in applied psycho-analysis. Ballou. 1921. I2175
6 Freud, S. Group psychology and the analysis of the ego. Hogarth. 1948. I2176
7-10 Freud, S. Collected papers. V. 1-4. Hogarth. 1924-25. I2177
11 Ferenczi, S. Further contributions to the theory and technique of psycho-analysis, comp. by Rickman. Hogarth. 1950. I2178

12 Freud, S. The ego and id. Clarke. 1951. I2179
13 Abraham, K. Selected papers. Hogarth. 1932. I2180
14 Rickman, J. Index psychoanalyticus. Ballou. 1928. I2181
15 Freud, S. The future of an illusion. Liveright. 1949. I2182
16 Money-Kyrle, R. E. The meaning of sacrifice. Hogarth. 1930. I2183
17 Freud, S. Civilization and its discontents. Hogarth. 1930. I2184
18 Flügel, J. C. The psychology of clothes. Ballou. 1930. I2185
19 Reik, T. Ritual. Norton. 1931. I2186
20 Jones, E. On the nightmare. Liveright. 1951. I2187
20 Also pub. as Nightmare, witches, and devils. Norton. 1931. I2188
21 Laforgue, R. The defeat of Baudelaire. Hogarth. 1932. I2189
22 Klein, M. The psychoanalysis of children. Norton. 1961. I2190
23 Deutsch, H. Psychoanalysis of the neuroses. Hogarth. 1932. I2191
24 Freud, S. New introductory lectures on psycho-analysis. Hogarth. 1933. I2192
25 Róheim, G. The riddle of the sphinx. Hogarth. 1934. I2193
26 Freud, S. An autobiographical study. Clarke. 1946. I2194
27 Reik, T. The unknown murderer. Hogarth. 1936. I2195
28 Freud, S. Inhibitions, symptoms and anxiety. Hogarth. 1936. I2196
29 Sharpe, E. F. Dream analysis. Hogarth. 1937. I2197
30 Freud, A. The ego and the mechanisms of defence. Hogarth. 1937. I2198
31 Laforgue, R. Clinical aspects of psycho-analysis. Hogarth. 1938. I2199
32 Reik, T. From thirty years with Freud. Hogarth. 1942. I2200
33 Freud, S. Moses and monotheism. Hogarth. 1951. I2201
34 Klein, M. Contributions to psycho-analysis, 1921-1945. Hogarth. 1948. I2202
35 Freud, S. An outline of psychoanalysis. Clarke. 1949. I2203
36 Sharpe, E. F. Collected papers on psycho-analysis. Clarke. 1950. I2204
37 Same as no. 7-10. V. 5. Clarke. 1950. I2205
38 Fliess, R. The psychoanalysis of the neuroses. Clarke. 1950. I2206
39 Brierley, M. Trends in psychoanalysis. Clarke. 1951. I2207
40-41 Jones, E. Essays in applied psycho-analysis. 2 v. Clarke. 1951. I2208
42 Freud, S. On dreams, tr. by Strachey. Clarke. 1952. I2209
43 Riviere, J., ed. Developments in psycho-analysis, by Klein and others. Clarke. 1952. I2210
44 Bálint, M. Primary love, and psycho-analytic technique. 1952. I2211
45 Ferenczi, S. First contributions to psycho-analysis. 1952. I2212
46 Greenacre, P. Trauma, growth and personality. 1953. I2213
47 Wisdom, J. O. The unconscious origin of Berkeley's philosophy. 1953. I2214
48 Ferenczi, S. Final contribution to the problems and methods of psycho-analysis. 1952. I2215
49 Abraham, K. Clinical papers and essays on psychoanalysis. 1955. I2216
50 Breuer, J. and Freud, S. Studies on hysteria, tr. by J. and A. Strachey. 1956. I2217
51 Balint, M. Problems of human pleasure and behaviour.

1957. I2218
52 Richman, J. Selected contributions to psycho-analysis. 1957. I2219
53 Sutherland, J. D., ed. Psycho-analysis and contemporary thought. 1958. I2220
54 Bálint, M. Thrills and regressions. 1959. I2221
55 Klein, M. Narrative of a child analysis. 1961. I2222
56 Guntrip, H. J. S. Personality structure and human interaction. 1961. I2223
57 Freud, S. Three essays on the theory of sexuality, tr. by Strachey. 1962. I2224
58 Eissler, K. R. Leonardo da Vinci. 1961. I2225
59 Freud, S. Psycho-analysis and faith, ed. by Meng and Freud, tr. by Mosbacher. 1963. I2226
60 Lidz, T. The family and human adaptation. 1964. I2227
61 Hartmann, H. Essays on ego psychology. 1964. I2228
62 Deutsch, H. Neuroses and character types. 1965. I2229
63 Searles, H. F. Collected papers on schizophrenia and related subjects. 1965. I2230
64 Winnicott, D. W. The maturational processes and the facilitating environment. 1965. I2231
65 Rosenfeld, H. A. Psychotic stages. 1965. I2232
66 New York. Mount Sinai Hospital. Evolution of psychosomatic concepts. 1965. I2233
67 Jacobson, E. The self and the object world. 1965. I2234
68 Freud, S. A psycho-analytic dialogue, ed. by Abraham and Freud, tr. by Marsh and Abraham. 1965. I2235
69 ____. Normality and pathology in childhood. 1966. I2236
70 Lampl-de Groot, J. The development of the mind. 1966. I2237
71 Lomas, P. The predicament of the family. 1967. I2238
72 Schnur, M. The id and the regulatory principles of mental functioning. 1967. I2239
73 Racker, E. Transference and counter-transference. 1968. I2240
74 Greenson, R. R. The technique and practice of psychoanalysis. V. 1. 1967. I2241
75 Rycroft, C. Imagination and reality. 1968. I2242
76 Milner, M. The hands of the living God. 1969. I2243
77 Guntrip. H. Schizoid phenomena. 1968. I2244
78 Modell, A. H. Object love and reality. 1969. I2245
79 Bowlby, J. Attachment and loss. 2 v. 1969. I2246
80 Freud, A. Indications for child analysis. 1969. I2247
81 Stoller, R. J. Sex and gender. 1969. I2248
82 McDougall, J. Dialogue with Sammy. 1969. I2249
83 Mahler, M. S. and Furer, M. On human symbiosis and the vicissitudes of individuation. 1968. (misnumbered 82) I2250
84 Freud, S., ed. The letters of Sigmund Freud & Arnold Zweig. 1970. I2251
85 Freud, A. Research at the Hampstead Child-Therapy Clinic. 1970. I2252
86 Zetzel, E. R. The capacity for emotional growth. 1970. I2253
87 Winnicott, D. W. Therapeutic consultation in child psychiatry. 1971. I2254
88 Wolf-Man. The Wolfman and Sigmund Freud, ed. by Gardner. 1972. I2255
89 Freud, S. Sigmund Freud and Lou Andreas - Salomé letters, ed. by Pfeiffer. 1972. I2256
90 Freud, A. Problems of psychoanalytic technique and therapy. 1972. I2257
91 Segal, H. Introduction to the work of Melanie Klein. 1973. I2258
92 Schur, M. Freud. 1972. I2259
93 Giovacchine, P. L., ed. Tactics and techniques in

psychoanalysis therapy. 1972. I2260
94 Laplanche, J. and Pontalis, J. B. The language of psychoanalysis, tr. by Nicholson-Smith. 1973. I2261
95 Bowlby, J. Attachment and loss. 1973. I2262
96 Freud, A. Infants without families. 1974. I2263
97 Stoller, R. J. Splitting. 1974. I2264
98 Khan, M. M. R. The privacy of self. 1974. I2265

INTERNATIONAL SCIENCE REVIEW SERIES (Gordon and Breach)

1 Klein, L., ed. Dispersion relations and the abstract approach to field theory. 1961. I2266
2 Morrison, H. L., ed. The quantum theory of many-particle systems. 1962. I2267
3 McIntyre, D. and Gornick, F., eds. Light scattering from dilute polymer solutions. 1964. I2268
4 Bogoliûbov, N. N., ed. The theory of superconductivity. 1962. I2269
5 Kabir, P. K., ed. The development of weak interaction theory. 1963. I2270
6 Rose, M. E., ed. Nuclear orientation. 1963. I2271
7 Meijer, P. H., ed. Group theory and solid state physics. 2 v. 1964. I2272
8:1 Truesdell, C. H., ed. Mechanical foundations of elasticity and fluid dynamics. 1965. I2273
8:2 ____. The rational mechanics of materials. 1965. I2274
8:3 ____. Foundations of elasticity theory. 1965. I2275
8:4 ____. Problems of non-linear elasticity. 1965. I2276
9 Weber, J., ed. Masers. 1967. I2277
10A-10B Weber, J., comp. Lasers. 1968. I2278
11 Kerner, E. H., comp. The theory of action-at-a-distance in relativistic particle dynamics. 1972. I2279
12 Kerner, E. H. Gibbs ensemble. 1972. I2280
13 Rossmann, M. G., ed. The molecular replacement method. 1972. I2281

INTERNATIONAL SERIES IN PURE AND APPLIED MATHEMATICS (McGraw)

Ahlfors, L. V. Complex analysis. 1953. I2282
Bellman, R. E. Stability theory of differential equations. 1953. I2283
Buck, R. C. Advanced calculus. 1956. I2284
Busacker, R. G. and Saatz, T. L. Finite graphs and networks. 1965. I2285
Cheney, E. W. Introduction to approximation theory. 1966. I2286
Chester, C. R. Techniques in partial differential equations. 1970. I2287
Chodorow, M. and Susskind, C. Fundamentals of microwave electronics. 1964. I2288
Coddington, E. A. and Levinson, N. Theory of ordinary differential equations. 1955. I2289
Cohn, H. Confirmal mapping on Riemann surfaces. 1967. I2290
Conte, S. D. and De Boor, C. Elementary numerical analysis. 1972. I2291
Dennemeyer, R. Introduction to partial differential equations and boundary value problems. 1968. I2292
Dettman, J. W. Mathematical methods in physics and engineering. 1962. I2293
Epstein, B. Partial differential equations. 1962. I2294
Golomb, M. and Shanks, M. E. Elements of ordinary differential equations. 1950. I2295
Graves, L. M. The theory of functions of real variables. 1956. I2296
Greenspan, D. Introduction to partial differential equations.

1961. I2297
Griffin, H. Elementary theory of numbers. 1954. I2298
Hamming, R. W. Numerical methods for scientists and engineers. 1962. I2299
Hildebrand, F. B. Introduction to numerical analysis. 1956. I2300
Householder, A. S. Principles of numerical analysis. 1953. I2301
Kalman, R. E. and others. Topics in mathematical system theory. 1969. I2302
Lass, H. Elements of pure and applied mathematics. 1957. I2303
____. Vector and tensor analysis. 1950. I2304
Leighton, W. An introduction to the theory of differential equations. 1952. I2305
LePage, W. R. Complex variables and the LaPlace transform for engineers. 1961. I2306
McCarty, G. S. Topology. 1967. I2307
Monk, J. D. Introduction to set theory. 1969. I2308
Moore, J. T. Elements of linear algebra and matrix theory. 1968. I2309
Mostow, G. D. and Sampson, J. H. Linear algebra. 1969. I2310
Moursund, D. G. and Duris, C. S. Elementary theory and application of numerical analysis. 1967. I2311
Nef, W. Linear algebra. 1967. I2312
Nehari, Z. Conformal mapping. 1952. I2313
Newell, H. E. Vector analysis. 1955. I2314
Newton, R. G. Scattering theory of waves and particles. 1966. I2315
Pearl, M. Matrix theory finite mathematics. 1973. I2316
Pipes, L. A. and Harvill, L. R. Applied mathematics for engineers and physicists. 1970. I2317
Present, R. D. Kinetic theory of gases. 1958. I2318
Ralston, A. A first course in numerical analysis. 1965. I2319
Ritger, P. D. and Rose, N. J. Differential equations with applications. 1967. I2320
Ritt, R. K. Fourier series. 1970. I2321
Rosser, J. B. Logic for mathematicians. 1953. I2322
Rudin, W. Principles of mathematical analysis. 1953. I2323
Saaty, T. L. and Bram, J. Non-linear mathematics. 1964. I2324
Sagan, H. Introduction to the calculus of variations. 1969. I2325
Simmons, G. F. Differential equations. 1972. I2326
____. Introduction to topology and modern analysis. 1963. I2327
Sneddon, I. N. Elements of partial differential equations. 1957. I2328
____. Fourier transforms. 1951. I2329
Stoll, R. R. Linear algebra and matrix theory. 1952. I2330
Struble, R. A. Nonlinear differential equations. 1962. I2331
Weinstock, R. Calculus of variations. 1952. I2332
Weiss, E. Algebraic number theory. 1963. I2333
Zemanian, A. H. Distribution theory and transform analysis. 1965. I2334

INTERNATIONAL SERIES IN PURE AND APPLIED PHYSICS (McGraw) (International Series in Physics prior to 1948)

Adler, R. and others. Introduction to general relativity. 1965. I2335
Allis, W. P. and Herlin, M. A. Thermodynamics and statistical mechanics. 1952. I2336
Bacher, R. F. and Goudsmit, S., comps. Atomic energy states. 1932. I2337
Becker, R. A. Introduction to

theoretical mechanics. 1954. I2338
Bitter, F. Introduction to ferromagnetism. 1937. I2339
Bjorken, J. D. and Drell, S. D. Realivistic quantum fields. 1965. I2340
____. Realivistic quantum mechanics. 1964. I2341
Brillouin, L. Wave propagation in periodic structures. 1946. I2342
Cady, W. G. Piezoelectricity. 1946. I2343
Chodorow, M. Fundamentals of microwave electronics. 1964. I2344
Clark, C. L. Applied x-rays. 1955. I2345
Collin, R. E. Field theory of guided waves. 1960. I2346
Condon, E. U. and Morse, P. M. Quantum mechanics. 1929. I2347
Curtis, H. L. Electrical measurements. 1937. I2348
Davey, W. P. A study of crystal structure and its applications. 1934. I2349
Edwards, H. M. Analytic and vector mechanics. 1933. I2350
Eldridge, J. A. The physical basis of things. 1934. I2351
Evans, R. D. The atomic nucleus. 1955. I2352
Fetter, A. L. and Walecka, J. D. Quantum theory of many particle systems. 1970. I2353
Feyman, R. P. and Hibbs, A. P. Quantum mechanics and path integrals. 1965. I2354
Finkelnburg, A. Atomic physics. 1950. I2355
Gamow, G. and Critchfield, C. L. Theory of atomic nuclear energy-sources. 1949. I2356
Ginzton, E. L. Microwave measurements. 1957. I2357
Green, A. E. S. Nuclear physics. 1955. I2358
Gurney, R. W. Introduction to statistical mechanics. 1949. I2359
Hall, C. E. Introduction to electron microscopy. 1966. I2360
Hardy, A. C. and Perrin, F. H. The principles of optics. 1932. I2361
Harnwell, G. P. Principles of electricity and electromagnetism. 1949. I2362
____ and Livingood, J. J. Experimental atomic physics. 1933. I2363
____ and Stephens, W. E. Atomic physics. 1955. I2364
Harrison, W. A. Solid state theory. 1970. I2365
Henley, E. M. and Thirring, W. Elementary quantum field theory. 1962. I2366
Householder, A. S. Principles of numerical analysis. 1953. I2367
Houston, W. V. Principles of mathematical physics. 1948. I2368
____. Principles of quantum mechanics. 1951. I2369
Hughes, A. L. and DuBridge, L. A. Photoelectric phenomena. 1932. I2370
Hund, A. High-frequency measurements. 1951. I2371
____. Phenomena in high frequency measurements. 1951. I2372
Ingersoll, L. R. and others. Heat conduction. 1948. I2373
Jammer, M. The conceptual development of quantum mechanics. 1966. I2374
Kemble, E. C. The fundamental principles of quantum mechanics. 1937. I2375
Kennard, E. H. Kinetic theory of gases. 1938. I2376
Koller, L. R. The physics of electron tubes. I2377
Lane, C. T. Superfluid physics. 1962. I2378
Leighton, R. B. Principles of modern physics. 1959. I2379
Lindsay, R. B. Mechanical radiation. 1960. I2380
Livingston, M. S. and Blewett, J. P. Particle accelerators. 1962. I2381
Marshak, R. E. Modern physics. 1952. I2382
Middleton, D. An introduction to statistical communication theory. 1960. I2383
Morse, P. M. Vibration and sound. 1948. I2384

____ and Fishbach, H. Methods of theoretical physics. 2 v. 1953. I2385
____ and Ingard, K. U. Theoretical acoustics. 1968. I2386
Muskat, M. The flow of homogeneous fluids through porous media. I2387
____. Physical principles of oil production. 1949. I2388
Newton, R. G. Scattering theory of waves and particles. 1966. I2389
Pauling, L. C. and Goudsmit, S. The structure of line spectra. 1930. I2390
Present, R. D. Kinetic theory of gases. 1958. I2391
Read, W. T. Dislocations in crystals. 1953. I2392
Richtmyer, F. K. Introduction to modern physics. 1955. I2393
Ritger, P. D. and Rose, N. J. Differential equations with application. 1968. I2394
Rossi, B. and Olbert, J. Introduction to the physics of space. 1970. I2395
Ruark, A. E. and Urey, H. C. Atoms, molecules and quanta. 1930. I2396
Schwartz, H. M. Introduction to special relativity. 1968. I2397
Schwartz, M. Principles of electrodynamics. 1972. I2398
Scjiff, L. I. Quantum mechanics. 1955. I2399
Seitz, F. The modern theory of solids. 1940. I2400
Slater, J. C. Introduction to chemical physics. 1939. I2401
____. Microwave transmission. 1942. I2402
____. Quantum theory of atomic structure. 2 v. 1960. I2403
____. Quantum theory of matter. 1951. I2404
____. Quantum theory of molecules and solids. 3 v. 1963-67. I2405
____ and Frank, N. H. Electromagnetism. 1947. I2406
____. Introduction to theoretical physics. 1933. I2407
____. Mechanics. 1947. I2408
Smythe, W. R. Static and dynamic electricity. 1950. I2409
Squire, C. F. Low temperature physics. 1953. I2410
Stratton, J. A. Electromagnetic theory. 1941. I2411
Thorndike, A. M. Mesons. 1952. I2412
Tinkham, M. Group theory and quantum mechanics. 1964. I2413
Townes, C. H. and Schlawlow, A. L. Microwave spectroscopy. 1955. I2414
Wang, S. Solid state electronics. 1966. I2415
White, H. E. Introduction to atomic spectra. 1934. I2416

INTERNATIONAL SERIES IN THE BEHAVIORAL SCIENCES (Houghton)

Ahmavaara, Y. Theory of behavioral dimension. 1968. I2417
Bonner, H. On being mindful of man. 1965. I2418
Eysenck, H. J. Crime and personality. 1964. I2419
Horrocks, J. E. and Jackson, D. The nature and development of the self. 1972. I2420
Lawson, C. A. Brain mechanisms and human learning. 1967. I2421
Manaster, G. J. and Havighurst, R. J. Cross-national research. 1972. I2422
Murphy, G. and Spohn, H. Encounter with reality. 1968. I2423
Sherif, M. In common predicament. 1966. I2424

INTERNATIONAL SERIES IN THE EARTH SCIENCES (McGraw)

Ager, D. V. Principles of paleoecology. 1963. I2425
Belousov, V. V. Basic problems of geotectonics, ed. by Maxwell. 1962. I2426
Berner, R. A. Principles of chemical sedimentology. 1971. I2427
Broecker, W. S. and Oversby, V. M. Chemical equilibria

in the earth. 1970. I2428
Cagniard, L. Reflections and refractions of progressive seismic waves, tr. by Flinn and Hewitt. 1962. I2429
Domenico, P. A. Groundwater hydrology. 1972. I2430
Ewing, G. W. and others. Elastic waves in layered media. 1960. I2431
Feynman, R. and Hibbs, A. R. Quantum mechanics. 1965. I2432
Grant, F. S. and West, G. F. Interpretation theory in applied geophysics. 1965. I2433
Griffith, J. C. Scientific method in analysis of sediments. 1967. I2434
Grim, R. E. Applied clay mineralogy. 1962. I2435
____. Clay mineralogy. 1953. I2436
Heinrich, E. W. Mineralogy and geology of radioactive raw materials. 1959. I2437
Heiskanen, W. A. and Vening Meinesz, F. A. The earth and its gravity field. 1958. I2438
Howell, B. F. Introduction to geophysics. 1959. I2439
Hyndman, D. W. Petrology of igneous and metamorphic rocks. 1972. I2439a
Jacobs, J. A. and others. Physics and geology. 1959. I2439b
Krauskopf, K. B. Introduction to geochemistry. 1967. I2439c
Krumbein, W. C. and Graybill, F. A. An introduction to statistical models in geology. 1965. I2439d
Koznet͡sov, S. I. and others. Introduction to geological microbiology, tr. by Broneer. 1963. I2439e
Legget, R. F. Geology and engineering. 1962. I2439f
Manskaia, S. M. and Drizdiva, T. V. Geochemistry of organic substances. 1968. I2439g
Menard, H. W. Marine geology of the Pacific. 1964. I2439h
Miller, V. C. and C. F. Photogeology. 1961. I2439i
Morisawa, W. Streams. 1968. I2439j
Morris, P. M. and Ingard, K. U. Theoretical acoustics. 1968. I2440
Officer, C. F. Introduction to the theory of sound transmission. 1958. I2441
Ramsay, J. G. Folding and fracturing of rocks. 1967. I2442
Robertson, E. The nature of solid earth. 1972. I2443
Rossi, B. and Olbert, S. Introduction to the physics of space. 1970. I2444
Shaw, A. B. Time in stratigraphy. 1964. I2445
Shrock, R. R. and Twenhofel, W. H. Principles of invertebrate paleontology. 1953. I2446
Sitter, L. U. de. Structural geology. 1964. I2447
Stanton, R. L. Ore petrology. 1972. I2448
Strangeway, D. W. The history of the earth's magnetic field. 1970. I2449
Starr, V. P. Physics of negative viscosity phenomena. 1968. I2450
Tolstoy, I. Fundamentals of wave propagation. 1973. I2451
Turner, F. J. Metamorphic petrology. 1968. I2452
____ and Verhoogen, J. Igneous and metamorphic petrology. 1960. I2453
____ and Weiss, L. E. Structural analysis of metamorphic tectonites. 1963. I2454
White, J. E. Seismic waves. 1965. I2455
Wood, J. A. Meteorites and the origin of the solar system. 1968. I2456

INTERNATIONAL SERIES OF MONOGRAPHS IN CHEMICAL ENGINEERING (Pergamon)

1 Wilkinson, W. L. Non-Newtonian fluids. 1960. I2457
2 Jamrack, W. D. Rare metal extraction by chemical engineering techniques. 1963. I2458
3 Nagiev, M. F. The theory of recycle processes in

chemical engineering, tr. by Harbottle, ed. by Nedderman. 1964. I2459
4 Bradley, D. The hydrocyclone. 1965. I2460
5 Sterbáček, Z. and Tausk, P. Mixing in the chemical industry, tr. by Mayer. 1965. I2461
6 Hobler, T. Mass transfer and absorbers, tr. by Bandrowski, tr. by Hartland. 1966. I2462
7 Rosenbrock, H. H. and Storey, C. Computational techniques for chemical engineers. 1966. I2463
8 Strauss, W. Industrial gas cleaning. 1966. I2464
9 King, M. B. Phase equilibrium in mixtures. 1967. I2465
10 Brown, R. L. and Richards, J. C. Principles of powder mechanics. 1970. I2466
11 Bretsnajder, S. Prediction of transport and other physical properties of fluids. 1971. I2467
12 Grassman, P. Physical principles of chemical engineering. 1970. I2468

INTERNATIONAL SERIES OF MONOGRAPHS IN EARTH SCIENCES (Pergamon)

1 Contributions in geophysics in honor of Beno Gutenberg, ed. by Benioff and others. 1958. I2469
2 Nat'l. Conf. on Clay and Clay Minerals. Clay and clay minerals. 1959. I2470
3 Ginzburg, I. I. Principles of geochemical prospecting, tr. by Sokoloff. 1960. I2471
4 Wait, J. R., ed. Overvoltage research and geophysical applications. 1959. I2472
5 Nat'l. Conference on Clay and Clay Minerals. Clay and clay minerals. 1962. I2473
6 Tíutiunov, I. A. An introduction to the theory of the formation of frozen rocks, tr. by Muhlhaus. 1964. I2474
7 Krinov, E. Principles of meteoritics, tr. by Vidzuinas. 1960. I2475
8 Nalivkin, D. V. The geology of the U. S. S. R., tr. by Richey. 1960. I2476
9 Same as no. 5. V. 2. 1961. I2477
10 Pokorný, V. Principles of zoological micropaleontology, tr. by Allen. V. 1. 1963. I2478
11-13 Same as no. 5. V. 3-5. 1962-63. I2479
14 Int'l. Clay Conference. Proceedings of the Conference held at Stockholm, Sweden, ed. by Rosenquist and Graff-Peterson. V. 1. 1963. I2480
15 Geochemical Society. Organic Geochemistry Group. Advances in organic geochemistry. 1964. I2481
16 Breger, I. A., ed. Organic chemistry. 1963. I2482
17 Helgeson, H. C. Complexing and hydrothermal ore disposition. 1964. I2483
18 Battey, M. H. and Tomkeieff, S. I., eds. Aspects of theoretical mineralogy in the U. S. S. R. 1964. I2484
19 Same as no. 5. V. 6. 1964. I2485
20 Same as no. 10. V. 2. 1964. I2486
21 Same as no. 14. V. 2. 1965. I2487
22 Ermakov, N. P. and others. Research on the nature of mineral-forming solutions, tr. by Sokoloff, ed. by Roedder. 1965. I2488
23 Same as no. 5. Index to volumes 1-10, ed. by Bridge. 1965. I2489
24 International Congress on Organic Geochemistry. Advances in organic geochemistry, ed. by Hobson and Louis. 1966. I2490
25 Same as no. 2. V. 2. 1966. I2491
26 Same as no. 5. 14th Conference. 1966. I2492
27 Same as no. 5. 15th Conference. 1967. I2493

28 Manskaia͡, S. M. and Drozdova, T. V. Geochemistry of organic substances. 1969. I2494

29 Dobri͡anskii, A. F. and others. Transformation of petroleum in nature, tr. by Barghoorn and Silverman. 1968. I2495

30 Origin and distribution of the elements, ed. by Ahrens. 1969. I2496

31 International Meeting on Organic Geochemistry. Advances in organic geochemistry, ed. by Schenk. 1969. I2497

32 International Congress on Organic Geochemistry. Advances in organic geochemistry, ed. by Hobson and Speers. 1969. I2498

33 ____. Advances in organic geochemistry. 1972. I2499

INTERNATIONAL SERIES OF MONOGRAPHS IN ELECTRICAL ENGINEERING (Pergamon)

1 Bean, A. R. and Simons, R. H. Light fittings. 1968. I2500

2 Wilson, D. R. Modern practice in servo design. 1969. I2501

3 Knight, U. G. Power systems engineering and mathematics. 1972. I2502

4 Jones, N. New approaches to the design and economics of EHV transmission plants. 1972. I2503

5 Bowdler, G. W. Measurements in high-voltage test circuits. 1973. I2504

6 Murphy, J. M. D. Thyristor control of AC motors. 1973. I2505

7 Mittra, R. Computer techniques for electromagnetics. 1973. I2506

INTERNATIONAL SERIES OF MONOGRAPHS IN ELECTROMAGNETIC WAVES (Pergamon)

1 Fok, V. A. Electromagnetic diffraction and propagation problems. 1965. I2507

2 Smith, E. K. and Matsushita, S., eds. Ionospheric sporadic E. 1962. I2508

3 Wait, J. R. Electromagnetic waves in stratified media. 1962. I2509

4 Beckmann, P. and Spizzichino, A. The scattering of electromagnetic waves from rough surfaces. 1963. I2510

5 Interdisciplinary Conf. on Electromagnetic Scattering. Electromagnetic scattering, ed. by Kerker. 1963. I2511

6 Symposium on Electromagnetic Theory and Antenna. Electromagnetic theory and antennas, ed. by Jordan. 2 v. 1963. I2512

7 Ginzburg, V. L. The propagation of electromagnetic waves in plasmas, tr. by Sykes and Tayler. 1964. I2513

8 DuCastel, F. Tropospheric radiowave propagation beyond the horizon, tr. by Sofaer and Wait. 1966. I2514

9 Baños, A. Dipole radiation in the presence of a conducting half-space. 1966. I2515

10 Keller, G. V. and Frischknecht, F. L. Electrical methods in geophysical prospecting. 1966. I2516

11 U. R. S. I. Symposium on Electromagnetic Wave Theory. Electromagnetic wave theory, ed. by Brown. 1967. I2517

12 Clemmow, P. C. The plane wave spectrum representation of electromagnetic fluids. 2 v. 1966. I2518

13 Kerns, D. M. and Beatty, R. W. Basic theory of wave guide junctions and introductory microwave network analysis. 1967. I2519

14 Watt, A. D. V L F radio engineering. 1967. I2520

15 Galejs, J. Antennas in inhomogeneous media. 1968. I2521

16 ____. Terrestrial propagation of long electromagnetic waves. 1972. I2522

17 Monteath, G. D. Applications on the electromagnetic reciprocity principle. 1972. I2523

INTERNATIONAL SERIES OF MONOGRAPHS IN EXPERIMENTAL PSYCHOLOGY (Pergamon)

1 Gray, J. A., ed. Pavlov's typology. 1964. I2524
2 Holland, H. C. The spiral after-effect. 1965. I2525
3 Lynn, R. Attention, arousal, and the orientation reaction. 1966. I2526
4 Claridge, G. S. Personality and arousal. 1967. I2527
5 Fellows, B. J. The discrimination process and development. 1968. I2528
6 Beech, H. R. and Fransella, F. Research and experiment in stuttering. 1968. I2529
7 Joffe, J. M. Prenatal determinants of behaviour. 1969. I2530
8 Martin, I. and Levy, A. B. Genesis of the classical conditioned response. 1969. I2531
9 Baird, J. C. Psychophysical analysis of visual space. 1970. I2532
10 Meldman, M. J. Diseases of attention. 1970. I2533
11 Shaw, L. and Sichel, H. S. Accident proneness. 1970. I2534
12 Lynn, R. Personality and national character. 1971. I2535
13 Stroh, C. M. Vigilance. 1971. I2536
14 Feldman, M. P. and MacCulloch, M. J. Homosexual behavior. 1971. I2537
15 Rachman, S. The effects of psychotherapy. 1971. I2538
16 Kolers, P. A. Aspects of motion perception. 1972. I2539
17 Levi, L., ed. Stress and distress in response to psychosocial stimuli. 1972. I2540
18 Claridge, G. S. and others. Personality differences and biological variations. 1973. I2541

INTERNATIONAL SERIES OF MONOGRAPHS IN HEATING, VENTILATION, AND REFRIGERATION (Pergamon)

1 Osborne, W. C. Fans. 1966. I2542
2 Ede, A. J. An introduction to heat transfer. 1967. I2543
3 Kut, D. Heating and hot water services in buildings. 1968. I2544
4 Amgus, T. C. The control of indoor climate. 1968. I2545
5 Down, P. G. Heating and cooling load calculations. 1969. I2546
6 Diamant, R. M. E. Total energy. 1970. I2547
7 Kut, D. Warm air heating. 1970. I2548

INTERNATIONAL SERIES OF MONOGRAPHS IN INTERDISCIPLINARY AND ADVANCED TOPICS IN SCIENCE AND ENGINEERING (Pergamon)

1 Sedov, L. I. Foundations of the non-linear mechanics of continua, tr. by Schoenfeld-Reiner. 1966. I2549
2 Eaton, J. R. Electrons, neutrons and protons in engineering. 1966. I2550
3 Chang, P. K. Separation of flow. 1970. I2551

INTERNATIONAL SERIES OF MONOGRAPHS IN NATURAL PHILOSOPHY (Pergamon)

1 Davydov, A. S. Quantum mechanics, tr. by ter Haar. 1965. I2552
2 Fokker, A. D. Time and space, weight and inertia, tr. by Bijl. 1965. I2553
3 Kaplan, S. A. Interstellar gas dynamics, ed. by Kahn. 1966. I2554
4 Abrikosov, L. P. and others. Quantum field theoretical methods in statistical physics, tr. by Brown. 1965. I2555
5 Okun', L. B. Weak interaction of elementary particles,

tr. by Nikolić, ed. by Bernstein. 1965. I2556
6 Shklovskiĭ, I. S. Physics of the solar corona, ed. by Beer, tr. by Meadows. 1965. I2557
7 Azhiezer, A. K. and others. Collective oscillators in a plasma, tr. by Massey. 1967. I2558
8 Kirzhnits, D. A. Field theoretical methods in many-body systems, tr. by Meadows, ed. by Brink. 1967. I2559
9 Klimontovich, I. L. The statistical theory of non-equilibrium processes in a plasma, tr. by Massey and Blunn. 1967. I2560
10 Kurth, R. Introduction to stellar statistics. 1967. I2561
11 Chalmers, J. A. Atmospheric electricity. 1967. I2562
12 Renner, B. Current algebras and their applications. 1968. I2563
13-14 Fain, V. M. and Khanin, Y. I. Quantum electronics. 2 v. 1969. I2564
15 March, N. H. Liquid metals. 1968. I2565
16 Hori, J. Spectral properties of disordered chains and lattices. 1968. I2566
17 Saint-James, D. and others. Type II superconductivity. 1969. I2567
18 Margenau, H. and Kestner, N. R. Theory of intermolecular forces. 1969. I2568
19 Jancel, R. Foundations of classical and quantum statistical mechanics. 1969. I2569
20 Takahashi, Y. An introduction to field organization. 1969. I2570
21 Yvon, J. Correlations and entropy in classical statistical mechanics, tr. by Massey. 1969. I2571
22 Penrose, O. Foundations of statistical mechanics. 1970. I2572
23 Visconti, A. Quantum field theory. V. 1. 1970. I2573
24 Furth, O. Fundamental principles of modern theoretical physics. 1970. I2574
25 Zhelezynakov, V. V. Radio emission of the sun and planets. 1970. I2575
26 Grindlay, J. Introduction to the phenomenological theory of ferroelectricity. 1970. I2576
27 Unger, H. F. Introduction to quantum electronics. 1970. I2577
28 Koga, T. Introduction to kinetic theory. 1970. I2578
29 Galasiewicz, Z. Superconductivity and quantum fluids. 1971. I2579
30 Constantinescu, F. and Magyari, E. Problems in quantum mechanics. 1971. I2580
31 Kotkin, G. L. and Serbo, V. G. Collection of problems in classical mechanics. 1971. I2581
32 Panchev, S. Random functions and turbulence. 1971. I2582
33 Talpe, J. Theory of experiments in paramagnetic resonance. 1971. I2583
34 Ter Haar, D. Elements of Hamiltonian mechanics. 1971. I2584
35 Clarke, D. Polarized light and optical measurements. 1971. I2585
36 Haug, A. Theoretical solid state physics. V. 1. 1972. I2586
37 Jordan, P. The expanding earth, tr. and ed. by Beers. 1971. I2587
38 Todorov, I. T. Analytic properties of Feynman diagrams in quantum field theory, tr. by Risk. 1971. I2588
39 Sitenko, A. G. Lectures on scattering theory. 1971. I2589
40 Sobel'man, I. I. Introduction to the theory of atomic spectra. 1972. I2590
41 Armstrong, B. H. and Nicholls, R. W. Emission, absorption and transfer of radiation in heated atmosphere. 1972. I2591

42 Brush, S. G. Kinetic theory. V. 3. 1973. I2592
43 Bogoliubov, N. N. A method for studying model hamiltonians, ed. by Shepherd. 1972. I2593
44 TStovich, V. N. An introduction to the theory of plasma turbulence. 1972. I2594
45 Pathria, R. K. Advanced statistical mechanics. 1972. I2595
46 Same as no. 36. V. 2. 1972. I2596
47 Nieto, M. M. The Titius-Bode law of planetary distance. 1972. I2597
48 Wagner, D. Theory of electromagnetism. 1972. I2598
49 Irvine, J. M. Nuclear structure theory. 1972. I2599
50 Strohmeier, W. Variable stars, ed. by Meadows. 1972. I2600
51 Batten, A. H. Binary and multiple systems of stars. 1972. I2601
52 Rousseau, M. and Mathieu, J. P. Problems in optics. 1973. I2602
54 Pomraning, G. C. The equations of radiation hydrodynamics. 1973. I2603
55 Belinfante, J. A survey of hidden-variable theories. 1973. I2604
56 Scheibe, E. The logical analysis of quantum mechanics, tr. by Sykes. 1973. I2605
57 Robinson, F. N. H. Microscopic electromagnetism. 1973. I2606
58 Gombas, P. and Kisdi, P. Wave mechanics and its applications. 1973. I2607
59 Kaplan, S. A. and Tsytovich, V. N. Plasma astrophysics. 1973. I2608
60 Kovács, I. and Zsoldos, L. Dislocations and plastic deformation. 1974. I2609
61 Auvray, J. Problems in electronics. 1974. I2610
62 Mathieu, J. P. Optics. 2 v. 1974. I2611
63 Atwater, H. A. Introduction to general relativity. 1974. I2612
64 Müller, A. Quantum mechanics, tr. by Rona. 1974. I2613
65 Bilen'ky, S. M. Introduction to Feynman diagrams. 1974. I2614
66 Voder, B. and others. Some aspects of vacuum ultraviolet radiation physics. 1974. I2615
67 Willett, C. S. Gas lasers. 1974. I2616
68 Akhiezer, A. I. Plasma electrodynamics. V. 2. 1974. I2617
69 Glasby, J. S. The nebular variables. 1974. I2618
70 Bialynicky-Birula, I. Quantum electrodynamics. 1974. I2619
71 Karpman, V. Non-linear waves in dispersive media. 1974. I2620
72 Cracknell, A. P. Magnetism in cryatalline materials. 1974. I2621
73 Pathria, R. K. Theory of relativity. 1974. I2622

INTERNATIONAL SERIES OF MONOGRAPHS IN SEMICONDUCTORS (Pergamon)

1 Hilsum, C. and Rose-Innes, A. C. Semiconducting III-V compounds. 1961. I2623
2 Tauc, J. Photo and thermoelectric effects in semiconductors, tr. by Laner. 1962. I2624
3 Blakemore, J. S. Semiconductor statistics. 1962. I2625
4 Drabble, J. R. and Goldsmid, H. J. Thermal conduction in semiconductors. 1961. I2626
5 Henisch, H. K. Electroluminescence. 1962. I2627
6 Rhodes, R. G. Imperfections and active centres in semiconductors. 1964. I2628
7 Frankl, D. R. Electrical properties of semi-conductor surfaces. 1967. I2629
8 Weiss, H. Structure and applications of galvanmagnetic devices. 1969. I2630

9 Wolf, H. F. Silicon semiconductor data. 1970. I2631
10 Wieder, H. H. Intermetallic transport in semiconductors. 1970. I2632

INTERNATIONAL SERIES OF MONOGRAPHS ON AERONAUTICS AND ASTRONAUTICS (Pergamon)

Early volumes published as: Int'l. Series of Monographs on Aeronautical Sciences and Space Flight.

Division 1: Solid and structural mechanics.
1 Savin, G. N. Stress concentration around holes. 1961. I2633
2 Gol'denveizer, A. L. Theory of elastic thin shells, ed. by Herrmann. 1961. I2634
3 Nowacki, W. Thermoelasticity. 1962. I2635
4 Cox, H. L. The buckling of plates and skills. 1963. I2636
5 Morley, L. S. B. Shew plates and structures. 1963. I2637
6 Mansfield, E. H. The bending and stretching of plates. 1964. I2638
7 Schuh, H. Heat transfer in structures. 1964. I2639
8 Cox, H. L. The design of structure of least weight. 1965. I2640
9 Washizu, K. Variational methods in elasticity and plasticity. 1969. I2641

Division 2: Aerodynamics.
1 Scorer, R. S. Natural aerodynamics. 1958. I2642
2 Landhahl, M. T. Unsteady transonic flow. 1961. I2643
3 Guderley, K. G. The theory of transonic flow. 1962. I2644
4 Martynov, A. K. Practical aerodynamics, tr. by Brix, ed. by Pankhurst. 1965. I2645
5 Irving, F. G. An introduction to the longitudinal static stability of low-speed aircraft. 1966. I2646
6 Loit͡sianskiĭ, L. G. Mechanics of liquids and gases. 1966. I2647
7 Carafoli, E. and others. Wing theory in supersonic flow. 1969. I2648

Division 3: Propulsion systems including fuels.
1 Penner, S. S. Chemistry problems in jet propulsion. 1957. I2649
2 Ducarme, J. and others, eds. Progress in combustion and technology. 1961. I2650
3 Ragozin, N. A. Jet propulsion fuels, tr. by Jones. 1961. I2651
4 Kholschevnikov, K. V. Some problems in the theory and assessment of turbo-jet engines, tr. by Jones. 1964. I2652
5 Zuev, V. S. and Skubachevskii, L. S. Combustion chambers for jet propulsion engines, tr. by Jones, ed. by Mullins. 1964. I2653
6 Goodger, E. M. Principles of space flight propulsion. 1970. I2654

Division 6: Flight testing.
1 Babister, A. W. Aircraft stability and control. 1961. I2655

Division 7: Astronautics.
1, 2 U.S. Air Force. Office of Scientific Research. Astronautics symposium. 2 v. 1957. I2656
3 Draper, C. S. and others. Inertial guidance. 1960. I2657
4 Nikolaev, B. A. Thermodynamics assessment of rocket engines, tr. by Jones. 1963. I2658
5 Gantmakher, F. R. and Levin, L. M. The flight of uncontrolled rockets, tr. by Blunn. 1964. I2659

Division 8: Materials, science and engineering.
1 Harris, W. J. Metallic fatigue. 1961. I2660

Division 9: Symposia.
Symposium on Naval Structural Mechanics. Structural mechanics; proceedings, ed. by Goodier and others. 1960.

1 Intl. Congress for the Aeronautical Sciences. Advances in aeronautical sciences; Proceedings, ed. by Von Kármán and others. 4 v. 1959-62. I2661
2 Advanced Propulsion Systems Symposium. Advanced propulsion systems; proceedings, ed. by Alperin and others. 1959. I2662
3 Intl. Symposium on Rarified Gas Dynamics. Proceedings. 1959- I2663
4 Durand Centennial Conference Aeronautics and Astronautics; proceedings, ed. by Hoff and Vincenti. 1960. I2664
5 Symposium on Full-Scale Fatigue Testing of Aircraft Structures. Full scale fatigue testing of aircraft structures; proceedings, ed. by Plantema and Schijve. 1961. I2665
6 Seminar on Astronautics. Current research in astronautical sciences; proceedings, ed. by Broglio. 1961. I2666
7-8 Same as no. 1. V. 3-4. 1962. I2667
9 Intl. Flight Test Instrumentation Symposium. Flight test instrumentation; proceedings. V. 1. 1960. I2668
10 European Congress of Aviation Medicine. Human problems of supersonic and hypersonic flight. 1962. I2669
11 Seminar on Astronautical Propulsion. Advances in astronautical propulsion. 1962. I2670
12 Symposium on Fatigue of Aircraft Structure. Fatigue of aircraft structures, ed. by Barrois and Ripley. 1963. I2671
13 Symposium on Network Theory. Recent development in network theory, ed. by Deards. 1963. I2672
14 Same as no. 9. V. 2. 1963. I2673
15 Ferrari, C. High temperatures in aeronautics. 1964. I2674
16 Space Engineering Symposium. Development of the Blue Streak satellite launchers, ed. by Samson. 1963. I2675
17 Seminario sui "combustibili e propellenti nuovi." Fuels and new propellants, ed. by Casci. 1964. I2676
18 Singer, S. F., ed. Interactions of space vehicles with an ionized atmosphere. 1965. I2677
19 Symposium on Current Aeronautical Fatigue Problems. Current aeronautical fatigue problems, ed. by Schijve and others. 1965. I2678
20 Fatigue design procedures, ed. by Gassner and Schütz. 1969. I2679

INTERNATIONAL SERIES OF MONOGRAPHS ON ANALYTICAL CHEMISTRY (Pergamon)

1 Weisz, H. Microanalysis by the ring oven technique. 1961. I2680
2 Crouthamel, C. E., ed. Applied gamma-ray spectrometry. 1960. I2681
3 Vickery, R. C. Analytical chemistry of the rare earths. 1961. I2682
4 Headridge, J. B. Photometric titrations. 1961. I2683
5 Buser, A. I. The analytical chemistry of indium, tr. by Greaves. 1962. I2684
6 Elwell, W. T. and Gidley, J. A. F. Atomic-absorption spectrophotometry. 1962. I2685
7 Erdey, L. Gravimetric analysis, tr. by Svehla, ed. by Buzás. 1963. I2686
8 Critchfield, F. E. Organic functional group analyses. 1963. I2687
9 Moses, A. J. Analytical chemistry of the actinide elements. 1963. I2688
10 Ri͡abchikov, D. I. and Gol'braikh, E. K. The analytical chemistry of thorium, tr. by Norris. 1963. I2689
11 Cali, J. P., ed. Trace analysis of semiconductor

materials. 1964. I2690
12 Zuma, P. Organic polargraphic analysis. 1964. I2691
13 Rechnitz, G. A. Controlled-potential analysis. 1963. I2692
14 Milner, O. I. Analysis of petroleum for trace elements. 1963. I2693
15 Alimarian, I. P. and Petrikova, M. N. Inorganic ultramicroanalysis. 1964. I2694
16 Moshier, R. W. Analytical chemistry of niobium and tantalum. 1964. I2695
17 Jeffery, P. G. and Kipping, P. J. Gas analysis by gas chromatography. 1964. I2696
18 Nielsen, A. E. Kinetics of precipitation. 1964. I2697
19 Caley, E. R. Analysis of ancient metals. 1964. I2698
20 Moses, A. J. Nuclear techniques on analytical chemistry. 1964. I2699
21 Pungor, E. Oscillometry and conductametry, tr. by Damokos, ed. by Townshend. 1965. I2700
22 Berka, A. and others. Newer redox titrants, tr. by Weisz. 1965. I2701
23 Moshier, R. W. and Sievers, R. E. Gas chromatography of metal chelates. 1965. I2702
24 Beamish, F. E. The analytical chemistry of the noble metals. 1966. I2703
25 I͡Atsimirskiĭ, K. B. Kinetic methods of analysis, tr. by Harvey. 1966. I2704
26 Szabadvary, F. History of analytical chemistry, tr. by Svehla. 1966. I2705
27 Young, R. S. The analytical chemistry of cobalt. 1966. I2706
28 Lewis, C. L. and others. The analysis of nickel. 1966. I2707
29 Braun, T. and Tölgyessy, J. Radiometric titrations, tr. by Finaly, ed. by Townshend. 1967. I2708
30 Ružička, J. and Starý, J. Substoichiometry in radiochemical analysis. 1968. I2709
31 Crompton, T. R. Analysis of organoaluminium and organozinc compounds. 1968. I2710
32 Schilt, A. A. Analytical applications of 1, 10-phen'-anthroline and related compounds. 1968. I2711
33 Bark, L. S. and S. M. Thermometric titrimetry. 1969. I2712
34 Guilbault, G. G. Enzymatic methods of analysis. 1970. I2713
35 Wainerdi, R. E. Analytical chemistry in space. 1970. I2714
36 Jeffery, P. G. Chemical methods of rock analysis. 1970. I2715
37 Weisz, H. Microanalysis by the ring-oven technique. 2d ed. 1970. I2716
38 Riemann, W. and Walton, H. Ion exchange in analytical chemistry. 1970. I2717
39 Gorsuch, T. T. The destruction of organic matter. 1970. I2718
40 Mukherji, A. R. Analytical chemistry of zirconium and hafnium. 1970. I2719
41 Adams, F. and Dams, R. Applied gamma-ray spectrometry. 2d ed. 1970. I2720
42 Beckey, H. D. Field ionization mass spectrometry. 1971. I2721
43 Lewis, C. L. Analytical chemistry of nickel. 1971. I2722
44 Silverman, L. The determination of impurities in nuclear grade sodium metal. 1971. I2723
45 Kuhnert-Brandstätter, M. Thermomicroscopy in the analysis of pharmaceuticals. 1971. I2724
46 Crompton, T. R. Chemical analysis of additives in plastics. 1971. I2725
47 Elwell, W. T. and Wood, D. F. Analytical chemistry of molybdenum and tungston. 1971. I2726
48 Beamish, F. E. and Van Loon, J. C. Advances in the analytical chemistry of

noble metals. 1971. I2727
49 Tölgyessy, J. and others. Isotope dilution analysis. 1972. I2728
50 Majumbar, A. K. N-benzoylphenylhydroxylamine and its analogues. 1972. I2729
51 Bishop, E., ed. Bishop indicators. 1972. I2730
52 Pribil, F. Analytical applications of EDTA and related compounds. 1972. I2731
53 Baker, A. D. and Betteridge, D. Photoelectron spectroscopy. 1972. I2732
54 Burger, K. Organic reagents in metal analyses, tr. by Mohacsy. 1973. I2733
55 Muzzarelli, R. A. A. Natural chelating polymers. 1974. I2734

INTERNATIONAL SERIES OF MONOGRAPHS ON AUTOMATION AND AUTOMATIC CONTROL (Pergamon)

1 Malov, V. S. Telemechanics, tr. by Inmirzi, ed. by Meltzer and Walker. 1964. I2735
2 Lossievskii, V. L. and Plishkin, L. J. Automation of continuous production processes, tr. by Froom, ed. by Ghosh. 1964. I2736
3 Polonnikov, D. Y. Electronic amplifiers for automatic compensators, tr. by Inston, ed. by Glass. 1965. I2737
4 Butusov, I. V. Automatic control measuring and regulating devices, tr. by Segal, ed. by Glass. 1965. I2738
5 Pugachev, V. S. Theory of random functions and its application to control problems, tr. by Blunn, ed. by Johnson. 1965. I2739
6 Meerov, M. V. Structural synthesis of high-accuracy automatic control systems, tr. by Ruban, ed. by Ashdown. 1965. I2740
7 Ginzburg, S. A. and others. Fundamentals of automation and remote control, tr. by Farkas and Schorr-Kon, tr. by Howl. 1966. I2741

INTERNATIONAL SERIES OF MONOGRAPHS ON CHILD PSYCHIATRY (Pergamon)

1 Harms, E., ed. Somatic and psychiatric aspects of childhood allergies. 1963. I2742
2 ____. Problems of sleep and dream in children. 1964. I2743
3 ____. Drug addiction in youth. 1965. I2744

INTERNATIONAL SERIES OF MONOGRAPHS ON ELECTRONICS AND INSTRUMENTATION (Pergamon)

No. 1 published as: ELECTRONICS AND WAVES: A SERIES OF MONOGRAPHS. No. 2-7 appeared as PERGAMON SCIENCE SERIES. ELECTRONICS AND WAVES.
1 Gillespie, A. B. Signal; noise and resolution in nuclear counter simplifiers. 1953. I2745
2 Birks, J. B. Scintillation counters. 1953. I2746
3 Woodward, P. M. Probability and information theory, with applications to radar. 1953. I2747
4 Bruining, H. Physics and applications of secondary electron emission. 1954. I2748
5 Lewis, I. A. D. Millimicrosecond pulse technique. 1959. I2749
6 Wass, C. A. A. Introduction to electronic analogue computers. 1955. I2750
7 Mentzer, J. R. Scattering and diffraction of radio waves. 1955. I2751
8 Beck, A. H. W. Space-change wave, and slow electro-magnetic waves. 1958. I2752
9 Helstrom, C. W. Statistical theory of signal detection. 1960. I2753
10 Holbrook, J. G. Laplace transforms for electronic

engineers. 1959. I2754
11 Fagot, J. and Magne, P. Frequency modulation theory. 1961. I2755
12 Gvozdover, S. D. and Hass, W. P. A. Theory of microwave valves. 1961. I2756
13 Kitov, A. I. and Krinitskii, N. A. Electronic computers, tr. by Froom, ed. by Booth. 1962. I2757
14 Nadler, M. Topics in engineering logic. 1962. I2758
15 Dummer, G. W. A. and Griffin, N. Environmental testing techniques for electronics and materials. 1962. I2759
16 Shevchik, V. N. Fundamentals of microwave electronics, tr. by Thompson. 1963. I2760
17 Rozhanskiĭ, L. L. Static electromagnetic frequency changers, tr. by Colin. 1963. I2761
18 Anempodistov, V. P. and others. Problems in the design and development of 750 M W turbogenerators, tr. by Urusov. 1963. I2762
19 Doganovskiĭ, S. A. and Ivanov, V. A. Controlled-delay devices, tr. by Blunn. 1963. I2763
20 Watt, D. E. and Ramsden, D. High sensitivity counting control. 1963. I2764
21 Botvinnik, M. M. Asychronized synchronous machines, tr. by Thompson, ed. by Westwood. 1964. I2765
22-23 T͡Sypkin, I͡A. Z. Sampling systems theory and its application, 1964. I2766
24 Venikov, V. A. Transient phenomena in electrical power systems, tr. by Adkins and Rutenberg. 1964. I2767
25 Shileiko, A. V. Digital differential analysers, tr. by Barrett, ed. by Booth. 1964. I2768
26 Thourel, L. The use of ferrites at microwave frequencies, tr. by Arthur. 1964. I2769
27 Birks, J. B. The theory and practice of scintillation counting. 1964. I2770
28 Bulgakov, A. A. Energetic processes in follow-up electrical control systems, tr. by Arthur, ed. by Ghosh. 1965. I2771
29 Ulanov, G. M. Excitation control, tr. by Thompson, ed. by Walker. 1964. I2772
30 Keropi͡an, K. K., ed. Electrical analogues of pin-jointed systems, tr. by Garfield. 1965. I2773
31 Vorob'eva, T. M. Electromagnetic clutches and couplings, tr. by Blunn, ed. by Booth. 1965. I2774
32 Bultot, E. Elements of theoretical mechanics for electronic engineers, tr. by Knowlson. 1965. I2775
33 Anismova, N. D. and others. Transient phenomena in electrical power systems, ed. by Venikov, tr. by Kaplan. 1965. I2776
34 Shevchik, V. N. and others. Wave and oscillatory phenomena in electron beams at microwave frequencies, tr. by Blunn, ed. by Meltzer. 1965. I2777
35 Benjamin, R. Modulation, resolution and signal processing in radar, sonar and related systems. 1966. I2778
36 Zelinger, A. Basic matrix analysis and synthesis. 1969. I2779

INTERNATIONAL SERIES OF MONOGRAPHS ON INORGANIC CHEMISTRY (Pergamon)

1 International Symposium on Chemistry of the Co-ordinate Compounds. Chemistry of the co-ordinate compounds. 1958. I2780
2 Vickery, R. C. The chemistry of yttrium and scadium. 1960. I2781
3 Graddon, D. P. An introduction to co-ordination chemistry. 1961. I2782
4 Ebsworth, E. A. V. Volatile

silicon compounds. 1963. I2783

INTERNATIONAL SERIES OF MONOGRAPHS ON LIBRARY AND INFORMATION SCIENCE (Macmillan)

1 White, C. M. Bases of modern librarianship. 1964. I2784
2 Anthony, L. J. Sources of information on atomic energy. 1966. I2785
3 Blaug, M. Economics of education. 1966. I2786
4 Saunders, W. L. The provision and use of library documentation services. 1966. I2787
5 Campbell, H. C. Metropolitan public library planning throughout the world. 1967. I2788
6 Baranson, J. Technology for underdeveloped areas. 1967. I2789
7 Yescombe, E. R. Sources of information in the rubber, plastics and allied industries. 1968. I2790
8 Saunders, W. L., comp. University and research library studies. 1968. I2791
9 Burkett, J. Special libraries and documentation centers in the Netherlands. 1968. I2792
10 Kimber, R. T. Automation in libraries. 1968. I2793
11 Bakewell, K. G. B. Industrial libraries throughout the world. 1969. I2794
12 Hale, B. M. The subject bibliography of the social sciences and humanities. 1970. I2795
13 Ellis, A. Library services for young people in England and Wales, 1830-1970. 1971. I2796
14 Bakewell, K. G. B. A manual of cataloguing practice. 1972. I2797
15 Hodson, J. H. The administration of archives. 1972. I2798

INTERNATIONAL SERIES OF MONOGRAPHS ON METAL PHYSICS AND PHYSICAL METALLURGY (Pergamon)

1-3 published as Metal Physics and Physical Metallurgy. Now called this series.
1 Kubaschewski, O. and Evans, E. L. Metallurgical thermochemistry. 1958. I2799
2 Jaswon, M. A. The theory of cohesion. 1954. I2800
3 Kubaschewski, O. and Catterall, J. A. Thermochemical data of alloys. 1956. I2801
4 Pearson, W. B. A handbook of lattice spacing and structure of metals and alloys. 1958. I2802
5 Raynor, G. V. The physical metallurgy of magnesium and its alloys. 1959. I2803
6 Weiss, R. J. Solid state physics for metallurgists. 1963. I2804
7 Christian, J. W. The theory of transformations in metals and alloys. 1965. I2805
8 Same as no. 4. V. 2. 1969. I2806

INTERNATIONAL SERIES OF MONOGRAPHS ON NUCLEAR ENERGY (Pergamon)

Division 1: Economics of nuclear power.
1 Allardice, C., ed. Atomic power. 1957. I2807
Division 2: Nuclear physics.
1 Hughes, D. J. Neutron cross sections. 1957. I2808
2 Soveschanie po fizike deleni͡ia atomnykh i͡ader Moscow? Physics of nuclear fission, tr. by Bradley. 1958. I2809
3 Atomna͡ia energi͡ia. Soviet reviews of nuclear science on the 40th anniversary of the October Revolution. 1959. I2810
4 Yiftah, S. and others. Fast reactor cross sections. 1960. I2811
5 Nelipa, N. F. The relation between the photo-production

and the scattering of π-mesons. 1961. I2812
6 Dzhelepov, B. S. and Dranitsyna, G. F. Systematics of beta-decay energies, tr. by Sykes. 1963. I2813
7 Zyryanova, L. N. Once-forbidden beta-transition, tr. by Basu. 1963. I2814
8 Dzhelepov, B. S. Isobaric nuclei with the mass number A= 74, tr. by Clarke. 1963. I2815
9 ____ and Zhukovskii, N. N. Isobaric nuclei with the mass number A= 110, tr. by Clarke. 1963. I2816
10 ____ and others. Isobaric nuclei with the mass number A= 140, tr. by Clarke. 1963. I2817
11 Grigoriev, Y. P. Isobaric nuclei with the mass number A= 73, tr. by Clarke. 1963. I2818
12 Alikhanov, A. I. Recent research on beta-disintegration, tr. by Jones. 1963. I2819

Division 3: Biology.
1 Burnaziân, A. I. and Lebeoinskii, A. V., eds. Radiation medicine. 1964. I2820

Division 4: Isotopes and radiation.
1 Atlas of γ- ray spectra from radiative capture of thermal neutrons, by Groshev and others, tr. by Sykes. 1959. I2821
2 Verkhovskii, B. I. and others. The use of radioactive isotopes for checking production processes. 1963. I2822
3 Shumilovskii, N. N. and Mel'ttser, L. V. Radioactive isotopes in instrumentation and control, tr. by Kelleher, ed. by Blaetus and Young. 1964. I2823
4 Atlas of γ-ray spectra from radiative capture of thermal neutrons, by Groshev and others, tr. by Sykes. 1959. I2824

Division 5: Health physics.
1 Handloser, J. S. Health physics instrumentation. 1959. I2825
2 Amphlett, C. B. Treatment and disposal of radio-active wastes. 1961. I2826

Division 6: Medicine.
1 Mead, J. F. and Howton, R. Radioisotope studies of fatty acid metabolism. 1960. I2827

Division 7: Reactor engineering.
1 Komarovskii, A. W. Shielding materials for nuclear reactors, tr. by Newton. 1961. I2828
2 Rydzewski, J. R. Introduction to structural problems in nuclear reactor engineering. 1962. I2829

Division 8: Materials.
1 Bellamy, R. G. and Hill, H. A. Extraction and metallurgy of uranium. 1963. I2830
2 Perel'man, F. M. Rubidium and caesium, tr. by Towndrow, ed. by Clarke. 1963. I2831

Division 9: Chemical engineering.
1 Galkin, N. P. and others. The technology of the treatment of uranium concentrates, tr. by Hegarty, ed. by Clarke. 1963. I2832
2 Patton, F. S. and others. Enriched uranium processing. 1963. I2833

Division 10: Reactor design physics.
1 Littler, D. J. and Raffle, J. F. Introduction to reactor physics. 1957. I2834
2 Price, B. T. and others. Radiation shielding. 1957. I2835
3 Galanin, A. D. Thermal reactor theory, tr. by Sykes. 1960. I2836
4 Dresner, L. Resonance absorption in nuclear reactors. 1960. I2837
5 Thie, J. A. Heavy water exponential experiments using ThO_2UO_2. 1961. I2838
6 Leĭpunskiĭ, O. I. and others. The propagation of gamma quanta in matter, tr. by Basu. 1965. I2839

Division 11: Reactor operational problems.
1 Russell, C. R. Reactor safeguards. 1962. I2840

Division 12: Chemistry.
1 Rabinowitch, E. I. and Belford, R. L. Spectroscopy and photochemistry of uranyl compounds. 1964. I2841
Division 14: Plasma, physics and thermonuclear research.
1 Simon, A. An introduction to thermonuclear research. 1959. I2842
102 Simmons, J. H. W. Radiation damage in graphite. 1968. I2843
103 Evans, P. V. Fast breeder reactors. 1969. I2844
104 Yemel-yanov, V. S. and Yevstyukhin, A. I. Metallurgy of nuclear fuel. 1970. I2845
105 Cember, H. Introduction to health physics. 1970. I2846
106 Egelstaff, P. A. and Pool, M. L. Experimental neutron thermalization. 1970. I2847
107 Cameron, J. F. and Clayton, C. G. Radioisotope instruments. V. 1. 1971. I2848
108 Thomas, A. F. Calculational methods for interacting arrays of fissile material. 1973. I2849

INTERNATIONAL SERIES OF MONOGRAPHS ON ORGANIC CHEMISTRY (Pergamon)

1 Waters, W. R., ed. Vistas in free-radical chemistry. 1959. I2850
2 Topchiev, A. V. and others. Boron fluoride and its compounds as catalysts in inorganic chemistry, tr. by Greaves. 1959. I2851
3 Janssen, P. A. J. Synthetic analgesics. V. 1. 1960. I2852
4 Williams, G. H. Homolytic aromatic substitution. 1960. I2853
5 Jackman, L. M. Applications of nuclear magnetic resonance spectroscopy in organic chemistry. 1959. I2854
6 Gefter, E. L. Organophosphorus monomers and polymers, tr. by Burdon. 1962. I2855
7 Scott, A. I. Interpretation of the ultraviolet spectra of natural products. 1964. I2856
8 Same as no. 3. V. 2. 1965. I2857
9 Hanson, J. R. The tetracyclic diterpenes. 1968. I2858
10 Jackman, L. M. and Sternhell, S. Applications of nuclear magnetic resonance spectroscopy in organic chemistry. 2d ed. 1969. I2859

INTERNATIONAL SERIES OF MONOGRAPHS ON PHYSICS (Oxford)

Abragam, A. The principles of nuclear magnetism. 1961. I2859a
____ and Bleaney, B. Electron paramagnetic resonance of transition ions. 1970. I2860
Afasofu, S. I. and Chapman, S. Solar-terrestrial physics. 1972. I2861
Alfvén, H. Cosmical electrodynamics. 1950. I2862
____. On the origin of the solar system. 1954. I2863
Bacon, G. E. Neutron diffraction. 1955. I2864
Born, M. and Huang, K. Dynamical theory of crystal lattices. 1954. I2865
Bowden, F. P. and Tabor, D. The friction and lubrication of solids. 1950. I2866
Chandraesekhar, S. Hydrodynamic and hydromagnetic stability. 1961. I2867
____. Radiative transfer. 1950. I2868
Chapman, S. and Bartels, J. Geomagnetism. 2 v. 1940. I2869
Cook, A. H. Interference of electromagnetic waves. 1971. I2870
Cottrell, A. H. Dislocation and plastic flow in crystals. 1953. I2871
Crowthers, J. A. Manual of physics. 1950. I2872
Davison, B. and Sykes, J. B. Neutron transport theory. 1957. I2873

DeGennes, P. G. The physics of liquid crystals. 1974. I2874
Dirac, P. A. M. The principles of quantum mechanics. 1958. I2875
Dyson, F. W. and Wooley, R. van der R. Eclipses of the sun and moon. 1937. I2876
Falkenhagen, H. Electrolytes. 1934. I2877
Flynn, C. P. Point defects and diffusion. 1972. I2878
Frenkel, I. I. Kinetic theory of liquids. 1946. I2879
____. Wave mechanics, advanced general theory. 1934. I2880
____. Wave mechanics, elementary theory. 1936. I2881
Gamow, G. Constitution of atomic nuclei and radioactivity. 1931. I2882
____. Structure of atomic and nuclear transformations. 1937. I2883
____ and Critchfield, C. I. Theory of atomic nucleus and energy sources. 1950. I2884
Goldman, M. Spin temperature and nuclear magnetic resonance in solids. 1970. I2885
Goldschmidt, V. M. Geochemistry. 1954. I2886
Guggenheim, E. A. Mixtures. 1952. I2887
Guild, J. The interference system of crossed diffraction grating. 1956. I2888
Hamilton, J. The theory of elementary particles. 1959. I2889
Hayes, W., ed. Crystals with the fluorite structure. 1974. I2890
Heitler, W. The quantum theory of radiation. 1954. I2891
Henisch, H. K. Rectifying semiconductor contracts. 1957. I2892
Hodgson, P. E. Nuclear reactions and nuclear structure. 1971. I2893
Jánossy, L. Cosmic rays. 1950. I2894
____. Theory and practice of the evaluation of measurement. 1965. I2895
Jeffreys, H. The theory of probability. 1972. I2896
Kolsky, H. Stress waves in solids. 1955. I2897
Konopinski, E. J. The theory of beta radio activity. 1966. I2898
Kourganoff, V. Basic methods in transfer problems. 1952. I2899
Lindenbaum, S. J. Particle-interaction physics of high energies. 1973. I2900
Linfoot, E. H. Recent advances in optics. 1955. I2901
Littler, T. S. The physics of the ear. 1965. I2902
Lovell, B. Meteor astronomy. 1954. I2903
Lynn, J. E. The theory of neutron resonance reactions. 1968. I2904
Marshall, W. and Lovesey, S. W. Theory of thermal neutron scattering. 1971. I2905
Massey, H. and others. Electronic impact phenomena. 2 v. 1969. I2906
Massey, H. S. W. and Burop, E. H. S. Electronic and ionic impact, phenomena. 1952. I2907
Meek, J. M. and Craggs, J. D. Electrical breakdown of gases. 1953. I2908
Milne, E. A. Kinematic relativity. 1948. I2909
____. Relativity, gravitation and world-structure. 1935. I2910
M'Lachlan, N. W. Theory and application of Mathieu functions. 1947. I2911
Møller, C. The theory of relativity. 1952. I2912
Mott, N. F. Electronic process in non-crystalline materials. 1971. I2913
Mott, N. F. and Gurney, R. W. Electronic processes in ionic crystals. 1949. I2914
____ and Jones, H. Theory of properties of metals and alloys. 1936. I2915
____ and Massey, H. S. W. The theory of atomic collisions. 1965. I2916

Nabarro, F. R. N. Theory of crystal dislocations. 1967. I2917
Peierls, R. E. Quantum theory of solids. 1955. I2918
Ramsey, N. F. Molecular beams. 1956. I2919
Rosseland, S. The pulsation theory of variable stars. 1949. I2920
____. Theoretical astrophysics. 1936. I2921
Ruhemann, M. The separation of gasses. 1949. I2922
Semenoff, N. Chemical kinetics and chain reactions. 1935. I2923
Stanley, H. E. Introduction to phase transitions and critical phenomena. 1971. I2924
Svedberg, T. and others. The ultra-centrifuge. 1940. I2925
Tolman, R. C. The principles of statistical mechanics. 1938. I2926
____. Relativity, thermodynamics and cosmology. 1934. I2927
Van Vleck, J. H. The theory of electric and magnetic susceptibilities. 1965. I2928
Wilks, J. The properties of liquids and solid helium. 1967. I2929
Winter, J. Magnetic resonance in metals. 1971. I2930
Woolley, R. v. d. R. and Stibbs, D. W. N. The outer layer of a star. 1953. I2931
Zeiger, H. and Pratt, G. Magnetic interactions in solids. 1973. I2932
Ziman, J. M. Electrons and phonons. 1960. I2933

INTERNATIONAL SERIES OF MONOGRAPHS IN PURE AND APPLIED BIOLOGY (Pergamon)

Biochemistry division.
1 Pitt-Rivers, R. and Tata, J. R. The thyroid hormones. 1959. I2934
2 Bush, I. E. The chromatography of steroids. 1961. I2935
3 Engel, L. L., ed. Physical properties of the steroid hormones. 1963. I2936
4 Bailey, R. W. Oligosaccharides. 1965. I2937
5 Parke, D. V. The biochemistry of foreign compounds. 1968. I2938
6 Glaz, E. and Vecsei, P. Aldosterone. 1971. I2939

Botany division.
1 Bor, N. L. The grasses of India, Burma and Ceylon. 1960. I2940
2 Turrill, W. B. Visitas in botany. 1959. I2941
3 Schultes, R. E. Native orchids of Trinidad and Tobago. 1960. I2942
4 Cooke, G. B. Cork and cork tree. 1961. I2943
5-7 Same as no. 2. V. 2-4. 1963-64. I2944
8 Viktorov, S. V. and others. Short guide to geo-botanical surveying, tr. by Maclennan, ed. by Proctor. 1964. I2945
9 Szafer, W. The vegetation of Poland. 2 v. 1966. I2946

Modern trends in physiological sciences division.
1 Florkin, M. Unity and diversity in biochemistry, tr. by Wood. 1960. I2947
2 Brachet, J. The biochemistry of development. 1960. I2948
3 Gerebtzoff, M. A. Cholinesterases. 1959. I2949
4 Brouha, L. Physiology in industry. 1960. I2950
5 Bacq, Z. M. and Alexander, P. Fundamentals of radiobiology. 1961. I2951
6 Florkin, M., ed. Aspects of the origin of life. 1960. I2952
7 Hollaender, A., ed. Radiation protection and recovery. 1960. I2953
8 Kayser, C. The physiology of natural hibernation. 1961. I2954
9 Françon, M. Progress in microscopy. 1961. I2955
10 Charlier, R. Coronary vasodilators. 1961. I2956
11 Gross, L. Oncogenic viruses. 1961. I2957

12 Mercer, E. H. Keratin and keratinization. 1961. I2958
13 Heath, D. F. Organophosphorus poisons. 1961. I2959
14 Chantrenne, H. The biosynthesis of proteins. 1961. I2960
15 Rivera, J. A. Cilia, ciliated epithelium and ciliary activity. 1962. I2961
16 Enselme, J. Unsaturated fatty acids in atherosclerosis, tr. by Crawford. 1962. I2962
17 Balabukha, V. S., ed. Chemical protection of the body against ionizing radiation, tr. by Greaves, ed. by Barnes. 1963. I2963
18 Peters, R. A. Biochemical lesions and lethal synthesis. 1963. I2964
19 Thomson, J. F. Biological effects of deuterium. 1963. I2965
20 Robertis, E. D. P. de. Histophysiology of synapses and neurosection. 1964. I2966
21 Kovács, E. The biochemistry of poliomyelitis viruses. 1964. I2967
22 McLaren, A. D. and Shugar, D. Photochemistry of protein and nucleic acids. 1964. I2968
23 Hermann, H. X. and Mornex, R. Human tumours secreting catecholamines, tr. by Crawford. 1964. I2969
24 Whitfield, I. C. Manual of experimental electrophysiology. 1964. I2970
25 Lissák, K. and Endröczi, E. The neuroendocrine control of adaptation. 1964. I2971
26 Troshin, A. S. Problems of cell permeability, ed. by Hell, tr. by Widdas. 1966. I2972
27 Bajusz, E. and others. Physiology and pathology of adaptation mechanisms. 1968. I2973
28 Schoffeniel, E. Cellular aspects of membrane permeability. 1967. I2974
29 LeClercq, M. Entomological parisitology. 1969. I2975
30 Kelemen, E. Physiopathology and therapy of human blood diseases. 1969. I2976
31 Strong, L. C. Biological aspects of cancer and aging. 1968. I2977
32 Turpin, R. A. and Lejeune, J. Human afflictions and chromosomal abberations. 1969. I2978
33 Von Cauwenberge, H. Assay of protein and polypeptide hormones. 1970. I2979
34 Goffart, M. Function and form in the sloth. 1971. I2980
35 Arvy, L. Histoenzymology of the endocrine glands. 1970. I2981
36 Bastenie, P. A. and Armans, A. M. Thyroiditis and thyroid function. 1972. I2982
37 Rocha e Silva, M. and Garcia Leme, J. Chemical mediators of the acute inflammatory reaction. 1972. I2983
38 Michelson, M. J. and Zeimal, E. V. Acetylchlorine. 1974. I2984

Plant physiology.

1 Sutcliffe, J. F. Mineral salts absorption in plants. 1962. I2985
2 Siegel, S. M. The plant cell wall. 1962. I2986
3 Mayer, A. M. The germination of seeds. 1963. I2987
4 Salisbury, F. B. The flowering process. 1963. I2988

Symposium.

1 Villee, C. A. and Engel, L. L., eds. Mechanism of action of steroid hormones. 1961. I2989

Zoology division.

1 Raven, C. R. An outline of developmental physiology, tr. by De Ruiter. 1959. I2990
2 ____. Morphogenesis. 1958. I2991
3 Savory, T. H. Instinctive living. 1959. I2992
4 Kerkut, G. A. Implications of evolution. 1960. I2993
5 Tartar, V. The biology of Stentor. 1961. I2994

6 Jenkin, P. M. Animal hormones. 1962. I2995
7 Corliss, J. O. The ciliated protozoa. 1961. I2996
8 George, F. H. The brain as a computer. 1961. I2997
9 Arthur, D. R. Ticks and disease. 1962. I2998
10 Raven, C. P. Oogenesis. 1961. I2999
11 Mann, J. H. Leeches (Hirudinea). 1962. I3000
12 Sleigh, I. A. The biology of cilia and flagella. 1962. I3001
13 Pitelka, D. R. Electron-microscope structure of protozoa. 1963. I3002
14 Fingerman, M. Control of chromatophores. 1963. I3003
15 Laverack, M. S. The physiology of earthworms. 1963. I3004
16 Hadzi, J. The evolution of the metazoa, tr. by Stanonik. 1963. I3005
17 Clements, A. N. The physiology of mosquitos. 1963. I3006
18 Raymont, J. E. G. Plankton and productivity in the oceans. 1963. I3007
19 Potts, W. T. W. and Parry, G. Osmotic and Ionic regulation in animals. 1964. I3008
20 Glasgow, J. P. The distribution and abundance of tsetse. 1963. I3009
21 Pantelouris, E. M. The common liver fluke, Fasciola hepatica L. 1965. I3010
22 Vandel, A. Biospeleology, tr. by Freeman. 1965. I3011
23 Biochemical Soc., London. Studies in comparative biochemistry, ed. by Munday. 1965. I3012
24 Robinson, R., ed. Genetics of the Norway rat. 1965. I3013
25 Needham, A. E. The uniqueness of biological materials. 1965. I3014
26 Bacci, G. Sex determination. 1965. I3015
27 Jørgensen, C. B. Biology of suspension feeding. 1966. I3016
28 Gabe, M. Neurosecretion. 1966. I3017
29 Apter, M. J. Cybernetics and development. 1966. I3018
30 Sharov, A. G. Basic arthropodan stock. 1966. I3019
31 Bennett, P. B. The aetiology of compressed air intoxication and inert gas narcosis. 1966. I3020
32 Pantelouris, E. M. Introduction to animal physiology and physiology genetics. 1967. I3021
33 Hahn, P. and Koldovsky, O. Utilization of nutrients during postnatal development. 1967. I3022
34 International Symposium on Cytoecology. The cell and environmental temperature, ed. by Prosser and others. 1967. I3023
35 Duncan, C. J. The molecular properties and evolution of excitable cells. 1967. I3024
36 Johnston, P. V. and Root, B. I. Nerve membranes. 1967. I3025
37 Threadgold, L. T. The ultrastructure of the animal cell. 1968. I3026
38 Griffiths, M. Echidnas. 1968. I3027
39 Rybak, B. Principles of zoophysiology. V. 1. 1968. I3028
40 Purchon, R. D. The biology of the Mollusca. 1968. I3029
41 Maupin, B. Blood platelets in man and mammals. 2 v. 1970. I3030
42 Brønsted, H. V. Planarian regeneration. 1970. I3031
43 Phillis, J. W. The pharmacology of synapses. 1970. I3032
44 Engelmann, F. The physiology of insect reproduction. 1970. I3033
45 Robinson, R. Genetics for cat breeders. 1970. I3034
46 ____. Lepidoptera genetics. 1971. I3035
47 Same as no. 6. V. 2. 1971. I3036

48 Culley, M. B. The Pilchard. 1972. I3037
49 Benyon, J. Physiology of echinoderms. 1972. I3038
50 Anderson, D. T. Embryology and phylogeny in annelids and arthropods. 1973. I3039
51 Boyden, A. A. Perspectives in zoology. 1973. I3040
52 Cushing, D. H. The detection of fish. 1973. I3041

INTERNATIONAL SERIES OF MONOGRAPHS ON PURE AND APPLIED MATHEMATICS (Pergamon)

1 Wallace, A. H. An introduction to algebraic topology. 1957. I3042
2 Pedoe, D. Circles. 1957. I3043
3 Spain, B. Analytical conics. 1957. I3044
4 Mikhlin, S. G. Integral equations and their applications to certain problems in mechanics, mathematical physics, and technology, tr. by Armstrong. 1957. I3045
5 Eggleston, H. G. Problems in Euclidean space. 1957. I3046
6 Wallace, A. H. Homology theory on algebraic topology. 1957. I3047
7 Noble, B. Methods based on the Wiener-Hopf technique for the solution of partial differential equations. 1959. I3048
8 Mikusiński, J. Operational calculus. 1959. I3049
9 Heine, V. Group theory in question mechanics. 1960. I3050
10 Bland, D. R. The theory of linear viscoelasticity. 1960. I3051
11 Kurth, R. Axiomatics of classical statistical mechanics. 1960. I3052
12 Fuchs, L. Abelian groups. 1960. I3053
13 Kuratowski, K. Introduction to set theory and topology, tr. by Boron. 1961. I3054
14 Spain, B. Analytical quadrics. 1960. I3055
15 Hartman, S. and Mikusinski, J. The theory of Lebesque measure and integration. 1961. I3056
16 Kuratowski, K. Introduction to calculus, tr. by Musielak. 1961. I3057
17 Kulczycki, S. Non-Euclidean geometry, tr. by Knapowski. 1961. I3058
18 Geronimus, I. L. Polynomials orthogonal on a circle and interval, tr. by Brown. 1960. I3059
19 El'sgol'ts, L. E. Calculus of variations. 1961. I3060
20 Alexits, G. Convergence problems of orthogonal series, tr. by Földes. 1961. I3061
21 Fuchs, B. A. and Levin, V. L. Functions of a complex variable. 2 v. 1962. I3062
22 Goodstein, R. L. Fundamental concepts of mathematics. 1962. I3063
23 Keene, G. B. Abstract sets and finite ordinals. 1961. I3064
24 Ditkin, V. A. and Prudnikov, A. P. Operational calculus in two variables and its applications. 1962. I3065
25 Vekua, I. N. Generalized analytic functions, tr. by Sneddon. 1962. I3066
26 Amir-Moéz, A. R. and Fass, A. L. Elements of linear spaces. 1962. I3067
27 Gradshtein, I. S. Direct and converse theorems, tr. by Boddington. 1963. I3068
28 Fuchs, L. Partially ordered algebraic systems. 1963. I3069
29 Postnikov, M. M. Foundations of Galois theory, tr. by Swinfen. 1962. I3070
30 Bermant, A. F. A course of mathematical analysis, tr. by Brosn. V. 2. 1963. I3071
31 Lukasiewicz, J. Elements of mathematical logic, tr. by Wojtasiewicz. 1963. I3072

32 Vulikh, B. Z. Introduction to functional analysis for scientists and technologists. 1963. I3073
33 Pedoe, D. An introduction to projective geometry. 1963. I3074
34 Timan, A. F. Theory of approximation of functions of a real variable, tr. by Berry. 1963. I3075
35 Császár, A. Foundations of general topology, tr. by K. Császár. 1963. I3076
36 Bronshtein, I. N. and Semendyayev, K. A. A guide book to mathematics, for technologists and engineers, tr. by Jaworowski and Bleicher. 1964. I3077
37 Mostowski, A. and Stark, M. Introduction to higher algebra, tr. by Musielak. 1964. I3078
38 Goddard, L. S. Mathematical techniques of operational research. 1963. I3079
39 Tikhonov, A. N. and Samarskii, A. A. Equations of mathematical physics, tr. by Robson and Basu. 1963. I3080
40 McLeod, E. B. Introduction to fluid dynamics. 1963. I3081
41 Moisil, S. The algebraic theory of switching structures. 1964. I3082
42 Otto, E. Nomography, tr. by Smolska. 1963. I3083
43 Rankin, R. A. An introduction to mathematical analysis. 1963. I3084
44 Same as no. 30. V. 1. 1963. I3085
45 Krasnoselskil, M. A. Topological methods in the theory of non-linear integral equations, tr. by Armstrong. 1964. I3086
46 Kantorovich, L. V. and Akilov, G. P. Functional analysis in normed spaces, tr. by Brown. 1964. I3087
47 Jones, D. S. The theory of electromagnetism. 1964. I3088
48 Fejes Tóth, L. Regular figures. 1964. I3089
49 Yano, K. Differential geometry on complex and almost complex spaces. 1965. I3090
50 Mikhlin, S. G. Variational methods in mathematical physics, tr. by Boddington, ed. by Chambers. 1964. I3091
51 Fuks, B. A. and Shabat, B. V. Functions of a complex variable and some of their applications, tr. by Berry. V. 1. 1964. I3092
52 Budak, B. M. and others. A collection of problems on mathematical physics, tr. by Robson, ed. by Brink. 1964. I3093
53 Giles, R. Mathematical foundations of thermodynamics. 1964. I3094
54 Saul'ev, V. K. Integration of equations of parabolic type by the method of nets, tr. by Tee, ed. by Stewart. 1964. I3095
55 Pontrîagin, L. S. and others. The mathematical theory of optimal processes, tr. by Brown. 1964. I3096
56 Sobolev, S. L. Partial differential equations of mathematical physics, tr. by Dawson, ed. by Broadent. 1964. I3097
57-62 Smirov, V. I. A course of higher mathematics, tr. by Brown, ed. by Sneddon. 5 v. in 6. 1964. I3098
63 Naĭmark, M. A. Linear representation of the Lorentz group, ed. by Snifen and Marstr and tr. by Farahat. 1964. I3099
64 Berman, G. N. A collection of problems on a course of mathematical analysis, tr. by Brown, ed. by Sneddon. 1965. I3100
65 Mashxherskii, I. V. A collection of problems of mechanics, tr. by Romicki. 1965. I3101
66 Arscott, F. M. Periodic differential equations. 1964. I3102

100 Saloma, A. Theory of automata. 1970. I3135
101 Kuratowski, K. Introduction to set theory and topology, ed. by Borón. 1972. I3136
102 Blyth, T. S. and Janowitz, M. F. Residuation theory. 1972. I3137
103 Kosten, L. Stochastic theory of service systems. 1973. I3138

INTERNATIONAL SERIES OF MONOGRAPHS ON SOCIAL AND BEHAVIOURAL SCIENCES (Pergamon)

1 Carter, M. P. Home, school and work. 1962. I3139
2 Lupton, T. On the shop floor. 1963. I3140

INTERNATIONAL SERIES OF MONOGRAPHS ON SOLID STATE PHYSICS (Pergamon)

1 Jona, F. and Shirane, G. Ferroelectric crystals. 1962. I3141
2 Schulman, J. H. and Compton, W. D. Color centers in solids. 1963. I3142
3 Friedel, J. Dislocations. 1964. I3143
4 Vonsovskiĭ, S. V., ed. Ferromagnetic resonance, tr. by Massey. 1966. I3144
5 Galasso, F. S. Structure, properties and preparation of perovskite-type compounds. 1969. I3145
6 Rose-Innes, A. C. Introduction to superconductivity. 1970. I3146
7 Galasso, F. F. Structure and properties of inorganic cells. 1971. I3147

INTERNATIONAL SERIES OF MONOGRAPHS ON THE ECONOMICS AND ASPECTS OF NUCLEAR ENERGY (Pergamon)

1 Allardice, C., ed. Atomic power. 1956. I3148

INTERNATIONAL STUDIES IN SOCIOLOGY AND SOCIAL ANTHROPOLOGY (Brill)

1 Mogey, J. M., ed. Family and marriage. 1963. I3149
2 Anderson, N., ed. Urbanism and urbanization. 1964. I3150
3 Piddington, R., ed. Kinship and geographical mobility. 1965. I3151
4 Ishwarsan, K., ed. Politics and social change. 1967. I3152
5 Buxbaum, D. C., ed. Traditional and modern legal institutions. 1967. I3153
6 Morioka, K. and Newell, W. H., comps. The sociology of Japanese religion. 1968. I3154
7 Case studies in social power, ed. by Evers. 1969. I3155
8 Studies in multilingualism. 1969. I3156
9 Duffy, N. F., ed. The sociology of the blue-collar worker. 1970. I3157
10 Gutkind, P. C. W., ed. The passing of tribal man in Africa. 1970. I3158
11 Family issues of employed women in Europe and America. 1971. I3159
12 Cross-national family research, ed. by Sussman and Cogswell. 1972. I3160
13 Symposium in Homadic Studies. Perspectives on nomadism. 1972. I3161
14 Inkeles, A. and Holsinger, D. B., eds. Education and individual modernity in developing countries. 1974. I3162
15 Korson, J. H. Contemporary problems of Pakistan. 1974. I3163

INTERNATIONAL TRACTS IN COMPUTER SCIENCE AND TECHNOLOGY AND THEIR APPLICATION (Pergamon)

1 Cashwell, E. D. and Everett, C. J. A practical manual on the Monte Carlo

method for random walk problems. 1959. I3164
2 Interdisciplinary Conference on Self-Organizing Systems. Self-organizing systems, ed. by Yovits and Cameron. 1960. I3165
3 Annual review in automatic programming. V. 1. 1960. I3166
4 Conference on Computing Methods. Computing methods and the phase problem in x-ray crystal analysis, ed. by Pepinsky and others. 1961. I3167
5 Barber, N. F. Experimental correlograms and Fourier transforms. 1961. I3168
6 Same as no. 3. V. 2. 1961. I3169
7 Smirov, G. D. Electronic digital computers, tr. by Segal. 1961. I3170
8 Akademiia nauk SSSR. Problems of the design and accuracy of complex continuous action devices and computer mechanisms, ed. by Bruyewick, tr. by Segal. 1964. I3171
9 Univ. of Illinois. Symposium on self-organization. Principles of self-organizations. 1962. I3172
10 Hall, J. A. P., ed. Computers in education. 1962. I3173
11-12 Same as no. 3-4. V. 3-4. 1962. I3174
13A Volynskiĭ, B. A. and Bukhman, V. Y. Analogues for the solution of boundary-value problems, tr. by Schorr-Kon, ed. by Michel. 1965. I3175
13B Same as no. 3. V. 5, ed. by Halpern and others. 1974. I3176

INTERPRETATIONS OF AMERICAN HISTORY (Harper)

Baltzell, E. D., ed. The search for community in modern America. 1968. I3177
Brock, W. R. The Civil War. 1969. I3178
Brody, D., comp. The American labor movement. 1971. I3179
Campbell, A. E., ed. Expression and imperialism. 1970. I3180
Davis, D. B., comp. Antebellum reform. 1967. I3181
Gleason, P., ed. Catholicism in America. 1970. I3182
Grantham, D. W., ed. The South and the sectional image. 1967. I3183
Greene, J. P., comp. The ambiguity of the American Revolution. 1968. I3184
Hill, M. S., ed. Mormonism and American culture. 1972. I3185
James, S. V., comp. The New England Puritans. 1968. I3186
Layton, E. T., ed. Technology and social change in America. 1973. I3187
Link, A. S. The impact of World War I. 1969. I3188
Lynd, S., ed. Reconstruction. 1967. I3189
Peterson, M. D., ed. Democracy, liberty and property. 1966. I3190
Pole, J. R., comp. The advance of democracy. 1967. I3191
Risjord, N. J. The early American party system. 1969. I3192
TePaske, J. J., comp. The American empires. 1967. I3193

INTERSCIENCE TRACTS IN PURE AND APPLIED MATHEMATICS (Interscience)

(Merged with Pure and Applied Mathematics to form Pure and Applied Mathematics, a Wiley Interscience Series of Texts, Monographs and Texts)
1 Montgomery, D. and Zippin, L. Topological transformation groups. 1955. I3194
2 John, F. Plane waves and spherical waves applied to partial differential equations. 1955. I3195

3 Artin, E. Geometric algebra. 1957. I3196
4 Richtmyer, R. D. Difference methods for initial value-problems. 1957. I3197
5 Lang, S. Introduction to algebraic geometry. 1958. I3198
6 Busemann, H. Convex surfaces. 1958. I3199
7 Lang, S. Abelian varieties. 1959. I3200
8 Ulam, S. M. A collection of mathematical problems. 1960. I3201
9 Gel'fand, I. M. Lectures on linear algebra, tr. by Shenitzer. 1961. I3202
10 Jacobsen, N. Lie algebras. 1962. I3203
11 Lang, S. Diophantine geometry. 1962. I3204
12 Rudin, W. Fourier analysis on groups. 1962. I3205
13 Nagata, M. Local rings. 1962. I3206
14 Niven, I. M. Diophantine approximations. 1963. I3207
15 Kobayashi, S. and Nomizu, K. Foundations of differential geometry. 1963. I3208
16 Plemelj, J. Problems in the sense of Riemann and Klein, ed. and tr. by Radok. 1964. I3209
17 Cohn, R. M. Difference algebra. 1965. I3210
18 Mann, H. B. Addition theorems. 1965. I3211
19 Ash, R. B. Information theory. 1965. I3212
20 Magnus, W. and Winkler, S. Hill's equation. 1966. I3213
21 Harris, Z. S. Mathematical structures of language. 1968. I3214
22 Corduneau, C. and others. Almost periodic functions, tr. by Bernstein and Tamer. 1968. I3215
23 Bucy, R. S. and Joseph, P. D. Filtering for stochastic processes with applications to guidance. 1968. I3216
24 Ribenboim, P. Rings and modules. 1969. I3217
25 Siegel, C. L. Topics in complex function theory. 3 v. 1969-70. I3218

INTERSCIENCE TRACTS ON PHYSICS AND ASTRONOMY (Interscience)

1 Hughes, D. J. Neutron optics. 1954. I3219
2 Livingston, M. S. High-energy accelerators. 1954. I3220
3 Spitzer, L. Physics of fully ionized gases. 1962. I3221
4 Cowling, T. G. Magnetohydrodynamics. 1957. I3222
5 Haar, D. ter. Introduction to the physics of many-body systems. 1958. I3223
6 Öpik, E. J. Physics of meteor flight in the atmosphere. 1958. I3224
7 Mendelssohn, K. Cryophysics. 1960. I3225
8 Delcroix, J. L. Introduction to the theory of ionized gases, tr. by Clark and others. 1960. I3226
9 Sterne, T. E. An introduction to celestial mechanics. 1960. I3227
10 Weber, J. General relativity and gravitational waves. 1961. I3228
11 Marshak, R. E. and Sudarsham, E. C. G. Introduction to elementary particle physics. 1961. I3229
12 Olsen, J. L. Electron transport in metals. 1962. I3230
13 Francon, M. Modern applications of physical optics, tr. by Scripta Technia, Inc. 1963. I3231
14 Jones, P. B. The optical model in nuclean and particle physics. 1963. I3232
15 Adair, R. K. and Fowler, E. C. Strange particles. 1963. I3233
16 Wilson, R. The nuclean-nucleon interaction. 1963. I3234
17 Denisse, J. F. and Delcroix, J. L. Plasma waves, by Weinrich and

INTER-UNIVERSITY COMMITTEE FOR RESEARCH ON CONSUMER BEHAVIOR. STUDIES IN CONSUMER SAVINGS. (Univ. of Illinois Pr.)

INTRODUCTION TO SYSTEMATIC GEOMORPHOLOGY SERIES (M. I. T. Pr.)

INVESTIGATIONS IN PHYSICS (Princeton Univ. Pr.)

INVESTIGATIONS IN THE BIOLOGICAL SCIENCES (Princeton Univ. Pr.)

1 Bonner, J. T. The cellular slime molds. 1959. I3269
2 Blum, H. F. Carcinogenesis by ultraviolet light. 1959. I3270

IOWA UNIVERSITY. STUDIES IN CHILD WELFARE.

1:1 Baldwin, B. T. The physical growth of children from birth to maturity. 1921. I3271
1:2 Seashore, C. E. A survey of musical talent in the public schools. 1920. I3272
1:3 Hawk, S. M. A preliminary study in corrective speech. 1920. I3273
1:4 Town, C. H. Analytic study of a group of five and six-year-old children. 1921. I3274
1:5 Daniels, A. L. and Byfield, A. H. Investigations in the artificial feeding of children. 1921. I3275
1:6 Horack, F. E. Child legislation in Iowa. 1920. I3276
1:7 Hart, H. N. Selective migration as a factor in child welfare in the United States. 1921. I3277
2:1 Baldwin, B. T. and Stecher, L. I. Mental growth curve of normal and superior children. 1922. I3278
2:2 Hart, H. N. Differential fecundity in Iowa. 1922. I3279
2:3 Bliss, A. I. Iowa child welfare legislation measured by Federal children's bureau standards. 1922. I3280
2:4 Hart, H. N. A test of social attitudes and interests. 1923. I3281
3:1 Whiting, P. W. A study of heredity and environmental factors determining a variable character. 1924. I3282
3:2 Wagoner, L. C. The constructive ability of young children. 1925. I3283
3:3 Marston, L. R. The emotions of young children. 1925. I3284
3:4 Wellman, B. L. The development of motor coordination in young children. 1925. I3285
3:5 Smith, M. E. An investigation of the development of the sentence and the extent of vocabulary in young children. 1926. I3286
3:6 Kirkwood, J. A. The learning process in young children. 1926. I3287
4:1 Baldwin, B. T. Anatomic growth of children. 1928. I3288
4:2 Berne, E. (Van Cleave). An experimental investigation of the wants of seven children. 1930. I3289
4:3 ____. An experimental investigation of social behavior patterns in young children. 1930. I3290
4:4 Updegraff, R. The visual perception of distance in young children and adults. 1930. I3291
4:5 Hicks, J. A. The acquisition of motor skills in young children. 1931. I3292
4:6 Manwell, E. S. (Moore). The development of mental health in a group of young children. 1930. I3293
5:1 Wallis, R. O. (Sawtell). How children grow. 1931. I3294
5:2 Wellman, B. L. and others. Speech sounds of young children. 1931. I3295
5:3 Chase, L. Motivation of young children. 1932. I3296
5:4 Scoe, H. F. Bladder control in infancy and early childhood. 1933. I3297
5:5 Johnson, W. The influence of stuttering on the personality. 1932. I3298
6 Researches in parent education, by Hatterdorf and others. 1932. I3299
7:1 The measurement of musical development by Williams and others. 1932. I3300
7:2 Skeels, H. M. A study of some factors in form

board accomplishments of preschool children. 1933. I3301
7:3 Roberts, K. E. Learning in preschool and orphanage children. 1933. I3302
7:4 Hagman, E. P. The companionships of preschool children. 1933. I3303
7:5 Kelly, H. G. A study of individual differences in breathing capacity in relation to some physical characteristics. 1933. I3304
8 Same as no. 6. V. 2. 1933. I3305
9:1 Horack, F. E. Legislation pertaining to women and children in Iowa. 1934. I3306
9:2 Francis, K. V. and Fillmore, E. A. The influence of environment upon the personality of children. 1934. I3307
9:3 Behavior of the preschool child, by Jack and others. 1934. I3308
9:4 Studies in infant behavior, by Irwin and others. V. 1. 1934. I3309
10 Same as no. 6. V. 3. 1934. I3310
11:1 Same as no. 9:4. V. 2. 1935. I3311
11:2 Same as no. 7:1. V. 2. 1935. I3312
11:3 Meredith, H. V. The rhythm of physical growth. 1935. I3313
11:4 Fillmore, E. A. Iowa tests for young children. 1936. I3314
12:1 Same as no. 9:4. V. 3. 1936. I3315
12:2 McCloy, C. H. Appraising physical status. 1936. I3316
12:3 Page, M. L. The modification of ascendant behavior in preschool children. 1936. I3317
12:4 Boynton, B. The physical growth of girls. 1936. I3318
12:5 Kelly, H. J. Anatomic age and its relations to stature. 1937. I3319
13:1 Crissey, O. L. Mental development as related to institutional residence and educational achievement. 1937. I3320
13:2 Williams, H. M. and others. Development of language and vocabulary in young children. 1937. I3321
13:3 Same as no. 9:4. V. 4. 1937. I3322
13:4 Studies in emotional adjustment by Brandt and others. V. 1. 1937. I3323
14 Studies in preschool education, by Updegraff and others. V. 1. 1937. I3324
15:1 Same as no. 13:4. V. 2. 1937. I3325
15:2 McCloy, C. H. Appraising physical status. 1938. I3326
15:3 Wellman, B. L. The intelligence of preschool children as measured by the Merrill-Palmer scale of performance tests. 1938. I3327
15:4 Skeels, H. M. and others. A study of environmental stimulation. 1938. I3328
16:1 Skodak, M. Children in foster homes. 1939. I3329
16:2 Same as no. 9:4. V. 5. 1939. I3330
16:3 Studies in topological and vector psychology, by Lewin and others. V. 1. 1939. I3331
17 Same as no. 6. V. 4. 1939. I3332
18:1 Same as no. 16:3. V. 2. 1941. I3333
18:2 Metheny, E. Breathing capacity and grip strength of preschool children. 1940. I3334
18:3 Knott, V. M. Physical measurement of young children. 1941. I3335
19 Meredith, H. V. Physical growth from birth to two years. 1943. I3336
20 Same as no. 16:3. V. 3. 1944. I3337

ISLAMIC SURVEYS (Aldine)

1 Watt, W. M. Islamic philosophy and theology.

1962. I3338
2 Coulson, N. J. A history of Islamic law. 1964. I3339
3 Cragg, K. Counsels in contemporary Islam. 1965. I3340
4 Watt, W. M. A history of Islamic Spain. 1965. I3341
5 Bosworth, C. E. The Islamic dynasties. 1967. I3342
6 Watt, W. M. Islamic political thought. 1968. I3343
7 Aziz Ahmad. An intellectual history of Islam in India. 1969. I3344
8 Bell, R. Introduction to the Qur'an, ed. by Watt. 1970. I3345
9 Watt, W. M. The influence of Islam on medieval Europe. 1972. I3346
10 Aziz Ahmad. A history of Islamic Sicily. 1974. I3347

ISLAMIC WORLD SERIES (Univ. of Calif. Pr.)

al-Jahif, 'A ibn B. The life and works of Jahiz, tr. by Pellet. 1970. I3348
Gabrieli, F., comp. Arab historians of the Crusades, tr. by Costello. 1969. I3349
Spuler, B., comp. History of Mongols, tr. by Drumond. 1972. I3350

ISTITUTO DI STUDI FILOSOFICA. EDIZIONE NAZIONALE DEI CLASSICI DEL PENSIERO ITALIANO (Vallecchi, Bocca 1951-)

1 Pico della Mirandola, G. F. De hominis dignitate, Heptaplus, De ente et uno, e scritta a cura di Eugenio Garin. 1942. I3351
2-3 ____. Disputationes adversus astrologiam divinatricem, libri I-V, ed. by Garin. 2 v. 1946-52. I3352
5 Pietro. Damiani, St. De divina omnipotentia e altri scritti, ed. by Nardi. 1943. I3353
6 Aconcio, G. De methode e opuscoli religiosi e filosifici, ed. by Radetti. 1944. I3354
7 ____. Stratagematum Satanae libri VIII, ed. by Radetti. 1946. I3355
8 Salutati, C. De nobilitate legum et medicinae. De verecundia, ed. by Garin. 1947. I3356
9 Garin, E., ed. La disputa delle arti nel Quattrocento. 1947. I3357
10-11 Campanella, T. Dio e la predestinazione, ed. by Amerio. 2 v. 1949-51. I3358

Serie 2:
1 Campanella, T. La prima e la seconda resurrezione. 1955. I3359
2 Crinito, P. De honesta disciplina. I3360
3-4 Nizzoli, M. De veris principiis et vera ratione philosophandi. 2 v. I3361
5 Campanella, T. Magia e teologia. I3362
6 Ficino, M. De triplici vita. I3363
7-8 Campanella, T. Cristologia. 2 v. 1958. I3364
9 ____. Della grazia gratificante. 1959. I3365
10-11 Canisio, E. Scechina e libellus de letteris hebraicis, ed. by Secret. V. 1-2. 1959. I3366
12 Campanella, T. Il peccato originale. 1960. I3367
13-14 ____. De homine, ed. by Amerio. 2 v. 1960. I3368
15-16 ____. Vita Chresti, ed. by Amerio. V. 1-2. 1962. I3369
17 ____. Cosmologia. 1964. I3370
26 ____. Escatalogia, ed. by Amerio. 1969. I3371
27 ____. Le creature sovrannaturali, ed. by Amerio. 1970. I3372
29 ____. Origine temporale di Cristo, ed. by Amerio. 1972. I3373

ISTITUTO ITALIANO PER GLI STUDI STORICI, NAPLES. PUBBLICAZIONI (1-5, Laterza; 6- Istituto...)